A Gui⟨
Major Trusts

2007/08 edition

Volume 2
A further 1,100 trusts

Alan French
Sarah Johnston
John Smyth

DIRECTORY OF SOCIAL CHANGE

A Guide to the Major Trusts
Volume 2
2007/08 edition

Published by
Directory of Social Change
24 Stephenson Way
London NW1 2DP
Tel: 08450 77 77 07; Fax: 020 7391 4804
email: publications@dsc.org.uk
www.dsc.org.uk
from whom further copies and a full publications list are available.

Directory of Social Change is a Registered Charity no. 800517

First Published 1993
Second edition 1995
Third edition 1997
Fourth edition 1999
Fifth edition 2001
Sixth edition 2003
Seventh edition 2005
Eighth edition 2007

ISBN 978 1 903991 78 7

British Library Cataloguing in Publication Data

A catalogue record for this book is available from the British Library

Cover designed by Keith Shaw
Text designed by Lenn Darroux and Linda Parker
Typeset by Marlinzo Services
Printed and bound by Page Bros., Norwich

Directory of Social Change Northern Office:
Federation House, Hope Street, Liverpool L1 9BW
Tel: 0151 708 0136; Fax: 0151 708 0139
email: research@dsc.org.uk

Contents

Introduction

Welcome to *A Guide to Major Trusts Volume 2*. This guide contains over 1,100 UK trusts, following on from the 400 largest detailed in *Volume 1*. The trusts in this book collectively give about £171 million a year (trusts in *Volume 1* gave a total of £2.3 billion).

The guide's main aim is to help people raise money from trusts. We aim to provide as much information as we can to enable fundraisers to locate relevant trusts and produce suitable applications. There is also a secondary aim: to be a survey of the work of grant-making trusts, to show where trust money is going and for what purposes.

What trusts do we include?

Our criteria are as follows: trusts must have the potential to give at least £30,000 a year in grants, and these grants should go to organisations in the UK. Many give far more than this, with over 500 giving at least £100,000. There are actually over 100 trusts giving £300,000 or more, which appear large enough to be included in *Volume 1*. However, in a number of cases the income of the trust was lower than the total given in grants for the latest financial year and the level of giving by such trusts may well decrease in future. Other reasons for *Volume 2* inclusion were that the majority of the trust's grants were distributed overseas, or in a particular part of the UK, or that its areas of work were too specific for *Volume 1*. For a full list of the trusts in size order see page ix. Some trusts were included regardless of the fact that they gave less than £30,000 as they have the potential to increase this grant total in the future.

What is excluded?

Trusts which appear large enough to warrant inclusion in this guide may be excluded for the following reasons:

- Some or all of their money is given to individuals, so that £30,000 a year is not available for organisations. The following two guides provide information on trusts which support individuals: *A Guide to Grants for Individuals in Need* and *The Educational Grants Directory*; or www.grantforindividuals.org.uk.
- They give exclusively to local causes in a particular geographical area of England. There are many very large trusts which restrict their grantmaking in this way. So if a trust restricts its giving to a single county or city (or smaller geographical area) it is generally excluded. In this way we hope that Volume 2 remains a national directory and therefore relevant to more people. Details of these trusts can be found in our local trust series.
- They only, or predominantly, support international charities. Such trusts were previously included in this guide, but information on these trusts can now be found in *The Directory of Grant Making Trusts*.
- They are company trusts, established as a vehicle for a company's charitable giving. These are detailed in *The Guide to UK Company Giving*; or www.companygiving.org.uk

DSC's subscription-based website www.trustfunding.org.uk contains details of over 4,200 including those that give UK-wide, locally and internationally.

The layout of this book

The layout of the entries is similar to that established in the previous editions of Volumes 1 and 2, illustrated on page viii. Please also see page vii for other information on how to use this guide.

We have used the word chair in preference to Chairman unless specifically requested to do so by the trust. We have also rounded off the financial figures to allow for easier reading of the guide, which explains why in some places the totals do not add up exactly.

Indexes

The trusts are listed alphabetically in this guide. To help you locate the most relevant trusts there are two indexes, which are a useful starting point.

- Subject index (page 379). This can be useful for identifying trusts with a particular preference for your cause. However, there are many trusts which have general charitable purposes (either exclusively or as well as other specific criteria) but there is no general category in the indexes. It would include so many trusts as to be useless. The index therefore should not be used as the definitive guide to finding the right trusts to apply to.
- Geographical index (page 411). Although trusts limiting their support to one particular area have been excluded, there are many which have some preference for one or more areas. These are listed in this index. Again, in a similar way to the subject index, care is needed. Many trusts state their beneficial area as UK so are not included in this index.

It is important to note that the trusts which appear under a particular index may have other criteria which exclude you. Please always read the entry carefully so you can be sure you fit in with all the trust's criteria. Don't just use the index as a mailing list.

How the guide was compiled

The following are the practical guidelines that were followed to produce this guide:

- concentrate on what the trust does in practice rather than the wider objectives permitted by its formal trust deed
- provide extensive information which will be of the most use to readers i.e. publish the trust's criteria and guidelines for applicants in full, where available
- include, where possible, details of the organisations which have received grants, to give the reader an idea of what the trust supports and the amounts it usually gives
- provide the most up-to-date information available at the time of the research
- include all trusts which meet our criteria for inclusion.

Availability of information

We believe that charities are public bodies not private ones and that charities should be publicly accountable. This view is backed up by Charity Commission regulations and the SORP (Statement of Recommended Practice), last updated in 2005.

SORP 2005 is a guidance document containing recommendations to charities on the preparation of their annual reports and accounts. The updated SORP was implemented for charities with accounting periods commencing 1 April 2005.

Many trusts recognise the importance of providing good, clear information about the work they do. However, there are some that wish to believe they are private bodies and ignore their statutory obligation to provide information to the public. Information held at the Charity Commission on them is sometimes many years out of date.

Failing to supply accounts on request

Charities are required to send their annual report and accounts to the Charity Commission and also to any member of the public who requests them in writing. They are obliged to send the information, although they can make a 'reasonable charge' for this (i.e. the costs of photocopying and postage).

Failure to disclose grants

In SORP 2005, there is a clear emphasis on transparency. The report section is designed to help interested parties understand the work of the charity, providing clarity and structure. It includes sections on: its aims and objectives and the strategies and activities undertaken to achieve them; its achievements and performance; and its plans for the future. SORP 2005 also provides guidance on how grants payable during the year should be analysed. This should be sufficient to give an understanding of how its grant-making activity fits in with its particular charitable objectives.

As in SORP 2000, the 2005 update requires trusts to detail at least 50 grants (if these are of £1,000 or more). Of the trusts listed in this guide, over 100 trusts did not provide any details of the grants they made during the year, where this is the case we have noted this in the 'information available' field.

Failing to provide a narrative report

All trusts should provide a narrative report describing the work of the trust. It is here the trust should give an account of their work during the year with an explanation and analysis of the grants they have made. Many trust reports are extremely brief giving very little away about their activities.

Good trust reports

On a positive note, there are some trusts which provide excellent reports, going beyond the basic 'The objective of this charity is to make grants to charitable institutions.' When they have been particularly interesting or informative for applicants we have reproduced them in the entries. Trusts like Lewis Family Charitable Trust, Rees Jeffreys Road Fund, The Yapp Charitable Trust and I A Ziff Charitable Foundation all provided well-presented and concise details of their activities in their annual reports and accounts.

What's new?

There are a number of trusts which are new to the series. There have also been trusts added from the previous edition of Volume 1 as they are no longer large enough to fit into the top 400, and some from the last edition of this guide have grown so they now warrant an entry in Volume 1. Others are newly established, or newly discovered and include the Country Houses Foundation, St Monica Trust Community Fund and Wallace and Gromit's Children's Foundation.

Applying to trusts

There is a lot of competition for grants. Many trusts in this guide receive more applications than they can support; for example, the Cotton Trust receives upwards of 700 applications each year, awarding about 80 to 100 grants, while in 2005/06 the W G Edwards Charitable Foundation received a total of 231 applications, of which 45 were successful. It is important to do the research: read the trust's criteria carefully and target the right trusts. This can only lead to a higher success rate and save you a lot of time on writing applications which are destined only for the bin. Applying to inappropriate trusts is bad practice and, as well as annoying trusts, can potentially cause problems for future applicants. Trusts tell us that around half of the applications they receive are from outside their stated areas of support.

Unsolicited applications

A number of trusts do not want to receive applications (and usually therefore do not want to appear in the guide). There can be good reasons for this. For example, the trust may do its own research, or support the same list of charities each year. There are some trusts, however, which believe they are a 'private' trust. No registered charity is a private body. We believe trusts should not resent applications but be committed to finding those charities most eligible for assistance.

We include these trusts for two reasons. First, they can state 'no unsolicited applications' simply as a deterrent, in an effort to reduce the number of applications they receive, but will still consider the applications they receive. The second reason relates to the secondary purpose of the guide; to act as a survey of grant-making trusts.

If you choose to write to one of these trusts, do so with caution, and only write to those where your organisation very clearly fits the trust's criteria. We would advise you not to include a stamped addressed envelope and to state that you do not expect a response unless you are eligible. If they do not reply, do not chase them.

Finally …

The research has been conducted as efficiently and carefully as possible. Many thanks to those who have made this easier; trust officers, trustees and others who have helped us. Since this guide was last updated two years ago, the availability of information on trusts has gone up considerably. Over 150 trusts in this guide now have their own websites. More importantly, the advances made by the Charity Commission since 2005 mean that trust accounts and annual reports are now easily accessible and can be downloaded from their website (www.charity-commission.gov.uk). The Charity Commission's 2005/06 Annual Report stated that the proportion of charities for which the most recent accounts and annual returns were held was 87.5%. Our extensive use of their site while researching this publication would generally bear this out.

We are aware that some of this information is incomplete or will become out of date. We are equally sure we will have missed some relevant charities. We apologise for these imperfections. If a reader comes across any omissions or mistakes, please let us know so they can be rectified in the future. We can be contacted at the Liverpool Office Research Department at the Directory of Social Change either by phone on 0151 708 0136 or by email: research@dsc.org.uk

The most up-to-date information will be available on our subscription website www.trustfunding.org.uk which contains all the information that we publish in any of our trust directories. We update as soon as we find new information.

To end on a positive note, there are more potential funders out there than you think, and some do not even receive enough relevant applications. Several trusts in this guide even had unspent surpluses – many complain that they don't receive enough interesting applications. We hope this gives you extra encouragement and wish you success in your fundraising.

How to use this guide

The contents

The entries are in alphabetical order describing the work of over 1,100 trusts. The entries are preceded by a listing of the trusts in order of size and are followed by a subject index and geographical index. There is also an alphabetical index at the back of the guide.

Finding the trusts you need

There are three basic ways of using this guide:

(a) You can simply read the entries through from A to Z (a rather time-consuming activity).

(b) You can look through the trust ranking table which starts on page ix and use the box provided to tick trusts which might be relevant to you (starting with the biggest).

(c) You can use the subject or geographical indexes starting on pages 379 and 411 respectively. Each has an introduction explaining how to use them.

If you use approaches (b) or (c), once you have identified enough trusts to be going on with, read each entry very carefully before deciding whether to apply. Very often their interest in your field will be limited and specific, and may require an application specifically tailored to their needs – or, indeed, no application at all.

Sending off applications which show that the available information has not been read antagonises trusts and brings charities into disrepute within the trust world. Carefully targeted applications, on the other hand, are usually welcomed by most trusts.

A typical trust entry

Name of the charity

The Fictitious Trust

Welfare
£180,000 (2006)
Beneficial area UK

The Old Barn, Main Street, New Town ZC48 2QQ

Correspondent Ms A Grant, Appeals Secretary

Trustees *Trustees Lord Great; Lady Good; A T Home; T Rust; D Prest.*

Charity Commission no. 123456

Information available Full accounts were on file at the Charity Commission.

General The trust supports welfare charities in general, with emphasis on disability, homelessness and ethnic minorities. The trustees will support both captial and revenue projects. 'Specific projects are preferred to general running costs.'

In 2006 the trust had assets of £2.3 million and an income of £187,000. Over 200 grants were given totalling £180,000. Grants ranged from £100 to £20,000, with about half given in New Town. The largest grants were to: New Town Disability Group (£20,000), Homelessness UK (£18,000) and Asian Family Support (£15,000). There were 10 grants of £2,000 to £10,000 including those to the Charity Workers Benevolent Society, Children without Families, New Town CAB and Refugee Support Group.

Smaller grants were given to a variety of local charities, local branches of national charities and a few UK welfare charities.

Exclusions

No grants to non-registered charities, individuals or religious organisations.

Applications

In writing to the correspondent. Trustees meet in March and September each year. Applications should be received by the end of January and the end of July respectively.

Applications should include a brief description of the project and audited accounts. Unsuccessful applicants will not be informed unless an sae is provided.

Summary of main activities
What the trust will do in practice rather than what its trust deed allows it to do.

Grant total (not income) for the most recent year available.

Geographical area of grant-giving including where the trust can legally give and where it gives in practice.

Contact address; telephone and fax numbers; email and website addresses if available.

Contact person

Trustees

Sources of information we used and which are available to the applicant.

Background/summary of activities
A quick indicator of the policy to show whether it is worth reading the rest of the entry.

Financial information
We try to note the assets, ordinary income and grant total, and comment on unusual figures.

Typical grants range to indicate what a successful applicant can expect to receive.

Large grants to indicate where the main money is going, often the clearest indication of trust priorities.

Other examples of grants – listing typical beneficiaries, and where possible the purpose of the grant. We also indicate whether the trust gives one-off or recurrent grants.

Exclusions – listing any area, subjects or types of grant the trust will not consider.

Applications including how to apply and when to submit an application.

Trusts ranked by grant total

Trust	Grants	Main grant areas
☐ Mental Health Foundation	£3.8 million	Mental health and learning disability research
☐ The National Gardens Scheme Charitable Trust	£2.9 million	Nursing, welfare, gardening
☐ B E Perl Charitable Trust	£2 million	Jewish, general
☐ BP Conservation Programme	£2 million	Wildlife and conservation.
☐ Bourneheights Limited	£1.7 million	Orthodox Jewish
☐ Help the Hospices	£1.3 million	Hospices
☐ The Rayne Trust	£1.2 million	Jewish organisations and charities benefiting children, older and young people, at risk groups and people disadvantaged by poverty or socially isolated
☐ Friends of Biala Ltd	£1 million	Jewish
☐ The Sigmund Sternberg Charitable Foundation	£1 million	Jewish, inter-faith causes, general
☐ Tomchei Torah Charitable Trust	£998,000	Jewish educational institutions
☐ Morgan Williams Charitable Trust	£982,000	Christian
☐ The Violet and Milo Cripps Charitable Trust	£980,000	Prison and human rights, general
☐ Truedene Co. Ltd	£916,000	Jewish
☐ The Moulton Charitable Trust	£803,000	Human health/welfare, clinical trials
☐ The Madeline Mabey Trust	£750,000	Medical research, children's welfare and education
☐ The Francis Winham Foundation	£722,000	Welfare of older people
☐ The Ruzin Sadagora Trust	£720,000	Jewish
☐ The Rootstein Hopkins Foundation	£716,000	Arts
☐ The M Bourne Charitable Trust	£713,000	Jewish and cancer related
☐ D D McPhail Charitable Settlement	£698,000	Medical research, disability, older people
☐ The Bernhard Heuberger Charitable Trust	£687,000	Jewish
☐ Largsmount Ltd	£684,000	Jewish
☐ The Law Society Charity	£680,000	Law and justice, worldwide
☐ The Cayo Foundation	£666,000	Crime, medical research, children
☐ The Leverhulme Trade Charities Trust	£662,000	Charities benefiting commercial travellers, grocers or chemists
☐ Royal Artillery Charitable Fund	£657,000	Service charities
☐ The Fawcett Charitable Trust	£654,000	Disability
☐ Premierquote Ltd	£594,000	Jewish, general
☐ The Christina Mary Hendrie Trust for Scottish and Canadian Charities	£593,000	Young and older people, general
☐ Alcohol Education and Research Council	£586,000	Educational and research projects concerning alcohol misuse
☐ The Tufton Charitable Trust	£581,000	Christian
☐ Newpier Charity Ltd	£574,000	Jewish, general
☐ Solev Co. Ltd	£567,000	Jewish charities
☐ Vyoel Moshe Charitable Trust	£561,000	Education, relief of poverty
☐ Dr Mortimer and Theresa Sackler Foundation	£557,000	Arts, hospitals
☐ Country Houses Foundation	£550,000	Preservation of buildings of historic or architectural significance
☐ Friends of Wiznitz Limited	£448,000	Jewish education
☐ Lewis Family Charitable Trust	£545,000	Medical research, health, education, Jewish charities
☐ The Schapira Charitable Trust	£535,000	Jewish

☐ John Laing Charitable Trust	£526,000	General
☐ The Priory Foundation	£513,000	Health and social welfare, especially children
☐ The Rothermere Foundation	£512,000	Education, general
☐ The Catholic Trust for England and Wales (formerly National Catholic Fund)	£498,000	Catholic
☐ The I A Ziff Charitable Foundation	£488,000	General, education, Jewish, arts, young and older people, medicine
☐ The Barbara Ward Children's Foundation	£481,000	Children, mental disability
☐ The Fowler, Smith and Jones Charitable Trust	£473,000	Social welfare
☐ The Grace Charitable Trust	£467,000	Christian
☐ The Kennel Club Charitable Trust	£466,000	Dogs
☐ DG Charitable Trust	£461,000	General
☐ Lloyd's Charities Trust	£452,000	General
☐ Gwyneth Forrester Trust	£450,000	General
☐ The Elizabeth Clark Charitable Trust	£450,000	Palliative care
☐ Melow Charitable Trust	£446,000	Jewish
☐ The Geoff and Fiona Squire Foundation	£433,000	General in the UK
☐ The Kohn Foundation	£432,000	Scientific and medical projects, the arts – particularly music, education, Jewish charities
☐ The Tanner Trust	£432,000	General
☐ The Christopher H R Reeves Charitable Trust	£431,000	Food allergies, disability
☐ The H P Charitable Trust	£430,000	Orthodox Jewish
☐ Mercury Phoenix Trust	£425,000	AIDS, HIV
☐ Alvor Charitable Trust	£422,000	Christian, humanitarian, 'social change'
☐ Epilepsy Research UK	£417,000	Epilepsy
☐ The Pestalozzi Overseas Children's Trust	£417,000	Children
☐ The Norman Family Charitable Trust	£413,000	General
☐ The David Lean Foundation	£412,000	Film production
☐ The Swire Charitable Trust	£412,000	General
☐ The George Cadbury Trust	£407,000	General
☐ The Rowlands Trust	£405,000	General
☐ Joshua and Michelle Rowe Charitable Trust	£402,000	Jewish
☐ J A Clark Charitable Trust	£394,000	Health, education, peace, preservation of the earth, the arts
☐ The Edith Winifred Hall Charitable Trust	£388,000	General
☐ The Ingram Trust	£387,000	General
☐ Lawrence Atwell's Charity	£386,000	Education, young people
☐ Newby Trust Limited	£384,000	Welfare
☐ Royal Masonic Trust for Girls and Boys	£380,000	Children, young people
☐ Gableholt Limited	£379,000	Jewish
☐ Brushmill Ltd	£373,000	Jewish
☐ Old Possum's Practical Trust	£371,000	General
☐ The John Coates Charitable Trust	£370,000	Arts, children, environment, medical, general
☐ Coutts and Co. Charitable Trust	£363,000	General
☐ The Essex Youth Trust	£361,000	Young people, education of people under 25
☐ The Children's Research Fund	£357,000	Child health research
☐ The Robert McAlpine Foundation	£357,000	Children with disabilities, older people, medical research, welfare
☐ The Panacea Society	£355,000	Christian religion, relief of sickness
☐ Keren Mitzvah Trust	£354,000	General
☐ The Locker Foundation	£350,000	Jewish
☐ The Weinstock Fund	£346,000	General
☐ Songdale Ltd	£344,000	Jewish
☐ The Comino Foundation	£343,000	Education

☐ The Persula Foundation	£343,000	Homelessness, disablement, human rights, animal welfare
☐ The W G Edwards Charitable Foundation	£342,000	Care of older people
☐ The Sir Steve Redgrave Charitable Trust	£336,000	Children and young people up to the age of 18 worldwide
☐ The Blueberry Charitable Trust	£333,000	Jewish, relief in need
☐ The Richard Desmond Charitable Trust	£333,000	General
☐ The Matt 6.3 Charitable Trust	£328,000	Christian
☐ The Ellerdale Trust	£326,000	Children
☐ The Millichope Foundation	£326,000	General
☐ The Platinum Trust	£325,000	Disability
☐ The Cecil Rosen Foundation	£322,000	Welfare, especially older people, infirm, people who are mentally or physically disabled
☐ The Richard Wilcox Welfare Charity	£321,000	Animal welfare, health, medical research, welfare of patients, hospitals
☐ The Stoller Charitable Trust	£320,000	Medical, children, general
☐ Woodlands Green Ltd	£319,000	Jewish
☐ Sino-British Fellowship Trust	£316,000	Education
☐ Children's Liver Disease Foundation	£315,000	Organisation benefiting children (up to the age of 18) with liver disease; medical, social and nursing research relating to disorders of the biliary tract
☐ Trumros Limited	£315,000	Jewish
☐ The Clive Richards Charity Ltd	£313,000	Churches, schools, arts, disability, poverty
☐ Fordeve Ltd	£312,000	Jewish, general
☐ The Laduma Dhamecha Charitable Trust	£312,000	General
☐ The Reta Lila Howard Foundation	£312,000	Children, arts, environment
☐ The Lotus Foundation	£307,000	Children and families, women, animal protection, addiction recovery, education.
☐ The Helene Sebba Charitable Trust	£306,000	Disability, medical, Jewish
☐ Salo Bordon Charitable Trust	£305,000	Jewish, some health-related
☐ The Philips and Rubens Charitable Trust	£305,000	General, Jewish
☐ The Breast Cancer Research Trust	£304,000	Research into breast cancer
☐ Ford Britain Trust	£303,000	Arts, community service, education, environment, disability, diversity, hospitals, professional and trade, schools, special schools, young people
☐ The Ward Blenkinsop Trust	£303,000	Medicine, social welfare, general
☐ The Yapp Charitable Trust	£301,000	Social welfare
☐ The Dellal Foundation	£300,000	General, Jewish
☐ The John Beckwith Charitable Trust	£300,000	Young people, general
☐ The R V W Trust	£298,000	Music education and appreciation, relief of need for musicians
☐ Lancashire Environmental Fund	£297,000	Environmental
☐ The Alan Evans Memorial Trust	£297,000	Preservation, conservation
☐ The Britten-Pears Foundation	£297,000	Arts, particularly music by living composers, Britten and Pears, some music education, the environment and occasionally humanitarian causes
☐ The Ulverscroft Foundation	£295,000	People who are sick and visually impaired, ophthalmic research
☐ The Alan and Babette Sainsbury Charitable Fund	£292,000	General
☐ The Constance Green Foundation	£292,000	Social welfare, medicine, health, general
☐ The Football Association National Sports Centre Trust	£292,000	Play areas, community sports facilities
☐ The Ireland Fund of Great Britain	£291,000	Welfare, community, education, peace and reconciliation, the arts
☐ Mrs Waterhouse Charitable Trust	£287,000	Medical, health, welfare, environment, wildlife, churches, heritage
☐ Coral Samuel Charitable Trust	£286,000	General, health, the arts

☐ The Carvill Trust	£285,000	General
☐ The Mr and Mrs F C Freeman Charitable Trust	£285,000	General
☐ SFIA Educational Trust Limited	£280,000	Education
☐ The W O Street Charitable Foundation	£280,000	Education, people with disabilities, young people, health, social welfare
☐ The Union of Orthodox Hebrew Congregation	£279,000	Jewish
☐ Jacobs Charitable Trust	£276,000	Jewish charities, the arts
☐ The Lynn Foundation	£276,000	General
☐ The Equity Trust Fund	£275,000	Theatre
☐ Talteg Ltd	£273,000	Jewish, welfare
☐ Norwood and Newton Settlement	£269,000	Christian
☐ The Fulmer Charitable Trust	£268,000	Developing world, general
☐ The Patrick Frost Foundation	£268,000	General
☐ The Peter Kershaw Trust	£268,000	Medical research, education, social welfare
☐ The Radcliffe Trust	£268,000	Music, crafts, conservation
☐ The Tony Bramall Charitable Trust	£267,000	Children, medical research, sickness
☐ John Coldman Charitable Trust	£266,000	General, Christian
☐ The Inman Charity	£265,000	See below
☐ Lindale Educational Foundation	£263,000	Roman Catholic; education
☐ Saint Sarkis Charity Trust	£262,000	Armenian churches and welfare, disability, general
☐ The Anchor Foundation	£262,000	Christian
☐ Sue Hammerson's Charitable Trust	£261,000	Medical research, relief in need
☐ The Laura Ashley Foundation	£260,000	Art and design, higher education, local projects in mid-rural Wales
☐ The Stone-Mallabar Charitable Foundation	£260,000	Medical, education
☐ Viscount Amory's Charitable Trust	£260,000	Welfare, older people, education
☐ The Whitley Animal Protection Trust	£259,000	Protection and conservation of animals and their environments
☐ Bud Flanagan Leukaemia Fund	£258,000	Leukaemia research and treatment
☐ Elshore Ltd	£256,000	Jewish
☐ The Philip Green Memorial Trust	£256,000	Young and older people, people with disabilities, people in need
☐ Anglo-German Foundation for the Study of Industrial Society	£255,000	Organisations benefiting academics and research workers in the UK and Germany
☐ Burdens Charitable Foundation	£255,000	General
☐ Rokach Family Charitable Trust	£225,000	Jewish, general
☐ The M A Hawe Settlement	£255,000	General
☐ The Batchworth Trust	£254,000	Medical, social welfare, general
☐ Stervon Ltd	£252,000	Jewish
☐ The Barnabas Trust	£252,000	Evangelical Christianity
☐ The Mole Charitable Trust	£252,000	Jewish, general
☐ Michael Marks Charitable Trust	£251,000	Culture, environment
☐ The Daiwa Anglo-Japanese Foundation	£250,000	Anglo–Japanese relations
☐ The Irish Youth Foundation (UK) Ltd (incorporating The Lawlor Foundation)	£250,000	Irish young people
☐ Wychville Ltd	£249,000	Jewish, education, general
☐ The English Schools' Football Association	£248,000	Association football
☐ The Sidney and Elizabeth Corob Charitable Trust	£248,000	General
☐ The Starfish Trust	£247,000	Sickness, medical
☐ The David Laing Foundation	£247,000	Young people, disability, mental health, the arts, general
☐ The Dinwoodie Settlement	£247,000	Postgraduate medical education and research
☐ The Lister Charitable Trust	£247,000	Water-based activities for young people who are disadvantaged

☐ Marbeh Torah Trust	£243,000	Jewish
☐ The Persson Charitable Trust (formerly Highmoore Hall Charitable Trust)	£243,000	Christian mission societies and agencies
☐ Extonglen Limited	£242,000	Orthodox Jewish
☐ J I Charitable Trust	£240,000	General
☐ The Sir Peter O'Sullevan Charitable Trust	£240,000	Animals worldwide
☐ The Duke of Devonshire's Charitable Trust	£239,000	General
☐ The Arnold Burton 1998 Charitable Trust	£236,000	Jewish, medical research, education, social welfare, heritage
☐ Women at Risk	£236,000	Women
☐ Child Growth Foundation	£235,000	Institutions researching child/adult growth disorders, and people with such diseases.
☐ The Geoffrey C Hughes Charitable Trust	£235,000	Nature conservation, environment, performing arts
☐ The Maureen Lilian Charitable Trust	£235,000	General
☐ Garvan Limited	£233,000	Jewish
☐ The Homelands Charitable Trust	£233,000	The New Church, health, social welfare
☐ The Michael and Morven Heller Charitable Foundation	£231,000	University and medical research projects, the arts
☐ The Austin and Hope Pilkington Trust	£229,000	
☐ The Hilda and Samuel Marks Foundation	£229,000	Jewish, general
☐ Lord Barnby's Foundation	£228,000	General
☐ R H Southern Trust	£228,000	Education, disability, relief of poverty, environment, conservation
☐ R S Charitable Trust	£228,000	Jewish, welfare
☐ The Thames Wharf Charity	£228,000	General
☐ The Dyers' Company Charitable Trust	£226,000	General
☐ Davidson Charitable Trust	£225,000	Jewish
☐ Philip Smith's Charitable Trust	£225,000	Welfare, older people, children
☐ The J R S S T Charitable Trust	£225,000	Democracy and social justice
☐ The George Elias Charitable Trust	£223,000	Jewish, general
☐ The James Weir Foundation	£222,000	Welfare, education, general
☐ The Paul Bassham Charitable Trust	£222,000	General
☐ Panahpur Charitable Trust	£221,000	Missionaries, general
☐ The Loftus Charitable Trust	£219,000	Jewish
☐ The Tisbury Telegraph Trust	£219,000	Christian, overseas aid, general
☐ The W F Southall Trust	£219,000	Quaker, general
☐ TJH Foundation	£219,000	General
☐ The Weavers' Company Benevolent Fund	£218,000	Young people at risk from criminal involvement, young offenders and rehabilitation of prisoners and ex-prisoners
☐ The Armourers' and Brasiers' Gauntlet Trust	£217,000	Organisations benefiting young adults, academics, research workers and students; materials science; general
☐ The William Allen Young Charitable Trust	£217,000	General
☐ The Chapman Charitable Trust	£216,000	Welfare, general
☐ The Second Joseph Aaron Littman Foundation	£216,000	General
☐ Menuchar Ltd	£215,500	Jewish
☐ Rees Jeffreys Road Fund	£215,000	Road and transport research and education
☐ The Nigel Moores Family Charitable Trust	£215,000	Arts
☐ The Thornton Foundation	£215,000	General
☐ The Oakdale Trust	£214,000	Social work, medical, general
☐ The Woodroffe Benton Foundation	£214,000	General
☐ The Cyril and Betty Stein Charitable Trust	£213,000	Jewish causes
☐ The Emmandjay Charitable Trust	£213,000	Social welfare, medicine, young people
☐ The Chevras Ezras Nitzrochim Trust	£212,000	Jewish
☐ H and L Cantor Trust	£211,000	Jewish, general
☐ The Coltstaple Trust	£210,000	Relief in need

☐ The John Swire (1989) Charitable Trust	£210,000	General
☐ The Ratcliff Foundation	£210,000	General
☐ The William Brake Charitable Trust	£210,000	General
☐ Carlee Ltd	£209,000	Jewish
☐ The Forest Hill Charitable Trust	£209,000	Mainly Christian causes and relief work
☐ The Cotton Trust	£208,000	Relief of suffering, elimination and control of disease, people who are disabled and disadvantaged
☐ The de Laszlo Foundation	£208,000	The arts, general

☐ The Roger Raymond Charitable Trust	£208,000	Older people, education, medical
☐ The Maurice Wohl Charitable Foundation	£207,000	Jewish, health and welfare
☐ The Steinberg Family Charitable Trust	£206,000	Jewish, health
☐ The Thomas Sivewright Catto Charitable Settlement	£206,000	General
☐ Jacqueline and Michael Gee Charitable Trust	£204,000	Health, education (including Jewish)
☐ The Bestway Foundation	£203,000	Education, welfare, medical
☐ The Eleanor Rathbone Charitable Trust	£203,000	Merseyside, women, unpopular causes
☐ The Simon Heller Charitable Settlement	£203,000	Medical research, science and educational research
☐ Mariapolis Limited	£202,000	Unity, ecumenism
☐ The C A Redfern Charitable Foundation	£202,000	General

☐ The Horne Trust	£201,000	Hospices
☐ The Janet Nash Charitable Settlement	£201,000	Medical, general
☐ The Odin Charitable Trust	£201,000	General
☐ Gordon Cook Foundation	£200,000	Education and training
☐ Ian Mactaggart Trust	£200,000	Education and training, culture, welfare and disability
☐ The Bay Tree Charitable Trust	£200,000	Development work, general
☐ The D W T Cargill Fund	£200,000	General
☐ The Edgar E Lawley Foundation	£200,000	Older people, disability, children, community.
☐ The Tay Charitable Trust	£200,000	General
☐ C B and H H Taylor 1984 Trust	£199,000	Quaker, general

☐ The Sir Edward Lewis Foundation	£199,000	General
☐ Tegham Limited	£197,000	Orthodox Jewish faith, welfare
☐ The Cotton Industry War Memorial Trust	£197,000	Textiles
☐ The Andrew Anderson Trust	£196,000	Christian, social welfare
☐ The Muriel and Gershon Coren Charitable Foundation	£196,000	Jewish, welfare, general
☐ The Saintbury Trust	£196,000	General
☐ The Mark Leonard Trust	£195,000	Environmental education, young people, general
☐ The A B Charitable Trust	£195,000	Promotion and defence of human dignity.
☐ The Barbour Trust	£195,000	Health, welfare
☐ The Holden Charitable Trust	£195,000	Jewish

☐ The Iliffe Family Charitable Trust	£195,000	Medical, disability, heritage, education
☐ The King/Cullimore Charitable Trust	£195,000	General
☐ The Russell Trust	£195,000	General
☐ The Weinberg Foundation	£195,000	General
☐ The British Council for Prevention of Blindness	£194,000	Prevention and treatment of blindness
☐ The Holst Foundation	£194,000	Arts
☐ Brian Mercer Charitable Trust	£192,000	Welfare, medical, visual arts in UK and overseas
☐ The Three Oaks Trust	£192,000	Welfare
☐ Buckingham Trust	£198,000	Christian, general
☐ The Normanby Charitable Trust	£191,000	Social welfare, disability, general

☐ Wallace and Gromit's Children's Foundation	£191,000	Children's healthcare
☐ The Christopher Laing Foundation	£190,000	Social welfare, environment, culture, health and medicine
☐ The Family Foundations Trust (also known as Mintz Family Foundation)	£190,000	General, Jewish
☐ R M Burton 1998 Charitable Settlement	£188,000	Jewish charities, social welfare, education, the arts

☐ The Ellinson Foundation Ltd	£188,000	Jewish
☐ The Stanley Kalms Foundation	£188,000	Jewish charities, general
☐ The William and Katherine Longman Trust	£188,000	General
☐ The George W Cadbury Charitable Trust	£187,000	Population control, conservation, general
☐ The Bassil Shippam and Alsford Trust	£186,000	Young and older people, health, education, learning disabilities, Christian
☐ The Scouloudi Foundation	£185,000	General

☐ Farthing Trust	£185,000	Christian, general
☐ Clover Trust	£184,000	Older people, young people
☐ The Eventhall Family Charitable Trust	£184,000	General
☐ The Holly Hill Charitable Trust	£184,000	Environmental education, conservation and wildlife
☐ The Pet Plan Charitable Trust	£184,000	Dogs, cats and horses
☐ The Toy Trust	£184,000	Children
☐ The Martin Laing Foundation	£183,000	General
☐ The Schmidt-Bodner Charitable Trust	£183,000	Jewish, general
☐ The Truemark Trust	£183,000	General
☐ Wakeham Trust	£183,000	Community development, education, community service by young people

☐ Cuby Charitable Trust	£182,000	Jewish
☐ Ranworth Trust	£182,000	General
☐ Double 'O' Charity Ltd	£181,000	General
☐ The Bernard Kahn Charitable Trust	£180,000	Jewish
☐ The Lauffer Family Charitable Foundation	£180,000	Jewish, general
☐ The Michael and Ilse Katz Foundation	£180,000	Jewish, music, medical, general
☐ The Craps Charitable Trust	£178,000	Jewish, general
☐ The Jean Shanks Foundation	£178,000	Medical research and education
☐ The Joseph and Annie Cattle Trust	£178,000	General
☐ The Jephcott Charitable Trust	£177,000	Alleviation of poverty in developing countries, general

☐ The Michael Bishop Foundation	£177,000	General
☐ AF Trust Company	£175,000	Higher education
☐ The Edith Murphy Foundation	£175,000	General; individual hardship; animals.
☐ The Jean Sainsbury Animal Welfare Trust	£175,000	Animal welfare
☐ Hospital Saturday Fund Charitable Trust	£174,000	Medical, health
☐ The Alchemy Foundation	£173,000	Health and welfare, famine relief overseas
☐ Garrick Charitable Trust	£172,000	Theatre, music, literature, dance
☐ The Lord Faringdon Charitable Trust	£172,000	Medical, general
☐ Lifeline 4 Kids	£170,000	Equipment for children with disabilities
☐ Melodor Ltd	£170,000	Jewish, general

☐ The Almond Trust	£170,000	Christian
☐ The Elsie Pilkington Charitable Trust	£170,000	Equine animals, welfare
☐ St Gabriel's Trust	£169,000	Higher and further religious education
☐ The Sir Victor Blank Charitable Settlement	£169,000	Jewish
☐ National Committee of The Women's World Day of Prayer for England, Wales, and Northern Ireland	£168,000	Christian education and literature
☐ The Broadfield Trust	£168,000	Education
☐ The Mitchell Charitable Trust	£168,000	Jewish, general
☐ The Sammermar Trust	£168,000	General
☐ The Thornton Trust	£167,000	Evangelical Christianity, education, relief of sickness and poverty
☐ The SMB Charitable Trust	£176,000	Christian, general

☐ Barchester Healthcare Foundation	£165,000	Health and social care
☐ Elizabeth Wolfson Peltz Trust	£165,000	Arts and humanities, education and culture, health and welfare, Jewish

☐ The Misses Barrie Charitable Trust	£165,000	Medical, general
☐ The Sir James Roll Charitable Trust	£165,000	General
☐ The Delves Charitable Trust	£164,000	Environment, conservation, medical, general
☐ The Wilfrid and Constance Cave Foundation	£164,000	Conservation, animal welfare, health, welfare
☐ Diana and Allan Morgenthau Charitable Trust	£163,000	Jewish, general
☐ The Bisgood Charitable Trust (registered as Miss Jeanne Bisgood's Charitable Trust)	£163,000	Roman Catholic purposes, older people
☐ The Bristol Charities	£163,000	General
☐ The Doris Field Charitable Trust	£165,000	General
☐ The Sir Jack Lyons Charitable Trust	£163,000	Jewish, arts, education
☐ Mazars Charitable Trust	£162,000	General
☐ Nicholas and Judith Goodison's Charitable Settlement	£162,000	Arts, arts education
☐ T F C Frost Charitable Trust	£161,000	Medical
☐ The Haymills Charitable Trust	£160,000	Education, medicine, welfare, young people
☐ The Leslie Mary Carter Charitable Trust	£160,000	Conservation/environment, welfare
☐ Marchig Animal Welfare Trust	£159,000	Animal welfare
☐ The Peggy Ramsay Foundation	£159,000	Writers and writing for the stage
☐ EMI Music Sound Foundation	£157,000	Music education
☐ John Martin's Charity	£157,000	Religious activity, relief in need, education
☐ The Anglian Water Trust Fund	£157,000	Money advice provision/ in need
☐ The Vandervell Foundation	£156,000	General
☐ East Kent Provincial Charities	£155,000	General, education, younger, older people
☐ The A H and E Boulton Trust	£155,000	Evangelical Christian
☐ The Ashe Park Charitable Trust	£155,000	Possible preference for child-related hospitals and hospices.
☐ The Lillie Johnson Charitable Trust	£155,000	Children, young people who are blind or deaf, medical
☐ The Cazenove Charitable Trust	£154,000	General
☐ Thackray Medical Research Trust	£153,000	History of medical products and of their supply trade
☐ The Leche Trust	£153,000	Preservation and restoration of Georgian art, music and architecture
☐ The Castang Foundation	£152,000	Medical professionals, research workers and people with physical or mental disabilities
☐ The Cecil Pilkington Charitable Trust	£152,000	Conservation, medical research, general on Merseyside
☐ The Elizabeth Casson Trust	£152,000	Oxford Brookes University, other occupational therapy schools and departments, and individual occupational therapists
☐ The Millfield House Foundation	£152,000	Social disadvantage, social policy
☐ The Schreiber Charitable Trust	£152,000	Jewish
☐ The Rock Foundation	£151,000	Christian ministries, see below
☐ The Hope Trust	£150,000	Temperance, Reformed Protestant churches
☐ The Incorporated Church Building Society	£150,000	Living churches benefiting Anglicans
☐ The Miller Foundation	£150,000	General
☐ The Sir Cliff Richard Charitable Trust	£150,000	Spiritual and social welfare
☐ Sir Siegmund Warburg's Voluntary Settlement	£149,000	Medicine and education
☐ Sueberry Ltd	£149,000	Jewish, welfare
☐ The Dumbreck Charity	£149,000	General
☐ The Leigh Trust	£149,000	Drug and alcohol rehabilitation, criminal justice, asylum seekers, racial equality
☐ Peltz Trust	£148,000	Arts and humanities, education and culture, health and welfare, Jewish
☐ The Cooks Charity	£148,000	Catering
☐ The Harbour Foundation	£148,000	Jewish, general
☐ The Paragon Trust	£148,000	General
☐ The R D Turner Charitable Trust	£147,000	General
☐ Calleva Foundation	£146,000	General

☐ Hockerill Educational Foundation	£146,000	Education, especially Christian education
☐ The Dorcas Trust	£146,000	Christian, general
☐ The Mayfield Valley Arts Trust	£145,800	Arts, especially chamber music
☐ The Astor Foundation	£145,000	General
☐ The Hawthorne Charitable Trust	£145,000	General
☐ The Wessex Youth Trust	£144,000	Young people, general
☐ The Marsh Christian Trust	£143,000	General
☐ Spar Charitable Fund	£142,000	Children
☐ The Charles Littlewood Hill Trust	£142,000	Health, disability, service, children (including schools)
☐ The Roger and Sarah Bancroft Clark Charitable Trust	£142,000	Quaker, general
☐ The Rowan Charitable Trust	£141,500	Overseas aid, social welfare, general
☐ British Institute at Ankara	£141,000	Arts, humanities and social sciences of Turkey and the Black Sea region
☐ The Pyke Charity Trust	£141,000	Prisoners and disadvantaged communities
☐ The Cooper Charitable Trust (206772)	£140,000	Medical, disability, Jewish
☐ The Doughty Charity Trust	£140,000	Orthodox Jewish, religious education, relief of poverty
☐ G M Morrison Charitable Trust	£138,500	Medical, education, welfare
☐ The A M Fenton Trust	£138,000	General
☐ The GRP Charitable Trust	£138,000	Jewish, general
☐ The Hugh and Ruby Sykes Charitable Trust	£138,000	General, medical, education, employment
☐ The John Slater Foundation	£138,000	Medical, animal welfare, general
☐ The Bacta Charitable Trust	£136,000	General
☐ The Viznitz Foundation	£136,000	General
☐ Beauland Ltd	£135,000	Jewish
☐ Sir Samuel Scott of Yews Trust	£135,000	Medical research
☐ The Gordon Fraser Charitable Trust	£135,000	Children, young people, environment, arts
☐ The Stella and Alexander Margulies Charitable Trust	£135,000	Jewish, general
☐ Wychdale Ltd	£135,000	Jewish
☐ The Sheldon Trust	£134,000	General
☐ Dischma Charitable Trust	£133,000	General
☐ The Benjamin Winegarten Charitable Trust	£133,000	Jewish
☐ The Billmeir Charitable Trust	£133,000	General, health and medical
☐ The Florence Turner Trust	£132,000	General
☐ The Haydan Charitable Trust	£132,000	Jewish, general
☐ The Helen Roll Charitable Trust	£132,000	General
☐ The Norman Whiteley Trust	£132,000	Evangelical Christianity, welfare, education
☐ The Wilfrid Bruce Davis Charitable Trust	£132,000	Health
☐ Vision Charity	£132,000	Children who are blind, visually impaired or dyslexic
☐ Onaway Trust	£131,000	General
☐ The Music Sales Charitable Trust	£131,000	Children and young people, musical education
☐ The Whitaker Charitable Trust	£131,000	Education, environment, music, personal development
☐ E and E Kernkraut Charities Limited	£130,000	General, education, Jewish
☐ The Mutual Trust Group	£130,000	Jewish, education, poverty
☐ The Sir Harry Pilkington Trust	£130,000	General
☐ The Stewards' Charitable Trust	£130,000	Rowing
☐ G R Waters Charitable Trust 2000	£129,000	General
☐ Seamen's Hospital Society	£129,000	Seafarers
☐ The Annandale Charitable Trust	£129,000	Major UK charities
☐ The Charles Dunstone Charitable Trust	£129,000	General
☐ The Star Charitable Trust	£129,000	General
☐ The Archbishop of Canterbury's Charitable Trust	£128,000	Christianity, welfare
☐ The Gunter Charitable Trust	£128,000	General

☐ The Ian Karten Charitable Trust	£128,000	Technology centres for people who are disabled
☐ The M D and S Charitable Trust	£128,000	Jewish
☐ Prison Service Charity Fund	£126,000	General
☐ Roger Vere Foundation	£125,000	General
☐ The Barbers' Company General Charities	£125,000	Medical and nursing education
☐ Oizer Dalim Trust	£124,000	General
☐ Salters' Charities	£123,000	General
☐ Stuart Hine Trust	£123,000	Evangelical Christianity
☐ The Cross Trust (298472)	£123,000	Christian work
☐ Foundation for Management Education	£122,000	Management studies

☐ St Monica Trust Community Fund	£122,000	Older people, disability
☐ The Baltic Charitable Fund	£122,000	Registered charities benefiting residents of the City of London, seafarers, fishermen, ex-service and service people
☐ The Charlotte Marshall Charitable Trust	£122,000	Roman Catholic, general
☐ The J E Joseph Charitable Fund	£122,000	Jewish
☐ The Linda Marcus Charitable Trust	£122,000	General
☐ Bear Mordechai Ltd	£121,000	Jewish
☐ Marc Fitch Fund	£121,000	Humanities
☐ The Idlewild Trust	£121,000	Performing arts, culture, restoration and conservation, occasional arts education
☐ The Kathleen Laurence Trust	£121,000	Heart disease, arthritis, older people, children with disabilities
☐ The Benham Charitable Settlement	£120,000	General

☐ The Beryl Evetts and Robert Luff Animal Welfare Trust	£120,000	Animal welfare
☐ The Forte Charitable Trust	£120,000	Roman Catholic, Alzheimer's disease, senile dementia
☐ The Leslie Silver Charitable Trust	£120,000	Jewish, general
☐ A M Pilkington's Charitable Trust	£119,000	General
☐ George A Moore Foundation	£119,000	General
☐ Riverside Charitable Trust Limited	£119,000	Health, welfare, older people, education, general
☐ The Burden Trust	£119,000	Christian, welfare, medical research, general
☐ The H and M Charitable Trust	£119,000	Seafaring
☐ The M and C Trust	£118,500	Jewish, social welfare
☐ The Joanna Herbert-Stepney Charitable Settlement (also known as The Paget Charitable Trust)	£118,000	General

☐ The Ogle Christian Trust	£118,000	Evangelical Christianity
☐ Golden Charitable Trust	£117,000	Preservation, conservation
☐ Henry Lumley Charitable Trust	£117,000	General, medical, educational, relief of poverty/hardship
☐ The Park House Charitable Trust	£117,000	Education, social welfare, ecclesiastical
☐ The Powell Foundation	£117,000	People who are elderly or mentally or physically disabled
☐ The Rainford Trust	£117,000	Social welfare, general
☐ The Raymond and Blanche Lawson Charitable Trust	£117,000	General
☐ The Van Neste Foundation	£117,000	Welfare, Christian, developing world
☐ Dromintree Trust	£116,000	General
☐ The C L Loyd Charitable Trust	£116,000	General

☐ The Muriel Edith Rickman Trust	£116,000	Medical research, education
☐ The Peter Minet Trust	£116,000	General
☐ The Vivienne and Samuel Cohen Charitable Trust	£116,000	Jewish, education, health, medical research and welfare
☐ The Batty Charitable Trust	£115,000	General
☐ The Earl of Northampton's Charity	£115,000	Welfare
☐ The John Thomas Kennedy Charitable Foundation	£115,000	General
☐ The Langdale Trust	£115,000	Social welfare, Christian, medical, general
☐ The Stanley Charitable Trust	£115,000	Jewish
☐ The Susanna Peake Charitable Trust	£115,000	General

☐ The Dugdale Charitable Trust	£114,000	Christian education, the advancement of Methodist education and the Catholic religion
☐ Saint Luke's College Foundation	£113,000	See below
☐ The Boltons Trust	£113,000	Social welfare, medicine, education
☐ The Edward and Dorothy Cadbury Trust	£113,000	Health, education, arts
☐ The Harry Bottom Charitable Trust	£113,000	Religion, education, medical
☐ The Moss Charitable Trust	£113,000	Christian, education, poverty, health
☐ Kirschel Foundation	£111,000	Jewish, medical
☐ The Sydney Black Charitable Trust	£111,000	Evangelical Christianity, social welfare, young people, older people and people who are disabled
☐ Rosalyn and Nicholas Springer Charitable Trust	£110,000	Welfare, Jewish, education, general
☐ The Inlight Trust	£110,000	Religion
☐ All Saints Educational Trust	£109,000	Religious education, home economics
☐ The Harding Trust	£109,000	Arts, welfare
☐ The Hyde Charitable Trust – Youth Plus	£109,000	Disadvantaged children and young people
☐ The Bowerman Charitable Trust	£108,000	General
☐ The Charles Skey Charitable Trust	£108,000	General
☐ The Cheruby Trust	£108,000	Welfare, education, general
☐ The Mrs C S Heber Percy Charitable Trust	£108,000	General
☐ EAGA Partnership Charitable Trust	£107,000	Fuel poverty
☐ London Law Trust	£107,000	Health and personal development of children and young people
☐ Ralph and Muriel Emanuel Charity Trust	£107,000	General, Jewish
☐ The Morris Charitable Trust	£107,000	Relief of need, education, community support and development
☐ Ambika Paul Foundation	£106,000	Education, young people
☐ The Ashworth Charitable Trust	£106,000	Welfare
☐ The Atlantic Foundation	£106,000	Education, medical, general
☐ The Phillips Family Charitable Trust	£106,000	Jewish charities, welfare, general
☐ The Ronald Cruickshanks' Foundation	£106,000	Welfare
☐ Kermaville Ltd	£105,000	Jewish
☐ The Charles Shorto Charitable Trust	£105,000	General
☐ The Gibbs Charitable Trust	£105,000	Methodism, international, arts
☐ The Marjorie Coote Animal Charity Fund	£105,000	Wildlife and animal welfare
☐ The Samuel and Freda Parkinson Charitable Trust	£105,000	General
☐ The Searchlight Electric Charitable Trust	£105,000	General
☐ Kollel Gur Trust	£104,000	Jewish
☐ P H Holt Charitable Trust	£104,000	General
☐ Ruth and Conrad Morris Charitable Trust	£104,000	Jewish, general
☐ The Archie Sherman Cardiff Foundation	£104,000	Health, education, Jewish
☐ The Dennis Curry Charitable Trust	£104,000	Conservation, general
☐ The Duke of Cornwall's Benevolent Fund	£104,000	General
☐ The Inland Waterways Association	£104,000	Inland waterways
☐ The Merchant Taylors' Company Charities Fund	£104,000	Education, church, medicine, general
☐ The Samuel Storey Family Charitable Trust	£104,000	General
☐ Hinchley Charitable Trust	£103,000	Mainly evangelical Christian
☐ Meningitis Trust	£103,000	Meningitis in the UK
☐ St James' Trust Settlement	£103,000	General
☐ The Association of Colleges Charitable Trust	£103,000	Further education colleges
☐ The Talbot Village Trust	£103,000	General
☐ The Colonel W H Whitbread Charitable Trust	£102,000	Health, welfare, general
☐ The Corona Charitable Trust	£102,000	Jewish
☐ The Laurence Misener Charitable Trust	£102,000	Jewish, general

☐ The Ouseley Trust	£102,000	Choral services of the Church of England, Church in Wales and Church of Ireland, choir schools
☐ The Sylvia Aitken Charitable Trust	£102,000	Medical research and welfare, general
☐ Ulting Overseas Trust	£102,000	Theological training
☐ Leslie Sell Charitable Trust	£101,000	Uniformed youth groups
☐ Mountbatten Festival of Music	£101,000	Royal Marines and Royal Navy charities
☐ The Follett Trust	£101,000	Welfare, education, arts
☐ The Leopold De Rothschild Charitable Trust	£101,000	Arts, Jewish, general
☐ The Leslie Smith Foundation	£101,000	General
☐ Access 4 Trust	£100,000	Children, welfare
☐ The Ampelos Trust	£100,000	General
☐ The Andrew Salvesen Charitable Trust	£100,000	General
☐ The Craignish Trust	£100,000	Arts, education, environment, general
☐ The Geoffrey Woods Charitable Foundation	£100,000	Young people, education, disability, health
☐ The Grand Order of Water Rats' Charities Fund	£100,000	Theatrical, medical equipment
☐ The Jack Goldhill Charitable Trust	£100,000	Jewish, general
☐ The Mary Webb Trust	£100,000	General
☐ The Michael Sacher Charitable Trust	£100,000	General
☐ The R J Larg Family Charitable Trust	£100,000	Education, health, medical research, arts particularly music
☐ The Richard Langhorn Trust	£100,000	Sport for children
☐ The Worshipful Company of Chartered Accountants General Charitable Trust (also known as CALC)	£100,000	General, education
☐ The Gerald Fogel Charitable Trust	£99,000	Jewish, general
☐ The South Square Trust	£99,000	General
☐ Gerald Micklem Charitable Trust	£98,000	General, health
☐ The Louis and Valerie Freedman Charitable Settlement	£98,000	General
☐ The P and C Hickinbotham Charitable Trust	£98,000	Social welfare
☐ Quercus Trust	£97,000	Arts, general
☐ The Bill Butlin Charity Trust	£97,000	General
☐ The Fitton Trust	£97,000	Social welfare, medical
☐ The Millward Charitable Trust	£96,500	Christian, general
☐ Dixie Rose Findlay Charitable Trust	£96,000	Children, seafarers, blindness, multiple sclerosis
☐ Localtrent Ltd	£96,000	Jewish, educational, religion
☐ Houblon-Norman/George Fund	£95,000	Finance
☐ The Fred and Della Worms Charitable Trust	£95,000	Jewish, education, arts
☐ The Heathcoat Trust	£95,000	Welfare, local causes to Tiverton, Devon
☐ The John Jarrold Trust	£95,000	social welfare, arts, education, environment/conservation, medical research, churches, developing countries
☐ The Oliver Morland Charitable Trust	£95,000	Quakers, general
☐ The Primrose Trust	£95,000	General
☐ Annie Tranmer Charitable Trust	£94,000	General, young people
☐ Princess Anne's Charities	£94,000	Children, medical, welfare, general
☐ The Jessie Spencer Trust	£94,000	General
☐ David Young Charitable Trust	£93,000	General, Jewish
☐ Edith and Ferdinand Porjes Charitable Trust	£93,000	Jewish, general
☐ International Bar Association Educational Trust	£93,000	Legal profession
☐ Lisa Thaxter Trust	£93,000	Children and adolescents with cancer in the UK
☐ The Construction Industry Trust for Youth	£93,000	Building projects benefiting young people
☐ The David Uri Memorial Trust	£93,000	Jewish, general
☐ The DLM Charitable Trust	£93,000	General
☐ The Noel Buxton Trust	£93,000	Child and family welfare, penal matters, Africa
☐ The Peter Samuel Charitable Trust	£93,000	Health, welfare, conservation, Jewish care
☐ Harbo Charities Limited	£92,000	General, education, religion

| ☐ Highcroft Charitable Trust | £92,000 | Jewish, poverty |
| ☐ The Bertie Black Foundation | £92,000 | Jewish, general |

☐ The Sir Jeremiah Colman Gift Trust	£92,000	General
☐ The George and Esme Pollitzer Charitable Settlement	£91,000	Jewish, health, social welfare, general
☐ The Nani Huyu Charitable Trust	£91,000	Welfare
☐ The Treeside Trust	£91,000	General
☐ British Humane Association	£90,000	Welfare
☐ Florence's Charitable Trust	£90,000	Education, welfare, sick and infirm, general
☐ Malbin Trust	£90,000	Jewish, general
☐ The Flow Foundation	£90,000	Welfare, education, environment, medical
☐ The Westcroft Trust	£90,000	International understanding, overseas aid, Quaker, Shropshire
☐ Educational Foundation of Alderman John Norman	£89,000	Education

☐ The Ironmongers' Foundation	£89,000	General
☐ The Moss Spiro Will Charitable Foundation	£89,000	Jewish welfare
☐ The Ormsby Charitable Trust	£89,000	General
☐ Truemart Limited	£89,000	General, Judaism, welfare
☐ The Morgan Charitable Foundation	£88,500	Welfare, hospices, medical, Jewish, general
☐ The H F Johnson Trust	£88,000	Christian education
☐ The Kreditor Charitable Trust	£88,000	Jewish, welfare, education
☐ The P Leigh-Bramwell Trust 'E'	£88,000	Methodist, general
☐ The Stanley Foundation Ltd	£88,000	Older people, medical, education, social welfare
☐ Mrs F B Laurence Charitable Trust	£87,000	Social welfare, medical, disability, environment

☐ SEM Charitable Trust	£87,000	Disability, general, Jewish
☐ The Nigel Vinson Charitable Trust	£87,000	General
☐ The Owen Family Trust	£87,000	Christian, general
☐ The Lyndhurst Trust	£86,200	Christian
☐ Grimmitt Trust	£86,000	General
☐ Malcolm Lyons Foundation	£86,000	Jewish
☐ Peter Barker-Mill Memorial Charity	£86,000	General
☐ The Arnold Lee Charitable Trust	£86,000	Jewish, educational, health
☐ The John Oldacre Foundation	£86,000	Research and education in agricultural sciences
☐ The Marjorie and Geoffrey Jones Charitable Trust	£86,000	General

☐ The Ruth and Lionel Jacobson Trust (Second Fund) No. 2	£48,000	Jewish, medical, children, disability
☐ The Ardwick Trust	£85,000	Jewish, welfare, general
☐ The Dwek Family Charitable Trust	£85,000	General
☐ The Jenour Foundation	£85,000	General
☐ The Joseph and Lena Randall Charitable Trust	£85,000	General
☐ The River Trust	£85,000	Christian
☐ The Thriplow Charitable Trust	£85,000	Higher education and research
☐ The Wyseliot Charitable Trust	£85,000	Medical, welfare, general
☐ Barclays Stockbrokers Charitable Trust	£84,000	General
☐ Marr-Munning Trust	£84,000	Overseas aid

☐ The Casey Trust	£84,000	Children and young people
☐ The N Smith Charitable Settlement	£84,000	General
☐ The Walter Guinness Charitable Trust	£84,000	General
☐ The Willie and Mabel Morris Charitable Trust	£84,000	Medical, general
☐ Famos Foundation Trust	£82,000	Jewish
☐ The Alborada Trust	£82,000	Veterinary causes, social welfare
☐ The Bagri Foundation	£82,000	General
☐ The Shipwrights' Company Charitable Fund	£82,000	Maritime or waterborne connected charities
☐ Blyth Watson Charitable Trust	£81,000	General, UK-based humanitarian organisations

☐ Mickleham Charitable Trust	£81,000	Relief in need
☐ The Animal Defence Trust	£81,000	Animal welfare
☐ The Neville and Elaine Blond Charitable Trust	£81,000	Jewish, education, general
☐ The Norton Foundation	£81,000	Young people under 25 years of age (currently restricted to the areas of Birmingham and the county of Warwick)
☐ The Simon Whitbread Charitable Trust	£81,000	Education, family welfare, medicine, preservation
☐ The Tory Family Foundation	£81,000	Education, Christian, medical
☐ Dame Violet Wills Charitable Trust	£80,000	Evangelical Christianity
☐ Laufer Charitable Trust	£80,000	Jewish
☐ R G Hills Charitable Trust	£80,000	General
☐ Scopus Jewish Educational Trust	£80,000	Jewish education
☐ The Lanvern Foundation	£80,000	Education and health, especially relating to children
☐ The Sydney and Phyllis Goldberg Memorial Charitable Trust	£80,000	Medical research, welfare, disability
☐ Balmain Charitable Trust	£79,000	General in the UK
☐ C and F Charitable Trust	£79,000	Orthodox Jewish charities
☐ The Evangelical Covenants Trust	£79,000	Christian evangelism
☐ The Kyte Charitable Trust	£79,000	Medical, disadvantaged and socially isolated people
☐ The Mason Porter Charitable Trust	£79,000	Christian
☐ The Matthews Wrightson Charity Trust	£79,000	Caring and Christian charities
☐ The Old Broad Street Charity Trust	£79,000	General
☐ The P and D Shepherd Charitable Trust	£79,000	General
☐ W W Spooner Charitable Trust	£79,000	General
☐ Jack Livingstone Charitable Trust	£78,300	Jewish, general
☐ The Edwina Mountbatten Trust	£78,200	Medical
☐ Michael Davies Charitable Settlement	£78,000	General
☐ The Richard and Christine Purchas Charitable Trust	£78,000	Medical research, medical education and patient care
☐ Peter Stormonth Darling Charitable Trust	£77,000	Heritage, medical research, sport
☐ The Llysdinam Trust	£77,000	General
☐ The Lord Cozens-Hardy Trust	£77,000	Medicine, health, welfare, general
☐ The Spear Charitable Trust	£77,000	General
☐ The Marchday Charitable Fund	£76,200	Education, health, social welfare, support groups, overseas aid
☐ David Solomons Charitable Trust	£76,000	Disability
☐ GMC Trust	£76,000	Medical research, healthcare, general
☐ REMEDI	£76,000	Research into disability
☐ The Gilbert and Eileen Edgar Foundation	£76,000	General
☐ The McKenna Charitable Trust	£76,000	Health, disability, education, children, general
☐ The Scurrah Wainwright Charity	£76,000	Social reform, root causes of poverty and injustice
☐ The Sutasoma Trust	£76,000	Education, general
☐ Adenfirst Ltd	£75,000	Jewish
☐ AM Charitable Trust	£75,000	Jewish, general
☐ The B G S Cayzer Charitable Trust	£75,000	General
☐ The Blair Foundation	£75,000	Wildlife, access to countryside, general
☐ The Harold and Alice Bridges Charity	£75,000	General
☐ The Kasner Charitable Trust	£75,000	Jewish
☐ The Richard Newitt Fund	£75,000	Education
☐ The Stanley Smith UK Horticultural Trust	£75,000	Horticulture
☐ The E H Smith Charitable Trust	£74,000	General
☐ The Friarsgate Trust	£74,000	Health and welfare of young and older people
☐ The Magen Charitable Trust	£74,000	Education, Jewish
☐ The Altajir Trust	£73,000	Islam, education, science and research
☐ The Amelia Chadwick Trust	£73,000	General

☐ The Audrey Sacher Charitable Trust	£73,000	Arts, medical, care
☐ The Elaine and Angus Lloyd Charitable Trust	£73,000	General
☐ The Millfield Trust	£73,000	Christian
☐ The Saints and Sinners Trust	£73,000	Welfare, medical
☐ The Eleni Nakou Foundation	£72,500	Education, international understanding
☐ Bill Brown's Charitable Settlement	£72,000	Health, social welfare
☐ The Nadezhda Charitable Trust	£72,000	Christian
☐ Macdonald-Buchanan Charitable Trust	£71,000	General
☐ The Ebenezer Trust	£71,000	Evangelical Christianity, welfare
☐ The Gough Charitable Trust	£71,000	Young people, Episcopal and Church of England, preservation of the countryside, social welfare
☐ The Seedfield Trust	£71,000	Christian, relief of poverty
☐ May Hearnshaw's Charity	£70,000	General
☐ The Charlotte Bonham-Carter Charitable Trust	£70,000	General
☐ The Christopher Cadbury Charitable Trust	£70,000	Nature conservation, general
☐ The Company of Actuaries' Charitable Trust Fund	£70,000	Actuaries, medical research, young and older people, disability, general
☐ The Earl Fitzwilliam Charitable Trust	£70,000	General
☐ The Elizabeth Frankland Moore and Star Foundation	£70,000	General in the UK
☐ The Humanitarian Trust	£70,000	Education, health, social welfare, Jewish
☐ The Pennycress Trust	£70,000	General
☐ The Aurelius Charitable Trust	£69,000	Conservation of culture and the humanities
☐ The Beaverbrook Foundation	£69,000	General
☐ The Hamamelis Trust	£69,000	Ecological conservation, medical research
☐ The Hammonds Charitable Trust	£69,000	General
☐ The Harebell Centenary Fund	£69,000	General, education, medical research, animal welfare
☐ Peter Storrs Trust	£68,000	Education
☐ The Francis Coales Charitable Foundation	£68,000	Historical
☐ The Inverforth Charitable Trust	£68,000	General
☐ The Isaac and Freda Frankel Memorial Charitable Trust	£68,000	Jewish, general
☐ The Naggar Charitable Trust	£67,400	Jewish, general
☐ Ashburnham Thanksgiving Trust	£62,000	Christian
☐ Leonard Gordon Charitable Trust	£67,000	Jewish religious, educational and welfare organisations
☐ Mabel Cooper Charity	£67,000	General
☐ The Barry Green Memorial Fund	£67,000	Animal welfare
☐ The Denise Cohen Charitable Trust	£67,000	Health, welfare, arts, humanities, education, culture, Jewish
☐ The Lambert Charitable Trust	£67,000	Health, welfare, Jewish, arts
☐ The Michael and Shirley Hunt Charitable Trust	£67,000	Prisoners' families, animal welfare
☐ The Ragdoll Foundation	£67,000	Children and the arts
☐ The Scott Bader Commonwealth Ltd	£67,000	
☐ The Artemis Charitable Trust	£66,000	Psychotherapy, parent education, and related activities
☐ The G D Herbert Charitable Trust	£66,000	Medicine, health, welfare, environmental resources
☐ The Leach Fourteenth Trust	£66,000	Medical, disability, environment, conservation, general
☐ The R J Harris Charitable Settlement	£66,000	General
☐ Criffel Charitable Trust	£65,000	Christianity, welfare, health
☐ J A R Charitable Trust	£65,000	Roman Catholic, education, welfare
☐ The Bernard Piggott Trust	£65,000	General
☐ The C J M Charitable Trust	£52,000	Social entrepreneurship
☐ The David and Ruth Behrend Fund	£65,000	General
☐ The Duncan Norman Trust Fund	£65,000	General
☐ The Joyce Fletcher Charitable Trust	£65,000	Music, children's welfare
☐ The Richard Cadbury Charitable Trust	£65,000	General

☐ The Richard Kirkman Charitable Trust	£65,000	General
☐ Minge's Gift and the Pooled Trusts	£64,250	Medical, education, disadvantage, disability
☐ Morris Family Israel Trust	£64,000	Jewish
☐ The Edinburgh Trust, No 2 Account	£64,000	Education, armed services
☐ The Horace and Marjorie Gale Charitable Trust	£64,000	General
☐ The JMK Charitable Trust	£64,000	Children's health
☐ The Lyons Charitable Trust	£64,000	Health, animals, children
☐ The Morel Charitable Trust	£64,000	
☐ The Sue Thomson Foundation	£64,000	Christ's Hospital School, education
☐ Triodos Foundation	£64,000	Overseas development, organics, community development
☐ Alexandra Rose Day	£63,000	Fundraising partnerships with 'people-caring' charities
☐ Matliwala Family Charitable Trust	£63,000	Islam, general
☐ The Exilarch's Foundation	£63,000	Jewish
☐ The Ian Askew Charitable Trust	£63,000	General
☐ The John and Freda Coleman Charitable Trust	£63,000	Disadvantaged young people
☐ A J H Ashby Will Trust	£62,000	Birds, wildlife, education and children
☐ Kinsurdy Charitable Trust	£62,000	General in the UK
☐ The Acacia Charitable Trust	£62,000	Jewish, education, general
☐ The Albert Reckitt Charitable Trust	£62,000	General
☐ The Clifford Howarth Charity Settlement	£62,000	General
☐ The Edgar Milward Charity	£62,000	Christian, humanitarian
☐ The Forbes Charitable Foundation	£62,000	Adults with learning disabilities
☐ The GNC Trust	£62,000	General
☐ The Homestead Charitable Trust	£62,000	See below
☐ The John Apthorp Charitable Trust	£62,000	General
☐ The Lawson Beckman Charitable Trust	£62,000	Jewish, welfare, education, arts
☐ The Salamander Charitable Trust	£62,000	Christian, general
☐ The Vernon N Ely Charitable Trust	£62,000	Christian, welfare, disability, children and young people, overseas
☐ The Peter Morrison Charitable Foundation	£61,100	Jewish, general
☐ Archbishop of Wales Fund for Children	£61,000	Children
☐ The Augustine Courtauld Trust	£61,000	General
☐ The Ian Fleming Charitable Trust	£61,000	Disability, medical
☐ The John Young Charitable Settlement	£61,000	Wildlife, general
☐ Cardy Beaver Foundation	£60,000	General
☐ CLA Charitable Trust	£60,000	Disabled facilities and training
☐ Coats Foundation Trust	£60,000	Textile and thread-related training courses and research
☐ Land Aid Charitable Trust	£60,000	Homelessness, relief of need
☐ Oppenheimer Charitable Trust	£60,000	General
☐ Sinclair Charitable Trust	£60,000	Jewish learning, welfare
☐ The Adamson Trust	£60,000	Children, under 16, who are physically or mentally disabled
☐ The Betterware Foundation	£60,000	Children
☐ The Chetwode Foundation	£60,000	Education, churches, general
☐ The Gamma Trust	£60,000	General
☐ The Merchants' House of Glasgow	£60,000	General
☐ The Michael and Anna Wix Charitable Trust	£60,000	Older people, disability, education, medicine and health, poverty, welfare, Jewish
☐ The Monica Rabagliati Charitable Trust	£60,000	Human and animal welfare, education and medical care and research in the UK
☐ The Spurrell Charitable Trust	£60,000	General
☐ Maranatha Christian Trust	£60,000	Christian, relief of poverty and education of young people
☐ The Jill Franklin Trust	£59,000	Overseas, welfare, prisons, church restoration
☐ The Peter Beckwith Charitable Trust	£59,000	Medical, welfare

☐ Mrs S K West's Charitable Trust	£58,000	General

☐ R S Brownless Charitable Trust	£58,000	Disabled, disadvantage, serious illness
☐ Rita and David Slowe Charitable Trust	£58,000	General
☐ Rofeh Trust	£58,000	General, religious activities
☐ The Alabaster Trust	£58,000	Christian Church and related activities
☐ The Burry Charitable Trust	£58,000	Medicine, health
☐ The James Trust	£58,000	Christianity
☐ Arthur James Paterson Charitable Trust	£57,000	Medical research, welfare of older people and children
☐ Grand Charitable Trust of the Order of Women Freemasons	£57,000	General in the UK and overseas
☐ Help the Homeless Ltd	£57,000	Homelessness
☐ Prairie Trust	£57,000	Third world development, the environment, conflict prevention

☐ The Barnsbury Charitable Trust	£57,000	General
☐ The Cleopatra Trust	£57,000	Health and welfare, disability, homelessness, addiction, children who are disadvantaged, environment
☐ The E L Rathbone Charitable Trust	£57,000	Education and welfare of women, alleviation of poverty
☐ The Harbour Charitable Trust	£57,000	General
☐ The J S F Pollitzer Charitable Settlement	£57,000	General
☐ The Seven Fifty Trust	£57,000	Christian
☐ The Wilkinson Charitable Foundation	£57,000	Scientific research, education
☐ St Michael's and All Saints' Charities	£56,000	Health, welfare
☐ The F H Muirhead Charitable Trust	£56,000	Hospitals, medical research institutes
☐ The Good Neighbours Trust	£56,000	People with mental or physical disabilities

☐ The Harry Dunn Charitable Trust	£56,000	Medical, general
☐ The Noon Foundation	£56,000	General, education, relief of poverty, community relations, alleviation of racial discrimination
☐ The Ove Arup Foundation	£56,000	Construction education and research
☐ The Stephen R and Philippa H Southall Charitable Trust	£56,000	General
☐ The Worshipful Company of Innholders General Charity Fund	£56,000	General
☐ The Bartlett Taylor Charitable Trust	£55,000	General
☐ The Buckinghamshire Masonic Centenary Fund	£55,000	General
☐ The Cripps Foundation	£55,000	Education, healthcare and churches in Northamptonshire, Cambridge University
☐ The Felicity Wilde Charitable Trust	£55,000	Children, medical research
☐ The Huggard Charitable Trust	£55,000	General

☐ The J G Hogg Charitable Trust	£55,000	Welfare, animal welfare, general
☐ The Mishcon Family Charitable Trust	£55,000	Jewish, social welfare
☐ The Modiano Charitable Trust	£55,000	Arts, Jewish, general
☐ The Shanti Charitable Trust	£55,000	General, Christian, international development
☐ The Violet M Richards Charity	£55,000	Older people, sickness, medical research and education
☐ Lord and Lady Lurgan Trust	£54,000	Medical, older people and the arts, in the UK and South Africa
☐ Michael and Leslie Bennett Charitable Trust	£54,000	Jewish
☐ The Adrienne and Leslie Sussman Charitable Trust	£54,000	Jewish, general
☐ The Anna Rosa Forster Charitable Trust	£54,000	Medical research, animal welfare, famine relief
☐ The B and P Glasser Charitable Trust	£54,000	Health, disability, Jewish, welfare

☐ The Catalyst Charitable Trust (formerly the Buckle Family Charitable Trust)	£54,000	Medical, general
☐ The Cuthbert Horn Trust	£54,000	Environment, people with disability/special needs, older people

☐ **The Educational Charity of the Stationers' and Newspaper Makers' Company**	£54,000	Printing education
☐ **The Late St Patrick White Charitable Trust**	£54,000	General
☐ **The Oliver Ford Charitable Trust**	£54,000	Mental disability, housing
☐ **The Scarfe Charitable Trust**	£54,000	Environment, churches, arts
☐ **The W L Pratt Charitable Trust**	£54,000	General
☐ **Blakes Benevolent Trust**	£53,000	General
☐ **Samuel William Farmer's Trust**	£53,000	Education, health, social welfare
☐ **The Charles Henry Foyle Trust**	£53,000	General
☐ **The Hudson Foundation**	£53,000	Older people, general
☐ **The Jewish Youth Fund**	£63,000	Jewish youth work
☐ **The Marina Kleinwort Charitable Trust**	£53,000	Arts
☐ **The Ruth and Jack Lunzer Charitable Trust**	£53,000	Jewish; children, young adults and students; education
☐ **The Searle Charitable Trust**	£53,000	Sailing
☐ **The Tabeel Trust**	£53,000	Evangelical Christian
☐ **Vivdale Ltd**	£53,000	Jewish
☐ **The E M MacAndrew Trust**	£52,500	Medical, children, general
☐ **The Balney Charitable Trust**	£52,000	Preservation, conservation, welfare, service charities
☐ **The David Brooke Charity**	£52,000	Young people, medical
☐ **The EOS Foundation**	£52,000	Money advice provision/ in need
☐ **The John Spedan Lewis Foundation**	£52,000	Natural sciences, particularly horticulture, ornithology, entomology
☐ **Montague Thompson Coon Charitable Trust**	£51,000	Children with disabilities
☐ **Philip Henman Trust**	£51,000	General
☐ **Richard Rogers Charitable Settlement**	£51,000	Housing, homelessness
☐ **The Bintaub Charitable Trust**	£51,000	Jewish, health, education, children
☐ **The Boris Karloff Charitable Foundation**	£51,000	General
☐ **Altamont Ltd**	£50,000	Jewish causes
☐ **Elizabeth Hardie Ferguson Charitable Trust Fund**	£50,000	Children, medical research, health, hospices
☐ **Ellador Ltd**	£50,000	Jewish
☐ **Forbesville Limited**	£50,000	Jewish, education
☐ **Limoges Charitable Trust**	£50,000	Animals, services, general
☐ **Morris Leigh Foundation**	£50,000	Jewish, general
☐ **Mrs H R Greene Charitable Settlement**	£50,000	General, particularly at risk-groups, poverty, social isolation
☐ **Nathan Charitable Trust**	£60,000	Evangelical Christian work and mission
☐ **Rosanna Taylor's 1987 Charity Trust**	£50,000	General
☐ **Stephen Zimmerman Charitable Trust**	£50,000	Jewish
☐ **The Albert Van Den Bergh Charitable Trust**	£50,000	Medical/disability, welfare
☐ **The Amanda Smith Charitable Trust**	£50,000	General
☐ **The Colin Montgomerie Charitable Foundation**	£50,000	General
☐ **The Daily Prayer Union Charitable Trust Ltd**	£50,000	Evangelical Christian
☐ **The Diana Edgson Wright Charitable Trust**	£50,000	Animal conservation, welfare, general
☐ **The Dorus Trust**	£50,000	Health and welfare, disability, homelessness, addiction, children who are disadvantaged, environment
☐ **The Elephant Trust**	£50,000	Visual arts
☐ **The Epigoni Trust**	£50,000	Health and welfare, disability, homelessness, addiction, children who are disadvantaged, environment
☐ **The John Wilson Bequest Fund**	£50,000	Health, welfare, women
☐ **The Kass Charitable Trust**	£50,000	Welfare, nursing homes, older people, education, cancer, Jewish
☐ **The Minos Trust**	£50,000	Christian, general
☐ **The Nyda and Oliver Prenn Foundation**	£50,000	Arts, education, health
☐ **The Puebla Charitable Trust**	£50,000	Community development work, relief of poverty

☐ The Simpson Education and Conservation Trust	£50,000	Environmental conservation, with a preference for the neotropics (South America)
☐ Belljoe Tzedoko Ltd	£49,000	Jewish
☐ Edwin George Robinson Charitable Trust	£49,000	Medical research
☐ Harry Bacon Foundation	£49,000	Medical, animal welfare
☐ Nesswall Ltd	£49,000	Jewish
☐ The Adnams Charity	£49,000	General
☐ The Carpenter Charitable Trust	£49,000	Humanitarian and Christian outreach
☐ The Golsoncott Foundation	£49,000	The arts
☐ The Grimsdale Charitable Trust	£49,000	Christian religion, education, poverty
☐ The National Manuscripts Conservation Trust	£49,000	Conserving manuscripts
☐ The Oikonomia Trust	£49,000	Christian
☐ The Rose Flatau Charitable Trust	£49,000	Jewish, general
☐ Moshal Charitable Trust	£48,000	Jewish
☐ Pearson's Holiday Fund	£48,000	Young people who are disadvantaged
☐ Sumner Wilson Charitable Trust	£48,000	General
☐ The DLA Piper Rudnick Gray Cary Charitable Trust (previously known as the DLA Charitable Trust)	£48,000	General
☐ The Frognal Trust	£48,000	Older people, disability, blindness/ophthalmological research, environmental heritage, youth development
☐ The Rest Harrow Trust	£48,000	Jewish, general
☐ The Sir William Coxen Trust Fund	£48,000	Orthopaedic hospitals or other hospitals or charities doing orthopaedic work
☐ The Solo Charitable Settlement	£48,000	Jewish, general
☐ The Weinstein Foundation	£48,000	Jewish, medical, welfare
☐ Blatchington Court Trust	£47,000	Supporting vision-impaired people under the age of 30
☐ Buckland Charitable Trust	£47,000	General, international development, welfare and health research
☐ The Anthony and Elizabeth Mellows Charitable Settlement	£47,000	National heritage, Church of England churches
☐ The Elmgrant Trust	£47,000	General charitable purposes, education, arts, social sciences
☐ The Emerton-Christie Charity	£47,000	Health, welfare, disability, arts
☐ The Geoffrey John Kaye Charitable Foundation	£47,000	Jewish, general
☐ The Lady Eileen Joseph Foundation	£47,000	General
☐ The Langley Charitable Trust	£47,000	Christian, general
☐ The Lord and Lady Haskel Charitable Foundation	£47,000	Jewish, social-policy research, arts, education
☐ The Max Reinhardt Charitable Trust	£47,000	Deafness, fine arts promotion
☐ WH Smith Group Charitable Trust	£47,000	General
☐ Mary Homfray Charitable Trust	£46,000	General
☐ Sir John and Lady Amory's Charitable Trust	£46,000	General
☐ The AS Charitable Trust	£46,000	Christian, development, social concern
☐ The Baker Charitable Trust	£46,000	Mainly Jewish, older people, sickness and disability, medical research
☐ The Barbara Whatmore Charitable Trust	£46,000	The arts and music and the relief of poverty
☐ The Cemlyn-Jones Trust	£46,000	See below
☐ The Emmanuel Kaye Foundation	£46,000	Medical research, welfare and Jewish organisations.
☐ The Kathleen Trust	£46,000	Musicians
☐ The Sandy Dewhirst Charitable Trust	£46,000	General
☐ The Whitecourt Charitable Trust	£46,000	Christian, general
☐ West London Synagogue Charitable Fund	£46,000	Jewish, general
☐ P G and N J Boulton Trust	£45,000	Christian
☐ Ryklow Charitable Trust 1992 (also known as A B Williamson Charitable Trust)	£45,000	Education, health and welfare

☐ The British Dietetic Association General and Education Trust Fund	£45,000	Dietary and nutritional issues
☐ The Crescent Trust	£45,000	Museums and the arts, occasionally health and education
☐ The Cumber Family Charitable Trust	£45,000	General
☐ The Dorothy Jacobs Charity	£45,000	Jewish care, medical
☐ The Hinrichsen Foundation	£45,000	Music
☐ The Loke Wan Tho Memorial Foundation	£45,000	Environment, medical causes, conservation organisations and overseas aid organisations
☐ Anona Winn Charitable Trust	£44,000	Health, medical, welfare
☐ Col-Reno Ltd	£44,000	Jewish
☐ Hartnett Charitable Trust	£44,000	Environmental issues
☐ The Alexis Trust	£44,000	Christian
☐ The Bothwell Charitable Trust	£44,000	Disability, health, older people, conservation
☐ The Demigryphon Trust	£44,000	Medical, education, children, general
☐ The Gretna Charitable Trust	£44,000	General
☐ The International Foundation for Arts and Culture	£44,000	Music
☐ The Loseley and Guildway Charitable Trust	£44,000	General
☐ The Red Rose Charitable Trust	£44,000	Older people and people with disabilities
☐ The Worshipful Company of Spectacle Makers' Charity	£44,000	Visual impairment, City of London, general
☐ William Dean Countryside and Educational Trust	£44,000	Education in natural history, ecology and conservation
☐ The D C Moncrieff Charitable Trust	£43,500	Social welfare, environment
☐ Candide Charitable Trust	£43,000	Music, visual arts
☐ Daisie Rich Trust	£43,000	General
☐ Panton Trust	£43,000	Animal wildlife worldwide; environment UK
☐ The A and R Woolf Charitable Trust	£43,000	General
☐ The E C Sosnow Charitable Trust	£43,000	Arts, education
☐ The Harry Crook Foundation	£43,000	Education, general
☐ The Linmardon Trust	£42,500	General
☐ The C S Kaufman Charitable Trust	£42,000	Jewish
☐ The Catholic Charitable Trust	£42,000	Catholic organisations
☐ The Hesed Trust	£42,000	Christian
☐ The Huxham Charitable Trust	£42,000	Christianity, churches and organisations, development work
☐ The Katzauer Charitable Settlement	£42,000	Jewish
☐ The M Miller Charitable Trust	£42,000	Jewish, general
☐ The P Y N and B Hyams Trust	£42,000	Jewish, general
☐ The Robert Clutterbuck Charitable Trust	£42,000	Service, sport and recreation, natural history, animal welfare and protection
☐ The Victor Adda Foundation	£42,000	Fan Museum
☐ William Arthur Rudd Memorial Trust	£42,000	General in the UK, and certain Spanish charities
☐ Miss M E Swinton Paterson's Charitable Trust	£41,000	Church of Scotland, young people, general
☐ Sir Alec Black's Charity	£41,000	Relief in need
☐ The Col W W Pilkington Will Trusts The General Charity Fund	£41,000	Welfare
☐ The John Feeney Charitable Bequest	£41,000	Arts, heritage and open spaces.
☐ The Manny Cussins Foundation	£41,000	Older people, children, health, Jewish, general
☐ The Personal Finance Society Charitable Foundation	£41,000	General
☐ The Smith Charitable Trust	£41,000	General
☐ The Torah Temimah Trust	£41,000	Orthodox Jewish
☐ The Willie Nagel Charitable Trust	£41,000	Jewish, general
☐ Alan and Sheila Diamond Charitable Trust	£40,000	Jewish, general
☐ Penny in the Pound Fund Charitable Trust	£40,000	Hospitals, health-related charities
☐ Roama Spears Charitable Settlement	£40,000	Welfare causes
☐ Stanley Spooner Deceased Charitable Trust	£40,000	Children, general

☐ The Dorothy Holmes Charitable Trust	£40,000	General
☐ The Fanny Rapaport Charitable Settlement	£40,000	Jewish, general
☐ The Huntly and Margery Sinclair Charitable Trust	£40,000	Medical, general
☐ The John Ritblat Charitable Trust No. 1	£40,000	Jewish, general
☐ The Rhododendron Trust	£40,000	Welfare, overseas aid and development, culture
☐ The Theodore Trust	£40,000	Christian education

☐ The Viscountess Boyd Charitable Trust	£40,000	Conservation, horticulture, education and preservation
☐ Audrey Earle Charitable Trust	£39,000	General, with some preference for animal welfare and conservation charities
☐ Briggs Animal Welfare Trust	£39,000	Animal welfare
☐ Cowley Charitable Foundation	£39,000	Registered charities
☐ The Beacon Trust	£39,000	Christian
☐ The Charter 600 Charity	£39,000	General charitable.
☐ The Cyril Shack Trust	£39,000	Jewish, general
☐ The Eva Reckitt Trust Fund	£39,000	Welfare, relief in need, extension and development of education, victims of war
☐ The Gould Charitable Trust	£39,000	General
☐ The Harold Joels Charitable Trust	£39,000	Jewish

☐ The ISA Charity	£39,000	See below
☐ The John M Archer Charitable Trust	£39,000	General.
☐ The Oak Trust	£39,000	General
☐ The Rayden Charitable Trust	£39,000	Jewish
☐ The William and Ellen Vinten Trust	£39,000	Industrial education, training and welfare
☐ A H and B C Whiteley Charitable Trust	£38,000	Art, environment, general
☐ Mrs Maud Van Norden's Charitable Foundation	£38,000	General
☐ Oppenheim Foundation	£38,000	General
☐ The Dennis Alan Yardy Charitable Trust	£38,000	General
☐ The Dorothy Hay-Bolton Charitable Trust	£38,000	Deaf, blind

☐ The Hare of Steep Charitable Trust	£38,000	General
☐ The Little Foundation	£38,000	Neurodevelopmental disorders
☐ The Moette Charitable Trust	£38,000	Education, Jewish
☐ The Ruth and Stuart Lipton Charitable Trust	£38,000	Jewish, general
☐ The Thistle Trust	£38,000	Arts
☐ Thomas Betton's Charity for Pensions and Relief-in-Need	£38,000	Disadvantage
☐ Tudor Rose Ltd	£38,000	Jewish
☐ William P Bancroft (No 2) Charitable Trust and Jenepher Gillett Trust	£38,000	Quaker
☐ Armenian General Benevolent Union London Trust	£37,000	Armenian education, culture and welfare
☐ Brian Abrams Charitable Trust	£37,000	Jewish/Israeli

☐ Eric Abrams Charitable Trust	£37,000	Jewish/Israeli
☐ The Astor of Hever Trust	£37,000	Young people, medical research, education
☐ The Berkeley Reafforestation Trust	£37,000	Reafforestation projects
☐ The Carron Charitable Trust	£37,000	Environment, education, medicine
☐ The Forces Trust	£37,000	Military charities
☐ The Glanrose Trust	£37,000	General
☐ The Kay Williams Charitable Foundation	£37,000	Medical research, disability, general
☐ The Leonard Trust	£37,000	Christian, overseas aid
☐ G S Plaut Charitable Trust	£36,000	Sickness, disability, Jewish, older people, Christian, general
☐ The Emily Fraser Trust	£36,000	Specific trades, older people

☐ The Fairway Trust	£36,000	General
☐ The Hellenic Foundation	£36,000	Greek, general
☐ The Linley Shaw Foundation	£36,000	Conservation

☐ The N B Johnson Charitable Settlement	£36,000	Education, older people
☐ The Oakmoor Charitable Trust	£36,000	General
☐ The Tillett Trust	£36,000	Classical music
☐ The Alan Sugar Foundation	£35,000	Jewish charities, general
☐ The Alex Roberts-Miller Foundation	£35,000	See below
☐ The Dickon Trust	£35,000	General
☐ The Nicholas Joels Charitable Trust	£35,000	Jewish, medical welfare, general
☐ The R M Douglas Charitable Trust	£35,000	General
☐ The Stone Ashdown Charitable Trust	£35,000	Equality and discrimination
☐ The Swan Trust	£35,000	General, arts, culture
☐ S C and M E Morland's Charitable Trust	£34,250	Quaker, sickness, welfare, peace and development overseas
☐ Paul Lunn-Rockliffe Charitable Trust	£34,000	Christianity, poverty, infirm people, young people
☐ Beatrice Hankey Foundation Ltd	£34,000	Christian
☐ Percy Hedley 1990 Charitable Trust	£34,000	General
☐ The Appletree Trust	£34,000	Disability, sickness, poverty
☐ The Beaufort House Trust	£34,000	Christian, education
☐ The Birmingham Hospital Saturday Fund Medical Charity and Welfare Trust	£34,000	Medical
☐ The Misselbrook Trust	£34,000	General
☐ The Oliver Borthwick Memorial Trust	£34,000	Homelessness
☐ Birthday House Trust	£33,000	General
☐ C J Cadbury Charitable Trust	£33,000	General
☐ D G Albright Charitable Trust	£33,000	General
☐ Lance Coates Charitable Trust 1969	£33,000	Biological and ecological approach to food production
☐ Mageni Trust	£33,000	Arts
☐ The A B Strom and R Strom Charitable Trust	£33,000	Jewish, general
☐ The Ann and David Marks Foundation	£33,000	Jewish charities
☐ The Annie Schiff Charitable Trust	£33,000	Orthodox Jewish education
☐ The Hanley Trust	£33,000	Social welfare and people who are disadvantaged
☐ The R H Scholes Charitable Trust	£33,000	Children and young people who are disabled or disadvantaged, hospices, preservation and churches
☐ Martin McLaren Memorial Trust	£32,000	General
☐ Sydney E Franklin Deceased's New Second Charity	£32,000	Development
☐ The Alderman Joe Davidson Memorial Trust	£32,000	Jewish, general
☐ The Cyril Taylor Charitable Trust	£32,000	Education
☐ The Ericson Trust	£32,000	See below
☐ The Millhouses Charitable Trust	£32,000	Christian, overseas aid, general
☐ The Mountbatten Memorial Trust	£32,000	Technological research in aid of disabilities
☐ The New Durlston Trust	£32,000	Christian, overseas development
☐ The Ripple Effect Foundation	£32,000	General
☐ Zephyr Charitable Trust	£32,000	Housing, health, environment, third world
☐ Mejer and Gertrude Miriam Frydman Foundation	£32,000	Jewish, Jewish education
☐ Mandeville Trust	£31,000	Cancer, young people and children
☐ Miss V L Clore's 1967 Charitable Trust	£31,000	General
☐ Peter Black Charitable Trust	£31,000	General
☐ The Barbara Welby Trust	£31,000	Animal welfare, medical, general
☐ The C B Trust	£31,000	General, Jewish
☐ The Halecat Trust	£31,000	General
☐ The T B H Brunner Charitable Settlement	£31,000	Heritage, arts, general
☐ The Sylvanus Charitable Trust	£30,000	Animal welfare, Roman Catholic
☐ Nazareth Trust Fund	£30,000	Christian, in the UK and developing countries
☐ The David Pickford Charitable Foundation	£30,000	Christian, general

☐ The Edith Maud Ellis 1985 Charitable Trust	£30,000	Quaker, ecumenical, education, peace and international affairs, general
☐ The Helen and Geoffrey de Freitas Charitable Trust	£30,000	Preservation of wildlife and rural England, conservation and environment, cultural heritage
☐ The Joseph and Queenie Gold Charitable Trust	£30,000	Jewish, general
☐ The Pallant Charitable Trust	£30,000	Church music
☐ The Rock Solid Trust	£30,000	Christian worldwide
☐ The Rural Trust	£30,000	Countryside
☐ Webb Memorial Trust	£30,000	Higher education (particularly economic and social sciences), the furthering of democracy and human rights, and development in Eastern Europe

☐ Mildred Duveen Charitable Trust	£29,000	General
☐ The F J Wallis Charitable Settlement	£29,000	General
☐ The John Rayner Charitable Trust	£29,000	General
☐ The Lady Tangye Charitable Trust	£29,000	Catholic, overseas aid, general
☐ The Lili Tapper Charitable Foundation	£29,000	Jewish
☐ Betard Bequest	£28,000	Welfare, disability, older people
☐ Premishlaner Charitable Trust	£28,000	Jewish
☐ The Constance Paterson Charitable Trust	£28,000	Medical research, health, welfare of children, older people, service people
☐ The Dorema Charitable Trust	£28,000	Medicine, health, welfare, education, religion
☐ The Late Sir Pierce Lacy Charity Trust	£28,000	Roman Catholics, general

☐ The Nancy Kenyon Charitable Trust	£28,000	General
☐ The TUUT Charitable Trust	£28,000	General, but with a bias towards trade-union-favoured causes
☐ Murphy-Neumann Charity Company Limited	£27,500	People who are older, very young with disabilities
☐ MYA Charitable Trust	£27,000	Jewish
☐ The Kessler Foundation	£27,000	General, Jewish
☐ The Macfarlane Walker Trust	£27,000	Education, the arts, social welfare, general
☐ The Mount 'A' Charity Trust	£27,000	General, children, arts
☐ St Andrew Animal Fund	£26,000	Animal welfare
☐ The Boughton Trust	£26,000	Elderly people, disability, youth groups, conservation projects
☐ The Eagle Charity Trust	£26,000	General, international, medicine, welfare

☐ The Geoffrey Burton Charitable Trust	£26,000	General
☐ The Mushroom Fund	£26,000	General
☐ The Pamela Champion Foundation	£26,000	General, disability
☐ The Roger Brooke Charitable Trust	£26,000	General
☐ Cobb Charity	£25,000	Sustainable development, green initiatives and related education
☐ Henry T and Lucy B Cadbury Charitable Trust	£25,000	Quaker causes and institutions, health, homelessness, support groups, developing countries
☐ Lord Forte Foundation	£25,000	Hospitality
☐ Mr and Mrs F E F Newman Charitable Trust	£25,000	Christian, overseas aid and development
☐ The Bluff Field Charitable Trust	£25,000	General
☐ The Calpe Trust	£25,000	Relief work

☐ The Camilla Samuel Fund	£25,000	Medical research
☐ The Delius Trust	£25,000	See below
☐ The John and Celia Bonham Christie Charitable Trust	£25,000	Local and national organisations
☐ Miss Doreen Stanford Trust	£24,000	General
☐ Miss S M Tutton Charitable Trust	£24,000	Music
☐ The Chownes Foundation	£24,000	Religion, relief-in-need, social problems
☐ The Green and Lilian F M Ainsworth and Family Benevolent Fund	£24,000	Young people, disability, health, medical research, disadvantage, older people, general
☐ The Mizpah Trust	£23,500	General

☐ **Maurice Fry Charitable Trust**	**£23,000**	Medicine, health, welfare, humanities, environmental resources, international
☐ **The Almshouse Association**	**£23,000**	Almshouses
☐ **The Linden Charitable Trust**	**£23,000**	General
☐ **The Maurice Wohl Charitable Trust**	**£23,000**	Jewish, health, welfare, arts, education
☐ **Wingfield's Charitable Trust**	**£23,000**	General
☐ **The Angela Gallagher Memorial Fund**	**£22,000**	Children and young people, Christian, humanitarian, education
☐ **The Malcolm Chick Charity**	**£22,000**	General
☐ **The Pat Allsop Charitable Trust**	**£22,000**	Education, medical research, children, relief of poverty
☐ **The Lind Trust**	**£21,200**	Social action, Christian service
☐ **Gerald Finzi Charitable Trust**	**£21,000**	Music
☐ **The Conservation Foundation**	**£21,000**	Environmental and conservation
☐ **The Peter Stebbings Memorial Charity**	**£21,000**	General
☐ **James and Grace Anderson Trust**	**£20,000**	Cerebral palsy
☐ **The Barbara A Shuttleworth Memorial Trust**	**£20,000**	Disability
☐ **The Geoffrey Berger Charitable Trust**	**£20,000**	General
☐ **Miss E B Wrightson's Charitable Settlement**	**£19,000**	Music education, inshore rescue, recreation
☐ **The Bedfordshire and Hertfordshire Historic Churches Trust**	**£19,000**	Churches
☐ **The Carlton House Charitable Trust**	**£19,000**	Bursaries, Jewish, general
☐ **The Chandris Foundation**	**£19,000**	Greek, shipping, children
☐ **The Daniel Rivlin Charitable Trust**	**£19,000**	Jewish, general
☐ **Jimmy Savile Charitable Trust**	**£18,000**	General
☐ **The Metropolitan Drinking Fountain and Cattle Trough Association**	**£17,000**	Provision of pure drinking water
☐ **The Keith and Freda Abraham Charitable Trust**	**£16,000**	General
☐ **Barbara May Paul Charitable Trust**	**£15,000**	Older people, young people, medical care and research, preservation of buildings
☐ **The Lionel Wigram Memorial Trust**	**£14,000**	General
☐ **Unity Charitable Trust**	**£11,000**	General
☐ **The Florian Charitable Trust**	**£10,000**	General
☐ **The Rowing Foundation**	**£8,800**	Water sports
☐ **The Gamlen Charitable Trust**	**£8,600**	Legal education, general
☐ **Sellata Ltd**	**£8,000**	Jewish, welfare
☐ **The Derek Crowson Charitable Settlement**	**£8,000**	General
☐ **Finnart House School Trust**	**£7,000**	Jewish children and young people in need of care
☐ **The A M McGreevy No 5 Charitable Settlement**	**£6,000**	General
☐ **The Ayrton Senna Foundation**	**£600**	Children's health and education

The A B Charitable Trust

Promotion and defence of human dignity

£195,000 (2004/05)

Beneficial area UK and developing world.

Macmillan House, 96 Kensington High Street, London W8 4SG

Correspondent T M Denham, Secretary

Trustees *Y J M Bonavero; D Boehm; Mrs A G M-L Bonavero; Miss C Bonavero; Miss S Bonavero; O Bonavero; P Bonavero.*

CC Number 1000147

Information available Accounts were on file at the Charity Commision.

General The trust gives grants for the promotion of human dignity. It is the trust's aim to make 'medium-sized' grants for a three-year period, subject to satisfactory reports and reapplication to the trustees.

In 2004/05 the trust had assets of £332,000 and an income of £206,000. Grants totalled £195,000.

From 507 applications received, grants to 51 organisations were made generally ranging from £500 to £5,000. The exceptions being £12,000 to Prison Reform Trust, £7,500 to a Kurdish human rights project and £6,000 to Link Community Development.

Other beneficiaries included Amber, Bethany Project, Detention Advice Service, Forth Sector, Holy Cross Centre Trust, Howard League for Penal Reform, Mustard Tree New Bridge, Portland College and Scottish Refugee Council (£5,000 each); Nurses' Welfare Trust (£4,000); Cancer Resource Centre, Kemp Hospice and Wells for India (£3,000 each); Ark Trust, Find Your Feet, Headway, Kurdish Cultural Centre, Rethink Disability and Theresa's House in Peterborough (£2,500 each); Gingerbread Centre and Voices for Ballet (£2,000); and St Mary's Church in Ilfracombe (£500).

Exclusions No support for medical research, animal welfare, expeditions, scholarships, conservation and environment.

Applications In writing to the secretary, up to a maximum of four A4 pages if appropriate, plus the most recent detailed audited accounts. The trustees meet on a quarterly basis in March, June, September and December.

Applications should be from UK registered charities only.

The Keith and Freda Abraham Charitable Trust

General

£16,000 (2004/05)

Beneficial area UK and local organisations in north Devon.

Church Farm, Yelland Road, Fremington, Devon EX32 3BU

Tel. 01271 345326

Correspondent C J Bartlett, Secretary

Trustees *K N Abraham; H J Purnell; C D Squire; C T Mill; G L Watts; J Sunderland; M J Ford.*

CC Number 288672

Information available Accounts were obtained from the Charity Commission website.

General The trust only supports major UK charities with which the trustees sympathise and local projects in north Devon.

In 2004/05 the trust had assets of £203,000 and an income of £29,000. Grants were made totalling £16,000. Donations included £7,000 to Barnstaple Rugby Football Club; £2,000 to Pilton Community College; £1,000 each to Park Community School and Headway – North Devon; £500 each to Barnstaple Male Voice Choir, Jigsaw Furniture Project, Salvation Army, West of England School for the Blind and Barnstaple Poverty Action Group; £250 to St Loye's Exeter; and £150 to 1st Chulmleigh Scouts.

Applications In writing to the correspondent.

Brian Abrams Charitable Trust

Jewish/Israeli

£37,000 (2004/05)

Beneficial area UK and Israel.

130–132 Nantwich Road, Crewe CW2 6AZ

Correspondent Robert Taylor

Trustees *Betty Abrams; Brian Abrams; Eric Abrams; Gail Gabbie.*

CC Number 275941

Information available Accounts were on file at the Charity Commission.

General In 2004/05 this trust had assets of £1 million, an income of £56,000 and made grants totalling £37,000.

Beneficiaries were Rabbi Nachman of Breslov Charitable Foundation (£5,300); Centre for Torah Education Trust, Halacha Lemoshe Trust and Friends of Ohr Akiva Institution (£5,000 each); United Jewish Israel Appeal (£4,100), the Heathlands Village (£2,600), Hale Adult Hebrew Education Trust (£1,600); Rainsough Charitable Trust (£1,300) and Manchester Jewish Federation; and UK Friends of Magen David Adom (£1,000 each).

Exclusions No grants to individuals.

Applications The trust has previously stated that its funds are fully committed and applications are not invited.

Eric Abrams Charitable Trust

Jewish/Israeli

£37,000 (2004/05)

Beneficial area UK and Israel.

130–132 Nantwich Road, Crewe CW2 6AZ

Correspondent Robert Talyor

Trustees *Brian Abrams; Eric Abrams; Steven Abrams.*

CC Number 275939

Information available Accounts were on file at the Charity Commission.

General In 2004/05 the trust had assets of just over £1 million and an income of £56,000. Grants to 29 organisations totalled £37,000.

There were 11 grants of £1,000 each or more listed in the accounts. Beneficiaries included Rabbi Nachman of Breslov Charitable Foundation (£5,300); Centre for Torah Education Trust, Friends of Ohr Akiva Institution and Halacha Lemoshe Trust (£5,000 each); United Jewish Israel Appeal (£4,300), the Heathlands Village (£2,500), Hale Adult Hebrew Education Trust (£1,600); Manchester Jewish Federation (£1,100);

and UK Friends of Magen David Adom (£1,000).

Other donations of less than £1,000 each totalled £3,800.

Exclusions No grants to individuals.

Applications The trust has previously stated that its funds are fully committed and applications are not invited.

The Acacia Charitable Trust

Jewish, education, general

£62,000 (2004/05)

Beneficial area UK and Israel.

5 Clarke's Mews, London W1G 6QN

Tel. 020 7486 1884 **Fax** 020 7487 4171

Correspondent Mrs Nora Howland, Secretary

Trustees K D Rubens; Mrs A G Rubens; S A Rubens.

CC Number 274275

Information available Full accounts were on file at the Charity Commission.

General In 2004/05 the trust had assets of £2.2 million and an income of £99,000. Grants to 31 organisations totalled £62,000. Grants ranged from £24 to £18,000, although most were for under £1,000 each. About half of the grants were recurrent. They were given in the following categories:

Community Care & Welfare – 11 grants totalling £14,000
Beneficiaries included Community Security Trust (£5,000), Jewish Care, Norwood Ltd and Spanish and Portuguese Jews Congregation (£2,000 each), World Jewish Aids (£1,800), Centre for Jewish-Christian Relations (£750), St John's Wood Society (£25).

Arts & Culture – 8 grants totalling £16,000
Beneficiaries included the Jewish Museum (£10,000), Royal National Theatre (£6,000), Painters and Stainers Charity (£100), Friends of the Royal Academy (£55) and JewisH Historical Society (£30).

Education – 5 grants totalling £20,000
Beneficiaries included University of Reading (£18,000), Institute for Jewish Policy Research (£1,000), British Friends of Haifa University (£500) and Friends of Israel Education Foundation (£100)

General – 1 grant totalling £500
United Jewish Israel Appeal was the sole beneficiary

Medical and Disability – 6 grants totalling £1,500
Beneficiaries included NSPCC (£1,000); Camphill Village Trust, Great Ormond Street Hospital for Children and King Edward VII Hospital (£100 each); and Cancer Research UK (£50).

Overseas – 1 grant totalling £10,000
World Jewish Relief was the sole beneficiary.

Exclusions No grants to individuals.

Applications In writing to the correspondent.

Access 4 Trust

Children, welfare

Around £100,000 (2005/06)
Beneficial area UK, Bangladesh, Ghana and Uganda.

Slater Maidment, 7 St James's Square, London SW1Y 4JU

Tel. 020 7930 7621

Correspondent C Sadlow

Trustees Miss S M Wates; J R F Lulham.

CC Number 267017

Information available Information was obtained from the Charity Commission website.

General Most grants, as in previous years, were to assist families in need with funds also going overseas to developing countries. In 2005/06 the trust had an income of £5,000 and a total expenditure of £125,000. Further information was not available.

In previous years the trust has supported WOMANKIND, Post-Adoption Centre; Entebbe All-Christian Women's Association; Action on Disability and Development, Friends of the Centre for the Rehabilitation of the Paralysed, Barnabus Tinkasmire – Uganda, Child Advocacy International, UNIFAT School – Uganda, Newham Bengali Community Trust, Concern Universal, Girls Growth and Development, Bawku Women's Development Association, Acid Survivors Foundation, Kuga Fong Community Association and Prisoners Abroad.

Exclusions No grants to individuals or sponsorships.

Applications In writing to the correspondent.

The Company of Actuaries' Charitable Trust Fund

Actuaries, medical research, young and older people, disability, general

£70,000 (2004/05)
Beneficial area UK and overseas, with a preference for the City of London.

Park Way, West Drive, Cheltenham GL50 4LB

Correspondent Graham Lockwood, Almoner

Trustees R Cobley, Chair; G Bannerman; A Benke; J Jolliffe; J Medlock; Fiona Morrison.

CC Number 280702

Information available Accounts were on file at the Charity Commission.

General The trust gives grants to registered charities working in the following areas:

- medical research and support
- young people
- people who are elderly or disabled
- general.

The trust believes that charities should be run efficiently and an indicator of efficiency is the level of administration expenses as a percentage of gross income. Therefore charities which can demonstrate effective expenditure will be preferred, with the ratio of volunteers to paid staff seen as an indicator of effectiveness.

There is also a preference for smaller charities where a comparatively small donation can be of real help, and for charities having a substantial connection with the City of London or surrounding boroughs.

In 2004/05 it had assets of £255,000 and an income of £66,000. Grants to organisations totalled £70,000.

Master's donations
Up to 20% of the funds are given solely

at the discretion of the Master of the Company each year. In 2004/05 grants totalling £8,900 were approved to four organisations. These were British Red Cross (£5,000), Reeds School Foundation (£1,800), Federation of London Youth Clubs (£1,500) and City of London SG Bursary Fund (£600).

Research
Under the research category, £13,500 went to the Chronic Disease Research Fellowship.

Education
Donations for educational purposes totalled £17,000, which was distributed in various bursaries and prizes.

City of London
In total, seven City charities were supported. Beneficiaries were Lord Mayor Appeal 2004 (£2,000), the City & Guilds of London Institute, Mansion House Scholarship Scheme and Sheriffs' and Recorder's Fund (£500 each) and Metropolitan Public Gardens' Association, Musicians Benevolent Fund and Royal British Legion – City Poppy Appeal (£100 each).

Other grants
Other grants, all for £500 each, went to 53 charities and totalled £27,000. Beneficiaries included ADD Family Support Centre, Brainwave, Central and East Housing Trust, the Children's Trust, Child Victims of Torture, Get Connected, Listening Ear, Marie Curie Cancer Care, New Bridge, the Pace Centre, St Barnabas Hospice, Teens in Crisis, Tower Hamlets Friends and Neighbours and Wells for India.

Exclusions No grants for the propagation of religious or political beliefs, the maintenance of historic buildings or for conservation. The trustees do not usually support an organisation which has received a grant in the previous 24 months.

The trust does not normally consider applications from individuals.

Applications In writing to the correspondent, including a copy of the most recent audited accounts, aims and purposes of the charity and details of the purposes for which the grant is needed.

The Adamson Trust

Children, under 16, who are physically or mentally disabled

£60,000 mostly to organisations (2005/06)

Beneficial area UK, but preference will be given to requests on behalf of Scottish children.

Barnshaw, Comrie Road, Crieff, Perthshire PH7 4BQ

Tel. 01764 656048

Correspondent K B Devine, Secretary

Trustees *R C Farrell; J W H Allen; Dr H Kirkwood; Dr M MacDonald Simpson; Mrs A Cowan.*

SC Number SC016517

Information available Limited information was provided by the trust.

General Formerly known as Miss Agnes Gilchrist Adamson's Trust, grants are made to organisations providing holidays for children under 16 who are mentally or physically disabled. Donations are usually one-off.

About £60,000 is given in grants each year, mostly to organisations.

Previous beneficiaries have included Barnardos Dundee Family Support Team, Children's Hospice Association Scotland, Lady Hoare Trust for Physically Disabled Children, Hopscotch Holidays, Over the Wall Gang Group, Peak Holidays, React, Scotland Yard Adventure Centre, Sense Scotland, Special Needs Adventure Play Ground and Scottish Spina Bifida Association.

Exclusions Unsolicited applications.

Applications On a form available from the correspondent. A copy of the latest audited accounts should be included together with details of the organisation, the number of children who would benefit and the proposed holiday. Applications are considered in January, May and September.

The Victor Adda Foundation

Fan Museum

£42,000 (2004/05)

Beneficial area UK, but in practice Greenwich.

c/o Kleinwort Benson Trustees, PO Box 57005, 30 Gresham Street, London EC2V 7PG

Correspondent The Trustees

Trustees *Mrs H E Alexander; R J Gluckstein; A Mosseri.*

CC Number 291456

Information available Full accounts were on file at the Charity Commission.

General Virtually since it was set up in 1984, the foundation has been a stalwart supporter of the Fan Museum in Greenwich. Both the foundation and the museum share a majority of the same trustees; the foundation also owns the property in which the museum is sited and has granted it a 999-year lease.

In 2004/05 the trust had assets stood at £1.1 million and an income of £32,000. The Fan Museum received all of the grant total (£42,000). In the previous year one other small grant was made to Child to Child Trust (£5,000).

Applications In writing to the correspondent. Only successful applications are notified of a decision.

Adenfirst Ltd

Jewish

£75,000 (2004)

Beneficial area Worldwide.

479 Holloway Road, London N7 6LE

Correspondent I M Cymerman, Governor

Trustees *Mrs H F Bondi; I M Cymerman; Mrs R Cymerman.*

CC Number 291647

Information available Accounts were on file at the Charity Commission.

General The trust supports mostly Jewish organisations, with a preference for education and social welfare. In 2004 it had an income of £92,000 and made 17 grants totalling £75,000.

Beneficiaries included Centre for Torah Education Trust, Friends of Harim

Establishments, Friends of Ponevez, Ohr Alciva Institutions and Torah Vechesed L'Ezra Vesa'ad (£8,000 each); Colel Polen Kupath Ramban (£5,700); Girls' School Zichron Yaakov, Pardes Chana Institutions and Yeshiva Gedola Zichron Yaakov (£5,000 each); Friends of Mosdos Bnei Brak (£4,000); Emunah Education Centre (£3,500); and Kollel Mesilath Yesharim and Ner Shimri Binyamina (£3,000 each).

Applications In writing to the correspondent.

The Adnams Charity

General

£49,000 (2004/05)

Beneficial area Southwold in Suffolk, and the area within 25 miles of Southwold Church, excluding Ipswich and Norwich.

Sole Bay Brewery, Southwold, Suffolk IP18 6JW

Tel. 01502 727200 **Fax** 01502 727267

Correspondent The Charity Administrator

Trustees *Simon Loftus; Jonathan Adnams; Melvyn Horn; Andrew Wood; Emma Hibbert; Guy Heald.*

CC Number 1000203

Information available Accounts were on file at the Charity Commission.

General Set up in 1990 the charity gives support to a wide variety of organisations including those involved with social welfare, education, recreation, the arts and historic buildings. The trust 'aims to make a real difference to the work of dozens of local organisations which have difficulty in attracting funds from elsewhere' and it prefers to give 'small sums to achieve specific ends'.

Grants are generally one-off for specific items. The trustees are reluctant to give grants to cover ongoing running costs. Grants are not made in successive years.

In 2003/04 the trust had an income of £53,000 and the charity made grants totalling £49,000. Grants were broken down as follows, shown with examples of beneficiaries in each category:

Education – 5 grants
Debenham High School (£3,000); Ashely

School – Lowestoft (£2,500); and Friends of Brampton Primary School (£500).

Health and social welfare – 13 grants
Warren Hill Prison (£5,000); Sailors' Families' Society (£1,000); St John's Housing Trust (£900); John Grooms Charity (£500); Suffolk Carers (£450); and John Turner House Day Centre (£350).

Arts – 5 grants
Nutmeg Puppet Company (£1,000), Beccles Choral Society (£500) and Sound of Wangford (£300).

Recreation – 6 grants
DanceEast (£1,800); Halesworth Dolphins (£860); Get-a-Life Gang (£740); and Ilkesthall St Lawrence Pre-School and Sizewell and Leiston Karate Club (£500 each).

Community facilities – 6 grants
Leiston Guide Hut (£3,900); St Andrew's Church – Walberswick (£1,000); Fortrey Heap Hall – Barnby (£940); and Middleton Village Hall (£500).

Exclusions No grants for UK organisations unless they are a local branch in the area of benefit. No grants to individuals, however public bodies and charities may apply on behalf of an individual. No grants for church bell repairs. The trust does not provide raffle prizes, nor does it provide sponsorship of any kind.

Applications In writing to the correspondent. Trustees meet quarterly.

AF Trust Company

Higher education

£175,000 (2004/05)

Beneficial area England.

34 Chapel Street, Thatcham, Berkshire RG18 4QL

Correspondent P D Welch, Secretary

Trustees *Anthony J Knapp; Jane Ross; Denise Everitt; Alison A Reid; Martin Wynne-Jones; David C L Savage; Graham E Raikes; Malcolm J Ace; Jeremy Lindley; David Leah; Sue McHugh; Andrew Murphy.*

CC Number 1060319

Information available Accounts were on file at the Charity Commission.

General Support is given for charitable purposes connected with the provision of higher education in England. The

company currently provides property services and leasing facilities to educational establishments on an at arms length basis.

In 2005/06 the trust had assets of £225,000. The total income and expenditure for the year was £5 million. However, it is worth noting that this relates to the funds used to lease buildings from educational establishments and then enter into lease-back arrangements rather than describing the size of funds available. Grants were made totalling £158.000.

Grants went to University of Nottingham (£36,000), Imperial College (£28,000), University of Southampton (£22,000), University of Reading (£18,000), University of Brighton (£17,000) and University of Surrey (£11,000).

Other donations of £10,000 or less totalled £27,000.

Exclusions No grants to individuals.

Applications In writing to the correspondent. However, unsolicited applications are only accepted from higher education institutions within England.

The Green and Lilian F M Ainsworth and Family Benevolent Fund

Young people, disability, health, medical research, disadvantage, older people, general

£24,000 (2005/06)

Beneficial area UK, with some preference for northwest England.

Royal Bank of Scotland plc, Trust Estate Services, Capital House, 2 Festival Square, Edinburgh EH3 9SU

Tel. 0131 523 2679

Correspondent The Senior Trust Officer

Trustee *The Royal Bank of Scotland plc.*

CC Number 267577

Information available Full accounts were on file at the Charity Commission.

General The trust states that each year it supports UK charities covering a wide range of interests mainly involving people of all ages who are disadvantaged by either health or other circumstances.

In 2005/06 the trust had assets of £76,000 and an income of £25,000. Grants totalled £24,000. The largest grant was awarded to Care International Tsunami Fund, whilst the majority of grants amounted to £1,000 or less each. Other beneficiaries included the Association of Blind Asians, Step By Step, Garden Science Trust, Edinburgh Young Carers, Everyman Cancer and the Shooting Star Trust (£1,000 each); Ayrshire Rolling Cougars, Barnardo's, Ting a Ling and the City of Exeter YMCA (£500 each); Arena Care & Repair (£350) and Dogs for the Disabled and FACT (£250 each).

Exclusions No grants to individuals or non-registered charities.

Applications On a form available from the correspondent.

The Sylvia Aitken Charitable Trust

Medical research and welfare, general

£102,000 (2005/06)
Beneficial area UK, with a preference for Scotland.

Fergusons Chartered Accountants, 24 Woodside, Houston, Renfrewshire PA6 7DD

Tel. 01505 610412 **Fax** 01505 614944

Correspondent Mrs N Ferguson, Administrator

Trustees *Mrs S M Aitken; Mrs M Harkis; J Ferguson.*

SC Number SC010556

Information available Full accounts were provided by the trust.

General Whilst this trust has a preference for medical projects, it has general charitable purposes, making small grants to a wide range of small local organisations throughout the UK, particularly those in Scotland. In 2005/06 the trust had assets of £4 million and an income of £273,000. Grants paid

during the year totalled £102,000, which were broken down as follows:

Grants of over £1,000 each included: Association for International Cancer Research, British Lung Foundation and Tenovus Scotland (£5,000 each); Motor Neurone Disease Association, the Roy Castle Lung Cancer Foundation and the Royal Scots Dragoon Guards Museum Trust (£3,000 each); Friends of the Lake District and Epilepsy Research Trust (£2,000 each); and Neurosciences Foundation and the Pain Relief Foundation (£1,000 each).

Grants of less than £1,000 each included: Sense Scotland (£750); British Stammering Association, Disabled Living Foundation, Network for Surviving Stalking, the Seeing Ear and Speakability (£500 each) and Young Minds, Tall Ships Youth Trust, Scottish Child Psychotherapy Trust, Sleep Scotland, the Barn Owl Trust and Wood Green Animal Shelters (£400).

Exclusions No grants to individuals: the trust can only support UK registered charities.

Applications In writing to the correspondent. Applicants should outline the charity's objectives and current projects for which funding may be required. The trustees meet at least twice a year, usually in March/April and September/October.

The Alabaster Trust

Christian Church and related activities

£58,000 (2004/05)
Beneficial area UK and overseas.

1 The Avenue, Eastbourne, East Sussex BN21 3YA

Tel. 01323 644579 **Fax** 01323 417643

Email john@caladine.co.uk

Correspondent J R Caladine, Accountant

Trustees *G A Kendrick; Mrs J Kendrick; Mrs A Sheldrake.*

CC Number 1050568

Information available Accounts were on file at the Charity Commission, without a list of grants.

General This trust was set up to make grants to evangelical Christian organisations in the UK and abroad. In

2004/05 it had an income of £48,000, mostly derived from Gift Aid donations and grants totalled £58,000. Further information was not available.

Exclusions No grants to individuals.

Applications In writing to the correspondent. The trustees meet to consider grants quarterly, in March, June, September and December.

The Alborada Trust

Veterinary causes, social welfare

£82,000 (2004/05)
Beneficial area Worldwide.

c/o Boodle Hatfield, 89 New Bond Street, London W1S 1DA

Correspondent The Trustees

Trustees *E M Garston; Miss K E Rausing; D J Way.*

CC Number 1091660

Information available Accounts were on file at the Charity Commission.

General This trust was established in October 2001 with an initial donation of £5 million being settled in April 2002.

Unsolicited applications are not requested as the trustees prefer to restrict the area of benefit to:

- Veterinary causes in the United Kingdom and Ireland with activities primarily devoted to the welfare of animals and/or in their associated research.
- Projects throughout the world associated with the relief of poverty, human suffering, sickness or ill health.

In 2004/05 the trust had assets of £5.5 million and an income of £241,000. Grants to 10 organisations totalled £82,000.

Beneficiaries were Emmaus (£25,000), Newmarket Upper School (£15,000), British Racing School (£10,000), Canine Partners (£8,000), Kilcloon Community Centre (£5,700), British Red Cross Society, Chellington Project and National Hospital for Neurology and Neurosurgery (£5,000 each) and Interact Reading Service (£1,000).

Applications Funds are fully committed. The trust does not accept unsolicited applications.

D G Albright Charitable Trust

General

£33,000 (2005/06)

Beneficial area UK, with a preference for Gloucestershire.

Old Church School, Hollow Street, Great Somerford, Chippenham, Wiltshire SN15 5JD

Correspondent Richard G Wood, Trustee

Trustees *Hon. Dr G Greenall; R G Wood.*

CC Number 277367

Information available Accounts were on file at the Charity Commission.

General In 2005/06 the trust had assets of £1.2 million and an income of £37,000. Grants were made totalling £33,000.

Donations included those to: Game Conservancy Trust and St Luke's Hospital for the Clergy (£3,000 each); Bromesberrow Parochial Church Council (£2,500); British Empire and Commonwealth Museum, the Children's Society, the Countryside Foundation for Education, Dean and Chapter – Gloucester Cathedral, the Family Haven – Gloucester, Gloucestershire Macmillan Cancer Service and SSAFA – Gloucester branch (£2,000 each); Butterfly Conservation, Gloucestershire County Association for the Blind, the Guild of Handicraft Trust and RNIB Talking Books (£1,000 each); and Bibles for Children (£300).

Exclusions Grants are not usually made to individuals.

Applications In writing to the correspondent.

The Alchemy Foundation

Health and welfare, famine relief overseas

£173,000 (2005/06)

Beneficial area UK and overseas.

Trevereux Manor, Limpsfield Chart, Oxted, Surrey RH8 0TL

Correspondent Annabel Stilgoe, Trustee

Trustees *Richard Stilgoe; Annabel Stilgoe; Revd Donald Reeves; Esther Rantzen; Alex Armitage; Andrew Murison; Holly Stilgoe; Jack Stilgoe; Rufus Stilgoe; Joseph Stilgoe; Dr Jemima Stilgoe.*

CC Number 292500

Information available Accounts were on file at the Charity Commission.

General This foundation was established in 1985 as The Starlight Foundation. It receives most of its income from a share of the royalties from the works of Richard Stilgoe and changed its name in 1987. It provides support for all forms of welfare, ranging from the material, mental and spiritual welfare of children, older people and people with disabilities or mental, physical or terminal illnesses to assisting those affected by famine. It also supports medical research. It shares the same board of trustees with The Orpheus Trust, a connected charity, which regularly receives large grants from this foundation.

In 2004/05 the total income was £330,000, of which £268,000 came from donations received and £62,000 was generated from the assets, which totalled £2.8 million. Grants were made totalling £173,000.

Applications In writing to the correspondent.

Alcohol Education and Research Council

Educational and research projects concerning alcohol misuse

£586,000 (2005/06)

Beneficial area UK.

Room 178, Queen Anne Business Centre, 28 Broadway, London SW1H 9JX

Tel. 020 7340 9502

Website www.aerc.org.uk

Correspondent Andrea Tilouche, Committees and Grants Manager

Trustees *Dr Noel Olsen, Chair; Prof. V Berridge; Ms J Craig; Prof. C Day; Ms R Emlyn-Jones; Prof. D Foxcroft; I Ford; Prof. I Gilmore; Prof. G Hastings; Prof. R Hobbs; Dr E Kaner; Mrs L King-Lewis; Dr P Li; D Munro.*

CC Number 284748

Information available Accounts were on file at the Charity Commission.

General Developing people and improving the evidence base

The main aims of the council are to increase the capacity of individuals and organisations to deal with alcohol issues and also to develop the evidence base.

Two types of projects will be considered. The first will be rigorous research projects that focus upon improving the evidence base. The second will aim to develop people and organisations.

Small grants

Funding is available for small projects up to a maximum of £5,000. Small grants could fund small research projects, pilot research studies or demonstration projects with a strong evaluation component. They could also fund projects that increase the capacity of individuals and organisations to deal with alcohol issues.

The council offers a limited number of studentships on a competitive basis to students who are working in the alcohol field and wish to acquire appropriate professional qualifications by following a taught course.

In 2005/06 it had assets of £13.2 million and an income of £660,000. Charitable expenditure totalled £586,000, of which research and action projects totalled £365,000, small grants totalled £116,000 and studentships totalled £105,000.

Applications An application form is available on request and can be downloaded from the website.

Full information about grant application procedures is available on the council's website.

Alexandra Rose Day

Fundraising partnerships with 'people-caring' charities

£63,000 (2005)

Beneficial area UK.

5 Mead Lane, Farmhan, Surrey GU9 7DY

Tel. 01252 726171 **Fax** 01252 727559

Email enquiries@alexandraroseday.org.uk

Website www.alexandraroseday.org.uk

Correspondent The Chief Executive

CC Number 211535

Information available Accounts were on file at the Charity Commission.

General Alexandra Rose Day was founded in 1912 by Queen Alexandra, as a practical way of marking the fiftieth anniversary of her first arrival in the UK from Denmark. The charity offers partnership in fundraising and other forms of support for smaller, people-caring charities. Its activities include an annual national Flag Day (Alexandra Rose Day) and regular raffles.

For Flag Days, this charity makes the arrangements and supplies equipment whilst the partner charity provides the flag sellers. Alexandra Rose Day makes an immediate grant to the partner equivalent to 90% of its gross collection. For raffles, Alexandra Rose Day organises the prizes and prints the tickets, which the partner charity sells and receives 80% of all gross sales.

The charity organises its own fundraising events including the Rose Ball and donates any surplus through its Special Appeal Fund, an annual programme of grants designed to bring immediate, practical benefits to people-caring charities and voluntary groups.

In 2005 the trust had assets of £635,000 and an income of £262,000. Grants were made during the year totalling £63,000.

The following organisations received grants in excess of £1,000 each during the year: Young Bristol (£2,700), League of Friends Rutland Hospital (£2,000), St Vincent de Paul Society – Woking (£1,400), League of Friends Shipston-on-Stour Hospitals and North Cotswold Volunteer Help Centre (£1,300 each), Every Link Counts (£1,200), Friends of Royal Brompton Hospital (£1,100) and Friends of Abbeyfield Orpington Society and Sea Cadets Corp – Reading (£1,000 each).

Exclusions Only charities participating in Flag Days or raffles are eligible to apply. Grants are not made to individuals or charities operating overseas.

Applications In writing to the correspondent.

The Alexis Trust

Christian

£44,000 (2004/05)

Beneficial area UK and overseas.

14 Broadfield Way, Buckhurst Hill, Essex IG9 5AG

Correspondent Prof. D W Vere, Trustee

Trustees *Prof. D W Vere; C P Harwood; Mrs E M Harwood; Mrs V Vere.*

CC Number 262861

Information available The information for this entry was provided by the trust.

General Support is given to a variety of causes, principally Christian. In 2004/05 the trust had an income of £45,000 and made grants totalling £44,000.

The sum of £29,000 was distributed to various missionary societies including County Workers Essex (£2,000), UCCF (£1,200); and Barnabas Fund, Epping Forest Youth for Christ and Scripture Gift Mission (£1,000 each). A further 93 unlisted beneficiaries received a total of £22,000.

A further £15,000 was distributed to 223 short-term missionary projects.

Exclusions No grants for building appeals, or to individuals for education.

Applications In writing to the correspondent, although the trust states that most of the funds are regularly committed.

All Saints Educational Trust

Religious education, home economics

£109,000 to organisations (2005/06)

Beneficial area UK and Commonwealth.

St Katharine Cree Church, 86 Leadenhall Street, London EC3A 3DH

Tel. 020 7283 4485 **Fax** 020 7621 9758

Email aset@aset.org.uk

Website www.aset.org.uk

Correspondent The Clerk

Trustees *The Rt Revd and Rt Hon. Richard Chartres, Bishop of London,*
Chair; Mrs M R Behenna; T L Guiver; Revd Canon P Hartley; Ms D McCrea; Miss A Philpott; Revd K G Riglin; Mrs A Rose; D Trillo; Mrs B Harvey; J K Hoskin; Dr C C A Pearce; Revd Canon D J Whittington.

CC Number 312934

Information available Accounts were on file at the Charity Commission.

General This trust was established from the proceeds of the closure of two teacher training colleges in London, one of which worked within a Christian framework and the other of which specialised in domestic science (now home economics and technology). Keeping in line with the former colleges, the trust's objectives are advancing higher or further education by:

- allowing individuals to attend a further education institute, or otherwise pursue a course of study to enable them to gain teaching qualifications
- promoting in other ways education and training
- promoting research and development of education, particularly in religious studies and home economics and similar subjects.

It achieves these aims by providing financial assistance to 'institutions that seek to undertake imaginative projects that enhance higher and further education', with the trustees distributing their grants in the way they feel will make the maximum possible difference to the institutions and their respective communities or spheres of influence.

In terms of grants to organisations, the trustees are keen to support proactive projects that promote the development of education, particularly in the areas of religious education, home economics and related areas, such as multi-cultural or inter-faith education. Priority is given to projects where teachers (particularly of religious studies, home economics or related areas) are helped directly or indirectly. Preference is given to 'pump-priming' projects and those which 'make a difference' through the intrinsic quality of new ideas or approach being put forward, or through the quantity of teachers and/or pupils who will benefit from it.

In 2005/06 the trust had assets totalling £11 million which generated an income of £478,000. Grants to organisations (*All Saints Corporate Awards*) totalled £109,000, with £91,000 going to individuals.

Beneficiaries of corporate awards included British Nutrition Foundation

(£40,000), Welsh National Centre for Religious Education – University of Wales (£24,000), Bible Reading Fellowship (£20,000), Culham Institute (£18,000), Southwark Cathedral Education Centre (£7,500) and Farming and Countryside Education (£6,000).

Exclusions The trust cannot support:

- general or core funds
- public appeals
- school buildings, equipment or supplies
- the establishment of courses or departments in universities or colleges
- general bursary funds.

Applications For applications from organisations (not individuals): applicants are invited to discuss their ideas informally with the clerk before requesting an application form. In some cases, a 'link trustee' is appointed to assist the organisation in preparing the application and who will act in a liaison role with the trust. Completed applications are put before the awards committee in April/May, with final decisions made in June.

Application forms are available on the trust's website, either in interactive or printable form.

The Pat Allsop Charitable Trust

Education, medical research, children, relief of poverty

£22,000 (2003/04)
Beneficial area UK.

c/o Monier Williams and Boxalls, 71 Lincoln's Inn Fields, London WC2A 3JF
Tel. 020 7405 6195 **Fax** 020 7405 1453
Correspondent J P G Randel, Trustee
Trustees *J P G Randel; A Collett; P W E Kerr; W J K Taylor.*
CC Number 1030950
Information available Accounts were on file at the Charity Commission.

General A number of educational grants are made each year, e.g. towards research and organising educational events. The founder of the trust was a partner in Allsop and Co. Chartered Surveyors, Auctioneers and Property Managers, therefore the trust favours supporting those educational projects and charities which have connections

with surveying and property management professions. The trustees have a policy of making a small number of major donations (over £2,500) and a larger number of smaller donations.

In 2003/04 it had an income of £41,000 and made grants totalling £22,000. Donations were in the range of £50 and £3,800.

Beneficiaries included the Story of Christmas (£3,800), Cambridge International Land Institute, RSPCA Educational Trust and Reading Real Estate Foundation (£2,500 each); Beis Brucha Mother and Babies Home and College of Estate Management and Lionheart (£1,000 each); Unicorn Children's Theatre (£940); Pardes House Grammar School (£600); British Friends of Asaf Harofeh Medical Centre, Norwood and Whizz-Kidz (£500 each); Moorfields Eye Hospital Development Fund (£300); GOSH Children's Charity, Liver Cancer Research, Macmillan Cancer Relief, NCH Action for Children and New Jumbulance Travel Trust (£250 each); Philip Green Memorial Trust (£200), Whizz-Kidz (£150); Strathcarron Hospice (£100); and In Ministry for Children (£50).

Exclusions No grants to individuals.

Applications In writing to the correspondent, but please note, the trust does not accept unsolicited applications.

The Almond Trust

Christian

£170,000 to organisations (2004/05)
Beneficial area UK and worldwide.

19 West Square, London SE11 4SN
Correspondent J L Cooke, Trustee
Trustees *J L Cooke; Barbara H Cooke; J C Cooke.*
CC Number 328583
Information available Full accounts were provided by the trust.

General The trust's aims are the support of evangelistic Christian projects, Christian evangelism and the translation, reading, study and teaching of the Bible.

In 2004/05 it had an income of £135,000 mainly from investments. Assets stood at £238,000. Grants were made to 16

organisations totalling £170,000. A further £16,000 went to two individuals.

Major beneficiaries of amounts over £10,000 each were Christian Youth and Schools Charitable Company (£60,000 in two grants); Christians in Sport (£21,000 in two grants); Wortegat Outreach Trust (£15,000), Lawyers' Christian Fellowship (£14,000 in five grants); and Overseas Missionary Fellowship (£12,000 in two grants).

Other beneficiaries included Agape (£6,000 in two grants); London Institute for Contemporary Christianity and Prison Fellowship (£5,000 each); Claypath Trust (£4,000); Friends of St Ebbe's Trust (£3,500); Jesus Lane Trust (£3,000); and St Ebbe's (£2,000).

Applications In writing to the correspondent, but please note that the trust states it rarely responds to uninvited applications.

The Almshouse Association

Almshouses

£23,000 (2005)
Beneficial area UK.

Billingbear Lodge, Carters Hill, Wokingham, Berkshire RG40 5RU
Tel. 01344 452922 **Fax** 01344 862062
Website www.almshouses.org
Correspondent Anthony De Ritter
Trustee *Executive Committee.*
CC Number 245668
Information available Annual report and quarterly *Almshouse Gazette.*

General The association makes grants and loans to almshouse charities after full advantage has been taken of statutory aid.

In 2005 the association had assets of £4.2 million, an income of £484,000 and made grants totalling £23,000.

Exclusions No grants to individuals.

Applications In writing to the director at any time.

The Altajir Trust

Islam, education, science and research

£73,000 (2006)

Beneficial area UK and Arab or Islamic states.

11 Elvaston Place, London SW7 5QG

Tel. 020 7581 3522 **Fax** 020 7584 1977

Correspondent The Trustees

Trustees *Prof. Alan Jones, Chair; Peter Tripp; Dr Roger Williams; Dr Charles Tripp; Richard Muir.*

CC Number 284116

Information available Information was provided by the trust.

General This trust makes grants for the advancement of science, education and research which is beneficial to the community in Britain or any Arab or Islamic state. Support is also given to students at universities in the UK and conferences and exhibitions are sponsored which promote understanding and the study of Islamic culture and arts throughout the world. Grants are made to both individuals and organisations.

In 2006 the trust had an income of £535,000 mostly from donations. Direct charitable expenditure totalled £544,000 of which £73,000 went on grants.

Beneficiaries of these grants were the Arab Women's Association, International Festival of Middle Eastern Spirituality and Peace, the Iran Heritage Foundation, Medical Aid for Palestinians, University of Birmingham, University of Nottingham, University of Stirling and University of York.

The trust also supported 27 students at various higher education institutions.

Applications The trust states that its resources are fully used without receiving applications.

Altamont Ltd

Jewish causes

£50,000 (2004/05)

Beneficial area Worldwide.

18 Green Walk, London NW4 2AJ

Correspondent David Last, Trustee

Trustees *D Last; H Last; Mrs H Kon; Mrs S Adler; Mrs G Wiesenfeld.*

CC Number 273971

Information available Accounts were on file at the Charity Commission.

General In 2004/05 the trust had an income of £1.7 million and made grants totalling £50,000. Two grants of £25,000 each were made to Pineoak Limited and Premierquote Limited.

Applications In writing to the correspondent.

Alvor Charitable Trust

Christian, humanitarian, 'social change'

£422,000 (2004/05)

Beneficial area UK, with a preference for Sussex, Norfolk and north east Scotland.

Monks Wood, Tompsets Bank, Forest Row, East Sussex RH18 5LW

Email wilkz@btopenworld.com

Correspondent I Wilkins, Chair

Trustees *C Wills; Mrs S Wills; M Atherton; Mrs F Atherton; I Wilkins; Mrs J Wilkins.*

CC Number 1093890

Information available Accounts were on file at the Charity Commission.

General Established in August 2002, this Christian and humanitarian charity predominately supports Christian social change projects in the UK and overseas. A proportion of its target funding goes to local projects around Sussex, Norfolk and north east Scotland where the trust has personal interests. The trust tends to support smaller projects where the grant will meet a specific need. It typically makes one large donation each year and a number of smaller grants.

In 2004/05 it had assets of £1.9 million and an income of £43,000. Grants totalled £422,000.

Beneficiaries of the largest grants included Salt Sussex Trading Ltd (£81,000 in 23 grants), Forest Row Baptist Church (£70,000), Anne Marie School – Ghana, Care for the Family, Kenward Trust and NSPCC (£25,000 each), Crusaders, Opera Brava and Saltmire Trust (£15,000 each) and East Grinstead CAB and Hope UK and Global Connections (£10,000 each).

Other beneficiaries included Interact (£8,000), Activenture, Bibles for

Children, Jabez and Maidstone Christian Care (£5,000 each), Worknet (£1,000) and Court Meadow School (£700).

Exclusions The trust does not look to support animal charities or medical charities outside the geographic areas mentioned above.

Applications In writing to the correspondent.

AM Charitable Trust

Jewish, general

£75,000 (2004/05)

Beneficial area UK and overseas.

Kleinwort Benson Trustees Ltd, 30 Gresham Street, London EC2V 7PG

Correspondent The Secretary

Trustee *Kleinwort Benson Trustees Ltd.*

CC Number 256283

Information available Accounts were on file at the Charity Commission.

General This trust supports a range of causes, particularly Jewish organisations but also medical, welfare, arts and conservation charities. Certain charities are supported for more than one year, although no commitment is usually given to the recipient. Grants range between £50 and £5,000 each, but are mostly of £200 to £400.

In 2004/05 it had assets of £1.8 million and an income of £81,000. Grants were made to 43 organisations totalling £75,000 and were divided between 'Jewish' and 'general' donations.

Jewish – 10 grants totalling 63,000
Beneficiaries were I Rescue (£15,000), Jerusalem Foundation, Weizmann Institute Foundation and World Jewish Relief (£10,000 each), Friends of the Hebrew University of Jerusalem (£8,000), British Friends of Boys Town Jerusalem (£5,000), Norwood Ltd and UK Friends of AWIS (£2,000 each), UK Jewish Aid and International Development (£500) and UK Society for the Protection of Nature in Israel (£100).

General donations – 33 grants totalling £12,000
Donation were in the range of £50 and £2,000 and included those to Cancer Research UK (£2,500), British Heart Foundation (£2,000), Blond Mclndoe Centre for Medical Research (£1,500), Anna Freud Centre (£500), Leonard

9

Cheshire Foundation (£300), Ability International of London, Deafblind UK, Kent Wildlife Trust and Royal Air Force & Dependents Disabled Holiday Trust (£200 each), Aquila Care Trust, Children with Leukaemia, Help the Aged, Royal College of Music and Westminster Association for Mental Health (£100 each) and Elizabeth Finn Trust and National Asthma Campaign (£50 each).

Exclusions No grants to individuals.

Applications Unsolicited applications are not welcomed. The trust stated that its funds are fully committed and only a small percentage of its income is allocated to new beneficiaries. Only successful applications are notified of the trustees' decision. Trustees meet in March and applications need to be received by January.

Ambika Paul Foundation

Education, young people

£106,000 to organisations and individuals (2004/05)

Beneficial area UK and India.

Caparo House, 103 Baker Street, London W1U 6LN

Tel. 020 7486 1417

Correspondent Lord Paul

Trustees *Lord Paul; Lady Paul; Hon. Angad Paul; Hon. Anjli Paul; Hon. Ambar Paul; Hon. Akash Paul.*

CC Number 276127

Information available Full accounts were on file at the Charity Commission.

General The trust supports large organisations, registered charities, colleges and universities benefiting children, young adults and students in the UK and India. Main areas of interest are to do with young people and education. Grants usually range from £100 to £3,000.

In 2004/05 it had an income of £723,000, mostly from donations received. Grants were made totalling £106,000. Assets stood at £5.2 million.

There were eight grants made of amounts over £1,000 each – two grants were made towards the Asian tsunami relief work: Prime Ministers National Relief – India (£60,000); and High Commission Disaster Relief Fund – Sri Lanka (£2,000).

Other beneficiaries listed in the accounts were: Shine (£20,000): Zoological Society of London (£10,500); The Bharatiya Vidya Bhavan (£5,000); PiggyBankKids (£2,700); Caritas UK (£1,500); and Women's India Association (£1,000).

Grants under £1,000 each unlisted in the accounts totalled £2,800.

Exclusions Grants are only available to children and young people's charities. No funding for individuals or DSS requests, nor for individuals' salaries/ running costs. Applications from individuals, including students, are mainly ineligible. Funding for scholarships are made direct to colleges/ universities, not to individuals. No expeditions.

Applications In writing to the trustees at the address above. Acknowledgements are sent if an sae is enclosed. However, the trust has no paid employees and the enormous number of requests it receives creates administrative difficulties.

Sir John and Lady Amory's Charitable Trust

General

£46,000 (2005/06)

Beneficial area Devon and elsewhere in the UK.

The Island, Lowman Green, Tiverton, Devon EX16 4LA

Tel. 01884 254 899

Correspondent Lady Heathcoat Amory, Trustee

Trustees *Sir Ian Heathcoat Amory; Lady Heathcoat Amory; William Heathcoat Amory.*

CC Number 203970

Information available Accounts were on file at the Charity Commission.

General The trust was set up in 1961 with a bequest from Sir John and Lady Amory. Its aim is to support charitable purposes principally by use of its annual income.

In 2005/06 the trust had assets of over £2 million and an income of £62,000. Grants totalled £46,000.

Donations in institutions exceeding £1,000 each included those to: National Trust (£5,300); Relief for the Elderly and Infirm (£2,700); Project Trust (£1,900);

Blundells School (£1,700); and BSES and Tiverton Opportunity Playgroup (£1,000 each).

Applications In writing to the correspondent.

Viscount Amory's Charitable Trust

Welfare, older people, education

£260,000 to organisations (2004/ 05)

Beneficial area UK, primarily in Devon.

The Island, Lowman Green, Tiverton, Devon EX16 4LA

Tel. 01884 254899 **Fax** 01884 255155

Correspondent The Trust Secretary

Trustees *Sir Ian Heathcoat Amory; Mrs Catherine Cavender; Paul Horsey.*

CC Number 204958

Information available Accounts were on file at the Charity Commission.

General 'The objectives of the trust are to donate the annual investment income to charitable institutions or other organisations primarily to benefit the inhabitants of the County of Devon; to assist young people, the poor and aged or in the advancement of education.'

In 2004/05 the trust had assets of £9.3 million and an income of £308,000. Grants were made totalling £272,000, broken down into the following categories:

Education – 25 grants totalling £116,000
Beneficiaries included: Blundells School (£44,000); Blundells Foundation (£20,000); Sands School (£6,700); Grenville College (£5,100); Stonar School (£4,200); Exeter School (£3,100); St Margaret's School (£3,000); Momson's Academy (£2,200); University of Bristol (£2,000); Urdang Academy (£1,700); Bicton College and Maynard School (£1,500 each); St John's School (£1,200); and Dame Hannah Rogers School, St Loye's Foundation and University College Dublin (£1,000 each).

General – 12 grants totalling £98,000
Organisations to benefit included: London Sailing Project (£71,000); Royal Horticultural Society (£11,000); Devon

FWAG (£4,750); Addaction and Tiverton Market Centre (£2,000 each); Project Gem (£1,500); Tiverton & District Scout Council (£1,100); and Church House, South Tawton and Coldharbour Mill (£1,000 each).

Religious – 4 grants totalling £5,800
Grants went to: St Peter's Music Fund (£2,800); and Exe Valley Team Ministry, Rockwell Green Christian Centre and St Giles Church, Little Torrington (£1,000 each).

Individuals
There were 21 grants made to individuals during the year totalling £12,000.

Exclusions No grants to individuals from outside south west England.

Applications In writing to the correspondent, giving general background information, total costs involved, amount raised so far and details of applications to other organisations.

The Ampelos Trust

General
About £100,000 (2004/05)
Beneficial area UK.

9 Trinity Street, Colchester, Essex CO1 1JN

Correspondent G W N Stewart, Secretary

Trustees *G W N Stewart; Baroness Rendell of Babergh; A M Witt.*

CC Number 1048778

Information available Accounts had been filed at the Charity Commission.

General In 2004/05 the trust had an income of £103,000 and a total expenditure of £109,000.

Previous beneficiaries have included Asian Elephant Survival Appeal, Book Trust, Chester Zoo, Ethiopaid, the Handel House Trust, Institute Trust Fund, Kids for Kids, Medical Foundation, National Literacy Trust, RNIB, Shelter and Teenage Cancer Trust.

Applications In writing to the correspondent.

The Anchor Foundation

Christian
£262,000 (2004/05)
Beneficial area UK.

PO Box 21107, Alloa FK12 5WA

Email secretary@theanchorfoundation.org.uk

Website www.theanchorfoundation.org.uk

Correspondent The Secretary

Trustees *Prudence Thimbleby; Michael Mitton; Revd Anker-Petersen.*

CC Number 1082485

Information available Accounts were on file at the Charity Commission.

General The foundation was registered with the Charity Commission in September 2000, it supports Christian charities concerned with social inclusion, particularly through ministries of healing and the arts. The grant range for a project is between £500 and £10,000. It is not the normal practice of the charity to support the same project for more than three years. Only in very exceptional circumstances will grants be given for building work.

In 2004/05 it had assets of £5.2 million generating an income of £213,000. Grants totalled £262,000.

Beneficiaries included Ark T Centre, Community House – Alloa and Kainos Community (£12,000 each), the Initiative and St Joseph Pastoral Care (£10,000 each), Going Public Trust (£9,900), CFM Trust (£9,600), Martha Trust, NCH Scotland and Scargill House (£8,000 each), East Belfast Mission (£7,500), Stepping Stones Trust (£7,000), Burrswood Hospital and the Well Christian Healing Centre (£6,000 each) and Bibles for Children, the St Columba's Fellowship, the Shaftesbury Society and Three Churches Project (£5,000 each).

Exclusions No grants to individuals.

Applications Application forms and information for applicants is available in pdf format on the foundation's website.

Applications are considered at twice-yearly trustees' meetings in April and November and need to be received by 28 February or 31 August each year.

The foundation regrets that applications cannot be acknowledged. Successful applicants will be notified as soon as possible after trustees' meetings.

Unsuccessful applicants may reapply after 12 months.

James and Grace Anderson Trust

Cerebral palsy
About £20,000 (2004/05)
Beneficial area UK.

32 Wardie Road, Edinburgh EH5 3LG

Tel. 0131 552 4062 **Fax** 0131 467 1333

Email tim.straton@virgin.net

Correspondent Tim D Straton, Trustee

Trustees *I K Ritchie; J Donald; J D M Urquhart; T D Straton.*

SC Number SC004172

Information available Information was obtained from the Scottish Charity Register and previous accounts supplied by the trust.

General The trust was established in 1974 and currently funds research into cerebral palsy. In 2004/05 the trust had a total income of £27,000. No further information was available from the Scottish Charity Register.

In 2003/04 the trust made grants to two organisations totalling £22,000. During the year the trust continued to support research in gait analysis with a view to alleviating the conditions arising from cerebral palsy.

The two grants were £19,000 to Lothian Primary Care NHS Trust towards gait analysis projects and £3,000 to Yorkhill NHS Trust. The sum of £500 was given to an individual.

Exclusions No grants are made: to individuals who do not have cerebral palsy; to projects not directly related to research into cure or alleviation of cerebral palsy; or as sponsorship of individuals.

Applications In writing to the correspondent. Trustees meet in May and October. Applications should be received by the previous month.

The Andrew Anderson Trust

Christian, social welfare

£196,000 to organisations (2005/ 06)

Beneficial area UK and overseas.

84 Uphill Road, Mill Hill, London NW7 4QE

Correspondent Miss M S Anderson, Trustee

Trustees *Miss A A Anderson; Miss M S Anderson; Revd A R Anderson; Mrs M L Anderson.*

CC Number 212170

Information available A full list of grants for 2005/06 was provided by the trust.

General The trust states in its trustees' report that it provides support to a wide range of charitable causes. Most of its money appears to go to evangelical organisations and churches, but it also makes a large number of small grants to health, disability and social welfare charities.

In 2005/06 this trust made 171 grants totalling £196,000. In 2004/05 it had assets approaching £8 million.

About 45 grants were made for amounts of £1,000 or more. Beneficiaries of larger grants included Proclamation Trust (£17,000), Fellowship of Independent Evangelical Churches (£15,000), St Ebbe's PCC – Oxford (£10,000), Aycliffe Evangelical Church, Concern Worldwide, Rehoboth Christian Centre – Blackpool, Trinity Baptist Church – Gloucester and Whitefield Christian Trust (£5,000 each), Christian Medical Fellowship (£3,500), Emmanuel Baptist Church – Sidmouth, Latin Link, St Helen's Church – Bishopsgate and Worldshare (£3,000 each), Kenward Trust and Weald Trust (£2,000 each) and DEC Niger Crisis Appeal, Good Shepherd Mission, Lawrence Weston Community Farm, Scientific Exploration Society, TNT Ministries and Wings (£1,000 each).

Beneficiaries of smaller grants included Activenture, Bible Society, Cancer Care, Drugscope, EMMS International, Friends of John Grooms, Global Care, Home Evangelism, Interserve, Keychange, Lifewords, Moorlands College, Open Air Mission, Prostate Cancer Charity, Richmond Fellowship, RNLI, Samaritans, Sightlink, Torch Trust for the Blind, Watford New Hope Trust and WWF.

A further £33,000 went to individuals in 2005/06.

Exclusions Individuals should not apply for travel or education.

Applications The trust states 'we prefer to honour existing commitments and initiate new ones through our own contacts rather than respond to applications.' It rarely responds to unsolicited appeals.

The André Christian Trust

Christian organisations

Nil (2005) see below

Beneficial area UK.

15 West Hill, Sanderstead, South Croydon, Surrey CR2 0SB

Correspondent Andrew K Mowll, Trustee

Trustees *Andrew K Mowll; Stephen Daykin.*

CC Number 248466

Information available Full accounts were on file at the Charity Commission.

General The trust makes grants towards the advancement of Christianity, either through printing and distributing Bible scriptures or through evangelistic work. A number of charities are listed in the trust deed, and they are its principle beneficiaries. Grants appear to be mainly ongoing.

In 2005 the trust had assets of £1.2 million and an income of £35,000. No grants were made during the year due to the death of one of the trustees. The sole trustee was unable to make any grants as two trustees were required to make executive decisions. A new trustee, Stephen Daykin was appointed on 12 August 2006.

In 2004 grants totalled £36,000. Beneficiaries were Strangers' Rest Mission (£27,000) and Overseas Missionary Fellowship, Scripture Gift Mission and Universities and Colleges Christian Fellowship (£3,000 each).

Applications In writing to the correspondent. However, the trust states: 'Applications are discouraged since grants are principally made to those organisations which are listed in the trust deed.' Funds are therefore fully committed and unsolicited requests cannot be supported.

The Anglian Water Trust Fund

Money advice provision/ individuals in need

£157,000 to organisations (2004/ 05)

Beneficial area Anglian Water region (Cambridgeshire, Lincolnshire, Norfolk, Suffolk, Peterborough, Milton Keynes and Hartlepool plus parts of Bedford, Buckinghamshire, Essex, Hertfordshire, Leicestershire, Northamptonshire, and Rutland).

PO Box 42, Peterborough PE3 8XH

Tel. 01733 421021 **Fax** 01733 421020

Email awtf@charisgrants.com

Website www.awtf.org.uk

Correspondent The Trust Liaison Officer

Trustees *Graham Blagden, Chair; Ms Barbara Ruffell; Ms Elizabeth Ingram; Stuart de Prochnow; John Sansby; Stephen Harrap; Ms Valerie Mansfield.*

CC Number 1054026

Information available Accounts were on file at the Charity Commission.

General 'The Anglian Water Trust is an independent charitable Trust established in 1996 which aims to contribute to the fight against poverty within the Anglian Water region.

'Grants are available to help individuals and families in need clear water and sewerage debt and other household bills and costs.

'The trust is also funding voluntary sector organisations to provide money and debt advice services and education projects.'

The trust currently receives an annual grant of £1 million from AWG plc and £7,000 from Three Valleys Water.

In 2004/05 grants to organisations totalled £157,000. Beneficiaries included: NCH Project (£78,000); Dough UK Project, Wymondham CAB and Youth Debt Project (£15,000 each); Great Yarmouth CAB (£9,800); Cambridge Independent Advice Centre (£9,100); Bedford CAB (£5,000); Northampton Welfare Rights Advice Service (£4,000); Basildon CAB (£3,300); East Lindsey CAB and Milton Keynes CAB (£2,500 each); Castle Point CAB (£2,300); and Buckingham CAB (£500).

The trust also operates a programme of grants to individuals and families in need, within the beneficial areas, helping them with arrears of water/sewerage charges, other priority bills and the purchase of essential household items. In 2004/05 grants to individuals and families totalled £842,000.

Applications Application forms are available from the trust.

Anglo-German Foundation for the Study of Industrial Society

Organisations benefiting academics and research workers in the UK and Germany

£255,000 (2005)

Beneficial area UK and Germany.

34 Belgrave Square, London SW1 8DZ

Tel. 020 7823 1123 **Fax** 020 7823 2324

Email info@agf.org.uk

Website www.agf.org.uk

Correspondent Dr Ray Cunningham, Director

Trustees *Bryan Rigby, Chair; Lord Croham; Simon Broadbent; Prof. Robert Leicht; Prof. Dr Anita B Pfaff; Dr Jürgen Oesterhelt; Prof. Dr Carl-Christian von Weizsäcker; John Edmonds; Dr Erika Mezger; Peter von Siemens; Dr Andrew Sentance; Prof Wendy Carlin; Prof. Dr Anita Pfaff.*

CC Number 266844

Information available Accounts were on file at the Charity Commission.

General **Creating Sustainable Growth in Europe programme**
This research initiative addresses the following core themes:

- innovation, productivity and growth
- environment and resources
- welfare, employment and social justice.

It aims to tackle the emerging economic, social and political challenges confronting governments not only in Germany and the UK, but across Europe and the industrialised world.

The objective is to fund applied comparative policy research, exchange and debate which can contribute to 'Creating sustainable growth in Europe'. The total budget for the initiative amounts to around £3 million, or €4.5 million.

To complement and support this research programme, the foundation provides around £40,000 each year in small grants to meet the costs of research events such as conferences, seminars or workshops (or less commonly for small, self-contained research projects) addressing one or more of the core themes of the research programme.

In 2005 the foundation paid a total of £235,000 in grants to 36 projects and £20,000 towards publications. Beneficiaries of the largest grants were: University of Sheffield/Institute for the Study of Labor (£32,000); UMIST/University of Bochum (£28,000); University of Leeds (£25,000); London School of Economics (£23,000); Institute for Fiscal Studies/German Institute for Economic Research – Berlin (£18,000); University of Portsmouth/IAT (£12,000); NIESR/German Institute for Economic Research – Berlin and Royal Institute of International Affairs/Hamburg Institute of International Economics (£11,000 each); and University of Essex (£10,000).

Exclusions The foundation does not provide grants of any kind for undergraduate or postgraduate study, fund academic posts, or pay overheads.

Applications In the first instance by email. A two-page outline is required before the formal application is submitted.

The Animal Defence Trust

Animal welfare

£81,000 (2004/05)

Beneficial area UK.

Horsey Lightly Fynn, Devon House, 12–15 Dartmouth Street, Queen Anne's Gate, London SW1H 9BL

Website www.animaldefencetrust.org/

Correspondent Alan Meyer, Honorary Treasurer and Secretary

Trustees *Miss M Saunders; Mrs B A McIrvine; Mrs C Bowles; Miss P Newton.*

CC Number 263095

Information available Accounts were on file at the Charity Commission.

General The trust makes grants for capital projects purely to animal welfare charities. In 2004/05 it had assets totalling £1.4 million and an income of £155,000, including £107,000 from donations and legacies. Grants were made to 42 organisations, including 21 that had previously been supported, totalling £81,000.

Beneficiaries included Woodside Animal Welfare Trust (£5,000), Thoroughbred Rehabilitation Centre (£3,000), Dumfries and Galloway Canine Rescue, Hart Wildlife Rescue, Prevent Unwanted Pets, Rotherham Dog Rescue, the Society for the Ferne Animal Sanctuary, Tree for Life for Animals and the Welfare of Horses and Ponies (£2,500 each), the Born Free Foundation, the Dartmoor Livestock Protection Society, Happy Landings Animal Shelter, International Otter Survival Fund, Lagos Animal Protection, the National Animal Welfare Trust, Perthshire Abandoned Dogs Society and Vet Aid (£2,000 each) and the Alternative Animal Sanctuary, Gower Bird Hospital, Maggies Pet Rescue, Mayhew Animal Home, Rainforest Concern (£1,000).

Exclusions No grants to individuals.

Applications In writing to the Grants Secretary at PO Box 44, Plymouth, PL7 5YW.

The Annandale Charitable Trust

Major UK charities

£129,000 (2004/05)

Beneficial area UK.

HSBC Trust Services, Norwich House, Nelson Gate, Commercial Road, Southampton SO15 1GX

Correspondent Stephen Gladwell

Trustees *Mrs C J Duggan; HSBC Trust Company (UK) Ltd.*

CC Number 1049193

Information available Accounts were on file at the Charity Commission.

General The trust supports a range of major UK charities. In 2004/05 the trust had assets of almost £5 million, an income of £190,000 and made 19 grants totalling £129,000.

Beneficiaries included: Motor Neurone Disease Association (£22,000 in three grants); Disasters Emergency Committee (£15,000); Christian Aid (£11,000 in two grants); the Terence Higgins Trust (£10,000); British Red Cross (£10,000 in two grants); Victim Support (£9,000 in three grants); Macmillan Cancer Relief (£8,000); the Blue Cross, Niger Crisis Appeal, Oxfam and RSPCA (£5,000 each); Cancer Research UK (£4,000 in two grants); Born Free (£3,000 in two grants); UNICEF (£2,000); and the Donkey Sanctuary (£1,000).

Applications In writing to the correspondent. The trust stated that it has an ongoing programme of funding for specific charities and all its funds are fully committed.

The Appletree Trust

Disability, sickness, poverty

£34,000 to organisations (2006/07)

Beneficial area UK and overseas, with a preference for Scotland and the north east Fife district.

The Royal Bank of Scotland plc, Trust and Estate Services, Eden Lakeside, Chester Business Park, Wrexham Road, Chester, CH4 9QT

Tel. 0131 523 2648

Correspondent The Royal Bank of Scotland plc, Administrator

Trustees *The Royal Bank of Scotland plc; Revd W McKane; Revd Dr J D Martin; Revd L R Brown.*

SC Number SC004851

Information available Accounts and a list of grants were provided by the trust.

General This trust was established in the will of the late William Brown Moncour in 1982 to relieve disability, sickness and poverty. The settlor recommended that Action Research for the Crippled Child, British Heart Foundation and National Society for Cancer Relief should receive funding from his trust, particularly for their work in the north east Fife district.

In 2006/07 the trust had assets of 1.2 million and an income of £35,000. Grants were made to 17 organisations totalling £34,000, the majority of which were concerned with palliative care.

Beneficiaries included the Prince and Princess of Wales Hospice (£5,000), Home Start East Fife and PDSA (£3,500 each), the Salvation Army (£3,000), 1st St Andrews Boys Brigade, Alzheimer Scotland, the Broomhouse Centre (£2,000 each), Scottish Spina Bifida Association (£1,800), Children's Hospice Association, Discovery Camps Trust and Scottish Motor Neurone Disease Association (£1,500 each), Arthritis Care In Scotland, Marie Curie Cancer Care and the Quarriers (£1,000 each) and RNID (£500).

Exclusions No grants to individuals.

Applications In writing to the correspondent. Trustees meet to consider grants in April.

The John Apthorp Charitable Trust

General

£62,000 to organisations (2006)

Beneficial area UK, with an interest in Greater London.

Myers Clark, Woodford House, Woodford Road, Watford, Hertfordshire WD17 1DL

Tel. 01923 224411 **Fax** 01923 235303

Correspondent The Trustees Accountant

Trustees *John Dorrington Apthorp; Dr D Arnold.*

CC Number 289713

Information available Full accounts were available from the Charity Commission website.

General The trust was established by its eponymous settlor in 1983. In 2006 the trust had assets of £21,000 and an income of £77,000. Grants were made to five organisations totalling £62,000. Recipients included the Tay Ghillies Association (£47,000), Radlett Choral Society (£5,400), Radlett Light Opera Society (£5,000) and the Radlett Art Society (£4,700).

Applications Unsolicited appeals are not welcome and will not be answered. The trustees carry out their own research into prospective grant areas.

The Archbishop of Canterbury's Charitable Trust

Christianity, welfare

£128,000 (2005)

Beneficial area Worldwide.

1 The Sanctuary, Westminster, London SW1P 3JT

Tel. 020 7222 5381

Correspondent D D Fullarton, Patronage Secretary – Archbishop of Canterbury

Trustees *Archbishop of Canterbury; Miss Sheila Cameron; Christopher Smith; Timothy Livesey.*

CC Number 287967

Information available Accounts were on file at the Charity Commission.

General This trust was established in 1983 by the former Archbishop of Canterbury, Lord Runcie, to advance the Christian religion and Christian education, in particular the objectives and principles of the Church of England, as well as supporting individuals working towards these goals. The trust deed states that trustees should hold particular interest towards:

- people training for the ministry and church work
- ministers, teachers and the church workers who are in need, and their dependants
- the extension of education in, and knowledge of, the faith and practice of the Church of England
- the development of work of any church, union of churches, denominations or sects which will further the Christian religion generally.

A proportion of the trust's funds are distributed through the Archbishop of Canterbury Trinity Church Fund, which can give support worldwide to Anglican projects at the discretion of the Archbishop of Canterbury. However, the correspondent states that there is much call on these funds and therefore the success rate of applications is very small.

There are also three smaller, restricted funds which are administered as part of this trust. (i) The Michael Ramsey Chair Fund, which finances the Michael Ramsey Chair in Anglican and Ecumenical Theology at the University of Kent. (ii) Dick and Sheila Stallard Fund, which supports church-related work in China and the Far East, rarely supporting work in the Middle East. (iii) Living Memory Rogers Harrison Lozo Relief Fund, which supports British-born retired Anglican bishops and priests, and their wives and widows living in England, as well as supporting people who are poor, blind, elderly or disabled in Greater London.

In 2005 it had assets of £2.5 million. The total income was £286,000, including £166,000 in donations received. Grants were made totalling £128,000.

Beneficiaries included: Lambeth Conference (£22,000); Bromley & Sheppards Colleges (£10,000); Windle Trust (£7,500); CMS (£6,500); Anglican Church South East Asia, Church of South India Synod, Diocese of Colombo, Diocese in Europe Apokrisarioi (£5,000 each); ACC (£4,000); Anglican Centre in Rome (£3,000); Lambeth Palace Library (£2,500); St Luke's Hospital Appeal and St Margaret's Restoration Fund (£2,000 each); UNICEF (£1,500); and INFORM, Word for Life Trust, St Hywyn's Church Restoration and Stepping Stones Trust (£1,000 each).

Applications Funds are allocated for several years ahead, therefore no new applications can be considered.

Archbishop of Wales Fund for Children

Children
£61,000 (2005)
Beneficial area Wales.

Church in Wales, 37–39 Cathedral Road, Cardiff CF11 9XF
Tel. 029 2034 8200
Email awfc@churchinwales.org.uk
Website www.churchinwales.org.uk/awffc
Correspondent The Secretary
Trustees *Revd J Michael Williams, Chair; Cheryl Beach; Ruth Forrester; Caroline Owen; James Tovey.*
CC Number 1102236
Information available Accounts were on file at the Charity Commission.

General This fund was established in 2004 to relieve hardship, sickness disability and distress amongst children and young persons in Wales. There is an opportunity for dioceses, Christian

bodies and other organisations including local authorities working with children in need in Wales to be part of this initiative.

The purpose of the fund is to support children in need and their families and local communities, through the work of organisations in this order of priority:

- Those in the Dioceses of the Church in Wales.
- Those associated with other Christian bodies which are members of Cytun (Churches Together in Wales).
- Other organisations working with children in Wales.

Over the last two years the fund has received substantial donations from Church in Wales congregations, particularly from collections at the annual Christingle services.

In 2005 it had an income of £70,000 and made grants totalling £61,000.

Successful applications in April 2005 included Aberdare Children's Contact Centre, Borth Out of School Club, Local Aid for Children, Maesgeirchen Healthy Living Centre, Penplas Family Centre Project, Salvation Army Risca Corps, Sennybridge Squirts and Youth Outreach Grosmont Group.

Applications Application forms can be requested from the correspondent in writing or by telephone. They can also be downloaded from the fund's website.

The John M Archer Charitable Trust

General
£39,000 (2006/07)
Beneficial area UK and overseas.

12 Broughton Place, Edinburgh EH1 3RX
Tel. 0131 556 4518
Correspondent Mrs W Grant, Secretary
Trustees *Gilbert B Archer; Mrs A Morgan; Mrs W Grant; Mrs C Fraser; Mrs I C Smith.*
SC Number SC010583
Information available Accounts were provided by the trust.

General The trust supports local, national and international organisations, in particular those concerned with:

- prevention or relief of individuals in need
- welfare of people who are sick, distressed or afflicted
- alleviation of need
- advancement of education
- advancement of religious or missionary work
- advancement of medical or scientific research and discovery
- preservation of Scottish heritage and the advancement of associated cultural activities.

In 2006/07 the trust had assets of over £1 million and an income of £46,000. There were 99 grants made totalling £39,000. Eight organisations received grants of £1,000 or more. They were: Erskine Stewarts Melville College – Arts Centre (£5,000); Mercy Corps Scotland (£4,000); Royal Liverpool University Hospital – Macular Degeneration Research (£3,000); Cambodian Hospital Siem Reap for Children (£2,500); Red Cross – Aberdeen Guest House (£2,000); Castlebrae School Tutoring Programme (£1,500); and the Canonmills Baptist Church and the Bobby Moore Fund (£1,000 each).

Applications In writing to the correspondent.

The Ardwick Trust

Jewish, welfare, general
£85,000 (2005/06)
Beneficial area UK, Israel and the developing world.

c/o Knox Cropper, 24 Petworth Road, Haslemere, Surrey GU27 2HR
Correspondent Janet Bloch, Trustee
Trustees *Mrs J B Bloch; Dominic Flynn; Miss Judith Portrait.*
CC Number 266981
Information available Accounts were on file at the Charity Commission.

General The trust supports Jewish welfare, along with a wide band of non-Jewish causes to include social welfare, health, education (especially special schools), older people, conservation and the environment, child welfare, disability and medical research. Although the largest grants made by the trust are to Jewish organisations, the majority of recipients are non-Jewish.

In 2005/06 it had assets of £951,000 and an income of £39,000. Grants were made to 240 organisations totalling £85,000. The main beneficiary, as in recent years, was Nightingale House which received three grants totalling £32,000.

The next largest grants were £5,000 to Jewish Care, £3,000 to Friends of Hebrew University, £2,000 each to Weizmann UK and World Jewish Relief and £1,000 each to British Technion Society, Jewish Museum, Langdon Foundation, Nightingale House (Howard Bloch Training Fund), Norwood Ltd and UJIA.

The remaining grants were all for £500, £200 or £100 each; there was no noticeable pattern between organisations receiving larger/smaller grants. Beneficiaries included Abbeyfield Society, Alexandra Rose Day, Alzheimer's Research Trust, Breast Cancer Care, British Red Cross, Centrepoint, Children in Crisis, Community Security Trust, Disabled Living Foundation, Friends of Israel Educational Foundation, Headway, Health Unlimited, Hope UK, Jewish Blind and Disabled, Lasers for Life, Magen David Adom UK, National Playing Fields Association, National Literacy Trust, Parkinson's Disease Society, Russian Immigrant Aid Fund, RNIB, Shaare Zedek UK, St Christopher's Hospice, Tree Aid, Uppingham Foundation, VSO and YWCA.

Exclusions No grants to individuals.

Applications In writing to the correspondent.

Armenian General Benevolent Union London Trust

Armenian education, culture and welfare

£37,000 to organisations (2005)
Beneficial area UK and overseas.

Armenian House, 25 Cheniston Gardens, London W8 6TG
Correspondent The Chair
Trustees *Bedros Aslanyan; Dr Berge Azadian; Berge Setrakian; Hampar*

Chakardjian; Mrs Annie Kouyoumjian; Aris Atamian; Harout Aghajanian; Mrs Annie Kouyoumdjian.
CC Number 282070
Information available Accounts were on file at the Charity Commission.

General The purpose of the trust is to advance education among Armenians, particularly those in the UK, and to promote the study of Armenian history, literature, language, culture and religion.

In 2005 it had assets of almost £3.4 million and an income of £134,000. Grants were made totalling £60,000 broken down as follows: £38,000 as student loans and grants, £22,000 in 'charitable and other grants'; £10,000 in humanitarian and medical aid to Armenia and £1,000 to AGBU London Branch.

Exclusions No support for projects of a commercial nature or for education for individual students.

Applications In writing to the correspondent. Applications are considered all year around.

The Armourers' and Brasiers' Gauntlet Trust

Organisations benefiting young adults, academics, research workers and students; materials science; general

£217,000 (2006/07)
Beneficial area UK, with some preference for London.

Armourers' Hall, 81 Coleman Street, London EC2R 5BJ
Tel. 020 7374 4000 **Fax** 020 7606 7481
Email info@armourersandbrasiers.co.uk
Website www.armourersandbrasiers.co.uk
Correspondent The Secretary
Trustees *R A Crabb, Chair; Prof. W Bonfield; P J Fenton; J S Haw; D E H Chapman; J P W Middleton.*
CC Number 279204
Information available Information was provided by the trust.

General The trust, which provides the charitable outlet for the Worshipful Company of Armourers and Brasiers, was set up in 1979. The majority of charitable giving is directed towards materials science education and research. The remaining funds are therefore quite limited and are directed towards 'people' rather than 'things', with the emphasis on youth and community projects. Grants are given in single payments, not on an ongoing basis. However organisations can still apply for grants each year.

In 2006/07 the trust had assets of £6.6 million, an income of £367,000 and made grants totalling £217,000.

Armourers' Novelis Scheme – £55,000
Beneficiaries at school, undergraduate and research student levels.

Armourers' Corus Scheme – £32,000
Beneficiaries at school, undergraduate and research student levels.

Armourers' Rolls-Royce Scheme – £35,000
Beneficiaries at school, undergraduate, research student and at post-doctoral levels.

Materials Science Scheme – £50,000
Beneficiaries at school, technical, undergraduate, research student and post-doctoral levels.

General Charitable Grants – £45,000
Beneficiaries in the following categories: armed forces, community and social care, children and young people, medical/health, general education, the arts and Christian mission.

Exclusions In general grants are not made to:

- organisations or groups which are not registered
- individuals
- organisations or groups whose main object is to fund or support other charitable bodies
- organisations or groups which are in direct relief of any reduction of financial support from public funds
- charities with a turnover of over £1 million
- charities which spend over 10% of their income on fundraising activities
- organisations whose accounts disclose substantial financial reserves.

Nor towards general maintenance, repair or restoration of buildings, including ecclesiastical buildings, unless there is a long-standing connection with the Armourers' and Brasiers' Company or unless of outstanding importance to the national heritage.

Applications In writing to the correspondent, with a copy of the latest annual report and audited accounts. Applications are considered quarterly.

The Artemis Charitable Trust

Psychotherapy, parent education, and related activities

£66,000 (2005)

Beneficial area UK.

Brook House, Quay Meadow, Bosham, West Sussex PO18 8LY

Tel. 01243 573475

Correspondent Richard Evans, Trustee

Trustees R W Evans; D S Bergin; W A Evans; D J Evans; M W Evans.

CC Number 291328

Information available Accounts were on file at the Charity Commission.

General The trust was set up in 1985, its 2005 trustees' report states: 'The policy of the trust has continued to be the making of grants to aid the provision of counselling, psychotherapy, parenting, human relationship training and related activities.'

In 2005 it had assets of £1.5 million and an income of £65,000. Grants totalled £66,000 and were categorised as follows, shown with examples of grants:

Social Welfare
Primhe (£20,000), Chichester Harbour Trust (£5,000) and Counselling in Primary Care Trust (£3,600 in three grants).

Research
University of Leeds (£33,000), West Sussex Health & Social Care Trust (£2,800) and Core System Trust (£1,400).

Applications The trust can only give grants to registered charities. 'We cannot entertain applications either from individuals or from organisations which are not registered charities. Applicants should also be aware that most of the trust's funds are committed to a number of major ongoing projects and that spare funds available to meet new applications are very limited.'

The Ove Arup Foundation

Construction – education and research

£56,000 (2004/05)

Beneficial area Unrestricted.

c/o 13 Fitzroy Street, London W1T 4BQ

Website www.theovearupfoundation. com

Correspondent The Secretary

Trustees M Shears; D Michael; R F Emmerson; R B Haryott; T M Hill; C Cole; R Hough; T O'Brien; R Yau.

CC Number 328138

Information available Accounts were on file at the Charity Commission.

General The trust was established in 1989 with the principal objective of supporting education in matters associated with the built environment, including construction-related academic research. The trustees are appointed by the board of the Ove Arup Partnership. It gives grants for research and projects, including start-up and feasibility costs.

In 2004/05 the foundation had assets of £2.4 million and an income of £42,000. Grants were made to 10 organisations totalling £56,000.

Beneficiaries were John Doyle Construction Ltd – 'Construclionadurn' (£15,000), London School of Economics (£10,000), Forum for the Future (£5,000), Architecture Centre Network (£4,700), XL Wales (£4,000), Architectural Association Foundation and Heriot-Watt Univesity (£2,000 each), Anglo-Danish Society (£1,600) and Construction Industry Trust for Youth (£1,000).

Exclusions No grants to individuals, including students.

Applications In writing to the correspondent, with brief supporting financial information. Trustees meet quarterly to consider applications (March, June, September and December).

The AS Charitable Trust

Christian, development, social concern

£46,000 (2004/05)

Beneficial area UK and developing countries.

Bix Bottom Farm, Henley-on-Thames RG9 6BH

Correspondent The Administrator

Trustees R Calvocoressi; C W Brocklebank; Mrs C Eady; G Calvocoressi.

CC Number 242190

Information available Full accounts were on file at the Charity Commission.

General This trust makes grants in particular to projects which combine the advancement of the Christian religion, with Christian lay leadership, with developing countries' development, with peacemaking and reconciliation or with other areas of social concern.

In 2004/05 the trust had assets of £6.7 million, an income of £182,000 and made 20 grants to 18 different organisations totalling £46,000.

Beneficiaries of grants of £1,000 or more were: Christian Engineers in Development, Langley House Trust and Traidcraft Exchange (£10,000 each); the Ferguson Charitable Trust (£10,000 in two grants); and the Dundas Foundation, GRACE, Oasis Trust and Trinity Fellowship (£1,000 each).

Exclusions Grants to individuals or large charities are very rare. Such applications are discouraged.

Applications In writing to the correspondent.

Ashburnham Thanksgiving Trust

Christian

£62,000 to organisations (2004/05)

Beneficial area UK and worldwide.

Agmerhurst House, Ashburnham, Battle, East Sussex TN33 9NB

Tel. 01424 892253

Correspondent The Trustees

Trustees *Mrs M Bickersteth; Mrs E M Habershon; E R Bickersteth; R D Bickersteth.*

CC Number 249109

Information available Full accounts were on file at the Charity Commission.

General The trust supports a wide range of Christian mission organisations and other Christian organisations which are known to the trustees, in the UK and worldwide. Individuals are also supported.

In 2004/05 the trust's assets, including properties owned, totalled £5.3 million, and generated an income of £147,000.

A total of £88,000 was distributed, of which £62,000 went to organisations. Further monies were distributed in restricted grants and grants to individuals.

There were 22 grants made of £1,000 or more. Beneficiaries included Genesis Arts Trust (£3,500), Ashburnham & Penhurst Church (£3,000), Prison Fellowship (£2,300), St Stephen's Society (£2,200), Open Doors (£2,000), Lawrence Barham Memorial Trust (£1,600), Lambeth Partnership and Stewards Trust (£1,500 each) Overseas Missionary Fellowship (£1,400), Operation Mobilisation (£1,300), Care Trust (£1,200), Latin American Missions, Micah Trust and Timothy Trust (£1,100 each) and Eden Christian Fellowship and Dorothy Kerin Trust (£1,000 each).

Other beneficiaries included Advantage Africa and International Nepal Fellowship (£650 each), Life & More Abundant Ministries (£550), International Fellowship of Evangelical Students, London City Mission and Spinnaker Trust (£500 each), Evangelical Alliance (£430), Scripture Union (£400), Nexus Trust (£200), L'Abri Fellowship (£120) and Emmanuel International and Oxford Community Church (£100 each).

Exclusions No grants for buildings.

Applications The trust has stated that its funds are fully committed to current beneficiaries. Unfortunately it receives far more applications than it is able to deal with.

A J H Ashby Will Trust

Birds, wildlife, education and children

£62,000 (2004/05)

Beneficial area UK, especially Lea Valley area of Hertfordshire.

HSBC Trust Company (UK) Ltd, Trust Services, Norwich House, Nelson Gate, Commercial Road, Southampton, Hampshire SO15 1GX

Tel. 023 8072 2243

Correspondent S J Gladwell, Trust Manager

Trustee *HSBC Trust Company (UK) Ltd.*

CC Number 803291

Information available Accounts were on file at the Charity Commission.

General The trust was established in 1990 to support birds and wildlife throughout the UK, as well as education projects and young people specifically in the Lea Valley area of Hertfordshire.

In 2004/05 the trust had an income from investments of £65,000. There were 14 grants made totalling £62,000.

Beneficiaries included RSPB (£25,000 in 4 grants), Bishops Stopfords School and Chase Community School (£5,000 each), Palmer Green High School (£4,500), Danemead Scout Campsite, Friends of West Lea School and St Georges Roman Catholic School (£4,000 each), St Andrews Church of England School (£3,500) and Holy Trinity Church of England School (£3,000).

Exclusions No grants to individuals or students.

Applications In writing to the correspondent.

The Ashe Park Charitable Trust

Possible preference for child-related hospitals and hospices

£155,000 (2004)

Beneficial area UK, with a possible preference for Hampshire, Isle of Wight and West Sussex.

Ashe Park, Steventon, Basingstoke, Hampshire RG25 3AZ

Correspondent Peter Scott, Trustee

Trustees *P J Scott; Mrs J M T Scott.*

CC Number 297647

Information available Accounts were obtained from the Charity Commission website.

General In 2004 the trust had assets of £15,000 and an income of £303,000 mainly from fundraising activities. Grants were made totalling £155,000. Beneficiaries were: the Honeypot Charity (£65,000); Breast Cancer Haven and the Prince's Drawing School (£40,000 each); Descent International (£16,000); Youth Clubs Hampshire (£10,000); and Head and Neck Cancer (£225). More recent information was not available.

Exclusions No funding towards salaries.

Applications In writing to the correspondent.

The Laura Ashley Foundation

Art and design, higher education, local projects in mid-rural Wales

£260,000 (2004/05)

Beneficial area Mostly Wales, other areas considered.

The Laura Ashley Foundation, Rhydoldog House, Cwmdauddwr, Rhayader, Powys LD6 5HB

Website www.laf.uk.net

Correspondent Wendy Abel

Trustees *Jane Ashley, Chair; Prof. Susan Golombok; Martyn C Gowar; Emma Shuckburgh; Lord Queensbury; Helena Appio; David Goldstone.*

CC Number 288099

Information available Accounts were on file at the Charity Commission.

General The foundation was set up in 1986 in memory of Laura Ashley by her family. It has a strong commitment to art and design and also to Wales, particularly Powys, where the Ashley business was first established.

The foundation is constantly reviewing its funding policies. Potential applicants are advised to check the website for the latest details and recent grants made.

The main areas of activity are:

Projects in mid-rural Wales
- to enhance the lives of families and communities
- rural regeneration
- welfare in the community.

Education
Special bursaries have been set up through institutions of the trustees' choice:

- music conservatoires – bursaries for talented musicians
- LSE – scholarship for a mature anthropology MA student
- Welsh colleges – bursary schemes for fashion/textile departments to Coleg Sir Gar and UWIC.

The arts in London
A pilot project set up by Jane Ashley called SLATE – a network of documentary film makers to encourage wider use of their talents.

In 2004/05 the trust had an income from investments of £269,000. Grants totalled £260,000.

There were 45 grants of £1,000 or more listed in the accounts. Donations included those to: Human Rights Watch (£24,000); Over the Wall Camp (£12,500); Beacon of Hope, Honeypot, Learning for Life, London School of Economics, Save the Children – Tsunami Appeal, Royal Academy and Royal Welsh College (£10,000 each); Mid Wales Opera (£8,300); Bracken Trust and Ponthafren Association (£7,500 each); Phoenix Community (£6,500); Bryn Helvyn-Lemm Sissay Group, Cruse Bereavement, Food & Land Trust, Gurkha Welfare Trust and Llanfyllin Music Festival (£5,000 each); Age Concern and Striking Attitudes (£4,000 each); the Seed (£3,000); Shakespeares Link (£2,600); Carno Community Council (£2,500); Notting Hill Carnival (£2,000); Young Carers (£1,500); and Carno Church (£1,000).

Exclusions The foundation does not fund the following:

- individuals
- new buildings
- medical research
- overseas travel/exchange visits
- private education
- purchase cost of property/land
- restoration of historic buildings or churches
- university or similar research
- projects concerned with domestic violence
- penal affairs

- sport
- general funds
- taking projects into schools
- outward bound-type courses
- newspapers/journals/publications/information packs
- video projects
- safety devices.

Applications Potential applicants are encouraged to telephone the trust to discuss eligibility before submitting an application. An initial application should be made in writing to the correspondent. It should include a summary of the organisation who are applying (activities and work), an outline of the actual project and for what specific purpose the grant is required and a financial summary of total project costs noting how much would be requested from the foundation. Please include details of any funds that have already been raised. It should be typed on one side of headed paper.

The Ashworth Charitable Trust

Welfare

£106,000 (2005/06)

Beneficial area UK and worldwide, with some preference for certain specific needs in Honiton, Ottery St Mary, Sidmouth and Wonford Green surgery, Exeter.

Foot Anstey, Senate Court, Southernhay Gardens, Exeter EX1 1NT

Tel. 01392 411221 **Fax** 01392 685220

Correspondent Mrs G Towner

Trustees *C F Bennett, Chair; Miss S E Crabtree; Mrs K A Gray; G D R Cockram.*

CC Number 1045492

Information available Accounts were on file at the Charity Commission.

General The trust was founded by Mrs C E Crabtree in 1995. The trust currently considers applications for and makes grants as appropriate to:

- Ironbridge Gorge Museum Trust
- people living in the areas covered by the medical practices in Honiton, Ottery St Mary, Sidmouth and Wonford Green surgery, Exeter. Such grants are to be paid for particularly acute needs
- humanitarian projects either to other charities or to individuals.

In 2005/06 the trust had assets of £3.9 million and an income of £138,000. Grants totalled £106,000.

As in the previous year the largest grants of £10,000 each went to Ironbridge Gorge Museum Trust and Hospiscare. Other beneficiaries included: Concern (£6,000); Cambodia's Dump Children and UNICEF (£5,000 each); King's World Trust for Children, Wells for India and World Medical Fund (£3,500 each) Aquila Care Trust, Barton Training Trust, Children in Crisis, Extreme Asylum, Kiloran Trust and Operation New World (£3,000 each); Chernobyl Children in Need (£2,500); Eyeless Trust and Happy Days (£2,000 each); Dressability, Hamlet Trust and NICHS (£1,500 each); and Newlife Foundation for Handicapped Children and Turntable Furniture (£500 each).

Please note these grant examples are not indicative of future giving.

Exclusions No grants for:

- research-based charities
- animal charities
- 'heritage charities' such as National Trust or other organisations whose aim is the preservation of a building, museum, library and so on (with the exception of the Ironbridge Gorge Museum)
- 'faith-based' charities, unless the project is for primarily humanitarian purposes and is neither exclusive to those of that particular faith or evangelical in its purpose.

Grants to individuals are strictly limited to the geographical area and purpose specified in the general section.

Applications In writing to the correspondent.

The Ian Askew Charitable Trust

General

£63,000 to organisations (2005/06)

Beneficial area UK, with a preference for Sussex, and overseas.

Hanover House, 18 Mount Ephraim Road, Tunbridge Wells, Kent TN1 1ED

Tel. 01892 511944

Correspondent Richard Lewis

Trustees *Mrs C Pengelley; R A R Askew; R J Wainwright; G B Ackery; J R Hecks; J B Rank.*

CC Number 264515

Information available Accounts were on file at the Charity Commission.

General Grants are given to a wide variety of charitable bodies throughout the country with a preference for those connected with the county of Sussex. In 2005/06 the trust had assets of almost £7 million and an income of £292,000. Grants to 120 organisations totalled £63,000. A further £11,000 was given in support costs.

The majority of grants to organisations were for £500 or less, with 24 for £1,000 or more. These included £2,000 to Sussex Heritage Trust, £1,000 to Glyndebourne Arts Trust and £1,000 each to Alzheimer's Society, the Anglo-Italian Society for the Protection of Animals Limited, the Art Fund, British Red Cross, Conservation Fund, Disaster Appeal Committee – Asia Quake, East Sussex Disability Association, Friends of Home Physiotherapy Service, Historic Churches' Preservation Trust, MACA, Rural Stress Information Network, St Anne's Church and the Stroke Association

In addition to the above-mentioned donations the trust maintains the woodlands at Plashett Estate, East Sussex, the main part of which is designated as a site of special and scientific interest. The woodlands are used principally for educational purposes.

Applications In writing to the correspondent. Applications are considered monthly.

The Association of Colleges Charitable Trust

Further education colleges

£103,000 (2005/06)

Beneficial area UK.

2–6 Stedham Place, London WC1A 1HU

Tel. 020 7827 4600

Email alice_thiagaraj@aoc.co.uk

Website www.aoc.co.uk

Correspondent Alice Thiagaraj, Trust Manager

Trustees *Alice Thiagaraj; Dr John Brennan; Peter Brophy; Sue Dutton; David Forrester; John Bingham.*

CC Number 1040631

Information available Accounts were on file at the Charity Commission. A prospectus can be downloaded from the trust's website.

General The Association of Colleges was created in 1996 as the single voice to promote the interests of further education colleges in England and Wales. It is responsible for administering two programmes; the largest of these is the Beacon Awards, which provide monetary grants to specific initiatives within further education colleges. The other programme that operates within the trust is the AoC Gold Awards.

Established in 1994, the Beacon Awards recognise and promote the interdependence of further education colleges and business, professional and voluntary sector organisations to their mutual advantage. The aim of the programme is to highlight the breadth and quality of education in colleges throughout the UK and increase understanding of colleges' contribution to UK educational skills policy and economic and social development.

The awards:

- recognise imaginative and exemplary teaching and learning practice in colleges
- draw attention to provision which encourages and supports learners to approach challenges positively and creatively
- support learning and continuous improvement through the dissemination of Award-bearing practice.

Applications may be for a programme, course, or project or for some other aspect of college provision – teaching, learning, guidance or support. To be eligible, initiatives should show evidence of imaginative yet sustainable teaching and learning practice or other relevant provision. It must also fulfil the following criteria:

- It must meet the specific requirements set out by the sponsors of the particular award (see relevant page in the Awards section of the Prospectus).
- It must be subject to evaluation/ quality assurance to influence the continuing development of the initiative.

- It must have been running for at least one academic session before the deadline for applications.
- It must have features which actively promote exemplary teaching and learning.
- It must be of benefit to one or more groups of students or trainees who will be identified and described in the application.
- It must have wider relevance and applicability making it of value to other colleges as an example of good practice and innovation.

Each award has separate criteria in the interests of the area of work of the sponsor. They range from broad educational development to the promotion of particular courses or subjects, covering most aspects of further education.

The other scheme operated by the trust is the AoC Gold Awards for Further Education Alumni, which reward former members of further education colleges who have since excelled in their chosen field or profession.

In 2004/05 the trust had an income of £325,000. Total expenditure for the year was £298,000, including £103,000 in Beacon Awards.

Applications Application forms can be downloaded form the trust's website.

Astellas European Foundation

Medical

See below

Beneficial area Worldwide.

Lovett House, Causeway Corporate Centre, Staines, Middlesex TW18 3AZ

Tel. 01784 419615

Correspondent The Trustees

Trustees *Dr Toichi Takenaka, Chair; Yasuo Ishii; Toshinari Tamura; Shinji Usuda; Wim Kockelkoren; Ken Jones.*

CC Number 1036344

Information available Full accounts were on file at the Charity Commission.

General The objectives of the foundation are to:

- commit long-term support to basic medical and related scientific programmes through organisations such as the SIU (Societe Internationale D'Urologie);

- support selected short, medium and long-term projects, aimed at integrating basic science and clinical research through interdisciplinary projects;
- provide facilities, promote or sponsor the exchange of ideas and views through lectures and discussions of an educational or cultural nature;
- promote, assist or otherwise support charitable institutions aimed at serving good causes.

The 2005/06 annual report stated: 'It is the long-term goal of the foundation to provide support for programmes and cultures that contribute to the advancement of an increasingly healthy society.

'The foundation's trustees believes this is best accomplished by providing funding for basic scientific research, for the examination of public health and environmental policy issues, and for the support of educational and cultural exchange programmes.'

The foundation administers the Astellas award and Lectureship, which grants US$50,000 given every year to reward people significantly contributing to the medical and medicinal disciplines. From 1994–2006 SIU has been the main beneficiary.

The Astellas Prize exists to support scientists or institutions of impeccable reputation to stimulate basic scientific and medical research in the fields that will be selected by the trustees.

The Astellas Fellowship is a scholarship to people studying these disciplines worth up to US$150,000 as a two-year support programme, with people supported being eligible to reapply for a maximum of three years.

In 2005/06 the trust had assets of US$14 million and an income of US$2.3 million. No grants were made to organisations during the year.

Previous beneficiaries have included: Departimento di Medicina Interna Universita di Pisa, the Department of Oncology at Helsinki University Central Hospital, Brauninger Stiftung GmbH Online Mouse Projekt, Connaître Les Syndromes Cérébelleux, Chase Children' Hospice, Foundation Sance at the Department of Hematooncology in Pediatric Faculty Hospital – Olomouc, Associacao De Amigos Da Criança E Da Familia for 'Chão Dos Meninos', Dyadis, Stichting VTV, Archipelago Cooperativa Sociale r.1. and Comitato Maria Letizia Verga.

Applications In writing to the correspondent.

The Astor Foundation

General

£145,000 (2005/06)

Beneficial area UK.

PO Box 3096, Marlborough SN8 3WP

Correspondent The Secretary

Trustees *R H Astor, Chair; Lord Astor of Hever; Lord Latymer; C Astor; Dr H Swanton; Prof J Cunningham.*

CC Number 225708

Information available Accounts were on file at the Charity Commission.

General The primary objective of the Foundation is medical research in its widest sense, favouring research on a broad front rather than in specialised fields. For guidance, this might include general medical equipment or equipment for use in research, or grants to cover travelling and subsistence expenses for doctors and students studying abroad.

In general, the foundation gives preference to giving assistance with the launching and initial stages of new projects and filling in gaps/shortfalls.

In addition to its medical connection, historically the foundation has also supported initiatives for children and youth groups, the disabled, the countryside, the arts, sport, carers groups and animal welfare.

The foundation does not favour the tying-up of large amounts in building projects, however expenditure on bricks and mortar need not be wholly excluded if it should consider this desirable in any particular case. The foundation does not favour the establishment or endowment of Chairs or Professorships. Grants are generally between £250 and £1,500.

In 2005/06 the trust had assets of £3.5 million generating an income of £126,000. Grants to 71 organisations totalled £145,000.

By far the largest grant was £45,000 to Royal Free and University College Medical School (2006–08). Other grants were in the range of £500 and £4,500 and included those to Invalids at Home and League of Friends – University College London Hospitals (£4,500), Help the Hospices (£3,500), Motor Neurone

Disease Association, the National Autistic Society and the Samaritans (£3,000 each), Save the Children (£2,700), British Paralympic Association, the Council of the Order of St John for Kent, the Cutty Sark Trust and Royal College Of Music (£2,500 each), Alzheimer's Disease Society and British School of Osteopathy (£2,000 each), Adventures Offshore, Arundel Castle Cricket Foundation, Meridian Trust Association, Painting in Hospital and Save the Rhino International (£1,000) and Alzheimer's Research Trust (£500).

Exclusions No grants to individuals or towards salaries. Grants are given to registered charities only.

Applications There are no deadline dates or application forms. Applications should be in writing to the correspondent and must include accounts and an annual report if available.

The trustees meet twice-yearly, usually in October and April. If the appeal arrives too late for one meeting it will automatically be carried over for consideration at the following meeting. An acknowledgement will be sent on receipt of an appeal. No further communication will be entered into unless the trustees raise any queries regarding the appeal, or unless the appeal is subsequently successful.

The Astor of Hever Trust

Young people, medical research, education

£37,000 (2005/06)

Beneficial area UK and worldwide, with a preference for Kent and the Grampian region of Scotland.

Frenchstreet House, Westerham, Kent TN16 1PW

Tel. 01959 565070 **Fax** 01959 561286

Correspondent The Trustees

Trustees *John Jacob, Third Baron Astor of Hever; Hon Camilla Astor; Hon. Philip D P Astor.*

CC Number 264134

Information available Accounts were on file at the Charity Commission.

General The trust gives grants UK-wide and internationally. It states that there is a preference for Kent and the

Grampian region of Scotland, although the preference for Kent is much stronger.

When Gavin Astor, second Baron Astor of Hever, founded the trust in 1955, its main areas of support were arts, medicine, religion, education, conservation, young people and sport. Reflecting the settlor's wishes, the trust makes grants to local youth organisations, medical research and educational programmes. Most beneficiaries are UK-wide charities or a local branch.

In 2005/06 the trust had assets of £1.1 million and an income of £37,000. Grants to 120 organisations totalled £37,000.

The nine largest grants of £1,000 or more went to: Migvie Church (£3,000); Rochester Cathedral Legacy Campaign and Rochester Cathedral Regeneration Campaign (£1,500 each); Macmillan Cancer Relief (£1,200); and Bryanston School, Rochester Cathedral Campaign, Royal Hospital Chelsea Appeal Ltd, St Thomas' Church – Aboyne and Take Heart (£1,000 each).

Other beneficiaries included: National Autistic Society, Riding for the Disabled Association – Wharton Bank Appeal and Woodend Arts (£750 each); Demelza House Children's Hospice and National Playing Fields Association (£500 each); Kent Community Foundation (£250); Animal Care Trust, Commonwork Land Trust, English Schools Orchestra, Invalids at Home, Sleep Scotland and Whizz-Kidz (£200 each); Fifth Trust and Royal Chapel Windsor (£150 each); Deal Festival of Music and the Arts, International Medical Corps UK, National Youth Orchestra of Scotland and Sea Cadets Stonehaven (£100 each); and Asthma UK (£50).

Exclusions No grants to individuals.

Applications In writing to the correspondent. Unsuccessful applications are not acknowledged.

The Atlantic Foundation

Education, medical, general

£106,000 (2004/05)

Beneficial area Worldwide, though with some preference for Wales.

Atlantic House, Greenwood Close, Cardiff Gate Business Park, Cardiff CF23 8RD

Tel. 029 2054 5680

Correspondent Mrs B L Thomas, Trustee

Trustees *P Thomas; Mrs B L Thomas.*

CC Number 328499

Information available Full accounts were on file at the Charity Commission.

General The trust supports a range of causes, with a strong interest in Wales. In 2004/05 it had an income of £952,000 from covenants. Grants totalled £106,000, broken down as follows:

- Independent school and colleges (37 grants totalling £42,000)
- Registered charities (50 grants totalling £36,000)
- Community Aid (38 grants totalling £24,000)
- Local authority support (5 grants totalling £3,900)
- Medical appeals and support (2 grants totalling £850)
- Religious foundations (2 grants totalling £400)

Beneficiaries of grants of £1,000 or more included Welsh National Opera (£8,000), Welsh College of Music and Drama (£7,100), Cathedral School (£5,100), Webber Douglas Dance School, Striking Attitudes and Teenage Cancer Trust (£5,000 each), Royal Academy of Music (£2,800), Hammond School and Raleigh International (£2,300 each), Marie Curie Cancer Care, Merthyr Shopmobility and Moorland Primary School – Splott (£2,000 each), Harvest Trust (£1,500) and Boys' and Girls' Clubs of Wales, Cardiff University, Christ College Brecon, Motability, Royal Ballet School, Tenovus, Vision Foundation, Voices Foundation – Dafen Primary School and Woodfield OAP Association (£1,000 each).

Applications In writing to the correspondent. Applications are considered throughout the year.

Lawrence Atwell's Charity

Education, young people

£386,000 to organisations and individuals (2004/05)

Beneficial area UK.

The Skinners' Company, Skinners' Hall, 8 Dowgate Hill, London EC4R 2SP

Tel. 020 7236 5629

Email atwell@skinners.org.uk

Website www.skinnershall.co.uk

Correspondent The Atwell Administrator

Trustee *The Worshipful Company of Skinners.*

CC Number 210773

Information available Accounts were on file at the Charity Commission.

General The purpose of the charity is to promote the education, including social and physical training, of young people who have reached the age of 16, but who are under the age of 27. Grants are made to schools, institutions and charities that undertake training and support with disadvantaged young people. The trust states that they do not publicise their grantmaking to organisations as they only give to organisations that they proactively contact.

In 2004/05 the charity had assets of £15 million and an income of £567,000. Grants totalled £386,000 of which £260,000 went to individuals and £110,000 to three Skinners' Company schools. The sum of £16,000 went to other organisations: Family Welfare Association – Educational Grants Advisory Service (£5,000); the Treloar Trust (£4,500); City and Guilds of London Art School (£4,200); and City and Guilds of London Institute (£1,200).

Exclusions No unsolicited applications.

Applications The trust states that they only give to organisations they proactively contact. Applications will therefore not be considered.

The Aurelius Charitable Trust

Conservation of culture and the humanities

£69,000 (2005/06)

Beneficial area UK.

Briarsmead, Old Road, Buckland, Betchworth, Surrey RH3 7DU

Tel. 01737 842186

Email philip.haynes@tiscali.co.uk

Correspondent P E Haynes, Trustee

Trustees *W J Wallis; P E Haynes.*

CC Number 271333

Information available Accounts were on file at the Charity Commission.

General During the settlor's lifetime, the income of the trust was distributed broadly to reflect his interests in the conservation of culture inherited from the past, and the dissemination of knowledge, particularly in the humanities field. Since the settlor's death in April 1994, the trustees have continued with this policy.

Donations are preferred to be for seed-corn or completion funding not otherwise available. They are usually one-off and range from £500 to £3,000.

In 2005/06 it had assets of £2.1 million, which generated an income of £72,000. Donations were made to 24 organisations totalling £69,000.

Beneficiaries included Canterbury Archaeological Trust – Dover excavations publication, the British Academy – Ceramic Petrology Workshop and St John on Bethnal Green – Soane Church restoration (£5,000 each), Bath Royal Literary and Scientific Institution – archive conservation (£4,700), Hampshire Archives Trust – Portsmouth Record Series (£4,000), The British Academy – towards a new polarising microscope for the Marc and Ismene Fitch Laboratory at the British School at Athens (£3,400), the Bristol Cathedral Trust – Diocesan and Cathedral Records (£3,000), Bletchley Park Trust – archive preservation (£2,000), University of Hull – 'Religion, Law & Philosophy: European Political Thought 1450–1700' (£1,000) and Trinity College of Music – East European students (£500).

Exclusions No grants to individuals.

Applications In writing to the correspondent. Donations are generally made on the recommendation of the trust's board of advisors. Unsolicited applications will only be responded to if an sae is included. Trustees meet twice a year, in January and July, and applications need to be received by May and November.

Harry Bacon Foundation

Medical, animal welfare

£49,000 (2005/06)
Beneficial area UK.

NatWest Bank plc, 153 Preston Road, Brighton BN1 6BD

Correspondent The Manager

Trustee *NatWest Bank plc.*

CC Number 1056500

Information available Accounts were on file at the Charity Commission.

General In 2005/06 the trust had assets of £1.9 million, an income of £77,000 and made grants totalling £49,000.

Ten grants were made to Age Concern, Breast Cancer Campaign, British Eye Research, Guide Dogs, GOS Hospital, Hope House, PBC Foundation, RNLI, SBCU and Wellchild.

Applications In writing to the correspondent.

The Bacta Charitable Trust

General

£136,000 (2004/05)
Beneficial area UK.

Bacta, Alders House, 133 Aldersgate Street, London EC1A 4JA

Tel. 020 7726 9826

Correspondent Linda Malcolm, Clerk

Trustees *R Higgins; C Daniels; M Horwood; S I Meaden; D Orton; J Stergides; M Gemson; J Thomas.*

CC Number 328668

Information available Accounts were on file at the Charity Commission.

General The trust only supports charities recommended by Bacta members. Bacta is the Trade Association for the Coin Operated Amusement Industry.

The trust's principal fundraising takes place at the annual Bacta Charity Ball through a prize raffle and pledges made by guests.

In 2004/05 the trust had assets of £240,000 and an income of £260,000. Grants totalled £136,000. The two main grant beneficiaries were Responsibility in Gambling Trust (£76,000) and BIBIC (£39,000).

Other grants included those to: DEC Tsunami Appeal (£11,000); Radcliffe Hospital (£5,000); BACTA North West, Fairbridge, Percy Hedley School and Christian Lewis Trust (£2,000 each); VICTA (£250); and Samaritans (£100).

Exclusions No grants for overseas charities or religious purposes.

Applications In writing to the correspondent, but via a Bacta member. Applications should be submitted by January, April or August, for trustees' meetings in February, May or September.

The Bagri Foundation

General

£82,000 to organisations (2004/05)
Beneficial area Worldwide.

80 Cannon Street, London EC4N 6EJ

Tel. 020 7280 0000

Correspondent The Hon. A Bagri, Secretary

Trustees *Lord Bagri; Hon. A Bagri; Lady Bagri.*

CC Number 1000219

Information available Accounts were on file at the Charity Commission, but without a list of grants.

General This trust was set up in 1990 with general charitable purposes. In 2004/05 it had assets of £2.2 million and an income of £100,000. Grants to organisations totalled £82,000, with a further £6,600 given to individuals. No further information was available, and a grants list was not on file at the Charity Commission.

Applications In writing to the correspondent.

The Baker Charitable Trust

Mainly Jewish, older people, sickness and disability, medical research

£46,000 (2005/06)
Beneficial area UK and overseas.

16 Sheldon Avenue, Highgate, London N6 4JT

Correspondent Dr Harvey Baker, Trustee

Trustees *Dr Harvey Baker; Dr Adrienne Baker.*

CC Number 273629

Information available Accounts were on file at the Charity Commission, without a list of grants.

General The trust makes grants in the areas of people who are elderly, chronically sick or disabled and people who have had limited educational opportunity. The trust also supports medical research related to the above groups. There is a preference for Jewish organisations.

In 2005/06 it had assets of £1.2 million and an income of £54,000. Grants to 30 organisations totalled £46,000. A list of grants was not included in the accounts filed at the Charity Commission.

Previous beneficiaries have included British Council Shaare Zedek Medical Centre, Chai Cancer Care, Community Security Trust, Disabled Living Foundation, Friends of Magen David Adom in Great Britain, Hillel Foundation, Institute of Jewish Policy Research, Jewish Women's Aid, Marie Curie Cancer Care, National Society for Epilepsy, Norwood Ltd, United Jewish Israel Appeal, St John's Hospice, United Synagogue, Winged Fellowship and World Jewish Relief.

Exclusions No grants to individuals or non-registered charities.

Applications In writing to the correspondent. The trustees meet to consider applications in January, April, July and October.

Balmain Charitable Trust

General in the UK

£79,000 (2005/06)
Beneficial area UK.

Pen Ridge House, Pen Selwood, Wincanton, Somerset BA9 8LN

Correspondent S Balmain, Trustee

Trustees *P G Eaton; A Tappin; S Balmain; I D S Balmain; Mrs L Balmain; C A G Wells.*

CC Number 1079972

Information available Accounts were on file at the Charity Commission.

General Registered with the Charity Commission in March 2000, in 2005/06 the trust had assets of £2.3 million, an income of £90,000 and made 37 grants totalling £79,000.

Organisations to receive grants in the year included: British Red Cross and Oxfam (£7,000 each); Royal Opera House Foundation and Royal Shakespeare Company (£5,000 each); the Suzy Lamplugh Trust (£3,500); the Game Conservancy Trust (£3,000); Association for International Cancer Research, Barnardos, the British Museum Friends, Leukaemia Research Fund, Second Chance, SSAFA Forces Help, the Wildfowl & Wetlands Trust, Wiltshire Wildlife Trust and the Zambezi Society (£2,000 each); Dorset & Somerset Air Ambulance Trust (£1,500); and Age Concern, Arthritis Research Campaign, Cancer Research UK, Crisis, the Lady Hoare Trust and Westcountry Rivers Trust (£1,000 each).

Applications In writing to the correspondent.

The Balney Charitable Trust

Preservation, conservation, welfare, service charities

£52,000 (2005/06)
Beneficial area UK, with a preference for north Buckinghamshire and north Bedfordshire.

The Chicheley Estate, Bartlemas Office, Pave ham, Bedford MK43 7PF

Tel. 01234 823663 **Fax** 01234 825058

Correspondent G C W Beazley, Clerk

Trustees *Maj. J G B Chester; R Ruck-Keene.*

CC Number 288575

Information available Accounts were on file at the Charity Commission.

General The objectives of the trust as stated in its accounts as follows:

- the furtherance of any religious and charitable purposes in connection with the parishes of Chicheley, North Crawley and the SCAN Group i.e. Sherington, Astwood, Hardmead and churches with a Chester family connection

- the provision of housing for persons in necessitous circumstances
- agriculture, forestry and armed service charities
- care of older people and the sick and disabled from the Chicheley area
- other charitable purposes.

In 2005/06 the trust had assets of £788,000 and an income of £70,000. Grants were made totalling £52,000. The trust makes 16 regular donations each year by standing order ranging from £25 to £1,000. In the year regular donations totalled £4,800. Beneficiaries included St Lawrence's Church – Chicheley, Buckinghamshire Historic Churches Trust, Friends of Tilsworth Church, Bedfordshire and Hertfordshire Historic Churches Trust and Gurkha Welfare Trust.

Other donations totalled £47,000 and included: British Red Cross – Responder Ambulance Appeal, Queen Alexandra Hospital Home and Stoke Mandeville Cancer & Haematology Fund; £3,000 to Lupus UK (£5,000 each); Age Concern – Milton Keynes, Emmaus – Carlton, National Playing Fields Association, Parkinson's Disease Society, Prostate Cancer Research and Wheel Power – Stoke Mandeville (£2,000 each); Leonard Cheshire Foundation – Enabling Project, National Missing Persons Helpline and Tree Aid (£1,000 each); and Brittle Bone Society and Elizabeth Finn Care – Buckinghamshire (£500 each).

Exclusions Local community organisations and individuals outside north Buckinghamshire and north Bedfordshire.

Applications In writing to the correspondent. Applications are acknowledged if an sae is enclosed, otherwise if the charity has not received a reply within six weeks the application has not been successful.

The Baltic Charitable Fund

Registered charities benefiting residents of the City of London, seafarers, fishermen, ex-service and service people

£122,000 (2004/05)
Beneficial area UK, with a preference for the City of London.

The Baltic Exchange, 38 St Mary Axe, London EC3A 8BH

Tel. 020 7623 5501

Correspondent The Company Secretary

Trustee *The Board of Directors.*

CC Number 279194

Information available Full accounts were on file at the Charity Commission.

General The trust aims to support applications relating to the sea, including training for professionals and children, the City of London, Forces charities and for sponsorship for Baltic Exchange members.

In 2004/05 the trust had assets of just over £1 million and an income of £49,000. Grants to 19 organisations totalled £122,000, of which the largest grants (£10,000 and over) went to: Reeds School Foundation Appeal (£42,000); City of London School for Boys (£39,000); City of London School for Girls (£21,000); and RNLI (£11,000).

Smaller grants included those to: St Paul's Cathedral (£5,000); Jubilee Sailing Trust (£2,500); Merchant Navy Falklands Memorial Trust (£2,000); British and International Sailors Society (£1,000); Royal British Legion Poppy Appeal (£500); Barnardos and Butlins Swimathon (£300 each); and the Mission to Seafarers (£250).

Exclusions No support for advertising or charity dinners, and so on.

Applications Unsolicited applications are not considered.

William P Bancroft (No. 2) Charitable Trust and Jenepher Gillett Trust

Quaker

£38,000 (2005)

Beneficial area UK and overseas.

Fernroyd, St Margaret's Road, Altrincham, Cheshire WA14 2AW

Correspondent Dr Roger Gillett, Trustee

Trustees *R Gillett; G T Gillett; D S Gillett; J Moseley; A J Yelloly.*

CC Number 288968

Information available Accounts were on file at the Charity Commission.

General This trust is unusual as it consists of two separate trusts which are operated as one. For historical reasons there is a William P Bancroft Trust giving in the UK and a Jenepher Gillet Trust giving in Delaware, USA which shared a common settlor/joint-settlor; the two trusts are now being run jointly with the same trustees and joint finances.

It makes grants towards charitable purposes connected with the Religious Society of Friends, supporting Quaker conferences, colleges and Friends' homes for older people.

In 2004/05 it had an income of £39,000 and gave grants totalling £38,000. Assets stood at £750,000.

Grants included those to Charney Manor Quaker Courses (£11,000), Woodbrooke College (£6,000), BYM – general funds/reserves (£5,000), Bootham School, Cape Town – Quaker Peace Centre, Chaigley Educational Centre, FWCC, Mount School York Foundation, Oxford Homeless Medial Fund, Quaker Voluntary Action, QUIET – Ramallah Friends School and Sibford School – bursaries (£1,000 each) and Alternates to Violence (£500).

Exclusions No appeals unconnected with Quakers. No support for individual or student grant applications.

Applications In writing to the correspondent. Trustees meet in May, applications must be received no later than April.

The Barbers' Company General Charities

Medical and nursing education

£125,000 (2004/05)

Beneficial area UK.

Barber-Surgeons' Hall, Monkwell Square, Wood Street, London EC2Y 5BL

Correspondent The Clerk

Trustees *A J Missen, Chair; J A H Bootes; J C Buckland-Wright; H H Harris Hughes; Sir Barry Jackson; J W L Last; F N Read; C W Sprague; J M Tomlinson.*

CC Number 265579

Information available Accounts were on file at the Charity Commission.

General The charities were registered in May 1973; grants are made to organisations and individuals. It no longer has direct contact with the hairdressing fraternity. However, a small amount is given each year to satisfy its historical links. Causes supported include those related to medicine education and nursing.

In 2004/05 it had assets of £1.1 million and an income of £125,000 including £82,000 from covenants and Gift Aid. Grants totalled £125,000.

Beneficiaries included: Royal College of Surgeons (£40,000); Phyllis Tuckwell Hospice (£22,000); BMA Medical Educational Trust (£19,000); Reed's School and the Royal Medical Foundation (£5,100 each); the Corporation of London School for Girls (£4,000); City of London Freeman's School (£3,600); St Thomas Lupus Trust (£2,000); and British Orthopaedic Association and Mansion House Scholarship Scheme (£1,000 each).

Applications The charities do not welcome unsolicited applications.

The Barbour Trust

Health, welfare

£195,000 (2005/06)

Beneficial area Mainly Tyne and Wear, Northumberland and South Tyneside.

J Barbour & Sons Ltd, Simonside, Tyne and Wear NE34 9PD

Tel. 0191 455 4444 **Fax** 0191 427 4259

Website www.barbour.com

Correspondent Harold Tavroges

Trustees *Dame Margaret Barbour, Chair; Henry Jacob Tavroges; Anthony Glenton; Miss Helen Barbour.*

CC Number 328081

Information available Accounts were on file at the Charity Commission.

General The objectives of the charity are to support any charitable institution (grants are not made directly to individuals) whose objectives include:

- The relief of patients suffering from any form of illness or disease, the promotion of research in to the causes and treatment of such illnesses or disease and the provision of medical equipment for such patients.

- The furtherance of education of children and young people by award of scholarship, exhibitions, bursaries or maintenance allowances tenable at any school, university or other educational establishment in England.
- The protection and preservation for the benefit of the public in England, such features of cities, towns, villages and the countryside as are of special environmental, historical or architectural interest.
- The relief of persons, whether resident in England or otherwise, who are in conditions of need, hardship or distress as a result of local, national or international disaster, or by reason of their social and economic circumstances.

In 2005/06 the trust had assets of £3.9 million and an income of £321,000. A total of 457 grants were made totalling £195,000 and were broken down by category as follows:

Community Welfare	£70,000
Youth/Children	£34,000
Medical care research and general health	£16,000
People with disabilities	£8,300
People who are older	£4,700
Conservation/horticultural	£2,000
Education/expeditions	£3,100
Service charities	£740
Arts	£4,600
Housing/homelessness	£26,000
Maritime charities	£2,100
Animal welfare	£6,000
Special appeals from overseas	£1,000
Deprivation	£16,000

There were 83 grants of £1,000 or more listed in the accounts. Beneficiaries included: Crisis (£24,000 in three grants); Animal Health Trust, Brian Roycroft Fund for Young People leaving Care, National Probation Service, Stepping Stones and Tyneside Cinema (£5,000 each); Sunderland University – Futures Fund (£3,000); Shelter (£2,500); Durham Wildlife Trust, Hebburn Neighbourhood Advice Centre, Refuge and YMCA Newcastle upon Tyne (£2,000 each); Inside Out Trust (£1,500); and Deafblind UK, Fairway in Tyne and Wear, Kids Kabin, NCH, North East Sailing Team, Pennywell Community Centre, St Vincent de Paul Society and Wansbeck Toy Library (£1,000 each).

Exclusions No support for:

- requests from outside the geographical area
- requests from educational establishments
- individual applications, unless backed by a particular charitable organisation
- capital grants for building projects.

Applications On an application form available from PO Box 21, Guisborough, Cleveland, TS14 8YH. The applications should include full back-up information, a statement of accounts and the official charity number of the applicant.

A main grants meeting is held every three to four months to consider grants of £500 plus. Applications are processed and researched by the administrator and secretary and further information may be requested.

A small grants meeting is held monthly to consider grants up to £500.

The trust always receives more applications than it can support. Even if a project fits its policy priority areas, it may not be possible to make a grant.

Barchester Healthcare Foundation

Health and social care

£165,000 to organisations and individuals (2005)

Beneficial area England, Scotland and Wales.

Suite 201, The Chambers, Chelsea harbour, London SW10 0XF

Tel. 0800 328 3328 **Fax** 020 7352 2229

Email info@bhcfoundation.org.uk

Website www.bhcfoundation.org.uk

Correspondent The Administrator

Trustees *Mike Parsons; Christine Hodgson; Prof. Malcolm Johnson; Elizabeth Mills; Nick Oulton; Janice Robinson; Chris Vellenoweth.*

CC Number 1083272

Information available Information is available on the foundation's website.

General The Barchester Healthcare Foundation was established by Barchester Healthcare to reinvest into the communities it serves.

It is a registered charity with independent trustees. The foundation was set up in 2003 with an initial grant of over £250,000. Barchester Healthcare has continued to make further contributions to the foundation and it is hoped that others will also donate.

'The charity's objective is to make grants to individuals and organisations, who have identified health and social care needs which cannot be met by the statutory public sector, or by the individual/s themselves.

'The trustees' emphasis is on supporting practical solutions that provide direct support to people in need. The foundation attaches importance to the assessment and dissemination of the results of work it has funded, so that others might benefit from lessons learned.'

Grants are available for work supporting:

- older people
- adults with physical disabilities
- adults with mental disabilities.

The focus is on adults over the age of 18 who live in England, Scotland or Wales.

Examples of instances where the foundation will provide funding include:

- Support to small community groups who provide activities for older people or disabled adults. These activities could include, for example, social events, outings, sports and education.
- Provision, for an individual, specialist care equipment or adaptations not the responsibility of the statutory services that will be important to the recipient(s).
- Support to community centres and volunteer groups who help, for example, people with dementia, multiple sclerosis or mental illness.
- Funding for course fees for disabled adults seeking to improve their quality of life by studying and obtaining a diploma or university degree.
- Support for innovative pilot projects and new schemes that will make a difference to older or disabled people.

The foundation can provide grants of any amount, up to a maximum of £10,000.

In 2005 grants totalled £165,000. Recent beneficiaries have included: 4 SIGHT, Alzheimer Scotland, Breasclete Community Association, the London Epilepsy Project, Music in Hospitals and VocalEyes.

Applications are welcomed from organisations, small groups or from individual applicants on behalf of the person who would benefit. They are not normally accepted from someone applying on their own behalf.

Exclusions The foundation will not normally provide ongoing support for a project following an initial grant. A further application for the same project will only be considered after a period of three years. Funds cannot be used to provide any services normally offered in a care home operated by the parent company or by any other group, nor to provide services for which the health and social care authorities have statutory responsibility. The foundation does not generally provide grants for indirect services such as helplines, newsletters, leaflets or research. No funding for core costs, salaries, general projects or major building projects.

Applications An online application form is available on the foundation's website. No additional documentation is required. A decision usually takes approximately ten weeks from the date of application.

Barclays Stockbrokers Charitable Trust

General

£84,000 (2004/05)

Beneficial area UK.

Barclays Bank Trust Co. Ltd, Osborne Court, Gadbrook Park, Rudheath, Northwich, Cheshire CW9 7UE

Correspondent The Trust Officer

Trustee *Barclays Bank Trust Company Ltd.*

CC Number 1093833

Information available Information was provided by the trust.

General Established in 2002, this charity makes grants to registered and exempt charities only. Preference is given to small and medium-sized charities and local branches of UK charities. Support is only given for capital projects and specific programmes rather than funding core or revenue costs.

Applications are considered in the following categories:

- physical and mental disability
- older people
- ill health/relief in need
- children/youth
- family and social welfare
- education and training
- blind/deaf
- poverty/homelessness.

Only one-off grants are made, grants are usually in the range of £10,000 and £50,000. Support will only be given for capital projects or specific programmes rather than core or revenue costs.

In 2004/05 the trust had an income of £86,000 and made grants totalling £84,000. Beneficiaries were L'Arche (£15,000), Children's Country Holiday Fund (£12,000), National Library for the Blind (£9,700), Newbury Community Resource Centre – Community Furniture Project (£7,400), Edinburgh Cyrenians (£6,800), Council for the Advancement of Communications with Deaf People (£6,600), Barrow and District Disability Association (£4,600), Penderyn Community Hall (£5,100), Cornwall Disability Arts Group, Oakridge Village Hall Trust and Orcadia Creative Learning Centre (£5,000 each) and Aquila Care Trust (£1,400).

Exclusions The following categories will not be considered for funding:

- large national charities
- individuals
- schools/colleges/universities
- religion/church buildings
- overseas charities/projects
- medical research
- animal welfare
- expenses that have already been incurred.

Applications In writing to the correspondent. Appeals are considered quarterly at trustees' meetings held at the end of February, May, August and November. If eligibility is established following receipt of an appeal letter, then an application form will be sent.

Peter Barker-Mill Memorial Charity

General

£86,000 (2005/06)

Beneficial area UK, with a preference for Hampshire, including Southampton.

c/o Longdown Management Ltd, The Estate Office, Longdown, Marchwood, Southampton SO40 4UH

Correspondent Christopher Gwyn-Evans, Administrator

Trustees *C Gwyn-Evans; T Jobling; R M Moyse.*

CC Number 1045479

Information available Accounts were on file at the Charity Commission website.

General In 2005/06 the trust had assets of £2.8 million and an income of £56,000. Grants were made to 20 organisations totalling £86,000.

Beneficiaries included: Furzey Gardens Charitable Trust (£20,000); Hounsdown School and Parish of Colbury (£10,000 each); Friends of Shepherds Down School (£5,500); Club Hampshire, Marchwood Parish Church Council, Treloars School and Trinity Centre Winchester (£5,000 each); Dreams Come True Charity and Homestart – Eastleigh (£3,000 each); Computer Aid International (£2,000); British Wireless for the Blind Fund (£1,000); and the Octopus Challenge (£500).

Exclusions No grants to individuals.

Applications In writing to the correspondent.

The Barnabas Trust

Evangelical Christianity

£252,000 to organisations and individuals (2005/06)

Beneficial area UK and overseas. Overseas projects are supported only if they are personally known by the trustees.

c/o 63 Wolsey Drive, Walton-on-Thames, Surrey KT12 3BB

Tel. 01932 220622

Correspondent Mrs Doris Edwards, Secretary

Trustees *K C Griffiths, Chair; D S Helden; N Brown.*

CC Number 284511

Information available Full accounts were on file at the Charity Commission.

General In 2005/06 the trust had assets of £3.4 million generating an income of £154,000. Grants to organisations and individuals totalled £252,000.

Community welfare – £33,000
Grants were given to local, UK and international medical institutions and charities concerned with the welfare of children, older people, prisoners, people experiencing poverty and the general community. Beneficiaries included: Yeldall Christian Centres (£4,500); Release International (£3,000); Bethany Children's Trust and Shaftesbury Society (£2,500 each); Brass Tacks and Oxford Overseas Student Housing (£2,000 each);

and Anglo-Peruvian Child Care Mission and the Exodus Project (£1,000 each).

Educational – £32,000

Grants were given to establishments in the UK and overseas, and general educational charities, including religious education. Beneficiaries included: Haggai Institute (£4,500); Schools Outreach (£2,500); All Nations Christian College, Church Pastoral Aid Society, Emmaus Bible School – Zimbabwe and the Stapleford Centre (£2,000 each); Danoko Training College (£1,500); and Operation Mobilisation and Tyndale House (£1,000).

Christian mission overseas – £121,000

The sum of £80,000 went to Scripture Gift Mission. Other beneficiaries included: Medical Missionary News (£4,500); Operation Mobilisation (£4,000 in two grants); United Mission to Nepal (£3,500); Echoes of Service (£3,000); WEC International (£2,500); Christian Youth Activities and On the Move (£1,500 each); and Arab Vision Trust (£1,000).

Christian mission in the UK – £51,000

Beneficiaries included: Naval, Military and Air Force Bible Society (£7,500 in two grants); Counties Evangelical Trust (£3,500 in two grants); Abernathy Trust and Open Air Mission (£2,000 each); Crusade for World Revival (£1,500); and Bible Reading Fellowship, Christian Viewpoint for Men, London City Mission, Radio Outreach and the Sycamore Project (£1,000 each).

Grants were made to individuals for: educational purposes (£10,000 in 13 grants); and for Christian mission overseas (£5,500 in four grants).

Exclusions 'The trust is no longer able to help with building, refurbishment or equipment for any church, since to be of any value grants need to be large.' On-going revenue costs such as salaries are not supported.

Applications In writing to the correspondent, giving as much detail as possible, and enclosing a copy of the latest audited accounts, if applicable. The trust states: 'Much of the available funds generated by this trust are allocated to existing donees. The trustees are willing to consider new applications, providing they refer to a project which is overtly evangelical in nature.' If in doubt about whether to submit an application, please telephone the secretary to the trust for guidance.

The trustees meet four times a year, or more often as required, and applications will be put before the next available meeting.

Please note it is likely that the trust will cease to exist by 2012. Very little money is available for unsolicited applications.

Lord Barnby's Foundation

General

£228,000 (2004/05)

Beneficial area UK.

PO Box 71, Plymstock, Plymouth PL8 2YP

Correspondent Mrs J A Lethbridge, Secretary

Trustees *Sir John Lowther; Lord Newall; Sir Michael Farquhar; Hon. George Lopes; Countess Peel.*

CC Number 251016

Information available Accounts were on file at the Charity Commission.

General The foundation has established a permanent list of charities that it supports each year, with the remaining funds then distributed to other charities.

Its priority areas include the following:

- heritage; the preservation of the environment; and the countryside and ancient buildings, particularly the 'great Anglican cathedrals'
- charities benefiting people who are ex-service and service, Polish, disabled or refugees
- welfare of horses and people who look after them
- youth and other local organisations in Ashtead – Surrey, Blyth – Nottinghamshire and Bradford – Yorkshire
- technical education for the woollen industry.

In 2004/05 the trust had assets of £4.5 million and an income of £214,000. Grants totalled £228,000 and were divided between 'permanent' and 'discretionary' donations.

Examples of the 68 organisation receiving 'discretionary' donations included: £15,000 to Barnby Memorial Fund; £10,000 each to Chillingham Wild Cattle Association Ltd, the Church Museum Appeal, the Evelina Children's Hospital Appeal, St Luke's Hospital for the Clergy and Royal Marsden Cancer Campaign; £5,000 each to Ashstead War Memorial, Martin Sailing Project, Merlin, Oxford Children's Hospital, Royal Commonwealth Ex-services

League and Toynbee Hall; £3,000 to countryside Foundation for Education; £2,500 to the Snowdon Award Scheme; £2,000 each to Alzheimer's Research Trust, Farms for City Children and Royal Hospital for Neuro-disability; £1,500 to Tall Ships Youth Trust; £1,000 each to the Brain Research Trust, Chicks, Hospice Homecare and Trinity Hospice; and £500 each to Worldwide Volunteering for Young People, Devon Red Cross and Winged Fellowship Trust.

Exclusions No grants to individuals.

Applications Applications will only be considered if received in writing accompanied by a set of the latest accounts. Applicants do not need to send an sae. Appeals are considered three times a year; in February, June and November.

The Barnsbury Charitable Trust

General

£57,000 (2003/04)

Beneficial area UK, but no local charities outside Oxfordshire.

26 Norham Road, Oxford OX2 6SF

Correspondent H L J Brunner, Trustee

Trustees *H L J Brunner; M R Brunner; T E Yates.*

CC Number 241383

Information available Accounts were on file at the Charity Commission website.

General In 2003/04 the trust had assets of £1 million and an income of £55,000. Grants were made to 36 organisations totalling £57,000.

The largest grants were £13,000 to Oxford Chamber Music Festival, £5,000 to Oxford Diocesan Board of Finance, £2,500 to Police Rehab Trust, £2,000 each to Cutteslowe Community Association and St Giles' PCC, £1,900 to Royal British Legion and £1,000 each to Blackfriars Overseas Aid, Charities Aid Foundation, Dorchester Abbey Preservation Trust, Oxfordshire Christian Institute for Counselling and Oxfordshire County Council.

Smaller grants included £500 each to Douglas House, Orchestra of St John, School of St Helen and St Catherine and St Mary's Chalgrove, £250 each to Friends Bodleian, Home Farm Trust and

New Road Baptist Church and £100 each to Didcot Unknown Donors Charity, Hampden Trust, Oxford Oratory Trust, Oxford Shire Museum, Thame Charities, Vale of Downland Museum Trust and Vale of White Horse District Charities.

Exclusions No grants to individuals.

Applications In writing to the correspondent.

Surrey, Queen Elizabeth's Foundation, Scottish Chamber Orchestra, Starlight Children's Foundation, Universal Beneficent Society and Wireless for the Bedridden (£1,000 each).

Exclusions No grants to individuals.

Applications In writing to the correspondent. Trustees meet three times a year; in April, August and December.

- Other – 8 grants were made ranging from £250 to £500 totalling £2,300

Individuals
- Medical – 7 grants were made ranging from £100 to £500 totalling £2,100
- Educational – 19 grants were made ranging from £100 to £750 totalling £5,600
- Other – 2 grants were made ranging from £100 to £250 totalling £350

Applications In writing to the correspondent. Trustees meet bi-monthly.

The Misses Barrie Charitable Trust

Medical, general

£165,000 (2004/05)
Beneficial area UK.

Messrs Raymond Carter and Co., 1b Haling Road, South Croydon CR2 6HS

Tel. 020 8686 1686

Correspondent Raymond Carter, Trustee

Trustees *R G Carter; R S Waddell; R S Ogg; Mrs R Fraser.*

CC Number 279459

Information available Full accounts were on file at the Charity Commission.

General In 2004/05 the income of the trust was £233,000 and grants to about 100 organisations totalled £165,000; assets stood at £5.1 million.

Beneficiaries of larger grants of £5,000 or more included: Eden Project and University of Oxford Weatherall Institute of Molecular Medicine (£10,000 each); Scottish Chamber Orchestra (£8,000); and Cobham Youth Trust – Worcestershire County Cricket Club (£5,000).

Other beneficiaries included: Princess Royal Trust for Carers (£3,750); University of Dundee Biomedical Research (£3,000); the Attic Charity, Edinburgh Young Carers Project, Glasgow City Mission and Eric Liddell Centre (£2,500 each); 1st Woldingham Scouts & Guides, Age Concern, Brighton and Hove Parents' and Children's Group, British Vascular Foundation, Wellbeing and Worshipful Company of Hackney Carriage Drivers (£2,000 each); Eastnor Brownies (£1,500); and Age Concern – Surrey, British Wheelchair Sports Foundation, CHICKS, Glasgow Old Peoples Welfare, Inspire Foundation, Life Education Centre

The Bartlett Taylor Charitable Trust

General

£55,000 (2004/05)
Beneficial area Preference for Oxfordshire.

24 Church Green, Witney, Oxfordshire OX8 6AT

Tel. 01993 703941 **Fax** 01993 776071

Correspondent G T Alty, Trustee

Trustees *Richard Bartlett; Gareth Alty; Mrs Katherine Bradley; Mrs Brenda Cook; James W Dingle; Mrs Rosemary Warner; Ian Welch; Mrs S Boyd.*

CC Number 285249

Information available Accounts were on file at the Charity Commission.

General In 2003/04 the trust had assets of £1.5 million and an income of £55,000. Grants were made totalling £55,000. There were 135 grants awarded during the year which were covered in the following categories:

International charities
- 7 grants were made ranging from £500 to £1,000 totalling £9,000

UK national charities
- Medical – 15 grants were made ranging from £100 to £1,000 totalling £7,400
- Educational – 2 grants of £500 each were made
- Other – 13 grants were made ranging from £250 to £500 totalling £5,500

Local organisations
- Community projects – 41 grants were made ranging from £100 to £750 totalling £13,000
- Medical – 12 grants were made ranging from £250 to £1,900 totalling £6,600
- Educational – 9 grants were made ranging from £200 to £700 totalling £3,700

The Paul Bassham Charitable Trust

General

£222,000 (2004/05)
Beneficial area UK, mainly Norfolk.

Howes Percival, The Guildyard, 51 Colegate, Norwich NR3 1DD

Tel. 01603 762103

Correspondent R Lovett, Trustee

Trustees *R Lovett; R J Jacob.*

CC Number 266842

Information available Accounts were on file at the Charity Commission.

General This trust was established in the early 1970s and in 2004/05 had assets of £7.5 million and an income of £250,000. During the year 191 donations were made totalling £222,000.

Beneficiaries during the year included: the Big C Appeal and Norfolk Community Foundation (£25,000 each); St Martins Housing Trust (£20,000); Norfolk County Council – 'The Supper at Emmaus' (£10,000); Victim Support Norfolk (£7,500); 1st Martham Scout Group, Assist Trust, British Trust for Ornithology, Dragon Hall Appeal, St Matthew Housing and World Land Trust (£5,000 each); Norfolk Family Mediation Service (£3,500); Whitlingham Charitable Trust (£3,000); 1st Cringleford Scout Group (£2,000 each); and Assist Trust, Brainwave, the Forum Trust Limited and Macmillan Cancer Relief (£1,000 each).

The trustees state that although they can give support to appeals from national charities, in practice all grants are given for work that has an involvement in Norfolk.

Exclusions Grant payments will not be made directly in favour of individuals.

Applications Only in writing to the correspondent – no formal application forms issued. Telephone enquiries are not invited because of administrative costs. 'The trustees meet quarterly (March, June, September, December) to consider general applications although additional meetings or discussions are held where major projects are the subject of an application or where there is some degree of urgency.'

The Batchworth Trust

Medical, social welfare, general

£254,000 (2005/06)

Beneficial area Worldwide.

CLB Gatwick LLP, Imperial Buildings, 68 Victoria Road, Horley, Surrey RH6 7PZ

Tel. 01293 776411

Correspondent M R Neve, Administrative Executive

Trustee Lockwell Trustees Ltd.

CC Number 245061

Information available Accounts were on file at the Charity Commission.

General The trust mainly supports nationally recognised charities, in the categories shown below.

In 2005/06 it had assets of £8.7 million, an income of £272,000 and made 40 grants totalling £254,000, broken down as follows:

Medical	24.8%
Humanitarian aid	20.8%
Welfare	19.5%
Education	12.5%
Conservation and environment	5.9%
Disabilities	3.9%
Drug and alcohol rehabilitation	3.9%
Housing	3.9%
Restoration	2.8%
Arts	2%

Grants ranged from £1,000 to £25,000, but were mainly for amounts of £5,000 or less. The beneficiaries of the 12 largest grants of £10,000 or more were: Disaster Emergency Fund (£25,000); New Hall College (£12,500); and Brick by Brick, the Clive Project, the Cure Parkinson's Trust, Energy & Vision, the Halo Trust, Hemel Hempstead Hospital, Hospice of St Francis, International Red Cross, the Mediae Trust and the Salvation Army (£10,000 each).

Other beneficiaries included: Epilepsy Action (£8,000); Oxford Credit Union (£7,500); the Dacorum Community Trust (£6,000); Cystic Fibrosis Association, Jubilee Sailing Trust, Merlin, Iain Rennie Hospice at Home, Scottish Wildlife Trust, SOS Children's Fund, Tithandizane Small Holder Farmers Association (£5,000 each); Raleigh Trust and Royal Marines Association (£3,000 each); and the Primary Club (£1,000).

Exclusions No applications from individuals can be considered.

Applications In writing to the correspondent. An sae should be included if a reply is required.

The Batty Charitable Trust

General

£115,000 (2004/05)

Beneficial area UK.

Rugby Chambers, 2 Rugby Street, London WC1N 3QU

Correspondent The Trustees

Trustees Michael Smith; Kathryn Skoyles.

CC Number 1094948

Information available Accounts were on file at the Charity Commission.

General This trust was registered with the Charity Commission in December 2002. Its policy is to support UK registered charities of every description with particular emphasis on small charities where a grant of £1,000 to £5,000 is likely to have a significant impact.

In 2004/05 it had an income of £2.4 million. Grants totalled £115,000. The sum of £2.6 million was carried forward at the end of the year.

There were 38 grants made in the year. Beneficiaries included Children with Cystic Fibrosis Dream Holidays, the Children's Adventure Farm Trust, Jewish Book Council, the Mzamowethu Pre-Primary School Appeal, Nightingale House, Regular Forces Employment Association, St Richard's Hospital Charitable Trust, Victim Support and Worcestershire and YWCA England and Wales (£5,000 each), Dressability (£3,000), City Escape, Earls Court Youth Club, Friends of the Hebrew University, Royal Academy of Music, Sedbergh Pepper-pot Club and the Wiener Library

(£2,500 each), British Friends of Ohel Sarah (£2,000), Oneg Youth Club and Winged Fellowship Trust (£1,000), Hampstead and Highgate Festival (£900) and Britain Tanzania Society (£500).

Applications Applicants should submit a letter stating when and for what purpose a grant is required and how a grant will make an impact on their work. Applicants must submit a copy of their latest accounts.

The Bay Tree Charitable Trust

Development work, general

£200,000 (2004)

Beneficial area UK and overseas.

c/o Payne Hicks Beach, 10 New Square, London WC2A 3QG

Correspondent The Trustees

Trustees I M P Benton; Miss E L Benton; P H Benton.

CC Number 1044091

Information available Accounts were on file at the Charity Commission.

General In 2004 the trust had assets of £2.6 million, an income of £90,000 and made 11 grants totalling £200,000. No grants were made in the previous year.

Beneficiaries were Crusaid, Marie Stopes International and Médecins Sans Frontières UK (£25,000 each), NSPCC and St Mungos (£20,000 each), Children of the Andes, EveryChild, Pesticide Action Network UK – Bhopal Medical Appeal, Tsunami Earthquake Appeal and Wessex Autistic Society (£15,000 each) and Schizophrenia Association of Great Britain (£10,000).

Exclusions No grants to individuals.

Applications In writing to the correspondent. No acknowledgements will be made to unsuccessful applications.

The Beacon Trust

Christian

£39,000 (2005/06)

Beneficial area Mainly UK, but also some overseas (usually in the British Commonwealth) and Spain and Portugal.

Unit 3, Newhouse Farm, Old Crawley Road, Horsham, West Sussex RH12 4RU

Correspondent Grahame Scofield

Trustees *Miss J Benson; Miss J M Spink; M Spink.*

CC Number 230087

Information available Accounts were on file at the Charity Commission.

General The trust's objectives are 'to advance the Christian faith, relieve poverty and advance education'.

In 2005/06 the trust had assets of £560,000, an income of £55,000 and made grants totalling £39,000.

The emphasis of the trust's support is on Christian work overseas, particularly amongst students, although the trust does not support individuals. The trust has previously stated that it has a list of charities that it supports in most years. This leaves very few funds available for unsolicited applications.

Principal donations in 2005/06 were: £10,000 each to IFES and Latin Link; £9,000 to Cascadas; £5,000 to Christian Heritage; and £1,000 to Trinity Church – Liphook.

Exclusions Applications from individuals are not considered.

Applications The trust does not respond to unsolicited applications.

Bear Mordechai Ltd

Jewish

£121,000 (2004/05)

Beneficial area Worldwide.

40 Fountayne Road, London N16 7DT

Correspondent Mrs Leah Benedikt, Secretary

Trustees *Y Benedikt; C Benedikt; E S Benedikt.*

CC Number 286806

Information available Accounts were on file at the Charity Commission.

General Grants are made to Jewish organisations. The trust states that religious, educational and other charitable institutions are supported.

In 2004/05 this trust had assets of £1.1 million, an income of £118,000 and made grants totalling £121,000.

Grant beneficiaries included NRST (£40,000 in two grants), Almat Limited (£26,000 in three grants), Yad Yemin (£17,000), Beis Minchas Yitzchok (£10,000), Tevini (£6,000), SOFT (£5,000 in two grants), Hod Yurushalaim Educational Centre (£4,800 in two grants), Lolev Charitable Trust (£3,600 in four grants), Yad Eliezer (£600), Yetev Lev Cong (£400) and ZBE Ltd (£250).

Applications In writing to the correspondent.

The Beaufort House Trust

Christian, education

£34,000 to organisations (2005)

Beneficial area UK.

Beaufort House, Brunswick Road, Gloucester GL1 1JZ

Correspondent Mrs R J Hall, Company Secretary

Trustees *M R Cornwall-Jones, Chair; W H Yates; Hon. N Assheton; N J E Sealy; H F Hart; M A Chamberlain; W N Stock.*

CC Number 286606

Information available Accounts were on file at the Charity Commission.

General The trustees make grants to promote the furtherance of education and the Christian religion. Appeals are considered from schools, colleges, universities or any other charitable body involved in this work. It receives an annual payment from the Ecclesiastical Insurance Group plc.

In 2005 the trust had assets of £105,000 and an income of £504,000, including £428,000 from their school fees scheme. After school fees were paid totalling £412,000, the sum of £79,000 was distributed in grants. In total 26 grants were given to educational organisations totalling £34,000 and 40 to individual bursaries totalling £45,000.

Exclusions No grants are made to organisations with political associations, UK-wide charities or individuals.

Applications On an application form. The following details will be required: the objectives of the charity; the appeal target; how the funds are to be utilised; funds raised to date; and previous support received from the trust.

Beauland Ltd

Jewish

£135,000 (2004/05)

Beneficial area Worldwide, possibly with a preference for the Manchester area.

309 Bury New Road, Salford M7 2YN

Correspondent M Neumann, Trustee

Trustees *F Neumann; H Neumann; M Friedlander; H Rosemann; J Bleier; R Delange; M Neumann; P Neumann; E Neumann; E Henry.*

CC Number 511374

Information available Accounts were on file at the Charity Commission.

General The trust's objectives are the advancement of the Jewish religion in accordance with the Orthodox Jewish faith and the relief of poverty. It gives grants to 'religious, educational and similar bodies'.

In 2004/05 the trust had assets of £3.7 million and an income of £456,000. Grants totalled £135,000 with 13 organisations receiving over £1,000 each listed in the accounts. Beneficiaries included: Noitzer Chesed (£36,000); Beis Yakov Institutions, Friends of Harim and Vayoel Moshe Charitable Trust (£20,000 each); Torah V'chesed (£10,000); Radford Education Trust (£4,000); Jewish Grammar School (£3,100); Asos Chesed (£2,200); and Torah V'emunah (£1,100).

Applications In writing to the correspondent.

The Beaverbrook Foundation

General

£69,000 (2004/05)

Beneficial area UK and Canada.

33 Lowndes Street, London SW1X 9HX

Website www.beaverbrookfoundation. org

Correspondent The Secretary

Trustees *Lord Beaverbrook, Chair; Lady Beaverbrook; Lady Aitken; T M Aitken; Hon. Laura Levi; J E A Kidd; Hon. M F Aitken.*

CC Number 310003

Information available Accounts were on file at the Charity Commission with an inadequate report and without a list of grants.

General This trust mostly supports its own work in the preservation and renovation of Cherkley Court. Grants are also made to other organisations as funds allow. In 2004/05 it had assets of £18 million and an income of £322,000. Out of a total expenditure of £2.2 million, grants to organisations totalled £69,000.

Exclusions Only registered charities are supported.

Applications In writing to the correspondent with an sae. Trustees meet in May and November.

The John Beckwith Charitable Trust

Young people, general

See below

Beneficial area UK and overseas.

124 Sloane Street, London SW1X 9BW

Correspondent Ms Sally Holder, Administrator

Trustees *Sir J Beckwith; H M Beckwith; C M Meech.*

CC Number 800276

Information available Unfortunately, although submitted by the trust to the Charity Commission, the accounts for these years had not made it to the public files for inspection.

General In 2005/06 the trust had an income of £16,000 (£455,000 in 2004/05) and a total expenditure of £303,000. Further information for this year was not available.

In recent years, very little information had been available on this trust and its work. Over the seven years to 2006, its income has been in the range of £9,400 and £1.1 million.

In 2001/02, the last year we were able to obtain accounts for this trust, it had assets of £2.4 million and an income of £30,000. Grants were made totalling £515,000. Unfortunately, no grants list was include in the accounts. The breakdown of the areas funded, however, was given as follows:

Sports	8 grants	£314,000
Arts	2	£106,000
Social welfare	16	£40,000
Education	1	£35,000
Medical research	10	£21,000

Previous beneficiaries have included Youth Sport Trust (founded by John Beckwith), Institute of Sport – Loughborough University, Royal Opera House Development Trust, Harrow Development Trust, Colon Cancer Care, Helen Rollason Cancer Care Centre, Leukaemia Research Fund, Release, National Literacy Trust, Alzheimer's Society, Hearing Research Trust and Research into Eating Disorders.

Applications In writing to the correspondent.

The Peter Beckwith Charitable Trust

Medical, welfare

£59,000 (2005/06)

Beneficial area UK.

Hill Place House, 55a High Street, Wimbledon Village, London SW19 5BA

Tel. 020 8944 1288

Correspondent The Trustees

Trustees *P M Beckwith; Mrs P G Beckwith; Mrs C T Van Dam; Miss T J Beckwith.*

CC Number 802113

Information available Accounts were on file at the Charity Commission but without a list of grants.

General This trust was established in 1989. In 2005/06 it had an income of

£74,000. Assets at the year end totalled £16,000. In this year grants came to £59,000 but unfortunately, no list of grants was included with the accounts that were on file at the Charity Commission.

Previous beneficiaries have included Burnbake Trust, Cara Trust, Carousel, Dartington International Summer School, Handy Aid to Independent Living, Queen Elizabeth Foundation for Disabled People, REAC, Royal School for Deaf Children and Rugby Mayday Trust.

Applications In writing to the correspondent.

The Bedfordshire and Hertfordshire Historic Churches Trust

Churches

£19,000 (2004/05)

Beneficial area Bedfordshire, Hertfordshire and that part of Barnet within the Diocese of St Albans.

31 Ivel Gardens, Biggleswade, Bedfordshire SG18 0AN

Tel. 01767 312966

Email ARussell@RussellsConsultants. com

Website www.bedshertshct.org.uk/

Correspondent Archie Russell, Grants Secretary

Trustees *A A I Jenkins; S C Y Farmbrough; C P Green; B A Hunt; P F D Lepper; P A Lomax; A J Philpott; A Russell; R H Tomlins.*

CC Number 1005697

Information available Information was available online from both the Charity Commission and trust's website.

General The trust gives grants for the restoration, preservation, repair and maintenance of churches in Bedfordshire, Hertfordshire and that part of Barnet within the Diocese of St Albans.

The aims of the trust are as follows:

- maintain a large, supportive membership whose annual committed income from subscriptions and donations will give the firm basis upon which to conduct its affairs

- foster an informed appreciation of the history, architecture and beauty of the churches and chapels in the two counties and so provide a way for the wider community to help to maintain that irreplaceable heritage
- raise substantial amounts of money, primarily through the annual sponsored bicycle ride, an event promoted by the trust and supported by other county trusts.

In 2004/05 the trust had assets of £174,000 and an income of £113,000. Grants were made to 10 beneficiaries totalling £19,000.

Grants to institutions included: £5,000 to Henlow St Mary the Virgin, for stonework repairs to buttresses, parapets of tower and south aisle; £2,500 to Bedford Park Road Methodist, for repairs to cracking ceiling; £2,000 each to Adeyfield St Barnabas, towards repairs to reinforced concrete window surrounds, Hexton St Faith, for stonework repairs to window surrounds, Houghton Conquest All Saints towards repairs to south aisle roof and Pavenham St Peter for replacement of copper on nave roof with lead. Grants of £1,000 each were given to Beeston Methodist towards fabric repairs, damp-proofing, decoration and repairs to rain water goods, Toddington Methodist for reappointing external brickwork, Watford Quaker Meeting towards repairs to windows, and Wyddial St Giles for repairs to west window and north aisle brickwork.

Exclusions No grants to individuals.

Applications In writing to the correspondent.

The David and Ruth Behrend Fund

General

£65,000 (2004/05)

Beneficial area UK, with a preference for Merseyside.

c/o Liverpool Charity and Voluntary Services, 14 Castle Street, Liverpool L2 0NJ

Tel. 0151 236 7728 **Fax** 0151 258 1153

Correspondent The Secretary

Trustees *David Bebb; Mark Blundell; Dil Daly; Charles Feeny; William Fulton; Prof. Philip Love; Andrew Lovelady; Shirley Mashiane-Talbot; Roger Morris; Sue Newton; Christine Reeves; Hilary Russell.*

CC Number 261567

Information available Accounts were obtained from the Charity Commission website.

General 'The trust was established to make grants for charitable purposes. Grants are only made to charities known to the settlors and unsolicited applications are therefore not considered.' Set up in 1969, it appears to give exclusively in Merseyside.

In 2004/05 the trust had assets of £1.4 million and an income of £82,000. Grants totalled £65,000 with 22 listed beneficiaries in receipt of grants of £1,000 or more including: Merseyside Development Foundation and PSS (£6,000 each); Liverpool School of Tropical Medicine (£5,200); Claire House Hospice (£5,000); EPA (£3,000); All Saints Church – Speke, the Basement Drop-in Centre, Sanctuary, Sefton Carers Centre, Toxteth Community Council Playgroup and Yellow House (£2,000 each); Marybone Youth & Community Association (£1,800) and British Refugee Council, Churches Together in the Merseyside Region and Whitechapel Centre (£1,000 each).

Exclusions Anyone not known to the settlors.

Applications This trust states that it does not respond to unsolicited applications.

Belljoe Tzedoko Ltd

Jewish

£49,000 to organisations (2005)

Beneficial area UK.

27 Fairholt Road, London N16 5EW

Correspondent H J Lobenstein, Trustee

Trustees *H J Lobenstein; Mrs B Lobenstein; D Lobenstein; M Lobenstein; Mrs S Falk; Mrs N Stern.*

CC Number 282726

Information available Full accounts were available from the Charity Commission.

General The trust's objectives are 'the advancement of religion in accordance with the orthodox Jewish faith and the relief of poverty'.

In 2005 the trust had assets of £86,000 and an income of £54,000. Grants were made to twelve organisations totalling £49,000.

Beneficiaries included Kupat Hair (£8,000), Hakallo, Society of Friends and Tzedoko (£5,000 each), Marbe Torah, Shomre Hachomos and Yeshivo Horomo (£4,000 each), the B & G Charitable Trust and Beer Miriam (£3,000 each), Adath Yisroel Synagogue (£1,400) and Yesodey Hatora and CWC (£1,000 each).

Applications In writing to the correspondent.

The Benham Charitable Settlement

General, see below

£120,000 (2005/06)

Beneficial area UK, with very strong emphasis on Northamptonshire.

Hurstbourne, Portnall Drive, Virginia Water, Surrey GU25 4NR

Correspondent Mrs M Tittle, Managing Trustee

Trustees *Mrs M M Tittle; Lady Hutton; E N Langley.*

CC Number 239371

Information available Accounts were on file at the Charity Commission.

General The charity was founded in 1964 by the late Cedric Benham and his wife Hilda, then resident in Northamptonshire, 'to benefit charities and other good causes and considerations'.

The objective of the charity is the support of registered charities working in many different fields – including charities involved in medical research, disability, elderly people, children and young people, disadvantaged people, overseas aid, missions to seamen, the welfare of ex-servicemen, wildlife, the environment, and the arts. The trust also supports the Church of England and the work of Christian mission throughout the world. Special emphasis is placed upon those churches and charitable organisations within the county of Northamptonshire [especially as far as new applicants are concerned].

In recent years the settlement has made a series of substantial donations, exceeding £1.9 million, to the Northamptonshire Association of Youth Clubs. These donations were principally for the purchase of a freehold site and to facilitate the financing and construction of an indoor sports arena. The trust stated its intention to continue to support certain operations of the association on a selected basis.

In 2005/06 the charity had assets of £4.7 million and an income of £140,000. It made 183 donations totalling £120,000 with the majority of grants ranging from £100 to £500. Grants of £1,000 or more were made to Northamptonshire Association of Youth Clubs (£30,000 in two grants), Progressive Supranuclear Palsy Association (£5,000), Coworth Flexlands School and Holy Trinity Church – Muheza Hospital, Tanzania (£3,000 each) Weekend Breakthrough Breast Cancer (£2,500) and Northampton Symphony Orchestra (£2,000).

Beneficiaries of grants under £1,000 each included Children with AIDS Charity and Holy Trinity Church (£900 each), Age Concern, Bibles for Children, Church Housing Trust, Electronic Aids for the Blind, Naomi House, National Library for the Blind, Royal British Legion, Suzy Lamplugh Trust, the Shaftesbury Society and Volunteer Reading Help (£500 each), AIDIS Trust, DEBRA, Asthma UK, Cathedral Camps, Combat Stress, Cued Speech Association, Friends of Northampton General Hospital, Living Paintings Trust, Marine Conservation Society, the Woodland Trust and VSO (£400 each) and Northampton Festival of Dance and the Willow Trust (£300 each).

Exclusions No grants to individuals.

Applications In recent years the trust has not been considering new applications.

Michael and Leslie Bennett Charitable Trust

Jewish

£54,000 (2005/06)
Beneficial area UK.

Bedggars Lea, Kenwood Close, London NW3 7JL

Correspondent Michael Bennett, Trustee

Trustees Michael Bennett; Lesley V Bennett.

CC Number 1047611

Information available Full accounts were on file at the Charity Commission.

General The trust supports a range of causes, but the largest donations were to Jewish organisations. In 2005/06 the trust had assets of £469,000 and an income of £43,000 including £20,000 from donations. There were 28 grants made totalling £54,000.

Grants of £1,000 or more were made to eight organisations: Jewish Care and United Jewish Israel Appeal (£11,000 each); World Jewish Relief (£10,000); Nightingale House (£5,000); Norwood Ravenswood (£4,000); Magen David Adom UK (£3,000); Chai Cancer Care (£2,750); and Jewish Care Scotland (£1,000).

Applications In writing to the correspondent.

The Geoffrey Berger Charitable Trust

General

About £20,000 (2005/06)
Beneficial area UK and overseas.

PO Box 12162, London NW11 7WR
Correspondent G D Berger, Trustee
Trustees G D Berger; N J Berger; Mrs A Berger; Ms L N Berger.
CC Number 1059991
Information available Information had been filed with the Charity Commission.

General In 2005/06 this trust had an income of £23,000 and a total expenditure of £22,000. Further information was not available for this year.

Exclusions No grants to individuals.

Applications The trust has stated that its funds are fully committed and that it does not accept unsolicited applications.

The Berkeley Reafforestation Trust

Reafforestation projects

£37,000 (2004/05)
Beneficial area Worldwide.

3 Harley Gardens, London SW10 9SW
Tel. 020 7370 1965
Correspondent R J B Portman, Trustee
Trustees Rodney Portman; Louise Cooke; Nicholas Foster; Rosalind Portman.
CC Number 297982
Information available Accounts were on file at the Charity Commission.

General The trust's aims are:

- the relief of poverty by promoting tree planting and effective tree management internationally as a means of combating land erosion and degradation, rural poverty and ecological and environmental deterioration
- the advancement of education in the importance of the role of forestry and in tree planting and tree management.

Its 2004/05 annual report stated that it largely supports ongoing projects in the Himalayan region of India and in Niger, alongside a new project in Uganda.

In 2004/05 it had an income of £40,000, almost entirely in donations received. Grants were made totalling £37,000. Other expenditure totalled £13,000, including fundraising events, newsletters, videos and computer software.

Applications In writing to the correspondent, although please note, the trust states that it 'does not solicit applications'.

The Bestway Foundation

Education, welfare, medical

£203,000 to organisations and individuals (2004/05)
Beneficial area UK and overseas.

Bestway Cash and Carry Ltd, Abbey Road, Park Royal, London NW10 7BW
Correspondent M Y Sheikh, Trustee

Trustees *A K Bhatti; A K Chaudhary; M Y Sheikh; Z M Chaudrey; M A Pervez.*

CC Number 297178

Information available Accounts were on file at the Charity Commission.

General In 2004/05 this trust had assets of £3.5 million, an income of £506,000 and made grants totalling £203,000.

Listed beneficiaries were: Save the Children (£50,000); Specialist Schools Trust – Allerton, Borderly Green, Mansion House Regency, Rhyddings Business and Enterprise (£30,000); Duke of Edinburgh's Awards (£15,000); Ancient India & Iran Trust (£13,000); City of Stoke on Trent – Blenheim High School (£2,500); the Calamus Foundation (£2,000); Bookpower, the EKFA Foundation, Imperial College Islamic Society, Volunteer Reading Help and Wines & Spirits Trades Benevolent Society (£1,000 each); and UCFA Aid (£100).

There were also 16 grants made to individuals during the year.

Exclusions No grants for trips/travel abroad.

Applications In writing to the correspondent, enclosing an sae. Applications are considered in March/April. Telephone calls are not welcome.

Betard Bequest

Welfare, disability, older people

£28,000 (2005)
Beneficial area UK.

CAF Grantmaking, Kings Hill, West Malling, Kent ME19 4TA

Tel. 01732 520334 **Fax** 01732 520159

Email grants@caf.online.org

Website www.cafonline.org/grants

CC Number 268369c

Information available Previous information was included in the *CAF Grant Programme Annual Review.*

General The trust gives support for holidays, specially adapted furniture, computers and medical aids for people with arthritis and rheumatism and to Scottish and French people who are old and lonely, and resident in the UK. Support is given only where it is not the duty of the DSS and other government departments.

In 2005 grants totalled about £28,000. No further financial information was available.

Previous beneficiaries have included Abilitynet, Arthritis Care, Leicester Charity Organisation Society, Mobility Trust, Ryder-Cheshire Foundation, Raynauds' Scleroderma Association, Lady Hoare Trust, 3H Fund, League of the Helping Hand and National Benevolent Fund for the Aged.

Exclusions Grants are not made directly to individuals but through an appropriate charity or social worker.

Applications Applications can be sent in at any time for quarterly consideration. Initial telephone calls by applicants are welcome. No application forms are necessary, but guidelines are issued. There are no deadlines for applications and no sae is required.

The Betterware Foundation

Children

£60,000 (2004/05)
Beneficial area UK.

Wood Hall Lane, Shenley, Hertfordshire WD7 9AA

Correspondent Iain Williamson

Trustees *Andrew Cohen; Wendy Cohen.*

CC Number 1093834

Information available Information was on file at the Charity Commission, without a list of grants.

General This foundation was established in September 2002. It receives most of its income directly from Betterware plc. In 2004/05 it had an income of £93,000 and made grants totalling £60,000.

Applications Grants are mostly given to children's charities which are of personal interest to the trustees.

Thomas Betton's Charity for Pensions and Relief-in-Need

Disadvantaged

£38,000 (2004/05)
Beneficial area UK.

Ironmongers' Hall, Barbican, London EC2Y 8AA

Tel. 020 7776 2311

Website www.ironhall.co.uk

Correspondent The Charities Administrator

Trustee *The Worshipful Company of Ironmongers.*

CC Number 280143

Information available Accounts were on file at the Charity Commission.

General In 2004/05 the trust had assets of £750,000 and an income of £57,000, including £31,000 from Thomas Betton's Estate Charity and £26,000 from investments. Grants totalled £38,000 and £2,200 was also spent on pensions to individuals.

Beneficiaries were Housing the Homeless Central Fund (£19,000), the Vivace Charitable Trust (£3,000), KIDS (£2,400), Aidis Trust, the Country Trust, Homestart – south east Essex, National Autistic Society, Rainy Day Trust, Sheriffs' and Recorder's Fund and Westminster Children's Society (£2,000 each) and Toynbee Hall (£1,000).

Exclusions Applications for grants to individuals are accepted only from registered social workers or other agencies, not directly from individuals.

Applications In writing to the correspondent.

The Billmeir Charitable Trust

General, health and medical

£133,000 (2004/05)
Beneficial area UK, with a preference for the Surrey area,

specifically Elstead, Tilford, Farnham and Frensham.

Messrs Moore Stephens, St Paul's House, Warwick Lane, London EC4M 7BP

Tel. 020 7334 9191

Correspondent Keith Lawrence

Trustees *B C Whitaker; M R Macfadyen; S Marriott; J Whitaker.*

CC Number 208561

Information available Accounts were on file at the Charity Commission.

General The trust states it supports a wide variety of causes. About a quarter of the grants are given to health and medical charities and about a third of the grants are given to local organisations in Surrey, especially the Farnham, Frensham, Elstead and Tilford areas.

In 2004/05 the trust had assets of £3.4 million and an income of £128,000. Donations were made to 36 charities totalling £133,000.

Beneficiaries included: Reed's School – Cobham (£10,000); Arundel Castle Cricket Foundation, Blaser, Lord Mayor Treloar School, the Meath Home and the New Ashgate Gallery (£7,000 each); Marlborough College (£6,000); Disability Challengers – Farnham, Farnham Maltings, Woodlarks Campsite Trust and Youth Sport Trust (£5,000 each); Fairbridge (£3,000); the Old Kiln Museum Trust (£2,500); Evelina Children's Hospital, Frensham Church, Milford and Villages Day Centre, the Royal Star and Garter Home, SPARKS and Surrey Community Development Trust (£2,000 each); and British Legion – Frensham (£1,000).

Applications The trust states that it does not request applications and that its funds are fully committed.

The Bintaub Charitable Trust

Jewish, health, education, children

£51,000 (2004/05)

Beneficial area Greater London, national and international.

29 Woodlands Close, London NW11 9QR

Correspondent Mrs Dahlia Rosenberg

Trustees *James Frohwein; Tania Frohwein; Daniel Frohwein.*

CC Number 1003915

Information available Accounts were on file at the Charity Commission.

General This trust was set up in 1991 and provides grants to mainly London organisations, towards 'the advancement of education in and the religion of the Orthodox Jewish faith'. Grants are also given for other charitable causes, mainly towards medical and children's work. In 2004/05 it had an income from donations of £58,000 and made grants totalling £51,000.

Beneficiaries of grants over £1,000 each were: Etz Chaim School (£9,000 in three grants); Yeshiva Tiferes Yaacov (£6,000 in two grants); Jewish Day School (£4,500 in three grants); Kupait Ha'ir (£1,100 in three grants); Menorah Foundation School (£3,400 in two grants); Va'ad Harabomin Le'irayonel Tzedaka (£1,400); and CJGH (£1,500).

Unlisted grants under £1,000 each totalled £25,000.

Applications In writing to the correspondent. However, the correspondent stated previously that new applications are not being accepted.

The Birmingham Hospital Saturday Fund Medical Charity and Welfare Trust

Medical

£34,000 (2005)

Beneficial area UK, but mostly centred around the West Midlands and Birmingham area.

Gamgee House, 2 Darnley Road, Birmingham B16 8TE

Tel. 0121 454 3601

Email charitabletrust@bhsf.co.uk

Correspondent Philip V Ashbourne, Secretary

Trustees *Dr R P Kanas; S G Hall; E S Hickman; M Malone; D J Read; J Salmons.*

CC Number 502428

Information available Accounts were on file at the Charity Commission.

General This trust supports the relief of sickness, with the trustees also holding an interest in medical research. The trustees continue to give priority to charities that benefit those living in the West Midlands area with some interest in the south west for historical reasons. The trust no longer receives an income from the parent company and so the trustees are now working purely with reserves and the interest from them. This has resulted in a more critical look at projects at each meeting and donations are now generally less than £2,000. Projects that are appropriate and reflect well thought through projects with realistic cost breakdowns are given greater consideration.

In 2005 it had assets of £533,000 and an income of £27,000. Grants totalled £34,000. There were 34 grants of £250 or more listed in the accounts.

Beneficiaries of grants of £1,000 or more included: NHS West Midlands – partnership for developing change (£3,900); Foundation for Nursing Studies – London (£2,600); the Birmingham Centre for Art Therapies (£2,000); Birmingham Disability Resource Centre and Shen Care Voluntary Transport – Birmingham (£1,900 each); Rehab UK – Birmingham (£1,700); Heart UK – Berkshire (£1,500); No Panic – Shropshire and St Richards Hospice – Worcester (£1,300 each); Christian Lewis Trust – Cardiff (£1,100); and Alzheimer Research Trust – Cambridge, Counsel and Care – London and Well Child – Cheltenham (£1,000 each).

Other beneficiaries included: Lord Mayor of Birmingham Charities (£800); the Foleshill Multicultural Open Forum, Coventry (£700); Institute of Orthopaedics – Oswestry (£600); British Dyslexics – Chester (£500); and Cornerstone, Birmingham (£250).

Exclusions The trust will not generally fund: direct appeals from individuals or students; administration expenditure including salaries; bank loans/deficits/mortgages; items or services which should normally be publicly funded; large general appeals; vehicle operating costs; or motor vehicles for infrequent use and where subsidised vehicle share schemes are available to charitable organisations.

Applications On a form available from the correspondent. The form requires basic information and should be submitted with financial details. Evidence should be provided that the project has been adequately considered through the provision of quotes or supporting documents, although the trust dislikes applications which provide too much general information or have long-winded descriptions of projects. Applicants should take great care to read the guidance notes on the application form. The trustees meet four times a year and deadlines are given when application forms are sent out.

Birthday House Trust

General

£33,000 to organisations (2004/05)

Beneficial area England and Wales.

Dickinson Trust Ltd, Pollen House, 10–12 Cork Street, London W1S 3LW

Trustee *Dickinson Trust Ltd.*

CC Number 248028

Information available Accounts were on file at the Charity Commission.

General Established in 1966, the main work of this trust is engaged with the running of a residential home for people who are elderly in Midhurst, West Sussex. In 2004/05 it had assets of £5.2 million and an income of £133,000. Grants to 14 organisations totalled £33,000 and grants to 15 pensioners totalled £66,000.

Beneficiaries were the Prince of Wales's Charitable Foundation (£20,000), Centre for Alternative Technology Charity Limited (£2.300), the Noon Foundation (£5,000), First Merton Scout Group (£2,000), Woodstock Research Trust (£1,000), the Boxgrove Priory Trust, Easebourne Scout & Guide Hut Committee and Fire Services National Benevolent Fund (£500 each), Breakspear Hospital Trust, Elsted with Treyford-cum Didling PCC and Healthlink Worldwide (£250 each), Orchid Cancer Appeal (£100) and Elm Farm Research Centre and the Murray Downland Trust (£50 each).

Exclusions No applications will be considered from individuals or non-charitable organisations.

Applications In writing to the correspondent, including a sae. No application forms are issued and there is no deadline. Only successful applicants are acknowledged.

The Bisgood Charitable Trust (registered as Miss Jeanne Bisgood's Charitable Trust)

Roman Catholic purposes, older people

£163,000 (2005/06)

Beneficial area UK, overseas and locally in Bournemouth and Dorset, especially Poole.

12 Waters Edge, Brudenell Road, Poole BH13 7NN

Tel. 01202 708460

Correspondent Miss J M Bisgood, Trustee

Trustees *Miss J M Bisgood; Miss P Schulte; P J K Bisgood.*

CC Number 208714

Information available Accounts were on file at the Charity Commission.

General This trust has emerged following an amalgamation of the Bisgood Trust with Miss Jeanne Bisgood's Charitable Trust. Both trusts had the same objectives.

The General Fund has the following priorities:

1 Roman Catholic charities
2 Charities benefiting people in Poole, Bournemouth and the county of Dorset
3 National charities for the benefit of older people.

No grants are made to local charities which do not fall under categories 1 or 2. Many health and welfare charities are supported as well as charities working in relief and development overseas.

In 2005/06 the trust had assets of £6.1 million, an income of £249,000 and made grants totalling £163,000. Previous beneficiaries from the general fund have included Apex Trust, ITDG, Horder Centre for Arthritis , Impact, St Barnabas' Society, St Francis Leprosy Guild, Sight Savers International and YMCA.

In considering appeals the trustees will give preference to charities whose fund-raising and administrative costs are proportionately low.

The trust was given 12 paintings to be held as part of the trust funds. Most of the paintings were sold and the proceeds were placed in a sub-fund, the Bertram Fund, established in 1998, the income of which is purely for Roman Catholic causes. It is intended that it will primarily support major capital projects. Most grants are made anonymously from this fund.

Exclusions Grants are not given to local charities which do not fit categories 1 or 2 above. Individuals and non-registered charities are not supported.

Applications In writing to the correspondent, quoting the UK registration number and registered title of the charity. A copy of the most recent accounts should also be enclosed. Applications should NOT be made directly to the Bertram Fund. Applications for capital projects 'should provide brief details of the main purposes, the total target and the current state of the appeal'. The trustees regret that they are unable to acknowledge appeals. The trustees normally meet in late February/early March and September.

The Michael Bishop Foundation

General

£177,000 (2004/05)

Beneficial area Worldwide, with a preference for Birmingham and the Midlands.

Donington Hall, Castle Donington, Derby DE74 2SB

Tel. 01332 854000

Correspondent Mrs P Robinson

Trustees *Sir Michael Bishop, Chair; Grahame N Elliott; John T Wolfe; John S Coulson.*

CC Number 297627

Information available Full accounts were on file at the Charity Commission.

General Sir Michael Bishop of British Midland set up the foundation in 1987 by giving almost £1 million of shares in Airlines of Britain (Holdings) plc, the parent company of British Midland. A further sum was given in 1992.

In 2004/05 it had assets of £2.5 million, which generated an income of £96,000. Grants were made to 34 organisatioins totalling £177,000.

There were 25 grants of £1,000 each or more listed in the accounts, the largest of which went to: the Foundling Museum (£35,000); Policy Exchange and the Royal Flying Doctor Service of Australia (£25,000 each); Terrence Higgins Trust (£20,000); ADAS (£15,000); and the Bobby Goldsmith Foundation and the D'Oyly Carte Opera Trust Limited (£10,000 each).

Other beneficiaries included: Reform Research and RNIB (£5,000 each); Barry and Martin's Trust, NAYC Pioneer Center, Steps and Stonewall (£2,500 each); the Camphill Village Trust (£1,500); and Addaction, Cancer Research UK, Debra, Elmhirst Ballet School Trust, Sane and Royal Academy of Dramatic Art (£1,000 each).

Grants of less than £1,000 each totalled £2,900.

Applications In writing to the correspondent. However, the long-term commitment mentioned above means that new applicants are not supported at present.

Peter Black Charitable Trust

General

About £31,000 to organisations (2005/06)

Beneficial area UK and overseas.

Peter Black Holdings Ltd, Airedale Mill, Lawkholme Lane, Keighley, West Yorkshire BD21 3BB

Tel. 01535 612247

Correspondent Kathleen M Bell

Trustees *T S S Black; G L Black; A S Black.*

CC Number 264279

Information available Accounts and grants list were provided by the trust.

General In 2005/06 the trust had an income of £13,000 and a total expenditure of £36,000. Further information was not available.

In 2003/04 the trust had assets of £280,000 and an income of £56,000. Grants totalled £31,000. Grants of £1,000 or over included Yorkshire Ballet Seminars (£2,000) and Leeds

International. Pianoforte Competition and The Ilkley Players – Lightning Appeal (£1,000). Other grants included Yorkshire Cancer Research (£300 in two grants), Leeds Jewish Welfare Board (£200 in two grants), Bradford WIZO, Ilkley Summer Festival Ltd, Leeds Teaching Hospitals Fund, Sport on Saturday Club – Ilkley and Yorkshire Wildlife Trust (£100 each), Ilkley Literature Festival (£50), and Bradford Jewish Benevolent Society (£25).

Exclusions No grants to individuals.

Applications In writing to the correspondent.

The Sydney Black Charitable Trust

Evangelical Christianity, social welfare, young people, older people and people who are disabled

£111,000 (2004/05)

Beneficial area UK.

75 Home Park Road, London SW19 7HS

Tel. 020 8946 1132

Correspondent The Secretary

Trustees *Mrs J D Crabtree; Mrs H J Dickenson; S J Crabtree; P M Crabtree.*

CC Number 219855

Information available Accounts were filed at the Charity Commission, without a grants list.

General In 2001 The Edna Black Charitable Trust and The Cyril Black Charitable Trust were incorporated into this trust. For the latest year the report stated that support is given to youth organisations, religious, medical and other institutions, such as those helping people who are disadvantaged or disabled.

In 2004/05 the trust had an income of £172,000 and total assets were £2.9 million. A substantial grant was made to Endeavour (£18,000); others totalled £93,000 and were of between £125 and £200 each. About 700 institutions benefited.

Applications Applications, made in writing to the correspondent, will be considered by the appropriate trust.

The Bertie Black Foundation

Jewish, general

£92,000 (2005/06)

Beneficial area UK, Israel.

Abbots House, 198 Lower High Street, Watford WDI7 2FG

Correspondent The Trustees

Trustees *I B Black; D Black; H S Black; Mrs I R Seddon.*

CC Number 245207

Information available Information was on file at the Charity Commission, without a list of grants.

General The trust tends to support organisations which are known to the trustees or where long-term commitments have been entered into. Grants can be given over a three-year period towards major projects.

In 2005/06 it had assets of £2.9 million and an income of £116,000. Grants were made totalling £92,000.

Previous beneficiaries have included British Friends of Assaf Harofeh Medical Centre, Community Security Trust, FMRC Charitable Trust, Friends of Ilan, Jewish Blind and Disabled, Jewish Care, Lubavitch UK, Magen David Adom UK, Norwood Ltd, UK Friends of AWIS, United Jewish Israel Appeal and Youth Aliyah.

Applications The trust states it 'supports causes known to the trustees' and that they 'do not respond to unsolicited requests'.

Sir Alec Black's Charity

Relief in need

£41,000 to individuals and organisations (2005/06)

Beneficial area UK, with a preference for Grimsby.

Messrs Wilson Sharpe and Co., 27 Osborne Street, Grimsby, North East Lincolnshire DN31 1NU

Correspondent Stewart Wilson, Trustee

Trustees *J N Harrison; P A Mounfield; G H Taylor; Dr D F Wilson; S Wilson.*

CC Number 220295

Information available Accounts were on file at the Charity Commission.

General The primary purposes of the trust are:

- the purchase and distribution of bed linen and down pillows to charitable organisations caring for people who are sick or infirm
- the provision of pensions and grants to people employed by Sir Alec Black during his lifetime
- the benefit of sick, poor fishermen and dockworkers from the borough of Grimsby.

In 2005/06 it had assets of £1.4 million and an income of £84,000. Grants to former employees of the settlor totalled £15,000. A further £25,000 went in grants to organisations, with £350 given to fishermen and dockworkers.

Applications In writing to the correspondent. Trustees meet in May and November; applications need to be received in March or September.

The Blair Foundation

Wildlife, access to countryside, general

£75,000 (2004/05)

Beneficial area UK, particularly southern England and Scotland; overseas.

Smith and Williamson, 1 Bishops Wharf, Walnut Tree Close, Guildford, Surrey GU1 4RA

Tel. 01483 407100

Correspondent The Trustees

Trustees *Robert Thornton; Jennifer Thornton; Graham Healy; Alan Thornton; Philippa Thornton.*

CC Number 801755

Information available Full accounts were on file at the Charity Commission.

General This foundation was originally established to create environmental conditions in which wildlife can prosper, as well as improving disability access to such areas. This work is focused on Scotland and southern England.

In 2004/05 the trust had assets of £1.9 million and an income of £90,000. Grants totalled £75,000.

There were 19 grants of £1,000 or more listed in the accounts with beneficiaries

including Ayrshire Wildlife Services (£26,000), National Trust for Scotland – Culzean Castle (£6,500), Ayrshire Fiddler Orchestra, Daily Amateur Football Club, Home Farm Trust and Queen Elizabeth Foundation for the Disabled (£5,000 each), RSAMD and Royal Naval Museum (£2,000 each), Royal School of Art (£1,500), and Bristol Cancer Help Centre, Live Music Now!, RSPB, RYA Sailability, Royal Scottish National Orchestra and the Scottish Society for Autism (£1,000 each).

Donations of less than £1,000 each totalled £3,600.

Exclusions Charities that have objectives the trustees consider harmful to the environment are not supported.

Applications In writing to the correspondent, for consideration at trustees' meetings held at least once a year. A receipt for donations is requested from all donees.

Blakes Benevolent Trust

General

£53,000 to organisations (2004/05)

Beneficial area UK.

2 Yew Tree Road, Huyton-with-Roby, Liverpool L36 5UQ

Correspondent Norman Silk, Trustee

Trustees *N K Silk; B Ball; P M Davies.*

CC Number 225268

Information available Accounts are on file at the Charity Commission, but with only a brief narrative report and without a grants list.

General In 2004/05 the trust had assets of £2.1 million and an income of £71,000. Grants were given to eight organisations totalling £53,000, with 33 individuals receiving £18,000.

Beneficiaries were Motor Trade Benevolent Fund (£25,000), Crisis, Front Line, Liverpool City Mission and Salvation Army (£5,000 each) and Nugent Care Society, the Universal Beneficent Society and Wirral Churches (£2,500 each). All of the organisations received the same grants in the previous year.

Applications This trust has previously stated that it only gives to 'private beneficiaries'.

The Sir Victor Blank Charitable Settlement

Jewish

£169,000 (2005/06)

Beneficial area Worldwide.

c/o Wilkins Kennedy, Bridge House, London Bridge, London SE1 9QR

Correspondent R Gulliver, Trustee

Trustees *Sir M V Blank; Lady S H Blank; R Gulliver.*

CC Number 1084187

Information available Accounts were on file at the Charity Commission.

General Registered with the Charity Commission in December 2000, in 2005/06 this charity had assets of £1.5 million generating an income of £40,000. Grants totalled £169,000.

There were 24 donations of £1,000 or more listed in the accounts. Beneficiaries included: Community Security Trust (£30,000); United Jewish Israel Appeal (£25,000); UCS Centennial Appeal (£20,000); Jewish Care (£17,000); Hillel Foundation (£10,000); the Lord Taverners (£9,100); Norwood Ltd (£7,500); Stockport Grammar School (£5,000); Nightingale House (£3,000); and Chai Cancer Care, Delamere Forest School, Israel Diaspora Trust, National Centre for Deaf and Blindness, the Roundhouse Trust and Unicorn Theatre (£1,000 each).

Other grants of less than £1,000 each totalled £14,000.

Applications In writing to the correspondent.

Blatchington Court Trust

Supporting vision-impaired people under the age of 30

£47,000 paid to organisations (2005/06)

Beneficial area UK, preference for Sussex.

Ridgeland House, 165 Dyke Road, Hove, East Sussex BN3 1TL

Tel. 01273 727222 **Fax** 01273 722244

Email enquiries@blatchington-court.co.uk

Website www.blatchington-court.co.uk

Correspondent Alison Evans, Excecutive Manager

Trustees *Richard J Martin, Chair; Geoffrey Lockwood; Roger F Jones; Bruce K McLeod; Colin W Finnerty; Ms Georgina James; Robert M Perkins; Alison Acason; Johnathon Wilson; Daniel Ellman-Brown.*

CC Number 306350

Information available Accounts were on file at the Charity Commission.

General This trust's initial income arose from the sale of the former Blatchington Court School for people who are partially sighted at Seaford. Its aim is 'the promotion of education and employment (including social and physical training) of blind and partially sighted persons under the age of 30 years'. There is a preference for Sussex.

In fulfilling its objects, the trust's aims are to:

- develop as a distinct trust with a primary role of an independent facilitator
- focus its resources on clearly defined needs and to avoid any duplication of provision
- initiate and develop working partnerships with statutory and voluntary organisations concerned with the care of the young people who are vision-impaired
- make grants in pursuance of its objectives
- listen to, and further the interests of, people who are vision-impaired relevant to the trust's objectives.

The trust helps by providing services including:

- counselling

- liaison with Local Educational Authorities and voluntary and statutory organisations
- selection, funding, purchase and training of educational support aids for the home, including IT equipment
- ongoing support and training with IT equipment
- assistance with the provision of leisure and social skills to enhance the lifestyle of the client
- help with the transition process from school to college
- regular contact upon leaving school with the student to offer practical and moral support in further education and career opportunities
- attendance with parents at school meetings/annual reviews concerning the educational needs of the student
- representation at meetings with the Local Education Authority
- awareness training at schools, colleges and with voluntary service providers
- help and advice regarding Benefit Entitlement, in particular Disability Living Allowance. 'We can help you to complete forms, help you to appeal if necessary; represent you at tribunals'
- if the diagnosis is recent, inform you of the services and facilities both local and national
- help make your contribution to a decision on a Statement of Special Educational Needs as effective as possible.

In 2005/06 the trust had assets of almost £11 million and an income mainly from investments of £497,000. Grants paid totalled £146,000, of which £47,000 went to organisations.

In 2003/04 the largest grants were made to Blatchington Court Trust Award Scheme (£37,000); AbilityNet (£10,000); Cambridge Foundation (£2,500); and Sport for Choice (£1,000).

Grants to individuals totalled £98,000.

Applications In writing to the correspondent from whom individual or charity grant application forms can be obtained. Applications can be considered at any time. An application on behalf of a registered charity should include audited accounts and up-to-date information on the charity and its commitments.

The Neville and Elaine Blond Charitable Trust

Jewish, education, general

£81,000 (2005/06)

Beneficial area Worldwide.

c/o H W Fisher and Co., Chartered Accountants, Acre House, 11–15 William Road, London NW1 3ER

Tel. 020 7388 7000

Correspondent The Trustees

Trustees *Dame Simone Prendergast; P Blond; Mrs A E Susman; S N Susman; Mrs J Skidmore.*

CC Number 206319

Information available Full accounts were on file at the Charity Commission.

General In 2005/06 the trust had assets of £1.5 million and an income of £72,000. Grants totalling £81,000 were made to 16 organisations, 10 of which had been supported in the previous year. The main beneficiaries were JPAIME (£30,000) and British WIZO (£13,000 in two grants).

The remaining grants were in the range of £250 and £8,000 and included those to: Community Security Trust (£8,000); Weizmann Institute Foundation (£7,000 in two grants); English Stage Co. (£5,000); Battle of Britain Historical Society (£4,250); Halle Orchestra (£4,000); Cotswold Care Hospital (£2,000); British ORT, Chicken Shed Theatre, Holocaust Educational Trust, Institute of Child Health and Jewish Lads and Girls Brigade (£1,000 each); the Stroke Association (£500); and the William Thyne Calendar Fund (£250).

Exclusions Only registered charities are supported.

Applications In writing to the correspondent. Applications should arrive by 31 January for consideration in late spring.

The Blueberry Charitable Trust

Jewish, relief-in-need

£333,000 (2004/05)
Beneficial area UK.

Third Floor, 345 Stockport Road, Manchester M13 0LF

Correspondent The Trustees

Trustees *Ian Aspinall; Johnathan Lyons.*

CC Number 1080950

Information available Accounts were on file at the Charity Commission

General Registered with the Charity Commission in May 2000, this trust describes it grant-making policy as follows: 'The charity is involved in giving grants at the trustees' discretion to community and voluntary organisations with a variety of objectives in accordance with its own charitable objectives.'

In 2004/05 it had an income of £399,000 mainly from donations of shares. It made grants totalling £333,000. Assets stood at £847,000.

There were seven grants made over £1,000 each. Beneficiaries were: the Quielle Trust (£165,000), the Chairman Charitable Trust (£93,000), Roots to Roots (£6,000), Council for Manchester and Salford Jews (£5,000), Outward Bound Trust (£3,500) and Lubavitch South Manchester (£2,500).

Applications In writing to the correspondent.

The Boltons Trust

Social welfare, medicine, education

£113,000 (2005/06)
Beneficial area Unrestricted.

c/o 1st Floor, Lynton House, 7–12 Tavistock Square, London WC1 H9LT

Correspondent Clive Marks, Trustee

Trustees *Clive Marks; Mrs C Albuquerque.*

CC Number 257951

Information available Accounts were on file at the Charity Commission.

General The main aims of the trust are:

- the pursuit of peace and understanding throughout the world, and the reduction of innocent suffering
- to support education.

The policy of the trust is to select and support a strictly limited number of projects, and it is at pains to deter unsolicited applications, emphasising its request for 'absolutely no personal callers or telephone enquiries', and stating that 'unsolicited applications are unlikely to be successful'.

In 2005/06 the trust had assets of £1.4 million, an income of £40,000 and made grants totalling £113,000. Beneficiaries were: World ORT Trust (£43,000 in two grants); Dartington International Summer School (£25,000 in two grants); London Philharmonic Orchestra (£25,000 in two grants); Global Health Foundation (£15,000); and University College London (£5,000).

Applications 'Sadly, the trust can no longer respond to unsolicited applications.'

The John and Celia Bonham Christie Charitable Trust

Local and national organisations

£25,000 (2004/05)
Beneficial area UK, with some preference for the former county of Avon.

PO Box 9081, Taynton, Gloucester GL19 3WX

Correspondent The Trustees

Trustees *Richard Bonham Christie; Robert Bonham Christie; Celia Bonham Christie; Peter Fitzgerald; Rosemary Kerr.*

CC Number 326296

Information available Accounts were obtained from the Charity Commission website.

General In 2004/05 the trust had assets of £927,000 and a total income of £30,000. Grants were made to 31 organisations totalling £25,000.

Beneficiaries included Sea Cadet Assocation (£1,800), Top UK (£3,500), BIBIC, Digestive Disorder Foundation,

Elizabeth Finn Trust, Frome Festival, Inspire Foundation, Ten of Us and Tsunami Appeal (£1,000 each), Butterwick Hospice and Royal Society for the Blind Winsley (£800 each), Cancer Research Campaign, Dorothy House, Foundation for the Study of Infant Cot Deaths, Home Start South Wiltshire and Kings Medical Trust (£500 each), Derby TOC and St John Ambulance (£400) and Care and Repair (£300).

Exclusions No grants to individuals.

Applications In writing to the correspondent. The trustees regret that the income is fully allocated for the foreseeable future. Only a small number of new applications are supported each year.

The Charlotte Bonham-Carter Charitable Trust

General

£70,000 (2005/06)
Beneficial area UK, with some emphasis on Hampshire.

66 Lincoln's Inn Fields, London WC2A 3LH

Correspondent Sir Matthew Farrer, Trustee

Trustees *Sir Matthew Farrer; Norman Bonham-Carter; Nicholas Wickham-Irving.*

CC Number 292839

Information available Accounts were on file at the Charity Commission.

General The trust is principally concerned with supporting charitable bodies and purposes which were of particular concern to Lady Bonham-Carter during her lifetime or are within the county of Hampshire.

In 2005/06 the trust had assets of £4 million, which generated an income of £137,000. It gave £70,000 in 53 grants, ranging from £500 to £10,000.

Beneficiaries included: the National Trust (£10,000); Wordsworth Trust (£5,750); Fitzwilliam Museum (£5,000); Abbot Hall and Ashmolean Museum (£4,000 each); the British Museum (£3,000); Holy Cross Church – Binsted and Public Catalogue Foundation (£2,500 each); McDonald Institute for Archaeological Research, Rambert Dance

Company and Walpole Society (£2,000 each); and Park Lane Group (£1,500).

Grants of £1,000 or less included those to: British Institute of Archaeology, British School of Archaeology in Iraq, Canine Partners for Independence, Enheduanna Society, Leonard Cheshire Foundation, Oakhaven Hospice Trust and Winchester Cathedral (£1,000 each); Harvest Trust Holidays for Children and Our Right to Read (£750 each); and 14th Eastleigh Scout Group, British Heart Foundation, Friends of Shepherds Down School, Jubilee Sailing Trust, London Children's Ballet, National Talking Newspapers and Magazines, One Parent Families, Rainbow Trust Children's Charity and Westminster Children's Society (£500 each).

Exclusions No grants to individuals or non-registered charities.

Applications In writing to the correspondent. The trust states that 'unsolicited general applications are unlikely to be successful and only increase the cost of administration'. There are no application forms. Trustees meet in January and July; applications need to be received by May or November.

Salo Bordon Charitable Trust

Jewish, some health-related

£305,000 (2004/05)
Beneficial area Worldwide.

78 Corringham Road, London NW11 7EB
Tel. 020 8458 5842
Correspondent S Bordon, Trustee
Trustees *S Bordon; Mrs L Bordon.*
CC Number 266439
Information available Full accounts were on file at the Charity Commission.

General This trust makes grants mainly to Jewish organisations, for social welfare and religious education. In 2004/05 it had assets amounting to £7.8 million and an income of £316,000. Grants were made to 56 organisations totalling £305,000.

Beneficiaries included: Mir (£38,000); Society of Friends of Torah (£25,000); Jaffa Institute (£19,000); Agudas Israel Housing Association Ltd (£10,000); Golders Green Beth Hamedrash

Congregation (£8,000); Brisk Yeshivas (£7,500); WST Charity (£6,700); London Academy of Jewish Studies (£5,200); Beth Jacob Grammar School (£5,000); Jewish Learning Exchange (£4,800); Baer Hatorah (£4,000); Shuvo Yisroel (£3,500); Menorah Primary School (£3,000); Beer Yaacov Yeshivah Trust (£2,500); Aish Hatorah U.K (£2,000); Horomo – Yeshivah (£1,600); Gertner Charitable Trust (£1,300); Gateshead Foundation for Torah (£1,200); and Irgun Yotzei Anglia, Reb Yechiel Kollel and Yeshivas Haran (£1,000 each).

Other grants of less than £1,000 each totalled £54,000.

Applications In writing to the correspondent.

The Oliver Borthwick Memorial Trust

Homelessness

£34,000 (2003/04)
Beneficial area UK.

c/o Donor Grants Department, Charities Aid Foundation, Kings Hill, West Malling, Kent ME19 4TA
Correspondent The Trustees
Trustees *Earl Bathurst; R Marriott; H L de Quetteville; M H R Bretherton; R A Graham; J MacDonald; J R Marriott; Mrs V Wrigley; Mrs J S Mace.*
CC Number 256206
Information available Accounts were on file at the Charity Commission.

General The intention of the trust is to provide shelter and help with homelessness. The trustees welcome applications from small but viable charities where they are able to make a significant contribution to the practical work of the charity, especially in disadvantaged inner-city areas.

In 2003/04 it had assets of £978,000, which generated an income of £35,000. Grants totalling £34,000 were made to 19 organisations, five of which were supported in the previous year.

Aside from the £6,500 to National Assocation of Almshouses, the grants were all of £1,500 each. Beneficiaries included Bethany Christian Trust, Caris – Islington, Dacorum Emergency Night Shelter, Haven Housing Trust, Humbercare Limited, Manna Society,

Mission in Hounslow Trust, E C Roberts Centre and St George Dragon Trust.

Exclusions No grants to individuals, including people working temporarily overseas for a charity where the request is for living expenses, together with applications relating to health, disability and those from non-registered charitable organisations.

Applications Letters should be set out on a maximum of two sides of A4, giving full details of the project with costs, who the project will serve and the anticipated outcome of the project. Meetings take place once a year in May. Applications should be received no later than April.

The Bothwell Charitable Trust

Disability, health, older people, conservation

£44,000 (2004/05)
Beneficial area England, particularly the South East.

14 Kirkly Close, Sanderstead, Surrey CR2 0ET
Tel. 020 8657 3369
Correspondent Angela Bothwell, Chair of Trustees
Trustees *Mrs Angela J Bothwell, Chair; Paul James; Crispian M P Howard.*
CC Number 299056
Information available Information was on file at the Charity Commission.

General The trust makes grants towards health, disability, conservation and older people's causes. In 2004/05 the trust had an income of £72,000 and made grants totalling £44,000 to 23 organisations.

Grants were for amounts of either £1,000 or £2,500. Beneficiaries included Arthritis Research Campaign, Blackthorn Trust, British Heart Foundation, British Home and Hospital for Incurables, ECHO International Health Services Ltd, Family Holiday Association, Friends of the Elderly, Invalid Children's Aid Nationwide and Macmillan Cancer Relief (£2,500 each) and British Trust for Conservation Volunteers, Children's Country Holiday Fund, Riding for the Disabled Association, Royal National Institute for Deaf People and South London YMCA Housing Association (£1,000 each).

Exclusions No grants for animal charities, overseas causes, individuals, or charities not registered with the Charity Commission.

Applications In writing to the correspondent. Distributions are usually made in March each year.

The Harry Bottom Charitable Trust

Religion, education, medical

£113,000 (2004/05)

Beneficial area UK, with a preference for Yorkshire and Derbyshire.

c/o Westons, Queen's Buildings, 55 Queen Street, Sheffield S1 2DX

Tel. 0114 273 8341

Correspondent D R Proctor

Trustees *J G Potter; J M Kilner; I G Rennie.*

CC Number 204675

Information available Accounts were on file at the Charity Commission.

General The trust states that support is divided roughly equally between religion, education and medical causes. Within these categories grants are given to:

- religion – small local appeals and cathedral appeals
- education – universities and schools
- medical – equipment for hospitals and charities concerned with disability.

In 2004/05 the trust had assets of £4.1 million. It had an income of £123,000 and made grants totalling £113,000 which were broken down as follows:

Medical

23 grants ranging from £500 to £10,000 totalled £38,000. Beneficiaries included Weston Park Hospital (£10,000), St Luke Hospice (£4,800), Sheffield Association for Cerebral Palsy (£3,300), Sheffield Mencap (£2,800), Arthritis Research Council, the Cavendish Centre, Defeating Deafness and RNIB (£1,000 each) and Alzheimer's Society (£500).

Religious

16 grants ranging from £500 to £25,000 totalled £36,000. Beneficiaries included Yorkshire Baptist Association (£25,000),

Hallam Methodist Church, Industrial Mission South Yorkshire and Mexborough Parish Rooms (£1,000 each), Christ Church Fulwood (£750) and Upper Wincobank Chapel (£500).

Education and other

34 grants ranging from £250 to £25,000 totalled £40,000. Beneficiaries included University of Sheffield (£5,500), Cherry Tree Children's Home (£3,250), RNLI (£3,000), Heeley City Farm (£2,000), Sheffield Family Holiday (£1,000), Sheffield Women's Aid (£750), Whizz-Kidz (£600), Croft House Settlement and St Vincent de Paul (£500 each) and Age Concern (£250).

Exclusions No grants to individuals.

Applications In writing to the correspondent at any time.

The Boughton Trust

Elderly people, disability, youth groups, conservation projects

£26,000 (2004/05)

Beneficial area UK.

c/o Kidd Rapinet Solicitors, 14 & 15 Craven Street, London WC2N 5AD

Tel. 020 7925 0303

Correspondent R D A Sweeting, Clerk to the Trustees

Trustees *P M Williams; G J M Wilding; C J T Harris.*

CC Number 261413

Information available Accounts were on file at the Charity Commission.

General The trust makes grants to organisations known to the trustees, benefiting elderly people, people with disabilities and environmental charities.

In 2004/05 the trust's assets totalled £709,000 and it had an income of £31,000. Grants were made totalling £26,000.

There were 17 grants given in this year, including those to Chase Hospice (£5,000), Highworth Recreation Centre (£3,000), St Andrew's Church and the Chaseley Trust – garden project (£2,500 each), the Chaseley Trust – Christmas party (£1,200), Mount Ephraim House – replacement of curtains and the Royal British Legion (£1,000 each), the Cherry Trees Project Limited, Crisis,

Christchurch – Leyton and Seven Springs and Cheshire Homes (£750 each) and Sargent Trust (£260).

Exclusions No individuals sponsored by the charity. Registered charities only.

Applications In writing only to the correspondent.

P G and N J Boulton Trust

Christian

£45,000 (2005/06)

Beneficial area Worldwide.

PO BOX 72, Wirral, Merseyside CH28 9AE

Website www.boultontrust.org.uk

Correspondent Mr Andrew L Perry, Trustee

Trustees *Miss N J Boulton, Chair; Miss L M Butchart; A L Perry; Mrs S Perry.*

CC Number 272525

Information available Accounts were on file at the Charity Commission.

General The trust's annual report states:

'The aims of the trust, as set out in the deed, are to provide assistance to the victims of disaster and to any charitable cause that the trustees consider worthy. The trustees are free to distribute both the capital and income of the trust as they see fit.

'The trustees fulfil these aims by making donations to other charities and by minimising administration costs. The trustees aim to target smaller charities, to whom a relatively small gift can make a significant difference.

'Whilst a substantial proportion of donations is allocated to Christian missionary work in accordance with the interests of the trustees, a wider interest is maintained by covering other areas such as poverty relief, medical research, healthcare and disability relief.'

In 2005/06 it had assets of £3.5 million, an income of £103,000 and made grants totalling £45,000.

Grants of £1,000 or more were made to seven organisations and were listed in the accounts: lntercessors For Britain (£14,000); New Life Centre (£12,000); Just Care (£4,500); Shalom Christian Fellowship (£4,000); Creation Research

Trust (£1,500); and Cedars School and Christian Institute (£1,000 each).

Other donations of £1,000 or less totalled £5,500.

Exclusions No grants to individuals or towards environment/conservation, culture, heritage, sports, leisure, church building repairs or animal welfare.

Applications In writing to the correspondent. Owing to the number of applications received the trustees cannot acknowledge all of them. Successful applicants will be contacted within two months.

The A H and E Boulton Trust

Evangelical Christian

£155,000 (2004/05)
Beneficial area Worldwide.

Moore Stephens, 47–49 North John Street, Liverpool L2 6TG
Correspondent J Glasby
Trustees *Mrs J R Gopsill; F P Gopsill.*
CC Number 225328
Information available Accounts were on file at the Charity Commission.

General The trust mainly supports the erection and maintenance of buildings to be used for preaching the Christian gospel, and teaching its doctrines. The trustees can also support other Christian institutions, especially missions in the UK and developing world.

In 2004/05 the trust had assets of £3.1 million and an income of £118,000. Grants totalled £155,000.

Beneficiaries of the largest grants were Charles Thompson Mission (£30,000), Slavic Gospel Association (£20,000), Holy Trinity Church and Pioneer People (£16,000 each), Liverpool City Mission (£15,000), Bethesda Church and Bridge Street Chapel (£10,000 each), Chile Mission Fund and Salvation Army (£3,000 each) and the Julius Trust and Leprosy Mission (£2,000 each).

A number of smaller grants were also made totalling £24,000.

Applications In writing to the correspondent. The trust tends to support a set list of charities and applications are very unlikely to be successful.

The M Bourne Charitable Trust

Jewish and cancer related

£713,000 (2004/05)
Beneficial area UK.

9 Lanark Square, London E14 9RE
Tel. 020 7536 6360
Correspondent Janet Bater
Trustees *C J Bourne; Mrs J H Bourne; Mrs K Cohen.*
CC Number 290620
Information available Full accounts were on file at the Charity Commission.

General The trust makes grants to Jewish individuals and institutions benefiting them. In 2004/05 the trust's assets totalled £3.6 million and it had an income of £149,000. Grants were made totalling £713,000.

By far the largest grant was £678,000 to Mossbourne Community Academy. Other beneficiaries included Prostate Cancer Research Foundation (£12,000), Cabrini New York (£9,700), Jewish Care (£2,500), World Jewish Relief (£1,100), Nofas UK (£1,000), Teenage Cancer Trust (£750), Transaid (£510), British ORT, Community Security Trust, Jewish Museum and Norwood Ltd (£500 each), Hadley Wood Jewish community (£400), Magen David Adom (£250) Drugscope and UJIA (£200 each), and Anne Frank Trust, Holocaust Educational Trust and Mill Hill Wizo (£100 each).

Applications In writing to the correspondent.

Bourneheights Limited

Orthodox Jewish

£1.7 million (2004/05)
Beneficial area UK.

Flat 10, Palm Court, Queen Elizabeth's Walk, London N16 5XA
Correspondent Schloime Rand, Trustee
Trustees *Chaskel Rand; Esther Rand; Erno Berger; Yechiel Chersky; Schloime Rand.*
CC Number 298359

Information available Accounts were on file at the Charity Commission.

General Registered with the Charity Commission in February 1998, in 2004/05 this charity had an income of £1.6 million including £1.2 million from donations and £441,000 from property income. Its assets stood at £3.7 million.

Grants were made totalling £1.7 million. There were 28 donations made. The beneficiaries of the five largest grants were Cosmon Belz Ltd (£358,000), Moreshet Hatorah (£307,000), College of Higher Rabbinical Studies (£200,000), BFOT (£160,000) and Telz Academy (£138,000).

Other grants included those to: Gevurath Air (£95,000), Chevra Mooz Ladol (£81,000), Forty Limited (£50,000), YHS Limited (£47,000), Tchabe Kollel (£31,000), Ohel Yehoshia (£16,000), Before Trust (£11,000), Yeshivath Hagrad (£8,000), Goan Tzvi (£5,300), Gur Community Free Loan Society (£5,000), North London Bikkur Cholim (£4,200), Chernobil Institutions (£3,600), JET (£3,500) and Lubavitch Mechina (£2,000).

Applications In writing to the correspondent.

The Bowerman Charitable Trust

General

£108,000 (2004/05)
Beneficial area UK, with a preference for West Sussex.

Champs Hill, Coldwatham, Pulborough, West Sussex RH20 1LY
Correspondent D W Bowerman, Trustee
Trustees *D W Bowerman; Mrs C M Bowerman; Mrs J M Taylor; Miss K E Bowerman; Mrs A M Downham; J M Capper.*
CC Number 289446
Information available Accounts were on file at the Charity Commission.

General The trust makes grants towards:

- church activities
- the arts, particularly music
- medical charities
- youth work
- charities concerned with relief of poverty and the resettlement of offenders.

In 2004/05 the trust had assets of £10.3 million and an income of £264,000. Grants were made totalling £108,000 and were distributed as follows:

Church activities – £22,000
Grants included £11,000 to Chichester Cathedral Trust, £5,000 to Titus Trust, £2,000 to UCCF and £1,000 to Coldwaltham PCC.

The arts – £64,000
Donations included £22,000 to Nash Concert Society, £13,000 each to Chichester Arts Festival and Music at Boxgrove, £7,400 to Elgar Foundation, £1,300 to Arundel Festival and £1,000 to City of London Festival.

Medical charities – £4,900
Donations included £1,800 to Royal Hospital Chelsea, £1,100 to 4 Sight and £1,000 to Chestnut Tree House.

Youth work – £8,400
Donations were £5,000 to St Mary's C of E Primary School and £3,400 to Mechilibi School Appeal.

Other – £670
Donations were £3,500 to National Gardens Scheme and £1,000 to Army Benevolent Fund.

A further £1,500 went to two individuals.

Applications In writing to the correspondent. The trustees said that they are bombarded with applications and unsolicited applications will not be considered.

The Viscountess Boyd Charitable Trust

Conservation, horticulture, education and preservation

About £40,000 (2003/04)
Beneficial area Worldwide, with a bias towards south west England, Devon and Cornwall.

c/o Smith and Williamson, 25 Moorgate, London EC2R 6AY
Correspondent The Administrator
Trustees *The Iveagh Trustees Ltd; Viscount Boyd; Viscountess Boyd; Hon. Dr Charlotte M Mitchell.*
CC Number 284270

Information available Information had been filed at the Charity Commission.

General In 2003/04 the trust had an income of £24,000 and a total expenditure of £54,000. The trust had stated that grants for this year totalled around £40,000.

Previous beneficiaries have included Abbey Restoration Fund (Onslow Tomb), Delaware Playgroup, East Cornwall Bach Festival, Eden Project, El Shaddai Trust, Gardeners' Benevolent Society, Historic Chapels Trust, Landulph Church, National Trust, Lichfield Cathedral Music Campaign, Mihai Eminescu Trust, National Asthma Campaign, Oxford Radcliffe Hospitals Charitable Fund, Parish Church of St Sampson Golant, St German's Under Fives, and World Cancer Research Fund.

Exclusions No grants to individuals.

Applications In writing to the correspondent; no application form is used. Please enclose an sae to ensure a reply. Applications are considered four times a year.

BP Conservation Programme

Wildlife and conservation

£2 million (2005)
Beneficial area Expeditions to and from anywhere in the world.

Birdlife International/FFI, Wellbrook Court, Girton Road, Cambridge CB3 0NA
Tel. 01223 277318 **Fax** 01223 277200
Email bp-conservation-programme@birdlife.org
Website conservation.bp.com
Correspondent Marianne Carter, BP Conservation Executive Programme Manager
Trustees *The Council: Dr Enrique Bucher (Argentina); Dr Jon Fjeldsa (Denmark); S A Hussain (India); Petar Iankov (Bulgaria); Anastasios P Leventis (UK); Prof. Yaa Ntiamoa-Baidu (Ghana); Baroness Young of Old Scone (UK).*
CC Number 1042125
Information available Full accounts were available from the Charity Commission.

General International conservation projects involving teams of interested

students, which address globally recognised priorities at a local level; projects must involve local counterparts. The programme is a partnership between Birdlife International, Fauna and Flora International, Conservation International, The Wildlife Conservation Society and BP. In 2005 the trust had an income of £8.5 million and a grant total of £2 million donated to various projects protecting endangered species and habitats.

An example of grants in 2005 included those made to: Tumbesian Forests – Nature and Culture International (£136,000); Cameroon Ngovayang Forest – Cameroon Biodiversity Conservation Society (£31,000); Seabirds Conservation Royal Society for the Protection of Birds (£30,000); Building Conservation and Environmental Networks in China Hong Kong Bird Watching Society (£20,000); and HOS Observatory Project Hellenic Ornithological Society – Greece (£17,000).

Other grants and awards amounted to £233,000.

Exclusions Only an entire expedition team will be funded: no applications will be considered from individuals applying for funding to join an expedition.

Applications Contact the programme manager for guidelines for applicants and application forms, or alternatively this can be found on the company website.

The William Brake Charitable Trust

General

£210,000 (2004/05)
Beneficial area UK, with a preference for Kent.

Gill Turner and Tucker, Colman House, King Street, Maidstone, Kent ME14 1JE
Tel. 01622 759051
Correspondent B Rylands, Solicitor
Trustees *Bruce Rylands; Philip Wilson; Mrs Deborah Isaac.*
CC Number 1023244
Information available Accounts were on file at the Charity Commission.

General The charity invites applications from the William Brake family for funding of worthy charitable causes each year, with a particular emphasis on local charities where the family know the charity's representative.

In 2004/05 the trust had assets of £8.4 million and an income of £208,000. The trust made 47 grants totalling £210,000 (£40,000 in 2003/04).

Beneficiaries of the largest grants were the Whitely Laing Foundation (£50,000), Myatt Garden Parent Teacher Association (£30,000), Royal Masonic Benevolent Institution (£25,000) and Canterbury and District Samaritans, Mike Collingwood Memorial Fund, Salisbury Diocesan Board of Finance and Society of Licensed Victuallers (£10,000 each)

Other beneficiaries included Christina Noble Children's Foundation (£5,000), NSPCC (£4,000), Cancer Research Campaign, Chase Children's Hospice Service, Elimination of Leukaemia Fund, Heart of Kent Hospice, Royal Agricultural Benevolent Institution, Vision Aid Overseas and the Wooden Spoon Society (£2,000 each) and Guildford Undetected Tumour Screening, the Lavender Trust, Lincolnshire & Nottingham Air Ambulance Trust, Maidstone & Tunbridge Wells NHS Charitable Fund, National Asthma Campaign, Portland College and Save the Children (£1,000 each).

Applications In writing to the correspondent.

The Tony Bramall Charitable Trust

Children, medical research, sickness

£267,000 (2004/05)

Beneficial area UK, with some preference for Yorkshire.

12 Cardale Court, Beckwith Head Road, Harrogate, North Yorkshire HG3 1RY

Correspondent The Trustees

Trustees *D C A Bramall; Mrs K S Bramall Odgen; Mrs M J Foody; G M Tate; Miss A Bramall.*

CC Number 1001522

Information available Full accounts were on file at the Charity Commission.

General 'The charity was established in 1988 by Mr D C A Bramall with an initial sum of £600,000. The charity's objectives are the promotion and supply of medical research mainly cancer focused and also assisting persons less able to finance their medical/health needs, particularly children and particularly those causes based in the northern part of the country.'

In 2004/05 the trust had assets of £3.8 million, an income of £217,000 and made grants totalling £267,000.

The largest donation went to Cancer Research UK (£200,000). Other beneficiaries included: Cookridge Cancer Centre and Henshaw's Society for Blind People (£5,000 each); BEN – Motor & Allied Trades Benevolent Association and the Hospital Heartbeat Appeal (£3,000 each); the Cavendish Centre for Cancer Care, Huntingdon's Disease Association and York Blind and Partially Sighted Society (£2,500 each); Association of Spina Bifida & Hydrocephalus, Children's Hospice Appeal Trust, Heartline Association, Motor and Allied Traders Benevolent Fund and Sue Ryder Care (£2,000 each); the Dystonia Society, the Helen Feather Memorial Trust, Mid-Yorkshire Hospital Trust and UNICEF (£1,000 each); and BLISS the Cavendish Centre and the Prince's Trust (£500 each).

Applications In writing to the correspondent.

The Breast Cancer Research Trust

Research into breast cancer

£304,000 (18 months ending April 2005)

Beneficial area UK.

48 Wayneflete Tower Avenue, Esher, Surrey KT10 8QG

Tel. 01372 463235 (J C Gazet); 01243 583143 (Rosemary Sutcliffe, Secretary)

Email bcrtrust@aol.com

Correspondent J C Gazet, Trustee

Trustees *Vera Lynn; Jean-Claude Gazet; Lady Delfont; Bob Potter; Prof T J Powles; Hon Mrs Justice Rafferty; Prof. Charles*

Coombes; R M Rainsbury; Dr Margaret Spittle.

CC Number 272214

Information available Information was provided by the trust.

General The trust supports medical research at a scientific and laboratory level within a recognised UK medical unit into the causation and diagnosis of breast cancer. Grants can be given for up to three years, ranging up to £35,000 a year.

In the 18 months to 5 April 2005 it had assets of £1.2 million, an income of £795,000 and made grants totalling £304,000.

By far the largest grant went to Imperial College (£162,000). Other beneficiaries were Winchester Cancer Research Trust (£48,000), St George's Hospital Medical School and Mary How Trust for Cancer Prevention (£29,000 each), Glasgow University Hospital (£9,500), Glasgow University Hospital (£9,000) and St George's Hospital (£5,000).

Exclusions No grants to students.

Applications On a form available from the correspondent.

The Harold and Alice Bridges Charity

General

£75,000 (2004/05)

Beneficial area South Cumbria and North Lancashire (as far south as Preston).

Messrs Senior Calveley and Hardy Solicitors, 8 Hastings Place, Lytham FY8 5NA

Tel. 01253 733333

Email rnh@seniorslaw.co.uk

Correspondent Richard N Hardy, Trustee

Trustees *Richard N Hardy; Jeffrey W Greenwood.*

CC Number 236654

Information available Accounts were obtained from the Charity Commission website.

General 'The trustees normally make grants to local causes in the Lancashire and South Cumbria area with special preference to the River Ribble area and northwards, the Blackburn area, and the

South Lakes area. Generally, grants are made to benefit the young and older people, are mainly towards capital projects in connection with rural and village life especially where there is associated voluntary effort.'

In 2004/05 the trust had assets of £2 million and an income of £88,000. Grants to 49 organisations totalled £75,000. Donations ranged between £500 and £5,000.

Beneficiaries included St John the Baptist, Broughton (£5,000), Parochial Church Council Ribby Cum Wrea (£3,000), Arkholme Village Hall, Boys Brigade North West, Chorley Adventure Youth Club, Deafway, Friends of Williamson Park, Rosemere Cancer Foundation, Slyne with Hest Memorial Hall, Tann Hill Trust and Walmer Bridge Village Hall Association (£2,000 each), Fleetwood Gymnasium Club, Mellor Junior Football Club – Blackburn, Langho Methodist Community Partnership, Over Kellet Indoor Bowling Club and Whitechapel Pre School Playgroup (£1,000 each) and Beetham Church Heritage Trust, Grange Bowling Club and Little Fish Parent and Toddler Group (£500 each).

Exclusions No grants to individuals.

Applications In writing to the correspondent, followed by completion of a standard application form.

Briggs Animal Welfare Trust

Animal welfare

£39,000 (2005/06)
Beneficial area UK and overseas.

Belmoredean, Maplehurst Road, West Grinstead, West Sussex RH13 6RN

Correspondent The Trustees

Trustee *Miss L M Hartnett and Mrs F Mathers.*

CC Number 276459

Information available Accounts were on file at the Charity Commission.

General This trust derives most of its income from shares in the company Eurotherm International plc. Although the original objectives of the trust were general, but with particular support for animal welfare, the trust's policy is to support only animal-welfare causes. There are five named beneficiaries in the trust deed: RSPCA, Reystede Animal

Sanctuary Ringmer, Brooke Hospital for Animals Cairo, Care of British Columbia House and the Society for the Protection of Animals in North Africa.

In 2005/06 it had assets of £843,000, an income of £35,000 and made grants totalling £39,000. No further information was available for this year.

Applications In writing to the correspondent.

The Bristol Charities

General

£163,000 to organisations (2005/06)
Beneficial area Within a 10-mile radius of Bristol city centre.

17 St Augustine's Parade, Bristol BS1 4UL

Tel. 0117 930 0301 **Fax** 0117 925 3824

Email info@bristolcharities.org.uk

Website www.bristolcharities.org.uk

Correspondent David Jones, Chief Executive

Trustees *J B Ackland; K Bonham; K Das; B R England; C A Halton; S Hampton; J Howard-Brown; D W P Lewis; A Morris; M Sisman; S W Thomas; S W Thomas; D L J Watts; Dr R Acheson; J Francis; N Hutchen; C Porter; V Stevenson.*

CC Number 1109141

Information available Accounts were available from the Charity Commission and information was available from the charity's website.

General The charity administers charities that, prior to the 1835 Municipal Corporations Act, were under the control of the Corporation of Bristol. Subsequently, many other charities have been brought under the administration of Bristol Charities. The oldest charity was founded in 1395 and the most recent was formed in 2004.

Bristol Charities focuses on three core areas:

- older people's residential and day care services
- grant-giving to individuals from a series of endowments and legacies left by Bristol benefactors
- professional management services to other charities.

'There are a number of grant-giving charities but the main ones are 'Relief in Need', 'Relief in Sickness', the 'Guild of the Handicapped' and the 'Miss Merchant Fund'. There are a number of smaller charities. Grants are made primarily to individuals, mainly in the form of vouchers that are used to acquire specific goods, although the trustees have, in recent years, created a 'retained ownership scheme', whereby items such as electric wheelchairs and scooters are acquired for named individuals but the ownership is retained so that the items can be recycled if the original recipient no longer requires those items.'

In 2005/06 the charities had assets of £21 million, an income of £2.3 million and made grants totalling £412,000, of which £249,000 consisted of over 1,400 grants to individuals.

Grants to organisations of £1,000 or more went to: Bristol Grammar School (£54,000); Bristol Charities Services Henbury Centre (£41,000); Badminton School and Orchard Homes (£11,000 each); the Red Maids' School (£7,500); Emmaus (£5,000); Dhek Bhal Elderly holiday break (£1,900); and Fairbridge West, St Michael on the Mount – Breakfast Club and St Peter's Hospice (£1,000 each).

Applications On an application form available from the correspondent.

The British Council for Prevention of Blindness

Prevention and treatment of blindness

£194,000 (2005/06)
Beneficial area Worldwide.

59–60 Russell Square, London WC1B 4HP

Tel. 020 7953 3777

Email info@bcpb.org

Website www.bcpb.org

Correspondent Jackie Webber

Trustees *A R Elkington; C Walker; S M Brooker; Prof. A Dick; Miss M Hallendorff; Dr C Harper; R Jackson; R Porter; R Titley; Lady J Wilson.*

CC Number 270941

Information available Full accounts were on file at the Charity Commission.

General The BCPB's mission statement is 'to help prevent blindness and restore sight in the UK and developing world by:

- funding research (including fellowships) in UK hospitals and universities into the causes and treatments of the major eye diseases
- supporting practical treatment programmes and research in the developing world
- promoting vital skills, leadership, awareness and demand for the expansion of community eye health in the developing world through the education of doctors and nurses within communities.'

The trust's policy is to divide its support equally between projects in the UK and abroad. Grants are given to hospitals, universities and health centres both in the UK and in developing countries. Grants are also given to individuals through the Boulter Fellowship Awards. Grants are usually for a maximum of £40,000 and given for a maximum of three years.

In 2005/06 the trust had assets of £414,000. It had an income of £103,000. Grants totalled £194,000.

Exclusions 'We do NOT deal with the individual welfare of blind people in the UK.'

Applications Applications can be made throughout the year.

The British Dietetic Association General and Education Trust Fund

Dietary and nutritional issues

£45,000 (2005/06)
Beneficial area UK.

5th Floor, Charles House, 148–149 Great Charles Street, Queensway, Birmingham B3 3HT

Tel. 0121 200 8080 **Fax** 0121 800 8081

Email info@bda.uk.com

Website www.bda.uk.com

Correspondent Secretary to the Trustees

Trustees P Brindley; Dame Barbara Clayton; Miss E T Elliot; W T Seddon; Mrs Pauline Douglas; Miss Una Martin.

CC Number 282553

Information available Accounts were on file at the Charity Commission.

General The trust supports the development of the scientific knowledge base for the discipline of dietetics through funding of relevant research; support to the profession's development of pre- and post-registration education structures and standards; an annual travel bursary for students and newly qualified dietitians.

In 2005/06 it had assets of £1.2 million and an income of £629,000. Grants were made totalling £45,000.

Exclusions Direct support of dietetic students in training or postgraduate qualifications for individuals, i.e. the trust will not pay postgraduate fees/expenses, or elective/MSc study for doctors.

Applications Guidelines, the grant-giving policy and an application form are sent to prospective applicants. All applications are acknowledged.

British Humane Association

Welfare

£90,000 (2005)
Beneficial area UK.

Priory House, 25 St John's Lane, Clerkenwell, London EC1M 4PP

Correspondent The Trustees

Trustees H Gould, Chair; B Campbell-Johnson; C Campbell-Johnston; Sir Anthony Grant; J M Huntington; H R Walduck; D J Williams; D J Eldridge; P Gee.

CC Number 207120

Information available Accounts were on file at the Charity Commission.

General In 2005 the trust had an income of £116,000 and made grants totalling £90,000. Assets stood at £3.4 million.

Grants were made totalling £89,000 in 2001. Grants included £36,000 to St John

of Jerusalem Eye Hospital, £10,000 to Professional Classes Aid Council, £5,700 to Ewe and You, £5,000 each to Friends of the Elderly, Guild of Aid for Gentlepeople, Home Start Herefordshire and St John in South Africa, £2,500 to Church Lads' and Girls' Brigade and £2,000 to Artists' General Benevolent Institution.

Applications The trust only supports one new cause each year and applications are unlikely to be successful.

British Institute at Ankara

Arts, humanities and social sciences of Turkey and the Black Sea region

£141,000 (2005/06)
Beneficial area UK, Turkey and the Black Sea region.

10 Carlton House Terrace, London SW1Y 5AH

Tel. 020 7969 5204 **Fax** 020 7969 5401

Email biaa@britac.ac.uk

Website www.biaa.ac.uk

Correspondent Gina Coulthard

Trustee Council of Management.

CC Number 313940

Information available Information was available on the institute's website.

General The charity describes its work by stating that it 'supports, promotes and publishes British research focused on Turkey and the Black Sea littoral in all academic disciplines within the arts, humanities and social sciences, whilst maintaining a centre of excellence in Ankara focused on the archaeology and related subjects of Turkey'.

As well as performing its own research and having a large research library in Ankara, the charity also provides a number of grants to individuals and organisations to undertake this work. In 2005/06 it gave grants totalling £141,000 from an income of £493,000. Please see the trust's website for further information.

Applications Initial telephone calls welcome. Application forms and guidelines are available on the website, along with exact deadlines.

The Britten-Pears Foundation

Arts, particularly music by living composers, Britten and Pears, some music education, the environment and occasionally humanitarian causes

£297,000 (2004/05)

Beneficial area UK, with a preference for East Anglia and Suffolk in particular.

The Red House, Golf Lane, Aldeburgh, Suffolk IP15 5PZ

Tel. 01728 451700

Email c.shepherd@brittenpears.org

Website www.brittenpears.org

Correspondent Cerys Shepherd

Trustees *Sir Robert Carnwath, Chair; Dr Colin Matthews; Noel Periton; Chris Banks; Peter Carter; Michael Berkeley; Mark Fisher; Stephen Oliver; Janis Susskind; John Evans.*

CC Number 295595

Information available Accounts were on file at the Charity Commission.

General The foundation was set up 'to promote public knowledge and appreciation of the musical works and writings of Benjamin Britten and Peter Pears and the tradition and principles of musical education and performance developed by them.'

It aims to promote new music, by way of grants to other charities or those whose objectives are of charitable intent, for commissions, live performances of contemporary music and, occasionally, recordings and innovatory musical education projects. It also makes occasional grants to local educational, environmental and peace organisations. Grants normally range from £100 to £1,000 with some projects being awarded from £1,000 to £2,000. An up-to-date guideline of eligible projects can be seen at the foundation's website.

The foundation owns and finances the Britten-Pears Library at Aldeburgh, and supports the Britten-Pears Young Artist Programme at Snape and the annual Aldeburgh Festivals in June and the autumn. Its annual income largely derives from the royalties from the performance worldwide of the works of Benjamin Britten, and is channelled to the foundation through its trading subsidiary, the Britten Estate Ltd, by Gift Aid.

In 2004/05 the foundation had assets of £16.9 million and an income of £1.2 million. Direct charitable expenditure totalled £651,000 of which £251,000 went to the Britten Pears Library and £104,000 went to the Red House Complex. There were 109 grants made totalling £297,000 with the largest grant of £200,000 being donated to Aldeburgh Productions. Other beneficiaries included: BMIC, NMC, RCM and SPNM (£5,000 each); Cheltenham Arts Festival (£2,000); London Sinfonietta and New London Chamber Choir (£1,500 each); BCMG (£1,200); Britten Sinfonia Ltd, Orchestra of St Johns, Scottish Opera and Stonewall (£1,000 each); and Buxton Festival (£500).

Exclusions No grants for: general charitable projects; general support for festivals other than Aldeburgh; requests from individuals for bursaries and course grants other than for the Britten-Pears Young Artist Programme; travel costs; or purchase or restoration of musical instruments or equipment, and of buildings other than at Snape Maltings/Aldeburgh.

The foundation does not consider applications for support for performances or recordings of the works of Benjamin Britten, of whose estate it is the beneficiary. Subsidy for works by Britten which, in the estate's view, need further promotion, can be sought from The Britten Estate Ltd, which is a subsidiary trading company.

Applications By plain text email only. Usually three deadlines per year. Applicants must consult the guidelines well in advance. These are published on the foundation's website (www.brittenpears.org).

The Broadfield Trust

Education

£168,000 (2004/05)

Beneficial area UK.

c/o Baker Tilly, Elgar House, Holmer Road, Hereford HR4 9SF

Correspondent Peter Johnston

Trustees *Hon. E R H Wills; J R Henderson; Sir Ashley Ponsonby; P N H Gibbs; C A H Wills; P J H Wills.*

CC Number 206623

Information available Accounts were on file at the Charity Commission.

General In 2004/05 the trust had assets of £5.6 million and an income of £178,000. One grant was made totalling £168,000 to the Farmington Trust, a regular beneficiary. Rendcomb College also receives regular support.

Exclusions No grants to individuals.

Applications In writing to the correspondent.

The Roger Brooke Charitable Trust

General

See below

Beneficial area UK, with a preference for Hampshire.

Withers, 16 Old Bailey, London EC4M 7EG

Tel. 020 7597 6123

Correspondent J P Arnold, Trustee

Trustees *J P Arnold; C R E Brooke; Mrs N B Brooke; Ms J R Rousso; S H R Brooke.*

CC Number 1071250

Information available Information was obtained from the Charity Commission.

General Established in 1998, this trust has general charitable purposes, including medical research, support for carers and social action.

In 2004/05 the trust had an income of £21,000 and a total expenditure of £157,000. Further information was not available.

Exclusions In general, individuals are not supported.

Applications In writing to the correspondent. Applications will only be acknowledged if successful.

The David Brooke Charity

Young people, medical

£52,000 (2005/06)

Beneficial area UK.

Cook Sutton, Billings House, Singer Lane, Henley-on-Thames, Oxfordshire RG9 1HB

Correspondent D J Rusman, Trustee

Trustees *D J Rusman; P M Hutt; N A Brooke.*

CC Number 283658

Information available Accounts were on file at the Charity Commission.

General The trust supports youth causes, favouring disadvantaged young people, particularly through causes providing self-help programmes and outdoor-activity training. Grants are also given to medical organisations.

In 2005/06 the trust had assets of £1.9 million generating an income of £63,000. Grants were given to 25 organisations and totalled £52,000.

Grants were broken down into the following two categories.

Children and young people

The eight beneficiaries in this category were: Great Ormond Street Hospital (£3,500); YMCA (£3,000); the Children's Society and Finchale Training College (£2,500 each); Lord Wandsworth College (£2,000); NSPCC (£1,500); and Berkshire Girl Guides and Berkshire Scouts (£750 each).

Other

Among the 17 beneficiaries in this category were: Arthritis Research Campaign, ASTO, the British Stammering Association, the Camphill Village Trust, the Fortune Centre of Riding Therapy and the Salvation Army (£2,700 each); RNIB (£2,500); Alzheimer's Society, the Samaritans and Yorkshire Dales Millennium Trust (£2,000 each); the Kennet & Avon Canal Trust (£1,500); and the Ramblers Association (£1,000).

Applications The correspondent stated that the trust's annual income is not for general distribution as it is committed to a limited number of charities on a long-term basis.

Bill Brown's Charitable Settlement

Health, social welfare

£72,000 (2004/05)

Beneficial area UK.

Payne Hicks Beach, 10 New Square, Lincoln's Inn, London WC2A 3QG

Tel. 020 7465 4300

Correspondent G S Brown, Trustee

Trustees *G S Brown; A J Barnett.*

CC Number 801756

Information available Full accounts were on file at the Charity Commission.

General This settlement supports health and welfare causes, including those for older people.

In 2004/05 the trust had assets of £2.9 million and an income of £602,000, including £500,000 from a legacy. Grants totalling £72,000 were made to 21 organisations, a number of which were recurrent. Administration and management costs totalled £17,000.

Beneficiaries included: Salvation Army (£10,000); Macmillan Cancer Relief (£7,000); Alzheimer's Disease Society, Holy Trinity Church Restoration Fund and the Princess Alice Hospice (£5,000 each); Disability Challengers, Scout Association and Treloar Trust (£4,000 each); Linden Lodge Charitable Trust (£3,000); Cancer Research UK and Leonard Cheshire Foundation (£2,500 each); RABMIND and St Christopher's Hospice (£2,000 each); Tuberous Sclerosis Association (£1,500); and Barnardos (£1,000).

Applications In writing to the correspondent, including as much detail as possible. Applications are considered every six months. The trust states that nearly all of its funds are allocated to charities known to the trust and new applications have little chance of receiving grants.

R S Brownless Charitable Trust

Disabled, disadvantage, serious illness

£58,000 (2005/06)

Beneficial area Mainly UK and occasionally overseas.

Hennerton Holt, Wargrave, Reading RG10 8PD

Tel. 0118 940 4029

Correspondent Mrs P M A Nicolai, Trustee

Trustees *Mrs F A Plummer; Mrs P M Nicolai.*

CC Number 1000320

Information available Accounts were on file at the Charity Commission, without a list of grants.

General The trust makes grants to causes that benefit people who are disabled, disadvantaged or seriously ill. Charities working in the fields of accommodation and housing, education, job creation and voluntary work are also supported. Grants are usually one-off, ranging between £100 and £2,000.

In 2005/06 the trust's assets totalled £1.3 million, it had an income of £57,000 and grants were made totalling £58,000.

Previous beneficiaries have included Alzheimer's Society, Camp Mohawk, Casa Allianza UK, Crisis, Foundation for Study of Infant Deaths, Prader-Willi Foundation, St Andrew's Hall, UNICEF, Wargrave PCC and Witham on the Hill PCC.

Exclusions Grants are rarely given to individuals for educational projects or to education or conservation causes or overseas aid.

Applications In writing to the correspondent. The trustees meet twice a year, but in special circumstances will meet at other times. The trust is unable to acknowledge all requests.

The T B H Brunner Charitable Settlement

Heritage, arts, general

£31,000 (2004/05)

Beneficial area UK.

2 Inverness Gardens, London W8 4RN

Correspondent T B H Brunner, Trustee

Trustees *T B H Brunner; Mrs H U Brunner.*

CC Number 260604

Information available Accounts were on file at the Charity Commission.

General In 2004/05 this trust had an income of £32,000 and made grants totalling £31,000. Assets stood at £1.2 million.

There were 58 grants made during the year, of which 13 were for £1,000 or more. Beneficiaries of these larger grants were Institute of Economic Affairs and Rotherfield Greys PCC (£2,500 each), Institute of Economic Affairs, Rotherfield greys PCC (£2,000), St Nicholas Appeal (£1,500), Live Music Now! (£1,300) and Harris Manchester College, the Minority Rights Group, Portobello Trust, Refresh, Ripon College Cuddesdon, Rotherfield Greys Village Hall and York Early Music (£1,000 each).

Applications In writing to the correspondent.

Brushmill Ltd

Jewish

£373,000 (2003/04)

Beneficial area Worldwide.

c/o Cohen Arnold and Co., New Burlington House, 1075 Finchley Road, London NW11 0PU

Correspondent Mrs M Getter, Secretary

Trustees *C Getter, Chair; J Weinberger; Mrs E Weinberger.*

CC Number 285420

Information available Information was on file at the Charity Commission, without a list of grants.

General In 2003/04 the trust had an income of £367,000, virtually all donation received. Grants totalled £373,000, but no grants list was available.

Previous beneficiaries have included Bais Rochel, Friends of Yeshivas Shaar Hashomaim and Holmleigh Trust.

Applications In writing to the correspondent.

Buckingham Trust

Christian, general

£198,000 (2004/05)

Beneficial area UK and worldwide.

17 Church Road, Tunbridge Wells, Kent TN1 1LG

Tel. 01892 774774 **Fax** 01892 774775

Correspondent Philip R Edwards, Trustee

Trustees *Philip R Edwards; Richard W D Foot.*

CC Number 237350

Information available Accounts were downloaded from the Charity Commission's website.

General In 2004/05 the trust had assets of £930,000 and an income of £152,000. Grants were made totalling £198,000 of which £113,000 was donated to churches, £78,000 was distributed to organisations and £4,500 was awarded to individuals.

Churches:
Grants included £65,000 to St Peter's Canary Wharf Trust, £8,000 to St John's – Tunbridge Wells, £6,400 to St Thomas' – Lancaster, £3,100 to Harpenden Methodist Church, £1,800 to Tonbridge Baptist Church and £1,500 to All Saints Crowborough.

Charities:
Grants included £13,000 to Tear Fund, £2,100 to Scripture Union, £1,900 to Leprosy Mission, £1,500 to Shambles PCC, £1,400 to Sudan Church Association, £1,300 each to the Bible Society and Titus Trust, £1,200 to Waltham Forest Youth for Christ, £1,100 each to Open Doors and Overseas Mission fellowship and £1,000 to Christians in Sport.

Applications Unsolicited applicants are not considered.

The Buckinghamshire Masonic Centenary Fund

General

£55,000 (2005/06)

Beneficial area Buckinghamshire.

51 Townside, Haddenham, Aylesbury, Buckinghamshire HP17 8AW

Tel. 01844 291275

Email alanwatkins590@btinternet.com

Website www.buckspgl.org

Correspondent A R Watkins, Hon. Secretary

Trustees *R Reed; E R Bunn; P N I Harborne; H N Hall.*

CC Number 1007193

Information available Accounts were on file at the Charity Commission.

General The fund was established in 1991 to aid non-Masonic charitable causes within Buckinghamshire. The fund makes donations to these causes on behalf of over 4,000 Buckinghamshire freemasons, who are the sole source of its financial support.

The fund will normally only give consideration to:

- Non-Masonic charitable causes within Buckinghamshire.
- Specific projects or facilities, rather than general appeals or requests to fund routine activities.
- Buckinghamshire charities that deal solely with cases in Buckinghamshire, and Buckinghamshire charities that also have connections in adjacent areas.
- Individual cases within Buckinghamshire, or outside Buckinghamshire if there is a strong Buckinghamshire connection, only if referred through, or supported by, community welfare or health agencies because of the implications for State and other welfare benefit provisions.

In 2005/06 the trust had assets of £749,000, an income of £49,000 and made 28 grants totalling £55,000.

Beneficiaries included: Chilterns Friends of the Endeavour (£5,000); Age Concern Milton Keynes (£4,900); Leonard Pullen Nursing Home (£4,700); 5th Aylesbury Scout Group (£4,000); High Wycombe Shopmobility (£3,800); Safety Centre – Milton Keynes (£3,500); Wycombe Rape

Crisis (£3,000); 1st Stokenchurch Scout Group (£2,800); Wendover Action Group (£2,200); Happy Days Children's Charity and Thames Valley Air Ambulance Trust (£2,000 each); Dogs for the Disabled (£1,500); Child Bereavement Trust, Hearing Dogs for Deaf People, Marlow Opportunities Playgroup and Princes Risborough Scouts and Guides (£1,000 each); Reactivate (£600); Invalids at Home (£500); and Chalfont St Giles Youth Club (£250).

Exclusions No grants to individuals for expeditions or for youth work overseas, no sponsorship of events or individuals. No grants to heritage, wildlife or conservation projects. No grants towards routine expenditure and activities, including staff costs.

Applications In writing to the correspondent, setting out aims and objectives on one page of A4 with a copy of the latest audited annual report and accounts if available. Details should be supplied of the specific facilities or projects for which funding is sought. The trustees meet three or four times a year to consider applications. The trust states that some grants are made after the organisation has been visited by a committee member.

Buckland Charitable Trust

General, international development, welfare and health research

£47,000 (2005/06)
Beneficial area UK and overseas.

1 Bishops Wharf, Walnut Tree Close, Guildford, Surrey GU1 4RA
Correspondent The Trustees
Trustees *E K M Afsari; A R Afsari.*
CC Number 273679
Information available Accounts were on file at the Charity Commission.

General In 2005/06 this trust made grants totalling £47,000. There were 34 grants made in the year.

Beneficiaries included: the Great North Air Ambulance Service (£5,000); Islamic Universal Association (£4,000); Macmillan Cancer Relief and Médecins Sans Frontières (£3,000 each); Eden Valley Hospice (£2,500); British Red

Cross and Children North East (£2,000 each); Alzheimer's Society, Inspire Foundation and Muslim Aid (£1,000 each); and Asthma UK, Project Trust and Samaritans (£500 each).

Applications In writing to the correspondent.

The Burden Trust

Christian, welfare, medical research, general

£119,000 (2005/06)
Beneficial area UK and overseas.

51 Downs Park West, Westbury Park, Bristol BS6 7QL
Tel. 0117 962 8611 **Fax** 0117 962 8611
Email p.oconor@netgates.co.uk
Correspondent Patrick O'Conor, Secretary
Trustees *A C Miles, Chair; Dr M G Barker; R E J Bernays; Prof. G M Stirrat; Bishop of Southwell and Nottingham; Prof. A Halestrap.*
CC Number 235859
Information available Accounts were on file at the Charity Commission.

General The trust operates in accordance with various trust deeds dating back to 1913. These deeds provide for grants for medical research, hospitals, retirement homes, schools and training institutions, homes and care for the young and people in need. The trust operates with an adherence to the tenets and principles of the Church of England.

In 2005/06 it had assets of £4.3 million, which generated an income of £125,000. Grants totalled £119,000, broken down as follows:

Neurological research – 1 grant of £45,000
This went to Burden Neurological Institute, which received the same amount in the previous year.

Homes and care for aged, infirm and disabled – 1 grant of £5,000
This went to Brunelcare, which received £6,000 in the previous year.

Clergy families' welfare – 1 grant totalling £1,000
This went to St Luke's Hospital for the Clergy, which received the same amount in the previous year.

Schools and training institutions – 8 grants totalling £64,000
All of these grants went to organisations supported in the previous year. Beneficiaries were Trinity College – Bristol (£14,500), Langham Research Scholarships (£12,500), Oxford Centre for Mission Studies and Union Biblical Seminary – Pune (£10,000 each), Association for Theological Education by Extension – Bangalore (£8,500), St Paul's Divinity College – Kenya (£2,000) and Redcliffe College (£1,500).

Organisations for care and training of young people – 1 grant of £4,000
This went to Easton Families Project, which received the same amount in the previous year.

Exclusions No grants to individuals.

Applications In writing to the correspondent to be received before 31 March each year. Financial information is required in support of the project for which help is requested. No application is responded to without an sae. Recipients of recurring grants are notified each year that grants are not automatic and must be applied for annually. Applications are considered at the annual trustees' meeting.

Burdens Charitable Foundation

General

£255,000 (2004/05)
Beneficial area UK, but mostly overseas, with special interest in Sub-Saharan Africa.

St George's House, 215–219 Chester Road, Manchester M15 4JE
Tel. 0161 832 4901 **Fax** 0161 835 3668
Correspondent Arthur J Burden, Trustee
Trustees *Arthur Burden; Godfrey Burden; Hilary Perkins; Sally Schofield; Dr A D Burden.*
CC Number 273535
Information available Annual report and accounts were available from the Charity Commission.

General The foundation was created in 1977 by Mr and Mrs W T Burden, who endowed it with shares in the business Mr Burden had created in 1929, WTB Holdings. This is a private company which employs about 1,000 people, many of whom also own shares in the company.

Whilst the trustees are not formally restricted by the Trust Deed as to the charitable activities which they are permitted to assist, their present main emphasis relates to the prevention and relief of poverty with particular reference to those people in countries such as those of Sub-Saharan Africa, whom they perceive to be substantially less fortunate than those in the UK. The particular elements of that relief to which the trustees currently give highest priority are the provision of safe water and sanitation and to education and access to information for visually impaired people. It is also increasingly the case that the trustees most favour the work of highly focused overseas projects capable of effective service delivery without either incurring significant costs in the UK or risking the diversion of funds from their key objectives.

Priorities overseas are:

- the geographical area of Sub-Saharan Africa, although consideration will be given to projects in other parts of Africa and other less developed countries;
- projects involving the provision of clean water, sanitation and combating visual impairment.

Priorities in the UK are:

- small local groups rather than large national/international charities;
- social outreach projects of local churches;
- groups where volunteers play a key role in the service delivered;
- low-cost umbrella agencies designed to facilitate the above.

Grants can relate to core costs, salaries, capital assets and so on without any exclusions in principle, save only that they really do make a difference. Large charities/projects and causes using professional fundraising costs to any substantial extent do not generally score particularly well.

In 2004/05 the foundation had assets of £12.2 million and made grants totalling £255,000.

Beneficiaries included La Renaissance School (£137,000), Harvest Help (£33,500) and Easton Christian Family Centre (£8,500).

Exclusions Causes which rarely or never benefit include animal welfare (except in less developed countries), the arts and museums, political activities, most medical research, preservation etc. of historic buildings and monuments, individual educational grants and sport, except sport for people with disabilities. No grants are made to individuals.

Applications In writing to the correspondent, accompanied by recent, audited accounts and statutory reports, coupled with at least an outline business plan where relevant. Trustees usually meet in March, June, September and December.

The Burry Charitable Trust

Medicine, health

£58,000 (2005/06)

Beneficial area UK, with a preference for Hampshire.

261 Lymington Road, Highcliffe, Christchurch, Dorset BH23 5EE

Correspondent N J Lapage, Trustee

Trustees *R J Burry; Mrs J A Knight; A J Osman: N J Lapage.*

CC Number 281045

Information available Accounts were on file at the Charity Commission.

General In 2005/06 the trust had assets of £108,000 and an income of £40,000. Grants to 14 organisations totalled £58,000.

Beneficiaries included: Oakhaven Hospital Trust (£30,000); Open Door Project, Not Forgotten Association, Salvation Army and Wessex Cardiac Trust (£5,000 each); John Grooms Association and Life Education Centres (£2,000 each); Disability Aid Fund and Wessex Autistic Society (£1,000 each); Mildmay Mission Hospital (£500); and Sway Welfare Aid Group (£250).

Exclusions No grants to individuals or students.

Applications This trust states that it does not respond to unsolicited applications.

R M Burton 1998 Charitable Settlement

Jewish charities, social welfare, education, the arts

£188,000 (2005/06)

Beneficial area England, with a preference for the Yorkshire and Humber area; also Israel.

c/o Trustee Management Ltd, 19 Cookridge Street, Leeds LS2 3AG

Correspondent The Trustees

Trustees *Arnold Burton; Jane Ingham; Harriet Coates.*

CC Number 1070588

Information available Accounts were on file at the Charity Commission, but without a list of grants.

General The trust has general charitable purposes, with particular interests in Jewish charities, social welfare, education, medicine, conservation and the arts, in Yorkshire and Humberside.

In 2005/06 the trust had assets of £1.1 million and an income of £104,000. Grants totalled £188,000, broken down as follows:

Arts	25 grants	£49,000
Conservation	18	£11,131
Education	6	£4,530
Health	18	£17,350
Jewish/Israel	39	£72,441
Social/Welfare	64	£33,725

The largest grants were distributed to Reform Foundation Trust (£25,000); University of York – library archive (£18,000); Community Security Trust and International Spinal Research (£10,000 each); Royal Opera House Foundation (£7,400); British ORT, Givat Havina, Selby Abbey Trust and Yorkshire Ballet Seminar Charitable Trust (£5,000 each); Together for Peace (£4,000); British Technion (£3,500); Yorkshire Bach Choir (£2,250); and Textile Industry Children's Trust (£2,000).

Exclusions Grants are not given to local charities outside Yorkshire or Humberside, individuals or to new charities where their work overlaps with already established organisations that are supported by the trust.

Applications In writing to the correspondent at any time. The trustees try to make a decision within a month.

Negative decisions are not necessarily communicated.

The Arnold Burton 1998 Charitable Trust

Jewish, medical research, education, social welfare, heritage

£236,000 (2005/06)

Beneficial area Worldwide.

c/o Trustee Management Ltd, 19 Cookridge Street, Leeds LS2 3AG

Correspondent The Trust Managers

Trustees *A J Burton; J J Burton; N A Burton; M T Burton.*

CC Number 1074633

Information available Accounts were on file at the Charity Commission.

General Established in 1998, this trust gives special consideration to appeals from Jewish charities and projects related to medical research, education, social welfare and heritage. No grants are made to individuals. In 2005/06 it had assets of £196,000, an income of £176,000 and made 37 grants totalling £236,000. Donations were broken down as follows:

Category	No. of grants	Amount
Education/arts	9	£54,000
Health	9	£7,500
Jewish/Israel	6	£151,000
Social welfare	13	£24,000

Organisations in receipt of grants of £1,000 or more included: United Jewish Israel Appeal (£100,000); JNF Charitable Trust (£45,000 in two grants); Royal Hall Restoration Trust (£20,000); Harrogate White Rose Theatre Trust Ltd and Leeds College of Art & Design (£10,000 each); University of Cambridge, Mitzvah Association Ltd, Roots Room, St John's College Cambridge and World Jewish Relief (£5,000 each); St George's Crypt and YMCA (£2,500 each); the Arnold Foundation (£2,000); Breakthrough Breast Cancer and Cambridge Expeditions Fund (£1,000 each); Barnardos (£500); and Children with Cystic Fibrosis (£250).

Applications In writing to the trust managers. Unsuccessful appeals will not necessarily be acknowledged.

The Geoffrey Burton Charitable Trust

General

£26,000 to organisations (2006)

Beneficial area UK, especially Suffolk and the Needham Market area.

Salix House, Falkenham, Ipswich IP10 0QY

Tel. 01394 448339 **Fax** 01394 448339

Email ericmaule@hotmail.com

Correspondent Eric Maule, Trustee

Trustees *Ted Nash; Eric Maule.*

CC Number 290854

Information available Full accounts were available from the Charity Commission website.

General In 2006 the trust had assets of £674,000 and an income of £33,000. Grants were made totalling £26,000. The trust continued to support the Green Light Trust with a contribution of £4,000 for general funding and the Mid Suffolk CAB with a donation of £1,500 towards the cost of a specialist advisor.

Other grant beneficiaries included RSPB – Berney Marshes (£2,000), Age Concern Suffolk – Saxon House Centre, Alzheimer's Research Trust and Bury St Edmunds Theatre Royal (£1,000 each) and Children's Country Holidays, Friends of the Suffolk Record Office and Gainsboroughs House towards the cost of a disabled access project (£500 each).

Exclusions No grants to individuals.

Applications In writing to the correspondent.

The Bill Butlin Charity Trust

General

£97,000 (2005/06)

Beneficial area UK.

Eagle House, 110 Jermyn Street, London SW1Y 6RH

Correspondent The Secretary

Trustees *Robert F Butlin; Lady Sheila Butlin; Peter A Hetherington; Trevor*

Watts; Frederick T Devine; Sonia I Meaden; Terence H North.

CC Number 228233

Information available Full accounts were provided by the trust.

General This trust was established by Sir William E Butlin in 1963. It has a preference for organisations working with children, especially those with disabilities, and older people. The trust has a list of regular beneficiaries, to which only a few charities may be added each year.

In 2005/06 it had assets of £2.4 million, which generated an income of £90,000. Grants were made totalling £97,000.

Beneficiaries included: Canadian Veterans Association of the UK and Petworth Cottage Nursing Home (£15,000 each); BIBIC, Cancer Research UK, CHICKS, Home Farm Trust, Dame Vera Lynne Trust for Children with Cerebral Palsy, the Marchant-Holliday School, Multiple Sclerosis Society and South Buckinghamshire RDA Group (£5,000 each); Friends of St Mary's Church – Pulburough, Grand Order of Lady Ratlings 'Cup of Kindness Fund', Grand Order of Water Rats and Lawrence Weston Community Farm (£3,000 each); the Lord's Taverners (£2,500); UK Antarctic Heritage Trust (£2,000); and Entertainment Artistes Benevolent Fund and Royal Marsden Hospital (£1,000 each).

Applications In writing to the correspondent. Trustees usually meet twice a year.

C and F Charitable Trust

Orthodox Jewish charities

£79,000 (2004/05)

Beneficial area UK and overseas.

c/o New Burlington House, 1075 Finchley House Road, London NW11 0PU

Correspondent The Trustees

Trustees *C S Kaufman; F H Kaufman; S Kaufman.*

CC Number 274529

Information available Accounts on file at the Charity Commission, without a list of grants.

General The trust income derives mainly from investment properties and other investments. Grants are made to Orthodox Jewish charities.

In 2004/05 the trust had assets of £1.3 million, an income of £118,000 and made grants totalling £79,000.

Previous beneficiaries have included Community Council of Gateshead, Ezras Nitrochim, Gur Trust, Kollel Shaarei Shlomo, SOFT and Yetev Lev Jerusalem Trust.

Exclusions Registered charities only.

Applications In writing to the correspondent.

The C B Trust

General, Jewish

About £31,000 to organisations (2004/05)

Beneficial area UK.

HSBC Trust Company UK Ltd, Trust Services, Norwich House, Nelson Gate, Southampton SO15 1GX

Tel. 02380 722 243

Correspondent Steve Gladwell

Trustees *Harold S Klug; Naomi S Klug; HSBC Trust Co. Ltd.*

CC Number 287180

Information available Information was obtained from the Charity Commission website.

General Registered with the Charity Commission in May 1983, in 2005 the trust had an income of £21,000 and a total expenditure of £40,000. A range of organisations are supported, including a number of Jewish charities.

Previously grant recipients have included Genesis Osteopathic Foundation (£15,000), Charities Aid Foundation (£10,000), The New North London Synagogue and British Friends of Neve Shalom (£1,000 each).

Applications In writing to the correspondent.

The C J M Charitable Trust

Social entrepreneurship

£52,000 (2004/05)

Beneficial area UK and overseas.

Messrs Farrer and Co., 66 Lincoln's Inn Fields, London WC2A 3LH

Correspondent The Trustees

Trustees *Christopher James Marks; Timothy John Marks; William Robert Marks; Rupert Philip Marks; Farrer and Co. Trust Corporation Ltd.*

CC Number 802325

Information available Full accounts were on file at the Charity Commission.

General In 2004/05 this trust had assets of £187,000, an income of £7,800 and made grants totalling £52,000. The charity will cease to exist in 2010.

Beneficiaries were: Network for Social Change (£40,000); the Mulberry Trust (£10,000) and Scottish Community Foundation (£2,600).

Applications In writing to the correspondent.

C J Cadbury Charitable Trust

General

£33,000 (2005/06)

Beneficial area UK.

Martineau Johnson, No. 1 Colmore Square, Birmingham B4 6AA

Correspondent The Clerk

Trustees *Hugh Carslake; Joy Cadbury; Thomas Cadbury: Lucy Cadbury.*

CC Number 270609

Information available Accounts were on file at the Charity Commission.

General In 2005/06 the trust had assets of £763,000 and an income of £40,000. Grants totalled £33,000.

Beneficiaries were: Island Conservancy Society UK (£23,000 in six grants); the Devon Wildlife Trust and Goodenough College (£3,000 each); and the Kingfishers Bridge Wetland and Plantlife International (£1,000 each).

Applications In writing to the correspondent. The trust does not generally support unsolicited applications.

Henry T and Lucy B Cadbury Charitable Trust

Quaker causes and institutions, health, homelessness, support groups, developing countries

About £25,000 to organisations (2005).

Beneficial area Mainly UK, but also the Third World.

B C M, Box 2024, London WC1N 3XX

Correspondent The Secretary

Trustees *E Rawlins; M B Gillett; C Carolan; C R Charity; V Franks; T Yates; T Hambly.*

CC Number 280314

Information available Information was obtained from the Charity Commission website.

General In the administration of this trust the trustees take it in turns to carry out the roles of the chair and secretary. Different trustees take responsibility for each area of concern to which grants are made. Each trustee is also separately allocated £1,500 in total to distribute to usually one to three charities, which relate to issues they are currently interested in.

In 2005 the trust had an income of £23,000 and a total expenditure of £30,000. Further information was not available.

Grant recipients are usually those that are personally chosen by one of the six trustees; who can award up to £1,500 to each beneficiary. In previous years, the following organisations have received grants ranging from £500 to £1,500: Dodford Children's Holiday Farm and Family Help, Battle Against Tranquillisers, Action for ME, Anaphylaxis Campaign, Bhopal Medical Appeal, Medical Foundation for Victims of Torture, Prisoners of Conscience, Quaker Opportunity Playgroup, Riverside Community Project, Tools for Self-Reliance and WOMANKIND Worldwide for Afghan Women.

Exclusions No grants to non-registered charities.

Applications The trust's income is committed each year and so unsolicited applications are not normally accepted. The trustees meet in March to consider applications.

The Christopher Cadbury Charitable Trust

Nature conservation, general

£70,000 (2005/06)

Beneficial area UK, with a strong preference for the Midlands.

New Guild House, 45 Great Charles Street, Queensway, Birmingham B3 2LX

Tel. 0121 212 2222

Correspondent Roger Harriman, Administrator

Trustees R V J Cadbury; Dr C James Cadbury; Mrs V B Reekie; Dr T N D Peet; P H G Cadbury; Mrs C V E Benfield.

CC Number 231859

Information available Accounts were on file at the Charity Commission.

General In 2005/06 the trust had assets of over £2 million and an income of £74,000. Grants totalled £70,000. The trustees have drawn up a schedule of commitments covering 19 charities which they have chosen to support. These charities can receive up to a maximum of £60,000 in any one year. Any surplus funds will be given to six other grant-making charitable trusts.

Beneficiaries included: Croft Trust – New Build Fund and Island Conservation Society UK – Aride (£11,000 each); Playthings Past Museum Trust (£7,500); P H G Cadbury Charitable Trust and Devon Wildlife Trust (£6,000 each); Norfolk Wildlife Trust (£5,000); Bower Trust, C James Cadbury Charitable Trust, R A and V B Reekie Charitable Trust and Sarnia Charitable Trust (£3,000 each); Fircroft College (£2,000); Berkshire Buckinghamshire and Oxfordshire Wildlife Trust and Survival International (£1,000 each); and Avoncroft Arts Society and Selly Oak Nursery School (£500 each).

Exclusions No support for individuals.

Applications The trustees have fully committed funds for projects presently supported and cannot respond positively to any further applications. Unsolicited applications are unlikely to be successful.

The George W Cadbury Charitable Trust

Population control, conservation, general

£187,000 (2005/06)

Beneficial area Worldwide.

New Guild House, 45 Great Charles Street, Queensway, Birmingham B3 2LX

Tel. 0121 212 2222 **Fax** 0121 212 2300

Correspondent Roger Harriman, Trust Administrator

Trustees Miss J C Boal; Mrs L E Boal; P C Boal; Miss J L Woodroffe; Mrs C A Woodroffe; N B Woodroffe.

CC Number 231861

Information available Accounts were on file at the Charity Commission.

General In 2005/06 the trust had assets of £6.5 million, generating an income of £221,000. Grants totalled £187,000, given in the following geographical areas:

USA	£92,000
UK	£80,000
Canada	£5,100
Africa	£10,000

There were 43 grants of £1,000 each or more listed in the accounts. Beneficiaries included Susan Kommen Foundation – Breast Cancer Research Centre, Fred Hutchinson Cancer Research Centre and Planned Parenthood of Western Washington (£4,300 each); Helen Bamber Association (£3,000); School of American Ballet and Westchester Children's Association (£2,800 each); Culpeper Community Garden and the Promise Fund (£2,000 each); Bridge the Gap and Seattle Art Museum (£1,700 each); One World Action (£1,100); and American Friends Service Committee, Winchester Foundation for Educational Excellence and WOMANKIND UK (£1,000 each).

There were a further 25 smaller grants made totalling £7,300.

Exclusions No grants to individuals or non-registered charities, or for scholarships.

Applications In writing to the correspondent. However, it should be noted that trustees' current commitments are such that no unsolicited applications can be considered at present.

The Richard Cadbury Charitable Trust

General

About £65,000 (2005/06)

Beneficial area UK, but mainly Birmingham, Coventry and Worcester.

26 Randall Road, Kenilworth, Warwickshire CV8 1JY

Correspondent Mrs M M Eardley, Trustee

Trustees R B Cadbury; Mrs M M Eardley; D G Slora; Miss J A Slora.

CC Number 224348

Information available Information had been filed at the Charity Commission.

General The trust has previously stated that the trust is 'people orientated' and supports projects such as playgroups, helping homeless people and the like and not arts and heritage-type causes. Grants range from £400 to £1,000 and are one-off. Grants are only given towards projects.

In 2005/06 the trust had an income of £17,000 and a total expenditure of £67,000.

Previous beneficiaries have included Birmingham Settlement, Centrepoint, Childline, Children's Society, Friends of Swanirvar, Help the Aged, Little Sisters of the Poor, National Children's Home, Oxfam, Salvation Army, VSO and YMCA.

Exclusions Grants are only given to organisations with charitable status and not to individuals and students. No grants for running costs or core funding.

Applications In writing to the correspondent giving reasons why a grant is needed and including a copy of the latest accounts if possible. Meetings are held in February, June and October.

The Edward and Dorothy Cadbury Trust

Health, education, arts

£113,000 (2005/06)

Beneficial area Preference for the West Midlands area.

Rokesley, University of Birmingham Selly Oak, Bristol Road, Selly Oak, Birmingham B29 6QF

Tel. 0121 472 1838 **Fax** 0121 472 7013

Correspondent Miss Susan Anderson, Trust Manager

Trustees *Mrs P A Gillett, Chair; Dr C M Elliott; Mrs P S Ward; Susan E Anfilogoff; Julia E Gillett.*

CC Number 1107327

Information available Accounts were on file at the Charity Commission.

General This trust was registered in December 2004, and is the recipient of funds transferred from the now defunct Edward and Dorothy Cadbury Trust (1928), registered charity number 221441. The objectives of the new trust remain the same, i.e. general charitable purposes in the West Midlands, with areas of work funded including music and the arts, children's charities, disadvantaged groups and support for the voluntary sector. The normal range of grants is between £500 and £2,500, with occasional larger grants made.

In 2005/06 it had assets of £4.5 million, which generated an income of £124,000. Grants totalled £113,000. Donations were broken down as follows:

Arts and culture – 12 grants totalling £10,000

Brornsgrove Festival (£3,800); Brornsgrove Concerts and City of Birmingham Symphony Orchestra and Council for Music in Hospitals (£1,000 each); Droitwich Concert Club (£750); Big Brum Theatre in Education Company and English Symphony Orchestra (£500 each); and Birmingham Festival Choral Society (£100).

Community projects and integration – 26 grants totalling £29,000

Herefordshire Riding for the Disabled – Wharton Bank Project (£10,000); South Birmingham Young Homeless Project (£3,000); Birmingham Children's Community Venture and Guide Association – Birmingham (£2,500 each); VSO and Willow Trust (£1,000 each); British Blind Sport and Whizz-Kidz (£750 each); and City of Birmingham Special Olympics, Jubilee Sailing Trust, Where Next Association and Worcester Action for Youth (£500 each).

Compassionate Support – 27 grants totalling £36,000

Cerebral Palsy Midlands (£10,000); Acorns Children's Hospice – Worcester and Pattaya Orphanage Trust (£5,000 each); Macmillan Cancer Relief (£1,100); Birmingham Institute for the Deaf, Brain Injury Rehabilitation Trust and CARE International UK, SENSE and WellChild (£1,000 each); Children's Liver Disease Foundation (£600); and British Institute for Brain Injured Children, Dystonia Society, Malvern Special Families, National Blind Children's Society and Sight Savers International (£500 each).

Education and training – 8 grants totalling £13,000

Dodford Children's Holiday Farm – Bromsgrove (£5,000); Living Paintings Trust and Queen Alexandra College – Birmingham (£2,500 each); Calibre Cassette Library (£500); and Population and Sustainability Network (£100).

Conservation and environment

Worcester Cathedral Development and Restoration Trust (£10,000); Woodland Trust (£2,500); Centre of the Earth – Wildlife Trust for Birmingham and the Black Country (£1,500); and RSPB (£500).

Research

Arthritis Research Campaign and British Heart Foundation (£500 each).

Exclusions No grants to individuals.

Applications In writing to the correspondent, giving clear, relevant information concerning the project's aims and its benefits, an outline budget and how the project is to be funded initially and in the future. Up-to-date accounts and annual reports, where available, should be included. Applications can be submitted at any time but three months should be allowed for a response. Applications that do not come within the policy as stated above may not be considered or acknowledged.

The George Cadbury Trust

General

£407,000 (2005/06)

Beneficial area Preference for the West Midlands, Hampshire and Gloucestershire.

New Guild House, 45 Great Charles Street, Queensway, Birmingham B3 2LX

Tel. 0121 212 2222 **Fax** 0121 212 2300

Correspondent Roger Harriman, Trust Administrator

Trustees *Mrs Anne L K Cadbury; Robin N Cadbury; Sir Adrian Cadbury; Roger V J Cadbury; Mrs A Janie Cadbury.*

CC Number 1040999

Information available Accounts were on file at the Charity Commission.

General The trust was set up in 1924 and maintains a strong financial interest in the Cadbury company. In 2005/06 the trust had assets of £10.1 million and an income of £333,000. Grants were made to 213 beneficiaries totalling £407,000.

The largest grants of £10,000 or more went to: St John of Jerusalem Eye Hospital (£60,000); National Youth Ballet (£35,000); Birmingham Settlement (£21,000); Friends of Bournville Carillon (£16,000); Dean and Chapter of Gloucester Cathedral (£15,000); and Bournville Junior and Infants School Acorns Hospice Trust, Gloucestershire Arthritis Trust, St Richard's Hospice and University of Cambridge Students Childcare Bursaries (£10,000 each).

Other beneficiaries included: James Cadbury Charitable Trust, R A and V B Reekie Trust and Sarnia Charitable Trust (£8,000); Avoncroft Museum of Buildings (£6,000); Books for Change, Anthony Nolan Trust and North Hampshire Medical Fund (£5,000 each); Duncraig, Grace of God Church Malawi and Symphony Hall Birmingham (£4,000 each); Outward Bound Trust (£3,000); Leonard Cheshire Home of Gloucestershire Refurbishment Appeal (£2,500); Bournville Parish Church and Jesus College Cambridge (£2,000 each); Royal British Legion (£1,500); and Alnwick Garden, Cornwall Community Foundation, Council for National Parks, Gosford Forest Guide House, Inventure Trust, Neptune Coast Line Campaign and Runnymede Trust and Uniaid Foundation (£1,000 each).

Exclusions No support for individuals for projects, courses of study, expedities or sporting tours. No support for overseas appeals.

Applications In writing to the correspondent to be considered quarterly. Please note that very few new applications are supported due to ongoing and alternative commitments.

Calleva Foundation

General

£146,000 (2004)
Beneficial area UK and worldwide.

PO Box 22554, London W8 5GN
Correspondent The Trustees
Trustees *S C Butt; C Butt.*
CC Number 1078808
Information available Accounts were on file at the Charity Commission, without a list of grants.

General Registered with the Charity Commission in January 2000, this trust can give in the UK and worldwide for the benefit of 'local communities'.

In 2004 it had assets of £24,000 and an income of £155,000. Grants totalled £146,000, broken down as follows:

- Education – £111,000
- Social Services – £17,000
- Children's Holidays and Social Services – £2,000
- Miscellaneous – £10,000
- Overseas Help – £5,000
- Ecological – £500
- Medical Care – £500
- Medical research – £200

Information on the size or type of grants, or the names of beneficiaries was not available.

Applications In writing to the correspondent.

The Calpe Trust

Relief work

£25,000 (2004/05)
Beneficial area Worldwide.

The Hideaway, Hatford Down, Faringdon, Oxfordshire SN7 8JH
Tel. 01367 870665
Email reggienorton@btinternet.com

Correspondent R Norton, Trustee
Trustees *R H L R Norton*, Chair; *B E M Norton; E R H Parks.*
CC Number 1004193
Information available Information was provided by the trust.

General The trust makes grants towards registered charities benefiting people in need including refugees, homeless people, people who are socially disadvantaged, victims of war, victims of disasters and so on.

In 2004/05 it made 31 grants totalling £25,000. The largest were £5,400 to Ecumenical Project, £2,500 to UNICEF, £1,800 to New Israel Fund for Reut-Sadaka, £1,500 to OXFAM and £1,000 each to Conciliation Resources and Family Rights Group.

Other grants included £940 to ORFA Natali Reyes, £700 to Christian Ecology Link for Ann Pettifor, £500 each to Caritas Social Action, Dhaka Ahsanta Mission, Intercare, LEPRA, Royal National Mission to Deepsea Fishermen, Survival International and Wells for India and £250 each to Acid Survivors Foundation and Riders for Health and St Francis Xavier Mission Society.

Exclusions No grants towards animal welfare or to individuals.

Applications In writing to the correspondent. Applicants must contact the trust before making an application.

Candide Charitable Trust

Music, visual arts

£43,000 (2005/06)
Beneficial area Worldwide

S G Kellys LLP, 52 Newtown, Lickfield, East Sussex TN22 5DE
Tel. 01825 746888 **Fax** 01825 746899
Correspondent Christopher Stebbing
Trustees *S H Schaefer; Ms O Ma; A Clark; M Kay.*
CC Number 1081134
Information available Accounts were on file at the Charity Commission.

General Established in 2000 this trust supports education and the advancement of promising young artists in the fields of visual arts and music by making grants and scholarships. The trust's annual report and accounts stated 'the

intention of the donors is to maintain a level of approximately £20,000 – £30,000 per annum for the foreseeable future, with the intention that the average grant should be in the range of £3,000 – £5,000'.

In 2005/06 the trust had an income of £51,000. Grants totalled £43,000, from which eight organisations benefited. Grants included: £23,000 to the London Symphony Orchestra – St Luke Appeal; £8,000 to the Royal Opera House Trust; £4,000 each to the London Philharmonic Orchestra and the Royal Opera House; £2,000 to the London Symphony Orchestra; and £1,250 to the Royal Academy Foundation.

Applications In writing to the correspondent.

H and L Cantor Trust

Jewish, general

£211,000 (2004/05)
Beneficial area UK, with some preference for Sheffield.

3 Ivy Park Court, 35 Ivy Park Road, Sheffield S10 3LA
Correspondent Mrs Lilly Cantor, Trustee
Trustees *L Cantor; N Jeffrey.*
CC Number 220300
Information available Information was on file at the Charity Commission.

General 'The principal objective of the trust is to provide benefit for charities, with particular consideration given to Jewish charities.'

In 2004/05 the trust had assets of £1 million and an income of £46,000. Grants totalled £211,000 with the largest grants being donated to Sheffield Jewish Congregation & Centre (£101,000) and Sheffield Galleries and Museum Trust (£100,000).

Other beneficiaries included Friends of Lubavitch UK and Royal Academy of Arts (£1,300 each), UJIA – Ethiopian project (£1,000), Magen David Adom (£500), British WIZO (£460), World Village for Children (£300), Friends of Jerusalem College of Technology, I Rescue and Meningitis Research Fund – Sheffield University (£250 each), Age Concern and Ben Gurion University Foundation (£200), British Friends of Shalva, Council of Christians & Jews,

Multiple Sclerosis Therapy Centre and United Jewish Israel Appeal (£100 each) and Jewish Blind & Disabled (£50).

Applications Unsolicited applications are not invited.

Cardy Beaver Foundation

General

£60,000 (2004/05)

Beneficial area UK.

Clifton House, 17 Reading Road, Pangbourne, Berkshire RG8 7LU

Correspondent G R Coia

Trustees *G R Coia, Chair; M G Cardy; S I Rice.*

CC Number 265763

Information available Accounts were on file at the Charity Commission.

General Registered with the Charity Commission in May 1973, in 2004/05 the foundation had assets of over £2 million and an income of £54,000. Grants totalled £60,000. The foundation's annual report stated that it supports 'national and local charities'.

During the year 21 grants were made. All were for £3,000 each, bar one. Beneficiaries included Action Medical Research, Alzheimer's Disease Society, Berkshire Multiple Sclerosis Society, Duchess of Kent House Trust, Macmillan Cancer Relief, Newbury & District Cancer Care, Prostate Cancer Research Campaign UK, Reading Hospital Cardiac Fund, RNLI, Samaritans – Reading, Dr Margaret Spittle Cancer Care, Thames Valley Air Ambulance, Trelor Trust, the Charlie Waller Memorial Trust and WAMSAD.

Applications In writing to the correspondent.

The D W T Cargill Fund

General

See below

Beneficial area UK, with a preference for the west of Scotland.

Miller Beckett and Jackson Solicitors, 190 St Vincent Street, Glasgow G2 5SP

Tel. 0141 204 2833 **Fax** 0141 248 7185

Email mail@millerbj.co.uk

Correspondent Norman A Fyfe, Trustee

Trustees *A C Fyfe; W G Peacock; N A Fyfe; Mirren Elizabeth Graham.*

SC Number SC012703

Information available Limited information was provided by the trust.

General This trust has the same address and trustees as two other trusts, W A Cargill Charitable Trust and W A Cargill Fund, although they all operate independently.

It supports 'any hospitals, institutions, societies or others whose work in the opinion of the trustees is likely to be beneficial to the community'.

In 2005/06 it had an income of £184,000. Grants have previously totalled around £200,000 a year. Despite providing accounts in the past, the administrators now make a charge for this information. No further information was available.

Previous beneficiaries include Greenock Medical Aid Society, City of Glasgow Society of Social Service, Glasgow and West of Scotland Society for the Blind, Scottish Maritime Museum – Irvine, Scottish Episcopal Church, Colquhoun Bequest Fund for Incurables, Glasgow City Mission, Scottish Motor Neurone Disease Association, Lead Scotland, Three Towns Blind Bowling/Social Club, North Glasgow Community Forum and Crathie Opportunity Holidays.

Exclusions No grants are made to individuals.

Applications In writing to the correspondent, supported by up-to-date accounts. Trustees meet quarterly.

Carlee Ltd

Jewish

£209,000 to organisations and individuals (2003/04)

Beneficial area Worldwide.

32 Pagent Road, London N16 5NQ

Correspondent The Secretary

Trustees *Hershel Grunhut; Mrs P Grunhut; Bernard Dor Stroh; Mrs B Stroh.*

CC Number 282873

Information available Accounts were on file at the Charity Commission, without a list of grants.

General The trust's principal activity is 'Jewish charitable purposes in the advancement of religion and the relief of need of persons, such as Talmudical students, widows and their families'.

In 2003/04 it had assets of £792,000 and an income of £81,000. Grants were made totalling £209,000 to individuals and organisations.

Previous beneficiaries have included Antryvale Ltd, Asos Cheshed, Egerton Road Building Fund, Glasgow Kollel, HTVC, Rav Chesed Trust, Tevini, Union of Hebrew Congregations, YHS and YHTC.

Applications In writing to the correspondent.

The Carlton House Charitable Trust

Bursaries, Jewish, general

£19,000 (2005/06)

Beneficial area UK and overseas.

Craven House, 121 Kingsway, London WC2B 6PA

Tel. 020 7242 5283

Correspondent Stewart S Cohen, Trustee

Trustees *Stewart S Cohen; Pearl C Cohen.*

CC Number 296791

Information available Accounts were on file at the Charity Commission.

General In 2005/06 it had assets of £637,000, which generated an income of £30,000. Grants were made to 26 organisations totalling £19,000.

Beneficiaries included: Western Marble Arch Synagogue (£5,700); Royal Institution (£5,000); Community Security Trust, Friends of Lubavitch UK and Girls Day School Trust (£1,000 each); Jewish Museum (£600); London Philharmonic Orchestra, National Trust, Royal Academy of Dramatic Art and United Jewish Israel Appeal (£500 each); Beth Shalom and Child Resettlement Fund (£250 each); British Technion Society (£300); Royal UK Benevolent Association (£250); Tel Aviv University Trust (£200) and Jewish Marriage Council (£100).

Applications In writing to the correspondent.

The Carpenter Charitable Trust

Humanitarian and Christian outreach

£49,000 (2005/06)

Beneficial area UK and overseas.

The Old Vicarage, Hitchin Road, Kimpton, Hitchin, Hertfordshire SG4 8EF

Correspondent M S E Carpenter, Trustee

Trustees *M S E Carpenter; Mrs G M L Carpenter.*

CC Number 280692

Information available Accounts were on file at the Charity Commission.

General In 2005/06 the trust's assets totalled £990,000 and it received an income of £44,000. Grants totalled £49,000.

Among the 29 beneficiaries listed in the accounts were: Christians Against Poverty, DEC – Asia Quake Appeal, Help in Suffering UK, MAF Mozambique Shuffle, ORBIS Charitable Trust and the Relationships Foundation (£5,000 each); Reach Out Projects (£2,500); British Heart Foundation, Brooke Hospital For Animals, Farm Africa, Salvation Army, Send a Cow, and UNICEF West Africa Famine Appeal (£1,000 each); and Blue Cross, Corrymeela Community, Fight for Sight, Gideons, Mercy Ships, Prison Fellowship and Scottish Wildlife Trust (£500 each).

Three grants were made to individuals from the designated Monica Fund totalling £90.

Exclusions 'The trustees will not consider applications for church repairs outside Hertfordshire, nor any application from an individual (other than in respect of the narrow criteria for the specially designated Monica Fund) nor any applications received from abroad unless clearly 'sponsored' by an established charity based in England and Wales.'

Applications In writing to the correspondent including sufficient details to enable a decision to be made. However, as about half the donations made are repeat grants, the amount

available for unsolicited applications remains small.

The Carron Charitable Trust

Environment, education, medicine

£37,000 (2005/06)

Beneficial area UK and overseas.

c/o Messrs Rothman Pantall and Co., 10 Romsey Road, Eastleigh, Hampshire SO50 9AL

Correspondent The Trustees

Trustees *P G Fowler; Mrs J Wells; W M Allen; D L Morgan.*

CC Number 289164

Information available Full accounts were on file at the Charity Commission.

General Applications from charities linked to wildlife, education, medicine, the countryside, printing and publishing will be considered, including charities working in the fields of health professional bodies, health campaigning and advocacy, conservation, wildlife parks and sanctuaries, natural history, endangered species, education and training, costs of study and academic research. Organisations benefiting academics, medical professionals, nurses and doctors, research workers and students are supported.

Grants are towards projects, research, running costs and salaries.

In 2005/06 the trust's income was £36,000 and it made grants totalling £37,000. Assets totalled £228,000 at the year end. Beneficiaries included: St Brides Church Appeal (£20,000); Optimum Mobility – Wheelchair (£6,000); Highland Health Board – Hip Replacement operation (£4,500) and Polar Charity Expedition and Curwen Print Study Centre – bursary (£1,000 each).

Exclusions No grants to individuals.

Applications Almost all of the charity's funds are committed for the foreseeable future and the trustees therefore do not invite applications from the general public.

The Leslie Mary Carter Charitable Trust

Conservation/ environment, welfare

£160,000 (2005)

Beneficial area UK, with a preference for Norfolk, Suffolk and North Essex.

c/o Birketts, 24–26 Museum Street, Ipswich IP1 1HZ

Correspondent The Trustees

Trustees *Miss L M Carter; S R M Wilson.*

CC Number 284782

Information available Information was provided by the trust.

General The trust has a preference for welfare organisations and conservation/environment causes, with an emphasis on local projects including those in Suffolk, Norfolk and North Essex. Grants generally range from £500 to £5,000, but larger grants are sometimes considered.

In 2005 the trust had assets of £3.1 million, an income of £123,000 and made grants totalling £160,000.

By far the largest grant in the year went to the National Trust – Shelford's Turf Farm (£50,000). Other beneficiaries included: East Anglia's Children's Hospices (£10,000); Norfolk Wildlife Trust – Pingo Project (7,500); British Heart Foundation, British Trust for Ornithology, Broughton House – Fit for the Future Appeal, Dawn Sailing Barge Trust, Essex Air Ambulance, Great Ormond Street Hospital – Orthopaedic and Spinal Surgery, Little Ouse Headwaters Project – River Link Appeal, Multiple Sclerosis Society MRI MS Research Programme and St Helena Hospice (£5,000 each); Motor Neurone Disease Association – Norfolk and Suffolk Visitors and Soil Association (£3,000 each); Barn Owl Trust and Plantlife – Norfolk (2,500 each); Thames Sailing Barge Trust (£2,000); Tall Ships Youth Trust (£1,500); and Age Concern Norwich (£1,000).

Exclusions No grants to individuals.

Applications In writing to the correspondent. Telephone calls are not welcome. There is no need to enclose an sae unless applicants wish to have materials returned.

The Carvill Trust

General

£285,000 (2004/05)
Beneficial area UK.

5th Floor, Minories House, 2–5 Minories, London EC3N 1BJ
Correspondent K D Tuson, Trustee
Trustees *R K Carvill; R E Pooley; K D Tuson.*
CC Number 1036420
Information available Accounts were on file at the Charity Commission.

General In 2004/05 the trust had assets of £297,000 an income of £122,000 and grants totalled £285,000. A major donation of £250,000 went towards Tsunami relief work.

Other beneficiaries included Irish Youth Foundation (£13,000), Warchild (£10,000) and the Lord's Taverners (£70).

Applications In writing to the correspondent, although the trust states that it only supports beneficiaries known to or connected with the trustees. Unsolicited applications from individuals will not be supported.

The Casey Trust

Children and young people

£84,000 (2004/05)
Beneficial area UK and developing countries.

27 Arkwright Road, London NW3 6BJ
Correspondent Kenneth Howard, Trustee
Trustees *Kenneth Howard; Edwin Green; Judge Leonard Krikler.*
CC Number 1055726
Information available Full accounts were on file at the Charity Commission.

General This trust was established to help children and young people in the UK and developing countries by supporting new projects, in a variety of countries.

In 2004/05 it had assets of £2.6 million, an income of £103,000 and made grants totalling £84,000.

Beneficiaries included: Norwood (£6,500); BMIE and Treloars (£2,500 each); SENSE (£2,300); Action for Kids, Angels International, Chailey Heritage

School, Changing Faces, Deafway, Henshaws Society for the Blind, PACE Centre and Youth At Risk (£2,000 each); Sightsavers (£1,800); Association of Wheelchair Children, Chernobyl Children In Need, Child Welfare Scheme, Motability, Opera North and War Child (£1,500 each); Rainbow Trust (£1,200); ACORNS, BLISS, Books Abroad, Computer Aid International, Defeating Deafness, Edinburgh Young Carers, Handicapped Childrens Action Group, National Youth Theatre, Pearson's Holiday Fund, Shooting Star Trust, Starlight Children's Foundation and UNICEF Tsunami Appeal (£1,000 each); Give Youth A Break (£800); Dream Connection and Strongbones Children's Charitable Trust (£750 each); and Leeds Women's Aid (£200).

Exclusions Grants are not given to 'individual applicants requesting funds to continue studies or travel'.

Applications 'Not being a reactive trust, it is regretted that the trustees will be unable to respond to the majority of requests for assistance. In order to both reduce costs and administration the trustees will respond mainly to those charitable institutions known to them. There is no application form.'

The Elizabeth Casson Trust

Oxford Brookes University, other occupational therapy schools and departments, and individual occupational therapists

£152,000 (2005/06)
Beneficial area Worldwide.

20 Chaundy Road, Tackley, Kidlington, Oxfordshire OX5 3BJ
Tel. 01869 331379
Email bernard.davies@btinternet.com
Correspondent B A Davies, Secretary
Trustees *Mrs C Rutland, Chair; K D Grevling; Prof. D T Wade; Mrs J S Croft; Mrs C A G Gray; Dr P L Agulnik; G A Paine; Mrs R Hallam.*
CC Number 227166
Information available Accounts were on file at the Charity Commission.

General Formerly known as the Dorset House School of Occupational Therapy, the primary object of the trust is to support occupational therapy education and training. Currently, grants are divided 60% to support Oxford Brookes University occupational therapy course and 40% to support other occupational therapy schools/departments and individual occupational therapists.

In 2005/06 the trust had assets of almost £6 million and an income of £224,000. Grants totalled £152,000. A further £39,000 was distributed in scholarships and prizes.

Exclusions No support for anything other than occupational therapy education and training.

Applications On the trust's application form which can be obtained from the correspondent.

The Castang Foundation

Medical professionals, research workers and people with physical or mental disabilities

£152,000 (2004/05)
Beneficial area UK.

c/o Carmelite House, 50 Victoria Embankment, Blackfriars, London EC4Y 0LS
Website www.castangfoundation.net
Correspondent The Trustees
Trustees *I A Burman; M B Glynn.*
CC Number 1003867
Information available Information was on file at the Charity Commission.

General 'The Castang Foundation was founded by Miss Hilda Castang who had a brother with cerebral palsy. When he died she decided to start a charity to provide funds for research into the causes of cerebral palsy and other neurodevelopmental disorders leading to their prevention so that others would not be faced with his problems.'

What do we do?
'The foundation funds research into the causes of neurodevelopmental disorders in children. It is one of the few non-government agencies in the UK sponsoring this type of research and trying to determine ways of preventing

such disorders. The foundation is concerned with conditions such as autism, learning disorders, cerebral palsy, specific learning disorders, attention deficit/hyperactivity disorders (ADHD) etc.

'The foundation provides direct grants in the area where Miss Castang lived (East Sussex) to help with services for disabled children.

'The foundation runs study groups and workshops for scientists from all over the world involved in research into neurodevelopmental disorders to discuss problems and plan research in the field. In association with this we run a number of research websites.'

In 2006 it was funding three research projects: (1) The Multicentre European Cerebral Palsy Study; (2) The Autism and Epilepsy Study; (3) The Human Placenta Study.

In 2004/05 the trust had assets of £2.4 million and an income of £119,000. Expenditure included: research projects (£149,000); and grants (£3,100).

Applications In writing to the correspondent.

The Catalyst Charitable Trust (formerly the Buckle Family Charitable Trust)

Medical, general

£54,000 to organisations (2005/06)

Beneficial area Mainly Suffolk and Essex.

9 Trinity Street, Colchester, Essex CO1 1JN

Correspondent G W N Stewart, Trustee

Trustees *Gillian Buckle; James Buckle; Joanna Thomson; Gavin Stewart.*

CC Number 1001962

Information available Accounts were on file at the Charity Commission.

General This trust has an interest in supporting small charities in the Suffolk/Essex area. It also funds a research

fellowship at Charing Cross and Westminster Hospital.

In 2005/06 the trust had assets of £53,000 and an income of £90,000 including £70,000 from donations. Grants to organisations totalled £54,000, with a further £5,000 going to an individual.

Donations included those to Oundle Schools Foundation and the Shakespeare Globe (£10,000 each).

Applications In writing to the correspondent although beneficiaries are normally selected through personal contact.

The Catholic Charitable Trust

Catholic organisations

£42,000 (2005)

Beneficial area America and Europe.

c/o Messrs Vernor, Miles and Noble, 5 Raymond Buildings, Gray's Inn, London WC1R 5DD

Correspondent J C Vernor Miles, Trustee

Trustees *J C Vernor Miles; R D D Orr; W E Vernor Miles.*

CC Number 215553

Information available Accounts were on file at the Charity Commission.

General The trust supports traditional Catholic organisations in America and Europe.

In 2005 it had assets of £1.4 million, which generated an income of £48,000. Grants were made to 12 organisations totalling £42,000.

Beneficiaries were: Society of Saint Pius X – England (£12,500); Little Sisters of the Poor (£6,000); Fraternity of St Pius X Switzerland (£5,000); Latin Mass Society, Society of St Catherine of Siena and Worth Abbey (£3,000 each); Society of the Grail, White Fathers and White Sisters (£2,000 each); and Cardinal Hume Centre (£1,500).

Two grants were made to American organisations: the Carmelite Monastery Carmel California and Oratorian Community Monterey California ($2,000 each).

Exclusions The trust does not normally support a charity unless it is known to the trustees. Grants are not made to individuals.

Applications Applications can only be accepted from registered charities and should be in writing to the correspondent. In order to save administration costs replies are not sent to unsuccessful applicants. For the most part funds are fully committed.

The Catholic Trust for England and Wales (formerly National Catholic Fund)

Catholic

£498,000 (2005)

Beneficial area England and Wales.

39 Eccleston Square, London SW1V 1BX

Tel. 020 7901 4810 **Fax** 020 7901 4819

Email secretariat@cbcew.org.uk

Website www.catholicchurch.org.uk

Correspondent Monsignor Andrew Summersgill

Trustees *Michael McKenna, Chair; Robin Smith; John Gibbs; Peter Lomas; Canon Nicholas Rothon; Dr James Whiston; Alison Cowdall; Ben Andradi.*

CC Number 1097482

Information available Accounts were on file at the Charity Commission.

General The fund was established in 1968 and is concerned with 'the advancement of the Roman Catholic religion in England and Wales'. The trust achieves its objectives through the work of the various Committees of the Bishops' conference and various agencies such as the Catholic Communications Service. Each committee is concerned with a different area of work of the Church. Grants are only given to organisations which benefit England and Wales as a whole, rather than local projects.

Five categories of grants have been agreed by the trustees:

1 'Small grants to charities that attract their major funding from other sources.

2 'Grants to organisations, charities and projects that have a national role recognised by the Bishops' Conference and are therefore considered as being

part of the national ecclesiastical structures.

3 'Grants to organisations, charities and projects that either contribute to the life and work of the Catholic community in more than one diocese and require significant funding or require initial funding in order to develop the work of the Bishops' Conference.

4 'Grants for purposes associated with social communications and media.

5 'Grants to fulfil the purposes of the Lisbon Trust Fund.'

In 2005 the trust had assets of £9.4 million and an income of £2.9 million, £1.7 million of which was from diocesan assessments. The majority of its income was spent on running the General Secretariat but £498,000 was also spent on Christian organisations.

A total of 31 grants and subscriptions were awarded ranging from £500 to £40,000. Examples of beneficiaries included: CARITAS Social Action (£40,000); University of York – research grant (£15,000); NBCW – Development Officer (£13,000); Young Christian Workers – Chaplaincy (£12,000); Catholic Chaplains in Higher Education and National Conference of Priests (£11,000 each); National Board of Catholic Women (£8,000); Churches Media Council (£7,000); Independent Catholic News (£2,000); and Catholic Evangelical Services (£1,000).

Exclusions No grants to individuals, local projects or projects not immediately advancing the Roman Catholic religion in England and Wales.

Applications In writing to the correspondent.

The Joseph and Annie Cattle Trust

General

£178,000 to institutions (2004/05)

Beneficial area Worldwide, with a preference for Hull and East Yorkshire.

Morpeth House, 114 Spring Bank, Hull HU3 1QJ

Tel. 01482 211198 **Fax** 01482 219772

Correspondent Roger Waudby, Administrator

Trustees *J A Collier; M T Gyte; P A Robins.*

CC Number 262011

Information available Full accounts were on file at the Charity Commission.

General The objective of the charity is to provide for general charitable purposes by making grants, principally to applicants in the Hull area. Older people and people who are disabled or underprivileged are assisted wherever possible, and there is a particular emphasis on giving aid to children with dyslexia.

In 2004/05 the trust had assets of £7.6 million and an income of £273,000. Grants totalled £234,000 with institutions receiving £178,000 and individuals a total of £56,000. Grants to institutions were broken down into four main categories.

Churches and Missions
Beneficiaries included: £10,000 to Newland Christian Trust; £2,000 each to St John's Baptist Church, Carnaby and Zion & Newland United Reform Church; and £1,000 to Church Housing Trust.

Local Societies and Activities
The largest grants were: £15,000 to Sobriety Project; £13,000 to Dyslexia Institute; and £7,000 to Anlaby Community Care Association.

National Societies
Grants included: £10,000 to Unicef UK; £3,000 each to Macmillan Cancer Appeal and Martin House; £2,000 to St Andrew's Hospice; and £1,500 to Norwood Ravenswood.

Sponsoring and Assisting Local Children and Adults with Disabilities and for Training
The largest grants were awarded to individuals through the following institutions, Hull Grammar school (£3,000), Hull City Social Services (£1,500), Boothferry Citizen's Advice and Multiple Sclerosis Society (£1,000 each).

Exclusions Grants are very rarely given to individuals and are only supported through social services or relevant charitable or welfare organisations.

Applications In writing to the correspondent. Meetings are usually held on the third Monday of each month.

The Thomas Sivewright Catto Charitable Settlement

General

£206,000 (2005/06)

Beneficial area Unrestricted, for UK-based registered charities.

PO Box 47408, London N21 1YW

Correspondent Miss Ann Uwins, Secretary to the Trustees

Trustees *Lord Catto; Mrs Olivia Marchant; Miss Zoe Richmond-Watson.*

CC Number 279549

Information available Accounts were on file at the Charity Commission.

General This trust has general charitable purposes, making a large number of smaller grants to a wide range of organisations and a few larger grants of up to £20,000. Despite the large number of grants made, there appears to be no strong preference for any causes or geographical areas.

In 2005/06 the trust had assets of £5.9 million, almost entirely from investments of £236,000. Grants totalled £206,000.

Previous beneficiaries have included Alone in London, British Liver Trust, British Museum, Haddo House Choral and Operatic Society, King Edward VII's Hospital, Leith Age Concern, London Immunotherapy Cancer Trust, Oxfam Partners Against Poverty, Pestalozzi Children's Village Trust, Royal Scottish National Orchestra, Tools for Self Reliance, Wiltshire Air Ambulance, Women's Aid Federation of England and World YWCA.

Exclusions The trust does not support non-registered charities, expeditions, travel bursaries and so on, or unsolicited applications from churches of any denomination. Grants are unlikely to be considered in the areas of community care, playschemes and drug abuse, or for local branches of national organisations.

Applications In writing to the correspondent, including an sae.

The Wilfrid and Constance Cave Foundation

Conservation, animal welfare, health, welfare

£164,000 (2005/06)

Beneficial area UK, with preference for Berkshire, Cornwall, Devon, Dorset, Hampshire, Oxfordshire, Somerset, Warwickshire and Wiltshire.

New Lodge Farm, Drift Road, Winkfield, Windsor SL4 4QQ

Correspondent Mrs Lorraine Olsen, Secretary

Trustees F Jones, Chair; Mrs T Jones; Mrs J Pickin; M D A Pickin; Mrs N Thompson; Mrs J Archer; R Walker; Mrs M Waterworth; Mrs K Faber; P Simpson; G Howells; W Howells.

CC Number 241900

Information available Accounts were on file at the Charity Commission.

General The trust supports local and UK-wide organisations for general charitable purposes.

In 2005/06 it had assets of £4.4 million which generated an income of £178,000. Grants to 42 organisations totalled £164,000 with donations ranging from £500 to £10,000.

Beneficiaries included: British Red Cross and Children in Crisis (£10,000 each); the Farmer's Club Pinnacle Award (£7,000); East Berkshire Women's Aid, Exmoor Natural History Society, Royal Agricultural Benevolent Institution, St Luke's Church School and Theatre Royal Plymouth (£5,000 each); ILPH (£4,000); Black Country Urban Industrial Mission, British Lung Foundation, the Thames Valley Adventure Playground Association and Winsford Village Hall (£3,000 each); Dorney Lake Trust, National Youth Music Theatre, Thames Valley Salmon Trust and Treloar Trust (£2,000 each); Battersea Dogs Home and Rare Breeds Survival Trust (£1,000 each); and Save the Children (£500).

Exclusions No grants to individuals.

Applications In writing to the correspondent a month before the trustees' meetings held twice each year, in May and October.

The Cayo Foundation

Crime, medical research, children

£666,000 (2004/05)

Beneficial area UK.

7 Cowley Street, London SW1P 3NB

Tel. 020 7248 6700

Correspondent Angela E McCarville

Trustees Angela E McCarville; Stewart A Harris.

CC Number 1080607

Information available Full accounts were on file at the Charity Commission.

General The trust supports the fight against crime, medical research and training and children's charities.

In 2004/05 it had assets of £81,000. The income was £673,000, almost entirely from donations received. Grants to 62 organisations totalled £666,000, beneficiaries included:

Crime fighting – £133,000
The sole beneficiary was Crimestoppers Trust.

Medical research and training – £202,000
Beneficiaries included Teenage Cancer Trust (£104,000), the Disability Foundation and the Elton John Aids Foundation (£25,000 each), Breakthrough and Wooden Spoon Society (£10,000 each), RAFT (£8,000), the Healing Foundation (£5,000), Wellbeing of Women (£2,500), SPARKS (£2,000), and National Autistic Society and the Ron Pickering Memorial Fund (£1,000 each).

Children's charities – £154,000
Grants included those to Cliff Richard Tennis Foundation (£70,000), Barnardos (£41,000), Wycombe Royal Grammar School Foundation (£22,000), Chain of Hope and Children in Crisis (£10,000 each) and the Children's Society (£1,000).

Other – £177,000
Beneficiaries included British Forces Foundation (£75,000), Policy Exchange (£20,000), the Royal Institute of International Affairs (£15,000), Addaction and the Police Memorial Trust (£10,000 each), Liberty Foundation (£6,100), the Lucy Faithfull Foundation, Hansard Society Limited, International Care and Relief and Students Partnership Worldwide (£5,000 each), Institute for Policy Research

(£4,000) and the Lawrence Barham Memorial Trust (£3,000).

Applications In writing to the correspondent.

The B G S Cayzer Charitable Trust

General

£75,000 (2004/05)

Beneficial area UK.

c/o Cayzer House, 30 Buckingham Gate, London SW1E 6NN

Correspondent The Trustees

Trustees Peter N Buckley; Peter R Davies.

CC Number 286063

Information available Full accounts were on file at the Charity Commission.

General In 2004/05 the trust had assets of £1.8 million, an income of £64,000 and made grants totalling £75,000.

There were 19 grants of £1,000 or more listed in the accounts, the largest was awarded to Royal Horticultural Society (£20,000).

Other beneficiaries included Christ Church, Feathers Club Association, Grange Park Opera, St Paul's Cathedral Foundation and Scottish Countryside Alliance Education Trust (£5,000 each), Game Conservancy Scottish Research Trust and Songbird Survival Trust (£3,000 each), Lawrance Messer Charitable Trust and Worshipful Company of Shipwright Charitable Fund (£2,500 each), Fergus Maclay Leukaemia Trust (£1,500) and Campaign to Protect Rural England and Oxford House (£1,000 each).

Grants of under £1,000 awarded totalled £5,400.

Exclusions No grants to organisations outside the UK. Unsolicited appeals will not be supported.

Applications In writing to the correspondent, although the trust tends to support only people/projects known to the Cayzer family or the trustees.

The Cazenove Charitable Trust

General

£154,000 (2005)
Beneficial area UK.

20 Moorgate, London EC2R 6DA
Correspondent The Secretary
Trustees *C R M Bishop; S R M Baynes; E M Harley.*
CC Number 1086899
Information available Accounts were on file at the Charity Commission.

General Established in 1969, this Trust primarily supports the charitable activities sponsored by current and Cazenove ex-employees. In 2005 the trust had assets of £1.3 million and an income of £33,000. Grants totalled £154,000.

Applications This trust does not respond to unsolicited applications.

The Cemlyn-Jones Trust

See below

£46,000 (2004/05)
Beneficial area North Wales and Anglesey.

59 Madoc Street, Llandudno LL30 2TW
Tel. 01492 874391
Correspondent P G Brown, Trustee
Trustees *P G Brown; Mrs J F. Lea; Mrs E G Jones.*
CC Number 1039164
Information available Accounts were on file at the Charity Commission.

General This trust was registered in 1994, and has a welcome preference for making grants to small local projects in North Wales and Anglesey. Its objectives, listed in the annual report, are:

1. conservation and protection of general public amenities, historic or public interests in Wales
2. medical research
3. protection and welfare of animals and birds
4. study and promotion of music
5. activities and requirements of religious and educational bodies.

In 2004/05 the trust's assets totalled £1.1 million, it received an income of £546,000 and grants were made totalling £46,000.

UCNW Development Trust received two grants, £25,000 towards its scholarship fund and £4,000 to its School of Ocean Sciences Research. Other beneficiaries were RSPB – Llanduno Junction Reserve (£5,500), St Mary's Church Menai Bridge (£5,000), Conwy Valley Civic Society and Macmillan Cancer Relief (£1,000 each) and Girl Guides Llanrwst and Neuro Muscular Centre (£500 each).

Exclusions No grants to individuals or non-charitable organisations.

Applications In writing to the correspondent.

The Amelia Chadwick Trust

General

£73,000 (2005/06)
Beneficial area UK, especially Merseyside.

Guy Williams Layton, Pacific Chambers, 11–13 Victoria Street, Liverpool L2 5QQ
Tel. 0151 236 7171 **Fax** 0151 236 1129
Correspondent J R McGibbon, Trustee
Trustees *J R McGibbon; J C H Bibby.*
CC Number 213795
Information available Accounts were on file at the Charity Commission.

General The trust supports a wide range of charities, especially welfare causes. Although grants are given throughout the UK, there is a strong preference for Merseyside.

In 2005/06 the trust had assets of £3.7 million, an income of £109,000 and made 36 grants totalling £73,000.

By far the largest grant was £22,000 to Merseyside Development Foundation. There were 19 further grants of £1,000 or more, including those to: Liverpool PSS (£8,500); Garston Adventure Playground and Liverpool Dyslexia Association (£5,000 each); Volunteer Reading Help (£3,000); Centrepoint and the Sylvia Fund (£2,000 each); Age Concern (£1,800); British Red Cross and Merseyside Holiday Service (£1,500 each); European Playwork Association (£1,200); and Alzheimer's Disease Society, Kensington Housing Trust, and Rotunda Community College (£1,000 each).

Applications All donations are made through Liverpool Council for Social Services. Grants are only made to charities known to the trustees, and unsolicited applications are not considered.

The Pamela Champion Foundation

General, disability

£26,000 (2004/05)
Beneficial area UK, with a preference for Kent.

Wiltons, Newnham Lane, Eastling, Faversham, Kent ME13 0AS
Tel. 01795 890233
Correspondent Elizabeth Bell, Trustee
Trustees *Miss M Stanlake; Mrs C Winser; Mrs E Bell; P M Williams.*
CC Number 268819
Information available Accounts were on file at the Charity Commission.

General Grants are made to all or any of the following: National Council for the Single Woman and Her Dependants, The Salvation Army, Church Army, Royal United Kingdom Beneficent Association, Wood Green Animal Shelter, Help the Aged, NSPCC, Marie Curie Memorial Foundation, and other charitable causes.

In 2004/05 the trust had assets of £740,000 and an income of £34,700. Grants were made totalling £26,000 and were distributed to Pattaya Orphanage Trust (£5,000), Blackthorn Trust, CHASE, Citizens Advice, Speakability and Wisdom Hospice (£2,000 each), DELTA, Help the Aged, Macmillan Nurses, Marie Curie and RDA – Bradbourne (£1,000 each) and Faversham Air Training Corps, the Peaceful Place, Smileys and Volunteer Reading Help (£500).

Exclusions No grants to non-registered charities.

Applications In writing to the correspondent.

The Chandris Foundation

Greek, shipping, children

£19,000 (2005)

Beneficial area UK and Greece.

Chandris Foundation Trustees Ltd, 17 Old Park Lane, London W1K 1QT

Correspondent R H Hall, Director

Trustee *Chandris Foundation Trustees Ltd.*

CC Number 280559

Information available Full accounts were on file at the Charity Commission.

General The trust makes grants mainly to Greek charities and secondarily in the area of shipping, reflecting respectively the nationality of the Chandris family and the core business of the connected company Chandris England Ltd. Smaller preference is given to other charities such as medical and health-related and Greek Orthodox organisations. Most beneficiaries are UK organisations, but Greek organisations elsewhere may also be considered.

In 2005 it had assets of £614,000, an income of £28,000 and made grants totalling £19,000.

Greek charities – 9 grants totalling £2,900
Beneficiaries included St Sophia's School Benevolent Fund (£1,000), Anglo Hellenic League (£550), Hellenic Centre (£250), Greek Orthodox Charity Organisation (£200) and Cypriot Estia of London (£150).

Children's charities – 11 donations totalling £3,400
Beneficiaries included Children's Safety Education Foundation (£750), Happy Days Children's Charity (£350), NSPCC (£300), Association of Wheelchair Children (£250) and Wellchild (£25).

Cancer relief charities – 5 grants totalling £1,200
Recipients were Teenage Cancer Trust (£350), Children's Cancer Care (£300), Christian Lewis Children's Cancer Care (£250), Breast Cancer Campaign (£200) and Royal Marsden Cancer Campaign (£100).

Maritime charities – 4 grants totalling £1,900
Beneficiaries were RNLI (£1,200), Seafarers UK (£300), Mercy Ships (£250) and Mission to Seafarers (£100).

Sundry – 22 grants totalling £9,200
Recipients included Cotswold Care Hospice (£2,000), Cranleigh Village

Hospital Trust (£1,300), London's Air Ambulance (£600), Almeida Theatre (£500), RADAR (£450), Age Concern, Help the Aged, National Eczema Society and Meningitis UK (£300 each), Friends of Africa (£250 each), British Heart Foundation (£200), Action Against Hunger (£150) and United Kingdom Thelasaemia Society (£25).

Exclusions No grants to individuals.

Applications The trustees allocate grants mainly to their existing beneficiaries, and prefer to seek new beneficiaries through their own research.

The Chapman Charitable Trust

Welfare, general

£216,000 (2005/06)

Beneficial area Eastern and south east England, including London, and Wales.

Crouch Chapman, 62 Wilson Street, London EC2A 2BU

Tel. 020 7782 0007 **Fax** 020 7782 0939

Email cct@crouchchapman.co.uk

Correspondent Roger S Chapman, Trustee

Trustees *Roger S Chapman; Richard J Chapman; Bruce D Chapman; Guy J A Chapman.*

CC Number 232791

Information available Accounts were on file at the Charity Commission.

General Established in 1963 with general charitable purposes, the trust mainly supports culture and recreation, education and research, health, social services, environment and heritage causes.

In 2005/06 the trust had assets of £6.6 million, an income of £433,000 and made grants totalling £216,000. A total of 164 grants were made totalling £216,000.

The seven largest grants of £10,000 each or more went to: Pesticide Action Network UK (£12,500 in two grants); and A Rocha, Aldeburgh Productions, Leonard Cheshire – St Bridgets, Methodist Homes for the Aged, NCH, Queen Alexandra's Hospital Home (£10,000 in two grants each).

Other beneficiaries included: Fragile X Society (£6,000 in two grants); Treehouse School (£5,000); Cherry Trees

(£4,000 in two grants); Arthritis Care (£3,000 in two grants); Barbican Centre Trust, Criccieth Festival, Grange Centre, National Endometriosis Society and Royal Academy of Arts (£2,000 each); Action for Blind People, Arthritis Care, British Liver Trust, Help the Hospices, Homestart, National Deaf Children's Society, National Talking Newspapers and Magazines, Porthmadog Maritime Museum, Surrey Community Development Trust, Women's Link (£1,000 each); Contact the Elderly, Crossroads, Inspire Foundation, Live Music Now!, Naomi House, Museum of Garden History, WellChild and Who Cares? Trust (£500 each); and Abinger Hammer Village School Trust (£250).

Exclusions No grants to or for the benefit of individuals, local branches of UK charities, animal welfare, sports tours or sponsored adventure holidays.

Applications In writing at any time. The trustees currently meet to consider grants twice a year at the end of September and in March. They receive a large number of applications and regret that they cannot acknowledge receipt of them. The absence of any communication for six months would mean that an application must have been unsuccessful.

The Charter 600 Charity

General charitable

£39,000 to organisations (2005)

Beneficial area UK.

Mercers' Hall, Ironmongers Lane, London EC2V 8HE

Tel. 020 7726 4991

Correspondent Charles H Parker, Clerk

Trustees *Robert Pope; Mrs Katherine Payne.*

CC Number 1051146

Information available Full accounts were available from the Charity Commission.

General The Charter 600 charity was established to commemorate the 600th anniversaries of the Grant of the Mercers' Company's first Charter in 1394 and of the first Mastership of Sir Richard Whittington in 1395. Established in 1994, it operates under a trust deed dated October 1995.

In 2005 the charity has assets of £652,000 and an income of £83,000.

Grants made during the year totalled £39,000 and were distributed for the following purposes:

- care for older people
- the church
- schools
- medical welfare
- special needs
- youth & community welfare and wildlife.

Grants were made to organisations fitting the purposes listed above and included: Active Planet (£2,500), Cardiac Risk in the Young and Springs Dance Company (£1,500), Housebound Learners Association (£1,200), Golden Bell Kindergarten, School Russian Orphan Opportunity Fund, Step by Step: A School for Autistic Children and the West London Churches Homeless Concern (£1,000 each) and the National Federation of Badger Groups (£500).

Exclusions Applications for charitable grants will only be accepted when put forward by a member of the Mercers' Company.

Applications The charity does not consider unsolicited applications.

The Worshipful Company of Chartered Accountants General Charitable Trust (also known as CALC)

General, education

£100,000 (2004/05)
Beneficial area UK.

Hampton City Services, Hampton House, High Street, East Grinstead, West Sussex RH19 3AW

Correspondent The Clerk to the Trustees

Trustees *Rachel Adams; John K Cardnell; William M T Fowle; Michael J Groom; The Rt Hon Sir Jeremy Hanley; William I D Plaistowe; Michael J Richardson; Adrian M C Staniforth.*

CC Number 327681

Information available Full accounts were on file at the Charity Commission.

General In general, the trust supports causes advancing education and/or benefiting disadvantaged people. It has a tendency to focus on a particular theme each year, as well as making grants to other causes and organisations of particular relevance to members of the company. In 2004/05 the trust's assets stood at £1.2 million. It had an income of £111,000 and made grants totalling £100,000, which were broken down as follows:

Grand Master's Charitable Project (£40,000)
Grants went to St Peter and St James Hospice – Sussex (£20,000), St Ann's Hospice – Manchester (£10,000), and Hospice At Home – Carlisle and North Lakeland and Hospice In The Weald – Tunbridge Wells Kent (£5,000 each).

Education project grants (£35,000)
Grants were made to 34 schools ranging from £2,000 – £500.

General (£2,000)
There were four minor donations made.

Other grants were listed under the following headings: Mango (£10,000), Lord Mayor's Appeal (£2,500) and Prizes (£1,000).

Applications Applications must be sponsored by a liveryman of the company.

The Cheruby Trust

Welfare, education, general

£108,000 (2005/06)
Beneficial area UK and worldwide.

62 Grosvenor Street, London W1K 3JF
Tel. 020 7499 4301

Correspondent Mrs S Wechsler, Trustee

Trustees *A L Corob; L E Corob; T A Corob; C J Cook: S A Wechsler.*

CC Number 327069

Information available Full accounts were on file at the Charity Commission.

General The trust's charitable objectives are the relief of poverty, the advancement of education and such other charitable purposes as the trustees see fit.

In 2005/06 the trust had assets of £128,000, an income of £80,000 and

made 35 grants totalling £108,000. Beneficiaries included: Save the Children (£10,000); Action Aid, Centrepoint, Child Hope, Children in Crisis, Family Welfare Association, the Hope Charity, Sight Savers, WaterAid and World Jewish Aid (£5,000 each); Help the Aged (£3,500); Alzheimer's Society, Amnesty International, Friends of the Earth, Medical Foundation and MIND (£3,000 each); British Deaf Association (£2,500); Friends of Alyn, One to One, SANE and Tibet Relief Fund (£2,000 each); Cruse Bereavement Care and Woodland Trust (£1,000 each); Trees for Life (£500); and Listening Books (£200).

Applications In writing to the correspondent.

The Chetwode Foundation

Education, churches, general

£60,000 (2005/06)
Beneficial area UK, with a preference for Nottinghamshire, Leicestershire and Derby.

Samworth Brothers (Holdings) Ltd, Chetwode House, 1 Samworth Way, Leicester Road, Melton Mowbray, Leicestershire LE13 1GA

Tel. 01664 414500

Correspondent J G Ellis, Trustee

Trustees *J G Ellis; R N J S Price.*

CC Number 265950

Information available Full accounts were on file at the Charity Commission.

General This trust has general charitable purposes, giving without exclusion across the UK. Whilst it has preferences for education, churches and work in Nottinghamshire, Leicestershire and Derby, this is not at the expense of other causes.

In 2005/06 the trust had assets of £1.5 million and an income of £197,000. Grants totalling £60,000 were made to 11 organisations.

The largest grant was £50,000 to Uppingham School. Other beneficiaries were Tythby and Cropwell Butler PCC (£2,000), Newark and Nottinghamshire Agricultural Society (£1,500), Hand in Hand Trust, Open Minds, Starlight Children's Foundation, Wheels on Fire and Vitalise (£1,000 each), St Mary

Magdalene Church Newark (£500), the National Trust for Scotland (£450) and Chance to Shine (£250).

Applications In writing to the correspondent.

The Malcolm Chick Charity

General

£22,000 to organisations (2006)
Beneficial area UK

White Horse Court, 25c North Street, Bishops Stortford, Hertfordshire CM23 2LD

Email charities@pwwsolicitors.co.uk

Website www.pwwsolicitors.co.uk/

Correspondent Mrs Jayne Day, The Trust Administrator

Trustees *D J L Mobsby; R S Fowler; N D Waldman.*

CC Number 327732

Information available Full accounts were provided by the trust.

General This trust has been in existence for some time with the trustees making small grants to organisations they were familiar with. On the death of one of the trustees, Malcolm Chick, the trust received part of his estate and has grown in size.

In 2006 the trust's assets stood at £791,000, with an income of £29,000. Grants were made to 13 organisations totalling £22,000; 54% of which went to organisations associated with youth character building.

Youth character building
There is an emphasis on grants towards sailing training. Grant recipients included Tall Ships Youth Trust – Hampshire (£2,500), Adventure Youth Sea Training, Grimsby & Cleethorpes Sea Cadets, and Stubbers Adventure Centre (£2,000 each), Andrew Marvell Youth Centre (£1,000) Sir Frances Chichester Trust (£800), Silo Central Youth Club (£700) and 8th Wimbledon Scout Group (£500)

Armed service charities
Grants are limited to those charities supporting ex-army personnel and to charities providing direct care for ex-army personnel, for example grants to homes and charities providing welfare services for such persons. A grant was awarded to SSAFA Forces Help – Kidderminster (£2,400).

Medical research and care
Grants are made towards research into causes and treatment of heart disease and for buying equipment suitable for the treatment and care of people recovering from coronary heart disease. A donation was made to CORDA (£5,000).

Other grants
Grants were made through charitable organisations to support individuals undertaking charity expeditions and voluntary work abroad. This included grants made to Project Trust (£2,000) and Raleigh International (£500).

Applications In the first place, applicants should write to ask for a copy of the criteria and application forms. Telephone calls are not welcomed. The trustees meet to consider applications in November and completed forms must be returned by the middle of October. There is a separate application form and guidance notes for individual applicants.

Child Growth Foundation

Institutions researching child/adult growth disorders, and people with such diseases

£235,000 (2004/05)
Beneficial area UK.

2 Mayfield Avenue, Chiswick W4 1PY

Tel. 020 8995 0257 **Fax** 020 8995 9075

Website www.childgrowthfoundation.org/

Correspondent T Fry, Hon. Chair

Trustees *Tam Fry, Chair; Nick Child; Russell Chaplin; Kay Grey; Simon Lane; Gillian Ward; Rachel Pidcock; Diana Turley.*

CC Number 274325

Information available Accounts were on file at the Charity Commission.

General The foundation seeks to: (a) ensure that the growth of every UK child is regularly assessed and that any child growing excessively slowly or fast is referred for medical attention as soon as possible; (b) ensure that no child will be denied the drugs they need to correct their stature; (c) support institutions researching the cause/cures of growth conditions; (d) maintain a network of families to offer support/advice for any

family concerned/diagnosed with a growth problem.

In 2004/05 the trust had an income of £345,000 and gave grants totalling £235,000. Beneficiaries included Kennedy Galton Centre and Royal London (£50,000 each), University of Wales (£40,000), Institute of Child Health (£32,000 in five grants), Manchester Hospital (£30,000), Leeds University (£28,000), Loughborough University (£25,000), Queen Mary's College (£23,000), University of Birmingham (£18,000), Central Council of Ohysical Recreation (£11,000) and Teenage Health Website (£8,000).

Applications In writing to the correspondent.

Children's Liver Disease Foundation

Organisation benefiting children (up to the age of 18) with liver disease; medical, social and nursing research relating to disorders of the biliary tract

£315,000 (2005/06)
Beneficial area UK.

36 Great Charles Street, Queensway, Birmingham B3 3JY

Tel. 0121 212 3839 **Fax** 0121 212 4300

Email info@childliverdisease.org

Website www.childliverdisease.org

Correspondent Mrs C Fleet, Office Manager

Trustees *Thomas Ross, Chair; Robert J Benton; Dr H Richard Maltby; Mrs Ann Mowat; Mrs Michele Hunter; Mrs Kellie Charge; Michael Sharp; Mrs Mairi Everard; Mrs Jayne Carroll.*

CC Number 1067331

Information available Accounts were on file at the Charity Commission.

General Children's Liver Disease Foundation (CLDF) funds medical research into all aspects of paediatric liver disease and disease of the biliary tract. CLDF is a member of the Association of Medical Research Charities (AMRC).

In 2005/06 CLDF had assets of £408,000 and an income of £849,000. Grants were made totalling £315,000. Beneficiaries were Institute of Biomedical Research – Birmingham, Liver Research Laboratories – University Hospital Birmingham, Royal Free and University College – London, University College Hospital and Institute of Liver Studies – King's College Hospital and University of Nottingham.

Exclusions The charity does not accept applications from organisations whose work is not associated with paediatric liver disease. No grants to individuals, whether medical professionals or patients. No grants for travel or personal education. No grants for general appeals.

Applications Applicants are strongly advised to look at the relevant pages on the CLDF website where there is information on making an application and the CLDF research strategy. All grant requests are subject to peer review and are assessed by the Medical Advisory Committee before submission to the trustees.

The Children's Research Fund

Child health research

£357,000 (2005/06)
Beneficial area UK.

668 India Buildings, Water Street, Liverpool L2 0RA

Tel. 0151 236 2844

Website www.childrensresearchfund.org.uk/

Correspondent The Trustees

Trustees *H Greenwood, Chair; G W Inkin; H E Greenwood; Elizabeth Theobald; Prof. D Lloyd; Lord Morris of Manchester.*

CC Number 226128

Information available Full accounts were on file at the Charity Commission.

General The trust supports research into children's diseases, child health and prevention of illness in children, carried out at institutes and university departments of child health. The policy is to award grants, usually over several years, to centres of research. It will also support any charitable project associated with the wellbeing of children.

In 2005/06 it had assets of £1.7 million, an income of £500,000 and made

research grants totalling £357,000. Beneficiaries included: British Association of Paediatric Surgeons (£90,000); University of London (£64,000); Royal College of Physicians of Edinburgh, Royal College of Physicians and Child Health and University of Leicester (£50,000 each); and Great Ormond Street Hospital (£48,000).

Exclusions No grants for capital projects.

Applications Applicants from child health research units and university departments are invited to send in an initial outline of their proposal; if it is eligible they will then be sent an application form. Applications are considered in March and November.

The Chownes Foundation

Religion, relief-in-need, social problems

£24,000 to organisations (2005/06)
Beneficial area UK.

The Courtyard, Beeding Court, Shoreham Road, Steyning, West Sussex BN44 3TN

Tel. 01903 816699

Correspondent Sylvia Spencer, Secretary

Trustees *Mrs U Hazeel; The Rt Revd S Ortiger; M Woolley.*

CC Number 327451

Information available Accounts were on file at the Charity Commission.

General The objectives of this trust are the advancement of religion, the advancement of education among the young, the amelioration of social problems, and the relief of poverty amongst older people and the former members of Sound Diffusion PLC who lost their pensions when the company went into receivership.

In 2005/06 the foundation had an income of £1.6 million, including £1.5 million from donations. Total charitable expenditure was £50,000 of which £24,000 went to 13 organisations. Beneficiaries included: Amnesty International (two grants totalling £5,000); Friends of the Samaritans, Howard League and St Anne's Convent (two grants each totalling £2,000); A&B Diocesan Trust and Burnside Amenity

Fund (two grants each totalling £1,500); LIFE (two grants totalling £1,200); and Burnside Social Club, the Imperial Cancer Research Fund, Mencap, NSPCC and Spinal Injuries Association (two grants each totalling £1,000).

Applications In writing to the correspondent.

CLA Charitable Trust

Disabled facilities and training

£60,000 (2003/04)
Beneficial area England and Wales only.

Caunton Grange, Caunton, Newark, Nottinghamshire NG23 6AB

Tel. 01636 636171 **Fax** 01636 636171

Website www.clacharitabletrust.org.uk/

Correspondent Peter Geldart

Trustees *A Duckworth-Chad; A H Duberly; G E Lee-Strong; G N Mainwaring.*

CC Number 280264

Information available Accounts were on file at the Charity Commission.

General The trust was founded in 1980. Its work includes support for education projects in the countryside (a) to provide sport and recreation facilities for disabled people, and (b) for children and young people with learning difficulties or who are disadvantaged.

It prefers to support smaller projects where a grant from the trust can make a 'real contribution to the success of the project'. It gives grants for specific projects or items rather than for ongoing running costs.

In 2003/04 it had assets of £348,000 and an income of £102,000. Grants totalled £60,000.

There were 22 grants of £1,000 or more listed in the accounts. Beneficiaries included Wheelyboat Trust (£5,500), Norfolk Museum of Rural Life (£5,300), Elizabeth Fitzroy Support (£3,300), Calvert Trust, Derbyshire Wildlife Trust, Growing Space and Lords House Farm (£2,000 each), Daisy Chain and Vauxhall City Farm Riding Therapy Centre (£1,900 each), Yorkshire Sculpture Park (£1,500), Royal Bath & West of England Society (£1,100) and Leonard Cheshire Homes (£1,000).

Other grants of less than £1,000 each totalled £13,000.

Exclusions No grants to individuals.

Applications In writing to the correspondent. Trustees meet four times a year.

J A Clark Charitable Trust

Health, education, peace, preservation of the earth, the arts

£394,000 (2004/05)

Beneficial area UK, with a preference for South West England.

PO Box 1704, Glastonbury, Somerset BA16 0YB

Correspondent Mrs P Grant, Secretary

Trustees Lance Clark; Tom Clark; William Pym; Aidan Pelly.

CC Number 1010520

Information available Full accounts were available from the Charity Commission.

General In 2004/05 the trust had assets of £13 million and an income of £392,000. Grants to 33 organisations totalled £394,000.

There were 17 donations of £10,000 or more, including those to: Eucalyptus Charitable Foundation (£54,000); Christian Aid (£51,000); New Economics Foundation (£35,000); Helix Arts (£29,000); Inner City Scholarship Fund and the National Youth Agency (£25,000 each); British Yearly Meeting – Geneva Process (£20,000); ASHOKA and Visions of Islam (£15,000 each); and Creative Health Network, Responding to Conflict, Sponsored Arts for Education, Theatre for Change, Woodstock Research Trust, UK Friends of Kwendo Kor (£10,000 each).

Other beneficiaries included: Contemporary Visual Arts Society (£6,000); DEC – Tsunami Earthquake Appeal and RNIB (£5,000 each); Watershed Arts Trust 1 (£2,000); and British Pugwash Trust (£1,000).

Applications This trust does not respond to unsolicited applications.

The Elizabeth Clark Charitable Trust

Palliative care

£450,000 (2005/06)

Beneficial area UK.

Allington House, 1st Floor, 150 Victoria Street, London SW1E 5AE

Tel. 020 7410 0330 **Fax** 020 7410 0332

Email info@sfct.org.uk

Correspondent Alan Bookbinder, Director

Trustees Miss J S Portrait; C T Stone.

CC Number 265206

Information available Full accounts were provided by the trust.

General This is one of the 18 Sainsbury Family Charitable Trusts, which collectively give over £75 million a year. The 2005/06 accounts describe the trust's work as follows: 'The trustees are free to apply funds for any charitable purpose. Bearing in mind the settlor's wish to bring about improvements in nursing, the trustees have decided to concentrate on supporting development of good practice in palliative care.'

'Trustees have earmarked their remaining resources for the Trinity Hospice redevelopment appeal, and therefore expect to make no new grants for the foreseeable future.'

In 2005/06 the trust had assets of £15,000 and an income of £23,000. Grants totalled £450,000, with the sole beneficiary being Trinity Hospice redevelopment appeal.

Applications 'Proposals are likely to be invited by the trustees or initiated at their request. Unsolicited applications are unlikely to be successful, even if they fall within an area in which the trustees are interested.' A single application will be considered for support by all the trusts in the Sainsbury family group.

The Roger and Sarah Bancroft Clark Charitable Trust

Quaker, general

£142,000 to organisations (2005)

Beneficial area UK and overseas, with preference for Somerset and Scotland.

c/o KPMG LLP, 100 Temple Street, Bristol BS1 6AG

Correspondent The Trustees

Trustees Mary P Lovell; Sarah C Gould; Roger S Goldby; Alice Clark; Robert B Robertson; Martin Lovell.

CC Number 211513

Information available Full accounts were on file at the Charity Commission.

General The objects of the trust are general charitable purposes with particular reference to:

- Religious Society of Friends and associated bodies
- charities connected with Somerset
- education (for individuals).

For historical reasons the accounts for this trust were split into two separate funds, although it is administered as one. This entry will break the trust down into the two funds, even though they are essentially the same.

ECR Fund
In 2005 this fund had assets of £1.2 million which generated an income of £43,000. Grants totalled £10,000.

Among the 18 beneficiaries were: South East Scotland Monthly Meeting (£2,000); OXFAM, Prisoners of Conscience and Refugee Council (£1,000 each); Amnesty International Charitable Trust (£600); Scottish Churches Housing Action (£500); YMCA (£400); and Age Concern (£100).

SBC Fund
In 2004/05 it had assets of almost £5 million, which generated an income of £186,000. Grants were made to 139 institutions totalling £132,000 and 274 individuals totalling £71,000.

By far the largest grant was £30,000 to Greenbank Swimming Pool. Other beneficiaries included: Quaker Peace & Social Witness (£9,500); Alfred Gillett Trust, Holburne Museum of Art and Oxfam (£5,000 each); Retreat York Ltd and Society for the Protection of Ancient

Buildings (£3,000 each); Ulster Quaker Service Committee (£2,500); Bury St Edmunds Meeting House Appeal and Session's Book Trust (£2,000 each); and Artlink Edinburgh, Médecins Sans Frontières, Wilmington Friends School and Woodbrooke Quaker Study Centre (£1,000 each).

Applications In writing to the correspondent. There is no application form and telephone calls are not accepted. Trustees meet about three times a year. Applications will be acknowledged if an sae is enclosed or an email address given.

The Cleopatra Trust

Health and welfare, disability, homelessness, addiction, children who are disadvantaged, environment

£57,000 (2005)
Beneficial area Mainly UK.

c/o Charities Aid Foundation, King's Hill, West Malling, Kent ME19 4TA
Correspondent C H Peacock, Trsutee
Trustees *Dr C Peacock; Mrs B Bond; C H Peacock.*
CC Number 1004551
Information available Accounts were on file at the Charity Commission.

General The trust has common trustees with two other trusts, the Dorus Trust and the Epigoni Trust (see separate entries), with which it also shares the same aims and polices. All three trusts are administered by Charities Aid Foundation. Generally the trusts support different organisations each year.

The trust makes grants in the following areas:

- mental health
- cancer welfare/education – not research
- diabetes
- physical disability – not research
- homelessness
- addiction
- children who are disadvantaged.

There is also some preference for environmental causes. It only gives grants for specific projects and does not give grants for running costs or general

appeals. Support is only given to national organisations, not for local areas or initiatives.

In 2005 it had assets of £3.1 million, which generated an income of £129,000. Grants were made to 12 organisations totalling £57,000.

Beneficiaries included: Macmillan Cancer Relief and Marine Conservation Society (£10,000 each); Over The Wall Gang Camp (£8,900); Wildfowl & Wetlands Trust (£5,300); Foundation for Conductive Education, Groundwork UK and Grasslands Trust (£5,000 each); National Library for the Blind (£4,900); Contact a Family Incorporated (£2,300); St Mary Magdalene Church (£100); and Leukaemia Research Fund (£30).

Exclusions No grants to individuals, expeditions, research, scholarships, charities with a local focus, local branches of UK-wide charities or towards running costs.

Applications On a 'funding proposal form' available from the correspondent. Applications should include a copy of the latest audited annual report and accounts. They are considered twice a year in mid-summer and mid-winter. Organisations which have received grants from this trust, the Dorus Trust or the Epigoni Trust should not reapply in the following two years. Usually, funding will be considered by only one of these trusts.

Miss V L Clore's 1967 Charitable Trust

General

£31,000 (2005/06)
Beneficial area UK.

Unit 3, Chelsea Manor Studios, Flood Street, London SW3 5SR
Tel. 020 7351 6061 **Fax** 020 7351 5308
Email info@cloreduffield.org.uk
Correspondent Sally Bacon
Trustees *Dame V L Duffield; David Harrel; Caroline Deletra.*
CC Number 253660
Information available Accounts were on file at the Charity Commission.

General The trust has general charitable purposes, but broadly speaking is concerned with the

performing arts, education, social welfare, health and disability. Grants usually range from £500 to £5,000. It is administrated alongside the much larger Clore Duffield Foundation, which gives well over 100 times more funds a year in grants.

In 2005/06 the trust had assets of £1.3 million, an income of £40,000 and made 15 grants totalling £31,000. A further £5,100 was paid to the Clore Duffield Foundation.

Beneficiaries included: Children's Hospice South West (£10,000); Maccabi GB and Tribe (£5,000 each); West London Synagogue (£2,500); Colon Cancer Care, English National Ballet School, Jewish Care, Macmillan Cancer Relief and NSPCC (£1,000 each); RHS Special Events (£580); Breakthrough Breast Cancer (£500); Wiener Library (£200); and United Synagogue (£60).

Exclusions No grants are given to individuals.

Applications In writing to the correspondent on one to two sides of A4, enclosing an sae.

Clover Trust

Older people, young people

£184,000 (2005)
Beneficial area UK, and occasionally overseas, with a slight preference for West Dorset.

c/o Suite 7, Messrs Herbert Pepper and Rudland, Accurist House, 44 Baker Street, London W1U 7BD
Tel. 020 7486 5535 **Fax** 020 7486 5545
Correspondent G F D Wright
Trustees *N C Haydon; S Woodhouse.*
CC Number 213578
Information available Accounts were on file at the Charity Commission.

General This trust supports organisations concerned with health, disability, children and Catholic activities. However, most grants are given to a 'core list' of beneficiaries and the trust states: 'the chances of a successful application from a new applicant are very slight, since the bulk of the income is earmarked for the regular beneficiaries, with the object of increasing the grants over time rather than adding to the number of beneficiaries.'

Grants are given towards general running costs, although no grants are given towards building work. Unsolicited applications which impress the trustees are given one-off grants, although only a tiny percentage of the many applications are successful.

In 2005 the trust had assets of £4.6 million and an income of £199,000. Grants to 35 organisations totalled £184,000. Grants ranged from £500 to £27,000, but were mainly for amounts of £5,000 or less. Beneficiaries of the largest grants were Friends of Children in Romania (£27,000) and Action Medical Research, CAFOD and Cotswold Care (£10,000 each).

Smaller grants were made to Peper Harrow Foundation (£7,500), Farms for City Children, Kate's Carers, Kidsactive, Orchard Vale Trust and West London Action for Children (£5,000 each), British Eye Research Foundation, Family Haven, Mary Hare Grammar School (£3,000), Disability Snowsport UK and National Eczema Society (£2,000 each) and Broadway Trust (£1,000).

Exclusions The arts, monuments and non-registered charities are not supported.

Applications In writing to the correspondent. Replies are not given to unsuccessful applications.

The Robert Clutterbuck Charitable Trust

Service, sport and recreation, natural history, animal welfare and protection

£42,000 (2005/06)

Beneficial area Mainly UK, with preference for Cheshire and Hertfordshire.

28 Brookfields, Calver, Hope Valley, Derbyshire S32 3XB

Email secretary@clutterbucktrust.org.uk

Website www.clutterbucktrust.org.uk

Correspondent G A Wolfe, Secretary

Trustees *Maj. R G Clutterbuck; I A Pearson; R J Pincham.*

CC Number 1010559

Information available Information was provided by the trust.

General The trust normally only makes grants to registered charities in the following areas: personnel and charitable activities within the armed forces, and ex-service men and women; charities associated with the counties of Cheshire and Hertfordshire; sport and recreational activities in Cheshire and Hertfordshire; natural history and wildlife; and the welfare and protection of domestic animal life in Cheshire and Hertfordshire.

In 2005/06 the trust had assets of £1.3 million, an income of £43,000 and made grants totalling £42,000. The trust prefers to make grants towards buying specific items.

Beneficiaries included: John Grooms (£5,000); Rochdale Special Needs Cycling Club (£2,500); Grimsby and Cleethorpes Sea Cadets (£2,100); Barbers Company General Charities, Care for the Wild International and Music in Hospitals (£2,000 each); National Gulf Veterans Association (£1,800); Cancer and Polio Research Fund and RAF Association (£1,600 each); Age Concern Cheshire, Bengeo Sports Association, Blacon High School, Henshaw's Society for the Blind, Royal British Legion and St Luke's Cheshire Hospice (£1,000 each); Whizz-Kidz (£800); Southern Wildlife Trust (£780); Lytham St Anne's Sea Cadets (£750); and Dogs Trust, Ethiopiaid and Scottish Wildlife Trust (£500 each).

Exclusions No grants to individuals.

Applications In writing to the correspondent. There are no application forms. Applications are acknowledged and considered by the trustees twice a year.

The Francis Coales Charitable Foundation

Historical

£68,000 (2005)

Beneficial area UK, with a preference for Bedfordshire, Buckinghamshire, Hertfordshire and Northamptonshire.

The Bays, Hillcote, Bleadon Hill, Weston-Super-Mare, Somerset BS24 9JS

Tel. 01934 814009

Email fccf45@hotmail.com

Correspondent T H Parker, Administrator

Trustees *J Coales, Chair; A G Harding; Revd B H Wilcox; H M Stuchfield.*

CC Number 270718

Information available Full accounts were on file at the Charity Commission.

General 'In 1885 Francis Coales and his son, Walter John Coales, acquired a corn merchant's business in Newport Pagnell, Buckinghamshire. Over the years similar businesses were acquired, but after a major fire it was decided to close down the business. From the winding-up was established The Francis Coales Charitable Trust in 1975.

'The nature of the foundation is to assist with grants for the repair of old buildings which are open to the public, for the conservation of monuments, tombs, hatchments, memorial brasses, etc., also towards the cost of archaeological research and related causes, the purchase of documents or items for record offices and museums, and the publication of architectural and archaeological books or papers. Assistance for structural repairs is normally given to churches and their contents in Buckinghamshire, Bedfordshire, Northamptonshire and Hertfordshire where most of the business of Francis Coales and Son was carried out with farmers. However, no territorial restriction is placed upon church monuments, etc.'

In 2004/05 it had assets of almost £2 million, an income of £90,000 and gave £68,000 in grants. Grants approved were in the range of £250 and £4,000 each.

Exclusions No grants for buildings built after 1875, hospitals or hospices. Ecclesiastical buildings cannot receive grants for 'domestic' items such as electrical wiring, heating, improvements or re-ordering.

Applications On a form available from the correspondent.

Applications should include a quotation for the work or the estimated cost, details of the amount of funds already raised and those applied for and other bodies approached. Applications for buildings or contents should include a copy of the relevant part of the architect/conservator's specification showing the actual work proposed. 'Photographs showing details of the problems often speak louder than words.'

The trust also states that receiving six copies of any leaflet or statement of finance is helpful so that each trustee can have a copy in advance of the meeting. Trustees normally meet three times a year to consider grants.

The John Coates Charitable Trust

Arts, children, environment, medical, general

£370,000 (2004/05)

Beneficial area UK, mainly southern England.

PO Box 529, Cambridge CB1 0BT

Correspondent Mrs R J Lawes, Trustee

Trustees *Mrs G F McGregor; Mrs C A Kesley; Mrs R J Lawes; Mrs P L Youngman.*

CC Number 262057

Information available Accounts were obtained from the Charity Commission website.

General This trust has general charitable purposes. Grants are made to large UK-wide charities, or small charities of personal or local interest to the trustees. In 2004/05 the trust continued to support projects that had been assisted in the past and also donated funds to charities not awarded grants previously.

In 2004/05 the trust had assets of £8.7 million, an income of £289,000 and made 69 grants totalling £370,000. About a third of organisations supported also received support in the previous year.

There were 14 grants of £10,000 each, beneficiaries were: Bart's Cancer Centre of Excellence Appeal, Evelina Children's Hospital Appeal, Fight for Sight, Jubilee Sailing Trust Limited, Mary Rose Trust, National Society for the Prevention of Cruelty to Children, National Trust – Neptune Campaign, Painshill Park Trust Limited, Royal Hospital for Neuro-Disability, Royal London Society for the Blind, Salvation Army, Scope, the South Bank Centre and Tommy's.

Beneficiaries of smaller grants included: Action on Addiction (£7,500); British Heart Foundation (£6,000); Alzheimer's Research Trust, Cancer Resource Centre,

Dulwich Picture Gallery, English National Opera, Linden Lodge Charitable Trust, Solent Protection Society and Welsh National Opera Limited (£5,000 each); Worldwide Volunteering for Young People (£2,500); Brain Research Trust and Farms for City Children Limited (£2,000 each); London Festival of Chamber Music (£1,500); Lymington United Reformed Church (£1,000); Suzie Lamplugh Trust (£500); and Mayday Trust (£250).

Exclusions Grants are given to individuals only in exceptional circumstances.

Applications In writing to the correspondent. Small local charities are visited by the trust.

Lance Coates Charitable Trust 1969

Biological and ecological approach to food production

£33,000 (2005/06)

Beneficial area UK.

Denham Lodge, Quainton, Aylesbury HP22 4AL

Correspondent E P Serjeant, Trustee

Trustees *H L T Coates; E P Serjeant.*

CC Number 261521

Information available Accounts were on file at the Charity Commission.

General The trust supports the promotion of ecological and integrated healthcare initiatives and practical holistic research projects. Projects deemed most important by the trust are funded on an annual basis with smaller grants given on a one-off basis.

In 2005/06 the trust had assets of £1.2 million, an income of £26,000 and a grant total of £33,000. Grant beneficiaries were International Therapeutic Institute (UK) Ltd (£20,000) and Country Trust (£12,500).

The above organisations also received support in the previous year, along with Farm Africa, Hearing Research Trust, Lawrence Home Nursing Team Trust and Westcare (£250 each).

Exclusions No grants to individuals.

Applications In writing to the correspondent including a summary of proposal.

Coats Foundation Trust

Textile and thread-related training courses and research

£60,000 (2005/06)

Beneficial area UK.

Coats plc, Pacific House, 70 Wellington Street, Glasgow G2 6UB

Tel. 0141 207 6821 **Fax** 0141 207 6856

Email jenny.mcfarlane@coats.com

Correspondent Jenny McFarlane

Trustee *The Coats Trustee Company Limited.*

CC Number 268735

Information available Accounts were on file at the Charity Commission, without a list of grants.

General Preference is given, but not specifically restricted, to applicants from textile and thread-related training courses.

In 2005/06 the foundation had assets of £2.1 million and an income of £60,000, all of which was given in grants. Donations were broken down as follows: education (£46,000); leisure and recreation facilities (£9,000); and relief in need (£5,700).

Applications Please write, enclosing a cv and an sae, giving details of circumstances and the nature and amount of funding required. There is no formal application form. Only applicants enclosing an sae will receive a reply. Applications are considered four times a year.

Cobb Charity

Sustainable development, green initiatives and related education

About £25,000 (2004/05)
Beneficial area UK.

108 Leamington Road, Kenilworth, Warwickshire CV8 2AA
Correspondent Eleanor Allitt, Trustee
Trustees *E Allitt; C Cochran; E Cochran; M Wells.*
CC Number 248030
Information available Information had been filed at the Charity Commission.

General The trust supports organisations involved in:

- Encouraging eco-friendly technology and appreciation of our natural environment, such as appropriate technology for the developing world, and cycle routes.
- Research for projects such as looking into the connection between food and health and the encouragement of organic gardening and food production.
- The preservation of tribal homelands and the preservation of country and traditional skills closer to home.
- Sustainable energy and recycling projects.

Funding is available for more than three years and can be for capital and core costs, feasibility studies, one-off projects, other projects, research, running costs, recurring costs, salaries and start-up costs.

Most beneficiaries are nationally based charities, but there are exceptions.

In 2004/05 it had an income of £20,000 and a total expenditure of £25,000.

Exclusions Grants are given to registered charities only, not to individuals. No support for medical organisations, student expeditions or building restorations.

Applications Funds are fully committed. New applications cannot be met.

The Denise Cohen Charitable Trust

Health, welfare, arts, humanities, education, culture, Jewish

£67,000 (2005/06)
Beneficial area UK.

Berwin Leighton and Paisner, Adelaide House, London Bridge, London EC4R 9HA
Correspondent Martin D Paisner, Trustee
Trustees *Mrs Denise Cohen; M D Paisner; Sara Cohen.*
CC Number 276439
Information available Full accounts were on file at the Charity Commission.

General In 2005/06 the trust had assets totalling £1.4 million and an income of £148,000. Grants were made to 84 charities totalling £67,000.

Grants of £1,000 or more were made to 25 organisations and included those to: Chai Cancer Care and Nightingale (£6,000 each); Royal Opera House (£4,100); Child Resettlement Fund (£3,300); Community Security Trust and Marie Curie Hospice (£2,000 each); Central Synagogue (£1,900); Cancer Research UK (£1,800); I Rescue (£1,500); and Ben Uri Gallery, British Technion Society, Donmar Warehouse Projects, Cancerkin, Hammerson House, Jewish Blind and Disabled, Magen David Adom, Royal Marsden Cancer Campaign, Shaare Zedek, Tate Gallery, Royal National Theatre and UJS Hillel (£1,000 each).

Applications In writing to the correspondent.

The Vivienne and Samuel Cohen Charitable Trust

Jewish, education, health, medical research and welfare

£116,000 (2004/05)
Beneficial area UK and Israel.

9 Heathcroft, Hampstead Way, London NW11 7HH
Correspondent Dr Vivienne Cohen, Trustee
Trustees *Dr V L L Cohen; M Y Ben-Gershon; J S Lauffer; Dr G L Lauffer.*
CC Number 255496
Information available Full accounts were on file at the Charity Commission.

General The majority of the trust's support is to Jewish organisations. In 2004/05 the trust had assets of £3.2 million and an income of £138,000. Grants totalled £116,000 and were donated to charities concerned with general charitable purposes.

There were 126 grants made in the year, donations of £1,000 or more were listed in the accounts. The largest donation went to University of Bristol (£17,000).

Other listed beneficiaries included: Ariel and Maaleh Hatorah School (£7,000 each); British Friends of Herzou Hospsital and World Jewish Relief (£5,000 each); B'nei B'rith Hillel Foundation, Jewish Care, National Galleries of Scotland and Yeshiva Birkat House (£3,000 each); Queen Mary and Westfield College and Yeshivat Zichron Yosef (£2,500 each); Friends of Neve Menas (£2,000); Chai Lifeline (£1,500); and Bachad Fellowship, Brighton and Hove Hebrew Congregation, Keren Klita and Norwood Child Care (£1,000 each).

Exclusions No grants to individuals.

Applications In writing only, to the correspondent.

John Coldman Charitable Trust

General, Christian

£266,000 (2005/06)

Beneficial area UK, with a preference for Edenbridge in Kent.

Polebrook, Hever, Edenbridge, Kent TN8 7NJ

Correspondent D Coldman, Trustee

Trustees *D J Coldman; G E Coldman; C J Warner.*

CC Number 1050110

Information available Information was on file at the Charity Commission.

General The trust gives grants to community and Christian groups in Edenbridge, Kent and UK organisations whose work benefits that community such as children's and medical charities.

This trust appears to have grown significantly over the last two years. In 2005/06 it had an income of £292,000, mainly from donations. Grants to 35 organisations totalled £266,000.

The beneficiary of the largest grant was Oasis Trust (£128,000). Other beneficiaries included the Prince's Trust (£20,000), Oasis India (£15,000), NSPCC – Penge Project, Oasis International – Tsunami project and St Luke's Hospital for the Clergy (£10,000 each), St Mary's Church Chiddingstone (£6,500), CAB – Edenbridge & Westerham (£6,000), Dan's Fund for Burns, Eden Christian Trust Edenbridge and the McCord Oesophageal Cancer Fund (£5,000 each), Cypress Junior School – South Norwood (£4,500), Duke Comprehensive Cancer Centre (£2,750), Charities Challenge, Kent Air Ambulance Trust and Little Havens Children's Hospice (£2,500 each), Spring House Family Support Centre (£2,000), Camphill Village Trust and Centrepoint (£1,000 each), Disability Challengers (£500), Little Havens Children's Hospice (£250) and Little Hearts Matter (£100).

Applications In writing to the correspondent.

The John and Freda Coleman Charitable Trust

Disadvantaged young people

£63,000 (2005/06)

Beneficial area Surrey and its surrounding area.

Alderney House, 58 Normandy Street, Alton, Hampshire GU34 1DE

Correspondent Paul Coleman, Administrator

Trustees *I Williamson; Mrs J L Bird; P H Coleman; B R Coleman.*

CC Number 278223

Information available Accounts were on file at the Charity Commission.

General The trust aims to provide: 'an alternative to an essentially academic education, to encourage and further the aspirations of young people with talents to develop manual skills and relevant technical knowledge to fit them for satisfying careers and useful employment. The aim is to develop the self-confidence of individuals to succeed within established organisations or on their own account and to impress upon them the importance of service to the community, honesty, good manners and self-discipline.'

The trust also noted that 'as a small family charitable trust we only help those who are situated near our base in Surrey'.

In 2004/05 the trust had assets of over £1 million, an income of £39,000 and made 13 grants totalling £63,000.

Beneficiaries were: Prince's Trust (£24,000); Guildford YMCA, Surrey Care Trust and Surrey SATRO (£5,000 each); Surrey Family Mediation Service (£4,000); NCPYE, Reigate and Redhill YMCA, Second Chance, Surrey Clubs for Young People and Surrey Community Development Trust (£3,000 each); Surrey Connections (£2,500); Skillway and Star Project – SCC Rodborough (£2,000); and Seeds of Hope Children's Garden (£1,000).

Exclusions No grants are made to students.

Applications In writing to the correspondent. Telephone calls are not welcome.

The Sir Jeremiah Colman Gift Trust

General

£92,000 (2004/05)

Beneficial area UK, with a preference for Hampshire, especially Basingstoke.

Malshanger, Basingstoke, Hampshire RG23 7EY

Correspondent Sir Michael Colman, Trustee

Trustees *Sir Michael Colman; Lady Judith Colman; Oliver J Colman; Cynthia Colman; Jeremiah M Colman.*

CC Number 229553

Information available Accounts were on file at the Charity Commission.

General The trust makes grants for general charitable purposes with special regard to:

- advancement of education and literary scientific knowledge
- moral and social improvement of people
- maintenance of churches of the Church of England and gifts and offerings to the churches
- financial assistance to past and present employees/members of Sir Jeremiah Colman at Gatton Park, J and J Colman Ltd or other clubs and institutions associated with Sir Jeremiah Colman.

In 2004/05 the trust had assets of £2.2 million and an income of £83,000. Grants to over 150 organisations totalled £92,000 and were broken down as follows: 'annual' donations (£54,000); 'special' donations (£37,000); and 'extra' donations (£1,100).

The trust made over 150 'annual' grants, with all the beneficiaries being supported in the previous year. Of these, just seven were for £1,000 or more: National Art Collection Fund (£2,000), Basingstoke and Northamptonshire Medical Trust and Church of England Pension Fund (£1,500 each), Bridges International (£1,250) and National Trust, See Ability and Youth for Christ (£1,000 each).

Smaller grants included those to Arthritis Care (£800), SCOPE (£750), Action Medical Research and NSPCC (£700 each), British School of Osteopathy (£500), Leukaemia Research Fund, Mental Health Foundation, Prison Research Trust and RUKBA (£400 each),

Marie Curie Memorial Foundation (£350), Children's Family Trust, Dyslexia Institute, Hampshire Buildings Preservation Trust, Historic Churches Preservation Trust, Music at Winchester and Rainbow Trust, (£250 each), the Honeypot Charity (£150), Falkland Island Memorial Chapel Trust, Scripture Union and VSO (£100 each) and Hampton Trust (£75).

During the year 31 'special' grants were made, including seven which were part of a long-term payments scheme. Examples of beneficiaries of 'special' grants included Youth with a Mission (£5,000), Landmarks (£4,000), Kew Foundation (£2,000), St Peter's Trust (£1,000), Alzheimer's Research Campaign and Positive Parenting (£500 each) and Canine Partners for Independence (£250).

Four 'extra' grants were awarded during the year. Beneficiaries were CIVITAS and Maggie's Cancer Caring Centre (£300 each) and CRPA and Great Music of the World (£250 each).

Exclusions Grants are not made to individuals requiring support for personal education, or to individual families for welfare purposes.

Applications The trust has stated that funds are fully committed – unsolicited applications are therefore not welcomed.

Col-Reno Ltd

Jewish

£44,000 (2005/06)

Beneficial area UK, Israel, USA.

15 Shirehall Gardens, Hendon, London NW4 2QT

Correspondent The Trustees

Trustees M H Stern; A E Stern; K Davies; Mrs R Davies.

CC Number 274896

Information available Accounts were on file at the Charity Commission.

General The trust appears to support only Jewish organisations, with a preference for medical aid organisations and education.

In 2005/06 it had assets of just over £1 million and an income of £144,000 including £86,000 from rental income and £42,000 from a covenant. Out of a total expenditure of £65,000, grants to 17 organisations totalled £44,000.

Grants included £13,000 to Agudas Yisroel of California, £12,000 to JSSM, £8,000 to Friends of Beis Yisroel Trust, £2,500 to SOFOT, £2,000 to American Friends of Israel College of Management, £1,800 to Emuna Women's Organisation, £1,400 to Jerusalem Municipality Parks Commission, £950 to Friends of Menorah Grammar School, £750 to Friends of Hebrew University, £500 to Hendon Adath Yisroel Congregation, £400 to Zionist Federation and £200 to British Friends of Chinuch Atzmai in Israel.

Applications In writing to the correspondent.

The Coltstaple Trust

Relief in need

£210,000 (2005/06)

Beneficial area Worldwide.

c/o Pollen House, 10–12 Cork Street, London W15 3NP

Correspondent Lord Oakshott of Seagrove Bay

Trustees Lord Oakshott of Seagrove Bay; Dr P Oakshott; Lord Newby of Rothwell; B R M Stoneham; Mrs E G Colville.

CC Number 1085500

Information available Accounts were on file at the Charity Commission.

General In 2005/06 the trust had assets of £5.8 million with an income of £212,000 and grants totalling £210,000.

The five grants issued went to: Oxfam (£110,000); Opportunity International (£40,000); St Mungo's (£20,000); and the Connection – St Martins-in-the-Field, Emmaus UK, North West University Whole School Development Programme and Students Partnership (£10,000 each).

Applications In writing to the correspondent.

The Comino Foundation

Education

£343,000 (2005/06)

Beneficial area UK.

29 Hollow Way Lane, Amersham, Buckinghamshire HP6 6DJ

Tel. 01494 722595

Email enquire@cominofoundation.org.uk

Website www.cominofoundation.org.uk

Correspondent A C Roberts, Administrator

Trustees Anna Comino-Jones; J A C Darbyshire; Dr W Eric Duckworth; Mike Tomlinson; Simon Bailey; J E Slater.

CC Number 312875

Information available Accounts were on file at the Charity Commission.

General The Comino Foundation is an educational charity and has two main purposes:

- to promote awareness that industry and commerce produce the basic goods, services and resources on which wellbeing and quality of life depend;
- to promote a clearer understanding of the basic processes involved in getting results, and thus improve people's power and will to create opportunities and achieve their purposes.

The foundation's vision is: 'that people in Britain should live more fulfilled lives within a prosperous and responsible society. The foundation contributes to the realisation of this vision through its educational activities by:

a) 'encouraging and enabling groups and individuals to motivate and empower themselves and to develop progressively their potential for the benefit of themselves and others,
b) 'encouraging a culture which affirms and celebrates both achievement and responsible practice in industry and commerce.'

The trust meets these aims through its patented GRASP approach, which offers a structure for thinking in a results-driven manner through a greater pattern, design and method of thinking. Most of the funds are given towards centres which promote the GRASP approach. Further information on this can be gathered from a leaflet prepared from the trust or on their extensive website.

In 2005/06 the foundation had assets of £6.9 million and an income of £277,000. Grants were made to 15 organisations totalling £343,000.

Beneficiaries were: Black County Partnership, Institute for Global Ethics UK Trust, Liverpool John Moores University, Sheffield Hallam University, University of Winchester and Wigan Borough Partnership (£30,000 each);

PACE Centre (£28,000); Homeground Project – Liverpool (£17,000); Bailey Comino Scholarship (£12,000); Ideas Foundation and Youth Leaders in STEM (£10,000 each); Potential Trust (£9,000); RSA Woman's Voices (£2,300); and Foundation for Science and Technology and Parenting Education and Support Forum (£2,000 each).

Exclusions No grants to individuals or for research projects.

Applications Requests for support should initially be sent to the administrator by email.

The Conservation Foundation

Environmental and conservation

£21,000 (2005)
Beneficial area UK and overseas.

1 Kensington Gore, London SW7 2AR
Tel. 020 7591 3111 **Fax** 020 7591 3110
Email info@conservationfoundation.co.uk
Website www.conservationfoundation.co.uk
Correspondent W F Moloney, Trustee
Trustees *J Senior, Chair; D A Shreeve; Prof. D J Bellamy; J B Curtis; W F Moloney.*
CC Number 284656
Information available Accounts were on file at the Charity Commission.

General The foundation is involved in the creation and management of environmental and conservation orientated projects funded by sponsorship. Income is generated to pay for the costs of managing charitable projects and supporting activities.

In 2005 the foundation had an income of £153,000. Out of a total expenditure of £153,000 grants totalled £21,000. Information about the foundation's current projects can be found on its website.

Applications In writing to the correspondent.

The Construction Industry Trust for Youth

Building projects benefiting young people

£93,000 to individuals and organisations (2004/05)
Beneficial area UK.

55 Tufton Street, London SW1P 3QL
Tel. 0207 227 4563
Email cyt@thecc.org.uk
Website www.constructionyouth.org.uk
Correspondent The Company Secretary
Trustees *Rod Bennion, Chair; Norman Critchlow; Doug Barrat; Michael Brown; Martin Davis; Anthony Furlong; Richard Haryott; Richard Laudy; Rob Oldham; Martin Scarth; John Taylor; Alistair Voaden; Denise Chevin; Paul Hyett; Andy Wates.*
CC Number 1094323
Information available Accounts were on file at the Charity Commission.

General The trust aims to increase access by young people to construction training and skills opportunity, with a particular focus on overcoming disadvantage and alleviating disadvantage. It achieves this through providing bursaries and scholarships to individuals and by funding voluntary projects.

It supports projects which arose from the initiative of local communities or charitable bodies. Consideration is given to local community trusts to initiate programmes of work placements and training with regeneration contractors. Training and placements should ideally be for people aged between 16 and 30, although applications for vocational skills training to disaffected 14- and 15-year-olds will also be considered.

In 2004/05 it had assets of £126,000 and an income of £309,000, mostly from donations received. New grant commitments totalled £93,000, with a further £135,000 spent on its own community-based projects.

Exclusions Training outside the construction industry and its associated trades and professions is not considered. Applications for building grants or the refurbishment of youth centres are not considered.

Applications In writing, or via email, to the correspondent for an application form, with an outline of the request. Forms can be downloaded from the trust's website.

Gordon Cook Foundation

Education and training

About £200,000
Beneficial area UK.

3 Chattan Place, Aberdeen AB10 6RB
Tel. 01224 571010 **Fax** 01224 571010
Email gordoncook@btconnect.com
Website www.gordoncook.org.uk
Correspondent Mrs Irene B Brown, Foundation Secretary
Trustees *G Ross, Chair; D A Adams; Prof. B J McGettrick; Dr P Clarke; Dr W Gatherer; J Marshall; C P Skene.*
SC Number SC017455
Information available Information was taken from the foundation's website.

General This foundation was set up in 1974 and is dedicated to the advancement and promotion of all aspects of education and training which are likely to promote 'character development' and 'citizenship'. The following information is taken from the foundation's website.

'In recent years, the foundation has adopted the term "Values Education" to denote the wide range of activity it seeks to support. This includes:

- 'the promotion of good citizenship in its widest terms, including aspects of moral, ethical and aesthetic education, youth work, cooperation between home and school, and coordinating work in school with leisure time pursuits
- 'the promotion of health education as it relates to values education
- supporting relevant aspects of moral and religious education
- helping parents, teachers and others to enhance the personal development of pupils and young people
- 'supporting developments in the school curriculum subjects which relate to values education
- 'helping pupils and young people to develop commitment to the value of work, industry and enterprise generally

• 'disseminating the significant results of relevant research and development.'

In 2006 the foundation had an income of £306,000. Previous research indicates that grants are made totalling around £200,000 each year. The foundation has previously stated that it supports projects, including 'consultations' organised by Institute of Global Ethics, Professional Ethics, Business Ethics, Enterprise Ethics and Values Education in the Four Home Nations. Grants usually range from around £1,000 to £30,000. Previous beneficiaries include Norham Foundation, Health Education Board for Scotland, Citizen Foundation, North Lanarkshire Council and Northern College.

Exclusions Individuals are unlikely to be funded.

Applications The trustees are proactive in looking for projects to support; however, unsolicited applications may be considered if they fall within the foundation's criteria and are in accordance with current programmes. Forms may be obtained from the correspondent.

The Cooks Charity

Catering

£148,000 (2004/05)

Beneficial area UK, especially City of London.

Coombe Ridge, Thursley Road, Churt, Farnham, Surrey GU10 2LQ

Correspondent M C Thatcher, Clerk and Solicitor

Trustees *M V Kenyon; H F Thornton.*

CC Number 297913

Information available Accounts were on file at the Charity Commission.

General The trust was established in 1989 to support educational and welfare projects concerned with people involved in catering, and then any charitable purposes (with some sort of catering connection) in the City of London.

In 2004/05 it had assets of £3.2 million and an income of £308,000. Grants to 11 organisations totalled £148,000. Beneficiaries included: Hackney College (£47,000); Academy of Culinary Arts (£37,000); Bournemouth University (£19,000); Springboard (£15,000); Treloar's Trust (£10,000); Royal

Marsden Cancer Fund (£7,300); City University (£6,500); Billingsgate Seafood Training School (£5,000); Kisharon College and Lakefield Residential Training Centre (£1,000 each); and St John Ambulance (£100).

Applications In writing to the correspondent. Applications are considered in spring and autumn.

The Cooper Charitable Trust (206772)

Medical, disability, Jewish

£140,000 (2004/05)

Beneficial area UK.

c/o Portrait Solicitors, 1 Chancery Lane, London WC2A 1LF

Correspondent The Trustees

Trustees *Mrs S Roter; Miss Judith Portrait; T Roter; Miss A Roter.*

CC Number 206772

Information available Accounts were on file at the Charity Commission.

General The trust was originally endowed with shares in Lee Cooper plc, which was taken over by Vivat Holdings plc. These shares were sold in 1990/91 and the assets of the trust are now invested in government stocks.

In 2004/05 it had assets of almost £2 million and income of £151,000. Grants to 14 organisations totalled £140,000.

The largest grant by far was £75,000 to Evelina Children's Hospital Appeal. Other beneficiaries included British Heart Foundation (£25,000), Paul Strickland Scanner Centre (£10,000), Jewish Care, Norwood Ravenswood and Prostate Cancer Research Centre (£5,000 each), Lifeline 4 Kids (£4,000) and Changing Faces, The Children's Trust – Tadworth, Royal Hospital for Neuro-disability and Teenage Cancer Trust (£2,000 each) and British Institute for Brain Injured Children, Independent Living Centre and the Speech Language and Hearing Centre (£1,000 each).

Exclusions No grants to individuals.

Applications In writing to the correspondent; applications are not acknowledged.

Mabel Cooper Charity

General

£67,000 (2004/05)

Beneficial area UK, with a possible interest in South Devon.

Lambury Cottage, East Portlemouth, Salcombe, Devon TQ8 8PU

Correspondent A E M Harbottle, Secretary

Trustees *A E M Harbottle; J Harbottle; I A Harbottle.*

CC Number 264621

Information available Accounts were obtained from the Charity Commission website.

General In 2004/05 the charity had assets of over £1 million, an income of £52,000 and grants were made totalling £67,000.

Beneficiaries included: Crisis and Devon Air Ambulance (£10,000 each); Kingsbridge Rotary Appeal (£5,000); Oxfam (£3,500); Arthritis Research, Cancer Research, Christian Aid, Help the Aged, McMillan Cancer Relief, National Children's Home, Parents United, St Luke's Hospice, St Peter's Hospice, St Petrock's – Exeter, Samaritans and UNICEF (£3,000 each); and Girls Workshop and MF Charitable Trust (£1,000 each).

Exclusions No grants to individuals.

Applications In writing to the correspondent, although the trust states that it does not welcome, or reply to, unsolicited applications.

The Marjorie Coote Animal Charity Fund

Wildlife and animal welfare

£105,000 (2004/05)

Beneficial area Worldwide.

Barn Cottage, Lindrick Common, Worksop, Nottinghamshire S81 8BA

Correspondent Sir Hugh Neill, Trustee

Trustees *Sir Hugh Neill; Mrs J P Holah; N H N Coote.*

CC Number 208493

Information available Accounts were on file at the Charity Commission.

General The trust was established in 1954 for the benefit of five named charities and any other charitable organisation which has as its main purpose the care and protection of horses, dogs or other animals or birds.

The trustees concentrate on research into animal health problems and on the protection of the species, whilst applying a small proportion of the income to general animal welfare, including sanctuaries.

In 2004/05 it had assets of £2.8 million and an income of £102,000. Grants to 44 organisations totalled £105,000.

Ongoing support (£73,000 in 21 grants) Grants were in the range of £1,000 and £10,000 and included those to: Animal Health Trust (£10,000); Friends of Conservation (£7,000); Guide Dogs for the Blind and World Wildlife Fund for Nature (£6,000 each); Whitely Wildlife Conservation Trust (£4,000); FRAME (£5,000); Mammals Trust UK (£2,000); and Greek Animal Welfare (£1,000).

One-off grants (£32,000 in 23 grants) Grants were in the range of £500 and £5,000 and included those to: Woburn Centre for Conservation & Education (£5,000); Brooke Hospital for Animals and Sheffield Wildlife Trust (£3,000 each); Fauna and Flora (£2,000); the Gambia Horse & Donkey Trust (£1,500); Veteran Horse Welfare (£1,000); and Dogs Trust, Dorset Wildlife Trust and Prevent Unwanted Pets (£500 each).

Exclusions No grants to individuals.

Applications In writing to the correspondent. Applications should reach the correspondent during September for consideration in October/November.

The Muriel and Gershon Coren Charitable Foundation

Jewish, welfare, general

£196,000 (2005/06)

Beneficial area UK and the developing world.

2 Tavistock Place, London WC1H 9SS

Correspondent G Coren, Trustee

Trustees G Coren; Mrs M Coren; A Coren.

CC Number 257615

Information available Full accounts were on file at the Charity Commission.

General The trust supports registered charities, particularly Jewish organisations. In 2005/06 its assets totalled £2.7 million and it received an income of £550,000. Grants to 49 organisations totalled £196,000.

Gategi Village Self Help Group (£37,000); Hadassah Medical Relief Association UK, Jewish Care, Nightingale House and North London Hospice (£10,000 each); Tzedek (£6,000); Alzheimer's Disease Society, B'nai B'rith UK, British Friends of Boys Town – Jerusalem, Cancer Research UK, Central British Fund for World Jewish Relief, Hope Charity and St Joseph's Hospice (£5,000 each); British Friends of Haifa University, Community Security Trust and Shelter (£4,000 each); UJIA (£2,500); Belarus School in Plinzk, British Friends of Hebrew University, Lubavitch Foundation and Prostate Cancer Charity (£2,000 each); British Friends Ramban Medical Centre and United Institution Arad (£1,000 each); and WIZO (£200).

Applications In writing to the correspondent.

The Duke of Cornwall's Benevolent Fund

General

£104,000 (2005/06)

Beneficial area UK, with a number of grants made in the Cornwall area.

10 Buckingham Gate, London SW1E 6LA

Tel. 020 7834 7346 **Fax** 020 7931 9541

Correspondent Robert Mitchell

Trustees Hon. James Leigh-Pemberton; W R A Ross.

CC Number 269183

Information available Accounts were on file at the Charity Commission.

General The fund receives donations from the Duke of Cornwall (Prince

Charles) based on amounts received by the Duke as Bona Vacantia (the casual profits of estates of deceased intestates dying domiciled in Cornwall without kin) after allowing for costs and ex-gratia payments made by the Duke in relation to claims on any estate.

The fund's objectives are the relief of people in need, provision of almshouses, homes of rest, hospitals and convalescent homes, advancement of education, advancement of religion, advancement of the arts and preservation for the benefit of the public of lands and buildings.

In 2005/06 the fund had assets of £3.1 million and an income of £198,000. Grants were made totalling £104,000.

There were 27 grants of £1,000 or more listed in the accounts. Beneficiaries included: Isles of Scilly Wildlife Trust (£20,000); Small Woods Association (£6,400); Business in the Community (£5,300); River Wye Preservation, St Agnes Sports and Leisure Group and Soil Association (£2,500 each); Cornwall Community Foundation and Lifebuoy Charitable Trust (£2,000 each); British Food Fortnight (£1,600); and ARC – Addington Fund, Boscastle and Crackington Gig Club, Cornwall County Council – Restormel Fort, Dorchester Town Council, Friends of St Mabyn Church, Newlyn Trinity Methodist Church, St Columb Minor Primary School, St Tudy's Church – Bodmin, the United Church of Princetown and West of England School and College (£1,000 each).

Other donations of less than £1,000 each totalled £40,000.

Applications In writing to the correspondent. Applicants should give as much detail as possible, especially information on how much money has been raised to date, what the target is and how it will be achieved. Applications can be made at any time.

The Sidney and Elizabeth Corob Charitable Trust

General

£248,000 (2005/06)

Beneficial area UK.

62 Grosvenor Street, London W1K 3JF

Tel. 020 7499 4301

Correspondent The Trustees

Trustees *A L Corob; E Corob; C J Cook; J V Hajnal; Ms S A Wechsler; S Wiseman.*

CC Number 266606

Information available Full accounts were on file at the Charity Commission.

General The trust has general charitable purposes, supporting a range of causes including education, arts, welfare and Jewish charities.

In 2005/06 the trust had assets of £1.1 million with an income of £104,000 and grants totalling £248,000.

There were 44 grants of £1,000 or more listed in the accounts; the largest of which went to: Oxford Centre for Hebrew and Jewish Studies (£45,000); University College London (£40,000); National Alliance for Autism Research (£20,000); and British Technion Society, the Hope Charity, Jewish Care and Magen David Adom (£10,000 each); and British ORT, Friends of Jerusalem Botanical Gardens, Norwood Ltd and Royal Holloway University of London (£5,000 each).

Other beneficiaries included: British Friends of the Art Museums of Israel (£3,400); Community Security Trust (£2,500); Chai Cancer Care, Friends of Ohel Torah Trust, the Jewish Quarterly, Royal National Theatre and World Jewish Relief (£2,000 each); and Alzheimer's Research Trust, Child Health Research Appeal Trust, Evelina Children's Hospital Appeal, Friends of Israel Educational Trust, Israel Diaspora Trust, Soho Theatre Company and UJIA (£1,000 each).

Other donations of less than £1,000 each totalled £35,000.

Exclusions No grants to individuals or non-registered charities.

Applications In writing to the correspondent. The trustees meet at regular intervals.

The Corona Charitable Trust

Jewish

£102,000 (2004/05)

Beneficial area UK and overseas.

16 Mayfield Gardens, Hendon, London NW4 2QA

Correspondent A Levy, Trustee and Secretary

Trustees *A Levy; A Levy; B Levy.*

CC Number 1064320

Information available Accounts were on file at the Charity Commission.

General In 2004/05 the trust had an income, mainly from donations of £74,000 and made grants totalling £102,000. Assets stood at £90,000 at the year end.

Beneficiaries included: Cosmos Belz Limited (£20,000); Ahavas Shalom Charitable Trust (£7,500); Yeshivas Kerem Beyaneh Foundation (£7,200); Achisomach Aid Co. (£6,300); Kiryat Chinuch Lebonim (£5,500); Gateshead Talmudical College and Kisharon (£5,000 each); Friends of Tashbar Chazon Ish (£4,900); Hasmonean High School (£4,500); WST Charity Limited (£4,300); Menorah Grammar School (£3,700); JSSM School, KZF and Sasson Vesimcha Charitable Trust (£3,000 each); Aaron Lazer and Tzirel Goorvith MT (£2,000); North London Talmudical College (£1,800); and NRST (£1,000).

Applications In writing to the correspondent.

The Cotton Industry War Memorial Trust

Textiles

£197,000 (2005/06)

Beneficial area UK.

5 Brampton Close, Platt Bridge, Wigan WN2 5HS

Correspondent R G Morrow, Trustee

Trustees *K R Garbett; R C Trotter; R G Morrow.*

CC Number 242721

Information available Full accounts were on file at the Charity Commission.

General This trust makes grants to educational bodies to assist eligible students in furtherance of their textile studies, to other bodies which encourage recruitment into or efficiency in the industry or organisations otherwise researching or benefiting the cotton industry.

In 2005/06 it had assets of almost £7 million and an income of £141,000. Grants totalled £197,000.

Beneficiaries included: University of Manchester (£65,000); Royal School for the Deaf and Communication Disorders (£55,000); Adventure Farm Trust (£30,000); Texprint (£25,000); and Samuel Crompton Fellowship Award (£500).

Applications In writing to the correspondent.

The Cotton Trust

Relief of suffering, elimination and control of disease, people who are disabled and disadvantaged

£208,000 (2004/05)

Beneficial area UK and overseas.

PO Box 6895, Earl Shilton, Leicester LE9 8ZE

Tel. 01455 440917 **Fax** 01455 440917

Correspondent Mrs J B Congdon, Trustee

Trustees *Mrs J B Congdon; Mrs T E Dingle; Ms E S Cotton; C B Cotton.*

CC Number 1094776

Information available Accounts were on file at the Charity Commission.

General The trust's policy is: the relief of suffering; the elimination and control of diseases; and helping people of any age who are disabled or disadvantaged. Grants are given for defined capital projects (excluding building construction and the purchase of new buildings). Running costs can be funded where there are identified projects. The trust receives upwards of 700 applications each year. It awards about 80 to 100 grants to UK-registered charities working both at home and overseas each year, ranging between £250 and £5,000.

In 2004/05 the trust had assets of £4.9 million, an income of £196,000 and made 86 grants totalling £208,000.

The 50 largest grants were listed in the accounts, the beneficiaries of the three largest grants were Leicester Charity Link (£30,000), British Red Cross – Tsunami appeal (£25,000) and Merlin (£10,000).

Other beneficiaries included: Motivation (£6,000); CmFed, Tree Aid (£5,000); Send A Cow (£4,700); Impact Foundation (£4,500); the Sycamore Project (£4,000); Earl Shilton Charity (£3,500); Hollybank Trust, Leicester Samaritans and the Pace Centre (£3,000); Break, Byker Bridge Housing

Association Ltd, Concern, LEPRA, TB Alert and Vet Aid (£2,500 each), Books Abroad, Kings World Trust for Children and the Wessex Autistic Society (£2,000 each); Defeating Deafness, Joliba Trust, International Service and Scottish Churches Housing Agency (£1,500 each); and Hopscotch and Tower Hamlets Mission (£1,200 each).

Exclusions Grants are only given to UK-registered charities that have been registered for at least one year. No grants to animal charities, individuals, students, further education, travel, expeditions, conservation, environment, arts, new building construction, the purchase of new buildings or 'circular' appeals. The trustees will only support the purchase of computer systems and equipment if it is to be directly used by people who are disadvantaged or have disabilities, but not general IT equipment for the running of organisations.

Applications In writing to the correspondent with latest accounts, evidence of charitable status, detailed budget, timetable and details of funds raised.

Guidelines are available with an sae. Deadlines for applications are the end of July and the end of January, with successful applicants being notified within three months of these dates. It is regretted that only successful applications can be answered. The trustees only accept one application in a 12-month period.

Country Houses Foundation

Preservation of buildings of historic or architectural significance
About £550,000 a year
Beneficial area England.

The Manor, Haseley Business Centre, Warwick CV35 7LS

Tel. 0845 402 4102 **Fax** 0845 402 4103

Email info@countryhousesfoundation.org.uk

Website www.countryhousesfoundation.org.uk/

Correspondent Amanda Witherall, Chief Executive/Secretary

Trustees *Oliver Pearcey; Nicholas Barber; Michael Clifton; Norman Hudson; Christopher Taylor; Sir John Parsons.*

CC Number 1111049

Information available Full guidelines are available on the foundation's website.

General Registered with the Charity Commission in August 2005, the main aims of the foundation are to support the preservation of buildings of historic or architectural significance together with their gardens and grounds, for the public benefit. Beneficiaries can include registered charities, building preservation trusts and private owners.

Total grants awarded in any one year total about £550,000.

Guidelines
'We aim to give grants for repairs and restoration work required to prevent loss or damage to historic buildings located in England, their gardens, grounds and any outbuildings. We would normally expect your building to be listed, scheduled, or in the case of a garden included in the English Heritage Register of Parks and Gardens. However, we may also make grants to projects which involve an unlisted building of sufficient historic or architectural significance or importance if it is within a conservation area.'

'In addition, to qualify for any grant you must be able to show the following:

- There is a compelling need for the work you want to undertake to be done within the next 2 to 3 years.
- The project will enhance our historic environment.
- There will be appropriate public access.
- The project will have a sustainable future.
- There is a financial need for the grant.
- The project can proceed within a reasonable time frame (i.e. 1–2 years).
- We aim to make grants for projects which are ready to proceed (i.e. can be started within 1–2 years) but which either do not qualify for funding from any of the mainstream sources or have been awarded only partial funding and require significant further funds to complete the resource package.'

'We will also consider making grants to effectively 'kickstart' a project but will expect your other funding to be completed within 1–2 years.'

Exclusions 'As a general rule we do not offer grants for the following:

- Projects which do not have a heritage focus.
- Alterations and improvements.
- Routine maintenance and minor repairs.
- General running costs.
- Demolitions.

- Rent, loan or mortgage payments.
- Buying furniture, fittings and equipment except where they have an historic relationship with the site and are relevant to the project.
- Work carried out before a grant offer has been made in writing and accepted.'

Applications Pre-Application Forms can be completed online, or in a hard copy and returned by post. The foundation tries to respond within 28 days of receipt. If a project fits the criteria then a unique reference number will be issued which must be quoted on the Full Application Form.

Applications can be made at any time.

The Augustine Courtauld Trust

General
£61,000 (2005/06)
Beneficial area UK, with a preference for Essex.

Number One, Legg Street, Chelmsford, Essex CM1 1JS

Tel. 01245 453800

Email mail@augustinecourtauldtrust.org

Website www.augustinecourtauldtrust.org

Correspondent Bruce Ballard, Clerk

Trustees *Lord Bishop of Chelmsford; Lord Lieutenant of Essex; Revd A C C Courtauld; Lord Braybrooke; J Courtauld; Lady Braybrooke; Derek Fordham.*

CC Number 226217

Information available Accounts were on file at the Charity Commission.

General This trust was founded in 1956 by Augustine Courtauld, an Arctic explorer who was proud of his Essex roots. His charitable purpose was simple: 'my idea is to make available something that will do some good.' Among the main areas of work supported before his death in 1959 were young people, people with disabilities, the countryside, certain churches, Arctic exploration and the RNLI. The current guidelines are to support organisations that are:

- working within the historical boundaries of the county of Essex
- involved in expeditions to the Arctic and Antarctic regions
- known to one of the trustees.

Within Essex, the preference is to support disadvantaged young people, conservation projects and certain charities that the founder specifically wanted to help. Grants range from £500 to £2,000 for projects and core costs and can be for multiple years, but only if the charity applies for a grant in consecutive years.

In 2005/06 the trust had assets of £1.3 million and an income of £61,000, all of which was given in grants.

Beneficiaries of larger grants included: Friends of Essex Churches (£8,000); the Cirdan Sailing Trust and Essex Association of Boys Clubs (£4,000 each); College of St Mark Audley End (£3,000); Prader Willi Syndrome Association UK and Refugee Council (£2,000 each); the Daws Hall Trust (£1,500); Rural Community Council of Essex (£1,400); and the Bishop of Chelmsford's Discretionary Fund, National Playing Fields Association – Essex branch, St Clare's Hospice – Harlow and St Luke's Hospital for the Clergy (£1,000 each).

Beneficiaries of smaller grants, all of £500 each included: Acorn Villages, Brentwood Catholic Children's Society, Brentwood Home Start, Chelmsford YMCA, Interact, Fishermen's Mission, Multiple Sclerosis Society, Ocean Youth Trust, Open Road, RNLI, St Francis Hospice and Victoria County History of Essex.

The trust also supported three expedition projects totalling £11,000.

Exclusions No grants to individuals. No grants to individual churches for fabric repairs or maintenance.

Applications In writing to the correspondent, or online via the trust's website. Applications are considered in spring. The closing date for applications each year is 1 March,

Coutts and Co. Charitable Trust

General

£363,000 (2005/06)

Beneficial area UK, specifically London.

440 Strand, London WC2R 0QS

Tel. 020 7753 1000 **Fax** 020 7753 1066

Email carole.attwater@coutts.com

Correspondent Mrs C Attwater, Administrator

Trustees *The Earl of Home; Nigel G C P Banbury; Mrs Sally Doyle; Gary Adlam; Anthony J Williams.*

CC Number 1000135

Information available Accounts were on file at the Charity Commission.

General The trust was set up by the company Coutts and Co. which provides banking and allied services. It is funded by the bank under a deed of covenant equivalent to one half of 1% of the bank's pre-tax profit with a minimum of £50,000. In 2005/06 it made 724 grants totalling £363,000.

Grants are given to UK organisations only and the trust prefers to support organisations in areas where the bank has a presence, mainly London.

The trust summarised its donations as follows:

Aged	£10,000
Alcohol/drug addiction	£5,500
Animal welfare	£5,300
Arts	£11,000
Arts/culture	£5,600
Benevolent	£1,400
Blind	£6,100
Building restoration/preservation	£5,200
Cancer care	£8,600
Cancer research	£14,000
Children	£13,000
Children/youth	£17,000
Deaf	£8,300
Disabled physical/mental	£20,000
Mental disability	£7,700
Disaster relief	£1,800
Education	£28,000
Emergency services	£2,300
Environment	£1,100
Heritage	£5,000
Homelessness	£24,000
Hospices	£14,000
Hospitals	£16,000
Housing	£250
Job creation/training	£500
Law and order	£1,000
Medical research	£19,000
Mental health	£4,000
Mentally handicapped	£1,000
Nursing home	£250
Overseas aid	£5,000
Pensioners	£50
Physically disabled	£4,000
Prison aid	£1,000
Rehabilitating offenders	£4,300
Religious	£13,000
Scientific research	£250
Service charities	£4,400
Social welfare	£36,000
Sundry	£5,000
Women	£250
Youth organisations	£6,800

Exclusions No response to circular appeals. No support for appeals from individuals or overseas projects.

Applications In writing to the correspondent, at any time. Applications should include clear details of the purpose for which the grant is required. Grants are made regularly where amounts of £500 or less are felt to be appropriate. The trustees meet quarterly to consider larger donations.

Cowley Charitable Foundation

Registered charities

£39,000 (2005/06)

Beneficial area Worldwide, with some preference for south Buckinghamshire and the Aylesbury area.

140 Trustee Co. Ltd, 36 Broadway, London SW1H 0BH

Tel. 020 7973 8044

Trustees *140 Trustee Co. Ltd; Mrs H M M Cullen.*

CC Number 270682

Information available Information was on file at the Charity Commission.

General In 2005/06 the trust had assets of £1.1 million and an income of £46,000. Grants to 39 organisations totalled £39,000.

Beneficiaries included: University of California – SETI@home (£10,000); International Dark Sky Association – USA (£8,000); Age Concern Buckinghamshire, Alzheimer's Society, Harrow Tsunami Relief Fund, Georgian Group, Keats Shelley Memorial Association, Médecins Sans Frontières, Public Catalogue Foundation, Wheelpower and Wordsworth Trust (£1,000 each); Association for International Cancer Research, Children with Leukaemia, Great Ormond Street Hospital Children's Charity, People's Trust for Endangered Species, Royal Court, Thinking Foundation, Venice in Peril Fund and YMCA (£500 each); Chelsea Pensioners' Fund (£200) and British Heart Foundation and NSPCC (£100 each).

Exclusions No grants to non-registered charities. No grants to individuals, or for causes supposed to be serviced by public funds or with a scope considered to be too narrow.

Applications The trust states that unsolicited applications are not invited, and that the trustees carry out their own research into charities.

The Sir William Coxen Trust Fund

Orthopaedic hospitals or other hospitals or charities doing orthopaedic work

£48,000 (2004/05)

Beneficial area England.

The Town Clerk's Office, Corporation of London, PO Box 270, Guildhall, London EC2P 2EJ

Correspondent The Trustees

Trustee *Six Aldermen appointed by the Court of Aldermen, together with the Lord Mayor.*

CC Number 206936

Information available Accounts were on file at the Charity Commission.

General This trust was established following a bequest from the late Sir William Coxen in 1940. Expenditure is mainly applied for the support of orthopaedic hospitals or other hospitals or charities doing orthopaedic work.

In 2004/05 the trust had assets of £1.6 million and an income of £61,000. Grants were made to 15 organisations totalling £48,000. Beneficiaries included: Association for Spina Bifida Hydrocephalus, Bobath Centre and Handicapped Children's Trust (£5,000 each); Bedfordshire and Northamptonshire Multiple Sclerosis Society, Diagnosis Investigation of Spinal Conditions and Neuromuscular Centre (£2,500 each); Brainwave, Brittle Bone Society, DEMAND, Institute of Orthopaedics, Osteopathic Centre for Children and Motability (£3,500 each); Friends of Valence School (£3,000); St Bartholomew Fellowship (£1,400); and Great Ormond Street Children's Appeal (£500).

Exclusions No grants to individuals or non-charitable institutions.

Applications In writing to the correspondent.

The Lord Cozens-Hardy Trust

Medicine, health, welfare, general

£77,000 (2005/06)

Beneficial area Merseyside and Norfolk.

PO Box 28, Holt, Norfolk NR25 7WH

Correspondent The Trustees

Trustees *Hon. Beryl Cozens-Hardy; J E V Phelps; Mrs L F Phelps; J J P Ripman.*

CC Number 264237

Information available Full accounts were on file at the Charity Commission.

General The trust supports a few UK charities in the fields of medicine, health and welfare and local groups in Merseyside and Norfolk. It gives both one-off and recurrent grants.

In 2005/06 the trust had assets of £2.7 million and an income of £117,000. Grants totalled £77,000.

Beneficiaries included: Norfolk and Norwich Association for the Blind (£21,000); BMA – Medical Education Trust Fund (£10,000); Letheringsett PCC (£1,400); Raleigh International Trust (£1,300); and Breast Cancer Campaign, East Anglia Children's Hospice, Liverpool School of Tropical Medicine, Princes Trust, Priory of England and the Islands – Hospital of St John, Salvation Army, St John of Jerusalem Eye Hospital and World Association of Girl Guides and Girl Scouts (£1,000 each).

Applications In writing to the correspondent. Applications are not acknowledged and are considered twice a year. Telephone calls are not invited.

The Craignish Trust

Arts, education, environment, general

Around £100,000 each year

Beneficial area UK, with a preference for Scotland.

Messrs Geoghegan and Co., 6 St Colme Street, Edinburgh EH3 6AD

Tel. 0131 225 4681 **Fax** 0131 220 1132

Email lachlan.fernie@geoghegans.co.uk

Correspondent Lachlan K Fernie, Treasurer

Trustees *Ms M Matheson; J Roberts; Ms C Younger.*

SC Number SC016882

Information available Accounts were provided by the trust.

General This trust was established in 1961 by the late Sir William McEwan Younger; its funding criteria is summarised as follows:

- no grants to large national charities
- there is a Scottish bias, but not exclusively
- arts, particularly where innovative and/or involved in the community
- education
- environment
- organisations/projects of particular interest to a trustee.

In 2006/07 the trust had assets of £5.2 million and an income of £151,000, generated mainly from investments. Grants were made totalling £89,000.

An example of grants in 2006/07 included those made to: Human Rights Watch Charitable Trust (£7,500); Soil Association Scotland (£6,000); Friends of the Earth Scotland (£5,000); Boilerhouse Theatre Company Ltd (£3,500); Edinburgh International Book Festival (£3,000); Art in Healthcare (£2,500); Butterfly Conservation – Scotland (£2,000); Centre for Alternative Technology (£1,500); Edinburgh Royal Choral Union (£1,000); and Cairndow Arts Promotions (£500).

Exclusions Running costs are not normally supported.

Applications There is no formal application form; applicants should write to the correspondent. Details of the project should be included together with a copy of the most recent audited accounts.

The Craps Charitable Trust

Jewish, general

£178,000 (2005/06)

Beneficial area UK, Israel.

3rd Floor, Bryanston Court, Selden Hill, Hemel Hempstead, Hertfordshire HP2 4TN

Correspondent The Trustees

Trustees J P M Dent; C S Dent; L R Dent.

CC Number 271492

Information available Accounts were on file at the Charity Commission.

General This trust supports mostly Jewish charities, although medical and other organisations are also supported. There is a list of eight charities mentioned in the trust deed, although not all of these are supported every year and other groups in the UK and overseas can be supported.

In 2005/06 it had assets of £3.7 million, which generated an income of £178,000. Grants totalled £178,000.

There were 27 grants made in the year, the largest of which went to: British Technion Society (£25,000); Jewish Care (£20,000); Friends of the Hebrew University of Jerusalem (£14,000); JNF Charitable Trust (£13,000); the Jerusalem Foundation (£11,000); and New Israel Fund and United Jewish Israel Appeal (£10,000 each).

Applications The trust states that 'funds of the trust are fully committed and the trust does not invite applications for its funds'.

The Crescent Trust

Museums and the arts, occasionally health and education

About £45,000 (2005/06)
Beneficial area UK.

9 Queripel House, 1 Duke of York Square, London SW3 4LY

Correspondent Ms C Akehurst

Trustees J C S Tham; R A F Lascelles.

CC Number 327644

Information available Information had been on file at the Charity Commission.

General The trust concentrates on arts (especially larger museums), heritage and ecology. Smaller grants are mainly given in the medical field. Only specific charities of which the trustees have personal knowledge are supported.

In 2005/06 the trust had an income of £19,000 and a total expenditure of £48,000.

Previous beneficiaries have included Addaction, the Attingham Trust, Burlington Magazine, Donhead St Mary Village Hall, PMSA, the National Society for Epilepsy, the Royal Collection Trust, Victoria and Albert Museum, the Wallace Collection and Wiltshire Wild Life Appeal.

Applications This trust states that it does not respond to unsolicited applications.

Criffel Charitable Trust

Christianity, welfare, health

£65,000 (2004/05)
Beneficial area UK and overseas.

Hillfield, 4 Wentworth Road, Sutton Coldfield, West Midlands B74 2SG

Correspondent Mr and Mrs J C Lees, Trustees

Trustees J C Lees; Mrs J E Lees; Mrs J I Harvey.

CC Number 1040680

Information available Accounts were on file at the Charity Commission.

General The objectives of the trust are the advancement of Christianity and the relief of poverty, sickness and other needs. In 2004/05 it had assets of £1.2 million and an income of £56,000. Grants totalled £65,000 and were broken down as follows:

- Relief of sickness £24,000
- Advancement of Christianity £21,000
- Relief of the poor and needy £7,600
- Miscellaneous £13,000

Included in the above were two donations of £10,000 each to the Monkton Campaign and Wellchild. All other donations were for amounts under £2,000 each.

Applications All funds are fully committed. The trust states that no applications are considered or acknowledged. Please do not apply.

The Violet and Milo Cripps Charitable Trust

Prison and human rights, general

£980,000 (2004/05)
Beneficial area UK.

2 Lambs Passage, London EC1Y 8BB

Correspondent The Trustees

Trustees Lord Parmoor; Anthony J R Newhouse; Richard J Lithenthal.

CC Number 289404

Information available Full accounts were on file at the Charity Commission.

General The trust supports large prison and human rights organisations.

In 2004/05 the trust had an income of £2.2 million and grants to seven organisations totalled £980,000. The sum of £1.3 million was carried forward.

Beneficiaries were Howard League for Penal Reform and Prison Reform Trust (£400,000 each), the Zoological Society of London (£100,000), St George's Parish – Warminster (£25,000), Man's Duty is to Serve Mankind and Treloar Trust (£20,000 each) and St George's School (£10,000).

Applications The trust states that unsolicited applications will not receive a response.

The Cripps Foundation

Education, healthcare and churches in Northamptonshire, Cambridge University

Around £55,000 (2005/06)
Beneficial area Northamptonshire, diocese of Peterborough and University of Cambridge.

CLB Littlejohn Fraser, Rocket Lifestyle Ltd, 1 Park Place, London E14 4HJ

Trustees Edward J S Cripps, Chair; D J T Cochrane; R W H Cripps.

CC Number 212285

Information available Limited information was obtained from the Charity Commission website.

General The foundation mainly supports schools and churches in Northamptonshire and colleges of Cambridge University. Almost all the money is given in a few very large awards to organisations. A minimal amount is reportedly available to unsolicited applications from organisations in Northamptonshire.

In 2005/06 the trust had an income of £20,000 and a total expenditure of £57,000. There was no further information available for this year. Previous beneficiaries included Peterborough Cathedral, Uppingham Parish Church and Northampton Volunteer Bureau.

Exclusions No grants are made to individual applicants or to organisations based outside the beneficial area.

Applications Applications should be by letter or by direct approach to the trustees. The trustees have a number of projects to which the majority of their funds are committed, but there is a relatively small amount open to unsolicited applications. Applications are filtered by assessing whether or not they strictly fit the areas of interest: Is it local? Is it a religious charity? Is it an educational charity? Suitable applications are then passed on to the council of management (the trustees) for consideration. Both applicants and recipients are visited by the foundation, particularly in the case of larger projects.

The Harry Crook Foundation

Education, general

£43,000 (2005/06)
Beneficial area Bristol.

Veale Wasbrough Lawyers, Orchard Court, Orchard Lane, Bristol BS1 5WS

Correspondent D J Bellow, Trustee

Trustees J O Gough, Chair; R G West; Mrs I Wollen; D J Bellew; M C Manisty.

CC Number 231470

Information available Full accounts were available from the Charity Commission.

General In 2007 the trust informed us that it had decided to 'close' the fund to external applications until further notice,

with all available funds 'directed towards a single identified charity'.

In 2005/06 the trust had assets of £1.4 million, an income of £33,000 and made grants totalling £42,000. Donations were broken down as follows:

Regular Donations Reviewed Annually – 6 grants totalling £26,000
Beneficiaries were: Salvation Army (£10,000); Boys Brigade and Harry Crook Activities Centre (£5,000 each); Westbury-on-Trym PCC and Young Bristol (£2,000 each); and Summerhill OAP Club (£1,500).

Discretionary Grants – 9 grants totalling £14,000
Recipients included: Nempnett Thrubwell Village Hall (£5,900); Harry Crook Youth Activities Centre (£3,300); Multiple Sclerosis Society Bristol Branch (£1,600); the Anchor Society and the Dolphin Society (£1,000 each); Kingswood Rotary Club and MacMillan Nurses Fund (£500 each); and Somerset Crimebeat (£100).

Adventurers – 9 grants totalling £2,800
Donations included those to: Borneo and the Oxford Medical Students Electives Trust (£1,000 each); Raleigh International (£200); and Bristol Volunteers for Development Abroad, Oasis Trust and Youth with a Mission (£100 each).

Exclusions Medical research charities and charities serving need outside the boundaries of the City of Bristol. No grants to individuals.

Applications In light of the foundation's 2007 resolution to 'close' the trust to external applications until further notice, any future applications to the trust will be ignored, 'no acknowledgement will be given, and, in particular, no consideration will be given to them.'

The Cross Trust (298472)

Christian work

£123,000 to organisations and individuals (2004/05)
Beneficial area UK and overseas.

Cansdales, Bourbon Court, Nightingale Corner, Little Chalfont, Buckinghamshire HP7 9QS

Tel. 01494 765428
Correspondent The Trustees

Trustees M S Farmer; Mrs J D Farmer; D J Olsen.

CC Number 298472

Information available Accounts were on file at the Charity Commission.

General The trust's objectives are:

- work for the furtherance of religious and secular education
- advancement of the Christian faith in the UK and overseas
- relief of Christian workers, their dependants, and other people who are poor, sick, elderly or otherwise in need
- support for any religious or charitable institution.

In 2004/05 the trust had assets of £167,000 and an income of £129,000 mainly from Gift Aid. Grants were made totalling £123,000 to organisations and individuals.

Beneficiaries included Oakhill College (£25,000), Friends of St Ebbe's Trust (£10,000), Proclamation Trust (£7,400), the Areopagus Trust, Friends International and the Rock Foundation (£5,000 each), Agape Missionaries (£2,400) and OMF Asia Interactive and St Andrews Partnership – summer school sponsorship (£1,000 each).

Applications No unsolicited applications are supported, with funds already fully committed.

The Derek Crowson Charitable Settlement

General

£8,000 to organisations (2005)
Beneficial area UK.

The Courtyard, River Way, Uckfield, East Sussex TN22 1SL

Tel. 01825 761555

Correspondent J R Hughes, Trustee

Trustees D C Crowson, Chair; J R Hughes; J E Eden.

CC Number 1027486

Information available Accounts were on file at the Charity Commission, but without a full narrative report.

General The trust was established in 1993, the trust's main priorities are to help relieve poverty, assist in the advancement of religion, the promotion of health and other such charitable purposes.

In 2005 the trust had assets of £26,000 and an income of £25,000. Grants totalled £8,200 and were made to the RNIB (£5,000), the River and Rowing Museum Foundation (£2,500) and the Horstead Keynes Pre-School Group (£700).

Applications In writing to the correspondent.

The Ronald Cruickshanks' Foundation

Welfare

£106,000 (2005/06)

Beneficial area UK, with some preference for Folkestone, Faversham and the surrounding area.

34 Cheriton Gardens, Folkestone, Kent CT20 2AX

Correspondent I F Cloke, Trustee

Trustees *I F Cloke, Chair; Jan Siemen Schilder; Mrs S Cloke.*

CC Number 296075

Information available Accounts were obtained from the Charity Commission website.

General The settlor of this trust died in 1995 leaving his shareholding in Howe Properties Ltd to the foundation, under the terms of his will. The trust's objectives are to provide general charitable and educational assistance as the trustees deem suitable with the knowledge of the wishes given to them by the settlor in his lifetime. The assistance is to include those in poverty and need in Folkestone and Faversham and their surrounding areas.

In 2005/06 the foundation had assets of £1.7 million and an income of £434,000. Over 100 grants were made totalling £106,000. Donations ranged from £250 to £6,000.

Beneficiaries included: Demelza House Children's Hospice, the Hospice on the Hill and the Pilgrims Hospice – Canterbury (£6,000 each); Parish Church of St Mary and St Eanswythe – Fabric Fund (£5,000); Kent Air Ambulance (£3,000); Parish of St Peter on the East

Cliff (£2,500); British Red Cross – Asian Earthquake Appeal, Holy Trinity Church and St George's Church (£2,000 each); Age Concern – Folkestone and the Folkestone Rainbow Centre (£1,500 each); and Arthritis Research Campaign, British Red Cross, Faversham Baptist Church, Lyminge Pre-School Playgroup, Park Farm Primary School, the Prostate Cancer Charity, Royal National Institute for the Blind, Sense and the Universal Beneficent Society (£1,000 each).

Applications In writing to the correspondent. Applications should be received by the end of September for consideration on a date coinciding closely with the anniversary of the death of the founder, which was 7 December.

Cuby Charitable Trust

Jewish

£182,000 (2004/05)

Beneficial area UK, overseas.

16 Mowbray Road, Edgware, Middlesex HA8 8JQ

Correspondent C B Cuby, Secretary

Trustees *S S Cuby, Chair; Mrs C B Cuby.*

CC Number 328585

Information available Accounts are on file at the Charity Commission, but without a list of grants.

General The main objectives of this charitable trust are 'providing charitable assistance in any part of the world and in particular for the advancement of Orthodox Jewish religious education'.

In 2004/05 the trust had assets of £128,000 and income of £187,000, mainly from donations. 'Payments for the purposes of charity' totalled £182,000. No list of grants was provided with the accounts to indicate the size or number of beneficiaries during the year.

Applications In writing to the correspondent.

The Cumber Family Charitable Trust

General

£45,000 (2005/06)

Beneficial area Worldwide, with a preference for the developing world and Berkshire and Oxfordshire.

Manor Farm, Marcham, Abingdon, Oxfordshire OX13 6NZ

Tel. 01865 391327

Correspondent Mrs M E Tearney, Trustee

Trustees *A R Davey; W Cumber; Mrs M J Cumber; Mrs M J Freeman; Mrs M E Tearney.*

CC Number 291009

Information available Accounts were on file at the Charity Commission.

General This trust has a preference for UK-wide needs, developing countries and local organisations in Oxfordshire and Berkshire. It favours the following causes: health, homelessness, disability, welfare, rural development, housing, overseas aid, Christian aid, agricultural development, youth and children's welfare and education. About 50% of the funding given is for work overseas.

In 2005/06 the trust had assets of £817,000, an income of £44,000 and a total of £45,000 was given in 53 grants. About 75% of grants were the result of repeat applications.

Beneficiaries included: Yatesbury Village Hall (£3,000); Hillforts of the Ridgeway and St John Ambulance – Theale (£2,500 each); Adventure Plus, Asylum Welcome, Esther Benjamin Trust, Find Your Feet, Hospice Care Kenya, the Matthew Trust, Mildmay Mission Hospital, Motor Neurone Disease Association and Prison Fellowship (£1,000 each); Books Abroad, Breast Cancer Care, Inkind Direct, Teenage Cancer Trust and Volunteer Reading Help (£500 each); and the Titus Trust (£250).

Exclusions No grants for animal welfare. Only very few to individuals with local connections and who are personally known to the trustees are supported. Local appeals outside Berkshire and Oxfordshire are not usually supported.

Applications In writing to the correspondent. The trustees usually meet twice a year.

The Dennis Curry Charitable Trust

Conservation, general

£104,000 (2004/05)
Beneficial area UK.

Messrs Alliotts, 5th Floor, 9 Kingsway, London WC2B 6XF

Tel. 020 7240 9971

Correspondent N J Armstrong, Secretary to the Trust

Trustees *M Curry; Mrs A S Curry; Mrs M Curry-Jones; Mrs P Edmond.*

CC Number 263952

Information available Accounts were on file at the Charity Commission.

General The trust has general charitable objectives with special interest in the environment and education; occasional support is given to churches and cathedrals.

In 2004/05 it had assets of £2.5 million and an income of £91,000. Grants were made to 10 organisations totalling £104,000.

Beneficiaries were Natural History Museum – Department of Palaeontology (£53,000), Durrell Wildlife Conservation Society (£14,000), Galapagos Conservation Trust and University of Oxford – Department of Zoology Wildlife Conservation Research Unit (£10,000 each), the Council for National Parks (£5,000), Oxford University Museum of Natural History (£4,000) and National Youth Wind Orchestra of Great Britain, Project Trust, Royal Botanic Gardens Kew Foundation and Satrosphere (£2,000 each).

Applications In writing to the correspondent.

The Manny Cussins Foundation

Older people, children, health, Jewish, general

£41,000 (2005/06)
Beneficial area Mainly UK, with some emphasis on Yorkshire.

c/o Ford Campbell Freedman, 34 Park Cross Street, Leeds, LS 1 2QH

Correspondent Arnold Reuben, Chair

Trustees A Reuben, Chair; A Cussins; A J Cussins; J R Cussins; Mrs A Reuben.

CC Number 219661

Information available Full accounts were on file at the Charity Commission.

General The trust's objectives are as follows:

- to support the welfare and care of older people
- welfare and care of children at risk
- health care in the Yorkshire region and abroad
- charities in Yorkshire and the former county of Humberside
- charitable need amongst Jewish communities in the UK and abroad
- and general charitable purposes.

In 2005/06 the trust had assets of over £1 million, an income of £140,000 and made grants totalling £41,000. Grants to 15 organisations totalled £41,000 with beneficiaries including: Leeds Jewish Welfare Board (£12,000); Martin House Hospice (£11,000); Angels International and Forgiveness Project (£4,000 each); Leeds International Piano Competition (£1,500); Donisthorpe Hall, United Jewish Israel Appeal and Lifeline for the Old Jerusalem (£1,000 each); Christie Hospital – Children Against Cancer and Women's International Zionist Organisation (£500 each); Wheatfields Hospice (£400); Leeds Jewish Education Authority (£200); and Hadassah Lodge (£20).

Exclusions Applications for the benefit of individuals are not supported.

Applications The correspondent states that applications are not sought as the trustees carry out their own research.

The Daily Prayer Union Charitable Trust Ltd

Evangelical Christian

£50,000 to organisations and individuals (2004/05)
Beneficial area UK.

10 Belitha Villas, London N1 1PD

Correspondent Sir Timothy Hoare, Trustee

Trustees *Revd G C Grinham; Canon J Tiller; Sir T Hoare; Mrs E Bridger; Mrs A Thompson; Mrs F M Ashton; Revd D Jackman; R M Horn; Mrs A J I Lines: Revd T J Sterry.*

CC Number 284857

Information available Accounts were on file at the Charity Commission.

General The trust supports evangelical Christian causes. Grants ranged from £1,000 to £7,000. In 2004/05 it had an income of £60,000 and made grants totalling £50,000. Grants are made to organisations and individuals.

There were 20 grants of £1,000 or more listed in the accounts. Organisations to benefit included Monkton Combe School (£7,000), Jesus Lane Trust (£2,000), UCCF (£1,200) and Martyn's Memorial Trust, St John's Winborne (£1,000 each).

There were 43 smaller grants under £1,000 each made totalling £32,000.

Exclusions No grants for bricks and mortar.

Applications The trust supports causes already known to the trustees. Unsolicited applications are unlikely to be successful. Trustees meet at different times throughout the year, usually around March, June and October.

The Daiwa Anglo–Japanese Foundation

Anglo-Japanese relations

£250,000 to organisations and individuals (2004/05)
Beneficial area UK, Japan.

Daiwa Foundation, Japan House, 13/14 Cornwall Terrace, London NW1 4QP

Tel. 020 7486 4348 **Fax** 020 7486 2914

Email office@dajf.org.uk

Website www.dajf.org.uk

Correspondent Prof. Marie Conte-Helm, Director General

Trustees *Nicholas Clegg, Chair; Masahiro Dozen; Lasy Adrian; Lord Broers; Lord Carrington; Hiroaki Fujii; John Gurdon; Yoshinari Hara; John Whitehead.*

CC Number 299955

Information available Accounts were on file at the Charity Commission; detailed website.

General The Daiwa Anglo-Japanese Foundation is a UK charity, established in 1988 with a benefaction from Daiwa Securities Co. Ltd. The foundation's purpose is to support closer links between Britain and Japan. It does this by:

- making grants available to individuals, institutions and organisations to promote links between the UK and Japan in all fields of activity
- enabling British and Japanese students and academics to further their education through exchanges and other bilateral initiatives
- awarding of Daiwa Scholarships for British graduates to study and undertake work placements in Japan
- organising a year-round programme of events to increase understanding of Japan in the UK.

In 2004/05 the trust had assets of £35 million and an income of £1.5 million. Charitable expenditure totalled £1.2 million, including £250,000 given in grants.

In 2003 the foundation introduced its restructured grants policy to bring a greater focus to its funding activities and to give encouragement to collaborations between British and Japanese partners.

The policy has been extended into 2006–07, with increased funding being made available for both Daiwa Foundation Small Grants and Daiwa Foundation Awards. In addition, funding bands and eligibility requirements have been adjusted to allow greater flexibility.

Grant-giving in 2006–07 will be carried out via the following programmes:

Daiwa Foundation Small Grants
'Daiwa Foundation Small Grants are available from £1,000–£5,000 to individuals, societies, associations or other bodies in the UK or Japan to promote and support interaction between the two countries. They can cover all fields of activity, including educational and grassroots exchanges, research travel, the organisation of conferences, exhibitions, and other projects and events that fulfil this broad objective. New initiatives are especially encouraged.'

Daiwa Foundation Awards
'Daiwa Foundation Awards are available from £5,000–£15,000 for collaborative projects that enable British and Japanese partners to work together, preferably within the context of an institutional relationship. Projects in all academic, professional, cultural and educational fields are eligible.'

Adrian Prizes
'Every three years, the foundation makes prizes available in recognition of significant scientific collaboration between Japanese and British research teams.'

Special projects
'The foundation wishes to be receptive to new initiatives and therefore endeavours to respond flexibly to proposals that meet its general objectives but may fall outside of the criteria for our Small Grants and Awards programmes. We hope to accommodate 2 or 3 significant projects per annum which require funding for a specified period.'

Applications Application forms are available online at www.dajf.org.uk.

Applications originating from the UK should be sent to the address listed here. Applications originating from Japan should be sent to The Daiwa Anglo-Japanese Foundation, TBR Bldg. 810, Nagat-cho2–10–2, Chiyoda-ku, Tokyo 100–0014.

Oizer Dalim Trust

General

£124,000 (2005/06)
Beneficial area UK.

68 Osbaldeston Road, London N16 7DR
Correspondent M Cik, Trustee
Trustees B Berger; M Freund; M Cik.
CC Number 1045296
Information available Accounts were on file at the Charity Commission, but without a list of grants.

General The trust has previously supported a wide range of charities throughout the UK, but without having been able to see a recent grants list we are unable to confirm this is still true.

In 2005/06 the trust had assets of £33,000, an income of £137,000 and made grants totalling £124,000. A list of grant beneficiaries was not available.

Applications In writing to the correspondent.

Davidson Charitable Trust

Jewish

£225,000 (2004/05)
Beneficial area UK.

58 Queen Anne Street, London W1G 8HW
Tel. 020 7224 1030
Correspondent Mrs E Winer, Trustee
Trustees G A Davidson; M Y Davidson; Mrs E Winer.
CC Number 262937
Information available Accounts were on file at the Charity Commission, without a list of grants.

General In 2004/05 this Jewish charity had an income, mainly from donations of £225,000. After very low adminstration costs of just £294, grants totalled £225,000, although a grants list was not included in the trust's annual report for that year.

Previous beneficiaries include British Friends of CBI, Imperial War Museum's Holocaust Project, Joint Jewish Charitable Trust, Norwood Ravenswood, and World Jewish Relief.

Applications In writing to the correspondent.

The Alderman Joe Davidson Memorial Trust

Jewish, general

£32,000 to organisations (2004/05)

Beneficial area UK, with a preference for Hampshire.

Chief Executive's Office, Civic Offices, Portsmouth PO1 2AL
Tel. 023 9283 4060 **Fax** 023 9283 4076
Email saskia.kiernan@portsmouthcc.gov.uk
Correspondent Saskia Kiernan, Secretary to the Trustees
Trustees Ald. Mrs M B E Leonard; C Davidson; P Gooch; Miss M A Ashton; K J Veness; J Klein; K Crabbe; M Thomas.
CC Number 202591

Information available Full accounts were available from the Charity Commission website.

General The trust was established in 1958 for 'dwellings for persons over 70 years of age in necessitous circumstances preferably resident in Portsmouth for more than 25 years'. Grants are also given to local and national charities that are named in the trust deed, deserving poor people (ten of whom should be Jewish) and for the provision of Christmas parties. The trust also presents watches to school children for regular attendance. Grants to organisations which are not named in the trust deed are limited.

In 2004/05 the trust had an income of £38,000 with assets standing at £607,000. Twenty-eight grants were made to organisations totalling £32,000 and were listed in two schedules.

Schedule 1
Grants were made to 15 organisations including Dr Barnardo's Homes, Hampshire County Council – Children's Cottage Homes, Portsmouth Council of Community Service, Portsmouth Association for the Blind and Portsmouth Voluntary Care Committee for Tuberculosis and Lung Diseases (£2,000 each), and Portsea Methodist Mission, Sussex Unity Lodge 4150 and the Tibet Relief Fund for the United Kingdom (£500 each).

Schedule 2
Portsmouth and Southsea Hebrew Congregation – Jewish Educational Committee (£8,000), Jewish Blind Society, Jewish Home and Hospital at Tottenham, Nightingale House-Home for Aged Jews and Norwood Home for Jewish Children (£1,000 each) and the British Technion Society, JNF Charitable Trust and Portsmouth Jewish Ladies Benevolent Society (£270 each).

Applications The trustees are only permitted to make grants to individuals or organisations that are specified in the Trust Deed.

Michael Davies Charitable Settlement

General

£78,000 to organisations (2005)
Beneficial area UK.

Lee Associates, 5 Southampton Place, London WC1A 2DA
Tel. 0207 025 4600
Correspondent K Hawkins, Administrator
Trustees *M J P Davies; G H Camamile.*
CC Number 1000574
Information available Full accounts were available from the Charity Commission.

General In 2004 the settlement had assets of £479,000 and an income of £90,000. Grants were made to 20 organisations totalling £78,000.

Recipients of grants included the following organisations Camp and Trek, the Jubilee Sailing Trust, the Royal Society of Arts and the Bright Red Dot Foundation (£10,000 each), Depford X, the Mount Everest Foundation and St Christopher's School (£5,000 each), Peter Rice Scholarship Fund – Havard University (£3,000), Trees for London (£1,500) and the Unicorn Children's Centre and the Woodside Retreat (£1,000 each).

Applications In writing to the correspondent.

The Wilfrid Bruce Davis Charitable Trust

Health

£132,000 (2005/06)
Beneficial area UK, but mainly Cornwall; India.

La Feock Grange, Feock, Truro, Cornwall TR3 6RG
Correspondent W B Davis, Trustee
Trustees *W B Davis; Mrs D F Davis; Mrs D S Dickens; Mrs C A S Pierce.*
CC Number 265421
Information available Accounts were on file at the Charity Commission.

General The trust was set up in 1967, the objectives being 'such charities as the settlor in his lifetime and the trustees after his death shall determine'. The trust presently concentrates on 'improving the quality of life for those who are physically disadvantaged and their carers'. The geographical area covered is almost exclusively Cornwall, however the main thrust of the trust's activities is now focused on India.

The trust is fully committed to its current beneficiaries.

In 2005/06 the trust had assets of £415,000 and an income of £81,000. Grants totalled £132,000.

Beneficiaries included: Pallium India (£35,000); Pain and Palliative Care Society Calicut (£31,000); Royal Cornwall Hospital's Trust (£20,000); Guwahati Pain Clinic (£11,000); Lieutenancy Trust Fund for Youth in Cornwall (£5,000); Christian Medical Association, Vellore (£2,500); Pathway (£2,000); Cornwall Macmillan Service (£1,600); Shelterbox Trust (£1,500); Prostate Cancer (£1,000); the British Kidney Patient Association and Jubilee Sailing Trust (£500 each); and the Jennifer Trust (£250).

Exclusions No applications from individuals are considered.

Applications No replies are made to unsolicited applications. The correspondent has stated that the budget for many years to come is fully committed and that the trust receives hundreds of applications, none of which can be supported.

The Helen and Geoffrey de Freitas Charitable Trust

Preservation of wildlife and rural England, conservation and environment, cultural heritage

Around £30,000 (2004/05)
Beneficial area UK.

c/o Speechly Bircham, 6–16 St Andrew Street, London EC4A 3LX
Tel. 020 7427 6400
Correspondent Richard Kirby, Trustee
Trustees *R C Kirby; Frances de Freitas; Roger de Freitas.*
CC Number 258597
Information available Information was obtained from the Charity Commission website.

General Most of the trust's income is designated for the conservation of countryside and environment in rural Britain, for the preservation of Britain's cultural heritage and for the assistance of disadvantaged people through community facilities and services, advice centres, community arts and recreation. Grants are usually one-off for feasibility studies, project and start-up costs and range from £500 to £5,000 each.

In 2004/05 the trust had an income of £22,000 and a total expenditure of £30,000. Further information was not available.

Previous beneficiaries have included the Rambler's Association for a social inclusion programme (£3,000), Gloucestershire Wildlife Trust towards acquiring a farm for wildlife conservation and Skippo Arts Team for creative visual arts work with community groups (£2,500 each), Friends of St Peter's – Sibton towards the creation of community facilities within the parish church (£2,000), Hanworth Park Preservation Trust for railing to protect the play area which is in a conservation area (£1,000) and Brighton Unemployed Workers Project for outings for the children of refugees (£500).

Exclusions No grants to non-registered charities, individuals, or to charities on behalf of individuals. Definitely no support for charities concerned with medical or health matters, or with physical, mental or sensory impairments.

Applications In writing to the correspondent. No application form or guidelines are available. No sae required. All applications are acknowledged by postcard. Trustees meet four times a year. Unsuccessful applicants are not notified.

The de Laszlo Foundation

The arts, general

£208,000 (2004/05)
Beneficial area UK and worldwide.

5 Albany Courtyard, London W1J 0HF
Correspondent Christabel Wood
Trustees *Damon P de Laszlo; Hon. Mrs Sandra de Laszlo; Lucy D de Laszlo; David C Dietz; Andrew Wilton.*
CC Number 327383

Information available Accounts were on file at the Charity Commission.

General Registered with the Charity Commission in March 1987, the foundation has the following objectives:

1 The advancement and promotion of education and interest in the visual arts with special reference to encouraging a knowledge of the works of contemporary painters, in particular those of the late Philip de Laszlo.
2 To encourage research into the restoration of works of art and their preservation and the location of suitable venues for them.
3 To acquire and maintain a collection of the works of art of the late Philip de Laszlo and of appropriate works of art of the same or any other period.
4 To advance education and research generally in the areas for arts science economics and medicine.
5 To encourage the study reproduction and cataloguing of works of art and the publication of books and literature in connection therewith.
6 To promote the founding of scholarships and prizes related to the above.

In 2004/05 it had assets of £2.4 million, an income of £286,000 and made grants totalling £208,000.

It is increasingly the policy of the trustees to make a small number of targeted large grants.

There were 24 grants of £1,000 or more listed in the accounts. Beneficiaries included: De Laszlo Archive Trust (£71,000); Foundation for Liver Research (£16,000); City and Guilds of London Art School – artists (£13,000) and prizes (£2,000); National Hospital Development Foundation – Multiple Sclerosis Society (£15,000); Durham University and Southampton University (£10,000 each); Royal Society of Portrait Painters (£6,800); Treloar Trust (£5,800); GAP – bursary fund and Royal Academy Trust (£5,000 each); Christchurch Primary School (£2,500); Bishop of Gibraltar Fund (£2,000); and Royal National Theatre, National Portrait Gallery and Save the Children Fund (£1,000 each).

Applications Grants tend to be made by personal recommendation. Unsolicited applications are unlikely to be successful.

The Leopold De Rothschild Charitable Trust

Arts, Jewish, general

£101,000 (2003/04)
Beneficial area UK.

Rothschild Trust Corporation Ltd, New Court, St Swithin's Lane, London EC4P 4DU
Correspondent Miss Norma Watson
Trustee *Rothschild Trust Corporation Ltd.*
CC Number 212611

Information available Accounts were on file at the Charity Commission.

General The trust gives most of its support to the arts and has some preference for Jewish organisations, with limited support to other causes covering heritage, welfare, medical and children.

In 2003/04 this trust had assets of just over £1 million and an income of £74,000. Grants totalled £101,000.

Two donations were made from capital, going to National Railway Museum (£25,000) and Exbury Gardens Limited (£20,000).

A further 88 were made from income. Beneficiaries of grants of £1,000 or more were Exbury Gardens Limited (£11,000), National Gallery and Royal National Theatre (£5,000 each), London Symphony Orchestra (£2,900), Liberal Jewish Synagogue (£2,600), Liberal Jewish Synagogue (£2,000) and English Chamber Orchestra and Genius of the Violin (£1,000 each).

Applications In writing to the correspondent.

William Dean Countryside and Educational Trust

Education in natural history, ecology and conservation

£44,000 (2005)

Beneficial area Principally Cheshire; also Derbyshire, Lancashire, Staffordshire and the Wirral.

St Mary's Cottage, School Lane, Astbury, Congleton, Cheshire CW12 4RG

Tel. 01260 290194

Email bellstmarys@hotmail.com

Correspondent Mrs Brenda Bell

Trustees *David Daniel, Chair; William Crawford; John Ward; David Crawford; Margaret Williamson.*

CC Number 1044567

Information available Information was provided by the trust.

General This trust gives grants towards enterprises in its immediate locality which promote education in natural history, ecology and the conservation of the natural environment.

In 2005 it had assets of £1.2 million, an income of £50,000 and made grants totalling £44,000.

There were 15 grants of £1,000 or more, including: £15,000 to Cheshire Wildlife Trust; £2,000 each to Derbyshire Wildlife Trust, Friends of Bridgnorth School, Groundwork Trust, North of England Zoological Society and the Woodland Trust; £1,200 in two grants to Bowland Pennine Mountain Rescue; and £1,000 each to the Albrighton Trust, Astbury Mere Trust, Congleton Museum Trust, the Countryside Foundation for Education Friends of Comberbach School and HDRA Conservation.

Other beneficiaries included Beeston Outdoor Education Centre, Blaen Wern Farm Trust, Buglife, Cheshire and Shropshire Wildlife Trust, the Children's Adventure Farm Trust, Mersey Basin Trust, Quinta School, Sandbach School, Shropshire Barn Owls, South Cheshire Barn Owl Group, St James Church and Weaver School Parents Association.

Exclusions The trust stated that education is not funded, unless directly associated with one of the eligible categories.

Applications In writing to the correspondent.

The Delius Trust

See below

£25,000 (2005)

Beneficial area UK and overseas.

16 Ogle Street, London W1P 6JA

Tel. 020 7436 4816 **Fax** 020 7637 4307

Email DeliusTrust@mbf.org.uk

Website www.delius.org.uk

Correspondent Marjorie Dickinson, Secretary to the Trust

Trustees *Musicians' Benevolent Fund (Representative: William Parker); David Lloyd-Jones; Martin Williams.*

CC Number 207324

Information available Accounts were on file at the Charity Commission.

General 'The trust promotes the music of Frederick Delius and of British composers born since 1860, by giving help towards the cost of performances, publications and recordings. In addition, assistance is occasionally offered to organisations and institutions active in this field. Priority is always given to the promotion of the works of Delius, especially those that are rarely performed.'

In 2005 the trust had an income of £133,000 and made grants totalling £25,000. Assets stood at £2.3 million.

Applications In writing for consideration by the trustees and the advisers. See the trust's website for further details.

The Dellal Foundation

General, Jewish

£300,000 (2005/06)

Beneficial area UK.

25 Harley Street, London W1G 9BR

Correspondent S Hosier, Administrator

Trustees *J Dellal; E Azouz; J Azouz; G Dellal.*

CC Number 265506

Information available Accounts were on file at the Charity Commission.

General The trust states that it continues to give 'a significant proportion of the grants towards charities whose aim is the welfare and benefit of Jewish people'.

In 2005/06 the trust had assets of £1.1 million and an income of £55,000. A total of £300,000 was given in grants.

Exclusions No grants to individuals.

Applications In writing to the correspondent.

The Delves Charitable Trust

Environment, conservation, medical, general

£164,000 (2004/05)

Beneficial area UK.

New Guild House, 45 Great Charles Street, Queensway, Birmingham B3 2LX

Tel. 0121 212 2222 **Fax** 0121 212 2300

Correspondent Roger Harriman, Trust Administrator

Trustees *Mary Breeze; John Breeze; George Breeze; Dr Charles Breeze; Elizabeth Breeze; Roger Harriman.*

CC Number 231860

Information available Accounts were on file at the Charity Commission.

General This trust has a list of 32 organisations that receive an annual subscription from the trust, and also provides a small number of grants to other organisations.

In 2004/05 the trust had assets of £5.4 million, which generated an income of £187,000. After management and administration costs of £23,000, grants totalled £164,000. These were broken down into 'subscriptions' (£144,000) and 'donations' (£20,000).

Beneficiaries of 'subscriptions' included British Heart Foundation (£25,000), Médecins Sans Frontières (£11,000), Sequal and Wateraid (£10,000 each), Survival International (£7,500), National Society for Cancer Relief – Macmillan Nurses and Quaker Peace and Social Witness (£6,500 each), Fairbridge (£6,000) and Action Medical Research and Liverpool School of Tropical Medicine (£5,500 each).

Those in receipt of smaller 'donations' included Médecins Sans Frontières –

Darfur Sudan (£5,000), Selly Oak Nursery School (£2,000), Centrepoint (£1,500), Big Issue Foundation (£750), Hospice in the Weald, Tree Aid and VSO – Malawi (£500 each) and Greenpeace Environmental Trust (£250).

Exclusions The trust does not give sponsorships or personal educational grants.

Applications 'The funds of the trust are currently fully committed and no unsolicited requests can therefore be considered by the trustees.'

The Demigryphon Trust

Medical, education, children, general

£44,000 (2005/06)
Beneficial area UK, with a preference for Scotland.

Pollen House, 10–12 Cork Street, London W1S 3LW
Correspondent The Secretary
Trustee *The Cowdray Trust Ltd.*
CC Number 275821
Information available Accounts were on file at the Charity Commission.

General The trust supports a wide range of organisations and appears to have a preference for education, medical, children and Scottish organisations.

In 2005/06 the trust had assets of £2.7 million and an income of £48,000. Grants were made to 14 organisations totalling £44,000.

There was one major beneficiary during the year, the Third Viscount Cowdray's Charity Trust, which received £34,000 (£50,000 in the previous year).

Other beneficiaries were: the Game Conservancy Trust (£5,000); Army Air Corps Fund, and Rhino Rescue Trust (£1,000 each); Echt, Skene and Midmar Agricultural Association (£300); Dunecht School PTA (£250); Strathdee Music Club and Wheel Power (£200); Royal Northern Countryside Initiative and Royal Scottish Agricultural Benevolent Institution (£500 each); and Breast Cancer Haven, and Cancer Research UK (£100 each).

A further £30,000 was distributed in 31 pensions.

Exclusions No grants to individuals; only registered charities are supported.

Applications In writing to the correspondent, including an sae. No application forms or guidelines are issued and there is no deadline. Only successful applications are acknowledged.

The Richard Desmond Charitable Trust

General

£333,000 (2004)
Beneficial area Worldwide.

The Northern and Shell Building, No. 10 Lower Thames Street, London EC3R 6EN
Correspondent Miss Charlie Slade
Trustees *R C Desmond; Mrs J Desmond.*
CC Number 1014352
Information available Accounts were on file at the Charity Commission.

General The trust gives one-off and recurrent grants for core, capital and project funding for general charitable purposes, especially for the relief of poverty and sickness amongst children.

In 2004 the trust had an income from donations of £337,000 and made 129 grants totalling £333,000.

Donations to 35 organisations were listed in the accounts. Beneficiaries of the largest amounts, over £10,000 each, were: Jewish Care (£52,000), the Disability Foundation (£50,000 in five grants), Fight for Sight (£50,000), the Variety Club Children's Charity (£24,000 in three grants), Community Security Trust and Wellbeing Trust (£15,000 each), Norwood Ravenswood (£14,000 in three grants) and the Hold My Hand Appeal Fund, Rays of Sunshine and World Jewish Relief (£10,000 each).

Other beneficiaries were Teenage Cancer Trust (£6,000), Jewish Blind & Physically Handicapped Society Ltd (£5,200), British ORT (£5,000), the Caron Keating Foundation (£4,000), Cystic Fibrosis Trust and World Jewish Affairs Funds (£3,000 each), SCOPE (£2,000), Cancer Research UK (£1,600), the Ireland Fund of Great Britain and Walk the Walk

Worldwide (£1,500 each), and Al Fayed Charitable Foundation, Kids Care London, Leukaemia Research Fund and Sargent Cancer Care for Children (£1,000 each).

A further 129 grants of less than £1,000 each totalled £52,000.

Applications In writing to the correspondent.

The Duke of Devonshire's Charitable Trust

General

£239,000 (2004/05)
Beneficial area UK, with a preference for Derbyshire.

Currey and Co., 21 Buckingham Gate, London SW1E 6LS
Tel. 020 7802 2700 **Fax** 020 7828 5049
Correspondent The Trustee Manager
Trustees *Marquess of Hartington; Sir Richard Beckett; Nicholas W Smith.*
CC Number 213519
Information available Accounts were on file at the Charity Commission.

General This trust has general charitable purposes giving grants ranging from £50 to £100,000 to a wide range of organisations, with a preference for those working in Derbyshire.

In 2004/05 the trust had assets of £8.8 million, which generated an income of £285,000. Grants were made to 102 organisations totalling £239,000. Management and administration expenditure was high at £31,000.

There were 45 grants of £1,000 or more listed in the accounts. By far the largest grant went to St George's Chapel Windsor (£100,000).

Other grants of £5,000 or more went to: Contact the Elderly (£11,000); NSPCC (£10,000); Countryside Foundation for Education (£9,000); Bolton Abbey PCC (£7,000); Bolton Abbey Village Hall (£5,800); Calow C of E VC Primary School (£5,700); and Abbeyfield Society Eastbourne and Queen Alexandra Cottage Homes (£5,000 each).

Other beneficiaries included: Edensor PCC (£4,000); Bakewell Church of England Infant School (£3,500); Ashgate Hospice, Doveridge Village Hall

Committee, Mary Hare Foundation and Silver Trust (£2,500 each); Nottingham Community Housing Association (£1,500); Christian Lewis Trust Children's Cancer Charity (£1,100); and British Heart Foundation, Hospital Heartbeat Appeal Fund, Martin House Children's Hospice and REACT (£1,000 each).

Grants of less than £1,000 each totalled £23,000.

Exclusions Grants are only given to registered charities and not to individuals.

Applications In writing to the correspondent.

The Sandy Dewhirst Charitable Trust

General

£46,000 (2003/04)

Beneficial area UK, with a strong preference for East and North Yorkshire.

Addleshaw Goddard, Sovereign House, PO Box 8, Sovereign Street, Leeds LS1 1HQ

Correspondent Ms Liz Jones, Trustees' Solicitor

Trustees T C Dewhirst; P J Howell; J A R Dewhirst.

CC Number 279161

Information available Accounts were obtained from the Charity Commission website.

General The trust was established in 1979, firstly for the welfare of people connected through employment with I J Dewhirst Holdings Ltd or the settlor of the trust and secondly for general charitable purposes, with a strong preference for East and North Yorkshire.

In 2003/04 the trust had assets of £1.7 million and an income of £56,000. Grants totalled £46,000 with £7,000 of this distributed in three grants to individuals.

Local grants
Beneficiaries included: York Minster Funds (£5,000); Project Newland – Hull (£2,500); Driffield Parochial Church Council (£2,000); Nafferton Parocial Church Council (£1,500); Driffield Rotary Club and St Catherine's Hospice

(£1,000 each); and All Saints Church – Kilham and Driffield Agricultural Society (£500 each).

National grants
Beneficiaries included: Sailors' Families' Society and St John the Baptist Church (£2,500 each); British Red Cross, Friends of Chernobyl, Sight Savers International, World Cancer Research Fund and YMCA (£1,000 each); Macmillan Cancer Relief (£500); and Starlight Children's Foundation (£250).

Applications In writing to the correspondent. The trust does not accept unsolicited applications.

DG Charitable Trust

General

£461,000 (2004/05)

Beneficial area UK.

PO Box 62, Heathfield, East Sussex TN21 8ZE

Correspondent Joanna Nelson

Trustees D J Gilmour; P Grafton-Green; Ms P A Samson.

CC Number 1040778

Information available Accounts are on file at the Charity Commission.

General This trust makes regular donations to a fixed list of charities. In 2004/05 the trust had assets of £443,000 and an income of £655,000. Grants totalled £461,000 with all beneficiaries except one, also receiving support in the previous year.

The largest grant was £200,000 to Oxfam. Other beneficiaries were Crisis (£50,000), Amnesty International, Environmental Investigation Agency Charitable Trust, Great Ormond Street Hospital, Medical Foundation for Victims of Torture and Shelter (£25,000 each), Age Concern and Greenpeace (£20,000 each), IPPF Europe (£15,000), Cancer Research UK and St Richard's Hospital Charitable Trust (£10,000 each), Prisoners of Conscience Appeal Fund (£5,000), Prisoners Abroad (£2,500), Terrence Higgins Trust (£2,000), Battersea Home for Dogs (£1,000) and Scope (£500).

Applications This trust does not consider unsolicited applications.

The Laduma Dhamecha Charitable Trust

General

£312,000 (2004/05)

Beneficial area UK and overseas.

Dhamecha Foods Ltd, Wembley Stadium Industrial Estate, First Way, Wembley, Middlesex HA9 0TU

Tel. 020 8903 8181

Correspondent Pradip Dhamecha, Trustee

Trustees K R Dhamecha; S R Dhamecha; P K Dhamecha.

CC Number 328678

Information available Accounts were on file at the Charity Commission, without a list of grants.

General The trust supports a wide range of organisations in the UK and overseas. The aims of the trust are listed in the annual report as being:

- to provide relief of sickness by the provision of medical equipment and the establishing or improvement of facilities at hospitals
- to provide an educational establishment in rural areas to make children self-sufficient in the long term
- other general charitable purposes.

In 2002/03 the trust had assets of £1.2 million and an income of £249,000, including £200,000 from donations. Grants totalled £312,000. No information was available on the size or number of beneficiaries during this year.

Applications In writing to the correspondent.

Alan and Sheila Diamond Charitable Trust

Jewish, general

£40,000 (2004/05)

Beneficial area UK.

Regency House, 3 Grosvenor Square, Southampton S015 2BE

Correspondent The Trustees

Trustees *A Diamond, Chair; Mrs S Diamond; P Rodney; Ms K Goldberg.*

CC Number 274312

Information available Accounts were on file at the Charity Commission but without a description of the trust's policy.

General About two-thirds of the trust's grant-making is to Jewish organisations. The trust supports the same organisations each year which are listed in its trust deed, and cannot consider other applications.

In 2005/06 the trust had assets of £1.3 million, an income of £48,000 and made grants totalling £40,000.

Regular beneficiaries include Community Centre in Israel Project, Youth Aliyah, Girton College – Cambridge, British School of Osteopathy, Anglo Israel Association, Jewish Care, Norwood, Community Security Trust and Holocaust Educational Trust.

Exclusions No grants to individuals.

Applications The trust states that it will not consider unsolicited applications. No preliminary telephone calls. There are no regular trustees' meetings. The trustees frequently decide how the funds should be allocated. The trustees have their own guidelines, which are not published.

The Dickon Trust

General

£35,000 (2005/06)

Beneficial area North East England and Scotland.

Dickinson Dees, St Anne's Wharf, 112 Quayside, Newcastle NE99 1SB

Tel. 0191 279 9698

Correspondent Helen Tavroges

Trustees *Mrs D L Barrett; Major-General R V Brims; R Y Barrett; M L Robson.*

CC Number 327202

Information available Accounts were on file at the Charity Commission.

General The trust has general charitable purposes, giving grants, as the trustees in their absolute discretion determine, to local groups in north east England (from the Tees in the south to Cumbria in the west) and Scotland. The

trustees in particular favour charities that are beneficial to children.

In 2005/06 the trust had assets of £1.4 million and an income of £50,000. Grants to 34 organisations totalled £35,000.

All grants but three were for £1,000 each. Beneficiaries included: Farm Crisis Network and Great North Air Ambulance (2,000 each); Alexandra Rose Day, British Red Cross – Northumbria Branch, Defeating Deafness, Families in Care, Horden Youth and Community Centre, Newcastle upon Tyne YMCA, Rainbow Trust Children's Charity Appeal, Rehab UK, RUKBA and Sense Scotland (£1,000 each); and Lothian Autistic Society (£500).

Exclusions No support for individuals, unregistered charities or churches.

Applications In writing to the correspondent.

The Dinwoodie Settlement

Postgraduate medical education and research

£247,000 (2005/06)

Beneficial area UK.

c/o Thomas Eggar, The Corn Exchange, Baffins Lane, Chichester, West Sussex PO19 1GK

Correspondent The Clerk to the Trustees

Trustees *William A Fairbairn; Dr John M Fowler; Miss Christian Webster; Rodney B N Fisher; John A Gibson.*

CC Number 255495

Information available Accounts were on file at the Charity Commission.

General 'The trustees endeavour to be proactive in pursuing the objectives of the Charity by supporting eligible projects in the field of postgraduate medical education and research in England.'

The maximum grant towards a Postgraduate Medical Centres (PMCs) project in any one area is normally £1 million. Medical research is for no more than the salary of two research workers in any one year.

In 2005/06 the trust had assets of £3.3 million and an income of £356,000. Charitable expenditure totalled £247,000.

Exclusions Anything falling outside the main areas of work referred to above. The trustees do not expect to fund consumable or equipment costs or relieve the NHS of its financial responsibilities.

Applications In writing to the correspondent. The trustees state they are proactive rather than reactive in their grant-giving. Negotiating for new PMCs and monitoring their construction invariably takes a number of years. The trust's funds can be committed for three years when supporting major projects. The accounts contain detailed reports on the development of centres under consideration.

Dischma Charitable Trust

General

£133,000 (2004/05)

Beneficial area Worldwide.

Rathbone Trust Company Ltd, c/o 159 New Bond Street, London W15 2UD

Tel. 020 7399 0820

Correspondent The Secretary

Trustees *Simon Manwaring Robertson; Edward Manwaring Robertson; Lorna Manwaring Robertson; Virginia Stewart Robertson; Selina Manwaring Robertson; Arabella Brooke.*

CC Number 1077501

Information available Accounts were on file at the Charity Commission.

General Registered with the Charity Commission in September 1999, in 2004/05 the trust had assets of £5 million and an income of £60,000. Grants to 50 organisations totalled £133,000.

Beneficiaries included: Treloar's (£8,000); Allavida, Family Friends, Multiple Sclerosis Society, World Society for the Protection of Animals, WWF – Mountain Gorilla's Project and Youth Culture Television (£5,000 each); Alton College (£4,000); National Library for the Blind and Sign (£3,500 each); Counsel and Care, Wild Things (£3,000 each); 3H Fund, British Association for Adoption and Fostering, Prisoner Conscience Appeal, Soundabout, the Cathja Project (£2,000 each); the Feminist Library, The Albert Kennedy Trust and St Martin's Christmas Appeal (£1,000 each); Independent Age (£500);

and the Julian Baring Scholarship and YJS Charitable Trust (£200 each).

Applications The trustees meet half-yearly to review applications for funding. Only successful applicants are notified of the trustees' decision. Certain charities are supported annually, although no commitment is given.

The DLA Piper Rudnick Gray Cary Charitable Trust (previously known as the DLA Charitable Trust)

General

£48,000 (2004/05)
Beneficial area UK.

Fountain Precinct, Balm Green, Sheffield S1 1RZ

Tel. 0114 267 5594

Email godfrey.smallman@wrigleys.co.uk

Correspondent G J Smallman, Secretary

Trustees *N G Knowles; P Rooney.*

CC Number 327280

Information available Accounts were on file at the Charity Commission.

General In 2004/05 this trust had an income of £76,000 and gave 88 grants totalling £48,000.

There were 10 grants made of £1,000 or more. Beneficiaries were Cayman Islands Hurricane Relief Appeal (£10,000), DEC Tsunami Earthquake Appeal (£5,000), Solicitors' Benevolent Association (£3,000), British Red Cross, Maggie's Centre, Manchester Children's Hospital and Sheffield Children's Hospital Charity (£2,500 each) and British Heart Foundation, the Industrial Trust and Sheffield Cathedral Chapter (£1,000 each).

Other donations of less than £1,000 each totalled £17,000.

Exclusions No grants to individuals.

Applications In writing to the correspondent, for consideration every three months.

The DLM Charitable Trust

General

£93,000 (2005/06)
Beneficial area UK, especially the Oxford area.

Messrs Cloke and Co., Warnford Court, Throgmorton Street, London EC2N 2AT

Tel. 020 7638 8992 **Fax** 020 7256 7892

Correspondent J A Cloke, Trustee

Trustees *Dr E A de la Mare; Mrs P Sawyer; J A Cloke; Miss J E Sawyer.*

CC Number 328520

Information available Accounts were available from the Charity Commission.

General The trust was established in 1990, after R D A de la Mare left 25% of the residue of his estate for charitable purposes. It supports charities that were supported by the settlor and local Oxford organisations 'where normal fundraising methods may not be successful'.

In 2005/06 the trust had assets of £4.8 million and an income of £136,000. The sum of £93,000 was distributed to 20 organisations.

Beneficiaries included: the Ley Community (£21,000); the Art Room, St Mary's Kidlington, See Saw and Wildlife Conservation Research Unit (£10,000 each); Driving for the Disabled Shifford Branch, National Listening Library, Nightingales Children's Project and Pathway Workshop (£5,000 each); British Red Cross and TRAX (£2,000 each); and Action for Blind People and Christians Against Poverty (£1,000 each).

Exclusions No grants to individuals.

Applications In writing to the correspondent. Trustees meet in February, July and November to consider applications.

The Dorcas Trust

Christian, general

£146,000 (2005/06)
Beneficial area UK.

Port of Liverpool Building, Pier Head, Liverpool L3 1NW

Tel. 0151 236 6666

Correspondent I Taylor

Trustees *J C L Broad; J D Broad; P L Butler.*

CC Number 275494

Information available Accounts were on file at the Charity Commission.

General The trust has a preference for Christian causes, although other charities have also been supported.

In 2005/06 the trust had assets of £1.1 million and an income of £34,000. Grants were made totalling £146,000 (£48,000 in 2004/05).

By far the largest grant went to Dorcas Developments Limited (£103,000). Other beneficiaries included Navigators (£15,000), Newmarket Day Centre (£14,000), World Vision (£5,000), Mildmay Mission (£3,000), Integra (£2,000), Shaftesbury Society and Moorlands Bible College (£1,000 each), Send a Cow (£500) Chernobyl Children's Lifeline (£100) and RNIB (£50).

Applications In writing to the correspondent, although the trust stated that applications cannot be considered as funds are already committed.

The Dorema Charitable Trust

Medicine, health, welfare, education, religion

£28,000 (2005)
Beneficial area UK.

4 Church Grove, Amersham, Buckinghamshire HP6 6SH

Correspondent D S M Nussbaum, Trustee

Trustees *D S M Nussbaum; Mrs K M Nussbaum; S Murray-Williams.*

CC Number 287001

Information available Information was available from the Charity Commission.

General This trust supports medicine, health, welfare, education and religion.

In 2005 the trust had an income of £9,000 and a total expenditure of £26,000. Grants totalled about £28,000. No further information was available.

Applications The trust strongly stated that unsolicited applications are not considered, describing such appeals as a waste of charitable resources.

The Dorus Trust

Health and welfare, disability, homelessness, addiction, children who are disadvantaged, environment

£50,000 (2005)

Beneficial area Mainly UK.

c/o Charities Aid Foundation, Kings Hill, West Malling, Kent ME19 4TA

Correspondent C H Peacock, Trustee

Trustees *C H Peacock; Mrs B Bond; A M Bond.*

CC Number 328724

Information available Full accounts were provided by the trust.

General The trust has common trustees with two other trusts, the Cleopatra Trust and the Epigoni Trust (see separate entries) with which it also shares the same aims and polices. All three trusts are administered by Charities Aid Foundation. Generally the trusts support different organisations each year.

The trust makes grants in the following areas:

- mental health
- cancer welfare/education – not research
- diabetes
- physical disability – not research
- homelessness
- addiction
- children who are disadvantaged.

There is also some preference for environmental causes. It only gives grants for specific projects and does not give grants for running costs or general appeals. Support is only given to national organisations, not local areas or initiatives.

In 2005 it had assets of £3.1 million, which generated an income of £129,000. Grants were made to 10 organisations totalling £50,000.

Beneficiaries were: British Association for Adoption and Fostering and National Council on Ageing (£10,000 each); Rehabilitation for Addicted Prisoners Trust (£5,800); Motor Neurone Disease (£5,400); Cardinal Hume Centre (£4,600); Camp and Trek and MDF the Bipolar Organisation (£5,000 each); Happy Days Children's Charity (£2,900); Disasters Emergency Committee (£2,500); and Rural Stress Information Network (£1,000).

Exclusions No grants to individuals, expeditions, research, scholarships, charities with a local focus, local branches of UK charities or towards running costs.

Applications On a 'funding proposal form' available from the correspondent. Applications should include a copy of the latest audited annual report and accounts. They are considered twice a year in mid-summer and mid-winter. Organisations which have received grants from this trust, the Cleopatra Trust or the Epigoni Trust should not reapply in the following two years. Usually, funding will be considered from only one of these trusts.

Double 'O' Charity Ltd

General

£181,000 (2004/05)

Beneficial area UK and overseas.

c/o 4 Friars Lane, Richmond, Surrey TW9 1NL

Correspondent The Trustees

Trustees *P D B Townshend; Mrs K Townshend; N R Goderson.*

CC Number 271681

Information available Accounts were on file at the Charity Commission.

General The primary objective of the trust is to make grants towards the relief of poverty, preservation of health and the advancement of education. The trust considers all requests for aid.

In 2004/05 the charity had an income of £46,000 and grants totalling £181,000.

Beneficiaries were Tsunami Earthquake Appeal (£50,000), Bedales School

(£25,000), Lifeworks Community (£17,000), Spirit of Recovery (£15,000), Chemical Dependency (£14,000), Oxford University (£6,500), Children of Chiswick and the Promise (£2,000 each), Arvon Foundation (£1,500) and Granada Disaster, Orleans House Gallery, SRLV 2004 Adventures and Yabsley Exhibitions (£1,000 each).

The sum of £3,900 was awarded to individuals.

Exclusions No grants to individuals towards education or for their involvement in overseas charity work.

Applications In writing to the correspondent.

The Doughty Charity Trust

Orthodox Jewish, religious education, relief of poverty

£140,000 (2004)

Beneficial area England, Israel.

22 Ravenscroft Avenue, Golders Green, London NW11 0RY

Tel. 020 8209 0500

Correspondent Gerald B Halibard, Trustee

Trustees *G Halibard, Chair; Mrs M Halibard.*

CC Number 274977

Information available Full accounts were on file at the Charity Commission.

General This trust appears to confine its giving to Orthodox Jewish causes. In 2004 the trust had an income of £168,000 and made grants totalling £140,000. Its assets stood at £65,000.

The largest grants went to Ponevez (£22,000), Tomchai (£12,000), Bobov Institute, Sunderland College and Lelov (£10,000), Kupat Hair Beitar (£6,000), Ezras Nitzrochim and Sharrei Torrah (£5,000 each) and Jewish Teachers' Training College (£4,000).

Other grants of less than £250 each totalled £3,000.

Exclusions No grants to individuals.

Applications In writing to the correspondent.

The R M Douglas Charitable Trust

General

£35,000 to organisations (2005/06)

Beneficial area UK with a preference for Staffordshire.

68 Liverpool Road, Stoke-on-Trent ST4 1BG

Correspondent J R T Douglas, Trustee

Trustees *J R T Douglas; Mrs J E Lees; F W Carder.*

CC Number 248775

Information available Accounts were on file at the Charity Commission, without a list of grants.

General The trust was set up for relief of poverty (including provision of pensions) especially for present and past employees (and their families) of Robert M Douglas (Contractors) Ltd, and for general charitable purposes especially in the parish of St Mary, Dunstall. In practice grants are only given to organisations previously supported by the trust. Grants range from £200 to £5,000, although only a few are for over £500.

In 2005/06 the trust had assets of £539,000 and an income of £44,000. Grants were made totalling £35,000. A further £8,400 was distributed to individuals connected with the company.

Previous beneficiaries have included Bible Explorer for Christian outreach, British Red Cross for general purposes, Burton Graduate Medical College to equip a new lecture theatre, Four Oaks Methodist Church for its centenary appeal, Lichfield Diocesan Urban Fund for Christian mission, St Giles Hospice – Lichfield for development, SAT-7 Trust for Christian outreach and John Taylor High School – Barton in Needwood for a performing arts block.

Applications The trust has previously stated that its funds were fully committed.

Dromintree Trust

General

£116,000 (2004/05)

Beneficial area Worldwide.

The Manor House, Main Street, Thurnby, Leicester LE7 9PN

Correspondent Hugh Murphy, Trustee

Trustees *Hugh Murphy; Margaret Murphy; Robert Smith; Paul Tiernan.*

CC Number 1053956

Information available Accounts were on file at the Charity Commission.

General Established in March 1996, in 2004/05 the trust had an income of £136,000 mainly from donations. Grants to 17 organisations totalled £116,000.

Beneficiaries included Consolata Fathers (£29,000), CAFOD (£20,000), Inter Care – Medical Aid for Africa, LOROS and Rainbows Children's Hospice (£10,000 each), Co-operation Ireland Foundation (£7,000), Coram Family, St Francis' Children's Society and Shelter (£5,000 each), Let The Children Live (£3,500), Samantha Dickson Research Trust (£2,500), Breast Cancer Campaign (£2,000), World Medical Fund (£1,000) and Macmillan Cancer Relief (£500).

Applications In writing to the correspondent.

The Dugdale Charitable Trust

Christian education, the advancement of Methodist education and the Catholic religion

£114,000 (2005/06)

Beneficial area UK, with a preference for Hampshire and West Sussex, and overseas.

Harmsworth Farm, Botley Road, Curbridge, Hampshire SO30 2HB

Correspondent R Dugdale, Trustee

Trustees *R A Dugdale; Mrs B Dugdale; J Dugdale; S Dugdale.*

CC Number 1052941

Information available Full accounts were on file at the Charity Commission.

General The trust has general charitable purposes and supports the advancement of the Methodist religion and Christian education in the UK. Increasingly, the trust supports overseas mission and relief work, particularly in the Indian subcontinent.

In 2005/06 the trust had assets of £448,000 and an income of £113,000. Grants were made totalling £114,000.

Beneficiaries included: Winchester Family Church (£34,000); OMS International (£15,000); Nambikkai Foundation (£11,000); Tear Fund (£10,000); CARE, Fair Trials Abroad, Marantha Family Village, Mission Aviation Fellowship, XLP Research Trust (£5,000 each); Insight (£2,600); Waltham Chase Methodist Church (£2,100); Door of Hope (£2,000); Africa Evangelical Fellowship (£1,800); International Nepal Fellowship (£1,200); Christian Blind Missionary (£1,000); and Antony Nolan Trust (£500).

Applications This trust only supports causes known personally to the trustees. Unsolicited applications are not considered.

The Dumbreck Charity

General

£149,000 (2005/06)

Beneficial area Worldwide, especially the West Midlands.

7 Bridge Street, Pershore, Worcestershire WR10 1AJ

Correspondent A C S Hordern, Trustee

Trustees *A C S Hordern; H B Carslake; Mrs J E Melling.*

CC Number 273070

Information available Accounts were on file at the Charity Commission.

General In 2005/06 the charity had assets of £3.4 million and an income of £100,000. Grants to organisations totalled £149,000. A small number of new grants are awarded each year to charities in Worcestershire, Warwickshire and West Midlands.

Grants were broken down as follows, shown here with examples of grants in each of the main categories.

Animal welfare/conservation

International/national – 15 grants totalling £15,000
Brooke Hospital for Animals Cairo (£3,000); International League for the Protection of Horses (£2,000); Blue Cross Animals Hospital, Greek Animal Welfare Fund, Horses and Ponies Protection Association and PDSA (£1,000 each); the Wildfowl Trust (£750); and World Wildlife Fund (£500).

Local – 8 grants totalling £7,800
Spear (£3,000); Redwing Horse Sanctuary (£1,000); the Worcester Farming and Wildlife Advisory Group (£750); and Avon Cats Home and Greyhound Rescue West of England (£500 each).

Children's welfare

National – 4 grants totalling £3,000
NSPCC and Save the Children Fund (£1,000 each); and Childline and World Villages for Children (£500 each).

Local – 6 grants totalling £4,500
The Jennifer Trust for Spinal Muscular Atrophy, Warwick Association of Youth Clubs and Warwickshire Clubs for Young People (£1,000 each); and Autism West Midlands and Coventry City Farm (£500 each).

Care of people who are elderly or have physical/mental disabilities

International/national – 11 grants totalling £7,500
The Injured Jockeys' Fund, the Royal Agricultural Benevolent Institution and the Royal British Legion Poppy Appeal (£1,000 each); Listening Books (£750); and Deafblind UK, the Gurkha Welfare Trust and RNIB Talking Book Service for the Blind (£500 each).

Local – 19 grants totalling £16,000
Myton Hospice (£2,000); Warwickshire Association for the Blind (£1,500); Birmingham Phab Camps, Dogs for the Disabled and Warwick Old People's Friendship Circle (£1,000 each); Disability Sport England and the Riding for the Disabled Association (£750 each); and the Birmingham Settlement, Coventry and Warwickshire Association for the Deaf and Mid Warwickshire Talking News (£500 each).

Medical

National – 3 grants totalling £2,500
Arthritis Research Capaign and British Red Cross (£1,000 each); and Marie Curie Cancer Care (£500).

Local – 11 grants totalling £11,000
County Air Ambulance and Shipston Home Nursing (£2,000 each); British Red Cross Association – Warwickshire Branch and St John Ambulance – Warwickshire Division (£1,000 each);

National Association for Crohns and Colitis (£750); and the Meningitis Trust (£500).

Miscellaneous

International/national – 6 grants totalling £5,800
Countryside Alliance (£2,000); Campaign to Protect Rural England and Hunt Servants Benefit Society (£1,000 each); the Leonard Cheshire Foundation (£750); and SSAFA (£500).

Extraordinary donations

Donations were given in the following categories:

Animal welfare/conservation	3 grants	£22,000
Care of older people and physically/mentally disabled	13 grants	£28,000
Medical	4 grants	£4,000
Miscellaneous	7 grants	£23,000

Exclusions No grants to individuals.

Applications In writing to the correspondent. The trustees meet annually in April/May. Unsuccessful applications will not be acknowledged. Organisations outside Worcestershire, Warwickshire or the West Midlands will not be supported.

The Harry Dunn Charitable Trust

Medical, general

£56,000 (2005/06)
Beneficial area UK, with a strong preference for Nottinghamshire.

Rushcliffe Developments, Tudor House, 13–15 Rectory Road, West Bridgford, Nottingham NG2 6BE
Correspondent The Trustees
Trustees *A H Dunn; N A Dunn; R M Dunn.*
CC Number 297389
Information available Full accounts were on file at the Charity Commission.

General This trust supports health, multiple sclerosis research, conservation, ecology and general community and voluntary organisations.

In 2005/06 it had assets of £1.8 million and a total income of £272,000. Grants totalled £56,000.

Beneficiaries included: Prostate Cancer Appeal (£5,000); Friends of Abbeyfield (£4,400); Abbeyfield UK and Nottingham Multiple Sclerosis Therapy Centre Ltd (£4,000 each); Disability Aid Fund (£3,500); RNLI, Support Dogs and

Wildfowl and Wetlands Trust RSPB (£3,000); Anvil Trust, the Ear Foundation and Multiple Sclerosis Society (£2,000 each); and Age Concern (£1,000).

Exclusions Only organisations known to the trustees are supported. No grants to individuals.

Applications In writing to the correspondent.

The Charles Dunstone Charitable Trust

General

£129,000 (2004/05)
Beneficial area UK and overseas.

c/o Withers, 16 Old Bailey, London EC4M 7EG
Correspondent The Trustees
Trustees *Denis Dunstone; Adrian Bott; Nicholas Folland.*
CC Number 1085955
Information available Accounts were on file at the Charity Commission.

General Registered with the Charity Commission in March 2001, in 2004/05 the trust had an income of £2.6 million, mostly from donations. Assets stood at £3.4 million at year end.

Grants to 29 organisations totalled £129,000 and were broken down into the following categories, shown here with examples of grants:

Conservation – £55,000
The sole beneficiary was Burnham Overy Harbour Trust.

Medical and disability – £37,000
Beneficiaries included Get Connected (£23,000), Thames Valley & Chiltern Air Ambulance (£1,000), National Autistic Society, Prostate Research Campaign UK, Sail 4 Cancer and the Wellbeing Trust (£500 each), DEBRA (£120), Cynthia Spencer Hospice (£100) and Cancer Research UK (£50).

Arts – £21,000
Beneficiaries were Serpentine Trust (£14,000) and Holkham Opera (£7,500).

Sport – £9,100
Grants went to Sail for Gold (£9,000) and British Sports Trust (£100).

Children and youth – £2,500
Organisations to benefit were St Joseph's College (£400) and Help a London Child (£100).

Education and training – £2,000
The sole beneficiary was Hounslow Action for Youth Association.

Maritime – £1,500
The sole beneficiary was RNLI.

General – £750
Beneficiaries included Chemical Dependency Unit (£250) and Challenge Yourself and Just Giving (£100 each).

Exclusions The trustees do not normally make grants to individuals.

Applications 'Proposals are usually requested by the trustees and unsolicited applications are not likely to be successful.'

Mildred Duveen Charitable Trust

General

£29,000 (2004/05)
Beneficial area Worldwide.

Devonshire House, 60 Goswell Road, London EC1M 7AD
Correspondent Peter Holgate, Trustee
Trustees *P Holgate; A Houlstoun; P Loose; J Shelford.*
CC Number 1059355
Information available Accounts were on file at the Charity Commission.

General Registered with the Charity Commission in November 1996, in 1999/2000 this trust received a substantial income of £1.3 million. In 2004/05 its assets stood at £1.1 million, generating an income of £32,000. After management and administration costs of £11,000, grants totalled £29,000.

There were 26 donations made in the range of £500 and £4,000. Beneficiaries included: St John's PCC and the Una Trust (£4,000 each); Friends of Oakley School and Lingfield and District Community Responders (£2,000 each); British Red Cross, Children's Discovery Centre, Emmaus Village Carlton, Hospice in the Weald Mind, Road Peace, the Shooting Star Children's Hospice and Charlie Waller Memorial Trust (£1,000); and Brighton and Hove Parents and Children Group, Care for the Elderly, the Respite Association, St

John Ambulance and Worthing and District Animal Rescue (£500 each).

Applications In writing to the correspondent.

The Dwek Family Charitable Trust

General

About £85,000 (2005/06)
Beneficial area UK, with a preference for the Greater Manchester area.

Suite One, Courthill House, 66 Water Lane, Wilmslow, Cheshire SK9 5AP
Correspondent J C Dwek, Trustee
Trustees *J C Dwek; J V Dwek; A J Leon.*
CC Number 1001456
Information available Information had been filed at the Charity Commission.

General In 2005/06 the trust had an income of £23,000 and a total expenditure of £89,000. Further information was not available for this year. In the previous year it had a high income of £630,000 and grants totalled £65,000.

Applications In writing to the correspondent.

The Dyers' Company Charitable Trust

General

£226,000 (2005/06)
Beneficial area UK.

Dyers Hall, Dowgate Hill, London EC4R 2ST
Correspondent The Clerk
Trustee *The Court of The Dyers' Company.*
CC Number 289547
Information available Full accounts were on file at the Charity Commission.

General In 2005/06 the trust had assets of £6 million generating an income of

£547,000. Grants totalled £226,000 and were given in the following categories:

The Craft – 8 grants totalling £42,000
Heriot-Watt University (£22,000); Royal College of Art (£6,000); the Salters' Institute and University of Manchester (£5,000 each); Stroudwater Textile Trust (£1,500); and Textile Conservation Centre (£1,000).

Local community/City/Inner London – 4 grants totalling £3,100
Lord Mayor's Appeal (£2,000); Mansion House Scholarship Scheme and Sheriffs' and Recorder's Fund (£500 each); and City of London Police Widows and Orphans (£100).

Norwich School – £25,000
This organisation has also received substantial donations in previous years.

Education and youth – 33 grants totalling £80,000
Boutcher C of E Primary School and St Saviour's (£26,000); St Olave's School (£13,000); Central Foundation Boys' School (£9,500); Gilwell Park Campaign (£2,500); Cirdan Sailing Trust, City & Guilds of London Arts School and London Youth (£2,000 each); Norwich Cathedral Choir Endowment and Young Enterprise (£1,000 each); Royal Scottish Trust (£500); and City of London Academy (£250).

The Church – 7 grants totalling £8,000
St James's Church, Garlickhythe (£2,000); and All Saints' Church – West Dulwich, Charterhouse-in-Southwark, Friends of St Paul's Cathedral, Norwich Cathedral Appeal and St Lawrence – Ventnor (£1,000 each).

The Services – 6 grants totalling £7,000
Ulysses Trust (£2,500); Airborne Forces Museum (£2,000); Combat Stress (£1,000); and RAF Benevolent Fund (£250).

The Arts – 17 grants totalling £15,000
Mary Hoare Foundation and Royal Overseas League Music Competition (£1,500 each); British Association for Performing Arts Medicine, Chelsea Opera Group, International Organ Festival Society, National Youth Orchestra and the Watermill Theatre Trust (£1,000 each); Ironbridge Gorge Museum Trust (£750); and the Actors' Charitable Trust, Becker Ensemble, Cotswold Players and Pimlico Opera (£500 each).

Health and Welfare – 41 grants totalling £37,000
Orchid Cancer Appeal (£5,000); HANDS (£2,500); Speak Ability (£2,000); Amber Trust, Community Links Trust, Hospice of St Francis – Berkhamsted, National

Library for the Blind, Oakhaven Hospice and Wessex Children's Hospice (£1,000 each); Centre 70 (£750); Bakewell and Eyam Community Transport, Fight for Sight, Huntingdon Disease Association, National Eczema Society, Theodora Children's Trust and Universal Beneficent Society (£500 each); and Royal Hospital – Chelsea and Take Heart (£250 each).

Other Appeals – 8 grants totalling £7,800

Swan Lifeline – Windsor, Swan Sanctuary – Egham and North Somerset Agricultural Society (£2,000 each); College of Arms Trust and Jubilee Sailing Trust (£1,000 each); and Frensham Pond Sailability (£500).

Exclusions No grants to individuals.

Applications The trust does not welcome unsolicited applications.

EAGA Partnership Charitable Trust

Fuel poverty

£107,000 (2005/06)

Beneficial area UK.

23 Macadam Gardens, Penrith, Cumbria CA11 9HS

Tel. 01768 210220 **Fax** 01768 210220

Email eagact@aol.com

Website www.eagagroup.com

Correspondent Dr Naomi Brown, Trust Manager

Trustees *J Clough; V Graham; A Harvey; Prof. G Manners; G Ritzema; Dr J Wade.*

CC Number 1088361

Information available Accounts were on file at the Charity Commission.

General The trust currently provides grants to fund research and other projects within two grant programmes:

- The first programme aims to clarify the nature, extent and consequences of fuel poverty and offer insights into the energy efficient and cost-effective relief of fuel poverty.
- The second programme aims to explore issues related to vulnerable consumers and their multiple needs and preferences. It explores the overlap between fuel poverty and wider deprivation, in order to develop a better understanding of different

groups of vulnerable and/or deprived consumers.

The trust gives priority to funding proposals that have the potential to inform or influence national perceptions and policies and have a wide geographic focus. A project that operates at a local level will only be considered for a grant if it: clearly demonstrates innovation; identifies the policy relevance of the project; has wide applicability; and has well developed and accurately costed evaluation and dissemination plans.

The work funded by the trust can be divided into four categories:

- rigorous, policy-related research
- action projects (such as practical, community-based initiatives which have wider applicability)
- the promotion of good practice (such as tool kits and workshops)
- practical resource materials and events (such as training and education resources).

In 2005/06 the trust had assets of £1.6 million, an income of £125,000 and approved new grants totalling £107,000. Grants included those to: Centre for Sustainable Energy; London School of Hygiene and Tropical Medicine; Energy Audit Company; and University of Aberdeen, in collaboration with Castlehill Housing Association and Aberdeen City Council Community Services.

Exclusions No grants to individuals. No grants for general fundraising appeals; no grants for projects that comprise solely of capital works; no retrospective funding; no funding for energy advice provision materials; no funding towards the maintenance of websites; no grants for local energy efficiency/warm homes initiatives.

Applications 'Applicants are requested to complete an application form. All applications that are completed in full and fulfil the main aims of [the trust] will be assessed at a formal meeting of trustees. Meetings are held three times a year. The trustees review applications against specific criteria and objectives.'

The Eagle Charity Trust

General, international, medicine, welfare

£26,000 (2005)

Beneficial area UK, in particular Manchester, and overseas.

Messrs Nairne Son and Green, 477 Chester Road, Cornbrook, Manchester M16 9HF

Tel. 0161 872 1701

Correspondent The Trustees

Trustees *Mrs L A Gifford; Miss D Gifford; Mrs E Y Williams; Mrs S A Nowakowski; R M E Gifford.*

CC Number 802134

Information available Information on file at the Charity Commission.

General The trust stated it supports a wide variety of charities, including UK and international charities and local charities in Manchester. There is a preference for those concerned with medicine and welfare. Grants are made on a one-off basis, with no commitment to providing ongoing funding.

In 2005 the trust had assets of £903,000, an income of £32,000 and made 19 grants totalling £26,000 (£46,000 in 2004).

Beneficiaries included: Oxfam (£4,500); UNICEF (£3,000); British Red Cross (£2,500); Alzheimer's Research Trust, Amnesty International, Macmillan Cancer Relief, New Hospitals Appeal, NSPCC, Rainbow Trust, Samaritans and WaterAid (£1,000 each); and RNLI, Sight Savers International and WWF UK (£500 each).

Applications In writing to the correspondent. However, please note, unsolicited applications are not invited.

Audrey Earle Charitable Trust

General, with some preference for animal welfare and conservation charities

£39,000 (2005/06)

Beneficial area UK.

24 Bloomsbury Square, London
WC1A 2PL

Tel. 020 7637 0661 **Fax** 020 7436 4663

Correspondent Paul Sheils, Trustee

Trustees *John Francis Russell Smith; Paul Andrew Shields; Roger James Weetch.*

CC Number 290028

Information available Accounts were on file at the Charity Commission.

General In 2005/06 this trust had an income of £50,000. Grants were made to 26 organisations totalling £39,000. Assets stood at £3.1 million. Most of the beneficiaries are supported year after year.

Beneficiaries included: St Clement's Church – fabric fund (£5,000); British Red Cross (£3,000); the Burnham Market & Norton Village Hall, League of Friends of Wells & District Hospital, the Royal British Legion, RNLI, RSPCA Norfolk Wildlife Hospital and Royal Star & Garter Home (£2,000 each); Burnham Overy Village Hall (£1,500); Action for Blind People, Age Concern, Battersea Dogs Home, International League for the Protection of Horses, PDSA, RSPB, St John Ambulance, the Salvation Army, Sense and the Wildfowl & Wetlands Trust (£1,000 each); and Wood Green Animal Shelters (£500).

Applications In writing to the correspondent.

East Kent Provincial Charities

General, education, younger, older people

£155,000 (2005/06)

Beneficial area UK, with a preference for Kent.

Masonic Centre, Tovil, Maidstone, Kent ME15 6QS

Website www.ekpca.org.uk

Correspondent Hugh Pierce, Trustee

Trustees *Noel Grout, Chair; Graham Smith; John Edmondson; Peter Daniels; Hugh Pierce; Patrick Thomas; Tony Denne.*

CC Number 1023859

Information available Accounts were obtained from the Charity Commission website.

General In 2005/06 the trust had assets of £6,700 and an income of £171,000. Grants to organisations totalled £155,000, broken down as follows:

Relief of poverty of children and older people	£65,000
Education	£5,500
Care of people who are sick and older people	£6,000
Other	£79,000

Beneficiaries included:

Registered Masonic charities
Provincial Grand Mark Lodge (£47,000); Grand Charity (£6,700); Kent Mark Benevolent Fund (£2,400); TLC Bears (£2,100); Royal Masonic Benevolent Institution (£1,100); and New Masonic Samaritan Fund (£1,000).

Non-Masonic registered charities
Tsunami Appeal (£57,000); Chatham Marine Cadets, East Kent Sea Cadets and Kent Hospices (£1,500 each); MacMillan Nursing Care (£710); and Demelza House (£600).

Applications In writing to the correspondent.

The Ebenezer Trust

Evangelical Christianity, welfare

£71,000 (2005/06)

Beneficial area UK and overseas.

31 Middleton Road, Shenfield, Brentwood, Essex CM15 8DJ

Correspondent Nigel Davey, Trustee

Trustees *Nigel Davey; Ruth Davey.*

CC Number 272574

Information available Accounts are on file at the Charity Commission.

General The trust gives grants to Evangelical Christian charities for education, medical, religion and welfare purposes.

In 2005/06 the trust had assets of £574,000, an income of £169,000 and made grants totalling £71,000.

Beneficiaries included: Brentwood Baptist Church (£8,400); TEAR Fund (£6,000); Baptist Missionary Society and Brentwood Schools Christian Worker Trust (£5,000 each); St Francis Hospice and Viz a Viz (£4,000 each); Spurgeon's College (£3,500); Gideons International (£2,700); Baptist Union Home Mission (£2,500); Alpha Partners, Evangelical

Alliance and Shaftesbury Society (£2,000 each); CARE Trust, Latin Link, Mildmay Mission Hospital and Salvation Army (£1,000 each); London City Mission (£750); Biblical Ministries Worldwide Christian Viewpoint for Men and Stepping Stones Trust (£500 each); and Leukaemia Research (£100).

Exclusions No grants to individuals.

Applications The trust states that they 'are most unlikely to consider unsolicited requests for grants'.

The Gilbert and Eileen Edgar Foundation

General – see below

£76,000 (2005)

Beneficial area UK (and a few international appeals).

c/o Chantrey Vellacott DFK, Prospect House, 58 Queens Road, Reading RG1 4RP

Website www.cvdfk.com

Correspondent Penny Tyson

Trustees *A E Gentilli; R S Parker.*

CC Number 241736

Information available Full accounts were on file at the Charity Commission.

General The settlor expressed the desire that preference be given to the following objectives:

- Medical research – the promotion of medical and surgical science in all forms.
- Care and support – helping people who are young, old and in need.
- Fine arts – raising the artistic taste of the public in music, drama, opera, painting, sculpture and fine arts.
- Education in fine arts – the promotion of education in fine arts.
- Religion – the promotion of religion.
- Recreation – the provision of facilities for recreation or other leisure time activities.

There is a preference for smaller organisations 'where even a limited grant may be of real value'. The majority of grants are around £500 each. Many of the organisations supported are regular beneficiaries.

In 2005 the foundation had assets of £1.8 million and an income of £76,000.

Grants were made totalling £76,000 and were broken down as follows:

Medical and surgical research

In this category there were 15 grants made totalling £8,500. Beneficiaries included: Cystic Fibrosis Trust and Prostate Cancer Research Charity (£1,000 each); and Arthritis Research Campaign, Blond McIndoe Centre, Fight for Sight, Leukaemia Research Fund and Royal College of Surgeons of England (£500 each).

Care and support

Children and young people

There were 17 grants in this category totalling £11,000. Beneficiaries included: Children in Crisis, Life Educational Centres, NSPCC, Operation New World and Weston Spirit (£1,000 each); and Childline, National Institute of Conductive Education, New Start Africa and Who Cares Trust (£500 each).

Elderly people

There were 3 beneficiaries in this category: Universal Beneficent Society (£1,000); and Gurkha Welfare Trust and Nightingale House (£500 each).

People with special needs

Donations totalled £14,000. Among the 26 beneficiaries were: National Missing Persons Helpline and Not Forgotten Association (£1,000 each); and Action for Blind People, Alone in London Service, British Home and Hospital for Incurables, Deafblind UK, Headway, Little Sisters of the Poor, Reading Community Welfare Rights Unit, Reading Voluntary Action, Victim Support and Willow Trust (£500 each); and Hambledon Surgery Medical Fund (£250).

Fine arts

Beneficiaries in this category were: Royal National Theatre (£4,000); English National Ballet (£2,000); and Living Paintings Trust (£500).

Education in fine arts

Grants went to: Royal College of Music – Junior Fellowship (£9,000); Royal Academy of Arts – Scholarship (£6,000); Royal Academy of Dramatic Art – Scholarship (£5,000); and Elizabeth Harwood Memorial Trust – scholarship (£1,000).

Religion and recreation including conservation

Among the 12 beneficiaries in this category were: the Worshipful Company of Clockmakers (£5,000); Arundel Cricket Foundation, Atlantic Salmon Trust and Landmine Action (£1,000 each); and B17 Charitable Trust, Intermediate Technology Development Group, Marine Conservation Society,

Sustrans and Warwickshire Association of Boys' Clubs (£500 each).

Exclusions Grants for education in fine arts are made by way of scholarships awarded by academies and no grants are made directly to individuals in this regard.

Applications In writing to the correspondent. There are no application forms.

Gilbert Edgar Trust

See below

Nil (2003/04) see below

Beneficial area Predominantly UK, limited overseas.

c/o Cave Harper and Co., North Lee House, 66 Northfield End, Henley-on-Thames, Oxfordshire RG9 2BE

Tel. 01491 572565

Correspondent The Trustees

Trustees *S C E Gentilli; A E Gentilli; Dr R E B Solomons.*

CC Number 213630

Information available Accounts were on file at the Charity Commission.

General In 2003/04 the trust had assets of £1 million and an income of £62,000. The trustees' decisions on grants to be awarded was made later than normal and hence only one grant was made in the year compared to 79 totalling £37,000 in 2002/03. Details of these grants are shown below.

Homelessness – 6 grants totalling £4,900

Grants of £1,000 were made to Centrepoint, Mind, Notting Hill Housing Trust and Shelter. The remaining grants were for £400 and £500.

Hospice – 6 grants of £500 each

Beneficiaries included Myton Hamlet Hospice and St Luke's Hospice.

Medical – 8 grants totalling £3,900

Grants included £1,000 to Cancer Relief Macmillan Fund and £500 to Multiple Sclerosis Society. Six grants of £400 were made to, for example, Quest for Test for Cancer and Scope.

Overseas – 5 grants totalling £2,800

Grants were £1,000 to British Red Cross, £500 each to Save the Children Fund and Impact Foundation and £400 to both Echo and Prisoners Abroad.

Research – 10 grants totalling £4,000

Grants included £400 each made to, for example, National Prostate Cancer Research to ME Association and Schizophrenia Association.

Social – 9 grants totalling £3,750

Grants were £1,000 to Samaritans, £500 to Police Foundation and St John Ambulance, £400 each to Homelife (DGAA), New Bridge, Prison Reform Trust, RABI and St John Ambulance, and £250 to Hambleden Church Council.

Youth – 3 grants totalling £1,300

Grants were £500 to YMCA and £400 each to National Association of Boys' Clubs and Venturers' Search and Rescue.

Children – 12 grants totalling £6,100

Grants included £1,000 to NSPCC and National Institute of Conductive Education, and £500 to Babes in Arms. Others were all for £400 including those to Action Research, Early Bird Fund and National Playbus Association.

Disabled – 14 grants totalling £5,900

Grants included those to Disabled Housing Trust and HAPA, Home Farm Trust Fund (£500 each) and £400 each to Robert Owen Foundation and Woodcraft Folk.

Deaf/Blind – 3 grants of £400 each

Grants went to Cambridge Learning Trust, Iris Fund and Sense.

Drug Abuse – 5 grants of £400 each

Grants included those to Accept Clinic, Re–Solv and Rhoserchan Project.

Exclusions No grants to individuals or non-registered charities.

Applications In writing to the correspondent, with a copy of a brochure describing your work.

The Edinburgh Trust, No. 2 Account

Education, armed services

£64,000 (2005/06)

Beneficial area UK and worldwide.

Buckingham Palace, London SW1A 1AA

Tel. 020 7930 4832

Correspondent The Secretary

Trustees *Sir Brian McGrath; C Woodhouse; Sir Miles Hunt-Davis.*

CC Number 227897

Information available Full accounts were on file at the Charity Commission.

General In 2005/06 the trust had assets of £1.7 million and an income of £71,000. Grants were made totalling £64,000, broken down as follows:

General	£42,000
Armed services	£15,000
Education	£5,700

There were 29 grants of £1,000 or more listed in the accounts. Beneficiaries included: Edwina Mountbatten Trust (£2,800); Commonwealth Ex-Serviceman's League (£2,500); King George Fund for Sailors and Royal Marines' General Fund (£2,500 each); Outward Bound Trust, the Award Scheme, the Federation of London Youth Clubs and the PP Trust for Windsor and Maidenhead (£2,000 each); and King Edward VII Hospital for Officers (£1,750); Burma Star Association, International Sacred Literature Trust, National Playing Fields Association, Royal Life Saving Society and SSAFA No. 1 Account (£1,500 each); and British Heart Foundation, the Game Conservancy Trust, Interact Worldwide, the Sail Training Association, WWF International and the Zoological Society of London (£1,000 each).

Exclusions No grants to individuals; only scientific expeditions are considered with the backing of a major society. No grants to non-registered charities.

Applications In writing to the correspondent. The trustees meet to consider grants in April each year. Applications must be submitted by January.

Educational Foundation of Alderman John Norman

Education

£89,000 to organisations (2005/06)

Beneficial area Norwich and Old Catton.

Brown and Co., Old Bank of England Court, Queen Street, Norwich NR2 4TA

Tel. 01603 629871

Email n.saffell@brown-co.com

Correspondent N F Saffell, Clerk

Trustees *Revd J Boston; R Sandall; Dr J Leach; Revd Canon M Smith; D S Armes; C D Brown; C I H Mawson; Mrs C I H Mawson; Mrs T Hughes; S Slack; J Hawkins; C Spinks.*

CC Number 313105

Information available Accounts were on file at the Charity Commission.

General The trust was originally founded by the terms of the will of Alderman Norman dated February 1720. It is currently regulated by schemes from 1972 and 1973. Grants made by the foundation are to assist the education of:

- young persons descended from Alderman John Norman;
- young persons resident in the parish of Old Catton;
- young persons resident in the city of Norwich and for the benefit of schools established for charitable purposes only or for the benefit of local authority schools for benefits not provided by local authority.

In 2005/06 the foundation had assets of £6.1 million and an income of £254,000. Grants were made totalling £127,000 and were broken down as follows:

- £118,000 to 355 descendants
- £11,000 to six residents living in Old Catton
- £7,400 for exhibitions/bursaries
- £89,000 in special awards to other charitable organisations.

Beneficiaries of the special awards included: West Earlham Middle School (£10,000); Leeway (£6,000); Norwich Cathedral Choir Endowment Fund (£5,800); Blyth-Jex School, Earlham High School, Eaton CNS School, Hewett School, Norfolk County Council – Pupil Access Support and Sprowston High School (£5,000 each); East Anglian Children's Hospices (£3,000); RAPT (£2,500); BUILD, Mancroft Advice Project and West Earlham Partnership (£2,000 each); Nancy Oldfield Trust (£1,500); and Britton Sinfonia, Norfolk and Norwich Chamber Music and RSPB (£1,000).

Exclusions No grants to non-registered charities. No applications from outside Norwich and Old Catton will be considered.

Applications In writing to the correspondent. The trustees meet three times each year, in February, May and October.

The W G Edwards Charitable Foundation

Care of older people

£342,000 (2005/06)

Beneficial area UK.

c/o 123a Station Road, Oxted, Surrey RH8 0QE

Tel. 01883 714412 **Fax** 01883 714433

Email janetbrown@ wgedwardscharitablefoundation.org.uk

Website www. wgedwardscharitablefoundation.org.uk

Correspondent Janet Brown, Clerk to the Trustees

Trustees *Mrs Margaret E Offley Edwards; Prof. Wendy D Savage; Mrs G Shepherd Coates; Ms Yewande Savage.*

CC Number 293312

Information available Accounts were on file at the Charity Commission.

General The foundation's policy statement is 'to assist with the provision of care for older people through existing charities, principally with capital projects but also innovative schemes for ongoing care.'

In 2005/06 the foundation had assets of £3.1 million and an income of £137,000. A total of 231 applications were received, of which 45 were successful. Grants totalled £342,000.

By far the largest grant went to Rockdale Housing Association – Sevenoaks towards the rebuilding of their residential home for older people (£200,000).

The average grant in the year was for about £3,000. Beneficiaries included: Abbeyfield – Clare and Bath Institute of Medical Engineering (£6,000 each); BEN – Motor and Allied Trades Benevolent Fund (£5,400); British Trust for Conservation Volunteers (£5,300); Abbots Hospital Guildford, Age Care London and the Community Reconciliation and Friends (£5,000 each); Age Concern Gillingham and Music in Hospitals – Scotland (£4,900 each); the Extracare Charitable Trust and Age Concern Mertsharn (£4,700 each); Preston Bethany Trust (£4,500); Age Concern Suffolk (£4,200); Bishop Creighton House Settlement (£3,600); Age Concern Canterbury (£3,500); Action on Elder Abuse and Age Concern

Slough (£3,000 each); Abbeyfield, Reading (£2,300); Beacon Centre for the Blind and Lindfield Christian Care Home (£2,000 each); Cleveland Housing Advice Centre (£1,500); Suffolk Deaf Association (£1,000); and Age Concern Knaresborough (£700).

Exclusions No grants to individuals.

Applications In writing to the correspondent, including: confirmation of charitable status (charity number on letterhead will suffice); brief details of the project; budget statement for the project; current fundraising achievements and proposals for future fundraising; items of expenditure within project costing approx £1,000 to £5,000 – trustees currently prefer to give towards a named item rather than into a pool building fund; copy of latest accounts if available.

There are no forms or deadlines for applications. If your project fulfils the foundation's policy criteria, your details will be passed on to the trustees for consideration at their next meeting.

The Elephant Trust

Visual arts

£50,000 to organisations (2005/06)

Beneficial area UK.

512 Bankside Lofts, 65 Hopton Street, London SE1 9GZ

Email ruth@elephanttrust.org.uk

Website www.elephanttrust.org.uk

Correspondent Ruth Rattenbury

Trustees Sarah Whitfield, Chair; Dawn Ades; Antony Forwood; Tony Penrose; Richard Wentworth; Polly Staple; Rob Tufnel.

CC Number 269615

Information available Accounts were on file at the Charity Commission.

General The trust makes grants to individual artists, arts organisations and publications concerned with the visual arts. It aims to extend the frontiers of creative endeavour, to promote the unconventional and the imaginative and, within its limited resources, to make it possible for artists and arts organisations to realise and complete specific projects.

In 2005/06 the trust's assets totalled £1.8 million and it received an income of £67,000. Grants to 20 organisations totalled £50,000. A further £11,000 was distributed to 7 individuals. Beneficiaries included: Arnolfini Gallery Ltd and Hayward Gallery (£4,000 each); Camden Arts Centre, De La Warr Pavilion, Electra and Triangle Arts Trust (£3,000 each); Ikon Gallery (£2,500); Art Works in Wimbledon and Milton Keynes Gallery (£2,000 each); and Gasworks Gallery (£1,500).

The trust also administers the George Melhuish Bequest, which has similar objectives.

Exclusions No education or other study grants.

Applications In writing to the correspondent. Guidelines are available. The trustees meet four times a year.

The George Elias Charitable Trust

Jewish, general

£223,000 (2005/06)

Beneficial area Some preference for Manchester.

Elitex House, 1 Ashley Road, Altrincham, Cheshire WA14 2DT

Tel. 0161 928 7171

Correspondent N G Denton, Charity Accountant

Trustees E C Elias; S E Elias.

CC Number 273993

Information available Accounts were obtained from the Charity Commission website.

General The trust states that it gives grants to charities supporting educational needs and the fight against poverty as well as organisations promoting the Jewish faith.

In 2005/06 the trust had assets of £557,000 and an income of £668,000, including £435,000 from a donation of investments. Grants totalled £223,000. There were 55 grants of £100 or more listed in the accounts.

Beneficiaries included: UK Friends of Nahat De Ah (£29,000); King David Schools Appeal (£20,000); Manchester Jewish Mesibra (£18,000); Hale Hebrew Adult Education Trust (£15,000); Aish Hatorah (£11,000); Yad Veachisomoch (£10,000); Community Security Trust and Horwich Shotter Charitable Trust (£6,000 each); South Manchester Mikva Trust (£4,000); Babylonian Jewry Heritage Centre and the Forum (£3,000 each); Manchester Jewish Chaplaincy (£2,200); Chai Network (£2,000); JNF (£1,100); and Kollel Machla David (£1,000).

Applications In writing to the correspondent. Trustees meet monthly.

The Elizabeth Frankland Moore and Star Foundation

General in the UK

Around £70,000 (2004/05)

Beneficial area UK.

Flat 23, Manor Fields, Putney Heath, London SW15 3LT

Correspondent J D Hewens, Trustee

Trustees Mrs J Cameron; R A Griffiths; J D Hewens; Dr David Spalton.

CC Number 257711

Information available Information was available from the Charity Commission website.

General Registered with the Charity Commission in February 1969, in 2004/05 the trust had an income of £19,000 and a total expenditure of £100,000. Further information was not available.

Previous grants have included those to John Muir Trust, National Trust for Scotland, Sir John Soames Museum, 3H Fund, Cystic Fibrosis Holiday Fund for Children, Abbeyfield North London Society Ltd, Alzheimer's Society, Crimestoppers Trust and Accord Hospice.

Applications In writing to the correspondent. Trustees meet twice a year.

Ellador Ltd

Jewish

£50,000 (2004/05)

Beneficial area UK.

Ellador Ltd, 20 Ashstead Road, London E5 9BH

Correspondent J Schrieber, Trustee and Governor

Trustees *J Schrieber; S Schrieber; Mrs H Schrieber; Mrs R Schrieber.*

CC Number 283202

Information available Accounts were on file at the Charity Commission, but without a grants list.

General The trust supports organisations benefiting Jewish people and also Jewish individuals. In 2004/05 its assets totalled £367,000 and it received an income of £55,000. Grants totalled £50,000. Types of charities which benefit from donations are educational, religious and other charitable organisations. Unfortunately a list of grants was not included in the accounts for this year.

Applications In writing to the correspondent.

The Ellerdale Trust

Children

£326,000 (2004/05)

Beneficial area Worldwide.

c/o Macfarlane and Co., Cunard Building, Water Street, Liverpool L3 1DS

Tel. 0151 236 6161

Correspondent The Trustees

Trustees *A T R Macfarlane; P C Kurthausen; S P Moores.*

CC Number 1073376

Information available Accounts were on file at the Charity Commission.

General This trust was established to relieve poverty, distress or suffering in any part of the world particularly children who are disadvantaged or in need.

In 2004/05 the trust had assets of £5.4 million and an income of £325,000. Grants paid to 35 organisations totalled £326,000.

By far the largest grant was £200,000 to NSPCC, the first year payment of a three year commitment. Other beneficiaries of grants of £1,000 or more included: Action for Kids and Rainbow Centre (£20,000 each); Barnardos and Mind (£15,000 each); Psychiatric Research Trust (£10,000); Childhope International (£7,000); Fairbridge Merseyside (£4,500); Brainwave, Break, Martin House, NAPAC and Young Minds Trust (£3,000 each); National Deaf Children's Society and Whirlow Hall Farm Trust (£2,500

each); Angels International (£1,200); and East Anglian Children's Hospice (£1,000).

Smaller grants included those to: BLISS, Children Today, Happy Days, Home Start – South Liverpool and the Sunflower Trust (£500 each); and City Escape (£300).

Applications In writing to the correspondent.

The Ellinson Foundation Ltd

Jewish

£188,000 (2005/06)

Beneficial area Worldwide.

Messrs Robson Laidler and Co., Fernwood House, Fernwood Road, Jesmond, Newcastle upon Tyne NE2 1TJ

Tel. 0191 281 8191

Correspondent The Trustees

Trustees *C O Ellinson; A Ellinson; A Z Ellinson; U Ellinson.*

CC Number 252018

Information available Full accounts were on file at the Charity Commission.

General The trust supports hospitals, education and homelessness in the UK and overseas, usually with a Jewish-teaching aspect. The trust regularly supports organisations such as boarding schools for boys and girls teaching the Torah.

In 2005/06 the trust had assets of £1.5 million and an income of £860,000. Grants totalled £188,000.

Beneficiaries of grants over £1,000 each were: Yeshivas Tushia Tifrach (£100,000); Mifaley Tzedoka Vechesed Jerusalem (£55,000); Friends of Yeshivas Brisk Jerusalem (£10,000); Kolel Ohel Torah (£9,000); Yeshiva Lezeirim Gateshead (£6,000); and Torah Ore Seminary Jerusalem and Yeshivas Ateres Yisrael (£2,000 each).

Grants of less that £1,000 each, unlisted in the accounts, totalled £3,900.

Exclusions No grants to individuals.

Applications In writing to the correspondent. However, the trust generally supports the same organisations each year and unsolicited applications are not welcome.

The Edith Maud Ellis 1985 Charitable Trust

Quaker, ecumenical, education, peace and international affairs, general

About £30,000 a year

Beneficial area UK, Ireland and overseas.

c/o Heckford Norton, 18 Hill Street, Saffron Walden, Essex CB10 1JD

Tel. 01799 522636

Email hf@heckfordnorton.co.uk

Correspondent Mrs H Fuff, Administrator

Trustees *A P Honigmann; E H Milligan.*

CC Number 292835

Information available Accounts were only available at the Charity Commission up to 1996/97.

General The trust supports general charitable purposes including religious and educational projects (but not personal grants for religious or secular education nor grants for church buildings) and projects in international fields especially related to economic, social and humanitarian aid to developing countries. Ecumenical and Quaker interests.

Unfortunately only information up to 1996/97 is available from the Charity Commission, when the trust had an income of £49,000 and a total expenditure of £35,000. Research confirms that the trust still exists. Grants appear to total about £30,000 each year. A recent beneficiary of this trust was University of Southampton Faculty of Law which received a contribution towards a conference entitled 'Restorative and Community Justice: Inspiring the Future'.

Exclusions No grants to individuals.

Applications In writing to the correspondent.

The Elmgrant Trust

General charitable purposes, education, arts, social sciences

£47,000 to organisations (2005/06)

Beneficial area UK, with a preference for the south west of England.

The Elmhirst Centre, Dartington Hall, Totnes, Devon TQ9 6EL

Tel. 01803 863160

Correspondent Angela Taylor, Secretary

Trustees *Marian Ash, Chair; Sophie Young; Paul Elmhirst; David Young; Mark Sharman.*

CC Number 313398

Information available Accounts were on file at the Charity Commission.

General This trust has general charitable purposes, but in particular aims to encourage local life through education, the arts and social sciences. Although there is a preference for south west England, grants to organisations are awarded throughout the UK.

In 2005/06 the trust had assets of £2 million and an income of £63,000. Grants paid to 59 organisations totalled £47,000. A further £5,200 was paid in 20 grants to individuals. Donations were broken down as follows, shown with examples of organisations receiving support in each category:

Education and educational research – 37 grants totalling £30,000)
The Second Chance Trust (£15,000); Farms for City Children, Sands School and Rudolph Steiner School South Devon (£750 each); Sir Robert Geffery's School (£700); Devon Development Education (£650); the Barn Owl Trust, Cornwall Blind Association, the Yarner Trust and Youth Action Wiltshire (£500 each); the English Speaking Union, the Friends of Ilsington School and the West of England School and College (£300 each); and Plymouth & District MIND Association (£150).

Arts and arts education – 15 grants totalling £7,500
Dartington International Summer School (£1,500); Awards for Young Musicians, the Dartington Hall Trust and Dawlish Repertory Company (£1,000); Double Elephant Print Workshop (£550); and Beaford Arts and the Devon Guild of Craftsmen (£500 each).

Social sciences and scientific grants – 18 grants totalling £9,100
Headway Devon, Swimbridge Jubilee Hall, Tiverton Adventure Play Association and the Towersey Foundation (£1,000 each); New Bridge (£600); Worlington Parochial Church Council and Totnes Community Family Trust (£500 each); Butleigh PCC and Ottervale One to One (£250 each); and Oxford Concert Party (£200).

Pensions, donations and compassionate grants – 9 grants totalling £5,500
Families and Carers Trust and Motor Neurone Disease Association (1,000 each); and Children's Clinic for Cornwall, Cruse Bereavement Care – South Devon and the Kiloran Trust (£500 each).

Exclusions The following are not supported:

- large-scale UK organisations
- postgraduate study, overseas student grants, expeditions and travel and study projects overseas
- counselling courses
- renewed requests from the same (successful) applicant within a two-year period.

Applications In writing to the correspondent, giving full financial details and, where possible, a letter of support. Initial telephone calls are welcome if advice is needed. There are no application forms. Guidelines are issued. An sae would be very helpful, although this is not obligatory. Currently, meetings are held three times a year in March, June and October. Applications need to be received one clear month prior to meeting.

Elshore Ltd

Jewish

£256,000 (2004/05)

Beneficial area Worldwide.

10 West Avenue, London NW4 2LY

Correspondent H Lerner, Trustee

Trustees *H M Lerner; A Lerner; S Yanofsky.*

CC Number 287469

Information available Accounts were on file at the Charity Commission, but without a list of grants.

General This trust appears to make grants solely to Jewish organisations. In 2004/05 it had an income of £259,000, mainly from donations. Grants were made totalling £256,000. The trust's assets came to £76,000. A grants list was not included with the accounts for this year.

Further information has been unavailable since 1994/95, when grants to 40 beneficiaries totalled £178,000. The larger grants were £26,000 to Eminor Educational Centre and £20,000 to Cosmon Belz. Grants of £10,000 were given to 10 organisations, including Gur Trust and Marbe Torah Trust. Most other grants were less than £1,000, although some were for up to £8,000.

Applications In writing to the correspondent.

The Vernon N Ely Charitable Trust

Christian, welfare, disability, children and young people, overseas

£62,000 (2005/06)

Beneficial area Worldwide, with a preference for London Borough of Merton.

Grosvenor Gardens House, 35–37 Grosvenor Gardens, London SW1W 0BY

Tel. 020 7828 3156

Correspondent Derek Howorth, Trustee

Trustees *J S Moyle; D P Howorth; R S Main.*

CC Number 230033

Information available Accounts were on file at the Charity Commission, but without a list of grants.

General The trust makes grants to Christian, welfare, disability, children, youth and overseas charities. Its 1997/98 annual report stated that the trust's policy had been reviewed during the year and it had been decided that the number of beneficiaries each year would be reduced, with larger grants being made.

In 2005/06 the trust had assets of £1.6 million and an income of £71,000. Grants were made totalling £62,000. Information regarding the size or number of beneficiaries was not available.

Exclusions No grants to individuals.

Applications In writing to the correspondent. Please note that the trust has previously stated that no funds are available.

Ralph and Muriel Emanuel Charity Trust

General, Jewish

£107,000 (2005/06)
Beneficial area UK.

61 Redington Road, London NW3 7RP

Correspondent Ralph N Emanuel, Trustee

Trustees *Ralph Neville Emanuel; Muriel Helena Emanuel; Maurice Seymour Emanuel; Sara Jane Emanuel.*

CC Number 266944

Information available Accounts were on file at the Charity Commission, without a list of grants.

General This trust was established in 1974; grants are made at the trustees' discretion. In 2005/06 it had assets amounting to over £1 million and an income of £463,000. Grants totalled about £107,000, broken down as follows.

Welfare	23 grants	£40,000
Health	16	£15,000
Arts	10	£13,000
General	1	£10,000
Religious	11	£8,300
Overseas	3	£7,750
Education	9	£5,800
Housing	1	£3,500
Research	4	£3,400

Previous beneficiaries have included Age Concern – Camden, Almedia Theatre, Brighton Jewish Film Festival, Hampstead and Highgate Festival, Institute of Jewish Studies, Jewish Care, Manchester Jewish Museum, Royal College of Music, University of the Third Age and Youth Aliyah.

Applications In writing to the correspondent.

The Emerton-Christie Charity

Health, welfare, disability, arts

£47,000 (2005/06)
Beneficial area UK.

c/o Cartmell Shepherd, Viaduct House, Carlisle CA3 8EZ

Tel. 01228 516666

Correspondent The Trustees

Trustees *A F Niekirk; Dr N A Walker; Dr C Mera-Nelson; Lt Col W D Niekirk; Dr S E Walker.*

CC Number 262837

Information available Accounts were on file at the Charity Commission.

General The Emerton Charitable Settlement was established in 1971 by Maud Emerton, with additional funds subsequently added by Vera Bishop Emerton. In April 1996, it became the Emerton-Christie Charity following a merger with another trust, The Mrs C M S Christie Will Trust.

In 2005/06 it had assets totalling £2.3 million and an income of £61,000. Grants totalled £47,000.

Beneficiaries included: Médecins Sans Frontières (£4,000); Arthur Rank Hospice – Cambridge, Brain Research Trust, Centre of the Cell, Halo Trust, Independence Dogs, Medical Foundation for Victims of Torture, National Eye Research Centre, Orpheus Centre Trust, RNLI and Save the Children and Sue Ryder Home – Ely (£2,000 each); and Poems in the Waiting Room, Royal College of Music and Women's Health in South Tyneside (£1,000 each).

Exclusions Generally no grants to: individuals; religious organisations; restoration or extension of buildings; start-up costs; animal welfare and research; cultural heritage; or environmental projects.

Applications In writing to the correspondent. A demonstration of need based on budgetary principles is required and applications will not be acknowledged unless accompanied by an sae. Trustees normally meet once a year in the autumn to select charities to benefit.

EMI Music Sound Foundation

Music education

£157,000 (2005/06)
Beneficial area UK.

27 Wrights Lane, London W8 5SW

Tel. 020 7795 7000 **Fax** 020 7795 7296

Email enquiries@ musicsoundfoundation.com

Website www.musicsoundfoundation. com

Correspondent Janie Orr

Trustees *Eric Nicoli, Chair; Jim Beach; John Deacon; Paul Gambaccini; Leslie Hill; David Hughes; Rupert Perry; Tony Wadsworth; Christine Walter.*

CC Number 1104027

Information available Accounts were on file at the Charity Commission.

General 'EMI Music Sound Foundation (EMI MSF) is an independent music education charity, established in 1997 to celebrate the centenary of EMI Records and to improve young peoples' access to music education in the UK and Ireland.

'We are now the single largest sponsor of Specialist Performing Arts Colleges and have created vital bursaries at seven music colleges to assist music students in need of financial support. We have also helped hundreds of schools and individual students improve their access to music through the purchase or upgrade of instruments and music making equipment.'

General Awards
'EMI MSF is dedicated to the improvement of music education with a focus on youth. Preference is given to full-time students under the age of 25.'

Support is given to:

- non-specialist schools to fund music education
- music students in full time education to fund instrument purchase
- music teachers to fund courses and training.

Bursary Awards
Every year EMI MSF awards bursaries to students at seven music colleges in the UK and Ireland. These bursaries are distributed at each college's discretion, based on criteria provided by EMI MSF. For more information, please contact the colleges directly (Birmingham Conservatoire, Drumtech/Vocaltech/

GuitarX – London, Institute of Popular Music – Liverpool, Irish World Music Centre – Limerick, Royal Scottish Academy of Music and Drama – Glasgow, Royal Academy – London and Royal Welsh College of Music and Drama – Cardiff).

In 2005/06 it had assets totalling £7.3 million and an income of £294,000. Grants totalled £157,000.

Exclusions No support for:

- applications from outside the United Kingdom
- non-school based community groups, music therapy centres, etc.
- applications over £2,500.

Applications On a form which can be downloaded from the foundation's website.

The Emmandjay Charitable Trust

Social welfare, medicine, young people

£213,000 (2005/06)

Beneficial area UK, with a special interest in West Yorkshire.

PO Box 88, Otley, West Yorkshire LS21 3TE

Correspondent Mrs A E Bancroft, Administrator

Trustees *Mrs Sylvia Clegg; John A Clegg; Mrs S L Worthington; Mrs E A Riddell.*

CC Number 212279

Information available Accounts were obtained from the Charity Commission website, but without a grants list.

General 'The trust gives most particularly to help disadvantaged people, but many different projects are supported – caring for the disabled, physically and mentally handicapped and terminally ill, work with young people and medical research. The trust likes projects which reach a lot of people. The trustees are keen that grants are actually spent.'

In 2005/06 the trust had assets of £4.5 million and an income of £194,000. Grants totalled £213,000. A grants list was not included in the accounts, although it contained a breakdown of the areas in which it gives grants as follows:

National charities	£62,000
Youth activities, schools	£26,000
Special overseas appeals	£26,000

Hospices, terminally ill, care	£25,000
Special schemes, workshops, disabled	£22,000
Medical research	£21,000
Local community groups	£16,000
Children's charities and care	£7,600
Homelessness	£3,400
Counselling services	£2,000
Advice centres	£1,500
Church, religious activities	£1,500
Social services, probation services	£1,200

Previous beneficiaries have included: Abbeyfield Bradford Society, Bradford's War on Cancer, British Heart Foundation, British Red Cross, Cancer Support Centre, Caring for Life – Leeds, Marie Curie Cancer Centre, Research into Ageing and West Yorkshire Youth Association.

Exclusions 'The trust does not pay debts, does not make grants to individual students, and does not respond to circulars.' Grants are only given, via social services, to individuals if they live in Bradford.

Applications In writing to the correspondent.

The English Schools' Football Association

Association football

£248,000 (2005)

Beneficial area England.

1–2 Eastgate Street, Stafford ST16 2NQ

Tel. 01785 785970

Email dawn.howard@schoolsfa.com

Website www.esfa.co.uk

Correspondent Ms D Howard

Trustees *P J Harding, Chair; G Smith; M R Duffield.*

CC Number 306003

Information available Accounts were on file at the Charity Commission.

General Support is given for the mental, moral and physical development and improvement of schoolchildren and students up to twenty years of age through the medium of association football. Assistance to teacher charities.

In 2005 the association had an income of £1.1 million with £248,000 given in grants.

Exclusions Grants are restricted to membership and teacher charities.

Applications In writing to the correspondent.

The EOS Foundation

Money advice provision/ individuals in need

£52,000 (2004/05)

Beneficial area England, Wales.

PO Box 42, Peterborough PE3 8XH

Tel. 01733 421021 **Fax** 01733 421020

Correspondent Kirstie Berridge, Trust Relationships Manager

Trustees *John Sansby, Chair; John Barratt; Graham Blagden; Anthony Jackson; Stuart de Prochnow.*

CC Number 1101072

Information available Full accounts were available from the Charity Commission.

General The foundation can help by giving grants to customers of the following companies Bournemouth and West Hampshire Water, Folkestone and Dover Water, Mid Kent Water, Portsmouth Water, South East Water and Tendring Hundred Water.

It can give grants to:

- clear or reduce arrears of domestic water charges
- help towards other essential domestic bills and costs. It is possible to apply for such help without applying for help with water charges.

Organisational grant programmes are also available. The direction of such programmes is dependent upon the availability of funds and the length of the commitment from donor companies. Many of the grants are awarded for money advice and debt management projects. In 2005 the trust had assets of £139,000 and an income of £252,000. It made 151 grants totalling £52,000, which were broken down as follows:

On behalf of individuals in respect of water and sewerage debt (£47,000) Grants included those made to South East Water (£20,000), Tendring Hundred Water (£9,000), Mid Kent Water (£6,000) and Folkestone and Dover Water (£2,000).

Further assistance payments (£5,000) Grants were made under the following headings: Bankruptcy (£1,500), Household (£1,300), Other (£1,000),

Water (£800), Electricity (£400) and Social Fund Loan (£100).

Exclusions No grants for: fines for criminal offences; educational or training needs; debts to central government departments; medical equipment, aids and adaptations; holidays; business debts; catalogues; credit cards; personal loans; deposits for secure accommodation; or overpayment of benefits.

Applications In writing to the correspondent.

The Epigoni Trust

Health and welfare, disability, homelessness, addiction, children who are disadvantaged, environment

£50,000 (2005)
Beneficial area UK.

c/o Charities Aid Foundation, King's Hill, West Malling, Kent ME19 4TA

Correspondent Charles Peacock, Trustee

Trustees *C H Peacock; Mrs B Bond; A M Bond.*

CC Number 328700

Information available Full accounts were on file at the Charity Commission.

General The trust has common trustees with two other trusts, the Cleopatra Trust and the Dorus Trust (see separate entries) with which it also shares the same aims and policies. All three trusts are administered by Charities Aid Foundation. Generally the trusts support different organisations.

The trust makes grants in the following areas:

- mental health
- cancer welfare/education – not research
- diabetes
- physical disability – not research
- homelessness
- addiction
- children who are disadvantaged.

There is also some preference for environmental causes. It only gives grants for specific projects and does not give grants for running costs or general appeals. Support is only given to

national projects, not local areas or initiatives.

In 2005 it had assets of £3.1 million, which generated an income of £132,000. Grants to 13 organisations totalled £50,000.

Beneficiaries included: Myasthenia Gravis Association (£9,700); National Children's Bureau (£8,400); Association for Spina Bifida and Hydrocephalus and Asthma UK (£5,000 each); Institute of Cancer Research (£4,700); Special Toys Educational Postal Service (£4,300); Movement Foundation (£3,400); Starlight Children's Foundation (£3,000); Lupus UK (£2,600); Ehlers Danlos Support Group (£1,700); and Disabled Living Foundation and Matthew Trust (£1,000 each).

Exclusions No grants to individuals, expeditions, research, scholarships, charities with a local focus, local branches of UK charities or towards running costs.

Applications On an application form available from the correspondent. Applications should include a copy of the latest audited annual report and accounts. They are considered twice a year in mid-summer and mid-autumn. Organisations which have received grants from this trust, the Cleopatra Trust or the Dorus Trust should not reapply in the following two years. Usually, funding will be considered from only one of these trusts.

Epilepsy Research UK

Epilepsy

£417,000 (2005/06)
Beneficial area UK.

PO Box 3004, London W4 4XT
Tel. 020 8995 4781 **Fax** 020 8995 4781
Email info@eruk.org.uk
Website www.epilepsyresearch.org.uk
Correspondent Isabella von Holstein, Research and Information Executive
Trustees *Dr R Appleton; B Akin; Prof C Binnie; Rt Hon D Cameron; Dr J H Cross; Dr R Elwes; J Hirst; S Lanyon; Dr J Mumford; Dr L Nashef; Prof B Neville; P Newman; Dr J Oxley; H Salmon; M Stevens; Dr H Wilkins.*

CC Number 1100394

Information available Accounts were on file at the Charity Commission.

General 'Epilepsy Research UK annually invites applications for grants to support basic, clinical and scientific research work in the UK into the causes, treatment and prevention of epilepsy. We encourage applications on all aspects of epilepsy including basic and social science, clinical management and holistic management of patients.'

In 2005/06 the trust had assets of £93,000 and an income of £683,000. Out of a total expenditure of £659,000, the sum of £417,000 was committed in research grants.

Exclusions Research not undertaken within a recognised institute in the UK.

Applications Applications are invited by advertisement in journals and through the Research Register (interested parties can register for updates at www.epilepsyresearch.org.uk).

The Equity Trust Fund

Theatre

£275,000 to organisations and individuals (2005/06)
Beneficial area UK.

222 Africa House, 64 Kingsway, London WC2B 6AH
Tel. 020 7404 6041
Correspondent Keith Carter, Secretary
Trustees *Milton Johns; Jeffrey Wickham; Nigel Davenport; Gillian Raine; Peter Plouviez; Derek Bond; Frank Williams; Ian McGarry; Colin Baker; Barbara Hyslop; Annie Bright; Graham Hamilton; Harry Landis; Frederik Pyne; Rosalind Shanks; Johnny Worthy; Frank Hitchman; James Bolam; John Rubinstein; Ian Talbot; Josephine Tewson; Robin Browne; Oliver Ford Davies; Jean Rogers.*

CC Number 328103

Information available Accounts were on file at the Charity Commission.

General The charity is a benevolent fund for professional performers and stage managers and their dependants. It offers help with welfare rights, gives free debt counselling and information and can offer financial assistance to those in genuine need. It also has an education fund to help members of the profession with further training provided they have at least 10 years' professional adult experience. It also makes grants and loans to professional theatres or theatre companies.

In 2005/06 the trust had assets of £9.4 million and an income of £351,000. Grants to organisations and individuals totalled £275,000.

Exclusions No grants to non-professional performers, drama students, non-professional theatre companies, multi-arts venues, community projects or projects with no connection to the professional theatre.

Applications In the first instance please call the office to ascertain if the application is relevant. Failing that, submit a brief letter outlining the application. A meeting takes place about every six to eight weeks. Ring for precise dates. Applications are required at least two weeks beforehand.

The Ericson Trust

See below

£32,000 (2005/06)

Beneficial area UK, developing countries, Eastern and Central Europe.

Flat 2, 53 Carleton Road, London N7 0ET

Correspondent The Trustees

Trustees *Miss R C Cotton; Mrs V J Barrow; Mrs A M C Cotton.*

CC Number 219762

Information available Full accounts were on file at the Charity Commission.

General The trust provides grants to previously supported organisations in the following fields: (a) older people; (b) community projects/local interest groups, including arts; (c) prisons, prison reform, mentoring projects, as well as research in this area; (d) refugees; (e) mental health; (f) environmental projects and research; and (g) aid to developing countries provided by a UK-registered charity.

In 2005/06 it had assets of £682,000 and an income of £46,000 including donations of £25,000. Grants were made to 12 organisations and totalled £32,000.

Beneficiaries were: Tools for Self Reliance (£7,000); Anti-Slavery International, Ashram International, CAMFED International, Psychiatric Rehabilitation Association, Quaker

Social Action and the Relatives and Residents Association (£3,000 each); St Mungo's Community Housing Association and Trail Blazers (£2,000 each); and Development Organisation of Rural Sichuan, Headway East London and Umanalini Mary Brahma Charitable Trust (£1,000 each).

Exclusions No grants to individuals or to non-registered charities. Applications from the following areas are generally not considered unless closely connected with one of the above: children's and young people's clubs, centres and so on; schools; charities dealing with illness or disability (except psychiatric); or religious institutions, except in their social projects.

Applications Unsolicited applications cannot be considered as the trust has no funds available. The correspondent stated: 'We are increasingly worried by the waste of applicants' resources when they send expensive brochures at a time when we are unable to consider any new appeals and have, indeed, reduced some of our long-standing grants due to the bad economic situation. It is particularly sad when we receive requests from small charities in Africa and Asia.'

The Essex Youth Trust

Young people, education of people under 25

£361,000 paid (2005/06)

Beneficial area Essex.

Gepp and Sons, 58 New London Road, Chelmsford, Essex CM2 0PA

Tel. 01245 493939 **Fax** 01245 493940

Correspondent J P Douglas-Hughes

Trustees *Richard Wenley; Julien Courtauld; Michael Dyer; Raymond Knappett; Revd Duncan Green; David Robson; Julia Denison-Smith; Claire Coltwell; Michael Biegel.*

CC Number 225768

Information available Accounts were on file at the Charity Commission.

General The Essex Youth Trust comprises four charities administered under a scheme dated 24 February 1993. The four charities are Essex Home School for Boys, The Charity of George Stacey Gibson, The Charity of George Cleveley and The Charity of Adelia Joyce Snelgrove.

The trust's objectives are the advancement of education for people under the age of 25 who are in need of assistance. Preference is given to those who are in need owing to 'being temporarily or permanently deprived of normal parental care or who are otherwise disadvantaged'.

'The trustees favour organisations which develop young people's physical, mental and spiritual capacities through active participation in sports and indoor and outdoor activities. As a result they are particularly supportive of youth clubs and other organisations which provide facilities for young people to take active part in an assortment of activities as well as single activity organisations.'

In 2005/06 the trust had assets of £8.5 million and an income of £493,000. Grants paid to 45 organisations in the year totalled £361,000.

Beneficiaries included: Stubbers Adventure Centre (£72,000 in three grants); Cirdan Sailing Trust (£69,000 in three grants); Essex Association of Boys Clubs (£39,000); St Mark's College (£20,000); Lambourne End Centre (£19,000 in two grants); Barnardos (£17,000); North Avenue Youth Centre (£16,000); Christian Adventure Trust (£15,000); St Mary's Church Saffron Walden (£9,000); Solid (£7,000); Voice for the Voiceless (£6,500); Ingatestone Boys Own Club (£5,000); Havering Motorvations and Listening Books (£3,000 each); Holy Cross Youth Club (£2,500); Out There (£2,000); and the Straight Talking Project (£1,000).

Exclusions No grants to individuals.

Applications On a form available from the correspondent. The trustees meet on a quarterly basis.

The Evangelical Covenants Trust

Christian evangelism

£79,000 (2005/06)

Beneficial area UK, with a preference for Devon.

Mardon, 188b Exeter Road, Exmouth, Devon EX8 3DZ

Correspondent Alfred W Tarring, Trustee

Trustees *C Desmond Gahan; Alfred W Tarring; Kathleen M Tarring.*

CC Number 285224

Information available Accounts were on file at the Charity Commission, without a list of grants.

General The objective of this trust is to distribute funds to Christian organisations of an evangelical nature, although any charitable cause will be considered. In 2005/06 the trust had assets of £27,000 and an income of £82,000, mostly from covenants and Gift Aid donations. A total of £79,000 was distributed in grants.

Grants are disbursed on a national basis, but, with the majority of donors living in Devon, the geographical spread of giving has reflected this interest (32% of all gifts were distributed to churches in the county).

Applications The trust stressed that unsolicited applications are NOT considered: 'Grants are made only on the request and recommendation of donors of the trust.'

The Alan Evans Memorial Trust

Preservation, conservation

£297,000 (2004/05)
Beneficial area UK.

Coutts and Co., Trustee Department, 440 Strand, London WC2R 0QS
Correspondent The Trust Manager
Trustees *Coutts and Co.; D J Halfhead; Mrs D Moss.*
CC Number 326263
Information available Full accounts were on file at the Charity Commission.

General The objectives of the trust 'are to promote the permanent preservation, for the benefit of the nation, of lands and tenements (including buildings) of beauty or historic interest and as regards land, the preservation (so far as practicable) of the natural aspect, features and animal and plant life'.

In 2004/05 the trust had assets of £2.4 million and an income of £72,000. After high administration and management costs of £53,000, grants to over 150 organisations totalled £297,000.

Beneficiaries included Calvert Trust – Exmoor, Gloucester Cathedral, Selby Abbey Restoration Appeal – Old Malton, St Mary de Haura – Shoreham-by-Sea and the John Rylands Library –

University of Manchester (£5,000 each), St Mary's, Cowbit – Spalding (£4,000) and Bletchley Park Trust, St Andrew's – Blo Norton and St Peter and St Paul – Wincanton (£3,000 each).

About two-thirds of the grants made were for amounts of £2,000, £1,500 or £1,000 each including those to Abbotts Hall Farm Coastal Realignment Project, Benjamin Franklin House – London, the Church of St Mary the Virgin – Rudford, Devon Wildlife Trust, the Friends of Grasmere, the Gaia Trust, Historic Chapels Trust, Middle St Synagogue – Brighton, People's Trust for Endangered Species, Raasay Heritage Trust, St Andrew's – Meonstoke, St Peter's – Ealing, Trees for Life and the Wessex Chalk Streams Project.

Exclusions No grants to individuals or for management or running expenses, although favourable consideration is given in respect of the purchase of land and restoration of buildings. Grants are given to registered charities only. Appeals will not be acknowledged.

Applications There is no formal application form, but appeals should be made in writing to the correspondent, stating why the funds are required, what funds have been promised from other sources (for example, English Heritage) and the amount outstanding. The trust also told us that it would be helpful when making applications to provide a photograph of the project. Trustees normally meet four times a year, although in urgent cases decisions can be made between meetings.

The Eventhall Family Charitable Trust

General

£184,000 (2005/06)
Beneficial area Preference for north west England.

PO Box 490, Altrincham WA14 22T
Correspondent The Trustees
Trustees *Julia Eventhall; David Eventhall.*
CC Number 803178
Information available Accounts were obtained from the Charity Commission website, but without a grants list.

General In 2005/06 the trust had assets of £2.9 million and an income of £116,000. Grants totalled £184,000 distributed to around 64 registered charities. A list of the beneficiaries was not available within the accounts.

In previous years other beneficiaries have included Aish Hatorah, ChildLine, Clitheroe Wolves Football Club, Community Security Trust, Greibach Memorial, Guide Dogs for the Blind, Heathlands Village, International Wildlife Coalition, JJCT, MB Foundation Charity, Only Foals and Horses Sanctuary, Red Nose Day, RNLI, Sale Ladies Society, Shelter and South Manchester Synagogue.

Exclusions No grants to students.

Applications In writing to the correspondent. Please note, however, previous research highlighted that the trust stated it only has a very limited amount of funds available. Telephone calls are not accepted by the trust. Trustees meet monthly to consider grants. A pre-addressed envelope is appreciated (stamp not necessary). Unsuccessful applicants will not receive a reply.

The Beryl Evetts and Robert Luff Animal Welfare Trust

Animal welfare

£120,000 (2004/05)
Beneficial area UK.

294 Earls Court Road, London SW5 9BB
Tel. 020 8954 2727
Correspondent The Administrator
Trustees *Sir R Johnson; Revd M Tomlinson; Mrs J Tomlinson; R P J Price; B Nicholson; Lady Johnson; Ms G Favot.*
CC Number 283944
Information available Full accounts were on file at the Charity Commission.

General The principal objective of the trust is the funding of veterinary research and the care and welfare of animals. It appears to make substantial commitments to a few organisations over several years, whether to build up capital funds or to establish fellowships. The trust gives priority to research projects and bursaries. In practice, the trust supports the same beneficiaries each year.

In 2004/05 the trust had assets of £1.4 million with an income of £50,000 and grants totalling £120,000.

Grants went to: Royal Veterinary College (£55,000); Animal Health Trust (two awards, a 'grant payment' of £35,000 and an additional £20,000); and Blue Cross (£10,000).

Applications 'No applications, thank you.' The trust gives grants to the same beneficiaries each year and funds are often allocated two years in advance.

The Exilarch's Foundation

Jewish

£63,000 (2005)
Beneficial area Mainly UK.

4 Carlos Place, Mayfair, London W1K 3AW
Correspondent N E Dangoor, Trustee
Trustees *N E Dangoor; D A Dangoor; E B Dangoor; R D Dangoor; M J Dangoor.*
CC Number 275919
Information available Information was on file at the Charity Commission.

General In 2005 the trust had assets of £40 million and it had an income of £3.4 million. After management and administration costs of £26,000, grants were made totalling £63,000.

The foundation's annual report states that: 'The trustees have built up a designated reserve of £10 million for the specific purpose of assisting the setting up of educational and religious institutions in a future re-established Jewish community in Iraq. Once the position and security of that country have been stabilised it is anticipated that some Jews may choose to live in Iraq when they will be free to pursue their religious faith without fear of persecution and discrimination.

'The funds now being specifically set aside are to be used to help rebuild synagogues and communal buildings, and to assist in providing Jewish schools in Iraq as and when the community's need arises, and when it becomes possible for Jews to live there again.'

Beneficiaries included: the Spanish and Portuguese Jews Congregation (£6,700); Spanish and Portuguese Burial Society

(£5,600); British Supports of Efrat (£5,000); Magen David Adom (£3,500); Jewish Chaplaincy Board, UCS Hardship Fund and the Simon Wiesenthal Centre in the UK (£3,000 each); Norwood (£2,500); Sassoon Memorial Fund (£1,400); and Community Security Trust, the Jerusalem Academy Trust and Menorah Grammar School (£1,000 each).

The sum of £3,300 was distributed to individuals.

Applications The trust stated that it does not respond to unsolicited applications for grants.

Extonglen Limited

Orthodox Jewish

£242,000 (2005)
Beneficial area UK.

New Burlington House, 1075 Finchley Road, London NW11 0PU
Correspondent The Trustees
Trustees *M Levine; Mrs C Levine; B B Rapaport; I Katzenberg.*
CC Number 286230
Information available Accounts were on file at the Charity Commission.

General Registered with the Charity Commission in January 1983, this trust accepts applications from representatives of Orthodox Jewish charities.

In 2005 it had assets of £13.4 million and an income of £260,000. Grants totalled £242,000 and included a major donation to Kol Halashon Education Programme (£176,000). Other listed beneficiaries were British Friends of Nishmat Yisrael (£38,000), Achisomoch Aid Society (£11,000), Children's Town Charity (£8,900), Kollel Shomrei Hachomoth (£5,000) and Keren Hatorah and Keren Hayoled (£1,000 each).

Donations under £1,000 each totalled £1,100.

Applications In writing to the correspondent.

The Fairway Trust

General

£36,000 (2005/06)
Beneficial area UK and worldwide.

The Gate House, Coombe Wood Road, Kingston-upon-Thames, Surrey KT2 7JY
Correspondent Mrs J Grimstone, Trustee
Trustees *Mrs Janet Grimstone; Ms K V M Suenson-Taylor.*
CC Number 272227
Information available Accounts were on file at the Charity Commission.

General The trust's accounts states it will continue support for charities engaged in the fields of education, religion and social welfare.

In 2005/06 the trust had an income almost entirely from donations of £36,000, all of which was given in grants. By far the largest grant was given to Family Education Trust (£20,000).

Other beneficiaries were: Sir John Soanes Museum (£5,000); Boys' and Girls' Clubs of Northern Ireland, the College of St George – Windsor Castle and Welsh National Opera (£2,000 each); Sight Savers (£1,500); Prayer Book Society (£1,250); KidsOut (£1,000); and Grantchester PCC (£750).

Exclusions No grants to medical charities.

Applications The trustees have an established list of charities which they support on a regular basis. Unsolicited applications are not therefore considered.

The Family Foundations Trust (also known as Mintz Family Foundation)

General, Jewish
See below
Beneficial area UK.

Gerald Edelman, 25 Harley Street, London W1G 9BR

Correspondent The Accountant to the Trustees

Trustees *R B Mintz; P G Mintz.*

CC Number 264014

Information available Information had been filed at the Charity Commission.

General In 2005/06 the trust had an income of £6,200 and a total expenditure of £194,000. No further information was available for this year. In the six years up to 2005/06 it had an income ranging between £112,000 and £243,000.

Previous beneficiaries have included Bar Ilan University, British ORT, Community Security Trust, JFS General Charitable Trust, Lubavitch Foundation, United Jewish Israel Appeal, Western Marble Arch Synagogue and World Jewish Relief.

Applications In writing to the correspondent.

Famos Foundation Trust

Jewish

£82,000 (2005/06)

Beneficial area UK and overseas.

4 Hanover Gardens, Salford, Lancashire M7 4FQ

Correspondent Rabbi S M Kupetz, Trustee

Trustees *Rabbi S M Kupetz; Mrs F Kupetz.*

CC Number 271211

Information available Accounts were on file at the Charity Commission.

General The trust supports a wide range of Jewish organisations, including those concerned with education and the relief of poverty. Many grants are recurrent and are of up to £5,000 each. In 2005/06 it had assets of £1.1 million and an income of £172,000. Grants totalled £82,000, broken down into the following categories: relief of poverty (£42,000); Education (£32,000); and places of worship (£8,500).

Exclusions No grants to individuals.

Applications In writing to the correspondent, at any time. The trust does not accept telephone enquiries.

The Lord Faringdon Charitable Trust

Medical, general

£172,000 (2004/05)

Beneficial area UK.

The Estate Office, Buscot Park, Oxfordshire SN7 8BU

Tel. 01367 240786

Correspondent J R Waters, Secretary to the Trustees

Trustees *A D A W Forbes, Chair; Hon. J H Henderson; R P Trotter.*

CC Number 1084690

Information available Accounts were on file at the Charity Commission.

General This trust was formed in 2000 by the amalgamation of the Lord Faringdon first and second trusts. It supports:

- educational objectives
- hospitals and the provision of medical treatment for the sick
- purchase of antiques and artistic objects for museums and collections that have public access
- care and assistance of people who are elderly or infirm
- development and assistance of arts and sciences, physical recreation and drama
- research into matters of public interest
- relief of poverty
- support of matters of public interest
- maintaining and improving the Faringdon Collection.

In 2004/05 it had assets of £5.1 million, which generated an income of £151,000. Grants to 48 organisations totalled £172,000.

Beneficiaries of the largest grants were: the Faringdon Collection (£35,000); Cotswold Care Hospice (£25,000); the National Trust (£18,000); and Autism Genome Project – NAAR UK and Royal Horticultural Society (£10,000 each).

Organisations in receipt of grants of £1,000 or more included: the Royal Choral Society (£7,500); St Luke's Hospital for the Clergy (£6,500); Harrow Club and the Royal Opera House (£5,000 each); the Hillier Gardens, Leicestershire Chorale and Lincoln Cathedral (£2,500 each); Everyman Theatre and Parkinson Society (£2,000 each); Crimestoppers Trust, Faringdon Arts Festival and Tall Ships Youth Trust (£1,500 each); and Dendrology Society,

Dressability and Victoria and Albert Museum (£1,000 each).

Organisations receiving smaller grants, under £1,000 each included Alzheimer's Society, Bridewell Organic Gardens, Eyeless Trust, Larkrise School Playgroup, Valiant Appeal and Wantage Independent Advice Centre.

Exclusions No grants to individuals, just to registered charities.

Applications In writing to the correspondent.

Samuel William Farmer's Trust

Education, health, social welfare

£53,000 (2005)

Beneficial area Mainly Wiltshire.

71 High Street, Market Lavington, Devizes, Wiltshire SN10 4AG

Correspondent Mrs M Linden-Fermor, Secretary

Trustees *Mrs J A Liddiard; W J Rendell; P G Fox-Andrews; B J Waight; C K Brockis.*

CC Number 258459

Information available Accounts were on file at the Charity Commission.

General The trust was established in 1928 for: the benefit of poor people who through ill health or old age are unable to earn their own livelihood; for educational purposes; and for the benefit of hospitals, nursing and convalescent homes or other similar objectives. The trustees apply a modern interpretation of these aims when assessing applications, supporting both individuals and organisations.

In 2005 the trust had assets of £2.1 million and an income of £76,000. 'Special' grants for this year totalled £53,000. An additional £6,000 was distributed in 'annual' grants: Royal Agricultural Benevolent Institution and Royal United Kingdom Beneficent (£3,000 each).

Special grants went to 27 organisations. Beneficiaries included: Dorothy House (£6,000); the Crown Centre – Devizes, Devizes and District Disabled Association, Devizes and District Guiding Building Fund and Wiltshire Air Ambulance Appeal (£5,000 each); Riding For the Disabled Association

113

(£2,500); 2nd Watlington Scouts, Canine Partners, Iknield Community College, Leonard Cheshire, the Oundle Society and Salisbury Arts Centre (£2,000 each); Age Concern – Salisbury District and National Osteoporosis Society (£1,000 each); Wiltshire Heritage (£750); and Happy Days and Help Counselling Services (£500 each).

Exclusions No grants to students, or for schools and colleges, endowments, inner-city welfare or housing.

Applications In writing to the correspondent. Trustees meet half-yearly.

Farthing Trust

Christian, general

£185,000 to organisations and individuals (2005/06)
Beneficial area UK and overseas.

48 Ten Mile Bank, Littleport, Ely, Cambridgeshire CB6 1EF
Correspondent The Trustees
Trustees C H Martin; Mrs E Martin; Miss J Martin; Mrs A White.
CC Number 268066
Information available Accounts were on file at the Charity Commission.

General In 2005/06 the trust had assets of £2.8 million, an income of £145,000 and made grants totalling £185,000. About £80,000 of this was given to organisations, including churches, in the UK.

Applications Applications and enquiries should be made in writing to the correspondent. Applicants, and any others requesting information, will only receive a response if an sae is enclosed. There would seem little point in applying unless a personal contact with a trustee is established.

The Fawcett Charitable Trust

Disability

£654,000 (2004/05) see below
Beneficial area UK with a preference for Hampshire and West Sussex.

Blake Lapthorn, Harbour Court, Compass Road, North Harbour, Portsmouth, Hampshire PO6 4ST
Tel. 023 9222 1122
Correspondent Céline Lecomte
Trustees D J Fawcett; Mrs F P Fawcett; D W Russell.
CC Number 1013167
Information available Accounts were on file at the Charity Commission.

General The trust was set up in 1991 by Derek and Frances Fawcett with an endowment of shares in their company with an initial value of £1.6 million.

According to the trust, it supports work aimed at increasing the quality of life of disabled people by facilitating and providing recreation opportunities. Preference is normally given to organisations and projects located in Hampshire and West Sussex.

In 2004/05 the trust had assets of £965,000, an income of £47,000 and made grants totalling £654,000 (£76,000 in the previous year).

By far the largest grant went to Tsunami Earthquake Appeal (£500,000). There were 14 other grants listed in the accounts in the range of £2,000 and £25,000. Beneficiaries included: Chichester Festive Theatre Trust, Chichester Harbour Trust and Jubilee Sailing Trust (£25,000 each); Khao Lak Community Appeal (£20,000); the Rowans Hospice, St Wilfred's Hospice and Naomi's House Children's Hospice (£10,000 each); Elizabeth Fitzroy Support and Sujeeva Humanitarian Association (£5,000 each); and Cobnor Activities Centre Trust (£2,000).

Exclusions Large national charities are excluded as a rule.

Applications In writing to the correspondent.

The John Feeney Charitable Bequest

Arts, heritage and open spaces

£41,000 (2005)
Beneficial area Birmingham.

Cobbetts Solicitors, One Colmore Square, Birmingham B4 6AJ

Tel. 0845 404 2404
Email martin.woodward@cobbetts.co.uk
Correspondent M J Woodward, Secretary
Trustees C R King-Farlow; D M P Lea; S J Lloyd; Mrs M F Lloyd; H B Carslake; J R L Smith; M S Darby; Mrs S R Wright.
CC Number 214486
Information available Accounts were on file at the Charity Commission.

General The trust was set up in 1907 when John Feeney directed that one-tenth of his residue estate be invested and the income used for the benefit of public charities in the city of Birmingham, for the promotion and cultivation of art in the city and for the acquisition and maintenance of parks, recreation grounds or open spaces in or near the city.

In 2004 it had assets of £1.5 million and an income of £63,000. There were 40 grants made totalling £41,000, broken down as follows and shown with examples of beneficiaries in each category:

Arts – 4 grants totalling £2,300
Royal Birmingham Society of Artists (£1,000); Artsense (£500); and Deep Impact Theatre Company (£300).

Music – 5 grants totalling £8,800
Birmingham Bach Choir (£5,000); Birmingham Festival Choral Society (£2,000); Three Choirs Festival (£1,000); and Operamus Birmingham Youth Opera (£300).

Open spaces – 2 grants totalling £3,000
Castle Bromwich Hall Gardens Trust (£2,000); and Birmingham Botanical Gardens and Glasshouses (£1,000).

Children and young people (medical) – 3 grants totalling £2,300
Edward's Trust (£1,000); the Norman Laud Association (£750); and BID Services with Deaf People (£500).

Children and young people (general) – 11 grants totalling £11,000
St Basil's Centre (£2,500); the Ackers and Birmingham Boys' and Girls' Union (£2,000); Birmingham Federation of Clubs for Young People (£1,000); Birmingham Phab Camps (£750); and 870 House and Friends of Birmingham Guiding (£500 each).

Medical – 4 grants totalling £2,500
Listening Books, the National Listening Library and Phoenix Sheltered Workshop (£750 each); and Birmingham Centre for Art Therapies (£500).

General – 11 grants totalling £11,000
Birmingham Rathbone Society (£1,500); City of Birmingham Special Olympics,

East Birmingham FSU, Open Door Youth Counselling and Samaritans Birmingham (£1,000 each); Access Committee for Birmingham and Cruse Bereavement Care (£500 each).

Exclusions Applications will not be accepted: from, or on behalf of, individuals; which do not directly benefit the Birmingham area or Birmingham charitable organisations; which could be considered as political or denominational.

Additionally, applications from large national charities, even with a Birmingham base, are unlikely to succeed.

Applications In writing to the correspondent by March of each year. There is no application form and no sae is required. However, letters in support must clearly set out for what purpose, or purposes, the funding is being sought and must enclose a copy of the charity's latest accounts.

The A M Fenton Trust

General

£138,000 (2005)

Beneficial area UK, preference for North Yorkshire, and overseas.

14 Beech Grove, Harrogate, North Yorkshire HG2 0EX

Correspondent J L Fenton, Trustee

Trustees *J L Fenton; C M Fenton.*

CC Number 270353

Information available Accounts were obtained from the Charity Commission website.

General The trust was created by Alexander Miller Fenton in 1975. After his death in 1977, the residue of his estate was transferred to the trust.

In 2005 the trust had assets of £4.3 million and an income of £137,000. Grants to 72 organisations totalled £138,000.

Beneficiaries of the four largest grants were: Yorkshire County Cricket Club Charitable Youth Trust (£20,000); and Hipperholme Grammar School, Hunsworth Scout Group HQ and St Mary Church Bosworth (£10,000 each).

Grants of £1,000 or more included those to: Dewsbury League of Friendship (£7,500); Norwood Green Village Hall

Charitable Trust and Tsunami Appeal (£5,000); Tweed Foundation and Yorkshire Air Ambulance (£3,000 each); Age Concern Knaresborough, Kenmore Leonard Cheshire Homes and Mid Yorkshire Hospital Laser Appeal (£2,500 each); Disability Action Yorkshire, Gurkha Welfare Trust and Salvation Army (£2,000 each); and Arthritis Research Campaign, British Red Cross and Yorkshire Children's Hospital Fund (£1,000 each).

Beneficiaries of smaller grants included Airedale Child Asthma Support Group, Association of WRENS, Dyslexia Institute, Help at Home, RNLI, Society for Abandoned Animals, Song Bird Survival, Time Together and War Memorials Trust.

Exclusions The trust is unlikely to support local appeals, unless they are close to where the trust is based.

Applications In writing to the correspondent.

Elizabeth Hardie Ferguson Charitable Trust Fund

Children, medical research, health, hospices

About £50,000

Beneficial area UK, with some interest in Scotland.

c/o 27 Peregrine Crescent, Droylsden, Manchester M43 7TA

Correspondent Paul Hardman, Trustee

Trustees *Sir Alex Ferguson; Cathy Ferguson; Huw Roberts; Ted Way; Les Dalgarno; Paul Hardman; Jason Ferguson.*

SC Number SC026240

Information available Limited information was provided by the trust.

General This trust was created by Sir Alex Ferguson in 1998 in memory of his mother. It supports a range of children's and medical charities. Grants range from £250 to £10,000 and can be recurrent. Various high-profile events have contributed to the trust's income in recent years. Grants are distributed in the areas where the income is raised. No recent financial information was

available from the correspondent, although previous research indicates that grants total around £50,000 each year.

Charities supported by the founder in his home town of Govan will continue to be supported through the trust. Recent beneficiaries have included the Govan Initiative and Harmony Row Boys' Club.

Exclusions Non-registered charities and individuals are not supported. The trust does not make grants overseas.

Applications An application form and guidelines should be requested in writing from the correspondent. The committee meets to consider grants at the end of January and July. Applications should be received by December and June respectively.

The Bluff Field Charitable Trust

General

See below

Beneficial area UK.

8 The Little Boltons, London SW10 9LP

Correspondent Peter Field, Trustee

Trustees *Peter Field; Sonia Field.*

CC Number 1057992

Information available Accounts were on file at the Charity Commission.

General Established in 1996, in 2005 this trust had an income of just £427 and a total expenditure of £29,000. In previous years it has received substantial income from donations and Gift Aid. In the six years up to 2005 it had an income of between £77,000 and £147,000.

Previous beneficiaries have included Emmanuel Church Billericay, Leukaemia Research Fund, Risk Waters' World Trade Centre UK Appeal, St George's Hospital Medical School and Wigmore Hall Trust.

Applications In writing to the correspondent.

The Doris Field Charitable Trust

General

£165,000 to organisations (2004/05)

Beneficial area UK, with a preference for Oxfordshire.

c/o Morgan Cole, Buxton Court, 3 West Way, Oxford OX2 0SZ

Correspondent The Trustees

Trustees *N A Harper; J Cole; Mrs W Church.*

CC Number 328687

Information available Accounts were on file at the Charity Commission.

General One-off and recurrent grants are given to large UK organisations and small local projects for a wide variety of causes. The trust states that it favours playgroups and local causes in Oxfordshire.

In 2004/05 the trust had assets of £6.1 million and an income of £310,000. Grants were made totalling over £166,000, of which £165,000 was donated to 139 organisations and £1,200 was awarded to two individuals.

Beneficiaries of larger grants included: the Pathway Workshop (£10,000); Hearing Dogs for Deaf People, Headway Oxford, Oxfordshire Historic Churches Trust and the Royal Society for the Protection of Birds (£5,000 each); St Peter's Church (£4,300); Mulberry Bush School (£3,500); St Andrew's Church and St Nicholas' PCC (£3,000 each); 4th Oxford Scout Group (£2,700); Bath Institute of Medical Engineering and Hinksey Sculling School and (£2,500 each); Oxfordshire Parents with Disabilities Network, Pennyhooks Project and Rose Hill and Donnington Advice Centre (£2,000 each); Asthma UK (£1,500); and Barnardos, BREAK, Church Housing Trust, Guideposts Trust, the Oxfordshire Touring Theatre Company, Trinity Sailing Trust, Watlington Bowls Club and Whizz-Kidz (£1,000 each).

Exclusions It is unlikely that grants would be made for overseas projects or to individuals for higher education.

Applications On a form available from the correspondent. Applications are considered three times a year or as and when necessary.

Dixie Rose Findlay Charitable Trust

Children, seafarers, blindness, multiple sclerosis

£96,000 (2004/05)

Beneficial area UK.

HSBC Trust Co. (UK) Ltd, Norwich House, Commercial Road, Southampton SO15 1GX

Correspondent Colin Bould

Trustee *HSBC Trust Co. (UK) Ltd.*

CC Number 251661

Information available Information was provided by the trust.

General This trust is concerned with children, seafarers, blindness, multiple sclerosis and similar conditions. In 2004/05 it had assets of £3.6 million and an income from investments of £108,000. A further £612,000 was received in funds from probate. Grants totalled £96,000

Beneficiaries of amounts of £1,000 or more were listed in the accounts and included Cassell Hospital, Children's Society, Glen Arun, Leukaemia Research, St John's Wood Church, the Mission to Seafarers, RNLI, Royal London Society for the Blind and Royal National Mission for Deep Sea Fishermen (£7,000 each in two grants), Action for Blind People, Multiple Sclerosis Therapy Centre, NSPCC and RNIB (£2,600 each in two grants) and Banardos, British Liver Trust, Deafblind UK, Elimination of Leukaemia Fund, King George's Fund for Sailors, Royal School for the Blind and Well Child (£1,300 each).

Applications In writing to the correspondent.

Finnart House School Trust

Jewish children and young people in need of care

£7,000 to organisations (2005/06)

Beneficial area Worldwide.

PO Box 603, Edgware, Middlesex HA8 4EQ

Tel. 020 3209 6006

Email info@finnart.org

Correspondent Peter Shaw, Clerk

Trustees *Dr Louis Marks, Chair; Robert Cohen; Hilary Norton; David Fobel; Lilian Hochhauser; Jane Leaver; Mark Sebba; Linda Peterson; Sue Leifer.*

CC Number 220917

Information available Financial information was provided by the trust.

General The trust supports the relief of children and young people who are of the Jewish faith and aged 21 and under. Bursaries and scholarships are given to Jewish secondary school pupils and university entrants who are capable of achieving, but would probably not do so because of family and economic pressures. Also supported is work concerned with people who are disaffected, disadvantaged socially and economically through illness or neglect or in need of care and education.

In 2005/06 it had assets of £4.6 million, which generated an income of £146,000. Grants were made to organisations totalling £7,000. A further £157,000 was given in total in 21 scholarships to individuals.

Applications There is an application form for organisations, which needs to be submitted together with a copy of the latest annual report and accounts.

For undergraduate students entering university there is a separate application form which has to be submitted with various supporting information.

Gerald Finzi Charitable Trust

Music

£21,000 to organisations and individuals (2004/05).

Beneficial area UK.

Benson Flynn & Co., Abbey House, 8 Abbey Square, Chester, CH1 2HU

Tel. 01244 320300 **Fax** 01244 341200

Email admin@finzi.org.uk

Website www.geraldfinzi.org/

Correspondent Elizabeth Pooley, Administator

Trustees *Robert Gower, Chair; Christian Alexander; Andrew Burn; Jean Finzi;*

Nigel Finzi; Jeremy Dale Roberts; Paul Spicer.

CC Number 313047

Information available Full accounts were on file at the Charity Commission.

General The trustees aim to reflect the ambitions and philosophy of the composer Gerald Finzi (1901–56), which included the general promotion of 20th-century British music through assisting and promoting festivals, recordings and performances of British music. A limited number of modest grants are also offered to young musicians towards musical training.

In 2005 the trust had assets of £117,000 and an income of £40,000. Donations were made totalling £21,000; these included those to the National Youth Orchestra (£3,500), Lontano (£3,000), Festivals of English Song (£2,250), St Mary's Cathedral Edinburgh (£1,250), the Kenneth Leighton Trust and the Three Choirs Festival (£1,000 each), the Royal College of Music (£400) and the Oxford University Press (£150).

Other activities included a contribution of £11,000 in scholarships and £2,100 to Reading University towards the Finzi bookroom.

Applications In writing to the correspondent.

Marc Fitch Fund

Humanities

£121,000 to organisations (2005/06)

Beneficial area UK.

PO Box 207, Chipping Norton OX7 3ZQ

Tel. 01608 811944

Email admin@marcfitchfund.org.uk

Website www.marcfitchfund.org.uk

Correspondent The Director

Trustees *A S Bell, Chair; Prof. D M Palliser; Prof. J Blair; Dr H Forde; A Murison; L Allason-Jones; Prof. D Hey.*

CC Number 313303

Information available Accounts were on file at the Charity Commission.

General The trust makes grants to organisations and individuals for publication and research in archaeology, historical geography, history of art and architecture, heraldry, genealogy, use and preservation of archives, conservation of artefacts and other

antiquarian, archaeological and historical studies. The primary focus of the fund is the local and regional history of the British Isles.

Grants range from relatively minor amounts to more substantial special project grants which may be paid over more than one year. In many cases, the awards enable work to be undertaken, or the results published either in print or on-line form, which would not otherwise be achieved.

In 2005/06 it had assets of £4.7 million and an income of £193,000. Grants to organisations totalled £121,000, whilst £41,000 was given in research grants to individuals.

Beneficiaries included: British School at Rome (£15,000); Staffordshire and Stoke-on-Trent Archives (£13,000); Bristol Cathedral Trust, Manorial Documents Register and Victoria County History – Middlesex (£10,000 each); University of Leicester (£9,900); Victoria County History (£7,500); Bowes Museum (£6,000); Corpus of British Medieval Library Catalogues and Lambeth Place Library (£5,000 each); Thomas Plume's Library (£2,500); Community Landscape and Survey Project and Monumental Brass Society (£2,000 each); Portsmouth Record Studies, Worcestershire Historical Society and York Archaeological Trust (£1,000 each); and Local Population Studies Society (£500).

Exclusions No grants are given towards foreign travel or for research outside the British Isles, unless the circumstances are very exceptional; no awards are made in connection with vocational or higher education courses or to people reading for higher degrees.

Applications In writing to the correspondent. The council of management meets twice a year, usually in April and September, to consider applications. The deadlines for receipt of completed applications and references are 1 March and 1 August.

The Fitton Trust

Social welfare, medical

£97,000 (2005/06)

Beneficial area UK.

PO Box 649, London SW3 4LA

Correspondent Mrs Rosalind Gordon-Cumming, The Secretary

Trustees *Dr R P A Rivers; D V Brand; R Brand; K J Lumsden; E M Lumsden; L P L Rivers.*

CC Number 208758

Information available Accounts were on file at the Charity Commission, but without a list of grants.

General In 2005/06 the trust had assets of over £2 million and an income of £165,000. The total amount given in 337 grants came to £97,000.

The majority of beneficiaries received £100–£250. Only six organisations received £1,000 or more: St Stephen's Restoration & Preservation Trust (£2,200); Kings Medical Research Trust (£2,100); Save the Baby Fund (£2,000); and Cancer Resource Centre, East Sussex Disability Association and Hertfordshire Building Preservation Trust (£1,000 each).

Exclusions No grants to individuals.

Applications In writing to correspondent. The trustees meet three times each year, usually in April, August and December. The trust states: 'No application considered unless accompanied by fully audited accounts. No replies will be sent to unsolicited applications whether from individuals, charities or other bodies.'

The Earl Fitzwilliam Charitable Trust

General

£70,000 (2005/06)

Beneficial area UK, with a preference for areas with historical family connections, chiefly in Cambridgeshire, Northamptonshire and Yorkshire.

Estate Office, Milton Park, Peterborough PE6 7AH

Correspondent J M S Thompson, Secretary to the Trustees

Trustees *Sir Philip Naylor-Leyland; Lady Isabella Naylor-Leyland.*

CC Number 269388

Information available Accounts were on file at the Charity Commission.

General The trust tends to favour charities that benefit rural communities, especially those with a connection to Cambridgeshire, Peterborough, South

Yorkshire and Malton in North Yorkshire where the Fitzwilliam family have held their landed estates for many centuries.

It was established in 1975 by the Rt Hon. Earl Fitzwilliam and has since had various capital sums and property gifted to it.

In 2005/06 it had assets of £7.2 million, an income of £219,000 and gave grants totalling £70,000.

A total of 53 grants were made in the year. Larger donations included those to: Bretton Parish Council, Royal Agricultural Benevolent Institution and St Michael's Church, Great Gidding (£5,000 each); the Countryside Foundation (£3,750); Cambridgeshire High Sheriffs Award Scheme, Fitzwilliam College, Cambridge, Chaplaincy Appeal and the Museum of Garden History (£2,500 each); and ASAP Foundation Trust, Little Gidding Trust Ltd, National Playing Fields Association, Westgate Church – Peterborough and York Minster Fund (£2,000 each).

Other beneficiaries of grants of £1,000 or less included: the Brainwave Centre, Concern Worldwide UK, Girl Guiding Northamptonshire, Marie Curie Cancer Care and Peterborough and District REMAP (£1,000 each); Yorkshire Museum (£900); Christ Church – Orton Goldhay, IMPACT, Macmillan Cancer Relief and the Red Stick Relief Fund (500 each); Glinton Vintage Working Weekend and Whizz-Kidz (£250 each); and Friends of Peterborough Cathedral (£50).

Exclusions No grants to individuals.

Applications In writing to the correspondent. Trustees meet about every three months.

Bud Flanagan Leukaemia Fund

Leukaemia research and treatment

£258,000 (2005)
Beneficial area UK.

c/o Abbots, Printing House, 66 Lower Road, Harrow HA2 0DH

Website www.bflf.org.uk

Correspondent Sandra Clark, General Secretary

Trustees S Coventry; K Kaye; A Rowden; G Till.

CC Number 1092540

Information available Accounts were on file at the Charity Commission.

General Established in 1969 from the estate of the late Bud Flanagan, the principle objects of the fund are 'the promotion of clinical research into the treatment and possible cure of leukaemia and allied diseases and the publication of the results of all such research'. The fund makes grants to hospitals and research institutions for research into the causes, diagnosis and treatment of leukaemia.

In 2005 it had assets totalling £432,000 and an income of £250,000, including £207,000 from fundraising events. Grants were made during the year totalling £258,000.

The main beneficiary of the trust has been Royal Marsden Hospital in Sutton, which received £206,000. Other grants were: £30,000 to Parkside Oncology Clinic; £5,500 to University of Southampton; and £2,750 to Christian Lewis Trust.

Exclusions The fund does not normally make grants to welfare charities or to individuals.

Applications In writing to the correspondent.

The Rose Flatau Charitable Trust

Jewish, general

£49,000 (2005/06)
Beneficial area UK.

5 Knott Park House, Wrens Hill, Oxshott, Leatherhead KT22 0HW

Correspondent M E G Prince, Trustee

Trustees M E G Prince; A E Woolf; N L Woolf.

CC Number 210492

Information available Accounts were on file at the Charity Commission.

General The trust supports Jewish organisations, although it also supports other organisations which particularly attract the interest of the trustees.

In 2005/06 it had assets of £1.5 million, which generated an income of £63,000. Grants were made to 22 organisations totalling £49,000.

Beneficiaries included: Brantwood Trust, Cherry Trees, Queen Elizabeth's Foundation and World Jewish Relief (£5,000 each); British Red Cross, Jewish Care, Queen Mary's Clothing Fund and Norwood Ltd (£2,500 each); Jewish Lads' and Girls' Brigade, Multiple Sclerosis Society, National Library for the Blind and Winged Fellowship Trust (£2,000 each); Anglo-Jewish Association (£1,000 each); West London Action for Children (£500); the Children's Trust (£250); and United Synagogues (£125).

Exclusions No grants to individuals.

Applications The trust stated: 'Our funds are fully committed to the foreseeable future'. Speculative applications will therefore be fruitless.

The Ian Fleming Charitable Trust

Disability, medical

£61,000 to organisations (2004/05)
Beneficial area UK.

haysmacintyre, Fairfax House, 15 Fulwood Place, London WC1V 6AY

Tel. 020 7969 5500

Correspondent A A I Fleming, Trustee

Trustees A A I Fleming; N A M McDonald; A W W Baldwin; A H Isaacs.

CC Number 263327

Information available Accounts were on file at the Charity Commission.

General This trust's income is allocated equally between: (a) UK charities actively operating for the support, relief and welfare of men, women and children who are disabled or otherwise in need of help, care and attention, and charities actively engaged in research on human diseases; and (b) Music Education Awards under a scheme administered by the Musicians' Benevolent Fund and advised by a committee of experts in the field of music.

In 2004/05 it had assets of £2.5 million, which generated an income of £99,000. Grants were made totalling £102,000, of which £61,000 was given in 35 grants to organisations and £41,000 in 12 music awards to individuals.

Beneficiaries included: Arthritis Care, Asthma UK, Brain Research Trust, Cancer Research UK, Combat Stress, Fight for Sight, Great Ormond Street

Hospital Children's Charity, Leonard Cheshire, Mencap, Parkinson's Disease Society, Raynaud's and Scleroderma Association and RNIB (£2,000 each); Action for Kids, Charterhouse-in-Southwark, Dystonia Society, LUPUS UK, Music in Hospitals, Seafarers UK and Spinal Injuries Association (£1,500 each); and ENABLE Scotland (£1,000).

Exclusions No grants to individuals except under the music education award scheme. No grants to purely local charities.

Applications In writing to the correspondent.

The Joyce Fletcher Charitable Trust

Music, children's welfare

£65,000 (2005/06)
Beneficial area England, almost entirely South West.

17 Westmead Gardens, Upper Weston, Bath BA1 4EZ

Tel. 01225 314355

Correspondent R A Fletcher, Trustee and Correspondent

Trustees *R A Fletcher; W D R Fletcher; S C Sharp; S P Fletcher.*

CC Number 297901

Information available Accounts were on file at the Charity Commission.

General The policy of the trust is to support institutions and organisations, usually registered charities, specialising in music in a social or therapeutic context, music and special needs, and children and young people's welfare. Other organisations which are supported outside these areas are usually known to the trustees and/or are in the south west. Grants usually range between £250 and £2,000. Occasionally more is given.

In 2005/06 the trust had assets of £2.2 million and an income of £82,000. Grants totalled £65,000. Of the 42 organisations receiving support, 31 were based in the south west.

Beneficiaries included: Live Music Now! (£7,500); Bath Festivals Trust (£5,000); Drake Music Project, Theatre Royal Bath and Welsh National Opera (3,000 each); Buxton Festival, For Ever Friends Appeal – Royal United Hospital, Holburne

Museum of Art, National Youth Orchestra, Quartet Community Foundation and Wiltshire Music Centre (£2,000 each); Bath International Guitar Festival (£1,500); 1st Wilton Scout Group, Bethlehem Link, Friends of Music at Wells Cathedral School, Hope and Homes for Children, National Theatre, Taunton School, the Voices Foundation and Wimborne Methodist Church (£1,000 each); and Corsley Festival Choir (£500).

Exclusions Grants to individuals and students are exceptionally rare; applications are not sought. No support for areas which are the responsibility of the local authority. No support is given to purely professional music/arts promotions. No support for purely medical research charities.

Applications In writing to the correspondent before 1 November each year. There are no application forms. Letters should include the purpose for the grant, an indication of the history and viability of the organisation and a summary of accounts. Preliminary telephone calls are accepted. Acknowledgements are only given if the application is being considered or if an sae is sent.

Florence's Charitable Trust

Education, welfare, sick and infirm, general

£90,000 (2005/06)
Beneficial area UK, with a preference for Rossendale in Lancashire.

E Suttons and Sons, PO Box 2, Riverside, Bacup, Lancashire OL13 0DT

Correspondent The Secretary to the Trustees

Trustees *C C Harrison; A Connearn; G D Low; J Mellows; R D Uttley; K Duffy; S Holding.*

CC Number 265754

Information available Accounts were on file at the Charity Commission, without a list of grants.

General 'The trust was formed to inter alia:

- establish, maintain and support places of education and to give scholarships and other awards to encourage proficiency in education;

- establish, maintain and support places providing relief for sickness and infirmity, and for the aged;
- relieve poverty of any person employed or formerly employed in the shoe trade; and
- provide general charitable public benefits.'

In 2003/04 the trust had assets of £1.2 million and an income of £54,000. Grants totalled £90,000, broken down as follows:

Educational support	38 grants	£44,000
General charitable public benefits	34	£35,000
Relief for sickness and infirmity	8	£9,400
Support for the aged and poverty	2	£1,600

Exclusions No grants to individuals' educational fees, exchange visits or gap year activities.

Applications In writing only to the correspondent (no telephone calls allowed). To save on administration costs, unsuccessful applications will not be acknowledged even if an sae is provided.

The Florian Charitable Trust

General

£10,000 (2005/06)
Beneficial area UK.

Thomas Eggar, The Corn Exchange, Baffins Lane, Chichester, West Sussex PO19 1GE

Correspondent R M G Thornely, Trustee

Trustees *V J Treasure; G A Treasure; R M G Thornely.*

CC Number 1043523

Information available Accounts were on file at the Charity Commission.

General The 2005/06 annual report stated that: 'The trustees meet bi-annually and are prepared to look at all applications received during the six months prior to the meeting, particular emphasis has been placed on funding specific projects, and where possible supporting those charities geographically local to one or more of the trustees, so there can be personal contact between a trustee and the charity benefited. The majority, but by no means all, of the donations have supported medical and allied charities, with a particular focus on those helping disabled children.'

In 2005/06 the trust had assets of £1.3 million and an income of £37,000. Grants totalled £10,000.

Grants of £2,500 were awarded to four organisations: Arthritis Research Campaign, BIME, the Brain Research Trust and Queen Elizabeth's Foundation.

Applications In writing to the correspondent.

The Flow Foundation

Welfare, education, environment, medical

£90,000 (2005/06)
Beneficial area UK.

22 Old Bond Street, London W1S 4PY
Correspondent Mrs Nita Sowerbutts, Trustee
Trustees *Mrs N Shashou; Mrs Nina Sowerbutts; H Woolf; Mrs J Woolf.*
CC Number 328274
Information available Full accounts were on file at the Charity Commission.

General In 2005/06 it had an income of £24,000 and a total expenditure of £92,000.

Previous beneficiaries have included After Adoption, Brain Research Trust, British Friends of Haifa University, British ORT, Chicken Shed Theatre Company, Honey Pot Charity, International Centre for Child Studies, Jewish Care, Norwood, Royal Pharmaceutical Society, Tate Gallery Foundation, Toynbee Hall Foundation, Unite for the Future, Variety Club Children's Charity, Weizmann Institute Foundation and West London Synagogue.

Applications In writing to the correspondent on one sheet of paper only.

The Gerald Fogel Charitable Trust

Jewish, general

£99,000 (2005/06)
Beneficial area UK.

Morley and Scott, Lynton House, 7–12 Tavistock Square, London WC1H 9LT
Correspondent J Clay, Accountant
Trustees *J G Fogel; B Fogel; S Fogel; D Fogel.*
CC Number 1004451
Information available Accounts were on file at the Charity Commission.

General The trust stated in its annual report that its policy is 'to make a wide spread of grants'. In practice it appears to support mainly Jewish organisations.

In 2005/06 the trust had assets of £898,000 and an income of £87,000, including £52,000 from donations. Grants totalled £99,000.

During the year 34 organisations received support of £1,000 or more, including: Chai Cancer Care (£11,000); Nightingale House (£8,400); Jewish Child's Day (£8,000); London Jewish Cultural Centre (£7,200); Jewish Care (£6,000); World Jewish Relief (£5,100); Oxford Centre for Hebrew and Jewish (£4,000); Jewish Blind and Disabled Trust and United Jewish Israel Appeal (£3,000 each); and Community Security Trust and Royal Academy of Arts (£2,500 each); Cancer Research and Jewish National Fund (£2,000); British Heart Foundation (£1,500); and Ben Gurion University, Friends of Israel Educational Foundation, King Edward Hospital, National Theatre, North London Hospice, Oxfam, Save the Children Fund and Variety Club of Great Britain (£1,000 each).

Small grants below £1,000 each totalled £5,800.

Exclusions No grants to individuals or non-registered charities.

Applications In writing to the correspondent.

The Follett Trust

Welfare, education, arts

£101,000 (2005/06)
Beneficial area UK and overseas.

17 Chescombe Road, Yatton, North Somerset BS49 4EE
Correspondent M D Follett, Trustee
Trustees *Martin Follett; Ken Follett; Barbara Follett.*
CC Number 328638
Information available Accounts were on file at the Charity Commission.

General The trust's policy is to: give financial assistance to organisations in the field of education and individual students in higher education including theatre; support organisations concerned with disability and health; support trusts involved with writers and publishing; respond to world crisis appeals for help.

In 2005/06 the trust had assets of £51,000 and an income of £81,000, mostly from donations. Grants totalled £101,000, including £8,800 given to individuals. Grants ranged from £50 to £26,000.

Beneficiaries of larger grants included: UCL Development Fund – Follett Scholarship (£26,000); Canon Collins Trust (£20,000); Stevenage CAB (£12,000); Stevenage Community Trust (£6,300); Dyslexia Action and Genesis Foundation (£5,000 each); Soho Family Centre (£2,000); One World Action (£1,500); Oxfam (£1,200); and John Clare Cottage Appeal, Home Start Stevenage, London Film Academy, Medical Aid for Palestinians, Youth Culture Television and York Minster Campaign (£1,000 each).

Smaller grants included those to Breast Cancer Care, Cancer Research UK, Dance for Fun, Hansard Society, Hope and Homes for Children, Human Rights Watch National Kidney Foundation and Volunteer Reading Help.

Applications The trust states, 'A high proportion of donees come to the attention of the trustees through personal knowledge and contact rather than by written application. Where the trustees find it impossible to make a donation they rarely respond to the applicant unless a stamped addressed envelope is provided'.

The Football Association National Sports Centre Trust

Play areas, community sports facilities

£292,000 (2005) see below
Beneficial area UK.

25 Soho Square, London W1D 4FA
Tel. 020 7745 4589 **Fax** 020 7745 5589
Email mike.appleby@TheFA.com

Correspondent Mike Appleby, Secretary to the Trustees

Trustees *G Thompson; W T Annable; R G Berridge; B W Bright; M M Armstrong.*

CC Number 265132

Information available Accounts were on file at the Charity Commission.

General The trust supports the provision, maintenance and improvement of facilities for use in recreational and leisure activities. Grants are made to county football associations, football clubs and other sports associations.

In 2005 the trust had assets of £4.5 million and an income of £181,000. Grants totalled £292,000.

A total of seven grants were made to grassroots football clubs totalling £42,000. Following the Tsunami in December 2004, the following organisations received grants: Tsunami Earthquake Appeal (£150,000) and FIFA/AFC Tsunami Solidarity (£100,000).

Applications In writing to the correspondent.

The Forbes Charitable Foundation

Adults with learning disabilities

£62,000 (2005/06)

Beneficial area UK.

9 Weir Road, Kibworth, Leicestershire LE8 0LQ

Correspondent The Secretary to the Trustees

Trustees *Col. R G Wilkes, Chair; Major Gen. R L S Green; I Johnson; J C V Lang; C G Packham; N J Townsend; J M Waite; R Warburton.*

CC Number 326476

Information available Accounts were on file at the Charity Commission.

General The trust supports charities involved with the care of adults with learning difficulties. It prefers to support capital rather than revenue projects.

In 2005/06 it had assets of £2.3 million, which generated an income of £72,000. Grants totalled £62,000.

Beneficiaries included: Down's Syndrome Association and Robert Owen

Communities (£10,000 each); Association for Real Change, Hansel Foundation and SeeAbility (£5,000 each); Cottage and Rural Enterprises Ltd (£4,500); Stockdales (£4,000); the Fifth Trust and St George's Association (£2,500 each); Merseyside Tuesday and Thursday Clubs (£2,000); and Okehampton and District Mencap Society (£1,000).

Applications In writing to the correspondent. Applications are considered in June and November.

Forbesville Limited

Jewish, education

£50,000 (2005)

Beneficial area UK and overseas.

Holborn House, 219 Golders Green Road, London NW11 9DD

Correspondent M Berger, Chair

Trustees *M Berger, Chair; Mrs J S Kritzler; D B Kritzler.*

CC Number 269898

Information available Brief information for this trust was available at the Charity Commission.

General The trust makes grants to Orthodox Jewish organisations, educational and charitable institutions.

In 2005 the trust had assets of £29,000 with an income of £65,000 and grants totalling £50,000. Unfortunately no grants list was available for this period.

Applications In writing to the correspondent.

The Forces Trust

Military charities

£37,000 (2005/06)

Beneficial area UK.

c/o Hunters, 9 New Square, London WC2A 3QN

Correspondent Col. A F Niekirk, Trustee

Trustees *Col. A F Niekirk; Capt. A P C Niekirk; Lieu. Col. W D Niekirk; Brig. R E Nugee; B E V Bowater.*

CC Number 211529

Information available Accounts were on file at the Charity Commission.

General The trust can only support military charities or institutions. The trustees currently prefer to support service charities that assist people rather than support buildings or property.

In 2005/06 it had assets of £1.2 million, which generated an income of £42,000. Grants totalling £37,000 were made to eight organisations, all of which were supported in the previous year.

Beneficiaries were: Ex-Services Mental Welfare Society – Combat Stress (£20,000); League of Remembrance (£4,800); and British Limbless Ex-Service Men's Association, Erskine Hospital, St David's Nursing Home, Scottish National Institution for the War Blinded, Scottish Veterans' Residences and Sir Oswald Stoll Foundation (£2,000 each).

Exclusions No grants to any non-naval or military charities, individuals, scholarships or education generally.

Applications In writing to the correspondent at any time, preferably on one side of A4.

Ford Britain Trust

Arts, community service, education, environment, disability, diversity, hospitals, professional and trade, schools, special schools, young people

£303,000 (2005/06)

Beneficial area Local to the areas in close proximity to Ford Motor Company Limited's locations in the UK. These are Essex, East London, South Wales, Southampton, Daventry and Leamington Spa.

Room 1/619, Ford Motor Company Limited, Eagle Way, Brentwood, Essex CM13 3BW

Tel. 01277 252551

Website www.ford.co.uk

Correspondent Andy Taylor

Trustees *M J Callaghan; J Calvert-Lee; S Dalvi; S Hochgreb; S McIlveen; D S Russell.*

CC Number 269410

Information available Accounts were on file at the Charity Commission.

General The objectives of the trust are the 'advancement of education, and other purposes beneficial to the community'. The trust supports organisations in the areas where the Ford Motor Company is based. When this is a town it will support the surrounding area, i.e. where the employees are likely to be living. There is also a preference for charities where a member of staff is involved. Grants are typically one-off. They normally range from £100 to £5,000 but some larger grants are made. The trust prefers to support projects run by registered charities.

Applications for new Ford vehicles are considered when two-thirds of the purchase price is available from other sources. These grants are not usually more than £2,000, but registered charities may be able to arrange a reduction from the recommended retail price. Grants are not available for second-hand vehicles.

In 2005/06 the trust had assets of £305,000 and an income of £367,000, mostly from voluntary income. Grants totalled £303,000, broken down as follows:

Community service	£64,000	67 grants
Schools/education	£32,000	42
Special needs education	£11,000	13
Disability	£34,000	54
Youth	£50,000	49

There were 11 grants of £3,000 or more listed in the accounts. Beneficiaries included: Thames Gateway Youth Football Programme – London Borough of Barking, Dagenham and East London (£20,000); Wheatsheaf Trust – Southampton (£10,000); All Saints Church – Hackney (£8,000); Childline – London (£5,400); Colchester and Tendring Women's Refuge and Essex County Scout Council (£5,200 each); YWCA Vineries Young Women's Centre (£5,000); the Cedar School – Southampton and SNAP – Brentwood (£4,000 each); Motor Neurone Disease Association – Northampton (£3,600); and Hampshire and Isle of Wight Youth Options – Southampton (£3,200).

Grants of £3,000 each or less totalled £117,000.

Exclusions National charities are assisted rarely and then only when the purpose of their application has specific benefit to communities located in close proximity to Ford locations.

Applications in respect of sponsorship, individuals, research, overseas projects, travel, religious or political projects are not eligible. Applications for core funding and/or salaries, revenue expenses, and major building projects are rarely considered.

Applications In writing to the correspondent. Applications should include the following:

- purpose of the project
- whom it is intended to help and how
- why the project is important and necessary (how things were done before)
- how the project is to be carried out
- the project's proposed starting time and time of completion
- total cost of the project
- how much has been raised so far, sources of funding obtained and expected
- examples of fundraising activities by the organisation for the project
- the amount being asked for.

A brief résumé of the background of the charity is appreciated. Where appropriate, copies of accounts should be provided.

Trustees meet in June and November each year. Applications are considered in order of receipt and it may take several months before an application is considered. The trust receives many more applications than it can help.

The Oliver Ford Charitable Trust

Mental disability, housing

£54,000 (2004/05)

Beneficial area UK.

Messrs Macfarlanes, 10 Norwich Street, London EC4A 1BD

Tel. 020 7831 9222

Correspondent Matthew Pintus

Trustees *Derek Hayes; Lady Wakeham; Martin Levy.*

CC Number 1026551

Information available Accounts were on file at the Charity Commission.

General The objectives of the trust are to educate the public and advance knowledge of the history and techniques of interior decoration, the designs of fabric and other decorative materials and landscape gardening including Oliver Ford's own work. Income and capital not used for these purposes is used for the Anthroposophical Society of Great Britain, Camphill Village Trust, Norwood or any other charity providing housing, educational or training facilities for children, young persons or adults who have learning disabilities or learning difficulties.

In 2004/05 it had assets of almost £2 million, which generated an income of £89,000. Grants were made totalling £54,000.

Beneficiaries were Martha Trust (£10,000), Mencap and the Wessex Autistic Society (£5,000 each), the Shaftesbury Society (£4,600), the Garden Science Trust (£4,500), the Norman Laud Associations (£3,900), Guideposts Trusts (£3,500), the Society of Antiquaries of London (£2,700) and Pentahact (£2,000).

Grants are given each year to students studying at the Victoria and Albert Museum (£13,000 in 2004/05).

Applications In writing to the correspondent. Trustees meet in March and October.

Fordeve Ltd

Jewish, general

£312,000 (2005/06)

Beneficial area UK.

c/o Gerald Kreditor & Co., Hallswelle House, 1 Hallswelle Road, London NW11 0DH

Correspondent J Kon, Trustee

Trustees *J Kon; Mrs H Kon.*

CC Number 1011612

Information available Accounts were on file at the Charity Commission

General The trust makes grants to Jewish causes and for the relief of need.

In 2005/06 it had assets of £506,000 and an income of £442,000, including £430,000 from voluntary income. Grants to six organisations totalled £312,000. Beneficiaries were: the Gertner Charitable Trust (£192,000); Lubavitch Foundation (£30,000); the Yom Tov Assistance Fund (£8,800); the Society of Friends of the Torah (£7,900); the Lolev Charitable Trust (£6,100); and Beth Jacob Grammar School for Girls (£5,500).

Applications In writing to the correspondent.

The Forest Hill Charitable Trust

Mainly Christian causes and relief work

£209,000 (2005)

Beneficial area UK and overseas.

104 Summercourt Way, Brixham, Devon TQ5 0RB

Correspondent Mrs P J Pile, Secretary to the Trustees

Trustees H F Pile, Chair; Mrs P J Pile; R S Pile; Mrs M S Tapper; M Thomas.

CC Number 1050862

Information available Accounts were on file at the Charity Commission.

General This trust gives grants mainly to Christian causes and for relief work (80%), although support is given to agencies helping people who are disabled, in need or sick.

In 2005 the trust had assets of £3.5 million and an income of £207,000. Grants to about 120 organisations were made totalling £209,000.

Beneficiaries included: LINX (£42,000 in eight grants); Barnabas Fund (£9,000 in three grants); Great Parks Chapel (£8,000 in four grants); Open Doors (£4,500 in two grants); Emmanuel Health Centre, Hand in Hand, Hope Now, Latin Link, Leprosy Mission, Life of the World, Plymstock Chapel, ROPE, SGA, Treasured In Heaven, USPG, Viz-a-Viz and WEC (£2,000 each); and Bible Network, Child Hope UK, Christian Blind Mission, Crossroad Christian Counsel, Ethiopaid, Everychild, Harvest Trust, Martha Trust, Medical Missionary News, Mission Aviation Fellowship, Pearson's Holiday Fund, Royal Star and Garter Home, Tiny Tim's Children's Centre, Tear Fund and Urban Vision (£1,000 each).

Applications The trustees have previously stated that their aim was to maintain regular and consistent support to the charities they are currently supporting. New requests for funding are therefore very unlikely to succeed.

Gwyneth Forrester Trust

General, see below

£450,000 (2004/05)

Beneficial area England and Wales.

231 Linden Hall, 162–168 Regent Street, London W1B 5TB

Correspondent C Perkins, Trustee

Trustees W J Forrester; A J Smee; M B Jones; C Perkins.

CC Number 1080921

Information available Information was on file at the Charity Commission.

General Established in May 2000, the trustees plan to support a specific charitable sector each year.

In 2004/05 this trust's assets stood at over £19 million and it had an income of £488,000 mainly from investments, but including £150,000 from Gift Aid. Grants totalled £450,000. Donations were made to nine hospices.

Exclusions No grants to individuals.

Applications The trust has previously stated that 'applications for aid cannot be considered'.

The Anna Rosa Forster Charitable Trust

Medical research, animal welfare, famine relief

£54,000 (2004/05)

Beneficial area Worldwide.

Floor E, Milburn House, Dean Street, Newcastle-upon-Tyne NE1 1LF

Tel. 0191 230 1819

Correspondent R Napier, Trustee

Trustees R Napier; Mr A Morgan.

CC Number 1090028

Information available Accounts were on file at the Charity Commission.

General Registered with the Charity Commission in January 2002, in 2004/05 the trust had assets of £1.8 million and an income of £70,000. Grants totalled £54,000 with a third of funds going in each of the following areas.

Animal welfare – 7 grants
Grants of £2,600 each included those to the Cats Protection League, the Dogs Trust, the Donkey Sanctuary, PDSA and World Society for the Protection of Animals.

Famine Relief – 7 grants
Grants of £2,600 each included those to British Red Cross, Farm Africa, Oxfam, World Emergency Relief and World Medical Fund.

Medical research – 10 grants
Grants of £1,800 each included those to Alzheimer's Research Trust, Cancer Research UK, Cystic Fibrosis Trust and Motor Neurone Disease Association.

Applications In writing to the correspondent.

The Forte Charitable Trust

Roman Catholic, Alzheimer's disease, senile dementia

£120,000 a year

Beneficial area UK and overseas.

Lowndes House, Lowndes Place, London SW1X 8DB

Correspondent Mrs Heather McConville

Trustees Hon. Sir Rocco Forte; Hon. Mrs Olga Polizzi di Sorrentino; G F L Proctor; Lowndes Trustees Ltd.

CC Number 326038

Information available Information was provided by the trust.

General The trust has recently narrowed its areas of work down to those relating to the Roman Catholic faith, Alzheimer's disease and senile dementia.

The trust stated that grants total about £120,000 a year.

Applications In writing to the correspondent.

Lord Forte Foundation

Hospitality

£25,000 (2005/06)

Beneficial area UK.

Lowndes House, Lowndes Place, Belgrave Square, London SW1X 8DB

Tel. 020 7235 6244 **Fax** 020 7259 5149

Correspondent Mrs Heather McConville

Trustees *Lord Janner, Chair; Hon Sir Rocco Forte; Hon. Mrs Olga Polizzi di Sorrentino; Viscount Montgomery of Alamein; G F L Proctor.*

CC Number 298100

Information available Accounts were on file at the Charity Commission.

General This trust was set up in 1987, 'to encourage excellence in the fields of hospitality encompassing the hotel, catering, travel and tourism industries'. It does this by giving grants directly to educational establishments which provide training courses or carry out research projects in these fields.

In 2005/06 it had assets of £2 million, which generated an income of £51,000. Grants were made totalling £25,000. Beneficiaries were: Training for Life – the Hoxton Apprentice (£15,000); and the University of Salford – Forte Foundation Scholar (£10,000).

Applications In writing to the correspondent.

Foundation for Management Education

Management studies

£122,000 (2004/05)
Beneficial area UK.

TBAC Business Centre, Avenue Four, Station Lane, Witney OX28 4BN

Website www.management-education. org.uk

Correspondent The Director

Trustees *Geoffrey Armstrong; Mary Chapman; James Watson; Paula Graham; Michael Jones; Tim Boswell; Dr Brian Alexander; William Redfern; Dr Charles Constable; David Thomas; Ellen Cockburn; John Wybrew; Robert Lintott; Valerie Boakes; Richard Hurd-Wood; Mike A Jones.*

CC Number 313388

Information available Accounts were on file at the Charity Commission.

General In 2004/05 the trust had assets of £901,000 and an income of £47,000. Charitable expenditure amounted to

£214,000, broken down into grants totalling £122,000 and support costs of £74,000. Grant beneficiaries included Aston University, the Universities of Aberdeen, Bath and Leeds and CRAC.

Exclusions Individual applications for further studies cannot be supported.

Applications Unsolicited applications are not encouraged.

The Fowler, Smith and Jones Charitable Trust

Social welfare

£473,000 (2005/06)
Beneficial area Essex.

c/o Messrs Tolhurst and Fisher, Malbrough House, Victoria Road South, Chelmsford, Essex CM1 1LN

Tel. 01245 216123 **Fax** 01245 494771

Email amason@tolhurstfisher.com

Correspondent Mrs A Mason, Secretary

Trustees *P J Tolhurst, Chair; W J Tolhurst; E C Watson.*

CC Number 259917

Information available Full accounts were on file at the Charity Commission.

General The trust supports a few nominated charities on an annual basis, with the balance given to local charities in Essex. The trust concentrates its giving as follows:

- charities nominated by the original benefactors
- overseas projects
- church projects
- other Essex-related projects.

There is a fundamental criterion that any funding made must be matched by other funding or contributions.

In 2005/06 the trust had assets of £11.1 million, which generated an income of £638,000. There were 144 grants made totalling £473,000, including those to the following beneficiaries:

Arts
New Empire Theatre Youth Project (£5,000); and Eastern Orchestral Band and Roman River Music Society (£1,000 each).

Churches
St Andrew's – Marks Tey (£8,000); St James' Church – Little Clacton (£5,500);

St Andrew's Church (£3,500); All Saints Church – Southend and Ferndale Baptist Church (£3,000 each); St Paul's Church (£1,500); and All Saints – High Roding (£1,000).

Community
John Grooms (£25,000); Salvation Army (£14,000); St Luke's Southend (£8,000); Arts for All (£5,000); Essex Community Foundation (£4,000); Age Concern, Basildon Community Resource Centre and EDPA (£3,000 each); Southend CAB (£2,500); Alzheimer's Society, Crossroads for Carers and React (£2,000 each); British Legion – Leigh-on-Sea (£1,500); and Mid Essex Respite Care Association (£1,000).

Major building
Farleigh Hospice (£60,000).

Medical/health
Headway Essex (£10,000); Marie Curie Cancer Care (£6,000); Cancer Research UK (£5,000); Dystonia Society (£2,000); and Together (£1,500).

Overseas
CAFOD (£20,000); Raleigh International (£13,000); and Zane and WaterAid (£5,000 each).

Youth
Essex Autistic Society (£15,000); Barnardos and Brentwood Catholic Children's Society (£8,000 each); Depaul Trust, First Step and Prince's Trust (£5,000 each); Essex Association of Boys' Clubs (£4,000); Football in the Community, InterACT and London Bus Theatre (£3,000 each); Witham Boys' Brigade (£2,000); Parent's Aid (£1,500); and Newport Youth Centre and PARC (£1,000 each).

Grants were also made under the heading 'miscellaneous and top up'.

Exclusions No grants to individuals.

Applications In writing to the correspondent.

The Charles Henry Foyle Trust

General

£53,000 (2004/05)
Beneficial area South west/central Birmingham and north Worcestershire.

c/o Birmingham Foundation, Suite 2A, St George's Court, 1 Albion Street, Birmingham B1 3AH

Tel. 0121 214 2080

Email team@bhamfoundation.co.uk

Website www.bhamfoundation.co.uk

Correspondent The Trust Administrator

Trustees *Michael Francis, Chair; Roger K Booth; Mrs Bridget Morris; Prof. Rae Mackay; Paul R Booth; Tom Morris.*

CC Number 220446

Information available Accounts were on file at the Charity Commission.

General The trust aims to provide grants to support organisations/activities operating within the south west/central Birmingham and north Worcestershire areas. The trustees are keen to receive applications from voluntary/community organisations that are able to demonstrate their project will bring benefit to the local community and in so doing meet at least one of the objectives listed below:

- to enhance the education and skills of local people, particularly the young – including the use of theatrical arts and music
- to assist communities in local regeneration programmes
- to protect and improve the local environment
- to support the improvement of sports and leisure facilities
- to celebrate and promote the cultural diversity of the City of Birmingham.

Preference will be given to projects or events promoting individual and community development, education and recreation for local residents. In particular, but not exclusively, the trust encourages applications from groups supporting activities for the 14–24 age group.

In 2004/05 the trust had assets of £2.6 million, an income of £61,000 and made grants totalling £53,000.

Major grant awards included those to: the Birmingham Foundation (£13,000); the Sydonia Pool and Recreational Appeal Fund (£10,000); Stitched Textile Award (£6,000); Birmingham University Botanic Gardens Winterbourne and Symphony Hall – Birmingham (£3,000 each); Acorn Children's Hospice (£2,500); Huntingdon's Disease Association and Whizz-Kidz (£2,000 each); Asian Welfare Association (£1,200); and the Birmingham Settlement, J T Memorial School and the Wildlife Trust for Birmingham and the Black Country (£1,000 each).

Exclusions Grants are not given for projects operating outside the specified beneficial areas, to large national charities (except where the local branch applies for their 'local' work), student costs or educational fees, organisations or individuals in the promotion of political or religious ideology.

Donations in aid of general appeals or to provide for an organisation's core costs are also unlikely to receive support.

The trust does not award grants to individuals.

Applications Applications should be made using the form that can be downloaded via the Birmingham Foundation's website.

Trustees meet quarterly to review applications.

The Isaac and Freda Frankel Memorial Charitable Trust

Jewish, general

£68,000 (2004/05)

Beneficial area UK and overseas, particularly Israel.

33 Welbeck Street, London W1G 8LX

Correspondent M D Frankel, Secretary

Trustees *M D Frankel; G Frankel; J Steinhaus; J Silkin.*

CC Number 1003732

Information available Accounts were on file at the Charity Commission, without a list of grants.

General The Isaac and Freda Frankel Memorial Charitable Trust was established in July 1991 by members of the Frankel family to support mainly Jewish causes.

In 2004/05 the trust had assets of £529,000. Its income of £51,000 included £25,000 from donations. Grants totalled £68,000. A list of beneficiaries was not included with the accounts filed at the Charity Commission.

Exclusions No grants to individuals or students, for expeditions or scholarships.

Applications In writing to the correspondent.

Sydney E Franklin Deceased's New Second Charity

Development

£32,000 (2005/06)

Beneficial area Worldwide; priority, but not exclusively, to developing world projects.

c/o 39 Westleigh Avenue, London SW15 6RQ

Correspondent Dr R C G Franklin, Trustee

Trustees *Dr R C G Franklin; Ms T N Franklin; Ms C Holliday.*

CC Number 272047

Information available Accounts were on file at the Charity Commission.

General The trust supports small charities with low overheads, focusing on developing world self-help projects, endangered species and people disadvantaged by poverty.

In 2005/06 the trust had assets of £609,000 and an income of £20,000. Grants totalled £32,000.

There were 19 grants of £1,000 or more. Beneficiaries included: Kerala Federation for the Blind (£4,000); Water for Kids (£3,000); Narwhal/Niaff (£2,000); United Charities Fund (£1,500); and Ashram International, Books Abroad, Children of the Andes, Kaloko Trust, Microloan Foundation, Tools for Self Reliance, Tree Aid and Window for Peace UK (£1,000 each).

Other smaller grants included those to: Forest Peoples Project (£750); African Initiatives, Lake Malawi Projects and World Medical Fund (£500 each); and Gwalior Children's Hospital (£250).

Applications Donations may only be requested by letter, and these are placed before the trustees at their meeting which is normally held at the end of each year. Applications are not acknowledged.

The Jill Franklin Trust

Overseas, welfare, prisons, church restoration

£59,000 (2005/06)

Beneficial area Worldwide.

Flat 5, 17–19 Elsworthy Road, London NW3 3DS

Tel. 020 7722 4543

Email info@jill-franklin-trust.org.uk

Website www.jill-franklin-trust.org.uk

Correspondent N Franklin, Trustee

Trustees *Andrew Franklin; Norman Franklin; Sally Franklin; Sam Franklin; Tom Franklin.*

CC Number 1000175

Information available Accounts were on file at the Charity Commission.

General Grants are typically £500 to £1,000, and the trust has four areas in which it is soliciting grant applications:

- Self-Help groups, advice, training, and employment; to support people with a mental illness or learning difficulties, and their carers (parents etc.).
- Respite care, and holidays (in the UK only). Grants for holidays are only given where there is a large element of respite care and only to registered charities, not to individuals.
- Organisations helping and supporting refugees and asylum-seekers coming to or in the UK.
- The restoration (not 'improvement') of churches of architectural importance (half a page in Pevsner's *Buildings*) and occasionally to other buildings of architectural importance. The church should be open to visitors every day.

In 2005/06 it had assets of £1.7 million, an income of £69,000 and made grants totalling £59,000, broken down as follows.

Bereavement counselling	1 grant	£9,000	16%
Church restoration, etc	20	£10,000	17%
Mental health and learning difficulties	19	£9,500	16%
Overseas	1	£500	1%
Prisoners, for education	15	£11,000	19%
Refugees	21	£10,000	17%
Respite/holidays	15	£8,000	14%
Other	1	£125	0%

The largest grants were £9,000 to Camden Bereavement Service, £8,700 to Prisoners' Educational Trust and £1,000 each to Age Concern York, Batley Self-Help Depression Group, Islington Carers Forum, One to One Enfield, Princess

Royal Trust – Knowsley, Refugee Survival Trust, South Leeds Health for All and Step Forward.

Exclusions Grants are not given to:

- appeals for building work;
- endowment funds;
- branches of national organisations, and to the centre itself (unless it is a specific grant, probably for training in the branches);
- replace the duties of government, local authorities or the NHS;
- encourage the 'contract culture', particularly where authorities are not funding the contract adequately;
- religious organisations set up for welfare, education etc. of whatever religion, unless the service is open to and used by people from all denominations;
- overseas projects;
- 'heritage schemes';
- animal charities;
- students, nor to any individuals nor for overseas travel;
- medical research.

Applications In writing to the correspondent, enclosing a copy of the latest annual report and accounts and a budget for the project. Organisations based outside the UK should provide the name, address and telephone number of a correspondent or referee in the UK.

'The trustees tend to look more favourably on an appeal which is simply and economically prepared: glossy, 'prestige' and mail sorted brochures do not impress the trustees.'

Unsolicited enquiries are not usually acknowledged. 'We have very little uncommitted cash, and so most applications are rejected, for the only reason that we have insufficient money.'

The Gordon Fraser Charitable Trust

Children, young people, environment, arts

£135,000 (2005/06)

Beneficial area UK, with a preference for Scotland.

Holmhurst, Westerton Drive, Bridge of Allan, Stirling FK9 4QL

Correspondent Mrs Margaret A Moss, Trustee

Trustees *Mrs Margaret A Moss; William F T Anderson.*

CC Number 260869

Information available Accounts were on file at the Charity Commission.

General Currently the trustees are particularly interested in supporting children/young people in need, the environment and visual arts (including performance arts). Most grants are given within these categories. The trust states that 'applications from or for Scotland will receive favourable consideration, but not to the exclusion of applications from elsewhere'.

In 2005/06 the trust had assets of £2.7 million and an income of £158,000. Grants were made to 123 organisations totalling £135,000.

The trustees rarely make donations to the same charity more than once in the same year and a donation rarely exceeds £20,000 or is less than £100 although there are no minimum or maximum amounts for donations.

There were 39 grants of £1,000 or more. Beneficiaries included: Scottish Museums Council (£12,000); Aberlour Child Care Trust (£6,000); MacRobert Arts Centre (£7,000); Braendam Family House and SANE (£5,000 each); Artlink Central (£4,500); Ballet West and Girlguiding Scotland (£4,000 each); London Children's Flower Society and Royal Scottish National Orchestra (£3,500 each); MacDougall Trust (£2,500); Music as Therapy and Tron Theatre Ltd (£2,000 each); Edinburgh International Festival Society (£1,500); and John Muir Trust and St Mungo Community Housing Association (£1,000 each).

Other beneficiaries of smaller grants under £1,000 each included Association of Wheelchair Children, Books Abroad, Craigmiliar Literacy Trust, Derma Trust, Inspire, Marine Conservation Society, Medical Foundation for the Care of Victims of Torture, Perth and District YMCA, Raynaud's and Scleroderma Association, Scottish Chamber Orchestra, Scottish Churches Architectural Heritage Trust, Strathearn Music Society, Tarbert Parish Church, Write Away and York Foundation for Conservation and Craftsmanship.

Exclusions No grants are made to organisations which are not recognised charities, or to individuals.

Applications In writing to the correspondent. Applications are considered in January, April, July and October. Grants towards national or international emergencies can be considered at any time. All applicants are acknowledged; an sae would, therefore, be appreciated.

The Emily Fraser Trust

Specific trades, older people

£36,000 to organisations (2003/04)

Beneficial area UK, with a preference for Scotland.

Turcan Connell WS, Princes Exchange, 1 Earl Grey Street, Edinburgh EH3 9EE

Tel. 0131 228 8111 **Fax** 0131 228 8118

Email lnk@turcanconnell.com

Correspondent Heather Thompson, Trust Administrator

Trustees *Dr Kenneth Chrystie, Chair; The Hon. Miss Ann Fraser; Miss Patricia Fraser; Blair Smith.*

SC Number SC007288

Information available Information was provided by the trust. Annual report and accounts are available for £10.

General The trust makes grants mainly to people in Scotland and their dependants who were or are engaged in the drapery and allied trades and the printing, publishing, books and stationery, newspaper and allied trades. Preference is given to people who are or were employed by House of Fraser Limited, Scottish Universal Investments Limited and Paisleys.

Grants are also made to Scottish organisations caring for older and infirm people with connections in the fields described above. It prefers to support small, community organisations which find it difficult to raise funds. It also prefers to support organisations in areas where there is little local funding available. The trustees 'consider that grants to large highly publicised national appeals are not likely to be as effective a use of funds as grants to smaller and more focused charitable appeals'.

In 2003/04 it had assets of £1.8 million and an income of £67,000. Grants to 16 organisations totalled £36,000, with a further £43,000 given to individuals.

The largest grant was £15,000 to Camphill Village Trust. Other grants included those to Brainwave (£3,000); and James Powell (UK) Trust, Wheelchair Sports Club, Maggie's

Cancer Caring Centre – Fife and Combat Stress (£2,000 each).

Exclusions Applicants already receiving grants from the Hugh Fraser Foundation will not be eligible.

Applications In writing to the correspondent. The trustees meet quarterly to consider applications, in January, April, July and October. The trustees of this trust are also the trustees of the much larger Hugh Fraser Foundation and applications are allocated to one or other of the trusts as appears appropriate.

The Louis and Valerie Freedman Charitable Settlement

General

£98,000 (2005/06)

Beneficial area UK, especially Burnham in Buckinghamshire.

c/o Bridge House, 11 Creek Road, East Molesey, Surrey KT8 9BE

Correspondent F H Hughes, Trustee

Trustees *M A G Ferrier; F H Hughes.*

CC Number 271067

Information available Accounts were on file at the Charity Commission.

General The trust supports health, welfare and equine interests in which the Freedman family have a particular interest. Local education and youth charities in Burnham are also supported.

In 2005/06 it had assets of £4.2 million, an income of £129,000 and made grants totalling £98,000.

Beneficiaries were: Burnham Parish Council (£52,000 in two grants); Burnham Health Promotion Trust (£15,000); Homestart – Slough and Victim Support (£10,000 each); and DEC Earthquake Appeal and Vitalise (£5,000 each).

Burnham Health Promotion Trust is a related charity, also established by Louis Freedman.

Exclusions No grants to individuals. Only registered charities are considered for support.

Applications There is no application form. Applications should be in writing to the correspondent and they will not be acknowledged. Notification of a failed application will only be given if an sae is enclosed.

The Mr and Mrs F C Freeman Charitable Trust

General

£285,000 (2005/06)

Beneficial area UK.

United Trusts, PO Box 14, Liverpool L69 7AA

Tel. 0151 709 8252

Correspondent F C Freeman, Trust Patron and Secretary

Trustees *J B Bibby; R S Freeman; J R McGibbon.*

CC Number 326462

Information available Accounts were on file at the Charity Commission.

General This trust was registered with the Charity Commission in November 1983. It has general charitable purposes.

In 2005/06 it had assets of £304,000 and an income of £129,000, including a £100,000 gift of cash. Grants totalling £285,000 were made to two organisations: United Trusts (£255,000); and Institute for the Study of Hierological Values (£30,000).

Applications In writing to the correspondent.

The Friarsgate Trust

Health and welfare of young and older people

£74,000 to organisations (2005/06)

Beneficial area UK, with a strong preference for West Sussex, especially Chichester.

The Corn Exchange, Baffins Lane, Chichester, West Sussex Po19 1GE

Tel. 01243 786111 **Fax** 01243 775640

Correspondent Miss Amanda King-Jones

Trustees *A C Colenutt; T J Bastow; Mrs V Higgins.*

CC Number 220762

Information available Accounts were on file at the Charity Commission.

General The objectives of the trust are:

- To provide funds for the academic and general education of orphans and children (whether infant or adult) whose parents are in poor or reduced circumstances.
- To promote the mental, moral, physical, technical and social education of children, young persons and adults.
- To provide, equip and maintain for the purposes referred to above camping grounds, holiday camps, playing fields, club rooms or other accommodation and facilities.
- To provide for the relief and care of impotent persons including in that expression all persons suffering either temporarily or permanently from disease or disability of any kind affecting their body or mind.
- To provide for the relief of persons over the age of sixty years by the provision of maintenance, food, clothing and housing.
- To promote and support or aid any charitable institutions, purposes or projects in any way connected with the objectives aforesaid or calculated to further such objects or any of them.

In 2005/06 the trust had assets of over £3 million and an income of £89,000. Grants totalled £75,000 of which £74,000 was donated to 51 organisations. A further £1,000 was donated to individuals.

Beneficiaries of the nine largest grants were: Petworth Cottage Nursing Home (£20,000); Chichester and Midhurst District Scout Council (£12,000); St Paul's Community Centre (£10,000); Horsham YMCA (£5,000); Chichester Community Transport (£2,000); and Parkinson's Disease Society, Sammy Community Support, St Barnabas Hospice and St Wilfrid's Hospice (£1,000 each).

The majority of grants were for £500. Beneficiaries included Bowel Cancer UK, Brighton and Hove Parents' and Children's Group, Deaf Sussex Today, the Field Lane Foundation, NCH, Over The Wall, Portfield Community Primary School, Rotary Club of Chichester, Talking Newspaper Association and Winston's Wish.

Exclusions Local organisations outside Sussex are unlikely to be supported.

Applications In writing to the correspondent. Applicants are welcome to telephone first to check if they fit the trust's criteria.

Friends of Biala Ltd

Jewish

£1 million (2005/06)

Beneficial area UK and overseas.

c/o Sugarwhite Associates, 5 Windus Road, London N16 6UT

Correspondent The Secretary

Trustees *B Z Rabinovitch; Mrs T Weinberg.*

CC Number 271377

Information available Accounts were on file at the Charity Commission, but without a list of grants.

General The trust supports religious education in accordance with the orthodox Jewish faith and registered welfare charities. In 2005/06 the trust had assets of £2.7 million and an income of £1.2 million, mostly from donations. Grants totalled just over £1 million. A list of beneficiaries was unfortunately unavailable.

Applications In writing to the correspondent.

Friends of Wiznitz Limited

Jewish education

£448,000 (2005/06)

Beneficial area UK and overseas.

8 Jessam Avenue, London E5 9UD

Correspondent E Gottesfeld

Trustees *H Feldman; E Kahan; R Bergmann; S Feldman.*

CC Number 255685

Information available Accounts were on file at the Charity Commission, without a list of grants.

General This trust supports major educational projects being carried out by orthodox Jewish institutions.

In 2005/06 the trust had assets of £806,000, an income of £597,000 and made grants totalling £548,000 divided between: education (£496,000); and relief of poverty (£52,000).

Previous beneficiaries have included: Ahavat Israel Synagogue, Beth Harnidrash Wiznitz Israel, Congregation Tzemach Tzadik USA, Chasidei Wiznitz Antwerp, CMA Trust, CMZ, Kollel Aron Yisroel, Imrei Chaim – Israel, Kollel Ateres Yeshiva, Mifal Chesed Tzemach Tzadik Israel, Shemtov Charitable Trust, Wiznitz Institution Belgium, Wiznitz Institution Israel, Wiznitz Synagogue and Yehivat Wiznitz.

Applications In writing to the correspondent.

The Frognal Trust

Older people, disability, blindness/ophthalmological research, environmental heritage, youth development

£48,000 (2004/05)

Beneficial area UK.

Charities Aid Foundation, 25 Kings Hill Avenue, Kings Hill, West Mailing, Kent ME49 4TA

Correspondent Donor Grants Officer

Trustees *Philippa Blake-Roberts; J P Van Montagu; P Fraser.*

CC Number 244444

Information available Accounts were on file at the Charity Commission.

General The trust supports smaller charities rather than national organisations or local branches of large national charities.

In 2004/05 it had assets of £1.7 million, which generated an income of £56,000. Grants were made to 34 organisations totalling £48,000.

Beneficiaries included: Canniesburn Research Trust, Samantha Dickson Research Trust and Royal Liverpool and Broad Green University Hospitals (£2,000 each); Aireborough Voluntary Services to the Elderly (£1,500); Elderly Accommodation Counsel and Leeds Society for Deaf and Blind People (£1,200 each); and Action Medical

Research, Adventure Farm Trust, Friends of the Elderly, Gloucestershire Disabled Afloat Riverboat Trust, Meningitis Research Foundation, National Rheumatoid Arthritis Society, Plantlife International, Stubbers Adventure Centre, Wireless for the Bedridden Society, Woodland Trust and Yorkshire Dales Millennium Project (£1,000 each).

Exclusions The trust does not support:

- any animal charities
- the advancement of religion
- charities for the benefit of people outside the UK
- educational or research trips
- branches of national charities
- general appeals
- individuals.

Applications In writing to the correspondent. Applications should be received by February, May, August and November, for consideration at the trustees' meeting the following month.

T F C Frost Charitable Trust

Medical

£161,000 (2004/05)

Beneficial area UK and overseas.

Holmes and Co. Accountants, 10 Torrington Road, Claygate, Esher, Surrey KT10 0SA

Tel. 01372 465378

Correspondent John Holmes

Trustees *T A F Frost; M D Sanders; M H Miller.*

CC Number 256590

Information available Accounts were on file at the Charity Commission.

General The trust supports research associates of recognised centres of excellence in ophthalmology, individuals and organisations benefiting academics, medical professionals, research workers and people with sight loss.

In 2004/05 it had assets of £2.2 million and an income of £97,000. Grants totalled £161,000.

'Our Founders' wish in establishing the Frost Charitable Trust was to foster research into the prevention of blindness by supporting programmes submitted by senior trainees and by enhancing their horizons by underwriting the costs of educational or research periods of

training at home or abroad at recognised centres.'

Donations in this year were £35,000 to Casey Eye Institute – Oregon, USA; £30,000 each to King's College – London and University of Southampton; £25,000 to University of Lancaster; £15,000 to Shirley Eye Center – San Diego, USA; £10,000 each to Institute of Ophthalmology and University of Bristol; and £5,000 to Massachusetts Eye and Ear Infirmary.

Exclusions There are no available resources for the relief of blind people or people suffering from diseases of the eye.

Applications In writing to the correspondent. Trustees meet twice a year.

The Patrick Frost Foundation

General

£268,000 (2004/05)

Beneficial area Worldwide, but only through UK charities.

c/o Trowers and Hamlins, Sceptre Court, 40 Tower Hill, London EC3N 4DX

Tel. 020 7423 8000 **Fax** 020 7423 8001

Correspondent Mrs H Frost, Trustee

Trustees *Mrs Helena Frost; Donald Jones; Luke Valner; John Chedzoy.*

CC Number 1005505

Information available Accounts were on file at the Charity Commission.

General The foundation makes general welfare grants to organisations and grants to help small charities that rely on a considerable amount of self-help and voluntary effort.

In 2004/05 the foundation's assets totalled £4.9 million and an income of £118,000 and grants were made to 34 organisations totalling £268,000. Legal and professional fees amounted to £31,000.

Beneficiaries of the three largest grants were Jubilee Sailing Trust, Lifestyle and London Narrow Boat Project (£20,000 each).

Remaining grants were mainly for £10,000 or £5,000 each and included those to Acorn Christian Foundation, Action for Blind People, Action on

Addiction, Motivation Charitable Trust, Opportunity International, SENSE, St Joseph's Pastoral Centre, Special Needs Advancement Project, Toynbee Hall and Write Away (£10,000 each), Camphill Village Trust, Chance for Children Trust, Contact the Elderly, the Gurkha Welfare Trust, John Groom's Association for Disabled People, Family Holiday Association, the Medical Foundation for the Care of Victims of Torture, Speakability, Tree Aid and Yeldall Christian Centres (£5,000 each) and Abergynolwyn Community Centre (£3,000).

Exclusions No grants to individuals or non-UK charities.

Applications In writing to the correspondent, accompanied by the last set of audited accounts. The trustees regret that due to the large number of applications they receive, they are unable to acknowledge unsuccessful applications.

Maurice Fry Charitable Trust

Medicine, health, welfare, humanities, environmental resources, international

£23,000 (2005)

Beneficial area UK and overseas.

98 Savernake Road, London NW3 2JR

Correspondent L E A Fry, Trustee

Trustees *L E A Fry; Mrs F Cooklin; Mrs L Weaks.*

CC Number 327934

Information available Accounts were on file at theCharity Commission.

General The trust's main areas of interest are welfare, humanities, environmental resources and international causes, but it is not restricted to these.

In 2005 the trust had assets of £1.1 million and a total income of £32,000. Grants to 15 organisations totalled £23,000. Beneficiaries included British Red Cross – Tsunami Appeal (£10,000), Berwick CAB, Friends of the Earth Trust and Medecins Sans Frontieres (£2,000 each), the Maltings Trust (£1,500), Alone in London, Amnesty International, Childline, Island Trust and Quaker Social Action (£1,000 each), Borders School for Life (£500) and Borders Exploration Group (£250).

Exclusions No grants to individuals.

Applications The trust states that it does not respond to unsolicited applications.

Mejer and Gertrude Miriam Frydman Foundation

Jewish, Jewish education

£32,000 (2006)

Beneficial area UK and overseas.

c/o Messrs Westbury Schotness and Co., 145–157 St John Street, London EC1V 4PY

Tel. 020 7253 7272

Correspondent G Frydman, Trustee

Trustees *L J Frydman; G B Frydman; D H Frydman.*

CC Number 262806

Information available Full accounts were on file at the Charity Commission.

General The trust supports new and established charitable projects for study and research, including scholarships, fellowships, professorial chairs, lectureships, prizes, awards and the cost of purchasing or erecting any building or land required for such projects.

In 2006 the foundation had an income of £35,000 and gave a total of £32,000 to organisations in charitable donations.

Recipients of these donations included: North West London Jewish Day School (£4,000), Jewish Care, Mizrachi Charitable Trust and Norwood Ravenswood (£3,500 each), Kisharon (£3,000), Chai Cancer Care (£2,000), Kesser Torah and SAGE (£1,500 each), Kerem B'Yavneh Foundation (£1,000), and Barnet Israel Group (£250).

Exclusions No grants to individuals for scholarships or any other purpose.

Applications In writing to the correspondent.

The Fulmer Charitable Trust

Developing world, general

£268,000 (2004/05)

Beneficial area Worldwide, especially the developing world and Wiltshire.

Estate Office, Street Farm, Compton Bassett, Calne, Wiltshire SN11 8SW

Tel. 01249 760410 **Fax** 01249 760410

Correspondent The Trustees

Trustees *J S Reis; Mrs S Reis; Mrs C Mytum; Miss E J Reis.*

CC Number 1070428

Information available Accounts were on file at the Charity Commission.

General Most of the support is given in the developing world, although UK charities are also supported, especially those working in Wiltshire.

In 2004/05 the trust had assets of £5.5 million and an income of £2.3 million, mostly from donations. Grants totalled £268,000.

Over 140 organisations received grants during the year. The largest grants were made to NSPCC, Save the Children, Sense and Shelter (£8,000 each), Sight Savers (£7,500), Age Concern and the Sequal Trust (£7,000 each), Macmillan Cancer Relief (£6,000) and the Brain Research Trust, Brainwave, Disasters Emergency Committee, Energy and Vision, Extracare (£5,000 each).

Other beneficiaries included TRAX (£4,000), Mercy Ships and World Medical Fund (£2,500 each), Ashram International, Children in Distress, Coventry Cathedral Development Trust, Haemophilia Society, Prison Fellowship, Tear Fund and Wiltshire Community Foundation (£2,000 each), British Heart Foundation and Sue Ryder Care (£1,500 each), Amnesty International, Compass Braille, Friends of the Gambia, Kurdish Human Rights Project, Raleigh International, Through the Roof and UNICEF (£1,000 each) and Brooke Hospital for Animals (£500).

Exclusions No support for gap year requests. Very few unsolicited applications are accepted.

Applications In writing to the correspondent.

Gableholt Limited

Jewish

£379,000 to organisations and individuals (2004/05)

Beneficial area UK.

115 Craven Park Road, London N15 6BL

Correspondent Mrs E Noe, Secretary

Trustees *S Noe; Mrs E Noe; C Lerner; P Noe; A E Bude.*

CC Number 276250

Information available Accounts were on file at the Charity Commission.

General Set up as a limited company in 1978, the trust gives practically all of its funds to Jewish institutions, particularly those working in accordance with the Orthodox Jewish faith.

In 2004/05 it had an income of over £1 million and made grants to organisations and individuals totalling £379,000. The sum of £14 million was carried forward to the next year.

Unfortunately no information on grants was included with the trust's accounts that were on file at the Charity Commission. In previous years beneficiaries have included: Afula Society, Child Resettlement, Friends of Harim Establishment, Friends of the Sick, Gur Trust, Mengrah Grammar School, Rachel Charitable Trust and Torah Venchased Le'Ezra Vasad.

Applications In the past this trust has stated that 'in the governors' view, true charitable giving should always be coupled with virtual anonymity' and for this reason they are most reluctant to be a party to any publicity. Along with suggesting that the listed beneficiaries might also want to remain unidentified, they also state that the nature of the giving (to orthodox Jewish organisations) means the information is unlikely to be of much interest to anyone else. Potential applicants would be strongly advised to take heed of these comments.

The Horace and Marjorie Gale Charitable Trust

General

£64,000 (2004/05)

Beneficial area UK, mainly Bedfordshire.

Garner Associates, Northwood House, 138 Bromham Road, Bedford MK40 2QW

Tel. 01234 354508 **Fax** 01234 349588

Email email@garnerassociates.co.uk

Correspondent G Garner

Trustees *G D Payne, Chair; J Tyley; J Williams; P H Tyley; K Fletcher.*

CC Number 289212

Information available Accounts were on file at the Charity Commission, without a list of grants.

General The trust gives support in three areas:

- for churches and church ministries, with emphasis on Bunyan Meeting Free Church in Bedford and the ministries of the Baptist Union in England and Wales
- donations to charities and organisations active in the community life of Bedford and Bedfordshire
- donations to UK charities and organisations active in community life.

In 2004/05 the trust had assets of £2.5 million and an income of £45,000. After high management and administration costs of £20,000, grants were made totalling £64,000. Unfortunately further information for this year was not available.

Previous beneficiaries have included Arthritis Care, Bunyan Meeting Free Church, the Baptist Union – Home Mission Fund, Cotton End Lower School, North Bedfordshire Hospice, Bedford Playing Fields Association, Bedford Philharmonic Orchestra, Bedfordshire Rural Communities Charity, Headway, Mayday Trust, Meningitis Research Foundation, Motor Neurone Disease Association, Starlight Children's Foundation, St Andrew's Church – Bedford, Warboys Orphanage Project and the Wishbone Trust.

Exclusions Grants are rarely given to individuals.

Applications In writing to the correspondent. Grants are distributed once a year and applications should be made by May for consideration in July.

The Angela Gallagher Memorial Fund

Children and young people, Christian, humanitarian, education

£22,000 (2005)

Beneficial area UK and international organisations based in the UK.

Church Cott, The Green, Mirey Lane, Woodbury, Devon EX5 1LT

Correspondent Mrs D R Moss, Secretary

Trustees *N A Maxwell-Lawford; P Mostyn; P A Wolrige Gordon; A Swan.*

CC Number 800739

Information available Full accounts were on file at the Charity Commission.

General The aim of the fund is to help children within the UK. The fund will also consider Christian, humanitarian and educational projects worldwide, although international disasters are only aided through British Red Cross or CAFOD. Small charities which do not have access to large corporate donors are given priority.

In 2005 the trust had assets of £1.1 million and an income of £33,000. Grants to 42 organisations totalled £22,000.

There were three grants made of £1,000 each to CAFOD for Tsunami, CAFOD for Pakistan and Microloan Foundation. remaining donation were all for £500 each and included those to 1st Eastnor Brownies, Acorn Christian Centre, Esther Benjamin Trust, Bibles for Children, Blaen Wern Farm Trust, Camp Trek Isle of Skye, Edinburgh University Children's Holiday Venture, Edinburgh Young Carers, the Eyeless Trust, Home-Start Torbay, Milton Keynes Lighthouse and Rochdale Special Needs Cycling Club.

Exclusions Donations will not be made to the following: older people; scientific research; hospitals and hospices; artistic and cultural appeals; animal welfare; or building and equipment appeals. No grants to individuals.

Applications In writing to the correspondent, for consideration at trustees' meetings twice a year. Applicants must include a set of accounts or the appeal will not be considered. Applications are not acknowledged without an sae.

The Gamlen Charitable Trust

Legal education, general

£8,600 (2005/06)

Beneficial area UK.

c/o Penningtons, Newbury House, 20 Kings Road West, Newbury, Berkshire RG14 5XR

Tel. 01635 571000

Correspondent R G Stubblefield, Trustee

Trustees *R G Stubblefield; I R Ponsford; J W M Chadwick.*

CC Number 327977

Information available Accounts were on file at the Charity Commission.

General Established in 1988, in 2005/06 this trust had assets of £1.5 million and an income of £40,000. Grants totalled £8,600.

There were six grants made in the year. Beneficiaries were the Law Charities Educational Trust and Newbury Spring Festival (£3,000 each), Garsington Opera (£1,000), Cancer Research UK (£800), Multiple Sclerosis Society (£500) and Bampton Classical Opera (£250).

Applications In writing to the correspondent.

The Gamma Trust

General

About £60,000

Beneficial area UK, with a possible preference for Scotland.

c/o Mazars CYB Services Limited, 90 St Vincent Street, Glasgow G2 5UB

Correspondent The Trust Secretary

SC Number SC004330

Information available Information was provided by the trust.

General This trust has general charitable purposes. It appears that new grants are only given to UK-wide organisations although most grants are ongoing commitments to local organisations in Scotland. It has a grant total of about £60,000 a year.

Previous beneficiaries have included British Red Cross, British Heart Foundation, Cancer Research Campaign and Erskine Hospital.

Exclusions No grants to individuals.

Applications In writing to the correspondent for consideration quarterly.

Garrick Charitable Trust

Theatre, music, literature, dance

£172,000 (2004/05)
Beneficial area UK.

15 Garrick Street, London WC2E 9AY
Tel. 020 7836 1737
Correspondent The Secretary
Trustees A Hammond, Chair; N Newton; G Palmer; Sir S Waley-Cohen; A H Doggart.
CC Number 1071279

Information available Accounts were on file at the Charity Commission.

General This trust supports institutions which are seeking to further the profession of theatre (including dance), literature or music. Grants are usually for amounts of £2,500, only in exceptional circumstances will they exceed £10,000.

In 2004/05 the trust had assets of £4.4 million and an income of £171,000. Grants totalled £172,000.

Beneficiaries included National Youth Orchestra, Nash Concert Society and Royal Court Theatre (£10,000 each), Roald Dahl Centre (£8,100), Park Lane Group (£7,500), Actors of Dionysus, City of Birmingham Symphony Orchestra, Eden Court Theatre, English National Opera, Hackney Music Development Trust, Opera Group, Shakespeare School Festival, Theatre Royal Plymouth and Vivace (£5,000 each) and Arion Orchestra, Arnolfini Gallery, Brighton Festival Youth Choir, Cheltenham Arts Festival, Leicester

Appeal for Music and Art and Living Picture Productions (£2,500 each).

Applications Initial applications are reviewed by the trustees who decide whether or not to send an application form. Trustees meet quarterly.

Garvan Limited

Jewish

£233,000 (2005/06)
Beneficial area UK.

Flat 9, Windsor Court, Golders Green Road, London NW11 9PP
Correspondent The Trustees
Trustees A Ebert; L Ebert.
CC Number 286110

Information available Accounts were on file at the Charity Commission, but without a list of grants.

General This trust makes grants to Jewish organisations. In 2005/06 it had assets of £588,000 and an income of £244,000. Grants totalled £233,000. Unfortunately, no further information was available on the size or number of beneficiaries for this year.

Applications In writing to the correspondent.

Jacqueline and Michael Gee Charitable Trust

Health, education (including Jewish)

£204,000 (2004/05)
Beneficial area UK.

27 Berkeley House, Hay Hill, London W1J 8NS
Tel. 020 7493 1904 **Fax** 020 7499 1470
Email trust@sherman.co.uk
Correspondent Michael J Gee, Trustee
Trustees M J Gee; J S Gee.
CC Number 1062566

Information available Accounts were on file at the Charity Commission.

General This charity's policy is to benefit almost exclusively health and

educational charities. In practice this includes many Jewish organisations.

It was created in 1997 by the settlement of £50 from the Archie Sherman Charitable Trust. In 2004/05 the trust had assets of £20,000, an income of £200,000 made up mostly from donations and made grants totalling £204,000. Grants were broken down as follows, shown here with examples of beneficiaries in receipt of grants of £1,000 or more:

Education and training – £128,000
Purcell School (£100,000), Pavilion Opera Educational Trust (£12,000), WJR (£6,400), Friends of the Hebrew University of Jerusalem (£3,000) and British WIZO (£1,000).

Arts and culture – £37,000
National Theatre (£23,000), Grange Park Opera (£5,000), Royal Academy (£2,000) and Garsington Opera (£1,000).

Medical, health and sickness – £24,000
Chai Cancer Care (£10,000), Norwood Ltd (£2,800), Prostate Cancer Research UK (£2,000), Nightingale House (£1,400) and MDA (£1,000).

Religious activities – £3,900
United Synagogue (£2,800).

General – £10,000
Tel Aviv Foundation (£10,000).

Applications In writing to the correspondent.

The Gibbs Charitable Trust

Methodism, international, arts

£105,000 (2005/06)
Beneficial area UK, with a preference for the south of England and worldwide.

8 Victoria Square, Clifton, Bristol BS8 4ET
Correspondent Dr James M Gibbs, Trustee
Trustees John N Gibbs, Chair; James Gibbs; Andrew Gibbs; Celia Gibbs; Elizabeth Gibbs; Jessica Gibbs; John E Gibbs; Juliet Gibbs; Patience Gibbs; Rebecca Gibbs; William Gibbs; James D Gibbs.
CC Number 207997

Information available Information was provided by the trust.

General The trust supports Methodist churches and organisations, other Christian causes (especially those of an ecumenical nature) and creative arts, education and social and international causes. It has a slight preference for projects which can be easily visited by the trustees and it also occasionally supports overseas applications.

In 2005/06 the trust had assets of £2.3 million, an income of £73,000 and made grants totalling £105,000 which were broken down as follows:

Methodist churches, circuits and districts – 9 grants totalling £4,600
Grants included Victoria Methodist Church – Bristol (£600) and Deeping St Nicholas Methodist Chapel, Lazells Methodist Church, Trinity Church – Gosforth and Winshill Methodist Church (£500 each).

Other Methodist initiatives – 9 grants totalling £15,000
Beneficiaries included Methodist Homes for the Aged (£5,000), Amelia Farm Trust and Oxford Institute for Methodist Theological Studies (£2,000 each), Lantern Arts (£1,000) and Second Step (£500).

Other Christian initiatives – 12 grants totalling £14,000
Beneficiaries included Church Army – 121 Appeal and Riding Lights (£2,000 each), Cambridge House, Corrymeela Trust, Greenbelt Festival and Riding Lights (£1,000 each) and Oasis and Sycamore Projects (£500 each).

International – 16 grants totalling £31,000
Grants included those to Christian Aid and Traidcraft (£5,000 each), Child to Child – Ecuador and Tree Aid (£3,000 each), MCSL Women's Skills Training Centre for Self Reliance and Sustainable Development – Sierra Leone and Practical Action (£2,000 each), Harvest Help, Kambia Hospital – Sierra Leone, Pump Aid, Tools for Self Reliance and VSO (£1,000 each) and CLEAR (£500).

Arts and Drama – 12 grants totalling £10,000
Beneficiaries included Mind Art – Cardiff University Psychology Department (£2,000), Hijinx Theatre Tour, National Theatre, Pegasus Opera and Streetwise Opera (£1,000 each), Circomedica (£700) and Brecon Theatre, CARAD Community Museum and Deep Impact Theatre Company (£500 each).

Social, educational and medical need – 2 grants totalling £2,000
Beneficiaries were British Empire and Commonwealth Museum (£1,000 each).

Designated fund – 1 grant totalling £30,000
One grant of £30,000 was donated to Methodist Church Fund for Ministerial Training.

Exclusions A large number of requests are received by the trust from churches undertaking improvement, refurbishment and development projects, but only a few of these can be helped. In general, Methodist churches are selected, sometimes those of whom the trustees have particular knowledge.

No unsolicited applications from individuals and no animal charities.

Applications The trust has no application forms, although an application cover sheet is available on the trust's website along with a policy and guidelines page. Requests should be made in writing to the correspondent. The trustees meet three times a year, after Christmas, near Easter and late summer. Unsuccessful applicants are not normally notified. The trustees do not encourage telephone enquiries or speculative applications. They also state that they are not impressed by applicants who send a huge amount of paperwork.

The Glanrose Trust

General

£37,000 (2004/05)
Beneficial area UK.

HSBC, Norwich House, Nelson Gate, Commercial Road, Southampton SO15 1GX
Correspondent Mr C Bould
Trustees *Wyn Howell Hughes; HSBC Trust Co. (UK) Ltd.*
CC Number 1079498
Information available Accounts were on file at the Charity Commission.

General Registered with the Charity Commission in February 2000, in 2004/05 the trust had an income of £259,000, including £220,000 from the sale of investments. Grants totalled £37,000.

There were 12 grants made during the year to three organisations: British Heart Foundation, Muscular Dystrophy and Oxfam.

Applications In writing to the correspondent.

The B and P Glasser Charitable Trust

Health, disability, Jewish, welfare

£54,000 (2004/05)
Beneficial area UK and worldwide.

Stafford Young Jones, The Old Rectory, 29 Martin Lane, London EC4R 0AU
Correspondent B S Christer
Trustees *J D H Cullingham; M J Glasser; J A Glasser.*
CC Number 326571
Information available Accounts were on file at the Charity Commission.

General This trust makes grants mainly to health and disability-related charities and Jewish charities, but also for other social-welfare purposes.

In 2004/05 the trust had an income of £71,000 with assets of £1.4 million. Grants to 27 organisations totalled £54,000.

Beneficiaries included Nightingale House (£7,000), RNIB (£5,000), Practical Action (£4,500), Sight Savers International (£4,000), British Council Shaare Zedek Medical Centre, Jewish Deaf Association, Macmillan Cancer Relief – Hertfordshire and UNICEF (£2,000 each), British Red Cross, Friends of St Francis Hospice, Help The Aged and SSAFA (£1,000 each) and Tring and District Patients Medical Fund (£500).

Exclusions No grant to individuals or students.

Applications In writing to the correspondent. To keep administrative costs to a minimum the trust is unable to reply to unsuccessful applicants.

GMC Trust

Medical research, healthcare, general

£76,000 (2005/06)
Beneficial area UK, predominantly in the West Midlands.

4 Fairways, 1240 Warwick Road, Knowle, Solihull, West Midlands B93 9LL
Tel. 01564 779971 **Fax** 01564 770499
Correspondent Rodney Pitts, Secretary

Trustees *Sir Adrian Cadbury; B E S Cadbury; M J Cadbury.*

CC Number 288418

Information available Accounts were on file at the Charity Commission.

General The trust supports medical research and causes related to inner-city disadvantage. Income is substantially committed to a range of existing beneficiaries.

In 2005/06 it had assets of £2.3 million and an income of £128,000. Grants totalling £76,000 were made to 54 organisations, only a quarter of which were not also supported in the previous year.

Grants of £1,000 or more included those to: Cancer Research at Birmingham and the Mental Health Foundation (£10,000 each); Acorns Children's Hospice Trust and Mind (£6,000 each); Macmillan Cancer Relief and St Giles Church (£5,000 each); Christ Church – India and Runnymede Trust (£2,500 each); Zane: Zimbabwe a National Emergency (£2,000); and Alzheimer's Research Trust, Arthritis Research Campaign, Coventry Cathedral, Cystic Fibrosis Trust, King's Lynn Arts Festival, Listening Books, Marie Curie Cancer Care, Oasis Trust, Prisoners of Conscience Appeal Fund, Salvation Army and SSAFA Forces Help (£1,000 each).

Smaller grants included those to: Dodford Children's Holiday Farm (£750); Fairbridge West Midlands and Myasthenia Gravis Association (£600 each); Age Concern, British Red Cross, Musicians Benevolent Fund, No Panic, READ Educational Trust, VSO and Youth Sports Association (£500 each); Shelter (£300); the ExtraCare Charitable Trust, Scope, Sight Savers and UNICEF (£250 each); and Friends of Birmingham Guiding (£100).

Exclusions No grants to individuals, or to local or regional appeals outside the West Midlands. The trust does not respond to national appeals, except where there are established links.

Applications In writing to the correspondent. The trust will only consider written applications, and applications outside the trust's remit will not be acknowledged.

The GNC Trust

General

£62,000 (2005)

Beneficial area UK, with preferences for Birmingham and Cornwall.

c/o Messrs PricewaterhouseCoopers, Cornwall Court, 19 Cornwall Street, Birmingham B3 2DT

Correspondent Mrs P M Spragg

Trustees *R N Cadbury; Mrs J E B Yelloly.*

CC Number 211533

Information available Accounts were obtained from the Charity Commission's website.

General In 2005 the trust had assets of £2.7 million and an income of £88,000. Grants were made totalling £62,000.

Support is given to registered charities which the trustees have special interest in, knowledge of or association with. Grants were broken down as follows:

Animal welfare
The sole beneficiary listed was Brooke Hospital receiving £3,000.

Conservation
Galapagos Conservation Trust received five grants totalling £1,100.

Disability
Beneficiaries included Association for Spina Bifida and Hydrocephalus, Enham Trust and Mary Hare Foundation Newbury (£1,000 each) and Treloar Trust (£960).

Furtherance of education
Grants included those to Conductive Education (£10,000), Sibford School (£1,800), Bourneville Junior and Infant School (£1,000), Venturers Search and Rescue (£750) and the Merlin Trust (£500).

Medical causes
The sole beneficiary listed was Primary Immune Deficiency Association receiving £5,000.

Performing arts
Grants in this category included those to the National Youth Ballet (£10,000) and St Barbe Museum and Art Gallery (£5,000).

Religious interests
Beneficiaries included St Mary's Church Doverdale (£1,500), St John Holy Trinity Division (£1,000) and Overseas Mission Fellowship (£750).

Social welfare
Grants in this category included: Action Aid (£3,500 in two grants), DEC Niger Appeal, Oakhaven Hospice Trust and

UNICEF (£1,000 each) and Tearfund (£750).

Other grants under £750 each totalled £8,700.

Exclusions No grants are made to national appeals, London-based charities or to individuals.

Applications In writing to the correspondent at any time. There are no application forms and applications are not acknowledged.

The Joseph and Queenie Gold Charitable Trust

Jewish, general

£30,000 (2005/06)

Beneficial area UK.

8 Blenheim Street, London W1S 1LQ

Correspondent Christopher Sills

Trustees *Lady C Djanogly; Sir H Djanogly; J Djanogly.*

CC Number 286351

Information available Full accounts were on file at the Charity Commission.

General The trust makes grants mainly to Jewish organisations, although other charities are also occasionally supported.

In 2005/06 the trust had assets of £1.2 million, an income of £64,000 and made grants totalling £30,000 to: United Jewish Israel Appeal (£27,000); Community Security Trust; and Food Life Line (£50).

Exclusions No grants to individuals.

Applications In writing to the correspondent.

The Sydney and Phyllis Goldberg Memorial Charitable Trust

Medical research, welfare, disability

£80,000 (2004/05)
Beneficial area UK.

Coulthards Mackenzie, 17 Park Street, Camberley, Surrey GU15 3PQ

Tel. 01276 65470

Correspondent M J Church, Trustee

Trustees *H G Vowles; M J Church; C J Pexton.*

CC Number 291835

Information available Full accounts were on file at the Charity Commission.

General The income for the trust comes from its investments which are mainly held in Syona Investments Limited. Phyllis Goldberg initially bequeathed her shareholding in Syona Investments Limited to the trust and since then the trust has bought the balance of the shares.

In 2004/05 the trust had assets of £2.4 million with an income of £74,000 and made grants totalling £80,000.

Grants were: £15,000 to Children of St Mary's Intensive Care Department of Child Health; £10,000 each to the British Stammering Association, the Dystonia Society, Children with Special Needs Foundation, Queen Alexandra Hospital Portsmouth and the Prostate Cancer Charity; £6,000 each to Cystic Fibrosis Trust and Life Centre; and £3,000 to the Isaac Goldberg Charity Trust.

Applications In writing to the correspondent. Telephone requests are not appreciated. Applicants are advised to apply towards the end of the calendar year.

Golden Charitable Trust

Preservation, conservation

£117,000 (2005/06)
Beneficial area UK with a preference for West Sussex.

Little Leith Gate, Angel Street, Petworth, West Sussex GU28 0BG

Correspondent Lewis Golden, Secretary to the Trustees

Trustees *Mrs S J F Solnick; J M F Golden.*

CC Number 263916

Information available Accounts were on file at the Charity Commission.

General The trust appears to have a preference in its grant-making for organisations in West Sussex in the field of the preservation and conservation of historic articles and materials.

In 2005/06 the trust had assets of over £1 million and an income of £160,000. Grants were made to 31 organisations totalling £117,000.

Beneficiaries included Petworth Cottage Nursing Home (£21,000), Westminster Synagogue (£16,000), the Wordsworth Trust (£14,000), the Airborne Forces Museum, Friends of the Parker Library, Lambeth Palace Library and Music Mind Spirit Trust (£10,000 each), British ORT (£5,000), Chichester Cathedral Restoration & Development Trust and Pallant House Gallery (£2,500 each), Petworth Festival and West Sussex Record Office (£2,000 each), Cowdray Heritage Trust, the Royal Star and Garter Home and Winston's Wish (£1,000 each), the Petworth Cottage Trust (£750), the Bowerman Charitable Trust (£700), Yvonne Arnaud Theatre Management Limited (£500) and British Heart Foundation and Langdon College (£100 each).

Exclusions No grants to individuals.

Applications In writing to the correspondent.

The Jack Goldhill Charitable Trust

Jewish, general

£100,000 (2005)
Beneficial area UK.

85 Kensington Heights, Campden Hill Road, London W8 7BD

Correspondent Jack Goldhill, Trustee

Trustees *G Goldhill; J A Goldhill; M L Goldhill.*

CC Number 267018

Information available Accounts were on file at the Charity Commission.

General In 2005 the trust had assets of £503,000 with an income of £80,000 and grants totalling £170,000. Unfortunately no grants list has been provided for recent years.

Previous beneficiaries have included CST, City and Guilds of London School of Art, Jack Goldhill Award Fund, JNF Charitable Trust, Jewish Care, Joint Jewish Charitable Trust, Nightingale House, Royal Academy of Arts, Royal London Hospital, Tate Gallery, Tricycle Theatre Co., West London Synagogue and Atlantic College.

Exclusions No support for individuals or new applications.

Applications The trustees have a restricted list of charities to whom they are committed and no unsolicited applications can be considered.

The Golsoncott Foundation

The arts

£49,000 (2005/06)
Beneficial area UK.

53 St Leonord's Rd, Exeter EX2 4LS

Tel. 01392 252855 **Fax** 01392 252855

Correspondent Hal Bishop, Administrator

Trustees *Penelope Lively, Chair; Josephine Lively; Stephen Wick; Dr Harriet Harvey Wood.*

CC Number 1070885

Information available Accounts were on file at the Charity Commission.

General The trust states its objects as follows: 'to promote, maintain, improve and advance the education of the public in the arts generally and in particular ... fine arts and music. The fostering of the practice and appreciation of the arts, especially amongst young people and new audiences, is a further specific objective.

'Grants vary according to context and are not subject to an inflexible limit, but they are unlikely to exceed £5,000 and are normally given on a non-recurrent basis.'

In 2005/06 the foundation had assets of £1.9 million and an income of £61,000. Grants to 44 organisations totalled £49,000. Among the 20 beneficiaries in receipt of grants of £1,000 or more were British Library, National Youth Orchestra and Rodhuish PCC (£5,000 each), Chamber Music 2000, National Children's Orchestra and TONIC (£2,000 each), Darwin Music Project and Two Moors Festival (£1,500 each) and Asham Trust, Friends of St Giles Cripplegate, Mrs Gaskell's House – Manchester Historic Buildings Trust, Music in Hospitals – Scotland and Walk the Plank Theatre (£1,000 each).

Other beneficiaries included Cobbe Collection, Cornwall Arts, Hobbs Factory Theatre, Phoenix Singers, Tunnel Trust, Worcester Concert Club and Young Actors' Theatre (£500 each), Luddesdownwe PCC (£50) and International Guitar Festival (£30).

Exclusions No grants to individuals.

Applications The trustees meet quarterly to consider applications, in February, May, August and November. Applications should be sent to the correspondent by the end of the month preceding the month of the trustees' meeting. They should include the following:

- 'A clear and concise statement of the project, whether the award sought will be for the whole project or a component part. Is the applicant organisation of charitable status?
- 'Evidence that there is a clear benefit to the public, i.e. does the project conform with the declared object of the trust.
- 'The amount requested should be specified, or a band indicated. Is this the only source of funding being sought? All other sources of funding should be indicated, including those that have refused funding.
- 'If the grant requested is part of the match-funding required by the Heritage Lottery Foundation (HLF) following an award, state the amount

of that award and the percentage of match-funding required by the HLF and the completion date.

- 'Wherever possible an annual report and accounts should accompany the application, as may other supporting information deemed relevant.

'Second or further applications will not be considered until a minimum of 12 months has elapsed since determination of the previous application, whether successful or not.'

The Good Neighbours Trust

People with mental or physical disabilities

£56,000 (2005)

Beneficial area UK, with preference for Bristol, Somerset and Gloucestershire.

16 Westway, Nailsea, Bristol BS48 2NA

Correspondent P S Broderick, Secretary

Trustees G V Arter, Chair; J C Gurney; P S Broderick; J L Hudd.

CC Number 201794

Information available Accounts were on file at the Charity Commission.

General The present policy of the trust is principally to support registered charities whose activities benefit people who are physically or mentally disabled. It mainly gives one-off grants for low-cost specific projects such as purchase of equipment or UK holidays for people with disabilities.

In 2005 the trust had assets of £2.5 million and an income of £80,000. Grants totalling £56,000 were made to 119 organisations; they ranged from £250 to £2,500. Donations were broken down as follows:

Local Grants (£23,000)
Beneficiaries included Avon Riding Centre for the Disabled, DeafBlind UK, HCPT Group 176, National Eye Research Centre and RICE (£1,000 each), Fosseway School (£750), Ability Sports Association, Brainwave, Dragon Club, Heartline, Listening Books, Royal Blind Society, Somerset Association for the Blind and Willow Trust (£500 each) and Multiple Sclerosis Research Unit (£300)

and Alzheimer's Society, Grateful Society and Toc H (£250 each).

National Grants (£33,000)
Beneficiaries included Help the Hospices (£2,500), the Children's Trust, Holidays with Help, Oakleigh Special School, Hedley Foundation and West of England and College for Children with Little or No Sight (£1,000 each), Blind in Business, Brecon & District disABLEd Club, British Blind Sport, DELTA, Derby Toc H Children's Camp, Hamlet Centre Trust, Hearing Dogs for the Deaf, West of England Residential School for the Deaf, Tools for Self Reliance and Yorkshire Spinal Injury Centre Appeal (£500 each) and Arthritis Care, Caring for Life, Children's Adventure Farm Trust, Disaway, Down Syndrome International Swimming Organisation, Handicapped Aid Trust, Henshaws Society for the Blind, Meadows School, MG Association Thursday Club and Where Next Association (£250 each).

Exclusions Support is not given: for overseas projects; general community projects*; individuals; general education projects*; religious and ethnic projects*; projects for unemployment and related training schemes*; projects on behalf of offenders and ex-offenders; projects concerned with the abuse of drugs and/ or alcohol; wildlife and conservation schemes*; and general restoration and preservation of buildings, purely for historical and/or architectural reasons. (* If these projects are mainly or wholly for the benefit of people who have disabilities then they may be considered.)

Ongoing support is not given, and grants are not usually given for running costs, salaries, research and items requiring major funding. Loans are not given.

Applications The trust does not have an official application form. Appeals should be made in writing to the secretary. Telephone calls are not welcome. The trust asks that the following is carefully considered before submitting an application:

Appeals must:

- be from registered charities
- include a copy of the latest audited accounts available (for newly registered charities a copy of provisional accounts showing estimated income and expenditure for the current financial year)
- show that the project is 'both feasible and viable' and, if relevant, give the starting date of the project and the anticipated date of completion
- include the estimated cost of the project, together with the appeal's

target figure and details of what funds have already been raised and any fundraising schemes for the project.

The trustees state that 'where applicable, due consideration will be given to evidence of voluntary and self-help (both in practical and fundraising terms) and to the number of people expected to benefit from the project'. They also comment that their decision is final and 'no reason for a decision, whether favourable or otherwise, need be given' and that 'the award and acceptance of a grant will not involve the trustees in any other commitment'.

Appeals are dealt with on an ongoing basis, but the trustees meet formally four times per year usually in March, June, September and December.

Nicholas and Judith Goodison's Charitable Settlement

Arts, arts education

£162,000 (2004/05)
Beneficial area UK.

PO Box 2512, London W1A 5ZP
Correspondent Sir N Goodison, Trustee
Trustees *Sir Nicholas Goodison; Lady Judith Goodison; Miss Katharine Goodison.*
CC Number 1004124
Information available Accounts were on file at the Charity Commission.

General The trust supports registered charities in the field of the arts and arts education. Grants are also given to institutions in instalments over several years towards capital projects.

In 2004/05 it had assets of £1.5 million, which generated an income of £211,000. Grants were made to 36 organisations totalling £162,000. Management and administration expenses for the year were very low at just £590.

The largest grants were £32,000 to Wigmore Hall, £27,000 to English National Opera, £25,000 to King's College, £14,000 to Fitzwilliam Museum, £13,000 to Burghers of Calais – NACF and £10,000 to National Gallery.

Other grants included £6,500 to Handel House Trust, £5,000 to Academy of Ancient Music, £3,600 to Victoria and Albert Museum, £2,000 each to National Art Collection Funds and Arvon Foundation, £1,000 each to Courtauld Institute of Art, Museum of Childhood – V and A and Tate Gallery, £500 each to Miriam Dean Refugee Trust, Furniture History Society and King Edward VII Hospital, £300 to Marfan Foundation, £200 each to Albanian Musicians' Trust and London Symphony Orchestra and £100 each to Arc and Worthing Society for the Blind.

Exclusions No grants to individuals.

Applications The trust states that it cannot respond to unsolicited applications.

Leonard Gordon Charitable Trust

Jewish religious, educational and welfare organisations

£67,000 (2005/06)
Beneficial area England and Wales.

17 Park Street, Salford M7 4NJ
Correspondent Leonard Gordon, Chair
Trustees *Leonard Gordon, Chair; Michael Gordon; Ian Fidler.*
CC Number 1075185
Information available Information was on file with the Charity Commission, without a list of grants.

General Established in 1999, in 2005/06 it had an income of £315,000, including £216,000 from Mr L Gordon. Grants were made totalling £67,000. No list of donations was included with the accounts.

Applications In writing to the correspondent.

The Gough Charitable Trust

Young people, Episcopal and Church of England, preservation of the countryside, social welfare

£71,000 (2004/05)
Beneficial area UK, with a possible preference for Scotland.

Lloyds TSB Private Banking Ltd, UK Trust Centre, 22–26 Ock Street, Abingdon OX14 5SW
Correspondent The Trust Manager
Trustees *Lloyds Bank plc; N de L Harvie.*
CC Number 262355
Information available Accounts were on file at the Charity Commission.

General The trust has previously shown a preference for Scotland, however it is not clear if this is still the case.

In 2004/05 the trust had an income of £65,000 and made grants totalling £71,000.

During the year the trust made grants to 16 organisations. No indication was given on the size of these donations. Beneficiaries were: Abberley Hall Foundation, Concordia Foundation, Crown and Manor Boys' Club, Household Brigade Benevolent Fund, Irish Guards Lieutenant Colonels Fun, the Lifeboat Service Memorial Book Trust, Lloyds Benevolent-Fund, Lloyds Charities Fund, National Army Development Trust, Prince of Wales Lodge No. 259 Benevolent Fund, Royal Hospital School, Royal Humane Society, St Peter's Hospice, Spa Pavilion Association, Trinity Hospice and Women Caring Trust.

Exclusions No support for non-registered charities and individuals including students.

Applications In writing to the correspondent at any time. No acknowledgements are sent. Applications are considered quarterly.

The Gould Charitable Trust

General

£39,000 (2004/05)

Beneficial area UK.

Cervantes, Pinner Hill, Pinner, Middlesex HA5 3XU

Correspondent S Gould, Trustee

Trustees *Mrs J B Gould; L J Gould; M S Gould; S Gould; S H Gould.*

CC Number 1035453

Information available Accounts were on file at the Charity Commission.

General In 2004/05 the trust had an income of £32,000 and made grants totalling £39,000. Assets stood at £740,000.

By far the largest grant was £25,000 to JPAIME. Other grants over £1,000 included LMT (£4,000), Childhope Asia Philippines and Diabetes UK (£3,300 each), Friends of Philharmonica, Médecins sans Frontières and Pattan (£2,000 each), National Medicines Society (£1,500) and World Jewish Relief (£1,100).

The accounts listed 45 donations. There were 14 organisations in receipt of grants of £1,000 or more, including Alzheimer's Research Trust (£4,000), FCED Foundation Philippines (£3,300), NSPCC (£3,000), Save the Children (£2,500), Centrepoint, Childhope, Médecins Sans Frontières and One to One (£2,000 each), Friends of Hebrew University (£1,300) and DEC Sudan Emergency, LMT Chamber Ensemble, Magen David Adom and World Jewish Relief (£1,000 each).

Exclusions No support for non-registered charities. No grants to individuals.

Applications In writing to the correspondent, although the trust states: 'We never give donations to unsolicited requests on principle.'

The Grace Charitable Trust

Christian

£467,000 to organisations (2005/06)

Beneficial area UK.

Rhuallt House, Rhuallt, St Asaph, Sir Ddinbych LL17 0TG

Tel. 01745 583141 **Fax** 01745 585243

Correspondent Mrs G J R Payne, Trustee

Trustees *Mrs G J R Payne; E Payne; Mrs G M Snaith; R B M Quayle.*

CC Number 292984

Information available Accounts were available from the Charity Commission, but without a list of beneficiaries.

General Established in 1985, the trust generally gives grants of £1,000 to £10,000 each with a preference for Christian organisations. In 2005/06 the trust had assets of £75,000 and an income of £117,000. Grants were made to organisations totalling £467,000, which were broken down as follows:

- £50,000–£99,999 – (3 grants totalling £175,000)
- £10,000–£49,999 – (7 grants totalling £162,000)
- £1,000–£9,999 – (35 grants totalling £127,000)
- Less than £1,000 – (10 grants totalling £3,000)

A further £6,000 was given in grants to seven individuals.

Applications The trust states: 'Grants are made only to charities known to the settlors and unsolicited applications are, therefore, not considered.'

Grand Charitable Trust of the Order of Women Freemasons

General in the UK and overseas

£57,000 to non-Masonic charities (2004/05)

Beneficial area UK and overseas.

27 Pembridge Gardens, London W2 4EF

Correspondent Mrs Joan Sylvia Brown, Trustee

Trustees *B I Fleming-Taylor; M J P Masters; B Wildman; H I Naldrett; J S Brown; I M Boggia-Black.*

CC Number 1059151

Information available Accounts were on file at the Charity Commission, but without a list of beneficiaries.

General This trust donates about half its grant total to causes related to the Order of Women Freemasons, including individual members and their dependants. The remaining half is donated to external charities.

In 2004/05 it had assets of £759,000 and an income of £207,000. A payment of £50,000 went to Adelaide Litten Charitable Trust, who provides support to individual Masons who are in need. Grants to other organisations totalled £57,000 while a total of £12,000 went directly to individuals.

Unfortunately there was no grants list included in the trust's accounts which makes it difficult to know which non-Masonic charities are supported.

Applications In writing to the correspondent. Applications should be submitted by the end of July each year for consideration by the trustees.

The Grand Order of Water Rats' Charities Fund

Theatrical, medical equipment

£100,000 (2004)

Beneficial area UK.

328 Gray's Inn Road, London WC1X 8BZ

Tel. 020 7407 8007

Website www.gowr.net

Correspondent John Adrian, Secretary

Trustees *Chas McDevitt, Chair; Wyn Calvin; Roy Hudd; Kaplan Kaye; Keith Simmons; Ken Joy.*

CC Number 292201

Information available Accounts were on file at the Charity Commission, but without a list of grants.

General The trust was established to assist members of the variety and light entertainment profession and their dependants who, due to illness or age, are in need. The fund also buys medical equipment for certain institutions and also for individuals who have worked with or who have been closely connected with the same profession.

In 2004 the trust had an income of £339,000 and a total expenditure of £144,000. The income mainly comes from the profit gained from functions organised by the members of the Grand Order of Water Rats. The assets at the year-end stood at £1.4 million. Grants totalled £100,000, which included £31,000 listed as donations, £62,000 in monthly allowances, grants and gifts, and £2,300 for fruit and flowers.

In 1997, the last year in which grant information was available, the largest grants went to Cause for Hope (£11,000), Bud Flanagan Leukaemia Fund (£6,700) and Queen Elizabeth Hospital for Children (£3,000). There were six grants of between £1,000 and £2,000 including those to Actors Church Union, British Legion Wales and Northwick Park Hospital.

Exclusions No grants to students.

Applications In writing to the correspondent. The trustees meet once a month.

The Constance Green Foundation

Social welfare, medicine, health, general

£292,000 (2005/06)

Beneficial area Mainly England, with a preference for West Yorkshire. Some grants are made to charities operating overseas.

Syon House, La Rue des Pallieres, St Ouen, Jersey JE3 2BB

Tel. 01534 487757 **Fax** 01534 485261

Email suzih@fcmtrust.com

Correspondent Mrs S Hall

Trustees *M Collinson; Col. H R Hall; Mrs M L Hall; Mrs S Collinson.*

CC Number 270775

Information available Accounts were on file at the Charity Commission.

General The foundation makes grants mainly in the fields of social welfare and medicine. There is a special emphasis on the needs of young people and people who are mentally or physically disabled. Preference is given to making grants to assist in funding special projects being undertaken by charities rather than

grants to supplement funds used for general purposes.

In 2005/06 the trust had assets of £8.1 million and an income of £362,000. Grants to 96 organisations totalled £292,000 and were broken down as follows:

- Children and young persons (£111,000)
- Medical and social care (£90,000)
- Disabled and aged (£58,000)
- People who are homeless (£17,000)
- Church and community projects (£15,000)

Beneficiaries included Marie Curie Cancer Care (£15,000), Children in Distress, the Sick Children's Trust and Whizz-Kidz (£10,000 each), CARIS – Islington (£7,000), Africa Equipment for Schools, Befriending Network, Care Alliance, Disability Equality in Education, Epiphany Trust, National Children's Bureau, NSPCC, Salvation Army, Save the Children – Pakistan Earthquake Appeal and Y Care International (£5,000 each), Action for Kids and UNICEF (£3,000 each) and Bikeability, the Broadway Trust, Centrepoint, Children's Heart Federation, Deafblind UK, Dream Holidays, INSPIRE, Motability, Peaceful Pace, Rochdale Cycling Club, Voluntary Action Calderdale and York Nightstop (£1,000 each).

Exclusions Sponsorship of individuals is not supported.

Applications At any time in writing to the correspondent (no special form of application required). Applications should include clear details of the need the intended project is designed to meet, plus an outline budget.

The Barry Green Memorial Fund

Animal welfare

£67,000 (2004/05)

Beneficial area UK, with a preference for Yorkshire and Lancashire.

Claro Chambers, Horsefair, Boroughbridge, York YO51 9LD

Correspondent The Clerk to the Trustees

Trustees *Richard Fitzgerald-Hart; Mark Fitzgerald-Hart.*

CC Number 1000492

Information available Accounts were on file at the Charity Commission.

General The trust was created under the will of Mrs E M Green. It supports animal welfare charities concerned with the rescue, maintenance and benefit of cruelly treated animals and also the prevention of cruelty to animals. There is a preference for small charities.

In 2004/05 the trust had assets of £1.3 million and an income of £199,000. After high management and administration costs of £83,000, grants to 56 organisations totalled £67,000.

Beneficiaries included the Royal Veterinary College (£6,000), HACK Horse Sanctuary and Wildlife in Need (£4,000 each), Eden Animal Rescue (£3,000), Brooke Hospital for Animals, Devon Horse and Pony Sanctuary, Horse World, Mossburn Animal Centre, Prevent Unwanted Pets and Sussex Horse Rescue Trust (£2,000 each) University of Glasgow Veterinary College (£3,000), the ARC Foundation, Mid-Cheshire Animal Welfare and Willows Animal Sanctuary (£1,500 each), Cats Protection League Wigan, Fairplace Animal Rescue, London Wildlife Trust, the Skye View Animal Home and Vale Wildlife Rescue (£1,000 each), Greyhounds in Need, New Life Parrot Rescue and Second Chances (£500 each) and St Mary's Horse Rescue (£100).

Exclusions No expeditions, scholarships, work outside the UK or individuals.

Applications In writing to the correspondent including a copy of the accounts.

The Philip Green Memorial Trust

Young and older people, people with disabilities, people in need

£256,000 (2004/05)

Beneficial area UK.

301 Trafalgar House, Grenville Place, Mill Hill, London NW7 3SA

Tel. 020 8906 8732 **Fax** 020 8906 8574

Email info@pgmt.org.uk

Website www.pgmt.org.uk

Correspondent The Committee

Trustees *C Paskin; M Campbell; S Paskin; I Rondel; P Green; M Parsons; D Calderhead.*

CC Number 293156

Information available Accounts were on file at the Charity Commission.

General The trust's 2004/05 accounts stated that the objectives of the charity are 'raising money to help young people, older people, people with disabilities, and the needy in the community at large'.

During the year it had an income of £578,000, mainly raised through means such as annual dinners, a quiz night and the London Marathon. Grants to 32 organisations totalled £256,000.

The beneficiary of the largest grant was CHAS Trading – Scottish Hospice (£93,000), which also received £127,000 in the previous year.

Other beneficiaries included: Fiveways School (£50,000); PACE Centre (£23,000); RAF Leuchars Service Fund (£11,000); the Stephen and Lorraine Trust (£10,000); AJEX (£9,000); Construction Trade Contractors Charity (£5,900); Service Funds MPA (£5,000); Searchlight Educational Trust (£4,000); Chai Lifeline Cancer Care Centre and Norwood Ltd (£3,000 each); I Rescue (£2,000); Atlantic Salmon Trust, London Ex-Boxers Association and Starlight Children's Foundation (£1,000 each); Jewish Care (£800); and Richard House Trust (£50).

Applications In writing to the correspondent.

Mrs H R Greene Charitable Settlement

General, particularly at risk-groups, poverty, social isolation

£50,000 (2004/05)

Beneficial area UK, with a preference for Norfolk and Wistanstow in Shropshire.

Birketts, 16 Queen Street, Norwich, Norfolk NR2 4SQ

Correspondent N G Sparrow

Trustees *A C Boston; Revd J B Boston; D A Moore.*

CC Number 1050812

Information available Accounts were on file at the Charity Commission.

General The founder of this trust lived in Wistanstow in Shropshire and the principal trustee was for many years based in Norwich. Both these factors influence the grant-making of the trust, with several grants given in both the parish of Wistanstow and in the Norfolk area. The trust has an additional preference for supporting organisations helping at-risk groups and people who are disadvantaged by poverty or socially isolated.

In 2004/05 the trust had assets of £1.8 million, an income of £69,000 and made grants totalling £50,000 which included £4,700 in Christmas donations for coal and poultry. This is the only information available for this year. The most recent grants list available comes from 1997/98, when it had an income of £61,000, a total expenditure of £72,000 and gave £60,000 in grants. This includes £6,700 given to individuals, plus £3,500 in Christmas gifts and poultry. The rest was given to 43 organisations, in grants ranging between £170 and £6,000.

The largest grant in 1997/98 was £6,000 to St Michael's Hospital Bartestree, followed by a grant of £2,500 to Norfolk and Norwich Clergymen's Widows' and Children's Charity. Grants of £2,000 were given to Brittle Bone Society, Children's Food Fund, Landau, Macmillan Cancer Relief, Muscular Dystrophy Group and Orbis.

The grants list did not mention the geographical location of most of the charities. It was possible to distinguish that some are based in Norfolk, as follows: Beeston Church Organ (£1,000), Friends of Norwich Cathedral (£500), Horsford and St Faith's Scout Group (£400) and Litcham Parochial Church Council (£300); also see the second largest grant, above. It was not obvious from the grants list that the trust gave any grants in Wistanstow, Shropshire in 1997/98, although a couple of charities appeared on the grants list that were in the bordering county of Herefordshire (such as the largest grant).

Applications The trust states that it does not respond to unsolicited applications.

The Gretna Charitable Trust

General

£44,000 (2005/06)

Beneficial area UK, with a preference for Hertfordshire and London.

Imperial London Hotels Limited, Russell Square, London WC1B 5BB

Correspondent The Trustees

Trustees *H R Walduck; Mrs S M C Walduck; A H E P Walduck; C B Bowles.*

CC Number 1020533

Information available Full accounts were on file at the Charity Commission.

General This trust gives grants to a wide range of voluntary organisations in the UK, with a preference for Hertfordshire.

In 2005/06 the trust had assets of just over £1 million, an income of £61,000 and made 52 grants totalling £44,000.

Beneficiaries included: Sports Hatfield (£5,000); St Alban's Cathedral (£2,000); Action on Addiction, Bridewell Foundation, Caribbean Women Equality Forum, Crimebeat Leicestershire and Rutland, Harcourt Group – Museum of London, Lymphena & Leukaemia Research, Marching Blues – Potters Bar Scouts Band, Royal Courts Robe Presentation, St Dunstans – Head of College, St John Museum Appeal and War Memorials Trust – Malta (£1,000 each); All Hallows by the Tower, Carers Islington, Hertfordshire Children's Fund, the Prince's Trust and Royal Overseas League (£500 each); Hertford Museum (£250); and Potters Bar Carnival (£100).

Exclusions The trust will not provide support to fund salaries or administration costs.

Applications This trust does not encourage applications.

Grimmitt Trust

General

£86,000 (2005/06)

Beneficial area Birmingham and district and areas where trustees have a personal connection.

43 Pembroke Croft, Hall Green, Birmingham B28 9EY

Correspondent The Secretary

Trustees *P W Welch; Mrs M E Welch; Revd C Hughes Smith; Dr A D Owen; Mrs S L Day; Ms R Keenleyside; L Murray.*

CC Number 801975

Information available Accounts were obtained from the Charity Commission website.

General Grants are given to organisations in the Birmingham area. Local branches of UK organisations are supported, but larger UK appeals are not. Over half of the grant total is given in grants of less than £500 each.

In 2005/06 it had assets of £7.2 million and an income of £153,000. There were 215 grants made in the year totalling £86,000, broken down as follows:

- community – £31,000 (78 grants)
- cultural and educational – £20,000 (35)
- overseas – £14,000 (10)
- children and youth £12,000 (44)
- medical and health – £7,300 (33)
- elderly – £1,000 (3)
- benevolent – £325 (4)

Beneficiaries included the Cantoris Trust (£10,000); Methodist Relief and Development Fund and WaterAid (£5,800 each); Birmingham International Student Homes (£5,000); Birmingham Money Advice and Grants (£3,200); St Basils (£2,000); City of Birmingham Symphony Orchestra – Contra Bassoon (£1,500); 870 House (£1,300); Birmingham Settlement and Royal Birmingham Society of Artists (£1,000 each); Birmingham St Mary's Hospice and A Voice for St Paul's (£750); Cerebral Palsy Midlands, Cruse Bereavement Care, Edward's Trust, Quinzone and Woodgate Valley Urban Farm (£700 each); and Action Medical Research, Birmingham Boys' & Girls' Union, Central Methodist Church Blackheath, Terence Higgins Trust, Life Education Centres, Macmillan Cancer Relief, Tall Ships Youth Trust, the Stroke Association, Walk Thru the Bible Ministries and Walsall Street Teams (£500 each).

Applications In writing to the correspondent.

The Grimsdale Charitable Trust

Christian religion, education, poverty

£49,000 (2002/03)

Beneficial area UK, with a preference for east and west Sussex, and overseas.

25 The Uplands, Gerrards Cross, Buckinghamshire SL9 7JQ

Correspondent Martin Grimsdale, Trustee

Trustees *Mrs M Grimsdale, Chair; Martin Grimsdale.*

CC Number 327118

Information available Accounts were on file at the Charity Commission website, only up to 2002/03.

General This trust has a preference for Methodist and other Christian charities. The trust also states that it has a preference for supporting 'reasonably local things' – it will therefore probably not support local organisations outside east or west Sussex and the surrounding area.

In 2002/03 the trust had assets of £695,000, an income of £31,000 and made grants totalling £49,000. The largest grant was £25,000 to Giant Leap Foundation. Other grants included £5,000 each to WaterAid, YMCA and Intermediate Technology Development, £1,300 to St George's URC Church, £1,000 each to Medical Missionary Association, Scripture Union, Bible Society, Voluntary Services Overseas, Tear Fund, Macmillan Cancer Relief and Africa Inland Mission and £500 to Misbourne School.

Exclusions No grants to individuals.

Applications In writing to the correspondent.

The GRP Charitable Trust

Jewish, general

£138,000 (2004/05)

Beneficial area UK.

Kleinwort Benson Trustees Ltd, PO Box 57005, 30 Gresham Street, London EC2V 7PG

Correspondent The Secretary

Trustee *Kleinwort Benson Trustees Ltd.*

CC Number 255733

Information available Full accounts were on file at the Charity Commission.

General The GRP of the title stands for the settlor, George Richard Pinto, a London banker who set up the trust in 1968. Most of the grants are given to Jewish organisations.

In 2004/05 the trust had assets of £4.5 million and an income of £211,000. A total of £138,000 was given in 24 grants, broken down as follows:

Jewish causes – 10 grants totalling £112,000
Beneficiaries included Oxford Centre for Hebrew & Jewish Studies (£50,000), British ORT and Jewish Care (£20,000 each), World Jewish Relief (£10,000), British Friends of the Israel Philharmonic Orchestra (£5,000), Community Security Trust (£3,000), Anglo-Israel Association (£2,000), Simon Marks Jewish Primary School Trust (£1,000) and British Technion Society (£350).

General – 14 grants totalling £26,000
Beneficiaries included Wallace Collection (£5,200), Barnabas Foundation, Council of Christians and Jews and Fresh Hope Trust (£5,000 each), Soil Association (£1,500), Friends of Courtauld Institute, Gurkha Regimental Trust and Hemihelp (£1,000 each), Chicken Shed Theatre Company (£500), Coventry Cathedral (£250) and Royal School for Deaf Children – Margate and Spotlight Appeal (£100 each).

Exclusions No grants to individuals.

Applications In writing to the correspondent. However, the trustees prefer to provide medium-term support for a number of charities already known to them, and unsolicited applications are not acknowledged. Trustees meet annually in March.

The Walter Guinness Charitable Trust

General

£84,000 (2004/05)

Beneficial area UK with a preference for Wiltshire and overseas.

Biddesden House, Andover, Hampshire SP11 9DN

Correspondent The Secretary

Trustees *Hon. F B Guinness; Hon. Mrs R Mulji; Hon. Catriona Guinness.*

CC Number 205375

Information available Accounts were on file at the Charity Commission.

General The trust was established in 1961 by Bryan Walter, the second Lord Moyne, in memory of his father, the first Lord Moyne. Most grants are given to a number of charities which the trust has been consistently supporting for many years. In 2004/05 the trust had assets of £4.1 million and an income of £124,000. Grants totalled £84,000.

Grants were broken down as follows:

- overseas – £13,000 (12 grants)
- communities/community £13,000 (11)
- education £12,000 (11)
- medical – £12,000 (13)
- youth – £9,510 (3)
- disability – £8,400 (14)
- culture – £3,900 (5)
- ecology – £2,500 (2)
- elderly – £2,500 (5)
- children – £2,100 (2)
- mental health – £1,500 (2)
- prisoners – £1,500 (2)
- other – £2,800 (4)

There were 34 grants of £1,000 or more listed in the accounts. Beneficiaries included: Fairbridge (£5,000); Ludgershall Scouts Hall, Oxford Medical Students Elective Trust, Relate Mid Wiltshire and Raleigh International (£3,000 each); Hawk and Owl Trust, Ockenden International, Oxfam, Rural Health Community Association, Samburu Aid in Africa, Share – Salisbury District Hospital, St John Ambulance Wiltshire and Winterbourne Stoke PCC (£2,000 each); Barnardos (£1,600); and Anti-Slavery International, British Youth Opera, Invalids at Home, Medical Foundation for the Care of Victims of Torture, New Bridge, Rainbow Centre for Conductive Education, Rose Road Association, University of Liverpool Faculty of Veterinary Science and VSO (£1,000 each).

Unlisted grants under £1,000 each totalled £22,000.

Exclusions No grants to individuals.

Applications In writing to the correspondent. Replies are only sent when there is a positive decision. Initial telephone calls are not possible. There are no application forms, guidelines or deadlines. No sae is required.

The Gunter Charitable Trust

General

£128,000 (2004/05)

Beneficial area UK.

c/o Forsters, 31 Hill Street, London W1J 5LS

Correspondent The Trustees

Trustees *J de C Findlay; R G Worrall.*

CC Number 268346

Information available Full accounts were on file at the Charity Commission.

General The trust gives grants to a wide range of local and UK organisations, including countryside, medical and wildlife causes.

In 2004/05 the trust had assets of £2.2 million, an income of £111,000 and made 46 grants totalling £128,000.

The largest grants were £22,000 each to the British Red Cross and Oxfam.

Other grants included: £8,600 to Liverpool School of Tropical Medicine; £8,000 to DEC Tsunami Earthquake Appeal; £7,000 to Marie Stopes International; £5,000 each to Dandelion Trust, Medical Foundation for the Care of Victims of Torture and Sustrans; £3,000 each to Médecins Sans Frontières and UNICEF; £2,000 to Underdog; £1,000 to World Emergency Relief; £500 to RUKBA; £300 to Camphill Village Trust; and £250 each to Campaign for the Protection of Rural England and Royal Mission for Deep Sea Fishermen.

Exclusions No support for unsolicited applications.

Applications No unsolicited applications are accepted by the trustees. All such applications are immediately returned to the applicant.

The Gur Trust

Jewish causes

Nil (2004/05)

Beneficial area Worldwide.

5 Windus Road, London N16 6UT

Correspondent The Trustees

Trustees *I M Cymerman; M Mandel; S Morgenstern.*

CC Number 283423

Information available Accounts were on file at the Charity Commission.

General In 2004/05 the trust had assets of £1.3 million and an income of £53,000. The trustees' report stated that: 'No grants were made as it was the intention of the trustees to make a further investment which would provide additional regular income.'

Previous beneficiaries have included Beis Yaacov Casidic Seminary, Beth Yaacov Town, Bnei Emes Institutions, Central Charity Fund, Gur Talmudical College, Kollel Arad, Yeshiva Lezeirim, Pri Gidulim, Maala and Mifal Gevura Shecehessed.

Applications In writing to the correspondent. The trust has previously stated that: 'Funds are raised by the trustees. All calls for help are carefully considered and help is given according to circumstances and funds then available.'

The H and M Charitable Trust

Seafaring

£119,000 (2005/06)

Beneficial area UK, with some preference for Kent.

19 Priory Close, London N20 8BB

Correspondent David Harris, Trustee

Trustees *I C S Lewis, Chair; Mrs P M Lister; D Harris.*

CC Number 272391

Information available Accounts were on file at the Charity Commission.

General The trust supports charities concerned with seamanship, divided between educational and welfare causes. In 2005/06 the trust had assets of £2.7 million and an income of £114,000. Grants to 14 organisations totalled £119,000.

Beneficiaries were: Arethusa Venture Centre (£43,000); Jubilee Sailing Trust, Royal Engineers Association and Royal Star and Garter Home (£10,000 each); Sail Trading Association (£8,000); Fairbridge in Kent (£6,000); Army Benevolent Fund, British Legion, North London Hospice and RNLI (£5,000 each); Kent Air Ambulance (£4,000); Missions to Seafarers and RSPCA (£3,000 each); and Hand in Gillingham (£2,000).

The trust has previously stated that 'resources are committed on a regular annual basis to organisations who have come to rely upon us for their funding'.

Applications The trustees said they do not wish their trust to be included in this guide since it leads to disappointment for applicants. Unsolicited applications will not be successful.

The H P Charitable Trust

Orthodox Jewish

£430,000 (2004/05)
Beneficial area UK.

26 Lingwood Road, London E5 9BN
Tel. 020 8806 2432
Correspondent Aron Piller, Trustee
Trustees *A Piller; Mrs H Piller; A Zonszajn.*
CC Number 278006
Information available Accounts were on file at the Charity Commission, but without a grants list.

General The H P Charitable Trust was created by Hannah Piller in 1979 and makes grants to orthodox Jewish charities. In 2004/05 its assets totalled £1.9 million and it had an income of £281,000. Grants totalled £430,000.

Previous beneficiaries included: Craven Walk Charities, Emuno Educational Centre Ltd, Gur Trust, Ponivez, Yad Eliezer, Yeshuas Caim Synagogue and Yetev Lev.

Applications In writing to the correspondent.

The Halecat Trust

General

£31,000 to organisations (2004)
Beneficial area UK, with a preference for north west England.

c/o Smith and Williamson Limited, Old Library Chambers, 21 Chipper Lane, Salisbury, Wiltshire SP1 1BG

Correspondent Jeremy Major, Administrator
Trustee *Smith Trustee Company Limited.*
CC Number 258157
Information available Accounts were on file at the Charity Commission.

General Grants are given to a wide range of UK and local organisations throughout the UK, although there was a slight preference for north-west England.

In 2004 the trust had assets of £238,000 and an income of £28,000. Donations were given to 50 organisations totalling £31,000. Grant recipients included Bristol University (£18,000), The Handel House (£4,000) and CT Scanner Appeal, Kirckman Concert Society and Witherslack Parochial Church Council (£1,000 each).

Applications In writing to the correspondent.

The Edith Winifred Hall Charitable Trust

General

£388,000 (2004/05)
Beneficial area UK.

Spratt Endicott, 52–54 South Bar Street, Banbury, Oxfordshire OX16 9AB
Correspondent D Endicott, Trustee
Trustees *D Reynolds; D Endicott; J R N Lowe; P P Reynolds; L C Burgess-Lumsden.*
CC Number 1057032
Information available Full accounts were on file at the Charity Commission.

General This trust has stated that it wants its funds to make a difference. It prefers to make a small number of large grants.

In 2004/05 the trust had assets of over £5 million and an income of £166,000. Grants totalled £388,000. Beneficiaries included: the Disaster Emergency Fund – Tsunami appeal (£100,000); the Chellington Project and Moggerhanger Preservation Trust (£55,000 each); Northamptonshire Community Fund – High Sheriff's Fund and Road Victims' Trust (£50,000 each); the Countryside Foundation and St Marys – Weekley (£30,000 each); St Peter's Independent School (£25,000); and Bedford School Foundation, Leicester and Rutland

Crimebeat and St John Ambulance Northampton (£5,000 each).

Applications In writing to the correspondent.

The Hamamelis Trust

Ecological conservation, medical research

£69,000 (2004/05)
Beneficial area UK, but with a special interest in the Godalming and Surrey areas.

c/o Penningtons Solicitors LLP, Highfield, Brighton Road, Godalming, Surrey GU7 1NS
Tel. 01483 791800
Correspondent Michael Fellingham
Trustees *Michael Fellingham; Dr A F M Stone; Mr R Rippengal.*
CC Number 280938
Information available Full accounts were available from the Charity Commission.

General The trust was set up in 1980 by John Ashley Slocock and enhanced on his death in 1986. The main areas of work are medical research and ecological conservation. Grants are occasionally made to other projects. Preference is given to projects in the Godalming and Surrey areas.

In 2004/05 the trust had assets of £2.2 million and an income of £72,000. Grants totalled £69,000, from which 29 organisations received grants ranging between £300 and £7,500. The largest grant went to Holy Cross for the cost of equipment re: Holy Cross Video (£7,500). Other beneficiaries included the Rodborough School Fund (£5,000), the Bat Conservation Trust, the Edward James Foundation and the Gaia Trust (£2,500 each) and the Normandy Community Therapy Garden (£400).

Exclusions Projects outside the UK are not considered. No grants to individuals.

Applications In writing to the correspondent. All applicants are asked to include a short summary of the application along with any published material and references. Unsuccessful appeals will not be acknowledged.

Dr Adam Stone, one of the trustees, who is medically qualified, assesses medical applications.

Sue Hammerson's Charitable Trust

Medical research, relief in need

£261,000 (2004/05)

Beneficial area UK, with a slight preference for London.

H W Fisher and Co., Acre House, 11–15 William Road, London NW1 3ER

Tel. 020 7388 7000

Correspondent R Watson

Trustees *Sir Gavin Lightman; A J Thompson; A J Bernstein; Mrs P A Beecham; D B Hammerson; P S Hammerson.*

CC Number 235196

Information available Accounts were on file at the Charity Commission.

General The objects of this trust are to advance medical learning and research and the relief of sickness and poverty; it also supports a range of other charities including a number of Jewish and arts organisations.

In 2004/05 it had assets of £7.5 million and an income of £264,000. Grants were made to almost 200 organisations totalling £261,000. Over half of the beneficiaries were also supported in the previous year.

By far the largest grant was £200,000 to Lewis W Hammerson Memorial Home, which also received the same amount in the previous year.

Other larger grants were: £5,000 each to English National Opera and Tsunami Earthquake Appeal; £4,000 to Royal Opera House; £3,000 to New Shakespeare Co. Ltd; £2,300 to West London Synagogue; and £1,000 each to Cheltenham College, Royal Academy Trust, Suzy Lamplugh Trust and the Martlets Hospice.

The remaining grants ranged between £50 and £750, with most being for less than £500. Beneficiaries included Age Concern, Brainwave, British Mexican Society, Children's Trust, Crisis, DEMAND, Dulwich Picture Gallery, Friends of the V & A, Institute of Jewish Policy research, JNF Charitable Trust, Leukaemia Research Fund, London Sumphony Orchestra, Nation Eczema Society, Oxfam, RAFT, Royal Albert Hall, RNIB, St John's Hospice, Treloar Trust and UNICEF.

Exclusions No grants to individuals.

Applications In writing to the correspondent. The trust states, however, that its funds are fully committed.

The Hammonds Charitable Trust

General

£69,000 (2004/05)

Beneficial area Mainly Birmingham, London, Leeds, Bradford and Manchester.

Hammonds, Rutland House, 148 Edmund Street, Birmingham B3 2JR

Correspondent Linda Sylvester

Trustees *R Burns; S M Gordon; J S Forrest; S R Miller; S P Levy.*

CC Number 1064028

Information available Full accounts were on file at the Charity Commission.

General This trust (formerly known as The Hammond Suddards Edge Charitable Trust) usually makes donations to charitable organisations based locally to the trust.

In 2004/05 the trust 'supported a number of national charities in a wide variety of areas, but in particular the trustees were pleased to support smaller charities working within the areas in which its firm's offices are based – situated in Birmingham, London, Leeds and Manchester'.

Income for the year 2004/05 was £99,000 with grants totalling £69,000.

Applications This trust does not accept unsolicited applications.

Beatrice Hankey Foundation Ltd

Christian

£34,000 to organisations (2005).

Beneficial area UK and overseas.

11 Staverton Road, Werrington, Peterborough, Cambridgeshire PE4 6LY

Tel. 01733 571794

Correspondent Mrs M Churchill, Secretary

Trustees *Revd S Barnes; E F Dawe; J G Green; Revd Canon P Gompertz; L Grafin zu Lynar; Mrs A Simpson; Revd D Savill; Mrs A Y Stewart; Mrs H Walker; Mrs G Vye.*

CC Number 211093

Information available Full accounts were on file at the Charity Commission.

General Grants are made to individuals and groups known personally to the foundation members and carrying out activities that will promote the values of Christian teaching. It gives small grants of between £50 and £500 each.

In 2005 the foundation had assets of £1.1 million and an income of £41,000. Grants were made to organisations totalling £34,000.

Beneficiaries included Lagan College (£12,500), St Alfege Schools Project (£5,000) Corrymeela Community (£2,500), Medical Foundation for the relief of victims of torture (£1,500), Village Services Trust (£1,250), the Dalitso Trust and the Humanitarian Aid Relief Trust – HART (£1,000 each), Christian Solidarity Worldwide, Jessie's Fund and Open Doors (£500 each) and EAPPI and the Sycamore Project (£100 each).

Exclusions No grants for buildings or equipment.

Applications Unsolicited applications cannot be considered.

The Hanley Trust

Social welfare and people who are disadvantaged

£33,000 to organisations (2005)

Beneficial area UK, with a preference for Corby and Rutland.

21 Buckingham Gate, London SW1E 6LS

Correspondent Hon. Mrs Sarah Price, Trustee

Trustees *Hon. Sarah Price, Chair; Hon. James Butler; Nicholas Smith.*

CC Number 299209

Information available Full accounts were available from the Charity Commission website.

General This trust states that it has various funding priorities, for social welfare and people who are disadvantaged. It makes grants to registered charities only, usually small, up to a maximum of £4,000.

In 2005 the trust had assets of £913,000 and an income of £31,000. Grants to organisations totalled £33,000 and included the following beneficiaries: the Butler Trust (£2,500), Irene Taylor Trust (£2,000), Ocean Youth Trust (£1,800), Cirdan Trust, Disability Aid Fund, Helen Arkell Dyslexia Centre, Help the Hospices, Howard League for Penal Reform, Kurdish Aid Foundation (£1,000 each), Defeating Deafness and Prader Willi Syndrome (£500 each), Corby Mind and the Prince's Trust (£250 each) and Local Solutions (£100).

Exclusions Grants are not made to individuals or to non-registered charities.

Applications In writing to the correspondent.

Harbo Charities Limited

General, education, religion

£92,000 (2004/05)
Beneficial area UK.

c/o Cohen Arnold and Co., New Burlington House, 1075 Finchley Road, London NW11 0PU
Correspondent The Trustees
Trustees *Harry Stern; Barbara J Stern; Harold Gluck.*
CC Number 282262
Information available Accounts were on file at the Charity Commission, but without a grants list.

General In 2004/05 the trust had assets of £1.1 million, an income of £174,000 and made grants totalling £92,000.

Previous beneficiaries have included Beis Chinuch Lebonos Girls School, Beth Rochel d'Satmar, Bobov Trust, Chevras Maoz Ladol, Craven Walk Charitable Trust, Edgware Yeshiva Trust, Keren Yesomim, Kollel Shomrei HaChomoth, Tevini Limited, Tomchei Shabbos, Yad Eliezer, Yesode Ha Torah School and Yeshiva Chachmay Tsorpha.

Applications In writing to the correspondent.

The Harbour Charitable Trust

General

£57,000 (2005/06)
Beneficial area UK.

c/o Barbican House, 26–34 Old Street, London EC1V 9QQ
Correspondent The Trustees
Trustees *Mrs B B Green; Mrs Z S Blackman; Mrs T Elsenstat; Mrs E Knobil.*
CC Number 234268
Information available Accounts were on file at the Charity Commission, but without a list of grants.

General The trust makes grants for the benefit of childcare, education and health research and to various other charitable organisations. In 2005/06 it had assets of £2.9 million and an income of £195,000. Grants were made totalling £57,000. These were categorised by the trust as follows: childcare (£20,000); healthcare (£20,000); Joint Jewish Charitable Trust (£15,000); and other donations (£2,000).

No further information was available on the charities supported.

Exclusions Grants are given to registered charities only.

Applications In writing to the correspondent.

The Harbour Foundation

Jewish, general

£148,000 (2004/05)
Beneficial area Worldwide, with a preference for London.

The Courtyard Building, 11 Curtain Road, London EC2A 3LT
Tel. 020 7456 8180
Correspondent The Trustees
Trustees *S R Harbour; A C Humphries; Mrs Z S Blackman; S Green; B B Green.*
CC Number 264927
Information available Accounts were on file at the Charity Commission.

General The principal activities of the trust are providing relief among refugees and people who are homeless, the advancement of education, learning and research, and to make donations to any institution established for charitable purposes throughout the world.

In 2004/05 the foundation had assets of £20.8 million and an income of £433,000. Grants totalled £148,000.

The following is taken from the trustees' report:

'The foundation's current and future charitable programme is directed towards general support for charities involved in work to aid those in need and to helping with programmes of education in technology especially in deprived areas both in London and elsewhere. Support will also be given to help musical organisations and musically talented individuals with their training.

'Educational support is directed both to university level and to those who have been failed by the educational system, including the inner boroughs of London. Rapid and continual innovation in this field and the attraction and retention of highly qualified teaching staff necessitate a high level of financial support on a consistent and ongoing basis. A carefully phased release of donations by the foundation to education providers at the leading edge acts as an incentive for them to maximise performance and enables them to plan ahead with some degree of confidence. It is, therefore, essential to continue to build up reserves of the foundation to a level sufficient to ensure a reliable high level of financial support to such providers.'

There were 14 grants listed in the accounts. Beneficiaries were Israel Guide Dog Center for the Blind (£45,000); SRF UK and Westminster Synagogue (£20,000 each); Les Azuriales Opera Trust (£7,000); Tel Aviv Foundation (£5,400); East London Business Alliance, Reform Club Conservation, UCLH and World Jewish Relief (£5,000 each); Save the Children (£3,000); Wigmore Hall Trust (£2,500); and Belsize Park Synagogue (£1,000).

Applications In writing to the correspondent. Applications need to be received by February, as trustees meet in March.

The Harding Trust

Arts, welfare

£109,000 (2004/05)

Beneficial area Mainly, but not exclusively, north Staffordshire and surrounding areas.

Brabners Chaffe Street, 1 Dale Street, Liverpool L2 2ET

Tel. 0151 600 3000

Correspondent The Administrator

Trustees *G G Wall; J P C Fowell; M N Lloyd; G B Snow.*

CC Number 328182

Information available Accounts were on file at the Charity Commission.

General The aim of this trust is 'to promote, improve, develop and maintain public education in, and appreciation of, the art and science of music, by sponsoring or by otherwise supporting public concerts, recitals and performances by amateur and professional organisations'.

In 2004/05 the trust had assets of £3.3 million, an income of £116,000 and made grants totalling £109,000 which were distributed as follows:

Music donations – 19 grants
The largest grants were £28,000 to Stoke-on-Trent Festival, £16,000 to Harding Trust Piano Recitals, £10,000 each to European Union Chamber Orchestra, Malvern Theatres Trust and Wolverhampton Civic Hall Orchestra, £5,000 to Stoke-on-Trent Music School – education scheme, £3,000 each to English Hadyn Festival and Stoke-on-Trent Repertory Theatre, £2,000 to Keele Concerts Society, £1,000 to Wolverhampton Recital Series and £500 to Kidderminster Lions – Midland Concert Orchestra.

Other donations
Donations were £2,500 each to Katharine House Hospice and Telegraph Merlin Appeal and £1,000 to St John Ambulance.

Applications In writing to the correspondent. The trustees meet annually in spring/early summer. Accounts are needed for recurrent applications.

The Hare of Steep Charitable Trust

General

£38,000 (2005/06)

Beneficial area UK, with preference for the south of England, especially Petersfield and East Hampshire.

56 Heath Road, Petersfield, Hampshire GU31 4EJ

Tel. 01730 267953

Correspondent Mrs S M Fowler

Trustees *P L F Baillon; V R Jackson; J R F Fowler; S M Fowler; S E R Johnson-Hill.*

CC Number 297308

Information available Accounts were on file at the Charity Commission.

General In 2005/06 the trust had assets of £995,000 and an income of £44,000. Grants were made to 41 organisations and totalled £38,000. There were no donations greater than 5% of the total distributed. There is a preference for local charities and other community projects in the south of England particularly in East Hampshire.

Unfortunately an exact breakdown of the grant beneficiaries was not provided by the trust. Previous grants have been made to Alzheimer's Disease Society, Arthritis and Rheumatism Council – Petersfield, British Heart Foundation, Rainbow House Trust and SSAFA.

Exclusions No funding for overseas charities, students, visits abroad or political causes.

Applications 'The trustees already support as many charities as they could wish and would certainly not welcome any appeals from others. Unsolicited requests are not acknowledged.'

The Harebell Centenary Fund

General, education, medical research, animal welfare

£69,000 (2005)

Beneficial area UK.

50 Broadway, London SW1H 0BL

Tel. 020 7227 7000

Correspondent Ms P J Chapman

Trustees *J M Denker; M I Goodbody; F M Reed.*

CC Number 1003552

Information available Accounts were on file at the Charity Commission.

General Established in 1991, this trust provides funding towards the promotion of neurological and neurosurgical research and the relief of sickness and suffering amongst animals, as well as holding an interest in the education of young people.

The current policy of the trustees is to concentrate on making donations to charities that do not receive widespread public support and to keep administrative expenses to a minimum. For this reason the trustees have decided to make donations only to registered charities and not to individuals.

In 2005 it had assets of £2.1 million, which generated an income of £75,000. Grants totalling £69,000 were made to 31 organisations, half of which were also supported in the previous year. Management and administration fees were high at £26,000.

All but three of the grants were for £2,000 each. Beneficiaries included: Association of Wheelchair Children and St Christopher's Hospice (£4,000 each); Crathie School (£2,500); and AbilityNet, Artificial Heart Fund, the Blackie Foundation, Council for Music in Hospitals, Helen House Hospice, Marine Conservation Society, Parkinson's Disease Society, the Stroke Association and Trinity Hospice (£2,000 each).

Exclusions No grants are made towards infrastructure or to individuals.

Applications In writing to the correspondent. Unsolicited applications are not requested, as the trustees prefer to make donations to charities whose work they have come across through their own research.

The R J Harris Charitable Settlement

General

£66,000 to organisations (2005/06)

Beneficial area UK, with a preference for west Wiltshire, with particular emphasis on Trowbridge – north Wiltshire south of the M4 verging into Bath and environs.

Messrs Thring Townsend, Midland Bridge, Bath BA1 2HQ

Tel. 01225 340098

Correspondent Miss S M Nutt, Secretary

Trustees *J L Rogers, Chair; A M Pitt; C I W Hignett; J J Thring.*

CC Number 258973

Information available Accounts were on file at the Charity Commission.

General This trust has general charitable purposes, supporting both individuals and organisations. Support is focused on west Wiltshire, with particular emphasis on Trowbridge, north Wiltshire south of the M4 verging into the environs of Bath. The main areas of work are social welfare, the arts, education, medical, mental health, conservation, environmental and youth organisations and projects.

In 2005/06 it had assets of £1.9 million, which generated an income of £55,000. Grants were made to 68 organisations totalling £66,000. A further £4,100 was distributed to 22 individuals.

Beneficiaries of grants of amounts of £1,000 or more in the year were: Holburne Museum – Bath (£15,000); Partis College – Bath (£8,000); Theatre Royal Bath (£5,500 in four grants); Dorothy House Foundation – Winsley (£5,000); Headway – Bath and district (£2,000 in two grants); National Eye Research Centre (£1,500); and Hope Nature Centre – Trowbridge, St John Ambulance – Wiltshire and Wiltshire Air Ambulance Appeal (£1,000 each).

Applications In writing to the correspondent. Trustees meet twice each year. An sae is required.

Hartnett Charitable Trust

Environmental issues

£44,000 to organisations (2006).

Beneficial area UK.

c/o Carpenter Box, Grafton Lodge, 15 Grafton Road, Worthing, West Sussex BN11 1QR

Correspondent The Trustees

Trustees *Mrs M Hartnett; D W Hartnett.*

CC Number 276460

Information available Full accounts were obtained from the Charity Commission website.

General Established in 1978, the trust stated it supports environmental issues. In 2006 the trust had assets of £1.1 million and an income of £46,000, all of which was accumulated from donations. Grants were made to eight organisations totalling £44,000, the largest grant was made in two awards to Exeter College-Oxford totalling £28,600.

Other beneficiaries included the Mary Rose Trust (£5,000), the International Otter Survival Trust (£2,300), the Great Bustard Group and the Wars Memorial Trust (£2,000 each) and Trees for Life (£1,800).

Exclusions No grants to individuals.

Applications In writing to the correspondent, enclosing an sae.

The Lord and Lady Haskel Charitable Foundation

Jewish, social-policy research, arts, education

£47,000 (2005)

Beneficial area UK.

12 Rosemont Road, Richmond-upon-Thames, Surrey TW10 6QL

Correspondent The Trustees

Trustees *A M Davis; J Haskel; M Nutman; Lord Haskel.*

CC Number 1039969

Information available Full accounts were on file at the Charity Commission.

General The charity funds projects concerned with social-policy research, Jewish communal life, arts and education.

In 2005 it had assets of £545,000 and an income of £37,000. Grants totalled £47,000 and were: £11,000 to Institute for Jewish Policy Research; £10,000 each to Aldeburgh Production and Liberal Judaism; £6,000 to the *Jewish Quarterly*; and £5,000 each to Jewish Council for Radical Equality and the Orange Tree Theatre.

Applications This trust states that it does not respond to unsolicited applications.

The M A Hawe Settlement

General

£255,000 to organisations (2005/06)

Beneficial area UK, with a preference for the north west of England, particularly the Fylde coast area.

94 Park View Road, Lytham St Annes, Lancashire FY8 4JF

Tel. 01253 796888

Correspondent M A Hawe, Trustee

Trustees *M A Hawe; Mrs G Hawe; M G Hawe.*

CC Number 327827

Information available Accounts were on file at the Charity Commission.

General In 2005/06 the trust had assets of £5.4 million and an income of £276,000. Grants to organisations totalled £255,000 with £10,000 being distributed to individuals.

As usual, the largest grant was to Kensington House Trust Ltd, which received £254,000. This company was established to run a property bought by the trust in 1993, as accommodation on a short-stay basis for young homeless people. It now also provides furniture and equipment to people in need, shelter for victims of domestic violence and holidays for children who are deprived.

The remaining grants ranged between £125 and £560. Beneficiaries were Holy Cross Church and Soup Kitchen (£560), Wear Valley CAB (£450), Supersigners (£150) and Jubilee Action (£125).

Applications In writing to the correspondent.

The Hawthorne Charitable Trust

General

£145,000 (2005/06)

Beneficial area UK, especially Hereford and Worcester.

c/o Baker Tilly, Lancaster House, 7 Elmfield Road, Bromley BR1 1LT

Correspondent Roger Clark, Trustee

Trustees *Mrs A S C Berington; R J Clark.*

CC Number 233921

Information available Full accounts were on file at the Charity Commission.

General The trust supports a wide range of organisations, particularly health and welfare causes but also charities concerned with animal welfare, disability, heritage and young people.

In 2005/06 it had assets of £6.9 million, which generated an income of £169,000. Out of a total expenditure of £192,000, grants to 67 organisations totalled £145,000. Donations were broken down into the following categories:

Medical, health and sickness	£42,000	17 grants
Caring for people with disabilities	£29,000	13 grants
Environment, conservation and heritage	£22,000	9 grants
Relief of poverty	£12,000	6 grants
Caring for animals	£8,000	5 grants
Other	£32,000	17 grants

Grants were in the range of £1,000 and £6,000 and included those to: the Society of Friends of Little Malvern Priory (£6,000); Save the Children Fund and St Richard's Hospice (£5,000 each); Acorn Children's Hospice Trust, Parish of St Wulstan – Little Malvern, Macmillan Cancer Relief – Malvern and the Royal Horticultural Society (£3,000 each); Alzheimer's Research Trust, Animal Health Trust, Army Benevolent Fund, Centrepoint Soho, Herefordshire Mind, Hospice Care Kenya, National Council for the Conservation of Plants and Gardens, the Pace Centre, Perennial – Gardens' Royal Benevolent Society, the Salvation Army and the Stroke Association (£2,500 each); Malvern Sea Cadets (£2,000); the Walpole Society (£1,500); and Digestive Disorders Foundation, Federation of City Farms and Community Gardens, Malvern Hills District CAB, National Eczema Society, People's Trust for Endangered Species and Worcester Rough Sleepers Project (£1,000 each).

A number of the above beneficiaries have been supported in previous years.

Exclusions Grants are given to registered charities only. No grants to individuals.

Applications In writing to the correspondent, including up-to-date accounts. Applications should be received by October for consideration in November.

The Dorothy Hay-Bolton Charitable Trust

Deaf, blind

£38,000 (2005/06)

Beneficial area UK, with a preference for the south-east of England and overseas.

c/o F W Stephens, 3rd Floor, 24 Chiswell Street, London EC1Y 4YX

Correspondent Brian E Carter, Trustee

Trustees *Brian E Carter; Stephen J Gallico.*

CC Number 1010438

Information available Accounts were on file at the Charity Commission.

General The trust makes grants towards charities working with people who are deaf or blind, particularly children and young people. In 2005/06 the trust had assets of £895,000, an income of £28,000 and made grants totalling £38,000.

Beneficiaries included Hearing Dogs for the Deaf (£3,000), Falconer Trust (£2,500), British Wireless for the Blind, SENSE, Sussex Lantern and Telephones for the Blind (£2,000 each), Country Holidays for Inner City Kids, Sheppard Trust and Tarabai Desai Eye Hospital and Research Centre (£1,500 each) and Eyeless Trust, Exsight and BBACT (£1,000 each).

Exclusions The trust states that it does not generally give to individuals.

Applications In writing to the correspondent.

The Haydan Charitable Trust

Jewish, general

£132,000 (2004)

Beneficial area UK.

c/o 1 Knightsbridge, London SW1X 7LX

Correspondent The Trustees

Trustees *Christopher Smith; Irene Smith; Anthony Winter.*

CC Number 1003801

Information available Full accounts were on file at the Charity Commission.

General This trust was set up in 1990, it has a clear relationship with its namesake company, Haydan Holdings Ltd. The trust states that it gives recurrent grants to a few organisations and does not invite applications.

In 2004 the trust had an income of £37,000 coming mostly from corporate donations. Grants totalled £132,000. Beneficiaries listed in the accounts were Jewish Communal Fund (£83,000), Babes in Arms, Greater London Fund For The Blind and Anthony Nolan Trust (£10,000 each), Beth Jacob Grammar School For Girls, Leukaemia Research Fund and Nordoff Robbins Music Trust (£5,000 each) and Cancer Research UK (£1,600).

Miscellaneous grants totalled £3,100.

Exclusions No grants are given for projects overseas.

Applications Unsolicited applications are not considered.

The Haymills Charitable Trust

Education, medicine, welfare, young people

£160,000 to organisations and individuals (2005/06)

Beneficial area UK, but particularly the west of London and Suffolk, where the Haymills Group is sited.

The Old Boiler House, Draymans Lane, Marlow, Buckinghamshire SL7 2FF

Correspondent I W Ferres, Secretary

Trustees *W G Underwood, Chair; E F C Drake; I W Ferres; K C Perryman; J A Sharpe; J L Wosner; I R Brown.*

CC Number 277761

Information available Accounts were on file at the Charity Commission, but without a list of grants.

General 'The trustees endeavour to make the best use of the monies available from the funds of the trust. In particular donations are made to projects they believe to be inadequately supported.'

In the past, grants have fallen into four main categories:

- education: grants to schools, colleges and universities
- medicine: grants to hospitals and associated institutions and to medical research
- welfare: primarily to include former Haymills' staff, and to those who are considered to be 'in necessitous circumstances' or who are otherwise distressed or disadvantaged
- youth: support for training schemes to assist in the education, welfare and training of young people.

In 2005/06 it had assets of £5.6 million and an income of £184,000. Grants totalled £160,000 and were broken down as follows:

Youth and welfare	£104,000
Medical	£35,000
Education	£22,000

Unfortunately no list of grants was included with the accounts on file at the Charity Commission, although they did state that it has agreed a five-year scholarship at Merchant Taylor's School, commencing in 2002, of £5,000 in the first year and increasing cumulatively in each of the following years.

In 1999/2000 beneficiaries in the three categories included the following:

Educational
Grants were given to various educational establishments, especially towards bursaries, prizes and scholarships. Grants included those to: Merchant Taylor's Company for the Dudley Cox Bursary Fund and the Dudley Cox Awards for engineering, design and technology; Anglia Polytechnic University for the Haymills Building Management Scholarship; Suffolk College; and Hammersmith and West London College.

Medical
Grants were mainly given to hospitals and hospital appeals, although grants were also given towards research. Beneficiaries included Central Middlesex Hospital League of Friends, Ealing Hospital League of Friends, Great Ormond Street Children's Hospital and Royal London Hospital.

Youth and welfare
Beneficiaries included Children's Hospice Eastern Region, East Suffolk Association for the Blind, Dyslexia Association, Friends of Samaritans – Ealing, Greater London Central Scout County, London Bible College, Macmillan Cancer Relief, Middlesex Young People's Clubs, Queen Elizabeth Hospital Children's Fund and West London Action for Children.

Exclusions No personal applications will be considered unless endorsed by a university, college or other appropriate authority.

Applications In writing to the correspondent, but note the comments in the general section. Trustees meet at least twice a year, usually in March and October. Applications are not acknowledged.

May Hearnshaw's Charity

General

About £70,000 (2004/05)

Beneficial area UK, particularly South Yorkshire, North Nottinghamshire, Derbyshire, East Lancashire or Cheshire areas.

Barber Harrison and Platt, 2 Rutland Park, Sheffield S10 2PD

Correspondent J Rowan, Trustee

Trustees *J Rowan; D C Law; Mrs M West; M Ferreday; R Law; W Munro.*

CC Number 1008638

Information available Accounts were on file at the Charity Commission.

General This trust was set up by the will of the late May Hearnshaw who died in 1988. It was her wish that the trust be used for the promotion of education, advancement of religion and relief of poverty and sickness. Support is mostly given to children's organisations within these themes. Grants are made to UK-wide charities or local charities working in the South Yorkshire, North Nottinghamshire, Derbyshire, East Lancashire or Cheshire areas.

In 2004/05 the trust had an income of £69,000 and grants totalled about £70,000. Previous beneficiaries have included Bluebellwood Hospice, Cavendish Centre and St Luke's Hospice.

Applications 'The trustees usually decide on and make grants to charitable organisations at least once a year but may decide to make grants at any time. They do not include in their consideration appeals received direct from individuals.'

The Heathcoat Trust

Welfare, causes local to Tiverton, Devon

£95,000 to organisations (2005/06)

Beneficial area Mainly Tiverton, Devon.

The Factory, Tiverton, Devon EX16 5LL

Tel. 01884 254949

Website www.heathcoat.co.uk

Correspondent Mr E W Summers, Secretary

Trustees *Sir Ian Heathcoat Amory; M J Gratton; Mrs B Hill; J Smith.*

CC Number 203367

Information available Accounts were on file at the Charity Commission.

General The trust was established in 1945. Its objectives as stated in the 2006 accounts are 'for the relief of financial hardship, for education and training, for building or making grants to health institutions, and in certain circumstances for making contributions to any charity but mostly in Tiverton in Devon and its neighbourhood or in places where the firms John Heathcoat and Company Limited and Lowman Manufacturing Company Limited and their subsidiaries carry on business. In so far as the income cannot be applied towards the objects specified in the trust deed, it may be applied for any charitable purpose.'

Over 100 grants a year, mostly under £1,000, are made to organisations and nearly all to local causes around the Tiverton area. Other grants are made to individuals, employees and pensioners of the Heathcoat group of companies. Educational grants are given to children of those employees or pensioners and also to local students attending schools and colleges in Tiverton, or beyond if courses are not available locally.

In 2005/06 the trust had assets of £19 million and an income of £610,000. Grants totalled £590,000 of which

£95,000 went to organisations and £505,000 to individuals.

Beneficiaries of organisational grants included: Coldharbour Mill Trust (£9,000); Tiverton Market Centre (£6,000); Old Heathcoat School (£3,000); National Trust – Knightshayes Court (£2,000); and British Forces Foundation, CLIC Sargent Cancer Care for Children, FORCE Cancer Research – Exeter, Tiverton Bowling Club and Tiverton & District Scout Council (£1,000 each).

Applications In writing to the correspondent. There are application forms for certain education grants.

Percy Hedley 1990 Charitable Trust

General

£34,000 (2005/06)

Beneficial area UK with a preference for Northumberland and Tyne and Wear.

10 Castleton Close, Newcastle-upon-Tyne NE2 2HF

Correspondent J Armstrong, Trustee

Trustees G W Meikle; J R Armstrong; Mrs F M Ruffman.

CC Number 1000033

Information available Accounts were on file at the Charity Commission.

General In 2005/06 the trust had assets of £1.4 million and an income of £43,000. Grants totalled £34,000 distributed to 52 institutions.

The largest grants went to the following 11 organisations: Theatre Royal Campaign (£5,000); Newcastle Royal Grammar School – Bursary Fund and Percy Hedley Foundation (£3,000 each); and Dame Allan's School – Newcastle, the Anaphylaxis Campaign, Macmillan Cancer Relief, Marie Curie Foundation – Conrad House, Northumberland Association of Clubs for Young People, Samaritans of Tyneside, St Oswald's Hospice – Gosforth and the Trinity Project – Gosforth (£1,000 each).

Other beneficiaries included: Alzheimer Research Trust, Beamish Museum Access Fund, the Calvert Trust, Koestler Trust for Arts Inside, Parkinson's Disease Society, National Trust for Scotland

Culloden Appeal, Prostate Cancer Research, RNLI Grace Darling Museum, Stroke Association, Whizz-Kidz – Tyne and Wear (£500 each); Baby Equipment Loan Services – Wallsend, Blyth Valley Northumberland Scouts – Walker Centre, Gosforth Sea Cadets, Newcastle Society for Blind People, the Anthony Nolan Trust, Plantlife – Northumberland Project, RNIB for Newcastle Talking Book Service, Washington Wildfowl and Wetlands Centre and University of Sunderland Development Trust (£250 each); and Bamburgh Church (£100).

Applications In writing to the correspondent. Trustees meet twice a year.

The Hellenic Foundation

Greek, general

£36,000 (2005)

Beneficial area UK.

St Paul's House, Warwick Lane, London EC4P 4BN

Tel. 020 7251 5100

Correspondent The Secretary

Trustees Stamos J Fafalios, Chair; George A Tsavliris; Nicos H Sideris; Irene M Monios; Dr Eleni Yannakakis; Zenon K Mouskos; Constantinos I Caroussis; Mary Bromley; Irene J Fafalios-Zannas; Angela K Kulukundis; George A Lemos; George D Lemos; Louisa Williamson; Despina M Moschos; Anna S Polemis-Alisafakis.

CC Number 326301

Information available Full accounts were on file at the Charity Commission.

General The foundation was set up in 1982 to 'advance and propagate education and learning in Great Britain in the cultural tradition and heritage of Greece and particularly in the subjects involving education, research, music and dance, books and library facilities and university symposia'.

In 2005 the trust's assets totalled £463,000 and it had an income of £33,000. Grants totalled £36,000 distributed to 18 organisations. The sum of £2,500 went to individuals.

Exclusions The foundation is unable to offer scholarships or grants to cover tuition fees and living expenses.

Applications In writing to the correspondent.

The Michael and Morven Heller Charitable Foundation

University and medical research projects, the arts

£231,000 (2004/05)

Beneficial area Worldwide.

Carlton House, 22a St James's Square, London SW1Y 4JH

Tel. 020 7415 5000 **Fax** 020 7415 0611

Correspondent M A Heller, Trustee

Trustees Michael Heller; Morven Heller; Pearl Livingstone.

CC Number 327832

Information available Accounts were on file at the Charity Commission.

General This trust was established in 1972, and funds specific projects relating to medical research, science and educational research. This usually involves making large grants to universities for research purposes, particularly medical research. In practice, there appears to be some preference for Jewish organisations.

In 2004/05 the trust had assets of £5.4 million and an income of £304,000. Grants totalled £231,000, broken down as follows: education (£119,000); humanitarian (£63,000); and research (£49,000).

Exclusions No support for individuals.

Applications In writing to the correspondent.

The Simon Heller Charitable Settlement

Medical research, science and educational research

£203,000 (2004/05)

Beneficial area Worldwide.

Carlton House, 22a St James' Square, London SW1Y 4JH

Tel. 020 7415 5000

Correspondent The Trustees

Trustees *M A Heller; Morven Heller; W S Trustee Company Limited.*

CC Number 265405

Information available Accounts were on file at the Charity Commission, without a list of grants.

General This trust was established in 1972, and funds specific projects relating to medical research, science and educational research. This usually involves making large grants to universities for research purposes, particularly medical research. In practice, there appears to be some preference for Jewish organisations.

In 2004/05 the trust had assets of £8.8 million and an income of £270,000. Grants were made totalling £203,000. Broken down as follows: humanitarian (£100,000); education (£74,000); and research (£30,000). No list of grants was included with the accounts filed at the Charity Commission.

The 2000/01 accounts listed 19 grants over £1,000 each. UJIA received the largest single grant of £35,000 with Institute for Jewish Policy Research receiving the same amount in two grants of £25,000 and £10,000. Other major beneficiaries were Jewish Care (£30,000), Aish Hatora (£15,000 in two grants), Spiro Institute (£13,000), Scopus (£12,000 in two grants) and Chief Rabbinate Charitable Trust (£10,000).

Exclusions No grants to individuals.

Applications In writing to the correspondent.

Help the Homeless Ltd

Homelessness

£57,000 (2005/06)
Beneficial area UK only.

5th Floor, Babmaes House, 2 Babmaes Street, London SW1Y 6HD

Email hth@help-the-homeless.org.uk

Website www.help-the-homeless.org.uk

Correspondent The Secretary

Trustees *F J Bergin; T S Cookson; L A Bains; T Rogers; P Fullerton; J Rose.*

CC Number 271988

Information available Accounts were on file at the Charity Commission.

General The trust makes small grants to smaller or new voluntary organisations, who are registered charities, for items of capital expenditure directly related to the provision of housing for people who are single and homeless. Grants do not normally exceed £3,000.

Trustees will also consider applications for larger pump priming grants for major and innovative projects. Applicants should enquire about the status of the Large Grants Programme before making an application.

In 2005/06 the trust had assets of £1.2 million and an income of £46,000. Grants were made totalling £57,000.

There were 11 grants made in the year. Beneficiaries were: Emmaus St Albans (£25,000); Touchstones 12 (£3,500); Cornerstone, Hammersmith Women's Aid and the Passage (£3,000 each); the Tab Centre (£2,700); Chelmsford Chess (£2,400); the Benjamin Foundation, Cirencester Housing for Young People and Spires (£2,000 each); and the Simon Community (£900).

Exclusions Charities with substantial funds are not supported. No grants to individuals.

Applications Application forms can be downloaded from the trust's website. Trustees meet to consider grants four times a year.

Help the Hospices

Hospices

£1.3 million (2005/06)
Beneficial area UK.

34–44 Britannia Street, London WC1 9JG

Tel. 020 7520 8200

Email grants@helpthehospices.org.uk

Website www.helpthehospices.org.uk

Correspondent David Praill, Chief Executive

Trustees *Rt Hon. Lord Newton of Braintree, Chair; Dr Helen Clayson; Suzy Croft; Dr Andrew Hoy; Terry Magee; Agnes Malone; George Miall; Hugh Scurfield; Sally Taylor; Alison Canning; David Clark; Rowena Dean; Bay Green; Jane Mason.*

CC Number 1014851

Information available Accounts were on file at the Charity Commission.

General The objectives of the charity are:

- to facilitate and promote the relief, care and treatment of the sick, especially of the dying, and the support and care of their families and carers and of the bereaved
- to facilitate and promote the charitable activities of independent hospices
- to provide or facilitate education and training for professionals and volunteers engaged in palliative care and increase awareness among the general public of the values, principles and practise of hospice and palliative care.

These objectives are met by providing education and training as well as funding hospices and palliative care units through a number of grant schemes. See website for up-to-date details of current programmes.

In 2005/06 the trust had assets of just under £6 million and an income of £6.5 million, including over £5 million from voluntary income. Grants to 148 hospices totalled £1.3 million. A further £314,000 was distributed among 314 individuals.

Applications Generally on a form available from the grants officer, from whom further information is also available. For major grant programmes, potential applicants should request details first as policies change. The trust's website contains detailed information of the grant-making policy and should be viewed before an application is considered. For emergency grants, applicants should write directly to the chief executive.

The Christina Mary Hendrie Trust for Scottish and Canadian Charities

Young and older people, general

£593,000 (2005/06)

Beneficial area Scotland and Canada.

Anderson Strathern Solicitors, 1 Rutland Court, Edinburgh EH3 8EY

Tel. 0131 270 7700 **Fax** 0131 270 7788

Correspondent Alan Sharp, Secretary

Trustees *Sir Alistair Irwin, Chair; Anthony Cox; Arabella Cox; Charles Cox; Ronald Cox; Mary-Rose Grieve; Susie Hendrie; Miss Caroline Irwin; John K Scott-Moncrieff.*

SC Number SC014514

Information available Full accounts were provided by the trust.

General The trust was established in 1975 following the death in Scotland of Christina Mary Hendrie. The funds constituting the trust originated in Canada. Grants are distributed to charities throughout Scotland and Canada, although the majority is now given in Scotland. There is a preference for charities connected with young or older people, although other groups to receive grants include cancer charities. In 2005/06 the trust had assets of £7 million and an income of £112,000. Grants were made totalling £593,000 and are broken down as follows:

The largest grants included those to: Queen Victoria School Appeal (£300,000); Friends of the Award In Edinburgh and the Lothians (£140,000); Cancer Relief (£25,000); St Andrews Hospice (£20,000); and Prison Phoenix Trust (£15,000).

Grants of £10,000 or less included those to: Canadian Mental Health Association (£10,000); Arberlour Child Care Trust (£5,000); Linlithgow Young People's Projects (£2,000); Seagull Trust (£1,000); and Cavalry Park Sports Club (£500).

Exclusions Grants are not given to individuals. Only organisations known to the trustees can be considered.

Applications In writing to the correspondent.

Philip Henman Trust

General

£51,000 (2004/05)

Beneficial area Worldwide.

16 Pembury Road, Tonbridge TN9 2HX

Tel. 01732 362227

Email info@pht.org.uk

Website www.djclark.com/pht/index.html

Correspondent D J Clark, Trustee

Trustees *J C Clark; D J Clark; J Duffey.*

CC Number 1054707

Information available Accounts were on file at the Charity Commission.

General The Philip Henman Trust offers grants to major UK-based overseas development organisations requiring partnership funding for projects lasting between three and five years. These grants are split into annual payments (normally between £3,000 and £5,000 per annum) with a maximum total of £25,000. Once the grant has been approved the organisation will be guaranteed an annual grant for the duration of the project, as long as receipts and reports are sent back to the Trust. Once a grant has been given, the organisation cannot apply for a grant in respect of a project for which they have already received funding.

The trust only has resources to guarantee an average of two new long-term grants a year, and therefore it is important to be sure any project fits our criteria before applying. Successful applications are normally those that prove the following:

- The project is being run professionally by an established major UK-registered charity (normally defined as having an income of over £100,000 per annum).
- The project is concerned with long-term overseas development.
- The project is a project and will start and finish within five years. We do not fund ongoing concerns.
- The funding from the Philip Henman Trust is important to the project (normally requires the grant funding to account for between 20% and 80% of the total project budget).

- The project will provide a lasting beneficial impact to the people or environment it seeks to help.
- The project is being partly funded by other sources. Voluntary work and central office administration costs can be counted as other source funding.

NOTE: from 2007 the trust is no longer offering one-off grants.

In 2004/05 the trust had assets of £1.5 million and an income of £54,000. Grants totalled £51,000.

There were 12 donations of £1,000 or more listed in the accounts. Beneficiaries were Tsunami Appeal (£10,000), Action Aid, Ark Trust, International Children's Trust, Oxfam, Scottish Catholic Fund, Sight Savers and WaterAid (£5,000 each), St Eanswythe's Mission (£1,500), and Action for Blind People, Move On Ltd and Zhaoging Slum (£1,000 each).

Unlisted grants totalled £1,700.

Applications Applications are only considered once a year – the deadline is always 10 September. Applications are no longer accepted by post. Please use the online form to submit applications.

The G D Herbert Charitable Trust

Medicine, health, welfare, environmental resources

£66,000 (2005/06)

Beneficial area UK.

Barnards Inn, 86 Fetter Lane, London EC4A 1EN

Correspondent J J H Burden, Trustee

Trustees *M E Beaumont; J J H Burden.*

CC Number 295998

Information available Full accounts were on file at the Charity Commission.

General The trust makes grants in the areas of medicine, health, welfare and environmental resources. It mainly gives regular grants to a set list of charities, with a few one-off grants given each year.

In 2005/06 this trust had assets of £1.9 million and an income of £52,000. Grants totalled £66,000, of which 26 were 'regular donations' totalling £56,000.

Beneficiaries of 'special donations' included: DEBRA, the Friends of

Warehorne Church, Great Ormond Street Hospital, Music in Hospital, National Playing Fields, Queen Elizabeth's Foundation for Disabled People, Treloar and Youth Action Wiltshire (£1,250 each).

Applications In writing to the correspondent. No applications are invited other than from those charities currently supported by the trust.

The Joanna Herbert-Stepney Charitable Settlement (also known as The Paget Charitable Trust)

General – see below

£118,000 (2005/06)

Beneficial area Worldwide, with an interest in Loughborough.

Old Village Stores, Dippenhall Street, Crondall, Farnham, Surrey GU10 5NZ

Correspondent Joanna Herbert-Stepney, Trustee

Trustees *Joanna Herbert-Stepney; Lesley Mary Blood; Meg Williams.*

CC Number 327402

Information available Information was on file at the Charity Commission.

General The trust supports both UK and local charities for general charitable purposes. Priorities include international aid and development, children who are disadvantaged, older people, animal welfare and environmental projects. The trust states that there is a preference for the 'unglamorous' and 'projects where a little money goes a long way'. In many cases ongoing support is given to organisations.

In 2005/06 the trust had assets of £4.4 million and an income of £250,000. Out of a total expenditure of £180,000, grants totalled £118,000.

Grants were made to 138 organisations of which 47 were for £1,000 or more. Beneficiaries included: RABI (£5,000);

1st Eastnor Brownies (£3,500); Oxfam, RSABI and Soil Association (£3,000 each); Family Holiday Association (£2,750); Children's Family Trust, Ethiopiaid, Harvest Help, Medical Foundation for Care of Victims of Torture, Pattaya Orphanage Trust, Stepney Children's Fund and John Storer House (£2,000 each); Impact (£1,500); Tibet Relief Fund of UK (£1,300); Leicestershire Care at Home Service (£1,200); and Angels International, Appropriate Technology Asia, Calcutta Rescue Fund, Children's Country Holidays Fund, Friends of Newcroft Primary School, Global Cancer Care, Peper Harow Foundation, Quaker Social Action, Southwark Community Education Council, Tree Aid and World Development Movement Trust (£1,000 each).

Smaller grants mainly of £500 each included those to 3H Fund, Action Aid, Asthma UK, British Humanitarian Aid, Brook Hospital for Animals, Caring for Life, Charity Education International, Childline Midlands, Deafway, Good Rock Foundation, Jubilee Action, Leprosy Mission, Mexico Child Link, Ockenden International, Seeds for Africa, St Andrew's Evangelical Mission, Tibet Watch and Wells for India.

Exclusions The trust states that 'sheer need is paramount, in practice, nothing else is considered'. Grants are only given to registered UK charities. Overseas projects can only be funded via UK charities; no money can be sent directly overseas. The trust does not support individuals (including students), projects for people with mental disabilities, medical research or AIDS/HIV projects.

Applications In writing to the correspondent; there is no application form. The trustees meet in spring and autumn. The trust regrets that it cannot respond to all applications.

The Hesed Trust

Christian

£42,000 to organisations (2005/06)

Beneficial area UK and overseas.

14 Chiltern Avenue, Cosby, Leicestershire LE9 1UF

Correspondent G Rawlings, Secretary

Trustees *P Briggs; R Eagle; G Rawlings; J C Smith.*

CC Number 1000489

Information available Accounts were on file at the Charity Commission.

General The trust's objectives are:

- the advancement of the Christian faith
- the relief of persons who are in conditions of need, hardship or distress or who are aged or sick
- the provision of instruction in the Christian faith at any educational establishment
- the provision of facilities for recreation for persons in need of, for the benefit of the public at large with the objective of improving the conditions of life for such persons.

In 2005/06 the trust had an income of £142,000 and out of a total expenditure of £154,000 gave grants to other charities totalling £42,000.

Organisations to benefit were: Ministries Without Borders (£26,000); Iglesia Cuba (£11,000); Covenant Life Church Melton and Rainbow Africa (£1,100 each); Arab World Ministries (£1,000); Covenant Life Church Leicester (£800); and All Nations Church Cardiff (£500).

Exclusions No support for expeditions and individual requests.

Applications The trust states that no applications are now being considered.

The Bernhard Heuberger Charitable Trust

Jewish

£687,000 (2005/06)

Beneficial area Worldwide.

12 Sherwood Road, London NW4 1AD

Correspondent The Trustees

Trustees *D H Heuberger; S N Heuberger.*

CC Number 294378

Information available Accounts were on file at the Charity Commission, but without a narrative report.

General This trust was established in 1986. In 2005/06 the trust had assets of £2.5 million and an income of £173,000. During the year 29 grants totalling £687,000 were approved compared with 18 grants totalling £167,000 in the previous year. Donations were broken down as follows (shown here with examples of beneficiaries in each category):

Education/training – £43,000
Gateshead Talmundical College, Simon Marks Jewish Primary School Trust and the Weinter Library (£10,000 each); the Hope Centre and Jewish Chaplaincy (£5,000 each); and Institute for Higher Rabbinical (£3,000).

Medical/health/sickness – £323,000
Hadassah UK and Share Zedek (£100,000 each); Alyn Orhopaedic Hospital and Great Ormond Street Hospital (£50,000 each); CHIZUK (£20,000); and Hatzolah Israel (£2,500).

General – £322,000
Jewish Care (£77,000); Friends of Horim Establishment (£50,000); British Emunah (£25,000); British Friends of Israel War Disabled, CMM, Jewish Women's Aid and Shuvo Yisroel (£20,000 each); North Hendon Adath Yisroel Synagogue (£13,000); Friends of Religious Settlements (£12,000); the Sunderland Kolel (£10,000); Kolel Shomrei Hachomoth (£7,500); and Hachzokas Torah Vechesed Charity (£5,000).

Applications In writing to the correspondent.

The P and C Hickinbotham Charitable Trust

Social welfare

£98,000 (2005/06)
Beneficial area UK, with a preference for Leicestershire and Rutland.

69 Main Street, Bushby, Leicester LE7 9PL
Tel. 0116 243 1152
Correspondent Mrs C R Hickinbotham, Trustee
Trustees *Catherine Hickinbotham; Roger Hickinbotham; Rachel Hickinbotham; Anna Hickinbotham.*
CC Number 216432
Information available Accounts were on file at the Charity Commission.

General Grants are generally not recurrent and are largely to social welfare organisations, with some churches and Quaker meetings also receiving support. Grants are mainly under £500, with some smaller grants made to a variety of registered charities. The trust gives occasional, one-off larger grants usually between £5,000 and £20,000.

In 2005/06 the trust had assets of £2.5 million and an income of £55,000. Grants were made totalling £98,000.

Beneficiaries included: Age Concern, Catherine House – Leicester and Voluntary Action – Rutland (£15,000 each); Leicester Money Advice Centre (£10,000); Centre for Alternative Technology, National Trust – Wales, Sibford School, St Andrews Church – Lyddington and Stamford Theatre (£5,000 each); Hope House, Children's Hospice (£2,000); British Red Cross – Leicestershire and Rutland; Leicester Credit Union, Ulster Quaker Service Committee and Uppingham Community College (£1,000 each); CRUSE Bereavement Care, Dove Cottage Day Hospice, Send a Cow and Snowdonia Society (£500 each); Community of Holy Peace, Royal Leicestershire Regiment Museum Trust and St Peters's Church – Shakestone (£250); African Children's Educational Trust (£100); Rainbows Children's Hospice (£50); and Anti-Slavery Society and Parkinson's Disease Society (£25 each).

Exclusions No grants to individuals applying for bursary-type assistance or to large UK charities.

Applications In writing to the correspondent, giving a brief outline of the purpose of the grant. Replies will not be sent to unsuccessful applicants.

Highcroft Charitable Trust

Jewish, poverty

£92,000 (2004/05)
Beneficial area UK and overseas.

15 Highcroft Gardens, London NW11 0LY
Correspondent Rabbi R Fischer, Trustee
Trustees *Rabbi R Fischer; Mrs S L Fischer.*
CC Number 272684
Information available Accounts were on file at the Charity Commission.

General The trust supports the advancement and study of the Jewish faith and the Torah, and also the relief of poverty and advancement of education among people of the Jewish faith. Grants range between £148 and £5,000.

In 2004/05 the trust had assets of £347,000 and an income of £128,000. Grants totalled £92,000.

The largest grants were £10,000 each to Chevras Maoz Ladal, Kol Yaacov, SOFT and Tevini.

Other beneficiaries included Friends of Beer Miriam, Institute For Higher Rabbinic Studies and Kollel Ohr Yechiel (£5,000 each), Kollel Chibas Yerushalayim (£4,200), Craven Walk Charity Trust (£2,500), London Friends of Kamenitzer (£2,000), Hachzakas Torah Vachesed Charity (£1,900), Amutat Shaarei Harama, Beis Yaacov High School and Tashbar Manchester (£1,000 each), Belt Haknesset Kehilat Yaacov (£700) and British Friends of College Technology and Delamere Forest School (£100 each).

Other donations of less than £100 each totalled £610.

Applications In writing to the correspondent.

The Holly Hill Charitable Trust

Environmental education, conservation and wildlife

£184,000 (2004/05)
Beneficial area UK.

Unit No. 525, Citibox Kensington Ltd, 2 Old Brompton Road, London SW7 3DQ
Correspondent The Trustees
Trustees *M D Stanley; A Lewis.*
CC Number 1044510
Information available Accounts were on file at the Charity Commission.

General This trust was established in 1995 to support environmental education, conservation and wildlife organisations.

In 2004/05 it had assets of £1.2 million and an income of £240,000, including £158,000 from donations. Grants were made to 18 organisations totalling £184,000.

Beneficiaries of the largest grants were Friends of the Earth (£28,000), Aberdeen University Darwin Initiative (£25,000), Rain Forest Concern (£23,000), Devon Wildlife Trust (£20,000), Kasanka Trust (£16,000), Wildcru Oxford University (£15,000) and Sussex Wildlife Trust (£13,000).

Smaller granst included those to Imperial College (£7,500), True Nature Films (£7,000), Woodland Trust

(£5,000), Plymouth University (£4,000), University of Sheffield (£1,000) and Kapal School Project (£600).

Exclusions No grants to individuals.

Applications In writing to the correspondent. Applications need to be received in April and September, and trustees meet in June and November.

The Charles Littlewood Hill Trust

Health, disability, service, children (including schools)

£142,000 (2005)

Beneficial area UK, with a preference for Nottinghamshire and Norfolk.

Berryman Shacklock LLP, Park House, Friar Lane, Nottingham NG1 6DN

Tel. 0115 945 3700 **Fax** 0115 948 0234

Correspondent W F Whysall, Trustee

Trustees *C W L Barratt; W F Whysall; T H Farr; N R Savory.*

CC Number 286350

Information available Accounts were on file at the Charity Commission.

General The trust supports schools, disability, health, service and children's organisations. It gives UK-wide, although particular preference is given to applications from Norfolk and Nottinghamshire.

In 2004 the trust had assets of £4 million, which generated an income of £174,000. Grants were made totalling £142,000 and were broken down as follows (shown here with examples of beneficiaries in each category):

Nottinghamshire – 20 grants
Rutland House School for Parents (£7,500); the Malt Cross Music Hall Trust Company (£6,000); Peter Le Marchant Trust, MacMillan Cancer Relief – Nottinghamshire and Nottingham City Hospital Charity (£5,000 each); Army Benevolent Fund – East Midlands and Life Education Centre – Nottingham (£3,000 each); Nottinghamshire Royal Society for the Blind (£2,000); and the Furniture Project, Nottinghamshire Regional Society for Autistic Children and Adults,

Nottingham Sea Cadet Unit and Stubbin Wood School (£1,000 each).

Norfolk – 12 grants
Norwich Cathedral Choir Endowment Fund (£30,000); the Norfolk Churches Trust (£6,000); the Prince's Trust (£5,000); Norfolk Eating Disorders Association (£3,000); the Church in the Plumsteads (£2,500); and All Hallows Hospital, How Hill Trust and Tapping House Hospice (£1,000 each).

Elsewhere – 21 grants
Hope & Homes for Children (£3,000); and Axess Information Association, British Heart Foundation, Royal Commonwealth Ex-Services League, the Epilepsy Research Foundation, Invalids at Home, Prostate Cancer Charity, the Royal Leicestershire Regiment Museum Appeal, the Royal Star and Garter Home, Soldiers and Airmen's Centres and War Widows Association of Great Britain (£1,000 each).

Exclusions Applications from individuals are not considered. Grants are seldom made for repairs of parish churches outside Nottinghamshire.

Applications In writing to the correspondent, including the latest set of audited accounts, at least one month before trustees' meetings in March, July and November. Unsuccessful applications will not be notified.

R G Hills Charitable Trust

General

£80,000 (2006/06)

Beneficial area UK and overseas.

Furley Page, 39 St Margaret's Street, Canterbury, Kent CT1 2TX

Tel. 01227 763939

Correspondent V E Barton, Trustee

Trustees *D J Pentin; V E Barton.*

CC Number 1008914

Information available Full accounts were on file at the Charity Commission.

General This trust was dormant until Mrs E M Hill's death in March 1996, when she left three-quarters of the residue of her estate to the trust. The balance was received in June 1999.

In 2005/06 the trust had assets of almost £3 million, an income of £109,000 and made 23 grants totalling £80,000.

Grant beneficiaries included: Demelza House (£4,000), British Executive Service Overseas, Bud Flanigan Leukaemia Fund, The Children's Trust, Coronary Artery Disease Research, Ex Services Mental Welfare Society, Greater London Fund for the Blind, Kent Air Ambulance, King George Fund for Sailors, Salvation Army and Spinal Injuries Association (£3,000) and Deaf Education through Listening and Talking, Hope UK, Impact Foundation, RNLI, RUKBA, Unicef and Wingate Special Children's Trust (£2,000 each).

Applications In writing to the correspondent.

Hinchley Charitable Trust

Mainly evangelical Christian

£103,000 (2004/05)

Beneficial area UK and overseas.

Watersmeet, 56 Barton Road, Haslingfield, Cambridge CB3 7LL

Tel. 01223 741120

Email bs217@cam.ac.uk

Correspondent Dr Brian Stanley, Chair

Trustees *Dr B Stanley; J D Levick; S P Dengate.*

CC Number 281178

Information available Accounts were on file at the Charity Commission.

General In 2004/05 the trust had an income of £144,000 and made grants totalling £103,000.

There were 31 grants of £1,000 or more listed in the accounts. Recipients of grants of £5,000 or more included the Crusaders' Union (£13,000), Associated Bus Ministries and Tear Fund (£10,000 each) and Shaftesbury Society, Spurgeon's College, Willowfield and Wycliffe Bible Translators (£5,000 each).

Other listed beneficiaries included Kulika (£4,000), Castle Hill Baptist Church and Scripture Union (£3,000 each), Arbury Road Baptist Church, Beauty from Ashes Trust, Homerton Space Project, Hope Now and Rural Ministries (£2,500 each), Mildmay Mission and Sycamore Project (£2,000 each) and Breadline, Primary Concern and Toxteth Vine Project (£1,000 each).

Other grants under £1,000 each totalled £2,800.

Applications The trust states that it does not respond to unsolicited applications. Replies will rarely, if ever, be made to applications for grants by post or on the telephone, as existing funds are all fully committed to charities which are regularly supported.

Stuart Hine Trust

Evangelical Christianity

£123,000 (2005/06)

Beneficial area UK and overseas.

'Cherith', 23 Derwent Close, Hailsham, East Sussex BN27 3DA

Correspondent Raymond Bodkin, Trustee

Trustees *Raymond Bodkin; Nigel Coltman; Amelia Gardner; Philip Johnson.*

CC Number 326941

Information available Accounts were on file at the Charity Commission.

General The trust gives grants to evangelical Christian organisations that have been supported by the trustees or by the settlor during his lifetime and that are known to the trustees. In 2005/06 the trust had an income of £128,000, mainly from royalties received from the song *How Great Thou Art* written by Stuart Hine. Grants totalled £123,000.

A detailed grants list was not available, although the trust did inform us that the bulk of the grant total was given to Wycliff Bible Translators (£97,000).

Applications The trust states that 'unsolicited requests for funds will not be considered'. Funds are basically distributed in accordance with the wishes of the settlor.

The Hinrichsen Foundation

Music

£45,000 approved (2005)
Beneficial area UK.

10–12 Baches Street, London N1 6DN

Website www.hinrichsenfoundation.org.uk/

Correspondent The Secretary

Trustees *P Standford, Chair; T Berg; Dr J Cross; Dr Linda Hirst; S Lubbock; K Potter; P Strang; Prof. S Walsh; Mrs T Estell.*

CC Number 272389

Information available Accounts were on file at the Charity Commission.

General The trust states: 'The Hinrichsen Foundation is a charity devoted to the promotion of music. Although the objects of the trust are widely drawn, the trustees have decided for the time being to concentrate on assisting in the areas of music to do with contemporary composition and its performance and musical research.'

The trust supports the public performance of living composers; grants include those to performing ensembles for concerts and festivals. Grants are not made retrospectively. Organisations supported include both UK organisations and local groups throughout the UK.

In 2005 it had assets of £87,000 and an income of £76,000, almost entirely from donations received. Grants were approved to 40 organisations totalling £45,000.

Beneficiaries included: Huddersfield Contemporary Music Festival (£10,000); English National Opera (£3,000); BMIC (£2,000); British Contemporary Piano Competition, London Sinfonietta and Spitalfields Festival (£1,500 each); and Birmingham Contemporary Music Group, Colourscape Music Festival, Kettle's Yard, Sligo New Music Festival and SPNM (£1,000 each).

Exclusions The trust does not support study courses, including those at postgraduate level. Grants are not given for instruments, equipment or recordings.

Applications On a form which can be downloaded from the foundation's website.

Hockerill Educational Foundation

Education, especially Christian education

£146,000 to organisations (2005/06)

Beneficial area UK, with a preference for the dioceses of Chelmsford and St Albans.

16 Hagsdell Road, Hertford, Hertfordshire SG13 8AG

Tel. 01992 303053 **Fax** 01992 425950

Email hockerill.trust@ntlworld.com

Correspondent C R Broomfield, Secretary

Trustees *Revd C W Herbert; Ven T P Jones. Four ex-officio trustees; four diocesan trustees; seven nominative trustees; one co-opted trustee.*

CC Number 311018

Information available Accounts were obtained from the Charity Commission website.

General The foundation was set up in 1978 following the closure of Hockerill College, which was established in 1852 to train women teachers who 'would go to schools in the service of humanity'. When the Secretary of State for Education and Science decided in 1976 to wind down Hockerill College, the proceeds of the sale of its assets were given to this foundation to use for the purposes for which the college was created.

The foundation's current priorities are:

- Grants to individual teachers and others in an educational capacity, either training to teach or seeking to develop their professional abilities and qualifications, particularly in Religious Education.
- Grants to individuals taking other first degree or further education courses, excluding courses which lead directly to careers other than teaching.
- Training and support for the church's educational work in the dioceses of Chelmsford and St Albans.
- Research, development and support grants to organisations in the field of religious education.

Grants are also made to organisations for projects and research likely to enhance the Church of England's contribution to higher and further education or religious education in schools. The trustees will normally consider applications from corporate bodies or institutions associated with education on Christian principles. There is a religious dimension to all education, but the trustees would expect any activity, course, project or research supported to be of real benefit to religious education and/or the church's educational work. They will give priority to imaginative new projects which will enhance the Church of England's contribution to higher and further education and/or promote aspects of religious education in schools.

In 2005/06 the foundation had assets of £6.5 million and a total income of £248,000. Grants were made totalling £184,000 which were distributed as follows:

Diocese of St Albans	£65,000
Diocese of Chelmsford	£61,000
Other	£20,000
Individuals	£38,000

Exclusions Grants are not given for general appeals for funds, 'bricks and mortar' building projects or purposes that are the clear responsibility of another body.

With regard to individuals, grants will not normally be considered for:

- teachers who intend to move out of the profession
- those in training for ordination or for other kinds of mission
- clergy who wish to improve their own qualifications, unless they are already engaged in teaching in schools and/or intend to teach in the future
- students of counselling, therapy or social work
- undergraduates or people training for other professions, such as accountancy, business, law or medicine
- people doing courses or visits abroad, including 'gap' year courses (except as an integral part of a course, or a necessary part of research)
- children at primary or secondary school.

Applications On a form available from the correspondent, to be submitted by 30 April each year. Results of applications will be communicated in June. Receipt of applications are not acknowledged. Applications which do not fit the criteria do not normally receive a reply.

The J G Hogg Charitable Trust

Welfare, animal welfare, general

About £55,000 (2005/06)

Beneficial area Worldwide.

Chantrey Vellacott DFK, Russell Square House, 10 -12 Russell Square, London WC1B 5LF

Correspondent C M Jones, Trustees' Accountant

Trustees *Sarah Jane Houldsworth; Joanna Wynfreda Turvey.*

CC Number 299042

Information available Information was on file at the Charity Commission

General The trust states that it has no set policy on the type of charity supported, but would give favourable consideration to those based primarily in the UK that support the relief of human and animal suffering.

In 2005/06 the trust had an income of £18,000 and a total expenditure of £57,000.

Previous beneficiaries have included Canine Partners for Independence, the Chemical Dependency Centre, Oxfam, Pets Placement, Quest, Royal Ballet School, Students Exploring Marriage Trust, Sue Ryder Care, Trust for Chernobyl Children and Variety Club of Great Britain.

Exclusions No grants to individuals. Registered charities only are supported.

Applications In writing to the correspondent. To keep administration costs to a minimum, the trust is unable to reply to unsuccessful applicants.

The Holden Charitable Trust

Jewish

£195,000 (2005/06)

Beneficial area UK, with a preference for the Manchester area.

c/o Lopian Gross Barnett and Co., Cardinal House, 20 St Mary Parsonage, Manchester M3 2IG

Correspondent The Clerk

Trustees *David Lopian; Marion Lopian; Michael Lopian.*

CC Number 264185

Information available Accounts were on file at the Charity Commission website.

General 'The Holden Charitable Trust exists to receive and distribute charitable donations to worthy causes primarily within the Jewish community.' In 2005/06 the trust had assets of £1.9 million and an income of £777,000 including £713,000 from donations. Grants totalled £195,000.

There were 30 grants of £1,000 or more listed in the accounts. Beneficiaries included: Hamachon L'Zichron Yoel Yaakov (£44,000); Friends of Beis Eliyohu Trust (£19,000); Broom Foundation (£13,000); Broughton Jewish Cassel Fox Primary School (£11,000); Asser Bishvil (£7,600); Manchester Jewish Grammar School (£5,000); British Friends of Zaka (£4,000); King David Schools and Talmud Torah Trust (£3,300 each); Manchester Charitable Trust (£3,000); Gateshead Jewish Boarding School (£2,600); UJIA (£2,500); British Friends of Mir Yeshiva (£2,000); Manchester Jewish Girls' School (£1,800); MDA (£1,500); and Gateshead Talmudical College and Zichron Chaim Simcha Foundation (£1,000 each).

Donations of less than £1,000 each totalled £23,000.

Applications In writing to the correspondent.

The Dorothy Holmes Charitable Trust

General

About £40,000 (2005/06)

Beneficial area UK, with a preference for Dorset.

Smallfield Cody and Co., 5 Harley Place, Harley Street, London W1G 8QD

Correspondent Michael Kennedy

Trustees *Mrs B M Cody; Miss M Cody; Dr S Roberts; J Roberts.*

CC Number 237213

Information available Accounts were on file at the Charity Commission.

General The trust's policy is to make a substantial number of relatively small donations to groups working in many charitable fields – including those involved in medical research, disability, older people, children and young people, churches, the disadvantaged, the environment and the arts. The trust can give throughout the UK but has a preference for Dorset, especially Poole. In practice nearly all grants are given to either national charities or those based in Dorset.

In 2005/06 the trust had an income of £25,000 and an expenditure of £47,000. Grants totalled about £40,000. Donations generally range from between £350 to £500, however some larger grants, up to £1,000, are made. Further information for this year was not available. Previous beneficiaries have included Crisis at Christmas, RAFT, St John's School – Wallingford and St Wilfrid's Hospice – Chichester.

Exclusions Only applications from registered charities will be considered.

Applications In writing to the correspondent, preferably in January to March each year.

The Holst Foundation

Arts

£194,000 to individuals and organisations (2004/05)
Beneficial area UK.

43 Alderbrook Road, London SW12 8AD
Tel. 020 8673 4215 (answerphone only)
Email holst@dpmail.co.uk
Correspondent The Grants Administrator
Trustees Rosamund Strode, Chair; Noel Periton; Prof. Arnold Whittall; Peter Carter; Andrew Clements; Julian Anderson.
CC Number 283668
Information available Accounts were on file at the Charity Commission.

General The trust has two objectives: first, to promote public appreciation of the musical works of Gustav and Imogen Holst; and second, to encourage the study and practice of the arts.

In practice the trust tends to be proactive. Funds are available almost exclusively for the performance of music by living composers. The trust has historical links with Aldeburgh in

Suffolk and is a major funder of new music at the annual Aldeburgh Festival. It also promotes the recording of new music by means of substantial funding to the recording label NMC, which the foundation also provided the funds to set up.

In 2004/05 it had assets of almost £2 million and an income of £269,000. Grants totalling £194,000 were made to individuals and organisations. There were 28 grants of £1,000 or more listed in the accounts.

By far the largest donation of £100,000 went to NMC Recordings. Other beneficiaries included Dartington International Summer School (£9,500), Vale of Glamorgan Arts Centre (£5,000), St Magnus Festival (£3,500), BEAST (£3,000), Adur Arts Forum and Deal Summer Music Festival (£2,500 each), Talisman/Karaoke Opera (£2,000), Roehampton Institute (£1,500) and BPF Composers, Bath Festivals Trust, Birmingham Symphonic Winds, Greenwich and Docklands Festivals and Thaxted Festival (£1,000 each).

A further 42 unlisted grants totalled £22,000.

Royalties from the Holst Estate have largely ceased since the copyright expired at the end of 2004. From 2006 both the number and the size of grants have been greatly reduced as a result.

Exclusions No support for the recordings or works of Holst that are already well supported, nor for capital projects. No grants to individuals for educational purposes.

Applications In writing to the correspondent. Trustees meet four times a year. There is no application form. Seven copies of the application should be sent. Applications should contain full financial details and be as concise as possible. Funding is not given retrospectively.

P H Holt Charitable Trust

General

£104,000 (2004/05)
Beneficial area UK, with a preference for Merseyside.

India Buildings, Liverpool L2 0RB
Tel. 0151 473 4693 **Fax** 0151 473 4693
Correspondent Roger Morris, Secretary

Trustees Neil Kemsley, Chair; Derek Morris; Tilly Boyce; Neil Kemsley; Martin Cooke; Nikki Eastwood; Gill Richards.
CC Number 217332
Information available Accounts were on file at the Charity Commission.

General The trust makes a large number of mostly small grants, about three-quarters of them in Merseyside. This trust is a welcome and exceptional example of Liverpool shipping money staying in and around the city. It continues to organise its giving in three established grant programmes concerned with Merseyside, 'Holt tradition' and elsewhere.

In 2004/05 the trust had assets of £11 million and an income of £375,000. Grants were made totalling £77,000, categorised as follows:

Activity 2004/05

	Merseyside	'Holt tradition'
No. of applications received	282	46
No. of grants made	67	24
of which		
recipients previously supported	47	23
recipients supported for the first time	17	1
consortium projects	3	nil
total value of commitments made	£90,000	£14,000
average size of grant	£1,300	£590

Grants by category 2004/05

	Total	Merseyside	'Holt' tradition
Community development and participation	£37,000	£34,000	£3,200
Social welfare	£19,000	£15,000	£3,800
Education	£30,000	£25,000	£5,000
Visual and performing arts	£15,000	£14,000	£500
Heritage and built environment	£1,800	£1,100	£750
Natural environment	£2,000	£950	£1,000
Medical research	Nil	Nil	Nil
Total committed in year	£104,000	£90,000	£14,000

Merseyside
Major grants included: Ariel Trust (£10,000); Plaza Community Cinema (£6,000); Liverpool JMU, Merseyside Dance Initiative and Rejects Revenge Theatre Company (£3,000 each); Liverpool Comedy Trust and Yellow House (£2,500 each); Basement Night Drop In Centre, Brouhaha International, Chrysalis, Merseyfest, New Everyman Youth Theatre and Unity (£2,000 each); and Active Drama Company, Arena Art and Design Association, Liverpool Lighthouse to help equip a room for its Harmonize project and Vivaee Charitable Trust (£1,500 each); and L'Arche, Campus Children's Holidays, Liverpool Council of Education and South Wirral High (£1,000 each).

Smaller grants included those to: Birkenhead Youth Club (£750); Action Force Africa, Liverpool Arts Interface, Loop Gallery and United Sikh Association (£500 each); Greenhouse Project (£300); and Liverpool Cathedral (£200).

There were also 19 routine grants to organisations with which the trust has regular contact.

The 'Holt Tradition'
Four one-off grants were made in this category. Beneficiaries were: University of Liverpool to assist the development of the Mercantile Liverpool Project (£4,000); GIFT (£1,000); Sailors' Families Society to help maintain its work (£500); and Global Women's Charity (£500).

There were also 20 routine grants to organisations with which the trust has regular contact.

Exclusions No grants to individuals. Grants are not usually given to organisations outside Merseyside.

Applications In writing to the correspondent at any time. Full and detailed guidance notes are available from the trust.

The Homelands Charitable Trust

The New Church, health, social welfare

£233,000 (2005/06)
Beneficial area UK.

c/o Alliotts, Ingersoll House, 5th Floor, 9 Kingsway, London WC2B 6XF
Correspondent N J Armstrong, Trustee
Trustees *D G W Ballard; N J Armstrong; Revd C Curry.*
CC Number 214322
Information available Accounts were on file at the Charity Commission.

General This trust was established in 1962, the settlors were four members of the Curry family and the original endowment was in the form of shares in the Curry company.

In 2005/06 it had assets of £6.7 million and a total income of £290,000. Grants were made totalling £233,000.

Over 70 grants were made during the year, beneficiaries included: General Conference of the New Church

(£45,000); Bournemouth Society of the New Church (£20,000); Broadfield Memorial Benevolent Trust (£11,000); New Church College (£7,500); Asbah (£5,000); RNLI (£4,000); Action Medical Research, Fellowship Afloat, Jubilee Sailing Trust, Manic Depression Fellowship and National Children Homes (£3,000 each); and Action for the Blind, Bliss, Child Accident Prevention Trust, Dreams Come True, Hope House, Mencap, RNID, Seeability, Survival International, Trinity Hospice, University College London, Wessex Children Hospice Trust and YMCA (£2,000 each).

The following was included under the heading 'Future plans and commitments':

'The trustees intend to continue supporting registered charities with a bias towards:

1 General Conference of the New Church
2 medical research
3 care and protection of children
4 hospices.

'The trustees are aware of the proposed extension and refurbishment of the New Church's residential centre in the Midlands at an estimated cost of £1.5 million and have set up a designated fund of £250,000 to contribute towards this project.'

Exclusions No grants to individuals.

Applications In writing to the correspondent.

The Homestead Charitable Trust

See below

£62,000 (2004/05)
Beneficial area UK.

Flat 7, Clarence Gate Gardens, Glentworth Street, London NW1 6AY
Correspondent Lady Nina Bracewell-Smith, Trustee
Trustees *Sir C Bracewell-Smith; Lady N Bracewell-Smith.*
CC Number 293979
Information available Accounts were on file at the Charity Commission.

General This trust makes grants towards medical, health and welfare, animal welfare, Christianity and the arts.

In 2004/05 it had assets of £4.5 million and an income of £1.8 million. The trust fund of the Sir Charles Bracewell-Smith Voluntary Settlement worth £1.6 million was transferred to the trust in October 2004. Grants given to individuals and institutions totalled £62,000.

Beneficiaries included: Cancer Research, CEF, Gurdwara Sri Guru Sigh and Unicef (£10,000 each); Hope and Homes for Children (£5,000); Oxfam (£3,000); Carthusians, Great Ormond Street Hospital, Matrix Music School, Missionaries of Charity, Oxfam and St James' Church and Tyburn Convent (£1,000 each); Great Dane Adoption Society (£500); Sport Relief (£250); Help the Aged (£120); and WaterAid (£50).

Applications In writing to the correspondent.

Mary Homfray Charitable Trust

General

£46,000 (2004/05)
Beneficial area UK, with a preference for Wales.

c/o Deloitte and Touche, Private Clients Ltd, Blenheim House, Fitzalan Court, Newport Road, Cardiff CF24 0TS
Correspondent Mrs A M Homfray, Trustee
Trustees *Mrs A M Homfray; G C S Gibson.*
CC Number 273564
Information available Accounts were on file at the Charity Commission.

General The trust supports a wide range of organisations, including many in Wales.

In 2004/05 it had assets of £1.6 million and an income of £57,000. Grants were made to 25 organisations totalling £46,000 and were mostly recurrent.

Beneficiaries included: Age Concern, Barnardos, Cathedral School Llandaff, Marie Curie Cancer Care, Meningitis Cymru, National Museum of Wales, PDSA, RUKBA, Salvation Army, Urdd Gobaith Cymru, Wallich Clifford Community and YMCA (£2,000 each); Dogs Trust (£1,000); and Maes-y-Dyfan and RSPB (£500 each).

Applications In writing to the correspondent. Applications should be made towards the end of the year, for consideration at the trustees' meeting in February or March each year.

The Hope Trust

Temperance, Reformed Protestant churches

About £150,000 (2004/05)

Beneficial area Worldwide, with a preference for Scotland.

Drummond Miller, 31–32 Moray Place, Edinburgh EH3 6BZ

Tel. 0131 226 5151

Email rmiller@drummond-miller.co.uk

Correspondent Robert P Miller, Secretary

Trustees *Prof. G M Newlands; Prof. D A S Ferguson; Revd G R Barr; Revd Dr Lyall; Carole Hope; Revd Gillean McLean.*

SC Number SC000987

Information available Basic information was available on this trust.

General This trust was established to promote the ideals of temperance in the areas of drink and drugs, and Protestant church reform through education and the distribution of literature. PhD students of theology studying at Scottish universities are also supported.

In 2004/05 its income was £164,000. Further information was not available for this year.

Previous beneficiaries have included Church of Scotland Priority Areas Fund, World Alliance of Reformed Churches, National Bible Society for Scotland, Feed the Minds and Waldensian Mission Aid.

Exclusions No grants to gap year students, scholarship schemes or to any individuals, with the sole exception of PhD students of theology studying at Scottish universities. No grants for the refurbishment of property.

Applications In writing to the correspondent. The trustees meet to consider applications in June and December each year. Applications should be submitted by mid-May or mid-November each year.

The Cuthbert Horn Trust

Environment, people with disability/special needs, older people

£54,000 (2005)

Beneficial area UK.

Capita Trust Company Limited, Phoenix House, 18 King William Street, London EC4N 7HE

Correspondent The Trustees

Trustees *Alliance Assurance Company Ltd; A H Flint.*

CC Number 291465

Information available Accounts were on file at the Charity Commission.

General The trust's main aims are to support charities helping older people and charities undertaking practical work in supporting the conservation and preservation of the environment.

In 2005 the trust had assets of £1.3 million and a total income of £256,000. Grants were made to 14 organisations totalling £54,000. Beneficiaries were Farms for City Children and Pesticide Action Network UK (£5,000 each), Elm Farm Research Centre, International Bee Research Association, Norfolk Wherry Trust, Bioregional Development Group, Prostate Research UK, 3H Fund and Crisis Recovery UK (£4,000 each) and Counsel and Care, the Island Trust, Mid Border Community Arts and Ovingdean Hall School (£3,000 each).

Exclusions No grants are made to individuals.

Applications There are no application forms to complete; applicants should provide in writing as much background about their charity or cause as possible. Applications need to be received by December as the trustees meet as soon as possible after the financial year end. Only successful applications will be notified.

The Horne Trust

Hospices

£201,000 (2004/05)

Beneficial area UK and the developing world.

Kingsdown, Warmlake Road, Chart Sutton, Maidstone, Kent ME17 3RP

Email mail.jh@horne-trust.org.uk

Correspondent J T Horne, Trustee

Trustees *J T Horne; J L Horne; N J Camamile.*

CC Number 1010625

Information available Accounts were on file at the Charity Commission.

General The trust supports homelessness charities and hospices, particularly children's hospices. Grants can also be given to medical support charities and organisations helping to develop self-reliant technology in Africa and the developing world.

In 2004/05 it had an income of £245,000, mostly from donations. Grants to 24 organisations totalled £201,000.

Beneficiaries included Lincolnshire Foundation (£40,000), Alzheimer's Society and Stroke Association (£15,000 each), Acorns Children's Hospice, Independent Age, St Richard's Hospice – Worcester and Whitby Network (£10,000 each), Association of Children's Hospices, Demelza House Children's Hospice, Heart of Kent Hospice, the Peaceful Place – Essex, St Gemma's Hospice – Leeds and Woodlands Hospice – Liverpool (£5,000 each) and Disability Aid Fund (£1,000).

Applications Normally in writing to the correspondent, although the trust has stated that currently unsolicited applications cannot be supported.

Hospital Saturday Fund Charitable Trust

Medical, health

£174,000 to organisations (2005/06)

Beneficial area UK, Republic of Ireland and overseas.

24 Upper Ground, London SE1 9PD

Tel. 020 7928 6662

Email trust@hsf.co.uk

Correspondent K R Bradley, Administrator

Trustees *Mrs P E Lee, Chair; K R Bradley, Mrs P G Boyle; Miss Z Richards; D L Sawers; Mrs L M C Warner; Miss I Racher.*

CC Number 327693

Information available Full accounts were on file at the Charity Commission.

General The Hospital Saturday Fund is a healthcare cash plan organisation, which was founded in 1873. In 1987 it established a charitable trust to support a wide range of hospitals, hospices and medical charities for care and research, as well as welfare organisations providing similar services. The trustees continue to provide support to smaller, lesser-known charities connected with diseases and disabilities about which there is little public awareness. Individuals can also be supported by the trust, usually for special equipment to relieve their condition or in cases where their health has contributed to their financial hardship, although sponsorship can be given to people studying for a medically-related career.

In 2005/06 it had assets of £982,000 and an income of £715,000, mostly through donations from its parent company. Grants were made to organisations totalling £174,000 and to individuals totalling £11,000. Grants to organisations were broken down geographically, as follows:

National (charities, hospitals and hospices) – 66 grants totalling £41,000
The largest grants went to Alzheimer's Society (£3,000); Teenage Cancer Trust and International Glaucoma Association (£1,500). Aside from these three grants, it gave 11 grants of £750 and 52 grants of £500 each. Recipients included Age Concern England, Brain Tumour UK, Childline, DEBRA, the Ear Foundation, Friends of the Elderly, the National Autistic Society, OCD Action, Rethink, the Shaftesbury Society, the Sunflower Trust, Terrence Higgins Trust and Wellbeing of Women.

South East and London – 48 grants totalling £31,000
These included 8 grants of £1,000 each to hospices and 12 grants of £500 each to hospitals. Other beneficiaries of grants of £750 and £500 each included 4Sight, Children's Trust, Connect, London Ambulance NHS Trust, Mildmay Mission Hospital, Parity for Disability, St Giles' Trust and the TreeHouse Trust.

South West and Wales – 9 grants totalling £5,500
There were 2 grants of £1,000 each made to hospices and 7 grants of £500 each made to hospitals. Other grants of £750 or £500 each included those to Brainwave, the Broadway Trust, Music Alive, Positive Action on Cancer, the Seeing Ear and Wiltshire Air Ambulance Appeal.

Midlands and North – 29 grants totalling £20,000
Grants included £1,000 each to 6 hospices and £500 each to 8 hospitals. Other grants of £750 or £500 each included those to Big C Appeal, Delamere Forest School, Hearing Help – Amber Valley, New Thresholds, Soundabout, Spinal Injuries Association and Volcare.

Scotland – 28 grants totalling £17,000
There were 8 grants made to hospitals mainly of £500 each and 3 grants made to hospices of £1,000 each. Other grants of £750 or £500 each included those to Borders Talking Newspaper, Cornerstone Community Centre, Edinburgh Young Carers Project, the Ness Foundation, the Scottish Society for Autism and Waverley Care.

Northern Ireland and Isle of Man – 8 grants totalling £5,800
There were 2 grants of £1,000 each made to hospices and 3 grants of £500 each made to hospitals. A further 3 grants of £750 each went to Northern Ireland Campaign for ME/CFS Healthcare.

Ireland – 61 grants totalling £40,000
There were 10 grants of £1,000 each made to hospices and 10 of £500 each made to hospitals. Others of £750 and £500 each included those to Age Action Ireland, Camphill Village Community, Debra Ireland, Eating Disorders Association Ireland, Irish Deaf Society, Miscarriage Association of Ireland, Muscular Dystrophy Ireland, Schizophrenia Ireland, Volunteer Stroke Scheme and Wexford Mental Health Association.

Overseas – 3 grants totalling £2,300
These were £750 to BasicNeeds UK Trust, LEPRA and Motivation Quality of Life.

Exclusions Unless there are exceptional circumstances, organisations are not supported in successive years.

Applications Hospitals, hospices and medically-related charities are invited to write detailed letters or to send a brochure with an accompanying letter. There is a form for individuals to complete available from the personal assistant to the trust administrator.

Houblon-Norman/George Fund

Finance
£95,000 (2005/06)
Beneficial area UK.

MA Business Support Unit HO-2, Bank of England, Threadneedle Street, London EC2R 8AH

Tel. 020 7601 3778 **Fax** 020 7601 4423

Email MA-HNGFund@bankofengland. co.uk

Website www.bankofengland.co. uk/education/fellowships

Correspondent The Secretary

Trustees *Rachel Lomax; Brendan Barber; Hon. Peter Jay.*

CC Number 213168

Information available Accounts were on file at the Charity Commission.

General The trust supports research into the interaction and function of financial and business institutions, the economic conditions affecting them, and the dissemination of knowledge thereof. Fellowships are tenable at the Bank of England. The research work to be undertaken is intended to be full-time work, and teaching or other paid work must not be undertaken during the tenure of the fellowship, without the specific consent of the trustees. In considering applications the trustees will pay particular regard to the relevance of the research to current problems in economics and finance.

In 2005/06 the trust had assets of £2.2 million, an income of £113,000 and made grants totalling £95,000 in the form of three fellowships.

Applications On an application form available from the website.

The Reta Lila Howard Foundation

Children, arts, environment

£312,000 (2005/06)

Beneficial area UK and Republic of Ireland.

Jamestown Investments Ltd, 4 Felstead Gardens, Ferry Street, London E14 3BS

Tel. 020 7537 1118

Email jamestown@btinternet.com

Correspondent The Company Secretary

Trustees *Emma Adamo; Nicolas Bauta; Geordie Dalglish; Sarah Eidson; Claudia Hepburn; Melissa Murdoch; Alannah Weston; Charles Burnett.*

CC Number 1041634

Information available Accounts were on file at the Charity Commission, without a list of grants, which was provided separately by the foundation.

General The founder of this trust had an interest in children's charities and the trust's grant-making focus is 'to support a few innovative projects that benefit children up to the age of 16 within the British Isles'. Funds are directed to selected projects, 'to support the education of young people or to ameliorate their physical and emotional environment'. In practice the trust also supports arts and environmental organisations. Donations are given over a finite period, with the aim that the project can be self-supporting when funding has ended.

In 2005/06 the trust had assets of £14.7 million and an income of £246,000. Grants to 15 organisations totalled £312,000. The annual report does not include a grants list, however, a list of beneficiaries was provided by the foundation on request.

Beneficiaries included: Farms for City Children (£45,000); Barnados and Dublin Zoo (£30,000 each); Institute of Economic Affairs (£27,000); the Tree Council (£25,000); Thames Explorer Trust (£23,000); Countryside Education Trust and the Woodland Trust (£20,000 each); Mactaggart Leisure Centre (£18,000); Greenhouse and Harnham Water Meadows Trust (£15,000); Bibles for Children (£10,000); and Battle of Britain Memorial Trust (£5,000).

Exclusions Grants are not given to individuals, organisations which are not registered charities, or towards operating expenses, budget deficits, (sole) capital projects, annual charitable appeals, general endowment funds, fundraising drives or events, conferences, or student aid.

Applications The trust states that it does not accept unsolicited applications, since the trustees seek out and support projects they are interested in.

The Clifford Howarth Charity Settlement

General

£62,000 (2005/06)

Beneficial area UK, with a preference for Lancashire (Burnley/Rossendale).

14A Hall Garth, Kelbeck, Barrow in Furness, Cumbria LA13 0QT

Correspondent James Howarth, Trustee

Trustees *James Howarth; Judith Howarth; Mary Fenton.*

CC Number 264890

Information available Accounts were on file at the Charity Commission

General The trust has general charitable purposes assisting local and UK charities supported by the founder. This is generally for work within Burnley and Rossendale.

In 2005/06 the trust had assets of £1.1 million, an income of £46,000 and made 11 grants totalling £62,000.

Grant beneficiaries included: Rampside Village Hall – Barrow (£15,000); Magdalene Project and RNLI (£10,000 each); Hospice Care for Burnley and Pendle and Hospice in Rossendale (£5,000 each); Sion Baptist Church and Tall Ships Youth Trust (£4,000 each); St Nicholas Church – Newchurch, Treloar Trust (£2,000); and Ulverstone Inshore Rescue (£1,000).

Exclusions Only registered charities will be supported. No grants to individuals, for scholarships or for non-local special projects.

Applications In writing to the correspondent. Grants are usually distributed in July.

The Hudson Foundation

Older people, general

£53,000 (2004/05)

Beneficial area UK, with a preference for the Wisbech area.

Whitegates, Barton Road, Wisbech, Cambridge PE13 1LE

Correspondent A D Salmon, Trustee

Trustees *A D Salmon, Chair; M A Bunting; H A Godfrey; D W Ball; S G Layton.*

CC Number 280332

Information available Accounts were obtained from the Charity Commission website.

General The objective of the foundation is the relief of infirm and/or older people, in particular the establishment and maintenance of residential accommodation for relief of infirm and/or older people and to make donations to other charitable purposes with a preference for the Wisbech area. The accounts state that 'whilst the trustees do make contributions to revenue expenditure of charitable organisations, they prefer to assist in the funding of capital projects for the advancement of the community of Wisbech and district'.

In 2004/05 the foundation had assets of £1.7 million and an income of £688,000. Grants were made totalling £53,000.

Beneficiaries included: Wisbech Grammar School (£22,000); Wisbech Swimming Club (£6,300); Royal Fleet Club (£6,000); Alexandra House (£5,200); the Historic Dockyard Chatham (£5,000); Methodist Homes for the Aged (£4,200); Wisbech Angles Theatre Council (£3,300); Wisbech Astroturf Committee (£1,600); and 1st Wisbech St Mary Guide Unit (£350).

Applications In writing to the correspondent. Trustees meet quarterly.

The Huggard Charitable Trust

General

£55,000 (2005/06)

Beneficial area UK, with a preference for South Wales.

8 Oakwood Road, Neath, West Glamorgan SA11 3DP

Correspondent S J Thomas, Trustee

Trustees *Mrs E M Huggard; T R W Davies; S J Thomas.*

CC Number 327501

Information available Accounts were on file at the Charity Commission.

General In 2005/06 the trust had assets of £1.8 million and an income of £63,000. Grants totalled £55,000.

Beneficiaries of the largest grants were: Amelia Methodist Trust – Vale of Glamorgan (£14,000); CURE Fund – Cardiff and Whitton Rosser Trust – Vale of Glamorgan (£6,000 each); and Bro Morgannwg NHS Trust (£4,000).

Other donations under £3,000 each totalled £25,000.

Applications The trustees are not inviting applications for funds.

The Geoffrey C Hughes Charitable Trust

Nature conservation, environment, performing arts

£235,000 (2005/06)
Beneficial area UK.

c/o Mills & Reeve, Francis House, 112 Hills Road, Cambridge CB2 1PH

Correspondent P C M Solon, Trustee

Trustees *J R Young; P C M Solon; W A Bailey.*

CC Number 1010079

Information available Accounts were on file at the Charity Commission, without a list of grants.

General This trust is essentially interested in two areas: nature conservation/environment and performing arts, particularly ballet or opera with a bias towards modern work.

In 2005/06 the trust had assets of £1.1 million and an income of £37,000. Grants totalled £235,000. no grants were made in the previous year.

Exclusions No grants to individuals.

Applications In writing to the correspondent.

The Humanitarian Trust

Education, health, social welfare, Jewish

£70,000 to organisations (2005/06)

Beneficial area Worldwide, mainly Israel.

27 St James' Place, London SW1A 1NR

Correspondent Mrs M Myers, Secretary

Trustees *M Jacques Gunsbourg; P Halban; A Lerman.*

CC Number 208575

Information available Accounts were on file at the Charity Commission.

General The trust was founded in 1946. In the early years donations were made overwhelmingly to educational causes in Israel. Nowadays the trust is giving to a wider range of causes, still mainly Jewish, but some smaller grants are given to non-Jewish organisations.

'The trustees consider grant applications from organisations and individuals in the UK and abroad, especially in the fields of education, health, social welfare, civil society, Jewish communal life and general charitable purposes.'

In 2005/06 it had assets of £4.2 million and an income of £98,000. Grants totalled £70,000 and were broken down as follows:

Academic and educational – 21 grants
The two largest grants went to one organisation, Friends of the Hebrew University of Jerusalem towards: the Humanitarian Trust Fellowship and the M Gunsbourg Memorial Scholarships (£10,000 each).

Other beneficiaries included: Isaiah Berlin Professorship in the History of Ideas (£4,500); Institute for Jewish Policy Research (£2,500); Leo Baeck College – London (£2,100); London Jewish Cultural Centre, British Friends of Neve Shalom and Yakar (£2,000 each); Friends of Israel Educational Foundation (£1,500); UJS Hillel (£1,000); Cambridge University Humanitarian Trust Studentship and Delamere Forest School (£500 each); Manchester Metropolitan University and University of Staffordshire (£200 each); and University of Southampton (£100).

Medical and charitable – 9 grants
Beneficiaries included: British Council of Shaare Zedek Medical Centre (£2,500); Cosgrove Care (£1,500); the Samaritans and Professor Yanko's Prevention of Blindness Research Project (£1,000 each); and Diabetes UK (£500).

Social service – 14 grants
New Israel Fund (£6,000); Beth Shalom Holocaust Memorial Centre and Centre for Jewish-Christian Relations (£2,000 each); A Step Forward, City University Olive Tree Educational Trust, European Association for Jewish Culture, Jewish Council for Racial Equality and New Israel Fund-Friendship Village (£1,000 each); and Abbeyfield Camden (£500).

Applications In writing to the correspondent, including annual report and accounts, projected budgets and future plans. Applications are considered at trustees' meetings in March and October.

The Michael and Shirley Hunt Charitable Trust

Prisoners' families, animal welfare

£67,000 (2005/06)
Beneficial area UK and overseas.

Ansty House, Henfield Road, Small Dole, West Sussex BN5 9XH

Tel. 01903 817116 **Fax** 01903 879995

Correspondent Mrs D S Jenkins, Trustee

Trustees *W J Baker; C J Hunt; S E Hunt; D S Jenkins; K D Mayberry.*

CC Number 1063418

Information available Accounts were on file at the Charity Commission.

General The trust makes grants for the benefit of prisoners' families, and also animals which are unwanted, sick or ill-treated.

In 2005/06 it had assets of £4.6 million and an income of £268,000. Grants were made totalling £67,000, broken down as follows and shown with examples of beneficiaries:

Relief of hardship of prisoners and prisoner's families – 8 grants totalling £18,500
Prisoners Abroad (£4,000); NCH – Dundee Intensive Support (£2,500); and New Bridge (£2,000).

163

Grants to 91 individuals totalled £10,000.

Relief of suffering of Animals – 15 grants totalling 21,000
Alternative Animal Sanctuary (£10,000); National Animal Welfare Trust (£2,000); and John Aspinall Foundation London Wildcare, Lincolnshire Trust for Cats and Vale Wildlife Hospital and Rehabilitation Centre (£1,000 each).

'Other deserving causes' – 5 grants totalling £17,000
Disasters Emergency Committee – Niger appeal fund, Martletts Hospice Hove and Miracles to Believe In (£5,000 each); and Task Force Romania (£2,000).

Exclusions No grants for fines, bail, legal costs, rent deposits and so on.

Applications In writing to the correspondent.

The Huxham Charitable Trust

Christianity, churches and organisations, development work

£42,000 to individuals and organisations (2005/06)
Beneficial area UK and Eastern Europe, especially Albania and Kosova.

Thatcher Brake, 37 Whidborne Avenue, Torquay TQ1 2PG
Correspondent Adrian W Huxham
Trustees *Revd Deryck Markham; Revd Percy; Mr Corney; Mrs Angela Huxham.*
CC Number 1000179
Information available Accounts were on file at the Charity Commission.

General In 2005/06 the trust had an income of £46,000 and a total expenditure of £42,000.

Applications The trust stated it has been unable to support any new organisations in recent years.

The Nani Huyu Charitable Trust

Welfare

£91,000 (2004/05)
Beneficial area UK, particularly but not exclusively within 50 miles of Bristol.

Rusling House, Butcombe BS40 7XE
Correspondent The Trustees
Trustees *S Whitmore; Ben Whitmore; Charles Thatcher; Maureen Whitmore.*
CC Number 1082868
Information available Accounts were on file at the Charity Commission, without a list of grants.

General The trust was registered with the Charity Commission in October 2000. In 2004/05 the trust had assets of £3.2 million and an income of £123,000. Grants totalled £91,000. No list of donations was included with the accounts on file at the Charity Commission.

The trust describes its work as: 'to assist people who are underprivileged, disadvantaged or ill, young people in matters of health, accommodation and training and those requiring assistance or medical care at the end of their lives'.

Applications In writing to the correspondent.

The P Y N and B Hyams Trust

Jewish, general

£42,000 (2004/05)
Beneficial area Worldwide.

610 Clive Court, Maida Vale, London W9 1SG
Correspondent Mrs M Hyams, Trustee
Trustees *N Hyams; Mrs M Hyams; D Levy; L Shebson.*
CC Number 268129
Information available Accounts were on file at the Charity Commission, but without a narrative report or a list of grants.

General In 2004/05 the trust had assets of £1.1 million and an income of £83,000. Grants to organisations totalled £42,000. No list of grants was included with the accounts.

In previous years, grants have been mostly given to Jewish organisations, although other causes are also funded.

Applications In writing to the correspondent, but please note, the trust states that funds are fully committed and unsolicited applications are not welcomed.

The Hyde Charitable Trust – Youth Plus

Disadvantaged children and young people

£109,000 (2005/06)
Beneficial area The areas in which the Hyde Group operates (currently London, Kent, Surrey, Sussex and Hampshire).

Youth Plus, Hyde Charitable Trust, Hollingsworth House, 181 Lewisham High Street, London SE13 6AA
Tel. 020 8297 7575
Email youthplus@hyde-housing.co.uk
Website www.youthplus.co.uk
Correspondent Janet Grant
Trustees *Brian Bishop; Richard Collins; Richard Finlison; Peter Matthew; Stephen Hill; Patrick Elliott; Geron Walker; Raymond Quintal; Martin Wheatley; Julian Saunders; Charmaine Odusina.*
CC Number 289888
Information available Information was on file at the Charity Commission.

General Hyde Charitable Trust is a company limited by guarantee established in 1984. It 'works to help improve the condition and quality of life of people from the poorest communities'.

Youth Plus works throughout the areas where the Hyde Group, one of the biggest housing association groups in the country, currently operates (London, Kent, Surrey, Sussex and Hampshire).

'Youth Plus aims to support disadvantaged children and young people in communities suffering high social deprivation in London and the South East of England. Each year, approximately £70,000 is available for distribution to projects that meet the Youth Plus objectives.

'Youth Plus is supported by Hyde Plus, Hyde's economic and community regeneration arm. Hyde Plus administers the grants and supports groups in the development of projects seeking Youth Plus funding.'

What have we funded previously and why?
'We are mainly interested in innovative projects seeking to address problems faced by children and young people in areas typified by social deprivation. These areas will often have high levels of unemployment and disenchantment within the community and offer very few prospects for young people.

'We are keen to hear about projects that demonstrate a partnership approach and which are committed to involving children and young people in both the planning and delivery of their services.'

Grants of up to £200 each can also be made to young Hyde residents (16 years or under) for education or development training and equipment under the Hyde Young Pride Award.

In 2005/06 the trust had assets of £3.1 million and an income of £97,000. Grants were made totalling £109,000.

Youth Plus grants approved in 2005/06 included: £16,000 to Swale Youth project – Faversham to provide an after school fun day; £5,200 to Friends of Kennington Park – Lambeth to fund a Saturday football club for 7- to 12-year-olds; £1,000 each to Ashmole Primary School – Lambeth towards gardening activities, Henry Fawcett Primary School – Lambeth towards completing work on the playground, Kender Community School – New Cross to extend sport-based after school clubs and Tollgate Primary School – Croydon to redevelop a memorial garden; £800 to Temple Hill C P School – Dartford to develop a sensory garden; £600 to Alphabets Nursery – Botley to purchase outdoor equipment; and £500 to St James C of E Primary School – Rochester to run after school sporting activities.

Exclusions No funding for:

- projects outside the area where Hyde is working. No areas outside the South East of England.
- sporting, social or fundraising events
- medical research, hospices, residential homes for older people
- any other projects which the trustees deem to fall outside our main criteria.

Applications Initial enquiries are welcomed by letter, email or telephone.

The Idlewild Trust

Performing arts, culture, restoration and conservation, occasional arts education

£121,000 (2005)
Beneficial area UK.

1a Taylors Yard, 67 Alderbrook Street, London SW12 8AD
Tel. 020 8772 3155
Email info@idlewildtrust.org.uk
Website www.idlewildtrust.org.uk
Correspondent Mrs Angela Hurst, Administrator
Trustees *Lady Judith Goodison, Chair; J C Gale; Mrs A C Grellier; J A Ford; M Wilson; J Ouvry; Dr T Murdoch.*
CC Number 268124
Information available Accounts were on file at the Charity Commission.

General The trust was founded in 1974 by Peter Brissault Minet, who had previously set up the Peter Minet Trust. Its policy is to support charities concerned with the encouragement of performing and fine arts and preservation for the benefit of the public of lands, buildings and other objects of beauty or historic interest. Occasionally support is given to bodies for educational bursaries in these fields or for conservation of the natural environment. The trust prefers to support UK charities and it is unlikely to support a project of local interest only.

In 2005 the trust had assets of £4.2 million, an income of £152,000 and made grants totalling £121,000.

Grants were categorised in the trust's annual report as follows:

Education	10 grants	£22,000
Performing arts	6	£13,000
Museums and galleries	8	£21,000
Preservation and restoration	21	£45,000
Fine art	4	£8,000
Nature conservation	7	£12,000

Grant beneficiaries included: Sir John Soane's Museum (£5,000); the Boxgrove Priory Trust, Dorset Opera, National Life Story Association, National Portrait Gallery, Royal Scottish National Orchestra, St Dunstan – Stepney, St John's Hospital Bakewell Almshouses, St Michael and All Angels, Great Whitley, Whitechapel Gallery and World Monuments Fund in Britain (£3,000 each); Academy of Ancient Music, Buxton Festival, Gainsborough's House

Society, Garsington Opera Ltd, National Trust and Pallant House Gallery Appeal (£2,500 each); Dawn Sailing Barge Trust, English National Opera, Lincoln Cathedral – the Wren Library, Charles Rennie Mackintosh Society and the Textile Conservation Centre Foundation (£2,000 each); and Buglife – the Invertebrate Conservation Trust, Hamilton Kerr Institute, National Trust for Scotland and Phoenix Singers (£1,500 each).

Exclusions Grants to registered charities only. No grants are made to individuals. The trust will not give to:

- repetitive UK-wide appeals by large charities
- appeals where all, or most, of the beneficiaries live outside the UK
- local appeals unless the artistic significance of the project is of more than local importance
- appeals whose sole or main purpose is to make grants from the funds collected
- endowment or deficit funding.

Applications On a form available from the correspondent, or as a download from the trust's website. This can be sent via post or emailed as a Microsoft Word file. Applications should include the following information:

- budget breakdown (one page)
- most recent audited accounts
- a list of other sponsors, including those applied to
- other relevant information.

Potential applicants are welcome to telephone the trust on Tuesdays or Wednesdays between 10am and 4pm to discuss their application and check eligibility. Trustees meet twice a year usually in March and November.

All eligible applications, which are put forward to the trustees, are acknowledged; other applications will not be acknowledged unless an sae is enclosed. Applications from organisations within 18 months of a previous grant will not be considered.

The Iliffe Family Charitable Trust

Medical, disability, heritage, education

£195,000 (2005/06)
Beneficial area UK and Worldwide.

Barn Close, Yattendon, Berkshire
RG18 0UX

Correspondent The Secretary to the
Trustees

Trustees *N G E Petter; G A Bremner;
Lord Iliffe; Hon. Edward Iliffe.*

CC Number 273437

Information available Full accounts
were on file at the Charity Commission.

General The trust gives grants towards
groups concerned with medical causes,
disability, heritage and education. The
bulk of the grants made are to charities
already known to the trustees, to which
funds are committed from year to year.
Other donations are made for a wide
range of charitable purposes in which
the trust has a special interest.

In 2005/06 the trust had assets of
£1.4 million and an income of £193,000.
Grants totalled £195,000 and were
broken down as follows, shown with
examples of beneficiaries in each
category:

Education – £29,000 in 5 grants
SCA Educational Trust (£12,500);
Bradfield Greek Theatre Project
(£10,000); Life Education Centres
(£5,000); Bishopsgate School/GOSH
(£1,000); and Basildon C of E Primary
School (£100).

Medical – £52,000 in 5 grants
Cystic Fibrosis Trust (£25,000);
Macmillan Cancer Relief (£12,750);
University of Cambridge Veterinary
School Trust (£7,500); Priors Court
Foundation (£5,000); Parkinsons Society
(£250).

Religious – £24,000 in 3 grants
St Bride's (£20,000); Yattendon and
Frilsham Christian Stewardship (£3,000);
and Norwich Cathedral Trust (£1,000).

Welfare – £42,000 in 10 grants
Berkshire Community Foundation
(£15,000); Jubilee Sailing Trust and
Arthur Rank Centre (£10,000 each);
Saxongate (£2,500); Marine Society &
Sea Cadets, Rural Housing Trust and
Save the Children Fund (£1,000 each);
NABS (£500); Lord Leycester's Hospital
(£300); and Royal British Legion (£100).

Conservation – £25,000 in 2 grants
Game Conservancy (£15,000); and Save
the Rhino International (£10,000).

Heritage – £22,500 in 2 grants
National Maritime Museum (£12,500);
and Royal Horticultural Society
(£10,000).

Exclusions No grants to individuals
and rarely to non-registered charities.

Applications In writing to the
correspondent. Only successful

applications will be acknowledged.
Grants are considered at ad hoc meetings
of the trustees, held throughout the year.

The Incorporated Church Building Society

Living churches benefiting Anglicans

£150,000 available (2007)

Beneficial area England, Wales, Isle
of Man and Channel Islands.

The Historic Churches Preservation
Trust, 31 Newbury Street, London
EC1A 7HU

Tel. 020 7600 6090 **Fax** 020 7796 2442

Email grants@historicchurches.org.uk

Correspondent The Grants Manager

Trustee *The Committee of Clergy and
Laymen.*

CC Number 212752

Information available Information was
provided by the trust.

General Providing grants to help
towards repair projects to Anglican
churches. Loans or grants towards the
building of new Anglican churches and
the enlargement of worship areas.

In 2006 it had assets of £815,000 and an
income of £49,000. Grants were made to
30 churches and totalled £127,500. The
majority were for repairs with two grants
awarded toward the building of new
Anglican churches.

In 2007 the sum of £150,000 was
available for distribution.

Exclusions Aid is limited to actual
church and chapel buildings. Repairs are
limited to essential fabric repairs.
Enlarging is restricted to the worship
area.

Applications By email or post to The
Historic Churches Preservation Trust
(HCPT) using their application forms.
Application packs are available on the
HCPT website at
www.historicchurches.org.uk.
Application packs are also available by
post.

In writing, by email or post. Applicants
are expected to submit a full set of

accounts and to show that they cannot
afford to carry out the work without the
society's help.

For churches looking for £15,000 or less
to complete their project, 'fast track'
grants are awarded at meetings held
every other month.

The Ingram Trust

General

£387,000 (2004/05)

Beneficial area UK and overseas,
especially Surrey.

c/o 8th Floor, 101 Wigmore Street,
London W1U 1QU

Correspondent Joan Major,
Administrator

Trustees *C J Ingram; Mrs J E Ingram; Ms
C M Maurice.*

CC Number 1040194

Information available Accounts were
on file at the Charity Commission.

General The trust's policies are as
follows:

- it selects a limited number of charities
  which it commits itself to support for
  three to five years
- it prefers to support specific projects
  which can include identifiable costs
  for special services provided by the
  charity or equipment that is required
- beneficiaries will generally be major
  UK-wide or international charities
  together with some local ones in the
  county of Surrey
- the majority of grants will be made for
  periods of 3–4 years at a time in order
  better to assess grant applications and
  monitor progress
- the only overseas aid charities which
  are considered are those dedicated to
  encouraging self-help and providing
  more permanent solutions to
  problems
- no animal charities are considered
  except those concerned with wildlife
  conservation.

In 2004/05 the trust had assets of
£13 million, an income of £399,000 and
made grants totalling £387,000.

There were 27 grants made in the year,
the beneficiaries of the 11 largest
donations went to Bart's Women's
Cancer Appeal (£90,000), WWF UK
(£50,000), Almeida Theatre and Shelter
(£35,000 each), NSPCC – West Sussex

Children's Services Team (£30,000), ACTIONAID and Queen Elizabeth Foundation for Disabled People (£25,000 each), Royal National Theatre – Education Department (£20,000) and Alzheimer's Society, the Howard League and St Mungos (£10,000 each).

Other beneficiaries included National Youth Orchestra of Great Britain (£8,000), Disasters Emergency Committee (£7,000), Disability Challengers, LEPRA, Rainbow Trust – respite care and SouthEast Cancer Care (£6,000 each), Cherry Trees – respite care (£5,000), and Countryside Foundation for Education, the Princess Alice Hospice and the Woodland Trust (£3,000 each).

Exclusions No grants to non-registered charities or to individuals. No charities specialising in overseas aid are considered except those dedicated to encouraging self-help or providing more permanent solutions. No animal charities except those concerned with wildlife conservation.

Applications In writing to the correspondent, although the trust states that it receives far more worthy applications than it is able to support.

The Inland Waterways Association

Inland waterways

£104,000 (2005)
Beneficial area UK and Ireland.

c/o IWA Head Office, PO Box 114, Rickmansworth WD3 1ZY
Tel. 01923 711114 **Fax** 01923 897000
Email iwa@waterways.org.uk
Website www.waterways.org.uk
Correspondent The Chairman of the IWA Restoration Committee
Trustee *The Council of the Association.*
CC Number 212342
Information available Accounts were on file at the Charity Commission.

General The trust supports organisations promoting the restoration of inland waterways (i.e. canal and river navigations).

It makes grants for:

1 construction, especially works relating to the restoration of navigation such as locks, bridges, aquaducts, culverts, weirs, pumps, excavation, dredging, lining and so on
2 administration – support for a particular purpose, such as a project officer, a funding appeal or for promotional literature or events
3 professional services, such as funding of feasibility studies or detailed work on engineering, economic or environmental issues
4 land purchase
5 research on matters affecting waterway restoration, including original research, reviews of research undertaken by others and literature reviews
6 education, such as providing information to local authorities or agencies to promote the nature and benefits of waterway restoration.

In 2005 the development fund made grants totalling £104,000.

Grant beneficiaries included: British Waterways – Froghall Basin Restoration (£21,000); Surrey and Hampshire Canal Society (£20,000); Cotswold Canals Trust (£15,000); Wendover Arm Trust (£14,000); Shropshire Union Canal Society (£10,000); Barnsley Dearne and Doves Canal Trust (£5,000); British Waterways – Bedford and Milton Keynes Link Study, Environment Agency – the Fens Waterways Link Study, Horncastle and Tattershall Canal and Inland Waterways Protection Society (£2,000 each); and Pocklington Canal Amenity Society General Restoration (£700).

Exclusions No grants to individuals. No retrospective grants for projects where expenditure has already been incurred or committed.

Applications In writing to the correspondent. Applications should comply with the *Guidelines for Applicants*, also available from the correspondent. Each applicant should provide a full description of its proposal, show that the organisation can maintain a satisfactory financial position and demonstrate that it is capable of undertaking the proposed project.

Applications for up to £2,000 are assessed under a simplified procedure – each application should demonstrate that the grant would be used to initiate or sustain a restoration scheme or significantly benefit a specific small project.

Applications for over £2,000 should demonstrate that the grant would be applied to one of the types of projects (1–6). Applicants should also demonstrate the extent to which the project satisfies one or more of the following conditions:

- the grant would unlock (lever) a grant several times larger from another body
- the grant would not replace grants available from other sources
- the project does not qualify for grants from major funding sources
- the grant would enable a key project to be undertaken which would have a significant effect on the prospect of advancing the restoration and gaining funds from other sources for further restoration projects
- the result of the project would have a major influence over the progress of a number of other restoration projects
- The Inland Waterways Association Restoration Committee would have a major influence in the management of the project, including monitoring of expenditure.

The Inlight Trust

Religion

£110,000 (2005/06)
Beneficial area UK.

PO Box 2, Liss, Hampshire GU33 6YP
Correspondent The Trustees
Trustees *Sir T Lucas; Mrs W Collett; M Meakin; S Neil; R Wolfe; D Hawkins; Mrs J Hayward.*
CC Number 236782
Information available Accounts were on file at the Charity Commission.

General The trust makes grants for the advancement of religion only. It states that its funding priorities are: 'To make donations on an undenominational basis to charities providing valuable contributions to spiritual development and charities concerned with spiritual healing and spiritual growth through religious retreats.'

Grants are usually one-off for a specific project or part of a project. Bursary schemes may also be supported. Core funding and/or salaries are rarely considered.

In 2005/06 it had assets of £5.3 million, which generated an income of £212,000. Grants were made to 18 organisations totalling £110,000.

The main beneficiaries were: UHB Charities, Birmingham (£25,000); Kagyu Samye Dzong – Sandhurst (£13,000); and Gaia House – Newton Abbot, the

Holy Island Project – Dumfriesshire and St Peter's Grange Appeal – Gloucester (£10,000 each).

Other beneficiaries included: Haughland House – Orkney and the Religious Society of Friends – Nottingham (£5,000 each); Prestbury and Pittville Youth, Cheltenham (£3,000); Atisha Buddhist Centre – Darlington and L'Arche – Keighley (£2,500 each); and King Edward Orthodox Trust – Woking (£1,000).

Exclusions Grants are made to registered charities only. Applications from individuals, including students, are ineligible. No grants are made in response to general appeals from large national organisations. Grants are seldom available for church buildings.

Applications In writing to the correspondent including details of the need the intended project is designed to meet plus an outline budget and the most recent available annual accounts of the charity. Only applications from eligible bodies are acknowledged. Applications must be accompanied by a copy of your trust deed or of your entry in the Charity Commission register. They are considered four times a year. Only successful applicants are informed.

The Inman Charity

See below

£265,000 (2005)
Beneficial area UK.

Payne Hicks Beech, 10 New Square, Lincoln's Inn, London WC2A 3QG

Correspondent The Trustees

Trustees *A L Walker; Miss B M A Strother; M R Matthews; Prof. J D Langdon.*

CC Number 261366

Information available Full accounts were on file at the Charity Commission.

General 'The directors operate a grant-giving policy, providing funds for such charitable objective or institution as the directors think fit. In addition to supporting a wide range of charitable organisations, the charity makes a regular payment (normally £15,000 per annum) to the Victor Inman Bursary Fund at Uppingham School of which the settlor had been a lifelong supporter.' The directors aim to make grants

totalling approximately £225,000 per year. Previously grants have been given in the areas of social welfare, disability, older people and hospices.

In 2005 it had assets of £5.2 million generating an income of £169,000. Grants to 71 organisations totalled £265,000.

By far the largest grant was £40,000 to DEC Tsunami Eathquake Appeal. After the grant of £14,000 to Uppingham School – Victor Inman Bursary Fund, remaining donations were in the range of £1,000 to £7,500. Beneficiaries included: Counsel & Care for the Elderly, Gurkha Welfare Trust, Help the Hospices and Vitalise (£7,500 each); Defeating Deafness – the Hearing Research Trust and St Richard's Hospice (£5,000 each); the Brain Research Trust, British Eye Research Foundation, CORE Fighting Gut and Liver Disease, Chronic Fatigue Syndrome Research Foundation and Kings College London Centre for Cell and Integrated Biology (£4,000 each), British Lung Foundation (£3,500); Parkinson's Disease Society, Petworth Cottage Nursing Home and Saffron Walden Day Centre (£3,000 each); Elizabeth Fitzroy Support, Lindfield Christian Care Home and the Prostate Cancer Charity (£2,500 each); Volunteer Link Scheme (£2,000); and the British Stammering Association and Write Away (£1,000 each).

Exclusions No grants to individuals.

Applications In writing to the correspondent accompanied by the charity's latest report and full accounts. Applications should contain the following: aims and objectives of the charity; nature of the appeal; total target if for a specific project; contributions received against target; registered charity number; any other relevant factors.

The Worshipful Company of Innholders General Charity Fund

General

£56,000 (2004/05)
Beneficial area UK.

Innholders' Hall, 30 College Street, London EC4R 2RH

Tel. 020 7236 6703 **Fax** 020 7236 0059

Email mail@innholders.co.uk

Correspondent The Clerk

Trustee *The Worshipful Company of Innholders.*

CC Number 270948

Information available Accounts were on file at the Charity Commission.

General This trust supports children and young people, older people and education and training, particularly regarding the hotel industry.

In 2004/05 it had assets of £145,000 and an income of £36,000, which included £20,000 in donations received. Grants were made totalling £56,000.

Most of the funds were given towards the 'welfare of the young' (£33,000) and Master Innholders' Scholarships (£20,000).

Exclusions No grants to individuals.

Applications In writing to the correspondent, including the reason for applying and current financial statements and so on.

International Bar Association Educational Trust

Legal profession

£93,000 to organisations (2005)
Beneficial area UK and developing countries.

1 Stephen Street, London, WIT 1AT

Email educationaltrust@int-bar.org

Website www.ibanet.org

Correspondent Elaine Owen, Executive Assistant

Trustees *Francis Neate; Julie Onslow-Cole; Keith Baker; Christopher Rees; Hugh Stubbs; Charles Lawton; Diana Benjamin.*

CC Number 287324

Information available Accounts were on file at the Charity Commission.

General The trust's objectives are to advance legal education, to promote the study of law, and to promote research into common legal problems and disseminate useful results, with an emphasis on grants to developing countries.

It describes its grant-making policy as follows: 'The trust funds scholarship programmes typically through institutions rather than by individual application; the production and dissemination of legal reports and newsletters where topical information is being addressed (such as the development of *legalbrief* electronic newsletter across Africa); and detailed investigations into worldwide legal matters (such as implementation of the death penalty).'

In 2005 the trust had assets of £121,000 and an income of £70,000, including £63,000 from donations. Grants totalled £122,000, of which £30,000 went to individuals. Grants to 11 organisations were broken down as follows:

Advancing legal education	£37,000
Promoting the study of law	£22,000
Promoting research into common legal problems	£34,000

Applications In writing to the correspondent. The trustees meet two or three times a year to consider applications.

The International Foundation for Arts and Culture

Music

£44,000 (2005)
Beneficial area UK.

36 High Street, Cobham, Surrey
KT11 3EB
Correspondent M Randerson, Trustee
Trustees *H Handa, Chair; M Randerson; N Osaki; Dr J L Breen.*
CC Number 1064735
Information available Accounts were on file at the Charity Commission.

General Established in October 1997, the objects of the foundation are to advance the education of the public in music.

In 2005 the foundation had an income of £48,000, mainly from donations. Just one grant was made in the year: £44,000 to SOAS/SISJAC.

Previous beneficiaries have included RNIB, St John Smith Square Concert, Soundscape, Theatre of Royal Holloway College.

Applications This trust does not accept unsolicited applications.

The Inverforth Charitable Trust

General

£68,000 (2005)
Beneficial area UK.

PO Box 6, 47–49 Chelsea Manor Street, London SW3 5RZ
Correspondent The Secretary
Trustees *Elizabeth Lady Inverforth; Lord Inverforth; Hon. Mrs Jonathan Kane.*
CC Number 274132
Information available Accounts were on file at the Charity Commission.

General 'For the three-year period commencing January 2008, the trustees have decided to support 12 selected charities with annual donations. The charities concerned have been notified. Charities supported in the past who have not been selected have also been notified, and for the next three years the funds of the Inverforth Charitable Trust will be fully committed. Charities which have not been selected for donations should not apply to the Inverforth Charitable Trust; any unsolicited applications made in 2008 and thereafter will be discarded and no acknowledgement will be sent.'

In 2004/05 it had assets of £3.6 million, which generated an income of £152,000. Grants were made to 119 organisations totalling £68,000.

Applications No applications are being accepted for the three-year period commencing January 2008.

The Ireland Fund of Great Britain

Welfare, community, education, peace and reconciliation, the arts

£291,000 (2005)
Beneficial area Ireland and Great Britain.

2nd Floor, Wigglesworth House, 69 Southwark Bridge Road, London SE1 9HH
Tel. 020 7378 8373 **Fax** 020 7378 8376
Email greatbritain@irlfunds.org
Website www.irlfunds.org/great_britain
Correspondent Aileen Ross, Director
Trustees *Peter Sutherland, Chair; Kingsley Aikins; Bryan Hayes; Susan Wildman; Seamus McGarry; Basil Geoghegan; Hugo MacNeill; Peter Kiernan; John Rowan; Hon. Kevin Pakenham.*
CC Number 327889
Information available Accounts were on file at the Charity Commission website.

General Founded in 1976 by Sir Anthony O'Reilly and a number of key American businessmen, The Ireland Fund is an international charitable organisation operating in 11 countries and has raised over $300 million for worthy causes in Ireland.

The Ireland Fund of Great Britain (IFGB) is dedicated to raising funds to support programmes of peace and reconciliation, arts and culture, education and community development in Ireland and the United Kingdom.

In 2005 the fund had assets of £420,000 an income of £637,000, mainly from fundraising events. Grants totalled £291,000.

Eligibility
IFGB supports projects in the following categories:

- arts and culture
- community development
- education
- peace and reconciliation.

Each category is accorded equal importance.

Arts and culture
IFGB wishes to support excellence and innovation in the arts and culture and especially projects that make the arts more accessible to the wider community. In particular, the IFGB will focus on the following:

- arts/cultural activities applied in settings of socio-economic disadvantage
- arts/ cultural activities applied in educational or health settings
- arts/ cultural activities promoting tolerance and reconciliation.

Community development
IFGB is seeking ways to promote an inclusive and integrated society and to ensure the regeneration of marginalised

sections of the Irish community. IFGB sees the following areas as priorities:

- increasing the capacity of the social economy
- promotion of social inclusion
- promotion of tolerance and diversity.

Education

Investment in education is investment in the future. Economic and social development depends on a well-educated population. For this reason, IFGB will focus on programmes supporting:

- access and progression to further education
- pre-school education
- lifelong learning
- tolerance through education.

Peace and reconciliation

IFGB seeks to support communities working together towards a shared future. The skills and culture of negotiation and compromise need to be honed politically and organisationally within and between communities. To this end, programmes supporting the following areas have been prioritised for assistance:

- citizenship and participation
- a greater understanding of cultural identity within and between communities
- social inclusion.

Typically, grants vary in size between £500 and £5,000.

Beneficiaries in 2005 included: Childline Northern Ireland and Tyneside Irish Social and Welfare Centre (£10,000 each); Greater Shantallow Community Arts (£7,500); London Irish Centre Charity – Missing Persons Service (£6,000); ICAP West Midlands, Irish Centre Housing and Irish Diaspora Foundation (£5,000 each); Irish in Greenwich (£4,000); Southwark Irish Arts and Culture Youth Project (£3,500); Irish Women's Theatre (£3,000); Camden Elderly Irish Network (£2,500); British Association for Irish Studies (£1,100); and Northern Ireland Outward Bound (£1,000).

Exclusions Grants are generally not given for: general administration costs; travel or accommodation costs; payments for buildings or land; general appeals i.e. applications must be made for clearly specified purposes; other grant-making trusts; payments for vehicles; medical expenses. No multi-annual awards.

Applications Application forms and full details of how to apply are available from the IFGB website.

The Irish Youth Foundation (UK) Ltd (incorporating The Lawlor Foundation)

Irish young people

£250,000 (2006)

Beneficial area UK.

The Irish Centre, Blacks Road, Hammersmith, London W6 9DT

Tel. 020 8748 9640

Email info@iyf.org.uk

Website www.iyf.org.uk

Correspondent The Administrator

Trustees *John O'Neill, Chair; John Dwyer; Fred Hucker; Colin McNicholas; Nessa O'Neill; Virginia Lawlor; Frank Baker; Mary Clancy; Mark Gilbert; David Murray; Jim O'Hara.*

CC Number 328265

Information available Accounts were on file at the Charity Commission.

General Irish Youth Foundation (UK) Ltd merged with the Lawlor Foundation (effective from 30 June 2005). The work of the Lawlor Foundation, towards the advancement of education in Northern Ireland, continues with support for Irish students and educational organisations.

This trust supports organisations anywhere in the UK working with young Irish people aged up to 25 who are socially, educationally or culturally disadvantaged.

A wide range of projects is supported which includes: help for homeless people; employment and training schemes; help for women and children escaping violence; repatriation schemes; help for young offenders; cross community initiatives; help to combat discrimination; professional counselling and advocacy; educational, cultural and social activities; and drug rehabilitation.

Grants range from £500 to £25,000 and are awarded annually. Grants for organisations in England, Scotland and Wales fall into the following three categories:

- Small grants for up to £2,500
- Medium grants for over £2,500 and under £12,000

- Large grants for one year or more ranging from £12,000 to £25,000.

The Irish Youth Foundation (UK) and the Irish Youth Foundation (Ireland) have established a joint fund to provide support for community and voluntary groups in Northern Ireland. Grants for organisations in Northern Ireland are up to £5,000.

In 2006 the trust had assets of £3.1 million and an income of£376,000. Grants totalled £250,000.

Beneficiaries in the UK (excluding Northern Ireland) included: Bristol Playbus, Camden Women's Aid , Irish Community Care – Merseyside, London Irish Centre and New Horizon Youth Centre – London (£12,000 each); Brent Irish Advisory Service (£10,000); London Irish Women's Centre (£9,000); Hammersmith and Fulham Irish Centre (£6,000); the Brandon Centre – London and St Michael's Irish Centre – Liverpool (£5,000 each); Irish Commission for Prisoners Overseas and Irish Music Project – Leeds (£4,000); Tyneside Irish Cultural Society – Newcastle-upon-Tyne (£2,000); and Artswave – Wales, Haringey Irish Cultural and Community Centre – London, London Irish Centre (£500 each).

Beneficiaries in Northern Ireland included: St Mary's Christian Brothers' Grammar School – Belfast (£6,000); Ardoyne Youth Club – Belfast (£4,000); and Corpus Christi Youth Centre – Belfast, Hazelwood Integrated College – Belfast, Lisneal College – Londonderry, REACH ACROSS – Derry, Voice of Young People in Care – Belfast (£3,000 each).

Exclusions The foundation generally does not support: projects for people over 25; general appeals; large/national charities; academic research; alleviating deficits already incurred; individuals; capital bids; or overseas travel.

Applications Applications are assessed on an annual basis and application forms are only available during the annual round either on the website or by request. The application period is short, with forms being available in October through to the end of November. Applications are considered in February and applicants notified in March/April. Applicants should photocopy and send six copies of the completed form if they are in Northern Ireland and seven copies if they are applying from elsewhere. Applications are considered in January and all applicants notified in February. Applications are assessed on the following requirements: need; continuity; track record/evaluation; disadvantaged young people; innovativeness; funding sources; and budgetary control. Faxed or emailed applications are not considered. Unsolicited applications outside the annual round of grant applications will not be considered or acknowledged.

The Ironmongers' Foundation

General, see below

£89,000 (2004/05)

Beneficial area UK with some preference for Inner London.

Ironmongers' Hall, Barbican, London EC2Y 8AA

Tel. 020 7776 2311 **Fax** 020 7600 3519

Email helen@ironhall.co.uk

Website www.ironhall.co.uk

Correspondent Helen Sant, Charities Administrator

Trustee *Worshipful Ironmongers' Company.*

CC Number 238256

Information available Accounts were on file at the Charity Commission.

General 'The Ironmongers' Company aims to help people who are disadvantaged to improve their ability to make the most of life. We wish to support projects that develop and nurture the motivation and skills necessary to take advantage of opportunities.'

Grants will be made for projects that meet all of the following criteria:

1 Children and young people up to the age of 25
2 Educational activities
3 Specific projects with clear aims and objectives to be met within a planned timescale.

Most grants are in the region of £1,000 to £5,000. The trustees will consider making grants over more than one year to longer-term projects, subject to a satisfactory evaluation of progress at the end of each year. The company's support should make a recognisable difference, therefore preference will be given to requests which cover a significant element of the cost and to those from smaller organisations.

In 2004/05 the fund had assets of £1.8 million, an income of £172,000 and made grants totalling £89,000.

The accounts listed beneficiaries in receipt of awards over £1,000 each, divided as follows:

Universities and industry – £13,000
Six universities received grants of either £6,000, £3,500 or £3,000 each. A grant of £2,100 was also made to British Institute of Foundrymen.

Restoration – £32,000
Grants included those to St Edmundsbury Cathedral (£11,000) and Ashburnham Furnace (£8,000).

Other organisations – £43,000
Beneficiaries included Saltash Community School (£15,000), Museum of London (£5,000), Lord Mayor's Appeal (£4,000), Sea Cadets (£3,700), Binoh Trust (£3,400), Guildhall School of Music and Drama (£2,100), Children's Adventure Farm Trust (£1,600), Arkwright Scholarship and Truro Cathedral (£1,500 each) and St Botolph's Church (£1,000).

In the previous year the sum of £2,000 was given towards 'crafts'.

Exclusions No grants towards:

• large projects towards which any contribution from the Company would have limited impact
• general appeals or circulars
• replacement of statutory funds
• general running costs (A reasonable proportion of overheads will be accepted as part of project costs.)
• counselling
• course fees for professionals
• medical research
• fundraising events and sponsorship
• retrospective appeals and projects starting before the date of the relevant committee meeting.

Applications The Company's 'Grant Application Summary Sheet' must be completed and returned including a description of the project, of no more than three A4 pages. Summary sheets can be downloaded from the fund's website.

The Appeals Committee meets twice a year in March and October. The deadlines for receipt of applications are 31 January and 31 August respectively. Please note that applications are not accepted by email.

Grants must be spent within twelve months from the date of the award.

The ISA Charity

See below

£39,000 (2005/06)

Beneficial area UK.

Bourton House, Bourton On The Hill, Moreton-In-Marsh, Gloucestershire GL56 9AE

Website www.isacharity.net/

Correspondent R Paice, Trustee

Trustees *R Paice; Mrs M Paice; Miss A Paice.*

CC Number 326882

Information available Accounts were on file at the Charity Commission, but without a list of grants. Detailed information is available on the charity's website.

General 'Founded in 1985 by Richard Paice, the ISA Charity supports causes related to the arts, health and education in the broadest sense. This can include both UK and overseas initiatives. The charity selects various organisations which help to find the individual beneficiaries. Up to £50,000 is distributed each year.'

In 2005/06 the charity had assets of £1.3 million, an income of £159,000, including £100,000 from ISA Holdings Limited. Grants totalled £39,000.

Applications The charity's website included the following statement: 'The charity adopts a venture philanthropy approach and identifies its own projects. It does not accept funding requests from individuals, organisations or other charities. As a consequence it will not acknowledge any unsolicited funding requests.'

J A R Charitable Trust

Roman Catholic, education, welfare

£65,000 (2005/06)

Beneficial area Worldwide.

c/o Vernor Miles and Noble, 5 Raymond Buildings, Gray's Inn, London WC1R 5DD

Correspondent Philip R Noble, Trustee

Trustees *Philip R Noble; Revd William Young; Revd Paschal Ryan.*

CC Number 248418

Information available Accounts were on file at the Charity Commission.

General The trust states in its annual report that it makes grants towards: Roman Catholic missionaries, churches and other causes; education for people under 30; and food and clothing for people over 55 who are in need. In practice, the trust gives regular grants to support mainly Roman Catholic organisations.

In 2005/06 the trust had assets of £2.3 million which generated an income of £75,000. Grants were made to 34 organisations totalling £65,000.

Beneficiaries included: Westminster Cathedral (£5,000); the Passage (£4,000); United Westminster Schools (£3,500); St Bede's School, St Joseph's Hospice, Venerable English College and Youth 2000 (£3,000 each); Liverpool Archdiocesan Youth Pilgrimage (£2,500); Cardinal Hume Centre, Catholic Children's Society Brentwood, Jesuit Missions, Nazareth House, Providence Row and White Sisters (£2,000 each); Archdiocese of Liverpool (£1,500); CAFOD, Little Sisters of the Poor and Society of Jesus (£1,000 each); and Dans La Rue (£500).

Exclusions The trust does not normally support a charity unless it is known to the trustees. It does not support individuals.

Applications In writing to the correspondent. Please note that the trust's funds are fully committed to regular beneficiaries and it states that there is very little, if any, for unsolicited appeals. In order to save administration costs replies are not sent to unsuccessful applicants.

J I Charitable Trust

General

£240,000 (2005)

Beneficial area England and Wales.

20 Tudor Close, Woodford Green, Essex IG8 0LF

Correspondent P Katz

Trustees *J M Isaacs: Mrs J M Isaacs; A R Isaacs.*

CC Number 1059865

Information available Accounts were on file at the Charity Commission.

General In 2004/05 this trust had an income of £1 million, mainly from donations. Grants totalled £240,000. Funds of £1.6 million were carried forward.

There were 19 grants made during the year. The two largest grants went to Jewish Care (£100,000) and Community Security Trust (£50,000).

Other beneficiaries included Lehman Brothers Foundation (£28,000), Drugsline Chabad (£15,000), Lubavitch of Edgeware (£12,000), Prep for Prep (£8,200), the Evelina Childrens Hospital Appeal, Princess Margarita of Romania Trust and the Royal Marsden Cancer Campaign (£5,000 each), Jewish National Fund Charitable Trust (£2,500), Community Trading Limited (£1,500), Sparks (£1,300), Community Concern (£1,000), the Mark Fisher Trust (£600) and British Heart Foundation (£250).

Applications In writing to the correspondent.

The J R S S T Charitable Trust

Democracy and social justice

£225,000 (2005)

Beneficial area UK.

The Garden House, Water End, York YO30 6WQ

Tel. 01904 625744 **Fax** 01904 651502

Email info@jrrt.org.uk

Website www.jrrt.org.uk

Correspondent Tina Walker

Trustees *Archibald J Kirkwood, Chair; Christine J Day; Christopher J Greenfield; Diana E Scott; David T Shutt (Lord Shutt of Greetland); Paedar Cremin; Mandy Cormack.*

CC Number 247498

Information available Accounts were on file at the Charity Commission.

General The trust was originally endowed by the non-charitable Joseph Rowntree Reform Trust Ltd. It will consider and sometimes instigate charitable projects which relate specifically to the work of The Joseph Rowntree Reform Trust Ltd in supporting the development of an increasingly democratic and socially just society in Great Britain.

In 2005 the trust had assets of £3.7 million and an income of £108,000. Grants totalled £225,000.

There were 27 grants made during the year. Beneficiaries of grants of £1,000 or more included: the POWER Inquiry (£91,000); Democratic Audit (£43,000); Searchlight Educational Trust (£25,000); Solent People's Theatre (£15,000); University College London (£14,000); Compass (£8,100); New Politics Network (£5,000); and New Zimbabwe.com and Zimbabwe Association Ltd (£3,000 each).

Grants of £1,000 or less were made to 15 organisations and totalled £6,100.

Exclusions No student grants are funded.

Applications The trustees meet quarterly. They do not invite applications.

Jacobs Charitable Trust

Jewish charities, the arts

£276,000 (2005/06)

Beneficial area Unrestricted.

9 Nottingham Terrace, London NW1 4QB

Correspondent The Rt Hon Lord Jacobs, Chair

Trustees *Lord Jacobs, Chair; Lady Jacobs.*

CC Number 264942

Information available Accounts were on file at the Charity Commission.

General In 2005/06 the trust had an income of £784,000, mostly from donations and gave grants totalling £276,000.

There were 56 grants made during the year, of which 31 were for £1,000 or more. Beneficiaries of the largest grants included: Central Synagogue Central Charities Fund (£36,000); Jewish Care (£30,000); Haifa University and London School of Economics (£28,000 each); Norton Museum of Art (£27,000); Tate Foundation (£25,000); and Community Security Trust (£20,000).

Other beneficiaries included: Israel Philharmonic Orchestra Foundation (£14,000); Royal Academy of Arts and Royal Opera House (£10,000 each); Norwood Ltd (£7,500); Board of Deputies of British Jews (£5,000); American Friends of the Israel Museum

(£2,900); Council for a Beautiful Israel (£1,800); and Barnardos, MDA UK, Princess Alice Hospice, Saving Faces and Tribe (£1,000 each).

There were 25 grants under £1,000 each totalling £8,400.

Applications In writing to the correspondent.

The Dorothy Jacobs Charity

Jewish care, medical

About £45,000 (2005)
Beneficial area UK.

Heywards, 6th Floor, Remo House, 310–312 Regent Street, London W1B 3BS
Correspondent R H Moss, Trustee
Trustees *R H Moss; A M Alexander.*
CC Number 328430

Information available Accounts were on file at the Charity Commission, but without a grants list or a narrative report.

General The trust was established in 1989 to provide 'relief of sickness by provision of medical aid and undertaking of medical research, advancement of education and relief of older people and infirm'.

The trust can only support the 15 nominated charities which are listed in the trust deed – three hospitals, four Jewish charities, three cancer-related charities and five others: Arthritis and Rheumatism Council, BBC Children in Need, British Red Cross, Oxfam and Scope. Other charities cannot be supported.

In 2004 the trust had an income of £14,000 and a total expenditure of £48,000.

Exclusions Any charity that is not listed in the trust deed.

Applications The trust states that it cannot accept unsolicited applications.

The Ruth and Lionel Jacobson Trust (Second Fund) No. 2

Jewish, medical, children, disability

£48,000 (2005/06)
Beneficial area UK, with a preference for north east England

14 The Grainger Suite, Dobson House, The Regent Centre, Newcastle-upon-Tyne NE3 3PF
Correspondent The Trustees
Trustees *Irene Ruth Jacobson; Malcolm Jacobson.*
CC Number 326665

Information available Accounts were on file at the Charity Commission.

General The trust supports UK charities and organisations based in the north east of England. The trust states that it supports the advancement of Jewish religious education and healthcare charities. Charities outside the north east of England are supported whenever possible.

In 2005/06 the trust had assets of £1.2 million, an income of £46,000 and made grants totalling £48,000.

The four main grants in the year went to: United Jewish Israel Appeal (£15,000); Hadassah Medical Relief Association UK (£3,000); Multiple Sclerosis Research Centre (£2,800); and Morbei Torah Trust (£2,500).

Grants to 102 other institutions not exceeding £500 each totalled £25,000.

Exclusions No grants for individuals. Only registered charities will be supported.

Applications In writing to the correspondent. Please enclose an sae. Applications are considered every other month.

The James Trust

Christianity

£58,000 (2005/06)
Beneficial area UK and overseas.

27 Radway Road, Upper Shirley, Southampton, Hampshire SO15 7PL
Tel. 023 8078 8249
Correspondent R J Todd, Trustee
Trustees *R J Todd; P Smith; G Blue.*
CC Number 800774

Information available Accounts were on file at the Charity Commission.

General Principally, the trust has a preference for supporting Christian organisations. It operates primarily as a channel for the giving of a small group of donors. Grants are primarily to churches and Christian organisations involved in overseas development and work with young people.

In 2005/06 it had an income of £31,000 and made grants to 52 organisations totalling £58,000. Donations were in the range of £30 and £10,000.

Beneficiaries of larger grants included Archbishops' Council (£10,000), Above Bar Church – Southampton (£7,700), Food for the Hungry (£5,100), Crusaders (£4,100), UCCF (£3,600), Interserve (£2,300), Christ Church Purley (£2,200), Tear Fund (£1,900), St John's – Copthorne (£1,400), Christian Aid (£1,300) and Ambassadors in Sport, Lamb Health Care Foundation and Speke Baptist Church (£1,000 each).

Other beneficiaries included Church Missionary Society, Lambeth Partnership and Scripture Union (£500 each), Langham Partnership (£300), Cancer Research and Mission Aviation Fellowship (£200 each), Feed the Minds, Kairos Trust and Toybox (£100 each), ReSource (£50) and Amnesty International (£30).

Exclusions No grants to individuals not personally known to the trustees.

Applications In writing to the correspondent. Unsolicited applications are not acknowledged.

The John Jarrold Trust

Social welfare, arts, education, environment/ conservation, medical research, churches, developing countries

£95,000 to organisations (2006).

Beneficial area UK and overseas, but mostly Norfolk.

Jarrold and Sons Ltd, Whitefriars, Norwich NR3 1SH

Tel. 01603 677360

Email caroline.jarrold@jarrold.com

Website www.jarrold.com

Correspondent Caroline Jarrold, Secretary

Trustees A C Jarrold, Chair; R E Jarrold; P J Jarrold; Mrs D J Jarrold; Mrs J Jarrold; K W Jarrold; Mrs W A L Jarrold; L C Jarrold.

CC Number 242029

Information available Full accounts were available from the Charity Commission.

General The trust supports a wide range of organisations including churches, medical, arts, environment/ conservation, welfare and overseas aid. It prefers to support specific projects, rather than contribute to general funding. In practice, most of the funds are given in Norfolk. In 2006 the trust had assets of £1.4 million and an income of £90,000. Grants were made to organisations totalling £95,000 and were broken down as follows:

Education
Grants were made to the BA Festival of Science (£2,600) and to the Friends of Norwich Museum (£200).

Special school status
Recipients included Earlham High School and Heartsease High School Trust (£1,000 each).

The arts
Recipients included the Norfolk and Norwich Festival (£4,000) and Northern Ballet and Maddermarket Theatre (£1,000 each).

Social and welfare
Beneficiaries included The Prince's Trust (£4,000), OPEN Norwich Youth Venue and the Big C (£2,000 each), SCOPE and Rotary House (£1,000 each), the Green Light Trust (£500), Norfolk Wildlife Trust (£300) and Picture Shotesham and the Sailors' Families Society (£100 each).

Environment
Grants were made to the Woodland Trust Trafalgar Woods Project (£1,000), British Trust for Ornithology (£500) and the Little Ouse Headwaters Project (£250).

Medical
Donations were made to Macmillan Cancer Relief (£2,000), the Arthritis Research Campaign and the Samantha Dickinson Research Trust (£1,000) and Brain Tumour UK (£500).

Developing countries
Beneficiaries were Basic Needs and WaterAid (£1,000 each) and Gurkha Welfare Trust (£250)

Churches and historic buildings
Recipients were St Peter's Church – Cringleford (£1,000) and St Thomas Church – Heigham (£100).

Exclusions Educational purposes that should be supported by the state will not be helped by the trust. Local groups outside Norfolk are very unlikely to be supported unless there is a personal connection to the trust. Individual educational programmes and gap year projects are not supported.

Applications Trustees meet in January and June each year and applications should be made in writing by the end of November and April respectively. Grants of up to £250 can be made between meetings.

Rees Jeffreys Road Fund

Road and transport research and education

£215,000 (2005)

Beneficial area UK.

Merriewood, Horsell Park, Woking, Surrey GU21 4LW

Tel. 01483 750758 **Fax** 01483 750758

Email briansmith@reesjeffreys.co.uk

Correspondent Brian Smith, Fund Secretary

Trustees David Bayliss, Chair; June Bridgeman; P W Bryant; M N T Cottell; Prof. S Glaister; M J Kendrick; Prof. J Wootton.

CC Number 217771

Information available Report and accounts with full grants list, explanation of grants, and descriptions of the trust's history and objects provided by the trust.

General The late William Rees Jeffreys established the trust in 1950, shortly after he wrote *The King's Highway*. He campaigned extensively for the improvement of better roads and transport and was described by Lloyd George as 'the greatest authority on roads in the United Kingdom and one of the greatest in the world', due to his unrivalled expertise in this field.

In 2005 the fund had assets of £6.9 million and an income of £164,000. Grants ranging between £100 to £24,000 totalled £215,000 and were broken down as follows:

- research and general – £67,000
- education – £133,300
- land adjoining highways – £22,700
- other education projects – £5,200.

The fund gives financial support for research to improve the quality and efficiency of roads and their use by vehicles, cyclists, pedestrians and public transport'.

The trust's priorities are:

- Education of transport professionals, largely through financial support for teaching staff and bursaries for postgraduate studies. The trust is concerned about the supply of trained professionals and has launched a study of future requirements.
- Appropriate research into all aspects of roads, road usage and road traffic, in accordance with the fund's objectives – this commands a large share of the fund's budget. The trust develops its own research programmes as well as responding to proposals from recognised agencies and researchers. Proposals are assessed against prevailing transport issues, such as environmental questions, congestion, modal choice and resource development.
- Roadside environment. Applications for the provision of roadside rests are welcome, while support for the work of country wildlife trusts for improving land adjoining main roads is also maintained. The trust is not normally able to buy land or to fund improvements to roads, footpaths or cycle tracks.

The trust will support projects and pump priming for longer-term ventures for up to a maximum of five years. Operational or administrative staff costs are rarely supported. In almost all cases applicants are expected to provide or arrange match funding.

Research and general

Grants from £2,000 to £24,000 examples included: £24,000 to PACTS Road Casualty Reduction in the UK; £5,000 to Council for National Parks – sustainable transport and Young TranNet website; £4,000 to Sports Turf Research Institute – roadside drainage; and £2,000 to Motorway Archive Trust Volume 3 – building the network.

Improvment of roadsides and environment

Grants were distributed as follows: £10,000 to Cairngorm National Park-lay-bye and entry points; £4,000 to The Lightbox – roadside garden; £3,000 to Cornwall Wildlife Trust – green routes; £2,500 to Bedfordshire Wildlife Trust – Glebe Meadows; £2,000 each to Devon Wildlife Trust – Bovey Heathfield and Norfolk Wildlife Trust – Weeting Heath; and £100 to the National Urban Forestry Unit Leesebrook.

Education

This category included a total £133,350 for academic funding; seven postgraduate studentships were awarded for the following institutions: Leeds University, Southampton University, Imperial College and Cardiff University. Grants were given through the Rees Jeffreys Senior Lectureship to the University of Oxford and the University of West of England. In addition, a research project at the University of West of England was given funding called 'The Interaction of non-motorised with other transport modes'. Unfortunately an individual breakdown of this academic funding total was unavailable.

Exclusions Grants are not given to environmental projects not related to highways, individual works for cycle tracks or works of only local application. Also, Operational and administrative staff costs are rarely considered.

Applications There is no set form of application for grants; brief details should be submitted initially to the trustees either by telephone or post. The trustees meet five times in the year, usually in January, April, July, September and November; Trustees 'favour proposals where the outcome will have a national impact rather than local application and where costs are shared with other funding partners'. In general, 'project expenditure (excluding overheads and core funding) is grant-aided'.

The Jenour Foundation

General

£85,000 (2004/05)

Beneficial area UK, with a special interest in Wales.

Deloitte and Touche, Blenhein House, Fitzalan Court, Newport Road, Cardiff CF24 0TS

Correspondent The Trustees

Trustees *Sir P J Phillips; G R Camfield; D M Jones.*

CC Number 256637

Information available Accounts were on file at the Charity Commission.

General This foundation has general charitable purposes, with a preference for Welsh causes.

In 2004/05 the foundation had assets of £2.5 million, an income of £86,000 and made 32 grants totalling £85,000.

Beneficiaries included Atlantic College (£7,000), Cancer Research Wales and Welsh National Opera (£6,000 each), British Heart Foundation, Macmillan Cancer Care Fund and Red Cross International (£5,000 each), Wales Millennium Centre (£4,600), Wales Council for the Blind (£3,500), Army Benevolent Fund, Barnardos, Provincial Grand Lodge of Monmouth and George Thomas Society (£3,000 each), Bath Institute of Medical Engineering (£2,500), British Deaf Association, RNLI – Welsh District and RUKBA (£2,000 each), DEC Tsunami Appeal, Leukaemia Research Fund and St John Ambulance in Wales (£1,000 each) and High Sheriffs Youth Awards and Society for Welfare of Horses and Ponies (£500 each).

Exclusions No support for individuals.

Applications Applications should be in writing and reach the correspondent by February for the trustees' meeting in March.

The Jephcott Charitable Trust

Alleviation of poverty in developing countries, general

£177,000 (2004/05)

Beneficial area UK, developing countries.

Cotley, Streatham Rise, Exeter, Devon EX4 4PE

Website www.jephcottcharitabletrust.org.uk

Correspondent Mrs Meg Harris, Secretary

Trustees *Lady Jephcott, Chair; Judge A North; H Wolley; K Morgan; J Bunnell; Mrs C Thomas.*

CC Number 240915

Information available Accounts were on file at the Charity Commission.

General The trust's funding priorities are:

• population control
• the natural environment
• education
• health.

The trust prefers to support projects which are pump-priming – helping to get an organisation up and running, or make a significant step forward. 'We like to make grants which will make a difference, preference will be given to charities or projects which are having difficulty getting started, or raising funds from other sources. This often means that the trust is funding capital projects, e.g. for equipment or materials, rather than running costs.' It is not usual to make more than one grant to any organisation, preferring to help many new projects to get started.

Grants are made in the range of £2,000 to £10,000, and in exceptional cases only, up to £20,000.

Population control
The trust is prepared to consider support for schemes, particularly educational ones, which help to control excessive growth in population.

The natural environment
The trust has supported a number of projects involved in conserving the natural environment. It does not support projects involving animal welfare or heritage sites or buildings.

Education
Projects will be considered benefiting people of all ages and backgrounds. They

may be able to provide formal education, to teach vocational skills to enhance the possibility of employment, to enhance computer skills, health awareness, distance learning.

Health

A wide range of healthcare projects is supported.

In 2004/05 the trust had assets of £5.3 million, an income of £283,000 and made 27 grants totalling £177,000. Examples of grants listed in the accounts included:

Health

Peru Shantytown (£15,000); Appropriate Technology (£14,000 in two grants); Icare (£12,000); Dental Project Peru (£12,000 in two grants); Devon Aid Korogwe, Goedgedacht Trust and MS Therapy Centre (£10,000 each); CAMDA (£7,000); Derbyshire Children's Holiday Centre and Highway Hospice (£5,000 each); and Eldoret Health and Tigre Trust (£2,000 each).

Educational

Karandusi School – Kenya (£10,000); ADPP Teacher Training College (£7,000); Bahia Street Trust and Dhaka Ahsania Mission (£6,000 each); Cape Academy, South Africa (£5,000); Hand in Hand (£4,500); and EDSA After-School Club (£3,700).

Environmental relief

Berkeley Reforestation Trust (£5,000).

Exclusions The trust does not support:

- organisations whose administrative expenses form more than 15% of their annual income
- individuals
- animal welfare
- heritage.

Projects which require long-term funding are not normally considered. The trust prefers to make one-off donations to get many projects started, rather than support fewer projects or charities over a long period.

Applications Full and detailed guidelines and application forms can be downloaded from the trust's website. Trustees meet twice a year (in April and October) and must have detailed financial information about each project before they will make a decision. Only applications from eligible bodies are acknowledged, when further information about the project may be requested. Monitoring of grant expenditure is usually required.

The Jewish Youth Fund

Jewish youth work

£63,000 (2005/06)

Beneficial area UK.

PO Box 603, Edgware HA8 4EQ
Tel. 020 3209 6006
Email info@jyf.org.uk
Correspondent Peter Shaw, Secretary
Trustees Jonathan Gestetner; Richard McGratty; Lady Morris of Kenwood; Miss Wendy F Pollecoff.
CC Number 251902
Information available Accounts were on file at the Charity Commission.

General The fund's objectives are to promote and protect religious, moral, educational, physical and social interests of young members of the Jewish community in the UK.

In 2005/06 the trust had assets of £2.5 million and an income of £155,000. Grants totalling £63,000 went to 12 organisations, 6 of which were also supported in the previous year.

Beneficiaries were Jewish Lads' and Girls' Brigade (£10,000), LJY Netzer and Redbridge Jewish Youth & Community Centre (£8,000 each), Limmud (£7,000), Bushey Youth Scene, B'nei Akiva, Brady Maccabi Youth and Community Centre and Reform Synagogue Youth Netzer (£5,000 each), AJ6 (£4,000) North Manchester Jewish Youth Project (£2,400), Maccabi Union (£2,000) and Friends of Jewish Servicemen (£1,500).

Exclusions Grants are not made in response to general appeals. Formal education is not supported.

Applications On an application form available from the correspondent, enclosing a copy of the latest accounts and an annual report.

The JMK Charitable Trust

Children's health

£64,000 (2005/06)

Beneficial area Worldwide.

Messrs Chantrey Vellacott DFK, Prospect House, 58 Queen's Road, Reading, Berkshire RG1 4RP

Correspondent The Trustees
Trustees Mrs J M Karaviotis; J Karaviotis.
CC Number 274576
Information available Accounts were on file at the Charity Commission.

General This trust supports registered charities, with a preference for those concerned with children's health.

In 2005/06 the trust had assets of £2.1 million and an income of £67,000. Grants to 14 organisations totalled £64,000.

The two largest grants went to: Royal College of Music (£20,000); and Philharmonia Trust (£10,000).

Other beneficiaries included: National Theatre (£7,500); World Jewish Relief (£6,400); Royal Academy Schools (£6,000); West London Synagogue (£5,000); Royal Academy of Arts (£2,500); Royal Opera House (£3,100); Second Junior Trust (£750); Association Des Amis De L'ope and Les Azuriales Opera Trust (£700 each); Salzburg Festival Trust (£350); and Onslow Neighbourhood Association (£50).

Applications In writing to the correspondent. No acknowledgement of receipt is given.

The Harold Joels Charitable Trust

Jewish

£39,000 (2005/06)

Beneficial area UK and overseas.

11a Arkwright Road, London NW3 6AA
Correspondent H Joels, Trustee
Trustees H Joels; Dr N Joels; Mrs V Joels; N E Joels.
CC Number 206326
Information available Full accounts were on file at the Charity Commission.

General The trust makes grants to Jewish organisations in the UK and US.

In 2005/06 the trust had assets of over £1 million. It had an income of £26,000 and made grants totalling £39,000.

In the UK, 51 grants totalling £19,000 were made. Beneficiaries included: World Jewish Relief (£5,100); David Joels Charitable Trust (£5,000); Jewish National Fund (£1,400); Norwood Ravenswood and Royal Academy Trust (£1,250 each); Royal National Theatre

(£1,000); the Tricycle Theatre Co. (£500); Chai Lifeline Cancer Care (£250); Hampstead Synagogue (£200); Jewish Blind and Disabled, Jewish Care, Jewish Women's Aid, Magen David Adom UK, Operation Wheelchairs Committee and Yad Vashem UK (£100 each); and Jewish Children's Holiday Fund, Macmillan Cancer Research and Shelter (£50 each).

In the US, 41 grants totalling £19,000 were made. Beneficiaries included: Temple Beth Shalom (£5,300); Women's Resource Centre of Sarasota County (£4,300); Florida Studio Theatre (£3,200); Emunah of America (£2,900); Jewish Theological Centre of America (£1,100); American Jewish Committee (£430); Flanzer Jewish Community Centre (£260); Jewish Theological Seminary (£100); Rally for A Cure (£60); and Habitat for Humanity International (£30).

Applications In writing to the correspondent.

The Nicholas Joels Charitable Trust

Jewish, medical welfare, general

About £35,000 (2005/06)
Beneficial area UK and overseas.

66 Wigmore Street, London W1U 2SB
Correspondent N Joels, Trustee
Trustees *N Joels; J Joels; H Joels; Mrs A Joels.*
CC Number 278409
Information available Information had been filed at the Charity Commission.

General The trust makes grants to registered charities only, and from the list of beneficiaries it appears to support Jewish causes and medical and welfare charities. In 2005/06 it had an income of £21,000 and a total expenditure of £36,000. No further information was available for this year.

Previous benficiaries have included Aspire, CMZ Trust, Great Ormond Street Hospital, Habad Orphan Aid Society, JNF Charitable Trust, Norwood, United Jewish Israel, Weizmann Institute, World Jewish Relief and Youth Aliyah Child Rescue.

Applications In writing to the correspondent.

The N B Johnson Charitable Settlement

Education, older people

£36,000 (2002/03)
Beneficial area UK, with a preference for Greater Manchester.

PO Box 165, Manchester M45 7XD
Correspondent Leslie Hyman
Trustees *L Hyman; N B Johnson; Mrs S J Johnson.*
CC Number 277237
Information available Accounts were on file at the Charity Commission up to 2002/03.

General In 2002/03 the trust had assets of £6,400, an income of £32,000 and made grants totalling £36,000. A list of grant beneficiaries was not available.

In 2000/01 beneficiaries included Heathlands (£5,100), Whitefield Hebrew Congregation (£3,500), Community Security Trust (£3,000), Manchester Charitable Trust (£2,000), Elliott Levy Memorial (£1,500) and Whitefield Kollel and Lubavitch Manchester (£1,000 each).

Smaller grants included those to Delamere School and League of Jewish Women (£500 each) and Bay Community and JNF (£250 each).

Applications In writing to the correspondent, however the trust has previously stated that unsolicited applications are not invited.

The Lillie Johnson Charitable Trust

Children, young people who are blind or deaf, medical

£155,000 (2005/06)
Beneficial area UK, with a preference for the West Midlands.

Heathcote House, 136 Hagley Road, Edgbaston, Birmingham B16 9PN
Tel. 0121 454 4141
Correspondent J W Desmond, Trustee
Trustees *V M C Lyttle; P W Adams; J W Desmond; Mrs V C Adams.*
CC Number 326761
Information available Accounts were obtained from the Charity Commission website.

General In 2005/06 the trust had assets of £5.7 million and an income of £191,000. Grants were made totalling £155,000.

There were 44 grants of £1,000 or more listed in the accounts. The largest grants went to: Home from Hospital Care (£30,000); MC Charitable Trust (£20,000); and Web Care (£15,000).

Other beneficiaries included: Birmingham and Midland Operatic Society – Youth (£9,400); Air Ambulance, Arthritis Research UK and Hearts of England Association (£3,500 each); Breast Cancer Campaign, Princes Trust and Pulse (£3,000 each); Family Care Trust and West House School (£2,500 each); Birmingham Focus on Blindness, Cystic Fibrosis Research Fund, Princes Royal Trust, Sense and UK Association for Braille Producers (£2,000 each); and Acorns Children's Hospice, Defeating Deafness, Pathway Project, Rathbone Society, Victim Support and Warwickshire Junior Tennis Foundation (£1,000 each).

Donations under £1,000 each totalled £14,000 and were made to 39 organisations.

Exclusions No support for individuals.

Applications Applications are only considered from charities which are traditionally supported by the trust. The trust stated that it is inundated with applications it cannot support and feels obliged to respond to all of these.

The H F Johnson Trust

Christian education

£88,000 (2005)
Beneficial area Worldwide, but mainly the UK.

PO Box 300, Kingstown Broadway, Carlisle, Cumbria CA3 0QS
Correspondent The Trustees

Trustees *Keith Danby; David Ryan; Libby Kelly; Ian Waterfield.*

CC Number 1050966

Information available Accounts were on file at the Charity Commission.

General Established by trust deed in 1962, the trust's main objective is the advancement of the Christian faith. Most of the funds are given towards distributing bibles and Christian products including books, videos and software to state schools.

In 2005 the sum of £88,000 was spent on supplying bibles and Christian products to schools and Christian organisations that work with schoolchildren.

In 2003 a donation of £125,000 was made to Challenge Literature Fellowship Ltd (a Christian charity that was established for the purpose of advancing Christian faith with an emphasis on literature).

Up until 2005 the trust's principal asset had been a freehold property in Langley near Slough. This was transferred to Send the Light Limited in July of that year.

Applications The trust stated that applications must be in writing enclosing an sae. Applicants should have direct involvement with the school for which the application is being made.

The Marjorie and Geoffrey Jones Charitable Trust

General

£86,000 (2005/06)

Beneficial area UK, preference south west of England.

Carlton House, 30 The Terrace, Torquay, Devon TQ1 1BS

Tel. 01803 213251

Email nigel.wollen@hooperwollen.co.uk

Correspondent N J Wollen, Trustee

Trustees *N J Wollen; W F Coplestone Boughey; P M Kay.*

CC Number 1051031

Information available Full accounts were on file at the Charity Commission.

General This trust was set up under the terms of the will of Rose Marjorie

Jones, who died in 1995, leaving the gross of her estate amounting to £2.2 million for grant-making purposes. In her will she donated amounts of £15,000 and £10,000 to charities based in Devon, such as the Donkey Sanctuary – Sidmouth, Paignton Zoological and Botanical Gardens Limited, the Rowcroft Hospital – Torquay, the Torbay Hospital League of Friends and RNIB – Torquay. Other organisations named in the will were UK-wide, such as RNLI, RSPCA and NSPCC – although grants were probably given to local branches.

In 2005/06 the trust had assets of £2 million and an income of £63,000. After management and administration costs of £18,000, grants to 46 organisations totalled £86,000.

Beneficiaries included: Torbay Boys' Grammar School Charitable Trust (£6,000); the National Trust (£5,000); National Playing Fields (£4,000); Dartington Hall Trust, Torbay Voluntary Service, Trinity Sailing and West of England School and College (£3,000 each); the Guinness Trust, Home Start – Torbay, National Coastwatch, Rowcroft Hospice and the Sir Francis Chichester Trust (£2,000 each); Association of Wheelchair Children (£1,900); Butterfly Conservation, Cornwall Blind Association, Hearing Dogs for Deaf People, Kids Out, Torbay Churches Homeless Trust and the Two Moors Festival (£1,000 each); and National Deaf Children's Society (£500).

Applications In writing to the correspondent. The trustees meet four times a year to consider applications.

The J E Joseph Charitable Fund

Jewish

£122,000 (2005/06)

Beneficial area London, Manchester, Israel, India and Hong Kong.

Flat 10, Compass Close, Edgware, Middlesex HA8 8HU

Correspondent Roger J Leon, Secretary

Trustees *F D A Mocatta, Chair; D Silas; J H Corre; P S Gourgey; J S Horesh; S Frosh.*

CC Number 209058

Information available Information was on file at the Charity Commission.

General The trust was established for the benefit of Jewish communities for

any purposes, mainly in the fields of education, disability and the relief of poverty. In 2005/06 it had assets of £4.3 million, an income of £153,000 and made grants totalling almost £122,000.

Grants were broken down as follows, shown with examples of beneficiaries in each category:

Home – general (13 grants totalling £49,000)

Od Yosef Hai Yeshiva and University Jewish Chaplaincy Board (£6,000 each); Spanish and Portuguese Synagogue Welfare Board (£5,500); Edinburgh House, Jacob Benjamin Elias Synagogue and Spanish and Portuguese Synagogue (£5,000 each); Aish Ha'Torah and Norwood (£4,000 each); Tribe (£3,000); Ezra U'Marpeh and Ilford Synagogue (£2,000 each); and Jewish Lads' and Girls' Brigade (£1,500).

Home – schools (4 grants totalling £16,000)

Jewish Free School and Kisharon Day School (£5,000 each); and Jewish Preparatory School and Simon Marks Jewish Primary School (£3,000 each).

'Eastern' (2 grants totalling £8,500)

Sir Jacob Sassoon Charity Trust (£6,500); and Ahva (£2,000).

'Israeli' (12 grants totalling £44,000)

The Future Generation Fund (£15,000); Alyn (£4,500); Tishma (£4,000); Melabev (£3,000); AKIM – Jerusalem and Common Denominator (£2,500 each); Mercaz Harmony and Yeshivat Dvar Yerushalayim (£2,000); and Or Chadash – Girls Town (£1,500).

Exclusions No grants to individuals. No support for capital projects.

Applications In writing to the correspondent, including a copy of the latest accounts. The trustees respond to all applications which are first vetted by the secretary. The trust stated that many applications are unsuccessful as the number of appeals exceeds the amount available from limited income.

The Lady Eileen Joseph Foundation

General

£47,000 (2004/05)

Beneficial area UK.

20 Smith Terrace, London SW3 4DL

Correspondent Judith M Sawdy, Trustee

Trustees *Judith M Sawdy; Thurlstan W Simpson; Ninette J Thornton.*

CC Number 327549

Information available Full accounts were available from the Charity Commission.

General The trust was registered in 1987. It supports people who are disadvantaged by poverty or who are socially isolated. Medical causes are also supported.

In 2004/05 the foundation had assets of £1 million and an income of £38,000. Grants totalled £47,000. Significant donations of £1,000 or more were made to Regalla Aid Project (£10,000), the National Art Collections Fund and the Rainbow Trust (£5,000 each), Corda, the Dove Cottage Day Hospice and the World Monuments Fund in Britain (£2,500 each), Prideaux House (£2,000) and Charlie's Challenge (£1,000).

Other grants of less than £1,000 amounted to £5,900.

Applications In writing to the correspondent, although the trust states that unsolicited requests will not be considered.

Company Limited and Jewish Educational Trust (£20,000 each); A B Charitable Trust (£13,000); and Achiezer and Friends of Be'er Miriam (£10,000 each).

Other beneficiaries included: Gateshead Jewish Primary School (£8,000); Menorah Primary School (£4,300); Bowden Charitable Trust (£3,000); Yeshivas Tiferes Yaakov (£2,000); Hasmonean High School (£1,700); Beth Hamedrash Elyon Golders Green Limited (£1,500); OJAS and Project SEED (£1,000 each); Knesset Hezeliah (£750); British Friends of Chinuch Atzmai Trust, Gateshead Jewish High School For Girls and Yeshivas Shaarei Torah (£500 each); Diaspora Yeshiva Toras Yisrael (£400); North West London Talmudical College (£250); Gateshead Talmudical College (£200); Yeshivas Imrei Shefer (£150); and Beis Yehudis Moscow and Wildfire Aid (£100 each).

Over half the grants were of under £1,000.

Applications In writing to the correspondent.

Grants were mainly to Jewish organisations (social and educational) with grants also going to the arts, education and health. Donations over £1,000 each were listed in the accounts and went to 29 organisations. The largest grants were to Dixons City Academy (£25,000), Milliken Community High (£23,000), Royal Opera House Foundation (£17,000), Jewish Care (£14,000) and Jewish National Fund (£12,000).

Other beneficiaries included Norwood (£7,600), British Friends of Haifa University (£7,200), Keren Klita (£7,000), Civitas, Centre for Social Justice, Institute of Economic Affairs, Jewish Policy Research, Royal Academy Trust (£5,000 each), and Stephen Wise Temple (£4,500), the Kabbalah Centre (£2,900), Anglo Israel Association (£2,000), British ORT (£1,500) and St James Conversation Trust (£1,000).

Smaller donations of less than £1,000 each totalled £4,000.

Applications In writing to the correspondent, but note that most of the trust's funds are committed to projects supported for a number of years.

The Bernard Kahn Charitable Trust

Jewish

£180,000 (2004/05)
Beneficial area UK and Israel.

18 Gresham Gardens, London NW11 8PD

Correspondent The Trustees

Trustees *Mrs C B Kahn; S Fuehrer; Y E Kahn.*

CC Number 249130

Information available Accounts were on file at the Charity Commission.

General In 2004/05 the trust had assets of £2 million and an income of £39,000 (£252,000 in the previous year including £177,000 in donations). Grants were made to 43 organisations totalling £180,000.

Beneficiaries of the largest grants were: Gateshead Academy for Torah Studies (£30,000); Orthodox Council of Jerusalem (£25,000); Marbeh Torah Trust (£21,000); Achisomoch Aid

The Stanley Kalms Foundation

Jewish charities, general

£188,000 (2005/06)
Beneficial area UK and overseas.

84 Brook Street, London W1K 5EH

Tel. 020 7499 3494

Correspondent Mrs Jane Hunt-Cooke

Trustees *Lord Stanley Kalms; Lady Pamela Kalms; Stephen Kalms.*

CC Number 328368

Information available Accounts were on file at the Charity Commission.

General Established in 1989 by Lord Stanley Kalms, the president of DSG International plc (formerly Dixons Stores Group plc), this charity states its objectives as the encouragement of Jewish education in the UK and Israel. Other activities include support for the arts and media and other programmes, both secular and religious.

In 2005/06 the foundation had assets of £841,000 and an income of £26,000. Grants were made totalling £188,000.

The Boris Karloff Charitable Foundation

General

£51,000 (2005/06)
Beneficial area Worldwide.

Peachey and Co., 95 Aldwych, London WC2B 4JF

Correspondent The Trustees

Trustees *Ian D Wilson; P A Williamson; O M Lewis.*

CC Number 326898

Information available Full accounts were on file at the Charity Commission.

General This foundation was set up in 1985, by Evelyn Pratt (Karloff), wife of the famous horror actor, Boris Karloff (whose real name was William Henry Pratt). When Evelyn Pratt died in June 1993, she bequeathed over £1.4 million to the assets of the foundation.

In 2005/06 the trust had assets of £2.2 million and an income of £64,000.

Grants totalled £51,000. Beneficiaries were: Royal Theatrical Fund, RADA – Boris Karloff Scholarship Fund and Save the Watermill Theatre Appeal (£10,000 each); Shakespeare Globe Trust (£6,500); LAMDA (£5,000); Royal National Theatre (£3,000); English Touring Theatre (£2,000); and Royal British Legion (£1,000).

Exclusions Charities with large resources are not supported.

Applications In writing to the correspondent.

The Ian Karten Charitable Trust

Technology centres for people who are disabled

£128,000 to organisations (2005/06)

Beneficial area Great Britain and Israel, with some local interest in Surrey and London.

The Mill House, Newark Lane, Ripley, Surrey GU23 6DP

Tel. 01483 225020 **Fax** 01483 222420

Email iankarten@btinternet.com

Correspondent Timothy Simon

Trustees *Ian H Karten, Chair; Mrs Mildred Karten; Tim Simon; Angela Hobbs.*

CC Number 281721

Information available Accounts were on file at the Charity Commission.

General The trusts states its objectives in its 2005/06 accounts:

'The objectives of the trust are to carry out legally charitable purposes for the relief of poverty, the advancement of education or religion or otherwise for the benefit of the community.

'The trust currently concentrates on:

- improving the quality of life and independence of people with severe physical, sensory, cognitive disability or mental health problems by providing for them Centres for Computer-aided Training, Education and Communication (CTEC Centres). These are typically established by and located in colleges of further education or (mainly residential) host charities concerned with rehabilitation and education, especially vocational,

of people with one or more of the above-mentioned disabilities.

- the support of higher education by funding studentships for postgraduate studies and research at selected universities in the UK.

'The trust also has a separate modest budget from which it makes small donations to other selected registered charities, mostly local to the trust (London or Surrey).'

In 2005/06 it had assets of £7.7 million and an income of £373,000. Grants to organisations totalled £128,000, broken down as follows and shown with examples of beneficiaries:

CTEC Centres – 6 grants totalling £105,000
Deaf Blind Tel Aviv (£48,000); Lauder College (£25,000); Aspire (£19,000); Keren – Haifa University (£11,000); Cantraybridge (£8,900); and Jewish Care – Stamford Hill (£1,800).

Large grants – 13 grants totalling £19,000
Jewish Care (£3,000); International Centre for Enhancement of Learning Potential (£2,300); Commonwealth Jewish Trust (£2,200); Yad Vashem UK Foundation (£2,000); UJIA Foundation for Education (£1,500); Spiro Ark (£1,400); Community Security Trust, Anne Frank Educational Trust and Institute for Jewish Policy Research (£900 each); Disability Aid Fund (£800); and Surrey Care Trust (£650).

The sum of £4,200 was given in small grants.

A further £51,000 was distributed to seven institutions for scholarships and £10,000 in six grants to individual scholars.

Exclusions No grants to individuals.

Applications The trust currently only considers grants to charities supported in the past. Individual scholarships are no longer available directly to students, instead the trust's chosen universities select the Karten Scholarships themselves.

The Kasner Charitable Trust

Jewish

£75,000 (2004/05)

Beneficial area UK and Israel.

1a Gresham Gardens, London NW11 8NX

Correspondent Josef Kasner, Trustee

Trustees *Elfreda Erlich; Baruch Erlich; Josef Kasner; Judith Erlich.*

CC Number 267510

Information available Accounts were on file at the Charity Commission.

General In 2004/05 the trust had assets of £705,000, an income of £65,000 and made grants to over 175 organisations totalling £75,000.

There were 13 grants of £1,000 or more each: Friends of Bar Ilan University and UJIA (£10,000 each), UTA (£5,100), Gateshead Academy for Jewish Studies, RS Trust and Yeshivat Maharash Engel Radomshitz (£5,000 each), Beth Abraham Synagogue and Emunoh Educational Trust (£3,000 each), British Friends of Bnei Brak Hospital and Friends of Arad (£2,000 each), Society of Friends of Torah (£1,500), Ponevez (£1,400) and Chevras Maoz Ladal (£1,200).

Other beneficiaries inlcuded Yesodey Hatorah School (£600), Friends of Sanz Institution and Marbei Torah Trust (£500 each), Achisomoch and Beis Yehudis (£400 each), Parshaim Ltd (£250), Magen David Adom and Orthodox Council of Jerusalem (£200 each), Hospital Kosher Meals Service (£175), Jewish Blind & Disabled (£150), Friends of Boys Town, Youth Aliyah Child Rescue and ZSV Trust (£100 each), Children's Welfare Committee and Manchester Jewish Girls School (£50 each) and Action for Kids and Ravenswood Village (£25 each).

Applications In writing to the correspondent.

The Kass Charitable Trust

Welfare, nursing homes, older people, education, cancer, Jewish

£50,000 (2004/05)

Beneficial area UK.

37 Sherwood Road, London NW4 1AE

Correspondent D E Kass, Trustee

Trustees *David Elliot Kass; Samuel Simcha Bunim Kass; Mrs Shulamith Malkah Sandler.*

CC Number 1006296

Information available Accounts were on file at the Charity Commission, but without a list of grants.

General The trust supports:

- provision of financial assistance without regard to any religious denominations to those who are in need or are suffering hardship
- provision and maintenance of nursing homes and other facilities for the benefit of older and infirm people
- promotion of education
- promotion of research into the causes of and cure for cancer and similar diseases
- promotion and advancement of the Jewish religion including the preservation and maintenance of Jewish cemeteries.

In 2004/05 the trust's assets stood at just £4,300. Its income was £54,000 mostly from donations received. Grants totalled £50,000.

Unfortunately a list of grant beneficiaries was not included with the accounts.

Applications In writing to the correspondent.

The Kathleen Trust

Musicians

£46,000 (2005/06)

Beneficial area UK, with a preference for London.

Currey and Co., 21 Buckingham Gate, London SW1E 6LS

Correspondent E R H Perks, Trustee

Trustees *E R H Perks; Sir O C A Scott; Lady P A Scott; Mrs CN Withington.*

CC Number 1064516

Information available Accounts were on file at the Charity Commission.

General Established in 1997, it is the policy of the trustees to 'assist young and impecunious musicians'.

In 2005/06 it had assets of £1.2 million and an income of £29,000. Grants were made totalling £46,000. Grants in the year were mainly to 11 individuals. One grant of £4,000 was made to Trinity College of Music.

Previous organisations to benefit have included Oxford Chamber Music Festival, Royal Academy of Music and Royal Northern College of Music.

Applications In writing to the correspondent.

The Michael and Ilse Katz Foundation

Jewish, music, medical, general

About £180,000 (2004/05)

Beneficial area Worldwide.

The Counting House, Trelill, Bodmin, Cornwall PL30 3HZ

Correspondent Osman Azis, Trustee

Trustees *Norris Gilbert; Osman Azis.*

CC Number 263726

Information available Information had been filed at the Charity Commission.

General Established in 1971, this foundation supports many Jewish organisations, although musical and medical charities also received funds.

In 2004/05 it had an income of £19,000 and a total expenditure of £197,000.

Previous beneficiaries have included Beth Shalom Memorial Centre, Leo Baeck College, Bournemouth Orchestral Society, British ORT, Community Security Trust, Hillel Foundation, Holocaust Educational Trust, Jewish Care, Jewish Child's Day, Norwood, Poole Arts Trust Ltd, Sharre Zedik Medical Centre, Tel Aviv Sourasky Medical Centre, UK Friends of the Association for the Wellbeing of Israel's Soldiers and WIZO.

Applications In writing to the correspondent.

The Katzauer Charitable Settlement

Jewish

£42,000 (2005/06)

Beneficial area UK, but mainly Israel.

c/o Devonshire House, 1 Devonshire Street, London W1W 5DR

Correspondent Gordon Smith, Trustee

Trustees *G C Smith; A Katzauer; Mrs E Moller; M S Bailey; W Lian.*

CC Number 275110

Information available Full accounts were on file at the Charity Commission.

General In 2005/06 the trust had assets of £882,000 with an income of £80,000 which was mainly derived from donations and investment income. Grants totalled £42,000.

Beneficiaries of grants over £1,500 each were: Chabad Ra'anana (£5,300); Moriah Synagogue (£5,000); Nahalat Yehiel (£4,300); Beit Kehillat Moriah (£4,000); Mishnalomedia (£3,000); Kollel Ra'anana and Mercaz Ora Vesimcha (£2,800 each); Mercaz Hatorah (£2,400); and Lag Baomer Chabad (£1,900).

Grants of under £1,500 each totalled £11,000.

Applications In writing to the correspondent.

The C S Kaufman Charitable Trust

Jewish

£42,000 (2005/06)

Beneficial area UK.

162 Whitehall Road, Gateshead, Tyne and Wear NE8 1TP

Correspondent C S Kaufman

Trustees *I I Kaufman; Mrs L L Kaufman; J J Kaufman; S Kaufman.*

CC Number 253194

Information available Accounts were on file at the Charity Commission.

General In 2005/06 this trust had an income of £69,000 and a grant total of £42,000. About 50 grants were made in the year.

Grant beneficiaries included: Mifaley Tzedaka Vechesed (£25,000); Craven Walk Charity Trust and Yeshiva Lezirim (£2,000 each); Shalom Banayial and SOFT (£1,000 each); BFOT (£600); Gateshead Foundation for Torah, Gateshead Jewish Boarding School, Institute for Higher Rabinnical Studies Gateshead, UTA and Va'ad Harabonim Linyonei Tzedaka (£500 each); Asos Chesed (£100); J & R Charities (£75); and Bnei Yisocher (£50).

Many organisations received more than one grant.

Exclusions No grants to individuals.

Applications In writing to the correspondent.

The Geoffrey John Kaye Charitable Foundation

Jewish, general

£47,000 (2005/06)

Beneficial area UK and overseas.

7 St John's Road, Harrow, Middlesex HA1 2EY

Correspondent R J Freebody, Accountant

Trustees G J Kaye; Mrs S Rose; J Pears.

CC Number 262547

Information available Accounts are on file at the Charity Commission.

General In 2005/06 the trust had assets of £897,000, an income of £100,000 and made grants totalling £47,000. Grants are largely recurrent and are made to Jewish organisations.

Beneficiaries included: UJIA (£23,000); Animal Shelter AC (£12,000); Zichron Menachem (£1,000); Lubavitch Foundation (£570); Mision San Pablo (£550); and Recibo di Donativo (£260).

Applications In writing to the correspondent, but please note that the foundation has previously stated that funds were fully committed.

The Emmanuel Kaye Foundation

Medical research, welfare and Jewish organisations

£46,000 (2004/05)

Beneficial area UK and overseas.

Oakleigh House, High Street, Hartley Wintney, Hampshire RG27 8PE

Tel. 01252 843773

Correspondent The Secretary to the Trustees

Trustees David Kaye; Lady Kaye; John Forster; Michael Cutler.

CC Number 280281

Information available Full accounts were provided by the trust.

General The trust supports organisations benefiting medical professionals, research workers, scientists, Jewish people, at risk groups, people who are disadvantaged by poverty and socially isolated people.

In 2004/05 it had assets of £1 million generating an income of £46,000. All of the income was given in grants.

Beneficiaries listed in the accounts were: Community Links (£20,000); Jewish Care, Imperial College London and St James' Conservation Trust (£5,000 each); Caius House (£1,900); and English Chamber Orchestra and Music Society, Friends of Bar Ilan University and Thrive (£1,000 each).

Unlisted grants of less than £1,000 each totalled £5,900.

Exclusions Organisations not registered with the Charity Commission are not supported.

Applications In writing to the correspondent.

The John Thomas Kennedy Charitable Foundation

General

£115,000 (2004/05)

Beneficial area Worldwide.

Reedham House, 31 King Street West, Manchester M3 2PJ

Correspondent The Trustees

Trustees J T Kennedy; Mrs V Kennedy; N J Shaw.

CC Number 1082421

Information available Accounts were on file at the Charity Commission.

General Registered with the Charity Commission in September 2000, in 2004/05 the foundation had assets of £1.5 million, an income of £124,000 and made grants totalling £115,000.

There were 28 grants listed in the accounts of £1,000 or more. Beneficiaries included: SMA Fathers (£20,000); Catholic Bishops Conference of England and Wales and Catholic Trust for England & Wales (£10,000 each); Jubilee Action (£7,700); Margaret Beaufort Institute of Theology (£7,000); Bnei Akiva (£6,000); Arundel and Brighton Dioceses, HCPT – The Pilgrimage Trust, St Columbian Fathers, Tsunami Appeal and Youth 2000 (£5,000 each); Restoration Ministries (£4,000); the Good Council Network (£3,000); Institute of Irish Studies (£2,500); Irish Abroad Charitable Trust (£2,000); and the Epiphany Trust and Gwalior Children's Hospital (£1,000 each).

Smaller donations under £1,000 each totalled £1,100.

Applications In writing to the correspondent.

The Kennel Club Charitable Trust

Dogs

£466,000 (2006)

Beneficial area UK.

1–5 Clarges Street, Piccadilly, London W1J 8AB

Email cas.oakes@thekennelclub.org.uk

Website www.mad4dogs.org.uk

Correspondent Cas Oakes, Administrator

Trustees M Townsend, Chair; M Herrtage; W H King; Mrs I E Terry; P Mann.

CC Number 327802

Information available Accounts were on file at the Charity Commission.

General The trust describes its objectives as 'science, welfare and support'. It supports the furthering of research into canine diseases and hereditary disorders of dogs and also organisations concerned with the welfare of dogs in need and those which aim to improve the quality of life of humans by promoting dogs as practical or therapeutic aids.

The trust gives both ongoing and one-off grants, generally up to £35,000 each a year for research and of up to £10,000 each for support of dogs and those who care for them or benefit from them.

In 2006 the trust had assets of £2.3 million and an income of £561,000. A total of 40 grants were made, totalling £466,000. These were divided into 'scientific and research project support' which amounted to £339,000, and 'education and other grants' totalling £127,000.

Beneficiaries of the largest grants were: Animal Health Trust – DNA research into canine eye conditions (£83,000); University of Liverpool – equipment for operating theatre (£52,000); Animal Health Trust – MRD in the Golden Retriever and Royal Veterinary College – equipment for operating theatre (£36,000 each); and Animal Health Trust – Cerebellar Ataxia in the Italian Spinone (£32,000).

Other beneficiaries included: Erasmus Wilson Dermatological Research Fund and Hearing Dogs for Deaf People (£10,000 each); Wood Green Animal Shelters (£8,000); Tia Greyhound and Lurcher Rescue (£5,000); Waggy Tails Rescue (£3,000); Animal Rescue Centre – Sidmouth and Prevent Unwanted Pets (£2,000 each); Dumfries & Galloway Canine Rescue Centre (£1,000); and British International Rescue and Search Dogs (£750).

Exclusions The trust does not give grants directly to individuals; veterinary nurses can apply to the British Veterinary Nursing Association where bursaries are available. The trustees tend not to favour funding the costs of building work.

Applications In writing to the Administrator, including latest accounts. Please state clearly details of the costs for which you are requesting funding, and for what purpose and over what period the funding is required. The trustees meet three or four times a year.

The Nancy Kenyon Charitable Trust

General
£28,000 (2005/06)
Beneficial area UK.

c/o Mercer and Hole, Gloucester House, 72 London Road, St Albans, Hertfordshire AL1 1NS
Correspondent The Trustees
Trustees *Lucy Phipps; Maureen Kenyon; Christopher Kenyon; Sally Kenyon; Peter Kenyon; Gillian Tallon.*
CC Number 265359
Information available Accounts were on file at the Charity Commission.

General The trust makes grants primarily for people and causes known to the trustees.

In 2005/06 the trust's assets totalled around £1.5 million. It had an income totalling £45,000 and made grants totalling £28,000.

Beneficiaries in the year included: Nancy Oldfield Trust (£11,000); St Nicholas Church – Ashchurch (£3,500); Cheltenham Youth for Christ (£2,000); Winston's Wish (£1,200); and Cheltenham Open Door, Cheltenham Community Projects, Church Mission Society, Earls Court Community Project, Epic Arts, the Haven Trust, National Star for Severely Handicapped Kids and Nehemiah Project (£1,000 each); and Christ Church Summerfield (£500).

Exclusions No grants to individuals.

Applications In writing to the correspondent at any time. Applications for causes not known to the trustees are considered annually in December.

Kermaville Ltd

Jewish
£105,000 (2004/05)
Beneficial area UK.

3 Overlea Road, London E5 9BG
Correspondent M Freund
Trustee *L Rabinowitz.*
CC Number 266075
Information available Accounts were on file at the Charity Commission.

General The trust makes grants to Jewish organisations and towards those concerned with general charitable purposes.

In 2004/05 the trust had assets of £242,000 and an income of £93,000, including £75,000 from donations. Grants totalled £105,000.

There were eight grants made over £1,000 each. Beneficiaries were: Yeshivas Imrei Chaim Spinka (£60,000); Bais

Rochel D'Satmar (£16,000); Keren Tzedoka Vechessed (£7,500); Kollel Congregation Yetev Lev (£6,100); Kollel Atzei Chaim (£5,000); United Talmudical Association (£4,000); Ponevez Beth Hamedrash (£4,000); and Lolev Charitable Trust (£3,000).

Applications In writing to the correspondent.

E and E Kernkraut Charities Limited

General, education, Jewish
£130,000 (2004/05)
Beneficial area UK.

c/o New Burlington House, 1075 Finchley Road, London NW11 0PU
Correspondent E Kernkraut, Chair
Trustees *E Kernkraut, Chair; Mrs E Kernkraut; Joseph Kernkraut; Jacob Kernkraut.*
CC Number 275636
Information available Accounts were on file at the Charity Commission, but without a list of grants.

General The trust states that it makes grants for educational, Jewish and other charitable purposes. It did not provide a list of grants with its accounts or further detail of its grant-making criteria, so we were unable to tell what type of educational charity is likely to be supported by this trust.

In 2004/05 it had an income of £250,000 from donations. Grants totalled £130,000.

Applications In writing to the correspondent.

The Peter Kershaw Trust

Medical research, education, social welfare

£268,000 (2005/06)

Beneficial area Manchester and the surrounding district only.

22 Ashworth Park, Knutsford, Cheshire WA16 9DE

Tel. 01565 651086

Email pkershawtrust@btinternet.com

Correspondent Bryan Peak, Secretary

Trustees *R P Kershaw, Chair; Mrs H F Kershaw; Mrs M L Rushbrooke; D Tully; Mrs R Adams; T Page.*

CC Number 268934

Information available Accounts were on file at the Charity Commission.

General The principal activities of the trust continue to be those of funding medical research, grants to medical and other institutions and to schools in respect of bursaries.

In 2005/06 the trust had assets of £6.3 million and an income of £230,000. Grants were made totalling £268,000 and were broken down as follows (shown here with examples of grants in each category):

Social welfare institutions – £130,000 in 31 grants
Copperdale Trust (£14,000); Bolton YMCA (£10,000); Autistic Society Greater Manchester (£7,800); Fairbridge and Spurgeons Child Care (£7,500 each); Emmaus Bolton (£6,300); DIAL Trafford (£6,000); Catholic Welfare Society (£4,500); Age Concern Stockport (£3,000); Old Moat Youth Outreach Project (£2,500); Life Centre – Salford (£1,000); Children with Leukaemia and English Churches Housing (£250 each); and English Church Housing (£250).

Memorial bursary – 58,000 in 4 grants
M13 Youth Project (£25,000); Ladybarn Community Centre (£15,000); Barlow Moor Community Association (£10,000); and Old Moat Youth Outreach Scheme (£7,500).

Medical research – £40,000 in 1 grant
Charnley Research Institute – hip replacement surgery research (£40,000).

School bursaries – £39,000 in 6 grants
King's School, Macclesfield (£11,000); Withington Girls' School (£8,400); William Hulme's Grammar School (£5,800); Manchester High School for Girls (£5,000); and Bury Grammar Schools (£3,800).

Exclusions No grants to individuals or for building projects.

Applications In writing to the correspondent, however the trust is always oversubscribed. The trustees normally meet twice a year in May and November to consider recommendations for grant aid which will be disbursed in June and December respectively.

The Kessler Foundation

General, Jewish

£27,000 (2004/05)

Beneficial area UK.

26–34 Old Street, London EC1V 9QR

Correspondent L R Blackstone

Trustees *L Blackstone, Chair; Mrs J Jacobs; Prof. M Geller; Lady Susan Gilbert; Mrs J F Mayers; P Morgenstern.*

CC Number 290759

Information available Accounts were on file at the Charity Commission.

General The foundation makes grants for general charitable causes, with particular emphasis on supporting Jewish organisations. Generally the trust will support relatively small institutions (with an income of less than £100,000 a year) which do not attract funds from the larger charities. In exceptional circumstances grants to individuals will be considered. The foundation's funds depend upon dividends from its shareholdings in the *Jewish Chronicle* and grants made by the newspaper. Grants generally range from £250 to £1,000 each, mostly at the lower end of this scale.

The foundation will assist organisations which may be devoted to:

- the advancement of Jewish religion, learning, education and culture
- the improvement of inter-faith, community and race relations, and the combating of prejudice
- the alleviation of the problems of minority and disadvantaged groups
- the protection, maintenance and monitoring of human rights
- the promotion of health and welfare
- the protection and preservation of records and objects with special significance to the Jewish and general community

- the encouragement of arts, literature and science including archaeology, natural history and protection of the environment with special reference to the Jewish community.

In 2004/05 the foundation had assets of £300,000 and an income of £40,000. Grants were made to 19 organisations totalling £27,000.

Beneficiaries included: Jewish Arts Festival (£10,000); DASH (£7,500); Institute of Jewish Studies UCL and Hannah Levy House Trust (£1,000 each); JCORE and Jewish East End Celebration Society (£750 each); Peace Child Israel (£600); AJEX, the Bath Recital Artists' Trust, British Friends of the Forgotten People, European Association of Jewish Studies, Friends of Ilan, Haifa Rape Crisis Centre, Holocaust Survivors Friendship Association and Jewish Aids Trust (£500 each); Colchester Furniture Project (£300); and the Chasunah Link (£180).

Exclusions In general the foundation will not support the larger well-known charities with an income in excess of £100,000, and will not provide grants for social, medical and welfare projects which are the responsibility of local or national government.

Applications On a form available from the correspondent. The trustees meet at least twice a year in June and December. Applicants will be notified of decisions as soon as possible after then.

The King/ Cullimore Charitable Trust

General

£195,000 (2005/06)

Beneficial area UK.

52 Ledborough Lane, Beaconsfield, Buckinghamshire HP9 2DF

Correspondent P A Cullimore, Trustee

Trustees *P A Cullimore; A G Cullimore; C J King; A G McKechnie.*

CC Number 1074928

Information available Accounts were on file at the Charity Commission.

General This trust has general charitable purposes and was registered with the Charity Commission on 30 March 1999.

In 2005/06 it had assets amounting to £5.5 million and an income of £341,000. Grants were made totalling £195,000.

Organisations to benefit in the year were: Aylesbury College (£100,000); Action for Brazil's Children (£40,000); St Peter and St James Hospice (£20,000); Duke of Edinburgh's Award (£10,000); and the Beaconsfield School (£4,500).

Applications In writing to the correspondent.

Kinsurdy Charitable Trust

General in the UK

£62,000 (2004/05)
Beneficial area UK.

UBS Laing and Cruickshank, 1 Curzon Street, London W1J 5UB
Correspondent The Trustees
Trustees *R P Tullett; A H Bartlett.*
CC Number 1076085
Information available Accounts were on file at the Charity Commission.

General Registered in June 1999, in 2004/05 this trust had assets of £1.2 million and an income of £133,000 including £84,000 from donations and £50,000 from investments.

Grants totalled £62,000 and were made to 10 organisations: Alzheimer's Society (£8,000); and Age Concern, the British Red Cross, Help the Aged, MacMillan Cancer Relief, Marie Curie Cancer Care, Multiple Sclerosis Society, Newbury Hospice Helpers League, Parkinson's Society and RNLI (£6,000 each).

Applications In writing to the correspondent.

The Richard Kirkman Charitable Trust

General

£65,000 (2005/06)
Beneficial area UK, with a preference for Hampshire.

Ashton House, 12 The Precinct, Wincester Road, Chandlers Ford, Eastleigh, Hampshire F053 2GB
Correspondent M Howson-Green, Trustee
Trustees *M Howson-Green; Mrs F O Kirkman; B M Baxendale.*
CC Number 327972
Information available Accounts were on file at the Charity Commission.

General This trust supports a range of causes with a preference for Hampshire, especially Southampton. The trustees have stated that they are considering financing various plans for alleviating drug addiction.

In 2005/06 the trust had assets of £1.6 million and an income of £61,000. Grants were made totalling £65,000.

There were 26 grants of £500 or more listed in the accounts. Beneficiaries included: British Limbless Ex-Servicemen Association, Enham Trust, Leukaemia Busters, Marwell Preservation Trust, Southampton Rotary Club Trust Fund and Southampton Youth Brass Band (£3,000 each); Southampton City and Regions Action to Combat Hardship (£2,500); Aidis Trust, Haemophilia Society, Dogs for the Disabled, Southampton Area Talking Echo, Streetscene and Stroke Association (£2,000 each); Alzheimer's Disease Society, Police Dependants Trust and Wessex Children's Hospice Trust (£1,000 each); and Clouds House (£580).

There were 36 further grants to institutions of £500 or less totalling £17,000.

Applications The trust carries out its own research for beneficiaries and does not respond to applications by post or telephone.

Kirschel Foundation

Jewish, medical

£111,000 (2003/04)
Beneficial area UK.

171 Wardour Street, London W1F 8WS
Tel. 020 7437 4372
Correspondent John Hoare, Trustee
Trustees *Laurence Grant Kirschel; John Hoare.*
CC Number 1067672

Information available Accounts were on file at the Charity Commission.

General This trust states its aims and objectives are 'to provide benefits to underprivileged persons, who may be either handicapped or lacking resources'. In practice this includes many Jewish organisations.

In 2003/04 the foundation had an income from donations of £102,000 and made grants totalling £111,000.

There were 26 grants of £1,000 or more listed in the accounts. Beneficiaries included: Friends of Ohr Somayach (£17,000); Lubavitch Foundation of Scotland (£13,000); Jewish Learning Exchange (£10,000); the Yakar Educational Foundation (£7,500); the Variety Club Children's Charity (£6,500); British Friends of Amedcbad Uni, Gateshead Academy for Torah Studies, Or Chadash and Tzedoko Trust (£5,000 each); I Rescue (£3,800; Norwood Ltd (£3,500); Palace for All (£3,000); Community Service Trust (£2,500); United Synagogue (£1,500); and Aharat Shalom Charity Fund, Deaf Blind UK, Friends of Marlborough School, Gateshead Jewish Family Service and the Lady Hoare Trust (£1,000 each).

The total of all other donations, individually less than £1,000 each was £9,200.

Applications In writing to the correspondent.

The Marina Kleinwort Charitable Trust

Arts

£53,000 (2005/06)
Beneficial area UK.

30 Gresham Street, London EC2V 7PG
Correspondent The Secretary
Trustees *Miss Marina Rose Kleinwort, Chair; David James Roper Robinson; Miss Zenaida Yanowsky; Mrs Tessa Elizabeth Bremmer.*
CC Number 1081825
Information available Accounts were on file at the Charity Commission.

General In 2005/06 it had assets of £1.5 million and an income of £58,000. Grants totalling £53,000 were made to 14 organisations.

Beneficiaries were: Royal Ballet School (£15,000); Almeida Theatre Co. Ltd and LAMDA (£5,000 each); Duke of Edinburgh's Award, Endymion Ensemble, Society for the Promotion of New Music, South Bank Centre and Theatre Royal Haymarket Master Class (£3,000 each); English Chamber Orchestra (£2,700); Live Music Now! North West (£2,500); Dance Umbrella, Gate Theatre Company Limited and London Symphony Orchestra (£2,000 each); and Carousel (£1,500).

Exclusions No grants to individuals.

Applications In writing to the correspondent.

The Kohn Foundation

Scientific and medical projects, the arts – particularly music, education, Jewish charities

£432,000 (2005)

Beneficial area UK.

c/o Wilkins Kennedy, Bridge House, London Bridge, London SE1 9QR

Correspondent Dr R Kohn, Trustee

Trustees *Dr Ralph Kohn, Chair; Zahava Kohn; Anthony A Forwood.*

CC Number 1003951

Information available Full accounts were on file at the Charity Commission.

General The foundation supports advancement of scientific and medical research, promotion of the arts – particularly music, general educational projects and Jewish charities.

In 2005 the foundation had assets of £1.7 million, an income of £38,000 and made grants totalling £432,000. Donations were broken down as follows, shown here with examples of beneficiaries in each category:

Medical and scientific – 9 grants totalling £267,000
The Royal Society (£184,000); Chai Cancer Care and the Royal Institution of Great Britain – Henry Dale Prize (£15,000 each); Royal College of Physicians (£13,000); University College of London – prize lecture (£12,000); Imperial College Ernst Chain Prize (£10,000); Imperial College (£6,900); and

Foundation for Science and Technology (£5,000).

Performing Arts – 14 grants totalling £107,000
Royal Academy of Music (£75,000); Peterhouse Development Fund (£10,000); Susan Chilcott Fund (£5,000); Schumanniade – Dresden (£3,500); Wigmore Hall Song Contest (£2,700); English Chamber Orchestra (£2,000); and Hampstead and Highgate Festival (£1,000).

Advancement of the Jewish religion, education and charitable institutions – 278 grants totalling £57,000
Israel Philharmonic Orchestra Foundation (£14,000); Emunah and Society for Friends of the Torah (£10,000 each); Hasmonean High School (£6,000); Friends of Ber-Ilan University (£5,000); North West London Jewish Day School (£3,500); Collel Chibath Yerushalayim (£1,200); and St John's Wood Synagogue and United Synagogue (£1,000 each).

Applications In writing to the correspondent.

Kollel Gur Trust

Jewish

£104,000 (2004/05)

Beneficial area Asia and Eurpoe.

16 Linthorpe Road, London N16 5RF

Correspondent The Trustees

Trustees *H Landau; A Zonszjan; J Margulies.*

CC Number 803762

Information available Accounts were on file at the Charity Commission, without a list of grants.

General Registered with the Charity Commission in July 1990, in 2004/05 the trust had an income of £94,000 and made grants totalling £104,000. No list of grants was included with the accounts on file at the Charity Commission.

Applications In writing to the correspondent.

The Kreditor Charitable Trust

Jewish, welfare, education

£88,000 (2004/05)

Beneficial area UK, with preferences for London and North East England.

Gerald Kreditor and Co., Chartered Accountants, Hallswelle House, 1 Hallswelle Road, London NW11 0DH

Tel. 020 8209 1535 **Fax** 020 8209 1923

Correspondent P M Kreditor, Trustee

Trustees *P M Kreditor; M P Kreditor.*

CC Number 292649

Information available Accounts are on file at the Charity Commission, without a list of grants.

General In 2004/05 the trust had assets of £59,000 with an income of £68,000, mostly from Gift Aid donations. Grants totalled £88,000, unfortunately a list of grants was not available for this period.

In previous years, grants have been mostly for less than £100 and have been given mainly to Jewish organisations working in education and social and medical welfare. Beneficiaries have been scattered across London and the north east of England. The vast majority of grants were for less than £100. Recipients have included Academy for Rabbinical Research, British Friends of Israel War Disabled, Fordeve Ltd, Jerusalem Ladies' Society, Jewish Care, Jewish Marriage Council Kosher Meals on Wheels, London Academy of Jewish Studies, NW London Talmudical College and Ravenswood. Non-Jewish organisations supported included British Diabetic Association, RNID and UNICEF UK.

Applications In writing to the correspondent.

The Kyte Charitable Trust

Medical, disadvantaged and socially isolated people

£79,000 (2004/05)

Beneficial area UK.

Business Design Centre, 52 Upper Street, London N1 0QH

Correspondent The Trustees

Trustees *D M Kyte; T M Kyte; A H Kyte.*

CC Number 1035886

Information available Accounts were on file at the Charity Commission, without a list of grants.

General The trust supports organisations benefiting medical professionals and research workers. Support may go to organisations working with at-risk groups, and people who are disadvantaged by poverty or socially isolated.

In 2004/05 the trust had an income of £80,000 from covenants and Gift Aid and made grants totalling £79,000. Assets stood at £18,000. No list of grants was included with the accounts filed at the Charity Commission.

Applications In writing to the correspondent.

The Late Sir Pierce Lacy Charity Trust

Roman Catholics, general

About £28,000 (2005/06)

Beneficial area UK and overseas.

Norwich Union, Trustee Department, Pitheavlis, Perth PH2 0NH

Tel. 01738 895590 **Fax** 01738 895903

Correspondent P Burke, Head of Trustee Management

Trustee *CGU Insurance plc*

CC Number 1013505

Information available Information was obtained from the Charity Commission website.

General In 2005/06 the trust has an income of £24,000 and a total expenditure of £21,000. Previously, grants totalled £28,000. Grants are only made to Roman Catholic and associated institutions. Newly established and UK organisations are supported, benefiting children, young adults, older people, Roman Catholics, at-risk groups, carers, people who are disabled and people disadvantaged by poverty.

Grants are made in the areas of medicine and health, welfare, education, religion and for general charitable purposes. The trust particularly supports charities working in the field of infrastructure development, residential facilities and services, Christian education, Christian outreach, Catholic bodies, charity or voluntary umbrella bodies, hospices, rehabilitation centres, advocacy, education and training, community services and community issues.

Recurrent small grants of £1,000 or less are made, and grants can be for buildings, capital, core costs, project, research and start-up costs. Funding for more than three years may be considered.

Previous grants have included the following: £1,400 to Crusade of Rescue, £920 to St Francis' Children's Society, £810 to Poor Mission Fund, £800 to St Cuthberts Mayne RC School – special donation, £720 to Society of St Vincent de Paul, £610 to Poor Mission Fund, £550 to Catholic Children's Society and £530 to St Francis' Leprosy Guild.

Exclusions The trust only supports the Roman Catholic Church or associated institutions.

Applications In writing to the correspondent, at any time.

John Laing Charitable Trust

General

£526,000 to organisations (2005)

Beneficial area UK.

33 Bunns Lane, Mill Hill, London NW7 2DX

Tel. 020 8959 7321

Email michael.a.hamilton@laing.com

Website www.laing.com/LCT.htm

Correspondent Michael Hamilton, Secretary

Trustees *C M Laing; Sir Martin Laing; D C Madden; R I Sumner; P Jones; D Whipp.*

CC Number 236852

Information available Accounts were on file at the Charity Commission.

General 'The first priority of the trust is to support existing and former employees of John Laing plc who face hardship. The second is to make general donations to organisations, not individuals, and in particular to support those organisations dealing with homelessness, disadvantaged young people, education and the environment'.

In 2005 the trust had an income of £1.6 million. The trust made grants totalling £526,000 to organisations, with a further £732,000 distributed to 785 individuals whom were either current or former employees of John Laing plc.

The largest 50 charitable donations were listed in the accounts. By far the largest grant of £100,000 was given to National Tenants Resource Centre. Other beneficiaries of larger grants included: ContinYou and Crime Concern (£25,000 each); Weston Spirit (£20,000); Atlantic College (£17,000); British Trust for Conservation Volunteers, Hertfordshire Groundwork, Homeless Link and Wastewatch (£15,000 each); 4Children (£14,000); and Big Issue Foundation, Church Action on Poverty, City Lit, Community Foundation Northern Ireland, Duke Of Edinburgh's Award, Groundswell and School Governors One Stop Shop (£10,000 each).

Other beneficiaries included: National Pyramid Trust (£7,500); Hertfordshire Community Foundation, Highlands School Enfield and Springboard for Children (£5,000 each); Watford New Hope Trust (£4,000) and the Abingdon Bridge, Colchester Furniture Project, Tower Hamlets Mission and Transport 2000 (£2,500).

Exclusions No grants to individuals (other than to Laing employees and/or their dependants).

Applications In writing to the correspondent. The trust says that all applications are acknowledged.

The Christopher Laing Foundation

Social welfare, environment, culture, health and medicine

£190,000 (2005/06)

Beneficial area UK, with an interest in Hertfordshire.

c/o TMF Management UK LTD, 400 Capability Green, Luton LU1 3LU

Correspondent Mrs Margaret R White, Senior Trust Consultant

Trustees *Christopher M Laing; Donald G Stradling; Peter S Jackson; Diana C Laing.*

CC Number 278460

Information available Accounts were obtained from the Charity Commission website.

General In 2005/06 the trust had assets of £6.3 million, which generated an income of £168,000. Grants were made totalling £190,000. Of this, £22,500 was given to Charities Aid Foundation for disbursement amongst smaller charities. Other grants were broken down as follows (shown here with examples of grants in each category):

Child and youth – £118,000
The Lord's Taverners (£50,000); Duke of Edinburgh's Award (£27,000); National Playing Fields Association (£25,000); NCH – Action for Children (£10,000); and Youth Create (£5,000).

Cultural and environmental – £12,500 in 2 grants
Global Action Plan (£10,000); and the St Albans Bach Choir (£2,500).

Health and medicine – £2,400 in 3 grants
Fight for Sight (£1,000); Leukaemia Research (£900); and GUTS (£500).

Religion – £1,000
The sole beneficiary was Ayot St Lawrence Church.

Social welfare – £30,000
Hertfordshire Community Foundation (£20,000); WINGS (£2,500); Action for Addiction, Leonard Cheshire and SportsAid Trust (£1,000); Hertfordshire Groundwork Trust (£520); and Home Farm Trust (£300).

Exclusions Donations are only made to registered charities.

Applications In writing to the correspondent.

The David Laing Foundation

Young people, disability, mental health, the arts, general

£247,000 (2005/06)

Beneficial area Worldwide.

Fermyn Woods Hall, Brigstock, Northamptonshire, NN 14 3JA

Correspondent David E Laing, Trustee

Trustees *David Eric Laing; John Stuart Lewis; Richard Francis Dudley Barlow; Frances Mary Laing.*

CC Number 278462

Information available Accounts were on file at the Charity Commission.

General This trust has general charitable purposes, with emphasis on youth, disability, mental health and the arts. It makes large grants to a wide and varied number of organisations as well as donating smaller grants through Charities Aid Foundation.

In 2005/06 the foundation had assets of almost £5 million and an income of £125,000. Grants totalled £247,000. They were broken down as follows and are shown here with examples of recipients of £1,000 or more:

General – £120,000
The sole beneficiary was Northamptonshire Community Foundation, receiving three grants.

Medical, health and sickness – £45,000
Grove House Hospice (£21,000); St John Ambulance (£6,000); Mind and Body Foundation (£2,000); and Great Ormond Street Hospital Children's Charity, Jimmy Goddard Trust, John Grooms, Marie Curie Cancer Care, Medical Emergency Relief International Charitable Trust and Wooden Spoon Society (£1,000 each).

Arts and culture – £25,000
International Organ Festival (£15,000); Grange Park Opera (£1,750); Bernewode Singers and St Albans Cathedral Music Trust (£1,500 each); and London Pro Arte Orchestra and New Shakespeare Company Ltd (£1,000 each).

Child and youth inc. education – £15,000
Lord's Taverners (£6,500 in four grants); and Rainbow Trust Children's Charity (£1,500).

Education/training – £14,000
Firfield Primary School PTA, Game Conservancy Trust and Hertfordshire Agricultural Society (£2,000 each); Canine Partners for Independence (£1,500); and International Students House (£1,250).

Social welfare – £11,000
Interact Reading Service (£2,000); Home Farm Trust £1,250 in two grants); and Event Mobility and Harpenden Lions Club (£1,000 each).

Sport and recreation – £9,700
British Olympic Foundation (£4,700 in three grants); and Pony Club Flamstead (£2,000).

Religion – £5,800
Peterborough Cathedral (£5,000).

Overseas aid – £1,500
Survival International Charitable Trust (£1,000).

Exclusions No grants to individuals.

Applications In writing to the correspondent. Trustees meet in March, June, October and December, although applications are reviewed weekly. Due to the large number of applications received, and the relatively small number of grants made, the trust is not able to respond to all requests.

The Martin Laing Foundation

General

£183,000 (2005/06)

Beneficial area UK and worldwide.

c/o TMF Management UK LTD, 400 Capability Green, Luton LU1 3LU

Correspondent Mrs Margaret R White, Senior Trust Consultant

Trustees *Sir John Martin Laing; Donald Stradling; Edward Charles Laing; Nicholas Gregory; Lady Stephanie Stearn Laing.*

CC Number 278461

Information available Accounts were on file at the Charity Commission.

General This trust makes a large number of small grants, given through the Charities Aid Foundation. Most of the support is given to organisations and projects with which the trustees have a personal connection. A small number of larger grants are also made.

In 2005/06 the foundation had assets of £6.3 million, which generated an income of £165,000. Management and administration charges totalled £13,000, while the investment manager's charges totalled £17,000. Grants were made totalling £183,000 of which £80,000 was distributed through CAF.

Grants made directly by the foundation were broken down as follows (shown with examples of grants in each category):

Overseas – £29,000 in 5 grants
Fondazzjoni Patrimonju Matti (£15,000); Air Battle of Malta Memorial Hangar Appeal and Little Sisters of the Poor (£5,000 each); and Hands Around the World and Hives Save Lives (£2,000 each).

Social welfare – £27,500 in 3 grants
Laing's Charitable Trust (£15,000);

Wessex Reinvestment Trust (£10,000); and WINGS (£2,500).

Cultural and environmental – £22,500 in 4 grants
WWF UK (£10,000); Marine Stewardship Council and Ponds Conservation Trust (£5,000 each); and St Albans Bach Choir (£2,500).

Health and medicine – £12,500 in 2 grants
Diabetes UK (£10,000); and the Dame Vera Lynn Trust (£2,500).

Child and youth – £1,000
Atlantic College was the sole beneficiary.

Applications 'The trustees receive an enormous and increasing number of requests for help. Unfortunately the trustees are only able to help a small proportion of the requests and consequently they limit their support to those charities where they have an interest in their activities.'

The Lambert Charitable Trust

Health, welfare, Jewish, arts

£67,000 (2005/06)
Beneficial area UK and Israel.

Mercer and Hole, 72 London Road, St Albans, Hertfordshire AL1 1NS
Tel. 020 7353 1597
Correspondent George Georghiou
Trustees M Lambert; Prof. H P Lambert; H Alexander-Passe; Jane Lambert; O E Lambert; D J R Wells.
CC Number 257803
Information available Full accounts were on file at the Charity Commission.

General This trust usually uses half of its funds supporting Jewish and Israeli causes and half for medical, welfare and arts causes.

In 2005/06 the trust had assets of £2.8 million and an income of £78,000. After administration costs of £20,000, grants totalled £67,000.

Donations were broken down as follows (shown here with examples of beneficiaries in each category):

Israel – £6,700 in 9 grants
Friends of Magen David Adom (£1,200); British Council of the Shaare Zedek Medical Centre and Sanz Medical Centre Laniado Hospital (£750 each); Boys

Town Jerusalem and British Friends of Ohel Sarah (£500 each); and Ponevez Yeshivah Israel (£250).

Jewish Faith in the United Kingdom – £22,000 in 7 grants
Jewish Care (£15,000); Nightingale House (£2,000); and Jewish Blind and Disabled, Jewish Children's Holiday Fund, Jewish Child's Day and Norwood Ravenswood (£1,000 each).

Other charitable purposes – £39,000 in 29 grants
Dorothy Gardner Centre (£4,000); 999 Group, Medical Foundation for the Care of Victims of Torture and New Horizon Youth Centre (£3,000 each); the Brandon Centre, Anne Frank Trust and Trinity Hospice (£2,000 each); Action for Blind People, Fiends of War Memorials, Headway, Hearing Dogs for the Deaf, Martin Sailing Project, National Library for the Blind, Parkinson's Disease Society, Riding for the Disabled Association, Royal London Society for the Blind, Streatham Youth and Community Trust, Tower Hamlets Old People's Welfare Trust and Winged Fellowship (£1,000 each).

Applications In writing to the correspondent before July for payment by 1 September.

Lancashire Environmental Fund

Environmental

£297,000 (2005)
Beneficial area UK, particularly Lancashire.

The Barn, Berkeley Drive, Bamber Bridge, Preston, Lancashire PR5 6BY
Tel. 01772 317247
Email andyrowett@lancsenvfund.org.uk
Website www.lancsenvfund.org.uk
Correspondent A Rowett, Administration Officer
Trustees A C P Martin, Chair; P Greijenberg; D Tattersall; P Taylor.
CC Number 1074983
Information available Accounts were on file at the Charity Commission.

General This fund was established in June 1998 from a partnership of four organisations: SITA (Lancashire) Ltd, Lancashire County Council, the Wildlife Trust for Lancashire, Manchester and

North Merseyside and Community Futures. The fund enables community groups and organisations throughout the country to take advantage of the funding opportunities offered by landfill tax credits. It achieves this by supporting organisations and projects based within Lancashire, or nationwide research or development with a relevance to Lancashire, which are managed by an Enrolled Environmental Body, as recognised by Entrust.

The fund operates two funding schemes:

Community Chest
'The Community Chest is available as a small grant for a small scheme usually to support groups who are seeking one-off funding for a project. Applications are accepted for grants between £3,000 and £15,000. The overall cost of the project should not exceed £30,000. The fund may act as Environmental Body for the project and administer the paperwork required by the regulator.

Strategic Fund
'The Strategic Fund is available to organisations who are registered as Environmental Bodies with Entrust, the scheme regulator. Applications are accepted for grants up to £25,000 but the overall cost should not exceed £250,000.

'The fund does not normally consider applications for 100% funding therefore, support from other grant sources is welcome.'

Full guidelines can be obtained from the fund's website.

In 2005 the fund had assets of £2.7 million, an income of £745,000 and made grants totalling £297,000, broken down as follows:

Bio-diversity projects	2 grants	£17,000
Community facility improvements	12	£122,000
Environmental education	3	£18,000
Environmental placements	3	£21,000
General environment improvements	5	£90,000
Habitat creation and management	6	£94,000
Parks, gardens and open spaces	4	£81,000
Play areas and recreational facilities	10	£138,000
Ponds, canals and rivers	2	£33,000

There were 18 grants made over £10,000 each. Major beneficiaries in the year included: Groundwork Rossendale (£45,000 in two grants); Groundwork Lancashire West (£44,000 in two grants); the Lancashire Wildlife Trust (£37,000 in two grants); Over Wyresdale Parish Hall Committee (£30,000); Groundwork East Lancashire (£28,000); Groundwork Rossendale, and the Village Initiative Environmental Group (£26,000 each); PCC Ribby cum Wrea, Sustrans, Tosside

PCC, Wildfowl and Wetlands Trust and Woodland Trust (£25,000 each); Baxenden Youth Action Group (£20,000 each); and Capernwray Missionary Fellowships of Torchbearers and RSPB (£15,000 each).

Other grants included those to: Bowland Penine Mountain Rescue Team, Cuerden Valley Park, Kelbrook and Sough Village Hall, the Lancashire Wildlife Trust and Salterforth Network (£7,500 each); Chipping Parish Council (£7,000); RSPB (£6,500); Pendle Environmental Network RE (£5,000); Sawley Village Hall Committee (£4,000); and Victoria Institute Caton (£2,500).

Exclusions All projects must satisfy at least one objective of the Landfill Tax Credit Scheme. For more information about the scheme contact Entrust, the regulatory body, by visiting their website at www.entrust.org.uk or telephoning 0161 972 0044.

Applications On a form available from the correspondent or the website. Completed forms should contain all possible relevant material including maps, photographs, plans, and so on if relevant. The board meets quarterly.

Staff are willing to have informal discussions before an application is made. Potential applicants are strongly advised to visit the website before contacting the trust.

Land Aid Charitable Trust

Homelessness, relief of need

£60,000 available (2006/07)
Beneficial area UK.

7th Floor, 1 Warwick Row, London SW1E 5ER
Tel. 020 7802 0117
Email enquiries@landaid.org
Website www.landaid.org
Correspondent The Chair, Policy & Grants Committee
Trustees Neil Richmond, Chair; Steven Ossack; Sherin Aminossehe; Carol Doughty; Michael Madden; Elana Overs; Derek Penfold; Michael Slade; Abi Broom; Stephen Yarnold; Mike Hussey; Liz Peace; Susan Freeman; Jeremy Newsum; David Taylor; Mike Slade.
CC Number 295157

Information available Information was provided by the trust.

General Land Aid's mission is to support homeless people by raising funds to help:

- provide accommodation
- assist with refurbishment projects
- run training and life skills programmes
- give start-up funding for schemes that might not otherwise get off the ground

In 2006/07 the charity planned to distribute £60,000 UK-wide to appropriate specialist agencies. Applications are invited for awards ranging from £1,000.00 to £60,000. The policy and grants committee will then consider whether to award several grants of different sizes or a single grant for the full amount available for an exceptional project.

Organisations supported have included Centrepoint, Empty Homes Agency, Hope and Homes for Children, Look Ahead Housing and Care's Hostel, New Horizon Youth Centre, the Kings Cross Furniture Project, the London Connection, St John at Hackney Community Space Centre and West London Day Centre.

Exclusions No grants to individuals.

Applications In writing to the correspondent, setting out the aims, objectives, outputs and outcomes of the project in no more than 500 words. (Please mark the envelope 'application for funding'.)

Applications should be submitted between 10 November and 31 January each year. A decision on grant allocation will be made by the committee towards the end of March. Before reaching a decision to fund the committee and/or its representatives may wish to visit the project/organisation.

The Langdale Trust

Social welfare, Christian, medical, general

£115,000 (2004/05)
Beneficial area Worldwide, but with a special interest in Birmingham.

c/o Cobbetts Solicitors, One Colmore Square, Birmingham B4 6AJ
Correspondent M J Woodward, Trustee

Trustees T R Wilson; Mrs T Whiting; M J Woodward.
CC Number 215317
Information available Full accounts were on file at the Charity Commission.

General The trust was established in 1960 by the late Antony Langdale Wilson. There is a preference for local charities in the Birmingham area and those in the fields of social welfare and health, especially with a Christian context.

In 2004/05 it had assets of £3.6 million, which generated an income of £126,000. Grants were made to 45 organisations totalling £115,000.

Beneficiaries included: Save the Children (£6,000); Deafblind UK, Friends of Cardigan Bay and the Leprosy Mission (£4,000 each); Addaction, Macmillan Cancer Relief, Marie Curie Cancer Care, Oxfam – Emergencies Fund, the Samaritans – Worcester, Y Care International, UNICEF – African Appeal and United Christian Broadcasters (£3,000 each); Apex Trust, Basildon Community Resource Centre, Deep Impact Theatre Co., Hope and Homes for Children, International Glaucoma Association, Mercy Ships, National Playing Fields Association, Open Door Youth Counselling, Prisoners Abroad, Quaker Social Action, Rainforest Foundation, Tree Aid and Woodland Trust (£2,000 each).

Applications In writing to the correspondent. The trustees meet in September/October.

The Richard Langhorn Trust

Sport for children

£100,000 (2004)
Beneficial area UK and overseas.

Stoop Memorial Ground, Langhorn Drive, Twickenham, Middlesex TW2 7SX
Tel. 020 8410 6030 **Fax** 020 8410 6014
Email polly@richardlanghorntrust.org
Website www.richardlanghorntrust.org/
Correspondent Polly Wiseman, Secretary
Trustees P Winterbottom, Chair; S Langhorn; Tony Copsey; Mark Evans.
CC Number 1046332
Information available Accounts were on file at the Charity Commission, without a list of grants.

General The trust makes grants towards sports charities for the benefit of children only, particularly in the areas of rugby, sailing, basketball and skiing.

In 2004 it had assets of £49,000 and an income of £71,000, mainly from donations. Grants totalled £100,000. Major grants were made to Great Britain Wheelchair Basketball Association junior championships, Harlequin Football Club's community initiative and the Meridian Trust's yacht project.

Applications In writing, or by email, to the correspondent.

The Langley Charitable Trust

Christian, general

£47,000 to individuals and organisations (2005)

Beneficial area UK and worldwide, with a preference for the West Midlands.

Wheatmoor Farm, 301 Tamworth Road, Sutton Coldfield, West Midlands B75 6JP

Tel. 0121 308 0165

Correspondent The Trustees

Trustees *J P Gilmour; Mrs S S Gilmour.*

CC Number 280104

Information available Accounts were available from the Charity Commission website, but without a list of grants.

General The trust makes grants to evangelical Christian organisations and to other charities in the fields of welfare, medicine and health. It makes grants in the UK and worldwide, but appears to have a small preference for the West Midlands. It operates My Word, a trading book shop and rents out the first floor of its offices to other charities to supplement its income.

In 2005 the trust had assets of £4.2 million and an income of £501,000. Grants were made to one individual and sixteen organisations totalling £47,000. Unfortunately, a list of beneficiaries was not included in the accounts.

Exclusions No grants to animal or bird charities.

Applications In writing to the correspondent. 'The trustees only reply where they require further information and so on. No telephone calls nor correspondence will be entered into concerning any proposed or declined applications.'

The Lanvern Foundation

Education and health, especially relating to children

£80,000 (2005)

Beneficial area UK.

P O Box 34475, London W6 9YB

Tel. 020 8741 2930

Correspondent J C G Stancliffe, Trustee

Trustees *J C G Stancliffe; A H Isaacs.*

CC Number 295846

Information available Accounts were on file at the Charity Commission.

General The foundation was established in 1986. The trustees state that it supports registered charities working primarily in the fields of education and health, with particular emphasis on children. There are never any grants to individuals.

In 2005 it had an income of £86,000 and made 10 grants totalling £80,000. Beneficiaries were Connect (£25,000), Childhood First and Joint Educational Trust (£10,000 each) and Bowel Cancer UK, Evelina Children's Trust, ICAN, IMS Prussia Cove, OCHRE, Wellbeing of Women and Winchester Young Carers (£5,000 each).

Exclusions Absolutely no grants to individuals.

Applications In writing to the correspondent.

The R J Larg Family Charitable Trust

Education, health, medical research, arts – particularly music

About £100,000

Beneficial area UK but generally Scotland, particularly Tayside.

Thorntons Law LLP, 50 Castle Street, Dundee DD1 3RU

Tel. 01382 229111 **Fax** 01382 202288

Email nbarclay@thorntons-law.co.uk

Correspondent Nick Barclay

Trustees *R W Gibson; D A Brand; Mrs S A Stewart.*

SC Number SC004946

Information available Information was provided by the trust.

General The trust has an annual income of approximately £127,000. Grants, which total about £100,000 each year, range between £250 and £6,000 and are given to a variety of organisations.

These include organisations concerned with cancer research and other medical charities, youth organisations, university students' associations and amateur musical groups. No further recent information was available.

Previous beneficiaries include High School – Dundee, Whitehall Theatre Trust, Macmillan Cancer Relief – Dundee and Sense Scotland Children's Hospice.

Exclusions Grants are not available for individuals.

Applications In writing to the correspondent. Trustees meet to consider grants in February and August.

Largsmount Ltd

Jewish

£684,000 (2004/05)

Beneficial area UK and overseas.

Cohen Arnold, New Burlington House, 1075 Finchley Road, London NW11 0PU

Tel. 020 8731 0777 **Fax** 020 8731 0778

Correspondent Jonathan Schwarz

Trustees *Z M Kaufman; Mrs N Kaufman; S Kaufman.*

CC Number 280509

Information available Accounts were on file at the Charity Commission.

General This trust supports Orthodox Jewish charities. In 2004/05 it had an income of £567,000 and a total expenditure of £1 million. Grants totalling £684,000 were made to beneficiaries including: MYR Charitable Trust (£349,000); Yetev Lev Jerusalem (£206,500); Friends of Ohr Akivah (£75,000); Gateshead Foundation for Torah (£5,000); Gateshead Junior Primary School (£2,200); and Soft Agudah Convention (£1,000).

Applications In writing to the correspondent.

Laufer Charitable Trust

Jewish

£80,000 (2006)

Beneficial area UK.

15 Leys Gardens, Cockfosters, Herts EN4 9NA

Tel. 020 8449 3432 **Fax** 020 8449 3432

Correspondent S W Laufer, Trustee

Trustees *S W Laufer; Mrs D D Laufer.*

CC Number 275375

Information available Accounts were on file at the Charity Commission, without a grants list.

General The trust makes grants mainly to Jewish organisations and has a list of charities to which it has a long-term commitment and supports annually or twice a year. It rarely adds new charities to the list.

In 2005/06 the trust had assets of £1.5 million, an income of £190,000 and an expenditure of £80,000 all of which went in grants. Unfortunately, we have no information regarding the beneficiaries.

Exclusions No grants to individuals, as grants are only made to registered charities.

Applications New beneficiaries are only considered by the trust in exceptional circumstances, as the trustees seek to maintain support for an existing group of charities. In view of this it is suggested that no applications be made.

The Lauffer Family Charitable Foundation

Jewish, general

£180,000 (2004/05)

Beneficial area Commonwealth countries, Israel and USA.

123 Hampstead Way, London NW11 7JN

Correspondent J S Lauffer, Trustee

Trustees *Mrs R R Lauffer; J S Lauffer; G L Lauffer; R M Lauffer.*

CC Number 251115

Information available Full accounts were on file at the Charity Commission.

General This trust has general charitable purposes, supporting Jewish causes in the Commonwealth, Israel and USA.

In 2004/05 it had assets of £5 million, which generated an income of £154,000. Grants totalled £180,000. Management and administration costs were high at £27,000.

Grants were broken down as follows:

Education	61 grants	£89,000
Welfare and care of children and families	72	£57,000
Medical healthcare	11	£13,000
Recreation and culture	27	£12,000
Religious activities	11	£4,300
Environment	9	£3,900

Beneficiaries included: British Friends of Ohr Someach (£13,500); British Friends of Sarah Herzog Memorial Hospital and Kollel Pardes Trust (£10,000 each); British Friends of Shvut Ami (£9,000); United Joint Israel Appeal (£7,500); Spiro Ark (£7,000); Society of Friends of Torah (£6,200); MESHI, Victoria Shasha Foundation and Zionist Federation (£5,000 each); Menorah Foundation School (£7,200); Community Security Trust, Friends of Mercaz Beth Jacob, University of Cambridge and Jewish Learning Exchange (£3,000 each); Kisharon School (£2,600); National Yad Vashem Charitable Trust (£2,500); Holocaust Educational Trust (£2,000); British Emunah (£1,500); and Home for Aged Jews, JNF Charitable Trust, Jewish Care, Jewish Child's Day, National Jewish Chaplaincy Board and World Jewish Relief (£1,000 each).

Exclusions No support for individuals.

Applications In writing to the correspondent; applications are considered once a year.

Mrs F B Laurence Charitable Trust

Social welfare, medical, disability, environment

£87,000 (2004/05)

Beneficial area Worldwide.

PO Box 28927, London SW14 7WL

Correspondent The Trustees

Trustees *M Tooth; G S Brown; D A G Sarre.*

CC Number 296548

Information available Accounts were on file at the Charity Commission.

General The trust produces guidelines which state: 'Our priority is for the care and/or improvement of conditions of the disadvantaged members of society within the United Kingdom or those overseas to whom the United Kingdom owes a duty of care.

'We mainly support charities that are known to the Trustees, or are established in their field and have a good track record. We do, however, consider small innovative charities with a hands-on approach, even if their work may be primarily devoted to a particular locality, or if they are likely to provide a model for wider application.'

This trust gives for general charitable purposes, including many service, medical and welfare charities as well as hospices and environmental groups.

In 2004/05 the trust had assets of £2.3 million, and a total income of £85,000. Grants were made totalling £87,000. Management and administration expenses were high at £19,000, including a payment of £13,000 to a firm in which one of the trustees is a partner. Whilst wholly legal, these editors always regret such payments unless, in the words of the Charity Commission, 'there is no realistic alternative'.

Major beneficiaries included: St Christopher's Hospice (£2,500); Breakthrough Breast Cancer (£2,000); and Dressability, Eve Charitable Trust, Extra Care Charitable Trust, Soundaround and SSFA (£1,5000 each). All other grants were for £1,000 or less, and totalled £75,000.

Exclusions No support for individuals. The following applications are unlikely to be considered:

- appeals for endowment or sponsorship
- overseas projects, unless overseen by the charity's own fieldworkers
- maintenance of buildings or landscape
- provision of work or materials that are the responsibility of the state
- where administration expenses, in all their guises, are considered by the trustees to be excessive
- where the fundraising costs in the preceding year have not resulted in an increase in the succeeding years' donations in excess of these costs.

Applications In writing to the correspondent, including the latest set of accounts, as filed with the Charity Commission. The guidelines state: 'Write to us on not more than two sides of A4 paper with the following information:

- who you are
- what you do
- what distinguishes your work from others in your field
- where applicable describe the project that the money you are asking for is going towards and include a business plan/budget
- what funds have already been raised and how?
- how much are you seeking from us?
- how do you intend to measure the potential benefits of your project or work as a whole?

'Trustees usually meet in April and November. Please submit your application by 1 February for the April meeting and by 1 August for the October meeting.

'To save on our administration costs, we will only notify the successful applicants.'

The Kathleen Laurence Trust

Heart disease, arthritis, older people, children with disabilities

£121,000 (2005/06)

Beneficial area UK.

Trustee Department, Coutts and Co., 440 Strand, London WC2R 0QS

Tel. 020 7753 1000 **Fax** 020 7753 1090

Correspondent David Breach, Assistant Trust Manager

Trustee Coutts and Co.

CC Number 296461

Information available Accounts were on file at the Charity Commission.

General Donations are given to a wide range of institutions, particularly favouring smaller organisations and those concerned with the treatment and care of individuals and research of heart disease and arthritis. Organisations concerned with older people and children who are mentally or physically disabled are also considered.

In 2005/06 the trust had assets of £3.2 million and an income of £50,000. Grants were made to 49 organisations totalling £121,000.

The largest grants were to Arthritis Research Campaign, British Heart Foundation, MENCAP, Elizabeth Finn Trust, Battersea Dogs Home, Cancer Research Campaign and NSPCC each of whom received £12,500.

Smaller grants included: Age Concern – England, Gynaecology Cancer Research Fund and Over the Wall (£1,000 each); CORDA – The Heart Charity, First Steps Scarborough and The Oxfordshire Befriending Network (£750 each); and Welsh Association of Youth Clubs, Narborough Pals and The Newlife Foundation – 1983 (£500 each).

Exclusions No donations are made for running costs, management expenses or to individuals.

Applications In writing to the correspondent. Trustees meet in January and June.

The Law Society Charity

Law and justice, worldwide

£679,810 (2005/06)

Beneficial area Worldwide.

113 Chancery Lane, London WC2A 1PL

Tel. 020 7320 5905

Correspondent Bill Bilimoria

Trustee The Law Society Trustees Ltd.

CC Number 268736

Information available Full accounts were on file at the Charity Commission.

General As the name suggests, this trust is concerned with causes connected to the legal profession, particularly in advancing legal education and access to legal knowledge. Organisations protecting people's legal rights and lawyers' welfare are also supported, as are law-related projects from charities without an identifiable legal connection.

In 2005/06 the trust had assets of £2 million and an income of £160,000. Grants totalling £680,000 were made to 23 organisations.

The largest grant was for £248,000 to LawCare Limited. Other major beneficiaries included: The Citizenship Foundation (£95,000); Solicitors' Benevolent Association (£80,000); BAILLI (£60,000); Diversity Access Scheme Scholarships (£50,000); Solicitors Pro Bono Group (£30,000); and Forest People's Project (£20,000).

Applications In writing to the correspondent. Applications are considered at quarterly trustees' meetings, usually held in April, July, September and December.

The Edgar E Lawley Foundation

Older people, disability, children, community

£200,000 (2005/06)

Beneficial area UK, with a preference for the West Midlands.

Lower Wakefield, 116 Foley Road, Claygate, Surrey KT10 0NA

Tel. 01372 805760 **Fax** 0121 445 3536

Email frankjackson1945@yahoo.com

Correspondent F S Jackson, Trustee

Trustees J H Cooke, Chair; Mrs G V H Hilton; P J Cooke; Mrs E E Sutcliffe; F S Jackson.

CC Number 201589

Information available Accounts were on file at the Charity Commission.

General The trust's primary objectives are 'the making of grants to charitable bodies for provision of medical care and services to children and the aged, the advancement of medicine and for educational purposes'. There is a preference for the West Midlands.

In 2005/06 the foundation had assets of £4.6 million and an income of just over £1 million. Some £945,000 of this was as a result of funds received from the will of the late Mrs V V Lawley. Grants were made to 110 organisations and totalled £200,000. Administration costs were very low at just £2,200.

Beneficiaries in the West Midlands included Age Concern – Sandwell, Birmingham Boys' & Girls' Union, Coventry Boys' Club, Family Care Trust – Solihull, Shakespeare Hospice and Yemeni Elderly in Small Heath.

Beneficiaries elsewhere included Age Concern – Sheffield, Belfast Central Mission, Brecon & District Disabled Club, Roy Castle Lung Cancer Foundation, Deafblind UK, Hartlepool & District Hospice, King's College – London, RNIB, Smile UK, South Bucks Hospice and Worcester MIND.

Exclusions No grants to individuals.

Applications In writing to the correspondent. Applications must be received during April.

The Lawson Beckman Charitable Trust

Jewish, welfare, education, arts

£62,000 (2004/05)

Beneficial area UK.

A Beckman plc, PO Box 1ED, London W1A 1ED

Tel. 020 7637 8412 **Fax** 020 7436 8599

Correspondent Maurice Lawson

Trustees *M A Lawson; J N Beckman; F C Katz; L R Stock.*

CC Number 261378

Information available Accounts were on file at the Charity Commission.

General The report for 2005 states that the trust gives grants for the 'relief of poverty, support of the arts and general charitable purposes'. Grants are allocated two years in advance.

In 2004/05 the trust had assets of £1.9 million and an income of £122,000. A total of £62,000 was distributed in grants broken down as follows:

Medical, health and sickness – £25,750 in 7 grants
Norwood Ravenswood (£13,500), Nightingale House (£5,000), UCH Hospital Charity (£2,500), Cystic Fibrosis (£2,000), The Mehran David Foundation (£1,500), Chai Lifeline Cancer Care (£1,000) and Aid for Alyn (£250).

Accommodation and housing – £16,000 in 1 grant
Jewish Care

Religious activities – £10,500 in 5 grants
UIA (£5,250), United Synagogue (£3,500), Conference of European Rabbis (£1,000), One Family UK (£500) and Hospital Kosher Meals (£250).

Overseas aid – £6,250 in 3 grants
World Jewish Relief (£5,000), Princess of Romania Trust (£1,000) and Friends of Lanioda UK (£250).

General charitable purposes – £1,200 in 2 grants
Bernard and Lucy Lyons Charitable

Trust (£750) and Central Synagogue General Charities Fund (£450).

Disability – £1,000 in 1 grant
Harrow MS Therapy Centre.

Education and training – £1,000 in 3 grants
British Tecion (£500) and Mill Hill Aviv and The University of Liverpool (£250 each).

Exclusions No grants to individuals.

Applications In writing to the correspondent, but please note that grants are allocated two years in advance.

The Raymond and Blanche Lawson Charitable Trust

General

£117,000 (2004/05)

Beneficial area UK, with an interest in West Kent and East Sussex.

28 Barden Road, Tonbridge, Kent TN9 1TX

Tel. 01732 352183 **Fax** 01732 352621

Correspondent Mrs P E V Banks, Trustee

Trustees *John V Banks; Mrs P E V Banks; Mrs Sarah Hill.*

CC Number 281269

Information available Accounts were on file at the Charity Commission.

General The trust has a preference for local organisations and generally supports charities within the following categories:

- local voluntary organisations
- preservation of buildings
- local hospices
- care in the community
- assistance for people who are disabled
- armed forces and benevolent funds.

In 2004/05 the trust had assets of £1.4 million, an income of £130,000 and made grants totalling £117,000. Administration and management costs were a low £1,900.

The largest grant was for £12,000 to Medway Valley Abbeyfield Home. Other large grants went to Tunbridge Wells Scouts Association (£5,000), Hadlow Village Hall and Hospice in the Weald (£4,000 each), British Legion Poppy

Appeal (£3,500) and the Heart of Kent Hospices (£3,000).

Smaller grants included £1,000 each to Cheshire Homes Seven Springs, The Dyslexia Institute and Winged Fellowship and £500 each to The Alfred Seafarers Society, Church Army and Motor Neurone Association.

Exclusions No support for churches or individuals.

Applications In writing to the correspondent.

The Leach Fourteenth Trust

Medical, disability, environment, conservation, general

£66,000 (2005/06)

Beneficial area UK, with some preference for south west England and overseas only via a UK charity.

Barron & Barron, Chartered Accountants, Bathurst House, 86 Micklegate, York Y01 6LQ

Tel. 01904 628551 **Fax** 01904 623533

Email info@barronyork.co.uk

Correspondent Guy Ward, Trustee

Trustees *W J Henderson; Mrs J M M Nash; R Murray-Leach; G S Ward.*

CC Number 204844

Information available Accounts were on file at the Charity Commission.

General Although the trust's objectives are general, the trustees tend towards medical and disability organisations. The trust also has a preference for conservation (ecological) organisations. In practice there is a preference for south west England and the Home Counties. In 2005/06 the trust had assets of £2.7 million, an income of £75,000 and gave 62 grants totalling £66,000.

A few charities receive regular donations. The trustees prefer to give single grants for specific projects rather than towards general funding and also favour small organisations or projects.

Beneficiaries for the year included: DEC Niger and The National Trust (£5,000 each); The Burned Children's Club, The Country Trust, Dorothy House Foundation and Durrell Wildlife

Conservation Trust (£2,000 each); 1st Felpham Sea Group, Hearts & Minds, Julian House, Trinity Hospice (£1,500 each); British Blind Sport and Wiltshire Bobby Van Trust (£1,000 each) and St John Ambulance and Wiltshire Air Ambulance (£500 each).

Exclusions Only registered charities based in the UK are supported (the trust only gives overseas via a UK-based charity). No grants to: individuals, including for gap years or trips abroad; private schools, other than for people with disabilities or learning difficulties; no pet charities.

Applications In writing to the correspondent. Applications for a specific item or purpose are favoured. Only successful appeals can expect a reply. A representative of the trust occasionally visits potential beneficiaries. There are bi-annual meetings of trustees in summer and late autumn. Grants tend to be distributed twice a year but exceptions are made.

The David Lean Foundation

Film production

£412,000 (2005)
Beneficial area UK.

Churchill House, Regent House, Stoke-on-Trent ST1 3RQ
Tel. 01782 202020 **Fax** 01782 266060
Email aar@kjd.co.uk
Website www.davidleanfoundation.org
Correspondent The Trustees
Trustees A A Reeves; J G Moore.
CC Number 1067074
Information available Accounts were on file at the Charity Commission.

General The foundation was registered on 23 December 1997 and was given rights to royalties of four of the major films directed by the late Sir David Lean. This provides the foundation's principal, current and future source of income.

The foundation's grant-making policy is to achieve its objectives by making awards:

- to other charitable institutions whose aims include aims similar to those of the foundation
- to National Film and Television School, Royal Holloway and Leighton

Park School for scholarship/chairs on recommendations of the school
- to institutions/individuals for film literature research/support in particular with Sir David Lean associations
- to individuals as scholarships for learning the film industry.

In 2005 the foundation had an income of £267,000 and distributed grants totalling £412,000.

The largest grants for the year were: £130,000 to National Film and Television School (NFTS); £98,000 to British Academy of Film and Television Arts (BAFTA); £34,000 to Leighton Park School; and £30,000 to British Kinematograph Sound and Television Society (BKSTS). These grants were mainly to support scholarships and educational training.

Other beneficiaries included: Royal Academy of Arts (£28,500); Royal Holloway University of London (£28,450); Literary research (two grants totalling £10,000); and to assist film-making (two grants totalling £6,500).

Future commitments totalling £342,000 were also made in 2005, including those to the following organisations – British Film Institute, BAFTA, BKSTS, NFTS and the Royal Academy of Arts.

Applications Scholarship grants for students attending the National Film and Television School, Royal Holloway or Leighton Park School, are normally only awarded on the recommendation of the course provider to the trustees.

Other applications for grants that would meet the aims of the foundation are invited in writing, enclosing full details of the project and including financial information and two references.

The Leche Trust

Preservation and restoration of Georgian art, music and architecture

£153,000 to organisations (2004/05)
Beneficial area UK.

84 Cicada Road, London SW18 2NZ
Tel. 020 8870 6233 **Fax** 020 8870 6233
Correspondent Mrs Louisa Lawson, Secretary

CC Number 225659
Information available Accounts were on file at the Charity Commission.

General The trust was founded and endowed by the late Mr Angus Acworth in 1950. It supports the following categories:

- assistance to students from overseas during the last six months of their postgraduate doctorate study in the UK
- assistance to academic, educational or other organisations concerned with music, drama, dance and the arts
- preservation of buildings and their contents and the repair and conservation of church furniture (including such items as monuments, but excluding structural repairs to the fabric) – preference is given to buildings and objects of the Georgian period
- assistance to conservation, including museums
- support with the charitable activities associated with the preservation of rural England
- the promotion of amity and good relations between Britain and the developing world or former 'Iron Curtain' countries by financing visits to such countries by teachers or other appropriate persons.

In 2004/05 the trust had assets of £6 million and an income of £227,000. 57 grants were approved totalling £180,000, broken down as follows:

Churches – 12 grants totalling £42,500
These included: £6,000 towards the restoration of the third Coalbrookedale cast iron-framed window at St Alkmund's Church in Shrewsbury; £5,000 towards the restoration of the carvings in the Redland Chapel in Bristol and £4,000 to help restore the organ in St George's Church in York.

Arts – 24 grants totalling £41,750
This category included modest grants given to promotions in the field of music, opera and dance. Examples include £3,000 to Central School of Ballet, £2,750 to Opera Circus and £1,500 to Lake District Summer Music.

Historic buildings – 9 grants totalling £38,000
These included: £5,000 to the restoration of the onion dome on the front range of the buildings at Castlemilk Stables, owned by the Glasgow Preservation Society; £5,000 for a feasibility study into

the future of Neuadd Fawr House at Cilyewm in Carmarthenshire and £5,000 to Painswick Roccoco Garden for the repainting of the extend of the Red House.

Education (institutions and museums) – 9 grants totalling £30,750

These included: £5,000 towards restoration of the frame of the Peter Lely picture, 'Nymphs by a Fountain', in the Dulwich Picture Gallery, £5,000 to the Fitzwilliam Museum in Cambridge for the restoration of their collection of Handel music manuscripts; and £2,750 to help with the restoration of the final two chairs in the set in the Henrietta Street Room at the Victoria and Albert Museum.

Overseas students – 27 grants totalling £18,750

Grants averaging £800 went to students from 18 separate countries who were in the final six month of their PhD degrees. The largest group of beneficiaries came from Bangladesh.

Education (individuals) – 3 grants totalling £8,000

These were given to individual students at Guildhall School of Music and West Dean College (£2,000 each) and London Contemporary Dance School (£4,000).

Exclusions No grants are made for: religious bodies; overseas missions; schools and school buildings; social welfare; animals; medicine; expeditions; or British students other than music students.

Applications In writing to the secretary. Trustees meet three times a year, in February, June and October; applications need to be received the month before.

The Arnold Lee Charitable Trust

Jewish, educational, health

£86,000 (2005/06)
Beneficial area UK.

47 Orchard Court, Portman Square, London W1H 9PD
Tel. 0207 486 8918
Correspondent A Lee, Trustee
Trustees *Arnold Lee; Helen Lee; Alan Lee.*
CC Number 264437

Information available Full accounts were on file at the Charity Commission, but without an up-to-date grants list.

General The policy of the trustees is to distribute income to 'established charities of high repute' for any charitable purpose or object. The trust supports a large number of Jewish organisations.

In 2005/06 the trust had assets of £1.8 million and an income of £96,000. Grants were made to 41 institutions totalling £86,000. No information regarding the beneficiaries was available.

Previous beneficiaries have included Joint Jewish Charitable Trust, Project SEED, Jewish Care, Lubavich Foundations, The Home of Aged Jews, Yesodey Hatorah School and Friends of Akim.

Exclusions Grants are rarely made to individuals.

Applications In writing to the correspondent.

Morris Leigh Foundation

Jewish, general

£50,000 (2005/06)
Beneficial area UK.

Adelaide House, London Bridge, London EC4R 9HA
Tel. 020 7353 0299
Correspondent M D Paisner, Trustee
Trustees *Martin D Paisner; Howard D Leigh.*
CC Number 280695

Information available Accounts were on file at the Charity Commission, but without an up-to-date grants list.

General The foundation has general charitable purposes, mostly supporting Jewish, welfare and arts organisations.

In 2005/06 the foundation had assets of £1.5 million and an income of £60,000. Grants totalling £50,000 were made during the year, but we have no details of the beneficiaries.

Previously, grants have been made to the Royal College of Music, London Business School, Rycolewood College, Institute for Jewish Policy Research, Ronald Raven Cancer Trust, London Symphony Orchestra, London Philharmonic Orchestra, Somerset House Arts Fund, Sussex University, Community Service Trust, Chicken Shed

Theatre, Holocaust Educational Fund, British ORT, Cancerkin – Women Gala, Commonwealth Jewish Trust, London Jewish Culture Centre, Reading Hebrew Congregation, UJIA, Medical Foundation and Inspire Foundation.

Applications In writing to the correspondent.

The Leigh Trust

Drug and alcohol rehabilitation, criminal justice, asylum seekers, racial equality

£149,000 (2004/05)
Beneficial area Unrestricted, but with some apparent London interest.

Begbies Chettle Agar, Epworth House, 25 City Road, London EC1Y 1AR
Tel. 020 7628 5801 **Fax** 020 7628 0390
Correspondent The Trustees
Trustees *Hon. David Bernstein; Dr R M E Stone; Caroline Moorehead.*
CC Number 275372

Information available Annual report and accounts on file at the Charity Commission.

General The Leigh Trust was established in 1976. In 2004/05 the trust had assets of £2.7 million and an income of £79,000. Grants totalled £149,000.

The current policy is to distribute investment revenue and a proportion of capital gains.

The trust makes grants to a variety of registered charities concerned with:

- drug and alcohol rehabilitation
- criminal justice
- asylum seekers/racial equality
- education.

The policy of the trustees is to support those organisations which they believe to be in greatest need. The trustees can respond favourably to very few applicants.'

Grants were categorised by the trust as follows:

Addiction	£37,000
Asylum seekers/racial equality	£38,000
Children/youth	£5,000
Community	£14,000
Criminal justice	£55,000

The trust gave 26 grants in 2004/05. The largest grants were £25,000 to Public Concern at Work, £15,000 to Churches Commission for Racial Justice and

£10,000 each to Chemical Dependency Centre, Clouds and Focus.

Other beneficiaries included Lord Ashdown Charitable Settlement (£8,000), Cariba Project, Children of Chernobyl, SIGN, Prison Advice and Care Trust, Prisoners Abroad, Trail-Blazers and Turkish Education Group (£5,000 each), Detainees Support Help Unit (£4,000), Ace of Clubs (£3,000), Lifebuoy Charitable Trust (£2,000) and Consequences and South Sudanese Community Association (£1,000 each).

Exclusions The trust does not make grants to individuals.

Applications Initial applications should be made in writing to the registered office of the trust.

Organisations should enclose the most recent audited accounts, a registered charity number, a cash flow statement for the next 12 months, and an sae.

Applicants should state clearly on one side of A4 what their charity does and what they are requesting funding for. They should provide a detailed budget and show other sources of funding for the project. The charity may be requested to complete an application form. It is likely that an officer of the trust will wish to visit the project before any grant is made. Trustees' meetings are held quarterly.

The P Leigh-Bramwell Trust 'E'

Methodist, general

£88,000 (2005/06)

Beneficial area UK, with a preference for Bolton.

W and J Leigh and Co., Tower Works, Kestor Street, Bolton BL2 2AL

Tel. 01204 521771

Correspondent P Morrison, Secretary

Trustees *Mrs H R Leigh-Bramwell; Mrs J L Hardyment; B H Leigh-Bramwell.*

CC Number 267333

Information available Accounts were on file at the Charity Commission.

General The objectives of the charity are to 'advance Christian religion, education, the RNLI and any other legal charitable institution'.

In 2005/06 the trust had assets of £2.3 million, an income of £103,000 and made grants totalling £88,000. The largest grant was given to Leigh-Bramwell Scholarship Fund (£40,000). Other large beneficiaries included The Methodist Church – Circuit (£11,000), Barnes Methodist Church (£5,500), The Unicorn School (£5,000), The Methodist Churches in Breightmet and Delph Hill (£3,400 each).

Smaller grant beneficiaries included YWCA, Royal Star and Garter Homes, The Samaritans, Bolton Choral Union, NCH Bypass and Trinity Hospice (£500 each).

Exclusions No grants to individuals.

Applications In writing to the correspondent; however, please note that previous research suggests that there is only a small amount of funds available for unsolicited applications and therefore success is unlikely.

The Leonard Trust

Christian, overseas aid

£37,000 to organisations (2004/05)

Beneficial area Overseas and UK, with a preference for Winchester.

18 Edgar Road, Winchester, Hampshire SO23 9TW

Tel. 01962 854 800

Correspondent Tessa E Feilden, Trustee

Trustees *Tessa Feilden; Dominic Gold; Carol Gold.*

CC Number 1031723

Information available Accounts were available from the Charity Commission, but without a narrative report.

General The trust informed us that it makes grants totalling about £30,000 each year, ranging between £1,000 and £5,000 each. It supports Christian and overseas aid organisations. In 2004/05 the trust had an income of £35,000 and made grants to 26 organisations totalling £37,000.

Grant recipients included Icthes World Care, Demand and L'Arche Overseas (£3,000 each), Glasgow Central Vineyard Church, MACA – now known as Together: Working for Well Being and Tear Fund (£2,000 each), the Bible Society, Evangelism Explosion and the Frontier Youth Trust (£1,000 each) and the Karen Hill Tribe Trust (£100).

Exclusions No grants to individuals. Medical research or building projects are no longer supported.

Applications Unsolicited applications cannot be considered.

The Mark Leonard Trust

Environmental education, young people, general

£195,300 (2004/05)

Beneficial area Worldwide, but mainly UK.

Allington House, 1st Floor, 150 Victoria Street, London SW1E 5AE

Tel. 020 7410 0330 **Fax** 020 7410 0332

Email info@sfct.org.uk

Correspondent Alan Bookbinder, Director

Trustees *Mrs Z Sainsbury; Miss Judith Portrait; J J Sainsbury; Mark Sainsbury.*

CC Number 1040323

Information available Accounts were on file at the Charity Commission.

General This is one of the 18 Sainsbury Family Charitable Trusts, which collectively give over £60 million a year. It mostly supports environmental causes and youth work, although it also gives towards general charitable purposes. The following descriptions of its more specific work are taken from its 2004/05 annual report:

Environment – 'Grants are made for environmental education, particularly to support projects displaying practical ways of involving children and young adults. The trustees rarely support new educational resource packs in isolation from the actual process of learning and discovering. They are more interested in programmes which help pupils and teachers to develop a theme over time (such as renewable energy), perhaps combining IT resources for data gathering and communication, with exchange visits and the sharing of information and ideas between schools.

'The trustees are particularly interested in projects that enable children and young people to develop a sense of ownership of the project over time, and that provide direct support to teachers to deliver exciting and high quality education in the classroom.

'The trustees are also interested in the potential for sustainable transport, energy efficiency and renewable energy in the wider society. In some cases the trustees will consider funding research, but only where there is a clear practical application. Proposals are more likely to be considered when they are testing an idea, model or strategy in practice.'

Youth work – 'The trustees aim to help projects that support the rehabilitation of young people who have become marginalised and involved in antisocial or criminal activities. They wish to apply their grants to overcome social exclusion. They are also interested in extending and adding value to the existing use of school buildings, enhancing links between schools and the community, and encouraging greater involvement of parents, school leavers and volunteers in extra-curricular activities.

In 2004/05 the trust had assets of £9.5 million and an income of £495,000. The management and administration charges included payments totalling £3,200 to a firm of solicitors in which one of the trustees is a partner. Whilst wholly legal, these editors always regret such payments unless, in the words of the Charity Commission, 'there is no realistic alternative'. Grants were approved totalling £195,300, broken down as follows:

Environment – 13 grants totalling £101,500
The largest grants were £15,000 each to Ashden Awards for Sustainable Energy and Sustainable Transport (Sustrans). Other grants included: £10,000 each to Envision, Global Generation, Pedestrians Association and the Woodland Trust; £8,000 to Global Action Plan; £7,500 each to BioRegional Development Group and Sustainability North West; and £4,500 to Green Beings Environmental Theatre.

Youth work – 5 grants totalling £87,300
The largest grant was £27,300 Groundwork Trust; Other beneficiaries were: £20,000 to Street Dreams; £18,000 to HMP/YOI Bullwood Hall; £15,000 to CJ's MediaWorkz and £7,000 to Leeds Action to Create Homes (LATCH).

General – 2 grants totalling £6,500
These were £5,000 to Reason Partnership and £1,500 to Sainsbury Archive.

Exclusions 'Proposals are generally invited by the trustees or initiated at their request. Unsolicited applications are not encouraged and are unlikely to be successful, even if they fall within an area in which the trustees are interested. The trustees' objective is to support innovative schemes with seed funding,

leading projects to achieve sustainability and successful replication. Grants are not normally made to individuals.'

Applications 'Proposals are likely to be invited by the trustees or initiated at their request. Unsolicited applications are unlikely to be successful, even if they fall within an area in which the trustees are interested.' A single application will be considered for support by all the trusts in the Sainsbury family group.

The Leverhulme Trade Charities Trust

Charities benefiting commercial travellers, grocers or chemists

£662,000 to organisations (2004/05)

Beneficial area UK.

1 Pemberton Row, London EC4A 3BG
Tel. 020 7822 6915
Correspondent Paul Read, Secretary
Trustees *Sir Michael Angus, Chair; Sir Michael Perry; N W A Fitzgerald; P J-P Cescau; A S Ganguly.*
CC Number 288404
Information available Accounts were on file at the Charity Commission.

General The Leverhulme Trade Charities Trust derives from the will of the First Viscount Leverhulme, who died in 1925. He left a proportion of his shares in Lever Brothers Ltd upon trust and specified the income beneficiaries to include certain trade charities. In 1983, the Leverhulme Trade Charities Trust itself was established, with its own shareholding in Unilever, and with grantmaking to be restricted to charities connected with commercial travellers, grocers or chemists, their wives, widows or children. The trust has no full-time employees, but the day-to-day administration is carried out by the director of finance at The Leverhulme Trust.

Grants are only made to:

- trade benevolent institutions supporting commercial travellers, grocers or chemists
- schools or universities providing education for them or their children.

In 2004/05 the trust had assets of £32 million and an income of £1.2 million. Grants to organisations totalled £662,000 of which £375,000 was for the benefit of individuals. A further £385,000 was given in 68 undergraduate bursaries.

The largest single grant of £185,000 went to Commercial Travellers' Institution. Other beneficiaries were Commercial Travellers of Scotland (£39,000 over three years), Provision Trade Institution (£63,000 over three years) and Royal Pinner School (£375,000 over three years).

Exclusions No capital grants. No response is given to general appeals.

Applications By letter to the correspondent. All correspondence is acknowledged. The trustees meet in February and applications need to be received by the preceding October.

Undergraduate bursary applications should be directed to the relevant institution.

Lewis Family Charitable Trust

Medical research, health, education, Jewish charities

£545,000 (2004/05)
Beneficial area UK and overseas.

Chelsea House, West Gate, London W5 1DR
Tel. 020 8991 4601
Correspondent The Secretary
Trustees *David Lewis; Bernard Lewis.*
CC Number 259892
Information available Accounts were on file at the Charity Commission.

General The trust's annual report stated that 'The Lewis Family Charitable Trust was established to give expression to the charitable intentions of members of the families of David, Bernard, Geoffrey and Godfrey Lewis and certain companies which they control. The legally permitted objectives are very wide and cover virtually every generally accepted charitable object. However, in practice the causes to which the trustees have devoted the bulk of their resources in recent years have been medical research and support with particular reference to the following:

- research into possible treatments for cancer specialising in gene therapy and leukaemia
- head injuries
- birth defects
- rehabilitation following amputation and physical disability
- jewish community general charities.

In 2004/05 the trust had assets of £5.2 million and an income of £1.5 million. Grants totalled £545,000.

Exclusions No grants to individuals.

Applications In writing to the correspondent.

The John Spedan Lewis Foundation

Natural sciences, particularly horticulture, ornithology, entomology

£52,000 (2005/06)
Beneficial area UK.

Partnership House, Carlisle Place, London SW1P 1BX

Tel. 020 7592 6121

Email bridget_chamberlain@johnlewis. co.uk

Correspondent Ms B M F Chamberlain, Secretary

Trustees *Sir Stuart Hampson, Chair; Ken Temple; Dr Vaughan Southgate; Simon Fowler; Cecily Watson.*

CC Number 240473

Information available Accounts were on file at the Charity Commission.

General The trust makes grants in the areas of horticulture, ornithology and entomology, and to associated educational and research projects. Donations are mainly one-off.

In 2005/06 it had assets of £2.5 million, which generated an income of £81,000. Grants were made to 14 organisations totalling £52,000.

Beneficiaries included York Foundation for Conservation and Craftmanship (£6,000), University of Oxford Botanic Garden (£5,300), St Mungos Community Housing Association (£5,000), Buglife and International Commission on Zoological Nomenclature (£4,700 each), National Council for the Conservation of Plants and Gardens (£4,100), Scottish

Native Woods (£3,500), University of Oxford Botanic Garden (£2,900), Clyde River Foundation (£2,000), Sussex Wildlife Trust (£1,800), Where Next Association? (£1,000) and Woodcroft Allotments Association (£950).

Exclusions No grants to individuals (including students), local branches of national organisations, or for salaries, medical research, welfare projects, building works or overseas expeditions.

Applications In writing to the correspondent with latest report and accounts and a budget for the proposed project.

The Sir Edward Lewis Foundation

General

£199,000 (2005/06)
Beneficial area UK and overseas, with a preference for Surrey.

Messrs Rawlinson and Hunter, The Lower Mill, Kingston Road, Ewell, Surrey KT17 2AE

Tel. 020 7451 9000

Correspondent Mrs Sandra Frankland

Trustees *R A Lewis; K W Dent; C J A Lewis; S J N Dorin.*

CC Number 264475

Information available Accounts were available from the Charity Commission website.

General The trust was established in 1972 by Sir Edward Roberts Lewis. In 2005/06 the foundation had assets of £7.1 million, an income of £234,000 and made grants to 101 organisations totalling £199,000.

The trust has revised its policy and now plans to make one substantial donation every two or three years to an appropriate cause as well as smaller donations on an annual basis. Therefore it will not distribute all its income every year. The trustees prefer to support charities known personally to them and those favoured by the settlor.

Beneficiaries of the largest grants were Fareshare (£25,000), the Children's Trust Tadworth and the Reconstruction Project (£20,000 each), the Arnold Foundation for Rugby School (£10,000) and King Edward VII's Hospital, Gurkha

Welfare Trust, the Rugby Clubs, SOS Children's Villages and the David Shepherd Wildlife Foundation (£5,000 each)

Other beneficiaries included Institute of Economic Affairs and Marie Curie Cancer Care (£3,000), Ophthalmic Aid to Eastern Europe (£2,500), CRISIS, Council for Music in Hospitals, Drake Music Project, Life Blood, Musician Benevolent Fund, National Osteoporosis Society, the Airey Neave Trust, the Purcell School, St Catherine Hospice, SeeAbility and UK Antarctic Heritage Trust (£2,000 each), Heatherley Cheshire Home, Reeds School and Shipwrecked Fishermans Society (£1,500 each), Blond McIndoe Centre for Medical Research, Familyline – Surrey, Goldsmiths Choral Union, the Haemophilia Society, MacMillan Fund Cancer Relief, National Asthma Campaign, Orchard Vale Trust, Research into Ageing, SSAFA, Surrey Opera, WaterAid and Young Concert Artists Trust (£1,000 each), Soundaround (£750) and Alzheimer's Disease Society, Barnardos, Compaid Trust, Counsel & Care for the Elderly, MIND and PDSA (£500 each).

Exclusions Grants are only given to charities, projects or people known to the trustees. No grants are given to individuals.

Applications In writing to the correspondent. The trustees meet every six months.

Lifeline 4 Kids

Equipment for children with disabilities

£170,000 to individuals and organisations (2005)
Beneficial area Worldwide.

215 West End Lane, London NW6 1XJ

Website www.lifeline4kids.org

Correspondent Roger Adelman, Trustee

Trustees *Jeffrey Bonn; Roger Adelman; Paul Maurice; Beverley Emden; Mrs Roberta Harris.*

CC Number 200050

Information available Accounts were on file at the Charity Commission, but without a list of grants. Information was available on its website.

General This charity supports children who are disabled up to 18 years old. The following description is taken from its website:

'We are a London-based children's charity established in 1961. Originally known as The Handicapped Children's Aid Committee, our working name has now changed to Lifeline 4 Kids. Our members work on an entirely voluntary basis and we have no paid staff.

'We were formed for one purpose – to provide essential equipment to help improve the quality of life for children with disabilities and special needs irrespective of their race or creed.

- 'We help equip hospital neonatal units with the latest incubators, infusion pumps and ultrasonic monitors amongst other life-saving equipment.
- 'Children's hospices, respite care homes and support centres throughout the UK also receive our help with equipment including beds, soft play and multi-sensory rooms.
- 'For the individual child we provide the full spectrum of specialised equipment such as electric wheelchairs, mobility aids and varying items including specialised computers. We are also one of the only UK charities prepared to help a special needs child from a low-income family with essential smaller items such as shoes, clothing, bedding and specialist toys.
- 'We are able to give emergency and welfare appeals immediate approval within the authorised limits of our welfare subcommittee.
- 'No appeal is too large or too small for us to consider.'

In 2005 it had assets of £709,000, an income of £238,000 and gave £170,000 in response to appeals.

Grants given in 2006 included those to: Central Middlesex Hospital, towards equipment for its outdoor play area (£5,000); the Living Paintings Trust, funding the production of 20 copies of a new Living Picture Book (£2,500); the New Jumbulance Travel Trust, providing two portable instant resuscitation packs (£2,400); Vision Aid, providing a specialised flat screen video magnifier (£2,000); and the Lothian Autistic Society, for equipment for its various play schemes (£1,500).

Exclusions Building projects, research grants and salaries will not be funded.

Applications Applications for help indicating specific requirements and brief factual information must initially be made in writing, addressed to the Investigations Officer, or by email (appeals@lifeline4kids.org). Each request will be acknowledged and provided it meets the charity's criteria, an application form will be sent by post.

Appeals are discussed and decided upon at monthly meetings. If appropriate, the appeal will be investigated personally by one of our members. If approved, a maximum sum is allocated and we take full responsibility for the purchase and safe delivery of the approved item.

Initial telephone calls from applicants are not welcome.

Limoges Charitable Trust

Animals, services, general

£50,000 (2005/06)

Beneficial area UK, with a preference for Birmingham.

Tyndallwoods Solicitors, 29 Woodbourne Road, Edgbaston, Birmingham B17 8BY

Tel. 0121 693 2222 **Fax** 0121 693 0844

Correspondent Mrs J A Dyke, Trustee

Trustees *Catherine Harriet Mary Bligh St George; Albert Kenneth Dyer; Judy Ann Dyke; Andrew Milner.*

CC Number 1016178

Information available Full accounts were on file at the Charity Commission.

General The trust has general charitable purposes, although there are preferences for animal and service organisations. Many of the beneficiaries are based in Birmingham.

In 2005/06 the trust had an income of £14,000 and an expenditure of £86,000. We have no information regarding grant recipients.

Previous beneficiaries of large grants have included Symphony Hall (Birmingham) Ltd, along with many other Birmingham-based organisations, such as Blue Coat School, University of Birmingham and Birmingham Parish Church (St Martin's) Renewal Campaign.

Smaller Birmingham grants included those to Birmingham and Midland Limbless Ex-Servicemen's Association, MSA for Midlands People with Cerebral Palsy, Birmingham Dogs Home and West Birmingham Scout Association.

Grants made elsewhere included those to Elizabeth Svendsen Trust, Arthritis Research Campaign, Dogs for the Disabled, Gloucester Three Choirs Appeal, Hope and Homes for Children and Live Music Now!

Applications In writing to the correspondent.

The Lind Trust

Social action, Christian service

£21,200 to organisations (2003/04)

Beneficial area UK.

Tithe Barn, Attlebridge, Norwich NR9 5AA

Tel. 01603 262626

Correspondent Graham Dacre

Trustees *Leslie C Brown; Dr Graham M Dacre; Gavin C Wilcock; Mrs Julia M Dacre; Russell B Dacre.*

CC Number 803174

Information available Accounts were on file at the Charity Commission.

General In 2003/04 this trust had assets of £4.8 million and an income of £695,000. Grants were made totalling £32,000, broken down as follows: Churches (£10,000); 'Other' charities (£11,200); and Individuals in full-time ministry (£11,200).

Applications In writing to the correspondent at any time. However, the trust commits most of its funds in advance, giving the remainder to eligible applicants as received.

Lindale Educational Foundation

Roman Catholic; education

£263,000 (2004/05)

Beneficial area UK and overseas.

1 Leopold Road, Ealing Common, London W5 3PB

Tel. 0207 229 7574

Correspondent J Valero

Trustees *Netherhall Educational Association; Dawliffe Hall Educational Foundation; Greygarth Association.*

CC Number 282758

Information available Accounts were on file at the Charity Commission.

General This foundation supports the Roman Catholic religion and the advancement of education. Its aims are to:

- train priests
- establish, extend, improve and maintain churches, chapels, oratories and other places of worship
- establish, extend, improve and maintain university halls and halls of residence for students of all nationalities
- arrange and conduct courses, camps, study centres, meetings, conferences and seminars
- provide financial support for education or research by individuals or groups of students
- provide financial support for other individuals or institutions which meet the trust's criteria, including the corporate trustees.

In 2004/05 the foundation had an income of £236,000 and a total expenditure of £263,000. Grants were made totalling £263,000 as detailed in the examples below.

The main emphasis was on the training of priests, with grants being made to Collegio Romano della Santa Croce (four grants totalling £90,000), Fondation Belmont (two grants totalling £80,000) and Pontificia Universitaria della Santa Croe (three grants totalling £1,700).

Other grants included those to: Wickenden Manor, the Netherhall Educational Association Centre for Retreats and Study, (five grants totalling £23,000); Thornycroft Hall (six grants totalling £25,000); and Dunreath, the Glasgow University residence of Netherhall Educational Association (£12,000).

Exclusions No grants to individuals.

Applications In writing to the correspondent, but note that most funds are already committed.

The Linden Charitable Trust

General

£23,000 (2003/04)

Beneficial area UK, with a preference for West Yorkshire.

Addleshaw Goddard, Sovereign House, PO Box 8, Sovereign Street, Leeds LS1 1HQ

Tel. 0113 209 2465 **Fax** 0113 209 2611

Email liz.jones@addleshawgoddard.co.uk

Correspondent Mrs M E Jones

Trustees *G L Holbrook; Miss M H Pearson; J F H Swales.*

CC Number 326788

Information available Information was obtained from the Charity Commission website.

General This trust supports a wide range of organisations including medical and healthcare charities and those related to the arts.

Further information was not available for 2004/05.

In 2003/04 the trust had an income of £79,000 and made grants totalling £23,000. Beneficiaries included Leeds International Pianoforte Competition (£10,000), Caring for Life, Kinkiizi Diocese and St Chad's PCC (£2,000 each) and Arthritis Care, Giving of Sight, Harrogate MRI Scanner, Jane's Appeal, Leeds Girls' Grammar School and Little Sisters of the Poor (£1,000 each).

Exclusions No grants to individuals.

Applications In writing to the correspondent.

The Linmardon Trust

General

£42,500 (2005/06)

Beneficial area UK, with a preference for the Nottingham area.

HSBC Trust Company Limited, Norwich House, Nelson Gate, Commercial Road, Southampton SO15 1GX

Tel. 023 8072 2223

Correspondent Isabella Salpagarova, Trust Manager

Trustee *HSBC Trust Company Limited.*

CC Number 275307

Information available Full accounts were on file at the Charity Commission.

General The trust supports charities in the UK with a preference for those in the Nottingham area. In 2005/06, it had assets of £1.3 million and an income of £153,000. Grants totalling £42,500 were made to 71 organisations.

The accounts grants list referred only to those beneficiaries receiving £1,000 or more each. These were: PDSA (£1,150 in two awards); and DeafBlind UK, Framework, Homestart, Nottingham City Hospital NHS Trust, Nottinghamshire Hospice, Nottinghamshire Coalition of Disabled People, Nottinghamshire Royal British legion, The Oaklands and CP Sport England and Wales (£1,000 each).

Exclusions Grants are made to registered charities only. No support to individuals.

Applications In writing to the correspondent. The trustees meet quarterly, generally in February, May, August and November.

The Ruth and Stuart Lipton Charitable Trust

Jewish, general

£38,000 (2004/05)

Beneficial area UK and overseas

Lewis Golden and Co., 40 Queen Ann Street, London W1M 9EL

Tel. 020 7580 7313

Correspondent N W Benson, Trustee

Trustees *Sir S Lipton; Lady Lipton; N W Benson.*

CC Number 266741

Information available Accounts were on file at the Charity Commission.

General The trust was founded by property/art mogul Stuart Lipton and his wife in 1973.

In 2004/05 the trust had assets of £470,000 and an income of £18,000 of which £6,000 was received in Gift Aid. Grants totalled £38,000.

Grant beneficiaries included: Royal Opera House (£11,000); Community Security Trust (£10,500); Western Marble Arch Synagogue (£8,100); Saving Faces – The Facial Surgery Research Foundation (£1,000); Architects Benevolent Society (£500); and, The Friends of Jewish Servicemen (£100).

Exclusions No grants to individuals.

Applications In writing to the correspondent.

The Lister Charitable Trust

Water-based activities for young people who are disadvantaged

£247,000 (2005/06)

Beneficial area UK.

c/o Apperley Limited, Maple House, High Street, Potters Bar, Hertfordshire EN6 5BS

Tel. 01707 828 692

Correspondent Mrs S J Sharkey

Trustees *Noel A V Lister; Benjamin Piers Cussons; Stephen John Chipperfield; D A Collingwood; David J Lister; P A Horne; R Horne; P A Lister; S J Lister.*

CC Number 288730

Information available Accounts were on file at the Charity Commission.

General This trust aims to help disadvantaged young people through sailing and other water-based activities. Grants are usually one-off for a specific project or part of a project. Core funding and/or salaries are rarely considered. Funding may be given for up to one year.

In 2005/06 the trust had assets of £11.4 million and an income of £249,000. Grants for the year totalled £247,000.

Major grant beneficiaries included: The Chemical Dependency Centre (£60,000); Children in Crisis (£54,000); UK Sailing Academy (£40,000); Sea Cadet Corps (£20,000); Stubbers Adventure Centre (£15,000); and Nancy Oldfield Trust, Reachout Project, Calvert Trust and Adventure Plus (£10,000 each).

Grants to other institutions during the year totalled £17,000.

Exclusions Applications from individuals, including students, are ineligible. No grants are made in response to general appeals from large UK organisations or to smaller bodies working in areas outside its criteria.

Applications In writing to the correspondent. Applications should include clear details of the need the intended project is designed to meet, plus an outline budget. Only applications from eligible bodies are acknowledged, when further information may be requested.

The Little Foundation

Neurodevelopmental disorders

£38,000 (2005)

Beneficial area UK.

30 Furnivel Street, London EC4A 1JQ

Tel. 020 7831 4918 **Fax** 020 7405 5365

Correspondent C Robinson, Chair

Trustees *C Robinson, Chair; Prof. M Crawford; Dr K Hameed; Prof. N Morris; Sara Cooke; DR J Singer; Mrs Peg Belson.*

CC Number 803551

Information available Accounts were on file at the Charity Commission.

General The foundation makes grants to established research bodies which will benefit future generations of children with neurodevelopmental disorders. It favours research projects recommended by its own Scientific Advisory Committee. These projects directly reflect the aims of the foundation to find the primary causes of such disorders and set up research with a view to prevention.

In 2005 the foundation had an income of £36,000 and issued grants for research purposes totalling £38,000. Although no beneficiaries were listed in the accounts, reference is made to an epilepsy/autism spectrum disorders study taking place at St George's Hospital, Tooting. We assume that at least some of the money given for research grants went towards this.

Exclusions No grants for individuals, training grants or scholarships.

Applications All available funds are committed.

The Second Joseph Aaron Littman Foundation

General

£216,000 (2004/05)

Beneficial area UK.

c/o Lawrence Graham, 190 Strand, London WC2R 1JN

Correspondent R J Littman, Trustee

Trustees *Mrs C C Littman; R J Littman.*

CC Number 201892

Information available Accounts were on file at the Charity Commission.

General This trust has general charitable purposes with special preference for academic and medical research. In 2004/05 it had assets of £5.1 million and an income of £280,000. Grants were made totalling £216,000.

The main beneficiary, as in previous years, was Littmann Library of Jewish Civilisation which received £185,000. There were 11 further donations of £1,000 or more listed in the accounts. Beneficiaries included Spiro Ark (£5,200), 45 Aid Society Holocaust Survivors and Foundation for Circulatory Health (£5,000 each), Lubavitch Senior Girls' School (£3,000), University London College (£2,000), Bournemouth Jewish Day School, Friends of Israel Educational Foundation, Friends of Lubavitch, the Jewish Museum (£1,000 each) and Westminster Synagogue (£500).

Sundry donations of less than £1,000 each totalled £2,500.

Exclusions Applications from individuals are not considered.

Applications The trust's funds are fully committed and no new applications are considered.

Jack Livingstone Charitable Trust

Jewish, general

£78,300 (2005/06)

Beneficial area UK and worldwide, with a preference for Manchester.

Westholme, The Springs, Park Road, Bowdon, Altrincham, Cheshire WA14 3JH

Correspondent Mrs Janice Livingstone, Trustee

Trustees *Mrs J V Livingstone; Brian White.*

CC Number 263473

Information available Accounts were on file at the Charity Commission.

General In 2005/06 the trust had assets of £1.9 million, an income of £99,500 and made grants totalling £78,000. The largest grant of £25,000 went to United

Jewish Israel Appeal. Other large grant beneficiaries included: Rainsough (£16,000); Community Security Trust, Jem and Lancashire County Cricket (£5,000 each); Christies (£3,200); and, Manchester Jewish Federation (£2,500).

Other grants of £1,000 or less each were made to Aish Hatorah UK Ltd, Brookvale, Lubavitch South, Norwood and Southport Jewish Aged Home.

Applications The trust does not respond to unsolicited applications.

The Elaine and Angus Lloyd Charitable Trust

General

£73,000 to organisations (2004/05)

Beneficial area UK, with a preference for Surrey, Kent and the south of England.

Messrs Badger Hakim Chartered Accountants, 10 Dover Street, London W1S 4LQ

Correspondent R Badger

Trustees C R H Lloyd; A S Lloyd; J S Gordon; Sir Michael Craig-Cooper; V E Best; J S Lloyd; P J Lloyd; R J Lloyd.

CC Number 237250

Information available Accounts were on file at the Charity Commission.

General In 1992, the Elaine Lloyd Charitable Trust and the Mr Angus Lloyd Charitable Settlement were amalgamated and are now known as the Elaine and Angus Lloyd Charitable Trust. Many grants are recurrent, some may be paid quarterly. Grants are mainly to UK charities and local organisations in the Surrey and Kent area and elsewhere in the south of England. Grants are given in practice to those charities known to one or more of the trustees. Donations are made to:

- any charitable institution whether incorporated or not
- any individual recipients to assist them in meeting education expenses either for themselves or their children
- any individual recipients whose circumstances are such they come within the legal conception of poverty.

In 2004/05 the trust had assets of £2.2 million and an income of £130,000.

Grants to organisations totalled £73,000 and grants to individuals totalled £6,000.

Donations included £5,000 to Salvation Army, £4,500 to EHAS, £4,000 to Rhemal Religious and Charitable Trust, £2,500 to Barry Vale Community Aid, £1,500 each to Waverley Youth Project and The Gospel Mission of India and £1,000 each to St Mary's Church Newport, Lotus Relief Charitable Trust, Surrey Clubs for Young People, Dans Fund for Burns and Teenage Cancer Trust.

Exclusions No support for overseas aid.

Applications In writing to the correspondent. The trustees meet regularly to consider grants.

Lloyd's Charities Trust

General

£452,000 (2005)

Beneficial area UK, with some interest in London.

One Lime Street, London EC3M 7HA

Tel. 020 7327 6075 **Fax** 020 7327 6368

Website www.lloyds.com

Correspondent Mrs Vicky Mirfin, Secretary

Trustees N Gooding, Chair; E Gilmour; J Lowe; Ms B Merry; Miss C Dandridge; B Pomeroy; A Townsend; G White; G Chilton; Ms H Bellingham.

CC Number 207232

Information available Accounts were available from the Charity Commission website.

General This charity was set up in 1953, and is the charitable arm of Lloyd's insurance market in London. In 2005 the trust had total assets of £2 million (including restricted and unrestricted funds). It had an income of £444,000 and made grants in the form of donations and grants and bursaries totalling £452,000. Grants were broken down as follows:

Lloyd's Partner Charities (2004–2007)
During the year, the trust continued to support Hopes and Homes for Children, Macmillan Cancer Relief and St Giles Trust. Donations were broken down as follows:

- Hope and Homes for Children: the charity received a second instalment of £75,000 to support its project based in Sierra Leone. The project aims to provide orphaned children with families and to prevent the abandonment of vulnerable children by giving help and support to young single mothers. A further £25,000 was awarded to Hope and Homes for Children as Lloyd's special 50th anniversary charity.
- Macmillan Cancer Relief: the charity received a second instalment of £50,000 to develop its national CancerLine. The project focuses on the provision of information and advice for children and young people affected by cancer and for minority ethnic groups where English is not the first language.
- St Giles Trust: the trust received a second instalment of £50,000 towards its housing advice and peer support project that aims to help prisoners break the cycle of homelessness and re-offending once they leave prison.

General donations
In addition to working with a smaller number of charities the trust also retains some funds in order respond to ad hoc appeals. During the year, grants were made to thirteen organisations totalling £41,000 and were broken down into the following categories:

- social welfare – housing, homelessness, community. Grants were made to five organisations totalling £14,000
- national medical – treatment, services, disability. Grants were made to three organisations totalling £11,000
- children. Grants were awarded to four organisations totalling £10,000
- other. One grant was made to RNLI totalling £5,000.

Cuthbert Heath Centenary Fund
This fund provides bursaries at nine schools, each are allocated £6,500 a year. During the year, the cost of funding the bursaries amounted to £52,000, as one school had not made an application and a donation had not been made by the trust.

Lloyd's Community Programme
The principal elements of this programme are support for projects in the fields of education, training and enterprise. The funds are raised predominantly by subscription from member companies from the Lloyd's market and are used to support organisations with which Lloyd's has had long working relationships.

In 2005 direct charitable expenditure totalled £114,000. The main beneficiaries were: Tower Hamlets Education Business Partnership – THEBP (£43,000); East

203

London Small Businesses Centre – ELSBC (£20,000); and East London Business Alliance, Royal National Theatre, the Children's Music Wworkshop and Tower Hamlets Summer University (£12,500 each).

Exclusions No grants for any appeal where it is likely that the grant would be used for sectarian purposes or to local or regional branches of charities where it is possible to support the UK organisation. Support is not given to individuals.

Applications Lloyd's Charities Trust makes ad hoc donations, however the majority of funds are committed to supporting the partnership charities the trust works with. The trust has previously stated that as funds are committed over a three-year period 'we are unable to respond positively to the numerous appeals we receive'. Applications are not being invited for partner charity status.

The Llysdinam Trust

General

£77,000 (2005/06)

Beneficial area Wales.

Rees Richards and Partners, Managing Agents, Druslyn House, De La Beche Street, Swansea SA1 3HH

Tel. 01792 650705 **Fax** 01792 468384

Email post@reesrichards.co.uk

Correspondent The Trustees

Trustees Mrs M J Elster; N O Tyler; Mrs E S Birkmyre.

CC Number 255528

Information available Full accounts were on file at the Charity Commission.

General In 2005/06 the trust had assets of £4.4 million and an income of £204,000. Grants totalled around £77,000.

Major beneficiaries included: University of Wales, Cardiff (£12,400); Christ College Scholarship (£8,000); British Ornithology Trust, CARAD, Harriet Davis Trust, Montgomery Youth Trust and National Waterfront (£5,000 each); and, Swansea Rugby Foundation (£4,000).

Exclusions No grants to individuals.

Applications The trust stated that it was overloaded with applications and does not welcome unsolicited applications.

Localtrent Ltd

Jewish, educational, religion

£96,000 (2004/05)

Beneficial area UK, with some preference for Manchester.

Lopian Gross Barnett and Co., 6th Floor, Cardinal House, 20 St Mary's Parsonage, Manchester M3 2LG

Tel. 0161 832 8721 **Fax** 0161 8353085

Correspondent A Kahan

Trustees Mrs M Weiss; B Weiss; P Weiss; Mrs J J Weissmandl; Mrs R Sofer; H Weiss.

CC Number 326329

Information available Full accounts were on file at the Charity Commission.

General The trust was established in 1983 for the distribution of funds to religious, educational and similar charities for the advancement of the Jewish religion.

'The governors have identified a number of Orthodox Jewish charities which carry out activities such as operating synagogues and providing Orthodox Jewish education so as to advance religion in accordance with the Orthodox Jewish faith.'

In 2004/05 the trust had assets of £272,500 and an income of £137,500. Grants totalled £96,000 with the largest amount being donated to Chasdei Yoel Charitable Trust (£39,000). Other major beneficiaries included: Congregation Chemed (£6,400); Tchabe Kollel (£6,000); UTA (£5,900); Asser Bishvil (£4,000); and, Yeshiva Ohel Shimon (£3,600).

Applications In writing to the correspondent.

The Locker Foundation

Jewish

£350,000 (2005/06)

Beneficial area UK and overseas.

28 High Road, East Finchley, London N2 9PJ

Tel. 020 8455 9280

Correspondent The Trustees

Trustees I Carter; M Carter; Mrs S Segal.

CC Number 264180

Information available Full accounts were on file at the Charity Commission.

General The trust mainly supports Jewish organisations. In 2005/06 it had assets of £3.7 million and an income of £336,000. It made 31 grants totalling £350,000.

The largest grant was £42,000 to Kahal Chassidim Bobov. Other major grant beneficiaries included: Magen David Adom (40,000); Ezer Mizion (£22,500); Operation Wheelchair (£20,500); British Emunah (£20,000); and Chai Cancer Care (£16,350).

Smaller grants between £100 and £1,000 were made to Bottoms Up, Friends of Luov, Phone and Learn, London Air Ambulance and United Jewish Appeal.

Applications In writing to the correspondent.

The Loftus Charitable Trust

Jewish

£219,000 (2004/05)

Beneficial area UK and overseas.

Asher House, Blackburn Road, London NW6 1AW.

Tel. 020 7604 5900

Correspondent Anthony Loftus, Trustee

Trustees R I Loftus; A L Loftus; A D Loftus.

CC Number 297664

Information available Full accounts were on file at the Charity Commission.

General The trust was established in 1987 by Richard Ian Loftus. Its objectives are:

- the advancement of the Jewish religion
- the advancement of Jewish education and the education of Jewish people
- the relief of the Jewish poor.

In 2004/05 the trust had an income of £52,000 of which £50,000 was in the form of a donation from Accurist Watches Ltd, based at the same address. Grants were made totalling £219,000.

The largest grants were: £37,500 to Jewish Care; £30,560 to CIS Development Fund; £17,000 to Immanuel College; £13,000 to Lubavitch Foundation; and £10,000 each to Ohr Torah Stone and Friends of Lubavitch UK.

Smaller grants of £1,000 each included those made to the following: I Rescue, Magen David Adom UK, Seed, Common

Denominator and Supporters of Laniado Hospital.

Applications The trustees state that all funds are committed and unsolicited applications are not welcome.

London Law Trust

Health and personal development of children and young people

£107,000 (2004/05)
Beneficial area UK.

Messrs Hunters, 9 New Square, Lincoln's Inn, London WC2A 3QN
Tel. 020 7412 0050
Correspondent G D Ogilvie, Secretary
Trustees *Prof. Anthony R Mellows; R A Pellant; Sir Michael Hobbs; Sir Ian Gainsford.*
CC Number 255924
Information available Information was on file at the Charity Commission.

General The trust's aims are to support charities which:

* prevent or cure illness and disability in children and young people – via seed-corn grants and grants towards small research projects
* alleviate or reduce the causes or likelihood of illness and disability in children and young people – via grants for new ventures and to small support groups for children and young people suffering less common syndromes
* encourage and develop in young people the qualities of leadership and service to the community – via grants to national organisations for specific purposes.

In 2004/05 the trust had assets of £3.6 million and an income of £123,000. Grants of between £500 and £5,000 (average £2,670) were made to 40 organisations and totalled £107,000.

Under the first category above, beneficiaries included: £5,000 each to British Lung Foundation, Great Ormond Street and St George's Hospital Medical School.

Under the second category above, beneficiaries included: £5,000 to BRIC; and £2,500 each to Activenture and Swan Syndrome.

Under the final category above, beneficiaries included: £5,000 to Deans & Canons of Windsor; £2,500 to Envision; and £1,000 to Circomedia.

Exclusions Applications from individuals, including students, are ineligible.

Applications In writing to the correspondent. The trustees employ a grant adviser whose job is to evaluate applications. Grant applicants are requested to supply detailed information in support of their applications. The grant adviser makes on-site visits to almost all applicants.

The trustees meet twice a year to consider the grant adviser's reports. Most grants are awarded in the autumn.

The William and Katherine Longman Trust

General

£188,000 (2004/05)
Beneficial area UK.

Charles Russell, 8–10 New Fetter Lane, London EC4A 1RS
Tel. 020 7203 5000
Correspondent W P Harriman, Trustee
Trustees *W P Harriman; J B Talbot; A C O Bell.*
CC Number 800785
Information available Accounts were on file at the Charity Commission.

General The trust supports a wide range of organisations with grants ranging from £500 to £18,000 each, mostly at the lower end of the scale.

In 2004/05 it had assets of £3.4 million, which generated an income of £71,000. Grants were made totalling £188,000. Management and administration charges were high at £23,000.

There were 43 grants made during the year, beneficiaries of the largest grants of £10,000 or more were International Centre for Reconciliation (£18,000), Chelsea Festival, Hope Education Trust and World Vision UK (£15,000 each), Vanessa Grant Memorial School (£13,000) and Care (£10,000).

Other beneficiaries included Macmillan Cancer Relief (£7,500), Action for ME, Cats Protection League and WSPA (£5,000 each), BAHIA Street Trust and

Royal British Legion (£4,000 each), Oxford Kilburn Boys Club (£3,500), Abbeyfield – Chelsea and Fulham, Age Concern – Kensington and Chelsea, British Association for Adoption and Fostering and Treloar Trust (£2,500 each), Helen Arkell Dyslexia Centre and London Philharmonic Orchestra (£2,000 each), British Refugee Council, CHCD Charitable Trust, St Giles Trust and Youth Sport Trust (£1,000) and Chelsea Old Church (£500).

Exclusions Grants are only made to registered charities.

Applications The trustees believe in taking a proactive approach in deciding which charities to support and it is their policy not to respond to unsolicited appeals.

The Loseley and Guildway Charitable Trust

General

£44,000 (2004/05)
Beneficial area International and UK, with an interest in Guildford.

The Estate Offices, Loseley Park, Guildford, Surrey GU3 1HS
Tel. 01483 405114 **Fax** 01483 302036
Email nicolacs@loseley-park.com
Correspondent Miss Nicola Cheriton-Sutton, Secretary
Trustees *Maj. James More-Molyneux, Chair; Mrs Susan More-Molyneux; Michael More-Molyneux; Adrian Abbott; Glye Hodson.*
CC Number 267178
Information available Accounts were available from the Charity Commission website.

General The trust was founded in 1973, when 'the More-Molyneux family injected private capital and transferred five of their own properties to the trust'. The rent of these properties provides about half the trust's present income. Two of these properties have now been sold in order to finance the purchase of land on which CHASE Children's Hospice has now been built.

The trust's accounts state that: 'The objectives of the charity are widely drawn to include making grants to charitable associations, trusts, societies and corporations whether they are local, national or international. The major part of the available funds tend to be distributed locally to charitable institutions which the trustees consider to be particularly worthy of support.' In effect this means that major grants tend to be given to charities with which various members of the More-Molyneux family and trustees are associated.

In 2004/05 the trust had assets of £1.2 million, an income of £49,000 and made grants totalling £44,000. Only the top ten grants were listed in the accounts. These were: Disability Challengers and Harriet Davis Trust (£5,000 each); CHASE (£2,500); Cherry Trees, Hope and Homes for Children, King George's Fund for Sailors, Medical Foundation, National Society for Epilepsy, Royal Agricultural Benevolent Institution and Task Force Romania (£1,000 each).

Exclusions No grants to individuals or non-registered charities.

Applications In writing to the correspondent. The trustees meet in February, May and September to consider applications. However, due to commitments, new applications for any causes are unlikely to be successful.

The Lotus Foundation

Children and families, women, animal protection, addiction recovery, education

£307,000 (2005)

Beneficial area UK, especially London and Surrey; occasionally overseas.

90 Jermyn Street, London SW1Y 6JD
Tel. 020 7930 5133
Email bridget@lotusfoundation.com
Website www.lotusfoundation.com
Correspondent Mrs B Starkey, Trustee
Trustees *Mrs B Starkey; R Starkey; Mrs E Turner.*
CC Number 1070111
Information available Accounts were on file at the Charity Commission.

General The trust was established in 1998 and aims to make grants to other established and newly formed charities.

The primary objectives of the trust are 'to offer financial aid and assistance to facilitate family and child welfare, women's issues, animal protection, addiction recovery and education'.

In 2005 the trust had assets of £137,000 and an income of £340,000. Grants totalling £307,000 were made to 50 organisations. Grants ranged from £500 to £30,000 and included the following major beneficiaries: Tsunami Earthquake Appeal (£30,000); British Red Cross and Chemical Dependency Centre – SHARP, Liverpool (£28,000 each); Crossroads, Antigua (£20,500); WaterAid (£20,000); and, WhizzKids (£11,150).

Beneficiaries of smaller grants included: British Heart Foundation (£500); The Beacon Appeal, CP Sport, Diane Fossey Gorilla Fund and Unicorn Theatre (£1,000 each).

Exclusions No response to circular appeals. No grants to individuals, non-registered charities, charities working outside the foundation's areas of interest, or for research purposes.

Applications In writing to the correspondent. Initial enquiries by email are welcome. Otherwise, give a brief outline of the work, amount required and project/programme to benefit. The trustees prefer applications which are simple and economically prepared rather than glossy 'prestige' and mail sorted brochures.

Note: In order to reduce administration costs and concentrate its efforts on the charitable work at hand, unsolicited requests will no longer be acknowledged by the foundation.

The C L Loyd Charitable Trust

General

£116,000 (2005/06)

Beneficial area UK, with a preference for Berkshire and Oxfordshire.

Betterton House, Lockinge, Wantage, Oxfordshire OX12 8QL
Tel. 01235 833 265
Correspondent C L Loyd, Trustee
Trustees *C L Loyd; T C Loyd.*
CC Number 265076
Information available Accounts were on file at the Charity Commission.

General The trust supports UK charities and local charities (in Berkshire and Oxfordshire) involved in welfare, animals, churches, medical/disability, children/youth and education.

In 2005/06 the trust had assets of £2.5 million, an income of £73,000 and made grants totalling £116,000.

The accounts only listed beneficiaries of grants of over £1,000. These were: Wantage Nursing Home Trust (£80,000); Country Buildings Protection Trust (£16,000); King Alfred's Education Charity (£3,000); W M Rowden Charitable Trust (£1,100); and, British Red Cross, Lockinge & Addington Relief in Need Charity and Burlington Magazine (£1,000 each).

Exclusions No support for individuals or medical research.

Applications In writing to the correspondent. Grants are made several times each month.

Henry Lumley Charitable Trust

General, medical, educational, relief of poverty/hardship

£117,000 (2005)

Beneficial area England and Wales.

Hargraves House, Belmont Road, Maidenhead, Berkshire SL6 6TB
Correspondent Peter Lumley, Trustee
Trustees *Henry Lumley; Peter Lumley; Robert Lumley; James Porter.*
CC Number 1079480
Information available Accounts were on file at the Charity Commission.

General Registered in February 2000, the income of the trust is derived from the dividends and interest received from shares in the private company Edward Lumley Holdings Ltd. Charities supported should be known to at least one trustee. Aside from the founder's initial list of beneficiaries, new charities have been added as funds permit and are usually of a one-off nature to assist medical or educational projects.

In 2005 the trust had an income of £122,000 and made grants totalling £117,000 to 37 organisations, most of which were recurring in nature. Although established as a general charitable trust, grants effectively cover three main areas, namely, medical, educational and relief of poverty and hardship. Examples of beneficiaries are given below.

Medical – 20 grants totalling £80,000, including: Action on Addiction, Prostate Cancer Charity and Wellbeing of Women (£5,000 each); Leukaemia Research Fund (£3,000); and, Friends of St Michael's Hospice and Meningitis UK (£2,500 each).

Educational – Five grants totalling £21,000, including: Royal Opera House Foundation, St Paul's Cathedral Foundation and University of Exeter (£5,000 each).

Relief of poverty and hardship – Five grants totalling £11,500, including: Parity, Royal British Legion and Royal Star and Garter Home for Disabled Ex-Service Men and Women (£2,500 each)

Other – Two grants totalling £4,500 to: Surrey Clubs for Young People (£2,500); and, Telephones for the Blind (£2,000).

Applications In writing to the correspondent.

Paul Lunn-Rockliffe Charitable Trust

Christianity, poverty, infirm people, young people

£34,100 (2005/06)

Beneficial area UK with a preference for Hampshire.

4a Barnes Close, Winchester, Hampshire SO23 9QX

Tel. 01962 852949 **Fax** 01962 852949

Correspondent Mrs J M Lunn-Rockliffe, Secretary

Trustees *Mrs Jacqueline Lunn-Rockliffe; Victor Lunn-Rockliffe; James Lunn-Rockliffe.*

CC Number 264119

Information available Accounts were on file at the Charity Commission.

General The 2005/06 annual report states that: 'the object of the charity is to make grants to any charity or for any charitable purpose, at the trustees' discretion, but preferably to those recipients likely to further Christianity, support the relief of poverty and assist

the aged and infirm'. Furthermore, that: 'the charity has supported 70 separate charities during the year … [and] maintains a database of details and financial data for the charities supported. The latest financial information for recipient charities is reviewed and their achievements assessed, prior to donating further funds'.

'The trustees have a policy of restricting the total number of recipient charities in order to ensure that each receives a more significant donations and has a preference for smaller and locally based charities, or those known to the trustees or members of their families.

'The trustees allocate a proportion of the funds for donations to be applied to charities not previously supported and for special one-off causes'.

In 2005/06 the trust had assets of £935,000 and an income of £190,000. Grants were made totalling £34,000 which were broken down as follows:

Aged – Two grants totalling £1,000. Frogmore Day Centre and Action for Elder Abuse (£500 each).

Children – Five grants totalling £2,600, including: Children Society (£600); Children Family Trust and Global Care (£500 each).

Disabled – Eight grants totalling £3,300, including: Spastics Society of India (£500); Combat Stress (£400); and Delta (£300).

Education and students – Five grants totalling £2,100, including: Fusion and Students Exploring Marriage (£500 each); and Darmaris (£300).

Family – Five grants totalling £2,700, including: Care (£800); AIM (£600); and Friends of the Family (£400).

Mission – Seven grants totalling £3,700, including: Bible Society (£800); AIM (£600); and Urban Expression (£500).

Needy people, drug addicts, homeless and unemployed people – 11 grants totalling £6,000, including: Christians Against Poverty (£1,000); Safe – Southampton (£600); and Society of St Dismas (£400).

Prisoners – Four grants totalling ££1,900, including: Koestler Awards, Langley House Trust and Prison Fellowship (£500 each).

Radio/Mission – Three grants totalling £1,400. Focus Radio and Hour of Revival (£500 each); and Way to Life (£400).

Third World – Nine grants totalling £4,600, including: Christian Aid and Tear Fund (£600 each); Africa Now (£400).

Youth – Five grants totalling £2,000, including: Fairbridge – Solent (£500); Boys' Brigade (£300); and Lee Abbey International Students Club (£200).

Others – Six grants totalling £2,800, including: Church Urban Fund (£600); The Magdalene Group (£500); and Carers Christian Fellowship (£300).

Exclusions The trustees will not fund individuals; for example, student's expenses and travel grants. Repair and maintenance of historic buildings are also excluded for support.

Applications The trust encourages preliminary phone calls to discuss applications. It will generally only reply to written correspondence if an sae has been included.

The Ruth and Jack Lunzer Charitable Trust

Jewish; children, young adults and students; education

£53,000 (2005/06)

Beneficial area UK.

c/o BDO Stoy Hayward, 8 Baker Street, London W1U 3LL

Tel. 020 7893 2499

Correspondent M D Paisner, Trustee

Trustees *J V Lunzer; M D Paisner.*

CC Number 276201

Information available Accounts were on file at the Charity Commission, but with only a brief narrative report.

General The trust says it makes grants to organisations benefiting children, young adults and students; primarily educational establishments. In practice many such beneficiaries are Jewish organisations.

In 2005/06 the trust had assets of £42,000 and an income of £55,000 with grants totalling £53,000.

The largest grants were £10,000 to Independent Jewish Day School and £6,000 to Kahal Chassidim Bobov.

Other grants included £3,000 to North West London Communal Mikvah, £2,000 to Hamayon, £1,000 to Medical Aid Trust, £500 to North London Hospice Proms, £250 to Friends of

Yeshiva Ohr Elchanan and £100 to Sunderland Talmudical College.

Applications In writing to the correspondent. Unsuccessful applicants are not acknowledged.

Lord and Lady Lurgan Trust

Medical, older people and the arts, in the UK and South Africa

£54,000 (2005)

Beneficial area UK and South Africa.

Pemberton Greenish (Ref MDB), 45 Pont Street, London SW1X 0BX

Tel. 020 7591 3333 **Fax** 020 7591 3300

Trustees *Simon David Howard Ladd Staughton; Andrew John Francis Stebbings; Diana Sarah Graves (partners Pemberton Greenish).*

CC Number 297046

Information available Accounts were on file at the Charity Commission.

General The registered objectives of this trust are:

- the relief and medical care of older people
- medical research, in particular cancer research and the publication of the useful results of such research
- the advancement of education including education in the arts for the public benefit by the establishment of educational and artistic bursaries
- other charitable purposes at the discretion of the trustees.

There is also special interest in: South Africa (due to the settlors spending the latter part of their lives there) with about one quarter of the funds available being distributed there; in music, and in Northern Ireland because of family origins.

In 2005 the trust had assets of £1.3 million and an income of £40,000. Grants totalling £54,000 were made to 49 beneficiaries.

Grant distribution is divided into two key areas:

Institutional grants in the UK – £10,000 to Royal College of Music, £5,000 to Queen's University of Belfast Foundation, £2,000 each to Help the Hospices and Independent Age, £1,000

each to Cornwall Disability Arts Group and Young Actors' Theatre.

South Africa – £523.81 each to BUSKAID, Forest Town School for Cerebral Palsy, The Nelson Mandela Children's Fund, Star Seaside Home, Tape Aids for the Blind and Woodside Sanctuary.

Applications In writing to the correspondent.

The Lyndhurst Trust

Christian

£86,200 (2005)

Beneficial area UK and overseas, with preferences for north east England and the developing world.

PO Box 615, North Shields, Tyne and Wear NE29 1AP

Correspondent The Secretary

Trustees *Revd Dr R Ward; Mrs J A L Hinton; M B Hinton ;Mrs J Brooks.*

CC Number 235252

Information available Accounts were on file at the Charity Commission.

General The 2003/04 accounts stated 'the trustees have sought opportunities for the promotion and advancement of the Christian religion in any part of the world … [They have] continued supporting regularly charities that are promoting the awareness of the Christian gospel, in those areas of the world where people are prevented from hearing it through normal channels of communication. Agencies operating in difficult circumstances are given special consideration'.

'The trustees have continued their policy of making funds available to the disadvantaged in the United Kingdom and Europe. Special attention continues to be given to those charities involved in meeting the needs of those with drug and alcohol problems through Christian rehabilitation programmes. Churches in the north east of England have been given increased support due to the particular needs of the communities where they are operating.'

In 2005 the trust had assets of £1.5 million and an income of £49,000. Grants totalled £86,200 and were broken down as follows:

Developing countries – 11 grants (25.6%)
Europe and rest of world – 0 grants (0%)
United Kingdom – 3 grants (8.7 %)
North East of England – 9 grants (65.7%)

Grants in the UK and north east of England included: £30,000 to N E 1 – Tyneside; £10,000 to Youth for Christ North East; £6,000 to St Barnabas Church, Middlesbrough; £5,000 to Blue Sky Trust; £1,500 to Edge Community Project, Selby; and £1,000 to Wydale Hall York Diocesan Centre.

Exclusions No support for individuals or buildings.

Applications In writing to the correspondent, enclosing an sae if a reply is required. Requests are considered half-yearly.

The Lynn Foundation

General

£276,000 (2005/06)

Beneficial area UK and overseas.

Blackfriars, 17 Lewes Road, Haywards Heath, West Sussex RH17 7SP

Tel. 01444 454773 **Fax** 01444 456192

Correspondent Guy Parsons, Chairman of the Trustees

Trustees *Guy Parsons, Chair; J F Emmott; Dr P E Andry; P R Parsons; Ian Fair.*

CC Number 326944

Information available Accounts were on file at the Charity Commission, but without any narrative.

General The trust has previously stated that it supports a very wide range of organisations, including those in the areas of music, the arts, Masonic charities, disability, older people and children.

In 2005/06 the trust had assets of £5.8 million and an income of £420,000. Grants during the year were made to 438 organisations and totalled £276,000. Details of individual beneficiaries was not available, although the total was broken down as follows:

Music and the arts – 136 grants totalling £90,200
Disabled children – 147 grants totalling £73,000

Disabled adults – 136 grants totalling £68,000
Youth sponsorship – 33 grants totalling £15,400
Medical research – 32 grants totalling £16,500
Hospices – 23 grants totalling £11,550
Sundry – two grants totalling £1,000.

Applications In writing to the correspondent.

The Lyons Charitable Trust

Health, animals, children

£64,000 (2005/06)
Beneficial area UK.

74 Broad Walk, London N21 3BX
Correspondent Michael Gibbon
Trustees M S Gibbon; J Gibbon; G Read.
CC Number 1045650
Information available Accounts were on file at the Charity Commission.

General The trust in particular makes grants in the fields of health, medical research, animals and children in need. The same 11 charities are supported each year.

In 2005/06 it had assets of £1.5 million and an income of £250,000. Grants were made totalling £64,000.

Major beneficiaries during the year were: the Royal Marsden Hospital, Macmillan Cancer Relief and St Thomas Hospital (£10,000 each); Helen House (£6,000); and Streetsmart and One25 Ltd (£5,000 each).

Applications The trust has stated that it is closed to new applications.

The Sir Jack Lyons Charitable Trust

Jewish, arts, education

£163,000 (2004/05)
Beneficial area UK and overseas.

Sagars, 3rd Floor, Elizabeth House, Queen Street, Leeds LS1 2TW
Correspondent The Trustees

Trustees Sir Jack Lyons; Lady Roslyn Marion Lyons; M J Friedman; D S Lyons; J S Lyons; P D Mitchell.
CC Number 212148
Information available Full accounts were on file at the Charity Commission.

General This trust shows a particular interest in Jewish charities and also a consistent interest in the arts, particularly music.

In 2004/05 the trust had assets of £2.9 million and an income of £170,000. Grants were made to 18 organisations totalling £163,000.

The four largest grants were £50,000 to Heslington Foundation, £48,000 (US $88,000) to Magen David Adom UK and £10,000 each to Friends of AWIS and London Symphony Orchestra.

Smaller grants included: £9,400 (CHF 20,000) to United Israel Appeal; £5,300 (US $10,000) each to Ben Gurion University and Weizmann Institute; £5,000 to Mariinsky Trust; £2,600 (US $5,000) each to Art Museum – Tel Aviv and Hadassah Hospital; £2,500 to City University – London; £1,000 to Community Security Trust; £700 to Jewish Care; £200 to Group Two WIZO; and £50 to ZVS Trust.

Exclusions No grants to individuals.

Applications In writing to the correspondent. In the past the trust has stated: 'In the light of increased pressure for funds, unsolicited appeals are less welcome and would waste much time and money for applicants who were looking for funds which were not available'.

Malcolm Lyons Foundation

Jewish

£86,000 (2004/05)
Beneficial area UK.

BDO Stoy Hayward, 8 Baker Street, London W1U 3LL
Correspondent J S Newman, Trustee
Trustees M S Lyons; Mrs J Lyons; J S Newman.
CC Number 1050689
Information available Full accounts were on file at the Charity Commission.

General This trust supports Jewish and Israeli organisations. In 2004/05 it had assets of £126,000. Total income was

£195,000 mainly from donations and grants totalled £86,000.

There were 17 grants listed in the accounts. Beneficiaries included Emuno Education Centre (£25,000), United Synagogue (£12,000), Kingsley Way Charitable Trust (£10,000), Mesorah Heritage Foundation (£7,000), Lubavitch Foundation (£6,000), British Friends of Ezer Mizion (£5,100), Jewish Learning Exchange (£3,800), Child Resettlement Fund (£2,900), Community Security Trust (£2,000), SAGE (£1,800), CIS Development Fund, Friends of Laniado UK, United Synagogue Eruv Committee (£1,000 each), OYH Primary and Kindergarten Schools (£750), United Jewish Israel Appeal (£500) and Lolev Charitable Trust (£100).

Applications The trust states that it will not consider unsolicited applications.

The M and C Trust

Jewish, social welfare

£118,500 (2004/05)
Beneficial area UK.

c/o Chantrey Vellacott DFK, Russell Square House, 10–12 Russell Square, London WC1B 5LF
Tel. 020 7509 9000 **Fax** 020 7509 9219
Correspondent A C Langridge, Trustee
Trustees A Bernstein; A C Langridge; Elizabeth J Marks; Rachel J Lebus.
CC Number 265391
Information available Accounts were on file at the Charity Commission.

General The trust's primary charitable objects are Jewish causes and social welfare.

In 2004/05 the trust had assets of £4.1 million and an income of £120,000. Grants totalled £118,500.

The three largest grants went to Jewish Care and Norwood (£20,000 each) and Jewish Children's Holiday Fund (£10,000).

Beneficiaries of smaller grants included: Community Security Trust, CSV and Deafblind UK (£5,000 each); Changing Faces and Chicken Shed Theatre (£3,000 each); and, Brady Maccabi Youth and Community Centre (£2,500).

The trust is connected with Quercus Trust, being under the same administration and having similar objectives.

Exclusions No grants to individuals.

Applications In writing to the correspondent, but the trust states that funds are currently earmarked for existing projects. In order to keep administration costs to a minimum, they are unable to reply to any unsuccessful applications.

The M D and S Charitable Trust

Jewish

£128,000 (2004/05)

Beneficial area UK and Israel.

15 Riverside Drive, Golders Green Road, London NW11 9PU

Tel. 020 7272 2255

Correspondent Martin D Cymerman, Trustee

Trustees *M D Cymerman; Mrs S Cymerman.*

CC Number 273992

Information available Full accounts were on file at the Charity Commission.

General The trust supports Jewish organisations in the UK and has general charitable purposes in Israel.

In 2004/05 the trust had assets of £2.4 million and an income of £280,000. Grants to 73 organisations totalled £131,000.

The largest grants were: United Torah Institutions of Gur (£17,500); Yetev Lev Jerusalem (£11,500); and Beis Yisroel Benevolence Trust (£11,000).

Other grants included: Ponevez Aid and Benevolence Fund (£6,850); Yeshivat Magen Avrohom (£5,500); Yeshivat Kolel Shaarei Shloime (£4,000); Agudat Torah V'Chessed Trust (£1,500); Kolel Beis Talmud L'Horaah (£1,150); and, Beit David Institutions (£1,000).

Applications In writing to the correspondent.

The Madeline Mabey Trust

Medical research, children's welfare and education

£750,000 (2005/06)

Beneficial area UK and overseas.

Mabey House, Floral Mile, Twyford, Reading RG10 9SQ

Tel. 0118 940 3921 **Fax** 0118 940 3675

Correspondent Joanna Singeisen, Trustee

Trustees *Alan G Daliday; Bridget A Nelson; Joanna L Singeisen.*

CC Number 326450

Information available Accounts were on file at the Charity Commission, but without a list of grants.

General The 2005/06 trustees report states: 'The principal areas of benefit continue to be the education and welfare of children both in the UK and overseas, and medical research into the causes of and cures for life-threatening illnesses. The trust favours identifying organisations itself, although it is willing to consider applications for grants. The intention is to fund organisations rather than individuals directly.'

During the year the trust had assets of nearly £600,000 and an income of £1.2 million (due primarily to an unexpected donation of ££85,000 in March 2006). Grants totalling £750,000 were made to 254 organisations. Regrettably, no further information was available.

Exclusions No grants to individuals.

Applications In writing to the correspondent. Please note, unsuccessful applications are not acknowledged.

The E M MacAndrew Trust

Medical, children, general

£52,500 (2005/06)

Beneficial area UK.

J P Thornton and Co., The Old Dairy, Adstockfields, Adstock, Buckingham MK18 2JE

Tel. 01296 714886 **Fax** 01296 714711

Correspondent J P Thornton, Administrator

Trustees *A R Nicholson; J K Nicholson; Mrs S Grant; Mrs V E Webster.*

CC Number 290736

Information available Accounts were on file at the Charity Commission.

General The trust is mainly interested in medical and children's charities. In 2005/06 it had assets of £1.3 million and an income of £52,000. Grants totalling £52,500 were made to 23 organisations.

Major beneficiaries included: Stoke Mandeville Burns and Reconstructive Surgery Research Trust (£7,000 in two grants); Buckingham and Winslow Crossroads Carers, and MERLIN (£5,000 each in four grants); and BLESMA, Childline and Marie Curie Cancer Care (£4,000 each).

Applications The trustees state that they do not respond to any unsolicited applications under any circumstances, as they prefer to make their own decisions as to which charities to support.

The Macdonald-Buchanan Charitable Trust

General

£71,000 (2005)

Beneficial area UK, with a slight preference for Northamptonshire.

Rathbone Trust Co. Ltd, 159 New Bond Street, London W1S 2UD

Tel. 020 7399 0820

Email linda.cousins@rathbone.com

Correspondent Miss Linda Cousins

Trustees *Capt. John Macdonald-Buchanan (chair); A J Macdonald-Buchanan; A R Macdonald-Buchanan; H J Macdonald-Buchanan; Mrs M C A Philipson.*

CC Number 209994

Information available Accounts were on file at the Charity Commission.

General The Hon. Catherine Macdonald-Buchanan set up this trust in 1952 for general charitable purposes and endowed it with 40,000 shares in the then Distillers Company.

In the 2005 trustees' report the following statement was made: 'The trustees' current policy is to make regular payments to a number of national and local charities with which they have long established connections. The trustees also reserve a proportion of their income to enable them to make ad hoc substantial donations when approached for funding from those charities with which they are more closely involved.'

In 2005 the trust had assets of £3 million and an income of £119,000. Grants were made totalling £71,000 of which the majority were for less than £500. Administration expenses were high at £20,000.

The largest grants were £15,000 to Carriejo Charity, £13,000 to Orrin Charitable Trust, and £2,000 each to Charities Aid Foundation and St Giles Church – Graffham.

Overall, grants by category of the recipient charity were broken down as follows:

- animal welfare £3,000
- disabled charities £5,500
- elderly welfare £2,700
- forces welfare charities £3,750
- hospices £1,950
- medical and research £11,050
- youth welfare £3,200
- general welfare £39,970.

Exclusions No grants to individuals.

Applications In writing to the correspondent, for consideration once a year. Appeals will not be acknowledged.

The Macfarlane Walker Trust

Education, the arts, social welfare, general

About £27,000 to organisations (2005)

Beneficial area UK, with priority for Gloucestershire.

50 Courthope Road, London NW3 2LD

Correspondent Mrs S V Walker, Secretary

Trustees *D F Walker; N G Walker; D Launchbury.*

CC Number 227890

Information available Information was obtained from the Charity Commission website.

General This trust has a particular interest in the provision of facilities for recreation and social welfare in Gloucestershire, the relief of poverty and hardship among employees and former employees of Walker Crosweller and Co. Ltd, the provision of educational facilities particularly in scientific research and the encouragement of music, drama and the fine arts. The trust also prefers to support small projects where they believe their 'contribution will be significant'.

In 2004/05 the trust had an income of £21,000 and a total expenditure of £27,000. Further information was not available.

In 2003/04 the trust had an income of £20,000. Grants to individuals totalled £1,600, with grants to organisations totalling £28,000. Beneficiaries included the Second World War Experience Centre (£5,000), Vita Nova (£3,000), Blackheath Concert Halls, Carlton Primary School, Charlton Kings Senior Citizens' Welfare, Dyslexia Institute, Gloucestershire Association for Mental Health, Gloucestershire Society, Listening Books and National Star College (£2,000 each), Brewery Arts, Perranzabuloe Rotary Club (Permuteran gamelan), St Peter's C of E Primary School (£1,000 each) and University of Gloucestershire (£900).

Exclusions No grants for expeditions, medical expenses, nationwide appeals, animal charities or educational fees.

Applications In writing to the correspondent giving the reason for applying, and an outline of the project with a financial forecast. An sae must accompany the initial application.

Ian Mactaggart Trust

Education and training, culture, welfare and disability

About £200,000

Beneficial area UK, with a preference for Scotland.

c/o Breeze Paterson and Chapman, 257 West Campbell Street, Glasgow G2 4TU

Correspondent The Trustees

Trustees *Sir John Mactaggart; P A Mactaggart; Jane L Mactaggart; Fiona M Mactaggart; Lady Caroline Mactaggart; Karin T Woodcock; Leora J Armstrong.*

SC Number SC012502

Information available Information was provided by the trust.

General The trust supports education and training, culture, the relief of people who are poor, sick, in need or disabled. No recent financial information was available from the correspondent, although previous research indicates that grants are made totalling around £200,000 each year.

Previous beneficiaries in Scotland include Bobath Scotland, Cantilena Festival on Islay, Royal One Scotland, Glasgow Social Work Department, Islay Pipe Band and Greater Glasgow Health Fund.

Applications In writing to the correspondent, although unsolicited requests for donations are discouraged.

The Magen Charitable Trust

Education, Jewish

£74,000 (2005/06)

Beneficial area UK.

New Riverside, 439 Lower Broughton, Salford M7 2FX

Tel. 0161 792 2626

Correspondent The Trustees

Trustees *Jacob Halpern; Mrs Rose Halpern.*

CC Number 326535

Information available Accounts were on file at the Charity Commission, but without a narrative report or list of grants.

General In the accounts the trust's aims were stated as making donations to charitable and educational institutions. In 2005/06 the trust had assets of £1.4 million and an income of £271,000. Grants were made totalling £74,000. Previous beneficiaries have included Manchester Yeshiva Kollel, Talmud Educational Trust, Bnos Yisroel School and Mesifta Tiferes Yisroel.

Applications In writing to the correspondent.

Mageni Trust

Arts

£33,000 (2004/05)

Beneficial area UK.

17 Hawthorne Road, Bromley, Kent BR1 2HN

Tel. 020 8295 0297

Correspondent G L Collins, Trustee

Trustees *G L Collins; Mrs G L Collins; S J Hoare.*

CC Number 1070732

Information available Accounts were on file at the Charity Commission.

General In 2004/05 the trust had assets of £1.2 million, an income of £53,000 and made grants totalling £33,000.

There were 13 donations made in the year, including those to DEC Tsunami Appeal (£10,000), BYMT Special Needs Music (£5,000), LPO Maestoso (£3,000), National Youth Orchestra (£2,500), Chicks, Foundation for Young Music and Halifax Charity Gala (£2,000 each), Greenworld, National Theatre and SDRF (£1,000 each), London Symphony Orchestra (£250) and SEKPA (£150).

Applications In writing to the correspondent.

Malbin Trust

Jewish, general

£90,000 (2004/05)
Beneficial area Worldwide.

8 Cheltenham Crescent, Salford M7 4FP
Correspondent B Leitner, Trustee
Trustees *B Leitner; M Leitner; J Waldman.*
CC Number 1045174
Information available Accounts were on file at the Charity Commission.

General Established in 1995, in 2004/05 this trust had assets of £342,000 and an income of £225,000. Grants totalled £90,000. Just one grant was made over £1,000 each and listed in the accounts: £10,000 to Chasidei Belz Institutions.

Applications In writing to the correspondent.

The Mandeville Trust

Cancer, young people and children

£31,000 (2004/05)
Beneficial area UK.

The Hockett, Hockett Lane, Cookham Dean, Berkshire SL6 9UF
Tel. 01628 484272
Correspondent R C Mandeville, Trustee

Trustees *Robert Cartwright Mandeville; Pauline Maude Mandeville; Peter William Murcott; Justin Craigie Mandeville.*
CC Number 1041880
Information available Accounts were on file at the Charity Commission.

General In 2004/05 the trust had an income of £30,500 and made grants totalling £31,000. Grant beneficiaries included: Research grants to University College London (£21,000) and Imperial College (£3,100); and, The Berkshire Community Foundation (£5,000). Other smaller grants totalled £1,850.

Applications In writing to the correspondent.

Maranatha Christian Trust

Christian, relief of poverty and education of young people

£59,750 (2004/05)
Beneficial area UK and overseas.

208 Cooden Drive, Bexhill-on-Sea, East Sussex TN39 3AH
Correspondent The Secretary
Trustees *A C Bell; Revd L Bowring; Rt Hon. Viscount Brentford.*
CC Number 265323
Information available Accounts were on file at the Charity Commission.

General The trust's objectives are the promotion of education among young persons and the relief of poverty, particularly among those professing the Christian religion or working to promote such religion.

In 2004/05 the trust had assets of £1 million and an income of £27,000. Grants were made totalling £60,000.

The largest grants were £10,000 to World Vision and £9,000 to International Reconciliation Centre. Other large grants included those to CARE (£6,000), Vanessa Grant Memorial School (£3,000), CMS – Restoring sight in Afghanistan (£2,000).

Grants of £1,000 each went to Bible Society, Stewards Trust, Ealing Christian Fellowship, Joshua Generation, Going Public, Ichthus Prayer House, Micah Trust, and World Youth Alliance.

Applications In writing to the correspondent, but please note, the trust does not consider unsolicited applications.

Marbeh Torah Trust

Jewish

£243,000 (2006)
Beneficial area UK and Israel.

116 Castlewood Road, London N15 6BE
Correspondent M C Elzas, Trustee
Trustees *Moishe Chaim Elzas; Jacob Naftoli Elzas; Simone Elzas.*
CC Number 292491
Information available Accounts were on file at the Charity Commission.

General The trust's objectives are to further and support Jewish education and religion as well as the relief of poverty.

In 2006 the trust had an income of £247,000, almost entirely comprised of donations received. Grants were made to 14 organisations and totalled £243,000. Major beneficiaries included: Yeshiva Marbeh Torah (£84,000), Chazon Avraham Yitzchak (£43,000), Kol Yaakov (£22,000) and Mishkenos Yaakov (£20,000).

Smaller grants included those to Matan Beseser (£7,500), Yoshvei Beth Hamedrash (£5,000) and Keren Ezra (£2,000).

Applications In writing to the correspondent.

The Marchday Charitable Fund

Education, health, social welfare, support groups, overseas aid

£76,200 (2005)
Beneficial area UK, with a preference for south east England.

c/o Marchday Group plc, Allan House, 10 John Princes Street, London W1G 0AH
Tel. 020 7629 8050 **Fax** 020 7629 9204

Correspondent Mrs Rose Leigh, Trustee

Trustees *Alan Mann; Lyndsey Mann; Dudley Leigh; Rose Leigh; Maureen Postles; Graham Smith; John Orchard; Priyen Gudka.*

CC Number 328438

Information available Accounts were on file at the Charity Commission.

General The trust was established in 1989 to support charities and projects in a broad spectrum of education, health, social welfare, support groups and overseas aid. The trustees wish to assist small charities where a grant will support a particular project or make a difference to the continuation of the charity. There is a preference for charities in the south east of England. The trust also prefers to commit itself to three years' support rather than give a one-off grant, and revenue funding is preferred. The trustees like to have continual involvement with supported charities.

In 2005 the fund had assets of £537,000 and an income of £100,000. Grants were made to 13 organisations and totalled £76,000.

The beneficiaries were: LEWA Trust (£8,000); REMAP (£7,500); Refugee Council and Pimlico Toy Library (£7,000 each); Tunbridge Wells Mental Health (£6,200);Camden and Westminster Citizen Advocacy, and Dyspraxia Foundation (£6,000 each); Kidscape, Red R, RAPT, Kids Can Achieve and the Living Paintings Trust (£5,000 each); and, Magic Lantern (£3,500).

The majority of beneficiaries have been supported in previous years.

Exclusions The trust prefers not to support local organisations outside the south east of England. No grants to individuals or towards building projects or for religious activities.

Applications In writing to the correspondent. Replies cannot be sent to all requests. Trustees meet quarterly.

Marchig Animal Welfare Trust

Animal welfare

£159,000 (2005)
Beneficial area Worldwide.

PO Box 9422, Carnwath ML11 8YG
Tel. 01555 840991 **Fax** 01555 840991
Email info@marchigtrust.org

Website www.marchigawt.org

Correspondent Les Ward, Managing Trustee

Trustees *Madame Jeanne Marchig; Les Ward; Bill Jorda; Colin Moor.*

CC Number 802133

Information available Accounts were on file at the Charity Commission. Further information is available via the website.

General The objectives of the trust are to protect animals and to promote and encourage practical work in preventing cruelty. There are no restrictions on the geographical area of work, types of grants or potential applicants, but all applications must be related to animal welfare and be of direct benefit to animals. Projects supported by the trust have included mobile spay/neuter clinics, alternatives to the use of animals in research, poster campaigns, anti-poaching programmes, establishment of veterinary hospitals, clinics and animal sanctuaries.

There are no restrictions on the geographical area of the work, the type of grant, or the applicant. All applications meeting the following criteria will be considered by the trust:

- those encouraging initiatives designed to improve animal welfare
- those promoting alternative methods to animal experimentation and their practical implementation
- those promoting and encouraging practical work in alleviating suffering and preventing cruelty to animals.

As well as giving grants, the trust also makes Marchig Animal Welfare Trust Awards. These awards, which take the form of a financial donation in support of the winner's animal welfare work, are given in either of the following two categories: (a) The development of an alternative method to the use of animals in experimental procedures and the practical implementation of such an alternative resulting in a significant reduction in the number of animals used in experimental procedures; (b) Practical work in the field of animal welfare resulting in significant improvements for animals either nationally or internationally.

In 2005 the trust had assets of £12.6 million, an income of £2.4 million and made grants totalling £159,000.

Grants in 2006
The trust's website give many examples of projects that have been supported worldwide recently, although the amounts awarded are not given. They include those to: Animal Help

Foundation – India, Animal India Trust – India, Beirut for the Ethical Treatment of Animals – Lebanon, Cat Welfare Society of Gibraltar, Centre for Animal Rehabilitation and Education – South Africa, Compassion Unlimited Plus Action – India, Concern for Helping Animals in Israel, Dog Rescue Centre – Samui, Dogs Trust – UK, Fethiye Hayvan Dostlari Dernegi – Turkey, Friends of the Ferals – UK, Little Ouse Headwaters Charity – UK, Maun Animal Welfare Society – Botswana, Montgomeryshire Cat Rescue – UK, Paws In Need – UK, PDSA – UK, SOS Almeria – Spain, Stray Animals Care Organisation – Greece, VITA – Russia, White River Cat Rescue – UK, Woodlands Animal Sanctuary – UK and Yorkshire Swan Rescue Hospital – UK.

Exclusions Applications which fail to meet the above criteria will be rejected. Additionally, those relating to: educational studies or other courses; expeditions; payment of salaries; support of conferences and meetings; and activities that are not totally animal welfare related.

Applications On an application form available from the correspondent or via the website.

The Linda Marcus Charitable Trust

General

£122,000 (2004/05)
Beneficial area UK and Israel.

9 Savoy Street, London WC2E 7ER

Correspondent Mrs Sarah Hunt

Trustees *Dame Shirley Porter; Mrs Linda Streit; Steven Nigel Porter; Brian Padgett; Andrew Peggie.*

CC Number 267173

Information available Accounts were on file at the Charity Commission.

General The trust states that it supports projects concerned with education, culture, the environment and welfare. In practice, most grants are made to Jewish or Israeli organisations.

In 2004/05 the trust had assets of £10.1 million, which generated an income of only £246,000. Grants were made totalling £122,000.

Major beneficiaries included: The Centre for Advancement of Family Therapy in Israel (£25,000); Federation of Jewish Relief Organisations (£13,350); British Friends of the Israel Philharmonic Orchestra (£13,220); Centre for the Advancement of Family Therapy and Tel Aviv University Trust (£10,000 each); and Tel Aviv Foundation – Carmeri Theatre (£6,000).

Exclusions Grants are only made to registered charities. No grants to individuals.

Applications In writing to the correspondent.

The Stella and Alexander Margulies Charitable Trust

Jewish, general

£135,000 (2004/05)

Beneficial area UK.

23 Grosvenor Street, London W1K 4QL

Tel. 020 7416 4160

Correspondent M J Margulies, Trustee

Trustees Marcus J Margulies; Martin D Paisner; Sir Stuart Lipton.

CC Number 220441

Information available Accounts were on file at the Charity Commission.

General This trust has general charitable purposes, with a preference for Jewish organisations.

In 2004/05 it had assets of £7.5 million, which generated an income of £279,000. Grants were made to 26 organisations totalling £135,000.

The two largest grants of the year went to UJIA (£69,000) and Royal Opera House (£25,000).

Other beneficiaries included B'nai Brith Hillel Foundation, British Technion Society, Hillel Foundation and the Shalom Foundation (£5,000 each), Nightingale House (£3,000), World Jewish Relief (£2,500), Central Synagogue (£2,000), Friends of Lubavitch UK (£1,800), United Synagogue Young Peoples Programmes (£1,200), Craven Walk Charitable Trust, Great Ormond Street, Parsha Limited and YMER (£1,000 each) and

Crimestoppers Trust and WellBeing (£250 each).

Applications In writing to the correspondent.

Mariapolis Limited

Unity, ecumenism

£202,000 (2005/06)

Beneficial area UK and overseas.

38 Audley Road, London W5 3ET

Tel. 020 8991 2022 **Fax** 020 8991 9053

Email timking@focolare.org.uk

Correspondent Tim King

Trustees Timothy M King; Bartolomé Mayans; Revd Charles Slipper; Peter Riepenhoff.

CC Number 257912

Information available Accounts were on file at the Charity Commission.

General The trust promotes the international Focolare Movement in the UK, and grantmaking is only one area of its work. It works towards a united world and its activities focus on peace and cooperation. It has a related interest in ecumenism and also in overseas development. Activities include organising conferences and courses, and publishing books and magazines.

In 2005/06 assets stood at £2.5 million and income, mostly from various donations received and earned income, at £508,000. Total expenditure was £523,000, of which £202,000 was given in four grants. These were broken down as follows: £196,000 to Pia Associazione Maschile Opera di Maria (PAMOM); £2,700 to Anglican Priests Training Fund; £2,500 in Educational grants; and, £660 in Family welfare grants.

Applications In writing to the correspondent.

Michael Marks Charitable Trust

Culture, environment

£251,000 (2005/06)

Beneficial area UK and overseas.

5 Elm Tree Road, London NW8 9JY

Tel. 020 7286 4633 **Fax** 020 7289 2173

Correspondent The Secretary

Trustees Marina, Lady Marks; Prof. Sir Christopher White.

CC Number 248136

Information available Full accounts were on file at the Charity Commission.

General The trust supports the arts (including galleries and museums), and environmental groups, with grants generally ranging from £150 to £25,000, although larger grants have been given.

In 2005/06 it had assets of £6.7 million, which generated an income of £195,000. Grants totalling £251,000 were made to 26 organisations.

Beneficiaries of the largest grants were the King's College University of London, Woodland Trust and the Zoological Society of London (£30,000 each), Museum of Childhood (£25,000), the Bach Choir and the Wallace Collection (£20,000 each) and Ecotrust Canada, London Philharmonic Orchestra, Museum Het Mauritshuis, National Trust, the Norfolk Churches Trust, Oxford Philomusica Trust and the Scottish Ensemble (10,000 each).

Other beneficiaries included Museum Het Rembrandthuis (£7,000), the Handel House Trust (£4,500), Benaki Museum and Royal Holloway University of London (£3,000 each), Polish Association of the Knights of Malta (£2,000), University of Oxford – Greek Society (£1,000) and Greek Archaeological Committee UK (£250).

Exclusions Grants are given to registered charities only. No grants to individuals or profit organisations.

Applications In writing to the correspondent before July. Applications should include audited accounts, information on other bodies approached and details of funding obtained. Requests will not receive a response unless they have been successful.

The Ann and David Marks Foundation

Jewish charities

£33,000 (2004/05)

Beneficial area Worldwide with a preference for Manchester.

Mutley House, 1 Ambassador Place, Stockport Road, Altrincham, Cheshire WA15 8DB

Tel. 0161 941 3183

Email davidmarks@mutleyproperties.co.uk

Correspondent D L Marks, Trustee

Trustees *D L Marks; Mrs A M Marks; Dr G E Marks; A H Marks.*

CC Number 326303

Information available Accounts were obtained from the Charity Commission website, but without a list of grants.

General The trust mainly supports Jewish charities, especially in the Manchester area. It has a number of regular commitments and prefers to distribute to charities known to the trustees. In 2004/05 the foundation had assets of £439,000 and an income of £50,000. Grants totalled £33,000, but unfortunately a list of grants was unavailable. Previous beneficiaries included the North Cheshire Jewish Primary School (£2,600), the United Jewish Israel Appeal (£2,500) and the Manchester Jewish Federation (£2,000).

Applications Previous research suggested that the trust's funds are mostly committed and unsolicited applications are not welcome.

The Hilda and Samuel Marks Foundation

Jewish, general

£229,000 (2005/06)

Beneficial area UK and Israel.

1 Ambassador Place, Stockport Road, Altrincham, Cheshire WA15 8DB

Tel. 0161 941 3183 **Fax** 0161 927 7437

Correspondent D L Marks, Trustee

Trustees *S Marks; Mrs H Marks; D L Marks; Mrs R D Selby.*

CC Number 245208

Information available Accounts were on file at the Charity Commission.

General The foundation mainly gives support to UK charities and to charities based in Israel. The 2005/06 annual report states that: 'The object of the foundation is to provide relief and assistance to poor and needy persons; for the advancement of education, religion or for other purposes beneficial to the community'.

Furthermore, that: 'The foundation intends following its existing policy of supporting organisations on a long-term basis with the trustees making major donations linked to specific projects. The foundation also believes it has a continuing responsibility to provide funds for maintenance of capital projects it has funded previously where appropriate and subject to availability of funds.'

In 2005/06 the foundation had assets of £3.3 million and an income of £177,000 – including a donation of £20,000 from Mutley Property (Holdings) Limited, a company in which all trustees are shareholders and directors. Grants totalling £229,000 were made during the year.

In line with the trustees' general rule, not to comment on individual donations, grants were broken down as follows:

- community £35,750 (15.62%)
- education £29,725 (12.99%)
- health £56,260 (24.58%)
- welfare £107,130 (46.81%).

However, notwithstanding this, the following observations were made.

Over the year in question donations totalling £109,535 were given to UK charities and £113,730 for Israel-based charities. The residue of £5,600 was given to projects in other countries.

The largest donations were for £25,000 each to the Child Resettlement Fund – Emunah and to Alyn Hospital in Jerusalem, both of whom the foundation has supported over a large number of years.

Donations totalling £12,650 were made to the Plymouth Synagogue which is the oldest Askanasi Synagogue in the English Speaking World. The Synagogue (which is a Grade I Listed Building) required funds for building repairs to assist in obtaining matched funds from English Heritage.

Exclusions No grants to individuals.

Applications The trust primarily supports projects known to the trustees and its funds are fully committed. Therefore unsolicited applications are not being sought.

The Marr-Munning Trust

Overseas aid

£84,000 (2005/06)

Beneficial area Worldwide, mainly developing world.

9 Madeley Road, Ealing, London W5 2LA

Tel. 020 8998 7747 **Fax** 020 8998 9593

Email dongleeson@tiscali.co.uk

Correspondent Donford Gleeson

Trustees *Glen Barnham; Marianne Elliott; Julian Kay; Guy Perfect; Richard Tomlinson; David Strachan; Pierre Thomas.*

CC Number 261786

Information available Accounts were on file at the Charity Commission.

General The Trust was founded in 1970 by the late Frank Harcourt-Munning. An extract from the trust deed encapsulates its purposes:

'To support charities giving overseas aid for the relief of poverty suffering and distress particularly those inhabitants so qualified of such territories as appear to the managing trustees to be economically underprivileged through want of development or of support of the necessities of life or of those commodities and facilities which enhance human existence enriched by education and free from the threat of poverty disease undernourishment or starvation.'

Income is derived primarily from the letting of property. The trustees have been addressing the historically low proportion of charitable expenditure by modernising the management of its assets and the effects are already being seen in an increased level of grants.

In 2005/06 the trust had assets of £9.8 million and an income of £411,000. Grants totalling £84,000 were made to 34 organisations working overseas and was broken down as follows:

Helping natural disaster victims (£28,000)
Providing shelter to destitute people (£30,000)
Supporting self-sustaining projects (£8,250)
Providing educational support (£8,500)
Providing healthcare to poor people (£10,000).

Major beneficiaries were: UNICEF – South Asia Earthquake Children's Appeal (£20,000); Marr-Munning Asram – India

(££15,000); Gram Niyojon Kendra – India (£6,300); and, Aysanew Kassa Trust – Ehiopia and Care International – Niger famine (£3,000 each).

Exclusions No grants to individuals or for work taking place within the UK.

Applications The trustees meet quarterly on average and usually review applications twice-yearly, in the spring and autumn. Sometimes a request may be carried forward to a later meeting. However, emergency appeals may be considered at any meeting.

Applications should be concise, ideally limited to no more than two sides of A4 plus a project description, budget and summary accounts or annual report. Clear financial information is essential, and applications from small or new organisations may benefit from reference to any better-known supporters or partners. Charitable or equivalent status of the applicant organisation should be made clear.

Please note: Any other supporting literature should be kept to a minimum. Do not waste stamps on an SAE; the trust regrets that it does not have the administrative resources at present to return papers or respond to telephone or email enquiries (a website is under consideration). A trustee has agreed to look at the requests each month and where necessary seek further information. Otherwise, applicants will normally only hear if their bid has been successful which may be more than six months from receipt of application.

The Marsh Christian Trust

General

£143,000 (2005/06)
Beneficial area UK.

Granville House, 132 Sloane Street, London SW1X 9AX

Tel. 020 7730 2626 **Fax** 020 7823 5225

Correspondent Millie Kenyon, Administrator

Trustees B P Marsh; R J C Marsh; N C S Marsh; L Ryan.

CC Number 284470

Information available Full accounts were available from the Charity Commission.

General The trust was established in 1981 and has increased steadily in size with each year. In 2005/06 the trust had assets of £5.7 million and an income of £227,000. Grants to organisations totalled £143,000.

Total charitable expenditure comprised of 14 awards and 220 grants made to organisations, of which 101 grants were to organisations supported in the previous year. Grants were broken down as follows:

- social welfare: £68,000
- literature, arts and heritage: £34,000
- environment causes and animal welfare: £24,000
- healthcare and medical research: £12,000
- education and training: £7,000
- overseas appeals: £5,000
- miscellaneous: £4,000.

Charitable donations
Grants range from £250 to £4,000, with responses to new applications being at the lower end of this scale. The trust engages in long-term core funding and prefers to build up the level of grantmaking over time.

Grants of £1,000 or more included: Wildlife Information Network (£6,000); In Kind Direct (£3,000); National Portrait Gallery (£2,500); Explore (£1,800); Industry and Parliament Trust, University of East Anglia and Royal College of Music (£1,500 each); Historic Chapels Trust (£1,400); Abbeyfield International (£1,250); and British Deaf Association, Christian Responsibility in Public Affairs, Christians Against Poverty, Friends of High Gate Cemetery, Lambeth Partnership, Tate Foundation, the Bible Reading Fellowship and the Leprosy Mission (£1,000 each).

Grants of under £1,000 each included: Prisoners Abroad (£900); Soho Family Centre and Soldiers', Sailors' and Airmen's Families Association (£750 each); Irish Peatland Conservation Society (£600); Rainbow Trust (£500); Marine Conservation Society (£400); Friends of Africa, Frontier Community Project and Resource Info Society (£300 each); Befriending Network and Birmingham Institute for the Deaf (£250 each); Royal Society for the Arts (£122); Royal Society of Literature (£40); and Order of the British Empire Chapel Fund (£15).

Awards
During the year, there were 21 awards running, of which fourteen were given out. In total, monies awarded ranged from £600 to £8,000 and are listed as follows:

- Marsh Biography Award: £8,000
- Marsh Ecology Award: £2,000
- Marsh Heritage Volunteer Award: £2,000
- Marsh Volunteer of the Year Award for Work with Children: £2,000
- Marsh Award for Conservation in Genetic Bio-diversity: £1,500
- Marsh Kent Nature Conservation Award: £1,500
- Marsh Award for Public Sculpture: £1,500
- Marsh Award for Volunteering in Support of Older People: £1,100
- Marsh Conservation Biology Award: £1,000
- Marsh Award for Insect Conservation: £1,000
- Marsh Award for Lifetime Achievement in Lepidoptera Conservation: £1,000
- The Thomas Henry Huxley Award: £600.

During the year, seven other awards were running, although they did not make awards at this time. These were: Authors' Club Best First Novel Award, Marsh Award for International Bird Conservation, Marsh Award for Children's Literature in Translation, Marsh Award for Volunteering in Support of Older People, Marsh Botany Award and Marsh Fountain of the Year Award.

Exclusions No grants can be made to individuals or for sponsorships. No start-up grants. No support for building funds, ordinary schools, colleges, universities or hospitals, or research.

Applications In writing to the correspondent. All applications for grants must be accompanied by a copy of the most recent audited accounts. The trustees currently receive about 8,000 applications every year, of which 7,800 are new. Decisions are made at monthly trustee meetings.

The trustees attempt to visit each long-term recipient at least once every three years to review the work done, to learn of future plans and renew acquaintance with those responsible for the charity.

The Charlotte Marshall Charitable Trust

Roman Catholic, general

£122,000 (2005/06)
Beneficial area UK.

c/o C and C Marshall Limited, 55–65 Castleham Road, Castleham Industrial Estate, St Leonards-on-Sea, East Sussex TN38 9NU

Tel. 01424 856058

Correspondent Kathy Porter

Trustees *Miss C C Cirket; E M Cosgrove; J Crosgrove; K B Page; J M Russell.*

CC Number 211941

Information available Accounts were on file at the Charity Commission.

General The trust has general charitable purposes in the UK, mainly supporting educational, religious and other charitable purposes for Roman Catholics.

In 2005/06 the trust had assets of £543,000 and an income of £111,000 – mainly derived from the dividend received from shares held in the C & C Marshall group of companies in which three of the trustees have an interest.

Furthermore, because of the cessation of trading of Marshall Tufflex Limited in May 2000 and the subsequent loss of dividend income, C. & C. Marshall Limited donated a further £60,000 (2005: £60,000) to the charity.

During the year, grants were made to 73 organisations and totalled £122,000. Of this, £81,000 went towards Roman Catholic activities and £41,000 towards other charitable activities. Grants were further broken down as follows:

Educational – seven grants totalling £28,000
Homelessness – eight grants totalling ££23,500
Disability and illness – 28 grants totalling £36,000
Parents, children and young people – twelve grants totalling £15,000
Needy and underprivileged – four grants totalling £3,500
Abuse, addiction, refugee and torture – six grants totalling £7,000
Elderly – four grants totalling £1,500
Other charitable activities – four grants totalling £7,500.

Exclusions No grants are given to individuals.

Applications On a form available from the correspondent. Completed forms must be returned by 31 December for consideration in March.

John Martin's Charity

Religious activity, relief-in-need, education

£157,000 to schools and organisations (2005/06)

Beneficial area Preference for the town of Evesham only.

16 Queen's Road, Evesham, Worcestershire WR11 4JP

Tel. 01386 765440 **Fax** 01386 765340

Email enquiries@johnmartins.org.uk

Website www.johnmartins.org.uk

Correspondent John Daniels, Clerk

Trustees *N Lamb, Chair; J Icke; Revd J Bomyer; Revd B Collins; A Bennett; Mrs J Turner; J Smith; C Scorse; R Emson; Mrs D Raphael; Mrs F S Smith; Mrs J Westlake.*

CC Number 527473

Information available Accounts were available from the Charity Commission.

General **Summary**
The charity was created following the death of John Martin of Hampton, Worcestershire in 1714. His property was left for the benefit of local residents, and over the years some of this property has been sold to generate income to enable the charity to carry out its objectives in accordance with his wishes. It was formally registered with the Charity Commission in 1981.

Aims and Objectives
Under the terms of the original will and the amended Charity Commission Scheme, the overall aim of the charity is to benefit the residents of the town and neighbourhood of Evesham, Worcestershire. It does this through the implementation of four specific aims:

- propagation of the Christian Gospel (religious support)
- relief in need
- promotion of education
- health.

Objectives
- religious support – To assist the Vicars and Parochial Church Councils within the town of Evesham
- relief in need – To assist individuals and organisations within the town of Evesham who are in conditions of need, hardship and distress
- promotion of education – To promote education to persons who are or have a parent residing within the town of

Evesham and to provide benefits to schools within Evesham
- health – The Trustees have wide-ranging authority within the scheme to provide such charitable purposes as they see fit, for either assisting beneficiaries within the town of Evesham or within the immediate neighbourhood. The Trustees currently utilise this authority to support people with chronic health problems and other related health issues.

Any unspent income at the end of the financial year can be used for the relief of conditions arising from health problems or medical needs either within the town of Evesham or certain designated villages.

Grant-making policy
Within the terms of the scheme, the trustees have the authority to make such policies as they see fit to meet the specific objectives. These policies are reviewed on an annual basis and this ensures that the grants awarded still meet the set objectives and also enables the policies to be adjusted to take account of new legislation, best practice, grant trends or other matters. The office assists with this process by making recommendations, although the final decision is a matter for the trustees.

The Charity invites applications for grants in line with the objectives by issuing public notices setting out the application criteria and closing dates for the receipt of an application. In addition, local agencies are made aware of the charity and numerous applications are referred from these sources.

Information about the charity is also available on the website, where application forms can be obtained. Upon receipt of an application the applicant is interviewed and a home visit may also be undertaken in some circumstances. The application is checked against the specific criteria for that type of grant request and then detailed on an agenda for the consideration of the trustees.

Applications falling outside the criteria are rejected unless there are strong mitigating circumstances that require further consideration.

The Pensioners' Heating Award and Student Grant have special timescales when applications can be made. With the Student Grant, this is to ensure the total number of applicants is known before the grant level is set. The overall budgeted amount for the grant is then divided equally between the applicants. Applications for all other types of grant can be made at any time throughout the year.

General

In 2005/06 the charity had assets of £20.2 million and an income of £657,000. Grants were made to organisations (including schools) totalling £157,000, broken down as follows:

Religious support – £57,000

Promotion of education – £54,000

Relief in need – £26,000

Health – £20,000

Beneficiaries included St Peter's PCC (£26,000), St Andrew's PCC (£16,000), Hampton 1st School (£11,000), Evesham Adventure Playground (£5,000) and Noah's Ark Trust (£3,000).

Grants were also made to individuals across all four categories totalling £378,000.

Exclusions No grants for the payment of rates or taxes, or otherwise to replace statutory benefits.

Applications On a form available from the correspondent on request. Initial telephone calls are welcomed. The trustees normally meet on the second and fourth Thursday in each month, with one meeting in June and December. The charity can make urgent grants in exceptional circumstances. Applicants for education grants should supply an sae and may obtain details of deadlines from the charity.

The Mason Porter Charitable Trust

Christian

£79,000 (2004/05)

Beneficial area UK.

Liverpool Charity and Voluntary Services, 14 Castle Street, Liverpool L2 0NJ

Tel. 0151 236 7728 **Fax** 0151 258 1153

Correspondent The Secretary

Trustees *William Fulton, Chair; David Bebb; Roger Morris; Mark Blundell; Dil Daly; Charles Feeny; Prof. Philip Love; Andrew Lovelady; Shirley Mashiane-Talbot; Sue Newton; Christine Reeves; Hilary Russell.*

CC Number 255545

Information available Accounts were on file at the Charity Commission.

General The trust appears to support mainly Christian causes in the UK, including those which provide relief or missionary work overseas.

In 2004/05 the trust had assets of £1.95 million and an income of £128,000. Grants to organisations totalled £79,000.

Grants of £1,000 and over included: Abernethy Trust Ltd (£13,500); ELIM International Missions (£10,000); Just Care (£8,000); Cliffe College (£5,400); Crossroads in Wirral Caring for Carers and New Creations (£5,000 each); Life Changing Ministries, Share Jesus International, and Sisters of Jesus Way (£2,500 each); The New Life Centre (£2,000); and St Luke's Methodist Church – Hoylake, and The Messengers (£1,000 each).

Applications The trust states that it only makes grants to charities known to the settlor and unsolicited applications are not considered.

Matliwala Family Charitable Trust

Islam, general

£63,000 (2004/05)

Beneficial area UK and overseas, especially Bharuch – India.

9 Brookview, Fulwood, Preston PR2 8FG

Tel. 01772 706501

Correspondent A V Bux, Trustee

Trustees *Ayub Vali Bux; Usman Salya; Abdul Aziz Vali Patel; Yousuf Bux; Ibrahim Vali Patel.*

CC Number 1012756

Information available Full accounts were on file at the Charity Commission.

General The trust's areas of giving are:

- the advancement of education for pupils at Matliwala School Of Bharuch in Gujerat – India, and other schools, including assisting with the provision of equipment and facilities
- the advancement of the Islamic religion
- the relief of sickness and poverty
- the advancement of education.

In 2004/05 the trust had an income of £1.7 million including £1.4 million from the sale of properties. The balance at the end of the year was £3.5 million. Grants

totalled £63,000. Of this, £55,000 was given to various causes in Bharuch, including hospital care, improvements to water supply, food, oil and housing construction for people who are disadvantaged. The accounts also stated that non-material grants were made during the year, totalling £7,600.

Applications In writing to the correspondent.

The Matt 6.3 Charitable Trust

Christian

£328,000 (2005/06)

Beneficial area UK.

Progress House, Progress Park, Cupola Way, Off Normanby Road, Scunthorpe, North Lincolnshire DN15 9YJ

Correspondent I H Davey

Trustees *C R Barnett; D Dibdin; T P Dibdin; R O Dauncey.*

CC Number 1069985

Information available Accounts were on file at the Charity Commission.

General Established in 1998, this trust mainly supports Christian organisations. In 2005/06 the trust had assets of £5.2 million and an income of £900,000. Grants totalling £328,000 were made to 12 organisations.

The beneficiaries were: Christian Centre (Humberside) Limited (£132,000); Centre for Justice & Liberty (£59,000); Shalom Centre – Grimsby Education (£29,000); Don Summers Evangelistic Association (£17,400); Caribbean Radio Lighthouse (£8,750); Hull University – Wilberforce Fund Education (£5,000); Kings Christian Bookshop (£4,000); Peace & Hope Trust (£3,000); and Evangelical Library (£500).

Other grants totalling £70,000 were made to individuals of which the largest was for Christian broadcasting (£63,520).

Applications The trust does not accept unsolicited applications. Funds are committed to ongoing projects.

The Maureen Lilian Charitable Trust

General

£235,000 (2005/06)

Beneficial area Worldwide.

Deloitte & Touche, Blenheim House, Fitzlan Court, Newport Road, Cardiff CF24 0TS

Tel. 02920 481111

Correspondent Steve Allan

Trustees *L H Wyndham; Mrs A E Daniels.*

CC Number 1078369

Information available Accounts were on file at the Charity Commission.

General Registered with the Charity Commission in November 1999, in 2005/06 the trust had an income of £70,000 and made grants totalling £235,000 (£90,000 in 2004/05). Assets stood at £1.7 million.

By far the largest grant was £100,000 to RNLI – Penarth. Grants of £10,000 each were made to 10 organisations: Cardiff & Vale NHS Charitable Trust, Cowbridge Physic Garden Trust, George Thomas Hospice, Jubilee Sailing Trust, Marie Curie – Wales, Sandville Self Help Centre, Society for the Welfare of Horses and Ponies, Teenage Cancer Trust, Ty Hafan and the Willow Trust.

Other beneficiaries included Bobath Cymru, Donkey Sanctuary, NSPCC – Whitchurch and Riding for the Disabled.

Applications In writing to the correspondent.

The Mayfield Valley Arts Trust

Arts, especially chamber music

£145,800 (2005/06)

Beneficial area Unrestricted, but with a special interest in Sheffield and South Yorkshire.

Hawsons, Pegasus House, 463a Glossop Road, Sheffield S10 2QD

Tel. 0114 266 7141

Correspondent P J Kennan, Administrator

Trustees *A Thornton; J R Thornton; Mrs P M Thornton; D Whelton; D Brown; J R Rider.*

CC Number 327665

Information available Accounts were on file at the Charity Commission.

General Established in 1987, the objectives of this trust are the advancement of education by the encouragement of art and artistic activities of a charitable nature, especially music and the promotion and preservation of concerts and other musical events and activities.

In 2005/06 the trust had assets of £2.5 million and an income of £112,000. Grants totalling £146,000 were made as follows: Wigmore Hall (£62,500); Sheffield Chamber Music in the Round (£30,000); Live Music Now (£25,800); York Early Music Foundation (£22,500); and Prussia Cove (£5,000).

Exclusions No grants to students.

Applications The trust states that no unsolicited applications are considered.

Mazars Charitable Trust

General

£162,000 (2005)

Beneficial area UK, overseas.

24 Bevis Marks, London EC3A 7NR

Tel. 020 7220 3462 **Fax** 0207377 9975

Correspondent Trust Management Committee

Trustees *Peter R Hyatt, Chair; John S Mellows; David J Evans.*

CC Number 287735

Information available Accounts were on file at the Charity Commission.

General The trust acts as a conduit for the charitable giving of the Mazars firm of chartered accountants (formerly Mazars Neville Russell). Up to 10% of the funds raised from each of the regional branches can be given to local organisations at the discretion of the managing partner; the rest of the funds are given by the trustees for general charitable causes. From April 2004 onwards, it was determined that grants will be broadly split between those received with a personal commendation of team members of Mazars LLP, the donor firm, and those which are aligned to the LLP's corporate ethos.

The trust states it prefers to support specific projects (e.g. capital expenditure, research, an event) rather than normal revenue expenditure, although the latter will be considered provided that the applicant appears to be launching a strategic initiative and is financially sound.

It also: 'supports charities which reflect the corporate ethos of our donor, the UK firm of Mazars. This ethos is being developed over time, but encapsulates the following sorts of charitable activity, associated with organisations which:

- will benefit significantly from receipt of a grant (i.e. the trust rarely supports large national charities)
- support professionals of whom our team are members (e.g. Chartered Accountants Benevolent Association)
- support disadvantaged people in the communities near which our offices are based
- seek to place people into employment and assist in housing (essential if a job is to be held down)
- seek to relieve hardship in deprived areas of the world in crisis situations
- our clients are encouraging us to support (subject always to careful adherence to independence criteria)'.

In 2005 the trust had assets of £60,000 and an income of £169,000. Grants were made to 95 organisations and totalled £162,000.

The largest grants were: UNICEF for tsunami disaster (£19,000); UNICEF for Kashmir earthquake (£10,700); John Grooms (£10,250); Royal Commonwealth Ex-services League and Sunfield (£10,000 each); and Tacade (£9,000).

In addition to the above, 76 other grants of between £50 and £1,500 each were made totalling £34,185.

Exclusions No grants to individuals, large national charities (rarely), applications from a particular national charity within three years of an earlier grant, or for ongoing funding. Unsolicited appeals are rarely considered.

Applications The trustees operate through a management committee which meets annually to consider applications for major grants which fit with the stated criteria. Some monies are allocated to five regional 'pot' holders who approve minor grant applications from within their own region. Applicants for a national grant must be known to the team members of Mazars LLP.

National and regional criteria are regularly reviewed but, in general, the trustees consider that the national grant-making policy should avoid core funding and other activities that require funding over a number of years. Most national grants are therefore made towards one-off projects.

A copy of these criteria is available upon request to the Trust Administrator.

The Robert McAlpine Foundation

Children with disabilities, older people, medical research, welfare

£357,000 (2004/05)
Beneficial area UK.

Eaton Court, Maylands Avenue, Hemel Hempstead, Hertfordshire HP2 7TR
Tel. 01442 233444
Correspondent The Trustees
Trustees Hon. David McAlpine; M H D McAlpine; Kenneth McAlpine; Cullum McAlpine; Adrian N R McAlpine.
CC Number 226646
Information available Full accounts were on file at the Charity Commission.

General This foundation generally supports causes concerned with children with disabilities, older people, medical research and social welfare. A small number of other charities are also supported, through a long-term connection with the foundation and therefore no new beneficiaries are considered from outside the usual areas.

In 2004/05 it had an income of £340,000 and made grants totalling £357,000.

There were 29 grants made during the year. The beneficiaries of the largest grants of £10,000 or more were The Ewing Foundation (£60,000), Stoke Mandeville Burns Research (£36,000), Contact the Elderly (£35,000), Fairbridge (£30,000), National Eye Research Centre (£19,000), Prostate Cancer Research Centre (£18,000), Community Self Build Agency (£15,000), University of Bristol – palliative care (£14,000), the Devas Club (£12,000) and Handicapped Children's Action Group and Kith and Kids (£10,000 each).

Other beneficiaries included the Brittle Bone Society and Eyeless Trust (£7,500 each), the Cai Dae Trust, the Grateful Society, Milton Keynes SNAP, Oxfordshire Befriending Network and Respite Association (£5,000 each) and Defeating Deafness (£3,400).

Exclusions The trust does not like to fund overheads. No grants to individuals.

Applications In writing to the correspondent at any time. Considered annually, normally in November.

The A M McGreevy No. 5 Charitable Settlement

General

£6,000 (2004/05)
Beneficial area UK, with a preference for the Bristol and Bath area.

KPMG, 100 Temple Street, Bristol BS1 6AG
Tel. 0117 905 4554
Correspondent Lisa Mirams
Trustees Avon Executor and Trustee Co. Ltd; Anthony M McGreevy; Elise McGreevy-Harris; Katrina Paterson.
CC Number 280666
Information available Accounts were on file at the Charity Commission.

General The trust was established in 1979 by Anthony M McGreevy. In previous years there has been a preference for charities based in the former county of Avon.

In 2004/05 the trust had assets of £1.7 million, generating an income of £37,000. Grants were made to two organisations totalling £6,000. The beneficiaries were: Fairbridge (£5,000) and Beckford Tower Trust (£1,000).

Exclusions No support for individuals.

Applications In writing to the correspondent.

The McKenna Charitable Trust

Health, disability, education, children, general

£76,000 to organisations (2005/ 06)
Beneficial area England and Wales.

c/o Buzzacoat, 12 New Fetter Lane, London EC4A 1AG
Tel. 020 7556 1200
Correspondent The Trustees
Trustees P A McKenna; Mrs M E A McKenna; J L Boyton; H R Jones.
CC Number 1050672
Information available Accounts were on file at the Charity Commission.

General The trust's aims are to:

- assist with education, medical welfare and relief of need amongst people with disabilities
- provide funds for education as a means of relieving poverty
- make grants to children's charities
- make grants for general charitable purposes.

In 2005/06 the trust had assets of £492,000 and an income of £760,000. However, as in previous years, this included an exceptional donation to the trust on behalf of the main beneficiary – Young Vic Theatre Company. It appears, therefore, that this grant of £760,000 has been given through the trust, rather than by it. As such, the grant balance of £76,000 which went to other organisations appears to describe better the nature of the trust's giving.

Aside from the grant of £760,000 to Young Vic Theatre Company, the other beneficiaries were: SNAP – Special Needs and Parents (£50,000); Elton John AIDS Foundation (£20,000); Downing College – Cambridge (£3,750); and Cystic Fibrosis Trust (£2,100). No grants were made to individuals during the year in question.

Applications In October 2005 we were advised by the trust that: 'Due to the excessive numbers of inappropriate applications, the trustees have decided that they will no longer consider any unsolicited appeals for grants of any size or nature'.

However, the 2005/06 trustees report and accounts state: 'The trustees will consider applications for grants from individuals and charitable bodies on their merits but will place particular emphasis on the educational needs and the provision of support for disabled people'.

Martin McLaren Memorial Trust

General

About £60,000 (2004/05)
Beneficial area UK.

c/o Charles Russell Solicitors, 8–10 New Fetter Lane, London EC4A 1RS

Tel. 020 7203 5000

Correspondent Alan Bryant

Trustees *Mrs Nancy Gordon McLaren; Nicholas Durlacher; Michael Robert Macfadyen; Revd Richard Francis McLaren; Sir Kenneth Carlisle.*

CC Number 291609

Information available Information was taken from the Charity Commission website.

General In 2004/05 the trust had an income of £21,000 and expenditure of £62,000. No further information was available.

Previously, in 2001/02, the trust's assets totalled £629,000 generating an income of £26,000. Grants were £11,900 to Art and Christianity Enquiry Trust, £10,000 to Horticultural Scholarships Fund, £4,800 to European Gardens and £2,000 to St John's Smith Square.

Further grants under £500 were to Combe PCC, ESU Music Scholarship Fund, (£500 each), Queen Mary's Clothing Guild (£200), Macmillan Cancer Relief, The PCC Busbridge Church (£100 each) and Fairbridge Garden Society (£50).

Applications In writing to the correspondent.

D D McPhail Charitable Settlement

Medical research, disability, older people

£698,000 (2005/06)
Beneficial area UK.

PO Box 285, Pinner, Middlesex HA5 3FB

Correspondent Mrs Sheila Watson, Administrator

Trustees *I McPhail; P Cruddas; J K Noble; Mrs C Charles-Jones.*

CC Number 267588

Information available Accounts were on file at the Charity Commission.

General This trust has been growing in size since 1997, when it began to receive sums from the Estate of the late Mr D D McPhail. Assets at the end of 1995/96 totalled £223,000 and grants were made in that year of £17,000. By 2005/06 the assets had risen to £8.7 million and it made grants totalling £698,000. In that year the trust had an income of £267,000.

In 2005/06 the four largest grants went to Demand (£450,000), Helen and Douglas House (£110,000), Association of Wheelchair Children (£90,000) and Sir William Burrough School (£18,000).

Other grants were either for £1,000 or £2,000 each and included those to the Barbara Bus Fund, Cancer Relief Macmillan Fund, County Air Ambulance, Friends of Northwood & Pinner Community Hospital, Harrow Blind Social Club, Harrow MENCAP, Mount Vernon Hospital Comforts Funds, RNID and Riding for the Disabled Association.

Applications In writing to the correspondent.

The Anthony and Elizabeth Mellows Charitable Settlement

National heritage, Church of England churches

£47,000 (2005/06)
Beneficial area UK.

22 Devereux Court, Temple Bar, London WC2R 3JR

Tel. 020 7583 8813

Correspondent Prof. A R Mellows, Trustee

Trustees *Prof. Anthony R Mellows; Mrs Elizabeth Mellows.*

CC Number 281229

Information available Accounts were on file at the Charity Commission.

General The trust gives support to charities in four main areas :

- the arts and national heritage
- churches of the Church of England
- hospitals and hospices
- the training and development of children and young people.

The trust states that it aims: 'To further the charitable work of the operational charities supported by grants. The grants for the arts and national heritage are made only to national institutions and, save in exceptional circumstances, grants for churches of the Church of England are only made on a recommendation from the Council for the Care of Churches.'

In 2005/06 the trust had assets of £43,000 and an income of £38,000. Grants were made totalling £47,000 and were broken down as follows: The arts and national heritage (£18,250); Churches – Council for the Care of Churches (£2,500); Church of England (£5,475); Hospitals, hospices and welfare (£21,000).

Major beneficiaries included: The Order of St John (£15,000); Royal Academy Trust, Royal Opera House Foundation and The Lambeth Fund (£5,000 each); The Sixteen (£3,000); and Help the Hospices (£2,500). Other grants included £1,000 each to National Gallery and St Margaret – Tatterford; and £470 to St John Ambulance.

Exclusions Applications from individuals, including students, are ineligible.

Applications Applications are considered when received, but only from UK institutions. No application forms are used. Grants decisions are made three times a year when the trustees meet to consider applications.

Melodor Ltd

Jewish, general

£170,000 (2005/06)
Beneficial area UK and overseas.

148 Bury Old Road, Manchester M7 4SE

Correspondent P Newnann, Secretary

Trustees *B Weiss; M Weiss; P Weiss; S Weiss; J L Weiss; H Weiss; R Sofer; H Neumann; M Neumann; E Neumann; P Neumann; J Bleier; E Henry; R De Lange; J Weissmandel; M Friedlander.*

CC Number 260972

Information available Full accounts were on file at the Charity Commission.

General This trust supports religious, educational and similar causes, with most grants going to Jewish organisations.

In 2005/06 it had assets of £924,000 and an income of £273,000. Grants to organisations totalled £170,000.

Beneficiaries of the largest grants were Centre for Torah Education Trust (£30,000), Beis Rochel (£19,000), Chasdei Yoel (£12,000).

Other beneficiaries included Beth Hamedrash Hachodosh (£6,100), Yeshivas Ohel Shimon (£5,300), Beis Minchas Yitzhok (£4,000), Talmud Torah Education Trust (£3,000), Dushinsky Trust (£1,900), Kollel Chelkas Yakov and Yetev Lev (£1,500 each), Delman Charitable Trust (£1,100) and Ovois Ubonim and Friends of Viznitz (£1,000 each).

Sundry donations under £1,000 each totalled £39,000.

Applications In writing to the correspondent.

Melow Charitable Trust

Jewish

£446,000 (2004/05)

Beneficial area UK and overseas.

21 Warwick Grove, London E5 9HX

Tel. 020 8806 1549 **Fax** 020 8806 9390

Correspondent J Low

Trustees *Miriam Spitz; Esther Weiser.*

CC Number 275454

Information available Accounts were on file at the Charity Commission.

General The trust makes grants to Jewish charities both in the UK and overseas. In 2004/05 it had assets of £3.9 million and an income of £400,000. Grants totalled £446,000 with many organisations receiving more than one grant during the year.

Grants were broken down as follows: Education (£219,000); Assisting the

needy (£157,500); Synagogues (£42,350); Religious education (£22,000); General charitable purposes (£3,120); Relief of poverty (£2,000); and Orphanages (£100).

Major beneficiaries were: Yetev Lev – Jerusalem (£120,500); Lolev Charitable Trust (£54,000); Interdam Ltd (£44,000); Craven Walk Charities (£36,000); and Ponovez Beth Hamedrash (£24,500).

Beneficiaries of smaller grants included: £2,500 to V'Yoel Moshe Charitable Trust; £2,450 to Yeshivas Metzuyonim; £1,250 to Ezras Yisroel Trust; and £1,000 each to London Bnois Jerusalem, Mesifta Talmundical College and Talmud Torah Beish Shlomo.

Applications In writing to the correspondent.

Meningitis Trust

Meningitis in the UK

£103,000 to organisations (2005/ 06)

Beneficial area UK.

Fern House, Bath Road, Stroud, Gloucestershire GL5 3TJ

Tel. 01453 768000 **Fax** 01453 768001

Email helpline@meningitis-trust.org

Website www.meningitis-trust.org

Correspondent Tracy Lewendon, Financial Grants & Helpline Administrator

Trustees *Albert Geoffrey Shaw; Lesley Green; Mrs Bernadette Julia McGhie; Mrs Beryl Anne Sutcliffe; Mrs Gillian Mae Noble; James William Edward Wilson; Dr Jane Wells; Michael Anthony Hall; Peter James Johnson; Robert Johnson; Suzanne Devine.*

CC Number 803016

Information available Accounts were on file at the Charity Commission.

General 'The Meningitis Trust is an international charity with a strong community focus, fighting meningitis through the provision of support, education and awareness and research.'

In 2005/06 the trust had an income of £3.5 million and a total expenditure of £3.2 million. Grants to organisations for research purposes totalled £103,000. The sum of £141,000 was distributed to individuals in support grants.

Applications Application forms are available from the correspondent. Requests for financial support are

reviewed regularly by the Financial Grants Review Panel.

Further information can be had by calling the helpline on 0800 028 1528.

Mental Health Foundation

Mental health and learning disability research

£3.8 million (2005/06)

Beneficial area UK.

9th Floor, Sea Containers House, 20 Upper Ground, London SE1 9QB

Tel. 020 7803 1100 **Fax** 020 7803 1111

Email mhf@mhf.org.uk

Website www.mentalhealth.org.uk

Trustees *Abel Hadden; Prof. Tony Thake; Dr Jocelyn Cornwell; Dr Philippa Russell; David Sachon; Prof. Daphne Statham; Michael O'Connor; Prof. Stephen Platt; Charles Walsh; Dr Mike Shooter.*

CC Number 801130

Information available Accounts were on file at the Charity Commission.

General The mission of the foundation is to generate new understanding, knowledge, support and services which are exemplary and replicable. These should promote emotional wellbeing and improve the lives of people with mental health issues and/or with learning disabilities. The foundation's objectives are to:

- increase knowledge and understanding about mental health across society
- combat the stigma associated with mental distress
- improve policy and practice in the field of mental health and learning disabilities
- empower users and carers
- build the confidence and competence of people working in the mental health/learning difficult field
- influence governments on issues relating to mental health/learning disability policies, practices and services.

Much of this work is carried out by the foundation itself. However, the 2005/06 accounts stated the following, under the heading 'Grant-making policy': 'The foundation has an internal process for identifying areas of work where it can make a useful contribution. For some projects this will involve the funding of other organisations through a grants programme. The foundation identifies such organisations through a tendering process. Organisations awarded a grant work to an agreed contact, which specifies the conditions. The monitoring of satisfactory delivery of the contract is in the first instance the responsibility of the project/programme manager.'

In 2005/06 the foundation had assets of £3.5 million. Total income was £4.1 million, mostly comprised of donations, gifts, legacies, charitable trading, fundraising events and grants from statutory and other sources. Although total expenditure on charitable activities amounted to £3.8 million, no figure was provided showing how much of this, if any, was given in the form of research grants.

Exclusions No grants for: individual hardship, education and training; travel; attendance at conferences; capital; expenses such as vehicles or property; general appeals; general running costs; overseas events.

Applications As at March 2007, research grant programmes were in abeyance. Please refer to the foundation's website for further information on programmes in the future.

Menuchar Ltd

Jewish

£215,500 (2004/05)
Beneficial area UK.

c/o Flack Stetson, Equity House, 128–136 High Street, Edgware HA8 7EL
Tel. 020 8381 2587
Correspondent The Trustees
Trustees N Bude; Mrs G Bude.
CC Number 262782

Information available Accounts were on file at the Charity Commission, but without a list of grants.

General The main objects of the trust are: the advancement of religion in accordance with the Orthodox Jewish faith and the relief of people in need.

In 2004/05 the trust had assets of £38,000 and an income of £39,000. Grants totalled £215,500 . Unfortunately, a list of beneficiaries was not available.

Exclusions No grants to non-registered charities or to individuals.

Applications In writing to the correspondent.

Brian Mercer Charitable Trust

Welfare, medical, visual arts in UK and overseas

£192,000 (2005/06)
Beneficial area UK and overseas.

Central Buildings, Richmond Terrace, Blackburn BB1 7AP
Tel. 01254 686600 **Fax** 01254 682483
Email arowntree@waterworths.co.uk
Correspondent A T Rowntree, Trustee
Trustees Mrs C J Clancy; K F Martin; K J Merrill; A T Rowntree.
CC Number 1076925

Information available Accounts were on file at the Charity Commission.

General The trust's objectives are:

- the advancement of education and in particular, but not restricted to, the provision of grants for the promotion of medical and scientific research and the dissemination of the useful results thereof
- the furtherance and promotion of any other exclusively charitable objects and purposes in any part of the world as the trustees may in their absolute discretion think fit.

However, in the 2005/06 report and accounts, the trustees state they have decided that: 'Amongst other objectives, the causes which they will most seek to benefit will be:

- the prevention, treatment and cure of diseases effecting eyesight
- the prevention, treatment and cure of cancer, particularly liver cancer
- the promotion of the visual arts.

'The trustees are seeking to develop close relationships with a number of charities with a view to working in partnership with those charities on specific projects and thus being in a position to influence the manner in which funds are expended in order to ensure that maximum benefit is derived from them. The trustees envisage that it may take some time yet to fully develop these relationships.'

In 2005/06 the trust had assets of £18.2 million and an income of £665,000. Grants totalling £192,000 were made to 13 organisations, including:

Fight for Sight and British Liver Trust (£50,000 each); Sight Savers International (£20,000); Macular Disease Society, East Lancashire Hospice and The Living Paintings Trust (£10,000 each); CanTreat (£5,000); and Blackburn College (£1,500).

Applications In writing to the correspondent. Trustees meet at least twice-yearly to allocate grants.

The Merchant Taylors' Company Charities Fund

Education, church, medicine, general

£104,000 (2004/05)
Beneficial area UK.

30 Threadneedle Street, London EC2R 8JB
Tel. 020 7450 4440
Email jbayford@merchant-taylors.co.uk
Website www.merchant-taylors.co.uk
Correspondent John Bayford, Deputy Clerk
Trustee The Master and Warden of the Merchant Taylor's Company.
CC Number 1069124

Information available Full accounts were available from the Charity Commission.

General Grants are considered for the arts, social care and community development, disability, older people, poverty, medical studies and research, chemical dependency, homelessness, children, and education, with priority for special needs.

In 2004/05 the trust had assets of £363,000 and an income of £161,000. Grants were made totalling £104,000 and were broken down as follows:

Educational awards
Grants totalling £20,000 included money for training awards, prizes, bursaries and other awards made via nine schools associated with Merchant Taylors' Company. The Schools included Merchant Taylors' Educational Trust, St John's School, Merchant Taylors' School Crosby – Boys, Merchant Taylors' School Crosby – Girls, Wolverhampton Grammar School, Foyle College –

Londonderry, Walingford School
Oxford, St Helen's School and Haymills.

Training awards

Grants were made to five organisations totalling £19,000. They went to Textile Conservation Centre (£10,000); Federation of Merchant Taylors for bursaries (£7,500); Guildhall School of Music (£6,000); and Royal School of Needlework – Merit Award and St Paul's Cathedral Choir School (£500 each).

Church and clergy

Grants to five organisations totalled £5,000. Beneficiaries were: St Helen's Church – Bishopgate (£2,000); St Paul's Cathedral of Friends and St Margaret's Church – Lee (£1,000 each); and St Michael's – Cornhill and St Paul's Church Swanley & St Peter's Huxtable (£500 each).

Miscellaneous

There were three grants made totalling £9,000. Beneficiaries were: St Mary Le Bow Young Homeless (£7,500); Voluntary Care Scheme (£2,500); and Brandram Road Community Centre Association (£300).

Livery and freemen fund

Grants were made to eleven organisations from this designated fund. Beneficiaries included Deafblind UK (£13,000); Blind in Business and Country Holidays for the Inner City Kids (£11,000 each); Epic Arts (£10,000); Teach First (£8,000 each); Dartford Methodist Mission (£7,500); Ready and St Margarets of Lee (£5,000); Thames Reach Bondway (£4,000); Cherry Garden School (£3,000); and St Mary Le Bow (£2,500).

Applications In writing to the correspondent.

The Merchants' House of Glasgow

General

£60,000 to organisations (2005)

Beneficial area Glasgow and the west of Scotland.

7 West George Street, Glasgow G2 1BA

Tel. 0141 221 8272 **Fax** 0141 226 2275

Email theoffice@merchantshouse.org.uk

Correspondent Roy Henderson, Assistant Collector

Trustee The Directors.

SC Number SC008900

Information available Accounts were provided by the trust.

General In 2005 the group celebrated its 400th anniversary. It's main activities included paying: 'pensions to pensioners, who may or may not have membership qualifications, and to provide assistance in the form of grants to charitable institutions within and around Glasgow'. It will normally consider applications from the following:

- organisations providing care and assistance to people with disabilities, older people, people who are terminally ill and people who have been socially deprived
- organisations providing for the care, advancement and rehabilitation of youth
- universities, colleges of further education and schools
- organisations connected with the arts, including music, theatre and the visual arts
- institutions that are connected with and represented by the Merchants' House.

In 2005 the group had assets of £6 million and an income of £742,000. Grants were made totalling £60,000, recipients included Erskine Hospital (£3,100), the National Youth Orchestra of Scotland – 4th of 4 (£1,500), Scottish Motor Neurone Disease (£1,250), and the Castle Howard Trust, Delta, the National Burns Memorial Homes, Quarriers Village and Shelter (£1,000 each).

Exclusions The trust will not, unless in exceptional circumstances, make grants to:

- individuals
- churches other than Glasgow Cathedral
- organisations that have received support in the two years preceding an application.

Applications In writing to the correspondent at any time, supported by copy of accounts and information about the organisation's principal activities.

Mercury Phoenix Trust

AIDS, HIV

£425,000 (2005/06)

Beneficial area Worldwide.

22 Cottage Offices, Latimer Park, Latimer, Chesham, Buckinghamshire HP5 1TU

Website www.mercuryphoenixtrust.com

Correspondent Peter Chant

Trustees M Austin; H J Beach; B H May; R M Taylor.

CC Number 1013768

Information available Accounts were on file at the Charity Commission.

General The trust was set up in memory of Freddie Mercury by the remaining members of the rock group, Queen, and their manager. It makes grants to 'help relieve the poverty, sickness and distress of people with AIDS and HIV and to stimulate awareness and education in connection with the disease throughout the world'.

'Since 1992 the Mercury Phoenix Trust have been responsible for donating more than £8 million in the fight against AIDS making over 600 grants to charities worldwide. Applications for grants have come in from many countries around the world and collaboration has been realised with groups as far removed as the World Health Organisation to grass-roots organisations run partly by voluntary workers in Uganda, Kenya, South Africa, Zambia, Nepal, India and South America. The trust is following the latest developments in drug therapies and adapting funding policy to the changing needs of those affected by HIV/AIDS, and currently concentrating its efforts on education and awareness in the Developing World.'

In 2005/06 the trust had assets of £1.4 million and an income of £362,000. Grants were made totalling £425,000.

Beneficiaries of the largest grants over £10,000 each included Care International – Ethiopia, Marie Stopes – Kenya and Oxfam – Thailand (£20,000 each), Concern Universal – Kenya, Echi Eteka – Nigeria and World Medical Fund – Malawi (£15,000 each) and I Cross – Kenya, International Care and Relief – Uganda and Teaching Aids at Low Cost – Angola (£10,000).

Applications In writing to the correspondent.

The Metropolitan Drinking Fountain and Cattle Trough Association

Provision of pure drinking water

£17,000 (2005)

Beneficial area UK, mainly London, and overseas.

Oaklands, 5 Queenborough Gardens, Chislehurst, Kent BR7 6NP

Tel. 020 8467 1261

Email ralph.baber@tesco.net

Website www.drinkingfountains.org

Correspondent R P Baber, Secretary

Trustees *J E Mills, Chair; R P Baber; Mrs S Fuller; J N King; Sir J Smith; M W Elliott; R E T Gurney; A King; M Bear; Mrs L Erith.*

CC Number 207743

Information available Accounts were on file at the Charity Commission.

General The objectives of the association are to promote the provision of drinking water for people and animals in the United Kingdom and overseas, and the preservation of the association's archive materials, artefacts, drinking fountains, cattle troughs and other installations.

Over the years the association has recognised a need for supplying fountains to schools throughout the United Kingdom. The association typically gifts a Novus drinking fountain to a school on the condition that the school pays £25 to join the association. Generally one fountain is donated per 100 children. The school is responsible for the installation and the maintenance of the fountain.

In 2005 the trust had assets of £725,000 and an income of £36,400. Grants totalling £17,000 were made to 33 organisations, including, Appropriate Technology Asia, Children of Fiji, Karen Hill Tribe Trust (£2,000 each), and The Friends of Hope (£1,500). 28 schools each received grants of not more than £1,000 each.

As of 2005, the total number of fountains and troughs supplied for use both in the UK and overseas was: 4,450

drinking fountains; 927 cattle troughs; 3,721 dog troughs; and 74 water wells/ storage tanks.

Applications In writing to the correspondent. In addition, in considering an application for a grant trustees also require the following information:

- a copy of the most recent audited accounts
- how has the cost of the project been ascertained, e.g. qualified surveyor?
- how many people/animals is it estimated would use the fountain/ trough in a day?
- will the charity supervise the project, if not who would?
- where is it anticipated the remainder of the funds to complete the project will come from?

Mickleham Charitable Trust

Relief in need

£81,000 (2004/05)

Beneficial area UK, with a preference for Norfolk.

c/o Hansells, 13–14 The Close, Norwich NR1 4DS

Correspondent The Trustees

Trustees *P R Norton; S F Nunney; Mrs J A Richardson.*

CC Number 1048337

Information available Accounts were on file at the Charity Commission.

General This trust was set up in 1995. Its main objectives are relief in need, particularly relating to young people and people who are blind.

In 2004/05 the trust had an income of £973,000, including £899,000 from an ex-trustee's legacy. Assets stood at £2.8 million at the end of the year.

Grants to 37 organisations totalled £81,000 (23 had been supported in the previous year). Beneficiaries included How Hill Trust (£19,000), Deafblind (£6,000) Orbis International (£5,000), Harvest Trust (£4,000), Musical Keys (£3,000), Age Concern, Barnardos, Leeway, National Library for the Blind and Nancy Oldfield Trust (£2,000 each), Whitlingham Charitable Trust (£1,500) and Action for Blind People, Alzheimer's Research Trust, British Wireless for the Blind, East Anglian Children's Hospice, Families House, Multiple Sclerosis

Society, Norwich Door to Door, RNIB, SENSE and Schizophrenia Association of Great Britain (£1,000 each).

Applications In writing to the correspondent.

Gerald Micklem Charitable Trust

General, health

£98,000 (2005)

Beneficial area UK.

Bolinge Hill Farm, Buriton, Petersfield, Hampshire GU31 4NN

Fax 01730 268515

Email ghmicklem.charitabletrust@ btinternet.com

Website www.peter.shone.btinternet.co. uk

Correspondent Mrs S J Shone, Trustee

Trustees *Susan J Shone; Joanna L Scott-Dalgleish; Helen Ratcliffe.*

CC Number 802583

Information available Information was provided by the trust.

General The trust was established in November 1989 with a bequest left in the will of Gerald Micklem. The trust states that it supports 'a wide range of activities' although most grants appear to be to health and welfare charities. Grants can be recurring or one-off and for revenue or capital purposes. Donations are generally for between £2,000 and £3,000.

In 2005 the trust had assets of £654,000 and an income of £215,000 though £80,000 of this sum was from Gift Aid payments and an exceptional; donation of £93,000. Grants totalling £98,000 were broken down as follows:

Carers/Older people – one grant of £3,000

Children/Young people – four grants totalling £11,000

Churches – one grant of £4,000

Disabled – four grants totalling £10,000

Drugs/Alcohol abuse/Counselling – one grant of £2,000

Environment/Wildlife – two grants totalling £4,000

General community – five grants totalling £11,000

Hospices – three grants totalling ££8,000

Medical conditions/Research/Hospitals – nine grants totalling £25,000

Mental disability – three grants totalling ££7,000

Museums/Galleries/Heritage – two grants totalling £4,000
Overseas aid/International – four grants totalling £7,000.

Major beneficiaries included: The Faith and Heritage Appeal – Ribchester, and The Society for Mucopolysaccharide Diseases (£4,000 each); Cecily's Fund and The Who Cares? Trust (£3,000 each); and Carousel and The New Jumbulance Travel Trust (£2,000 each).

Exclusions No grants to, or sponsorship arrangements with, individuals or to organisations that are not UK-registered charities.

Applications In writing to the correspondent. Interested applicants should note that the organisations which have received grants in the past should not be taken as indicative of a geographical or other bias.

The trustees meet informally a few times each year, but the dates are not fixed. They usually meet once only to decide on grants in January or February. Applications can be sent at any time, but preferably not later than the preceding November.

The M Miller Charitable Trust

Jewish, general
Possibly around £42,000 a year
Beneficial area UK.

41 Harrogate Road, Chapel Allerton, Leeds, West Yorkshire LS7 3PD
Tel. 0113 228 4000
Correspondent Richard Ellis, Trustee
Trustees *Matthew Miller; Renee B Miller; Richard Ellis.*
CC Number 1014957
Information available Recent accounts have not been filed at the Charity Commission.

General The M Miller Charitable Trust was set up by Matthew and Renee Miller and Richard Ellis in 1992 with general charitable objects. Unfortunately no financial information has been provided in recent years. However, from information held at the Charity Commission we can confirm the contact details to be correct.

In 1998/99 it had an income of £43,000 and made grants totalling £42,000. The

trust had no assets. Grants are directed predominantly at Jewish causes.

Applications In writing to the correspondent.

The Miller Foundation

General
About £150,000
Beneficial area UK, with a preference for Scotland, especially the west of Scotland.

Maclay Murray and Spens, 151 St Vincent Street, Glasgow G2 5NJ
Tel. 0141 248 5011 **Fax** 0141 248 5819
Email jean.galloway@mms.co.uk
Correspondent Andrew S Biggart, Secretary
Trustees *C Fleming-Brown; G R G Graham; J Simpson; G F R Fleming-Brown.*
SC Number SC008798
Information available Basic information provided online at OSCR.

General The foundation supports a wide range of charitable activities, primarily in Scotland, but also in other parts of the UK. Grants previously ranged from £500 to £2,000, with the majority of them recurrent.

In 2006/07 the foundation had a gross income of £182,000. No other financial information was available, although previous research indicates that grants are made totalling around £150,000 each year.

Exclusions No grants to individuals.

Applications On a form available from the secretary, although the trust has previously stated that its funds were fully committed. Trustees meet once a year to consider grants in October. Applications should be received by the end of September.

The Millfield House Foundation

Social disadvantage, social policy
£152,000 (2005/06)
Beneficial area North east England particularly Tyne and Wear.

19 The Crescent, Benton Lodge, Newcastle-upon-Tyne NE7 7ST
Tel. 0191 266 9429 **Fax** 0191 266 9429
Email finley@lineone.net
Website www.mhfdn.org.uk
Correspondent Terence Finley, Administrator
Trustees *Rosemary Chubb; George Hepburn; Grigor McClelland; Jenifer McClelland; Stephen McClelland; Sheila Spencer; Jane Streather.*
CC Number 271180
Information available Full accounts were available from the Charity Commission.

General This foundation aims to 'tackle poverty, disadvantage and exclusion, and to promote social change in Tyne and Wear. It funds selected initiatives and research that inform debate and influence public policy and attitudes, with the intention of improving social provision and empowering communities.'

Projects supported may, for example:

- give a voice to excluded groups
- bring first-hand experience of poverty to opinion formers and policy makers
- promote social-policy debate in the region
- campaign on local social issues.

The financial resources available to the foundation are a tiny fraction of the total available for charitable activity in Tyne and Wear. The trustees therefore wish to concentrate their resources on objects that most other funding bodies cannot or will not support.

As a charity, the foundation must confine its grants to purposes accepted in law as charitable. However, official guidance makes it clear that charities may include a variety of political and campaigning activities to further their purposes.

The foundation wishes to promote equal opportunities through its grantmaking. It will do its best to ensure that applications are dealt with fairly and that nobody is denied access to information or funding on grounds of race, colour, ethnicity or national origin, religious affiliation, gender, sexual orientation, age or disability. If appropriate, the foundation will offer help with the completion of an application.

The foundation welcomes applications from stand-alone projects, from organisations which sponsor or manage projects, or from two or more projects applying jointly.

In certain cases, and strictly subject to compliance with Section 6 of the Charity Commission's guidance on Political Activities and Campaigning (CC9), the foundation may be willing to support proposals that involve non-violent direct action.

The trustees may consider an additional element of grant to allow for support from a consultant to assist with campaigning, lobbying, media and public relations.

The trustees are willing to take some risks in funding projects which strongly reflect the stated priorities. The administrator is available to discuss and give guidance on the submission of innovative proposals.

The guidance notes go on to state that the foundation: 'aims to provide, alone or in partnership with other funders, significant and medium-term support to a small number of carefully selected projects or organisations.

The foundation is unlikely to have more than about 6 to 12 grants in payment at the same time and can therefore approve only a small number of new grants in any one year. One-off grants may be between £5,000 and £50,000. Grants for more than one year could be between £20,000 and £30,000 a year for two or three years'

In 2005/06 the foundation had assets of £6.2 million and an income of £168,000. Grants were made to seven organisations totalling £152,000. Beneficiaries were: Institute for Public Policy Research (£60,000); Black and Ethnic Minority Community Organisations Network (£40,000); Prison Reform Trust – Smart Justice (£31,000); North East Women's Forum (£10,000); Institute for Public Policy Research – environmental conference (£7,000); and North of the Tyne Patients' Voice and Northumbria University – Sustainable Cities Research Institute (£2,000 each).

'The Foundation's grants increasingly reflect the trustees' preference for making fewer and larger grants.'

Exclusions The foundation 'will not fund straightforward service provision, nor mainline university research, nor the wide range of other projects that are eligible for support elsewhere'.

Applications Initial outline proposals should be made in writing to the correspondent. If the application meets the stated guidelines the administrator may request further information or arrange a meeting. Applications unconnected with Tyne and Wear are not acknowledged.

The trustees meet twice a year, in May and November so completed applications should arrive by the end of March or end of September. The administrator is willing to provide guidance for the preparation of final applications, but not without first receiving an outline proposal.

Applications should include:

- contact details, including an email address if possible
- a detailed description of the project, its aims and intended outcomes
- a budget for the project, giving a breakdown of the total expenditure and of any other sources of expected income
- a copy of the most recent annual report and audited accounts for the project and/or the sponsoring body
- the constitution of the responsible body
- details of the organisation's equal opportunities policy and procedures
- if appropriate, plans for the dissemination of the results of the project
- details of arrangements for monitoring and evaluation
- a job description if funding is sought for a salaried post
- the names of two independent referees (these may not be taken up in every case).

For further information potential applicants are strongly advised to visit the trust's website.

The Millfield Trust

Christian

£73,000 (2005/06)
Beneficial area UK and worldwide.

Millfield House, Bell Lane, Liddington, Swindon, Wiltshire SN4 0HE

Tel. 01793 790181 **Fax** 01793 710437

Correspondent D Bunce, Trustee

Trustees D Bunce; P W Bunce; S D Bunce; A C Bunce; R W Bunce.

CC Number 262406

Information available Accounts were on file at the Charity Commission.

General The trust was set up to provide grants to Christian organisations, and has supported a number of missionary societies for the last 50 years. Grants are given solely to organisations known to the trust and new applications are not considered.

In 2005/06 the trust had assets of £135,000 and an income of £68,000, including £46,000 in Gift Aid donations from two of its trustees and a further £5,000 from Bunce (Ashbury) Ltd. Grants to organisations totalled £73,000. A further £3,800 was given in grants to individual missionaries, evangelists and older people.

Major beneficiaries included: Gideon's International (£14,500); Gospel Mission of South America (£6,500); Tear Fund (£5,000); Mark Gillingham Charitable Trust (£4,000); Ashbury Evangelical Free Church (£3,500); and Overseas Council for Theological Education and Mission (£2,500).

A further 61 organisations received grants of up to £1,000 each, including: Swindon Youth for Christ (£1,000); Gospel Printing Mission (£800); Barnabus Fund (£700); Liverpool School of Tropical Medicine (£500); Anglo Peruvian Childcare Mission (£350); and Soap Box (£100).

Applications No replies to unsolicited applications.

The Millhouses Charitable Trust

Christian, overseas aid, general

£32,000 (2004/05)
Beneficial area UK and overseas.

c/o MacFarlane and Co., Cunard Building, Water Street, Liverpool L3 1DS

Correspondent The Trustees

Trustees Revd J S Harcus; Dr A W Harcus; J L S Alexander; P A Thornton; F J van Nieuwkerk.

CC Number 327773

Information available Accounts were on file at the Charity Commission.

General In 2004/05 the trust had assets of £511,000 and an income of £45,000. Grants to 20 organisations totalled £32,000.

Beneficiaries included NSPCC and UNICEF UK (£5,000 each), Amnesty International UK Section, Medical Foundation for the Victims of Torture and Save the Children (£2,500 each), Christian Aid and Oxfam (£2,000 each), Barabas Fund, Crisis, Operation Mobilisation, Release International, Send a Cow, Shelter and Tear Fund (£1,000 each), Children in Crisis (£750), Rehab UK (£500) and the Camphill Village Trust and the Leprosy Mission (£250 each).

Exclusions Grants are made to registered charities only; no grants to individuals.

Applications In writing to the correspondent, but note that most of the grants given by this trust are recurrent. If new grants are made, they are usually to organisations known to the trustees.

The Millichope Foundation

General

£326,000 (2005/06)

Beneficial area UK, especially the West Midlands and Shropshire.

Millichope Park, Munslow, Craven Arms, Shropshire SY7 9HA

Tel. 01584 841234

Correspondent Mrs S A Bury, Trustee

Trustees *L C N Bury; Mrs S A Bury; Mrs B Marshall.*

CC Number 282357

Information available Accounts were on file at the Charity Commission.

General The foundation makes donations to a wide range of different organisations including:

- UK charities
- local charities serving Birmingham and Shropshire
- arts and culture
- conservation/heritage
- education.

In 2005/06 the foundation had assets of £7.4 million and an income of £419,000. Grants were made to organisations totalling £326,000.

The two largest grants given during the year were in support of the Foundation of Ludlow College and Moor Park RC School – Ludlow (£25,000 each).

The next largest grants were £20,000 to Oxfam and £10,000 each to Hope and Homes for Children, Lady Forester Trust and St Catherine's – Tugford.

Smaller grants included: £3,500 to the Royal Opera House Trust; £2,000 to Wildscreen Trust; £1,000 to Midland Spinal Injuries; £500 to Beambridge Clubroom; £200 to National Gardens Scheme; and, £100 to Craven Arms Methodist Church.

Exclusions No grants to individuals or non-registered charities.

Applications In writing to the correspondent.

The Millward Charitable Trust

Christian, general

£96,500 (2005/06)

Beneficial area UK and overseas.

Burgis and Bullock, 2 Chapel Court, Holly Walk, Leamington Spa, Warwickshire CV32 4YS

Tel. 01926 451000

Correspondent John Hulse, Trustee

Trustees *Maurice Millward; Sheila Millward; John Hulse.*

CC Number 328564

Information available Accounts were on file at the Charity Commission.

General The trust has general charitable purposes and during the year supported a variety of causes including Christian, social welfare, performing arts, medical research and animal welfare.

In 2005/06 the trust had assets of £2.2 million and an income of £69,500. Grants were made totalling £96,500 which were broken down as follows:

- social welfare – 19 grants totalling £38,000
- performing arts – 11 grants totalling £55,000
- medical research – one grant of £250
- animal welfare – two grants totalling £2,000.

A further two social welfare grants were made to individuals totalling £1,200

Institutional grants greater than £1,000 each included: Birds Eye View (£24,000 in two grants); Music in the Round (£11,350 in two grants); CORD Sudan Appeal and City of Birmingham Symphony Orchestra (£10,000 each); St Paul's Church (£8,000 in two grants); and Warwick Arts Society (£6,700 in two grants).

Applications In writing to the correspondent.

The Edgar Milward Charity

Christian, humanitarian

£62,000 (2005/06)

Beneficial area UK and overseas.

16 Cufelle Close, Chineham, Basingstoke, Hampshire RG24 8RH

Correspondent Mrs J C Austin, Trustee

Trustees *J S Milward, Chair; T Pittom; Mrs M V Roberts; G M Fogwill; Mrs J C Austin; Mrs E M Smuts; S M W Fogwill.*

CC Number 281018

Information available Accounts were on file at the Charity Commission.

General The objective of the charity is to distribute all of its income as it arises as follows:

- one-half for the furtherance of the Christian religion within the UK and throughout the world
- two-fifths for general charitable purposes
- one-tenth for educational purposes within a 15-mile radius of the Civic Centre in Reading.

Within this, the trust's grant-making policy is to support a limited number of causes known to the trustees, particularly those supported by the settlor.

In 2005/06 the charity had assets of £1.2 million and an income of £63,000. Grants were made totalling £62,000 and were distributed as follows:

Christian religion – 43 grants totalling £32,250, including those to: Redcliffe College (£2,000); Ripon College (£1,700); and, Interserve (£1,500). Grants of under £1,000 each were made to 29 other institutions and totalled £15,000.

General charitable purposes – 53 grants totalling £27,000, including those to: Tear Fund (£2,000); A Rocha Trust (£1,500); and, N:Quire (£1,000). Grants of under £1,000 each were made to 47 other institutions and totalled £18,000.

Educational purposes – three grants of £1,000 each were made to: Arab Vision, Churches Together with Schools, and E P Collier College.

Exclusions No new applications will be supported.

Applications Unsolicited applications cannot be considered.

The Peter Minet Trust

General

£116,000 (2004/05)

Beneficial area Mainly south east London boroughs, particularly Lambeth and Southwark.

1a Taylors Yard, 67 Alderbrook Road, London SW12 8AD

Tel. 020 8772 3155

Email info@peterminet.org.uk

Website www.peterminet.org.uk

Correspondent Angela Hurst, Administrator

Trustees *J C B South, Chair; N McGregor-Wood; Mrs R L C Rowan; Ms P C Jones; R Luff; Revd Bruce Stokes; Mrs L Cleverly.*

CC Number 259963

Information available Accounts were on file at the Charity Commission.

General In the mid-sixties, the Minet family sold much of their property to local councils. Part of the proceeds were used by Peter Brissault Minet to set up the trust in 1969.

The trust gives priority to registered charities working with people in the boroughs of Lambeth and Southwark, particularly those working in the areas of social welfare, health and the community, with people who are young, sick, disabled, disadvantaged or elderly.

In 2004/05 the trust had assets of £4.2 million, an income of £167,000 and made grants totalling £116,000. Grants were distributed in the following categories:

Children and youth – £49,000 in 48 grants
For playschemes, holidays, youth clubs, adoption agencies and sports programmes.

Health and disability – £24,000 in 18 grants
For counselling projects, holidays for people with disabilities, medical education and information and access projects.

Community projects – £367,000 in 33 grants
For projects providing information, advice and support to various groups including ex-offenders, homeless people, single parents and unemployed people.

General and cultural – £7,500 in 2 grants
The accounts listed 53 grants made of £1,000 or more. Beneficiaries included: DEC Tsunami Earthquake (£5,000); Angell Eco Self Build (£3,000); Dulwich Helpline, Futures Theatre Company, Happy Faces Community Nursery, Streets Alive Theatre Company and Studland Village Appeal for Pitwal (£2,500 each); Downside Fisher Youth Club, Inside Out Trust, Lambeth Play Association, Listening Books, Southwark Day Centre for Asylum Seekers (£2,000 each); Age Concern Theatre Trust and Women's Link (£1,500 each); and the Drake Music Project (£1,000).

Exclusions Grants to registered charities only. No grants are made to individuals. The trust will not give to: local appeals, other than those within or directly affecting the trust's immediate locality; repetitive nationwide appeals by large charities for large sums of money; appeals where all, or most of the beneficiaries live outside the UK; appeals whose sole purpose is to make grants from collected funds; endowment or deficit funding; or medical or other research.

Applications For further information or to discuss your project, please contact the administrator at the address below on Tuesday or Wednesday between 10am and 4pm. A form is available with a leaflet giving guidelines for applicants, either by post or from the trust's website as a Microsoft Word file. The form should be submitted including audited accounts, details of the project (no more than two sides of A4), a budget breakdown, money raised so far, and a list of other bodies to whom you have applied for funding. Meetings are usually held in February, June and October. Unsuccessful applicants will not be acknowledged unless an sae is enclosed.

Minge's Gift and the Pooled Trusts

Medical, education, disadvantage, disability

£64,250 to organisations (2004/05)

Beneficial area UK.

The Worshipful Company of Cordwainers, Dunster Court, Mincing Lane, London EC3R 7AH

Tel. 020 7929 1121 **Fax** 020 7929 1124

Email office@cordwain.co.org

Website www.cordwainers.org

Correspondent Lt Col. J R Blundell, Clerk

Trustee *The Master and Wardens of the Worshipful Company of Cordwainers.*

CC Number 266073

Information available Accounts were on file at the Charity Commission.

General Minge's Gift – The trust was established for general charitable purposes as directed by the Master and Wardens of the Worshipful Company of Cordwainers. The income of Minge's Gift is generally allocated for the support of educational and medical establishments with which the company has developed long term relationships, ex-service organisations and towards assistance for disabled and/or disadvantaged youth.

In 2004/05 the trust had assets of £745,000 and an income of £81,000. Grants were made to organisations totalling £64,250, broken down as follows:

Standard grants – 25 totalling £48,750, the largest of which were: £15,000 to Cordwainers Educational Trust, £6,500 to London College of Fashion (for scholarships and prizes); £5,000 to University College of Northampton; £2,500 to Royal London Society for the Blind; and, £2,000 each to RFH Nurses Midwifery Education Development Fund and St Dunstan-in-the-West Church.

Master's gifts – six totalling £1,200, including those to: Hedley Foundation, St John Ambulance and City of London Fusiliers (£200 each).

Special grants – three totalling £15,000 as follows: £10,000 to Cordwainers Educational & Training Trust; £4,500 to University College Northampton; and £1,000 to Friends of Galle.

In addition to the above, £4,925 was spent on the upkeep of company almshouses and £580 on 'trophies and engraving'.

Pooled Trusts – Also included in the accounts for Minge's Gift, were details of the giving of the Common Investment Fund (Pooled Trusts). This combines a number of small trusts which are administered by the Worshipful Company of Cordwainers for the benefit of scholars, the blind, deaf, clergy widows, spinsters of the Church of England, ex-servicemen and their widows and those who served in the merchant services. It also provides for the upkeep of the Company's five almshouses in Shorne, Kent.

In 2004/05 the trusts had assets of £1.2 million and an income of £31,000. Pensions to individuals totalled £9,400, whilst a total of £3,000 went to three organisations. Grants were for £1,000 each and went to King George's Fund for Sailors, Royal Free Hospital School of Medicine Scholarship and SSAFA.

Exclusions Grants to individuals are only given through the Pooled Trusts. Generally, only UK-based charitable organisations are supported.

Applications In writing to the correspondent.

The Minos Trust

Christian, general

£50,000 (2002/03)

Beneficial area UK and overseas.

Kleinwort Benson Trustees Ltd, PO Box 57005, 30 Gresham Street, London EC2V 7PG

Tel. 020 8207 7336 **Fax** 020 8207 7665

Correspondent The Trustees

CC Number 265012

Information available Accounts were on file at the Charity Commission

General Previously we were advised that the trust gives most of its support to Christian charities in grants ranging up to £15,000. Remaining funds are given to other causes, with a preference for animals and wildlife, although these grants tend to be less than £1,000. Many of the organisations receiving the larger grants are regularly supported by the trust.

In 2004/05 the trust had an income of £13,000 and a total expenditure of £36,000. This is in line with previous years when its expenditure has regularly

exceeded its income. Further information was not available.

In 2002/03 the trust had assets of £277,000 and an income of £23,000. The total amount given as grants was £50,000.

The largest grants were £3,000 each to Care Trust and Tigers Club Project. Other large grants included those to Care Trust (£2,500), Tearfund (£2,000) and Ashburnham Christian Trust (£1,500), with £1,000 each to Bible Society, Friends of the Elderly and Youth with a Mission.

80% of the grants were under £1,000 and were given to Christian organisations in the UK and overseas including: Africa Christian Press (£400), Aid to Russian Christians (£300) and Gideons International (£100). Other grants included those to Worldwide Fund for Nature (£450) and Sussex Farming Wildlife Advisory Group and RSPB (£50 each).

Applications In writing to the correspondent, for consideration on an ongoing basis.

The Laurence Misener Charitable Trust

Jewish, general

£102,000 (2005/06)

Beneficial area UK.

Messrs Bourner Bullock, Sovereign House, 212–224 Shaftesbury Avenue, London WC2H 8HQ

Tel. 020 7240 5821

Correspondent David Lyons

Trustees J E Cama; Capt. G F Swaine

CC Number 283460

Information available Accounts were on file at the Charity Commission.

General In 2005/06 the trust had assets of £3 million and an income of £145,000. Grants were made totalling £102,000.

The largest grants were £10,000 to Richard Dimbleby Cancer Fund, £7,500 each to Jewish Care, Jewish Association for Physically Handicapped and Home for Aged Jews – Nightingale House, and £6,000 to Robert Owen Foundation.

Other grants include £4,500 to Imperial Cancer Research Fund; £3,500 to Great Ormond Street Children's Hospital

Fund; £3,000 to Age Concern; £2,500 to Imperial War Museum Trust; £2,000 to Royal Marsden Hospital; and £1,350 to RNLI – Salcombe Lifeboat.

Applications In writing to the correspondent.

The Mishcon Family Charitable Trust

Jewish, social welfare

£55,000 (2003/04)

Beneficial area UK.

Summit House, 12 Red Lion Square, London WC1R 4QD

Correspondent The Trustees

Trustees Lord Mishcon; P A Cohen; P Mishcon; R Mishcon; J Landau.

CC Number 213165

Information available Full accounts were on file at the Charity Commission.

General The trust supports mainly Jewish charities, but also gives grants to general social welfare and medical/disability causes, especially children's charities.

In 2003/04 the trust had assets of £1.7 million, which generated an income of £78,000. Grants were made to over 100 organisations totalling £55,000.

The largest grant went to UJIA (£17,000). There were seven further grants of £1,000 or more made to United Synagogue (£4,400), North Western Reform Synagogue (£2,700), Youth Aliyah Child Rescue (£1,500), Chai Cancer Care (£1,200) and Alone in London, Amnesty International UK Section Charitable Trust and UK Friends of Awis (£1,000 each).

Remaining grants were in the range of £2.50 and £850. Beneficiaries included the Art Room (£800), Friends of Alyn (£590), Institute for Jewish Policy Research (£500), British Friends of Neve Shalom and Electronic Aids for the Blind (£250 each), Cancer Bacup, Children in Crisis, Dreams Come True Charity, Friends of the Hebrew University of Jerusalem, Jewish Marriage Council, National Jewish Chaplaincy, NSPCC, Pearsons Holiday Fund, the Willow Trust and Young Minds (£100 each), the David Adams Leukaemia Appeal Fund (£90), Avondale Extra, Great Ormond Street Hospital for Children and Marie

Curie Cancer Care (£50) and Maccabeans (£2.50).

'Donations for the relief of poverty', presumably made to individuals, totalled £11,000.

Applications In writing to the correspondent.

The Misselbrook Trust

General

£34,000 to organisations (2006).

Beneficial area UK with a preference for the Wessex area.

Ashton House, 12 The Precinct, Winchester Road, Chandlers Ford, Eastleigh, Hampshire, SO53 2GB

Tel. 023 8027 4555

Correspondent M Howson-Green, Trustee

Trustees *Miss M J Misselbrook; M Howson-Green; B M Baxendale.*

CC Number 327928

Information available Full accounts were available from the Charity Commission.

General In 2006 the trust had assets of £561,000 and an income of £35,000. Grants were made totalling £34,000.

Grants of more than £500 went to D E C Tsunami Earthquake Appeal (£5,000), Enham Trust and the Marwell Preservation Trust (£3,000 each), Haemophilia Society, Rose Road Association, Southampton Rotary Club Trust Fund and Southampton Action to Combat Hardship (£1,000 each), and St Michael & All Angels Church (£600).

Other grants of £500 or less were made to 62 institutions.

Applications In writing to the correspondent.

The Mitchell Charitable Trust

Jewish, general

£168,000 (2003/04)

Beneficial area UK, with a preference for London and overseas.

28 Heath Drive, London NW3 7SB

Tel. 020 7794 5668 **Fax** 020 7794 5680

Correspondent Ashley Mitchell, Trustee

Trustees *Ashley Mitchell; Elizabeth Mitchell; Antonia Mitchell.*

CC Number 290273

Information available Full accounts were on file at the Charity Commission.

General The trust was established in 1984. It has general charitable purposes but in practice appears to have a strong preference for welfare charities, Jewish organisations and health charities.

In 2005/06 the trust had assets of £1.25 million and an income of £376,000. Grants were made totalling £168,000 and were broken down as follows:
Community and welfare – three grants totalling £79,500
Education – four grants totalling £8,500
Ethnic organisations – three grants totalling £1,700
Medical and disability – 10 grants totalling £32,500
Overseas – one grant of £46,000
General – two grants totalling £350.

Major beneficiaries included: Jewish Care (£76,000 in two grants); World Jewish Relief (£46,000 in three grants); Macmillan Cancer Relief and Marie Curie Cancer Care (£10,000 each); and London School of Economics and The National Organisation for Foetal Alcohol Syndrome (£6,000 each in two grants).

Exclusions No grants to individuals or for research, education, overseas appeals or non-Jewish religious appeals. Applicants from small charities outside London are unlikely to be considered.

Applications In writing to the correspondent. Applications must include financial information. The trust does not reply to any applications unless they choose to support them. Trustees do not meet on a regular basis, thus applicants may not be advised of a grant for a considerable period.

Keren Mitzvah Trust

General

£354,000 (2004)

Beneficial area UK.

c/o 1 Knightsbridge, London SW1X 7LX

Correspondent The Trustees

Trustees *C J Smith; Manny Weiss; Moishe Weiss.*

CC Number 1041948

Information available Accounts were on file at the Charity Commission.

General In 2004 the trust had an income of £1.3 million from donations. Grants totalled £354,000. The sum of £968,000 was carried forward to the next year.

Grants of £5,000 or more were made to 14 organisations and were listed in the accounts. Beneficiaries included CML (£47,000), Society of Friends of the Torah (£40,000), Side by Side (£18,000), Achisomoch (£37,000), Project Seed (£15,000), Beis Hamedrash Beis Yisroel (£14,000), Friends of Toras Haim Torah, Jewish Care and Chesed Limited (£10,000 each), Beskiv World Centre (£6,600), Friends of the Jewish Secondary Schools Movement (£6,000), Lezion (£5,300) and Chevras and Nach Alas Shai (£5,000 each).

Unlisted smaller grants totalled £118,000.

Applications The trust stated that the trustees support their own personal choice of charities.

The Mizpah Trust

General

£23,500 (2005/06)

Beneficial area UK and overseas.

Foresters House, Humbly Grove, South Warnborough, Hook, Hampshire RG29 1RY

Correspondent A C O Bell, Trustee

Trustees *A C O Bell; Mrs J E Bell.*

CC Number 287231

Information available Full accounts were on file at the Charity Commission.

General The trust is proactive and makes grants to a wide range of organisations in the UK and, to a lesser extent, overseas.

In 2005/06 the trust had assets of £245,000 and an income of £222,000. Grants were made to nine organisations totalling £23,500. A further £4,200 was given to individuals.

Major beneficiaries were: Warham Trust, World Vision and CARE (£5,000 each). Smaller grants of £1,000 each went to:

Cloud Trust; Lambeth Partnership; Oasis Trust; and, Action for ME.

Applications The trust has stated that 'no applications will be considered'.

The Modiano Charitable Trust

Arts, Jewish, general

£55,000 (2005/06)

Beneficial area UK and overseas.

Broad Street House, 55 Old Broad Street, London EC2M 1RX

Tel. 020 7012 0000

Correspondent G Modiano, Trustee

Trustees *G Modiano; Mrs B Modiano; L S Modiano.*

CC Number 328372

Information available Accounts are on file at the Charity Commission.

General In 2005/06 the trust had an income of £101,000 and made grants totalling £55,000. Although in previous years around 30–40% of the trusts income has been given in grants to Jewish organisations, this year saw support mainly going to arts organisations. However, its core charities were not neglected, whilst a number of new recipients were added.

The largest grants were: £22,000 to Philharmonia Orchestra; £7,500 to Weiznam Institute Foundation; £5,445 to Royal College of Music; and £5,000 to World Jewish Relief. Smaller grants went to: The Samaritans (£600); Contact the Elderly (£500); Friends of Christ Church – Spitalfields (£250); The Landmark Trust (£200); The Keyboard Charitable Trust (£100); and St John's Eye Hospital (£50).

Applications In writing to the correspondent.

The Moette Charitable Trust

Education, Jewish

About £85,000 (2005/06)

Beneficial area U K and overseas.

1 Holden Road, Salford M7 4NL

Tel. 0161 832 8721

Correspondent Simon Lopian, Trustee

Trustees *Simon Lopian; Pearl Lopian; David Haffner.*

CC Number 1068886

Information available Accounts were on file at the Charity Commission.

General 'The principal activity of the trust is the provision of support of the poor and needy for educational purposes.'

In 2005/06 the trust had an income of £18,500 (2004/05: £100,000) and an expenditure of £96,000.

In 2002/03 the trust's assets comprised cash at the bank totalling £158,000. Its income was £27,000, mostly from donations received. Grants totalled £38,000.

Larger grants to beneficiaries were £15,000 to Finchley Road Synagogue, £2,500 each to King David Schools (Manchester) and Manchester Charitable Trust, £2,000 to The Purim Fund and £1,000 each to Yad Voezer and Yeshivas Lev Aryeh.

Smaller grants included £500 each to Hakalo and London School of Jewish Studies, £400 to Manchester Jewish Federation and £50 to Manchester Seminary for Girls.

Applications In writing to the correspondent.

The Mole Charitable Trust

Jewish, general

£252,000 (2005/06)

Beneficial area UK, with a preference for Manchester.

2 Okeover Road, Salford M7 4JX

Correspondent Martin Gross, Trustee

Trustees *M Gross; Mrs L P Gross.*

CC Number 281452

Information available Accounts were on file at the Charity Commission.

General The objectives of the charity are to make donations and loans to educational institutions and charitable organisations, and for the relief of poverty.

In 2005/06 the trust had assets of £2.1 million and an income of £147,000. Grants totalled £252,000 which was broken down as follows:

- education (£85,850)
- religious institutions and charitable organisations (£155,000)

- relief of poverty (£11,000).

The largest grant beneficiaries included: Three Pillars Charity (£60,000); Manchester Jewish Grammar School (£26,000); and Chasdei Yoel Charitable Trust and United Talmudical Associates Limited (£20,000 each).

Other beneficiaries included: Binoh of Manchester (£6,000); Beis Ruchel Girls School (£3,000); Manchester Jewish Federation (£2,500); and Our Kids (£1,000).

Applications The trust has stated that it does not wish to receive any new applications.

The D C Moncrieff Charitable Trust

Social welfare, environment

£43,500 (2005/06)

Beneficial area UK and worldwide, with a preference for Norfolk and Suffolk.

8 Quinnell Way, Lowestoft, Suffolk NR32 4WL

Tel. 01502 564613

Correspondent Mr Friston, Secretary

Trustees *D J Coleman; R E James; M F Dunne.*

CC Number 203919

Information available Accounts were on file at the Charity Commission.

General The trust was established in 1961. It supports a number of large UK organisations but tends to concentrate on charities local to the Norfolk and Suffolk areas.

In 2005/06 the trust had assets of £1.6 million and an income of £40,000. Grants were made to 53 organisations totalling £43,500.

Beneficiaries included: East Anglia's Children's Hospices (£2,000); Friends of the Norwich Museums (£1,500); Norfolk Autistic Society (£1,000); The Suffolk Punch Trust (£800); The Magdalene Group – Norwich (£600); and REACT (£500).

Exclusions No grants for individuals.

Applications In writing to the correspondent. The trust has previously stated that demand for funds exceeded available resources, therefore no further requests are currently invited.

Montague Thompson Coon Charitable Trust

Children with disabilities

£51,000 (2005/06)

Beneficial area UK.

Bay Tree House, 8 Oak Lawn, Newton Abbot, Devon TQ12 1QP

Correspondent John Lister, Trustee

Trustees *P A Clarke, Chair; J P Lister; Mrs A Purser.*

CC Number 294096

Information available Accounts were on file at the Charity Commission.

General This trust was registered with the Charity Commission in 1986. Grants are made to projects involving children with disabilities, particularly those providing opportunities for recreation and access to the countryside.

In 2005/06 the organisation had assets of £1.2 million and an income of £48,000. There were 16 grants made in the year totalling £51,000.

Beneficiaries included: The Wildfowl and Wetlands Trust, to support the creation of a new visitor entrance at the Welney reserve (£8,000); Muscular Dystrophy Group, to support research into muscular dystrophy (£7,500); Holton Lee, to provide a replacement 'Mule' for the reserve (£5,500); Scope, to fund the purchase of new laptop computers and wireless printers (£5,500); The Wildfowl and Wetlands Trust, to part-fund new facilities at the Barnes reserve (£5,000); the Pace Centre, to provide equipment for new nursery classroom (£4,100); the Sayers Croft Environmental Educational Trust, to provide access for disabled visitors (£1,750); 3H Fund, to assist with holidays for people who are disabled (£2,000); Soundabout, to provide musical instruments for therapy of children who are disabled (£1,500); London Youth Clubs, to provide a shelter for canoes used by visiting children with disabilities (£1,500); and Caring and Sharing Trust, to assist with facilities for disabled children (£1,000).

Exclusions No grants to individuals.

Applications In writing to the correspondent.

The Colin Montgomerie Charitable Foundation

General

Around £50,000 to organisations (2005)

Beneficial area UK.

c/o IMG, Pier House, Strand on the Green, Chiswick, London W4 3NN

Correspondent John Murray, Trustee

Trustees *Colin Montgomerie; Guy Kinnings; John Murray; Eimear Montgomerie.*

CC Number 1072388

Information available Information was obtained from the Charity Commission, but was limited.

General Set up in November 1998, the foundation aims to support the relief of poverty, the advancement of education and religion, and any other charitable purposes as decided by the trustees.

In 2005 the trust had an income of £14,000 and a total expenditure of £67,000. Grants totalled around £50,000. Details on beneficiaries were not available for the year, however previous recipients have included British Lung Foundation, Cancer Vaccine Institute, NSPCC for the Full Stop Campaign and University of Glasgow MRI Scanner Fund.

Applications In writing to the correspondent.

George A Moore Foundation

General

£119,000 (2005/06)

Beneficial area Principally Yorkshire and the Isle of Man.

Mitre House, North Park Road, Harrogate, North Yorkshire HG1 5RX

Website www.gamf.org.uk

Correspondent Mrs A L James, Chief Administrator

Trustees *George A Moore; Mrs E Moore; J R Moore; P D Turner.*

CC Number 262107

Information available Accounts were on file at the Charity Commission

General The trustees of the foundation select causes and projects from applications received during the year, as well as using independent research to identify specific objectives where they wish to direct assistance.

In 2005/06 the trust had assets of £9.3 million and an income of £509,000. A total of £119,000 was distributed in 48 grants, the majority of which were for £1,000 or less.

Major beneficiaries were: Macmillan Cancer Relief (£50,000); and HMS Illustrious and Tockwith Show (£12,000 each). Smaller grants included those to: St Stephens Church – Sulby (£4,200); Cystic Fibrosis Trust (£2,500); CLIC Sargent, High Street Centre, National Library for the Blind and St John Ambulance – IOM (£2,000 each); Project 21 (£1,900); and Childline Yorkshire and North East, Knaresborough Feva Festival and Pinewoods Conservation Group (£1,500 each).

Further donations of between £100 and £1,000 were made to various organisations including Action Medical Research, British Deaf Association, Manx Flower Festival, and Wetherby Arts Festival

Exclusions No assistance will be given to individuals, courses of study, expeditions, overseas travel, holidays, or for purposes outside the UK. Local appeals for UK charities will only be considered if in the area of interest. Because of present long-term commitments, the foundation is not prepared to consider appeals for religious property or institutions.

Applications In writing to the correspondent. No guidelines or application forms are issued. The trustees meet approximately four times a year, on variable dates, and an appropriate response is sent out after the relevant meeting.

The Nigel Moores Family Charitable Trust

Arts

£215,000 (2005/06)

Beneficial area UK, but mostly Wales and Liverpool.

233

c/o Macfarlane and Co., 2nd Floor, Cunard Building, Water Street, Liverpool L3 1DS

Tel. 0151 236 6161 **Fax** 0151 236 1095

Correspondent P Kurthausen, Accountant

Trustees *J C S Moores; Mrs P M Kennaway.*

CC Number 1002366

Information available Accounts were on file at the Charity Commission.

General The trustees have determined that their principal objective should be the raising of the artistic taste of the public, whether in relation to music, drama, opera, painting, sculpture or otherwise in connection with the fine arts, the promotion of education in the fine arts and academic education, the promotion of the environment, the provision of facilities for recreation or other leisure time occupation and the advancement of religion.

In 2005/06 the trust had assets of £505,000 and an income of £570,000. During the year the sole beneficiary was the A Foundation which received a grant of £215,000. (The trustees of the foundation are also trustees of The A Foundation.)

Applications In writing to the correspondent.

The Morel Charitable Trust

See below

£64,000 (2001/02)

Beneficial area UK and the developing world.

34 Durand Gardens, London SW9 0PP

Tel. 020 7582 6901

Correspondent S E Gibbs, Trustee

Trustees *J M Gibbs, Chair; W M Gibbs; S E Gibbs; B M O Gibbs; Thomas Gibbs; Dr E Parry; Mrs S Coan.*

CC Number 268943

Information available No accounts on file at the Charity Commission since 2003.

General The trust supports: the arts, particularly drama; organisations working for improved race relations; inner-city projects and developing-world projects. Also supported are: culture and recreation; health; conservation and environment; education and training; and social care and development.

In 2002/03 the trust had an income of £43,000 and expenditure of £69,000. No further information was available.

In 2001/02 the trust had assets of £1.3 million with an income of £81,000 and grants totalling £64,000.

The largest grants were £5,000 each to Child to Child, African Initiatives and Oxfam, £4,000 each to Child to Child (Ecuador) and Action Aid (Peace Building), £3,000 each to Jubilee Plus, Oxfam (BRAC in Bangladesh), Oxfam (Maharashtra), Tree Aid, Walls of Llangynidr and Hope and Homes for Children, £2,000 each to Walworth Methodist Church, Ockenden Ventures, Book Aid International and Sightsavers.

Grants of £1,000 or less were awarded to International Planned Parenthood, Healthlink Worldwide, Ghana School Aid, Achimota Trust, Hospice Care, Mildmay Mission Hospital, Harvest Help, Royal West of England Academy, Northumberland Community Trust, Corrymeela, Pecan, Greenwich Committee Against Racist Attacks, Llangynidr Church Fabric Fund and Rainbow Trust.

Exclusions No grants to individuals.

Applications In writing to the correspondent. The trustees normally meet three times a year to consider applications.

Although accounts have not been filed at the Charity Commission since March 2004 (for year end March 2003), we have contacted the trustees and been advised that applications are still being accepted.

The Morgan Charitable Foundation

Welfare, hospices, medical, Jewish, general

£88,500 (2004)

Beneficial area UK.

Courts and Co., 15 Wimpole Street, London W1G 9SY

Tel. 020 7637 1651 **Fax** 020 7637 0205

Correspondent Sarah Scott

Trustees *The Morgan Charitable Foundation Trustees Ltd. (A Morgan; L Morgan; T Morgan).*

CC Number 283128

Information available Accounts were on file at the Charity Commission.

General The Morgan Charitable Foundation (previously known as The Erich Markus Charitable Foundation) was established in 1979 when, following Erich Markus's death, half of his residual estate was left to the trust. The original capital was made up of 355,000 ordinary 25p shares in Office and Electronic Machines Ltd.

In 2004 the foundation had assets at £3.1 million and an income of £330,000. Of this, £200,000 was donated by Durbin Plc, a company connected to two of the trustees. Grants were made to 42 organisations and totalled £88,500. Management and administration costs were quite high at £29,000.

The three largest grants went to World Jewish Relief (£10,500), Spanish and Portuguese Jews Congregation (£6,000) and In Kind Direct (£5,000). All other grants were of £4,000 or less.

Grants of £4,000 were given to: Chai Lifeline Cancer Care; Jewish Blind and Disabled; Jewish Care; Magen David Adom UK; St Christopher's Hospice and UK Friends of Megan and David.

Smaller grants of £1,000 each included those to Age Care, Delamere Forest School, Gurkha Welfare Trust, Mobility Trust, Soundaround and The Bran Research Trust.

Exclusions No grants to individuals..

Applications In writing to the correspondent. Applications will only be considered if accompanied by a copy of the charitable organisation's latest report and accounts. Trustees meet twice a year, usually in April and October. No telephone enquiries please.

Morgan Williams Charitable Trust

Christian

£982,000 (2005/06)

Beneficial area UK.

43 Chelsea Square, London SW3 6LN

Tel. 020 7352 6592 **Fax** 020 7568 0912

Correspondent K J Costa, Trustee

Trustees *K J Costa; Mrs A F Costa.*

CC Number 221604

Information available Full accounts were on file at the Charity Commission.

General In 2005/06 the trust had assets of £140,000 and an income of £1 million derived mostly from donations. Grants were made totalling £990,000, including £5,500 to individuals

The largest grants were: £580,000 to Holy Trinity Church Brompton, St Paul's, and £330,000 to Holy Trinity Church.

Other grants were: £25,000 to Great Ormond Street; £10,000 to Reg Com Charity; £7,500 to The Message Trust; and, £5,000 each to Chasah Trust, Soul Survivor, The Cardinall's Musick and P C West Family Trust.

Applications The trust states that only charities personally connected with the trustees are supported and absolutely no applications are either solicited or acknowledged.

Diana and Allan Morgenthau Charitable Trust

Jewish, general

£163,000 (2004/05)
Beneficial area Worldwide.

26 Redington Road, London NW3 7RB
Correspondent Allan Morgenthau, Trustee
Trustees *Allan Morgenthau; Diana Morgenthau.*
CC Number 1062180
Information available Accounts were on file at the Charity Commission.

General Registered with the Charity Commission in April 1997, grants are made to a range of Jewish, medical, education and arts organisations. In 2004/05 the trust had an income of £95,000 and made grants totalling £163,000.

Beneficiaries of the four largest grants were Nightingale House (£50,000), British Friends of the Jaffa Centre (£30,000), London Jewish Cultural Centre (£25,000) and UJIA (£10,000).

Other beneficiaries included Belsize Square Synagogue (£8,500), World Jewish Relief (£6,000), World Jewish Aid (£5,000), Rays of Sunshine (£4,000), Cambridge Chaplaincy Board (£3,000), British Pigmentosa Society (£1,300) and

Ben Uri Gallery, British Friends of the Jaffa Centre, Rays of Sunshine, Sussex University German Jewish Department, Tate Foundation (£1,000 each).

Applications In writing to the correspondent.

The Oliver Morland Charitable Trust

Quakers, general

£95,000 (2005/06)
Beneficial area UK.

Thomas's House, Stower Row, Shaftesbury, Dorset SP7 0QW
Tel. 01747 853524
Correspondent J M Rutter, Trustee
Trustees *Priscilla Khan; Stephen Rutter; Joseph Rutter; Jennifer Pittard; Kate Lovell; Charlotte Jones; Simon Pittard.*
CC Number 1076213
Information available Accounts were on file at the Charity Commission.

General The trustees state that the majority of funds are given to Quaker projects or Quaker-related projects, which are usually chosen through the personal knowledge of the trustees. In 2005/06 the trust had an income of £91,000 and made grants totalling £95,000. Assets stood at £1.3 million.

Grants were broken down as follows:

Quaker and schools – 21 grants totalling £69,000
Beneficiaries included Quaker Peace and Service (£28,000), Quaker Home Service – children and young people (£10,000), Woodbrooke Bursary Fund (£5,000), Hlekweni RT Centre Zimbabwe and Ulster Quaker Service (£3,000 each), Quaker Social Action (£2,500), Sibford School and Waterford School Kambala (£2,000 each), Peter Bedford Trust and Leap Confronting Conflict (£1,000 each) and the Leaveners (£500).

Health and social care – 14 grants totalling £10,000

Beneficiaries included Refugee Council (£2,000), Sightsavers International (£1,500), Living Again and Ockenden International (£1,000 each), Fairfield Opportunity Farm (£800), Robert Barton Trust, ICAN, KidsActive and National Deaf Children's Society (£500 each) and Stonham Housing (£200).

International and environment – 6 grants totalling £6,600
Beneficiaries included Pakistan Environmental Protection Foundation (£2,500), Magdalen Project and University of York – technical education in Russia (£1,000 each), Intermediate Technology Development (£800) and Tools for Self Reliance (£500).

Animals and Nature – 5 grants totalling £2,800
Beneficiaries included National Trust and Somerset Wildlife Trust (£1,000 each) and Blue Cross Animal Hospital and PDSA (£250 each).

Meeting house appeals – 5 grants totalling £2,800
Meeting houses in Muswell Hill, Norwich, Nottingham, Salisbury and Wrexham recieved grants.

Sundry – 6 grants totalling £3,300
Beneficiaries included Sessions Book Trust (£1,000) and Medical Aid for Palestine (£500).

Exclusions No grants to individuals.

Applications 'Most of our grants are for continuing support of existing beneficiaries (approx 90%) so there is little left for responding to new appeals. We receive unsolicited applications at the rate of six or seven each week, 99% are not even considered.'

S C and M E Morland's Charitable Trust

Quaker, sickness, welfare, peace and development overseas

£34,250 (2005/06)
Beneficial area UK.

Gable House, Parbrook, Glastonbury, Somerset BA6 8PB
Tel. 01458 850804
Correspondent J C Morland, Trustee
Trustees *J C Morland; Ms J E Morland; Ms E Boyd; H N Boyd.*
CC Number 201645
Information available Accounts were on file at the Charity Commission.

General The trust states in its annual report and accounts that it 'gives to Quaker, local and national charities which have a strong social bias, and also to some UK-based international charities'. Also, that it supports those charities concerned with the relief of poverty and ill health, and those promoting peace and development overseas.

The trust generally makes grants to charities it has supported on a long-term basis, but each year this list is reviewed and new charities may be added.

In 2005/06 the trust had assets of £990,000 and an income of £35,000. Grants to 102 charities totalled £34,250. Only two grants of £1,000 or over were made and thus required listing in the accounts. These were to Britain Yearly Meeting (£6,500) and Oxfam (£1,000).

Exclusions The trust does not usually give to animal welfare, individuals or medical research.

Applications In writing to the correspondent. The trustees meet twice a year to make grants, in March and December. Applications should be submitted in the month before each meeting.

Ruth and Conrad Morris Charitable Trust

Jewish, general

£104,000 (2004/05)

Beneficial area UK and Israel.

c/o MRI Moores Rowland, 3 Sheldon Square, Paddington, London W2 6PS

Tel. 020 7470 0000

Correspondent Conrad Morris, Trustee

Trustees Mrs R S Morris; C J Morris.

CC Number 276864

Information available Full accounts were on file at the Charity Commission.

General The trust has Jewish charitable purposes. In 2004/05 the trust had an income of £246,000 and made grants totalling £104,000.

The largest grants were: £46,000 to Yeshivat Kerem B Yavne and £10,000 to Lubavitch Foundation.

Other grants included those to: Bar Iian (£6,000); Aish Hotorah and Chief Rabbinate Trust (£5,000 each); ORT (£3,000); Kisharon (£2,000); and Yesoday Hatora (£1,500).

Donations of £1,000 or less totalled £11,350.

Applications In writing to the correspondent.

The Morris Charitable Trust

Relief of need, education, community support and development

£107,000 (2003/04)

Beneficial area UK, with a preference for Islington.

c/o Management Office, Business Design Centre, 52 Upper Street, London N1 0QH

Tel. 020 7288 6200

Email info@morrischaritabletrust.com

Website www.morrischaritabletrust.com

Correspondent The Trustees

Trustees J A Morris, chair; P B Morris; A R Stenning.

CC Number 802290

Information available Accounts were on file at the Charity Commission.

General The Morris Charitable Trust was established in 1989 to provide support for charitable causes. It was founded by the Morris Family, whose principal businesses – City Industrial Limited, The Business Design Centre, CIL International, CIL Securities, City North Islington and Portland Design Associates – are based in Islington, London. The companies contribute a proportion of their annual profits to facilitate the trust's charitable activities.

The trust has general charitable purposes, placing particular emphasis on alleviating social hardship and deprivation, supporting national, international and local charities. There is a preference for supporting causes within the borough of Islington.

In 2005/06 the trust had assets of £155,000 and an income of £127,000 mainly from donations received from the above mentioned companies. Grants totalling £107,000 were made to 160 beneficiaries.

Only the three largest grants were listed in the accounts, namely: £25,000 to Age Concern – Islington; £5,000 to The Bridge School – Islington; and £1,000 to the Islington Senior Citizens Fund.

Exclusions No grants for individuals. No repeat donations are made within 12 months.

Applications By application form available from the trust or downloadable from its website. The completed form should be returned with any supporting documentation and a copy of your latest report and accounts.

The trustees generally meet monthly.

The Willie and Mabel Morris Charitable Trust

Medical, general

£84,000 (2004/05)

Beneficial area UK.

41 Field Lane, Letchworth Garden City, Hertfordshire SG6 3LD

Correspondent Angela Tether

Trustees Michael Macfadyen; Joyce Tether; Peter Tether; Andrew Tether; Angela Tether; Suzanne Marriott.

CC Number 280554

Information available Full accounts were on file at the Charity Commission.

General The trust was established in 1980 by Mr and Mrs Morris. It was constituted for general charitable purposes and specifically to relieve physical ill-health, particularly cancer, heart trouble, cerebral palsy, arthritis and rheumatism. Grants are usually only given to registered charities.

In 2004/05 the trust had assets of £2.8 million and an income of £104,000. Grants were made totalling £84,000.

There were 94 donations made in the range of £100 to £10,000. Beneficiaries of larger grants included St Thomas' Lupus Trust (£10,000), British Diabetic Association and Maidstone and Tunbridge Wells NHS Trust (£2,500 each), Centre for Cancer Treatment – Mount Vernon Hospital, CIRCA, Elimination of Leukaemia Fund, Islet Research Laboratory, the Meningitis Research Foundation, Muscular Dystrophy Campaign, Motor Neurone Disease Foundation, the Primrose Appeal and the Stroke Association (£2,000 each), Balham Nursery School Out of School Care (£1,500) and Alzheimer's Society, British Lung Foundation, Cerebral Palsy Care, Covent Garden Cancer Research Trust, the

Genesis Appeal, the Hearing Research Trust, Happy Days Children's Charity and Tuberous Sclerosis Association (£1,000 each).

Smaller grants under £1,000 each included those to 1st Sandy Scouts, Cancer Research UK, Combat Stress, Dogs for the Disabled, Farm Africa, Listening Books, Music in Hospitals, NSPCC, the Royal British Legion, Safety Net for Children and WaterAid.

Exclusions No grants for individuals or non-registered charities.

Applications The trustees 'formulate an independent grants policy at regular meetings so that funds are already committed'.

Morris Family Israel Trust

Jewish

£64,000 (2004/05)
Beneficial area UK and Israel.

Flat 90, North Gate, Prince Albert Road, London NW8 7EJ

Tel. 020 7722 0252

Correspondent Conrad J Morris, Trustee

Trustees *Conrad Morris; Ruth Morris; David Morris.*

CC Number 1004976

Information available Accounts were on file at the Charity Commission.

General In 2004/05 the trust had an income of £66,000 from donations. Grants were made to 15 organisations and totalled £64,000.

Major beneficiaries included: Manhigut Yehudit (£14,000); and, Mosdot Neu Zvia (£5,600).

Other beneficiaries were: Kollel Maarat Hamachpela (£3,700); Ohr Sameach Institute – Jerusalem (£3,500); Beit Yisrael Synagogue (£3,000); Mercaz Hatorah (£2,750); Ascent Institute (£2,500); and, Israel Trauma Care (£1,000).

Sundry donations not exceeding £1,000 amounted to £21,000.

Applications In writing to the correspondent.

The Peter Morrison Charitable Foundation

Jewish, general

£61,100 (2004/05)
Beneficial area UK.

Begbies Chettle Agar, Chartered Accountants, Epworth House, 25 City Road, London EC1Y 1AR

Tel. 020 7628 5801

Correspondent J Payne

Trustees *M Morrison; I R Morrison.*

CC Number 277202

Information available Full accounts were on file at the Charity Commission.

General In the trust's annual report it states that, 'The trustees are concerned to make donations to charitable institutions which in the opinion of the trustees are most in need and which provide a beneficial service to the needy.'

In 2004/053 the trust had assets of £1.1 million and an income of £60,000. Grants totalling £61,100 were made during the year, mostly for less than £500 each.

The largest grants were those to: Ramsbury Recreation Centre (£4,600); Kingston Hospital Cancer Unit (£4,000); West London Synagogue (£3,500); and Barnfield Riding for the Disabled (£3,000).

Smaller grants went to: Royal National Institute for Blind People (£1,000); Hawk Conservancy (£500); Prostate Research Campaign UK (£250); Newbury Spring Festival (£100); Cup of Kindness (£50); and Great Totham Primary School (£20).

Applications In writing to the correspondent.

G M Morrison Charitable Trust

Medical, education, welfare

£138,500 (2004/05)
Beneficial area UK.

Currey and Co., 21 Buckingham Gate, London SW1E 6LS

Tel. 020 7802 2700

Correspondent A E Cornick, Trustee

Trustees *G M Morrison, Chair; N W Smith; A E Cornick.*

CC Number 261380

Information available Full accounts were on file at the Charity Commission.

General Grants are given to a wide variety of activities in the social welfare, medical and education/training fields. The trust maintains a list of beneficiaries that it has regularly supported.

In 2004/05 the trust had assets of £5.5 million and a total income of £172,000. Grants were made to 245 organisations totalling £138,500 and ranged from £350 to £10,000 each. The average size of grant was £570. Grants were categorised by the trust as follows:

- medical and health – 115 grants totalling $60,900
- social welfare – 73 grants totalling £23,900
- education and training – 20 grants totalling £35,800
- others (including churches, conservation, environment and sport) – 37 grants totalling £19,700.

By far the largest grant was £10,000 to University of Aberdeen Development Trust. Other smaller grants included those to: Royal College of Surgeons (£2,200); Kurt Hahn Trust – Cambridge German students (£1,200); Northwick Park Institute of Medical Research (£1,000); St Mungo's Association – Down and Out (£650); Musicians Benevolent Fund (£400); and Possum Trust (£350).

Exclusions No support for individuals, charities not registered in the UK, schemes or activities which are generally regarded as the responsibility of statutory authorities, short-term projects or one-off capital grants.

Applications The trust's annual report states: 'Beneficiaries of grants are normally selected on the basis of trustees' personal knowledge and recommendation. The trust's grantmaking is however of a long-term recurring nature and is restricted by available income. The trustees have decided that for the present, new applications for grants will only be considered in the most exceptional circumstances; any spare income will be allocated to increasing the grants made to charities currently receiving support. In the future this policy will of course be reviewed. Applicants who understanding this policy and nevertheless wish to apply for a grant should write to the correspondent.'

Monitoring is undertaken by assessment of annual reports and accounts which are required from all beneficiaries, and by occasional trustee visits.

Moshal Charitable Trust

Jewish

About £70,000 (2004/05)

Beneficial area UK.

c/o S Yodaiken & Co., 14 Castlefield Avenue, Salford M7 4GQ

Correspondent The Trustees

Trustees *D Halpern; L Halpern.*

CC Number 284448

Information available Accounts were on file at the Charity Commission.

General In 2004/05, the trust had an income of £24,000 and a total expenditure of £82,000. No further information was available.

In 2002/03 the trust's assets totalled £95,000 and it had an income of £37,000. Grants were made totalling £48,000, but no grants list for that year was included in the file at the Charity Commission.

Applications In writing to the correspondent.

Vyoel Moshe Charitable Trust

Education, relief of poverty

£561,000 (2004/05)

Beneficial area UK and overseas.

2–4 Chardmore Road, London N16 6HX

Correspondent J Weinberger, Secretary

Trustees *Y Frankel; B Berger; S Seidenfeld.*

CC Number 327054

Information available Accounts were on file at the Charity Commission, but without a list of grants or a narrative report.

General In 2004/05 the trust's assets totalled only about £1,400 and it had an income from donations of £519,000. Grants were made totalling around £561,000. The sum of £504,000 was given overseas and £20,000 in the UK (a further £37,000 was given towards Zorchei Yom Tov – UK).

Applications In writing to the correspondent.

The Moss Charitable Trust

Christian, education, poverty, health

£113,000 (2004/05)

Beneficial area Worldwide, with an interest in Dorset, Hampshire and Sussex.

7 Church Road, Parkstone, Poole, Dorset BH14 8UF

Tel. 01202 730002

Correspondent P D Malpas

Trustees *J H Simmons; A F Simmons; P L Simmons; D S Olby.*

CC Number 258031

Information available Information was provided by the trust.

General The objectives of the trust are to benefit the community in the county borough of Bournemouth and the counties of Hampshire, Dorset and Sussex, and also the advancement of religion in the UK and overseas, the advancement of education and the relief of poverty, disease and sickness.

The trust achieves this by providing facilities for contributors to give under Gift Aid or direct giving and redistributes them according to their recommendations. The trustees also make smaller grants from the general income of the trust.

In 2004/05 the trust had assets of £55,000, an income of £96,000 and made grants totalling £113,000. Beneficiaries receiving grants of over £1,000 included: Emmanuel Christian Fellowship (£10,000); Christ Church – Westbourne (£6,400); Tabitha Trust (£5,000); Revelation TV (£4,000); Tear Fund (£2,000); and Juniper Tree Charitable Foundation (£1,000).

Applications No funds are available by direct application. Because of the way

in which this trust operates it is not open to external applications for grants.

The Moulton Charitable Trust

Human health/welfare, clinical trials

£803,000 (2005/06)

Beneficial area UK.

The Mount, Church Street, Shoreham, Sevenoaks, Kent TN14 7SD

Tel. 01959 524008

Email jon.moulton@btopenworld.com

Correspondent J P Moulton, Trustee

Trustees *J P Moulton; Mrs P M Moulton.*

CC Number 1033119

Information available Accounts were on file at the Charity commission.

General The trust stated in 2005/06 that its objectives are: 'to improve human health, by supporting principally clinical trials, and to promote human welfare generally'.

In 2005/06 the trust had assets of £490,000 and an income of £47,000. Grants were made to 16 organisations totalling £803,000, of which £663,000 went towards supporting clinical trials.

Excluding grants for clinical trials, the major beneficiary was South Manchester University Hospital which received £100,000. Other grants were: £10,000 to the Stuart Low Trust; £7,000 to the Bipolar Organisation; £5,000 to Children's Investment Fund Foundation; and £1,000 to Compassion UK.

Exclusions No grants for individuals, students or animal charities.

Applications 'The trustees award grants on the perceived merits of applications which are made to the charitable trust in writing.'

The Mount 'A' Charity Trust

General, children, arts

£27,000 (2004/05)
Beneficial area Jersey.

Abacus (CI) Limited, La Motte Chambers, St Helier, Jersey C.I JE1 1BJ

Tel. 01534 602000

Email karen.stoker@abacusglobal.com

Correspondent Karen Stoker

Trustees *Stephanie Berni; Catherine Rosa Cava; Abacus (CI) Limited.*

CC Number 264127

Information available Accounts were available from the Charity Commission website.

General In the past the trust has stated that 'only appeals from children's charities are considered by the trustees', however the current list of grants shows some deviation from this policy. Grants are only made to organisations associated with Jersey and the majority were for £1,000 or less.

In 2004/05 the trust had net assets of £839,000 and an income of £36,000. Grants totalled £27,000 to 26 organisations.

The largest grants included: £5,000 to the Tsunami Appeal; £2,500 each to The Caesarea Association, and the University of Oxford – Optima Unit; £2,000 each to HOPE, and the Jersey Pastoral Centre, £1,500 each to Howard Leopold Davis Scholarship Trust and The Durrell Wildlife Conservation Trust; and £1,000 each to Diabetes Action Jersey, Family Nursing and the GOSH Jersey Appeal.

Smaller grants ranged between £100 and £500, and included: Brig-Y-Don Children's Home; British Heart Foundation; Cancer BACUP and Cystic Fibrosis Research Trust.

Applications In writing to the correspondent.

Mountbatten Festival of Music

Royal Marines and Royal Navy charities

£101,000 (2005/06)
Beneficial area UK.

The Corps Secretariat, HMS Excellent, Whale Island, Portsmouth PO2 8ER

Tel. 02392 547 201 **Fax** 02392 547 207

Email royalmarines.charities@charity. vfree.com

Website www.royalmarinesregimental. co.uk

Correspondent Lt Col I W Grant, Corps Secretary

Trustees *Commandant General Royal Marines; Director of Royal Marines; Deputy Chief Staff Manpower.*

CC Number 1016088

Information available Information was on file at the Charity Commission.

General The trust was set up in 1993 and is administered by the Royal Marines. It raises funds from band concerts, festivals of music and beating retreat. Unsurprisingly, the main beneficiaries are service charities connected with the Royal Marines and Royal Navy. The only other beneficiaries are those hospitals or rehabilitation centres and so on, which have recently directly aided a Royal Marine in some way and Malcolm Sergeant Cancer Care. Both one-off and recurrent grants are made.

In 2005/06 the trust had assets of £156,000 and an income of £271,000. Grant were made totalling £101,000.

Major beneficiaries during the year were: Malcolm Sergeant Cancer Fund (£20,000); RM Benevolent Fund (£12,000); The 1939 War Fund, RN Benevolent Fund and RM Museum (£10,000 each); and RN/RM Children's Home (£6,000).

Beneficiaries of smaller grants included: Wrens Benevolent Trust, King George's Fund for Sailors, Royal British Legion, St Dunstan's Home, The 'Not Forgotten' Society, and Scottish Veterans Residences (£1,000 each).

Exclusions Charities/organisations unknown to the trustees.

Applications Unsolicited applications are not considered as the trust's income is dependent upon the running and success of various musical events. Any money raised by this means is then disbursed to a set of regular beneficiaries.

The Mountbatten Memorial Trust

Technological research in aid of disabilities

£32,000 (2004/05)
Beneficial area Mainly UK, but some overseas.

The Estate Office, Broadlands, Romsey, Hampshire SO51 9ZE

Tel. 01794 518885

Correspondent John Moss, Secretary

Trustees *HRH The Prince of Wales, Chair; Lady Pamela Hicks; Hon. Michael-John Knatchbull; Countess Mountbatten of Burma.*

CC Number 278691

Information available Full accounts were on file at the Charity Commission, with a detailed description of the trust's grant policy.

General The trust was set up in 1979 to honour the ideals of the Admiral of the Fleet, the Earl Mountbatten of Burma. It supports charities and causes 'working to further the humanitarian purposes with which he was associated in his latter years'. The trust mainly focuses on making grants towards the development of technical aids for people with disabilities. A previous focus has also been to support the United World Colleges movement, which has the aim of providing a broad education to students from around the world and grants continue to be given to Atlantic College.

The trustees state that they, 'wish to provide grants as seed money acting in the form of a catalyst for projects rather than to fund a given project in total'.

In 2004/05 the trust had assets of £740,000 and an income of £32,500. Grants totalling £32,000 were made to the following organisations: £14,800 to Atlantic College; £5,000 each to Children and Families of the Far East Prisoners of War and Diagnostic Investigation of Spinal Conditions and Sciatica; £3,900 to Defeating Deafness – The Hearing Research Trust; and £3,000 to Medical Engineering Resource Unit.

Exclusions No grants are made towards the purchase of technology to assist people with disabilities.

Applications In writing to the correspondent, at any time.

The Edwina Mountbatten Trust

Medical

£78,200 (2004/05)

Beneficial area UK and overseas.

Estate Office, Broadlands, Romsey, Hampshire SO51 9ZE

Tel. 01794 518885 **Fax** 01794 529755

Correspondent John Moss, Secretary

Trustees *Countess Mountbatten of Burma, Chair; Noel Cunningham-Reid; Lord Faringdon; Peter H T Mimpriss; Mrs Mary Fagan.*

CC Number 228166

Information available Full accounts were on file at the Charity Commission.

General The trust was established in 1960 to honour the causes Edwina, Countess Mountbatten of Burma was involved with during her lifetime. Each year support is given to St John Ambulance (of which she was superintendent-in-chief) for work in the UK and its Commonwealth, and Save the Children (of which she was president) for the relief of children who are sick, distressed or otherwise in need. Nursing organisations are also supported, as she was the patron or vice-president of a number of nursing organisations. Grants, even to the core beneficiaries, are only given towards specific projects rather than core costs.

In 2004/05 the trust had assets of £3 million and an income of £81,000. Grants totalling £78,000 were made to 14 organisations.

The two major beneficiaries were: Save the Children Fund (£30,000) and Order of St John (£20,200).

Other grant recipients included: National Osteoporosis Society and The St Jerusalem Eye Hospital (£5,000 each); Evelina's Children's Hospital and Swinfen Charitable Trust (£3,000 each); and Alabare Christian Care Centre and Home Start – Eastleigh (£1,000 each).

Exclusions No grants for research or to individual nurses working in the UK for further professional training.

Applications In writing to the correspondent. The trustees meet once a year, generally in September/October.

The F H Muirhead Charitable Trust

Hospitals, medical research institutes

£56,000 (2003)

Beneficial area UK.

51 Perrymount Road, Haywards Heath, West Sussex RH16 3BN

Tel. 01444 411333 **Fax** 01444 440604

Correspondent S J Gallico

Trustees *M J Harding; S J Gallico; Dr R C D Staughton.*

CC Number 327605

Information available Information was previously provided by the trust.

General The trust makes grants for specific items of medical equipment for use in hospitals and medical research institutes. Priority is given to applications from smaller organisations.

In 2005/06 the trust had an income of £24,000 and an expenditure of £93,000. No further information was available.

In 2002/03 the trust had assets of £461,000, an income of £23,000 and made grants totalling £56,000. Grant beneficiaries included Defeating Deafness (£11,000), Cystic Fibrosis Trust (£9,300), Bath Institute of Medical Engineering (£9,100), Ehlers-Danlos Support Group (£8,000), The David Tolkien Trust for Stoke Mandeville NBIC (£7,700), Covent Garden Cancer Research Trust (£6,400) and High Blood Pressure Foundation (£4,700).

Exclusions No grants to non-charitable bodies. No grants for equipment for diagnostic or clinical use.

Applications On a form available from the address below. This should be returned with details of specific items of equipment for which a grant is required. Trustees meet twice a year in March and October. Application forms to be received at least three weeks before the meeting.

The Edith Murphy Foundation

General; individual hardship; animals

£175,000 (2005/06)

Beneficial area UK with some preference for Leicestershire.

c/o Crane and Walton, 113–117 London Road, Leicester LE2 0RG

Tel. 0116 2551901

Correspondent David L Tams, Trustee

Trustees *David L Tams; Pamela M Breakwell; Christopher P Blakesley; Richard F Adkinson.*

CC Number 1026062

Information available Accounts were on file at the Charity Commission.

General The foundation was set up in 1993 by the late Mrs Murphy in memory of her late husband, Mr Hugh Murphy, with the following objectives:

- to assist those who by reason of their age, youth, infirmity, disablement, poverty or social and economic circumstances are suffering hardship or distress or are otherwise in need
- to provide relief of suffering of animals of any species who are in need of care and attention and the provision and maintenance of facilities of any description for the reception and care of unwanted animals and the treatment of sick or ill-treated animals
- to make donations for general charitable purposes.

Following the death of Mrs Murphy in 2005, her will provided for the foundation to receive certain benefits including a proportion of the residue of her estate. The value of the benefits received to date following the year end, amounts to £28.2 million. A further amount due relating to the balance of the residue of the estate is likely to be in the order of £1 million.

In view of the stated intention of the trustees, 'that all funds which are received should be paid out in furtherance of the charity as soon as appropriate causes can be evaluated', it seems likely that the foundation's level of grantmaking will increase substantially in the coming years.

In 2005/06 the foundation had assets of £28.4 million. Grants were made to organisations totalling £175,000 and was broken down as follows:

Education – £59,000
Animal charities – £30,000
Welfare – £25,000
Help for the disabled – £58,000
Children's charities – £2,500

The beneficiaries were: Vitalise (£43,000); Wreake Valley Community College (£34,000); Leicester and Leicestershire Animal Aid Association (£30,000 in two grants); Army Benevolent Fund and University of Leicester – Library Development (£25,000 each); Skillshare International – Lesotho Disability Project (£15,000); and ADAPT (£2,500).

Applications In writing to the correspondent.

Murphy-Newmann Charity Company Limited

People who are older, very young with disabilities

£27,500 (2005/06)
Beneficial area UK, predominantly the south, the south east and the Midlands.

Hayling Cottage, Upper Street, Stratford-St-Mary, Colchester, Essex CO7 6JW

Tel. 01206 323685 **Fax** 01206 323686

Email mnccl@aol.com

Correspondent Mrs T R Lockett, Secretary

Trustees *M J Lockett; Mrs T R Lockett; M Richman.*

CC Number 229555

Information available Accounts were on file at the Charity commission

General The trustees state that: 'The objectives of the charity are to support projects aimed at helping those in society who suffer economic or social disadvantages; aid charities working to alleviate chronic illness and disabling diseases among all age groups; and help fund research into medical conditions for which there is not yet a cure.'

In 2005/06 the trust had assets of £800,000 and an income of £33,000.

Grants were made totalling £27,500 and ranged between £200 and £2,000. Most, however, were for between £500 and £1,500.

Major beneficiaries included: Contact the Elderly and Evening Argus Christmas Appeal (£1,750 each); Invalids at Home Trust (£1,500); and Gentlefolks Aid Association, Haemophilia Society, Vitalise, RUKBA, Norwood Children and Families Trust, and Hospice in the Weald (£1,000 each).

Smaller grants included those to: UCan Do It (£200); Bag Books (£250); SCBU – Hope Hospital (£400); and Raynaud's and Scleroderma Association (£500).

Exclusions No grants to individuals, or non-registered charities.

Applications In writing to the correspondent, in a letter outlining the purpose of the required charitable donation. Telephone calls are not welcome. There are no application forms, guidelines or deadlines. No sae required. Grants are usually given in November and December.

The Mushroom Fund

General

£26,000 (2004/05)
Beneficial area UK and overseas, with a preference for St Helens.

Liverpool Charity and Voluntary Services, 14 Castle Street, Liverpool L2 ONJ

Tel. 0151 236 7728

Correspondent Marjorie Staunton

Trustees *William Fulton, Chair; D F Pilkington; Mrs R Christian; Mrs J Wailing; J Pilkington; including 11 other LCVS trustees.*

CC Number 259954

Information available Accounts were obtained from the Charity Commission website.

General The trust has general charitable purposes, usually supporting causes known to the trustees.

In 2004/05 the trust had assets of £931,000 and an income of £33,000, gained from investments. Grants totalled £26,000, and included the following donations: £3,000 to Intermediate Technology Development Group; £2,500 to Born Free Foundation; £2,000 to the

Wildlife Trust for Lancashire, Manchester and North; £1,500 to Claremont Fan Court School; £1,250 to Buckley and Mold Lions Club; and £1,000 each to Compass, Extracare Charitable Trust, Macmillan Cancer Relief, Marie Curie Cancer Care, Roy Castle Lung Cancer Foundation, St Helens Housing Association, the Basement Night Drop-in Centre and Trinity Hospice London.

Other grants during the year totalled £7,700.

Exclusions No grants to individuals, or to organisations that are not registered charities.

Applications The trust does not consider or respond to unsolicited applications.

The Music Sales Charitable Trust

Children and young people, musical education

£131,000 (2005)
Beneficial area UK, but mostly Bury St Edmunds and London.

Music Sales Ltd, Dettingen Way, Bury St Edmunds, Suffolk IP33 3YB

Tel. 01284 702600 **Fax** 01284 768301

Email neville.wignall@musicsales.co.uk

Correspondent Neville Wignall, Clerk

Trustees *Robert Wise; T Wise; Ian Morgan; Christopher Butler; David Rockberger; Mrs Mildred Wise.*

CC Number 1014942

Information available Accounts were on file at the Charity Commission, but without a list of grants.

General The trust was established in 1992 by the company Music Sales Ltd. It supports registered charities benefiting children and young adults, musicians, people who are disabled and people disadvantaged by poverty, particularly those resident in London and Bury St Edmunds. The trust is also interested in helping to promote music and musical education, again with a particular interest in children attending schools in London and Bury St Edmunds.

In 2005 the trust had an income of £76,000 which we understand came as a donation from Music Sales Ltd. During the year grants were made to 83 organisations totalling £131,000. These were broken down as follows:

Animals – two grants totalling £350
Arts and culture – 18 grants totalling £28,000
Education/training – 19 grants totalling £69,700
Medical, health, sickness – 40 grants totalling £17,200
Overseas aid/famine relief – two grants totalling £6,000
Religion – two grants totalling £10,000.

Major beneficiaries were: The Purcell School Scholarship (£45,000 in three grants); Suffolk County Council, Music Department (£15,000); Westminster Synagogue (£!0,000 in two grants); and St Edmundsbury Borough Council 2005 Festival (£6,000).

Exclusions No grants to individuals.

Applications In writing to the correspondent. The trustees meet quarterly, generally in March, June, September and December.

The Mutual Trust Group

Jewish, education, poverty

£130,000 (2005).
Beneficial area UK.

12 Dunstan Road, London NW11 8AA
Tel. 020 8458 7549
Correspondent B Weisz, Trustee
Trustees *B Weisz; M Weisz.*
CC Number 1039300
Information available Brief accounts were on file at the Charity Commission.

General In 2005 the trust had an income of £147,000 and made grants totalling £130,000. The largest beneficiary was Yeshivat Shar Hashamaym which received £72,300. Other grants went to: Rescue Committee for Families in Distress (£24,000); Chevras Mooz Ladal £11,000); and Slabodka Yeshiva Trust (£9,000).

Applications In writing to the correspondent.

MYA Charitable Trust

Jewish

£27,000 (2004/05)
Beneficial area Worldwide.

25 Egerton Road, London N16 6UE
Correspondent M Rothfield, Trustee
Trustees *M Rothfeld; Mrs E Rothfeld; Mrs H Schraiber; J D Pfeffer.*
CC Number 299642
Information available Accounts were on file at the Charity Commission.

General In 2004/05 this trust had assets of £641,000 and an income of £74,000. Grants totalled £27,000 (£155,000 in 2003/04).

There were nine grants listed in the accounts of £1,000 each or more. Beneficiaries were ZSV Trust (£3,500), KZF (£3,300), Beis Rochel and Keren Zedoko Vochesed (£2,500 each), London Friends of Kamenitzer Yeshiva and Maos Yesomim Charitable Trust (£2,000 each), Bikkur Cholim De Satmar (£1,100) and Keren Mitzva Trust and Wlodowa Charity Rehabilitation Trust (£1,000 each).

A further nine smaller grants to organisations of under £1,000 each totalled £1,200. The sum of £7,200 was distributed to nine 'poor and needy families'.

Applications In writing to the correspondent.

The Nadezhda Charitable Trust

Christian

£72,000 (2005/06)
Beneficial area UK and worldwide, particularly Zimbabwe.

c/o Ballard Dale Syree LLP, Oakmore Court, Kingswood Road, Hampton Lovett, Droitwich Spa WR9 0GH
Correspondent The Trustees
Trustees *William M Kingston; Mrs Jill M Kingston; Anthony R Collins.*
CC Number 1007295
Information available Accounts were on file at the Charity Commission.

General The trust makes grants to projects for the advancement of Christianity in the UK and overseas, especially Zimbabwe.

In 2005/06 the trust had an income of £78,000 and made grants totalling £72,000. Of this £40,000 came from restricted funds which are designated for use in Zimbabwe. The beneficiaries from this were, Theological College of Zimbabwe (£21,000) and Evangelical Fellowship of Zimbabwe (£19,000).

Grants totalling £31,300 were made from the unrestricted fund, including those to: Worcester Area Schools Project (£12,000); Friends of George Whitfield College (£4,600); Community of the Holy Fire and the Mark Trust (£3,000 each); ISAAC – International Substance Abuse and Addiction Coalition (£2,000); and A P Shaw Trust (£1,900).

Exclusions No grants to individuals.

Applications The majority of funds are presently directed to supporting the Christian Church in Zimbabwe. The trust does not, therefore, respond to unsolicited applications.

The Willie Nagel Charitable Trust

Jewish, general

£41,000 (2004/05)
Beneficial area UK.

Lubbock Fine, Russell Bedford House, City Forum, 250 City Road, London EC1V 2QQ
Correspondent A L Sober, Trustee
Trustees *W Nagel; A L Sober.*
CC Number 275938
Information available Accounts were available at the Charity Commission, but without a full narrative report or a grants list.

General The trust makes grants to registered charities, committing its income before the funds have been generated.

In 2004/05 it had assets of £29,000. Total income was £51,000, almost entirely from donations. Grants were made totalling £41,000. No further information on the size or type of grants, or any details of the beneficiaries, was available.

The most recent grants information available was for 1989/90, when grants generally ranged from £20 to £2,000, but were mostly for £100 or less. There were five larger grants made, one of which was for £20,000, the others for £5,000 or less. These went to Board of Deputies Charitable Trust, Friends of Wiznitz, Israel Music Foundation, National Children's Home and Victoria and Albert Museum.

Applications In writing to the correspondent.

The Naggar Charitable Trust

Jewish, general

£67,400 (2005/06)

Beneficial area UK and overseas.

15 Grosvenor Gardens, London SW1W 0BD

Tel. 020 7834 8060

Correspondent Mr and Mrs Naggar, Trustees

Trustees *Guy Naggar; Hon. Marion Naggar; Marc Zilkha.*

CC Number 265409

Information available Accounts were on file at the Charity Commission.

General The trust mainly supports Jewish organisations and a few medical charities. Arts organisations also receive some support.

In 2005/06 the trust had an income of £67,000 and made grants totalling £67,400.

Major grant beneficiaries included: British Friends of the Art Museums of Israel (£23,600); Western Marble Arch Synagogue (£8,000); British Aid Committee Vahad Hayeshivot for Maoz Labbione (£7,300); JNF (£5,750); Friends of Israel Sports Centre for the Disabled (£5,400); and London Jewish Cultural Centre (£3,000).

Smaller grants included those to: British Wizo, RAD/RBS Billy Elliot Gala and Cancer Research UK (£500 each); and North West London Jewish Day School, The Holocaust Educational Trust and Venice in Peril (£250 each).

Applications In writing to the correspondent.

The Eleni Nakou Foundation

Education, international understanding

£72,500 (2003/04)

Beneficial area Worldwide, mostly continental Europe.

c/o Kleinwort Benson Trustees, PO Box 191, 10 Fenchurch Street, London EC3M 3LB

Tel. 020 7475 5093

Correspondent C Gilbert, Secretary

Trustees *E Holm; Y A Sakellarakis; L St John T Jackson; H Moller.*

CC Number 803753

Information available Full accounts were on file at the Charity Commission.

General The main aim of the trust is to advance the education of the people of Europe in each other's culture. The four trustees include two Danes, one Briton and one Greek.

In 2003/04 the foundation had an income of £79,000 and made grants totalling £72,500.

The beneficiaries during the year were: Danish Institute at Athens (£45,000); Hellenic Foundation (£17,500); Elein Nakou Scholarship Athens (£9,000); and Scandinavian Society for Modern Greek Studies (£1,100).

Applications In writing to the correspondent. Applications are considered periodically. However, the trustees state: 'It is unusual to respond favourably to unsolicited appeals.'

The Janet Nash Charitable Settlement

Medical, general

£201,000 to organisations (2004/05)

Beneficial area UK.

Ron Gulliver and Co. Ltd, The Old Chapel, New Mill Lane, Eversley, Hampshire RG27 0RA

Correspondent R Gulliver, Trustee

Trustees *Ronald Gulliver; M S Jacobs; Mrs C E Coyle.*

CC Number 326880

Information available Full accounts were on file at the Charity Commission.

General The trust has general charitable purposes, although it mostly supports medical and social welfare organisations.

In 2004/05 the trust ha an income of £421,000, almost entirely from donations received. Grants to 16 organisations totalled £201,000. A further £159,000 was given in grants to 21 individuals.

Four major beneficiaries received the following grants: £51,000 to Shirley Medical Centre; £50,000 to Aide Au Pere Pedro Opeka; £31,400 to The International School – Monaco; and £25,000 to The Royal Air Force Museum.

Smaller grants included those to: Bobath Children's Therapy Centre – Wales (£3,000); REACT (£2,500); Crimestoppers Trust (£2,000); and St Peter and St James Charitable Trust (£1,000).

Applications Absolutely no response to unsolicited applications. In 2007, the trustees stated: 'The charity does not, repeat not, ever consider any applications for benefit from the public.' Furthermore, that: 'Our existing charitable commitments more than use up our potential funds and were found personally by the trustees themselves, never as a result of applications from third parties.'

Nathan Charitable Trust

Evangelical Christian work and mission

£60,000 (2005/06)

Beneficial area UK and overseas.

The Copse, Sheviock, Torpoint, Cornwall PL11 3EL

Correspondent T R Worth, Trustee

Trustees *T R Worth; Mrs P J Worth; G A Jones.*

CC Number 251781

Information available Accounts were on file at the Charity Commission.

General In 2005/06 the trust made grants totalling £60,000.

Current beneficiaries include Bridges for Peace, Care, Carrot Tops, Christian Friends of Israel, Leprosy Mission, Open

Air Campaigners, Open Doors, Operation Mobilisation, Mission Aviation Fellowship, Prayer for Israel and Riding Lights.

Applications Funds are fully committed to current beneficiaries.

National Committee of The Women's World Day of Prayer for England, Wales, and Northern Ireland

Christian education and literature

£168,000 (2004)
Beneficial area UK and worldwide.

Commercial Road, Tunbridge Wells, Kent TN1 2RR

Tel. 01892 541411 **Fax** 01892 541745

Email office@wwdp-natcomm.org

Correspondent Mrs Lynda Lynam, Administrator

Trustees *Mrs J Hackett; Mrs Emma Wilcock.*

CC Number 233242

Information available Full accounts were available from the Charity Commission website.

General The trust makes grants to charitable Christian educational projects and Christian organisations publishing literature and audiovisual material designed to advance the Christian faith.

The main object of the trust is to unite Christians in prayer, focused in particular on a day of prayer in March each year. The trust's income is mainly from donations collected at this event. After the trust's expenses, including the costs of running the day of prayer, the income can be used for grantmaking

Themes for the Day of Prayer have been set as:
2007: United Under God's Tent – Paraguay
2008: God's Wisdom Provides New

Understanding – Guyana
2009: In Christ There Are Many Members But Only One Body – Papua New Guinea
2010: Let Everything That Has Breath Praise God – Cameroon
2011: How Many Loaves Have You? – Chile

In 2004 the trust had assets of £181,000 and an income of £329,000. Grants were made totalling £168,000 and were broken down as follows:

Charitable grants
Grants were made to 16 organisations totalling £109,000. Beneficiaries were: Bible Society, Feed the Minds and United Society for Christian Literature (£18,000 each); Scripture Gift Mission (£12,000); Bible Reading Fellowship and International Reading Association (£7,500 each); CAFOD, Royal National Institute for the Blind, Scripture Union and Society for Promoting Christian Knowledge (£4,000 each); the Salvation Army – the Missionary Literature Fund (£3,000); St John's Guild for the Blind, the Leprosy Mission and United Christian Broadcasters (£2,000 each); Northern Ireland Bible Society (£1,500); and Mission to Deep Sea Fishermen (£1,000).

International donations
Two grants were made in this category and were World Day of Prayer International Committee – Annual (£14,000) and World Day of Prayer European Committee (£200).

One-off grants
One-off grants were made to 19 to organisations totalling £41,000. The WDP National committees of India, Indonesia, Malaysia, Myanmar, Sri Lanka and Thailand each received £1,700. Other grants made included: Christian Deaf Link UK, Compass Braille and WDP National Committee of Panama (£5,000 each); SEAN International (£3,000); Cross Winds Prayer Trust and Mission India (£2,000 each); and Greenwich School of Theology (£1,000).

Grants to Welsh-speaking Churches
There were ten grants made in this category. Beneficiaries included: Wales Sunday Schools Council (£700); Christians against Torture – Wales (£600); Alcoholic and Drug Council – Wales Bangor Diocese Mothers' Union, Christian Aid – Wales, and the Reconciliation and Peace – Wales (£500 each); CAFOD and Churches Together in Wales (£300 each); and Bible Society – Wales (£200).

Exclusions No grants to individuals.

Applications In writing to the correspondent, before the end of June. Grants are made in November.

The National Gardens Scheme Charitable Trust

Nursing, welfare, gardening

£2.9 million (2004/05)
Beneficial area UK.

Hatchlands Park, East Clandon, Guildford, Surrey GU4 7RT

Tel. 01483 211535

Email ngs@ngs.org.uk

Website www.ngs.org.uk

Correspondent The Chief Executive

Trustees *Nick Payne, Chair; Jill Cowley; John Ainley; Jane Baldwin; Harriet Boileau; Fred Carr; Patricia Elkington; Elizabeth Fleming; Anthea Foster; Anthony Frost; Joanna Kerr; Martin McMillan; George Plumptre.*

CC Number 279284

Information available Full accounts were available from the Charity Commission website.

General This trust has, since 1927, raised funds by 'opening gardens of quality, character and interest to the public' and through the sale of a publication called *The Gardens of England and Wales*, known as *The Yellow Book.*

In 2004/05 the trust had assets of £385,000 and an income of £2.9 million. Grants were made to organisations totalling £2.9 million. Beneficiaries included Macmillan Cancer Relief (£1 million); Marie Curie Cancer Care (£500,000); NGS Gardeners' Bursaries (£400,000); the Nurses' Welfare Service (£180,000); the Queen's Nursing Institute (£170,000); Help the Hospices and Crossroads (£124,000 each); Perennial – Gardeners' Royal Benevolent Society and the Royal Gardeners' Orphan Fund (£95,000); RHS (£25,000); and County Nursing Associations (£24,000).

Applications The trust's website states: 'We donate money only to charities selected by council. We regret that we can not accept or acknowledge unsolicited applications for funds.'

The National Manuscripts Conservation Trust

Conserving manuscripts

£49,000 (2005)

Beneficial area UK.

c/o The National Archives, Kew, Surrey TW9 4DU

Tel. 020 8392 5218

Email nmct@nationalarchives.gov.uk

Website www.nationalarchives.gov. uk/preservation/trust/

Correspondent The Secretary

Trustees *Lord Egremont; B Naylor; C Sebag-Montefiore.*

CC Number 802796

Information available Full accounts were available from the Charity Commission website.

General The objective of the trust is to make grants towards the costs of conserving manuscripts and archives that are of historic or educational value, and of national importance.

Grants are made towards the cost of repair, binding and other preservation measures, including reprography and may cover the cost of contract preservation and conservation or the salaries and related expenses of staff specially employed for the project, as well as expendable materials required for the project.

In 2005 the trust had assets of £1.8 million and an income of £79,000.

Grants were made to eight organisations totalling £49,000 and are listed as follows: St Paul's Cathedral towards the conservation and preservation of the Architectural Archive (£18,000); Shropshire Archives towards the conservation of the Lilleshall Collection (£15,000); the National Trust towards conservation of Wimpole architectural drawings (£7,000); two grants to Royal Academy of Music, one towards the conservation of letters from the Royal Academy of Music's library (£5,000) and one towards the conservation of items in the Novello Collection (£1,000); London Metropolitan Archives towards conservation of the First Minute Book of the Surrey and Kent Commission of Sewers – 1569 to 1601 (£750); and Edinburgh University Library – Lothian Health Services Archive towards the conservation of Four Manuscripts (£650).

The trust is administered by the National Archives.

Exclusions The following are not eligible: public records within the meaning of the Public Records Act; official archives of the institution or authority applying except in the case of some older records; loan collections unless exempt from capital taxation or owned by a charitable trust; and photographic, audiovisual or printed materials.

Applications Applicants must submit six copies of the application form including six copies of a detailed description of the project. The applicant should also submit one copy of their most recent annual reports and accounts and details of its constitution.

Grants are awarded bi-annually, each June and December, for 50% of the cost of conservation of manuscripts held by any record office, library or by an owner of manuscript material that is exempt from capital taxation or owned by a charitable trust. The trustees take into account the significance of the manuscript or archive, the suitability of the storage conditions, the applicants' commitment to continuing good preservation practice, and the requirement for the public to have reasonable access to it.

Visit the trust's website for full details of how to apply.

Nazareth Trust Fund

Christian, in the UK and developing countries

£28,000 to organisations (2005/06)

Beneficial area UK and developing countries.

Barrowpoint, 18 Millennium Close, Salisbury, Wiltshire SP2 8TB

Tel. 01722 349322

Correspondent R W G Hunt, Trustee

Trustees *R W G Hunt; E M Hunt; David R Gainer Hunt; Elma R L Hunt; Philip R W Hunt; Nicola Mhairi Hunt.*

CC Number 210503

Information available Full accounts were available from the Charity Commission website.

General This trust funds churches, Christian missionaries, Christian youth work and overseas aid. Grants are only made to people or causes known personally to the trustees.

In 2004/05 the trust had an income of £38,000 and made grants totalling £30,000. Grants made to organisations totalled £28,000. Beneficiaries included Bible Society, Crusaders, IREF – UK, NHEC, Harnham Free Church, Mission Aviation Fellowship, London City Mission, Scripture Union, Sight Savers, WaterAid and World Vision.

Exclusions No support for individuals not known to the trustees.

Applications In writing to the correspondent, although the trust tends to support only organisations it is directly involved with.

Nesswall Ltd

Jewish

£49,000 (2005/06)

Beneficial area Worldwide.

28 Overlea Road, London E5 9BG

Tel. 020 8806 2965

Correspondent Mrs R Teitelbaum, Secretary

Trustees *I Teitelbaum, Chair; Mrs R Teitelbaum; I Chersky; Mrs H Wahrhaftig.*

CC Number 283600

Information available Accounts were on file at the Charity Commission but without a recent list of grants.

General In 2005/06 the trust had assets of £456,000 and an income of £137,000. Grants and donations totalled £49,000. A list of grants was not available. Previous beneficiares have included Friends of Horim Establishments, Torah Vochesed L'Ezra Vesaad and Emunah Education Centre.

Applications In writing to the correspondent, at any time.

The New Durlston Trust

Christian, overseas development

£32,000 to individuals and organisations (2005)

Beneficial area UK and developing countries.

98 Reading South Road, Fleet, Hampshire GU52 7UA

Correspondent N A H Pool, Trustee

Trustees *Nigel Austen Hewitt Pool; Alister John Mogford; Alexandra Louise Moon.*

CC Number 1019028

Information available Full accounts were available from the Charity Commission website.

General The trust supports charities and individuals involved in Christian-based projects. In 2005 the trust had assets of £98,000, an income of £28,000 and made grants to individuals and organisations totalling £32,000.

Recipients of the largest grants included the Church on the Heath (£5,000), Gateway Charity (£2,500), Elam Ministries and the Urban Sanctuary (£1,500 each) and Breacon Centre Trust, Caring for Life and Toxteth Vine Project (£1,000 each).

Other grants of £300 or less each totalled £13,000.

Exclusions No grants for work other than for Christian-based work. Overseas grants are only given through UK-based charities.

Applications In writing to the correspondent.

Newby Trust Limited

Welfare

£384,000 to organisations and individuals (2005/06)

Beneficial area UK.

Hill Farm, Froxfield, Petersfield, Hampshire GU32 1BQ

Tel. 01730 827557 **Fax** 01730 827938

Email info@newby-trust.org.uk

Website www.newby-trust.org.uk

Correspondent Miss W Gillam, Secretary, Secretary

Trustees *Mrs S A Charlton; Mrs J M Gooder; Dr R D Gooder; Mrs A S Reed; R B Gooder; Mrs A L Foxell.*

CC Number 227151

Information available Full accounts were available from the Charity Commission website.

General This trust has a specific theme for its funding for organisations each year, usually within social welfare. In 2007/08 this was:

- extra-curricular training for those aged 16 and under.

Grants range from £100 to £10,000 each. In addition to the funding for organisations, it also provides welfare grants to individuals for medical or relief in need purposes and funding to postgraduate students. These are made generally regardless of the theme for organisations. (Full details of the funding available to individuals can be found on the trust's website.)

In 2005/06 the trust had assets of £13 million and an income of £361,000. Grants were made to 476 organisations and individuals totalling £384,000. Grants made to institutions and individuals were broken down into the following categories:

Medical – £15,000

Grants included Medical Foundation for the Care of Victims of Torture and St Thomas' Lupus Trust (£5,000 each); Brae Partnership (£3,000); and Hope in the Valley Riding Group (£1,000). Other grants of less than £1,000 each were made to 56 institutions totalling £10,000.

Education, training and research – £209,000

Grants were made to 46 institutions totalling £209,000, forty-three of which were of £1,000 or more each. Three of the largest grants were made to Bedales School and Ditchling Museum (£25,000 each) and Pegasus Opera Company (£10,000). Other beneficiaries were Changing Faces, Citizenship Foundation, Community of Holy Fire, InterAct Network, Royal Academy of Arts, the Earthworks Trust and the Whitechapel Art Gallery (£5,000 each); Newham Music Trust, Oval House, the Multiple Sclerosis Society and Wells Cathedral Girl Chorister Trust (£3,000 each); Chain Reaction Theatre, North End Young Peoples' Project, Royal Society for the Blind and St Vincent de Paul Society (£2,000 each); and British Athletics Charitable Trust (£1,200).

In addition, grants of less than £1,000 each were made to three institutions totalling £1,300 and grants to 136 individuals totalled £65,000.

Relief of poverty – £58,000

Beneficiaries included Camphill Village Trust (£5,000 each) and Derby Playhouse (£1,000).

Other grants included 178 grants, none exceeding £550 (£24,000) and two grants from restricted funds (£24,000).

Applications In writing to the correspondent, on no more than two sides of A4 with details of costings and amounts raised so far. All applicants must provide a copy of the latest annual report/accounts, along with an sae (the trust will not reply unless this is enclosed). Applications need to be received by the end of September or January for consideration in November or March respectively. Applicants are advised of the outcome approximately three weeks after the meeting. (There is a separate application procedure for individuals, please see the trust's website for further information).

The Richard Newitt Fund

Education

£75,000 (2005/06)

Beneficial area UK.

Kleinwort Benson Trustees Ltd, PO Box 191, 10 Fenchurch Street, London EC3M 3LB

Tel. 020 7475 5093

Correspondent Chris Gilbert, The Administrator

Trustees *Kleinwort Benson Trustees Ltd; D A Schofield; Prof. D Holt; Baroness Diana Maddock.*

CC Number 276470

Information available Full accounts were on file at the Charity Commission.

General In 2005/06 the trust had assets of £2.3 million and an income of £57,000. Grants made to charitable institutions totalled £75,000. Beneficiaries were University of Southampton for existing bursaries (£65,000) and Bristol Old Vic Theatre School and Royal Northern School of Music (£5,000 each).

Exclusions No grants to individuals.

NEWITT / NEWMAN / NEWPIER / NITZROCHIM •

Applications Requests for application forms should be submitted by 1 April in any one year; applicants will be notified of the results in August. Unsolicited applications are unlikely to be considered, educational institutional applications by invitation only.

Mr and Mrs F E F Newman Charitable Trust

Christian, overseas aid and development

£25,000 (2005/06)
Beneficial area UK, Republic of Ireland and overseas.

c/o David Quinn Associates, Southcroft, Caledon Road, Beaconsfield, Buckinghamshire HP9 2BX
Tel. 01494 674 396
Correspondent David Quinn, Administrator
Trustees *Frederick E F Newman; Margaret C Hayes; David M F Newman; Michael R F Newman; George S Smith.*
CC Number 263831
Information available Full accounts were on file at the Charity Commission.

General In 2005/06 the trust had assets of £232,000 and an income of £26,000. Grants were made totalling £25,000 and were distributed from two funds as follows:

Donations – 'A' Fund
Grants were made to 22 organisations, ranging from £25 to £400. Beneficiaries included: Thal Village Project (£400); Samaritans – Guildford (£300); Christian Aid (£200); Church Housing Trust (£150); Music as Therapy and N W Surrey Chest Hospital (£100 each); Parkinson's Disease Society (£50); and Help the Aged and Horsell Common Preservation Society (£25 each).

Donations – 'B' Fund
Grants were made to 31 organisations, ranging from £100 to £2,000. Beneficiaries included: Bible Society, Building Relationships, Children's Society and Tear Fund (£2,000); Church Mission Society, Orpington Church PCC and St Luke's (£1,000 each); Africa Enterprise, CARE, Friends of the Clergy, Riding Lights Trust, Winged Fellowship Trust and World Development Mission

(£500 each); Acorn (£250); and Cyfa/Pathfinder Ventures (£100).
Exclusions No grants to individuals.
Applications In writing to the correspondent.

Newpier Charity Ltd

Jewish, general

£574,000 (2004/05)
Beneficial area UK.

115 Craven Park Road, London N15 6BL
Correspondent Charles Margulies, Trustee
Trustees *C M Margulies; Mrs H Knopfler; Mrs R Margulies.*
CC Number 293686
Information available Accounts were on file at the Charity Commission, but without a list of grants.

General The main objectives of the charity are the advancement of the orthodox Jewish faith and the relief of poverty.

In 2004/05 it had an income of £660,000 mainly from donations (£372,000) and rent (£265,000) and made grants totalling £574,000. Assets stood at £4.8 million.

No grants list was included with the accounts. The last available list was from 1997/98 when grants were made to 23 organisations totalling £80,000. All the beneficiaries were Jewish organisations and nine had also received a grant the year before. The largest donation was to SOFT for redistribution to other charities. Other beneficiaries have included BML Benityashvut, Friends of Biala, Gateshead Yeshiva, KID and Mesdos Wiznitz.

Applications In writing to the correspondent. The address given is effectively a PO Box, from where letters are passed on to the trustees and telephone calls are not invited.

The Chevras Ezras Nitzrochim Trust

Jewish

£47,000 to organisations (2005)
Beneficial area UK, with a preference for London.

53 Heathland Road, London N16 5PQ
Tel. 020 8800 5187
Correspondent H Kahan, Trustee
Trustees *J Stern; K Stern; H Kahan.*
CC Number 275352
Information available Full accounts were on file at the Charity Commission.

General 'The objectives of the charity are the relief of the poor, needy and sick and the advancement of Jewish religious education.' There is a preference for Greater London, but help is also given further afield. Grants can also be made to individuals.

In 2005 the trust had assets of £2,000 and an income of £221,000. Grants totalled £212,000, of which £47,00 went to organisations and £165,000 to individuals.

Grants were made to 75 organisations. Beneficiaries included: Mesifta (£4,000); Kupas Tzedoko Vochesed (£3,000); Beis Chinuch Lenonos , Yad Eliezer and Yeshias Hatorah School (£2,000 each); Hachzokas Torah Vochesed Trust (£1,000); Ezras Hakohol Trust and Woodstock Sinclair Trust (£600 each); Side by Side (£500); Yeshivas Panim Meiros and Yeahuas Chaim Synagogue (£300 each); TYY Trust (£200); and Square Yeshiva and Stanislow (£100 each).

Grants were made to 825 individuals who were needy and sick, unemployed, widowed or incapacitated totalling £165,000. Grants were also given in the form of food, medical supplies and clothing.

Applications In writing to the correspondent.

The Noel Buxton Trust

Child and family welfare, penal matters, Africa

£93,000 (2005)

Beneficial area UK, eastern and southern Africa.

PO Box 393, Farnham, Surrey GU9 8WZ

Website www.noelbuxtontrust.org. uk/index.htm

Correspondent Ray Waters, Secretary

Trustees *Richenda Wallace; Joyce Morton; Simon Buxton; Paul Buxton; Jon Snow; Jo Tunnardr; John Littlewood; Brendan Gormley.*

CC Number 220881

Information available Accounts were on file at the Charity Commission.

General Grants are made for the following:

- The welfare of children in disadvantaged families and of children in care. This will normally cover families with children of primary school age and younger, although work with children in care will be considered up to the age at which they leave care. (Grants are NOT given for anything connected with physical or mental disability or any medical condition.)
- The prevention of crime, especially work with young people at risk of offending; the welfare of prisoners' families and the rehabilitation of prisoners (housing of any kind is excluded).
- Education and development in eastern and southern Africa.

The trust is a small one and seldom makes grants of more than £4,000, often considerably less. The average grant in 2004 was about £1,250. The trust will fund core costs and will consider making a series of annual grants for up to three years. Due to the size of grant, appeals whose major component is salary costs will not be considered.

The trustees very much welcome appeals from small local groups in England, Scotland and Wales. The emphasis of their giving is on areas outside London, south-east England and Northern Ireland. The trust does not respond to appeals from large and well-supported charities or to general appeals.

In 2005 the trust had assets of £2.5 million and an income of £107,000. Donations were made totalling £93,000.

They were broken down as follows and are shown here with examples of beneficiaries:

Africa – 11 grants totalling £31,000
APT Enterprise Development – Tanzania, Find Your Feet – Malawi and Harvest Help – Zambia (£4,000 each), Bugosa Trust – Uganda (£3,000), African Initiatives – Tanzania (£2,000) and Mango Tree – Tanzania (£1,000).

Family – 37 grants totalling £30,000
Church Housing Trust, Respect and Voice for the Child in Care (£1,500 each), Asylum Aid, Friendship Project for Children, Shaftesbury Homes and Arethusa, Sheffield Mind, Who Cares? Trust and Wybourn Youth Trust (£1,000 each), British Bengali Welfare Association, Homestart Dundee and Tower Hamlets Women's Aid (£500 each) and Brighton and Hove Unwaged Advice and Rights Centre (£250).

Penal – 20 grants totalling £32,000
Howard League for Penal Reform (£4,000), Prisoners Abroad (£3,500) IQRA Trust (£3,000), Consett Churches Detached Youth Project, New Bridge and St Giles Trust (£2,000 each), Fair Shares, Inside Our Trust and Prison Reform Trust (£1,000 each) and Door UK (£500).

Exclusions The trust does not give to: academic research; advice centres; animals; the arts of any kind; buildings; conferences; counselling; development education; drug and alcohol work; older people; the environment; expeditions, exchanges, study tours, visits, and so on, or anything else involving fares; housing and homelessness; human rights; anything medical or connected with illness or mental or physical disability; anywhere overseas except eastern and southern Africa; peace and disarmament; race relations; youth (except for the prevention of offending); and unemployment. Grants are not made to individuals for any purpose.

Applications By letter, setting out the reasons why a grant is being requested. Applications should include the applicant's charity registration number and the name of the organisation to which cheques should be made payable if different from that at the head of the appeal letter. Applications should include: budget for current and following year; details of funding already received, promised or applied for from other sources; latest annual report/accounts in the shortest available form.

Applications may be made at any time and are not acknowledged. Successful applicants will normally hear from the trust within six months. The trust will

not discuss applications on the telephone or correspond about rejected appeals.

The Noon Foundation

General, education, relief of poverty, community relations, alleviation of racial discrimination

£56,000 to institutions (2005)

Beneficial area England and Wales.

25 Queen Anne's Gate, St James' Park, London SW1H 9BU

Tel. 020 7654 1600

Email grants@noongroup.co.uk

Correspondent The Trustees

Trustees *Gulam Kanderbhoy Noon; Akbar Shirazi; Zeenat Harnal; A M Jepson; D Robinson; Zarmin N Sekhon.*

CC Number 1053654

Information available Full accounts were available from the Charity Commission website.

General This trust was set up in 1996 by Gulam Kaderbhoy Noon, the founder of Noon Products. In 2005 the trust had assets of £3.7 million and an income of £199,000. Grants were made totalling £56,000 and are summarised as follows:

- **education:** £42,000.
- **sickness:** £8,000
- **poverty:** £6,000
- **community relations:** £250.

Those of more than £1,000 each were made to 11 institutions: Tower Hamlets College (£25,000); University of Derby – Multi-Faith Centre, NHS Doctors – Integrated Medicine in India and Help the Aged (£5,000 each); National Institute for Conductive Education and University of Dundee – Faculty of Law (£4,000 each); Imperial college London (£2,500); and Bliss – the Premature Children's Charity, Well Being of Women, WZO – Pakistani Earthquake Appeal and University of Birmingham – UCE (£1,000 each).

Other grants made to institutions of less than £1,000 each totalled £1,250.

Applications All applications and queries should be made by email.

The Norman Family Charitable Trust

General

£413,000 (2005/06)

Beneficial area Primarily south west England.

14 Fore Street, Budleigh Salterton, Devon EX9 6NG

Tel. 01395 446699 **Fax** 01395 446698

Email enquiries@nfct.org

Website www.nfct.org

Correspondent R J Dawe, Chairman of the Trustees

Trustees *R J Dawe, Chair; Mrs M H Evans; M B Saunders; Mrs M J Webb; Mrs C E Houghton.*

CC Number 277616

Information available Full accounts were available from the Charity Commission website.

General In 2005/06 the trust had assets of £7.2 million and an income of £428,000. Grants were made to 331 organisations totalling £413,000. Grants of over £1,000 each were listed as follows:

Medical grants including those for research – £137,000
The largest grants made were those awarded to: Brain Research Trust (£20,000); Diabetes Research and Education Centre, FORCE and North Devon Hospice (£15,000 each); Dr Hadwen Trust (£11,000); and Exeter Hospice (£10,000). Smaller grants made included those to: Chestnut Appeal for Prostate Cancer and Devon Air Ambulance (£5,000 each); Motor Neurone Disease (£2,500); R D and E League of Friends (£2,000); and ASBAH, Lee Smith Research Foundation, National Society for Epilepsy, Prostate Research Campaign and Stroke Association (£1,000 each). Other grants totalled £10,000.

Community, sport and leisure – £63,000
Beneficiaries included: Budleigh Salterton Town Council (£10,000); Exeter Community Transport Association, Norman Lockyer Observatory and Shelter Box Trust (£5,000 each); Exmouth and District Community Transport (£3,000); Sir Francis Chichester Trust (£2,000); and Exmouth Beach Rescue Lions Club – Budleigh Salterton and Royal Albert

Memorial Museum (£1,000 each). Other grants totalled £9,000.

Blind, deaf and physically disabled – £50,000
Beneficiaries included: West of England School (£10,000); Devon and Exeter Spastics Society and Talking Newspaper for the Blind (£5,000 each); Devon County Association for the Blind (£2,500); South West MS Centre (£1,500); and Bath Institute of Medical Engineering, British Wireless for the Blind Foundation, Calibre Cassette Library and Seeability (£1,000 each). Other grants of less than £1,000 each totalled £17,000.

Children's welfare – £45,000
Grant recipients included: Children's Hospice South West and CLIC (£5,000 each); Bristol Royal Hospital for Children and Great Ormond Street Hospital (£2,000 each); and Gingerbread, Happy Days Children's Charity, Springboard Opportunity Group and Whizz Kids (£1,000 each). Other grants of less than £1,000 each totalled £20,000.

Youth – £33,000
Grants included those made to: Sports Aid South West (£10,000); 1st Budleigh Salterton Scout Group and Rotary Club Exmouth (£5,000 each); VSO (£3,000); Adventure Trust for Girls (£2,000); and Tall Ships Youth Trust (£1,000). Other grants totalled £6,000, all of which were for less than £1,000 each.

Environment and conservation – £27,000
Grant recipients included: Devon Wildlife Trust (£20,000); and National Coastwatch Institution (£3,000). Other grants totalled £2,000.

Animal welfare – £18,000
Beneficiaries included: Cats Protection League (£2,500); Alternative Animal Sanctuary, Blue Cross, RSPB, RSPCA Cornwall and RSPCA Little Valley (£2,000 each); and Cinnamon Trust and RSPCA North Devon (£1,000 each). Other grants of less than £1,000 each totalled £3,250.

Homelessness – £15,000
Grant recipients included: St Petrock's Centre (£5,000); Exeter Homeless Action Group (£2,000); and Foyer Federation, Homestart, Open Door Centre, Shelter and St Mungo's Association (£1,000 each). Other grants of less than £1,000 each totalled £3,000.

Mentally disabled – £10,000
Grants were made to 13 organisation and included Devon Sheltered Homes (£2,500); and Bipoplar Organisation, DASS and Samaritans (£1,000 each).

Other grants of less than £1,000 each totalled £4,000.

Drugs, alcohol and prison – £7,000
Grants included those made to Addaction, Broadreach House, Crimestoppers and Freedom Trust (£1,000 each). Other grants of less than £1,000 each totalled £3,000.

Other – £7,000
There were 18 grants made in this category.

Senior – £3,000
There were seven grants made to organisations, all of which were for less than £1,000 each.

Exclusions No grants to individuals. No funding for religious buildings or to assist any organisations using animals for live experimental purposes or generally to fund overseas work.

Applications In writing to the correspondent. A subcommittee of trustees meets regularly to make grants of up to £5,000. Grants in excess of £5,000 are dealt with at one of the quarterly meetings of all the trustees.

The Duncan Norman Trust Fund

General

£65,000 (2004/05)

Beneficial area UK, with a preference for Merseyside.

Liverpool Charity and Voluntary Services, 14 Castle Street, Liverpool L2 0NJ

Tel. 0151 236 7728

Correspondent The Trustees

Trustees *J A H Norman; R K Asser; Mrs C Chapman; Mrs V S Hilton; Mrs C E Lazar; W Stothart.*

CC Number 250434

Information available Accounts were obtained from the Charity Commission website.

General This trust has general charitable purposes, particularly supporting organisations in the Merseyside area. In 2004/05 the trust fund had assets of £792,000 and an income of £29,000.

Grants to charities were made totalling £65,000, those of over £1,000 each went to: Oundle School Foundation (£25,000); St Jude's Centenary Appeal (£10,000); DEC Tsunami Earthquake Appeal (£5,000); Hospice of the Good Sheperd (£2,000); Macmillan Cancer (£1,300); and Tadmarton PCC, the Nicholas Knatchbull Memorial Fund and Wadham College University of Oxford (£1,000 each).

Exclusions No grants to individuals.

Applications The trust states that it only makes grants to charities known to the settlor and unsolicited applications are not considered.

The Normanby Charitable Trust

Social welfare, disability, general

£191,000 to organisations (2005/06)

Beneficial area UK, with a special interest in north east England.

Lythe Hall, Nr Whitby, North Yorkshire YO21 3RL

Correspondent The Trustees

Trustees *The 5th Marquis of Normanby; The Dowager Marchioness of Normanby; Lady Lepel Kornicka; Lady Evelyn Buchan; Lady Peronel Phipps de Cruz; Lady Henrietta Burridge.*

CC Number 252102

Information available Accounts were available from the Charity Commission website.

General 'The trustees have decided that only exceptionally will they help individuals in the future, and that they will confine their assistance for the moment, to mainly North Yorkshire and the North East of England.' The trust concentrates its support upon general charitable purposes, however previous research has suggested a preference for supporting social welfare, disability and the arts. The trust has occasionally considered giving grants for the preservation of religious and secular buildings of historical or architectural interest.

In 2005/06 the trust had assets of £9 million and an income of £260,000. Grants to 43 organisations were made totalling £191,000. The largest grants included those to: Scarborough Museums Trust and the York Minster Fund (£20,000 each); Abbeyfield UK and

Scarborough Blind and Partially Sighted Association (£15,000 each); and Clymping Village Hall and Whitby Mission and Seafarers' Trust (£10,000 each).

Other grants were made to: Ruswarp Village Hall (£7,500); Dragon School – Oxford, National Library of the Blind and Sleights Village Sports Field Pavilion Fund (£5,000 each); Marie Curie Cancer Care (£4,000); Ocean Youth Trust – North East, St Patrick's Cathedral – Dublin and Whitby & District Voluntary Action – Musicport (£2,000 each); Elizabeth Finn Care, Inter Active Whitby and District and Tom Carpenter Centre (£1,000 each); and Billingham players and Whitby Civic Society (£500 each).

Exclusions No grants to individuals, or to non-UK charities.

Applications In writing to the correspondent. There are no regular dates for trustees' meetings. Please note, only successful applications will be acknowledged.

The Earl of Northampton's Charity

Welfare

£115,000 to organisations (2005/06)

Beneficial area England, with a preference for London and the South East.

Mercers' Company, Mercers' Hall, Ironmonger Lane, London EC2V 8HE

Tel. 020 7726 4991 **Fax** 020 7600 1158

Email mail@mercers.co.uk

Website www.mercers.co.uk

Correspondent Charles H Parker, The Clerk

Trustee *The Mercers Company.*

CC Number 210291

Information available Full accounts were on file at the Charity Commission.

General In 2005/06 the charity's assets stood at £21,000. It had an income of £4.3 million and an expenditure of £434,000, most of which was for the cost of running its almshouses. Grants were made to 11 organisations totalling £115,000.

The largest grant was to the Charity of Sir Richard Whittington to distribute through its Relief in Need Programme.

The remaining grant recipients were: Trinity Hospital Clun (£24,000); Trinity Hospital Castle Rising (£10,000); Hornsey Management Agency (£7,500); Age Concern – Southwark, Southwark Churches Care and WPF Counselling and Psychotherapy (£5,000 each); Elderly Accommodation Councel and Furzedown Project (£3,000 each); Jubilee Trust Almshouses (£2,000); and St Michael's Church Framlingham (£250).

Applications In writing to the correspondent.

The Norton Foundation

Young people under 25 years of age (currently restricted to the areas of Birmingham and the county of Warwick)

£81,000 to organisations (2006)

Beneficial area UK, with a preference for Birmingham and the county of Warwick.

PO Box 10282,, Redditch, Worcestershire B97 5ZA

Email correspondent@ nortonfoundation.org

Website www.nortonfoundation.org

Correspondent Richard C Perkins, Correspondent

Trustees *R H Graham, Suggett Chair; Peter Adkins; Alan Bailey; Michael R Bailey; Parminder Singh Birdi; Mrs Jane Gaynor; Mrs Sarah V Henderson; Richard G D Hurley; Dr Dev Khosla; Brian W Lewis; Robert K Meacham; Richard C Perkins; Mrs Louise Sewell.*

CC Number 702638

Information available Accounts were obtained from the Charity Commission website.

General The trust was created in 1990. Its objectives are to help children and young people under 25 who are in 'need of care or rehabilitation or aid of any kind, particularly as a result of delinquency, deprivation, maltreatment or neglect or who are in danger of lapsing or relapsing into delinquency'.

In 2006 the trust had assets of £4 million, which generated an income of £122,000. Grants were made to both individuals (£53,000) and organisations

(£81,000) totalling £134,000. Grants were made to 19 institutions for the following purposes: education and training, housing, leisure activities, social work and holidays.

Beneficiaries of grants larger than £1,000 included City of Coventry Scout Country (£60,000), Happy Days, Furnace Fields Parents Centre, Tall Ships Youth Trust – Coventry and Warwickshire Branch and the Warwickshire Association of Youth Clubs (£2,000 each), Emmanuel Young People's Trust West (£1,500) and VCC Midlands, Depaul Trust, 870 House, the Foundation for Conductive Education, Emmanuel Community Church, Friendship Project for Children, Adventure Camps City Kids – Country Places, Birmingham Focus on Blindness and Whizz-Kidz (£1,000 each).

Exclusions No grants for the payment of debts that have already been incurred. Grants are not made for further education (except in very exceptional circumstances).

Applications By letter which should contain all the information required as detailed in the guidance notes for applicants. Guidance notes are available from the correspondent or from the foundation's website. Applications from organisations are normally processed by the trustees at their quarterly meetings. Application forms may be obtained from the correspondent or from the trust's website.

Norwood and Newton Settlement

Christian

£269,000 to organisations (2006)
Beneficial area England and Wales.

126 Beauly Way, Romford, Essex RM1 4XL

Tel. 01708 723670

Correspondent David M Holland, Trustee

Trustees *P Clarke; D M Holland; Mrs Stella Holland; W W Leyland.*

CC Number 234964

Information available Full accounts were on file at the Charity Commission.

General The trust supports Methodist and other mainline Free Churches and some other smaller UK charities in

which the founders had a particular interest. As a general rule, grants are for capital building projects which aim to improve the worship, outreach and mission of the church.

Where churches are concerned, the trustees take particular note of the contribution and promised contributions towards the project by members of the church in question.

In 2006 the settlement had assets of £8.4 million and an income of £317,000. Grants and donations were made to 43 organisations totalling £269,000.

The largest grants made included those to: Trinity Methodist Church – Romford (£30,000); Church on the Heath – Hampshire (£15,000); and Headington Baptist Church – Oxford, Holtwood Methodist Church – Dorset, Ingleton Methodist Church – North Yorkshire, St Marks Methodist Church – Gloucestershire (£10,000 each).

Other grants made included those to: Abbey URC – Romsey (£7,500); Hawkshead Hill Baptist Church – Cumbria (£5,000); Kelvedon URC – Essex and Moat URC – East Grinstead (£4,000 each); Bromborough Methodist Church – Wirral and Broomfield Methodist Church – Chelmsford (£2,000 each); and Ambassadors in Sport – Bolton (£1,000).

Exclusions Projects will not be considered where an application for National Lottery funding has been made or is contemplated. No grants to individuals, rarely to large UK charities and not for staff/running costs, equipment, repairs or general maintenance.

Applications In writing to the correspondent. In normal circumstances, the trustees' decision is communicated to the applicant within seven days (if a refusal), and if successful, immediately after the trustees' quarterly meetings.

The Sir Peter O'Sullevan Charitable Trust

Animals worldwide

£240,000 (2005/06)
Beneficial area Worldwide.

c/o NP Racing, 26 The Green, West Drayton, Middlesex UB7 7PQ

Website www.thevoiceofracing.com

Correspondent Nigel Payne, Trustee

Trustees *Christopher Spence; Lord Oaksey; Sir Peter O'Sullevan; Nigel Payne; Geoffrey Hughes; Bob McCreery.*

CC Number 1078889

Information available Accounts were on file at the Charity Commission.

General Registered with the Charity Commission in January 2000, in 2005/06 it had an income of £327,000 mainly from fundraising events. Grants were made totalling £240,000.

There were six grants of £40,000 each. Beneficiaries were Blue Cross, Brooke Hospital for Animals, Compassion in World Farming, International League for the Protection of Horses, the Racing Welfare Charities and the Thoroughbred Rehabilitation Centre.

Applications In writing to the correspondent.

The Oak Trust

General

£39,000 to organisations (2006).
Beneficial area UK.

Birkett Long, Red House, Colchester Road, Halstead, Essex CO9 2DZ

Tel. 01787 272231

Email bruce.ballard@birkettlong.co.uk

Correspondent Bruce Ballard, Clerk

Trustees *Revd A C C Courtauld; J Courtauld; Dr E Courtauld; Mrs C M Courtauld.*

CC Number 231456

Information available Full accounts were available from the charity Commission website.

General The trust has a preference for supporting those charities that it has a special interest in, knowledge of or association with. In 2006 the trust had assets of £615,000 and an income of £28,000. Grants were made to 44 organisations totalling £39,000, of which 47% received £500 each.

Grant recipients included the Cirdan Sailing Trust, Christian Aid and Save the Children (£3,000 each), Prader-Willi Syndrome Association – UK (£2,000), St Luke's Hospital for the Clergy, Ataxia – Telangiectasia Society, Back to Work for the Over 40s, Dhaka Ahansia Mission and the Marine Conservation Society

(£500 each) and the Manranta Orphanage Ministries – Malawi (£250).

Exclusions No support to individuals.

Applications In writing to the correspondent. Trustees meet twice a year. Unsuccessful applications are not replied to.

The Oakdale Trust

Social work, medical, general

£214,000 (2004/05)

Beneficial area Worldwide, especially Wales.

Tansor House, Tansor, Oundle, Peterborough PE8 5HS

Email oakdale@tanh.demon.co.uk

Correspondent Rupert Cadbury

Trustees *B Cadbury; Mrs F F Cadbury; R A Cadbury; F B Cadbury; Mrs O Tatton-Brown; Dr R C Cadbury.*

CC Number 218827

Information available Accounts were on file at the Charity Commission.

General This trust's main areas of interest include:

- Welsh-based social and community projects
- medical – support groups operating in Wales and UK-based research projects
- UK-based charities working in the third world
- environmental conservation in the UK and overseas
- penal reform.

Some support is also given to the arts, particularly where there is a Welsh connection. The average grant is approximately £900.

In 2004/05 the trust had assets of £5.2 million and an income of £286,000, including Gift Aid of £153,000. Grants were made to over 220 organisations and totalled £214,000.

There were 94 grants of £1,000 or more, beneficiares included: CARE International UK (£10,000); British Red Cross and Oxfam (£7,000 each); the Brandon Centre, CARE International UK, Concern Universal and Medical Foundation for Care of Victims of Torture (£5,000 each); the Council for National Parks (£4,500); International Children's Trust (£4,000); the Magic of

Life Trust (£3,000); Cambridge Female Education Trust, International Childcare Trust, Medical Aid for Palestinians, Quaker Peace Studies Trust and St John Ambulance in Wales (£2,000 each); Howard League for Penal Reform (£1,500), Quaker Peace and Social Witness (£1,200); and Breast Cancer Campaign, Brecknockshire Citizen Advocacy, Cardiff CAB, Dhaka Ahsania Mission, Great Ormond Street Children's Charity, Health Unlimited, Hearing Dogs for Deaf People, Kurdish Human Rights Project, L'Arche Brecon Community, Newport Action for the Single Homeless, Pembrokeshire Mind, Research Institute for Care of the Elderly and Simon Community (£1,000 each).

Other beneficiraies included Community Action Machynlleth and District and Dewi Sant Housing Association (£750 each), Africa Equipment for Schools, Appropriate Technology Asia, CRUSE Bereavement Care, Carmarthen Youth Project, Child Health International , Cinnamon Trust, Eating Disorders Association, Groundwork Greater Nottingham, Maun Animal Welfare Society, Positive Vision, Refugee Support Centre, Starlight Children's Foundation and Welsh Association Youth Clubs (£500 each), Crest Co-operative, the Disabled Drivers Association, Gwent Epilepsy Group, the New Forest Owl Sanctuary, Rural Stress Information Network and Welshpool Community Transport (£250 each) and Macular Disease Society Support Group (£100).

Exclusions No grants to individuals, holiday schemes, sports activities or expeditions.

Applications An application form is available from the trust; however, applicants are free to submit requests in any format, providing they are clear and concise, covering aims, achievements, plans and needs, and supported by a budget. Applications for grants in excess of £1,000 are asked to submit a copy of a recent set of audited accounts (these can be returned on request). The trustees meet twice a year in April and October to consider applications. The deadline for these meetings is 1 March and 1 September respectively; no grants are awarded between meetings. Unsuccessful applicants are not normally notified and similarly applications are not acknowledged even when accompanied by an sae.

The Oakmoor Charitable Trust

General

£36,000 (2005)

Beneficial area UK.

Rathbone Trust Company Limited, 159 New Bond St, London W1S 2UD

Tel. 020 7399 0000 **Fax** 020 73990 013

Correspondent Kevin Custis, Administrator

Trustees *Rathbone Trust Company Ltd; P M H Andreae; Mrs R J Andreae.*

CC Number 258516

Information available Full accounts were available from the Charity Commission website.

General Established in 1969 the trust receives regular donations from the settlor, Peter Andreae.

In 2005 the trust had assets of £1.2 million and an income of £33,000. Grants were made to organisations totalling £36,000.

The largest grants made to organisations included Save Britain's Heritage (£7,500), the Institute of Economic Affairs (£6,000) Catholic Bishops' Conference of England & Wales and CAFOD (£5,000 each) and the Royal Academy Trust (£2,500).

Smaller grants of £1,000 or less included the Brompton Association, Hampshire County Learning, Gilbert White's House (£1,000 each), Dean & Chapter Winchester and Friends of the Elderly (£500 each), Dan's Fund for Burns and the Institute of Economic Affairs (£250 each) and Grange Park Opera (£150).

Exclusions No grants to individuals.

Applications The trust states that it does not respond to unsolicited applications.

The Odin Charitable Trust

General

£201,000 (2005/06)

Beneficial area UK.

PO Box 1898, Bradford-on-Avon, Wiltshire BA15 1YS

Correspondent Mrs S G P Scotford, Trustee

Trustees *Mrs S G P Scotford; Mrs A H Palmer; Mrs D L Kelly; Mrs P C Cherry.*

CC Number 1027521

Information available Accounts were on file at the Charity Commission.

General In 2004/05 the trust had assets of £3.9 million and an income of £173,000. Grants were made to 53 organisations, some of whom have been awarded recurrent grants up to 2006. A total of £201,000 was given during the year, including £91,000 to be distributed between four of the beneficiaries up to 2006.

Although the objectives of the charity are wide, the trust has a preference for making grants towards: furthering the arts; providing care for people who are disabled and disadvantaged; supporting hospices, homeless people, prisoners' families, refugees, gypsies and 'tribal groups'; and furthering research into false memories and dyslexia.

The trustees are more likely to support small organisations and those that by the nature of their work find it difficult to attract funding.

Beneficiaries receiving recurrent grants were British False Memory Society (£117,000 in three grants to 2006), Cardiff Gypsy and Traveller Project (£9,000 in three grants to 2006), Interact Reading Service (£6,000 in three grants to 2006) and Action for Prisoners' Families (£4,500 in three grants to 2006).

Other beneficiaries included Royal West of England Academy (£8,000), St Giles Trust (£3,000), Edinburgh Young Carers Project, Hope for the Homeless, Hospice Homecare, Julian House, New Bridge and Prison Fellowship (£2,000 each), Detainees Support and Help Unit and Harvest Trust (£1,500 each), Acorns Children's Hospice Trust and Music in Hospitals (£1,000 each) and AbilityNet, Asylum Welcome, Lewisham Churches for Asylum Seekers and Women in Prison (£500 each).

Exclusions Applications from individuals are not considered.

Applications In writing to the correspondent.

The Ogle Christian Trust

Evangelical Christianity

£118,000 (2004)

Beneficial area Worldwide.

43 Woolstone Road, Forest Hill, London SE23 2TR

Correspondent Mrs F J Putley, Trustee

Trustees *D J Harris, Chair; R J Goodenough; S Proctor; Mrs F J Putley; Mrs L M Quanrud.*

CC Number 1061458

Information available Accounts were on file at the Charity Commission.

General This trust mainly directs funds to new initiatives in evangelism worldwide, support of missionary enterprises, publication of Scriptures and Christian literature, pastor training and famine and other relief work.

In 2004 it had assets of £2.5 million and an income of £110,000. Grants totalled £118,000. There were 78 grants made in the year of which 35 were for £1,000 or more and were listed in the accounts.

By far the largest grant went to Operation Mobilisation (£22,000). Other beneficiaries included Elam Ministries and the Translation Trust (£6,000 each), Nambikkai Foundation (£4,500), CCSM and Middle East Media (£4,000), All Nations Christian College, International Christian College and London School of Theology (£3,500 each), Dehra Dun, France Mission Trust and Siliguri (£3,000 each), Friends of China, IFES, PECAN, Tearfund and Thane HIV/AIDS Project (£2,000 each), Off the Fence (£1,500) and 3P Ministries, Albanian Evangelical Mission, Chessington Evangelical Church, Christian Viewpoint for Men, Middle East Concern and the XL Project (£1,000 each).

Unlisted grants totalled £18,000.

Exclusions Applications from individuals are discouraged; those granted require accreditation by a sponsoring organisation. Grants are rarely made for building projects. Funding will not be offered in response to general appeals from large national organisations.

Applications In writing to the correspondent, accompanied by documentary support and an sae. Trustees meet in May and November, but applications can be made at any time.

The Oikonomia Trust

Christian

£49,000 (2005/06)

Beneficial area UK and overseas.

98 White Lee Road, Batley, West Yorkshire WF17 8AF

Correspondent Colin Mountain, Trustee

Trustees *D H Metcalfe; R H Metcalfe; S D Metcalfe; C Mountain; R O Owens.*

CC Number 273481

Information available Full accounts were on file at the Charity Commission.

General The trust supports evangelical work, famine and other relief through Christian agencies. The trust is not looking for new outlets as those it has knowledge of are sufficient to absorb its available funds.

In 2005/06 it had assets of £407,000 and an income of £86,000. Grants were made to 24 organisations and totalled £49,000.

Beneficiaries included Bethel Church (£5,000), Arab Christian Ministry (£3,500), Asia Link, Association of Evangelists, BCH Hospital, Barnabus Trust, Caring for Life, Drumchapel Church and Leeds City Mission (£3,000 each), Slavic Gospel Association (£2,500), AWM, Japan Mission and Outreach Workers Fund (£2,000 each), the Faith Mission (£1,500), Christian Blind Mission and Soldiers and Sailors Scripture RA (£1,000 each) and Mission India (£500).

Exclusions No grants made in response to general appeals from large national organisations.

Applications In writing to the correspondent, although the trust has previously stated that known needs are greater than the trust's supplies. If an applicant desires an answer, an sae should be enclosed. Applications should arrive in January.

The Old Broad Street Charity Trust

General

£79,000 to organisations (2005/06)

Beneficial area UK and overseas.

Eagle House, 110 Jermyn Street, London SW1Y 6RH

Tel. 020 7451 9000

Correspondent The Secretary to the Trustees

Trustees *Mrs Evelyn J Franck; Mrs Martine Cartier-Bresson; Adrian T J Stanford; Peter A Hetherington; Christopher J Sheridan.*

CC Number 231382

Information available Accounts were on file at the Charity Commission.

General The objects of the trust are general, although most of the funds are given towards the arts. It was the wish of Louis Franck, the founder, that part of the income should be used to fund scholarships, preferably for UK citizens to reach the highest levels of executive management in banking and financial institutions. It gives around half of its grant total each year to the Louis Franck Scholarship Fund for this purpose (£35,000 in seven scholarships in 2005/06).

In 2005/06 it had assets of £2.2 million and an income of £178,000. Grants totalling £79,000 were made to eleven organisations, all but four were supported in the previous year.

Beneficiaries were Foundation Henri Cartier-Bresson (£45,000), Société Française le Lutte contre la Cecite et contre le Tranchome (£10,000), Bezirksfursorge – Saanen (£8,900), International Menuhin Music Academy (£4,500), English Speaking Union in Lebanon and Royal Academy of Arts (£2,500), Fondation de Bellerive (£2,300), the National Gallery Trust (£2,000), Tate Gallery Foundation (£1,000) and Artangel and Whitechapel Art Gallery (£400 each).

Exclusions The trustees only support organisations of which they personally have some knowledge.

Applications In writing to the correspondent. Unsolicited applications are not considered.

Old Possum's Practical Trust

General

£371,000 to organisations and individuals (2005/06)

Beneficial area UK and overseas.

Baker Tilly, 5th Floor, Exchange House, 446 Midsummer Boulevard, Milton Keynes MK9 2EA

Tel. 01908 687800 **Fax** 01908 687801

Website www. old-possums-practical-trust.org.uk

Correspondent Mrs Judith Hooper, Trustee

Trustees *Mrs Esme Eliot; Mrs Judith Hooper; Mrs D Simpson.*

CC Number 328558

Information available Full accounts were on file at the Charity Commission.

General The primary objective of the trust is to increase knowledge and appreciation of any matters of historic, artistic, architectural, aesthetic, musical or theatrical interest. The trust however is not limited to that primary object and considers all worthwhile causes carefully.

The trust states that grants are more likely to be given to projects that involve children or young people; disabled or disadvantaged people and communities.

In 2005/06 the trust had assets of £7.3 million and an income of £487,000. Grants were made £371,000 and were broken down into the following categories:

Educational support

Grants were awarded to 12 organisations in this category totalling £49,000. The largest grant was awarded to Merchant Halliday School (£20,000). Other grant recipients included InterAct Reading Service (£6,000); Wildlife Trusts, National Association for Gifted Children and Kings College London (£3,000 each); Books Abroad and Inspire (£2,000 each); and the Greenwich Toy library Association (£1,000).

The arts and historical conservation

Grants were made to 20 organisations and two individuals. The two largest grants in this category were given to London Library (£25,000); Royal Academy of Music (£20,000); Friends of Little Gidding (£16,000); and Museum of Childhood (£10,000). Other beneficiaries included National Portrait Gallery and Wordsworth Trust (£6,000 each); Anglican Centre and London's Children's Ballet (£5,000 each); Living Archive, Poetry Trust and Young Vic (£3,000 each); British Youth Opera (£2,500); Royal Society of Literature (£1,500); Historian Theatre Co. (£1,000); and TS Eliot Poetry Prize (£250).

Support for the disabled and disadvantaged

Grants were awarded to 32 organisations totalling £190,000. The largest grant by far was awarded to Book Trade Benevolent Society BTBS (£110,000). Other grant recipients included Farms for City Children, Hearing Dogs for Deaf People, Louis Barclay Leukaemia Fund and Motor Neuron Disease Association (£5,000 each); Tuberous Sclerosis Society (£3,000); Peaceful Place Day Care Centre (£2,500); Islington Carers Forum and React (£2,000); Winged Fellowship Trust, Brainwave, Summer Dreams and Children's Fire and Burn Trust (£1,500 each); and the Ark Charity and Waggy Tails Rescue (£1,000 each).

Exclusions The trust does not support the following:

- activities or projects already completed
- capital building projects
- personal training and education e.g. tuition or living costs for college or university
- projects outside the UK
- medical care or resources feasibility studies, national charities having substantial amounts of potential funding likely from other sources.

Applications On an application form available on the trust's website The trust has stated: 'The trustees wish to continue the policy of using the trust's income to support a few carefully chosen cases, generally located in the UK, rather than make a large number of small grants. The emphasis will be on continued support of those institutions and individuals who have received support in the past. Unfortunately we have to disappoint the great majority of applicants who nevertheless continue to send appeal letters. The trustees do not welcome telephone calls from applicants soliciting funds.' For further information please refer to the trust's website.

The John Oldacre Foundation

Research and education in agricultural sciences

£86,000 (2005/06)

Beneficial area UK.

Hazleton House, Hazleton, Cheltenham, Gloucestershire GL54 4EB

Correspondent Henry Shouler, Trustee

Trustees H B Shouler; S J Charnock; D G Stevens.

CC Number 284960

Information available Full accounts were on file at the Charity Commission.

General Grants are made to universities and agricultural colleges towards the advancement and promotion, for public benefit, of research and education in agricultural sciences and the publication of useful results.

In 2005/06 it had assets of £3.5 million and an income of £108,000. Grants were made totalling £86,000.

Beneficiaries were University of Bristol (£28,000), Royal Agricultural College (£20,000), Nuffield Fanning Trust (£23,000) and Arable Research Centre (£13,000).

A grant to an individual was made totalling £2,500.

Exclusions No grants towards tuition fees.

Applications In writing to the correspondent.

Onaway Trust

General

£131,000 (2005)

Beneficial area UK, USA and worldwide.

275 Main Street, Shadwell, Leeds LS17 8LH

Tel. 0113 265 9611

Email david@onaway.org

Website www.onaway.org

Correspondent David Watters, Trust Administrator

Trustees J Morris; A Breslin; C Howles; Elaine Fearnside; Annie Smith; Ms V A Worwood; D Watters.

CC Number 268448

Information available Full accounts were available from the Charity Commission website.

General This trust's objectives are stated on its website as follows: 'To relieve poverty and suffering amongst indigenous peoples by providing seed grants for (small) self-help, self-sufficiency and environmentally sustainable projects. This is expressed in many areas and includes the protection of the environment, the support of children and adults with learning difficulties, the assistance of smaller charities whose aim is to safeguard sick, injured, threatened or abandoned animals and emergency relief for victims of disaster.'

In 2005 the trust had assets of £4.6 million and an income of £167,000. Grants were made to 32 organisations totalling £131,000 and awarded in the following categories:

Indigenous – America totalling £36,000
Beneficiaries in this category included Plenty USA who received 5 grants for separate projects totalling £17,000. Other beneficiaries were Care International (£5,000) and American Indian Institute (£1,000).

Indigenous – Rest of the world £42,000
The largest grant was given to Centre for Rural Education and Economic Development for India Tsunami Response (£14,000). Other grant recipients included St Nicholas Home for the Aged – Middle East (£8,000), Forest Peoples Programme Africa and SOBTI – India (£5,000 each) and Wells for India (£2,000).

Environmental – £18,000
Beneficiaries were the Woodland Trust and Earth Action Network (£8,000 each) and Magic of Life Butterfly Trust (£2,000).

Animal welfare – £9,000
One-off grants were made to Dian Fossey Gorilla Fund – Africa and Durrell Wildlife Conservation Trust (£4,000) and Romania Animal Rescue (£1,000).

Other Onaway projects – £27,000
Beneficiaries were DEC – Asian Earthquake Appeal (£10,000), Jeel Al Amal – Middle East (£8,000), Oakhaven Hospice Trust (£3,000), Welfare Association – Middle East (£2,500) and Khadeejeh Ayyad – Middle East, the Simon Community and St Gemma's Hospice (£1,000 each).

Exclusions No grants for administration costs, travel expenses or projects considered unethical or detrimental to the struggle of indigenous people.

Applications In writing to the correspondent, enclosing an sae.

Oppenheim Foundation

General

Around £38,000 (2005/06)

Beneficial area UK.

33 King Street, London EC2V 2DQ

Tel. 020 7600 7900

Correspondent Peter Smith, Trustee

Trustees J N Oppenheim; T S Oppenheim; P A Smith.

CC Number 279246

Information available Information was available from the Charity Commission website.

General In 2005/06 the trust had an income of £181 and a total expenditure of £43,000. No further information was available.

Applications The trust stated that it does not consider applications from organisations with whom it has had no previous contact.

Oppenheimer Charitable Trust

General

£60,000 (2004/05)

Beneficial area UK.

17 Charterhouse Street, London EC1N 6RA

Tel. 020 7404 4444

Correspondent The Secretary to the Trust

Trustees Michael Farmiloe; Michael Page; Brian MacDonald.

CC Number 200395

Information available Full accounts were available from the Charity Commission website.

General This trust has general charitable purposes for the wellbeing and benefit of people living in areas where companies of the De Beers group operate. The following areas are particularly supported: medicine and health; children and youth; older people; general welfare; and the arts.

In 2004/05 the trust's assets stood at £4,000. It had an income of £60,000, which it paid out in grants to 99 charitable bodies.

The majority of grants awarded were for £350 each. The largest grants were made to: Royal Opera House Foundation (£7,000); Evelina Sick Children's Hospital and the Victoria and Albert Museum (£5,000 each); the Council of Commonwealth Societies (£3,000); the English Speaking Union and Macmillan Cancer Relief (£1,500 each); and Action for Children in Conflict, Moorfield's Development Fund, the Art Fund and Heritage of London Trust (£1,000 each).

Grants of less than £1,000 each included Brainwave, Children's Fire and Burn Trust, Debra, the National Autistic Society, South of Scotland Youth Awards Trust and the Children's Heart Foundation (£500 each) and Age Concern – Southwark, Christian Lewis Trust, Coram Family, Lowe Syndrome Trust, Raynaud's & Scleroderma Association, Women's Health Concern and Queen Elizabeth's Foundation (£350 each).

Exclusions No educational grants are given.

Applications In writing to the correspondent. Trustees meet in January, April, July and October.

The Ormsby Charitable Trust

General

£89,000 (2005/06)

Beneficial area UK, London and the South East.

Wasing Old Rectory, Shalford Hill, Aldermaston, Reading RG7 4NB

Correspondent Mrs K McCrossan, Trustee

Trustees *Rosemary Ormsby David; Angela Ormsby Chiswell; Katrina Ormsby McCrossan.*

CC Number 1000599

Information available Full accounts were on file at the Charity Commission.

General In 2005/06 the trust had assets of £1.7 million and an income of £749.000. Donations were made to 28 organisations totalling £89,000, 35% of which were for £2,000 each. The largest grant was made to Breast Cancer Haven (£22,000).

Other beneficiaries included Hammersmith & Fulham Carers Centre, the Home Farm Trust and Wessex Children's Hospice Trust (£4,000 each), Galapogos Conservation Trust (£3,500), Action on Addiction, British Heart Foundation, Thames Valley & Chiltern Air Ambulance Trust and Phyllis Tuckwell Hospice (£2,000), the Living Paintings Trust, St Mungo's Community housing Association and the Royal Marsden Cancer Campaign (£500).

Exclusions No grants to individuals, animals or religious causes.

Applications In writing to the correspondent.

The Ouseley Trust

Choral services of the Church of England, Church in Wales and Church of Ireland, choir schools

£102,000 (2005/06)

Beneficial area England, Wales and Ireland.

127 Coleherne Court, London SW5 0EB

Tel. 020 7373 1950 **Fax** 020 7341 0043

Email clerk@ouseleytrust.org.uk

Website www.ouseleytrust.org.uk

Correspondent Martin Williams, Clerk

Trustees *Dr Christopher Robinson, Chair; Dr J A Birch; Rev Canon Mark Boyling; Dr S M Darlington; Prof B W Harvey; Mrs Gillian Perkins; Martin Pickering; Adam Ridley; Dr John Rutter; Revd A F Walters; Richard White; Sir David Willcocks.*

CC Number 527519

Information available Full accounts were available from the Charity Commission website.

General The trust administers funds made available from trusts of the former St Michael's College, Tenbury. Its objective is 'projects which promote and maintain to a high standard the choral

services of the Church of England, the Church in Wales and the Church of Ireland', including contributions to endowment funds, courses, fees and the promotion of religious, musical and secular education for pupils connected to the churches and observing choral liturgy.

In 2005 the trust had assets of £3.3 million and an income of £119,000. Grants were made totalling £95,000, broken down as follows:

Endowments – 6 Grants totalling £64,000
Grants awarded will usually be paid in one sum to provide an immediate contribution to an endowment fund. Beneficiaries were Hereford Cathedral (£25,000), Carlisle Cathedral (£15,000), Abbey School – Tewkesbury (£14,000), St Thomas the Apostle – Wigston (£5,000), and St Mary the Virgin (£2,000).

Fees for individuals – 9 grants totalling £23,000
Applications must be submitted by an institution. Grants awarded will be paid in one sum as an immediate contribution. The trustees may require an assurance that the sum offered will achieve the purpose for which help has been requested. Beneficiaries by institution were York Minster in two grants (£6,000), Abbey School – Tewkesbury, St James's School – Grimsby and Well Cathedral School (£4,000 each), Salisbury Cathedral School (£3,000) and Christ Church Cathedral School and Wells Cathedral School (£2,000 each).

Other – 3 grants totalling £8,000
Grants were made to Bradford Cathedral and Oundle International Organ Festival (£3,000 each) and Thomas Attwood Project (£2,000).

Grants will be awarded only where there is a clear indication that an already acceptable standard of choral service will be raised. Under certain circumstances grants may be awarded for organ tuition. Each application will be considered on its merits, keeping in mind the specific terms of the trust deed. Unique, imaginative ventures will receive careful consideration.

The trust does not normally award further grants to successful applicants within a two-year period. The trustees' policy is to continue making grants to cathedrals, choral foundations and parish churches throughout England, Wales and Ireland.

Exclusions Grants will not be awarded to help with the cost of fees for ex-choristers, for chant books, hymnals or psalters. Grants will not be made for the purchase of new instruments or for the installation of an instrument from another place of worship where this involves extensive reconstruction. Under normal circumstances, grants will not be awarded for buildings, cassettes, commissions, compact discs, furniture, pianos, robes, tours or visits. No grants are made towards new organs or the installation of one which involves extensive reconstruction.

Applications Applicants are strongly advised to obtain a copy of the trust's guidelines (either from the correspondent or their website, currently under construction at the time of writing) before drafting an application. Applications must be submitted by an institution on a form available from the correspondent. Closing dates for applications are 31 January for the March meeting and 30 June for the October meeting.

The Owen Family Trust

Christian, general

£87,000 (2005/06)
Beneficial area UK, with a preference for West Midlands.

Mill Dam House, Mill Lane, Aldridge, Walsall WS9 0NB

Tel. 0121 526 3131

Correspondent A D Owen, Trustee

Trustees *Mrs H G Jenkins; A D Owen.*

CC Number 251975

Information available Full accounts were available from the Charity Commission website.

General Grants are given to independent and church schools, Christian youth centres, churches, community organisations, arts, conservation and medical charities. Support is given throughout the UK, with a preference for the West Midlands.

In 2005/06 the trust had assets of £1.1 million and an income of £68,000. During the year 36 grants were made totalling £87,000.

The largest grants were made to Oundle School Foundation (£15,000), Walsall Museum and Art Galleries Development Trust (£8,000) and Lozells Project, Frontier Youth Trust, Lichfield

Cathedral Music Campaign, the Shakespeare Centre and Black Country Museum Development Trust (£5,000 each).

Other beneficiaries included Parish of Bilston Special Projects and St Matthew's Church PCC – Wolverhampton (£3,000 each), Symphony Hall Birmingham Ltd and Friends of Whitchurch Heritage (£2,500 each), Walk Thru the Bible Ministries and Explore (£1,000 each), St John's Church – Wimborne (£500) and the Chicken Shed Theatre Trust (£100).

Exclusions The trust states 'No grants to individuals unless part of a charitable organisation.'

Applications In writing to the correspondent including annual report, budget for project and general information regarding the application. Organisations need to be a registered charity, however an 'umbrella' body which would hold funds would be acceptable. Only a small number of grants can be given each year and unsuccessful applications are not acknowledged unless an sae is enclosed. The trustees meet quarterly.

The Pallant Charitable Trust

Church music

£30,000 to organisations and individuals (2005/06)
Beneficial area UK, with a preference for areas within 50 miles of Chichester.

c/o Thomas Eggar, The Corn Exchange, Baffins Lane, Chichester, West Sussex PO19 1GE

Tel. 01243 786111 **Fax** 01243 532001

Correspondent The Clerk to the Trustees

Trustees *A J Thurlow; S A E Macfarlane; C Smyth; C J Henville.*

CC Number 265120

Information available Full accounts were available from the Charity Commission website.

General The trust's objective is to promote mainstream church music both in choral and instrumental form. Consideration will be given for schemes that provide training and opportunities for children or adults in the field of church music and with an emphasis on

traditional services. Such schemes may include:

- vocal or instrumental (in particular organ) training
- choral work in the context of church services
- the training of choir leaders, organists or directors
- the provision and the purchase of equipment necessary for the above.

In 2005/06 the trust had assets of £1.2 million and an income of £52,000. Grants were made totalling £30,000.

Beneficiaries were: Choristers Scholarships, Prebendal School – School Fees (£12,000); Guildford Cathedral Music Development (£5,000); Arundel Cathedral Music and St Nicholas Church Arundel PCC (£3,000 each); Dean and Chapter of Chichester (£2,900) and RSCM Sussex Area (£750).

Exclusions No grants to individuals, nor for computer equipment or sponsorship for concerts.

Applications In writing to the correspondent. Applications should be submitted by recognised organisations such as churches, schools, colleges or charities working in the field of church music.

The Panacea Society

Christian religion, relief of sickness

£355,000 (2005)
Beneficial area UK, with a strong preference for Bedford and its immediate region.

14 Albany Road, Bedford MK40 3PH

Tel. 01234 359737

Email admin@panacea-society.org

Website www.panacea-society.org

Correspondent David McLynn, Business Administrator

Trustees *Miss G Powell; J L Coghill; Mrs R Klien; L Aston; Revd Jane Shaw.*

CC Number 227530

Information available Full accounts were available from the Charity Commission website.

General The work of this Christian charity, established in 1926, is informed by the teachings of Joanna Southcott. In meeting its charitable objectives the society from time to time makes grants out of its income.

Funding criteria

The trustees have agreed the following policy criteria should apply in all cases for a funding application to be selected for further consideration. The purpose of the funding should be:

- Work related to the advancement of the religious beliefs of the society as defined by its original charitable objects.
- Sponsoring the writing, publication, and distribution of religious works associated with the visitation.
- Undertaking the duties and responsibilities incumbent on being the custodian of Joanna Southcott's Box of Sealed Writings.
- Sponsoring research by recognised academic institutions into the history and theology of the society and its antecedents.
- Supporting the work of the Church of England in advancing the Christian religion especially in the Bedford area, or in aspects of theology or liturgy that relate to the society's specific interests.
- Supporting recognised local organisations dealing with the relief of sickness within the Bedford area.

The trust states that grants will only be made for charitable purposes to UK-based organisations only. Priority will be given to funding requests that promote the religious aims of the society, benefit large numbers of people and are made on behalf of organisations rather than individuals.

In 2005 the society had assets of £22.3 million and an income of £754,000. Grants were made totalling £355,000, broken down into the following categories:

Oxford Prophecy Project – 2 grants totalling £202,000

Both grants were made to the University of Oxford. The first totalled £200,000 and the second £2,000.

Educational projects – 3 grants totalling £71,000

Grants were made to Doctoral scholarship funding (£54,000), University of Cambridge (£16,000) and Liverpool Hope University (£1,000).

Health/medical projects – 7 grants totalling £55,000

Grant recipients were Bedfordshire and Northamptonshire MS Therapy Centre (£12,000), Macmillan Nursing, Macmillan Hospice, Age Concern – Guild House and Leonard Cheshire Enabling Project (£10,000 each),

BedCHAR Bedford (£2,000) and Cruise Bedford (£1,000).

Religious projects – 4 grants totalling £28,000

Grant recipients were St Paul's Church Bedford who received two grants for separate projects (£13,000), BELIEF Bedford (£10,000) and Bishop of Salisbury (£5,000).

Exclusions The society will not consider funding:

- to political parties or political lobbying
- to pressure groups which support commercial ventures
- for non-charitable activities which could be paid out of central or local government funds.

Applications The trust has previously stated that it receives many applications that they are unable or unwilling to support. Please read the grant criteria carefully before submitting an application. Unsolicited applications are not responded to.

Any organisation considering applying for funding support should make a formal application in writing to the correspondent. The application should set out the purpose for which the funding is required, and explain how it falls within the funding criteria and complies with their requirements. Full information on the work of the applicant body together with details of how the proposed funding will be applied should be given.

The correspondent will acknowledge receipt of an application, and indicate if the application falls within their parameters. At this point the society may call for additional information, or indicate that it is unable to consider the application further. Most applications fail because they fall outside the criteria, however the society does not provide additional reasons why it is unable to support a particular application.

When all relevant information has been received the application will be discussed at the next meeting of the society's trustees together with other valid applications. The trustees may at that meeting refuse or defer any application or request further information without giving reasons. Applicants will be advised in writing of the trustees' decision. For full details visit the society's website.

Panahpur Charitable Trust

Missionaries, general

£221,000 to organisations and individuals (2005)

Beneficial area UK, overseas.

Jacob Cavenagh and Skeet, 5 Robin Hood Lane, Sutton, Surrey SM1 2SW

Tel. 020 8643 1166

Correspondent The Trust Department

Trustees *P East; Miss D Haile; D Harland; A Matheson; A E Perry; J Perry.*

CC Number 214299

Information available Full accounts were on file at the Charity Commission.

General The trust's 2005/06 accounts stated that: 'the trust was established for the distribution of funds to Christian charities and other Christian organisations and individuals, both in the UK and overseas. In the past the trust has sought to support a wide range of Christian missionary organisations. Over the last few years it has sought not only to form partnerships with a small number of organisations and people, but to work with them in a more meaningful relationship and over a greater period of time.'

In 2005/06 the trust had assets of £5.8 million and an income of £1.5 million. Grants totalled £221,000, broken down into the following categories:

- Missionary work – overseas totalled £169,000
- Mission work – UK totalled £42,000
- Relief work totalled £6,000
- Direct preaching of the Gospel totalled £4,000.

The largest grants were received by Operation Agape (£50,000), Oasis International (£33,000), Panahpur Kandi Christian Trust (£19,000), Global Connections (£15,000), Emmanuel Healthcare (£12,000) and All Nations Christian College (£11,000).

Other grants included those to Inheritors and Viva Network (£8,000 each), On the Move, People International, South Asian Concern and Vision Tarpuy (£5,000 each), the Gathering (£3,000), Link Charitable Trust (£2,000), Redcliffe College (£1,000) and UCB (£500).

Applications The trustees do their own research and do not respond to unsolicited applications.

Panton Trust

Animal wildlife worldwide; environment UK

£43,000 to organisations (2005)
Beneficial area UK and overseas.

Ramsay House, 18 Vera Avenue, Grange Park, London N21 1RB
Tel. 020 8370 7700
Correspondent Laurence Slavin, Trustee
Trustees *L M Slavin; R Craig.*
CC Number 292910
Information available Full accounts were on file at the Charity Commission.

General The trust states that it is 'concerned with any animal or animals or with wildlife in any part of the world, or with the environment of the UK or any part thereof. The trustees consider applications from a wide variety of sources and favour smaller charities which do not have the same capacity for large-scale fundraising as major charities in this field.'

The trust had assets of £208,000 and an income of £46,000. Grants were made totalling £43,000. Beneficiaries included Flora and Fauna International (£4,500), Royal Botanic Garden Kew and St Tiggywinkles Wildlife Hospital (£4,000 each), PDSA and the Whales and Dolphin Conservation Society (£3,000 each), British Trust for Conservation Volunteers and Canine Partner (£2,000 each).

Other grants of less than £1,000 totalled £11,000.

Applications In writing to the correspondent.

The Paragon Trust

General

£148,000 (2004/05)
Beneficial area UK.

c/o Thomson Snell and Passmore, Solicitors, 3 Lonsdale Gardens, Tunbridge Wells, Kent TN1 1NX
Tel. 01892 510000
Correspondent The Trustees
Trustees *Rt Hon. J B B Wrenbury; Revd Canon R F Coppin; Miss L J Whistler; P*

Cunningham; P Bagwell-Purefoy; Dr F E Cornish.
CC Number 278348
Information available Full accounts were on file at the Charity Commission.

General In 2004/05 the trust had assets of £2.1 million and an income of £91,000. Grants to over 70 organisations totalled £148,000. The majority of donations are standing orders.

The beneficiaries if the largest grants were Tsunami Earthquake Appeal (£50,000) and British Red Cross (£20,000).

Grants of £1,000 or more included those to Compassion in World Farming (£4,000), Demelza House Children's Hospice and Médicins Sans Frontières (£2,000 each), SSAFA (£1,500), Newnham College and Salvation Army Trust (£1,100 each) and Army Benevolent Fund, Church of England Pensions Board, the Divert Trust, Friends of the National Libraries, L'Arche Kent Community, Mildmay Mission Hospital, Polish Air Force Benevolent Fund, Send a Cow, Sussex Air Ambulance, Sight Savers International and Sussex Bells Restoration Fund (£1,000 each).

Grants of less than £1,000 included those to The Children's Society (£910), Church Housing Trust (£750), Barnardos (£600), NSPCC (£550) and Action Health, Amnesty International, Arthritis Care, Pestalozzi International Village, Winged Fellowship, the Woodland Trust and YMCA West London (£500 each).

Applications The trust states that it does not respond to unsolicited applications; all beneficiaries 'are known personally to the trustees and no attention is paid to appeal literature, which is discarded on receipt. Fundraisers are therefore urged to save resources by not sending literature.'

The Park House Charitable Trust

Education, social welfare, ecclesiastical

About £130,000 (2006)
Beneficial area UK and overseas, with a preference for the Midlands, particularly Coventry and Warwickshire.

Dafferns, Queen's House, Queen's Road, Coventry CV1 3DR
Tel. 024 7622 1046
Correspondent Paul Varney
Trustees *N P Bailey; M M Bailey; P Bailey; M F Whelan.*
CC Number 1077677
Information available Information was available from the Charity Commission website.

General This trust was established in September 1999. In 2006 the trust had an income of £8,000 and a total expenditure of £131,000. Further information was not available.

Previously, grants have been made to a variety of donees mainly for ecclesiastical, education and social welfare purposes. Past beneficiaries have included the Ark of the Covenant, Equestrian Order of the Holy Sephulchre of Jerusalem, Walsingham Trust, Margaret Beaufort Institute of Theology, Cambridge Nazareth Trust, Tall Ships Youth Trust – Coventry and Warwickshire Branch, Holy Ghost Fathers, Helen Ley Charitable Trust, Bible Alive and Survive Mia.

Exclusions No grants to individuals.

Applications In writing to the correspondent. The trust has stated that it does not expect to have surplus funds available to meet the majority of applications.

The Samuel and Freda Parkinson Charitable Trust

General

£105,000 (2004/05)
Beneficial area UK.

Thomson Wilson Pattinson, Trustees' Solicitors, Stonecliffe, Lake Road, Windermere, Cumbria LA23 3AR
Tel. 01539 442233 **Fax** 01539 488810
Correspondent J R M Crompton, Trust Administrator
Trustees *D E G Roberts; Miss J A Todd; M J Fletcher.*
CC Number 327749
Information available Accounts were on file at the Charity Commission.

General This trust was established in 1987 with £100. The fund stayed at this level until 1994/95 when £2.1 million worth of assets were placed in the trust on the death of the settlor. It supports the same eight beneficiaries each year, although for varying amounts.

In 2004/05 it had assets of £2.7 million, an income of £116,000 and made grants totalling £105,000. Beneficiaries were the Leonard Cheshire Foundation (£25,000), the Church Army and the Salvation Army (£23,000 each), RNLI (£15,000) and Animal Concern, Animal Rescue, Animal Welfare and RSPCA (£5,000 each).

Applications The founder of this charity restricted the list of potential beneficiaries to named charities of his choice and accordingly the trustees do not have discretion to include further beneficiaries, although they do have complete discretion within the stated beneficiary list.

Arthur James Paterson Charitable Trust

Medical research, welfare of older people and children

£57,000 (2005/06)
Beneficial area UK.

Royal Bank of Canada Trust Corporation Limited, 71 Queen Victoria Street, London EC4V 4DE

Tel. 020 7653 4337

Email susan.cooper@rbc.com

Correspondent Susan Cooper

Trustee *Royal Bank of Canada Trust Corporation Ltd.*

CC Number 278569

Information available Accounts were on file at the Charity Commission.

General In 2005/06 the trust had assets of £1.1 million with an income of £54,000. Grants to 14 organisations totalled £57,000.

Grants included £11,000 each to Glenalmond College and Worcester College, £3,500 each to Elizabeth Finn Trust and Triscope, £3,000 each to Alzheimer's Research Trust, NSPCC, OXPIP and the Wingate Special Children's Trust, £2,500 to Orthopaedic Institute Limited and £2,000 each to Age Concern and Clubs for Young People.

Applications There are no application forms. Send your application with a covering letter and include the latest set of report and accounts. Deadlines are February and August.

The Constance Paterson Charitable Trust

Medical research, health, welfare of children, older people, service people

£28,000 (2006)
Beneficial area UK.

Royal Bank of Canada Trust Corporation Limited, 71 Queen Victoria Street, London EC4V 4DE

Tel. 020 7653 4756

Email anita.carter@rbc.com

Correspondent Miss Anita Carter, Administrator

Trustee *Royal Bank of Canada Trust Corporation Ltd.*

CC Number 249556

Information available Full accounts were on file at the Charity Commission.

General The trust makes grants in support of medical research, healthcare, welfare of elderly people and children (including accommodation and housing) and service people's welfare.

In 2006 the trust had assets of £866,000 and an income of £14,000. Grants were made to 9 organisations totalling £28,000. Grant recipients included the National Playing Fields Association (£4,000), the Cancer Vaccine Institute, Independent Age, Move On and NAPAC (£3,500 each) and Down's Syndrome (£2,500).

Exclusions No grants to individuals.

Applications In writing to the correspondent, including covering letter and the latest set of annual report and accounts. The trust does not have an application form. Deadlines for applications are June and December.

Miss M E Swinton Paterson's Charitable Trust

Church of Scotland, young people, general

£41,000 (2004/05)
Beneficial area Scotland.

Lindsays' Solicitors, Calendonian Exchange, 19a Canning Street, Edinburgh EH3 8HE

Correspondent Callum S Kennedy, Trustee

Trustees *Michael A Noble; J A W Somerville; C S Kennedy; R J Steel.*

SC Number SC004835

Information available Full accounts were provided by the trust.

General The trust was set up by the will of Miss M E Swinton Paterson who died in October 1989. The objectives of the trust are the support of charities in Scotland, specifically including schemes of the Church of Scotland.

In 2004/05 the trust had an income of £46,000. Grants totalling £41,000 were made to 47 organisations. Just one beneficiary received over £1,000, L'Arche Edinburgh Community (£2,000).

All other grants were for either £1,000 or £500. Beneficiaries receiving £1,000 included Livingstone Baptist Church, Lloyd Morris Congregational Church, Haddington West Parish Church, Acorn Christian Centre, Stranraer YMCA, Care for the Family, Boys' and Girls' Clubs of Scotland, Fresh Start, Friends of the Elms, Iona Community, Edinburgh Young Carers' Project and Epilepsy Scotland.

Beneficiaries receiving £500 included Stoneykirk Parish Church, Scotland Yard Adventure Centre, Atholl Centre, Scottish Crusaders, Disablement Income Group Scotland and Artlink.

Exclusions No grants to individuals or students.

Applications In writing to the correspondent. Trustees meet once a year in July to consider grants.

Barbara May Paul Charitable Trust

Older people, young people, medical care and research, preservation of buildings

About £15,000 (2004/05)

Beneficial area East Anglia and UK-wide.

Lloyds TSB Private Banking Ltd, UK Trust Centre, 22–26 Ock Street, Abingdon, Oxon OX14 5SW

Tel. 01235 232731

Correspondent C Shambrook, Trust Manager

Trustee *Lloyds TSB Private Banking Ltd.*

CC Number 256420

Information available Information was obtained from the Charity Commission.

General Lloyds TSB Bank plc is the sole trustee for this and two other trusts, each founded by a different sister from the Paul family. This trust is the largest and makes larger grants but they all appear to have very similar grant-making policies. There is a preference throughout the trusts for Suffolk and some organisations have been supported by all three trusts.

This trust has stated in recent years that it is increasingly focusing its grantmaking on local organisations in East Anglia, and East Anglian branches of UK charities. UK-wide organisations can, and do, receive funding, although local groups outside East Anglia do not.

In 2004/05 the trust had an income of £15,000 (£14,000 2003/04) and a total expenditure of £48,000 (£17,000 2003/04). Further information for this year was not available.

Previous beneficiaries have included Bus Project, Cancer Research Campaign, Essex County Youth Service, East Suffolk Mines, Essex Voluntary Association for the Blind, Ipswich Disabled Advice, Ipswich Scouts and Guides Council, Malcolm Sargent Cancer Fund, Norfolk Millennium Trust for Carers, Norfolk and Norwich Scope, One-to-One, Queen Elizabeth's Foundation for Disabled People, Rotary Club of Ipswich, Shelter, Suffolk Association for Youth, Suffolk Preservation Society, Tannington Church and Whizz-Kidz. Previously, grants have ranged from £500 to £5,000.

Exclusions No grants to overseas charities.

Applications In writing to the correspondent at any time.

The Susanna Peake Charitable Trust

General

£115,000 (2005/06)

Beneficial area UK, with a preference for the south west of England, particularly Gloucestershire.

Rathbone Trust Company Limited, 159 New Bond Street, London W1S 2UD

Correspondent Miss L J Cousins, Secretary

Trustees *Susanna Peake; David Peake.*

CC Number 283462

Information available Full accounts were on file at the Charity Commission.

General This is one of the Kleinwort family trusts. It was set up by Susanna Peake in 1981 for general charitable purposes and has a preference for charities based in the Gloucestershire area. In addition, non-local appeals when received are accumulated and considered by the trustees annually.

In 2005/06 the trust had assets of £5 million and an income of £153,000. Grants were made to 42 organisations totalling £115,000, broken down as follows:

- medical, cancer and hospices – £39,000
- local charitable organisations – £28,000
- international and overseas organisations – £18,000
- general charitable organisations – £15,000
- education and children – £11,000
- older people – £4,000.

Grants ranged from £250 to £5,000. Beneficiaries included: St James' Church Longborough (£6,000 in three grants); Brainwave, Gloucestershire Life Education Centre, National Star Centre for Disabled Youth, Pioneer and Royal Ballet School-White Lodge Development Appeal (£5,000 each); APT Enterprise Development and Riding for the Disabled Knightsbridge Group (£3,000 each); Action for Blind People,

Campaign to Protect Rural England, Campden Home Nursing, Hepatitis C Trust and WaterAid (£2,000 each); British Heart Foundation, Oxford Childrens Hospital, the Gloucestershire Society, Victim Support – Gloucestershire and Well Being of Women (£1,000 each); the Cats Protection League and Canine Partners (£500 each); and Ashmolean Museum (£250).

Exclusions No grants to individuals.

Applications In writing to the correspondent. 'The trustees meet on an ad hoc basis to review applications for funding, and a full review is undertaken annually when the financial statements are available. Only successful applications are notified of the trustees' decision.'

Pearson's Holiday Fund

Young people who are disadvantaged

£48,000 to organisations (2006)

Beneficial area UK.

PO Box 3017, South Croydon CR2 9PN

Tel. 020 8657 3053

Website www.pearsonsholidayfund.org

Correspondent The General Secretary

Trustees *A John Bale, Chair; John S Bradley; David P Golder; John F Gore; Mark A Hutchings; Andrew Noble.*

CC Number 217024

Information available Accounts were available from the Charity Commission website.

General The following is taken from the trust's guidelines:

'Pearson's Holiday Fund provides financial grants towards helping disadvantaged children and young people to have holidays, outings or take part in group respite activities, that take them away for a little while from their otherwise mundane or restricted environment which would not be possible without some external financial support.

'We regard children and young people as being disadvantaged who may have:

- learning difficulties
- physical disabilities or other health-related problems

experienced abuse or violence in the home or are regarded as being at risk

● disabled or elderly parents to care for

● other problems, e.g. living in the 'poverty trap', refugees, homelessness, etc.

'The following conditions must also be met in all cases:

● The child/children/young person(s) must live in the United Kingdom

● The holiday, outing or group activity must be in the United Kingdom

● The child/children/young person(s) must be aged 4 to 16 years (inclusive) at the time of the holiday or activity.

'Where a family with disadvantaged child/young person are taking a holiday together, we normally regard all the children/young people in the family, within our age range, participating in the holiday as meeting our criteria for grants.'

These grants can go to individuals or to groups and are to a maximum of £75 per person and £750 per group.

In 2006 the fund had assets of £124,000 and an income of £82,000, all of which came from donations. Grants were made totalling £114,000 of which 229 grants were made to individuals totalling £66,000 and 72 grants were made towards group activities totalling £48,000.

Applications In writing to the correspondent. However due to the trust's low income in recent years, the trust may not be able to provide some activities. Potential applicants are strongly advised to visit the trust's website where full details of the trust's position are posted.

Full guidelines are available from the correspondent (upon receipt of an sae) or downloadable from the website. Completed forms must be returned with an sae. Applications will not be accepted by email.

Applications must include evidence that the criteria and conditions of the fund are being met, the number of children/young people expected to benefit from the activity, the amount requested and details of to whom the cheque should be made payable. Applications for individuals must be supported by a referring agency, such as social workers, health visitors, teachers, doctors, ministers of religion and so on.

Peltz Trust

Arts and humanities, education and culture, health and welfare, Jewish

£148,000 (2005/06)

Beneficial area UK and Israel.

Berwin Leighton Paisner, Adelaide House, London Bridge, London EC4R 9HA

Tel. 020 7760 1000

Correspondent Martin D Paisner, Trustee

Trustees *Martin D Paisner; Daniel Peltz; Elizabeth Julia Natasha Wolfson Peltz.*

CC Number 1002302

Information available Full accounts were available from the Charity Commission website.

General In 2005/06 the trust had assets of £48,000 and an income of £90,000, including £70,000 from Gift Aid. Grants were made to 39 organisations totalling £148,000, broken down into the following categories:

Education and training – 13 grants totalling £36,000
Beneficiaries included Emmanuel College and Holocaust Educational Trust (£10,000 each), British Ort (£5,000), British Technion Society (£3,000), Institute of Jewish Studies (£1,500), the Jerusalem Foundation (£1,000) and Cancerkin (£250).

Medical, health and sickness – 3 grants totalling £29,000
Grants recipients were Royal Marsden Hospital (£28,000), Cancer Research (£500) and Sparks Trust (£250).

Relief of poverty – 2 grants totalling £15,000
Grants were made to Jewish Care (£10,000) and British Friends of Jaffa Institute (£5,000).

Arts and culture – 3 grants totalling £14,000
Beneficiaries were Royal National Theatre (£10,000 in two payments), the Chicken Shed Theatre Trust (£3,000) and Hampstead Theatre Foundation (£1,000).

Religious activities – 3 grants totalling £6,000
Grants were awarded to Central Synagogue (£5,000) and Central Synagogue Minister's Fund and United Synagogue (£300 each).

Accommodation and housing – 1 grant totalling £3,000
The sole grant in this category was made to Nightingale House.

Sport and recreation – 1 grant totalling £2,500
There was one grant made to Rowley Lane Recreational Trust.

Exclusions No grants to individuals for research or educational awards.

Applications In writing to the correspondent. The trustees meet at irregular intervals during the year to consider appeals from appropriate organisations.

Elizabeth Wolfson Peltz Trust

Arts and humanities, education and culture, health and welfare, Jewish

£165,000 (2004/05)

Beneficial area UK and Israel.

Berwin Leighton Paisner, Adelaide House, London Bridge, London EC4R 9HA

Tel. 020 7760 1000

Correspondent Martin D Paisner, Trustee

Trustees *Martin D Paisner; Daniel Peltz; Hon. Elizabeth Wolfson Peltz; Lord Wolfson of Marylebone.*

CC Number 1070064

Information available Accounts were on file at the Charity Commission.

General In 2004/05 the trust had an income of £200,000 and made grants totalling £165,000. Assets stood at £36,000.

Grants approved in the year included those to Immanuel College and Royal Marsden Hospital (£25,000 each), Ben Gurion University Foundation, Friends of the Hebrew University of Jerusalem, Jewish Care and Weizmann Institute Foundation (£20,000 each), Norwood Ltd (£15,000), UK Friends of Magen David Adom (£10,000) and British ORT (£5,000).

Exclusions No grants to individuals for research or educational awards.

Applications In writing to the correspondent. The trustees meet at irregular intervals during the year to consider appeals from appropriate organisations.

Penny in the Pound Fund Charitable Trust

Hospitals, health-related charities

About £40,000 (2005)

Beneficial area UK, but mostly around the Merseyside region.

Medicash Health Benefits Limited, Merchants Court, 2–12 Lord Street, Liverpool L2 1TS

Tel. 0151 702 0202 **Fax** 0151 702 0250

Email sweir@medicash.org

Website www.medicash.org

Correspondent Susan Weir, Trustee

Trustees *K W Monti; W Gaywood; S Weir; W Tubey; A Hill.*

CC Number 257637

Information available Information obtained from the Charity Commission website.

General This trust was established in 1968 by a health benefits insurance company, from which the trust continues to receive donations each year. The objectives of the trust are to provide amenities to patients in hospital or under the care of health-related charities by reimbursing them with the cost of facilities purchased to make their patients' stays more comfortable and enjoyable. Grants are given throughout the UK, although centred on the north west of England.

In 2005 the trust had an income of £14,000 and a total expenditure of £43,000. Further information was not available.

Previous grants have been given to hospitals in Merseyside including Aintree Hospitals NHS Trust, Royal Liverpool, Broadgreen University Hospitals NHS Trust, Countess of Chester Hospital NHS Trust, Southport and Ormskirk Hospital NHS Trust, Robert Jones, A Hunt Hospital NHS Trust, The Yorkhill NHS Trust, Halton Primary Care NHS Trust and Bolton Hospitals NHS Trust.

Other grants were previously awarded to Mersey Neurological Trust, Children's Adventure Farm Trust, Toggs Centre, Woodlands Hospice Charitable Trust, Action Medical Research, Brainwave, Myasthenia Gravis Association, Abbeyfield North Mersey Society Ltd and the Liver Group.

Exclusions No grants towards medical equipment.

Applications There is a separate application form for hospitals and charities available from the trust.

Applications need to be received by the end of September and trustees meet in October. Successful applicants are notified in November.

The Pennycress Trust

General

£70,000 (2005/06)

Beneficial area UK and worldwide, with a preference for Cheshire and Norfolk.

15d Millman Street, London WC1N 3EP

Correspondent Mrs Doreen Howells, Secretary to the Trustees

Trustees *Lady Aline Cholmondeley; Anthony J M Baker; C G Cholmondeley; Miss Sybil Sassoon.*

CC Number 261536

Information available Accounts were available from the Charity Commission website.

General The trust's policy is to make donations to smaller charities and especially those based in Cheshire and Norfolk, with some donations to UK and international organisations.

In 2005/06 the trust had assets of £2.1 million and an income of £73,000. During the year 213 donations were made totalling £70,000. These were mostly between £100 and £500, with one of £2,000, one of £1,200 and six of £1,000 each.

Previous beneficiaries have included All Saints' Church – Beeston Regis, Brain Research Trust, Brighton and Hove Parents' and Children's Group, British Red Cross, Crusaid, Depaul Trust, Elimination of Leukaemia Fund, Eyeless Trust, Genesis Appeal, Help the Aged, Matthew Project, RUKBA, St Peter's – Eaton Square Appeal, Salvation Army,

Tibet Relief Fund, West Suffolk Headway, Women's Link and Youth Federation.

Exclusions No support for individuals.

Applications In writing to the correspondent. 'No telephone applications please.' Trustees meet regularly. They do not have an application form as a simple letter will be sufficient.

The Mrs C S Heber Percy Charitable Trust

General

£108,000 (2005/06)

Beneficial area Worldwide, with a preference for Gloucestershire.

Rathbones, 159 New Bond Street, London W1S 2UD

Tel. 020 7399 0812

Correspondent Miss L J Cousins

Trustees *Mrs C S Heber Percy; Mrs J A Prest.*

CC Number 284387

Information available Full accounts were on file at the Charity Commission.

General The trust has a stated preference for Gloucestershire. In addition to local appeals, non-local applications are accumulated and considered annually by the trustees. In 2005/06 the trust had assets of £5 million and an income of £157,000. Grants were made to 38 organisations totalling £108,000. Categories of charities supported are as follows:

- medical, cancer and hospices – £29,000
- general charitable organisations – £28,000
- education and children – £20,000
- international charities – £18,000
- local organisations – £9,000
- animal welfare and the local environment – £5,000.

Grants recipients included Royal Ballet School – White Lodge development Appeal (£18,000 in two grants), Independent Age (£7,000), Marie Curie Cancer Care (£6,000 in two grants), Dumfries and Galloway Action Centre, Friends of Aphrodisias, Healing Hands Network, Upper Slaughter Village Hall Appeal and Venice in Peril (£5,000 each), British Yemeni Society – Soqotra Training Centre Appeal (£2,500), Everyman's Theatre, Hunt Servant Fund and Oxford Children's Hospital (£2,000 each), SongBird Survival (£1,000); and Save the Children and Stroke Association (£500 each).

Exclusions No grants to individuals.

Applications The correspondent stated that unsolicited applications are not required.

B E Perl Charitable Trust

Jewish, general

£1.9 million (2004/05)
Beneficial area UK.

Fofoane House, 35–37 Brent Street, Hendon, London NW4 2EF

Correspondent B Perl, Chair

Trustees *B Perl, Chair; Mrs S Perl; S Perl; J Koval; Jonathan Perl; Joseph Perl; Naomi Sorotzkin.*

CC Number 282847

Information available Accounts were on file at the Charity Commission.

General The trust says it makes grants for the advancement of the Orthodox Jewish faith as well as for other charitable purposes.

In 2004/05 the trust had assets of £9.5 million and an income of £1.6 million. Grants totalled £1.9 million. The largest grant was for £1.6 million and was donated to the Huntingdon Foundation Limited.

Other grants of £1,000 or more were made to 31 organisations including Kisharon, Gateshead Yeshiva, Talmud Torah School, Hertsmere Jewish High School, The Harav Lord Jacobovits Torah Institute of Contemporary Issues, Gateshead Jewish Academy for Girls, Or Chadash Children's Town, British Friends of Shuvu and the Before Trust.

Applications In writing to the correspondent.

The Personal Finanace Society Charitable Foundation

General

£41,000 (2004/05)
Beneficial area UK.

Personal Finance Society, 20 Aldermanbury, London EC2V 7HY

Tel. 020 7417 4467

Email lyn.new@thepfs.org

Website www.thepfs.org

Correspondent The Trustees

Trustees *K Carby, Chair; G Tisshaw; I Green; Ms A T McIlvenny; J Butler; M Bamford.*

CC Number 1071492

Information available Recent accounts are not on file at the Charity Commission. Copy requested from foundation.

General Established in September 1998, the foundation raises funds for UK-wide and local causes through the efforts of its 35 branches.

In 2004/05 the foundation had assets of £59,000 and an income of £54,000. Grants were made totalling £41,000. The largest beneficiary was the Wheelchair Foundation, which received £12,000. The remaining £30,000 was donated to different charities elected by local Life Insurance Association regions. A full list of these donations is available on request from the trustees.

Applications Beneficiaries are elected by local PFS regions.

The Persson Charitable Trust (formerly Highmoore Hall Charitable Trust)

Christian mission societies and agencies

£243,000 (2005/06)
Beneficial area UK and overseas.

Long Meadow, Dark Lane, Chearsley, Aylesbury, Buckinghamshire HP18 0DA

Correspondent P D Persson, Trustee

Trustees *P D Persson; Mrs A D Persson; J P G Persson; A S J Persson.*

CC Number 289027

Information available Basic accounts were on file at the Charity Commission.

General 'The trustees have a policy of awarding grants to charitable, not-for-profit, organisations which are predominantly involved in promoting the Christian faith and in humanitarian aid.'

In 2005/06 it had an income of £273,000, including £200,000 from Gift Aid. Grants totalled £243,000, broken down as follows:

home missions	£140,000
overseas missions	£102,000
other charities	£1,800

The seven largest grants of £10,000 or more were listed in the accounts. Beneficiaries were: Bible Reading Fellowship – 'Foundations21' (£50,000); Alpha International (£40,000); Tearfund – Christian relief (£38,000); Micah Network (£30,000); Jubilee Centre Trust (£15,000); the Relationship Foundation (£11,000) and Christian Solidarity Worldwide – No Boh Bible School (£10,000).

Other smaller grants totalled almost £50,000.

Exclusions No grants to non-registered charities.

Applications The trust states that it does not respond to unsolicited applications. Telephone calls are not welcome.

The Persula Foundation

Homelessness, disablement, human rights, animal welfare

£343,000 (2005/06)

Beneficial area Predominantly UK; overseas grants are given, but this is rare.

Unit 3/4, Gallery Court, Hankey Place, London SE1 4BB

Tel. 020 7357 9298 **Fax** 020 7357 8685

Email info@persula.org

Website www.persula.org

Correspondent Mrs Fiona Brown, Chief Executive

Trustees *Julian Richer; David Robinson; David Highton; Mrs R Richer; Mrs H Oppenheim.*

CC Number 1044174

Information available Accounts were available from the Charity Commission website.

General The trust works in collaboration with organisations to support projects that are innovative and original in the UK and worldwide. The trust researches new projects and charities to support, listing their core interest as being in the following areas:

1 animal welfare
2 blind and visually impaired
3 bullying
4 deaf and hard of hearing
5 human rights and welfare
6 mental health
7 learning disabilities
8 physical disabilities
9 youth.

'The Persula Foundation is able to introduce the commercial expertise of our sponsoring organisation to charities.' The trust is able to offer professional help with:

1 communications
2 PR and marketing
3 customer service
4 staff motivation
5 sales
6 financial management.

The foundation prefers to use these resources to provide an added value aspect to its collaboration with organisations. It also offers support in the form of time and resources.

In 2005/06 the trust had assets of £1 million and an income of £747,000.

Grants were made to ten organisations £343,000. The largest grant went to Tapesense (£93,000), the trust's mail-order service, which offers subsidised equipment and acessories to blind and visually impaired people.

Other monies were distributed among the following causes:

- charities for human rights – £47,000
- storytelling tours for the blind – £44,000
- charities for animal welfare – £29,000
- charities for the deaf – £16,000
- charities for the blind – £3,500
- sufferers from leprosy – £3,000
- sufferers from mental health – £2,000.

Grants also went to Spinal Injuries Association (£12,000) and On the Right Track (£10,000). Other donations totalled £5,000.

Exclusions No grants to individuals, including sponsorship, for core costs, buildings/building work or to statutory bodies.

Applications In writing to the correspondent.

The Pestalozzi Overseas Children's Trust

Children

£417,000 (2005)

Beneficial area Worldwide, especially Asia and Africa.

70 Sandy Lane, Hartley Wintney, Hook, Hampshire, RG27 8DU

Tel. 01252 844 485

Correspondent Caroline E Winchurch, Charity Correspondent

Trustees *Lady Butler; J J Dilger; S P Pahlson-Moller; F Von Hurter.*

CC Number 1046599

Information available Accounts were available from the Charity Commission website.

General Pestalozzi Overseas Children's Trust – POCT is the coordinating entity of PestalozziWorld – the working alliance of several organisations working in Africa and Asia.

The 2005 accounts stated that: 'The Trust's mission is to provide a practical secondary education (aged about 10 upwards) to deprived children in some

of the poorest countries in Africa and Asia. It focuses on the brightest children, especially girls. The uniqueness of the programme is that the children once educated by Pestalozzi help provide education for the other children similar to themselves. This produces an ongoing ripple effect.'

The accounts continued to detail the trust's work as follows:

The Trust and the Pestalozzi US Children's Charity Inc. now fund the education of over 300 children in Nepal, India, (including exiled Tibetans in India), Malawi and Zambia. The education of an additional 93 children is funded through Pestalozzi overseas foundations in Thailand, Nepal and India.

The primary focus for expansion continues to be the Asian Village in Northern India where there are now 50 children.

The trust operates Centres (hostels and skills centres) built by the trust in India, Nepal and Zambia. The Centres are run in conjunction with local schools.

In addition, the trust has provided funding for the acquisition of land for the Asian Village in Dehraddun, India to accommodate up to 200 children of three or four nationalities. The children selected for the village are Indians, Nepalese and Tibetans.

The Pestalozzi alumni hosted the annual Pestalozzi Asian Reunion in Dehradum, which was attended by delegates from India (including Tibetans), Nepal, Thailand and Europe.

Pestalozzi graduates from India, Nepal, Tibet and Zambia attended International Baccalaureate courses provided by the Pestalozzi International Village trust in England and the United World College in India.

In 2005 the trust had assets of £1.3 million and an income of £1.2 million. Donations were made totalling £417,000 including capital expenditure of £230,000 for the Asian Village and also for school fees totalling £121,000.

Exclusions The trust emphasised that funding is not available to individuals, including students.

Applications Applications cannot be made to this trust. It works in partnerships with local organisations it identifies through its own research and networks and grants are given proactively by the trust. The trust will contact organisations it wants to support proactively.

The Pet Plan Charitable Trust

Dogs, cats and horses

£185,000 (2005)
Beneficial area UK.

Great West Road, Brentford, Middlesex TW8 9EG

Tel. 020 8580 8013 **Fax** 020 8580 8186

Website www.petplantrust.org/

Correspondent Catherine Bourg, Administrator

Trustees *David Simpson, Chair; Clarissa Baldwin; Patsy Bloom; John Bower; Gareth Jones; Roz Haywood-Butt; Nicholas Mills; George Stratford.*

CC Number 1032907

Information available Full accounts were available from the Charity Commission website.

General This trust was established by a pet insurance company by adding an optional £1 a year to the premiums paid by its members. The trust provides grants towards the welfare of dogs, cats and horses by funding clinical veterinary investigation, education and welfare projects. Funding is sometimes given for capital projects. Educational grants are given to fund projects aimed at both the general public and the welfare industry.

In 2005 the trust had assets of £803,000 and an income of £448,000. There were 23 grants made totalling £185,000.

The largest grants were awarded to two research teams in Liverpool, to investigate tissue engineering for osteochondral repair (£67,000) and to research an understanding of the genetic basis of canine osteoarthritis (£40,000). Research was also funded in Cambridge to study equine cartilage repair (£32,000).

Scientific grants were made varying from £2,000 to £40,000; most were between £5,000 and £6,000. Grants were made to Animal Health Trust, the Royal Veterinary College and institutions in Liverpool, Cambridge, Bristol, St Barts and Glasgow for a variety of investigations and projects.

Welfare and educational grants were made to SLL to fund a humanitarian ride across France and England for horses for disabled children (£5,000), CSWCT Sanctuary for a dog and cat welfare programme (£1,000), Joseph Clarke School Trust in an annual grant for school pets (£500) and

Loughborough Women's Aid for a pet project 'Families in Crisis' (£250).

In addition, an individual received an overseas bursary grant (£2,000).

Exclusions No grants to individuals or non-registered charities. The trust does not support or condone invasive procedures, vivisection or experimentation of any kind.

Applications In writing, or by telephone or email, to the correspondent. Application forms are available from the trust's website, where full guidelines can also be found. Closing dates for scientific and welfare applications vary so please check first. Grants are generally announced at the end of the year.

The Phillips and Rubens Charitable Trust

General, Jewish

£305,000 (2005/06)
Beneficial area UK.

Berkeley Square House, Berkeley Square, London W1X 5PB

Tel. 020 7491 3763 **Fax** 020 7491 0818

Correspondent M L Phillips, Trustee

Trustees *Michael L Philips; Mrs Ruth Philips; Martin D Paisner; Paul Philips; Gary Philips; Carolyn Mishon.*

CC Number 260378

Information available Full accounts were on file at the Charity Commission.

General The trust supports a wide range of causes, including medical research, education, disability, old age, poverty, sheltered accommodation and the arts. In practice, almost all the grants are made to Jewish/Israeli organisations.

In 2005/06 the trust had assets of £10.1 million and an income of £123,000. Grants were made totalling £305,000.

The largest grants were made to United Jewish Israel Appeal (£79,000 in 6 grants), the Philips Family Charitable Trust (£65,000 in three grants), Charities Aid Foundation (£25,000), Jewish Care (£13,000) and Holocaust Educational Trust and Yesoday Hatorah Grammar School (£10,000 each).

Other grants were made to London Jewish Cultural Centre (£8,000 in two

grants), the Jerusalem Foundation and Simon Wiesenthal Centre (£7,000 each), Lubavitch Foundation (£5,000), Aleh Charitable Foundation (£3,000), Bar llan University (£2,500) and British Technion Society and Child Resettlement Fund (£1,000 each).

Grants to organisations of less than £1,000 each totalled £33,200.

Exclusions No grants are made to individuals.

Applications In writing to the correspondent at any time.

The Phillips Family Charitable Trust

Jewish charities, welfare, general

£106,000 (2005/06)
Beneficial area UK.

Berkeley Square House, Berkeley Square, London W1J 6BY

Tel. 020 7491 3763 **Fax** 020 7491 0818

Email psphillipsbsh@aol.com

Correspondent Paul S Phillips, Trustee

Trustees *Michael L Phillips; Mrs Ruth Phillips; Martin D Paisner; Paul S Phillips; Gary M Phillips.*

CC Number 279120

Information available Full accounts were available from the Charity Commission website.

General This trust stated that it makes grants to Jewish organisations and to a range of other organisations, including elderly, children and refugee charities and educational establishments.

In 2005/06 the trust had assets of £45,000 and an income of £66,000. Grants were made totalling £106,000.

The largest grants were made to UJIA (£15,000 in two grants), the London Carlbach Shul Trust (£11,000 in two grants) and Holocaust Educational Trust (£10,000).

Other grants were made to British Friends of the Jaffa Institute (£6,000), Chief Rabbinate Trust, Community Security Trust and Tel Aviv University Trust (£5,000 each), the Lubavitch Foundation (£3,000), Friends of the Hebrew University of Jerusalem (£2,000) and Camp Simcha, Greenhouse Schools

Project Limited, Royal Marsden Cancer Campaign, Royal National Theatre Foundation and World Jewish Relief (£1,000 each).

Exclusions No grants to individuals.

Applications In writing to the correspondent. Please note, the trust informed us that there is not much scope for new beneficiaries.

The David Pickford Charitable Foundation

Christian, general

£30,000 to organisations (2005/ 06)

Beneficial area UK (with a preference for Kent and London) and overseas.

Elm Tree Farm, Mersham, Ashford, Kent TN25 7HS

Tel. 01233 720200 **Fax** 01233 720522

Correspondent D M Pickford, Trustee

Trustees *D M Pickford; C J Pickford; Mrs E J Pettersen.*

CC Number 243437

Information available Information was obtained from the Charity Commission website, but was limited.

General The general policy is to make gifts to Christian organisations especially those helping youth, and those helping with special needs in overseas countries. In 2005/06 the foundation had an income of £25,000 and a total expenditure of £34,000. Grants totalled around £30,000. Further information for this year was not available.

Exclusions No grants to individuals. No building projects.

Applications In writing to the correspondent. Trustees meet every other month from January. Applications will not be acknowledged. The correspondent states: 'It is our general policy only to give to charities to whom we are personally known.' Those falling outside the criteria mentioned above will be ignored.

The Bernard Piggott Trust

General

£65,000 (2005/06)

Beneficial area North Wales and Birmingham.

4 Streetsbrook Road, Shirley, Solihull, West Midlands B90 3PL

Tel. 0121 744 1695 **Fax** 0121 744 1695

Correspondent Miss J P Whitworth

Trustees *D M P Lea; N J L Lea; R J Easton; Ven. M L Williams.*

CC Number 260347

Information available Full accounts were available from the Charity Commission website.

General This trust provides one-off grants for Church of England, Church of Wales, educational, medical, drama and youth organisations in Birmingham and North Wales only. In 2005/06 the trust's assets stood at £1.2 million. It had an income of £91,000 and made grants totalling £65,000. Grants ranged from £250 to £5,000, 50% of grants totalled £1,000 each.

Grant recipients included Christ Church – Selly Park (£5,000), St Mary's Church – Dolgellau (£4,000), St Peter's Church – Aberdyfi, Epilepsy Research Foundation, Sunfield Childrens Home, St Mary's Church Caernarfon and Royal Blind Society (£2,000 each) 870 House, the Gurkha Welfare Trust, Jubilee Sailing Trust, St Luke's Hospital for the Clergy and the Stroke Association (£1,000 each), Birmingham Centre for Arts Therapies (£750), Deep Impact Theatre Company and Masquerade – Llanfyllin (£500 each) and City Can Cycle Scheme (£200).

Exclusions No grants to individuals.

Applications The trustees meet in May/June and November. Applications should be in writing to the secretary including annual accounts and details of the specific project including running costs and so on. General policy is not to consider any further grant to the same institution within the next two years.

The Cecil Pilkington Charitable Trust

Conservation, medical research, general on Merseyside

£152,000 (2003/04)

Beneficial area UK, particularly Sunningwell in Oxfordshire and St Helens.

c/o McFarlane & Co., Cunard Building, Water Street, Liverpool L3 1DS

Tel. 0151 236 6161

Correspondent Mr McFarlane, The Administrator

Trustees *A P Pilkington; R F Carter Jonas; M R Feeny.*

CC Number 249997

Information available Full accounts were available from the Charity Commission website.

General This trust supports conservation and medical research causes across the UK, supporting both national and local organisations. It also has general charitable purposes in Sunningwell in Oxfordshire and St Helens.

In 2003/04 the trust's assets stood at £5.8 million. It had an income of £214,000 and made grants to organisations totalling £152,000. More recent information was not available. The largest grants were made to Psychiatric Research Trust (£60,000), Covent Garden Cancer Research Trust (£25,000) and Exeter University Foundation (£10,000).

Other grant recipients were: Royal Agricultural Benevolent Institute (£6,000); Alzheimer's Research Trust, Handel House Museum and Willowbrook Hospice (£5,000 each); BTCV and Global Canopy Foundation (£3,000 each); Marine Conservation Society and Mental Health Foundation (£2,000 each); Arthritis Care, Barn Owl Trust, BBO Wildlife Trust, Green Alliance, Rare Breeds Survival Trust and Sunningwell School of Art (£1,000 each); and Countryside Foundation for Education (£500).

Exclusions No grants to individuals or non-registered charities.

Applications The trust does not respond to unsolicited appeals.

The Elsie Pilkington Charitable Trust

Equine animals, welfare

£170,000 (2005/06)

Beneficial area UK.

Taylor Wessing, Carmelite, 50 Victoria Embankment, London EC4Y 0DX

Correspondent Lord Brentford

Trustees *Mrs Caroline Doulton, Chair; Mrs Tara Economakis; Richard Scott; Mrs Helen Timpany.*

CC Number 278332

Information available Accounts were available from the Charity Commission website.

General This trust supports small specific projects of a capital nature which benefit equines and older people in need.

In 2005/06 the trust's assets stood at £3.3 million. It had an income of £85,000 and made grants totalling £170,000, broken down as follows:

- to prevent cruelty to equine animals – £91,000
- to provide help for aged infirm or poor – £79,000.

A list of beneficiaries was not available, however the 2005/06 accounts stated that: '27 [grants] were made by the trustees during the year: 12 were made for the protection and relief of suffering equines; 15 to provide social services and help for older people.'

Applications In writing to the correspondent.

The Austin and Hope Pilkington Trust

See below

£229,000 (2005)

Beneficial area Unrestricted, but see exclusions field.

PO Box 124, Stroud, Gloucestershire GL6 7YN

Email admin@austin-hope-pilkington. org.uk

Website www.austin-hope-pilkington. org.uk

Correspondent Karen Frank, Administrator

Trustees *Jennifer Jones; Deborah Nelson; Penny Shankar.*

CC Number 255274

Information available Full accounts were available from the Charity Commission website.

General The trust usually gives about 100 grants to mainly national organisations through its regular programme. In a refreshing change from conventional practice, this changes each year:

- 2007: children, young and older people and medical
- 2008: music and the arts
- 2009: community and disability.

'The trustees welcome applications for projects within the [above] areas for the next three years. These categories are then repeated in a three-year rotation. Please note that the trustees have decided no longer to consider applications that deal solely with religion or poverty.'

Grants are usually between £1,000 and £10,000, with most being for £5,000 or less. Exceptionally, grants for up to £20,000 can be made for medical research projects. Grants are usually one-off.

In 2005 the trust had assets of £7.9 million and an income of £225,000. Grants were made totalling £229,000, grants are broken down as follows:

Arts and music – 53 grants totalling £91,000
Beneficiaries included Centrepoint, Great Ormond Street Hospital and Sir John Soane Museum (£5,000 each), Academy of St Martin in the Fields, Bournemouth Symphony Orchestra, Derby Playhouse, Live Arts in Pembrokeshire, Tate Modern and Youth at Risk (£3,000 each) and Buxton Opera House, Deep Impact Theatre Company, Handel House Museum, Opera North, Orcadia Creative Learning Centre, Opheus Centre and Reach Inclusive Arts (£1,000 each).

Overseas – 45 grants totalling £86,000
Grant recipients included Learning for Life (£9,000), Interact Worldwide and Oxfam (£5,000 each), Care International, Farm Africa, Plan and St Dunstan's (£3,000 each) and Harvest Help, Target Tuberculosis, Tools for Self Reliance, Tree Aid, War Child, WaterAid and Wells for India (£1,000 each).

Music commitments
There were two scholarships awarded to Purcell School totalling £49,000.

Exclusions Grants only to registered charities. No grants to individuals, including individuals embarking on a trip overseas with an umbrella organisation. Overseas projects can only be supported in the stated year.

National organisations are more likely to be supported than purely local organisations.

Applications In writing to the correspondent. Only overseas applications are considered for the stated years: 2007, 2008 and 2009. Applicants are strongly advised to visit the trust's website as projects supported and eligibility criteria change from year to year.

There is no application form. Applications should include an A4 summary of the project, a budget for the project and the applicant's most recent annual report and accounts. Necessary supporting information should be kept to a minimum as the trust will request further information if required.

Grants are made twice a year, with deadlines for applications being 1 June and 1 November. With the increased level of applications, the trust has stated that all successful applicants will in future be listed on their website on the 'recent awards' after each trustee meeting. All applicants will still be contacted by letter in due course.

The Sir Harry Pilkington Trust

General

£130,000 (2004/05)

Beneficial area UK and Merseyside, with a preference for the St Helens area.

Liverpool Charity and Voluntary Services, 14 Castle Street, Liverpool, Merseyside L2 0NJ

Tel. 0151 236 7728 **Fax** 0151 258 1153

Correspondent The Trustees

Trustee *Liverpool Charity and Voluntary Services.*

CC Number 206740

Information available Accounts were obtained from the Charity Commission website.

General This trust has general charitable purposes, giving most of its grants in and around St Helens.

In 2004/05 the trust had assets of £4.9 million and an income of £172,000. Grants were made totalling £130,000.

Grants of £1,000 or more were made to 30 organisations and were listed in the accounts. Beneficiaries included Liverpool Charity and Voluntary Services (£40,000), the Millennium Centre St Helens Ltd (£20,000), Sefton Carers Centre (£10,000), Barnardos (£8,000), PERC (£4,000), NCH (£3,000), Pilkington Horticultural Society and Southport Flower Show (£2,500 each), Compass, Liverpool Personal Service Society, Merseyside Youth Association, Oasis Centre and Tuesday Club (£2,000 each), L'Arche (£1,500) and the Civic Centre and Newton-le-Willows Family and Community Association (£1,000 each).

Other unlisted grants totalled £1,200.

Applications In writing to the correspondent.

The Col W W Pilkington Will Trusts – The General Charity Fund

Welfare

£47,000 (2004/05)

Beneficial area UK, with a preference for Merseyside.

Rathbones, Port of Liverpool Building, Pier Head, Liverpool L3 1NW

Tel. 0151 236 6666 **Fax** 0151 243 7003

Correspondent Sarah Nicklin

Trustees *Arnold Pilkington; Hon. Mrs Jennifer Jones; Neil Pilkington Jones.*

CC Number 234710

Information available Full accounts were available from the Charity Commission website.

General The trust gives grants to registered charities only, with a preference for the Merseyside area. In 2004/05 the trust had assets of £1.4 million and an income of £42,000. Grants were made to organisations totalling £47,000 and were broken down into the following categories:

Medical – 11 grants totalling £30,000 Beneficiaries included Institute of Psychiatry (£10,000), Exeter University Postgraduate Medical School (£8,000), Mental Health Foundation, Richmond Fellowship and Sane (£2,000 each) and Anxiety Care, Dystonia Society and No Panic (£1,000 each).

Environment – 4 grants totalling £5,000 Grant recipients were the Mersey Forest (£2,000) and Children's Adventure Farm Trust, Tree Aid and Wildlife Trust (£1,000 each).

International – 4 grants totalling £5,000 Grants were awarded to Médicins Sans Frontières (£2,000) and Farm Africa, Mary Stopes International and Minority Rights Group (£1,000 each).

Drugs – 2 grants totalling £4,000 Beneficiaries were Drugscope and Resolve (£2,000 each).

Arts – 3 grants totalling £3,000 Grant recipients were Action Factory, Music Space North West and Windows Project (£1,000 each).

Exclusions No support for non-registered charities, building projects, animal charities or individuals.

Applications In writing to the correspondent. Grant distributions are made in January and July.

A M Pilkington's Charitable Trust

General

£119,000 (2005/06)

Beneficial area UK, with a preference for Scotland.

Carters, Chartered Accountants, Pentland House, Saltire Centre, Glenrothes, Fife, KY6 2AH

Tel. 01592 630055 **Fax** 01592 623200

Email info@cartersca.co.uk

Trustee *The Trustees*

SC Number SC000282

Information available Accounts were provided by the trust, but without a list of grants.

General The trust supports a wide variety of causes in the UK, with few causes excluded (see exculsions). In practice there is a preference for Scotland – probably half the grants are given in Scotland. There is a preference

for giving recurring grants, which normally range from £500 to £1,500.

In 2005/06 the trust's assets stood at £3.3 million. It had an income of £132,000, generated mainly from investment income. Grants were made to 146 organisations totalling £119,000.

Exclusions Grants are not given to overseas projects or political appeals.

Applications The trustees state that, regrettably, they are unable to make grants to new applicants since they already have 'more than enough causes to support'. Trustees meet in June and December.

The Platinum Trust

Disability

£325,000 (2003/04)

Beneficial area UK.

Langham House, 1b Portland Place, London W1B 1GR

Correspondent The Secretary

Trustees *G K Panayiotou; A D Russell; C D Organ.*

CC Number 328570

Information available Accounts were on file at the Chaity Commission.

General This trust gives grants in the UK for the relief of children with special needs and adults with mental or physical disabilities 'requiring special attention'.

In 2003/04 the trust had an income of £328,000 mainly from donations. Grants to 12 organisations totalled £325,000. More recent information was not available.

Beneficiaries included: Alliance for Inclusive Education (£69,000); Parents for Inclusion (£59,000); British Council of Disabled People (£50,000); Disability, Pregnancy and Parent International (£40,000); Centre for Studies on Inclusive Education (£35,000); Independent Panel for Special Education Advice (£15,000); Birmingham Institute for the Deaf (£10,000); Greater London Action on Disability (£7,500); and Hampshire Centre for Independent Living and Signed Performances in Theatre (£5,000 each).

Exclusions No grants for services run by statutory or public bodies, or from mental-health organisations. No grants for: medical research/treatment or equipment; mobility aids/wheelchairs; community transport/disabled transport schemes; holidays/exchanges/holiday playschemes; special-needs playgroups; toy and leisure libraries; special Olympic and Paralympics groups; sports and recreation clubs for people with disabilities; residential care/sheltered housing/respite care; carers; conservation schemes/city farms/horticultural therapy; sheltered or supported employment/ community business/social firms; purchase/construction/repair of buildings; and conductive education/ other special educational programmes.

Applications The trust does not accept unsolicited applications; all future grants will be allocated by the trustees to groups they have already made links with.

G S Plaut Charitable Trust

Sickness, disability, Jewish, older people, Christian, general

£36,000 (2003/04)

Beneficial area Predominantly UK.

39 Bay Road, Wormit, Newport-on-Tay, Fife DD6 8LW

Correspondent Dr R A Speirs

Trustees Dr G S Plaut, Chair; Mrs A D Wrapson; Dr H M Liebeschuetz; K A Sutcliffe; W E Murfett; Miss T A Warburg.

CC Number 261469

Information available Accounts were on file on at the Charity Commission, without a list of grants.

General This trust appears to make grants across the whole spectrum of the voluntary sector, however it may have some preference for charities in those fields listed above. In 2003/04 the trust's assets totalled £573,000, it had an income of £33,000 and grants totalled £36,000.

Previous beneficiaries have included Book Aid International, British Deaf Association, Down's Syndrome Association, Friends of Meals on Wheels Service – Liverpool, Gurkha Welfare Trust, Hull Jewish Community Care, Liverpool School of Tropical Medicine, Nightingale Home for Aged Jews, Rehearsal Orchestra, RNIB Talking Book Services, St George's Crypt – Leeds,

Southend Riding Club for the Disabled, TOC H and VSO.

Exclusions No grants to individuals or for repeat applications.

Applications In writing to the correspondent. Applications are reviewed twice a year. An sae should be enclosed. Applications will not be acknowledged.

The George and Esme Pollitzer Charitable Settlement

Jewish, health, social welfare, general

£91,000 (2005/06)

Beneficial area UK.

Saffery Champness, Beaufort House, 2 Beaufort Road, Clifton, Bristol B58 2AE

Tel. 0117 915 1617

Correspondent J Barnes, Trustee

Trustees J Barnes; B G Levy; R F C Pollitzer.

CC Number 212631

Information available Full accounts were on file at the Charity Commission.

General This trust has general charitable purposes with no exclusions. Most funds are given to Jewish causes.

In 2005/06 the settlement's assets stood at £3 million. It had an income of £105,000 and made grants to 53 organisations totalling £91,000. A large proportion of grants were for £1,000 and £1,500 each.

Beneficiaries included: Employment Resource Centre, John Grooms, Nightingale House and Prime Trust Cymru (£5,000 each); Royal Hospital for Neuro Disability (£4,000); Breast Cancer Care and Norwood (£3,000 each); the Royal British Legion, the Royal College of Surgeons of England and the Prostate Cancer Charity (£2,000 each); Listening Books, Magen David Adom UK, Marie Curie Cancer Care and Multiple Sclerosis Society (£1,500 each); Alzheimer's Research Trust, the Delamere Forest School, the Elizabeth Finn Trust and Independent Age (£1,000 each); and the Suzy Lamplugh Trust (£500).

Applications In writing to the correspondent.

The J S F Pollitzer Charitable Settlement

General

£57,000 (2005/06)

Beneficial area UK and overseas.

c/o H W Fisher and Co., 11–15 William Road, London NW1 3ER

Tel. 020 7388 7000

Correspondent P Samuel, Accountant

Trustees Mrs J F A Davis; Mrs S C O'Farrell; R F C Pollitzer; J S Challis.

CC Number 210680

Information available Full accounts were on file at the Charity Commission.

General The trust supports a range of UK and local charities. In 2005/06 the trust had assets of £706,000 and an income of £51,000. Grants were made to 57 organisations totalling £57,000, all grants were for amounts of £1,000 each, with the exception of one grant totalling £500. Grants were broken down into the following categories:

Health – 11 grants totalling £11,000 Grants were made to Bath Institute of Medical Engineering, Befriending Network, Epilepsy Research Foundation, Changing Faces, Core, Myasthenia Gnavis Association, Octopus Oxford Colon Cancer Trust, Teenage Cancer Trust, the British Eye Research Foundation, the Lee Smith Research Foundation and the Royal Air Forces Association.

Disabled – 9 grants totalling £9,000 Grants were made to Assist, Cherished Memories Support Group, Hearing Help (Amber Valley), Leonard Cheshire Northern Ireland, Sign, Spadework Ltd, the Dystonia Society, the Vassall Centre Trust and the Thomas Morley Trust Bikeability South Coast.

Conservation and environment – 6 grants totalling £6,000 Beneficiaries were 9 Lives Furniture, Clyde River foundation, Excellent Development, Forest Peoples Project, Open Spaces Society, the Wildlife Trust Staffordshire and Chichester Cathedral.

Cultural – 6 grants totalling £5,500 Grant recipients were Absolute Theatre, Brewery Arts, Interact, the Young Vic Theatre Company, Wychwood Music Festival (£1,000 each) and Quenington Sculpture Trust (£500).

Children and Youth – 4 grants totalling £4,000

Grants were awarded to Childlink Adoption Society, Every Child, Happy and Sunfield Children's Home Ltd.

Social, community and Welfare – 4 grants totalling £4,000

Grants were made to Coram Family, East Belfast Mission, the Foyer Foundation and Senior Citizens of Scotland.

Education, science and technology – 3 grants totalling £3,000

Grants were awarded to HDRA, National Literacy Trust and Young Enterprise Education.

Overseas aid – 3 grants totalling £3,000

Beneficiaries were African Equipment for School, Concern Universal and Concern Worldwide.

Religion – 2 grants totalling £2,000

Grant recipients were the Parish of Harnham and WHCM.

Blind – 1 grant £1,000

The sole beneficiary in this category was the Guide Dogs for the Blind Association.

Hospices – 1 grant £1,000

A grant was awarded to Hospice of Hope Romania Ltd.

Sport and recreation – 1 grant £1,000

Mulgrave Community Sports Association received the sole grant in this category.

Other – 6 grants totalling £6,000

Beneficiaries were Alexandra Rose Day, Glosaid Youth Action, Royal British Legion, the British Red Cross Society, the Fishermen's Mission and the Yard.

Other categories included Animals and Museums, although neither had grants awarded.

Exclusions No grants to individuals or students, i.e. those without charitable status.

Applications In writing to the correspondent. Grants are distributed twice a year, usually around April/May and November/December.

Edith and Ferdinand Porjes Charitable Trust

Jewish, general

£93,000 (2004/05)

Beneficial area UK and overseas.

Adelaide House, London Bridge, London EC4R 9HA

Correspondent M D Paisner, Trustee

Trustees *M D Paisner; A H Freeman; A S Rosenfelder.*

CC Number 274012

Information available Full accounts were on file at the Charity Commission.

General Although the trust has general charitable purposes, the trust is inclined to support applications from the Jewish community in the UK and overseas. The trustees have set aside a fund, referred to as the 'British Friends of the Art Museums of Israel Endowment Fund' with the specific aim of supporting the British Friends of the Art Museums of Israel.

In 2004/05 the trust had assets of £1.6 million and an income of £55,000 with grants totalling £93,000.

There were 12 grants made in the year. Beneficiaries included Oxford Centre for Hebrew and Jewish Studies (£18,000), Queen Mary and Westfield College and Royal Academy Trust (£10,000 each), Ben-Gurion University Foundation, Centre for Jewish-Christian Relations, Chi-Lifetime Cancer Care, Council for Christians and Jews and the Hope Charity, the Hope Charity, New Israel Fund and Royal Marsden (£5,000 each), B'nai B'rith First Lodge Charitable Trust (£2,500) and British Friends of Ohel Sarah (£1,500).

Applications In writing to the correspondent.

The Powell Foundation

People who are elderly or mentally or physically disabled

£117,000 (2005/06)

Beneficial area Within the Milton Keynes Unitary Council area.

c/o Milton Keynes Community Foundation, Acorn House, 381 Midsummer Boulevard, Central Milton Keynes MK9 3HP

Tel. 01908 690 276 **Fax** 01908 233 635

Email information@ mkcommunityfoundation.co.uk

Website www.mkcommunityfoundation.co.uk

Correspondent Julia Seal, Chief Executive

Trustees *R W Norman; R Hill.*

CC Number 1012786

Information available Full accounts were available from the Charity Commission website.

General The foundation supports general charitable purposes; however, according to the wishes of Margaret Powell, the trustees restrict the activities of the trust to providing grants for the benefit of people who are older or disabled living in the Milton Keynes area.

In 2005/06 the trust had assets of £3.7 million and an income of £136,000. Grants were made totalling £117,000, £90,000 of which was designated to Milton Keynes Community Foundation, an annual grant for distribution to voluntary groups that meet the foundation's criteria of benefiting older people or people who are physically or mentally disabled, regardless of age. Direct grants can be considered for groups. Small grants can be considered for disabled individuals in exceptional circumstances; they must be residents of Milton Keynes.

Other beneficiaries were the Pace Centre and Milton Keynes Theatre Pantomime Trip (£14,000 each).

Applications Please visit the trust's website for full guidelines and details of how to apply. Application forms are available on request from the grants team who can either post or email the forms.

Prairie Trust

Third world development, the environment, conflict prevention

£57,000 (2005/06)

Beneficial area Worldwide.

83 Belsize Park Gardens, London NW3 4NJ

Tel. 020 7722 2105 **Fax** 020 7483 4228

Correspondent The Administrator

Trustees *Dr R F Mulder; Ms Fenella Rouse; Mrs Hannah Mulder.*

CC Number 296019

Information available Accounts were available from the Charity Commission, but without a list of grants.

General The trust does not consider unsolicited applications and instead develops its own programme to support a small number of organisations working on issues of third world development, the environment and conflict prevention, particularly to support policy and advocacy work in these areas. The trustees are also interested in supporting innovative and entrepreneurial approaches to traditional problems.

In 2005/06 the trust had assets of £284,000 and an income of £37,000. Grants were made totalling £57,000, a list of beneficiaries was not available.

Previously grants have been made to Funding Network, Linacre College, Centre for Social Markets, Network for Social Change, FINCA, Nicol Society, Oxfam, Action for ME, New Economics Foundation, Salts of the Earth and RESULTS Education.

Exclusions No grants to individuals, for expeditions or for capital projects.

Applications The trust states: 'As we are a proactive trust with limited funds and administrative help, we are unable to consider unsolicited applications'.

The W L Pratt Charitable Trust

General

£54,000 (2005/06)

Beneficial area UK, particularly York, and overseas.

Messrs Grays, Duncombe Place, York YO1 7DY

Tel. 01904 634771 **Fax** 01904 610711

Email christophergoodway@ grayssolicitors.co.uk

Correspondent C C Goodway, Trustee

Trustees *J L C Pratt; C M Tetley; C C Goodway.*

CC Number 256907

Information available Full accounts were available from the Charity Commission website.

General The trust divides its grant-giving between overseas charities, local charities in the York area and UK national charities. UK and overseas grants are restricted to well-known registered charities. In 2005/06 the trust's assets stood at £1.8 million. It had an income of £57,000 and made grants totalling £54,000, broken down into the following categories:

Local charities – 19 grants totalling £20,000

Grant recipients included York Diocesan Board of Finance (£4,000), St Leonard's Hospice and Wilberforce Trust (£2,000), York CVS (£1,000), Martin House Hospice (£500), Riding for the Disabled (£400) and Abbeyfield York Society and York Sea Cadets (£300 each).

One-off donations – 7 grants totalling £16,000

The largest grant was awarded to York Minister Development Campaign (£12,000). Other grants were made to Yorkshire Air Ambulance and Asia Earthquake Appeal (£1,000 each) and the Lord Mayor's Charities, York and District Mind, Baghdad Hospital for Children and Kohima Educational Trust (£500 each).

Overseas charities – 7 grants totalling £10,000

Beneficiaries included Christian Aid and Sight Savers International (£2,000 each), British Humanitarian Aid Limited and British Red Cross – Overseas (£1,000 each) and Oxfam (£700).

Exclusions No grants to individuals. No grants for buildings or for upkeep and preservation of places of worship.

Applications In writing to the correspondent. Applications will not be acknowledged unless an sae is supplied. Telephone applications are not accepted.

Premierquote Ltd

Jewish, general

£594,000 (2003/04)

Beneficial area Worldwide.

18 Green Walk, London NW4 2AJ

Correspondent D Last, Trustee

Trustees *D Last; Mrs L Last; H Last; M Weisenfeld.*

CC Number 801957

Information available Accounts were on file at the Charity Commission, but without a list of grants.

General The trust was established in 1985 for the benefit of Jewish organisations, the relief of poverty and general purposes. In 2003/04 it had an income of £923,000 from investments and Gift Aid. Grants totalled £594,000.

Previous beneficiaries have included Achisomoch, Belz Yeshiva Trust, Beth Jacob Grammar School for Girls Ltd, British Friends of Shuvu, Friends of Ohel Moshe, Friends of Senet Wiznitz, Friends of the United Institutions of Arad, Kehal Chasidel Bobov, Meadowgold Limited, Menorah Primary School, North West London Communal Mikvah and Torah Vedaas Primary School.

Applications In writing to the correspondent.

Premishlaner Charitable Trust

Jewish

£28,000 (2003/04)

Beneficial area UK and worldwide.

186 Lordship Road, London N16 5ES

Correspondent C M Margulies, Trustee

Trustees *H C Freudenberger; S Honig; C M Margulies.*

CC Number 1046945

Information available Accounts were on file at the Charity Commission.

General This trust was founded in 1995; its principal objectives are:

- to advance orthodox Jewish education
- to advance the religion of the Jewish faith in accordance with the Orthodox practice
- the relief of poverty.

In 2003/04 it had an income of £98,000 and awarded grants totalling £28,000 (£58,000 in the previous year). Assets stood at £414,000.

Gateshead Jewish Primary School received £20,000, this was the only donation listed. Grants of £5,000 and under each totalled £8,400.

Applications In writing to the correspondent.

The Nyda and Oliver Prenn Foundation

Arts, education, health

About £50,000 (2005)
Beneficial area UK, with a preference for London.

Moore Stephens Chartered Accountants, St Paul's House, Warwick Lane, London EC4M 7BP

Correspondent T Cripps

Trustees *Oliver Prenn; Mrs Nyda Prenn; Stanley Lee; Alexis Prenn; Ms Natasha Prenn; Mrs Ann Cavanagh.*

CC Number 274726

Information available Information was obtained from the Charity Commission website.

General This trust supports arts, education and health organisations, usually based in London, which have been identified by the trustees through their own research.

In 2005 the foundation had an income of £13,000 and a total expenditure of £61,000. Further information was not available.

However, previous beneficiaries have included UCL Development, Contemporary Art Society, Cancer Care UK, the Speech, Language and Hearing Centre, Amadeus Scholarship Fund, the Serpentine Trust, Hearing Dogs for the Deaf, Age Concern, Motability, Wigmore Hall Trust, Royal Ballet School, Help the Hospices and Streatham Youth Centre.

Exclusions Local projects outside London are unlikely to be considered.

Applications Unsolicited applications are not acknowledged.

The Primrose Trust

General

£95,000 (2005/06)
Beneficial area UK.

Field View, Old Park, Devizes, Wiltshire SN10 5JR

Correspondent M G Clark, Trustee

Trustees *M G Clark; Susan Boyes-Korkis.*

CC Number 800049

Information available Full accounts were on file at the Charity Commission.

General The trust was established in 1986 with general charitable purposes. In 2005/06 the trust had assets of £4 million and an income of £124,000. Grants were made to four organisations totalling £95,000.

Grant recipients were National Federation of Badger Groups (£55,000), Swan Rescue Sanctuary (£20,000) and the Vegan Society and the Bill Jordan Foundation for Wildlife (£10,000 each).

Exclusions Grants are given to registered charities only.

Applications In writing to the correspondent, including a copy of the most recent accounts. The trust does not wish to receive telephone calls.

Princess Anne's Charities

Children, medical, welfare, general

£94,000 (2005/06)
Beneficial area UK.

Buckingham Palace, London SW1A 1AA

Correspondent Capt. N Wright

Trustees *Hon. M T Bridges; Commodore T J H Laurence; B Hammond.*

CC Number 277814

Information available Accounts were available from the Charity Commission website.

General This trust has general charitable purposes, with a preference for charities or organisations in which the Princess Royal has a particular interest. In 2005/06 the trust had assets of £4.7 million and an income of £176,000. Grants were made to 31 organisations totalling £94,000, broken down as follows:

- social welfare: 14 grants totalling £37,000
- children and youth: 3 grants totalling £24,000
- medical: 7 grants totalling £19,000
- environment: 3 grants totalling £6,000
- animal: 2 grants totalling £4,000
- armed forces: 1 grant totalling £2,000
- general: 1 grant totalling £2,000

Grant recipients were the Butler Trust, the Canal Museum Trust Cranfield Trust, Dogs Trust, Dorothy House Foundation, Durrell Wildlife Conservation Trust, the Evelina Children's Hospital Appeal Farms for City Children, Farrer and Co. Charitable Trust, Fire Services National Benevolent Fund, the Home Farm Trust, Intensive Care Society, International League for the Protection of Horses, King Edward VIII Hospital – Sister Agnes, National Autistic Society, Minchinhampton Centre for the Elderly, Mission to Seafarers, Princess Royal Trust for Carers, REDR, RYA Sailability, Save the Children Fund, Scottish Field Studies Association, Scottish Motor Neurone Disease Association, SENSE, Spinal Injuries Association, Strathcarron Hospice, Transaid, London Bombing Relief Charitable Fund, Victim Support, VSO (formerly British Executive Service Overseas) and Women's Royal Navy Benevolent Trust.

Exclusions No grants to individuals.

Applications Trustees meet to consider applications in January, and applications need to be received by November. 'The trustees are not anxious to receive unsolicited general applications as these are unlikely to be successful and only increase the cost of administration of the charity.'

The Priory Foundation

Health and social welfare, especially children

£513,000 (2005)
Beneficial area UK.

c/o Cavendish House, 18 Cavendish Square, London W1G 0PJ

Correspondent The Trustees

Trustees *N W Wray; L E Wray; T W Bunyard; D Poutney.*

CC Number 295919

Information available Accounts were on file at the Charity Commission.

General The trust was established in 1987 to make donations to charities and appeals that directly benefit children.

In 2005 it had assets of £2.4 million and an income of £543,000. Grants totalled £513,000.

There were 48 grants listed in the accounts of £1,000 or more. The largest grants went to Saracens Foundation (£29,000), Sir Jai Sankara Education School (£25,000), London Borough of Barnet (£24,000), Arundel Castle Cricket Foundation and Ravenscroft School (£20,000 each), Lord's Taverners (£17,000), Watford Place Theatre (£16,000), ABCD and Ivybridge Community College (£15,000 each), BIRD and RAFT (£11,000 each) and Sports Leader UK, University of Bristol Boat Club and Wellbeing (£10,000 each).

Other beneficiaries included Barnet Primary Care NHS Trust (£9,600), Cricket Federation for People with Disabilities and London Irish Amateur RFC (£7,500 each), Aplastic Anaemia Trust (£6,000), British Paralympic Association (£4,000), Making A Difference (£3,000), Aspire (£2,500), Shooting Star Children's Hospice (£1,600) and Crimestoppers and Rotary Club of London (£1,000 each).

Other smaller grants of less than £1,000 each totalled £82,000.

A grant of £15,000 was made to an individual.

Applications In writing to the correspondent.

Prison Service Charity Fund

General

£126,000 (2005)

Beneficial area UK.

68 Hornby Road, Walton, Liverpool
L9 3DF

Tel. 0151 530 4000 Ext. 4502

Correspondent The Trustees

Trustees *A N Joseph, Chair; P Ashes; J Goldsworthy; R Howard; P McFall; Ms C F Smith; K Wingfield.*

CC Number 801678

Information available Full accounts were available from the Charity Commission website.

General The trust's accounts included the following narrative, describing how the trust was started: 'Having started a cash collection to assist in the treatment of a very sick local child, Liverpool's [prison] staff were obliged to seek help from other prisons nationwide, in order to achieve their financial goal. This resulted in us receiving considerably more money than we needed for our appeal and we used the spare cash to launch the Prison Service Charity Fund.' The charity is now an established fundraiser and grant-making trust.

The trust stated that the fund is 'for the staff, run by the staff'; the staff comprises 5,000 to 6,000 members of the Prison Service.

In 2005 the fund's assets stood at £501,000. It had an income of £128,000 and made grants to 144 organisations totalling £126,000, the majority of which were for less than £1,000 each.

The beneficiaries of the largest grants included Andrew Barkess Appeal – Frankland and the Callum Mardy Fund – Leeds (£5,000 each), Vista (£4,000), Callum Mardy Fund – AGM, Daniel Norton Appeal, Rainbow Children's Hospice and Top to Bottom Appeal (£3,000 each), Breathing Space, Kidney Care Appeal and Martin Coston Fund (£2,000 each), Help the Hospices, MS Society, FSID and St Cuthbert's Hospice (£1,000 each).

Other grants included those to Anthony Nolan Trust and Cancer Research UK – Ranby and Elmley (£800 each), Action Medical Research, Make a Wish Foundation, Farleigh Hospice and See Ability (£500 each), Walk the Walk Worldwide and Special Needs Group – Liverpool (£300 each), Cystic Fibrosis Trust (£200) Clic/Sargent (£150) and Hospice of the Good Shepherd (£50).

Applications The trust does not accept outside applications – the person making the application has to be a member of staff.

The Puebla Charitable Trust

Community development work, relief of poverty

£50,000 (2005/06)

Beneficial area Worldwide.

Ensors, Cardinal House, 46 St Nicholas Street, Ipswich IP1 1TT

Tel. 01473 220 022

Correspondent The Clerk

Trustees *J Phipps; M A Strutt.*

CC Number 290055

Information available Full accounts were available from the Charity Commission website.

General The trust has stated that: 'At present, the council limits its support to charities which assist the poorest sections of the population and community development work – either of these may be in urban or rural areas, both in the UK and overseas.'

Grants are normally in the region of £5,000 to £20,000, with support given over a number of years where possible. Most of the trust's income is therefore already committed, and the trust rarely supports new organisations.

In 2005/06 the trust's assets stood at £2.8 million. It had an income of £108,000 and made grants to two organisations totalling £50,000.

Grant recipients were Shelter (£20,000) and Zimbabwe Benefit Foundation (£30,000).

Exclusions No grants for capital projects, religious institutions, research or institutions for people who are disabled. Individuals are not supported and no scholarships are given.

Applications In writing to the correspondent. The trustees meet in July. The trust is unable to acknowledge applications.

The Richard and Christine Purchas Charitable Trust

Medical research, medical education and patient care

£78,000 (2004/05)
Beneficial area UK.

46 Hyde Park Gardens Mews, London W2 2NX

Correspondent Daniel Auerbach, Trustee

Trustees *Daniel Auerbach; Mrs Pauline Auerbach; Dr Douglas Rossdale; Robert Auerbach.*

CC Number 1083126

Information available Accounts were on file at the Charity Commission.

General Registered with the Charity Commission in October 2000, in 2004/05 this trust had assets amounting to £2.5 million and an income of £113,000. Grants totalled £78,000.

No list of grants was included with the accounts filed at the Charity Commission. Previously the trust has part-funded the post of Consultant Speech Therapist at the Charing Cross Hospital in association with Macmillan Cancer Relief.

Applications In writing to the correspondent.

The Pyke Charity Trust

Prisoners and disadvantaged communities

£141,000 (2006)
Beneficial area UK.

The Shieling, St Agnes, Cornwall TR5 0SS

Tel. 01871 553822

Correspondent Martin Ward, Administrator

Trustees *J N Macpherson; T Harvie-Clark.*

CC Number 296418

Information available Full accounts were available from the Charity Commission website.

General The trustees have recently reviewed the aims and objectives of the trust. The trust will now concentrate the grants it awards to assisting small UK charities whose work does not readily attract popular support and where a grant from the trust can make a significant difference. The charities that will be considered for grants include those working for the rehabilitation of prisoners, before and after release and support for prisoners' families. The trust will also consider small local charities whose primary aim should be to improve the quality of life for the most severely disadvantaged communities.

In 2006 the trust's assets stood at £4.1 million. It had an income of £160,000 and made grants totalling £141,000. Grants were made in five categories as follows:

Support for those working with prisoners and their families – 24 grants totalling £95,000
Grants included Lancaster and District YMCA, Little Hay Prison Visitors Centre and NEPACS (£6,000), HM Prison Eastwood Park, New Bridge and the Prison Education Trust (£5,000 each), PEOPLE and HAPPY (£4,000 each), Inside Out Trust and Open Gate (£3,000 each) and Prisoners' Advice Service and HM Prison Barlinnie (£1,000 each)

Youth – 3 grants totalling £11,000
Beneficiaries were Venture Trust (£5,000), Warrington Youth Club and Castlemilk Youth Services (£3,000 each).

Homelessness and poverty – 5 grants totalling £22,000
Grants included St Giles Trust (£9,000), Hertfordshire Youth Homeless (£5,000) and Family Project Coventry (£2,000).

General – 3 grants totalling £8,000
Grant recipients were Basildon Community Resource Centre and Aberdare Children's Contact Centre (£3,000 each) and Family Mediation Scotland (£2,000).

Asylum seekers and refugees – 1 grant of £3,000
The sole beneficiary in this category was Leeds Christian Community (£3,000).

Disabled – 1 grant of £2,500
There was one grant made to Clough's (£2,500).

Another category listed was 'school fees', although no grants were made in this category during the year.

Exclusions The trust does not accept applications from individuals, applications for assistance with school fees, charities or organisations involved in medical projects, or those whose aim is solely to promote religious beliefs.

Applications Applications from charities and organisations that feel they meet the criteria set out by the trustees should be made in writing to the correspondent. The application should set out clearly the work undertaken by the applicant charity or organisation and should be accompanied by an up-to-date annual report and abridged accounts where possible.

Quercus Trust

Arts, general

£97,000 (2004/05)
Beneficial area UK.

Chantrey Vellacott, Russell Square House, 10–12 Russell Square, London WC1B 5LF

Correspondent A C Langridge, Trustee

Trustees *Lord Bernstein of Craigwell; Alan C Langridge; Kate E Bernstein; Lady Bernstein.*

CC Number 1039205

Information available Full accounts were on file at the Charity Commission.

General In February 1999 the trustees declared by deed that distributions would in future be directed principally (but not exclusively) to the arts and any other objectives and purposes which seek to further public knowledge, understanding and appreciation of any matters of artistic, aesthetic, scientific or historical interest.

In 2004/05 the trust had assets of £4.7 million and an income of £139,000. Grants totalled £97,000 with the beneficiary of the two largest grants being Random Dance Company (£40,000 and £30,000).

Other beneficiaries included Pluto Productions (£5,000), Royal Opera House Foundation (£3,100), Royal Academy of Dance and University of Cambridge (£3,000 each), Guggenheim UK Charitable Trust (£2,700), Friends of Bolivia (£1,500), Royal Academy Trust (£1,250), Donmar Warehouse Projects and the Howard League (£1,000 each) and Almeida Theatre Company (£550).

Exclusions No grants to individuals.

Applications In writing to the correspondent, but please note, the trust states: 'All of the trust's funds are currently earmarked for existing projects. The trust has a policy of not making donations to individuals and the trustees regret that, in order to keep administrative costs to a minimum, they are unable to reply to any unsuccessful applicants.'

R S Charitable Trust

Jewish, welfare

£228,000 (2005/06)
Beneficial area UK.

138 Stamford Hill, London N16 6QT
Correspondent Max Freudenberger, Trustee
Trustees M Freudenberger; Mrs M Freudenberger; H C Freudenberger; S N Freudenberger; C Margulies.
CC Number 1053660
Information available Full accounts were available from the Charity Commission website.

General Established in 1996, this trust states that it supports Jewish organisations and other bodies working towards the relief of poverty. In 2005/06 the trust had assets of £2 million and an income of £597,000. Grants were made to 15 organisations totalling £228,000.

The largest grant went to British Friends of Tshernobil (£145,000), NRST (£13,000), Society of Friends of the Torah (£11,000) and Forty Ltd (£10,000).

Other grants included Viznitz (£7,000), Yeshiva Horomo (£5,000), Yeshivas Luzern (£2,500) and Talmud Hochschule (£1,500).

Applications In writing to the correspondent.

The R V W Trust

Music education and appreciation, relief of need for musicians

£298,000 (2005)
Beneficial area UK.

16 Ogle Street, London W1W 6JA
Tel. 020 7255 2590 **Fax** 020 7255 2591
Correspondent Ms Helen Faulkner, Secretary/Administrator
Trustees Dr Michael Kennedy, Chair; Lord Armstrong of Ilminster; Sir John Manduell; Mrs Ursula Vaughan Williams; Hugh Cobbe.
CC Number 1066977
Information available Accounts were available from the Charity Commission website.

General The trust's current grant-making policies are as follows:

1 To give assistance to British composers who have not yet achieved a national reputation.
2 To give assistance towards the performance and recording of music by neglected or currently unfashionable 20th century British composers, including performances by societies and at festivals which include works by such composers in their programmes.
3 To assist UK organisations that promote public knowledge and appreciation of 20th and 21st century British music.
4 To assist education projects in the field of music.

In 2005 the trust's assets stood at £1.4 million with an income of £332,000. Grants were made totalling £298,000, broken down as follows:

- Public performance – 69 grants (£116,000)
- Music festivals – 24 grants (£80,000)
- Public education – 16 grants (£35,000)
- Education grants – 9 grants (£67,000).

The largest grants went to: British Music Information Centre and Huddersfield Contemporary Music Festival (£25,000 each); Vaughan Williams Memorial Library/English Folk Dance and Song Society (£23,000); Society for the Promotion of New Music (£22,000); Chandos (£11,000); and Park Lane Group and Bournemouth Symphony Orchestra/Kokoro (£10,000 each).

Other grants went to: Maecenas Contemporary Composers and Spitalfields Festival (£5,000 each); Orchestra of St John's, Birmingham Contemporary Music Group, Britten Sinfonia and Royal Over-Seas League (£3,000 each); and Endymion Ensemble, New London Children's Choir, City of London Festival Opera Group, Madestrange, Dorset Guild of Singers and Music Past and Present (£2,000 each).

Exclusions No grants for local authority or other government-funded bodies, nor degree courses, except first Masters' degrees in musical composition. No support for dance or drama courses. No grants for workshops without public performance, private vocal or instrumental tuition or the purchase or repair of musical instruments. No grants for concerts that do not include music by 20th and 21st century composers or for musicals, rock, pop, ethnic, jazz or dance music. No grants for the construction or restoration of buildings.

Applications In writing to the correspondent, giving project details, at least two months before the trustees meet. Trustees' meetings are held in February, June and October. Masters in Music Composition applicants will only be considered at the June meeting; applications must be received by the middle of April. Further details are available from the trust.

The Monica Rabagliati Charitable Trust

Human and animal welfare, education and medical care and research in the UK

£60,000 (2005/06)
Beneficial area UK.

S G Hambros Trust Company Limited, S G House, 41 Tower Hill, London EC3N 4SG
Tel. 0207 597 3061 **Fax** 0207 702 9263
Correspondent Mrs Shirley Baines, Administrator
Trustees S G Hambros Trust Company Limited; R C McLean.
CC Number 1086368
Information available Accounts were available from the Charity Commission website.

General This trust was registered with the Charity Commission in April 2001. In 2005/06 the trust had assets of £2 million and an income of £45,000. Grants were made to 14 organisations totalling £60,000 and were broken down into the following categories:

Medical – nine grants totalling £18,000 Grant recipients were Deafness Research

UK (£3,000), DEBRA, International Childcare Trust, PEACH, Sebastian's Action Trust, Surrey Care Trust and St Chris Topers Hospice (£2,000) and Demelza House Children's Hospice and Little Havens Children's Hospice (£1,500 each).

General – 3 grants totalling £22,000
Beneficiaries were Ironmongers Quincentenary Charity and Sir Joseph Priestly Scholarships (£10,000 each) and Toc H Children's Camp (£2,000).

Animal welfare – 1 grant of £10,000
The sole beneficiary in this category was Cats Protection League (£10,000).

Humanitarian – 1 grant of £10,000
There was one grant made to the RNLI (£10,000).

Applications 'The charity does not solicit applications, but considers all relevant applications and the trustees give such applications fair consideration.'

The Radcliffe Trust

Music, crafts, conservation

£268,000 (2004/05)
Beneficial area UK.

Vizards Tweedie, 42 Bedford Row, London WC1R 4JL

Correspondent John Burden, Secretary to the Trustees

Trustees *Rt Hon. John Tapling; Dr Ivor F Guest; Rt Hon. Robert Bruce Balfour of Burleigh; Christopher Butcher; Hon. Felix Warnock.*

CC Number 209212

Information available Accounts were on file at the Charity Commission.

General The Radcliffe Trust was founded in 1714 by the will of Dr John Radcliffe, the most prominent physician of his day, who left his residuary estate for the income to be applied for general charitable purposes.

The trustees' present grant-making policy is concentrated in two main areas – music and the crafts – but they may consider applications which do not fall within those two categories.

In 2004/05 it had assets of £11.1 million, which generated an income of £341,000. Grants were made totalling £268,000,

broken down as follows and shown with examples of beneficiaries:

Crafts – £159,000 in 22 grants
The Type Museum – education officer (£23,000), Mansfield Traquair Trust – conservation internship (£16,000); West Dean College – staff costs for a building conservation project (£12,000); Council for the Care of Churches – Church upkeep (£11,000); Whitchurch Silk Museum – vocational training (£10,000); Tate Gallery London – frames conservation (£9,000); Imperial War Museum – conservation of military equipment (£8,300); National Portrait Gallery – frame conservation internship training (£8,000); Meridian Trust Association – apprentice shipwrights (£7,000); Hopetoun House – tapestry and textile conservation workshop (£6,000); University of Nottingham – conservation and cataloguing of Archdeaconry Bill (£5,000); and Chester Archaeological Society – archival programme (£1,500).

Music – £106,000 in 26 grants
Allegri String Quartet – educational music purposes and Royal Academy of Music – maintenance of historic piano collection (£14,000 each); Aldeburgh Productions – music festivals, City of Birmingham Symphony Orchestra – youth orchestra and Drake Music Project – progressive music workshop for disabled people, National Library for the Blind and National Youth Orchestra of Great Britain – music grant (£5,000 each); London Philharmonic Orchestra – 'Future First' project and Royal College of Music – printing costs of the museum catalogue (£4,000 each); British Youth Opera – support for youth orchestra and the North East Scotland Music School – travel costs of tutors (£3,000 each); Kings College London – contemporary music (£2,500); and the School Fund – music teaching (£1,000).

'Miscellaneous' grants to three organisations totalled £2,100.

Exclusions No grants to individual applicants. No grants to non-registered charities, or to clear or reduce past debts.

Applications 'Applications for music grants are short-listed for consideration by a panel of musicians who make recommendations, where appropriate; recommended applications are then placed before the trustees for decision. The music panel usually meets in March and October in advance of the trustees' meetings in June and December, and applications should be submitted by the end of January and the end of August respectively to allow time for any further

particulars (if so required) to be furnished.'

Applications for miscellaneous grants should be in writing and received by the end of April for consideration at the June meeting, or by October for consideration at the December meeting.

The Ragdoll Foundation

Children and the arts

£67,000 (2004/05)
Beneficial area UK and worldwide.

Timothy's Bridge Road, Stratford upon Avon, Warwickshire CV37 9NQ

Tel. 01789 404100

Email KarenN@ragdollfoundation.org. uk

Website www.ragdollfoundation.org.uk

Correspondent Karen Newell, Development Co-ordinator

Trustees *Katherine Wood, Chair; Peter Hollingsworth; Peter Thornton; Anne Wood.*

CC Number 1078998

Information available Full accounts were available from the Charity Commission website.

General The foundation's website states:

'The Ragdoll Foundation is dedicated to developing the power of imaginative responses in children through the arts. It owns 15% of its parent company and springs from the same philosophical roots. This can be summed up by the quotation from Sylvia Ashton-Warner in her book *Teacher*, which has greatly influenced Anne's work: I see the mind of a five-year-old as a volcano with two vents; destructiveness and creativeness. And I can see that to the extent that we widen the creative channel, we atrophy the destructive one.

Ragdoll Foundation Guidelines
'The primary purpose of the Ragdoll Foundation is to make grants for charitable purposes around the world that:

1 promote the development of children through their imaginative thinking
2 encourage innovative thinking and influence good practice elsewhere
3 offer creative solutions that deal with the causes of problems in childhood

4 ensure effective evaluation of projects to promote sharing and learning
5 above all demonstrate how the voices of children can be heard.

'Preference will be given to innovative projects that share the same values of imagination and creativity as the Ragdoll Foundation. In particular, those projects which show a true understanding of how to listen to children and allow the voices of children themselves to be heard. We will focus mainly on applications which involve children during their early years, but appropriate projects for older children will not be dismissed without consideration.

'Grants will also be made to projects, organisations or individuals through personal recommendation or knowledge of those connected with Ragdoll Foundation. The Trustees wish to make a range of grants available. We will consider a large-scale grant, but it is anticipated that the majority will range from £500 upwards.

'Foundations can be truly innovative when they retain a capacity for thinking and working outside the box. In order to achieve this we have re-structured the application and monitoring process. We have replaced it with a process that we hope will encourage new ways of thinking and working. We aim to develop and establish governance models that treat innovation as a process.'

The website goes on to state that: 'We wish to encourage people who seek to facilitate new partnerships and promote new ways of working through:

1 sharing ideas and contacts
2 working across boundaries
3 supporting pilot projects

Research and advocacy

'We wish to develop our advocacy role and will therefore take an active role in projects where appropriate and aim to:

1 Pioneer new work, support innovative ideas, learning and new ways of thinking.
2 Work with hard-to-reach children.'

Projects

The trust supports various projects that include the following – What Makes Me Happy – Ragdoll and Save the Children, Sun and Shadow, Whole New Worlds, Clown Doctors, Feeling Safe, Listening to Children, Dis Life, The Little Mermaid, Blue Eyed Soul, DigIT and Kids Aloud.

In 2004/05 the trust had assets of £303,000 and an income of £90,000, which was mainly from donations, gifts and legacies. Grants were made totalling £67,000. The largest grants went to 'What Makes Me Happy' – a project between Ragdoll and Save the Children (£14,000), Redcar and Cleveland Women's Aid (£10,000), Women's Aid Federation of England (£7,500) and Le Rire Médecin – Clown Doctors and 104 Films – 'Special People' (£6,000 each).

Other grants made included those to Queen's Park Media Centre (£3,500), Feeling Safe (£3,000), the Cartoon Art Trust Museum (£2,000) and the Royston Trust/Fischy Music (£450).

Exclusions Grants are not given for: replacement of statutory funding; work that has already started or will have been completed whilst the application is being considered; promotion of religion; animal welfare charities; vehicles; emergency relief work; general fundraising or marketing appeals; open-ended funding arrangements; loans or business advice; charities which are in serious deficit; holidays; any large capital, endowment or widely distributed appeal; specialist schools; school fees for people over 17 years of age; and gap-year funds.

Applications On a short form available from the correspondent, preferably by email if possible (sent to karenN@ragdollfoundation.org.uk). Completed forms should be submitted with an 'inspirational paragraph' summarising the project (one side of A4 maximum). See the foundation's website for further details.

The Rainford Trust

Social welfare, general

£117,000 (2005/06)

Beneficial area Worldwide, with a preference for areas in which Pilkington plc have works and offices, especially St Helens and Merseyside.

c/o Pilkington plc, Prescot Road, St Helens, Merseyside WA10 3TT

Tel. 01744 20574 **Fax** 01744 20574

Correspondent W H Simm, Secretary

Trustees Dr F Graham; A L Hopkins; Mrs A J Moseley; H Pilkington; Lady Pilkington; D C Pilkington; R G Pilkington; S D Pilkington; Mrs I Ratiu; Mrs L F Walker.

CC Number 266157

Information available Accounts were obtained from the Charity Commission website.

General The trust's accounts stated that its objectives are to: 'apply money for charitable purposes and to charitable institutions within the St Helens MBC area, and other places in the UK or overseas where Pilkington has employees. This does not prejudice the trustees' discretion to help charities that operate outside those areas.'

Further to this the trust's charitable purposes are to support:

- the relief of poverty, the aged, the sick, helpless and disabled, and the unemployed
- the advancement of education including the arts, and other purposes with wide benefit for the community such as environmental and conservation projects.

In 2005/06 the trust had assets of £6.7 million and an income of £188,000, generated from investments. Grants were made totalling £117,000 and were broken down into the following categories:

Welfare – 59 grants totalling £67,000
Grant recipients included: Bristol Cancer Help (£4,000 in two grants); Local Solutions (£3,000); British Wireless for the Blind, the Eyeless Trust and the Prince's Trust (£2,000 each); Charity Search, ExtraCare Charitable Trust and the British Stammering Association (£1,500 each); CommunicAbility, Compaid Trust, Demand, Motability, Target Tuberculosis, the Neuromuscular Centre and the Spinal Injuries Association (£1,000 each); Back Care, Diabetes UK North West, the Mary Hare Foundation and the Nancy Oldfield Trust (£500 each); and Derbyshire Hill Bowling Club (£250).

Education – £21,000
Beneficiaries included Clonter Farm Music Trust (£12,000); Book Aid International and Eccleston Mere Primary School (£2,000 each); and Kings World Trust for Children (£1,000 each)

Humanities – £13,000
Grants made included those to St Helens Open Art Exhibition (£10,000), the Koester Awards Trust (£1,000) and the Pilkington Choir (£500).

Medical – £13,000
Beneficiaries included Prostrate Cancer Charity (£2,000), International Disfigurement Guidance Centre (£1,500), Derma Trust (£1,000) and National Eczema Society (£750).

Environmental – £2,000

Grants went to Marine Conservation Society (£1,000) and International Otter Survival Fund and Little Ouse Headwater Project (£500).

Exclusions Funding for the arts is restricted to St Helens only. Applications from individuals for grants for educational purposes will be considered only from applicants who are normally resident in St Helens.

Applications On a form available from the correspondent. Applications should be accompanied by a copy of the latest accounts and cost data on projects for which funding is sought. Applicants may apply at any time. Only successful applications will be acknowledged.

The Peggy Ramsay Foundation

Writers and writing for the stage

£159,000 (2005)

Beneficial area British Isles.

Harbottle and Lewis Solicitors, Hanover House, 14 Hanover Square, London W1S 1HP

Tel. 020 7667 5000 **Fax** 020 7667 5100

Email laurence.harbottle@harbottle.com

Website www.peggyramsayfoundation. org

Correspondent G Laurence Harbottle, Trustee

Trustees *Laurence Harbottle; Simon Callow; Michael Codron; Sir David Hare; Baroness (Genista) McIntosh of Hudnall; John Tydeman; Harriet Walker; John Welch.*

CC Number 1015427

Information available Accounts were obtained from the Charity Commission website.

General This trust was established in 1992, in accordance with the will of the late Peggy Ramsey.

Peggy Ramsay was one of the best-known play agents in the United Kingdom during the second half of the Twentieth Century. When she died in 1991 her estate was left for charitable purposes to help writers and writing for the stage.

The objects of the trust are:

- the advancement of education by the encouragement of the art of writing
- the relief of poverty among those practising the arts, together with their dependants and relatives, with special reference to writers
- any charitable purpose which may, in the opinion of the trustees, achieve, assist in, or contribute to, the achievement of these objectives.

Grants are made to:

- writers who have some writing experience who need time to write and cannot otherwise afford to do so
- companies which might not otherwise be able to find, develop or use new work
- projects which may facilitate new writing for the stage.

The main priority of the trust is to support semi-professional writers who fulfil the trust's application criteria. The trust also supports organisations and projects, which they review annually. Please visit the trust's website for further information.

In 2005 the trust had assets of £5.1 million and an income of £231,000. Grants were made totalling £159,000.

The largest grants went to the Actors Centre (£12,000) and Queen's Theatre Hornchurch, Northwest Playwrights and Liverpool and Merseyside Theatre Trust (£10,000 each).

Grants of less than £10,000 each went to Pearson Management (£6,500), the George Devine Memorial Fund, Kali Theatre and Alfred Fagon Award (£5,000 each), the Hall of Cornwall Trust (£3,000), the Operating Theatre Company Trust (£2,500), Traverse Society and Society of Authors (£1,500), the Gate theatre (£1,000) and Magnetic North Theatre Productions (£650).

Grants were made to 44 individuals totalling £86,000 (£112,000 to 56 individuals in 2004).

Exclusions No grants are made for productions or writing not for the theatre. Commissioning costs are often considered as part of production costs. Course fees are not considered. Aspiring writers without some production record are not usually considered.

Applications Applications should be made by writing a short letter, when there is a promising purpose not otherwise likely to be funded and which will help writers or writing for the stage. Grants are considered at four or five meetings during the year, although urgent appeals can be considered at other times. All appeals are usually acknowledged.

The Joseph and Lena Randall Charitable Trust

General

£85,000 (2005/06)

Beneficial area Worldwide.

Europa Residence, Place des Moulins, Monte-Carlo

Tel. 00 377 93 50 03 82

Fax 00 377 93 25 82 85

Correspondent D A Randall, Trustee

Trustees *D A Randall; Mrs B Y Randall; Ms A Randall.*

CC Number 255035

Information available Accounts were on file at the charity Commission.

General It is the policy of this trust to provide regular support to a selection of charities.

In 2005/06 the trust's assets totalled £1.8 million, it had an income of £90,000 and 41 grants were made totalling £85,000.

Beneficiaries included Downe House 21st Century Appeal and Jewish Care (£10,000 each), LSE Foundation (£8,000), ROH Foundation (£7,400), LPO (£5,000), Diabetes UK, Nightingale House and Transplant Trust (£3,000 each), Community Security Trust and Norwood Ltd (£2,500 each), Cancer research UK (£2,000), Jewish Deaf Association (£1,200), Bournemouth War Memorial Homes (£1,000), Christies Against Cancer and Motor Neurone Disease Association (£750 each), AJEX (£700), Blonde McIndoe Centre (£700) and Holocaust Educational Trust and Not Forgotten Association (£500 each).

Exclusions No grants to individuals.

Applications In writing to the correspondent. The trust stated that funds were fully committed and that it was 'unable to respond to the many worthy appeals'.

Ranworth Trust

General

£182,000 (2005)

Beneficial area UK and developing countries, with a preference for Norfolk.

The Old House, Ranworth, Norwich NR13 6HS

Correspondent Hon. Mrs J Cator, Trustee

Trustees *Hon. Mrs J Cator; F Cator; C F Cator; M Cator.*

CC Number 292633

Information available Accounts were obtained from the Charity Commission website.

General The trust gives regular support to:

- Cancer Research UK (but not to any other cancer research charity)
- Cancer care organisations working locally
- Organisations working in developing countries, specifically WaterAid, Practical Action and Médecins Sans Frontières
- People with physical disabilities via the Jubilee Sailing Trust
- Its local wildlife trust
- Local prison and victim charities.

In 2005/06 the trust's assets stood at £7.5 million. It had an income of £2.8 million and made grants to 31 organisations totalling £182,000.

Exclusions No grants to non-registered charities.

Applications The trust does not respond to unsolicited applications.

The Fanny Rapaport Charitable Settlement

Jewish, general
Around £40,000 (2005/06)
Beneficial area North west England.

Kuit Steinart Levy, 3 St Mary's Parsonage, Manchester M3 2RD

Tel. 0161 832 3434

Correspondent J S Fidler, Trustee

Trustees *J S Fidler; N Marks.*

CC Number 229406

Information available Information was obtained from the Charity Commission website.

General The trust supports mainly, but not exclusively, Jewish charities and health and welfare organisations, with preference for the north west of England.

In 2005/06 the settlement had an income of £25,000 and a total expenditure of £43,000. Further information was not available.

However, previous beneficiaries included: King David Schools; The Heathlands Village; South Manchester Synagogue; Christie Hospital NHS Trust; Community Security Trust; Delamere Forest School; United Jewish Israel Appeal; Brookvale; Manchester Jewish Federation; and World Jewish Relief.

Exclusions No grants to individuals.

Applications Trustees hold meetings twice a year in March/April and September/October with cheques for donations issued shortly thereafter. If the applicant does not receive a cheque by the end of April or October, the application will have been unsuccessful. No applications are acknowledged.

The Ratcliff Foundation

General
£210,000 (2005/06)
Beneficial area UK, with a preference for local charities in the Midlands, North Wales and Gloucestershire.

36 Great Charles Street, Birmingham B3 3RQ

Tel. 0121 456 4456 **Fax** 0121 200 1614

Email chris.gupwell@feltonandco.co.uk

Correspondent C J Gupwell, Secretary

Trustees *David M Ratcliff, Chair; Edward H Ratcliff; Carolyn M Ratcliff; Gillian Mary Thorpe; James M G Fea; Christopher J Gupwell.*

CC Number 222441

Information available Accounts were on file at the Charity Commission.

General The trust was established in 1961, by Martin Rawlinson Ratcliff. In 2005/06 the foundation had assets of £3.8 million and an income of £239,000. Grants were made totalling £210,000, 52 of which were for £2,000 or more each.

The largest grants went to: Bishop Vesey Grammar School (£12,000); Cancer Research Campaign – Kemerton (£6,000); and Asian Earthquake Appeal, Manor Green Primary School Fund Trust, Tewkesbury Welfare and Volunteer Centre, Warwick School

Development Campaign and Windsor Nursery School (£5,000).

Smaller grants included those to the: Air Ambulance, Fire and Rescue – Coventry (£4,000); Avoncroft Museum of Historic Buildings and Movement Foundation (£3,500 each); and Equal 4 All, Great Bridge Community Forum and St David's Hospice (£3,000 each); Youth Sports Association (£2,500); and Climate Outreach and Information Network, Cruse Bereavement Care – Birmingham and Devon Wildlife Trust (£2,000 each).

There were 40 grants of less than £2,000 each that totalled £45,000.

Exclusions No grants to individuals.

Applications In writing to the correspondent, by 30 November for consideration by trustees in following January. Grants made once a year only, by 31 March.

The E L Rathbone Charitable Trust

Education and welfare of women, alleviation of poverty
£57,000 (2004/05)
Beneficial area UK, with a strong preference for Merseyside.

Rathbone Investment Management Ltd, Port of Liverpool Building, Pier Head, Liverpool L3 1NW

Tel. 0151 236 6666

Email pederson@cybase.co.uk

Website merseytrusts.org.uk

Correspondent Barbara Pederson, Secretary

Trustees *J B Rathbone; Mrs S K Rathbone; Mrs V P Rathbone; R S Rathbone.*

CC Number 233240

Information available Accounts were on file at the Charity Commission, without a list of grants.

General There is a strong preference for Merseyside with local beneficiaries receiving the major funding. The trust has a special interest in social work charities. In 2005/06 the trust had assets of £1.8 million and an income of £73,000. Grants were made to 48 organisation totalling £57,000.

Previous beneficiaries have included Action for ME, Brunswick Boys' Club, Crosby Victim Support, FWAG, Garston CAB, Sheila Kay Fund, Liverpool Deaf Children's Society, Liverpool Playhouse, LPSS, Rathbone Society, River Mersey Inshore Rescue, St John's Hospice, Walton and District Family Support Group and YMCA.

Exclusions No grants to individuals seeking support for second degrees.

Applications In writing to the correspondent.

The Eleanor Rathbone Charitable Trust

Merseyside, women, unpopular causes

£203,000 (2005/06)

Beneficial area UK, with the major allocation for Merseyside; also women-focused international projects.

546 Warrington Road, Rainhill, Merseyside L45 4LZ

Email eleanor.rathbone.trust@tinyworld.co.uk

Website www.eleanorrathbonetrust.org

Correspondent Mrs Liese Astbury, Administrator

Trustees W Rathbone; Ms Jenny Rathbone; A Rathbone; Lady Morgan.

CC Number 233241

Information available Accounts were available from the Charity Commission website.

General The trust concentrates its support largely on the following:

- charities and charitable projects focused on Merseyside (48% in 2005/06)
- charities benefiting women and unpopular and neglected causes but avoiding those with a sectarian interest
- special consideration is given to charities with which any of the trustees have a particular knowledge or association or in which it is thought Eleanor Rathbone or her father William Rathbone VI would have had a special interest
- a small number of grants are made to charities providing holidays for disadvantaged people from Merseyside.

In 2005/06 the trust's assets stood at £7.6 million. It had an income of £244,000 and made grants totalling £203,000, which are broken down as follows:

- Merseyside: 56 grants totalling £121,000
- International: 30 grants totalling £47,000
- National/Regional: 30 grants totalling £34,000
- Holidays: 2 grants totalling £1,500.

Grants were made between £1,000 to £2,000, with most of the grants totalling less than £1,000 each.

As listed in the trust's 2005/06 accounts, exceptional grants were made to Liverpool Personal Service Society (PSS) towards the Larry and Patrick Rathbone Memorial Fund (£25,000), Liverpool and Merseyside Theatres Trust for an Eleanor Rathbone Women's Commission Award (£4,000) and Care International to provide access to water for vulnerable populations in West Bank and Gaza (£2,500).

Exclusions Grants are not made in support of: any activity which relieves a statutory authority of its obligations; individuals, unless (and only exceptionally) it is made through a charity and it also fulfils at least one of the other positive objectives mentioned above; overseas organisations without a sponsoring charity based in the UK.

The trust does not generally favour grants for running costs, but prefers to support specific projects, services or to contribute to specific developments.

Applications There is no application form. The trust asks for a brief proposal for funding including costings, accompanied by the latest available accounts and any relevant supporting material. It is useful to know who else is supporting the project.

To keep administration costs to a minimum, receipt of applications is not usually acknowledged. Applicants requiring acknowledgement should enclose an sae.

Trustees currently meet three times a year on varying dates.

The Rayden Charitable Trust

Jewish

£39,000 (2004/05)

Beneficial area UK.

c/o Vantis Group Ltd, 82 St John Street, London EC1M 4JN

Correspondent The Trustees

Trustees S Rayden; C Rayden; P Rayden.

CC Number 294446

Information available Accounts were on file at the Charity Commission.

General In 2004/05 the trust had an income from donations of £35,000 and made grants totalling £39,000. Assets stood at £8,800.

Over 120 grants were made in the year, of which 16 were for £1,000 or more. Beneficiaries of these larger grants included: Northwest London Jewish Day School (£5,000); British Friends of Or Chadash (£4,300), Lubavitch Foundation (£3,250); Yesoday Hatorah School (£2,400); London Carlebach Shul Trust and Norwood Challenges (£2,000 each); One Family UK (£1,600); British Friends of Ascent of Safed and Magen David Adom UK (£1,500 each); Community Security Trust (£1,250); and Central London Mikveh, Children's Adventure Farm Trust, CAF – South East Asia Disaster, LCS Trust and London School of Economics Annual Fund (£1,000 each).

Applications In writing to the correspondent.

The Roger Raymond Charitable Trust

Older people, education, medical

£208,000 (2004/05)

Beneficial area UK (and very occasionally large, well-known overseas organisations).

Suttondene, 17 South Border, Purley, Surrey CR8 3LL

Tel. 020 8660 9133

Email russell@pullen.cix.co.uk

Correspondent R W Pullen, Trustee

Trustees *R W Pullen; P F Raymond; M G Raymond.*

CC Number 262217

Information available Accounts were on file at the Charity Commission.

General In 2004/05 the trust had assets of £9.7 million and an income of £213,000. After management and administration costs of £42,000, grants were made totalling £208,000.

The principal beneficiary during the year, as in previous years, was Bloxham School, which received a donation of £143,000.

Beneficiaries during the year included Rangen School of Dance (£7,500), Sight Savers (£5,000), Nanyuki Children's Home (£3,500), UNICEF (£2,500), Brain Research, Haste, Leonard Cheshire and St Mary's Wrestwood Trust (£2,000 each) and Swanage Hospital and VSO (£1,500 each).

Exclusions Grants are rarely given to individuals.

Applications The trust stated that applications are considered throughout the year, although funds are not always available.

The Rayne Trust

Jewish organisations and charities benefiting children, older and young people, at risk groups and people disadvantaged by poverty or socially isolated

£1.2 million (2005/06)

Beneficial area Israel and UK.

Carlton House, 33 Robert Adam Street, London W1U 3HR

Tel. 020 7487 9637 **Fax** 020 7935 3737

Email info@raynefoundation.org.uk

Website www.raynefoundation.org.uk

Correspondent Tim Joss, Director

Trustees *Lady Jane Rayne; the Hon. Robert A Rayne.*

CC Number 207392

Information available Accounts were available at the Charity Commission.

General The Rayne Trust was established by Lord Rayne to support

organisations in which its trustees have a close personal interest and it shares the Rayne Foundation's overall theme of bridge-building. The trust focuses its contributions on the following areas:

- projects in Israel;
- social welfare and arts charities working in the UK to help young and older people and others disadvantaged by poverty or social isolation.

In 2005/06 the trust had assets of £20 million and an income of £549,000. Grants to 87 organisations totalled £1.2 million. The sum of £168,000 was given in the UK. Grants were categorised as follows:

Grants to organisations relating to Israel – totalling over £1 million
Beneficiaries included: Jerusalem Foundation (£1 million), receiving by far the largest grant for the Max Rayne Hand in Hand School for Jewish and Arab Education; and Ezer Mizion (£50,000), for the Lloyd Gerard Donor Pool.

Grants to organisations relating to the UK – totalling £168,000
The sole beneficiary of a grant over £25,000 was the UN World Food Programme (£25,000), for South Africa Appeal. Smaller grants totalled £143,000.

Exclusions No grants to individuals or non-registered charities.

Applications If you are considering applying to the trust you should first discuss your proposal with the Grants Manager, Susan O'Sullivan (tel. 020 7487 9630 or email: sosullivan@raynefoundation.org.uk).

The John Rayner Charitable Trust

General

£29,000 (2004/05)

Beneficial area England, with a preference for Merseyside and Wiltshire.

Manor Farmhouse, Church Street, Great Bedwyn, Marlborough, Wiltshire SN8 3PE

Tel. 01672 870362 **Fax** 01672 870362

Email raynertrust@hotmail.co.uk

Correspondent Mrs J Wilkinson, Trustee

Trustees *Mrs J Wilkinson; Dr J M H Rayner; Mrs A L C de Boinville.*

CC Number 802363

Information available Full accounts were available from the Charity Commission.

General This trust has general charitable purposes in the UK, with a preference for Merseyside. Support is given to small organisations. In 2004/05 the trust had an income of £25,000 and made grants totalling £29,000. Beneficiaries included the Bath Institute of Medical Engineering, the British Kidney Association, the Community Foundation, the Countryside Foundation for Education, Crossroads, Delta, the Haven Trust, Live Music Now! – North West and Trinity College of Music (£3,000 each).

Exclusions No grants to individuals or non-registered charities.

Applications In writing to the correspondent by 31 January each year. Trustees meet to allocate donations in February/March. Only successful applicants will be contacted. There are no application forms or guidelines.

The Albert Reckitt Charitable Trust

General

£62,000 (2005/06)

Beneficial area UK.

13 Risborough Street, London SE1 0HF

Correspondent John Barrett, Secretary

Trustees *Mrs S C Bradley, Chair; Sir Michael Colman; Mrs G M Atherton; J Hughes-Reckitt; P C Knee; Dr A Joy; W Russell.*

CC Number 209974

Information available Accounts were on file at the Charity Commission, without a list of grants.

General The trust states its objectives are 'to make grants to a wide variety of registered charities, including non-political charities connected with the Society of Friends. It tends to support UK organisations rather than local groups, giving grants of £250 to £750 each.

In 2005/06 it had assets of £2.6 million, which generated an income of £73,000. Grants totalled £62,000, given as £42,000 in subscriptions (annual grants), the rest in donations (one-off grants). No further information for the year was available.

Exclusions No support to individuals. No grants for political or sectarian charities, except for non-political charities connected with the Society of Friends.

Applications In writing to the correspondent. Trustees meet in June/July and applications need to be received by the end of March.

Eva Reckitt Trust Fund

Welfare, relief in need, extension and development of education, victims of war

£39,000 (2005)

Beneficial area UK and overseas.

1 Somerford Road, Cirencester, Gloucestershire GL7 1TP

Tel. 01285 659383

Correspondent David Birch, Trustee

Trustees *Anna Bunney; Chris Whittaker; David Birch; Diana Holliday.*

CC Number 210563

Information available Accounts were on file at the Charity Commission.

General Registered in October 1962, in 2005 the trust had an income from investments of £34,000. Grants totalled £39,000.

Beneficiaries included: Afghan Educational Trust, Child Hope, Christian Engineers in Development, Fistula Hospital – Ethiopia, Médecins Sans Frontières, Medical Foundation for the Care of Victims of Torture and Penha (£2,000 each); Medical Support in Romania (£1,500); Asian Women's Helpline (£1,200); Chernobyl Children in Need, Canon Collins Education Trust for Southern Africa, the Cog Wheel Trust, the Community College, the Matthew Trust, Prisoners of Conscience Appeal Fund, Quaker Social Action, Rise and Shine Primary School – Nairobi and WOMANKIND Worldwide (£1,000 each); and Send a Cow and St Giles Trust (£500 each).

Grants are also made towards the relief of poverty amongst persons who have been in the service of the family of the founder.

Applications In writing to the correspondent.

The Red Rose Charitable Trust

Older people and people with disabilities

£44,000 (2005/06)

Beneficial area UK with a preference for Lancashire and Merseyside.

c/o Rathbones, Port of Liverpool Building, Pier Head, Liverpool L3 1NW

Tel. 0151 236 6666 **Fax** 0151 243 7003

Correspondent J N L Packer, Trustee

Trustees *Miss Olwen Seddon; James N L Packer; Mrs Jane L Fagan.*

CC Number 1038358

Information available Full accounts were available from the Charity Commission website.

General This trust was registered with the Charity Commission in June 1994. It has a preference for supporting charities working with older people and people who are physically or mentally disabled. Grants are also made to individuals within these categories. In 2005/06 the trust's assets stood at £1 million. It had an income of £45,000 and made grants totalling £44,000.

The largest grants were made to S R J Services (£10,000) and Liverpool Cathedral Centenary Fund (£5,000). Other grant recipients included Henshaw Society for the Blind, Motor Neurone Disease, the Richard Overall Trust and Spinal Research (£2,000 each) and Arc, Ex-Servicemen Mental Welfare Society, and the Rathbone Society (£1,000 each).

Applications In writing to the correspondent.

The C A Redfern Charitable Foundation

General

£202,000 (2005/06)

Beneficial area UK.

PricewaterhouseCoopers, 9 Greyfriars Road, Reading, Berkshire RG1 1JG

Tel. 0118 959 7111

Correspondent The Trustees

Trustees *C A G Redfern, Chair; Sir R A Clark; William Maclaren; D S Redfern; T P Thornton; S R Ward.*

CC Number 299918

Information available Accounts were available from the Charity Commission website.

General This trust supports a wide range of organisations with some preference for those concerned with health and welfare. In 2005/06 the foundation had assets of £5.4 million and an income of £169,000. Grants were made totalling £202,000. Grants ranged from £250 to £30,000, with the majority of grants totalling less than £5,000 each.

The largest grants included those to: South Buckinghamshire Riding for the Disabled and Saints and Sinners (£30,000 each); White Ensign (£10,000); Gurkha Welfare Trust (£6,500); and Cancer Resource Centre, Canine Partners for Independence, Chase Children's Hospice Services, Farms for City Children, Foundation for the Study of Infant Deaths and Historic Royal Palaces (£5,000 each).

Smaller grants included those to: Chicks Country Hospital for Inner City Kids (£4,000); BEN, Little Sisters of the Poor, Meath Home and Royal National Institute for the Blind (£3,000 each); Boys' and Girls' Clubs of Scotland, British Limbless Ex-Servicemen's Association – Buckinghamshire and Fund for Epilepsy (£2,000 each); British Sports Trust, Child Bereavement Trust and Institute of Hepatology (£1,000 each); Motor Neurone Disease Association, Noah's Ark Trust and SADA (£500 each); and New Heart New Start Appeal, MIND and County Air Ambulance (£250 each).

Exclusions No grants for building works or individuals.

Applications The trust does not accept unsolicited applications.

The Sir Steve Redgrave Charitable Trust

Children and young people up to the age of 18 worldwide

£336,000 (2005/04)

Beneficial area UK.

PO Box 200, Petersfield, Hampshire GU32 2ZX

Correspondent Adrian Milne, Administrator

Trustees *Paul Richardson, Chair; Sir Steve Redgrave; Dr Lady Ann Redgrave; Wallace Dobbin; Andrew Wigmore; Athole Still; Lizzy Pearce.*

CC Number 1086216

Information available Accounts were available from the Charity Commission website and further information was obtained from the trust's website.

General Five times Olympic champion Steve Redgrave established this trust in 2001.The trust's main priority is to raise and distribute over £5 million in five years to small charities and groups and individuals.

The aim of the trust is to improve and enhance the quality of young people's lives, particularly in relation to medical, social, educational and economic needs within the UK.

Potential applicants should:

• be Children/Youth/Community-based
• be UK-based
• have low administrative costs: less than 25% of revenues per annum
• have an income less than £200,000 per annum
• have low public profile
• applicants must prove the tangible outcome of their work and how it makes a real difference, for example work in the following areas:
  (a) Buildings/equipment;
  (b) Research; (c) Drugs/crime Prevention; (d) Nationwide (e) Up to age 18

For full details of the trust's grant application criteria, please visit their website.

In 2004/05 the trust had assets of £639,000 and an income of £828,000. Grants were made totalling £336,000, which were broken down as follows:

• education and training: nine grants totalling £217,000

• medical and disability: eight grants totalling £59,000
• miscellaneous: three grants totalling £32,000
• poverty and hardship: two grants totalling £6,000

Ten of the largest grants were made to: Bobath Scotland (£126,000 in two grants); Birmingham City Council (£100,000); Cosmic (£40,000); Stroke Rowing Association (£10,000); Camp Quality UK (£9,000); Ashgate croft School Swimming Pool and St Michael's Community Nursery (£5,000 each); Grantham Journal Children's Appeal (£4,800) and Alana Marie Memorial Fund (£3,000).

Applications In writing to the correspondent. The recipient shall report within six months of receipt of the grant detailing how the money was used and the difference it has made. This will be published in the Sir Steve Redgrave Charitable Trust's annual report/website.

The Christopher H R Reeves Charitable Trust

Food allergies, disability

£431,000 (2005)

Beneficial area UK.

Hinwick Lodge, Nr Wellingborough, Northamptonshire NN29 7JQ

Tel. 01234 781090 **Fax** 01234 781090

Correspondent E M Reeves, Trustee

Trustees *E M Reeves; V Reeves; M Kennedy.*

CC Number 266877

Information available Accounts were provided by the trust.

General The trust states that it is 'holding about 75% of its income and capital for application in the limited area of food allergy and related matters. Nearly all the income in this section has already been committed to Allergy Research and Environmental Health at King's College, London and to the production and distribution of a database of research references under the title of Allergy and Environmental Medicine Database'.

'New appeals related to food allergy and intolerance are invited and a response will be made to applicants.'

'The remaining 25% of the trust's income and capital will be held for general donations. The main area of interest is in disability. Donations will largely be made to charities already associated with the trust. Only successful applicants will receive a response.'

In 2005 the trust had assets of £4.1 million and an income of £3.7 million. Grants were made totalling £431,000, which were divided between the following two categories:

Research – 3 grants totalling £350,000
The trust has funding commitments to Kings College London and University of Surrey, which it met through two donations to FAIR totalling £70,000. There were four other grants made totalling £280,000.

Other – 24 grants totalling £81,000
The largest grants made included those to: Uppingham School (£50,000); Timespan (£9,000); Campaign to Protect Rural England (£5,000); Solicitors Benevolent Fund (£2,000); and Northamptonshire Association of Youth Clubs and the Anaphylaxis Campaign (£1,000 each).

Smaller grants of £500 or less each included those to: the Wildlife Trust, Autism Bedfordshire, Bedfordshire and Northamptonshire and MS Therapy Centre Rutland House Community Centre (£500 each); and Countryside Foundation for Education and Christopher Reeves VA School – Governors (£300 each).

Exclusions No grants for: individuals; overseas travel and expeditions; animal charities; church/community hall/school appeals outside the north Bedfordshire area; overseas aid; children's charities; drugs/alcohol charities; mental health charities; or education.

Applications In writing to the correspondent, including a copy of the latest annual report and accounts. Trustees meet five times a year in March, May, July, September and November. Only successful applicants will receive a reply.

The Max Reinhardt Charitable Trust

Deafness, fine arts promotion

£47,000 (2005/06)
Beneficial area UK.

c/o BSG Valentine, Lynton House, 7–12 Tavistock Square, London WC1H 9BQ

Tel. 0207 393 1111

Correspondent The Secretary

Trustees *Joan Reinhardt; Veronica Reinhardt; Belinda McGill.*

CC Number 264741

Information available Accounts were available from the Charity Commission website.

General The trust supports organisations benefiting people who are deaf and fine arts promotion. In 2005/06 the trust had assets of £485,000 and an income of £37,000. Grants were made totalling £47,000. Grants were made to 18 organisations totalling £47,000.

The largest grants were those made to Paintings in Hospitals (£24,000), St George's Medical School (£11,000), Top Banana (£8,000) and RNID (£1,500).

Other grants made included those to Delta (£750), Art in Healthcare and NDCS (£250 each), Salvation Army (£200), Sound Seekers and Concern Worldwide (£100 each) and the Art Fund (£28).

Exclusions No grants to individuals.

Applications In writing to the correspondent.

REMEDI

Research into disability

£76,000 (2005/06)
Beneficial area UK.

14 Crondace Road, London SW6 4BB

Tel. 020 7384 2929 **Fax** 020 7731 8240

Email rosie.wait@remedi.org.uk

Website www.remedi.org.uk

Correspondent Mrs Rosie Wait, Director

Trustees *Dr Anthony K Clarke, Chair; James Mosley; Brian Winterflood; Dr Adrian H M Heagerty; Colin Maynard; Dr I T Stuttaford; Dr Anthony B Ward.*

CC Number 1063359

Information available Accounts were available from the Charity Commission website.

General REMEDI supports pioneering research into all aspects of disability in the widest sense of the word, with special emphasis on the way in which disability limits the activities and lifestyle of all ages.

The trust receives most of its income from companies and other trusts, which is then given towards researchers carrying out innovative and original work who find it difficult to find funding from larger organisations. Grants are generally for one year, although funding for the second year is considered sympathetically and for a third year exceptionally. There is a preference for awarding a few sizeable grants rather than many smaller grants.

The trust has a number of current projects; one main funding priority is a five-year Cerebral Palsy project which began in January 2006. The trust is in collaboration with Cerebra, with the trust funding the time and research element of the project.

In 2005/06 the trust's assets stood at £192,000. It had an income of £204,000 and made grants totalling £70,000.

Research grants made included those to the following institutions and projects: Frenchay Hospital for Speech and Language – 'Children's participation in speech and language therapy' (£35,000); University of Birmingham – 'Effects on external-focus feedback on motor skill acquisition' (£22,000); University of Nottingham – 'Psychological treatments for depression in Aphasic patients' (£11,000); and St Augustine's Medical Practice – 'storytelling for pain study' (£9,000).

Exclusions Cancer and cancer-related diseases are not supported.

Applications By email to the correspondent. Applications are received throughout the year. They should initially include a summary of the project on one side of A4 with costings. The Chair normally considers applications on the third Tuesday of each month with a view to inviting applicants to complete an application form by email. For further information please visit the trust's website.

The Rest Harrow Trust

Jewish, general

£48,000 (2005/06)
Beneficial area UK.

c/o Portrait Solicitors, 1 Chancery Lane, London WC2A 1LF

Tel. 020 7320 3890

Correspondent Miss Judith S Portrait

Trustees *Mrs J B Bloch; Miss J S Portrait; HON and V Trustee Limited.*

CC Number 238042

Information available Accounts were available from the Charity Commission website.

General This trust was established in 1964, its main objectives are to distribute grants from its income for education, housing and to assist the deprived and older people.

In 2005 the trust had an income of £60,000 and made grants totalling £48,000. Its assets stood at £920,000. There were 323 grants made totalling £48,000, of which 75% were for £100 each.

The largest grants were those made to: Nightingale House (£5,500); Friends of the Hebrew University – Jerusalem (£1,500); and Cheltenham Ladies College – for bursaries fund, Council of Christian and Jews, Jewish Blind and Disabled, Jewish Care, JNF Charitable Trust, St Christopher's Hospice, Weizmann Institute Foundation and World Jewish Relief (£1,000 each).

Smaller grants included those made to: Friends of Israel Educational Foundation, Norwood, Pinhas Rutenberg Educational Trust and Spiro Ark (£500 each); Merlin (£400); New Israel Fund (£300); Africa Now, Book Aid International, Breast Cancer Care, City Escape, Drug and Alcohol Foundation, Dermatrust, Interfaith Network for the UK, Medical Foundation, Notting Hill Housing Trust, Scope and Sightsavers International (£200 each); and Childhope UK, British Blind Sport, Prison Phoenix Trust and Quaker Social International (£100).

Exclusions No grants to non-registered charities or to individuals.

Applications In writing to the correspondent. Appeals are considered quarterly. Only applications from eligible bodies are acknowledged.

The Rhododendron Trust

Welfare, overseas aid and development, culture

£40,000 (2005/06)

Beneficial area UK and overseas.

c/o 12 Main Street, Howsham YO60 7PH

Correspondent P E Healey, Trustee

Trustees *Peter Edward Healey; Dr Ralph Walker; Mrs Sarah Ray; Mrs Sarah Oliver.*

CC Number 267192

Information available Accounts were available from the Charity Commission website.

General It is the current policy of the trustees to divide donations as follows: (i) 50% to charities whose work is primarily overseas; (ii) 40% for UK social welfare charities; and (iii) 10% for UK cultural activities.

Grants of £500 or £1,000 are made generally to charities which have been supported in the past although a few new beneficiaries are included each year. In 2005 the trust made 58 grants totalling £40,000.

Grant recipients included Ashram International, British Deaf Association, Cambodia Trust, Find Your Feet, Mine Advisory Group, Survival International and WOMANKIND Worldwide (£1,000 each) and Angels International, Brandon Centre, Children in Crisis, Excellent Development Trust, Joliba Trust and the Karuna Trust (£500 each).

Exclusions The trust does not support medical research, individual projects, or local community projects in the UK.

Applications In writing to the correspondent. The majority of donations are made in March. Applications are not acknowledged.

Daisie Rich Trust

General

£43,000 to organisations (2005/06)

Beneficial area UK, with a priority for the Isle of Wight.

The Hawthorns, School Lane, Arreton, Isle of Wight PO30 3AD

Email daisierich@yahoo.co.uk

Correspondent The Secretary

Trustees *M R Oatley; A H Medley.*

CC Number 236706

Information available Accounts were on file at the Charity Commission.

General This trust has a priority for supporting organisations and individuals on the Isle of Wight, with any available surplus given in the UK or elsewhere.

In 2005/06 the trust had assets of £2.7 million, which generated an income of £113,000. Grants totalled £76,000 of which £33,000 went to ex-employees of Upward and Rich Ltd and their dependants.

Grants to 56 organisations totalled £43,000. Beneficiaries of donations of £1,000 or more included: Earl Mountbatten Hospice (£9,800); Macmillan Nurses (£2,200); Isle of Wight Rural Community Council – Helping Hands Fund, Isle of Wight Youth Trust, SSAFA and St Helens Youth Club (£1,500 each); and Carisbrooke Castle Museum, Carisbrooke Priory Trust, Hampshire and Wight Trust for Maritime Archaeology, Hampshire and Wight Wildlife Trust, Island Women's Refuge, Isle of Wight Society for the Blind, Macmillan Cancer Relief and Portsmouth Hospitals Rocky Appeal (£1,000 each).

Smaller grants included those to: Holy Trinity Church – Ryde, Hospital Broadcasting Corporation, Isle of Wight CAB, Isle of Wight Spina Bifida and Hydrocephalus Association, Motor Neurone Disease Association, Multiple Sclerosis Society, NCH Action for Children and St Johns Ambulance (£500 each); Salvation Army – Newport (£350); Brighton and Hove Parents' and Children's Group, Julia Margaret Cameron Trust, CRUSE Bereavement Care, Isle of Wight Deaf Children's Association and Samaritans (£250 each); Saturday Club for Deaf Children (£200); and Rope Walk Social Club (£150).

Applications In writing to the correspondent.

The Sir Cliff Richard Charitable Trust

Spiritual and social welfare

Around £150,000 (2005/06)

Beneficial area UK.

Harley House, 94 Hare Lane, Claygate, Esher, Surrey KT10 0RB

Tel. 01372 467752 **Fax** 01372 462352

Correspondent Bill Latham, Trustee

Trustees *William Latham; Malcolm Smith.*

CC Number 1096412

Information available Information was obtained from the Charity Commission website.

General This trust has general charitable purposes, with a preference for causes seeking to improve spiritual and social welfare.

In 2005/06 the trust had an income of £16,000 and a total expenditure of £169,000. Further information was not available. Previous beneficiaries included British Lung Foundation, Cliff Richard Tennis Development Trust, Genesis Art Trust and Arts Centre Group.

Exclusions Capital building projects, church repairs and renovations are all excluded. No support for individuals.

Applications Applications should be from registered charities only, in writing, and for one-off needs. All applications are acknowledged. Grants are made quarterly in January, April, July and October.

The Violet M Richards Charity

Older people, sickness, medical research and education

£55,000 (2005/06)

Beneficial area UK, with a preference for East Sussex, West Kent and around Tunbridge Wells and Crowborough.

c/o Wedlake Bell (ref CAH), 52 Bedford Row, London WC1R 4LR

Tel. 0207 395 3155 **Fax** 0207 406 1601

Correspondent Charles Hicks, Secretary

Trustees Mrs E H Hill; G R Andersen; C A Hicks; Miss M Davies; Mrs M Burt; Dr J Clements.

CC Number 273928

Information available Full accounts were available from the Charity Commission website.

General The trust's objectives are relief of age and sickness, through advancement of medical research (particularly into geriatric problems), medical education, homes and other facilities for older people and those who are sick. The trustees are happy to commit themselves to funding a research project over a number of years, including 'seedcorn' projects. Applications from East Sussex, West Kent and around Tunbridge Wells and Crowborough are especially favoured by the trustees.

In 2005/06 the trust had an income of £69,000 and made grants totalling £55,000. Its assets stood at £2.3 million.

Grants made to ten organisations were as follows: British Neurological Research Trust (£30,000); British Eye Research Foundation, Brain Tumour UK and Derma Trust (£4,000 each); Hospice in the Weald (£3,000); British Liver Trust and Crossroads (£2,000 each); and Caring for Carers and St Christopher's Hospice (£1,000 each).

Exclusions No support for individuals.

Applications In writing to the correspondent, however the trust stated in the 2005/06 accounts that they 'prefer to be proactive with charities of their own choice, rather than reactive to external applications.' The trustees generally meet to consider grants twice a year in the spring and the autumn. There is no set format for applying and only successful applications are acknowledged.

The Clive Richards Charity Ltd

Churches, schools, arts, disability, poverty

£313,000 (2005/06)

Beneficial area UK, with a preference for Herefordshire.

Lower Hope, Ullingswick, Herefordshire HR1 3JF

Tel. 01432 820557 **Fax** 01432 820772

Email anna@crco.co.uk

Correspondent Miss Anna Lewis, Trustee

Trustees W S C Richards; Mrs S A Richards; Miss Anna Lewis.

CC Number 327155

Information available Accounts were available from the Charity Commission website.

General The area of this trust's interest is people with disabilities and those disadvantaged by poverty. Priority has been given to education, the arts and sport. In 2005/06 the trust had assets of £27,000 and an income of £136,000. Grants were made totalling £313,000.

The largest grants made included those to: St Mary's RC High School (£50,000); Woodland Trust (£33,000); Chance to Shine Appeal and Kingstone High School (£25,000 each); Belmont Abbey General Fund (£12,000); and Nelson's Column Hereford (£10,000).

Grants of less than £10,000 each included those made to: St Joseph's Church (£5,000); the Guide Dog for the Blind Association (£2,500); the Welsh National Opera Development Fund (£2,000); and National History Museum and Royal Shakespeare Society (£1,000 each).

Other grants of less than £1,000 each totalled £15,000.

Exclusions No grants for political causes.

Applications In writing to the correspondent. However, the trust states that 'the charity's resources are almost fully committed and thus it is extremely selective in accepting any requests for funding'.

The Muriel Edith Rickman Trust

Medical research, education

£116,000 (2004/05)

Beneficial area UK.

12 Fitzroy Court, 57 Shepherds Hill, London N6 5RD

Correspondent H P Rickman, Trustee

Trustees H P Rickman, Chair; M D Gottlieb; R Tallis.

CC Number 326143

Information available Accounts were on file at the Charity Commission.

General The trust makes grants to medical research organisations towards equipment. The trust prefers to support physical disabilities rather than mental illnesses.

In 2004/05 it had assets of £138,000 and an income of £112,000, mostly from donations. Grants to eight organisations totalled £116,000.

Beneficiaries were Fight for Sight (£30,000), Technion – Israel Institute of Technology (£25,000), Cystic Fibrosis Trust (£19,000), the Anthony Nolan Trust (£18,000), Myasthenia Gravis Association (£13,000), Liver for Life Appeal (£10,000), the Rockinghorse Appeal (£1,000) and the Guide Dogs for the Blind Association (£250).

Exclusions The trustees will not respond to individual students, clubs, community projects or expeditions.

Applications There are no guidelines for applications and the trust only replies if it is interested at first glance; it will then ask for further details. Trustees meet as required.

The Ripple Effect Foundation

General

£32,000 (2004/05)

Beneficial area UK.

Marlborough Investment Consultants Ltd, Wessex House, Oxford Road, Newbury, Berkshire RG14 1PA

Correspondent Miss Caroline D Marks, Trustee

Trustees *Miss Caroline D Marks; I R Marks; I S Wesley.*

CC Number 802327

Information available Accounts were on file at the Charity Commission.

General The accounts of this charity state: 'The objectives of the trustees are to support a range of charitable causes over a few years that meet their funding criteria. They proactively seek out projects that meet their criteria and do not respond to unsolicited applications.'

In 2004/05 the trust had assets of £1.4 million, which generated a low income of £36,000. Grants to two organisations totalled £32,000.

Network for Social Change received £25,000, which was passed on to other charities. A grants of £7,000 went to Devon Community Foundation Friends.

Applications The trust states that it does not respond to unsolicited applications.

The John Ritblat Charitable Trust No. 1

Jewish, general

£40,000 (2004/05)

Beneficial area UK.

Baker Tilly, 46 Clarendon Road, Watford WD17 1JJ

Tel. 01923 816400

Correspondent The Clerk

Trustees *J H Ritblat; N S J Ritblat; C B Wagman; Miss S C Ritblat; J W J Ritblat.*

CC Number 262463

Information available Full accounts were on file at the Charity Commission.

General In 2004/05 the trust had assets of £308,000 and an income of £74,000. Grants to 20 organisations totalled £40,000.

Beneficiaries included United Jewish Israel Appeal (£11,000), Lubavitch Foundation and Skiers Trust of Great Britain (£5,000 each), Royal Academy of Music (£3,800), Tate Foundation (£3,500), Gertner Foundation (£3,000), JNF Charitable Trust (£2,300), Ascent (£2,000), Central Synagogue (£1,000), United Synagogue (£800), Music of Modern Art and Jewish National Fund (£500 each), Western Marble Arch Synagogue (£350), Anglo-Israel Association (£300), the Prince's Trust (£250) and International Students Home (£50).

The trust makes grants primarily to long-established organisations.

Exclusions No grants to individuals.

Applications Please do not apply as all funds are committed.

The River Trust

Christian

£85,000 (2004/05)

Beneficial area UK, with a preference for Sussex.

c/o Kleinwort Benson Trustees Ltd, PO Box 57005, 30 Gresham Street, London EC2V 7PG

Tel. 020 3207 7336

Correspondent Chris Gilbert, Secretary

Trustee *Kleinwort Benson Trustees Ltd.*

CC Number 275843

Information available Accounts were obtained from the Charity Commission website.

General Gillian Warren formed the trust in 1977 with an endowment mainly of shares in the merchant bank Kleinwort Benson. It is one of the many Kleinwort trusts. The River Trust is one of the smaller of the family trusts. It supports Christian causes. In 2004/05 the trust had assets of £543,000 and an income of £99,000. There were 42 grants made towards Evangelical Christian faith causes totalling £85,000, these were divided into the following categories:

Advancement of Christian Faith – 12 grants totalling £33,000
Grant recipients included: Youth with a

Mission (£14,000); Timothy Trust (£8,000); Tear Fund and Ashburnham Christian Trust (£2,000 each); Micah Trust and Release International (£1,000 each); and Beauty from Ashes (£500).

Religious education – 10 grants totalling £23,000
Beneficiaries included: Care Trust (£7,000); Genesis Arts Trust (£5,000 each); and Interprayer Charitable Trust (£500).

Church funds – 7 grants totalling £16,000
Grants awarded include those made to: Barcombe Parochial Church (£7,000); St Luke's Prestonville Church (£2,500); All Souls Church Eastbourne (£1,500); and St Barnabus Church (£750).

Religious welfare work – 7 grants totalling £8,000
Grants made included those to: Care for the Family (£4,000); Encounter (£2,000); Open Doors UK and the Society of Mary and Martha (£500 each).

Missionary work – 6 grants totalling £5,000
Beneficiaries included: On the Move (£1,800); St Stephen's Society (£1,000); and African Enterprise and International Films (£500 each).

Exclusions Only appeals for Christian causes will be considered. No grants to individuals. The trust does not support 'repairs of the fabric of the church' nor does it give grants for capital expenditure.

Applications In writing to the correspondent. Unsolicited appeals are considered as well as causes which have already been supported and are still regarded as commitments of the trust. Only successful applicants are notified of the trustees' decision. Some charities are supported for more than one year, although no commitment is usually given to the recipients.

Riverside Charitable Trust Limited

Health, welfare, older people, education, general

£119,000 to individuals and organisations (2005/06)

Beneficial area Mainly Lancashire.

Riverside, Bacup, Lancashire OL13 0DT

Correspondent F Drew, Trustee

Trustees *B J Lynch; I B Dearing; J A Davidson; F Drew; H Francis; A Higginson; G Maden; L Clegg; B Terry.*

CC Number 264015

Information available Accounts were obtained from the Charity Commission website.

General The trust's objectives are to support the following: poor, sick and older people; education; healthcare; the relief of poverty of people employed or formerly employed in the shoe trade; and other charitable purposes.

In 2005/06 the trust had an income of £112,000 and made 192 grants totalling £119,000. Its assets stood at £2.4 million. Grants were broken down into the following categories:

- Relief for sickness, infirmity and for older people – 27 grants totalling £31,000
- General charitable public benefits – 74 grants totalling £49,000
- Relief of poverty – 72 grants totalling £38,000
- Death grants – 18 grants totalling £580
- Educational support – 1 grant of £350

Exclusions No grants for political causes.

Applications In writing to the correspondent.

The Daniel Rivlin Charitable Trust

Jewish, general

£19,000 (2005/06)

Beneficial area UK.

Manor House, Northgate Lane, Linton, Wetherby, West Yorkshire LS22 4HN

Tel. 01937 589645

Correspondent D R Rivlin, Trustee

Trustees *D R Rivlin; N S Butler; M Miller.*

CC Number 328341

Information available Accounts were available from the Charity Commission website.

General In 2005/06 the trust had assets of £65,000 and an income of £62,000. Grants were made totalling £19,000.

There were ten grants made during the year to: UJIA (£16,000); Friends of Israel and Hay-on-Wye Festival of Literature (£1,000 each); Makor Charitable Trust (£750); JNFCT (£225 in two grants); Make a Dream and Donisthorpe Hall (£200 each); Pocklington and Market Weighton Rotary Club (£50); and Yad Vashem (£18).

Applications The trust states that funds are fully committed and does not welcome unsolicited applications.

The Alex Roberts-Miller Foundation

See below

£35,000 (2005/06)

Beneficial area UK.

PO Box 104, Dorking, Surrey RH5 6YN

Fax 01306 741356

Email alexrmfoundation@mac.com

Website www.alexrmfoundation.org.uk

Trustees *Will Armitage; David Avery-Gee; Emma Balkwill; Richard Roberts-Miller; Fiona Roberts-Miller; Jo Roberts-Miller; Beth Roberts-Miller.*

CC Number 1093912

Information available Accounts were available from the Charity Commission and further information was taken from the trust's website.

General The foundation was established in 2002. Its main goal is to help provide educational, sporting and social opportunities for disadvantaged young people. It aims to target funds where they will have a direct and significant impact on the lives of the people they are trying to help. The foundation also promotes road safety and its education.

In 2005/06 the trust had an income of £29,000 and made grants totalling £35,000. Its assets stood at £136,000.

Grants were made to nine organisations: Starlight Children's Foundation (£6,000); Children's Country Holiday Fund, Springboard for Children, CCB and H Young Carers, RoadPeace, the Sutton Trust, the Elizabeth Foundation, and Red Balloon (£4,000 each); and SAFE Justice Foundation (£1,000).

Exclusions No grants to individuals.

Applications The foundation researches its own beneficiaries.

Edwin George Robinson Charitable Trust

Medical research

Around £49,000 (2005/06)

Beneficial area UK and developing countries.

71 Manor Road South, Hinchley Wood, Surrey KT10 0QB

Tel. 020 8398 6845

Correspondent E C Robinson, Trustee

Trustees *E C Robinson; Mrs S C Robinson.*

CC Number 1068763

Information available Information was obtained from the Charity Commission website.

General The trust makes grants for specific research projects. Grants are not usually made to fund general operating costs. In 2005/06 the trust had an income of £12,000 and a total expenditure of £53,000. Further information was not available.

Previous beneficiaries included British Red Cross, Marie Curie Cancer Care, Diabetes UK, National Society for Epilepsy, Brainwave, Spencer Dayman Meningitis Laboratory, Elimination of Leukaemia Fund, Fight for Sight, Research into Ageing, RNLI.

Exclusions No grants to individuals or for general running costs for small local organisations.

Applications In writing to the correspondent.

The Rock Foundation

Christian ministries, see below

£151,000 to organisations (2004/05)

Beneficial area Worldwide.

Park Green Cottage, Barhatch Road, Cranleigh, Surrey GU6 7DJ

Tel. 01483 274 556

Correspondent The Trustees

Trustees *Richard Borgonon; Andrew Green; Irene Spreckley; Kevin Locock; Jane Borgonon; Colin Spreckley.*

CC Number 294775

Information available Accounts were on file at the Charity Commission.

General Formed in 1986, this charity seeks to support charitable undertakings which are built upon a clear biblical basis and which, in most instances, receive little or no publicity. It is not the intention of the foundation to give widespread support, but rather to research and invest time and money specifically in the work of a few selected Christian ministries. As well as supporting six such ministries, grants are also made to registered charities.

In 2004/05 the foundation had an income of £192,000 and made grants totalling £197,000 of which £151,000 went to 32 organisations.

There were 11 grants of £1,000 or more listed in the accounts: TNT Ministries (£53,000), Proclamation Trust (£38,000), Cranleigh Baptist Church (£24,000), the Simon Trust (£9,600), International Student Christian Society/Friends International (£7,800), Great St Helen's Trust and Oasis Charitable Trust (£5,000 each), St Andrew's Partnership (£2,300), Agape (£1,500) and Diocese of Ruaha and James Harrington Memorial Trust (£1,000 each).

The sum of £45,000 was distributed to 22 individuals.

Applications 'The trust identifies its beneficiaries through its own networks, choosing to support organisations it has a working relationship with. This allows the trust to verify that the organisation is doing excellent work in a sensible manner in a way which cannot be conveyed from a written application. As such, all appeals from charities the foundation do not find through their own research are simply thrown in the bin. If an sae is included in an application, it will merely end up in the foundation's waste-paper bin rather than a post box.'

The Rock Solid Trust

Christian worldwide

£30,000 to organisations (2004/05)

Beneficial area Worldwide.

7 Belgrave Place, Clifton, Bristol B58 3DD

Correspondent J D W Pocock, Trustee

Trustees *J D W Pocock; T P Wicks; T G Bretell.*

CC Number 1077669

Information available Accounts were on file at the Charity Commission.

General This trust supports:

- Christian charitable institutions and the advancement of Christian religion
- the maintenance, restoration and repair of the fabric of Christian churches
- the education and training of individuals
- relief of need.

In 2004/05 it had assets amounting to £737,000, an income of £36,000 and made grants totalling £47,000.

The sum of £30,000 was distributed to organisations. Beneficiaries were Changing Tunes (£7,000), Tearfund (£3,500 in two grants), Bristol Dyslexia Trust and NCH Action for Children (£3,000 each), Save the Children Fund (£2,500), Care for the Family, Christian Aid and Young Voices (£2,000 each), NSPCC (£1,500), NeuroBlastoma and SKI (£1,000 each), CLIC and Rotary Club of Sherborne (£500 each), Cancer Research (£250) and Mencap (£100).

There were eight grants to individuals made totalling £17,000.

Applications In writing to the correspondent.

Rofeh Trust

General, religious activities

£58,000 (2005/06)

Beneficial area UK.

44 Southway, London NW11 6SA

Correspondent The Trustees

Trustees *Martin Dunitz; Ruth Dunitz; Vivian Wineman; Henry Eder.*

CC Number 1077682

Information available Accounts were on file at the Charity Commission, but without a list of grants.

General In 2005/06 the trust had an income of £73,000 and made grants totalling £58,000. Its assets stood at £805,000. Unfortunately no list of grants was included with accounts on file at the Charity Commission.

Applications In writing to the correspondent.

Richard Rogers Charitable Settlement

Housing, homelessness

£51,000 (2003/04)

Beneficial area UK.

Lee Associates, 5 Southampton Place, London WC1A 2DA

Correspondent K A Hawkins

Trustees *Lord R G Rogers; Lady R Rogers; G H Camamile.*

CC Number 283252

Information available Accounts were available from the Charity Commission website.

General In 2003/04 the trust had assets of £873,000 and an income of £151,000. Grants were made to 38 organisations totalling £51,000. More recent information was not available.

The largest grant went to: Gulbenkian Trust (£10,200); Dyslexia Institute (£10,000); the Serpentine Trust (£8,000); Peter Rice Scholarship Fund – Harvard University (£6,000); Royal Academy (£5,000); and Medical Aid for Palestinians and Royal Academy of Arts (£1,000 each).

Smaller grants of less than £1,000 each went to: British Heart Foundation (£800); Afrikids, Harmabee Schools Kenya and Training for Life (£500 each); National Tenants Resource Centre and Natural History Museum (£100 each); and River Thames Society (£25).

Applications In writing to the correspondent.

Rokach Family Charitable Trust

Jewish, general

£225,000 (2004/05)
Beneficial area UK.

20 Middleton Road, London NW11 7NS

Tel. 020 8455 6359

Correspondent Norman Rokach, Trustee

Trustees *N Rokach; Mrs H Rokach; Mrs E Hoffman; Mrs M Feingold; Mrs A Gefilhaus; Mrs N Brenig.*

CC Number 284007

Information available Full accounts were on file at the Charity Commission.

General This trust supports Jewish and general causes in the UK. In 2004/05 the trust had an income of £302,000 and made grants to 15 organisations totalling £255,000. Its assets stood at £3.6 million.

The largest grant recipients were Before Trust (£166,000), Kisharon Charitable Trust (£20,000) and Cosmon Limited (£19,000).

Smaller grants included those to Moreshet Hatorah Ltd (£5,000), Belz Synagogue (£3,000) and Friends of Wiznitz.

Other grants were made of £1,000 or less each, totalling £19,000.

Applications In writing to the correspondent.

The Helen Roll Charitable Trust

General

£132,000 (2005/06)
Beneficial area UK.

30 St Giles, Oxford OX1 3LE

Correspondent F R Williamson, Trustee

Trustees *Christine Chapman; Paul Strang; Christine Reid; Jennifer Williamson; Dick Williamson; Stephen G Williamson.*

CC Number 299108

Information available Accounts were available from the Charity Commission website.

General 'One of the trustees' aims is to support work for charities, which find it difficult or impossible to obtain funds from other sources. Some projects are supported on a start-up basis, others involve funding over a longer term.'

The charities supported are mainly those whose work is already known to the trustees and who report on both their needs and achievements. Each year a handful of new causes is supported. However the trust has stated that 'the chances of success for a new application are about 100–1'.

In 2005/06 the trust had assets of £1.7 million and an income of £61,000. Grants were made totalling £132,000.

Beneficiaries of the largest grants were: Friends of Home Farm Trust (£12,000); Pembroke College – Oxford and the John R T Davies Collection (£10,000 each); European Men's Health Development Foundation (£9,000); Oxford University Ashmolean Museum (£8,600); Community of the Holy Fire (£8,000); Trinity College of Music (£6,000); and Berkshire, Buckinghamshire and Oxon Wildlife Trust, Greenhouse Trust and Purcell School (£5,000 each).

Beneficiaries of smaller grants included: Canine Partners for Independence (£4,000); Dartington Summer School (£3,000); Dream Holidays (£2,000); Thames Valley and Chilterns Air Ambulance Trust (£1,000); and Susy Lamplugh Trust (£500).

Exclusions No support for individuals or non-registered charities.

Applications In writing to the correspondent during the first fortnight in February. Applications should be kept short, ideally on one sheet of A4. Further material will then be asked of those who are short-listed. The trustees normally make their distribution in March.

The Sir James Roll Charitable Trust

General

£165,000 (2004/05)
Beneficial area UK.

5 New Road Avenue, Chatham, Kent ME4 6AR

Tel. 01634 830111

Correspondent N T Wharton, Trustee

Trustees *N T Wharton; B W Elvy; J M Liddiard.*

CC Number 1064963

Information available Full accounts were on file at the Charity Commission.

General The trust's main objectives are the:

- promotion of mutual tolerance, commonality and cordiality in major world religions
- furtherance of access to computer technology as a teaching medium at primary school levels
- promotion of improved access to computer technology in community-based projects other than political parties or local government
- funding of projects aimed at early identification of specific learning disorders.

In 2004/05 the trust had assets totalling just under £4 million and an income of £189,000. Grants were made to over 180 beneficiaries totalling £165,000. Grants ranged from £500 to £20,000, although most were for either £500 or £750 each.

The largest grants were: £20,000 to DEC Asia Earthquake Appeal; £10,000 to DEC Sudan Emergency; £5,000 each to Africa Appeal – Comic Relief, Crisis at Christmas; £2,500 each to Hackney Quest, Howard League for Penal Reform, Open Age Project, Prison Reform Trust and Shelter; £1,500 each to Dyslexic Computer Training Charity and LIFT; and £1,000 each to DIAL – Kent and Prisoners Abroad.

Beneficiaries of smaller grants of either £500 or £750 included 4Sight, Action for Blind people, Amnesty International, British Dyslexia Association, Children in Crisis, Christian Aid, City Escape, Contact a Family, Fairbridge in Kent, Headway, Hope and Homes for Children, Kids Care London, Manna Society, Mobility Trust, NSPCC, Open Age Project, Parkinson's Disease Society, PDSA, Refugee Support Centre, SCOPE, Tall Ships Youth Trust, Volunteer Reading Help and Who Cares? Trust.

Applications In writing to the correspondent.

The Rootstein Hopkins Foundation

Arts

£716,000 to organisations (2005)
Beneficial area UK.

PO Box 14720, London W3 7ZG

Tel. 020 8746 2136

Correspondent The Secretary

Trustees *M J Southgate, Chair; I G Cole; G L Feldman; Mrs D J Hopkins; Prof E M Hogan; Mrs J C Morreau.*

CC Number 1001223

Information available Accounts were available from the Charity Commission website.

General The trust's objectives are described as follows:

- To promote fine and applied arts by providing grants, bursaries and other financial assistance to schools of art, other art educational establishments, arts organisations, artists or groups of artists, and students or groups of them, art teachers and lecturers and groups of them, and any body which runs a school or arts school or otherwise promotes or develops for public benefit the development, study, research and practice of art in all its branches, but in particular painting, drawing, sculpture, photography and fine and applied art.
- To promote and develop the study and research of fine arts in all branches (particularly painting and drawing).
- To promote and develop the study and research into improved methods of display and visual mechanisms.

In 2005 the trust had assets of £5.4 million and an income of £179,000. Grants were made totalling £740,000.

There were two grants made to National Life Story Collection. The larger of the two was a special grant for future recordings of Artists' Lives (£400,000), whilst the second was a capital grant for equipment (£27,000).

Other grants made included those to Wimbledon School of Art – a special grant to preserve and collate the Jocelyn Herbert Archive (£100,000) and Victoria and Albert Museum – a special grant for collation and transfer of Hugh Casson Archives to the museum (£40,000).

Other grants included grants made to individuals totalling £24,000.

Applications Application forms are available from the correspondent or can be downloaded from the trust's website. Application forms should be returned by December by post only.

The Cecil Rosen Foundation

Welfare, especially older people, infirm, people who are mentally or physically disabled

£322,000 (2005/06)

Beneficial area UK.

118 Seymour Place, London W1H 1NP

Tel. 020 7262 2003

Correspondent M J Ozin, Trustee

Trustees *M J Ozin; J A Hart; P H Silverman.*

CC Number 247425

Information available Accounts were on file at the Charity Commission, but without a list of grants and only a limited review of activities.

General Established in 1966, the charity's main object is the assistance and relief of the poor, especially older people, the infirm or people who are disabled.

The correspondent has previously stated that almost all the trust's funds are (and will always continue to be) allocated between five projects. The surplus is then distributed in small donations between an unchanging list of around 200 organisations. 'Rarely are any organisations added to or taken off the list.'

In 2005/06 the foundation had an income of £318,000 and had assets of £6.3 million. Grants were made totalling £322,000. Unfortunately, a list of grants was not included in the accounts.

The foundation has previously made grants to Jewish Blind and Disabled and The Cecil Rosen Charitable Trust (a charity with the same trustees as this foundation).

Exclusions No grants to individuals.

Applications The correspondent stated that 'no new applications can be considered'. Unsuccessful applications are not acknowledged.

The Rothermere Foundation

Education, general

£512,000 (2004/05)

Beneficial area UK.

Beech Court, Canterbury Road, Challock, Ashford, Kent TN25 4DJ

Correspondent V P W Harmsworth, Secretary

Trustees *Rt Hon. Viscount Rothermere; Viscountess Rothermere; V P W Harmsworth; J G Hemingway; Hon. Esme Countess of Cromer.*

CC Number 314125

Information available Information was on file at the Charity Commission.

General This trust was set up for: the establishment and maintenance of 'Rothermere Scholarships' to be awarded to graduates of the Memorial University of Newfoundland to enable them to undertake further periods of study in the UK; and general charitable causes.

In 2004/05 the foundation had assets of £33 million and an income of £585,000. Grants totalled £512,000, broken down in the following categories:

Medical research
Beneficiaries included the Royal Marsden Hospital (£35,000), Mesotheliorna Cancer Research (£20,000), Barrett's Oesophagus Foundation, Moorfields Eye Hospital and WISE Communities (£10,000 each) and Cancer Research UK, St John Ambulance and World Swim for Malaria (£1,000 each).

Environmental/conservation and maintenance
Beneficiaries included Royal Parks Foundation (£4,900), Hinton Hall (£2,000) and the Landmark Trust (£1,000).

Educational/children's charities
Beneficiaries included Francis Holland School (£50,000), St Mary's Wantage School (£42,000), Harvard Business School (£28,000), Children in Crisis and Dragon School Trust (£10,000 each), Brunel University (£5,000) and Barnados and Endres Foundation (£1,000 each).

Religious organisations
Beneficiaries included St George's Chapel (£25,000) and St Bride's Church (£10,000).

The arts/sport
Beneficiaries included Cabinet War Rooms/Churchill Museum (£150,000), London Symphony Orchestra (£85,000), Cherubim Music Trust (£50,000),

Guildhall Drama School (£43,000), Coram's Field and Royal Academy of Dramatic Art (£10,000 each), Victoria and Albert Museum (£5,000), Elmhurst Ballet School (£4,000), Imperial War Museum (£2,400) and St Martin's College (£1,100).

Other charitable donations
Beneficiaries included Dorset Police Welfare (£10,000) and Eden Court (£1,000).

Grants to assist two individuals in education totalled £12,000.

Applications In writing to the correspondent.

The Rowan Charitable Trust

Overseas aid, social welfare, general

£141,500 to UK organisations
(2004/05)

Beneficial area UK, especially Merseyside, and overseas.

Mr Jonathan C M Tippett, c/o Morley Tippett, White Park Barn, Loseley Park, Guildford GU3 1HS

Tel. 01483 575193

Correspondent Mr Jonathan C M Tippett

Trustees *C R Jones; Revd J R Pilkington; Mrs M C Pilkington.*

CC Number 242678

Information available Accounts were available from the Charity Commission.

General The trust focuses on projects that will benefit disadvantaged groups and communities and generally allocates two-thirds of its grant funds to overseas projects and one-third to United Kingdom-based projects. It gives a mix of one-off and recurrent grants. It has regularly given grants to a limited number of large national organisations and development agencies, but also gives grants to smaller organisations and locally based projects.

Beneficiary organisations overseas included:

- Practical Action (formerly I DG) – £50,000
- Christian Aid – £33,000
- African Initiatives – £2,000
- Anti-Slavery – £3,000

- Child Soldiers Coalition Educational and Research Trust – £3,000
- Church Mission Society – £10,000
- Concordis International – £10,000
- Drama and Music in Tanzania – £1,000
- Fair Trade – £3,000
- Habitat for Humanity – £5,000
- Hope and Homes for Children – £1,000
- Labour Behind the Label – £3,000
- Marine Stewardship Council – £2,000
- Positive Help – £3,000
- UK Food Group – £10,000
- World Jewish Relief – £2,000.

Beneficiary organisations in the UK included:

Tranmere Alliance – £7,000; Asylum Link Merseyside – £5,000; Christians Against Poverty – £3,500; Foundation for the Study of Infant Deaths – £1,200; Leicestershire AIDS Support Services – £2,000; and Whizz-Kidz – £3,000.

Exclusions The trust does not give grants for:

- individuals
- buildings, building work or office equipment (including IT hardware)
- academic research and medical research or equipment
- expeditions
- bursaries or scholarships
- vehicle purchases
- animal welfare charities.

Applications In writing to the correspondent. No application forms are issued.

Applications should include:

- a brief description (two sides of A4 paper) of, and a budget for, the work for which the grant is sought
- the organisation's annual report and accounts (this is essential).

The applications need to provide the trustees with information about:

- the aims and objectives of the organisation
- its structure and organisational capacity
- what the funds are being requested for and how much is being requested
- how progress of the work will be monitored and evaluated.

Trustees meet twice a year. The closing dates for applications are 30 June and 15 December.

Unfortunately the volume of applications received precludes acknowledgement on receipt or notifying unsuccessful applicants. The trust emphasises that it is unable to make donations to applicants who are not, or

do not have links with, a UK-registered charity.

Joshua and Michelle Rowe Charitable Trust

Jewish

£402,000 (2005/06)

Beneficial area UK and worldwide.

84 Upper Park Road, Salford M7 4JA

Tel. 0161 720 8787

Correspondent J Rowe, Trustee

Trustees *J Rowe; Mrs M B Rowe.*

CC Number 288336

Information available Accounts were available from the Charity Commission website.

General In 2005/06 the trust had assets of £456,000 and an income of £138,000. Grants were made to 63 organisations totalling £402,000.

Beneficiaries of the largest grants included: King David (£156,000); UJIA (£102,000); Aish Hatorah Rabbi Schiff, Chrel Rab Trust, MCR Charitable Trust and United Synagogue Kehillah Project (£10,000 each).

Beneficiaries of smaller grants included: CST (£7,000); Barr Llan University – Israel (£5,000); Heathlands Village (£2,000); Holocaust Centre Pears Foundation and Institute for Jewish Policy Research (£1,000 each); Sasson V Simcha (£500); Friends of Beis Elryahv Rabbi Klyne (£250); and Kollel Zichron (£20).

Applications In writing to the correspondent.

The Rowing Foundation

Water sports

£8,800 to organisation (2005)

Beneficial area UK.

6 Lower Mall, Hammersmith, London W6 9DJ

Tel. 0208 878 3723 **Fax** 0208 878 6298

Email p.churcher@sky.com

Website www.ara-rowing.org

Correspondent Pauline Churcher, Secretary

Trustees *D W Parry, chair; J Buchan; S Goodey; P J Phillips; I Reid; R S Smith.*

CC Number 281688

Information available Full accounts were available from the Charity Commission website.

General The Rowing Foundation was set up in 1981 to generate and administer funds for the aid and support of young people (those under 18 or still in full-time education) and people who are disabled of all ages, through their participation in sport and games, particularly water sports. Its income is mainly dependent on donations from the rowing fraternity.

Grants are made in the range of £500 and £2,000 to pump-prime projects. The foundation is anxious to help organisations and clubs whose requirements may be too small or who may be otherwise ineligible for an approach to the National Lottery or other similar sources of funds. It has also helped to get rowing started in areas where it did not exist or was struggling. Beneficiaries have included: Headington School – Oxford to purchase single sculling boats, designed specifically for juniors; Doncaster Schools Rowing Association to help provide equipment; Merchant Taylors' School – Crosby with their joint scheme with the Birkdale School for the Hearing Impaired; the Rees Thomas School – Cambridge for children with special needs; and Iffley Mead School – Oxford.

In 2006, a grant was made jointly to the London Docks Regatta Centre, Brunel University and the Royal National Orthopaedic Hospital to develop a rowing machine which assists patients with severe spinal cord injuries. Grants have also been made towards the purchase of buoyancy aids, splash suits, canoes and the promotion of taster rowing courses for youth clubs, sailing and other water sports clubs.

In 2005 the trust had assets of £272,000 and an income of £31,000. Grants were made totalling £8,800. Beneficiaries included Walton Rowing club (£2,000 each), St Cuthbert's Society and Curlew Rowing Club (£1,500 each), Bristol Ariel Rowing Club, Claires Court School and Eton Excelsior (£1,000 each) and ARA – Hill Bursary (£500).

Exclusions The foundation does not give grants to individuals, only to clubs and organisations, and for a specific purpose, not as a contribution to general funds.

Applications In writing to the correspondent.

The Rowlands Trust

General

£405,000 (2005)

Beneficial area The geographical area of benefit is the West Midlands and South Midlands, including Hereford and Worcester, Gloucester, South Shropshire and Birmingham.

c/o Mills and Reeve, 78–84 Colmore Row, Birmingham B3 2AB

Tel. 0121 454 4000 **Fax** 0121 200 3028

Correspondent Ms N Fenn, Clerk to the Trustees

Trustees *A C S Hordern, Chair; Mrs F J Burman; Mrs A M I Harris; G B G Hingley; K G Mason.*

CC Number 1062148

Information available Accounts were available from the Charity Commission website.

General This trust makes grants for 'research, education and training in the broadest sense so as to promote success' and to 'support charities providing for medical and scientific research, the sick, poor, handicapped, elderly, music, the arts and the environment'.

In 2005 the trust had assets of £6 million and an income of £199,000. Grants were made totalling £405,000.

Research, education and training – 32 grants totalling £345,000
The largest grants went to: St Richard's New Hospice Appeal (£250,000); Shenley Court Specialist Arts College (£15,000); Baverstock Foundation School (£14,000); and City Technology College (£12,000).

Grants of £5,000 or les included those to: Friends of Chantry School and Holy Trinity Catholic School (£5,000 each); Inside Out Trust (£3,000); Children's Liver Disease Foundation (£2,500); Coventry City Farm and Dyslexia Institute (£2,000 each); Gordon Russell Trust and Metamorphosis of the Martineau Gardens (£1,000 each); and St John Ambulance – Youth Service (£500).

Medical and scientific research – 2 grants totalling £17,000
Grants went to Worcester Acute Hospitals NHS Trust – Islet Research Laboratory (£15,000) and Leukaemia Research Fund (£2,000).

'The sick, the poor, the handicapped and the elderly' – 38 grants totalling £69,000
Grant recipients included: Thomas Morley Trust – Martin Sailing Project (£7,500); Birmingham Rathbone Society Living Springs Family Centre (£5,000); Alzheimer's Society – Coventry Branch, POD Charitable Trust and Roundabout (£2,500 each); Friends of Bettridge, Rowington Almshouse Charity and St Andrew's House – Coventry and Worcester City Mind (£2,000 each); Lydney Playgroup and Dudley Rethink – Volunteers Project (£1,000 each); Karis Neighbour Scheme (£500); and Home from Hospital Care and WellBeing of Women (£250).

Music – 1 grant of £10,000
The sole beneficiary in this category was the Royal College of Organists.

The arts – 4 grants totalling £8,000
Grants went to Belgrave Theatre Trust (£5,000), Roses Theatre Trust (£2,000), Three Choirs Festival – Worcester (£1,000) and Lichfield Festival (£250).

The environment – 9 grants totalling £13,000
Grant made included those to Ironbridge Gorge Museum Trust Limited (£5,000), Groundwork Black Country Trust (£2,000), Cotswolds Canals Trust (£1,000) and Lansallos Church (£250).

Exclusions No support for individuals or to charities for the benefit of animals. No support is given for revenue funding.

Applications Applications should only be made for capital funding. Forms are available from the correspondent, to be returned with a copy of the most recent accounts. The trustees meet to consider grants four times a year.

Royal Artillery Charitable Fund

Service charities

£657,000 (2005)

Beneficial area UK and overseas.

Front Parade, Royal Artillery Barracks, Woolwich, London SE18 4BH

Tel. 020 8781 3004 **Fax** 020 8654 3617

Email welfsec.rhgra@army.mod.uk.net

Correspondent The Welfare Secretary

CC Number 210202

Information available Accounts were available from the Charity Commission website.

General In 2005 the trust had an income of £770,000 and made grants totalling £657,000. Its assets stood at £12 million.

Grants were made to six organisations as follows: Gunner Magazine (£43,000); Royal Artillery Institution (£38,000); Regiment and Batteries (£18,000); Not Forgotten Association and King Edward VII Hospital (£2,500 each) and Ex-Service Fellow Centre (£1,000).

Applications In writing to the correspondent.

Royal Masonic Trust for Girls and Boys

Children, young people

£380,000 to non-Masonic charities (2005)
Beneficial area UK.

31 Great Queen Street, London WC2B 5AG
Tel. 020 7405 2644 **Fax** 020 7831 4094
Website www.rmtgb.org
Correspondent Clive Andrews, Chief Executive
Trustees *Col G S H Dicker; Rt Hon. the Lord Swansea; M B Jones; P A Marsh.*
CC Number 285836
Information available Accounts were available from the Charity Commission website.

General This trust was established in 1982. It predominantly makes grants to individual children of Freemasons who are in need. Grants are also made to UK non-Masonic organisations working with children and young people and it also supports bursaries at cathedrals and collegiate chapels.

In 2005 the trust had assets of £141 million and an income of £7 million. Grants made to non-Masonic charities totalled £380,000. Grants made to organisations connected with the trust totalled £6 million.

Other grants included those to individuals through two programmes as follows: TalentAid (£317,000) and UndergradAid (£1,000).

A list of beneficiaries was not available. In previous years beneficiaries have included: Newman School – Rotherham; Winston's Wish; British Blind Sport; Endeavour Training; Norman Laud Association; Side by Side; Christ's Hospital Band; Nigel Clare Network; Plymouth Hospital School; Henry Spink Foundation; Fleet Air Arm Officers; Ormskirk Grammar School; Reeds School; Royal Wolverhampton School; and Wolverhampton Grammar School.

Applications In writing to the correspondent.

William Arthur Rudd Memorial Trust

General in the UK, and certain Spanish charities

£42,000 (2004/05)
Beneficial area UK and Spain.

12 South Square, Gray's Inn, London WC1R 5HH
Correspondent Miss A A Sarkis, Trustee
Trustees *Miss A A Sarkis; D H Smyth; R G Maples.*
CC Number 326495
Information available Accounts were on file at the Charity Commission, without a narrive report or a list of beneficiaries.

General This trust makes grants in practice to UK charities and certain Spanish charities. In 2004/05 the trust had assets of £747,000, an income of £42,000 and made grants totalling £42,000. The trust's accounts have previously stateed that donations have been made to registered charities in the UK and to certain Spanish charities; however, no grants list was provided.

Applications As the trust's resources are fully committed, the trustees do not consider unsolicited applications.

The Rural Trust

Countryside

About £30,000 to organisations (2005)
Beneficial area UK.

73 Collier Street, London N1 9BE
Tel. 020 77138685
Email cgw@medarc-limited.co.uk
Correspondent Dr Charles Goodson-Wickes, Chair
Trustees *Dr C Goodson-Wickes, Chair; The Earl of Stockton; R Mathew QC.*
CC Number 1060040
Information available Information was provided by the trust.

General The trust makes grants towards the protection, maintenance or preservation of the countryside, and to educate the public and promote any objective that will benefit the countryside.

In 2005 the trust had an income of £171, with previous grants totalling £30,000. During the year, beneficiaries included the Chillingham Wild Cattle Association, Forest Stewardship Council, Grasslands Trust, Moor Trees, National Council for the Conservation of Plants and Gardens, the Rural Buildings Trust, Scottish Native Woods and the Soil Association – Poultry.

Exclusions No support for individuals, non-charitable bodies or of new buildings works. The trustees tend not to make grants to other wildlife trusts, as in their experience they found these organisations had larger assets than themselves. However, the trustees will consider all grant applications equally.

Applications In writing to the correspondent.

The Russell Trust

General

£195,000 (2005/06)
Beneficial area UK, especially Scotland.

Markinch, Glenrothes, Fife KY7 6PB
Tel. 01592 753311
Email russelltrust@trg.co.uk

Correspondent Ms Iona Russell, Administrator and Trustee

Trustees *Fred Bowden; Mrs Cecilia Croal; Graeme Crombie; David Erdal; Don Munro; Ms Iona Russell; Alan Scott.*

SC Number SC004424

Information available Accounts were provided by the trust.

General This family trust was established in 1947 in memory of Capt. J P O Russell who was killed in Italy during the Second World War. The trustees prefer to make grants to pump-prime new projects, rather than giving on an ongoing basis. Grants of up to £10,000 can be distributed; however, generally the amounts given are for between £250 and £2,000. Three or four larger grants of up to £20,000 may be awarded annually.

In 2005/06 the trust had assets of £9.8 million and an income of £265,000. Grants were made totalling £195,000, broken down as follows:

- music and the arts – £36,000
- education – £26,000
- St Andrew's University – £24,000
- archaeology – £21,000
- health and welfare – £19,000
- National Trust for Scotland – £15,000
- youth work – £15,000
- preservation work – £12,000
- local – £9,000
- church – £7,000
- general – £5,500
- The Iona Community – £5,000

Exclusions Only registered charities or organisations with charitable status are supported.

Applications On a form available from the correspondent. A statement of accounts must be supplied. Trustees meet quarterly, although decisions on the allocation of grants are made more regularly.

Ryklow Charitable Trust 1992 (also known as A B Williamson Charitable Trust)

Education, health and welfare

£45,000 (2004/05)

Beneficial area Worldwide.

c/o Robinsons Solicitors, 10–11 St James Court, Friar Gate, Derby DE1 1BT

Tel. 01332 254105

Email stephen.marshall@ robinsons-solicitors.co.uk

Correspondent Stephen F Marshall

Trustees *J V Woodward; A Williamson; E J S Cannings.*

CC Number 1010122

Information available Accounts were on file at the Charity Commission.

General The trust says that its notes for applicants: 'have been compiled to help applicants understand how best it is felt the trust can be operated and the constraints of time under which the (unpaid) trustees must work. It will help enormously if you try to ensure that your application follows these guidelines if at all possible.'

Applications will only be considered for activities if they meet the following descriptions:

- medical research, especially that which benefits children
- assistance to students from overseas wishing to study in the UK or for UK students volunteering for unpaid work overseas
- projects in the developing world – especially those which are intended to be self-sustaining or concerned with education
- help for vulnerable families, minorities and the prevention of abuse or exploitation of children
- conservation of natural species, landscape and resources.

In 2004/05 the trust had assets of £912,000 and an income of £38,000. Grants totalled £45,000, all of which were for £500 each.

Beneficiaries included Africa Mission, Ark Trust, BLISS, Books Abroad, Cambodia Trust, Care International UK, Children in Crisis, Children with Leukaemia, Community Self Build Agency, Farm Africa, Hand in Hand, Interact Worldwide, International Otter Survival Fund, Lake Malawi Project, Motor Neurone Research, Nepal Trust, Parents for Children, Soil Association, Sun Seed (Tanzania) Trust, University of Cape Town, WaterAid, Wildlife Conservation Research Unit, Wolf Trust and Young Minds.

Two grants were made to individuals totalling £900.

Applications 'Applications should be brief. We are a small charity with few trustees and there is little time for all in turn to read numerous or long documents.

'A statement of your finances is a must, or better still, an audited financial report. Individual applicants unable to provide either should send details of the precise purpose for which help is required with reputable back-up evidence.

'The trustees read all applications (of which there are many) over the months of January and February because they feel that this is the only fair way of comparing the merits of one against another. To allow us to arrive at a fair distribution of available monies we ask that all applications reach us between 1 September and 31 December in any calendar year. Trustees can then devote January and February to the study of the needs before them. When decisions have been reached cheques are despatched at the end of March.

'Unfortunately we are unable to help every applicant no matter how deserving the cause may be. To keep down costs we do not write to unsuccessful applicants. Therefore if you have not heard from us before the end of April you will know that your application has been unsuccessful in that year.'

The Audrey Sacher Charitable Trust

Arts, medical, care

£73,000 (2005/06)

Beneficial area UK.

c/o H W Fisher and Co., 11–15 William Road, London NW1 3ER

Tel. 020 7388 7000

Correspondent The Trustees

Trustees *Mrs Nicola Shelley Sacher; Michael Harry Sacher.*

CC Number 288973

Information available Accounts were on file at the Charity Commission.

General The trust states its main areas of work as the arts, medical and care. Grants are only made to charities known personally to the trustees and generally range from £250 to £30,000.

In 2005/06 the trust had assets of £2 million and an income of £66,000. Grants totalled £73,000 and were broken down into these key areas:

Culture and arts – £45,000
Among the 13 beneficiaries were National Gallery Trust (£15,000), Royal National Theatre (£7,500), Royal Opera House Foundation (£6,300), Royal Ballet School – White Lodge Redevelopment Scheme (£5,000), British Friends of the Art Museums of Israel (£2,500), English Chamber Orchestral and Music Society (£2,000), Tate Gallery Foundation (£1,000), the Almeida Theatre Company (£500) and the 999 Club Trust (£250).

Overseas aid – £8,700 in 3 grants
Beneficiaries were New Israel Fund (£5,000), Venice in Peril Fund (£2,000) and UJIA (£1,700).

Education – £5,900 in 3 grants
Beneficiaries were Goldsmith College (£4,400), Kisharon (£1,000) and One to One (£500).

Community care – £3,500 in 2 grants
Grants went to Jewish Care (£2,500) and Nightingale House (£1,000).

Animals – £3,300
One grant was made to Whale and Dolphin Conservation Society.

Children and youth – £3,000
Norwood Ltd received the sole grant in this category

Health – £1,750 in 3 grants
Beneficiaries were MDA UK (£1,000), Chain of Hope (£500) and Charlie Waller Memorial Trust (£250).

Religious organisations – £1,600
Beneficiaries were West London Synagogue (£1,000) and United Synagogue Membership (£630).

Exclusions No grants to individuals or organisations which are not registered charities.

Applications In writing to the correspondent.

The Michael Sacher Charitable Trust

General

£100,000 (2005/06)
Beneficial area UK and Israel.

16 Clifton Villas, London W9 2PH

Tel. 020 7289 5873

Correspondent Mrs Irene Wiggins, Secretary

Trustees *Simon John Sacher; Jeremy Michael Sacher; Hon. Mrs Rosalind E C Sacher; Mrs Elisabeth J Sacher.*

CC Number 206321

Information available Full accounts were on file at the Charity Commission.

General This trust supports a wide range of organisations, with an interest in Jewish/Israeli organisations. In 2005/06 the trust had assets of £4.4 million and an income of £198,000. Grants were made totalling £100,000 and were broken down into the following seven categories:

Medical and disability – 10 grants totalling £32,000
The largest grants went to Anna Freud Centre (£20,000) and Oxford Children's Hospital (£5,000). Other grants included the Royal Marsden Cancer Campaign (£2,500), Walk the World Worldwide (£1,000) and Tetbury Hospital Trust (£100).

Arts, culture and heritage – 13 grants totalling £21,000
The largest grant was made to Royal Opera House (£9,000). Other grants included Nicholas Boas Trust (£2,000), the Courtauld Institute of Art Fund and Victoria and Albert Museum (£1,000 each) and Wigmore Hall Trust (£50).

Community and welfare – 3 grants totalling £10,000
Grants were made to Friends of the Hebrew University and Community Security Trust (£5,000 each) and Friends of Elderly (£100).

Overseas aid – 1 grant of £10,000
This grant went to Share Foundation-Tsunami.

Education, science and technology – 5 grants totalling £8,000
Grants made included those to Royal Philatelic Society – London (£3,000), Weizmann Institute Foundation (£1,000) and Beaminster Playgroup Ltd (£250).

Children and youth – 3 grants totalling £840
Grants were made to NSPCC (£790 in two grants) and Child Bereavement Trust (£50).

General – 3 grants totalling £400
Beneficiaries were Avondale Extra (£250), Wherever the Need (£100) and Elizabeth Finn Trust (£50).

Applications In writing to the correspondent at any time.

Dr Mortimer and Theresa Sackler Foundation

Arts, hospitals

£557,000 (2004)
Beneficial area UK.

15 North Audley Street, London W1K 6WZ

Tel. 020 7493 3842

Correspondent Christopher B Mitchell, Trustee

Trustees *Dr Mortimer Sackler; Theresa Sackler; Christopher Mitchell; Robin Stormonth-Darling; Raymond Smith.*

CC Number 327863

Information available Accounts were on file at the Charity Commission.

General The foundation was set up in 1985 by Mortimer Sackler of Rooksnest, Berkshire for general charitable purposes and 'the advancement of the public in the UK and elsewhere in the fields of art, science and medical research generally'.

The assets of the foundation stood at £5.2 million in December 2004 and it had an income of £720,000. Grants were made totalling £557,000.

There were 14 grants made of £10,000 or more. Beneficiaries were Royal Opera House (£100,000), Dulwich Picture Gallery Centre for Arts Education (£70,000), State Hermitage Museum (£65,000), Tate Foundation (£57,000), National Gallery of Scotland – Sackler Sculpture Hall and V & A Museum (£50,000 each), the Bradfield Foundation (£20,000), Western Eye Hospital – Corneal Polarisation (£11,250) and Capital City Acadamy, Hermitage Development Trust, Royal Horticultural Society Bicentenary Glass House, St

Peter's College, Serpentine Gallery, UCL Development Fund – Panopticon Project (£10,000 each).

Donations under £10,000 each totalled £74,000.

Applications In writing to the correspondent.

The Ruzin Sadagora Trust

Jewish

£720,000 (2004/05)

Beneficial area UK and Israel.

269 Golders Green Road, London NW11 9JJ

Correspondent Rabbi I M Friedman, Trustee

Trustees *Rabbi I M Friedman; Mrs S Friedman.*

CC Number 285475

Information available Accounts were on file at the Charity Commission.

General In 2004/05 the trust had assets of £482,000 with an income of £724,000 and grants totalling £720,000.

Grants listed in the accounts were £380,000 to Friends of Ruzin Sadagora, £213,000 to Beth Israel Ruzin Sadagora, £61,000 to Chevras Moaz Ladol, £38,000 to Igud Yehudi Zito Mir, £18,000 to Knesset Mordechai and £8,600 to Sadagora Institute Jerusalem.

'Sundry donations' totalled £910.

Applications In writing to the correspondent.

The Jean Sainsbury Animal Welfare Trust

Animal welfare

£175,000 (2004/05)

Beneficial area UK-registered charities.

PO Box 50793, London NW6 9DE

Website www. jeansainsburyanimalwelfare.org.uk

Correspondent Mrs Madeleine Orchard, Administrator

Trustees *Jean Sainsbury; Colin Russell; Gillian Tarlington; James Keliher; Mark Spurdens; Evelyn Jane Winship.*

CC Number 326358

Information available Accounts were on file at the Charity Commission.

General The trust was established in 1982 with the objective of benefiting and protecting animals from suffering. Around £3 million had been donated by 2001. The policy of the trustees is to support smaller charities concerned with animal welfare and wildlife. Some organisations receive regular donations. Seven overseas organisations were supported during the year.

In 2005 the trust had assets of £7.8 million and an income of £508,000. Grants totalled £175,000. A total of 69 animal charities were supported.

Beneficiaries of larger grants of £1,000 or more included: Leicester and Leicestershire Animal Aid, North Clwyd Animal Rescue and Royal Veterinary College (£10,000 each); Lincolnshire Trust (£8,000); Three Owls (£7,500); Thoroughbred Rehabilitation Centre (£7,000); Brent Lodge Bird and Wildlife Trust, Caring for Cats – East Yorkshire, FAITH, Happy Landings, Proteus Reptile Trust, Waggy Tails, Worcestershire Animal Rescue Shelter and Willows Animal Sanctuary (£5,000 each); Cottontails Sanctuary and Wildlife Rescue and Ambulance (£4,000 each); Julie's Trust and HART Wildlife Rescue (£3,000 each); Haworth Animal Rescue, Hounslow Animal Welfare and Jigsaw (£2,500 each); Shropshire Cat Rescue (£2,000); and Associagao dos Amigos dos Animais Abandonados and Island Farm Donkey Sanctuary (£1,000 each).

Smaller grants, of £1,000 or less, included those to Broomfield Sanctuary – Cornwall and Petcare Network – Edinburgh (£750 each), Greyhounds in Need – Surrey, Safe Haven for Donkeys in the Holy Land, Southern Wildlife Ambulance Network – Kent and Westlea Animal Rescue – Gloucstershire (£500 each), Lord Whisky Sanctuary Fund – Kent (£300) and Compassion in World Farming (£250).

Exclusions No grants are made to individuals or non-registered charities and no loans can be given.

Applications In writing to the correspondent, including a copy of accounts. There are three trustees' meetings every year, usually in March,

July and November. Application information is now available by visiting the website.

The Alan and Babette Sainsbury Charitable Fund

General

£292,000 (2005/06)

Beneficial area Worldwide.

Allington House, 1st Floor, 150 Victoria Street, London SW1E 5AE

Tel. 020 7410 0330 **Fax** 020 7410 0332

Email info@sfct.org.uk

Correspondent Alan Bookbinder, Director

Trustees *The Hon. Simon Sainsbury; Miss Judith Portrait.*

CC Number 292930

Information available Accounts were on file at the Charity Commission.

General This is one of the Sainsbury Family Charitable Trusts, which share a joint administration and have a common approach to grantmaking.

The following information about the trust's grantmaking in 2005/06 is taken from the annual report. 'The trustees concentrate their resources on a small number of programmes which are built on themes of the trust's earlier grantmaking. At present these include support for ethnic minority and refugee groups, community-based mental health initiatives, human rights and encouraging participation in the arts.'

Its assets in 2005/06 stood at £12.4 million, generating an income of £330,000. Grants were paid during the year totalling £292,000. Beneficiaries were:

Education
Writers and Scholars Education Trust (£25,000).

Health and social welfare
Loonscape (£30,000); Asylum Advocacy (£8,000); Vernon House School (£1,600); and Rye Lane Community Cycling Project (£500).

Overseas
Canon Collins Educational trust for South Africa (£28,000); Ashden Awards for Sustainable Energy (£15,000); Anglo-

Israel Association (£7,500); and British Friends of Neve Shalom (£6,000).

Scientific and medical research
Restoration of Appearance and Function Trust (£50,000); UK Intensive Care Society (£30,000); and Juvenile Diabetes Research Foundation (£20,000).

The arts
Islington Music Centre (£70,000).

General
The Sainsbury Archive (£800).

Exclusions Grants are not normally made to individuals.

Applications 'Proposals are likely to be invited by the trustees or initiated at their request. Unsolicited applications are unlikely to be successful, even if they fall within an area in which the trustees are interested.' A single application will be considered for support by all the trusts in the Sainsbury family group.

Saint Luke's College Foundation

See below

£113,000 (2005/06)

Beneficial area UK and overseas, with some preference for Exeter and Truro.

Heathayne, Colyton, Devon EX24 6RS
Tel. 01297 552281 **Fax** 01297 552281

Correspondent Professor Michael Bond, Director

Trustees *The Bishop of Exeter; The Dean of Exeter; Diocesan Director of Education; Chairman of Diocesan Board of Finance; one nominated by the Bishop of Exeter; three nominated by the University of Exeter; four co-optative trustees.*

CC Number 306606

Information available Accounts were available from the Charity Commission website.

General This foundation encourages original work and imaginative new projects by educational and training bodies. Grants are only made for research or studies in theology and religious education and normally only at postgraduate level.

In 2005/06 the foundation had assets of £4 million and an income of £140,000.

Grants were made totalling £113,000, which was broken down as follows:

- Chapel and chaplaincy (£41,000)
- University of Exeter – Chair of Theology (£31,000)
- Personal and corporate grants (£40,000).

Exclusions Grants are not made for studies or research in fields other than religious studies, or for buildings or schools (except indirectly through courses or research projects undertaken by RE teachers). Block grants to support schemes or organisations are not made. Grants are not normally made for periods in excess of three years.

Applications Requests for application packs, and all other correspondence, should be sent to the correspondent. Applications are considered once a year and should be received by 1 May.

Saint Sarkis Charity Trust

Armenian churches and welfare, disability, general

£262,000 (2005/06)

Beneficial area UK and overseas.

98 Portland Place, London W1B 1ET
Tel. 020 7636 5313

Correspondent Louisa Hooper, Secretary

Trustees *Martin Sarkis Essayan; Boghos Parsegh Gulbenkian; Paul Curno; Robert Brian Todd.*

CC Number 215352

Information available Accounts were available from the Charity Commission website.

General 'The principal objectives of the trust are the support of the Armenian Church of St Sarkis in London and Gulbenkian Library at the Armenian Patriarchate in Jerusalem. In addition, the trustees support other charities concerned with the Armenian community in the UK and abroad, and to the extent that funds are available, grants are also made to small registered charities concerned with social welfare and disability.'

In 2005/06 the trust had an income of £152,000 and made grants totalling £266,000. Its assets stood at £7.2 million. Grants were divided into two categories:

Armenian projects – £227,000
The largest grants were made to: Judge Business School at Cambridge University – Eurasia Programme (£62,000); Armenian Church of Saint Sarkis and Everychild Foster Care (£58,000 each); Surp Pirgic Hospital (£27,000); and London Armenian Poor Relief Society Trust (£10,000).

Smaller grants of less than £10,000 each included those made to: the Armenian Institute (£6,500) and the Oriental Institute – University of Oxford (£1,500).

Individual grants of £1,000 or less totalled £500.

Other projects – £35,000
Beneficiaries included the Hand Partnership (£3,000), Axess Information Association (£2,500) and Family Meditation Lothian (£2,000).

Two individual grants of £1,000 totalled £2,000.

Exclusions No grants to individuals.

Applications In writing to the correspondent. Trustees meet monthly.

The Saintbury Trust

General

£196,000 (2005)

Beneficial area West Midlands and Warwickshire (which the trust considers to be postcode areas B, CV, DY, WS and WV), Worcestershire, Herefordshire and Gloucestershire (postcode areas WR, HR and GL).

P O Box 464, Abinger Hammer, Dorking RH4 9AF

Correspondent Mrs J P Lewis, Trustee

Trustees *Victoria K Houghton; Anne R Thomas; Jane P Lewis; Amanda E Atkinson-Willes; Harry O Forrester.*

CC Number 326790

Information available Accounts were on file at the Charity Commission.

General The trust gives grants for general charitable purposes, although the trust deed states that no grants can be given to animal charities. Grants are made to registered charities in Gloucestershire, West Midlands and Worcestershire.

In 2005 the trust had assets of £7.7 million and an income of £254,000.

Grants were made to 52 organisations totalling £196,000. Grants ranged from £500 to £50,000.

Beneficiaries included Birmingham Boys and Girls Union (£50,000), RAPt (£15,000), Birmingham Women's Hospital and St Richard's Hospice Foundation (£10,000 each), Acorns Children's Hospice (£7,000), Berkeley Castle Charitable Trust, Birmingham Symphony Orchestra, Cirencester Brewery Arts, Coventry and Warwickshire Family Mediation, Family Care Trust, the Stroud Preservation Trust and Sunfield Children's Homes Limited (£5,000 each), FSU East Birmingham (£4,000), Cotswold Villages Old People's Housing Association and Victoria Road Multi Use Centre (£3,000 each), Rehab UK and Roundabout (£2,000 each), Dementia Care Trust and Elizabeth Fitzroy Support (£1,000 each) and Parkinson's Disease Society of the UK, Tall Ships Youth Trust and Youth Sports Association (£500 each).

Exclusions No grants to animal charities, individuals (including individuals seeking sponsorship for challenges in support of charities), 'cold-calling' national charities or local branches of national charities. The trust only gives grants to charities outside its beneficial area if the charity is personally known to one or more of the trustees.

Applications In writing to the correspondent. Applications are considered in April and November and should be received by 28 February and 30 September respectively.

The Saints and Sinners Trust

Welfare, medical

£73,000 (2004/05)
Beneficial area Mostly UK.

Lewis Golden and Co., 40 Queen Anne Street, London W1G 9EL
Tel. 020 7580 7313
Correspondent N W Benson, Trustee
Trustees *N W Benson; Sir Donald Gosling; N C Royds; I A N Irvine.*
CC Number 200536
Information available Accounts were available from the Charity Commission website.

General This trust supports welfare and medical causes through the proceeds

of its fundraising efforts. In 2004/05 the trust had assets of £273,000 and an income of £82,000. Grants were made totalling £73,000.

Beneficiaries included: South Bucks Riding for the Disabled and White Ensign Association Limited (£5,000 each); Crusaid, Marine Conversation Society and National Osteoporosis Society (£4,000 each); Alastair Hignell Multiple Sclerosis and Saints and Sinners Club of Scotland (£3,000 each); and Refresh and British Eye Research Foundation (£1,000 each).

Exclusions No grants to individuals or non-registered charities.

Applications Applications are not considered unless nominated by members of the club.

The Salamander Charitable Trust

Christian, general

£62,000 (2005/06)
Beneficial area Worldwide.

Threave, 2 Brudenell Avenue, Canford Cliffs, Poole, Dorset BH13 7NW
Tel. 01202 706661
Correspondent John R T Douglas, Trustee
Trustees *J R T Douglas; Mrs Sheila M Douglas.*
CC Number 273657
Information available Accounts were available from the Charity Commission website.

General Founded in 1977, the principal objects of the trust are the:

- relief and assistance of people who are poor or in need, irrespective of class, colour, race or creed
- advancement of education and religion
- relief of sickness and other exclusively charitable purposes beneficial to the community.

In 2005/06 the trust had assets of £2 million and an income of £69,000. Grants were made to 97 organisations totalling £62,000, ranging from £250 to £3,000. A list of beneficiaries was not available.

Previous beneficiaries included: SAT-7 Trust, All Nations Christian College, All Saints in Branksome Park, Birmingham Christian College, Christian Aid,

Churches Commission on overseas students, FEBA Radio, International Christian College, London Bible College, Middle East Media, Moorland College, St James PCC in Poole, SAMS, Trinity College and Wycliffe Bible Translators.

Exclusions No grants to individuals. Only registered charities are supported.

Applications The trust's income is fully allocated each year, mainly to regular beneficiaries. The trustees do not wish to receive any further new requests.

Salters' Charities

General

£123,000 (2005/06)
Beneficial area Greater London or UK.

The Salters' Company, Salters' Hall, 4 Fore Street, London EC2Y 5DE
Tel. 020 7588 5216 **Fax** 020 7638 3679
Email diane@salters.co.uk
Website www.salters.co.uk
Correspondent The Charities Administrator
Trustee *The Salters' Company: Master, Upper Warden and Clerk.*
CC Number 328258
Information available Accounts were available from the Charity Commission website.

General The trust supports UK-wide charities concerned with children and young people, health, Christian aid, the developing world, the environment and members of the armed forces. Grants are also available to local charities connected with the City of London. As a livery company, the trust pays particular interest to charities a liveryman is involved with. In previous years, grants of around £2,000 have been given to around 80 charities each year where such sums can make a difference, placing less emphasis on giving small grants to large organisations. Many beneficiaries have received grants over a number of years.

In 2005/06 the trust had an income of £138,000 and made grants totalling £123,000. Its assets stood at £3,000.

Armed forces – 3 grants totalling £5,500
These went to London Sea Cadet Corps – District 5 – NE and the King's Royal Hussars Regimental Association (£2,000

each) and South West London Army Cadet Force (£1,500).

Children, schools and youth – 10 grants totalling £22,000

Beneficiaries included the Federation of London Youth Clubs (£3,000), British Wheelchair Sports Foundation, Honourable The Irish Society – step-up appeal, King's Corner Project and Rainbow Trust (£2,000 each) and the National Deaf Children's Society (£1,000).

Christian Aid – 1 grant of £1,000

The sole beneficiary was WPF Westminster Pastoral Foundation.

City of London – 9 grants totalling £20,000

Grant recipients included City and Guilds of London Institute (£3,000), Community Links (£2,500), Mansion House Scholarship Scheme (£2,000) and St John Ambulance – City Branch and Teacher Training Scheme (£1,000).

Environment/Third World – 3 grants totalling £10,000

Grants were made to UNEP – WCMC (£7,000), TEAR Fund (£2,000) and the African Scholars' Fund (£1,000).

Medical – 19 grants totalling £33,000

Beneficiaries included Blind in Business, Diabetes UK, Eating Disorders Association, Fight for Sight, Motor Neuron Disease Foundation, Restoration of Appearance and Function Trust – RAFT, Rehabilitation for Adults Prisoners Trust – RAPT (£2,000 each) and Prostate Cancer Charity, the Royal United Kingdom Beneficent Association – RUKBA and Thames Hospice Care (£1,000 each).

Homelessness – 3 grants totalling £6,000

Grants went to Centrepoint – for the Salters' City Foyer Project, Providence Row/Just Ask – Counselling & Advisory Service and the Passage (£2,000 each).

Other donations – 12 grants totalling £21,000

Grants made included those to Tsunami Appeals (£10,000 in three grants), the Lord Todd Memorial Bursary (£3,000), Chelsea Pensioners Appeal (£2,000), Training for Life, Trinity Winchester and University of Ulster step up programme (£1,000 each), Arundel Castle Cricket Foundation, and Ironbridge Gorge Museum Trust (£500 each) and Royal British Legion – City of London poppy appeal (£150).

Exclusions Grants are not normally made to charities working with people who are homeless unless there is some connection with a liveryman of the company or with the Salters' City Foyer and the charities involved.

Applications In writing to the correspondent.

The Andrew Salvesen Charitable Trust

General

About £100,000

Beneficial area UK, with a preference for Scotland.

c/o Meston Reid and Co., 12 Carden Place, Aberdeen AB10 1UR

Tel. 01224 625554

Correspondent Mark Brown

Trustees *A C Salvesen; Ms K Turner; V Lall.*

SC Number SC008000

Information available Limited information was available from the trust.

General The trust gives grants for general charitable purposes, in particular it will support the arts, education/training, medical sciences and welfare of people who are young, elderly or ill.

In previous years grants have been made totalling around £100,000. Unfortunately we were unable to obtain further up-to-date information.

Previous beneficiaries have included Bield Housing Trust, William Higgins Marathon Account, Multiple Sclerosis Society in Scotland, Royal Zoological Society of Scotland, Sail Training Association, Scottish Down's Syndrome Association and Sick Kids Appeal.

Exclusions No grants to individuals.

Applications The trustees only support organisations known to them through their personal contacts. The trust has previously stated that all applications sent to them are 'thrown in the bin'.

The Sammermar Trust

General

£172,000 (2005)

Beneficial area UK and overseas.

Swire House, 59 Buckingham Gate, London SW1E 6AJ

Tel. 020 7834 7717

Correspondent Mrs Yvonne Barnes

Trustees *Lady Judith Swire; M Dunne; M B Swire; Sir Kerry St Johnson; Mrs M.V.Allfrey.*

CC Number 800493

Information available Accounts were available from the Charity Commission website.

General The trust, formerly known as The Adrian Swire Charitable Trust, was established in 1988 with general charitable purposes. In 2005 the trust had assets of £5.4 million and an income of £1.3 million. Grants were made totalling £172,000.

The largest grants were those made to: University College Oxford (£53,000), Wantage Nursing Home Charitable Trust (£50,000), Mango Tree Orphan Support Programme (£10,000), the Spitfire Society (£5,500); and Children-in-Crisis, Combined Trusts Scholarship Trust, Oxfordshire Nature Conservation Forum, Prior's Court Foundation (£5,000 each).

Smaller grants of less than £5,000 each were made to: Nilgiris Adivasi Welfare Association (£2,500); Myton Hamlet Hospice, National Rheumatoid Arthritis Society, Second Space, Somerville College, Warwick Hospital Cancer Ward Appeal and Warwickshire Association of Youth Clubs (£2,000 each); Wycombe Air Centre Ltd (£1,800); and Deafway, Flying Scholarships for the Disabled and Sporting Chance Appeal (£1,000 each).

Other grants were made totalling £11,000 and were for less than £1,000 each.

Applications In writing to the correspondent. The trustees meet monthly.

Coral Samuel Charitable Trust

General, health, the arts

£286,000 (2004/05)

Beneficial area UK.

c/o Great Portland Estates plc, 33 Cavendish Square, London W1G 0PW

Correspondent Mrs Coral Samuel, Trustee

Trustees *Coral Samuel; P Fineman.*

CC Number 239677

Information available Accounts were on file at the Charity Commission.

General This trust was established in 1962, it makes grants of £10,000 or more to educational, cultural and social welfare charities plus a number of smaller donations to other charities.

In 2004/05 the trust's assets totalled £4.3 million. The income was £279,000 and grants to charities totalled £286,000.

Grants were made to 39 organisations, 11 of which were supported in the previous year. The largest grants were Royal Academy of Arts and South Bank Centre (£50,000 each), Victoria & Albert Museum (£25,000), DEBRA and Imperial College of Science & Technology (£20,000) and the Mary Rose Trust, Royal Opera House Foundation and SAVE (£10,000 each).

The remaining, smaller grants ranged from £500 to £7,000. A wide variety of organisations were supported including: RNLI (£7,000); Academy of St Martin in the Fields, Animal Care Trust, British ORT, the Burlington Magazine Foundation, Central School of Ballet Charitable Trust, Chicken Shed Theatre Company, the Anthony Nolan Bone Marrow Trust, Friends of the Israel Aged and World Jewish Relief (£5,000 each); Attingham Trust and the London Symphony Orchestra Endowment Trust (£3,000 each); Alexandra Rose Day and the Alnwick Garden (£2,000 each); Elias Ashmole Trust and Ben Uri Art Society, British WIZO, the Council of Christians and Jews, Leeds Jewish Welfare, National Eczema Society and Wellbeing (£1,000 each); and the Kensington Society (£500).

Exclusions Grants are only made to registered charities.

Applications In writing to the correspondent.

The Peter Samuel Charitable Trust

Health, welfare, conservation, Jewish care

£93,000 (2005/06)

Beneficial area South Berkshire, Highlands of Scotland and East Somerset.

The Estate Office, Castle Road, Farley Hill, Berkshire RG7 1UL

Tel. 0118 973 0047 **Fax** 0118 973 0385

Correspondent Miss Emma Chapman, Trust Administrator

Trustees *Hon. Viscount Bearsted; Hon. Michael Samuel.*

CC Number 269065

Information available Full accounts were available from the Charity Commission website.

General The trustees' report states: 'The trust seeks to promote the family's interest in medical sciences, and the quality of life in local areas, heritage and forestry/land restoration.' In 2005/06 the trust had assets of £3.6 million and an income of £109,000. Grants were made totalling £93,000.

The largest grants were those made to: University College of London – Development Fund (£20,000); Game Conservancy and Pippin (£15,000 each); and Anna Freud Centre (£12,000).

Other grants made included those to: Child Bereavement Trust and Oxford Children's Hospital for Thomas (£5,000 each); Cancer Research (£3,000); Jewish Care and Norwood Ravenswood (£2,500 each); Community Security Trust and St John Ambulance (£2,000); Langley House Trust, New Bridge and Tribe(£1,000 each); Talking Newspaper Association and Woodland Trust (£500 each); and Thames River Restoration Trust (£250).

Exclusions No grants to purely local charities outside Berkshire or to individuals.

Applications In writing to the correspondent. Trustees meet twice-yearly.

The Camilla Samuel Fund

Medical research

Around £25,000 (2005/06)

Beneficial area UK.

40 Berkerly Square, London W1J 5AL

Correspondent The Secretary to the Trustees

Trustees *Sir Ronald Grierson; Hon. Mrs Waley-Cohen; Dr Hon. J P H Hunt.*

CC Number 235424

Information available Information was obtained from the Charity Commission website.

General The trust supports medical research projects in a discipline agreed by the trustees at their annual meetings.

In 2005/06 the trust had an income of £19,000 and a total expenditure of £30,000. Further information was not available. Previous beneficiaries were Imperial Cancer Research Fund and EORTC.

Exclusions No grants to individuals, general appeals or any other charitable institution.

Applications The trustees will request written applications following the recommendation of a suitable project by the medical trustees. However, please note as all the money available, together with the fund's future income, has been earmarked for four years for an important research project, the fund will not be in a position to consider any applications for grants during this period.

Jimmy Savile Charitable Trust

General

£18,000 (2005/06)

Beneficial area UK.

Stoke Mandeville Hospital, Mandeville Road, Aylesbury, Buckinghamshire HP21 8DL

Trustees *Sir James Savile; James Collier; Luke Lucas.*

CC Number 326970

Information available Accounts were available from the Charity Commission website.

General The trust's annual report has previously stated that the objectives of the charity are 'to provide funds for the relief of poverty, the relief of sickness and other charitable purposes beneficial to the community including the provision of recreational and other facilities for people with disability'. In 2005/06 the trust had assets of £3.3 million and an income of £199,000. Grants were made totalling £18,000.

Grants of £1,000 or more went to Buckinghamshire NHS Trust (£2,500) and Disability Aid Fund, HSBC Asian Appeal and Benedictine Nuns of Minster Abbey (£1,000 each).

Other grants made included those to Women Supporting Women (£700), National Children's Home (£500), Bradford Gingerbread (£250) and Aids Trust (£200).

Applications The trust does not respond to unsolicited applications.

The Scarfe Charitable Trust

Environment, churches, arts

£54,000 (2005/06)
Beneficial area UK, with an emphasis on Suffolk.

Salix House, Falkenham, Ipswich, Suffolk IP10 0QY
Tel. 01394 448 339 **Fax** 01394 448 339
Email ericmaule@hotmail.com
Correspondent Eric Maule, Trustee
Trustees *N Scarfe; E E Maule.*
CC Number 275535
Information available Accounts were available from the Charity Commission website.

General The trust was established in 1978 by W S N Scarfe. In 2005/06 the trust had an income of £62,000 and made grants totalling £54,000. Its assets stood at £1.3 million. Grants were made as follows:

Churches – 17 grants
Beneficiaries included: St Mary PCC – Syleham (£1,500); All Saints – Bentley, St Helen PCC – Bishopsgate and St Michael PCC – Lowestoft (£1,000 each); King Charles the Martyr PCC – Shelland (£700); All Saints, Bury St Edmunds (£500); St Mary PCC – Stratford St Mary

(£400); and St Peter PCC – Thurston and All Saints – Gazeley (£200).

Organisations – 51 grants
Grant recipients included: Aldeburgh Productions (£9,000); Music in Country Churches (£5,000); Greenlight Trust and Woodbridge Town Trust (£2,000 each); Red Rose Chain Theatre (£1,250); Friends of the Suffolk Record Office, Gainsboroughs House Suffolk Institute of Archaeology and History and Theatre Royal Bury St Edmunds (£1,000 each); Cedar House Trust (£500); EACH (£750); Eastern Angles, Fry Art Gallery and Terrence Higgins Trust (£500.each); Aldeburgh Music Club (£300); Prisoners of Conscience, Dance Umbrella and Wymondham Abbey Book project (£250 each); and Bury St Edmunds Quaker Meeting House (£200).

Other grants included two grants made to individuals (£1,500).

Applications In writing to the correspondent.

The Schapira Charitable Trust

Jewish

£535,000 (2005)
Beneficial area UK.

2 Dancastle Court, 14 Arcadia Avenue, Finchley, London N3 2JU
Tel. 020 8371 0381
Correspondent The Trustees
Trustees *Issac Y Schapira; Michael Neuberger; Suzanne L Schapira.*
CC Number 328435
Information available Accounts were available from the Charity Commission website.

General This trust appears to make grants exclusively to Jewish charities. In 2005 the trust had assets of £7 million and an income of 1.5 million. Grants were made totalling £535,000.

The largest grants made included those to: Friends of Tashbar Chazon Ish (£198,000); Mercaz Hatorah Vehachinuch Limited (£39,000); British Friends of Migdal Ohr (£38,000); Emuno Educational Centre Limited (£31,000); Friends of Horim (£23,000); Keren Association Limited (£18,000); Society of Friends of Torah (£12,000); and T and S Trust Fund (£10,000).

Smaller grants of less than £10,000 each included those made to: Rowanville Limited (£7,000); British Friends of Mosdos Tchernobel (£4,500); Hatzola Northwest Trust (£2,000); Talmud Centre Trust (£1,700); Support (£1,500); Keren Hatorah and Side by Side Kids Ltd (£1,000 each); and Kol Yehuda Synagogue (£500).

Applications In writing to the correspondent.

The Annie Schiff Charitable Trust

Orthodox Jewish education

£33,000 (2005/06)
Beneficial area UK, overseas.

8 Highfield Gardens, London NW11 9HB
Tel. 020 8458 9266
Correspondent J Pearlman, Trustee
Trustees *J Pearlman; Mrs R Pearlman.*
CC Number 265401
Information available Full accounts were on file at the Charity Commission.

General The trust's objectives are:

- relief of poverty, particularly amongst the Jewish community
- advancement of education, particularly the study and instruction of Jewish religious literature
- advancement of religion, particularly Judaism.

In 2005/06 the trust had assets of £244,000 and an income of £32,000. Grants were made to 11 organisations totalling £33,000.

Grant recipients were: Friends of Beis Yisrael Trust (£10,000); Chevras Mo'oz Ladol (£6,000); Menorah Grammar School Trust (£5,300); Yeshivo Horomo Talmudical College (£4,000); Yesodey Hatorah Schools (£2,000); Centre for Torah Education Trust (£1,800); Law of Truth Talmudical College (£1,200); Institute for Higher Rabbinical Studies (£1,000); Talmud Torah Tiferes Shlomo (£750); Parsha Ltd (£550); and North West Sephardish Synagogue (£500).

Exclusions No support for individuals and non-recognised institutions.

Applications In writing to the correspondent, but grants are generally made only to registered charities. The

303

trust states that presently all funds are committed.

The Schmidt-Bodner Charitable Trust

Jewish, general

£183,000 (2004/05)

Beneficial area Worldwide.

8 Baker Street, London W1U 3LL

Tel. 020 7486 5888

Correspondent Daniel Dover

Trustees *Daniel Dover; Martin Paisner; Mrs E Schmidt-Bodner.*

CC Number 283014

Information available Full accounts were on file at the Charity Commission.

General This trust mainly supports Jewish organisations though it has also given a few small grants to medical and welfare charities. In 2004/05 the trust had assets of £1.3 million and an income of £49,000. Grants were made to 14 organisations totalling £183,000.

The largest grants went to Yesodey Hatorah Trust (£125,000) and SAGE – Service to the Aged, Friends of Lubavitch UK and British Friends of Or Chadash (£10,000 each).

Smaller grants of less than £10,000 each included those made to: World Jewish Relief (£6,000); Community Security Trust and Jewish Care (£5,000 each); One Family UK (£4,000); Simon Marks Jewish Primary School Trust (£3,000); United Synagogue Kehillah Project (£2,000); CHAI Cancer Care and Institute for Higher Rabbinical Studies (£1,000 each); and UJIA (£250).

Applications In writing to the correspondent.

The R H Scholes Charitable Trust

Children and young people who are disabled or disadvantaged, hospices, preservation and churches

£33,000 (2005/06)

Beneficial area England.

Fairacre, Bonfire Hill, Southwater, Horsham, West Sussex RH13 9BU

Email roger@rogpat.plus.com

Correspondent R H C Pattison, Trustee

Trustees *R H C Pattison; Mrs A J Pattison.*

CC Number 267023

Information available Accounts were available from the Charity Commission website.

General This trust currently only supports organisations in which the trustees have a special interest, knowledge of or association with. Both recurrent and one-off grants are made depending upon the needs of the beneficiary. Core costs, project and research grants are made. Funding for more than three years will be considered.

In 2005/06 the trust had assets of £584,000 and an income of £32,000. Grants were made to 108 organisations totalling £33,000.

Grants of £1,000 each went to the Church of England Pensions Board, the Friends of Lancing Chapel, Historic Churches Preservation Trust, St Catherine's Hospice, St Luke's Hospital for the Clergy and the Children's Country Holidays Fund. All other grants were between £100 and £800 each.

Exclusions Grants only to registered charities. No grants to individuals, animal charities, expeditions or scholarships. The trust tries not to make grants to more than one charity operating in a particular field, and does not make grants to charities outside England.

Applications In writing to the correspondent, although due to a lack of funds it is not currently accepting unsolicited applications from organisations it is not already supporting.

The Schreiber Charitable Trust

Jewish

£152,000 (2005/06)

Beneficial area UK.

PO Box 35547, The Exchange, 4 Brent Cross Gardens, London NW4 3WH

Correspondent G S Morris, Trustee

Trustees *Graham S Morris; David A Schreiber; Mrs Sara Schreiber.*

CC Number 264735

Information available Full accounts were available from the Charity Commission website.

General In 2005/06 the trust had assets of £3.2 million and an income of £220,000. Grants were made totalling £152,000.

The largest grants went to Friends of Rabbinical College Kol Tora Jerusalem (£52,000) and Gateshead Talmudical College (£11,000).

Smaller grants included those made to North West London Communal Mikvah (£5,000), British Committee for P'eilim in Israel (£2,500), Chai Charitable Trust and Collel Chibath Yerushalayim (£2,000 each), Shaare Zedek UK (£1,500), Aleph Society Trust Friends of Mir and the Spiro Ark (£1,000 each), World Jewish Aid (£250) and Achisomoch Aid Society (£180).

Other grants of less than £1,000 totalled £28,000.

Applications The trust states that all funds are currently committed. No applications are therefore considered or replied to.

Scopus Jewish Educational Trust

Jewish education

Around £80,000 (2005)

Beneficial area UK.

52 Queen Anne Street, London W1G 8HL

Tel. 020 8906 4455

Trustees *P Ohrenstein, Chair; J Kramer; S Cohen; Mrs B Hyman.*

CC Number 313154

Information available Information was obtained from the Charity Commission website.

General This trust makes grants to Jewish day schools, associations, societies and institutions, calculated to benefit directly or indirectly Jewish education. In 2005 the trust had an income of £5,000 and a total expenditure of £93,000. Further information was not available.

Previously Simon Marks Jewish Primary School has been a grant recipient.

Applications In writing to the contact address.

The Scott Bader Commonwealth Ltd

See below

£67,000 (2005)
Beneficial area UK and overseas.

Wollaston, Wellingborough, Northamptonshire NN29 7RL

Tel. 01933 666755 **Fax** 01933 666608

Email commonwealth_office@ scottbader.com

Website www.scottbader.com

Correspondent Sue Carter, Commonwealth Secretary

Trustees *The Board of Management: Sylvia Brown; Conon Burrell; Bob Coxon; Phillipe Dembicki; Julianne Field; Jeffery Legg; Jackie Long; Paul Palmer; Mark Stanion.*

CC Number 206391

Information available Accounts were available from the Charity Commission website.

General This commonwealth supports projects, activities or charities which: find difficulty raising funds; are innovative, imaginative and pioneering; or are initiated and/or supported by local people. Each year there is a particular area of focus, so applicants should check current focus before applying.

Grants are given for the assistance of distressed and needy people of all nationalities and the establishment and support of charitable institutions whose objects may include the advancement of education. The commonwealth looks for projects, activities or charities which: respond to the needs of those who are most underprivileged, disadvantaged, poor or excluded; encourage the careful use and protection of the earth's resources (those which assist poor rural people to become self-reliant are particularly encouraged); or promote peace-building and democratic participation. The commonwealth also supports the research, development and advancement of education in industrial participation of a nature beneficial to the community.

In 2005 the trust had assets of £305,000 and an income of £170,000. Grants were made totalling £67,000. Larger grants were made in the following categories:

UK – 3 grants totalling £10,000
Grants went to St Mary's Parochial Church Council and the Hope Project (£5,000 each) and KIDS (£260).

International – 7 grants totalling £19,000
Grant recipients included Scott Bader Company Limited – Tsunami Dubai Round Table (£5,000), InterAct (£3,000), SBCL – Payment for Fulton School for the Deaf (£2,500) and Tigre Trust (£1,000).

President's fund
Beneficiaries included Forum for the Future (£1,500), Quaker Peace and Social Witness (£750), Peace Child International, Oxford Research Group and Victoria Centre (£500 each) and TREAT (£250).

Exclusions No support for charities concerned with the wellbeing of animals, individuals in need or organisations sending volunteers abroad. It does not respond to general appeals or support the larger well-established national charities. It does not provide educational bursaries or grants for academic research. It does not make up deficits already incurred, or support the arts, museums, travel/adventure, sports clubs or the construction, renovation or maintenance of buildings.

Applications In writing or by email to the correspondent. Trustees meet quarterly in January, April, July and October.

Sir Samuel Scott of Yews Trust

Medical research

£135,000 (2005/06)
Beneficial area UK.

c/o Currey and Co., 21 Buckingham Gate, London SW1E 6LS

Tel. 020 7802 2700 **Fax** 020 7828 5049

Correspondent The Secretary

Trustees *Lady Phoebe Scott; Hermione Stanford; Edward Perks.*

CC Number 220878

Information available Accounts were available from the Charity Commission website.

General In 2005/06 the trust had assets of £5.4 million and an income of £133,000. There were 47 grants made to organisations totalling £135,000.

The largest grants made included those to: Alzheimers Research Trust and Great Ormond Street Hospital Children's Charity (£10,000 each); University College London Hospitals Charitable Foundation (£6,000); and Ataxia Telangiectasia Society, Children with Leukaemia, Parkinson's Disease Society, Prostrate Cancer Charity and Institute of Cancer Research (£5,000 each).

Smaller grants of less than £5,000 each included those made to: British Eye Research Foundation (£4,000); Brain Research Trust, Ear Nose and Throat Department – Leicester Royal Infirmary (£3,000 each); FSID – Foundation for Study of Infant Deaths, Muscular Dystrophy Campaign SPARKS – Sport Aiding Medical Research for Kids and WellBeing of Women (£2,000 each); British Lung Foundation, Dermatrust, Diabetes UK, DISCS – Diagnostic Investigation of Spinal Conditions and Sciatica, National Tremor Foundation, Neuro-Disability Research Trust, Raynaud's and Scleroderma Association, Research Institute for the Care of the Elderly and University of Bath – Centre for Orthopaedic Biomechanics (£1,000 each).

Exclusions No grants for: core funding; purely clinical work; individuals (although research by an individual may be funded if sponsored by a registered charity through which the application is made); research leading to higher degrees (unless the departmental head concerned certifies that the work is of real scientific importance); medical students' elective periods; or expeditions (unless involving an element of genuine medical research); No core funding; no support for purely clinical work; no grants to individuals (although research by an individual may be funded if sponsored by a registered charity through which the application is made); no support for research leading to higher degrees (unless the departmental head concerned certifies that the work is of real scientific importance); no grants for medical students' elective periods; no grants for expeditions (unless involving an element of genuine medical research).

Applications In writing to the correspondent. Trustees hold their half-yearly meetings in April and October and applications have to be submitted two months before. There are no special forms, but applicants should give the following information: the nature and purpose of the research project or programme; the names, qualifications and present posts of the scientists involved; reference to any published results of their previous research; details of present funding; and if possible, the budget for the next 12 months or other convenient period.

All applications are acknowledged and both successful and unsuccessful applicants are notified after each meeting of the trustees. No telephone calls.

The Scouloudi Foundation

General

£185,000 (2005/06)
Beneficial area UK charities working domestically or overseas.

c/o Haysmacintyre, Fairfax House, 15 Fulwood Place, London WC1V 6AY
Tel. 020 7969 5500 **Fax** 020 7969 5529
Correspondent The Administrators
Trustees *Miss Sarah E Stowell, Chair; David J Marnham; James R Sewell.*
CC Number 205685
Information available Full accounts were available from the Charity Commission website.

General The foundation has three types of grants:

- historical grants are made each year to the Institute of Historical Research at University of London for research and publications, to reflect the interests of the settlor, Irene Scouloudi, who was a historian

- regular grants, generally of £1,000 each, are made to organisations on a five-year cycle
- special grants are one-off grants in connection with capital projects.

In 2005/06 the foundation had assets of £6 million and an income of £217,000 generated mostly from income investment. Grants were made totalling £185,000, broken down as follows:

- humanities – £84,000
- medicine, health and hospices – £20,000
- disability – £16,000
- famine relief and overseas aid – £11,000
- social welfare – £11,000
- children and youth – £9,000
- environment – £8,000
- aged – £7,000
- welfare of armed forces and sailors – £6,000.

By far the largest grant was a historical grant made to the University of London – Institute of Historical Research (£80,000).

Other grants included those made to: British Red Cross Disaster Fund (£10,000); Save the Children (£6,000); and Action for Prisoners Families, British and International Sailor's, British Records Association, British Trust for Conservation Volunteers, Christina Noble Children's Foundation, Council for the Protection of Rural England, Crisis Working for Homeless People, Ex-Services Mental Welfare Society, Family Welfare Association, Habitat Scotland, Historical Association, Invalid Children's Aid Nationwide, Leonard Cheshire Foundation, London Connection, Multiple Sclerosis Society, Professional Classes Aid Council, Queen Elizabeth's Foundation for Disabled People, Royal Commonwealth Society for the Blind, St Francis Leprosy Guild, Stroke Association, Sue Ryder Foundation, Terence Higgins Lighthouse, Trust Tree, Council, UK Youth, Vision and Voluntary Service Overseas (£1,000 each).

Exclusions Donations are not made to individuals, and are not normally made for welfare activities of a purely local nature.

The trustees do not make loans or enter into deeds of covenant.

Applications Only Historical grants are open to application. Copies of the regulations and application forms for Historical Awards can be obtained from: The Secretary, The Scouloudi Foundation Historical Awards Committee, c/o Institute of Historical

Research, University of London, Senate House, London WC1E 7HU.

Seamen's Hospital Society

Seafarers

£129,000 to organisations (2004)
Beneficial area UK.

29 King William Walk, Greenwich, London SE10 9HX
Tel. 020 8858 3696
Email admin@seahospital.org.uk
Website www.seahospital.org.uk
Correspondent Peter Coulson, General Secretary
Trustees *J Allen; Capt. D Glass; Capt. P M Hambling; J C Jenkinson; Dr J F Leonard; P McEwan; Capt. G W S Miskin; A R Nairne; Capt. A J Speed; S Todd.*
CC Number 231724
Information available Accounts were on file at the Charity Commission.

General This trust makes grants to medical, care and welfare organisations working with seafarers and to individual seafarers and their dependants. In 2004 the society distributed over £129,000 to organisations helping seafarers, with a further £70,000 to individuals.

Beneficiaries were Royal Alfred Seafarers' Society (£38,000), NUMAST Welfare Fund – Mariners' Park (£33,000), Merchant Seamen's War Memorial Society (£25,000), Royal National Mission to Deep Sea Fishermen (£12,000), Queen Victoria Seamen's Rest (£10,000), Scottish Nautical Welfare Society (£4,000), Mission to Seafarers (£3,500), Royal Merchant Navy School Foundation (£3,000) and International Seafarers' Centre at Great Yarmouth (£1,300).

Other grants totalled £100.

The society also operates the Seafarers' Benefits Advice Line, which provides free confidential advice and information on welfare benefits, housing, consumer problems, legal matters, credit and debt, matrimonial and tax.

Applications On a form available from the correspondent. Grants are awarded in November of each year.

The Searchlight Electric Charitable Trust

General

£105,000 (2005/06)

Beneficial area UK, with a preference for Manchester.

Searchlight Electric Ltd, 900 Oldham Road, Manchester M40 2BS

Correspondent H E Hamburger, Trustee

Trustees *D M Hamburger, Chair; H E Hamburger; M E Hamburger.*

CC Number 801644

Information available Accounts were obtained from the Charity Commission website.

General This trust has general charitable purposes, although most grants are given to Jewish organisations. A large number of grants are made in the Manchester area. In 2005/06 the trust had assets of £1 million and an income of £290,000. Grants were made totalling £105,000.

The largest grants included those made to: UJIA (£49,000); Heathlands (£6,000); Manchester Jewish Federation (£4,000); Rainsough Charitable Trust (£3,000); and JNF Charitable Trust, King David School and Laniado (£2,000 each).

Smaller grants of £1,000 or less included those made to: Manchester Jewish Care, Magen David Adom, Victim Support and WIZO (£1,000 each); RESHET (£750); and Effrat Emergency Medical Centre Charity, Manchester Charitable Trust and RNIB (£500 each).

Exclusions No grants for individuals.

Applications In writing to the correspondent, but note that in the past the trustees have stated that it is their policy to support only charities already on their existing list of beneficiaries or those already known to them.

The Searle Charitable Trust

Sailing

£53,000 (2004/05)

Beneficial area UK.

c/o Apperley Limited, Maple House, High Street, Potters Bar EN6 5BS

Correspondent A D Searle, Trustee

Trustees *Andrew D Searle; Victoria C Searle.*

CC Number 288541

Information available Full accounts were on file at the Charity Commission.

General This trust was established in 1982 by Joan Wynne Searle. Following the death of the settlor in 1995 the trust was split into two. One half is administered by the son of the settlor (Searle Charitable Trust) and the other half by her daughter (Searle Memorial Trust).

The Searle Charitable Trust only supports projects/organisations for youth development within a nautical framework.

In 2004/05 the trust had assets of £2.9 million and an income of £72,000. Grants totalled £53,000. By far the largest grant was £52,000 to RONA Trust, also a major beneficiary in previous years. Two small grants of £500 each were made to National Hospital Development and Teenage Cancer Trust.

Exclusions No grants for individuals or for appeals not related to sailing.

Applications In writing to the correspondent.

The Helene Sebba Charitable Trust

Disability, medical, Jewish

£306,000 (2005/06)

Beneficial area UK, Canada and Israel.

PO Box 326, Bedford MK40 3XU

Tel. 01234 266657

Correspondent David L Hull

Trustees *Mrs N C Klein; Mrs J C Sebba; L Sebba.*

CC Number 277245

Information available Full accounts were available from the Charity Commission website.

General The trust supports disability, medical and Jewish organisations and in the past has made grants to causes in the UK, Canada and Israel. In 2005/06 the trust had assets of £3 million and an income of £246,000. Grants were made totalling £306,000 divided between two categories:

Welfare, health including medical research – 30 grants totalling £298,000
The largest grants in this category went to Friends of the Neurim Home for the Mentally Handicapped (£200,000) and Friends of Israel Sports Centre for the Disabled and Ehlers-Danlos and Connective Tissue Disorders Research Fund (£15,000 each).

Smaller grants included those made to: Norwood (£6,000); Ferring Country Centre and the Relatives and Residents Association (£5,000 each); Beis Brucha (£4,000); the Prostate Cancer Charity (£3,500); Jewish Care and Mencap (£2,500 each); Alzheimer's Society, British Friends of Ohel Sarah and Scope (£2,000 each); Breakthrough Breast Cancer, Age Concern and RNIB Trust (£1,000 each); and AKIM, BIBIC and Brainwave (£500 each).

Other – 5 grants totalling £8,000
Grants went to: Ashwell Village Hall (£3,000); Jersey Heritage Trust (£2,000); Royal Geographical Society (£1,500); Bridge Quartet (£1,000); and National Jewish Chaplaincy (£500).

Applications In writing to the correspondent.

The Seedfield Trust

Christian, relief of poverty

£71,000 (2004)

Beneficial area Worldwide.

3 Woodland Vale, Lakeside, Ulverston, Cumbria LA12 8DR

Correspondent The Trustees

Trustees *John Atkins; Keith Buckler; David Ryan; Revd Lionel Osborn; Janet Buckler; D Heap.*

CC Number 283463

Information available Accounts were on file at the Charity Commission.

General The trust's main objectives are the furthering of Christian work and the relief of poverty. In 2004 the trust had assets of £2.1 million and an income of £81,000. Grants to 24 organisations totalled £71,000.

A number of the beneficiaries had been supported at the same or similar levels in previous years, these included some of the recipients of the largest grants: European Christian Mission (£15,000) and Dorothea Trust and Overseas Missionary Fellowship (£10,000 each).

Other grants included those to the Gideons International, the Muller Homes and New English Orchestra (£5,000 each), Churches Child Protection Advisory (£4,000), Keswick Convention (£3,500), Crusaders, Leprosy Mission, Open Door Gospel and Social Ministries – India, Walk Thru the Bible Ministries, Wycliffe Bible Translators and YWAM – Kenya (£1,000 each) and Anglo Peruvian Childcare Mission and Riding Lights (£500 each).

Exclusions No grants to individuals.

Applications In writing to the correspondent, for consideration by the trustees who meet twice each year. Please enclose an sae for acknowledgement.

Leslie Sell Charitable Trust

Uniformed youth groups

£101,000 (2005/06)
Beneficial area UK and worldwide.

Ashbrittle House, 2a Lower Dagnall Street, St Albans, Hertfordshire AL3 4PA
Tel. 01727 843603 **Fax** 01727 843663
Website www.lesliesellct.org.uk
Correspondent The Secretary
Trustees *P S Sell, Chair; Mrs M R Wiltshire; A H Sell; J Byrnes.*
CC Number 258699
Information available Accounts were on file at the Charity Commission.

General Established in 1969 by the late Leslie Baden Sell, the trust supports youth groups, mainly Scouts and Guides, but also community groups.

In 2005/06 the trust had an income of £155,000 and assets totalling £3.1 million. Grants were made totalling £101,000.

Applications In writing to the correspondent. Applications should include clear details of the project or purpose for which funds are required, together with an estimate of total costs and total funds raised by the group or individual for the project.

Sellata Ltd

Jewish, welfare

£8,000 (2005/06)
Beneficial area UK.

29 Fontayne Road, London N16 7EA
Correspondent E S Benedikt, Trustee
Trustees *E S Benedikt; Mrs N Benedikt; P Benedikt.*
CC Number 285429
Information available Accounts were on file at the Charity Commission, but without a list of grants.

General The trust says it supports the advancement of religion and the relief of poverty. In 2005/06 the trust had assets of £442,000 and an income of £163,000. Grants were made totalling £8,000. A list of beneficiaries was not available.

Applications In writing to the correspondent.

SEM Charitable Trust

Disability, general, Jewish

£87,000 (2005/06)
Beneficial area Mainly South Africa, Israel and UK.

Reeves and Neylan, 37 St Margaret's Street, Canterbury, Kent CT1 2TU
Tel. 01227 768231
Correspondent The Trustees
Trustees *Mrs Sarah E Radomir; Michael Radomir.*
CC Number 265831
Information available Accounts were available from the Charity Commission website.

General In 2005/06 the trust had an income of £210,000 and made grants totalling £87,000. Its assets stood at £1.2 million.

Grants went to: Natal Society for Arts (£52,000); Friends of the Earth (£10,000); Vuka Community Environment Project (£9,000); The Valley Trust (£2,900); Entrust Foundation (£2,700); CET and School Leavers Opportunity Trust (£2,000); West London Synagogue (£1,600); Play Action Ltd (£1,500); UK Trust (£1,250); Disabled Living Foundation, and DVHC

Masada Trust (£1,000) and Dressability (£500).

Exclusions No grants to individuals.

Applications In writing to the correspondent.

The Ayrton Senna Foundation

Children's health and education

£600 (2005)
Beneficial area Worldwide, with a preference for Brazil.

Eagle House, 10 Jermyn Street, London SW1Y 6RH
Tel. 020 7451 9000
Correspondent Christopher Bliss, Trustee
Trustees *Viviane Lalli, President; Milton Guerado Theodoro da Silva; Neyde Joanna Senna da Silva; Leonardo Senna da Silva; Christopher Bliss.*
CC Number 1041759
Information available Accounts were available from the Charity Commission website.

General The trust was established in 1994 by the father of the late Ayrton Senna, in memory of his son, the racing driver. The trust was given the whole issued share capital of Ayrton Senna Foundation Ltd, a company set up to license the continued use of the Senna trademark and copyrights.

In 2005 the trust had assets of £3 million and an income of £257,000. The trust had an expenditure of £242,000, which was listed in the accounts as 'management and administration, including foreign exchange movements'. There was one grant made to CEDES totalling £600.

Exclusions No grants to individuals.

Applications In writing to the correspondent.

The Seven Fifty Trust

Christian

£57,000 (2004/05)
Beneficial area UK and worldwide.

All Saints Vicarage, Chapel Green, Crowborough, East Sussex TN6 1ED

Tel. 01892 667384

Correspondent Revd Andrew C J Cornes, Trustee

Trustees *Revd Andrew C J Cornes; Katherine E Cornes; Peter N Collier; Susan M Collier.*

CC Number 298886

Information available Full accounts were on file at the Charity Commission.

General This trust is for the advancement of the Christian religion in the UK and throughout the world. In 2004/05 it had assets of £1.5 million and an income of £52,000. Grants totalled £57,000.

Beneficiaries included All Saints Church – Crowborough (£14,000), Aquila Care Trust (£7,900), St Matthew's Fulham (£4,100), the Langham Partnership (£3,500), Overseas Missionary Fellowship (£2,300), C S Lewis Institute (£2,200), Christian Solidarity Worldwide (£2,000), Care for the Family (£1,400), CPAS (£1,000) and Cliff College (£500).

Exclusions No support for unsolicited requests.

Applications It should be noted that the trust's funds are fully committed and unsolicited requests are not entertained. No reply is sent unless an sae is included with the application, but even then the reply will only say that the trust does not respond to unsolicited applications.

SFIA Educational Trust Limited

Education

£280,000 (2005/06)
Beneficial area UK.

39 Queen Street, Maidenhead, Berkshire SL6 1NB

Tel. 01628 502040 **Fax** 01628 502049

Email admin@plans-ltd.co.uk

Website www.plans-ltd.co.uk/trusts

Correspondent Mrs Anne Feek, Chief Executive

Trustees *Mrs Beatrice Roberts; Anthony Hastings; D Prince John Rees; Hugh Monro.*

CC Number 270272

Information available Full accounts were available from the Charity Commission website.

General Associated with charity SFIA Educational Trust Limited. Since 1959 over £13 million has been paid out in grants.

Grants are only awarded to schools/educational organisations towards bursaries to cover part fees for pupils with the following needs:

- special learning difficulties
- social deprivation
- emotional/behavioural difficulties
- physical disabilities
- gifted in a specialist area
- boarding need.

Grants are also given towards educational projects, books, equipment and school trips to promote the advancement of learning. Grants will only be considered for specific projects. Recipients will be asked to complete a declaration confirming that the funds will be used for the nominated purpose. No applications will be considered from individuals or from schools/organisations in respect of pupils/students over the age of 18.

In 2004/05 the trust had assets of £5.5 million and an income of £222,000. Grants were made totalling £280,000 and were divided as follows:

Educational organisations – 2 grants totalling £4,500
Grants went to Youth Music Theatre UK (£2,500) and Arkwright Scholarships (£2,000).

Schools – 30 grants totalling £281,000
The largest grants included those to: Lord Wandsworth, Reed's and Royal Wolverhampton (£30,000 each); Haberdashers and Purcell (£24,000); Kingham Hill (£20,000); and Small School and Stanbridge Earls (£10,000 each).

Smaller grants of £5,000 or less each included those to St Christopher's School and Shepherds Spring Infant School (£5,000 each); Aughton Christ Church School, Cox Green and Treehouse (£2,000 each); Downton School, Thriftwood Special School, Manor Infant School and Milton Hall Primary School (£1,000 each); and Cranbourne Primary School (£500).

Exclusions No applications will be considered from individuals or from schools/organisations in respect of pupils/students over the age of 18.

Applications Application forms are available on the trust's website. All applications should be received by 31 January accompanied by the most recent set of audited accounts. Applications are considered in March/April each year. After the meeting, all applicants will be informed of the outcome as soon as possible.

The Cyril Shack Trust

Jewish, general

£39,000 (2004/05)
Beneficial area UK.

c/o Lubbock Fine, Chartered Accountants, Russell Bedford House, City Forum, 250 City Road, London EC1V 2QQ

Correspondent The Clerk

Trustees *J Shack; C C Shack.*

CC Number 264270

Information available Accounts were on file at the Charity Commission, but without a list of grants.

General In 2004/05 the trust's assets totalled £586,000. It had an income of £150,000 and made grants totalling £39,000. Mainly Jewish organisations are supported.

There was no grants list available for that year. The most recent list of beneficiaries in the public files at the Charity Commission was from 1996/97. Jewish organisations supported have included Finchley Road Synagogue, Nightingale House and St John's Wood Synagogue. UK organisations to benefit have included Breakthrough Breast Cancer, Crisis, Golf Aid, Hampstead Theatre, Hartsbourne Ladies Charity, London Library, Prisoners of Conscience, Samaritans, St John's Hospice and University of the Third Age – London.

Exclusions No grants for expeditions, travel bursaries, scholarships or to individuals.

Applications In writing to the correspondent.

The Jean Shanks Foundation

Medical research and education

£178,000 (2005/06)

Beneficial area UK.

3 Ridgeway, Wargrave, Reading RG10 8AS

Correspondent Mrs B Sears

Trustees *Prof. Sir Dillwyn Williams; Prof. Charles Hales; Eric Rothbarth; Prof. Dame Lesley Rees; Prof. Andrew Carr; Prof. Sir James Underwood; Prof. Sir Nicholas Wright.*

CC Number 293108

Information available Accounts were on file at the Charity Commission.

General Registered with the Charity Commission in November 1985 this trust supports medical research and education. In 2005/06 it had assets amounting to £16 million and an income of £3.4 million. Grants totalled £178,000.

The largest grants went to University College London (£41,000), University of Cambridge (£39,000), Barts and University of London (£19,000) and University of Oxford (£10,000).

Grants of £6,300 each went to the universities of Birmingham, Bristol, Leeds, Leicester, London and Southampton with £5,000 going to National Bureau for Disabled Students.

Applications In writing to the correspondent.

The Shanti Charitable Trust

General, Christian, international development

£55,000 (2005/06)

Beneficial area UK, with preference for West Yorkshire, and developing countries (especially Nepal).

53 Kirkgate, Silsdon, Keighley, Bradford BD20 0AQ

Tel. 01535 65311

Correspondent J E Brown

Trustees *Miss J B Gill; T F X Parr; R K Hyett.*

CC Number 1064813

Information available Accounts were available from the Charity Commission website.

General This trust's main interest is in supporting the International Nepal Fellowship, although other funding is given. The trust states that most of the beneficiaries are those with which the trustees already have links with and this priority also influences them in giving to local branches of national organisations.

In 2005/06 the trust had assets of £223,000 and an income of £99,000. Grants were made to 15 organisations totalling £55,000. The largest grant was made to International Nepal Fellowship (£20,000).

Other grants included those made to Protac/Theotac – Nepal (£6,000), CBRS and St John's Church (£5,000 each), Urban Vision (£2,500), Sue Ryder – Manorlands (£2,000), Nepal Leprosy Trust (£1,000), CMS (£500) and Belle Vue Boys School (£100).

Exclusions No grants to gap-year students, or political or animal welfare causes.

Applications In writing to the correspondent. Please note, most beneficiaries are those the trustees already has contact with.

The Linley Shaw Foundation

Conservation

£36,000 (2005/06)

Beneficial area UK.

Natwest Trust Services, 5th Floor, Trinity Quay 2, Avon Street, Bristol BS2 0PT

Tel. 0117 940 3283 **Fax** 0117 940 3275

Correspondent The Trust Section

Trustee *National Westminster Bank plc.*

CC Number 1034051

Information available Non-financial information was provided by the trust.

General The trust supports charities working to conserve, preserve and restore the natural beauty of the UK countryside for the public benefit.

Generally the trust prefers to support a specific project, rather than give money

for general use. In his will, Linley Shaw placed particular emphasis on those charities, which organise voluntary workers to achieve the objects of the trust. This may be taken into account when considering applications. Grants can be given towards any aspect of a project. Previous examples include the cost of tools, management surveys and assistance with the cost of land purchase.

In 2005/06 the trust had assets of £1.2 million and an income of £46,000. Grants were made to seven organisations totalling £36,000. Beneficiaries were Northumberland Wildlife, Gloucestershire Wildlife, London Wildlife, World Land Trust, Grasslands Trust, Cumbria Wildlife and Mersey Forest.

Exclusions No grants to non-charitable organisations, or to organisations whose aims or objectives do not include conservation, preservation or restoration of the natural beauty of the UK countryside, even if the purpose of the grant would be eligible. No grants to individuals.

Applications In writing to the correspondent. All material will be photocopied by the trust so please avoid sending 'bound' copies of reports and so on. Evidence of aims and objectives are needed, usually in the forms of accounts, annual reports or leaflets, which cannot be returned. Applications are considered in February/early March and should be received by December/early January.

The Sheldon Trust

General

£134,000 (2004/05)

Beneficial area West Midlands.

White Horse Court, 25c North Street, Bishop's Stortford, Hertfordshire CM23 2LD

Email charities@pothecary.co.uk

Correspondent The Trust Administrator

Trustees *A Bidnell; Revd R S Bidnell; R V Wiglesworth; J C Barratt; Mrs R M Bagshaw.*

CC Number 242328

Information available Full accounts were on file at the Charity Commission.

General The trust's geographical area of giving is the West Midlands, with particular emphasis on the areas of

Birmingham, city of Coventry, Dudley, Sandwell, Solihull, Warwickshire and Wolverhampton. The main aims continue to be relieving poverty and distress in society, concentrating grants on community projects as well as those directed to special needs groups, especially in deprived areas. The trustees review their policy and criteria regularly. 'Although they have a central policy, a certain flexibility is ensured in reacting to changes in the environment and the community alike.'

In 2004/05 it had assets of £3.3 million, which generated an income of £178,000. Management and administration costs were high at £32,000 an increase of £8,000 on the previous year. Grants were made to 54 organisations totalling £134,000.

Grants were broken down in the accounts as follows:

Grants to individuals
'To regionalise their interest in the Midlands, the trustees have continued to make an annual grant of £13,000 to Birmingham Money Advice and Grants (Personal Services) in Birmingham, who make many small grants to individuals for clothing, furniture and travel expenses for visiting the sick, as well as providing a debt-counselling service.

Holiday projects
An annual sum of £6,000 is allocated for holiday projects and during the year grants were awarded to: the Harvest Trust, Peak (National Asthma Joint Holidays), 3H Fund, BREAK, Bethany Christian Fellowship, Vitalise, Birmingham Phab Camps, Children's Heart Federation, Happy Days, Birmingham Young Volunteers Adventure Camps and Barton Training Trust.

Grants for special needs groups
Organisations supported during the year included: Sense, 870 House, Where Next Association, Birmingham St Mary's Hospice, Kinmos Volunteer Group Ltd, SNAP, The Norman Laud Association, Birmingham Institute for the Deaf, Headway Black Country, Warwickshire Domestic Violence Support Services and Deafblind UK.

Community projects
Organisations supported during the year included: St Barnabus Family Centre, The Light House Trust, All Saints' Women's Resource Centre, the Handsworth Group Youth Project, Ladywood Furniture Project, DebtCred, the Vine Trust – Walsall, the Springfield Project, SAFE and Contact the Elderly.

Continuing grants
Several continuing grants came to an end during the year and two new awards were approved by the trustees: Shenley Green Centre and Parkinson's Disease Society (both three-year funding).

Exclusions 'The trustees will not consider appeals in respect of the cost of buildings, but will consider appeals where buildings have to be brought up-to-date to meet health, safety and fire regulations. The trustees will not consider general appeals from national organisations or individual appeals.'

Applications On a form available from the correspondent. The trustees meet three times a year, in March, July and November, making 10 to 15 grants depending on income. The trust's report stated that they will 'for the present be committing a good proportion of their income to continuing grants which means that they will have less income for other charitable purposes'. If acknowledgement of receipt is required an sae must be included with the application.

P and D Shepherd Charitable Trust

General

£79,000 to organisations (2004/05)

Beneficial area Worldwide, particularly the north of England and Scotland.

5 Cherry Lane, Dringhouses, York YO24 1QH

Correspondent The Trustees

Trustees *Mrs P Shepherd; Mrs J L Robertson; Patrick M Shepherd; D R Reaston; I O Robertson; Mrs C M Shepherd; Michael James Shepherd.*

CC Number 272948

Information available Full accounts were on file at the Charity Commission.

General The trust makes grants through charitable organisations to benefit people in need and society in general. There is a preference for supporting charities in the north of England and Scotland, or those connected with the trustees, particularly those involving young people.

In 2004/05 it had assets of £505,000 and an income of £104,000. Grants were made to 151 organisations totalling £79,000, with a further £2,600 given in total to 11 individuals.

The following institutions received £1,000 or more during this period: United Response (£6,000); Yorkshire Air Museum (£14,000); York Against Cancer (£5,400); Clifton Parish Church Council (£5,000); the York Waggon Plays (£4,000); York Early Music Festival (£2,500); Rotary Club of York Vikings (£1,500); Dringhouses Primary School (£1,200); and Huntington's Disease Association, York Museums Trust and Yorkshire Cancer Research (£1,000 each).

Applications In writing to the correspondent.

The Archie Sherman Cardiff Foundation

Health, education, Jewish

£104,000 (2005/06)

Beneficial area UK, Canada, Australia, New Zealand, Pakistan, Sri Lanka, South Africa, India, Israel, USA and other parts of the British Commonwealth.

Archie Sherman Administration Limited, 27 Berkeley House, Hay Hill, London W1J 8NS

Correspondent The Trustees

Trustee *Rothschild Trust Corporation Ltd.*

CC Number 272225

Information available Full accounts were available from the Charity Commission website.

General Established in 1976, this foundation supports health and educational charities. Most of the beneficiaries are Jewish or Israeli organisations. In 2005/06 the foundation had assets of £2.5 million and an income of £162,000. Grants were made totalling £104,000, broken down as follows:

Education and training – 2 grants totalling £74,000
These went to Friends of the Hebrew University (£71,000) and Akim (£3,000).

Overseas aid – 3 grants totalling £20,000
Beneficiaries were UJIA (£14,000),

British Red Cross – Beslan (£10,000) and Tel Aviv Foundation (£6,000).

Community – 1 grant of £7,500
This went to Bradplace Charitable Foundation.

Health – 1 grant of £3,000
The sole beneficiary was JNF Charitable Trust.

Exclusions No grants to individuals.

Applications In writing to the correspondent.

The Bassil Shippam and Alsford Trust

Young and older people, health, education, learning disabilities, Christian

£186,000 to organisations and individuals (2005/06)

Beneficial area UK, with a preference for West Sussex.

Messrs Thomas Eggar, The Corn Exchange, Baffins Lane, Chichester, West Sussex PO19 1GE

Tel. 01243 786111 **Fax** 01243 537672

Correspondent S A E MacFarlane, Clerk to the Trustees

Trustees J H S Shippam; C W Doman; S A E MacFarlane; S W Young; Mrs M Hanwell; R Tayler; Mrs S Trayler.

CC Number 256996

Information available Full accounts were available from the Charity Commission website.

General This trust supports charities active in the fields of care for young and older people, health, education and religion. Many of the organisations supported are in West Sussex. In 2005/06 the trust had assets of £4.4 million and an income of £154,000. Grants were made totalling £186,000.

The largest grants included those made to: Lodge Hill (£70,000 in two grants); Chichester Boys Club (£12,500); Aldingbourne County Centre (£10,000); St Wilfrids Hospice (£5,000); Canine Partners (£3,800); Chichester Counselling Services (£2,500); Tall Ships Youth Trust (£1,700); and Fishbourne Roman Palace, Wessex Cancer Help

Centre, West Sussex Learning Link and West Wittering Parish Council (£1,000 each).

Grants of £500 or less included those made to: Abinger Hammer Village School, Ann Sutton Foundation, CARE, Chichester Area Mind, Dame Vera Lynn, Rainbow Trust Childrens Charity, Ro Ro Sailing Project Limited, St Luke's Hospital for the Clergy and Whizz-Kidz (£500 each); Chichester Festival for Music Dance & Speech (£350); Manhood Mobility Volunteer Service Limited, Dreams Come True Charity and Fair Play for Children (£300 each); the Bambolulu Fund, Chichester Art Trust Limited, Liverpool School of Tropical Medicine and Saturday Venture Association (£250 each); the Not Forgotten Association and Scripture Gift Mission (£200 each); Brighton and Hove Unwaged Advice & Rights Centre and the Motor Neurone Disease Association (£100).

Applications In writing to the correspondent, including a copy of the latest set of reports, accounts and forecasts. Applications are considered in May and November.

The Shipwrights' Company Charitable Fund

Maritime or waterborne connected charities

£82,000 (2005/06)

Beneficial area UK.

Ironmongers' Hall, Barbican, London EC2Y 8AA

Tel. 020 7606 2376 **Fax** 020 7600 8117

Email clerk@shipwrights.co.uk

Website www.shipwrights.co.uk

Correspondent The Clerk

Trustee The Worshipful Company of Shipwrights

CC Number 262043

Information available Accounts were available from the Charity Commission website.

General The Shipwrights' Company is a Livery Company of the City of London and draws its members from all the various aspects of marine commerce and

industry in the UK. Its charitable interests therefore focus on the maritime, with an emphasis on young people and the City. There is a preference for salt water over fresh. In 2005/06 the trust had assets of 2.4 million and an income of £423,000. Grants were made totalling £82,000 and were broken down as follows:

- general donations – £60,000
- outdoor activity bursaries – £22,000
- special donations – £200.

Grant recipients included Apostleship of the Sea – RC Mission to seafarers, British and International Sailor's Society (welfare), City of London Unit, Sea Cadet Corps, HMS *Belfast* – Fairbridge, George Green's School, Jubilee Sailing Trust, Lord Mayor's Appeal, Ocean Youth Trust, Royal Alfred Seafarers' Society, Royal Hospital School, Holbrook (bursaries), Sail Training Association, St Paul's Cathedral (Refurbishment Project) and Sea Cadet Association.

Applications from individuals or, for example, schools to join sail training voyages are considered. It supports sailing for people with disabilities, with both the Jubilee Sailing Trust and the Challenger class.

Exclusions Any application without a clear maritime connection.

Applications In writing to the correspondent. Applications and guidelines are available from the trust's website. Applications are considered in February, June and November.

The Charles Shorto Charitable Trust

General

£105,000 (2004/05)

Beneficial area UK.

Lancaster House, 67 New Hall Street, Birmingham B3 1NR

Tel. 0121 233 6900

Correspondent T J J Baxter

Trustees Joseph A V Blackham; Brian M Dent.

CC Number 1069995

Information available Accounts were on file at the Charity Commission.

General This trust was established under the will of Edward Herbert Charles Shorto with general charitable purposes. Whilst welcoming applications, the trustees also like to identify causes that they know Charles Shorto had an interest in.

In 2004/05 the trust had assets of £4.2 million, which generated an income of £179,000. Management and administration expenses were high at £56,000. Grants totalled £105,000.

The beneficiary of the largest grant was Oxford Youth Works – director project (£36,000). Cumnor PCC received two grants totalling £25,000.

Other beneficiaries were Brecon Cathedral Choir Endowment Appeal, East Budleigh PCC and Exmouth District Community Transport Appeal (£5,000 each), East Budleigh Village Hall (£3,000) and Age Concern – Budleigh Salterton, Blind in Business, Brainwave, British Wheelchair Sports Foundation, Kids Company, Lincoln Toy Library and Tall Ships Youth Trust (£1,000 each).

Applications In writing to the correspondent at any time.

The Barbara A Shuttleworth Memorial Trust

Disability

About £20,000 (2005/06)

Beneficial area UK, with a preference for West Yorkshire.

Baty Casson Long, Shear's Yard, 21 Wharf Street, The Calls, Leeds LS2 7EQ

Tel. 0113 242 5848 **Fax** 0013 247 0342

Email baty@btinternet.com

Correspondent John Baty, Chair

Trustees *John Alistair Baty, Chair; Miss Barbara Anne Shuttleworth; John Christopher Joseph Eaton; Frank Ramsay Fenton.*

CC Number 1016117

Information available Information was obtained from the Charity Commission website.

General The trust gives grants to organisations that aim to improve the circumstances of people who are disabled generally and particularly children. Grants are given for equipment to facilitate the work of qualified

professionals in treating the problems. In 2005/06 the trust had an income of £22,000 and a total expenditure of £24,000. Further information was not available.

Previous beneficiaries included Corner – Airedale CDC, Leeds Teaching Hospitals for ultrasound equipment, Martin House Hospice for scanbeta cots, Cot Death Society towards an infant respirator, Highbury School for classroom equipment, the Ear Trust for specialist equipment, Reactivate, Edwards' Trust for toys and therapy items and Bradford and District Autistic Support Group for medical equipment.

Applications In writing to the correspondent.

The Leslie Silver Charitable Trust

Jewish, general

£120,000 (2005/06)

Beneficial area UK, but mostly West Yorkshire.

Bentley Jennison, 2 Wellington Place, Leeds LS1 4AP

Tel. 0113 244 5451 **Fax** 0113 242 6308

Correspondent Ian J Fraser, Trustee

Trustees *Leslie H Silver; Mark S Silver; Ian J Fraser.*

CC Number 1007599

Information available Full accounts were available from the Charity Commission website.

General This trust principally supports Jewish-based charities and appeal funds launched in the West Yorkshire area. In 2005/06 the trust had assets of £748,000 and an income of £35,000. Grants were made totalling £120,000.

The largest grants included those made to: Jewish Welfare Board (£50,000); Leeds Centre for Deaf and Blind People (£16,000); Opera North Development Appeal (£10,000); the Zone (£8,000); and Leeds Jewish Welfare Board, Leeds International Pianoforte Comp and Jewish National Fund (£5,000 each).

Other grants included those made to: Leeds College of Art & Design and St George's Crypt Leeds (£3,000 each); Learning Partnerships (£2,000); Caring for Children, Donisthorpe Hall and World War II Experience (£1,000 each) and Holocaust Education Trust (£500).

Exclusions No grants to individuals or students.

Applications The trustees state that 'the recipients of donations are restricted almost exclusively to the concerns in which the trustees take a personal interest and that unsolicited requests from other sources, although considered by the trustees, are rejected almost invariably'.

The Simpson Education and Conservation Trust

Environmental conservation, with a preference for the neotropics (South America)

£50,000 (2005/06)

Beneficial area UK and overseas, with a preference for the neotropics (South America).

Honeysuckle Cottage, Tidenham Chase, Chepstow, Gwent NP16 7JW

Tel. 01291 689423 **Fax** 01291 689803

Correspondent N Simpson, Chair

Trustees *Dr R N F Simpson, Chair; Prof. D M Broom; Dr J M Lock; Prof. S Chang; Dr K A Simpson.*

CC Number 1069695

Information available Accounts were on file at the Charity Commission.

General Established in 1998, the main objectives of this trust are:

1 the advancement of education in the UK and overseas, including medical and scientific research
2 the conservation and protection of the natural environment and endangered species of plants and animals with special emphasis on the protection of forests and endangered avifauna in the neotropics (South America).

The trust receives its income from Gift Aid donations, which totalled £61,000 in 2005/06. Its priority for that year was to support the Jocotoco Foundation in Ecuador. This charity is dedicated to the conservation of endangered special birds through the acquisition of forest habitat. The chair of this trust, an expert in

313

ornithology and conservation, is also on the board of trustees for Jocotoco Conservation Foundation.

In 2005/06 JCF received a grant of £40,000 from the trust. Other grants were: £5,600 to American Bird Conservancy; £2,000 to Liverpool School of Tropical Medicine; £1,400 to Linnean Society – Tanzania and £1,000 to Lord Trealor Trust.

Exclusions No grants to individuals.

Applications In writing to the correspondent. The day-to-day activities of this trust are carried out by email, telephone and circulation of documents, since the trustees do not all live in the UK.

Sinclair Charitable Trust

Jewish learning, welfare

£60,000 (2003)
Beneficial area UK.

6th Floor, 54 Baker Street, London W1U 7BU

Tel. 020 7034 1940

Correspondent Dr M J Sinclair, Trustee

Trustees *Dr M J Sinclair; Mrs P K Sinclair; E J Gold.*

CC Number 289433

Information available Accounts were on file at the Charity Commission, but without a list of grants.

General The objectives of the trust are to support organisations concerned principally, although not necessarily exclusively, with Jewish learning and welfare. Most of the income derives from substantial donations received from a company controlled by two of the trustees.

In 2003 the trust had an income of £90,000, all of which came from donations and gifts. Grants were made totalling £60,000, although a list of beneficiaries was not available.

Applications In writing to the correspondent.

The Huntly and Margery Sinclair Charitable Trust

Medical, general

£40,000 to organisations (2006)
Beneficial area UK.

c/o Vernor-Miles and Noble Solicitors, 5 Raymond Buildings, Gray's Inn, London EC1R 5DD

Tel. 020 7423 8000 **Fax** 020 7423 8001

Email wilfridvm@vmn.org.uk

Correspondent Wilfrid Vernor-Miles, Administrator

Trustees *Mrs A M H Gibbs; Mrs M A H Windsor; Mrs J Floyd.*

CC Number 235939

Information available Full accounts were available from the Charity Commission website.

General This trust has general charitable purposes at the discretion of the trustees, although it does not respond to unsolicited applications. In 2006 the trust had assets of £1.4 million and an income £44,000. Grants were made to 28 organisations totalling £40,000.

Recipients of the largest grants included Rendcombe College (£10,000), the National Trust (£4,500) and the Parkinson's Disease Society, West Highland Museum, Scottish Wildlife Trust and Gloucester Cathedral (£2,000 each). Two awards amounting to £1,500 were also given to the National Parrott Sanctuary.

Smaller donations of £1,000 or less included PDSA and the Council for the Preservation of Rural England (£1,000 each) and Charlie Waller Memorial Trust, the Institute of Cancer Research, Elkstone Church PCC and Country Side Alliance (£500 each).

Applications This trust does not respond to unsolicited applications.

Sino-British Fellowship Trust

Education

£316,000 (2005)
Beneficial area UK and China.

23 Bede House, Manor Fields, London SW15 3LT

Correspondent Mrs Anne Ely

Trustees *Prof. M N Naylor, Chair; Prof. H D R Baker; Mrs A E Ely; P J Ely; Prof. Sir B Heap; Dr J A Langton; Prof. Sir D Todd; Lady P Youde.*

CC Number 313669

Information available Full accounts were available from the Charity Commission website.

General The trust makes grants to institutions benefiting individual postgraduate students. It does this through: scholarships to Chinese citizens to enable them to pursue their studies in Britain; grants to British citizens in China to educate/train Chinese citizens in any art, science, profession or handicraft; grants to Chinese citizens associated with charitable bodies to promote their education and understanding of European methods.

In 2005 the trust had assets of £11.5 million and an income of £362,000. Grants were made totalling £316,000. Grants were divided between two categories:

UK Institutions – 7 grants totalling £180,000
Grants went to: Royal Society (£82,000); British Library (£22,000); British Academy and Great Britain China Educational Trust (£20,000 each); Universities China Committee (£15,000); Institute of Archaeology (£12,500); Needham Research Institute (£8,500).

Overseas Institutions – 7 grants totalling £94,000
Grants went to: China Scholarship Council (£23,000); Chinese University of Hong Kong, Hong Kong University and Open University of Hong Kong (£16,500 each); Hong Kong Nurses Training and Education Foundation (£9,000); Lingnan University (£7,500) and Vocational Training Council Shatin Technical College (£5,000).

Applications On a form available by writing to the address below.

The Charles Skey Charitable Trust

General

£108,000 (2005/06)

Beneficial area UK.

Flint House, Park Homer Road, Colehill, Wimborne, Dorset BH21 2SP

Correspondent J M Leggett, Trustee

Trustees *C H A Skey, Chair; J M Leggett; C B Berkeley; Revd J H A Leggett.*

CC Number 277697

Information available Accounts were available from the Charity Commission website.

General The trust's 2005/06 annual report states: 'The trustees support causes on an annual basis, irregularly and on a one-off basis. For those charities receiving annual donations, the amount to be given is reviewed annually. For those receiving periodic donations, the trustees are the judge of when a further grant should be made. For one-off donations, the trustees examine the requests which have been received and have sole authority as to which to support. In general, the trust supports those causes where the grant made is meaningful to the recipient.'

In 2005/06 the trust had assets of £3 million and an income of £267,000. Grants were made totalling £108,000 and were broken down as follows:

Education, training, medical, health, sickness and disability – 17 grants
Beneficiaries included: Lloyds Patriotic Fund (£10,000); Trinity Hospice (£7,500); Christ Church School – Chelsea (£5,000); Careforce and Stepping Stones Trust (£4,500 each); Camphill Village Trust (£3,000); Cleft Lip and Palate Trust Fund (£2,500); St Philip's Community Worker Project (£1,500); King Edward VII Hospital for Officers and StreetSmart (£1,000 each); and Gurkha Welfare Trust (£500).

General purposes – 3 grants
Grants went to the Fusiliers' Museum (£10,000), Christian Care Association (£2,000) and the Royal British Legion (£1,000).

Environmental, conservation and heritage – 4 grants
Grants went to War Memorials Trust (£34,000), Roses Charitable Trust (£4,000); WaterAid (£2,000) and Heritage of London Trust (£1,000).

Religious activities – 1 grant
The sole beneficiary was the Dagenham Gospel Trust (£1,000).

Applications No written or telephoned requests for support will be entertained.

The John Slater Foundation

Medical, animal welfare, general

£138,000 (2004/05)

Beneficial area UK, with a strong preference for the north west of England especially West Lancashire.

HSBC Trust Services, Norwich House, Nelson Gate, Commercial Road, Southampton SO15 1GX

Tel. 023 8072 2231 **Fax** 023 8072 2250

Correspondent Colin Bould

Trustee *HSBC Trust Co. Ltd.*

CC Number 231145

Information available Accounts were obtained from the Charity Commission website.

General The foundation gives grants for £1,000 to £5,000 to a range of organisations, particularly those working in the fields of medicine or animal welfare. In 2004/05 it had assets of £3.4 million and an income of £152,000. Grants were made totalling £138,000.

The largest grants included those made to: Blackpool Ladies Sick Poor Association (£10,000); Adlington Community Centre, Bury Grammar School for Girls and Macmillan Cancer Relief (£6,000 each); and RSPCA and the NW Air Ambulance Trust (£5,000 each).

Other grants included those made to: Royal National Mission to Deep Sea Fishermen, St Gemma's Hospice – Leeds and Thornton Clevelys Old People's Welfare (£4,000 each); Grand Theatre Blackpool and St John's Church – Levens (£3,000 each); Blackpool and Fylde Society for the Blind (£2,500); Battersea Dogs Home, Bingley Flower Fund Homes, Duchess of York Hospital for Babies, Mersey Inshore Rescue, Liverpool School of Tropical Medicine and Muscular Dystrophy Shipley (£2,000 each); Bispham Parish Church and Life Education Centre for Lancashire (£1,000 each); and Freckleton Music Festival and

Rivington and Alington Brass Band (£500 each).

Exclusions No grants to individuals.

Applications In writing to the correspondent, including accounts. Applications are considered twice a year, on 1 May and 1 November.

Rita and David Slowe Charitable Trust

General

£58,000 (2005/06)

Beneficial area UK and overseas.

32 Hampstead High Street, London NW3 1JQ

Correspondent R L Slowe, Trustee

Trustees *R L Slowe; Mrs E H Douglas; J L Slowe; G Weinberg.*

CC Number 1048209

Information available Full accounts were available from the Charity Commission.

General The trust makes grants to a range of registered charities. In 2005/06 the trust had an income of £61,000 and made grants to nine organisations totalling £58,000. Its assets stood at £614,000.

Grants went to: Maasai Conservation and Development Organisation Shelter (£10,000 each); APT Enterprise Development and Computer Aid International (£7,500 each); Practical Action (£6,500); Books Abroad, Excellent Development and Wells for India (£5,000 each); and Action Aid (£1,800).

Exclusions No grants are made to individuals (including gap-year students) or religious bodies.

Applications In writing to the correspondent.

The SMB Charitable Trust

Christian, general

£176,000 (2004/05)

Beneficial area UK and overseas.

15 Wilman Rd, Tunbridge Wells, Kent TN4 9AJ

Tel. 01892 537301 (after 6pm)
Fax 01892 618202

Correspondent Mrs B M O'Driscoll, Trustee

Trustees E D Anstead; P J Stanford; Mrs B O'Driscoll; J A Anstead.

CC Number 263814

Information available Accounts were on file at the Charity Commission.

General The trust supports charities which meet one of the following criteria:

- support of the Christian faith
- provision of social care in the UK and abroad
- provision of famine or emergency aid
- protection of the environment and wildlife
- support of education or medical research.

Grants are generally of £1,000 each, although this can vary. The founder's preferences are taken into account when deciding which of the applicants will be supported.

In 2004/05 it had assets of £5.1 million and an income of £124,000. Grants totalled £176,000. About 140 grants were made, about a third of which were recurrent.

Beneficiaries included: London City Mission and Pilgrim Homes (£4,000 each); Salvation Army (£3,000); Baptist Missionary Society, British Red Cross and Tear Fund – Tsunami appeal (£2,500 each); All Nations Christian College, Bible Society, Leprosy Mission, Mildmay Mission Hospital, Mission Aviation Fellowship, Oasis Trust, Scripture Union and Tear Fund (£2,000 each); Gideons International, Hope Now, Impact, Liverpool City Mission, OMF, St john Ambulance, Shaftesbury Society and YMCA (£1,500 each); and Action for Kids, the Bridge, British Red Cross – Philippines Typhoon Appeal, Church Army, Crisis Recovery UK, Fairtrade Foundation Ltd, Home Evangelism, International Media for Ministry, Mercy Ships, Moorlands Bible College, National Listening Library, Scripture Gift Mission, Soul in the City, Tower Hamlets Mission, Tree Aid and World Wildlife Fund and Young Minds (£1,000 each).

Exclusions Grants to individuals are not normally considered, unless the application is made through a registered charity which can receive the cheque.

Applications In writing to the correspondent, including the aims and principal activities of the applicant, the current financial position and details of any special projects for which funding is sought. Application forms are not used. Trustees met in March, June, September and December and applications should be received before the beginning of the month in which meetings are held. Because of the volume of appeals received, unsuccessful applicants will only receive a reply if they enclose an sae. However, unsuccessful applicants are welcome to reapply.

The N Smith Charitable Settlement

General

£84,000 (2005/06)
Beneficial area Worldwide.

Linder Myers, Phoenix House, 45 Cross Street, Manchester M2 4JF

Tel. 0161 832 6972 **Fax** 0161 834 0718

Correspondent Anne E Merricks

Trustees T R Kendal; P R Green; J H Williams-Rigby; G Wardle.

CC Number 276660

Information available Full accounts were available from the Charity Commission website.

General This trust was established in 1978, in 2005/06 the trust had assets of £4.2 million and an income of £142,000. Grants were made totalling £84,000 and were broken down into the following categories:

Social work – £27,000
Beneficiaries included Action For Kids, Addiction Recovery Centre, Changing Faces, Children's Country Holidays Fund, Compass, Operation New World, Phoenix Sheltered Workshop, the Prison Phoenix Trust, Raven House Trust Limited, the Stroke Association, Strongbones Children's Charitable Trust, the Thomas Morley Trust and Woodlands Hospice Charitable Trust (£500 each).

Overseas aid – £25,000
Grants made included those to Disasters Emergency Committee (£5,000) and Anseba Development, Appropriate Technology Asia, Link Community Development, the Nehemiah Project, Send a Cow, Sightsavers International, Tools For Self Reliance and Victoria Climbie Charitable Trust (£750 each).

Medical research – £15,000
Grant recipients included British Eye Research Foundation, Christie Hospital NHS Trust, Cystic Fibrosis Trust, Neuro-disability Research Trust, the Prostrate Cancer Charity, the Roy Castle Lung Cancer Foundation and Society for Mucopolysaccharide Diseases (£1,000 each).

Education – £8,000
Grants made included those to British Dyslexics, Broomley Grange, Chantry High School and Sixth Form Centre, Punch & Judy Family Centre, Scottish Council, the Scout association, Spadework Limited and Stables Theatre Limited (£750 each).

Arts – £3,500
Grants went to Addison Group of Singers, Dance Base National Centre for Dance, English National Opera, Hampstead Theatre, Isle of Jura Music Festival, Music Alive and National Youth Orchestras of Scotland – NYOS (£500 each).

Environment and animals – £3,500
Grants went to Archerfield Wildlife Centre, the Civic Trust, Devon Wildlife Trust, the Dian Fossey Gorilla Rescue, Mountain Rescue Council, University of Glasgow and WWF-UK (£500 each).

Exclusions Grants are only made to registered charities and not to individuals.

Applications In writing to the correspondent. The trustees meet in October and March.

The Smith Charitable Trust

General

£41,000 (2005/06)
Beneficial area UK and overseas.

Messrs Moon Beever, Solicitors, 24 Bloomsbury Square, London WC1A 2PL

Tel. 020 7637 0661

Correspondent Paul Shiels, Trustee

Trustees A G F Fuller; P A Sheils; R I Turner; R J Weetch.

CC Number 288570

Information available Accounts were available from the Charity Commission website.

General The trust supports registered charities, which are usually larger well-known UK organisations. Beneficiaries are chosen by the settlor and he has a set list of charities that are supported twice a year. Other charities are unlikely to receive a grant.

In 2005/06 the trust had assets of £44,000 and an income of £70,000. Grants were made totalling £41,000. Grants included those made to: Sue Ryder Care (£12,000); Research Institute for the Care of the Elderly and St Mary's Convent and Nursing Home (£4,000 each); British Red Cross (£3,000); and the Marine Society and Sea Cadets, YMCA England, Artists' General Benevolent Institution and Providence Row Charity (£2,000 each).

Exclusions No grants to animal charities or to individuals.

Applications Unsolicited applications are not considered.

The Amanda Smith Charitable Trust

General

Around £50,000 (2005)
Beneficial area UK.

c/o Manro Haydan Trading, 1 Knightsbridge, London SW1X 7LX
Tel. 020 7823 2200
Correspondent Neil Bradley
Trustees *C Smith, Chair; Ms A Smith.*
CC Number 1052975
Information available Information was obtained from the Charity Commission website.

General This trust was established in 1996. The trust's income is derived mainly from the rent of a shopping centre and a housing estate. The trust stated that this is gradually decreasing. The trust makes grants irregularly.

In 2005 the trust had an income of £2,000 and a total expenditure of £76,000. Further information was not available. Previous beneficiaries have included Cedar School and Nordoff Robbins Music Therapy.

Applications In writing to the correspondent.

The E H Smith Charitable Trust

General

£74,000 (2005/06)
Beneficial area UK, some preference for the Midlands.

Westhaven House, Arleston Way, Shipley, West Midlands B90 4LH
Tel. 0121 706 6100
Correspondent K H A Smith, Trustee
Trustees *K H A Smith; Mrs B M Hodgskin-Brown; D P Ensell.*
CC Number 328313
Information available Full accounts were available from the Charity Commission website.

General This trust supports a wide and varied range of causes throughout the UK, concentrating mainly on the Midlands. It tends to give a large number of smaller grants, which average around £250 each, although they have been made of over £1,000 to £2,000 each. In 2005/06 the trust had assets of £167,000 and an income of £86,000. There were 137 grants made to organisations totalling £74,000.

The largest grant by far was made to Christadelphian Care Home (£23,000).

Other grants included: Cancer Research UK (£850); Marie Curie Cancer Centre (£600); Bettridge (£500); Leafield Athletic FC (£450); Golf Promotion (£400); Grove House Charity (£300); Castle Bromwich Hall Gardens Trust, Changing Faces, Chicks, Compton Hospice, Derma Trust, Opportunity International UK, Osteopathio Centre For Children, Samantha Dickinson Research Trust, the Add Action Project and the Albrighton Trust (£250 each); Dogs for the Disabled, Dream Holidays, Food Lifeline, the Association for Post Natal Illness, the Barn Owl Trust, the Peter Pan Nursery for Children With Special Needs and the Pied Piper Appeal (£200 each); Child Victim Support, Contact A Family, Endeavour Training, Everychild, the Eyeless Trust, the Northampton Soup Kitchen, the Royal British Legion, VLA Grove House, Wm Baxter Community School (£150 each); Watford New Hope Trust (£50); and Caistor Town CC (£40).

Exclusions No grants to political parties. Grants are not normally given to individuals.

Applications In writing to the correspondent. Apply at any time.

The Leslie Smith Foundation

General

£101,000 (2005/06)
Beneficial area UK with a preference for the south of England, especially Wiltshire, Norfolk, Middlesex, London and Dorset.

The Old Coach House, Sunnyside, Bergh Apton, Norwich NR15 1DD
Correspondent The Directors
Trustees *M D Willcox; H L Young Jones.*
CC Number 250030
Information available Accounts were obtained from the Charity Commission website.

General The foundation, which regularly reviews its grant-making policy, is currently focusing on:

- children with illnesses, both terminal and non-terminal, in the UK, excluding respite care and research
- orphans
- schools, specifically special needs schools based in the UK.

In 2005/06 the trust had an income of £122,000 and made grants totalling £101,000. Its assets stood at £4.5 million. Grants were broken down as follows:

- health and allied services – £55,000
- children's welfare – £24,000
- counselling services – £13,000
- ex-servicemen's welfare – £7,000
- miscellaneous – £1,500

Grants included those made to Gaddum Centre (£14,000); Cystic Fibrosis Holiday Fund for Children (£10,000); Dorothy House Hospice, Manna House Counselling Services, and Shooting Star (£5,000 each); Norfolk Accident Rescue Service (£3,000); UK Youth and Wooden Spoon Society (£2,000 each); Norwich Door to Door (£1,000 each); and St Peter and St Paul – Bergh Apton (£500).

Exclusions Grants are given to registered charities only; no grants are available to individuals.

Applications In writing to the correspondent. Only successful applications are acknowledged.

WH Smith Group Charitable Trust

General

£47,000 (2004)

Beneficial area UK.

WH Smith plc, Nations House, 103 Wigmore Street, London W1H 0WH

Correspondent The Secretary

Trustees *Sarah Durham; Jim Woodcock; Alex Walker; Stuart Thomas; Nicky Fleming; Jenny Burns; Jo Koster; Kevin Hall; Richard Ryan; Sue Beaumont.*

CC Number 1013782

Information available Full accounts were on file at the Charity Commission.

General This trust is unusual in that although it is connected to a company, it is totally independent and controlled by the employees rather than the management. Employees of WH Smith Group have effectively established their own trust for which they raise funds, making grants to the organisations which inspired them to solicit those donations.

In 2004 the trust had assets of £174,000 and an income of £92,000. Grants totalled £47,000.

The accounts listed 13 donations of £1,000 or more. Beneficiaries were Camden School Community Association (£2,500), Prostate Cancer Charity and University Hospital North Staffordshire (£2,000 each) and Darlington CAB, East Kent Rapeline, Friends of Mandeville, Home-Start – Chorley and South Ribble, Marshlands PTFA, Meningitis Research Foundation, Parkinson's Disease Society – Leicester & District Branch, the Daniel Parry Foundation and the Sophie Centre (£1,000 each).

Applications Due to the proactive nature of the trust, it is a waste of time applying for a grant.

The Stanley Smith UK Horticultural Trust

Horticulture

£75,000 (2005/06)

Beneficial area UK and, so far as it is charitable, outside the UK.

Cory Lodge, PO Box 365, Cambridge CB2 1HR

Tel. 01223 336299 **Fax** 01223 336278

Correspondent James Cullen, Director

Trustees *C D Brickell; Lady Renfrew; J B E Simmons; A De Brye; P R Sykes; Dr D A H Rae; E Reed.*

CC Number 261925

Information available Accounts were on file at the Charity Commission.

General Established by deed in 1970, the trust's objectives are the advancement of horticulture. In particular, the trustees have power to make grants for the following purposes:

- horticultural research
- the creation, development, preservation and maintenance of public gardens
- the promotion of the cultivation and wide distribution of plants of horticultural value/other value to mankind
- the promotion of the cultivation of new plants
- publishing books and work related to horticultural sciences.

In 2005/06 the trust's assets totalled £3.2 million and it had an income of £122,000. Grants to 21 organisations and individuals totalled £75,000.

Beneficiaries from the general fund included: Strawberry Hill and University of Bristol Botanic Garden (£5,000 each); Gateway Garden Trust, the Merchant's House, National Trust for Scotland and Scottish Sculpture Workshop (£2,500 each); Oxford University Botanic Gardens (£1,500); and Glasgow Allotments Forum (£1,000).

The director continues to provide advice to actual and potential applicants, and to established projects which have already received grants. Any grant provided by the trust bears the condition that the recipient should provide within six months, or some other agreed period, a report on the use of the grant.

Exclusions Grants are not made for projects in commercial horticulture (crop production) or agriculture, nor are they made to support students taking academic or diploma courses of any kind, although educational institutions are supported.

Applications In writing to the correspondent. Detailed *Guidelines for Applicants* are available from the trust. The director is willing to give advice on how applications should be presented.

Grants are awarded twice a year, in spring and autumn. To be considered in the spring allocation, applications should reach the director before 15 February of each year; for the autumn allocation the equivalent date is 15 August. Potential recipients are advised to get their applications in early.

Philip Smith's Charitable Trust

Welfare, older people, children

£225,000 (2004/05)

Beneficial area UK with a preference for Gloucestershire.

Bircham Dyson Bell, 50 Broadway, London SW1H 0BL

Tel. 020 7227 7039 **Fax** 020 7222 3480

Correspondent Mrs D'Monte

Trustees *Hon. P R Smith; Mrs M Smith.*

CC Number 1003751

Information available Accounts were obtained from the Charity Commission website.

General The trust makes grants to UK-wide charities, principally in the fields of welfare, older people and children. In 2004/05 the trust had assets of £1 million and an income of £28,000. Grants were made totalling £225,000.

Grants included those made to: Gloucester Community Foundation (£150,000); GRCC (£10,000); Gloucester Cathedral and the Gordon Russell Trust (£5,000 each); the Connection at St Martins (£2,500); Oxford Children's Hospital Campaign, Scottish Countryside Alliance Educational Trust and the Gloucestershire Society (£1,000 each); the Gloucestershire Historic Churches Trust (£500); Shakespeare Hospice (£250); and Royal Green Jackets (£100).

Applications In writing to the correspondent. The trustees meet regularly to consider grants. A lack of response can be taken to indicate that the trust does not wish to contribute to an appeal.

Solev Co. Ltd

Jewish charities

£567,000 (2004/05)
Beneficial area UK.

Romeo House, 160 Bridport Road, London N18 1SY
Correspondent R Tager, Trustee
Trustees R Tager; C M Frommer.
CC Number 254623
Information available Accounts were on file at the Charity Commission, but without a grants list.

General In 2004/05 the charity had an income of £408,000 and made grants totalling £567,000. No information on beneficiaries has been included in the accounts in recent years.

In 1996/97 the following two donations were mentioned in the annual report: '£100,000 to the Dina Perelmam Trust Ltd, a charitable company of which Mr Perelman and Mr Grosskopf are governors; and £40,000 to Songdale Ltd, a charity of which Mr M Grosskopf is a governor.'

A comprehensive grants list has not been included in the accounts since 1972/73, when £14,000 was given to 52 Jewish charities. Examples then included Society of Friends of the Torah (£3,900), Finchley Road Synagogue (£2,300), NW London Talmudical College (£1,500), Yesodey Hatorah School (£700) and Gateshead Talmudical College (£400).

Applications In writing to the correspondent.

The Solo Charitable Settlement

Jewish, general

£48,000 to organisations (2006)
Beneficial area UK and Israel.

c/o Randall Greene, 32–34 London Road, Guildford, Surrey GU1 2AB
Tel. 01483 230440
Correspondent The Trustees
Trustees Peter D Goldstein; Edna A Goldstein; Paul Goldstein; Dean Goldstein; Jamie Goldstein; Tammy Ward.
CC Number 326444
Information available Full accounts were obtained from the Charity Commission website.

General Peter David Goldstein established the trust in 1983. The main object of the trust is to support Jewish charities, and where possible, to concentrate their efforts on the relief of suffering and poverty, and on education. The majority of grants were given to organisations that focused on Jewish-related causes, medical research and palliative care.

In 2006 the trust had assets of £5.5 million and an income of £194,000. Grants were made to 23 organisations totalling £48,000, which were broken down as follows:

The largest grants of £1,000 or more went to: Community Security Trust (£14,000); Norwood Ravenswood (£8,000); UJIA (£6,000); English Stage Company (£2,500); the Eve Appeal and the Heart Cells Foundation (£2,000 each); and to the Dulwich College Bursary Appeal and the Royal Marsden Cancer Campaign (£1,000 each).

Other beneficiaries included Chelsea Synagogue (£900); Cancer Research (£500); Nightingale House (£400); Philip Green Memorial Trust (£300); British Friends of Haifa University (£250); St Lukas Hospice (£200); and Jewish National Fund (£100).

Applications In writing to the correspondent.

David Solomons Charitable Trust

Disability

£76,000 (2004/05)
Beneficial area UK.

Jasmine Cottage, 11 Lower Road, Breachwood Green, Hitchin, Hertfordshire SG4 8NS
Tel. 01438 833254
Correspondent Graeme Crosby, Administrator

Trustees J L Drewitt; J J Rutter; W H McBryde; Dr R E B Solomons; M T Chamberlayne.
CC Number 297275
Information available Accounts were on file at the Charity Commission.

General This trust supports research into the treatment and care of people with mental disabilities, with a preference for smaller or localised charities. Most grants range from £1,000 to £2,000, although larger and smaller amounts are given. Administrative expenses and large building projects are not usually funded, although grants can be made towards furnishing or equipping rooms.

In 2004/05 the trust had assets of £2.1 million, an income of £249,000 and made grants to over 60 organisations totalling £76,000.

By far the largest grants were £20,000 to Solden Hill House. Other grants included £8,000 to Down's Syndrome Association, £2,000 each to Acorn Villages Ltd, Daisy Chain, Disabled Afloat Riverboats Trust, Martha Trust, Mencap and the Tree House Trust, £1,500 each to Community Linkup, Scotland Yard Adventure Trust and Stockport Cerebral Palsy Society and £1,000 each to the Albrighton Trust, BIBIC, the Garden Science Trust, Kids Care, Peter Pan Nursery, Sussex Autistic Association, and Welsh Initiative for Conductive Gardening.

Smaller donations of £500 or £250 each included those to Chanctonbury Community Play Scheme, Fiveways School, Friends of Mulberry, Invalids at Home, the New Life Foundation, Property Housing Association, Sarum Chamber Orchestra, Spadework and the Thomas Telford Trust.

Exclusions No grants to individuals.

Applications In writing to the correspondent. Meetings are in May and November and applications should be received the previous month.

Songdale Ltd

Jewish

£344,000 (2005/06)
Beneficial area UK and Israel.

6 Spring Hill, London E5 9BE
Correspondent M Grosskopf, Governor
Trustees M Grosskopf; Mrs M Grosskopf; Y Grosskopf.

CC Number 286075

Information available Accounts were on file at the Charity Commission.

General In 2005/06 the trust had assets of £2.3 million and an income of £252,000. Grants were made totalling £344,000.

Ten of the largest grants went made to Cosmon Belz Ltd (£53,000), Kollel Belz (£50,000), BFOT (£27,000), Ezras Yisroel (£20,000), Forty Limited (£17,000), Darkei Ovois (£10,400), Germach Veholachto and Keren Nedunnia Lchasanim (£10,000 each), Belz Nursery (£9,500) and Bais Chinuch (£9,000).

Applications In writing to the correspondent.

The E C Sosnow Charitable Trust

Arts, education

£43,000 (2005/06)

Beneficial area UK and overseas.

PO Box 13398, London SW3 6ZL

Correspondent The Trustees

Trustees *E R Fattal; Mrs F I M Fattal.*

CC Number 273578

Information available Full accounts were on file at the Charity Commission.

General The trust informed us that it makes grants mainly to educational charities, including arts organisations. Other areas mentioned in its annual report are welfare, education, the arts, the underprivileged, healthcare and emergency relief. In 2005/06 the trust had assets of £2 million and an income of £64,000. Grants were made totalling £43,000.

Grants included those made to: London School of Economics (£5,000); Holocaust Education Trust (£4,500); Hammerson House Charitable Trust and the Royal Marsden Cancer Campaign (£3,000 each); City of London School Bursary Trust (£2,500); the Chicken Shed Theatre Campaign (£2,000); British Friends of the Jaffa Institute (£1,500); Pembroke College Oxford (£1,000); and the Skiers' Trust of Great Britain and Trinity College Music (£500 each).

Exclusions No grants are made to individuals.

Applications In writing to the correspondent.

The South Square Trust

General

£99,000 to organisations (2004/05)

Beneficial area UK, with a preference for London and the Home Counties.

PO Box 67, Heathfield, East Sussex TN21 9ZR

Tel. 01435 830778 **Fax** 01435 830778

Correspondent Mrs Nicola Chrimes, Clerk to the Trustees

Trustees *A E Woodall; W P Harriman; C P Grimwade; D B Inglis.*

CC Number 278960

Information available Accounts were on file at the Charity Commission.

General General donations are made to registered charities working in the fields of the arts, culture and recreation, health, social welfare, medical, disability and conservation and environment.

The trust also gives grants to students for full-time postgraduate or undergraduate courses within the UK connected with the fine and applied arts, including drama, dance, music, but particularly related to gold and silver work. Students should be over 18 years old. Courses have to be of a practical nature. Help is given to various colleges in the form of bursary awards. A full list is available from the correspondent. Where a school is in receipt of a bursary, no further assistance will be given to individuals as the school will select candidates themselves.

In 2004/05 it had assets of £3.7 million, which generated an income of £157,000. Grants were made totalling £121,000, broken down as follows:

Annual donations to charities – £19,000
These consisted of 3 grants of £1,000 each and 32 grants of £500 each. Further information was not available.

General charitable donation – £24,000
A total of 37 grants were made, of which 2 were for amounts over £1,000 each: Merlin – Tsunami Disaster Appeal (£5,000) and Sir John Soane's Museum (£1,500).

Bursaries and scholarships to schools/colleges – £56,000
Five institutions were supported by these schemes: St Paul's School (£21,000); Textile Conservation Centre (£20,000); Royal Academy of Music (£15,000);

Guildhall School of Music & Drama (£13,000); and Royal College of Art (£12,000).

Directly aided students and single payment grants – £22,000
These were made to 23 individuals.

Exclusions No grants given to individuals under 18 or those seeking funding for expeditions, travel, courses outside UK, short courses or courses not connected with fine and applied arts.

Applications **Registered charities:** In writing to the correspondent with details about your charity, the reason for requesting funding, and enclosing a condensed copy of your accounts. Applications are considered three times a year, in spring, summer and winter. It is advisable to telephone the correspondent for up-to-date information about the criteria for funding.

Individuals: Standard application forms are available from the correspondent. Forms are sent out between January and April only, to be returned by the end of April for consideration for the following academic year.

The Stephen R and Philippa H Southall Charitable Trust

General

£56,000 to organisations (2005)

Beneficial area UK, but mostly Herefordshire.

Porking Barn, Clifford, Hereford HR3 5HE

Tel. 01497 831243

Correspondent Mrs P H Southall, Trustee

Trustees *Stephen Readhead Southall; Mrs Philippa Helen Southall; Ms Anna Catherine Southall; Mrs Candia Helen Compton.*

CC Number 223190

Information available Accounts were obtained from the Charity Commission website.

General This trust has general charitable purposes, with a large number of grants made in Herefordshire.

In 2005 the trust had assets of £2 million and an income of £48,000. Grants were made to organisations totalling £56,000.

Beneficiaries included the Hereford Waterworks Museum Trust (£23,000), Oxfam and the National Museums & Galleries of Wales (£10,000 each) and the Taste for Adventure Centre and the Walk the Walk Worldwide (£1,000 each).

Applications The trust has previously stated: 'No applications can be considered or replied to.'

The W F Southall Trust

Quaker, general

£219,000 (2005/06)

Beneficial area UK and overseas.

c/o Rutters Solicitors, 2 Bimport, Shaftesbury, Dorset SP7 8AY

Tel. 01747 852377 **Fax** 01747 851989

Email southall@rutterslaw.co.uk

Correspondent Stephen T Rutter, Secretary

Trustees *Donald Southall, Chair; Joanna Engelkamp; Claire Greaves; Mark Holtom; Daphne Maw; Annette Wallis.*

CC Number 218371

Information available Accounts were available from the Charity Commission website.

General This trust prefers to support smaller charities where the grant will make a more significant difference. Areas of work supported are: Society of Friends; peace and reconciliation; alcohol, drug abuse and penal affairs; environmental action; homelessness; community action; and overseas development.

In 2005/06 the trust had assets of £8.6 million and an income of £278,000. Grants were made totalling £219,000 and were broken down as follows:

Quaker and Society of Friends Charities – £97,000
Grant recipients included Yearly Meeting – Society of Friends (£50,000), Jordans Monthly Meeting (£7,500) and Friends World Committee for Consultation (£6,000). There were fifteen other grants between £300 and £3,000 made totalling £28,000.

Peace and reconciliation – £34,000
Beneficiaries included International Voluntary Services (£6,500), Corrymeela Community (£4,000), Peaceworkers UK (£3,000), Oxford Research Group and Responding to Conflict (£2,500 each). There were five other grants between £500 and £2,000 made totalling £8,000.

Overseas Development – £34,000
Beneficiaries included Oxfam (£6,000), International Services (£3,000) and Money for Madagascar (£2,500). There were twelve other grants between £500 and £2,000 totalling £17,000.

Environmental action – £20,000
Grants included those to Worcestershire Wildlife Trust (£8,000) and Green Light Trust (£5,000). There were six other grants between £1,000 and £2,000 totalling £7,000.

Community action – £22,000
Grants included Refugee Council (£3,500), Ark-T Centre (£1,500) and Youth At Risk (£1,000). There were nine other grants between £500 and £2,000 totalling £11,000.

Alcohol and drug abuse and penal affairs – £9,000
The St Giles Trust was a beneficiary in this category (£2,500). There were five other grants between £750 and £2,000 totalling £7,000.

Homelessness – £4,000
There were two grants between £1,000 and £2,000 totalling £4,000.

Exclusions No grants to individuals or large national charities.

Applications In writing to, or email, the correspondent requesting an application form. Applications are considered in February/March and November. Applications received between meetings are considered at the next meeting.

R H Southern Trust

Education, disability, relief of poverty, environment, conservation

£228,000 (2005/06)

Beneficial area Worldwide.

23 Sydenham Road, Cotham, Bristol BS6 5SJ

Tel. 0117 942 5834

Correspondent The Trustees

Trustees *Marion Valiant Wells; Charles Sebastian Rivett Wells; Charles James Long Brugel; Colkin Trustee Company Limited.*

CC Number 1077509

Information available Accounts were on file at the Charity Commission.

General This trust was registered with the Charity Commission on 31 March 1999. In 2000 substantial funds were settled totalling £6.9 million. Its objectives are:

- the advancement of education (including medical and scientific research)
- the relief of poverty
- disability
- the preservation, conservation and protection of the environment.

In 2005/06 the trust had assets of £3.5 million and an income of £184,000. Grants were made to 36 organisations totalling £228,000 and were broken down as follows:

Education – £66,000
Grants made to Feasta amounted to £27,000. Other grants made included Corporate Europe Observatory (£10,000) and Panos (£5,000).

Environment – £62,000
Global Commons Institute (£30,000), Soil Association (£15,000 in two grants) and Friends of the Earth (£10,000).

Poverty – £54,000
Grants included those made to Salt of the Earth (£15,000), Action Village India and Just Change – Oxfam (£10,000 each) and E I Rural Links – West Dean (£8,500).

Disabilities – £47,000
There were four grants made to Interventure (£31,500) and one made to Motivation (£15,000).

Applications In writing to the correspondent.

Spar Charitable Fund

Children

£142,000 (2005/06)

Beneficial area UK.

Mezzanine Floor, Hygeina Building, 66 – 68 College Road, Harrow, Middlesex HA1 1BE

Correspondent P W Marchant, Director and Company Secretary

Trustee *The National Guild of Spar Ltd.*

CC Number 236252

Information available Full accounts were on file at the Charity Commission.

General This trust tends to choose one main beneficiary, which receives most of its funds, with smaller grants being made to the same beneficiaries each year. In 2005/06 the trust had an income of £140,000 and made grants totalling £142,000. Its assets stood at £1 million.

The main beneficiaries were the British Heart Foundation (£77,000) and Childline (£32,000). Other grants included those made to Caravan NGBF (£12,000), Business in the Community (£7,500) and SGBF (£3,000).

Applications In writing to the correspondent.

The Spear Charitable Trust

General

£77,000 to organisations (2005)

Beneficial area UK.

Roughground House, Old Hall Green, Ware, Hertfordshire SG11 1HB

Tel. 01920 823071 **Fax** 01920 823071

Correspondent Hazel E Spear, Secretary

Trustees *P N Harris; F A Spear; H E Spear; N Gooch.*

CC Number 1041568

Information available Full accounts were provided by the trust.

General Established in 1994 with general charitable purposes, this trust has particular interest in helping employees and former employees of J W Spear and Sons plc and their families and dependants.

In 2005 the assets totalled £4.7 million and generated an income of £130,000. Grants were made to 65 organisations totalling £77,000, whilst ex-employees received £31,000 in total. Management and administartion charges were high at £21,000.

Beneficiaries included RSPCA – Enfield (£8,000), Fenland Archaeological Trust and New College Oxford – Martin Hall (£5,000 each), Demelza House (£3,500), Camphill Village Trust and NSPCC Enfield Ridgeway (£3,000 each) East-Side Educational Trust (£2,500), the Institute of Development Studies, Gift of Life Commemorative Trust and Marine

Conservation Society (£2,000 each), Dr Graham's Homes (£1,800) and Devon Wildlife Trust, Barn Owl Trust, Computer Aid International, Greyhounds' Compassion, Kehillah Project, National Library for the Blind, Parkinson's Disease Society and Pekinese Rescue (£1,000 each).

Exclusions Appeals from individuals are not considered.

Applications In writing to the correspondent.

Roama Spears Charitable Settlement

Welfare causes

Around £40,000 (2005/06)

Beneficial area Worldwide.

4 More London Riverside, London SE1 2AU

Correspondent Glenn Hurstfield

Trustee *Mrs R L Spears.*

CC Number 225491

Information available Information was obtained from the Charity Commission website.

General This trust states that it makes grants to organisations towards the relief of poverty worldwide. In practice it appears to support a range of organisations including a number of museums and arts organisations. It has some preference for Jewish causes.

In 2005/06 the trust had an income of £19,000 and a total expenditure of £94,000. Further information was not available.

Previous beneficiaries included Cancer Macmillan Fund, Royal Opera House, Royal College of Music, Ackerman Institute for the Family, Wellbeing, North West London Jewish Day School.

Applications In writing to the correspondent.

The Worshipful Company of Spectacle Makers' Charity

Visual impairment, City of London, general

£44,000 to organisations (2004/05)

Beneficial area Worldwide.

Apothecaries Hall, Blackfriars Lane, London EC4V 6EL

Tel. 020 7236 2932

Email clerk@spectaclemakers.com

Website www.spectaclemakers.com

Correspondent John Salmon, Administrator

Trustees *Michael Barton; David Burt; John Marshall; Brian Mitchell; Paul Southworth; Christine Tomkins.*

CC Number 1072172

Information available Accounts were on file at the Charity Commission.

General Registered with the Charity Commission in October 1998, this livery company stated that it tends to support causes related to visual impairment and City of London, however it has supported a wide range of projects worldwide.

In 2004/05 the charity had assets of £486,000 and an income of £130,000. Grants were made to organisations totalling £44,000. During the year, the trust celebrated 375 years since the company was granted Royal Charter status; a fund was set up in the name of the charity to assist the work of St John's Eye Hospital in Jerusalem.

Grants from the general fund included the following organisations: 16 Close Support Medical Regiment RAMC, Blind in Business, Henshaw's Society for the Blind People, the Company of Hackney Carriage Drivers – Magical Taxi Fund, Look, the Lord Mayor's Appeal, the Sheriff's and Recorder's Fund, Talking Newspapers and Vision Aid Overseas.

Exclusions No grants are made to individuals.

Applications The trustees do their own research; unsolicited applications are unlikely to be successful.

The Jessie Spencer Trust

General

£94,000 to organisations (2005/06)

Beneficial area UK, with a preference for Nottinghamshire.

Berryman Shacklock LLP, Park House, Friar Lane, Nottingham NG1 6DN

Tel. 0115 945 3700 **Fax** 0115 948 0234

Correspondent The Trustees

Trustees *V W Semmens; R S Hursthouse; Mrs J Galloway; Mrs B Mitchell.*

CC Number 219289

Information available Accounts were available from the Charity Commission website.

General The trust supports a range wide of causes, including welfare, religion and the environment amongst others. Whilst grants are made UK-wide, there is a preference for work in Nottinghamshire.

In 2005/06 the trust had assets of £3.6 million and an income of £140,000. Grants were made totalling £98,000 and were broken down as follows:

Medical and disabled – £35,000
Beneficiaries included: Nottingham City Hospital Charity (£5,000); Nottinghamshire Hospice (£4,000); Rainbows Children's Hospice (£2,000); CLIC Sargent (£1,000); St Luke's Hospital for the Clergy (£750); and Orbis, the National Autistic Society, Talking Newspaper Association and Tapping House Hospice (£500 each).

Welfare – £22,000
Grants included those made to: the Malt Cross Music Hall Trust Company (£4,000); Fundays in Nottinghamshire (£2,000); St John Ambulance – Nottingham (£1,000); and Coram Family, Horizons, St John's Day Centre for the Elderly and Starlight Children's Foundation (£500 each).

Churches – £12,000
Grant recipients included: Nottinghamshire Historic Churches Trust (£8,000); St Edmund's Church – Holme Pierrepont (£1,500); St Mary and All Saints Church – Bingham; and St Stephen with St Paul's Church Centre (£500 each); and Lincoln Cathedral (£250).

Education – £8,000
Beneficiaries included: Rutland House School for Parents (£2,500); Rutland House School (£1,500); Community of

the Holy Fire (£1,000); Eastwood Junior School (£750); The Greenfield Centre Limited (£500); and Barbara London Trust (£250).

Other – £6,000
Grants included those made to: the Haven (£2,000); Clifton Village Hall Trust (£1,000); Project Trust (£750); and National Playing Fields Association (£500).

Accommodation – £4,500
Grants went to: Abbeyfield UK Nottingham (£2,500); Shelter – Nottinghamshire (£1,000); and the Oaklands and St Mungo's (£500 each).

Groups and Clubs – £2,000
Grant recipients included: Arnold St Mary's Community Youth Club (£1,000); Oliver Hind Club (£500); and Ollerton and Boughton Scout and Guide Group (£250).

Arts – £2,000
Grants went to the National Youth Orchestra of Great Britain (£1,000) and Magdala (£750).

Environment – £1,000
Grants went to: FWAG – Notts and Nottinghamshire Wildlife Trust (£500 each).

Services – £1,000
Grant recipients were the Gurkha Welfare Trust and SSAFA (£500 each).

Heritage – £1,000
The sole beneficiary was Cathedral Camps.

Individuals – £4,000
Grants totalled £4,000.

Exclusions Grants are rarely made for the repair of parish churches outside Nottinghamshire.

Applications In writing to the correspondent, including the latest set of audited accounts, at least three weeks before the trustees' meetings in March, June, September and December. Unsuccessful applications will not be notified.

The Moss Spiro Will Charitable Foundation

Jewish welfare

£89,000 (2005/06)

Beneficial area UK.

Crowndean House, 26 Bruton Lane, London W1J 6JH

Tel. 020 7491 9817 **Fax** 020 7499 6850

Correspondent Trevor Spiro, Trustee

Trustees *Trevor David Spiro; Melvin Clifford Kay; David Jeremy Goodman.*

CC Number 1064249

Information available Information was obtained from the Charity Commission website.

General The trust makes grants towards Jewish welfare. In 2005/06 the trust had an income of £17,000 and a total expenditure of £90,000. Further information was not available.

Previous beneficiaries included American Friends of Yershivas Birchas Ha Torah, Lubavitch Foundation, J T Tannenbaum Jewish Cultural Centre, Friends of Neve Shalom, Jewish Care and HGS Emunah.

Applications In writing to the correspondent.

W W Spooner Charitable Trust

General

£79,000 (2005/06)

Beneficial area UK, with a preference for Yorkshire especially West Yorkshire.

c/o Addleshaw Booth and Co., Sovereign Street, Leeds LS1 1HQ

Tel. 0113 209 2000

Correspondent M H Broughton, Chair and Trustee

Trustees *M H Broughton, Chair; Sir James F Hill; J C Priestley; T J P Ramsden; Mrs J M McKiddie; J H Wright.*

CC Number 313653

Information available Accounts were obtained from the Charity Commission website.

General The trust will support charities working in the following areas:

- youth – for example, welfare, sport and education including school appeals and initiatives, clubs, scouting, guiding, adventure training, individual voluntary service overseas and approved expeditions
- community – including churches, associations, welfare and support groups
- healing – including care of people who are sick, disabled or underprivileged,

welfare organisations, victim support, hospitals, hospices and selected medical charities and research

- the countryside – causes such as the protection and preservation of the environment including rescue and similar services and preservation and maintenance of historic buildings
- the arts – including museums, teaching, performing, musical and literary festivals and selective support for the purchase of works of art for public benefit.

It has a list of regular beneficiaries that receive grants each year and also supports around 40 to 50 one-off applications. Grants can range from £200 to £2,000, although they are usually for £250 to £350.

In 2005/06 the trust had assets of £1.9 million and an income of £78,000. Grants were made totalling £79,000 and were broken down as follows:

- Wordsworth Trust Projects (£21,000)
- Hard core grants and donations (£41,000)
- Single appeals (£18,000).

Previous beneficiaries have included Wordsworth Trust – Grasmere, Parish of Tong and Holme Wood, Guide Dogs for the Blind, St Margaret's PCC – Ilkley, Abbeyfield Society, All Saints' Church – Ilkley, Ardenlea, Hawksworth Church of England School, Leith School of Art, Martin House Hospice, North of England Christian Healing Trust, St Gemma's Hospice, St George's Crypt, Wheatfield House and Yorkshire Ballet Seminar.

Exclusions 'No grants for high-profile appeals seeking large sums.' Most donations are for less than £500.

Applications In writing to the correspondent.

Stanley Spooner Deceased Charitable Trust

Children, general

£40,000 (2005/06)

Beneficial area UK.

The Public Trustee (Ref. G5361), Official Solicitor and Public Trustee, 81 Chancery Lane, London WC2A 1DD

Correspondent G J W Cunliffe

CC Number 1044737

Information available Accounts were on file at the Charity Commission.

General The trust mainly makes grants to charities listed in the trust deed and only a small part of its grantmaking is discretionary. In 2005/06 the trust had an income of £48,000 and made grants totalling £40,000. Its assets stood at £1.3 million. A list of grants was not available.

In previous years the three regular beneficiaries have been the Children's Society, Docklands Settlement and Metropolitan Police Courts Poor Boxes (Drinan Bequest). Each of these beneficiaries received three-tenths of the income. The remaining tenth was divided equally between Barnardos and National Children's Home. It appears as if both of these charities also receive grants on an ongoing basis.

Applications In writing to the correspondent.

Rosalyn and Nicholas Springer Charitable Trust

Welfare, Jewish, education, general

£110,000 (2005/06)

Beneficial area UK.

Flat 27, Berkeley House, 15 Hay Hill, London W1J 8NS

Tel. 020 7493 1904

Correspondent Nicholas Springer, Trustee

Trustees Mrs R Springer; N S Springer; J Joseph.

CC Number 1062239

Information available Full accounts were on file at the Charity Commission.

General This trusts supports the relief and assistance of people in need, for the advancement of education, religion and other purposes. Grants were made in the following categories: medical, health and sickness, education and training, arts and culture, religious activities, relief of poverty and for general charitable purposes. In 2005/06 the trust had assets of £51,000 and an income of £125,000. Grants were made totalling £110,000.

Ten of the largest grants made included those to UJIA (£31,000), UK Friends of MDA (£9,000), King Alfred School and JNF (£5,000 each), Jewish Care and Norwood Ravenswood (£4,000 each), the Royal Opera House Foundation (£3,000), Chai Lifeline Cancer Care (£2,000) and the Jaffa Institute (£1,000).

Applications The trust states that it only supports organisations it is already in contact with. 99% of unsolicited applications are unsuccessful and because of the volume it receives, the trust is unable to reply to such letters. It would therefore not seem appropriate to apply to this trust.

The Spurrell Charitable Trust

General

£60,000 (2005/06)

Beneficial area UK, with some preference for Norfolk.

16 Harescroft, Moat Farm, Tunbridge Wells, Kent TN2 5XE

Tel. 01892 541565

Correspondent A T How, Trustee

Trustees Alan T How; Richard J K Spurrell; Mrs Inge H Spurrell; Martyn R Spurrell.

CC Number 267287

Information available Accounts were on file at the Charity Commission.

General This trust's funds are only distributed to charities known personally to the trustees. There appears to be a preference for supporting causes in Norfolk. The trust states that funds are fully committed.

In 2005/06 the trust had assets of £2.3 million, an income of £72,000 and made grants totalling £60,000. Larger grants were £5,000 to East Anglian Air Ambulance, £4,000 each to Parkinson's Disease Society and Royal Agricultural Benevolent Institution, £3,000 to Friends of Norwich Cathedral – restoration appeal and £2,500 to Big C Appeal – Cancer Research Norfolk Trust.

Smaller grants included £1,000 each to Alzheimer's Research Trust, Brooke Hospital for Animals, East Anglia Children's Hospice, Norfolk and Norwich Association for the Blind, RAF Benevolent Fund and St Luke's Hospital for the Clergy, £500 each to Church Mission Society, Cued Speech

Association UK, Headway, North Norfolk Riding for the Disabled, Queen Elizabeth Foundation, St Dunstans, Samaritans – Norwich, Wireless for the Bedridden and Woodland Trust and £250 each to Aircrew Association Archive Trust, Fern Street Settlement and Sheringham & Cromer Choral Society.

Applications Unsolicited applications are not considered.

The Geoff and Fiona Squire Foundation

General in the UK

£433,000 (2005/06)
Beneficial area UK.

Home Farm House, Hursley, Winchester, Hampshire SO21 2JL

Correspondent Fiona Squire, Trustee

Trustees *G W Squire; F P Squire; B P Peerless.*

CC Number 1085553

Information available Accounts were on file at the Charity Commission.

General Registered with the Charity Commission in March 2001. In 2005/06 the trust had assets of £14 million and an income of £843,000. Grants were made totalling £433,000.

The largest grants included those made to: SENSE Holiday Fund (£80,000); Starlight (£66,000); Oxford Brookes University (£55,000); Changing Faces (£45,000); Naomi House (Wessex Children's Hospice Trust) (£40,000); the Lord's Taverners (£31,000); Shepherds Down School (£20,000); Evelina Children's Hospital (£18,000); Colon Cancer Research (£12,000) and British Paralympic Association (£10,000).

Other grants included those made to: Multiple Sclerosis Resource Centre, the Sequel Trust and the royal Society for the Blind (£5,000 each); Royal Opera House (£2,000); Motor Neurone Disease (£750); Music at Winchester Trust, Shooting Star Childrens Hospice and Great Ormond Street Hospital (£500 each); and Marine and Sea Cadets (£250).

Applications 'The trustees have in place a well-established donations policy and we do not therefore encourage unsolicited grant applications, not least

because they take time and expense to deal with properly.'

St Andrew Animal Fund

Animal welfare

£26,000 (2004)
Beneficial area UK and overseas, with a preference for Scotland.

10 Queensferry Street, Edinburgh EH2 4PG

Tel. 0131 225 2116 **Fax** 0131 220 6377

Email info@advocatesforanimals.org

Website www.advocatesforanimals.org

Correspondent Ross Minett, Secretary

Trustees *Murray McGrath, Chair; David Martin; Dr Jane Goodall; Heather Petrie; Rebecca Ford; Shona McManus; Stephen Blakeway; Emma Law, Audrey Fearn; Duchess of Hamilton; Virginia Hay; Les Ward; Sheelagh Graham.*

SC Number SC005337

Information available Annual report and accounts were provided by the trust.

General The fund was formed in 1969 to carry out charitable activities for the protection of animals from cruelty and suffering. Grants are awarded only to fund or to part-fund a specific project, e.g. building work, renovation, repairs and so on; an animal project – spaying/neutering, re-homing and so on; animal rescue/animal sanctuary – providing care for unwanted, ill or injured animals.

The activities during 2004 included making grants and awards to further animal welfare projects in the UK and overseas. The fund continued its involvement in a project dealing with the force-feeding of ducks and geese in the production of foie gras, and with Focus on Alternatives, a group promoting the development, acceptance and use of humane alternatives to animals in research.

The trustees consider that the priorities for the charity in the next few years are support for the development of non-animal research techniques, funding farm animal and companion animal and wildlife projects to improve and enhance the welfare of animals.

In 2004 the assets of the fund stood at £572,000. Income totalled £63,000, including £22,000 from donations and legacies, £20,000 from investments and

£18,000 from rent. Grants totalled £26,000 with other charitable expenditure amounting to £68,000.

There were 19 grants made in the year, the largest of which was made to Lawrence and Beavan Website Project (£11,000). Other beneficiaries receiving over £1,000 were Tinto Kennels (£3,000), InterNICHE and Uist Hedgehog Rescue (£2,000 each) and Captive Animals Protection Society and Norwegian School of Veterinary Science (£1,200 each).

Beneficiaries of smaller grants included ATLA Abstracts, Friends of the Ferals – Devon, Muirhead Animal Fund – Edinburgh, Cat Register and Rescue Centre – Falkirk and The Sanctuary – Morpeth.

Exclusions No support for routine day-to-day expenses.

Applications In writing to the correspondent. The trustees meet in April and applications must reach the fund by 28 February for consideration at the next meeting. Applications should include a copy of the latest accounts, the name and address of a referee (e.g. veterinary surgeon or an animal welfare organisation), the purpose for which any grant will be used and, where relevant, two estimates. Receipts for work carried out may be requested and the fund states that visits by representatives of the fund to those organisations receiving grants will be made at random.

St Gabriel's Trust

Higher and further religious education

£169,000 (2005)
Beneficial area Mainly in the UK.

Ladykirk, 32 The Ridgeway, Enfield, Middlesex EN2 8QH

Tel. 020 8363 6474

Correspondent Peter Duffell, Clerk

Trustees *General Secretary of the National Society; nine co-optative trustees and two nominated trustees.*

CC Number 312933

Information available Full accounts were available from the Charity Commission website.

General The trust is concerned with the advancement of higher and further education in one or more of the following ways:

- promotion of the education and training of people who are, or intend to become, engaged as teachers or otherwise in work connected with religious education
- promotion of research in, and development of, religious education
- promotion of religious education by the provision of instruction, classes, lectures, books, libraries and reading rooms
- granting of financial assistance to institutions of higher or further education established for charitable purposes only.

In 2005 the trust had assets of £6.5 million and an income of £237,000. Grants totalling £169,000 were made comprising £74,000 in corporate awards, £89,000 to St Gabriel's Programme (see below) and £7,000 in total to 11 individuals.

Six corporate grants were made, the largest being to ACCT Virtual RE Centre – RE online (£23,000), King's College – London for RE in Church of England School (£21,000) and ACCT – Teach RE (£7,500).

The trustees have committed funds for several corporate projects including:

- an initiative to recruit RE teachers, in conjunction with other trusts
- the St Gabriel's Programme, an ongoing venture which has been run jointly with The Culham Institute, 'to develop thought and action in support of RE teachers'.

Awards to individuals are given towards course fees and expenses for teachers taking part-time RE courses whilst continuing their teaching jobs. Occasional grants have been given to those undertaking specialist research that will clearly benefit the religious education world.

Exclusions Grants are not normally available for: any project for which local authority money is available, or which ought primarily to be funded by the church – theological study, parish or missionary work – unless school RE is involved; and research projects where it will be a long time before any benefit can filter down into RE teaching. No grants are made to schools as such; higher and further education must be involved.

Applications In writing to the correspondent with an sae. Applicants are asked to describe their religious allegiance and to provide a reference from their minister of religion.

Applications need to be received by the beginning of January, April or September as trustees meet in February, May and October.

St James' Trust Settlement

General
£103,000 (2005/06)
Beneficial area Worldwide.

Epworth House, 25 City Road, London EC1Y 1AR
Trustees *Jane Wells; Cathy Ingram; Simon Taffler.*
CC Number 280455
Information available Full accounts were on file at the Charity Commission.

General The trust's main aims are to make grants to charitable organisations that respond to areas of concern in which the trustees are involved or interested. In the UK, the main concerns are health, education and social justice; in the USA the main areas are in education, especially to the children of very disadvantaged families, and in community arts projects.

Grants are made by the trustees through their involvement with the project. Projects are also monitored and evaluated by the trustees.

In 2005/06 the trust had assets of £3.7 million and an income of £93,000. Grants were made totalling £103,000. Grants were paid totalling £313,000, which went to five organisations in the UK amounting to £41,000 and fifteen in the USA amounting to £62,000.

In the UK grants went to Caris Islington and Aegis Trust (£10,000 each), Homeopathy Action Trust (£8,500), Elizabeth House Play and Youth Service (£7,500) and Marie Curie Cancer Care (£5,000).

In the USA, grants included those to Theatre for a New Audience (£14,000), Human Rights Watch (£4,000), Theatre Aspen (£3,000), International Women's Health Coalition (£2,000), Barnes and Noble Head Start (£800) and the Sarcoma Foundation Ame (£600).

Exclusions No grants to individuals.

Applications 'The trust does not seek unsolicited applications to grants, the trustees do not feel justified in allocating administrative costs to responding to

applications. If you do send an application you must send an sae.'

St Michael's and All Saints' Charities

Health, welfare
£56,000 (2005)
Beneficial area City of Oxford.

St Michael's Church Centre, St Michael at the North Gate, Cornmarket Street, Oxford OX1 3EY
Tel. 01865 240940 **Fax** 01865 728095
Correspondent Robert J Spencer Hawes
Trustees *P Beavis; C Burton; Rev H Lee; P Eldridge; Prof. P Langford; M Lear; Sir John Krebs; The Ven J Morrison; A Paine.*
CC Number 202750
Information available Accounts were obtained from the Charity Commission website.

General Income of the charity is applied to relieve, either generally or individually, persons resident in the city of Oxford who are in conditions of need, hardship or distress. Grants may be made to institutions or organisations which provide services or facilities for such people.

In 2005 the trust had assets of £988,000 and an income of £63,000. Grants were made totalling £56,000. Beneficiaries included the Porch (£5,000), the Leys Youth Programme (£4,000), RESTORE (£3,000), Oxford Parent-Infant Project (£2,000) and Wood Farm Youth Club (£1,000).

Exclusions Individuals are very rarely supported.

Applications In writing to the correspondent.

St Monica Trust Community Fund

Older people, disability

£122,000 (2006)

Beneficial area Preference for the south west of England, particularly Bristol and the surrounding area.

Cote Lane, Westbury-on-Trym, Bristol BS9 3UN

Tel. 0117 949 4003 **Fax** 0117 949 4058

Email community.fund@stmonicatrust. org.uk

Website www.communityfund. stmonicatrust.org.uk

Correspondent Emma Beeston, Community Fund Manager

Trustees *Revd Robert Grimley Dean Of Bristol; Timothy Thom; Robert Bernays; Revd Ian Gobey; D'arcy Parkes; Peter Sherwood; Trevor Smallwood; Mrs Mary Prior; Sir David Wills; Gillian Camm; Charles Hunter; Mrs Judith Pearce; Prof. Patricia Broadfoot.*

CC Number 202151

Information available Accounts were on file at the Charity Commission.

General This trust has provided accommodation, care and support for older and disabled people for over 80 years. Another branch of its work, the St Monica Trust Community Fund, gives grants to individuals and organisations to help improve the daily lives of people with a physical or long-term physical health problem.

Grants of up to £10,000 each are available to organisations. Grants may be awarded for capital items and/or for running costs. To be considered, organisations must meet all five of the following criteria:

To be considered for a grant from the St Monica Trust Community Fund your organisation must meet all five of the following criteria:

1 Benefit people (over 16 years old) who have a physical or sensory impairment or long-term physical health problem, including those with infirmities due to old age.
2 Benefit people living in Bristol or the surrounding area (North Somerset, Somerset, South Gloucestershire, Gloucestershire, Bath and North East Somerset and Wiltshire).
3 Make a real difference to people's daily lives.

4 Be both properly constituted and a not-for-profit organisation.
5 Be working to reduce the loneliness and isolation of people with a physical or sensory impairment or long-term physical health problem by bringing people together.

Each year has a different theme – the 2007 grants scheme being open to organisations working to bring together people with a physical or sensory impairment or long-term physical health problem. Please see the fund's website for up-to-date information.

The fund is keen to receive applications from organisations that 'enable people to get together, to connect with others and the wider community. This could include: befriending schemes, social clubs, support groups or computer training projects.'

In 2006 the trust gave grants to 41 organisations totalling £122,000, beneficiaries included: Age Concern Somerset, Alzheimer's Society – North Somerset, Centre for Deaf People and the Mede Community and Learning Centre (£10,000 each); Disabled Living Centre (£7,000); Coney Hill Neighbourhood Project – People Together, Dressability and Gloucestershire Dance (£5,000 each); SWAN Advice Network (£3,500); Arts Together and St Mary's Church (£1,000 each); and Melksham Phab (£500).

The trust accepts applications from organisations that it has previously funded.

Exclusions No grants to fund buildings, adaptations to buildings or minibus purchases.

Applications On a form available from the correspondent, or as a download from the fund's website. All applicants must submit a form together with additional information that is requested, for example, an annual report.

Please see the fund's website for deadline dates.

All applications will be considered by the Community Fund Committee of the trust. Notification of the outcome will be made in writing.

'We receive many more requests than we have funds available. For example, in 2006 we received 76 applications with requests totalling over £514,000: well above the £122,000 we had available. In practice this means that we do not give grants to organisations which do not fully meet our criteria; please make sure that your organisation is eligible before applying. If you are in any doubt or have

any questions about our application form or process, please contact us.'

The Late St Patrick White Charitable Trust

General

£54,000 (2005/06)

Beneficial area UK, with a possible preference for Hampshire.

HSBC Trust Co. UK Ltd, Norwich House, Nelson Gate, Commercial Road, Southampton SO15 1GX

Tel. 023 8072 2223

Correspondent Barry Sims, Trust Manager

Trustee *HSBC Trusts Co. (UK) Ltd.*

CC Number 1056520

Information available Accounts were available from the Charity Commission website.

General The objects of the charity are in perpetuity to pay or to apply the income from the trust fund for the benefit of Barnardo's, Guide Dogs for the Blind, The Salvation Army, Age Concern and other charities benefiting the blind, cancer research, arthritis and rheumatism research.

In 2005/06 the trust had assets of £2 million and an income of £83,000. Grants were made totalling £54,000. Beneficiaries included Dr Barnardo's (£6,000 in three awards); Age Concern and Arthritis Care (£5,500 each in three awards); Cancer Research UK (£5,000 in three awards); the Guide Dogs for the Blind Association (£3,500 in two awards); Arthritis Research Campaign, Sense and Worcestershire Association for the Blind (£1,500 each); and Prostate Cancer (£1,250 in two awards).

Applications In writing to the correspondent. Applications are considered in February, May, August and November.

Miss Doreen Stanford Trust

General

£24,000 to organisations and individuals (2005)
Beneficial area UK.

26 The Mead, Beckenham, Kent BR3 5PE

Tel. 020 8650 3368

Correspondent Mrs G M B Borner, Secretary

Trustees *T Carter; R S Borner; T Butler; D Valder; Miss M Winter.*

CC Number 1049934

Information available Full accounts were available from the Charity Commission.

General The trust states that its aims are to provide grants to individuals in need through charities, to further their education and help them or the public in the appreciation of the learned arts or sciences, to help towards holidays and to help those in conditions of hardship or distress.

In 2005 the trust had assets of £666,000 and an income of £33,000. Grants were made totalling £24,000. Beneficiaries included the Aidis Trust (£2,500), Deathblind, Happy Days and Motability (£2,000 each), Multiple Sclerosis and Talking Newspaper (£1,000 each), Invalids-at-Home (£1,500), Vitalise (£1,300) and the British Legion (£350).

Exclusions No grants are given towards building repairs, alterations to property, electrical goods, floor coverings, holidays for individuals or towards household furniture or equipment.

Applications In writing to the correspondent, enclosing an sae. Allocations of grants are made once a year in March at the trustees' meeting.

The Stanley Charitable Trust

Jewish

£115,000 (2003/04)
Beneficial area UK, with a preference for Greater Manchester.

32 Waterpark Road, Salford M7 4ET
Correspondent David Adler, Trustee

Trustees *D Adler; I Adler; J Adler.*
CC Number 326220

Information available Accounts were obtained from the Charity Commission website.

General The trust supports Jewish religious charities, with a preference for those in Greater Manchester and for projects and people known to the trustees.

In 2003/04 the trust had assets of £1.9 million and an income of £115,000. Grants were made totalling £115,000.

The largest grant was £50,000 to AMA Memorial Trust. Other beneficiaries were Chasidei Square (£8,000), Craven Walk Charitable Trust, Torah Learning Centre and SAYSER Charity (£5,000 each) and Broughton Charitable Trust (£1,800).

Exclusions Only registered charities are supported.

Applications The trust has said that it gives regular donations and does not consider new applications.

The Stanley Foundation Ltd

Older people, medical, education, social welfare

£88,000 (2005/06)
Beneficial area UK.

Flat 3, 19 Holland Park, London W11 3TD
Correspondent The Secretary

Trustees *N Stanley, Chair; S R Stanley; Mrs E Stanley; S H Hall.*

CC Number 206866

Information available Full accounts were on file at the Charity Commission.

General The trust has traditionally supported charities helping older people and medical, educational and social welfare charities. In 2005/06 it had assets of £3.4 million and an income of £101,000. Grants were made to 50 organisations totalling £88,000.

Grants included: £8,000 to Bristol Cancer Care; £5,000 each to AMBER and Victoria & Albert Museum; £4,500 to Holbourne Museum; £3,500 each to Cystic Fibrosis Trust and TATE Foundation; £3,000 each to Gainsborough House, Raynaud's and Sclerodesura Association, Royal Hospital for Neuro Disability, St Mary's Church

Welsham and Woodrow Hugh House; £2,500 each to Moorfield Eye Hospital, Prostate Cancer Charity and Worldwide Volunteering Young; £2,000 each to Alzheimer's Society and UK Friends of Hospital (£2,000 each); and Arthritis Research Campaign and Walk the Walk (£1,000 each).

Donations of less than £1,000 each totalled £5,800 (19 charities).

Exclusions No grants to individuals.

Applications In writing to the correspondent.

The Star Charitable Trust

General

Around £129,000 (2005/06)
Beneficial area UK.

2nd Floor, 16–18 Hatton Garden, London EC1N 8AT

Tel. 020 7404 2222 **Fax** 020 7404 3333

Trustees *D D Fiszman; P I Propper.*
CC Number 266695

Information available Information was obtained from the Charity Commission website.

General Connected to the Star Diamond Group of companies, this trust was established in March 1974. In 2005/06 the trust had an income of £14,000 and a total expenditure of £129,000. Further information was not available.

Applications In writing to the correspondent.

The Starfish Trust

Sickness, medical

£247,250 to organisations (2005/06)
Beneficial area Within a 25-mile radius of Bristol.

PO Box 213, Patchway, Bristol BS32 4YY
Tel. 0117 970 1756 **Fax** 0117 970 1756
Correspondent Robert N Woodward
Trustees *Charles E Dobson; Mary Dobson.*

CC Number 800203

Information available Full accounts were on file at the Charity Commission

General Priority is given to appeals from individuals and charitable organisations living or based within a 25-mile radius of central Bristol in the following areas:

- direct assistance to people who are disabled
- direct assistance to people for the relief of illness or disease
- medical research and welfare in the above areas.

Furthermore, according to the trust's 2005/06 report and accounts:

It is the trustees' policy that they should give priority to providing direct assistance to individuals and to identifying and evaluating specific projects when giving to charitable organisations. Where appropriate, matched funding is encouraged.

It is the trustees' future policy that they will not make grants in excess of £10,000 to capital projects.

It will be the trustees' future policy not to provide grants to NHS Trusts.

In 2005/06 the trust had assets of £1.5 million and an income of £104,000. Grants totalling £271,000 were made, of which £23,750 was paid to 14 individuals. Grants to organisations included the following:

Direct assistance to the disabled – £150,000 to The Vassall Centre; £27,000 to Hop, Skip and a Jump (The Seven Springs Foundation); £10,000 to Springboard Opportunity Group; £5,000 to Woodspring Association for Blind People; £2,500 to Paul's Place; and, £1,500 to Visually Handicapped Self Help Association.

Medical research and welfare – £40,000 to Meningitis UK; £5,000 to Computers for Life; £1,300 to Centre for Deaf People; £1,000 to Brislington Neighbourhood Centre; £800 to Tyndall Circle Centre; and £100 to NSPCC.

Exclusions Individuals and charitable organisations outside a 25-mile radius of Bristol or not working in the areas defined above.

Applications In writing to the correspondent.

The Educational Charity of the Stationers' and Newspaper Makers' Company

Printing education

£54,000 to organisations (2004/ 05)

Beneficial area UK.

The Old Dairy, Adstockfields, Adstock, Buckingham MK18 2JE

Tel. 01296 714586 **Fax** 01296 714711

Correspondent P Thornton, Secretary

Trustee *Stationers' and Newspaper Makers' Company.*

CC Number 312633

Information available Accounts were available from the Charity Commission website.

General This trust was set up in 1985 primarily to support the education of people under 25 wishing to enter the stationers' or newspaper makers' trades. It has close links with Reeds School and King Edward's School – Witley. However, possibly reflecting the changing technological nature of the business, the trust also funds the installation of printing departments at schools. The trust stated that grants to schools towards fitting out a printing department vary from year to year and may be for more than £30,000 a year. In 2004/05 the trust had assets of £2.8 million and an income of £127,000. Grants were made totalling £79,000, of which £54,000 went to organisations.

Grants were made to Treloar College and Catford Girls' School towards the cost of desktop publishing equipment. There were two postgraduate bursaries awarded to students in Electronic Publishing at the City University CASS Business School.

Exclusions No grants towards anything not related to printing, stationery or papermaking.

Applications Application forms can be obtained from the correspondent. They are considered monthly.

The Peter Stebbings Memorial Charity

General

£21,000 to institutions (2005)

Beneficial area UK and developing countries.

45 Pont Street, London SW1X 0BX

Tel. 020 7591 3333

Correspondent Andrew Stebbings, Trustee

Trustees *A J F Stebbings; N F Cosin; Mrs J A Clifford.*

CC Number 274862

Information available Accounts were available from the Charity Commission website.

General The trust makes grants for a range of charitable purposes and the objectives of the trust are to fund, in particular, medical research and education, and the welfare of those who are poor, old or sick.

In 2005 the charity had assets of £3.1 million and an income of £99,000. Grants were made to institutions totalling £21,000.

Beneficiaries included Welcare Community Projects (£2,000), CanSupport (£1,500), Alzheimer's Society, Amnesty International, Farm Africa, the National Pyramid Trust, Rethink, Tools for Self-Reliance and Women at Risk (£1,000 each) and Computer Aid International, Marie Curie Cancer Care and Westminster Pastoral Foundation (£500 each).

Exclusions No grants to individuals, non-registered charities or for salaries.

Applications This trust states that it does not respond to unsolicited applications and that its funds are fully committed.

The Cyril and Betty Stein Charitable Trust

Jewish causes

£213,000 (2005/06)
Beneficial area UK and Israel.

c/o Clayton Stark and Co., 5th Floor, Charles House, 108–110 Finchley Road, London NW3 5JJ

Tel. 020 7935 4999

Correspondent The Trustees

Trustees *Mrs B Stein; C Stein; D Stein; L Curry.*

CC Number 292235

Information available Accounts were on file at the Charity Commission.

General The trust makes a small number of substantial grants each year, primarily for the advancement of the Jewish religion and the welfare of Jewish people.

In 2005/06 the trust had an income of £121,000 and made grants totalling £213,000. Its assets stood at £79,000. Beneficiaries included the Institute for the Advancement of Education in Jaffa (£76,000); Bar Amana (£25,000); Friends of Bnei David (£16,000); British Friends of Machon Meir (£10,500); Taylor Schechter Genizah Research Unit (£8,000); Western Marble Arch Synagogue (£7,000); the Hope Charity (£5,000); Friends of Ma'alot Education Centre (£2,500); Manchester Jewish Federation (£1,000); and Community Security Trust (£500).

There were 104 other grants made totalling £13,000 of less than £1,000 each.

Applications In writing to the correspondent.

The Steinberg Family Charitable Trust

Jewish, health

£206,000 (2004/05)
Beneficial area UK, with a preference for Greater Manchester.

Stanley House, 151 Dale Street, Liverpool L2 2JW

Correspondent The Trustees

Trustees *D Burke, Chairman; Mrs B Steinberg; J Steinberg; Mrs L R Ferster; D K Johnston; M Sampson; B Davidson.*

CC Number 1045231

Information available Full accounts were on file at the Charity Commission.

General 'Whilst the objects of the founding deed are very wide, the trust is primarily concerned with the support of charities located in the North West region or active within the Jewish Community (whether in the North West or Israel), particularly those involved with the provision of social or health services. There is a particular emphasis on the needs of children and young people within those areas.'

In 2004/05 the trust had assets of £6.7 million, an income of £190,000 and made 94 grants totalling £206,000.

The 13 largest grants of £5,000 or more went to: Manchester Jewish Federation and Manchester Kashrus (£25,000 each); the Heathlands Village Foundation Fund (£13,000); Community Security Trust, North West Cancer Research Fund and WIZO (£10,000 each); Chief Rabbinate Trust and the Joseph & Fay Tannenbaum 'Hamesorah' Institutions (£8,000 each); and King David High School, Laniado, Manchester City Galleries, Merkaz Lechinuch Torani and the Rainsough Charitable Trust (£5,000 each).

Other beneficiaries included: Wingate Institute for Physical Education & Sport (£4,000); Council of Manchester & Salford Jews (£3,400); Other beneficiaries included DEBRA (£2,500); RAFT (£2,000); the Institute for the Advancement of Education in Jaffa (£1,000); Alzheimer's Society, the British Technion Society, One Family UK and Shining Faces in Africa (£500 each); the British Kidney Patient Association, Gertener Charitable Trust and the Police Memorial Trust (£250 each); and Food Lifeline, Kidsout and Willowfield Parish Community Association (£100 each).

Exclusions Registered charities only.

Applications In writing to the correspondent, including evidence of charitable status, the purpose to which the funds are to be put, evidence of other action taken to fund the project concerned, and the outcome of that action.

The Sigmund Sternberg Charitable Foundation

Jewish, inter-faith causes, general

£1 million (2005/06)
Beneficial area Worldwide.

Star House, Grafton Road, London NW5 4BD

Tel. 020 7485 2538

Correspondent Sir S Sternberg, Trustee

Trustees *Sir S Sternberg; V M Sternberg; Lady Sternberg; Rev M C Rossi Braybrooke; M A M Slowe; R Tamir; M D Paisner.*

CC Number 257950

Information available Full accounts were on file at the Charity Commission.

General This trust supports Jewish and Israeli charities, with a preference for organisations that address inter-faith issues and cooperation. It makes a small number of large grants, generally of £10,000 to £50,000 each, and a large number of smaller grants. In 2005/06 the trust had an income of £294,000 and made 220 grants totalling £1 million. Its assets stood at £5.1 million.

The ten largest grants included those made to: Three Faiths Forum (£94,000); the Reform Synagogues of Great Britain (£70,000); the Board of Deputies Charitable Foundation (£37,000); Friends of the Hebrew University of Jerusalem (£32,000); Council for Christians and Jews (£14,000); International Council for Christians and Jews and Dartmouth Street Trust (£12,000 each); the Interreligious Coordinating Council in Israel (£11,000); Leo Baeck College Centre for Jewish Education (£6,000); and Centre for Jewish-Christian Relations (£5,000).

Exclusions No grants to individuals.

Applications The foundation stated in April 2004 that its funds are fully committed.

Stervon Ltd

Jewish

£252,000 (2004)
Beneficial area UK.

c/o Stervon House, 1 Seaford Road, Salford, Greater Manchester M6 6AS

Tel. 0161 737 5000

Correspondent A Reich, Secretary

Trustees *A Reich; G Rothbart.*

CC Number 280958

Information available Accounts were on file at the Charity Commission.

General 'The principal objective of the company is the distribution of funds to Jewish, religious, educational and similar charities.' In 2004 the trust had an income of £307,000 and made grants totalling £252,000. Its assets stood at £130,000.

Beneficiaries included: Eitz Chaim (£18,000); Rehabilitation Trust and Chasdei Yoel (£11,000); Beis Yoel (£8,000); Friends of Horeinu (£6,500); Beis Hamedrash Hachadash (£3,500); Tashbar (£3,000); Tov V' Chessed (£2,500); Beth Sorah Schneirer (£1,700); and Asser Bishvil (£1,000).

Applications In writing to the correspondent.

The Stewards' Charitable Trust

Rowing

£130,000 (2004/05)
Beneficial area Principally the UK.

Regatta Headquarters, Henley-on-Thames, Oxfordshire RG9 2LY

Tel. 01491 572153 **Fax** 01491 575509

Correspondent Daniel Grist, Secretary

Trustees *M A Sweeney; C G V Davidge; C L Baillieu; R C Lester.*

CC Number 299597

Information available Accounts were on file at the Charity Commission.

General The trust makes grants to organisations and clubs benefiting boys and girls involved in the sport of rowing. It supports rowing at all levels, from grassroots upwards; beneficiaries should be in full-time education or training. Support is also given to related medical and educational research projects. Grants

range from £1,000 to £60,000. They are preferably one-off and are especially made where matched funds are raised elsewhere.

In 2004/05 the trust had assets of £4 million and an income of £557,000, including £421,000 in donations received from various aspects of the Henley Regatta and Henley Festival. Grants were made totalling £130,000.

Beneficiaries were ARA Scholarships (£92,000), River and Rowing Museum (£15,000), Philip Henman Foundation and Rowing Foundation (£10,000 each) and Ball cup Regatta (£3,200).

Exclusions No grants to individuals or for building or capital costs.

Applications In writing to the correspondent. Applications are usually first vetted by Amateur Rowing Association.

The Stoller Charitable Trust

Medical, children, general

£320,000 (2005/06)
Beneficial area UK, with a preference for the Greater Manchester area.

PO Box 164, Manchester M24 1XA

Tel. 0161 653 3849 **Fax** 0161 653 6874

Correspondent Alison M Ford, Secretary

Trustees *Norman K Stoller, Chair; Roger Gould; Jan Fidler; Sheila M Stoller.*

CC Number 285415

Information available Accounts were available from the Charity Commission website.

General The trust supports a wide variety of charitable causes, but with particular emphasis on those that are local, medically related or supportive of children. There is a bias towards charities in Greater Manchester where the trust is based. It also endeavours to maintain a balance between regular and occasional donations and between the few large and many smaller ones.

In 2005/06 the trust had assets of £7.1 million and an income of £305,000. Grants were made totalling £320,000.

Grants can be considered for buildings, capital costs, projects, research costs,

recurring costs and start-up costs. As well as one-off grants, funding may also be given for up to three years.

Grants included those made to: Broughton House (£20,000); Army Benevolent Fund and Live Music Now! (£10,000 each); the Prince's Trust – Get Off The Bench (£9,000); Community Security Trust (£7,500); St John Ambulance (£5,000); Manchester Cathedral (£3,000); Church Housing Trust (£2,000); National Youth Orchestra and Salford Sailing Group (£1,000 each); and Listening Book and British Blind Sport (£250 each).

Exclusions No grants to individuals.

Applications In writing to the correspondent. Applications need to be received by February, May, August or November and the trustees meet in March, June, September and December.

The Stone Ashdown Charitable Trust

Equality and discrimination

£35,000 (2004/05)
Beneficial area UK, mainly London, and, to a limited extent, overseas.

4th Floor, Barkat House, 116–118 Finchley Road, London NW3 5HT

Tel. 020 7472 6060

Email trust@stoneashdown.org

Website www.stoneashdown.org

Correspondent The Grants Manager

Trustees *Richard Stone; Lutfur Ali; Leroy Logan.*

CC Number 298722

Information available Accounts were on file at the Charity Commission.

General The Stone Ashdown Trust was created in 2000 from the Joe Stone Charitable Trust, renamed Stone Ashdown, and with funding from the Lord Ashdown Charitable Settlement. The trust received a donation of £4 million from the Lord Ashdown Charitable Settlement in 2000/01, its first year of operation, which accounted for almost all its income. In 2004/05 it had assets of £2.1 million and an income of £99,000. Grants totalled £35,000.

The trustees have skill and expertise in the areas of the trust's activity. These are:

- relief of poverty
- advancement of education
- inter-religious dialogue
- asylum and immigration
- black and minority ethnic voluntary sector support
- promoting equalities and anti-racism
- outward-looking Judaism in the UK
- other charitable purposes.

Grants included £15,000 to Uniting Britain Trust, £10,000 to 1990 Trust, £2,600 to Youth Cultural Television, £2,000 to Asylum Aid, £1,000 to Tricycle Theatre and £250 each to Age Exchange Theatre Trust, Family Planning Association, Miracle of Life, Open trust and Yan Asantewaa Arts and Community Centre.

Exclusions The trust does not generally support individuals.

Applications The trust has a full list of existing commitments and anticipated programmes to support. It does not respond to applications from organisations outside its current programme in any year. To reduce costs, the trust will not respond to unsolicited applications.

Trustees meet at least three times a year.

The Stone-Mallabar Charitable Foundation

Medical, education

£260,000 (2004/05)
Beneficial area UK.

41 Orchard Court, Portman Square, London W1H 6LF
Correspondent Jonathan M Stone, Trustee

Trustees *Jonathan Stone; Thalia Stone; Robin Paul.*

CC Number 1013678

Information available Accounts were on file at the Charity Commission.

General In 2004/05 the foundation had assets of £981,000 and an income of £40,000. Grants were made totalling £260,000.

There were 24 donations of £1,000 or more listed in the accounts. Beneficiaries of amounts of £10,000 or more were St Christopher's Hospice (£100,000), Royal Northern College of Music (£40,000 in four grants), Opera North & Leeds Grand Theatre (£25,000), Motor Neurone Disease Association (£14,000 in two grants), Thomley Hall Centre Ltd (£14,000), Hardman Trust (£10,000 in two grants) and British Red Cross Society (£10,000).

Other beneficiaries included Deafblind UK and Zimbabwe Benefit Foundation (£5,000 each), Kingston University – Faculty of Healthcare (£3,000), Wigmore Hall Trust (£1,700), Pearsons Holiday Fund (£1,300) and British Epilepsy Association, Dorset Opera , Royal Philharmonic Orchestra Ltd, West London Mission and Woodlands Hospice Charitable Trust (£1,000 each).

Unlisted grants of less than £1,000 each totalled £2,200.

Exclusions No grants to individuals.

Applications The trustees regret that they cannot respond to applications as all funds have been allocated.

The Samuel Storey Family Charitable Trust

General

£104,000 (2004/05)
Beneficial area UK, with a preference for Yorkshire.

21 Buckingham Gate, London SW1E 6Ls
Tel. 020 7802 2700
Correspondent Hon. Sir Richard Storey, Trustee

Trustees *Hon. Sir Richard Storey; Wren Hoskyns Abrahall; K Storey.*

CC Number 267684

Information available Accounts were obtained from the Charity Commission website.

General This trust has general charitable purposes, supporting a wide range of causes, including the arts, gardens and churches. The grants list shows a large number of beneficiaries in Yorkshire. In 2004/05 the trust had assets of £4 million and an income of £126,000. Grants were made totalling £104,000.

The largest grants went to Hope and Homes for Children (30,000) and York University (£20,000). Other grants went to Abba Light Foundation (£3,000), St Gregory's Foundation (£2,000), Opera North & Leeds Grand Theatre Development Trust (£1,000); Social Affairs Unit (£500); and Scottish Community Foundation (£250).

Exclusions The trust does not support non-registered charities or individuals.

Applications In writing to the correspondent.

Peter Stormonth Darling Charitable Trust

Heritage, medical research, sport

£77,000 (2006)
Beneficial area UK.

7 Swan Walk, London SW3 4JJ
Correspondent Peter Stormonth Darling, Trustee

Trustees *Tom Colville; J F M Rodwell; Peter Stormonth Darling.*

CC Number 1049946

Information available Full accounts were on file at the Charity Commission.

General The trust makes grants towards heritage, education, healthcare and sports facilities. In 2006 the trust had assets of £2.2 million and an income of £245,000. Grants were made totalling £77,000.

The largest grants included those made to the London Library, Treloar and World Monuments Fund in Britain (£10,000 each) and Canterbury Cathedral Trust Fund, Chailey Heritage School and Chelsea Physio Garden (£5,000).

Other grants included those to Reed's School (£3,000), Crown and Manor Club – Hoxton (£2,000) and King Edward VII's Hospital, Southwell Minister and Unicorn Theatre (£1,000 each).

Applications This trust states that it does not respond to unsolicited applications.

Peter Storrs Trust

Education

£68,000 (2005/06)
Beneficial area UK.

Smithfield Accountants, 117 Charterhouse Street, London EC1M 6AA

Tel. 020 7253 3757

Correspondent J A Fordyce, Trustee

Trustees G V Adams; A R E Curtis; J A Fordyce.

CC Number 313804

Information available Accounts were on file at the Charity Commission, but without a list of beneficiaries.

General The trust makes grants to registered charities working for the advancement of education in the UK. In 2005/06 the trust had assets of £2.5 million and an income of £440,000. Grants were made totalling £68,000, unfortunately further information including a list of grant beneficiaries was not available.

Applications In writing to the correspondent. Applications are considered every three to six months. Please note, the trust receives far more applications than it is able to support, many of which do not meet the criteria outlined above. This results in a heavy waste of time and expense for both applicants and the trust.

The W O Street Charitable Foundation

Education, people with disabilities, young people, health, social welfare

£280,000 (2005)
Beneficial area Worldwide. In practice UK, with a preference for the north west of England and Jersey.

c/o Barclays Bank Trust Company Ltd, PO Box 15, Osborne Court, Gadbrook Park, Northwich CW9 7UR

Correspondent Sue Wakefield, Trust Officer

Trustees Barclays Bank Trust Co. Ltd; Mr C D Cutbill.

CC Number 267127

Information available Accounts were available at the Charity Commission.

General In considering grants the trustees pay close regard to the wishes of the late Mr Street who had particular interests in education, support for people with financial difficulties (particularly older people, people who are blind or who have other disabilities), health and social welfare generally. Special support is given to the north west of England and Jersey.

A limited number of educational projects have been selected to which significant grants are being given over a relatively short period (usually no more than three years), to enable the projects to establish themselves. This policy is kept under review but it is likely that a programme of supporting projects of this nature will be sustained (at least for the foreseeable future). As a result the trustees will not be able to devote as much of their resources as they have in the past to smaller 'one-off' grants.

A proportion of the available income annually, not exceeding 10%, is paid by grant to the W O Street Jersey Charitable Trust. Arrangements have also been made for a limited number of small local grants to be made, particularly in the Bury area of the north west. In addition the foundation supports the Combined Trusts Scholarship Trust (a separate registered charity – numbered 295402). It also provides grants to assist with fee-paying schooling where there is unexpected financial difficulty.

In 2005 the trust had assets of £16 million and an income of £430,000. 38 grants were made totalling £280,000. Of this £47,000 was paid to the W O Street Jersey Charitable Trust, £59,000 was spent on educational bursaries and the remaining £170,000 was given in grants.

Beneficiaries included: Combined Trusts Scholarship Trust (£35,000); the Fusiliers Museum (£15,000); Answer Project Limited and Disability Action (£10,000 each); Christian Concern – Crewe, the Fairbridge Society, Lattendales, Rainbow House for Conductive Education and the Add Action Project (£5,000 each); Derby Toc H Children's Camp and Easy Go Travel Service (£3,000 each); Age Concern – East Cheshire, Children's Heart Foundation and Disability Action (£2,500 each); Conquest Art (£2,000); and Cambridge Cyrenians, Multiple Sclerosis Society, No Panic and Oakleigh Special School PSA (£1,000 each).

Exclusions No grants towards:

- schools, colleges or universities
- running or core costs
- religion or church buildings
- medical research
- animal welfare
- hospices
- overseas projects or charities
- NHS trusts.

Applications directly from individuals are not considered.

Applications In writing to the correspondent. Applications are considered on a quarterly basis, at the end of January, April, July and October.

The A B Strom and R Strom Charitable Trust

Jewish, general

£33,000 (2004/05)
Beneficial area UK.

c/o 11 Gloucester Gardens, London NW11 9AB

Correspondent Mrs R Strom, Trustee

Trustee Mrs R Strom.

CC Number 268916

Information available Accounts were on file at the Charity Commission.

General According to the correspondent 'the trust only supports a set list of charities working with elderly people, schools/colleges, hospitals and Christian causes. It does not have any money available for any charities not already on the list.'

In 2004/05 the trust had assets of £400,000 with an income of £114,000. Grants totalled £33,000.

Grants in excess of £1,000 each went to Yeshivas Hanegev (£10,000), JRRC (£10,000 in two grants) and Redcroft and Russian Immigrants (£5,000 each).

Applications Please note that the same organisations are supported each year, therefore the trust does not want to receive any applications for funding.

Sueberry Ltd

Jewish, welfare

£149,000 (2004/05)

Beneficial area UK and overseas.

29 Reisel Close, London N16 5GZ

Correspondent Mrs M Davis, Trustee

Trustees *J Davis, Chair; Mrs H Davis; Mrs M Davis; D S Davis; C Davis.*

CC Number 256566

Information available Accounts were on file at the Charity Commission but without a list of beneficiaries.

General The trust makes grants to Jewish organisations and also to other UK welfare, educational and medical organisations benefiting children and young adults, at risk groups, people who are disadvantaged by poverty, or socially isolated people.

In 2004/05 the trust had an income of £141,000 and made grants totalling £149,000. A list of beneficiaries was not available. In previous years the trust has supported educational, religious and other charitable organisations.

Applications In writing to the correspondent.

The Alan Sugar Foundation

Jewish charities, general

£35,000 (2005/06)

Beneficial area UK.

Brentwood House, 169 Kings Road, Brentwood, Essex CM14 4EF

Tel. 01277 201333 **Fax** 01277 208006

Correspondent Colin Sandy, Trustee

Trustees *Sir Alan Sugar; Colin Sandy; Simon Sugar; Daniel Sugar; Mrs Louise Baron.*

CC Number 294880

Information available Accounts were available from the Charity Commission website.

General This trust was established by the well-known ex-chair of Tottenham Hotspur FC, and gives a small number of substantial grants each year. Grants are made to registered charities that are of current and ongoing interest to the trustees.

In 2005/06 the trust had assets of £119,000 and an income of £81,000. Grants were made to five organisations totalling £35,000. Grants went to: Ravenswood (£22,000); the Drugs Line and Manchester Jewish Community Care (£5,000 each); Prostate Cancer Charitable Fund (£2,000) and 45 Aid Society (£1,000).

Exclusions No grants for individuals or to non-registered charities.

Applications This trust states that it does not respond to unsolicited applications. All projects are initiated by the trustees.

The Adrienne and Leslie Sussman Charitable Trust

Jewish, general

£54,000 (2005/06)

Beneficial area UK, in practice Greater London, particularly Barnet.

25 Tillingbourne Gardens, London N3 3JJ

Correspondent Mrs A H Sussman

Trustees *A H Sussman; L Sussman; M D Paisner.*

CC Number 274955

Information available Accounts are on file at the Charity Commission, without a list of grants.

General The trust supports a variety of Jewish, medical and social welfare organisations, including many in the Greater London area. In 2005/06 the trust's assets stood at £1.9 million. It had an income of £247,000 and made grants totalling £54,000.

A list of beneficiaries was not available, however previous beneficiaries have included BF Shvut Ami, Chai – Lifeline and B'nai B'rith Hillel Fund, Child Resettlement, Children and Youth Aliyah, Finchley Synagogue, Jewish Care, Nightingale House, Norwood Ravenswood and Sidney Sussex CLL.

Exclusions No grants to branches of UK charities outside Barnet, non-registered charities and individuals.

Applications In writing to the correspondent.

The Sutasoma Trust

Education, general

£76,000 (2004/05)

Beneficial area UK and overseas.

Kett House, Station Road, Cambridge CB1 2JY

Tel. 01223 443 817

Correspondent Anna Brand

Trustees *Dr A R Hobart; M A Burgauer; J M Lichtenstein; Prof. B Kapferer.*

CC Number 803301

Information available Full accounts were available from the Charity Commission website.

General The trust's objectives are 'to advance education in particular by providing grants to graduate students in the social sciences and humanities' and general charitable purposes. In 2004/05 the trust had assets of £2.6 million and an income of £209,000. Grants were made totalling £76,000. The largest grants went to Lucy Cavendish College Fellowship (£15,000) and University of Bergen (£10,000).

Other grants included those made to Emslie Horniman Fund and School of Oriental and African Studies (£5,000 each), Kerala Council for Historical Research (£3,000), Amnesty International and the Corporation of Haverford (£2,000 each), Guildhall School Trust and Lewa Wildlife – Conservancy (£1,000 each) and Link Community – Kongo Primary (£250).

Applications In writing to the correspondent.

The Swan Trust

General, arts, culture

£35,000 (2004/05)

Beneficial area Overseas and the UK, with a preference for East Sussex, Kent, Surrey and West Sussex.

Pollen House, 10–12 Cork Street, London W1S 3LW

Tel. 020 7439 9061

Correspondent Laura Gosling

Trustee *The Cowdray Trust Limited.*

CC Number 261442

Information available Accounts were on file at the Charity Commission.

General The trust makes grants to a range of organisations including a number that are arts and culture related. Priority is given to grants for one year or less; grants for up to two years are considered.

In 2004/05 the trust had assets of £969,000, it had an income of £126,000 and 63 grants were made totalling £35,000. Grants were in the range of £20 and £5,000.

Grants included £5,000 each to St Paul's Church – Covent Garden and the Magdalen College Development Trust, £1,800 to Friends of Covent Garden, £1,500 to Royal National Theatre, £1,300 to Royal Academy Trust, £1,000 each to the Yehudi Menuhin School Limited, Withyham Parochial Church Council, Royal Horticultural Society, the National Portrait Gallery, Harrow Development Trust and Caryl Jenner Productions Ltd, £600 to English National Opera, £500 to the Chelsea Physic Garden Company, and £200 each to Campaign to Protect Rural England and Royal United Kingdom Beneficent Association and NSPCC.

Exclusions No grants to individuals or non-registered charities.

Applications In writing to the correspondent. Acknowledgements will only be sent if a grant is being made. The trust stated in January 2007 that it was fully subscribed until 2009.

The John Swire (1989) Charitable Trust

General

£210,000 (2005)
Beneficial area UK.

John Swire and Sons Ltd, Swire House, 59 Buckingham Gate, London SW1E 6AJ

Correspondent B N Swire, Trustee

Trustees *Sir John Swire; J S Swire; B N Swire; M C Robinson; Lady Swire.*

CC Number 802142

Information available Full accounts were on file at the Charity Commission.

General Established in 1989 by Sir John Swire of John Swire and Sons Ltd, merchants and ship owners, the trust supports a wide range of organisations including some in the area of arts,

welfare, education, medicine and research.

In 2005 the trust had assets of £11 million and an income of £1.7 million. Grants were made totalling £210,000. The largest grants included those to Selling PCC (£12,500), Selling Village Hall (£8,000) and the Canterbury Festival Foundation and the Soil Association Limited (£6,000 each).

Other grants included those to Prior's Court Foundation and the Rural Housing Trust(£5,000 each), the Royal Caledonian Ball Trust and University College Oxford (£2,500 each) and Atlantic Salmon Trust, Down's Syndrome Association, Irish Guards Benevolent Fund, Pavilion Opera Education Trust and Prostate Research Campaign UK (£1,000 each).

Applications In writing to the correspondent.

The Swire Charitable Trust

General

£412,000 (2005)
Beneficial area Worldwide.

John Swire and Sons Ltd, Swire House, 59 Buckingham Gate, London SW1E 6AJ

Tel. 020 7834 7717

Correspondent Michael Todhunter, Charities Administrator

Trustees *Sir J Swire; Sir Adrian Swire; B N Swire; M J B Todhunter; P A Johansen; J S Swine; J W J Hughes-Hallett.*

CC Number 270726

Information available Full accounts were on file at the Charity Commission.

General In 2005 the trust had an income of £402,000 almost entirely from donations received from John Swire & Sons Ltd. Grants totalled £412,000.

The trust made 78 grants of £1,000 or more, these were listed in the accounts. Beneficiaries of the eight largest grants were: Motor Neurone Disease Association (£72,000); St George University of London (£38,000); Wantage Nursing Home Charitable Trust (£50,000); Air League Educational Trust (£21,000); Priors Court Foundation (£15,000); and Book Aid International, Cystic Fibrosis Trust, and Project Trust (£10,000 each).

Other beneficiaries included: Shipwrights Ark Appeal – Worshipful Company of Shipwrights (£8,000); Voluntary Service Overseas (7,500); Combat Stress (£6,000); the Black Watch Association, Breast Cancer Haven, Brooklands Museum Trust Limited, International Care & Relief Limited, Marine Stewardship Council, the Salvation Army, the Stroke Association and the Trinity Sailing Trust (£5,000 each); Oxford Children's Hospital (£4,000); the Heritage of London Trust Limited (£3,000); All Saints Leighton Buzzard Preservation Trust, Commonwealth War Graves Commission, Head First, National Maritime Museum and Watermill Theatre Trust (£2,500 each); British Lung Foundation and Sightsavers International (£2,000 each); the English-Speaking Union and Save the Rhino (£1,500 each); and the Britain–Australian Society, British Eye Research Foundation, Dame Vera Lynn Trust for Children with Cerebral Palsy, Fight for Sight, the Kenyan Children's Project, King George's Fund for Sailors, REGAIN, Talking Newspapers Association of the United Kingdom and Westminster Children's Society (£1,000 each).

Grants of less than £1,000 each totalled £12,000.

Applications In writing to the correspondent. Applications are considered throughout the year.

The Hugh and Ruby Sykes Charitable Trust

General, medical, education, employment

£138,000 (2005/06)
Beneficial area Principally South Yorkshire, also Derbyshire.

The Coach House, Brookfield Manor, Hathersage, Hope Valley, Derbyshire S32 1BR

Tel. 01433 651190

Correspondent Brian Evans, Administrator

Trustees *Sir Hugh Sykes; Lady Sykes.*

CC Number 327648

Information available Accounts were on file at the Charity Commission, but without a list of grants.

General This trust was set up in 1987 for general charitable purposes by Sir Hugh Sykes and his wife Lady Sykes. It supports local charities in South Yorkshire and Derbyshire, some major UK charities and a few medical charities.

In 2005/06 the trust had an income of £128,000 and made grants totalling £138,000. Its assets stood at £2.3 million. A list of beneficiaries was not included in the accounts.

Exclusions No grants are made to individuals. Most grants are made to organisations which have a connection to one of the trustees.

Applications Applications can only be accepted from registered charities and should be in writing to the correspondent. In order to save administration costs, replies are not sent to unsuccessful applicants. If the trustees are able to consider a request for support, they aim to express interest within one month.

The Sylvanus Charitable Trust

Animal welfare, Roman Catholic

£30,000 in Europe (2005)
Beneficial area Europe and North America.

Vernor Miles and Noble, 5 Raymond Buildings, Gray's Inn, London WC1R 5DD
Tel. 020 7242 8688
Correspondent John C Vernor Miles, Trustee
Trustees *John C Vernor Miles; Alexander D Gemmill; Wilfred E Vernor Miles; Gloria Taviner.*
CC Number 259520
Information available Full accounts were on file at the Charity Commission.

General This trust was established in 1968 by the Countess of Kinnoull, who spent the last 40 years of her life in California, and supports the animal welfare, prevention of animal cruelty and the teachings and practices of the Roman Catholic Church. Organisations in North America and Europe are supported, with the trust splitting its finances into two sections, the sterling section (Europe) and the dollar section (North America) to avoid currency troubles.

As the dollar section focuses on US giving only (and information on it was unavailable) only the sterling section is described here. It had assets of £1.7 million, which generated an income of £50,000. Grants were made to 16 organisations totalling £30,000.

These were: £10,000 to Fraternity of Saint Pius X, £6,000 to Mauritian Wildlife Foundation, £7,500 to University College Oxford, £2,000 each to FRAME, Help in Suffering and SPCA Zimbabwe, £1,000 each to Blue Cross, Born Free Foundation, Care for the Wild, Durrell Wildlife Conservation Trust, Environmental Investigation Agency, Fauna & Flora International and World Society for the Protection of Animals and £500 each to Quintinha dos Animais Abandonados and Refugio dos Burro de Estombar.

Exclusions No grants for expeditions, scholarships or individuals.

Applications In writing to the correspondent. The trustees meet once a year.

The Tabeel Trust

Evangelical Christian

£53,000 (2004/05)
Beneficial area Worldwide.

Dairy House Farm, Great Holland, Frinton-on-Sea, Essex CO13 0EX
Tel. 01255 812130
Correspondent D K Brown, Secretary
Trustees *K A Brown, Chair; D K Brown; Mrs P M Brown; Mrs B J Carter; Dr M P Clark; Mrs J A Richardson; J Davey; Mrs H M Hazelwood; Mrs S Taylor.*
CC Number 266645
Information available Full accounts were on file at the Charity Commission.

General In 2004/05 this trust had assets amounting to £1.1 million and an income of £42,000. Grants were made to 34 organisations totalling £53,000.

Beneficiaries included Tabernacle Baptist Church – Generation Bangladesh Project (£3,000), Barnabas Fund and Frontier Youth Trust (£2,000 each), Christian Viewpoint for Men, Kingdom Trust, OICCU – mission expenses and TWR – Africa (£1,000 each) and Evangelical Alliance, Christian Institute, London City Mission and On The Move (£500).

Applications In writing to 'the trustee who has an interest in the project', i.e.

only charities with which a trustee already has contact should apply. Grants are considered at trustees' meetings in May and November.

The Talbot Village Trust

General

£103,000 authorised and paid (2005)
Beneficial area The boroughs of Bournemouth, Christchurch and Poole; the districts of east Dorset and Purbeck.

Dickinson Manser, 5 Parkstone Road, Poole, Dorset BH15 2NL
Tel. 01202 673071
Email garycox@dickinsonmanser.co.uk
Correspondent Gary S Cox, Clerk
Trustees *C J Lees, Chair; Sir T E Lees; J R G Fleming; Sir G C C T G Meyrick; H W Plunkett-Ernle-Erle-Drax; Sir T M J Salt; J R Gibson.*
CC Number 249349
Information available Accounts were obtained from the Charity Commission's website.

General As well as making grants, this trust also gives extensive support to charities in the form of loans. In addition, the charity owns and manages land and property at Talbot Village, Bournemouth, including almshouses which it maintains through an associated trust. There is a strong property focus to much of the trust's work.

In 2005 the trust had assets of almost £30 million and an income of £1.5 million of which £807,000 was obtained from rents. Grants authorised and paid during the year totalled £103,000 whilst donations authorised but left unpaid totalled £405,000.

Grants authorised and paid during the year went to:

- Mental After Care Association, towards refurbishment of Kings House Westbourne (£50,000)
- Christ Church – Creekmoor, towards alternations to the main church to increase space, modernisation of the kitchen, provision of toilets for people who are disabled and the replacement of furnishings (£15,000)

- SWOP – Cherry Tree Nursery, towards building a new room (£10,000)
- Whizz-Kidz, towards the purchase of specialist mobility equipment for up to six children within the trustees' area of benefit (£8,000)
- Christian Association for Youth, towards the replacement of equipment (£5,000)
- St Luke's Church – Winton, towards the provision of toilets for the people who are disabled (£5,000)
- Canford Heath First School, towards new play equipment and sheltered area (£4,000)
- Motor Neurone Disease Association, towards the purchase of computers (£3,000)
- St Mary's Church – Winterbourne Zelston, towards repairs to the tower roof (£2,500).

Exclusions No grants for individuals.

Applications In writing to the correspondent.

Talteg Ltd

Jewish, welfare

£273,000 (2005)

Beneficial area UK, with a preference for Scotland.

90 Mitchell Street, Glasgow G1 3NQ

Correspondent F S Berkeley, Trustee

Trustees *F S Berkeley, Chair; M Berkeley; A Berkeley; A N Berkeley; M Berkeley; Miss D L Berkeley.*

CC Number 283253

Information available Accounts were on file at the Charity Commission, but without a grants list or a narrative report.

General In 2005 the trust had assets totalling £3.2 million and an income of £381,000. Grants were made during the year totalling £273,000. Unfortunately a list of grants has not been available since 1993.

Previous beneficiaries include British Friends of Laniado Hospital, Centre for Jewish Studies, Society of Friends of the Torah, Glasgow Jewish Community Trust, National Trust for Scotland, Ayrshire Hospice, Earl Haig Fund – Scotland and RSSPCC.

Applications In writing to the correspondent.

The Lady Tangye Charitable Trust

Catholic, overseas aid, general

£29,000 (2005/06)

Beneficial area UK and worldwide, with some preference for the Midlands.

55 Warwick Crest, Arthur Road, Birmingham B15 2LH

Correspondent The Clerk

Trustees *Gitta Clarisse Gilzean Tangye; Colin Ferguson Smith.*

CC Number 1044220

Information available Accounts are on file at the Charity Commission.

General This trust has general charitable purposes, with a preference for work in the Midlands or developing world. Christian and environmental causes are well-represented in the grants list.

In 2005/06 it had assets of £451,000, which generated an income of £30,000. Grants were made to 20 organisations totalling £29,000.

Beneficiaries included: West Midland Urban Wildlife Trust (£3,000); Aid to the Church in Need, Childline Midlands, Father O'Mahoney Memorial Trust and Tettenhall Horse Sanctuary (£2,000 each); Amnesty International, Crew Trust, Friends of the Royal Botanical Gardens – Kew, Priest Training Fund and St Giles Hospice (£1,500 each); European Children's Trust, Leonard Cheshire Foundation, Middlemore Homes, Walsall and District Samaritans and VSO (£1,000 each); and St Saviours Church (£500).

Applications In writing to the correspondent.

The Tanner Trust

General

£432,000 (2005/06)

Beneficial area UK, with a slight preference for the south of England, and overseas.

c/o Blake Lapthorn Linnell, Harbour Court, Compass Road, Portsmouth PO6 4ST

Correspondent The Trust Administrator

Trustees *Mrs Alice P Williams; Mrs Lucie Nottingham; Robert Foster.*

CC Number 1021175

Information available Full accounts were on file at the Charity Commission.

General This trust has general charitable purposes, supporting organisations worldwide. The grants list shows no cause or geographical regions favoured or missing, although there appear to be many organisations concerned with youth, welfare and relief work.

In 2005/06 the trust had assets of £5.2 million, an income of £380,000 and made about 150 grants totalling £432,000.

Beneficiaries included: Shelterbox Appeal (£15,000); Greenhouse Schools Project (£6,000); Alzheimer's Society, Chase Hospice Care for Children, Community Action Nepal, Cornwall Community Foundation, DEC – Niger, Friends of Royal Cornwall Hospital, Independent Age, Hedgerely Parish Church Council, Historic Chapels Trust, Listening Books, Lord Lieutenants fund for Youth in Cornwall, Oxfordshire Community Foundation, Mango Tree Orphan Support Programme and National Trust (£5,000 each); Cornwall Trust for Nature Conservation (£4,900); Christ The Worker Church Centre, Cornwall Mobility Centre, Country Holidays for Inner City Kids and Deafblind UK (£4,000 each); 3 Villages Youth Project, Helford River Children's Sailing Trust, and the Industrial Trust (£3,000 each); Abbeyfield, Action for Children in Conflict, Elizabeth Finn Care, Gurkha Welfare Trust, Leprosy Mission, National Children's Homes and Schizophrenia Society (£2,000 each); Museum of Garden History (£1,500); Cinnamon Trust, Living Paintings, St Christopher's Fellowship and Society for the Protection of Animals Abroad (£1,000 each); Gurkha Museum (£750); and Oxfordshire Deaf and Hard of Hearing Centre (£200).

Exclusions No grants to individuals.

Applications The trust states that unsolicited applications are, without exception, not considered. Support is only given to charities personally known to the trustees.

The Lili Tapper Charitable Foundation

Jewish

£29,000 (2004/05)

Beneficial area UK.

c/o KPMG LLP, St James' Square, Manchester M2 6DS

Correspondent The Trustees

Trustees M Webber; J Webber.

CC Number 268523

Information available Accounts were on file at the Charity Commission.

General The trust supports organisations benefiting Jewish people.

In 2004/05 it had assets of £2.6 million, which generated an income of £118,000. Grants were made to eight organisations totalling £29,000. Beneficiaries were: UJIA (£10,000); CST and Manchester Jewish Foundation (£5,000 each); Teenage Cancer Trust (£3,000); Keshet Eilon (£2,600); Israel Educational Foundation (£2,500); Chicken Shed Theatre Company (£1,000); and Jewish Representation Council (£120).

Exclusions No grants to individuals.

Applications The trust states that it does not respond to any unsolicited applications.

The Tay Charitable Trust

General

About 200,000 (2004/05)

Beneficial area UK, with a preference for Scotland, particularly Dundee.

6 Douglas Terrace, Broughty Ferry, Dundee DD5 1EA

Correspondent Mrs Elizabeth A Mussen, Trustee

Trustees Mrs E A Mussen; Mrs Z C Martin; G C Bonar.

SC Number SC001004

Information available Basic information was available on this trust.

General This trust has general charitable purposes and supports a wide range of causes. Grants are generally made to UK-wide charities or organisations benefiting Scotland or Dundee, although local groups elsewhere can also be supported.

In 2004/05 the trust had an income of £213,000. No further information was available for this year. In the previous year it had assets of £4.2 million and an income of £176,000. Grants were made to 210 charities totalling £178,000, including 126 smaller grants of less than £1,000 totalling £62,000.

The largest grants were made to Dundee Congregational Church (£7,000) and Dundee Heritage Trust, LINK and RNLI (£5,000 each). Other beneficiaries included Dermatrust (£3,000) and Bobath Scotland, Byre Theatre, John Muir Trust, Little Sisters of the Poor and TICR (£2,000 each).

Recipients of £1,000 each included the following: Amnesty International, Alzheimer's Scotland, Breakthrough Breast Cancer, Camphill Village Trust, CSC Scotland, Drugscope, Dundee West Church, Edinburgh International Festival, Great Ormond Street Hospital, Marine Conservation, National Counselling Service Dundee, National Youth Choir of Scotland, Prison Fellowship Trust, Scottish Centre for Motor Impairments, Trees for Life and Tay Sailing Association.

Exclusions Grants are only given to charities recognised by the Inland Revenue. No grants to individuals.

Applications No standard form; applications in writing to the correspondent, including a financial statement. An sae is appreciated.

C B and H H Taylor 1984 Trust

Quaker, general

£199,000 (2005/06)

Beneficial area West Midlands, Ireland and overseas.

c/o Home Farm, Abberton, Worcestershire WR10 2NR

Correspondent W J B Taylor, Trustee

Trustees Mrs C H Norton; Mrs E J Birmingham; J A B Taylor; W J B Taylor; Mrs C M Penny; T W Penny; R J Birmingham; S B Taylor.

CC Number 291363

Information available Accounts were on file at the Charity Commission.

General The trust's geographical areas of benefit are:

- organisations serving Birmingham and the West Midlands
- organisations outside the West Midlands where the trust has well-established links
- organisations in Ireland
- UK-based charities working overseas.

The general areas of benefit are:

- the Religious Society of Friends (Quakers) and other religious denominations
- healthcare projects
- social welfare: community groups; children and young people; older people; disadvantaged people; people with disabilities; homeless people; housing initiatives; counselling and mediation agencies
- education: adult literacy schemes; employment training; youth work
- penal affairs: work with offenders and ex-offenders; police projects
- the environment and conservation work
- the arts: museums and art galleries; music and drama
- Ireland: cross-community health and social welfare projects
- UK charities working overseas on long-term development projects.

About 60% of grants are for the work and concerns of the Religious Society of Friends (Quakers). The trust favours specific applications. It does not usually award grants on an annual basis for revenue costs. Applications are encouraged from minority groups and women-led initiatives. Grants, which are made only to or through registered charities, range from £500 to £3,000. Larger grants are seldom awarded.

In 2005/06 it had assets of £7.4 million and an income of £258,000. Grants to 132 organisations totalled £199,000.

The largest grant, of £25,000, went to Britain Yearly Meeting. Other beneficiaries included: Quaker Peace and Social Witness (£8,000 in two grants); Warwickshire Monthly Meeting (£7,000); FWCC (£5,000); Cape Town Quaker Peace Centre, Family Service Unit and Quaker Social Action (£4,000 each); CYPC (£3,500); Family Service Unit, Friends House Library, Fry Housing Trust, FWCC Ramallah, Money for Madagascar and Worcester Snoezelen (£3,000 each); Salvation Army (£2,500); Amnesty International and Responding to Conflict (£2,000 each); Leap and Relate Birmingham (£1,500 each); Anti

Slavery Project Sudan, Caring for the Carers Northern Ireland, Life Education Centre and Refugee Council (£1,000 each); and Dhaka Ahsania Mission, Settle Friends, Traidcraft Exchange and Wells for India (£500 each).

Exclusions The trust does not fund: individuals (whether for research, expeditions, educational purposes and so on); local projects or groups outside the West Midlands; or projects concerned with travel or adventure.

Applications There is no formal application form. Applicants should write to the correspondent giving the charity's registration number, a brief description of the charity's activities, and details of the specific project for which the grant is being sought. Applicants should also include a budget of the proposed work, together with a copy of the charity's most recent accounts. Trustees will also wish to know what funds have already been raised for the project and how the shortfall will be met.

The trust states that it receives more applications than it can support. Therefore, even if work falls within its policy it may not be able to help, particularly if the project is outside the West Midlands.

Trustees meet twice each year, in May and November.

Applications will be acknowledged if an sae is provided.

The Cyril Taylor Charitable Trust

Education

£32,000 to organisations (2005/06)

Beneficial area Generally in Greater London.

Penningtons, Bucklersbury House, 83 Cannon Street, London EC4N 8PE

Tel. 020 7457 3000 **Fax** 020 7457 3240

Email lintottcj@penningtons.co.uk

Correspondent Christopher Lintott, Trustee

Trustees *Sir Cyril Taylor, Chair; Clifford D Joseph; Robert W Maas; Peter A Tchereprine; M Stephen Rasch; Christopher Lintott.*

CC Number 1040179

Information available Accounts were on file at the Charity Commission.

General This trust makes grants to organisations benefiting students in particular those studying at Richmond College and the American International University in London.

In 2005/06 the trust had an income of just £3 (£39,000 in 2004/05). Grants totalled £32,000. Beneficiaries included: Richmond Foundation (£25,000); Institute of Economic Affairs and the British Friends of Harvard Business School (£3,000 each); RHS Kew Appeal (£1,000 each) and the Cornwallis School Voluntary Fund (£500).

Applications In writing to the correspondent.

Rosanna Taylor's 1987 Charity Trust

General

£50,000 (2005/06)

Beneficial area UK and overseas, with a preference for Oxfordshire and West Sussex.

Pollen House, 10–12 Cork Street, London W1S 3LW

Correspondent The Secretary

Trustee *The Cowdray Trust Limited.*

CC Number 297210

Information available Accounts were on file at the Charity Commission.

General This trust has general charitable purposes, including support for medical, cancer, child development and environmental charities.

In 2005/06 the trust had assets of £1.2 million, an income of £29,000 and made grants totalling £50,000. Donations were made to Charities Aid Foundation (£28,000) and Pearson Taylor Trust (£22,000).

Exclusions No grants to individuals or non-registered charities.

Applications In writing to the correspondent. Acknowledgements are not sent to unsuccessful applicants.

Tegham Limited

Orthodox Jewish faith, welfare

£197,000 (2004/05)

Beneficial area UK.

1 Hallswelle Road, London NW11 0DH

Correspondent Mrs S Fluss, Trustee

Trustees *Mrs S Fluss; Miss N Fluss.*

CC Number 283066

Information available Accounts were on file at the Charity Commission but without a list of grants.

General This trust supports the promotion of the Jewish Orthodox faith and the relief of poverty.

In 2004/05 the trust had assets of £1.6 million, an income of £227,000 and made grants totaling £197,000. Unfortunately no grants list was available for this period.

Applications In writing to the correspondent, although the trust stated that it has enough causes to support and does not welcome other applications.

Thackray Medical Research Trust

History of medical products and of their supply trade

£153,000 (2005/06)

Beneficial area Worldwide.

c/o Thackray Museum, Beckett Street, Leeds LS9 7LN

Correspondent Martin Schweiger, Chair of the Trustees

Trustees *Martin Schweiger, Chair; Richard Keeler; Christin Thackray; Stanley Warren; Matthew Wrigley; William Mathie.*

CC Number 702896

Information available Accounts were on file at the Charity Commission.

General This trust is concerned with two aspects of medical products: their history with particular emphasis on the medical supplies trade; and their charitable supply and development for third world countries. The trust initiated and supported the establishment of the award-winning Thackray Museum in Leeds, one of the largest medical museums in the world, and continues to support the research resource there, to provide a unique information centre for the history of medical products and the medical supplies trade worldwide.

The 2005/06 annual report states that: 'The trust wishes to encourage grant applications from international medical supply charities for pump-priming funds or project launch funds.'

Medical supply organisations

'Grants are provided for charitable organisations which specialise in supplying medical equipment to or within the developing world. Support is unlikely to be for actual funding of equipment purchases but instead may be for 'pump-priming', start-up or organisational expenses where alternative funding is not available. Preference will be given where the charity is involved in value-for-money projects e.g. the supply of used rather than new equipment.

'The likely maximum grant for any one applicant in a single year is £10,000.'

Research into the history of medicine

'The trust supports high quality research by experienced individuals and groups into the history of medicine and medical products. Applicants should be within recognised relevant units in universities in the UK, EU and Commonwealth. They will be expected to possess a doctorate or clinical qualification and preference will be given to applicants who have already had some work published in an appropriate field. A senior member of the relevant unit must sponsor the application and undertake to monitor progress on the project.

'Support is available in the form of reimbursement of expenses, and in some cases subsistence costs over a maximum period of three years. Grants will not normally exceed £20,000 in cases where subsistence costs are to be covered and £2,000 in other cases.'

In 2005/06 it had assets of almost £6 million and an income, of £204,000. Grants awarded totalled £153,000, of which £150,000 went to the Thackray Museum. A further £3,000 went to the Liverpool School of Tropical Medicine.

Applications In writing to the correspondent. The trustees usually meet twice a year.

The Thames Wharf Charity

General

£228,000 (2004/05)

Beneficial area UK.

c/o Lee Associates, 5 Southampton Place, London WC1A 2DA

Correspondent G H Camamile, Trustee

Trustees *P H Burgess; G H Camamile; G C Stirk; A Lotay.*

CC Number 1000796

Information available Accounts were on file at the Charity Commission.

General In 2004/05 the charity had assets of £258,000, an income of £115,000 and made grants to about 150 organisations totalling £228,000.

The largest grants went to Goldschmied Foundation (£62,000), Glebe Court Residents Support Group (£16,000) and Architectural Association – Stephen Lawrence Scholarship Fund (£10,000).

There were over 50 further grants of £1,000 or more. Other beneficiaries included Mossbourne Community Academy (£8,500), Cancer Research UK (£5,400), Serpentine Gallery (£4,200), Special Trustees of Moorfields Eye Hospital (£4,500), Disasters Emergency Committee (£4,100), Indian Gymkhana Club Trust 2004 (£4,000), Médecins Du Monde – UK (£3,900), Friends of Vineyard School (£3,800), Integrated Neurological Services (£3,000), Addenbrookes Hospital – Liver Transplants Department (£2,800), BUKKA Education and Research Trust (£1,800), Mark Lees Foundation (£1,500), Music Space Trust (£1,100) and Drukpa Kargyud Trust and Sir Steve Redgrave Charitable Trust (£1,000 each).

Beneficiaries of smaller grants included Oxfam (£800), London Cyclists Trust (£500), Royal Marsden Hospital Charity (£430), National Gallery (£400), Trinity Hospice (£300) Parkinson's Disease Society (£280) and Woodland Trust (£100).

Exclusions No grants for the purchase of property, motor vehicles or holidays.

Applications In writing to the correspondent.

Lisa Thaxter Trust

Children and adolescents with cancer in the UK

£93,000 (2005/06)

Beneficial area UK.

1 Betjeman Close, Coulson, Surrey CR5 2LU

Website www.lisathaxter.org

Trustees *Mrs Gillian Lesley Thaxter, Chair, Andrew Day; Anthony James Kirk; Mrs Denise Clarke; Geoffrey Gordon Thaxter; Dr Michael Stevens.*

CC Number 1056017

Information available Full accounts were available from the Charity Commission website.

General Established in 1996, the trust provides grants to organisations that provide support to children and adolescents with cancer and their families. In 2005/06 the trust had assets of £163,000. Its income totalled £116,000, of which 38% came from It's A Wrap charity gift-wrapping service. Other sources of income included monies from fundraising, sponsorship and Gift Aid. Grants totalled £93,000 and were broken down as follows:

Grants to organisations – 3 grants totalling £16,000

Grants went to Theodora Trust (£8,000), Over the Wall Gang (£7,000) and Martin House (£500).

Sponsorship of Research – 3 grants totalling £40,000

Royal Marsden Children's Cancer Unit (£23,000), Coventry University study (£12,000) and Burkitt's Lymphoma – Africa Project (£4,000).

Advice and Information – 1 grant of £36,000

The sole beneficiary was *Contact* Magazine.

The trust specialises in 'pump-priming' programmes that advance both treatment and care. Grants of up to £20,000 per annum are considered. Organisations who may apply can include research and hospital units, or other organisations helping children and adolescents with cancer, for example parent groups.

Programmes need to be able to demonstrate an end result, or be capable of continuation beyond the grant period. The trust will not normally consider requests to support individual treatment or hardship grants.

Applications In writing to the correspondent.

The Theodore Trust

Christian education

Income of £40,000 a year
Beneficial area UK.

3 Upper King Street, Norwich NR3 1RL
Tel. 01603 610 481
Correspondent G W Woolsey Brown
Trustees *Revd D J Baker, Chair; Revd J E Barnes; Right Hon. J S Gummer MP; G W Woolsey Brown.*
CC Number 1008532
Information available Accounts were on file at the Charity Commission, but only up to 1996 on the public screen and up to 1995 in the public files.

General The trust aims to support the advancement of Christianity by way of education.

The trust previously told us that its income is around £40,000 each year. It did not state its grant total, but said that during the three years 1999 to 2001 grants had included: £30,000 in three grants to Sarum College for Institute of Liturgy; £15,000 each to Anglican Centre in Rome for their library and to Catholic Central Library; £10,000 to Let the Children Live to help fund a Christian television station in South America; £5,000 to St Dimitry's Orphanage in Moscow; £3,000 to Catholic Student Council; £2,500 to International Theological Institute; and £1,400 to Newman Conference at Oxford for attenders' expenses.

This list of grants shows that the grant total must have risen considerably since 1995, when grants totalled £6,300.

Exclusions No grants to individuals.

Applications In writing to the correspondent.

The Thistle Trust

Arts

£38,000 (2005/06)
Beneficial area UK.

PO Box 57005, 30 Gresham Street, London EC2P 2US
Correspondent Nicholas Robert Kerr-Sheppard, Secretary
Trustees *Madeleine, Lady Kleinwort; Nigel Porteous; Neil Morris; Donald McGilvray; Nicholas Kerr-Sheppard.*
CC Number 1091327
Information available Accounts were on file at the Charity Commission.

General This trust was established in 2002, and during the following year it received a £1 million endowment from the settlor.

Its main objectives are to promote study and research in the arts and to further public knowledge and education of art.

In 2005/06 the trust had assets of £1.4 million and an income of £46,000. Grants totalled £38,000.

Grants were made to: Sir John Soane's Museum and Tate Modern (£10,000 each); Whitechapel Auto Gallery Trustee Ltd (£5,000); London Symphony Orchestra (£4,200); Gate Theatre (£3,000); Pursued by a Bear (£2,800); Menagerie Theatre Co. Ltd (£2,000); and Sussex Chorus (£1,000).

Exclusions No grants to individuals.

Applications In writing to the correspondent including most recent report and financial accounts. The trustees meet at least once a year with only successful applicants notified of the trustees' decision.

The Loke Wan Tho Memorial Foundation

Environment, medical causes, conservation organisations and overseas aid organisations

£45,000 (2004/05)
Beneficial area Worldwide.

Abacus Financial Services Ltd, La Motte Chambers, St Helier, Jersey, Channel Islands JE1 1BJ
Tel. 01534 602000 **Fax** 01534 602002
Correspondent Irene Fadden, Administrator

Trustees *Lady Y P McNeice; Mrs T S Tonkyn; A P Tonkyn.*
CC Number 264273
Information available Accounts were obtained from the Charity Commission website.

General In 2004/05 it had assets of £3.4 million and an income of £703,000. Grants totalled £45,000. The trust supports environment/conservation organisations, medical causes and overseas aid organisations.

Grants included £10,000 to Animals Asia, £6,000 to Wildfowl & Wetlands Trust, £5,000 each to Merlin, Reed's School Foundation Appeal, Health Unlimited, World Land Trust and Bio Regional Development Group, £2,000 to The Royal Veterinary College Animal Care Trust, £1,000 to Contact the Elderly and £500 each to the Fishermen's Mission and the Children's Adventure Farm Trust.

Applications In writing to the correspondent.

The Sue Thomson Foundation

Christ's Hospital School, education

£64,000 (2005/06)
Beneficial area UK with a particular interest in Sussex and London.

Furners Keep, Furners Lane, Henfield, West Sussex BN5 9HS
Tel. 01273 493461 **Fax** 01273 495139
Email susanmitchell@macdream.net
Correspondent Mrs S M Mitchell, Trustee
Trustees *Mrs S M Mitchell; C L Corman; Susannah Holliman; Timothy Binnington.*
CC Number 298808
Information available Accounts were on file at the Charity Commission.

General The foundation exists to support children in need in the UK, mainly by helping Christ's Hospital and the school in Horsham which caters specifically for children in need. Other areas of support include educational and self-help organisations and projects. Grants are awarded within one of three levels of financial support:

- Major grants which can be above £3,000 in any one year;
- Medium grants which can be from £500 to £3,000 in any one year;
- Special grants which can be up to £3,000 per year for periods of 1 to 3 years.

In 2005/06 the trust had assets of £2.6 million and an income of £142,000. Grants paid totalled £64,000, divided between education (£46,000); and welfare (£18,000).

Major grants
The majority of the funds went to Christ's Hospital, which received £43,000. The foundation nominates one new entrant each year from a needy background to the school, subject to the child meeting Christ's Hospital's own admissions criteria academically, socially and in terms of need. The foundation commits to contributing to the child's costs at a level agreed with Christ's Hospital for as long as each of them remains in the school.

Medium grants
It is the policy of the trustees to provide up to 10% of the foundation's available income each year for grants in this category, subject to the foundation's commitments to Christ's Hospital having been satisfied. Charities eligible for consideration for grants at this level include:

- Charities related to Christ's Hospital including the sister school, King Edward's – Witley;
- UK booktrade charities, including the charities of the Worshipful Company of Stationers and Newspaper Makers;
- Suitable grant-making charities selected in recognition of pro-bono professional work done for the foundation by its trustees or others;
- Special situations or other applications at the trustees' discretion.

Grants in this category may be spread over a period of years.

Special grants
It is the policy of the trustees to set aside a further 10% of available income each year for this programme, subject to its commitments in the major and medium categories and other financial needs having been met. Special grants are awarded to up to four small charities at any one time. They are confined to charities that support young and older people in need through no fault of their own, often via well run small self-help organisations, usually at a local level in Sussex or London.

Donations included: £4,300 to Dechert Charitable Trust; £2,500 to LOGOS –

Oregon; £2,000 to the Book Trade Benevolent Society; £1,600 to King Edward's School – Witley; £750 to the Publishing Training Centre; £550 to National Blind Children's Society; £500 each to British Ethnic Health Awareness Foundation, Discovery Camps Trust, Homestart – Eastleigh, Let's Face It, the Stationers' Benevolent Fund and the Wildlife Trust; £300 to the Children's Adventure Trust; and £250 each to the Highfield Centre, Operation New World, Threshold Women's Mental Health Initiative, Strongbones Children's Charitable Trust, Tiny Tim's Children's Centre and Unity Conductive Education.

Exclusions No grants to large, national charities (except Christ's Hospital) or individuals, except as part of a specific scheme. No research projects, charities concerned with animals, birds, the environment, gardens or historic buildings. Unsolicited applications are not acknowledged, unless accompanied by an sae.

Applications In writing to the correspondent, or preliminary telephone enquiry.

The Thornton Foundation

General
£215,000 (2005/06)
Beneficial area UK.

Stephenson Harwood, 1 St Paul's Churchyard, London EC4M 8SH
Tel. 020 7329 4422
Correspondent A H Isaacs
Trustees R C Thornton, Chair; A H Isaacs; H D C Thornton; Mrs S J Thornton.
CC Number 326383
Information available Accounts are on file at the Charity Commission.

General The objective of the foundation is to make grants to charities selected by the trustees. The principal guideline of the trust is to use the funds to further charitable causes where their money will, as far as possible, act as 'high powered money', in other words be of significant use to the cause. Only causes that are known personally to the trustees and/or that they are able to investigate thoroughly are supported. The trust states it is proactive rather than reactive in seeking applicants.

In 2005/06 the trust had assets of £4.7 million, which generated an income of £57,000. Grants totalling £215,000 were made to 19 organisations, of which many were supported in the previous year.

The largest grants were £50,000 to Peper Harrow, £40,000 in two grants to the National Gallery, £32,000 to Institute of Cancer Research, £17,000 to HMS Trincomolee Trust and £10,000 each to the Cirdan Sailing Trust, Keble College – Oxford and Stowe School Foundation.

Other beneficiaries included Achievement Trust (£8,000), Action for Blind People and Books Abroad (£5,000 each), the Handel Society and Museum of London (£1,000 each) and Prostate Campaign UK (£500).

Applications The trust strongly emphasises that it does not accept unsolicited applications, and, as it states above, only organisations that are known to one of the trustees will be considered for support. Any unsolicited applications will not receive a reply.

The Thornton Trust

Evangelical Christianity, education, relief of sickness and poverty
£167,000 (2004/05)
Beneficial area UK and overseas.

Hunters Cottage, Hunters Yard, Debden Road, Saffron Walden, Essex CB11 4AA
Correspondent D H Thornton, Trustee
Trustees D H Thornton; Mrs B Y Thornton; J D Thornton.
CC Number 205357
Information available Accounts were on file at the Charity Commission.

General This trust was created in 1962 for 'the promotion of and furthering of education and the Evangelical Christian faith, and assisting in the relief of sickness, suffering and poverty'.

In 2004/05 it had assets of £1.3 million and an income of £66,000. Grants were made to over 70 organisations totalling £167,000.

The two largest grants went to Saffron Walden Baptist Church (£35,000) and Africa Inland Mission (£17,000).

Other beneficiaries included Keswick Convention (£7,500), Beulah Trust (£6,100), Redcliffe Missionary College (£6,000), Bible Society, London City Mission and Tyndale House (£5,000 each), Youth with a Mission (£4,500), Mildmay Mission Hospital (£3,500), Tear Fund (£3,000), Care for the Family, Crusaders Union, Mission Aviation Fellowship, Scripture Union and Stort Valley Schools Trust (£2,500 each), DEC Tsunami Earthquake Appeal, London School of Theology and Middle East Christian Outreach Ltd (£2,000 each), Evangelical Alliance (£1,600) and International Fellowship of Evangelical Students (£1,500).

Grants of £1,000 or less included those to Bishops Down Baptist Church, Christian Theatre Company, Church of Scotland – Killin, Hertfordshire Community Foundation, National Library for the Blind, National Prayer Breakfast and Stroud Green Baptist Church (£1,000 each), World Trumpet Mission (£550), Christian Viewpoint for Men and RAF Benevolent Fund (£500 each), Carers Christian Fellowship (£250), All Nations Christian College (£300), Help a Local Child (£100) and Young Life Hertford (£100).

Applications The trust states: 'Our funds are fully committed and we regret that we are unable to respond to the many unsolicited calls for assistance we are now receiving.'

The Three Oaks Trust

Welfare

£192,000 to organisations (2005/06)

Beneficial area Overseas, UK, with a preference for West Sussex.

The Three Oaks Family Trust Co. Ltd, PO Box 243, Crawley, West Sussex RH10 6YB

Email contact@thethreeoakstrust.co.uk

Website www.thethreeoakstrust.co.uk

Correspondent The Trustees

Trustees *Mrs M E Griffin; Mrs C A Johnson; Mrs P A Wilkinson; Dr P Kane; Mrs S A Kane.*

CC Number 297079

Information available Accounts were on file at the Charity Commission.

General The trust regularly supports the same welfare organisations in the UK and overseas each year. Grants are also to individuals via statutory authorities or voluntary agencies.

In 2005/06 the trust had assets of £6.1 million and a total income of £230,000. Grants were made totalling £247,000 of which £192,000 was donated to organisations and £44,000 to individuals. Grants were broken down as follows, shown here with examples of beneficiaries:

Within the UK – 26 grants totalling £122,000
HCS (£12,000); Crawley Open House and NCYPE (£10,000 each); Raynaud's Association (£7,500); Back to Work (£7,000); Parkinson's Disease Association, the Hardman Trust, Norton House, Let's Face it and Mankind UK (£5,000 each); Manor Gardens Welfare Trust (£2,000); and Disability Aid Fund (£2,000 in four grants).

Overseas aid – 22 grants totalling £71,000
Kaloko Trust – Zambia (£17,000 in four grants); ICT Shilpa (£10,000 in two grants); SAIDIA – Kenya and Wells for India (£5,000 each); and Computer Aid International – Zambia (£3,000).

Exclusions No direct applications from individuals. Applications from students for gap-year activities are not a priority and will not be funded.

Applications The trust's 2005/06 annual report stated: 'The directors intend to continue supporting the organisations that they have supported in the past and are not planning to fund any new projects in the near future. To save administration costs, the directors do not respond to requests, unless they are considering making a donation.'

The Thriplow Charitable Trust

Higher education and research

£85,000 (2005/06)

Beneficial area Preference for British institutions.

PO Box 243, Cambridge CB3 9PQ

Correspondent Mrs E Mackintosh, Secretary

Trustees *Sir Peter Swinnerton-Dyer; Dr Harriet Crawford; Prof. Karen Sparck Jones; Prof. Christopher Bayly.*

CC Number 1025531

Information available Accounts were on file at the charity Commission.

General The charity was established by a trust deed in 1983. Its main aims are the furtherance of higher and further education and research, with preference given to British institutions.

Projects that have generally been supported in the past include contributions to research study funds, research fellowships, academic training schemes, computer facilities and building projects. Specific projects are preferred rather than contributions to general running costs. The trust prefers to support smaller projects where grants can 'make a difference'.

In 2005/06 it had assets of £3.6 million, an income of £82,000 and gave 21 grants totalling £85,000.

Beneficiaries included: Foundation of Research Students (£10,000); Cambridge University Library and Fitzwilliam Museum (£8,000 each); Centre of South Asian Studies and University of Reading (£6,000 each); Computer Aid International (£5,000); Loughborough University (£3,800); Fight for Sight, Foundation for Prevention of Blindness, Hearing Research Trust, Royal Botanic Gardens and Transplant Trust (£3,000 each); Inspire Foundation and, Transplant Trust and Royal College of Music (£2,000 each); and Marie Curie Cancer Care (£1,900).

Exclusions Grants can only be made to charitable bodies or component parts of charitable bodies. In no circumstances can grants be made to individuals.

Applications There is no application form. A letter of application should specify the purpose for which funds are sought and the costings of the project. It should be indicated whether other applications for funds are pending and, if the funds are to be channelled to an individual or a small group, what degree of supervision over the quality of the work would be exercised by the institution. Trustee meetings are held twice a year – in spring and in autumn.

The Tillett Trust

Classical music

£36,000 (2005/06)
Beneficial area UK.

Courtyard House, Neopardy, Crediton, Devon EX17 5EP

Tel. 01363 777844 **Fax** 01363 777845

Email tilletttrust@tiscali.co.uk

Website www.thetilletttrust.org.uk

Correspondent Miss K Avey, Secretary to the Trust

Trustees *Paul Strang, Chair; Miss Fiona Grant; Miss Yvonne Minton; David Stiff; Miss Clara Taylor; Howard Davis; Paul Harris.*

CC Number 257329

Information available Accounts were on file at the Charity Commission.

General The trust supports young classical musicians of outstanding ability in the UK. Funds are directed at the start of their professional careers to help them obtain performing experience. It is not normally available to individuals for the support of study courses, either undergraduate or postgraduate, although postgraduate bursaries are awarded annually to nominees from each of the main UK conservatoires. Grants are also made to organisations which provide opportunities for young performers and money is put into the trust's own performance scheme, Young Artists' Platform.

In 2005/06 the trust had assets of £718,000, an income of £25,000 and made grants totalling £36,000.

Exclusions Funding for the purchase of musical instruments, for study courses, for commercial recordings or for the commissioning of new works. Applications for ordinary subsistence costs are also not considered.

Applications In writing to the correspondent. No application form is used and there are no deadlines. Enclose a CV or biography and references, also a performance cassette and budget for the project.

The Tisbury Telegraph Trust

Christian, overseas aid, general

£219,000 (2005/06)
Beneficial area UK and overseas.

35 Kitto Road, Telegraph Hill, London SE14 5TW

Correspondent Mrs E Orr, Trustee

Trustees *John Davidson; Alison Davidson; Eleanor Orr; Roger Orr; Sonia Phippard.*

CC Number 328595

Information available Accounts were on file at the Charity Commission.

General In 2005/06 it had assets of £131,000 and an income of £232,000, mostly from donations. Grants were made totalling £219,000.

There were 25 organisations in receipt of grants of £1,000 or more, including: World Vision (£125,000 in two grants); Romania Care (£20,000); Agape Trust – Uganda (£13,000); St Mary's PCC (£7,000 in three grants); Church Mission Society (£4,500 in two grants); Pecan (£4,000 in two grants); Tear Fund (£5,000); St Mary's Building Fund (£3,000); Bible Society (£2,500); Christian Aid (£2,000); CMJ (£1,500); Soteria Trust (£1,200); and Habitat for Humanity, Sightsavers and Traidcraft Exchange (£1,000 each).

A further 26 smaller grants were made totalling £12,000.

Exclusions Grants are only made to registered charities. No applications from individuals for expeditions or courses can be considered.

Applications In writing to the correspondent. However, it is extremely rare that unsolicited applications are successful and the trust does not respond to applicants unless an sae is included. No telephone applications please.

TJH Foundation

General

£219,000 (2005/06)
Beneficial area England and Wales with some preference for organisations based in the north west of England.

Gleadhill House, Dawbers Lane, Euxton, Chorley, Lancashire PR7 6EA

Tel. 01257 269400

Correspondent J C Kay, Trustee

Trustees *T J Hemmings, Chair; Mrs M Catherall; J C Kay; Ms K Revitt.*

CC Number 1077311

Information available Accounts were obtained from the Charity Commission website.

General The TJH Foundation was established in 1999. In 2005/06 it had assets of £2.7 million and an income of £114,000. Grants to 39 organisations totalled £219,000. They were broken down into the following categories, shown here with examples of beneficiaries:

Medical
Cardiff University – Diabetes Research Unit (£100,000); St Catherine's Hospice (£51,000 in two grants); the Alzheimer's Society (£5,000); the Marina Dalglish Appeal (£2,500); Cancer Research UK Cambridge Centre Appeal and Macmillan Cancer Relief (£1,000 each); Lancashire and Cumbria Kidney Patients Association (£900); Leukaemia Research (£650); and Alder Hey Imagine Appeal (£250).

Education
St George's Hall Charitable Trust (£25,000); and University of Central Lancashire Foundation (£8,000).

Social welfare
The Princess Royal Trust for Carers (£7,400 in two grants); the Disability Foundation (£2,500); British Red Cross (£2,000 in two grants); Riding for the Disabled Association (£1,000); the Karl Alexander Tumour Appeal, the Hyndburn Mayoral Charity Fund, Little Sisters of the Poor and the Sportsman's Charity Limited and Wheelpower (£500 each); RNLI and Starlight Children's Foundation (£250); and Royal British Legion (£100).

Racing welfare
Moorcroft Racehorse Welfare Centre (£500).

Applications In writing to the correspondent.

Tomchei Torah Charitable Trust

Jewish educational institutions

£998,000 (2004/05)
Beneficial area UK.

c/o Harold Everett Wreford, Second Floor, 32 Wigmore Street, London W1U 2RP

Correspondent A Frei, Trustee

Trustees *I J Kohn; S M Kohn; A Frei.*

CC Number 802125

Information available Full accounts were on file at the Charity Commission.

General This trust supports Jewish educational institutions. Grants usually average about £5,000.

In 2004/05 the trust's assets were £504,000 and it had an income of £1.3 million mainly from donations. Grants totalled £998,000 and were made to mainly Jewish organisations.

There were 15 grants made over £10,000 each. Beneficiaries of the three largest grants were British Friends of Nehora (£259,000), British Friends of Gesher (£212,000) and Friends of Mir (£117,000).

Other beneficiaries included Menorah Grammar School (£57,000), Gateshead Yeshiva L'zeirim Tiferes Yaacov (£41,000) Menorah Primary School (£35,000), Achisomoch (£24,000), MST College (£20,000), Gertner Charitable Trust (19,000), WST Charity (£18,000) and Friends of Shekel Hakodesh (£15,000).

Other smaller grants under £10,000 each totalled £153,000.

Applications In writing to the correspondent at any time.

The Torah Temimah Trust

Orthodox Jewish

£41,000 (2003/04)
Beneficial area UK.

16 Reizel Close, Stamford Hill, London N16 5GY

Correspondent Mrs E Bernath, Trustee

Trustees *Mrs E Bernath; M Bernath; A Grunfeld.*

CC Number 802390

Information available Accounts were on file at the Charity Commission, without a list of grants.

General This trust was set up in 1980 to advance/promote Orthodox Jewish religious education and religion. In 2003/04 it had an income from donations of £46,000. Grants totalled £41,000.

Applications In writing to the correspondent.

The Tory Family Foundation

Education, Christian, medical

£81,000 (2005/06)
Beneficial area Worldwide, but principally Folkestone.

The Estate Office, Etchinghill Golf, Folkestone, Kent CT18 8FA

Correspondent Paul N Tory, Trustee

Trustees *P N Tory; J N Tory; Mrs S A Rice.*

CC Number 326584

Information available Full accounts were on file at the Charity Commission.

General The trust's 2005/06 annual report stated: 'The charity was formed to provide financial help to a wide range of charitable needs. It is currently supporting causes principally in the locality of Folkestone. These causes include education, religious, social and medical subjects and the donees themselves are often registered charities.'

The charity does not normally aim to fund the whole of any given project, and thus applicants are expected to demonstrate a degree of existing and regular support. Some beneficiaries receive more than one grant during the year and many have been supported in previous years.

In 2005/06 the foundation had assets of £3.1 million, an income of £116,000 and made grants totalling £81,000. These were broken down as follows, shown here with examples of beneficiaries in each category:

Education – 16 grants totalling £32,000
Uppingham Foundation (£25,000 in two grants); Compaid Trust (£750); Foresight (£590); Amherst Heritage, Bletchley Park and St Lawrence CEP (£500 each); and MAD Foundation and Youth Action Wiltshire (£250 each).

Local – 20 grants totalling £19,000
Hawkinge Youth Centre (£10,000); Folk Rainbow Club (£1,000); Deal Festival, RABI, Strange Cargo and Theatre Royal (£500 each); Ashford YMCA, Causeway and Shepway Blind Support (£250 each); and Royal British Legion (£100).

Churches – 7 grants totalling £11,000
St Mary Virgin (£4,500); All Saints Stanford and St Matthews Warehorne (£2,000 each); Canterbury Cathedral (£1,000); and Shine (£250).

Health – 15 grants totalling £6,700
Kent Cancer Trust and VSO (£1,000 each); the Aldis Trust (£600); East Kent Hospitals (£500 in 2 grants); Let's Face It, Odyssey and RABI (£250 each); and Kedra Goodal (£100).

Overseas – 32 grants totalling £11,000
Friends of Birzett (£2,000); Trekforce (£1,400 in seven grants); the Project Trust (£1,200 in 8 grants); Gurkha Welfare (£1,000); Changing Worlds (£600 in 3 grants); Pump Aid (£600); Concern Worldwide, Pattaya Orphans and Sight Savers (£500 each); and BSES (£250 in 2 grants).

Others – 4 grants totalling £1,900
Blue Cross, Disability Law Service and RNLI (£500 each).

Exclusions Grants are given to registered charities only. Applications outside Kent are unlikely to be considered. No grants are given for further education.

Applications In writing to the correspondent. Applications are considered throughout the year. To keep costs down, unsuccessful applicants will not be notified.

The Toy Trust

Children

£184,000 (2006)
Beneficial area UK.

British Toy and Hobby Association, 80 Camberwell Road, London SE5 0EG

Tel. 020 7701 7271

Email karen@btha.co.uk

Website www.btha.co.uk/

Correspondent Ms Karen Baxter

Trustees *The British Toy and Hobby Association; N Austin; P Brown; R Dyson; K Jones; D Hawtin.*

CC Number 1001634

Information available Accounts were on file at the Charity Commission.

General This trust was registered in 1991 to centralise the giving of the British Toy and Hobby Association. Prior to this, the association raised money from the toy industry, which it pledged to one charity on an annual basis. It was felt that the fundraising activities of the association were probably more than matched by its individual members, and that the charitable giving of the toy industry to children's charities was going unnoticed by the public. The trust still receives the majority of its income from fundraising activities, donating the proceeds to children's charities and charitable projects benefiting children.

In 2006 the trust had assets of £145,000 and an income of £228,000, mostly in donations received. Grants were made totalling £184,000.

The eight beneficiaries listed in the accounts were: Kidscape (£30,000); National Association of Toy and Leisure Libraries (£20,000); Findels (£15,000); Toy Box Charity (£10,000); Birmingham Focus on Blindness (£8,800); International Child Care Trust (£6,600); and Action for Kids and the Rainbow Centre for Conductive Education (£5,000 each).

Other grants totalled £184,000.

Applications Application forms can be downloaded from the British Toy and Hobby Association website.

Annie Tranmer Charitable Trust

General, young people

£94,000 to organisations (2005/06)

Beneficial area UK, particularly Suffolk and adjacent counties.

51 Bennett Road, Ipswich IP1 5HX

Correspondent Mrs M R Kirby

Trustees *J F F Miller; V A Lewis.*

CC Number 1044231

Information available Accounts were obtained from the Charity Commission website.

General The objectives of the trust are to:

- make grants in the county of Suffolk and adjacent counties
- make grants to national charities according to the wishes of Mrs Tranmer during her lifetime
- advance education and historical research relating to the national monument known as Sutton Hoo burial site and Sutton Hoo estate
- protect and preserve the Sutton Hoo burial site
- further the education of children and young people in Suffolk
- make grants for general charitable purposes.

In 2005/06 the trust had assets of £3.7 million and an income of £117,000. Grants were made totalling £107,000 of which £94,000 was donated to organisations and £7,100 to individuals.

Beneficiaries of the largest grants included: East Anglian Air Ambulance and East Anglia's Children's Hospices (£10,000 each); Felixstowe Ferry Youth Sailing (£6,000); and Cancer Research, Great Ormond Street Hospital, MacMillan Cancer Relief, Marie Curie Cancer, Mid Essex Hospital NHS Burns Unit, the Ipswich Hospital NHS Trust and the Suffolk Punch Trust (£5,000 each).

Other beneficiaries included: Independent Age and Motor Neurone Disease (£3,000 each); the Blue Cross, Brainwave and RNIB (£2,000 each); Against Breast Cancer, Brittle Bone Disease, Combat Stress and Wellbeing (£1,000 each); Listening Books (£600); Defeating Deafness and Wellchild (£500 each); and Bowel Cancer, Canine Partners for Independence, RSPB and Scope (£250 each).

The 2005/06 annual report stated that: 'the trustees have agreed to provide in future years a one-off grant, of at least £45,000, to the National Trust to facilitate the building of a full-scale replica of the Saxon Burial Ship at Sutton Hoo.'

Applications This trust does not accept unsolicited applications.

The Treeside Trust

General

£91,000 (2004/05)

Beneficial area UK, but mainly local.

4 The Park, Grasscroft, Oldham OL4 4ES

Correspondent John Gould, Trustee

Trustees *C C Gould; J R B Gould; J R W Gould; D M Ives; R J Ives; B Washbrook.*

CC Number 1061586

Information available Accounts were on file at the Charity Commission, but without a list of grants.

General The trust supports mainly small local charities, and a few UK-wide charities which are supported on a regular basis. It states: 'In the main the trustees' policy is to make a limited number of substantial grants each year, rather than a larger number of smaller ones, in order to make significant contributions to some of the causes supported.'

In 2004/05 the trust had assets of £762,000 and an income of £142,000. Grants totalled £91,000. A list of grants for this year was not available.

Applications In writing to the correspondent, however, the trust has stated that they 'do not welcome unsolicited applications'.

Triodos Foundation

Overseas development, organics, community development

£64,000 (2005)

Beneficial area UK and developing countries.

Brunel House, 11 The Promenade, Clifton, Bristol BS8 3NN

Correspondent The Trustees

Trustees *P Blom; M Robinson; D Hawes; C Middleton.*

CC Number 1052958

Information available Accounts were on file at the Charity Commission, without a list of grants.

General This trust, registered in 1996, makes grants both nationally and overseas, through its own networks. Wherever possible it prefers to act in partnership with existing charitable organisations to provide benefits.

The objectives of the foundation are to support charitable needs which have been identified through, but which are unable to be fully supported by, the work of Triodos Bank in the UK. It works closely with individuals, organisations and depositors of the bank to support projects that work in charitable areas.

In 2005 the trust had an income of £18,000 comprised mainly of donations and made grants totalling £64,000.

Previous grants have included those to a leading micro-finance institution, K-Rep Bank in Kenya and support for the first organic research conference in the UK, in Aberystwyth.

Exclusions No grants to individuals or students.

Applications 'Triodos Foundation receives many more applications than it can respond to positively. The Foundation Board can only consider approaches from charities whose goals closely match those of Triodos Bank. Applications should be made in writing, outlining the purpose of the project and providing any relevant supporting information. The Triodos Foundation Board meets on an ad hoc basis throughout the year to assess the applications and make decisions about specific grants. Unfortunately we are not able to reply to applications that are unsuccessful.'

Truedene Co. Ltd

Jewish
£916,000 (2004/05)
Beneficial area UK and overseas.

c/o Cohen Arnold and Co., 1075 Finchley Road, London NW11 0PU
Correspondent The Trustees
Trustees Samuel Berger; Solomon Laufer; Sije Berger; Mrs S Klein; Mrs Z Sternlicht.
CC Number 248268
Information available Accounts were on file at the Charity Commission.

General In 2004/05 this trust had assets of almost £5 million and an

income of £268,000. Grants were made totalling £916,000.

There were 43 grants made during the year, of which 28 were for £10,000 or more. The beneficiary of by far the largest grant was United Talmudical Associates Limited (£285,000). Other larger grants went to Cosmon Belz Limited (£55,000), Beis Ruchel D'Satmar Girls' School Ltd (£53,000), Congregation Mosdos Toldos Aharon Institution (£50,000), Kollet Avreichim of UTA (£33,000), Chevras Mo'oz Ladol and Kolel Shomrei Hachomoth (£25,000 each), Congregation Saad V'ezer (£22,000), Mosdos Ramou (£21,000), British Friends of Tchernobyl, Orthodox Council of Jerusalem and VMCT (£20,000 each), Congregation Paile Yoetz and Machene Sva Rotzohn (£16,000 each), Koltel Tiferes Yaakov Yosef (£14,000) and Mesifta Talmudical College and Yeshivo Horomo Talmudical College (£10,000 each).

Smaller grants included those to Friends of Mir (£5,500), Chasdei Shlomo (£5,000), Beth Hamedrash Satmar Trust (£1,800) and Tevini Limited (£1,000).

Applications In writing to the correspondent.

The Truemark Trust

General
£183,000 (2005/06)
Beneficial area UK only.

PO Box 2, Liss, Hampshire GU33 6YP
Correspondent The Trustees
Trustees Sir Thomas Lucas; Mrs W Collett; S Neil; M Meakin; R Wolfe; Mrs J Hayward; D Hawkins.
CC Number 265855
Information available Accounts were on file at the Charity Commission.

General The trust favours small organisations with a preference for innovatory projects, particularly neighbourhood-based community projects and less popular groups. Current main areas of interest are: disability, older people and people otherwise disadvantaged, including counselling and community support groups in disadvantaged areas and alternative or complementary health projects.

Grants are usually one-off for a specific project or part of a project. Core funding and/or salaries are rarely considered. The average size of grants is £1,000.

In 2005/06 it had assets of £9.5 million which generated an income of £357,000, including £257,000 from rental income. Grants totalled £183,000.

There were 115 grants made in the year. The largest were £3,000 each to the Burnbake Trust – Salisbury, Girlguiding Lymington and District – Lymington, the Hanworth and Feltham Project, the Light House Christian Care Ministry – Coventry, New Approaches to Cancer – Chertsey, Reality at Work in Scotland – Glasgow, Special Needs Adventure Playground – Calderwood and Touchstones 12 – Colwyn Bay.

Other beneficiaries included: Rehabilitation for Addicted Prisoners Trust, London (£2,500); Colchester Furniture Project, Coventry Boys' Club, GlosAid Youth Action, Folkestone Rainbow Centre, Friends of Mulberry – Chester, Orcadia Creative Learning Centre – Edinburgh, Positive Lifestyle – Newton Abbot and Toys in Motion – Eastbourne (£2,000 each); Lothian Autistic Society – Edinburgh, Marches Family Network – Leominster and Southwark Homeless Information Project (£1,500 each); and Barham Park Veterans' Club – Wembley, Bridewell Organic Gardens – Wilcote, Kestrel Sports Club for the Disabled – Hertford, Safe and Sound – Derby, Saffron Walden Day Centre – Saffron Walden and St Michael's Community Renewal – London (£1,000 each).

Exclusions Grants are made to registered charities only. Applications from individuals, including students, are ineligible. No grants are made in response to general appeals from large national charities. Grants are seldom available for churches or church buildings or for scientific or medical research projects.

Applications In writing to the correspondent, including the most recent set of accounts, clear details of the need the project is designed to meet and an outline budget. Trustees meet four times a year. Only successful applicants receive a reply.

Truemart Limited

General, Judaism, welfare

£89,000 (2005/06)

Beneficial area UK-wide and overseas, with a preference for Greater London.

34 The Ridgeway, London NW11 8QS

Correspondent Mrs S Heitner, Secretary

Trustees *I Heitner; I M Cymerman: B Hoffman.*

CC Number 1090586

Information available Accounts were on file at the Charity Commission, without a list of grants.

General The trust was set up to promote:

- the advancement of religion in accordance with the Orthodox Jewish faith
- the relief of poverty
- general charitable purposes.

In 2005/06 it had an income from donations of £94,000. Grants totalled £89,000. Unfortunately a list of beneficiaries was not included with the accounts.

Applications In writing to the correspondent.

Trumros Limited

Jewish

£315,000 (2004)

Beneficial area UK.

282 Finchley Road, London NW3 7AD

Correspondent Mrs H Hofbauer, Trustee

Trustees *R S Hofbauer; Mrs H Hofbauer.*

CC Number 285533

Information available Full accounts were on file at the Charity Commission.

General In 2004 the trust had assets of £4.3 million and a total income of £1.5 million, of which £804,000 came from rental income and £662,000 from a trading subsidiary. A total of £315,000 was given in about 150 grants.

Beneficiaries of the largest grants of £10,000 or more were Chevras Mo'oslodol (£34,000), Beis Joseph Zvi

Jerusalem (£29,000), Menorah Primary School (£25,000), BEFORE Trust (£20,000), Yeshiva Orah Yehoshua (£18,000), Shomrei Emunim (£12,000) and Chevras Ezros Nizrochim (£10,000).

Other beneficiaries included London Academy of Jewish Studies (£9,600), Toldos Aharon (£9,000), Jewish Learning Exchange (£8,500), AV Trust (£5,600), Bayis Cheshem Idlefires, Friends of Sanz Institutions, Gateshead Talmudic College, Golders Charitable Trust and Yeshiva Mechino (£1,000 each), Friends of Covent Garden Chessed Trust (£770), Torah Bal Peh and Woodstock Sinclair Trust (£500 each), Lolev Charitable Trust (£480), Comet Charities (£250) and Jewish Centre for Special Education (£100).

Applications In writing to the correspondent, but note that the trust states it is already inundated with applications.

Tudor Rose Ltd

Jewish

£38,000 (2003/04)

Beneficial area UK.

c/o Martin and Heller, Accountants, 5 North End Road, London NW11 7RJ

Correspondent Samuel Taub, Secretary

Trustees *M Lehrfield; M Taub; A Taub; S Taub; S L Taub.*

CC Number 800576

Information available Full accounts were on file at the Charity Commission.

General This trust works for the promotion of the Orthodox Jewish faith and the relief of poverty.

In 2003/04 it had assets of £1.3 million. Total income was £269,000, mainly from property income (the sum of £107,000 was spent during the year on these properties). Grants were made totalling £38,000.

Beneficiaries were Beis Yakov (£16,000), Yetev Lev (£9,100), Parsha (£4,700), CWCT (£2,500), Yad Eliezer (£2,000), Torah Temimah (£1,600), LAJS (£1,500) and Tiferes Zvi (£500).

Applications In writing to the correspondent.

The Tufton Charitable Trust

Christian

£581,000 (2005)

Beneficial area UK.

Slater Maidment, 7 St James's Square, London SW1Y 4JU

Correspondent The Trustees

Trustees *Sir Christopher Wates; Lady Wates; J R F Lulham.*

CC Number 801479

Information available Accounts were on file at the Charity Commission.

General This trust supports Christian organisations, by providing grants as well as allowing them to use premises leased by the trust for retreats.

In 2005 the trust had assets of £581,000 an income of £542,000, including £339,000 from Gift Aid and other donations. Grants totalled £581,000.

There were 18 grants listed in the accounts. Beneficiaries included: the Church of England (£374,000 in 14 grants); Prison Fellowship (£90,000 in 12 grants); Nuffield Hospitals (£50,000); Off the Fence (£15,000); the Zoological Society of London (£10,000); the Tropical Health and Education Trust (£9,800); Relationship Foundation (£7,500); the Cambridge Foundation (£3,000); On the Move, the Story of Christmas, RSPB and Treloar Trust (£2,500 each); All Souls Clubhouse and Christians Against Poverty (£2,000 each); the Dame Vera Lynne Trust (£1,500); Old Town Community Church (£1,300); and Send a Cow (£1,000).

There were 13 smaller grants of less than £1,000 each made totalling £3,200.

Exclusions No grants for repair or maintenance of buildings.

Applications In writing to the correspondent, including an sae.

The R D Turner Charitable Trust

General

£147,000 (2005/06)

Beneficial area UK, with a preference for the Worcestershire area.

1 The Yew Trees, High Street, Henley-in-Arden B95 5BN

Tel. 01564 793085

Correspondent J E Dyke, Administrator

Trustees *D P Pearson; J M Del Mar; S L Preedy; P J Millward; J M G Fea.*

CC Number 263556

Information available Accounts were on file at the Charity Commission.

General This trust has general charitable purposes, particularly in the West Midlands area, with a specific preference for the villages of Arley and Upper Arley in Worcestershire.

In 2005/06 it had assets of £25 million, which generated an income of £630,000. Most of this was spent on the upkeep of the Ardley Estate (£418,000), with grants to 31 organisations totalling £147,000. Grants were broken down by the trust as follows:

Elderly – 2 grants
Elizabeth Fitzroy Homes (£4,000); and Friends of the Elderly (£2,000).

Children and young people – 6 grants
Sunfield Children's Homes (£20,000); Kidderminster and District Scouts (£5,000); and Cheltenham Sea Cadets and Evesham Adventure Playground (£2,000 each).

Environment and heritage – 4 grants
Worcester and Dudley Historic Churches Trust (£12,000); Ironbridge Gorge Museum (£10,000) and St Bartholomew's Bayton (£2,000).

The arts – 5 grants
The Barber Institute (£12,000); Worcester Cathedral Music and Light (£10,000); and Huntingdon Arts (£5,000).

Community and social work – 8 grants
British Red Cross Hereford and Worcester (£12,000); Trimpley Village Hall (£5,000); Kidderminster RNLI and Relate Worcestershire (£2,000 each) and Stensham Village Hall (£1,000).

Disabled and health – 6 grants
Kidderminster Disabled Club (£7,000); Macmillan Worcestershire (£5,000); Worcestershire Association for the Blind (£4,000); Acquired Aphasia Trust (£2,000); and Listening Books (£1,000).

Hospices – 1 grant
St Richard's Hospice (£25,000).

Exclusions No grants to non-registered charities or to individuals.

Applications In writing to the correspondent with a copy of your latest annual report and accounts. There are no application forms. The trustees meet in February, May, August and December to consider applications, which should be submitted in the month prior to each meeting. Telephone enquiries may be made before submitting an appeal.

The Florence Turner Trust

General

£132,000 (2005/06)

Beneficial area UK, but with a strong preference for Leicestershire.

c/o Harvey Ingram Owston, 20 New Walk, Leicester LE1 6TX

Correspondent The Trustees

Trustees *Roger Bowder; Allan A Veasey; Caroline A Macpherson.*

CC Number 502721

Information available Full accounts were provided by the trust.

General This trust has general charitable purposes, giving most of its support in Leicestershire.

In 2005/06 it had assets of £5.1 million which generated an income of £160,000. Grants totalled £132,000.

There were 139 grants made in the year, of which 48 were listed in the accounts. Beneficiaries included: Leicester Charity Organisation Society (£11,000); Leicester Grammar School – bursaries (£8,000); British Red Cross Leicestershire/Rutland Branch Ambulance Appeal (£5,000); Age Concern Leicester, the Care Fund, Leicestershire Scout Council, Leicester Society for Mentally Handicapped Children and Leicester YMCA (£2,100 each); National Autistic Society (£2,000); RNLI (£1,600); Barnardos, VISTA and Young People First (£1,100 each); and Cornerstone Project – Whitwick and Skillshare International (£1,000 each).

A further 91 grants below £ 1,000 each totalled £42,000.

Exclusions The trust does not support individuals for educational purposes.

Applications In writing to the correspondent. Trustees meet every eight or nine weeks.

Miss S M Tutton Charitable Trust

Music

£24,000 to organisations (2005/06)

Beneficial area UK.

BDO Stoy Hayward, 8 Baker Street, London W1U 3LL

Correspondent The Trustees

Trustees *Susan Diane Dolton; Peter G G Miller; Rosemary Pickering; Richard Van Allen; Susan M Bullock.*

CC Number 298774

Information available Accounts were on file at the Charity Commission.

General The trust provides financial support to young singers (through the Sybil Tutton Awards) for postgraduate opera studies and selected music colleges, charities and training opera companies benefiting adults aged 20 to 30. Assistance is generally provided only where students are recommended by organisations with which the trust has a close working relationship.

In 2005/06 the trust had assets of £2.7 million and an income of £68,000. Grants to organisation totalled £24,000 with a further £33,000 given via the Sybil Tutton Awards.

The main focus of the funds was towards the Sybil Tutton Awards, with £16,000 given for this purpose. Other beneficiaries, all also supported in the previous year, were National Opera Studio (£10,000), British Youth Opera (£7,500), Clonter Farm Music Trust (£3,000), Young Concert Artists Trust (£2,000) and Britten-Pears School (£1,500).

Applications Individuals seeking grants for opera studies should consider applying directly to the Musicians' Benevolent Fund (charity no: 228089) which administers the Sybil Tutton Awards. Organisations should submit full details of projects to the correspondent. The trust has some funds available for occasional discretionary grants, but they are very limited. Assistance is generally provided only where students are recommended by organisations with which the trust has a close working relationship.

The TUUT Charitable Trust

General, but with a bias towards trade-union-favoured causes

£28,000 (2005/06)

Beneficial area Worldwide.

Congress House, Great Russell Street, London WC1B 3LQ

Tel. 020 7637 7116 **Fax** 020 7637 7087

Email info@tufm.co.uk

Correspondent Ann Smith, Secretary

Trustees *Lord Christopher; A Tuffin; M Walsh; M Bradley; B Barber; Lord Brookman; E Sweeney.*

CC Number 258665

Information available Accounts and a newsletter were provided by the trust.

General Established in 1969 by the trade-union movement to ensure the profits of the company would go to good causes rather than individual schareholders. In previous years, the trust has had no particular areas of interest, with the trust deed requiring all trustees to be trade unionists so the giving of the funds represents the interests of the membership. Due to the large number of applications the trust is receiving but is unable to support, it has now decided to have specific areas of interest to enable it to make fewer, but more worthwhile, grants than it has been able to in recent years.

Preference is given to:

- charities established by the TUC or an affiliated trade union for the benefit of its members
- charities formally supported by the TUC or an individual trade union at national or branch level
- charities demonstrating a direct and active link with one or more unions (for instance, those that recognise an individual union for bargaining purposes)
- overseas applications accompanied by a letter of support on behalf of the ICFTU, CTUC, ETUC or a member organisation.

The trustees still also consider applications outside these categories from small to medium-sized non-religious charities in the UK that benefit a wide range of people, with reference to one of the following:

- medical research

- support for victims of war or natural disaster
- relief of poverty, age or mental or physical illness or disability
- influencing public policy on human rights, welfare or employment issues
- education
- promoting economic and social development in developing countries.

In 2005/06 the trust had assets of almost £2 million and an income of £30,000. Grants were made totalling £28,000. A Fellowship Award of £6,800 was made.

Beneficiaries included: the Esther Benjamins Trust (£7,000); Cares (£5,000); Second Chance (£3,000); Macmillan Cancer Relief and People in Aid (£2,500 each); Medical Aid for Palestinians (£2,000); BLISS and Motor Neurone Disease (£1,000 each); ABC, Big Brother Big Sisters of South Africa, Ceylon Plantation Union, Evelina Childrens Hospital Appeal, Prisoners of Conscience and World Development Movement Trust (£500 each); and Bedfordshire and Northamptonshire MS Centre, British Retinitis Pigmentosa Society, Contact the Elderly, Global Care, Tydden Bach Trust and Zenzele (£250 each)

Exclusions No grants to individuals or to charities based overseas.

Applications In writing to the correspondent. Applications should be submitted from a head office (where appropriate) and include latest accounts, purpose for donation and details of trade-union links. Trustees meet three times a year.

Ulting Overseas Trust

Theological training

£102,000 (2004/05)

Beneficial area The developing world (mostly, but not exclusively, Asia, Africa and South and Central America).

Pothecary & Barratt, Talbot House, 8–9 Talbot Court, London EC3V 0BS

Correspondent T B Warren, Trustee

Trustees *Dr J A B Kessler; J C Heyward; J S Payne; A J Bale; Dr D G Osborne; Mrs M Brinkley; D Ford; N W H Sylvester; T B Warren; Revd J Kapolyo.*

CC Number 294397

Information available Accounts were on file at the Charity Commission.

General The trust exists solely to provide bursaries, normally via grants to Christian theological training institutions or organisations with a training focus, for those in the developing world who wish to train for the Christian ministry, or for those who wish to improve their ministry skills. It gives priority to the training of students in their home countries or continents.

In 2004/05 it had assets of £3.2 million and an income of £113,000. There were 33 grants in the year totalling £102,000.

Beneficiaries included IFES, Langham Trust and Scripture Union International (£14,000 each), Interserve and Oxford Centre for Mission Studies (£6,100 each), Pan African Christian College (£4,800), Asian Theological Seminary and Discipleship Training College – Singapore (£4,600 each), Latin Link (£3,400), London Institute (£2,600), Cornerstone Christian College and Theological College Central Africa (£1,800 each), Bangkok Bible College (£1,500), All Nations Christian College (£1,400) and Christian Service College (£1,000).

Exclusions No grants are given for capital projects such as buildings or library stock, nor for training in subjects other than Biblical, theological and missionary studies. Grants are only made to institutions to pass on to their students; direct grants to individuals cannot be made.

Applications The funds of the trust are already committed. Unsolicited applications cannot be supported.

The Ulverscroft Foundation

People who are sick and visually impaired, ophthalmic research

£295,000 (2004/05)

Beneficial area Worldwide.

1 The Green, Bradgate Road, Anstey, Leicester LE7 7FU

Tel. 0116 236 1595 **Fax** 0116 236 1594

Email foundation@ulverscroft.co.uk

Website www.foundation.ulverscroft.com/

Correspondent Joyce Sumner

Trustees *A W Leach, Chair; P H F Carr; M K Down; D Owen; R Crooks.*

CC Number 264873

Information available Accounts were on file at the Charity Commission.

General Ulverscroft Large Print Books Limited, was formed in 1964. The company republished existing books in large type to sell to libraries and donate the profits to sight-related charitable causes. In 1972 The Ulverscroft Foundation was created.

The foundation supports projects which will have a positive effect on the quality of life of visually impaired people (blind and partially sighted). Funding is channelled via recognised organisations which help the visually impaired, for example, libraries, hospitals, clinics, schools and colleges, and social and welfare organisations.

In 2004/05 Ulverscroft Group (as the trading company is known) generated an income of £16.8 million. The foundation had an income of £1.8 million. Out of a total expenditure of £1.5 million, grants were made totalling £295,000.

Beneficiaries included: Moorfields Eye Hospital (£84,000); University of Leicester (£53,000); St Mary's (£50,000); Society of Chief Librarians (£25,000); Institute of Opthalmology (£11,000); COTIS (£10,000); National Blind Children's Society and Second Sight (£5,000 each); Swinfen Charitable Trust (£4,000); VSO (£3,400); Action for Blind People, Birmingham Focus on Blindness, British Retinitis Pigmentosa Society, Lindsay Blind Society, Royal London Society for the Blind, Suffolk County Council and Visibility (£2,000 each); and Appropriate Technology Asia, Association of Blind Asians, Brighton Society for the Blind, Iris Vision Resource Centre, LEPRA, NLB and Nystagmus Network (£1,000 each).

Grants under £1,000 each totalled £5,800.

Exclusions Applications from individuals are not encouraged. Generally, assistance towards salaries and general running costs are not given.

Applications In writing to the correspondent including latest annual report and accounts. Applicants are advised to make their proposal as detailed as possible, to include details of the current service to people who are visually impaired, if any, and how the proposed project will be integrated or enhanced. If possible the trust asks for an estimate of how many people who are visually impaired use/will use the service, the amount of funding obtained to date,

if any, and the names of other organisations to whom they have applied. The success of any appeal is dependent on the level of funding at the time of consideration. The trustees meet four times a year to consider applications.

The Union of Orthodox Hebrew Congregation

Jewish

£279,000 (2005)

Beneficial area UK.

140 Stamford Hill, London N16 6QT

Correspondent The Administrator

Trustees *B S F Freshwater; I Cymerman; C Konig; Rabbi A Pinter.*

CC Number 249892

Information available Accounts were on file at the Charity Commission.

General The operational charity works to protect and to further in every way the interests of traditional Judaism in Great Britain and to establish and support such institutions as will serve this object.

In 2005 it had assets of £1.7 million and an income of £1.2 million comprising principally 'grants and donations and community levies'. Out of a total charitable expenditure of £1.1 million, grants to organisations totalled £279,000.

There were 50 grants listed in the accounts, including £25,000 to Atereth Shau, £18,000 to Chesed Charity Trust, £16,000 to Mutual Trust, £14,000 to Beis Malka, £12,000 each to Achieve Trust and Belz Nursery, £11,000 to Maoz Ladol, £10,000 each to Addas Yisoroel Mikva Foundation and North West London Mikvah, £9,000 each to Needy Families and Poor Families Pesach, £7,800 to ZSV, £7,000 to Talmud Centre Trust, 6,000 to Kollel Shomrei Hachomos, £5,000 to London Board of Schechita, £4,800 to Beis Shmuel, £2,000 to Society of Friends of the Torah, £1,900 to Bnos Yerushaim and £1,500 to VMCT.

Other Donations of less than £1,000 each totalled (£11,000).

Applications In writing to the correspondent.

Unity Charitable Trust

General

£11,000 (2004/05)

Beneficial area UK.

5 Accommodation Road, London NW11 8ED

Correspondent R Baron, Trustee

Trustees *R Baron; S Raymond; A Epton.*

CC Number 1057710

Information available Accounts were on file at the Charity Commission, but without a list of grant beneficiaries.

General This trust tends to give one large grant each year rather than making a number of smaller grants; as such it stated that it has no extra funds to give. In 2004/05 it had an income of £39,000 mainly from donations and made grants totalling £11,000. No further information was available.

Applications The trustees do their own research. Unsolicited applications are not considered.

The David Uri Memorial Trust

Jewish, general

£93,000 (2005/06)

Beneficial area Worldwide.

Suite 511, 78 Marylebone High Street, London W1U 5AP

Correspondent The Trustees

Trustees *Mrs S Blackman; Mrs B Roden; B Blackman.*

CC Number 327810

Information available Accounts were on file at the Charity Commission, but without a list of grants since 1991/92.

General In 2005/06 the trust's assets totalled £2.3 million, it had an income of £236,000, mainly from property investment revenue and made grants to organisations totalling £93,000.

Unfortunately, no grants list or information was available on the beneficiaries of the trust since 1991/92. In that year, grants totalled £28,000, with most grants to Jewish organisations. The largest were £15,000 to Yakar Education Foundation and £2,500 to the National Jewish Chaplaincy Board. All the other grants to Jewish organisations were under £500.

Grants to non-Jewish organisations included £5,000 to the Jefferies Research Wing Trust, with all the others receiving under £500, including Age Concern, Crisis at Christmas and NSPCC.

Exclusions No grants to individuals.

Applications In writing to the correspondent.

The Albert Van Den Bergh Charitable Trust

Medical/disability, welfare

£50,000 (2004/05)
Beneficial area UK and overseas.

TWM Solicitors, Broadoak House, Horsham Road, Cranleigh, Surrey GU6 8DJ

Tel. 01483 273515
Correspondent G R Oliver, Trustee
Trustees *P A Van Den Bergh; G R Oliver; Mrs J M Hartley.*
CC Number 296885

Information available Accounts were on file at the Charity Commission, without a list of grants.

General The trust was established in 1987. In 2004/05 its assets stood at £2.1 million. It had an income of £68,000 and gave £50,000 in grants. Unfortunately there was no grants list on file at the Charity Commission for that year.

Previous beneficiaries BLISS, Bishop of Guildford's Charity, British Heart Foundation, Counsel and Care for the Elderly, Leukaemia Research Trust, Multiple Sclerosis Society, Parentline Surrey, National Osteoporosis Society, RNID , Riding for the Disabled – Cranleig Age Concern, SSAFA, St John Ambulance and United Charities Fund – Liberal Jewish Synagogue.

Most grants went to national charities in the fields of health, welfare and disability. Some went to Jewish

organisations and some to Surrey-based charities. A few grants went to local charities elsewhere, but mainly in the London area.

Applications In writing to the correspondent, including accounts and budgets.

The Van Neste Foundation

Welfare, Christian, developing world

£117,000 (2005/06)
Beneficial area UK, especially the Bristol area, and overseas.

15 Alexandra Road, Clifton, Bristol BS8 2DD

Correspondent Fergus Lyons, Secretary
Trustees *M T M Appleby, Chair; F J F Lyons; G J Walker; J F Lyons; B M Appleby.*
CC Number 201951

Information available Full accounts were available from the Charity Commission website.

General The trustees currently give priority to the following:

- developing world
- people who have disabilities or are elderly
- advancement of religion and respect for the sanctity and dignity of life
- community and Christian family life.

These objectives are reviewed by the trustees from time to time but applications falling outside them are unlikely to be considered. In 2005/06 the trust had assets of £6.7 million and an income of £191,000. Grants were made totalling £117,000.

Grants included those made to: Clifton RC Cathedral towards an audio system (£12,000); Tiny Lives Campaign to refurbish Neonatal Intensive Care Unit Bristol (£10,000); Bristol Mind towards mental health advocacy project and John Grooms to refurbish the local residential care home (£5,000 each); African Initiatives for development work in Ghana (£4,000); Inter Care towards help for HIV/Aids patients in Africa (£1,700); Fairbridge West for supporting excluded young people (£1,000); the Inter Faith Network to help raise awareness of the importance of interfaith understanding (£500); and the Dolphin Society towards

helping the housebound and disabled (£250).

Exclusions No grants to individuals or to large, well-known charities. Applications are only considered from registered charities.

Applications Applications should be in the form of a concise letter setting out the clear objectives to be obtained, which must be charitable. Information must be supplied concerning agreed funding from other sources together with a timetable for achieving the objectives of the appeal and a copy of the latest accounts. The foundation does not normally make grants on a continuing basis. To keep overheads to a minimum, only successful applications are acknowledged. Even then it may be a matter of months before any decision can be expected, depending on the dates of trustees' meetings.

Mrs Maud Van Norden's Charitable Foundation

General

£38,000 (2005)
Beneficial area UK.

Messrs Payne Hicks Beach, 10 New Square, Lincoln's Inn, London WC2A 3QG

Tel. 020 7465 4300 **Fax** 020 7465 4393
Correspondent N J Wingerath, Secretary and Trustee
Trustees *Mrs Ena M Dukler; John Strahearn Gordon; Mrs Elizabeth A Humphryes; Neil J Wingerath.*
CC Number 210844

Information available Full accounts were available from the Charity Commission website.

General Established in 1962, in 2005 the trust had assets of £1 million and an income of £40,000. Grants were made totalling £38,000.

Grants included those made to the Friends of the Chelsea and Westminster Hospital (£2,500), Gurkha Welfare Trust (£2,000), Victim Support (£1,500), and British Association for Adoption and Fostering, Carers National Association, Humane Slaughter Association Royal Hospital for Neuro-disability Katherine

Low Settlement and National Benevolent Fund for the Aged (£1,000 each).

Exclusions No grants to individuals, expeditions or scholarships.

Applications The trustees will only consider applications if accompanied by a copy of the applicant's latest reports and accounts. The trustees make donations to registered charities only. The trustees meet to consider applications in May each year.

The Vandervell Foundation

General

£156,000 to organisations (2005)
Beneficial area UK.

Bridge House, 181 Queen Victoria Street, London EC4V 4DZ

Correspondent Ms Sheila Lawler

Trustee *The Vandervell Foundation Limited Trustee Company.*

CC Number 255651

Information available Full accounts were on file at the Charity Commission.

General This trust has general charitable purposes, supporting both individuals and organisations. A wide range of causes has been supported, include schools, educational establishments, hospices and other health organisations, with the trust stating there are no real preferences or exclusions. Grants generally range from £1,000 to £5,000 each.

In 2005 the trust had assets of £8 million and an income of £303,000. Grants were made totalling £373,000, of which £156,000 went to organisations.

Advancement of education	8 grants	£54,000
Medical research	4	£22,500
Performing arts	6	£23,000
Environmental regeneration	4	£5,000
Social welfare	32	£52,000

The largest grants included those made to: Royal College of Surgeons (£20,000); Royal National Lifeboat Institution (£17,000); and Gap Activity Project, Project Trust, PMS Foundation, and The Arts Educational School (£10,000 each).

Other grants of less than £10,000 each included those made to: Lucy Cavendish College (£8,000) Royal National Theatre and St George's Youth Club (£5,000 each); Voice for the Child in Care (£3,000) and Buxton Mountain Rescue

Team and Contact the Elderly (£1,000 each).

Applications In writing to the correspondent. Trustees meet every two months to consider major grant applications; smaller grants are considered more frequently.

Roger Vere Foundation

General

£125,000 to organisations (2005/06)

Beneficial area UK and worldwide, with a special interest in High Wycombe.

19 Berwick Road, Marlow, Buckinghamshire SL7 3AR

Correspondent Peter Allen, Trustee

Trustees *Mrs Rosemary Vere, Chair; Mrs Marion Lyon; Peter Allen.*

CC Number 1077559

Information available Accounts were on file at the Charity Commission.

General This trust was established in September 1999 and supports:

- the relief of financial hardship in and around, but not restricted to, High Wycombe
- advancement of education
- advancement of religion
- advancement of scientific and medical research
- conservation and protection of the natural environment and endangered plants and animals
- relief of natural and civil disasters
- general charitable purposes.

In 2005/06 the trust had assets of £3.8 million and an income of £174,000. Grants were made totalling £128,000, of which £3,500 went to individuals. No single grant exceeded £500. The trustees' report stated that 'the foundation does not have any ongoing commitments to any organisation'.

Previous beneficiaries have included Cord Blood Charity, the Leprosy Mission, Claire House Children's Hospice, Angels International, Signalong Group, Changing Faces, Women's Aid, St John Water Wing, UK Youth and Jubilee Plus.

Applications In writing to the correspondent.

The Nigel Vinson Charitable Trust

General

£87,000 (2005/06)

Beneficial area UK, with a preference for north east England.

Messrs Hoare Trustees, 37 Fleet Street, London EC4P 4DQ

Tel. 020 7353 4522

Correspondent The Trustees

Trustees *Mrs Rowena A Cowan; Rt Hon Lord Vinson of Roddam Dene; Thomas O C Harris; Hon Miss Bettina C Witheridge; Hon Mrs Antonia C Bennett.*

CC Number 265077

Information available Full accounts were on file at the Charity Commission.

General This trust was established in 1972. It makes grants towards the encouragement and development of business and industry, the arts and education.

In 2005/06 the trust had assets of £3.7 million and an income of £193,000.

Grants were made totalling £87,000. Beneficiaries of the largest grants were: Institute for Policy Research (£23,000); Civitas (£20,000); Institute of Economic Affairs (£12,000); Educational Research Trust (£4,000); Hampden Trust and Renewable Energy Fund (£3,300 each); Ilderton PCC (£2,700); Christian Institute (£2,000); Songbird Survival (£1,500); and Northumbria Historic Churches Trust (£1,100).

Grants of £1,000 or less totalled £14,000.

Applications In writing to the correspondent. Applications are considered throughout the year.

The William and Ellen Vinten Trust

Industrial education, training and welfare

£39,000 (2005/06)

Beneficial area UK, but mostly Bury St Edmunds.

353

Greene and Greene Solicitors, 80 Guildhall Street, Bury St Edmunds, Suffolk IP33 1QB

Correspondent The Chairman of the Trustees

CC Number 285758

Information available Accounts were obtained from the Charity Commission website.

General The 2005/06 trustee's report stated that: 'The trustees continued to consider and to implement initiatives to increase the interest of school students in science and technology subjects in the Bury St Edmunds area of Suffolk, with a view to increasing the numbers who might consider careers related to these subjects.'

In 2005/06 the trust had assets of £1.5 million and an income of £51,000. Grants were made totalling £39,000 of which £32,000 was given towards education and £7,000 towards training.

Applications The trust stated that as a proactive charity it does not seek unsolicited applications. Such applications are now so significant in number that the trust has decided not to respond to them, however discourteous this may seem.

Vision Charity

Children who are blind, visually impaired or dyslexic

£132,000 (2004/05)

Beneficial area UK.

PO Box 729, Aylesbury HP22 9AS

Email Peter.Thompson@VisionCharity.co.uk

Website www.visioncharity.co.uk

Correspondent Peter Thompson

Trustees *Bill Bohanna; John Carpenter; David Coupe; David Pacy.*

CC Number 1075630

Information available Accounts were on file at the Charity Commission.

General The objectives of the charity are to combine the fundraising efforts of companies and individuals who use or benefit from, or work in, the visual communications industry for the benefit of children who are blind, visually impaired or dyslexic.

In 2004/05 it had assets of £231,000 and an income of £390,000, most of which

came from donations received and various fundraising events organised by the charity. A total of £194,000 was spent on organising these events. Grants were made totalling £132,000.

There were 12 grants of £1,000 or more listed in the accounts. Beneficiaries of the largest grants were: Joseph Clark School towards a minibus (£27,000); Dyslexia Institute towards computer monitors and a virtual private network project (£26,000); Blind in Business towards specialist computer software (£22,000); Royal London Society for the Blind – Dorton House towards specialist computer equipment (£11,000); and UNICEF tsunami appeal (£10,000).

Other beneficiaries included: the Eyeless Trust towards a research project at Moorfield Hospital and a family support project in Northern Ireland (£8,400); the Vision Foundation towards computer software (£2,700); and Cherry Orchard School towards sensory toys (£2,000).

Other donations of up to £1,000 each totalled £2,000.

Applications A brief summary of the request should be sent to the correspondent. If the request is of interest to the trustees, further details will be requested. If the request has not been acknowledged within three months of submission, the applicant should assume that it has not been successful. The charity is interested to receive such applications but regrets that it is not able to acknowledge every unsuccessful submission.

Vivdale Ltd

Jewish

£53,000 (2004/05)

Beneficial area UK.

17 Cheyne Walk, London NW4 3QH

Correspondent D H Marks, Trustee

Trustees *D H Marks; L Marks; F Z Sinclair.*

CC Number 268505

Information available Accounts were available at the Charity Commission.

General In 2004/05 the trust's assets totalled £1.2 million, it had an income of £133,000 and donations totalled £53,000.

There were 15 grants over £1,000 each listed in the accounts. Beneficiaries included Education and Torah Establishment Arad (£9,000), Beis Yisroel Tel Aviv (£6,000), Emuno

Educational Centre Ltd. (£4,500), Friends of Harim Bnei Brak (£3,500), Beis Yaakov Town and Mosdos Bnei Brak (£3,000 each), Jewish Teachers Training College Gateshead (£2,900), Achisomach Aid Company Ltd (£2,500), Comet Charities Ltd and Torah Vechesed Ashdod (£2,000 each), Hendon Adath (£1,800), Woodstock Sinclair Trust (£1,500) and Beis Soroh Schneirer (£1,100).

Donations of not more than £1,000 each totalled £7,700.

Applications In writing to the correspondent.

The Viznitz Foundation

General

£136,000 (2004/05)

Beneficial area Worldwide.

23 Overlea Road, London E5 9BG

Correspondent H Feldman, Trustee

Trustees *H Feldman; E Kahan.*

CC Number 326581

Information available Accounts were on file at the Charity Commission, without a list a grants.

General In 2004/05 the foundation had assets of £1.5 million, an income of £175,000 and made grants totalling £136,000. Unfortunately no grant list was available for this period.

Applications In writing to the correspondent.

The Scurrah Wainwright Charity

Social reform, root causes of poverty and injustice

£76,000 (2005/06)

Beneficial area Preference for Yorkshire, South Africa and Zimbabwe.

16 Blenheim Street, Hebden Bridge, West Yorkshire HX7 8BU

Tel. 01422 845085

Website www.wainwrighttrusts.org.
uk/swc3.html

Correspondent Kerry McQuade,
Administrator

Trustees *M S Wainwright, Chair; J M
Wainwright; H A Wainwright; T M
Wainwright; P Wainwright; H Scott; R
Bhaskar.*

CC Number 1002755

Information available Full accounts
were available from the Charity
Commission website.

General The trust supports a wide
range of charitable projects with an
emphasis on social reform and tackling
the root causes of poverty and injustice.
Applications from the north of England,
particularly Yorkshire, will generally be
given strong priority; the trustees also
have an interest in Zimbabwe.

Grants have ranged from less than £100
to over £25,000, but there is no
minimum or maximum. Support may be
given in stages, for example a £30,000
grant over three years via three annual
payments of £10,000. A brief progress
report must be sent within a year of
receiving a grant. In 2005/06 the trust
had an income of £68,000 and made
grants totalling £76,000. Its assets stood
at £1.7 million.

Grants included those made to: Aldwych
Campaign (£11,000); Pay and
Employment Rights Service and Oxford
Research Group (£5,000 each); Bicycling
Empowerment Network and Omega
(£4,000 each); RETAS (£3,000), and
AMRIT, CHAS Housing Aid Kirklees,
the Grove Foundation Housing, Keighley
Voluntary Services and RJC Dance
(£1,000 each).

Exclusions No grants for individuals,
buildings, medical research or the
welfare of animals.

Applications In writing to the
correspondent. Applicants are expected
to provide background information
about their organisation, the work they
wish to pursue and their plans for its
practical implementation, which will
involve an outline budget and details of
any other sources of finance. The most
recent income and expenditure and
balance sheets should be included.
Trustees meet in March, July and
November. Applications should be
received by the first day of the preceding
month. For further information please
visit the trust's website.

Wakeham Trust

Community development, education, community service by young people

£183,000 (2005/06)

Beneficial area UK.

Wakeham Lodge, Rogate, Petersfield,
Hampshire GU31 5EJ

Tel. 01730 821748

Email wakehamtrust@mac.com

Website www.wakehamtrust.org

Correspondent The Trustees

Trustees *Harold Carter; Barnaby
Newbolt; Tess Silkstone.*

CC Number 267495

Information available Accounts were
on file at the Charity Commission. Full
and detailed guidelines can be found at
the trust's website.

General 'We provide grants to help
people rebuild their communities. We
are particularly interested in
neighbourhood projects, community arts
projects, projects involving community
service by young people, or projects set
up by those who are socially excluded.

'We also support innovative projects to
promote excellence in teaching (at any
level, from primary schools to
universities), though we never support
individuals.'

Grants are normally given where an
initial £75 to £750 can make a real
difference to getting the project up and
running.

In 2005/06 the trust's assets totalled
£1.9 million and it had an income of
£45,000. Grants to 90 organisations were
made totalling £183,000.

Beneficiaries of the largest grants were:
Charities Aid Foundation (£100,000);
CADECOM (£20,000); Lansallos Parish
Church (£10,000); Glebe Charitable
Trust (£6,000); Dean and Canons of
Christ Church (£3,500); Find Your Feet,
Lighthouse Education Centre and Values
Education for Life (£2,000 each);
Romanian Children's Homes (£1,500);
and INSEAD Trust Europe, Hewa Bora
Community Development and
Merseyfest Festivities (£1,000 each).

Smaller grants included those to Age
Concern – Southwark, BREAK, Brighton
and Hove Unemployed Centre, Cruise
Bereavement Care, Jill Franklin Trust,
London Tigers, Manyangwa Church,
Pelican Children's Centre, Pestalozzi

International Village Trust, St Cleopas'
Urban Project Aid, Streatham Darby and
Joan Club and Youth Action Flintshre.

Exclusions No grants to individuals or
large, well-established charities, or
towards buildings and transport.

Applications By letter or by filling in
the online form. The trust prefers online
applications.

Wallace and Gromit's Children's Foundation

Children's healthcare

£191,000 (2004/05)

Beneficial area UK.

PO Box 2186, Bristol BS99 7NT

Email info@wrongtrousersday.org

Website www.
wallaceandgromitfoundation.org

Correspondent Nicola Masters

Trustees *David Sproxton; Ian Hannah;
Jocelyn Moule; David Simons; Simon
Cooper; Nicholas Park; Peter Lord.*

CC Number 1096483

Information available Accounts were
on file at the Charity Commission.

General Wallace and Gromit's
Children's Foundation raises money to
improve the quality of life for children
in hospitals throughout the UK. It
provides funds for projects such as:

- arts, music and entertainment
  programmes
- providing welcoming and accessible
  environments
- funding education and information
  programmes
- helping to fund the acquisition of
  medical facilities
- sustaining family relationships
- helping to meet the cost of care in a
  children's hospice
- supporting children with physical and
  emotional difficulties.

In 2004/05 it had an income of £610,000
mainly arising from the Wrong Trousers
Day. Grants to 21 organisations totalled
£191,000.

All but two of the grants made were for
£10,000 each. Beneficiaries included the
Archie Foundation – Aberdeen,
Butterwick Children's Hospice –

Stockton on Tees, the Children's Appeal – Sheffield, Martin House Children's Hospice, Noah's Ark Art Project at the Children's Hospital for Wales, the Rockinghorse Appeal – Brighton and Yorkhill Children's Foundation – Glasgow.

Applications Grants are distributed on an annual basis. Application forms and guidelines are posted on the website from October.

The F J Wallis Charitable Settlement

General

£29,000 (2005/06)

Beneficial area UK, with some interest in Hampshire and Surrey.

c/o Bridge House, 11 Creek Road, Hampton Court, East Molesey, Surrey KT8 9BE

Email francis@hughescollett.co.uk

Correspondent F H Hughes, Trustee

Trustees F H Hughes; A J Hills; Revd J J A Archer.

CC Number 279273

Information available Accounts were obtained from the Charity Commission website.

General The trust was established for two broad purposes:

1 to build up an endowment fund for a significant project or donation to be made in memory of the founder
2 to make charitable donations to those causes that the trustees consider in need of assistance.

In 2005/06 the settlement had assets of £1.3 million and an income of £58,000. Grants to 23 organisations totalled £29,000 (£47,000 in the previous year). The majority of grants given were for £1,000.

In 2005/06 the settlement introduced a criteria-based approach to grantmaking. The trustees intend to rotate the areas of charitable activity that will receive grants. In 2006/07 these areas were disability, children charities and medical research/health and sickness, moving onto animal charities, community charities and hospices in 2007/08.

Exclusions No grants to individuals or to local charities except those in Surrey

or in Hampshire. The same organisation is not supported twice within a 24-month period.

Applications In writing to the correspondent. No telephone calls. Applications are not acknowledged and unsuccessful applicants will only be contacted if an sae is provided. Trustees meet in March and September and applications need to be received the month prior to the trustees' meeting.

Sir Siegmund Warburg's Voluntary Settlement

Medicine and education

£149,000 (2005/06)

Beneficial area UK, especially London.

33 St Mary Axe, London EC3A 8LL

Correspondent The Trustees

Trustees Hugh A Stevenson, Chair; Doris E Wasserman; Dr Michael J Harding; Christopher Purvis.

CC Number 286719

Information available Full accounts were available from the Charity Commission website.

General In 2005/06 the trust had an income of £385,000 and made grants totalling £133,000, with support costs of £16,000. Grants were given in two categories as follows:

Health and medicine – two grants (£125,000)
Beneficiaries were Royal Botanical Gardens Kew (£105,000) and Julia Polak Research Trust (£20,000).

Education – One grant (£7,500)
The sole beneficiary was King Edward's – School Warburg Science School (Witley) who were in receipt of an annual grant.

Exclusions No grants to individuals.

Applications In writing to the correspondent.

The Ward Blenkinsop Trust

Medicine, social welfare, general

£303,000 to organisations (2005/06)

Beneficial area UK, with a special interest in Merseyside and surrounding counties.

PO Box 28840, London SW13 0WZ

Correspondent Charlotte Blenkinsop, Trustee

Trustees A M Blenkinsop; J H Awdry; S J Blenkinsop; C A Blenkinsop; F A Stormer; H E Millin.

CC Number 265449

Information available Accounts had been filed with the Charity Commission.

General The trust currently supports charities in the Merseyside area and charities of a medical nature, but all requests for funds are considered.

In 2005/06 the trust had an income of £282,000 and made grants totalling £303,000.

By far the largest grant was £100,000 to Clatterbridge Cancer Research.

Other beneficiaries of larger grants included: the Clod Ensemble (£21,000); Royal Academy of Dance (£20,000); Comic Relief (£12,000); and Action on Addiction, Chase Children's Hospice, Hope HIV, George Martin Music Foundation, St Joseph's Family Centre (£10,000 each).

Other beneficiaries included: BID (£9,000); Church of the Holy Spirit Clapham, Fairley House, Infertility Network, NSPCC Trading Company, Rainbow House and Winchester Visitors Group (£5,000 each); Blackburn with Darwen Education Development Trust, Brainwave, Deafway, Depaul Trust, Fairfield Housing Trust, Give Youth a Break, Halton Autistic Family Support Group, Listening Books, St John's Leyland Division, Strongbones Children's Charitable Trust and Wirral Holistic Care Services (£1,000); and BIRD and Walk the Walk (£500 each).

Exclusions No grants to individuals.

Applications In writing to the correspondent.

The Barbara Ward Children's Foundation

Children, mental disability

£481,000 (2005)

Beneficial area England and Wales.

5 Great College Street, London
SW1P 3SJ

Website www.bwcf.org.uk

Correspondent The Trustees

Trustees *Mrs B I Ward, Chair; J C Banks; K R Parker; A M Gardner; B Walters.*

CC Number 1089783

Information available Accounts were on file at the Charity Commission.

General This foundation makes grants to organisations working with children who are seriously or terminally ill, disadvantaged or otherwise. In 2005 it had assets of £7.8 million and an income of £429,000. Grants to 43 organisations totalled £481,000.

The largest grants were made to Rainbow Trust Children's Charity (£67,000), the PACE Centre (£37,000), Starlight Children's Foundation (£35,000), Tree House (£26,000), BIBIC (£26,000), MERU (£25,000), DEBRA (£22,000) and the Elizabeth Foundation, Martin House and the Reedham Trust (£20,000 each).

Other beneficiaries included the Shooting Star Trust (£18,000), the Sick Children's Trust (£15,000), Royal London School for the Blind (£10,000), Lisa Thaxter Trust (6,400), AFASIC, the Bridge School, CHICKS, Deafway, Greenwich Toy & Leisure Library Association, Hopscotch and the Who Cares? Trust (£5,000 each), Ability Sports Association (£2,500), the Nursery Playgroup (£1,500), Threshers Day Nursery (£1,000), Side by Side (£900) and Rochdale Special Needs Cycling Club (£800).

Applications In writing to the correspondent including latest set of audited financial statements. The trustees usually meet quarterly.

Mrs Waterhouse Charitable Trust

Medical, health, welfare, environment, wildlife, churches, heritage

£287,000 (2005/06)

Beneficial area UK, with an interest in Lancashire.

25 Clitheroe Road, Whalley, Clitheroe
BB7 9AD

Correspondent D H Dunn, Trustee

Trustees *D H Dunn; E Dunn.*

CC Number 261685

Information available Accounts were on file at the Charity Commission.

General Support is given to organisations working in the Lancashire area or UK-wide. It mostly makes small recurrent grants towards core costs of small organisations to enable them to maintain and improve their services. Larger grants can also be made towards capital projects.

In 2005/06 the trust had assets of £7.4 million, which generated an income of £291,000. Grants were made to 69 organisations, of which 58 were recurrent, totalled £287,000. Grants included £83,000 to Lancashire charities and £33,000 to Lancashire branches of UK-wide organisations and were broken down as follows:

Medical and health – general	16 grants	£94,000
Medical and health – research	10	£55,000
Medical and health – children	10	£36,000
Welfare in the community – children and youth	8	£27,000
Welfare in the community – blind and deaf	5	£19,000
Welfare in the community – general	11	£23,000
Environment and wildlife	7	£28,000
Church and heritage	2	£5,000

There were seven grants of £10,000 each, beneficiaries were: AMEND, Cancer BACUP, Christie Hospital NHS Trust, East Lancashire Hospice Fund, Marie Curie Cancer Care, Macmillan Cancer Relief and National Trust Lake District Appeal.

Other beneficiaries included: National Eczema Society (£8,000); National Youth Orchestra (£7,000); Arthritis Research Campaign, Breakthrough Breast Cancer, Cancer Research UK, Lancashire Wildlife Trust, Multiple Sclerosis Society and National Osteoporosis Society (£5,000 each); Asthma UK, Brainwave, National Autistic Society and Whizz-Kidz (£3,000 each); Accrington and District Blind Society, ERIC, Home Start Ribble Valley,

Jennifer Trust and Leonora Trust (£2,000 each); and Community Gardening Ribble Valley (£1,000).

Exclusions No grants to individuals.

Applications In writing to the correspondent. There is no set time for the consideration of applications, but donations are normally made in March each year.

G R Waters Charitable Trust 2000

General

£129,000 (2004/05)

Beneficial area UK. Also North and Central America.

Finers Stephens Innocent, 179 -185 Great Portland Street, London W1W 5LS

Correspondent Michael Lewis

Trustees *M Fenwick; A Russell.*

CC Number 1091525

Information available Accounts were on file at the Charity Commission.

General This trust was registered with the Charity Commission in 2002, replacing Roger Waters 1989 Charitable Trust (Charity Commission number 328574), which transferred its assets to this new trust. (The 2000 in the title refers to when the declaration of trust was made.) Like the former trust, it receives a share of the Pink Floyd's royalties as part of its annual income. It has general charitable purposes throughout the UK, as well as North and Central America.

The following financial information (as well as the list of trustees) refer to the former, now extinct, trust. As the new trust stated that it will work in exactly the same manner as the one it has replaced, it can be assumed it is typical of how this trust will operate.

In 2004/05 the trust had assets of £1.2 million, total income was £134,000 and grants were made totalling £129,000.

Beneficiaries included Mandeville School Fund (£50,000), Kingston Grammar School (£13,000), Chaucer Clinic (£10,000), React (£5,000) and Bear and Ragged Staff Pumpkin Club (£500).

Applications In writing to the correspondent.

Blyth Watson Charitable Trust

General, UK-based humanitarian organisations

£81,000 (2004/05)

Beneficial area UK.

50 Broadway, Westminster, London SW1H 0BL

Correspondent The Trustees

Trustees *Edward Nicholas William Brown; Ian Hammond McCulloch.*

CC Number 1071390

Information available Accounts were on file at the Charity Commission.

General The trust dedicates its grant-giving policy in the area of humanitarian causes based in the UK.

In 2004/05 the trust had assets of £2.5 million and an income of £76,000. Grants to 28 organisations totalled £81,000.

Grants were in the range of £500 and £5,000 and included those to Army Benevolent Fund, King Edward VII Hospital, St Martin in the Fields Christmas Appeal, St Martin-in-the-Fields Building Project and Society for the Relief of Distress (£5,000 each), Breast Cancer Haven, Children's Fire and Burns Trust, St John of Jerusalem Eye Hospital and St Luke's Hospital (£3,000 each), Breast Cancer Haven, Over the Wall Gang Camp, Pace Centre, St John's Hospice and Waterways Trust (£2,500 each), Regalla Aid, St Leonard's Hospice and Vision Aid Overseas (£2,000 each), Progressive Supranuclear (£1,500) and Wavemakers (£1,000).

Applications In writing to the correspondent. Trustees usually meet twice during the year.

The Weavers' Company Benevolent Fund

Young people at risk from criminal involvement, young offenders and rehabilitation of prisoners and ex-prisoners

£218,000 (2005)

Beneficial area UK.

The Worshipful Company of Weavers', Saddlers' House, Gutter Lane, London EC2V 6BR

Tel. 020 7606 1155 **Fax** 020 7606 1119

Email charity@weaversco.co.uk

Website www.weavers.org.uk/

Correspondent John Snowdon, Clerk

Trustee *The Worshipful Company of Weavers.*

CC Number 266189

Information available Accounts were on file at the Charity Commission. *Guidelines for Applicants* can be found on the Weaver's Company website.

General This benevolent fund was set up in 1973 with funds provided by the Worshipful Company of Weavers, the oldest of the City of London Livery Companies. Its priorities are:

1. Helping disadvantaged young people

'The object of the fund is to support projects working with disadvantaged young people to ensure that they are given every possible chance to meet their full potential and to participate fully in society. We normally define young people as being aged from 5 to 30 years.'

2. Offenders and ex-offenders, particularly those under 30 years of age

'Many offenders and ex-offenders suffer from a variety of difficult and complex problems and they are amongst the most vulnerable members of society. We will fund work that addresses the social and economic problems faced by this group and their families, and provide them with support, life skills training and a way back into education, training and/or employment, so that they may

reintegrate and make a positive contribution to society.'

'We are especially interested in helping smaller organisations which offer direct services. They must be registered charities or in the process of applying for registration. Our grants are relatively modest, usually with an upper limit of £15,000 per annum, and to make sure grants of this size have an impact, we will not fund large organisations.'

'Applicants must show that they have investigated other sources of funding and made plans for the future, which should include replacement funding if appropriate.'

In 2005 the trust had assets of £6.4 million, an income of £258,000 and made grants totalling £218,000.

Grant beneficiaries included Prisoners Penfriends (£19,000), Fine Cell Work and Townsend Youth Project (£15,000 each), HOPE (£10,000), HMP Cardiff (£7,800), Prison Reform Trust Lecture (£7,000), Futures Theatre Company and Nomad (£6,000 each) and Just Drop-In Youth Info and Advice Centre, Kings Corner Project, Mercian Trust and Sobriety Project (£5,000 each).

Exclusions No grants to individuals. Applicants must be registered charities, in the process of registering, or qualified as charitable.

No grants for: long-term support; general appeals, endowment funds; grant-giving charities; retrospective funding; work that should be covered by statutory funding; building projects; capital projects to provide access in compliance with the Disability Discrimination Act; umbrella bodies or large, established organisations; organisations outside the UK.

Applications Detailed *Guidelines for Applicants* are available from the Weaver's Company website.

Application forms can be downloaded from the fund's website, or be requested by post or email.

The grants committee meets in February, June and October of each year, it may take up to four months for your application to be processed.

Webb Memorial Trust

Higher education (particularly economic and social sciences), the furthering of democracy and human rights, and development in Eastern Europe

About £30,000 to organisations

Beneficial area UK and Eastern Europe.

Mount Royal, Allendale Road, Hexham, Northumberland NE46 2NJ

Fax 01434 601846
Correspondent Michael J Parker, Honorary Secretary

Trustees *M D Bailey; D Gladwin; D Hayter; J Miller; M J Parker; R N Rawes.*

CC Number 313760

Information available Information was provided by the trust.

General This trust was set up to run a conference centre for the 'advancement of education and learning with respect to the history and problems of government and social policy'. In the 1950s and 1960s it became an important base for education and discussion for bodies such as the Fabian Society and many trade unions. However, following the decline in demand for such a facility, the trust decided to sell the house; the proceeds provided the funds for the trust's present grant-making activities.

The trust's grants policy reflects its original values and grants are made in the areas of higher education (particularly economic and social sciences), the furthering of democracy and human rights, and development in Eastern Europe. Grants are made to both individuals and universities. Other projects can also be supported, 'including international conferences and think tanks to increase the understanding of individuals and groups resident in Eastern Europe of democracy and how its institutions and political parties function and behave, as well as the development of social and economic policies within the UK'.

Beneficiaries have included Ruskin College, Fabian Society, Institute of Contemporary British History, Socialist Health Association, Transport 2000, Westminster Foundation for Democracy and Unison. Amounts awarded by the trust in the past have ranged between £500 and £10,000 for a single project.

The trust states that it distributes about £60,000 to £65,000 each year in grants, half of which goes towards funding students from Eastern Europe attending Ruskin College – Oxford to study courses relevant to the trust's objectives. The rest goes on projects either within the UK or overseas in Europe.

Exclusions No grants in support of any political party.

Applications On a form available from the correspondent, outlining the nature of the project – costs, timing and how the project fits in with the trust's objectives as outlined above. Applications for grants in the trust's financial year, which begins on 1 August, must be submitted by 31 January in the previous financial year (i.e. in the same calendar year). A copy of your latest annual report and accounts should be submitted with the application form.

The Mary Webb Trust

General

Around £100,000 (2005/06)
Beneficial area UK and overseas.

Cherry Cottage, Hudnall Common, Berkhamsted HP4 1QN

Correspondent Mrs C M Nash, Trustee
Trustees *Martin Ware; Mrs Jacqueline Fancett; Mrs Cherry Nash.*

CC Number 327659

Information available Information was obtained from the Charity Commission website.

General The trust states that it generally supports only smaller charities and will continue to do so. In 2005/06 the trust had an income of £22,000 and a total expenditure of £111,000. Further information was not available.

Previous beneficiaries have included the National Trust for Bre Pen, NSRA for Apeldoorn Blind Shooting, Fenland Archaeological Trust and Jubilee Appeal for Commenwealth Veterans.

Exclusions No grants to individuals or non-registered charities.

Applications The trust's annual report says that the trustees are: 'concerned by the large number of appeals received during the year. They prefer to make their own enquiries and find it difficult to handle the large volume of documents and unsolicited accounts sent to them'. Trustees normally meet quarterly, in March, May, August and December; applications need to be received by the month prior to the trustees' meeting.

The Weinberg Foundation

General

£195,000 (2004/05)
Beneficial area UK and overseas.

2nd Floor, Manfield House, 1 Southampton Street, London WC2R 0LR

Tel. 020 7845 7500
Correspondent N A Steinberg
Trustees *N H Ablitt; C L Simon.*

CC Number 273308

Information available Accounts were on file at the Charity Commission.

General In 2004/05 the trust had assets of over £1 million, which generated an income of £39,000. Grants were made totalling £195,000.

There were 30 donations of £1,000 or more listed in the accounts. Beneficiaries of the largest grants were: New College Development Fund (£30,000); Blenheim Foundation (£16,000); Haste and TATE Foundation (£15,000 each); Tikkun UK (£13,000); and Amnesty International UK Charitable Trust, Community Security Trust, Jennifer d'Abo Memorial Scholarship, the Royal Shakespeare Theatre and the University of the Witwatersrand Foundation (£10,000 each).

Other beneficiaries included the St James's Place Foundation (£7,400), Action on Addiction (£5,800), Evelina Children's Hospital and Elton John AIDS Foundations (£5,000 each), Institute for Policy Research (£2,500), International Spinal research Trust (£2,000) and Battle of Britain London (£1,000).

Other donations under £1,000 each totalled £4,600.

Applications In writing to the correspondent.

The Weinstein Foundation

Jewish, medical, welfare

£48,000 (2004/05)

Beneficial area Worldwide.

32 Fairholme Gardens, Finchley, London N3 3EB

Correspondent M L Weinstein, Trustee

Trustees *E Weinstein; Mrs S R Weinstein; M L Weinstein; P D Weinstein.*

CC Number 277779

Information available Full accounts were on file at the Charity Commission.

General This trust mostly supports Jewish organisations, although it does have general charitable purposes and supports a wide range of other causes, notably medical-related charities.

In 2004/05 the foundation had assets of £1.4 million, an income of £38,000 and made grants totalling £48,000.

There were 15 grants of £1,000 each or more listed in the accounts, beneficiaries included Chevras Ezras Nitzrochim Trust (£7,300), Friends of Mir (£5,000), Woodstock Sinclair Charitable Trust (£2,800), United Jewish Israel Appeal (£2,700), Hachzokas Torah Vechesed Charity (£1,800), Chesed Charitable Trust (£1,500), Friends of Haifa University (£1,300), Jewish Care (£1,200), Halev Charitable Trust and Nightingale House (£1,100 each) and Child Resettlement Fund, National Jewish Chaplaincy Board and Torah and Chesed Ltd (£1,000 each).

Donations under £1,000 each totalled £16,000.

Exclusions No grants to individuals.

Applications In writing to the correspondent.

The Weinstock Fund

General

£346,000 (2005/06)

Beneficial area Unrestricted, but with some local interest in the Wiltshire and Newbury area.

PO Box 17734, London SW18 3ZQ

Correspondent Miss Jacqueline Elstone, Trust Administrator

Trustees *Susan G Lacroix; Michael Lester; Laura H Weinstock.*

CC Number 222376

Information available Accounts were on file at the Charity Commission.

General 'The trustees support a wide range of charitable causes, particularly in the field of welfare, children, education, medicine and the arts. Only UK-registered charities are considered.'

In 2005/06 the fund had assets of £9 million, a total income of £355,000 and made 191 grants totalling £346,000.

The largest grant was £100,000 to Winchester College Development Fund, also a major beneficiary in the previous year.

Other beneficiaries included: St Paul's Girls School Development Trust (£20,000); Community Security Trust (£10,000); Ashmolean Museum, Royal Opera House Foundation, Save the Children Fund and St Hilda's College, Oxford (£5,000 each); CLIC Sargent (£3,000); British ORT, Holocaust Educational Trust, Jewish Care Oxford Synagogue and Jewish Centre (£2,500 each); Chicken Shed Theatre Company, Dorothy House Foundation and National Gallery Trust (£2,000 each); Army Benevolent Fund, British Friends of Hatzolah Israel, Donmar Warehouse, Garsington Opera, Hampstead Theatre, Home Warmth for the Aged and London Symphony Orchestra (£1,000 each); Delamere Forest School, Multiple Sclerosis Society, NICHS and Rainbow Trust (£500); UK Youth (£750); and Yetev Lev Youth Club (£250).

Exclusions No grants to individuals or unregistered organisations.

Applications In writing to the correspondent. There are no printed details or applications forms. Previous information received stated 'Where nationwide charities are concerned, the trustees prefer to make donations centrally.' Donations can only be made to registered charities, and details of the registration number are required before any payment can be made.

The James Weir Foundation

Welfare, education, general

£222,000 (2005)

Beneficial area UK, with a preference for Ayrshire and Glasgow.

84 Cicada Road, London SW18 2NZ

Tel. 020 8870 6233

Correspondent The Secretary

Trustees *Simon Bonham; William J Ducas; Elizabeth Bonham.*

CC Number 251764

Information available Accounts were on file at the Charity Commission.

General The foundation has general charitable purposes, giving priority to schools and educational institutions; Scottish organisations, especially local charities in Ayrshire and Glasgow; and charities with which either James Weir or the trustees are particularly associated. These preferences, however, do not appear to be at the expense of other causes, UK-wide charities or local organisations outside of Scotland. The following six charities are listed in the trust deed as potential beneficiaries:

- The Royal Society
- The British Association for Advancement of Science
- The RAF Benevolent Fund
- The Royal College of Surgeons
- The Royal College of Physicians
- The University of Strathclyde.

In 2005 the trust had an income of £213,000 and made 126 grants totalling £222,000. Assets stood at £6.8 million.

The largest grants were for £3,000 each, given to the six organisations listed in the trust deed. Other beneficiaries included: Boys' and Girls' Clubs Scotland, Chelsea Pensioners' Appeal, Elimination of Leukaemia Fund, Fairbridge in Scotland, Kidney Kids Scotland, National Deaf Children's Society, North Ayr Resource Centre, Prince's Trust Scotland, RNIB Scotland and Victim Support London (£2,000 each); and Brain Tumour UK, Dalmarnock Centre, Scottish Deaf Association, Visibility and Wiltshire Wildlife Trust (£1,000 each).

Exclusions Grants are given to recognised charities only. No grants to individuals.

Applications In writing to the correspondent. Distributions are made twice-yearly in June and November when the trustees meet. Applications should be received by May or October.

The Barbara Welby Trust

Animal welfare, medical, general

£31,000 (2005/06)

Beneficial area UK, with a small preference for Lincolnshire.

9 New Square, Lincoln's Inn, London WC2A 3QN

Correspondent The Trustees

Trustees *N J Barker; C W H Welby; C N Robertson.*

CC Number 252973

Information available Full accounts were on file at the Charity Commission

General The trust states that it considers supporting a range of charities, but has a preference for those of which the founder had special knowledge and for charities which have objectives with which she was especially associated. This was not defined any further by the trust, but from the list of grant beneficiaries it would appear that support is given mainly to animal welfare and medical charities. A number of beneficiaries were based in Lincolnshire.

In 2005/06 it had an income of £41,000 and made grants to 38 organisations totalling £31,000. The 13 largest grants went to: Stroxton Church (£3,000); Lincoln Cathedral Fabric Fund and Lincolnshire Agricultural Society – Lincfarms (£2,500 each); and Cafod, Cancer Research UK, ILPH, Ponies Association UK, RUKBA, St Luke's Hospital for the Clergy, St Wulfram's Church, the Connection at St Martin's, Westminster Cathedral and Wytham Hall (£1,000 each).

Other grants, all of £500 each, included those to British Red Cross, Depaul Trust, Farms for City Children, the Farmers' Benevolent Institution, FRAME, Grantham and District Mencap, Great Ormond Street Hospital – Samaritan's Fund, Lincolnshire Rural Stress Network, Rutland House School for Parents, St Barnabas Hospice, the Salvation Army and UNICEF.

Exclusions Applications for individual assistance are not normally considered unless made through an established charitable organisation.

Applications In writing at any time to the above address, although the trustees meet to consider grants in March and October.

The Wessex Youth Trust

Young people, general

£144,000 (2004/05)

Beneficial area Worldwide.

Farrer and Co., 66 Lincoln's Inn Fields, London WC2A 3LH

Tel. 020 7242 2022

Correspondent Jenny Cannon

Trustees *Mark Foster-Brown; Abel Hadden; Denise Poulton; Robert Clinton; Malcolm Cockren.*

CC Number 1076003

Information available Accounts were on file at the Charity Commission.

General 'The charity's primary aim is to assist other registered charities and charitable causes and in particular those with which Their Royal Highnesses have personal connection or interests. The charity is particularly, although not exclusively, interested in supporting projects which provide opportunities to help, support and advance young people.'

Most grants are one-off, although substantial grants may be made for up to five years.

In 2004/05 the trust had an income of £138,000 mainly from donations. Assets stood at £88,000. Grants totalled £144,000.

Beneficiaries included Bath Institute of Medical Engineering Limited, Blind in Business, Cambodia's Dump Children, Caring for Life, Chase Hospice Care for Children, Children's Adventure Farm Trust, Children's International Summer Villages, Duke of Edinburgh's Award International, East Anglia Children's Hospices 2000, Friends of Beverley School, Hoxton Hall, Invalids-at-Home, Jessie May Trust, Nancherrow Centre, National Youth Orchestra of Scotland, North Wiltshire Holiday Club for Children, Piggy Bank Kids, Playaway, Royal Scottish Academy of Music and Drama and Shawbury Scout and Guide Management.

The accounts stated: 'The Charities [sic] Commission has been supplied with details of amounts given to each charity together with an explanation of the reasons for the non-disclosure of individual amounts in the financial statements.' Non-disclosure of grants information should only be made where the information being made public may be potentially harmful to the trust or its recipients; failing to disclose information without providing an explanation in the public sphere may prompt unjustified speculation about the nature of grants made.

Exclusions No grants are made to:

- non-registered charities or causes
- individuals, including to people who are undertaking fundraising activities on behalf of a charity
- organisations whose main objects are to fund or support other causes
- organisations whose accounts disclose substantial financial resources and that have well-established and ample fundraising capabilities
- fund research that can be supported by government funding or that is popular among trusts.

Applications In writing to the correspondent in the first instance. A response will be made within two weeks in the form of an application form and guidelines to eligible applicants or a letter of rejection if more appropriate. Completed forms, which are not acknowledged upon receipt, need to be submitted by 1 May or 1 November, for consideration by the end of the month. Clarity of presentation and provision of financial details are among the qualities which impress the trustees. Successful applicants will receive a letter stating that the acceptance of the funding is conditional on an update being received before the next meeting. The trust's criteria state other correspondence cannot be entered into, and organisations cannot reveal the size of any grants they receive.

West London Synagogue Charitable Fund

Jewish, general

£46,000 (2006)

Beneficial area UK.

33 Seymour Place, London W1H 5AU

Tel. 020 7723 4404

Correspondent The Fund Coordinator

Trustees *Alan Bradley; Jane Cutter; Michael Cutter; Francine Epstein; Vivien Feather; Sarah Gluckstein; Ruth Jacobs; Hermy Jankel; Monica Jankel; Phyllis Levy; Caroline Marx; Elaine Parry; Jean Regen; Elizabeth Shrager; Anthony Stewart. Four ex-officio trustees.*

CC Number 209778

Information available Accounts on file at the Charity Commission.

General The trust stated that it makes grants to both Jewish and non-Jewish organisations. It prefers to be involved with charities which synagogue members are involved with or helped by. In 2006 it had an income of £50,000 and made 53 grants totalling £46,000.

Beneficiaries included: Save a Child's Heart and Strongbones (£8,000 each); MS Trust (£7,500); Berkeley Street Club and West London Synagogue (£2,000 each); MS Therapy Centre Harrow, Rabbi Freeman's Discretionary Fund and Rabbi Winer's Discretionary Fund (£1,000 each); Hammerson House, Magen David Adom and Norwood (£750 each); Action for Kids, Jewish Child's Day, Motor Neurone Disease, Oasis of Peace and World Jewish Relief (£500 each); Akiva School, Bet Shalom, Centrepoint – Soho, Downs Syndrome Association, Fortune Riding Centre for the Disabled, Jewish Youth Orchestra, Psoriasis Society and Winston's Wish (£250 each); and World Union of Progressive Judaism (£200).

Exclusions No grants to individuals.

Applications In writing to the correspondent.

Mrs S K West's Charitable Trust

General

£58,000 to organisations (2005)

Beneficial area UK.

20 Beech Road, Garstang, Preston PR3 1FS

Correspondent P J Schoon, Trustee

Trustees *P Schoon; Chris Blakeborough; J Grandage.*

CC Number 294755

Information available Full accounts were available from the Charity Commission website.

General Established in 1986, the trust has come to distribute roughly half of their available funds between charities promoting the Christian faith and those charities 'having people as their main concern'. The majority of support given to organisations is recurrent from previous years.

In 2005 the trust had assets of £441,000 and an income of £26,000. Grants amounted to £58,000 and were given to thirteen organisations.

Beneficiaries of the largest grants included Tear Fund (£17,000), Churchfields Hall (£12,000) and the Otley Meeting Room (£5,000).

Other grants made included BLESMA and the Holme Christian Care Centre (£4,000 each) and Age Concern, the Bible Society, Save the Children and Shaftesbury Society (£1,000 each).

Applications The trust states that it does not respond to unsolicited applications and would prefer not to receive any such applications asking for support.

The Westcroft Trust

International understanding, overseas aid, Quaker, Shropshire

£90,000 (2004/05)

Beneficial area Unrestricted, but with a special interest in Shropshire – causes of local interest outside Shropshire are rarely supported.

32 Hampton Road, Oswestry, Shropshire SY11 1SJ

Correspondent Mary Cadbury, Managing Trustee

Trustees *Mary C Cadbury; Richard G Cadbury; James E Cadbury; Erica R Cadbury.*

CC Number 212931

Information available Accounts were obtained from the Charity Commission website.

General Currently the trustees have five main areas of interest:

- international understanding, including conflict resolution and the material needs of the developing world
- religious causes, particularly social outreach, usually of the Society of Friends (Quakers) but also for those originating in Shropshire
- development of the voluntary sector in Shropshire
- needs of people with disabilities, primarily in Shropshire
- development of community groups and reconciliation between different cultures in Northern Ireland.

Medical education is only helped by support for expeditions overseas that include pre-clinical students. Medical aid, education and relief work in developing countries is mainly supported through UK-registered organisations. International disasters may be helped in response to public appeals.

The trust favours charities with low administrative overheads and that pursue clear policies of equal opportunity in meeting need. Grants may be one-off or recurrent; recurrent grants are rarely made for endowment or capital projects.

In 2004/05 it had assets of £2.1 million, which generated an income of £95,000. Grants were made totalling £90,000, broken down as follows:

Religious Society of Friends Central Committees – 1 grant of £6,900
This grant was donated to Britain Yearly Meeting.

Meeting Houses – 10 grants totalling £5,100
Grants included £750 to Bury St Edmunds Friends Meeting House, £550 to Alton Preparative Meeting, £500 each to Amis Quakers, Norwich Meeting Friends Building Fund and Stourbridge Friends Meeting House and £250 to Bristol and Frenchay Monthly Meeting.

Other funds, institutions and appeals – 14 grants totalling £13,000
The largest grants were £2,700 to Northern Friends Peace Board, £1,300 to Woodbrooke, £1,100 to The Retreat – York and £1,000 to Friends World Committee for Consultation. Other grants were £860 to Friends Therapeutic Community, £750 each to Young Friends General Meeting and West Midlands Quaker Peace Educational Trust and £450 to Quaker Social Action.

Shropshire Social Service in the county – 22 grants totalling £10,000
The largest grants were £1,500 to HOAP in two payments and £1,100 to

Community Council of Shropshire. Other grants included £670 to Citizen Advocacy, £500 each to Gordana House, Home Start South Shropshire and Bridgnorth, PCAS Shropshire Peer Counselling and Advocacy Service and Willowdene Farm and £300 to The Rock Spring Trust.

Education in the county – 1 grant totalling £160
This grant was donated to Shropshire Playbus.

Disability, health and special needs – 6 grants totalling £3,500
Donations included £1,100 to Macmillan Shropshire in two payments, £610 to Hope House, £500 to North Shropshire Special Olympics and £390 to Headway Shropshire.

Medical and surgical Research – 6 grants totalling £4,000
Grants were £970 to Institute of Orthopaedics, £950 to Remedi, £740 to Liverpool School of Tropical Medicine, £600 to Staffordshire University, £430 to Pain Relief Foundation and £300 to Bacup Cancer.

National Disabilities and special needs – 5 grants totalling £4,000
The largest grant was £2,200 to British Epilepsy Association. Other donations were £530 each to Mobility Information Service and Re-Solv, £440 to SANDS and £260 to Sequal Trust.

Social Services (England, Wales and Scotland) – 7 grants totalling £4,800
The largest grant was £1,100 to Hoxton Hall. Other grants included £670 to London Connection, £600 to HOPE for Children, £550 to Campus, £300 to Two Saints, £280 to Chaplaincy Fund of Walton Prison and £240 to Cheshire Foundation.

Social Services (Northern Ireland) – 2 grants totalling £960
These were £610 to Positive Ethos Trust and £350 to Forthspring Community Group.

Overseas Medical aid – 10 grants totalling £5,600
The largest grant was £1,100 to St John's Ophthalmic Hospital. Other donations included £670 to Impact Foundation, £650 to Orbis, £550 to Bethesda Leprosy Hospital, £500 each to The Tigre Trust, ROPE Relief for Oppressed People Everywhere and British Palawan Trust and £440 to Marie Stopes International.

Education – 10 grants totalling £8,900
The largest grants were £2,800 to Budiriro Trust and £1,500 to Canon Collins Trust. Other grants included

£750 to Community of The Holy Fire, £620 to Harambee Educational Fund, £550 to Womenkind Worldwide and £440 each to British Friends of Neve Shalom and The Friends of Students' Education Trust.

Relief work – 18 grants totalling £14,000
The largest grants were £2,200 to Oxfam, £1,500 to Action Village Trust Tsunami Appeal, £1,200 to Miriam Dean Trust Fund and £1,000 each to British Red Cross Phillipines Typhoon, Concern Sudan and DEC Tsunami Appeal. Smaller grants included £790 to Find Your Feet, £670 to Save the Children and £400 to UNICEF.

International understanding – 11 grants totalling £9,500
The largest grants were £4,000 to Bradford University Department of Peace Studies and £1,000 to Peace Direct. Other grants included £730 to Development Education Project, £500 each to Y Care International and Omega Foundation, £400 to The Iona Community and £390 to World University Service.

Exclusions Grants are given to charities only. No grants to individuals or for medical electives, sport, the arts (unless specifically for people with disabilities in Shropshire) or armed forces charities. Requests for sponsorship are not supported. Annual grants are withheld if recent accounts are not available or do not satisfy the trustees as to continuing need.

Applications In writing to the correspondent. There is no application form or set format but applications should be restricted to a maximum of three sheets of paper, stating purpose, overall financial needs and resources together with previous years' accounts if appropriate. Printed letters signed by 'the great and good' and glossy literature do not impress the trustees, who prefer lower-cost applications. Applications are dealt with about every two months. No acknowledgement will be given. Replies to relevant but unsuccessful applicants will be sent only if an sae is enclosed. As some annual grants are made by Bank Telepay, details of bank name, branch, sort code, and account name and number should be sent in order to save time and correspondence.

The Barbara Whatmore Charitable Trust

The arts and music and the relief of poverty
£46,000 (2005/06)
Beneficial area UK.

Spring House, Priors Way, Aldeburgh, Suffolk IP15 5EW

Correspondent Mrs P M Cooke-Yarborough, Chair

Trustees *Patricia Cooke-Yarborough, Chair; David Eldridge; Denis Borrow; Gillian Lewis; Luke Gardiner; Sally Carter; Stephen Bate.*

CC Number 283336

Information available Accounts were on file at the Charity Commission.

General This trust was registered with the Charity Commission in October 1981. In 2005/06 it had assets of £1.3 million. It had an income of £51,000 and made 31 grants totalling £46,000.

Beneficiaries included St Mary the Virgin – Holne (£3,500), Campaign for Drawing and Leather Conservation Centre (£3,000 each), Park Lane Group and Polka Theatre (£2,500 each), Britten-Pears Young Artist Programme, City & Guilds of London Art School, Museum of East Anglian Life, National Youth Orchestra, Pro Corda, St Mary's, Stratford St Mary, Textile Conservation Centre and Watts Gallery – Compton (£2,000 each), Foundation for Young Musicians and St Mary the Virgin – Huntingfield (£1,500 each), Britten Sinfonia, Coldharbour Mill, St Botolph's – Banningham and St Peter & St Paul – Fressingfield (£1,000 each), Fry Art Gallery (£650), Opera North (£500) and New Lanark Conservation (£250).

Applications In writing to the correspondent.

The Whitaker Charitable Trust

Education, environment, music, personal development

£131,000 (2005/06)

Beneficial area UK, but mostly east Midlands and Scotland.

c/o Currey and Co., 21 Buckingham Gate, London SW1E 6LS

Correspondent The Trustees

Trustees *Edward Ronald Haslewood Perks; David W J Price; Lady Elizabeth Jane Ravenscroft Whitaker.*

CC Number 234491

Information available Accounts were on file at the Charity Commission.

General The trust has general charitable objects, although with stated preferences for music education, agricultural and silvicultural education, countryside conservation, Scottish charities and prison-related charities.

Grants are made to UK-wide organisations and local organisations in Nottinghamshire and the east Midlands.

In 2005/06 the trust had assets of £7.3 million, which generated an income of £169,000. Grants to 48 organisations totalled £131,000.

A substantial grant of £35,000 was made to Atlantic College. Other beneficiaries included: Glenalmond College (£10,000); Leith School of Art (£8,000); Harworth Parochial Church Council (£7,000); St John Ambulance (£6,000); Opera North and Royal Forestry Society (£5,000 each); Game Conservancy – Scotland and Jasmine Trust (£3,000 each); Bassetlaw Hospice and Lincoln Cathedral Fabric Fund (£2,000 each); Prison Phoenix Trust (£1,500); Arboreum Trust, Focus on Young in Bassetlaw, the Zibby Garnett Travelling Fellowship, Music in Hospitals and Tree Aid (£1,000 each).

Exclusions Support is given to registered charities only. No grants are given to individuals or for the repair or maintenance of individual churches.

Applications In writing to the correspondent. Trustees meet half-yearly. Applications should include clear details of the need the intended project is designed to meet plus a copy of the latest accounts available and an outline budget. If an acknowledgement of the application, or notification in the event of the application not being accepted, is required, an sae should be enclosed.

The Colonel W H Whitbread Charitable Trust

Health, welfare, general

£102,000 (2005)

Beneficial area UK, with an interest in Gloucestershire.

Fir Tree Cottage, Worlds End, Sinton Green, Worcestershire WR2 6NN

Email sysan@whitbread-trust.fsnet.co.uk

Correspondent Mrs Susan M Smith

Trustees *H F Whitbread, Chair; J R Barkes.*

CC Number 210496

Information available Full accounts were on file at the Charity Commission.

General 'The trustees have resolved to support charitable organisations and general areas of charitable activity which were, or in the opinion of the trustees would have been, of interest to the trust's founder, the late Colonel William Henry Whitbread, which comprise the following:

1 'The promotion of education and in particular: (a) the provision of financial assistance towards the maintenance and development of Aldenham School, and (b) the creation of Colonel W.H. Whitbread scholarships or bursaries or prizes to be awarded to pupils at Aldenham School.
2 'Charitable organisations within Gloucestershire.
3 'The preservation, protection and improvement for the public benefit of places of historic interest and natural beauty.'

The trustees will only in exceptional circumstances consider grant applications for purposes which fall outside those described above. Within this framework the trustees will distribute a minimum of £500 per distribution.

The trustees make charitable distributions on an arbitrary basis, having reviewed all applications and considered other charities that they wish to benefit.

In 2005 the trust had assets of £6.4 million and an income of £214,000. Grants were made to 33 organisations totalling £102,000.

The three largest grants went to DEC Tsunami Earthquake Appeal, Hunt Servants' Fund and St Peter and St Paul Northleach Charitable Trust (£10,000 each).

Other beneficiaries included: 1st Queen's Dragon Guards Regimental Trust and Great Ormond Street Hospital Children's Charity (£5,000 each); Friends of Alderman Knights School, Gloucestershire Historic Churches Trust, Gloucestershire Hospitals NHS Trust, Queen Mary's Clothing Guild and St Richard's Hospice (£3,000 each); Army Benevolent Fund, Household Cavalry Museum Appeal, National Deaf Children's Society and Royal Star and Garter Home (£2,000 each); Stroud Autistic Support Group (£1,500); Abbey School Tewkesbury (£1,000); the Chelsea Pensioners (£800); Royal Hospital Chelsea (£300); and CLIC Sargent (£200).

Applications A brief summary (no more than one side of A4) in writing (by email if possible) to the correspondent. It is not necessary to send any accompanying paperwork at this stage. Should the trustees wish to consider any application further, then an application form would be sent out.

The Simon Whitbread Charitable Trust

Education, family welfare, medicine, preservation

£81,000 (2004/05)

Beneficial area UK, with a preference for Bedfordshire.

Hunters, 9 New Square, Lincoln's Inn, London WC2A 3RZ

Correspondent E C A Martineau, Administrator

Trustees *Mrs H Whitbread; S C Whitbread; E C A Martineau; Mrs E A Bennett.*

CC Number 200412

Information available Accounts were on file at the Charity Commission.

General The trust supports general causes in Bedfordshire, and education, family welfare, medicine, medical research and preservation UK-wide.

In 2004/05 the trust had assets of £3.1 million and an income of £87,000. Grants were made to 58 organisations totalling £81,000.

Beneficiaries included Bedfordshire Music Trust (£6,500), Chillingham Wild Cattle (£5,000), Countryside Foundation for Education (£4,000), Gravenhurst Parish Council, St Luke's Hospital for the Clergy and Spurgeons Child Care (£3,000 each), Royal Green Jackets and Retirement Education Centre Bedfordshire (£2,500 each), Army Benevolent Fund and Bedfordshire Historical Records Society (£2,000 each), All Saints Church, Mencap, RSPB and St Mungo's (£1,000 each) and Arthritis Care, National Association of Widows and SCOPE (£500 each).

Exclusions Generally no support for local projects outside Bedfordshire.

Applications In writing to the correspondent. Acknowledgements are not given. Please do *not* telephone.

The Whitecourt Charitable Trust

Christian, general

£46,000 (2005/06)

Beneficial area UK and overseas, with a preference for Sheffield.

48 Canterbury Avenue, Fulwood, Sheffield S10 3RU

Correspondent Mrs G W Lee, Trustee

Trustees *P W Lee; Mrs G W Lee; M P W Lee.*

CC Number 1000012

Information available Accounts were on file at the Charity Commission.

General Most of the grants given by the trust are recurrent and to Christian causes in the UK and overseas. Other grants are given to a few Christian and welfare causes in Sheffield.

In 2005/06 the trust had an income of £79,000. Grants were made totalling £46,000.

There were 115 grants made in the year of which 3 totalling £10,500 were made to Christ Church Fulwood: General Fund (£4,500); Missionary Fund (£4,500); and the Vicar's Discretionary

Fund (£1,000). This organisations has also received substantial support in previous years.

Other beneficiaries of grants over £1,000 each were: University of Sheffield (£5,000); Monkton Combe School Bursary Fund (£3,000); South Yorkshire Community Foundation (£2,100); and Church Mission Society, DEC Asia Quake Appeal, DEC Niger Crisis Appeal and Whirlow Grange Ltd (£1,000 each).

Beneficiaries of smaller grants included African Child Trust, the Claypath Trust, Church Army, Greenhouse Trust, Interserve, Jubilee Centre, National Trust, Phoenix House Trust, Royal Society of Arts, Scripture Union, Sheffield YMCA, TEAR Fund, Youth for Christ and Yorkshire Cadet Trust.

Exclusions No support for animal or conservation organisations or for campaigning on social issues.

Applications In writing to the correspondent, at any time. However, the trust states very little money is available for unsolicited applications, due to advance commitments.

A H and B C Whiteley Charitable Trust

Art, environment, general

£38,000 (2005/06)

Beneficial area England, Scotland and Wales, with a special interest in Nottinghamshire.

Marchants, Regent Chambers, Regent Street, Mansfield, Nottinghamshire NG18 1SW

Tel. 01623 655111

Correspondent E G Aspley, Trustee

Trustees *E G Aspley; K E B Clayton.*

CC Number 1002220

Information available Accounts were obtained from the Charity Commission website.

General The trust was established in 1990 and derives most of its income from continuing donations. The trust deed requires the trustees to make donations to registered charities in England, Scotland and Wales but with particular emphasis on charities based in Nottinghamshire.

In 2005/06 the trust had assets of £1.3 million and an income of £44,000. Grants were made to five organisations totalling £38,000.

Beneficiaries were Cardothoracic Centre Liverpool and Portland College (£10,000 each), Macmillan Cancer Relief and Mansfield Cat Protection League (£7,500 each) and Terry Marsh Bird Rescue (£3,000).

Applications The trust does not seek applications.

The Norman Whiteley Trust

Evangelical Christianity, welfare, education

£132,000 (2005/06)

Beneficial area Worldwide, although in practice mainly Cumbria.

Lane Cove, Grassgarth Lane, Ings, Cumbria LA8 9QF

Correspondent D Foster

Trustees *Mrs B M Whiteley; P Whiteley; D Dickson; J Ratcliff.*

CC Number 226445

Information available Accounts were available from the Charity Commission website.

General This trust supports the furtherance of the Gospel, the relief of poverty and education. Grants can be made worldwide, but in practice are usually restricted to Cumbria and the surrounding areas. In 2005/06 the trust had assets of £2.5 million and an income of £136,000. Grants were made totalling £132,000.

The largest grants included those made to: Osterreichische Evangelische Allianz (£16,000); Full Life Church and Alpha Osterreich (£15,000 each); Agape Osterreich (£12,000); and Bibellesbund (£10,000).

Grants of less than £10,000 each included those made to: Sports Reach (£6,500); Before the Throne Ministries (£5,000); Bootle Evangelical Church and Millom Methodist Church (£3,000 each); Assemblies of God (£2,000); and Tottlebank Baptist Church (£1,000).

Exclusions Whilst certain overseas organisations are supported, applications from outside Cumbria are not accepted.

Applications In writing to the correspondent. Trustees meet to consider applications twice a year.

The Whitley Animal Protection Trust

Protection and conservation of animals and their environments

£259,000 (2005)

Beneficial area UK and overseas, with a preference for Scotland.

Edgbaston House, Walker Street, Wellington, Telford, Shropshire TF1 1HF

Tel. 01952 641651

Correspondent M T Gwynne

Trustees *E Whitley, Chair; Mrs P A Whitley; E J Whitley; J Whitley.*

CC Number 236746

Information available Full accounts were on file at the Charity Commission.

General This trust supports the prevention of cruelty to animals and the promotion of their conservation and environment. Grants are made throughout the UK and the rest of world, with about 20% of funds given in Scotland.

In 2005 the trust had assets of £8.8 million and an income of £336,000. Grants totalled £259,000.

Beneficiaries were Whitley Fund for Nature (£133,000), Rivers and Fisheries Trust for Scotland (£40,000), Fauna and Flora International (£30,000), Edinburgh Zoo (£20,000), the Wildlife Conservation Research Unit of the Department of Zoology in the University of Oxford (£15,000), Orangutan Foundation and RSPB Scotland (£5,000 each), Eden Rivers Trust, Shropshire Wildlife Trust and the Wye and Usk Foundation (£3,000 each) and British Small Animal Vets and Hawk and Owl Trust (£1,000 each).

Exclusions No grants to non-registered charities.

Applications In writing to the correspondent. The correspondent stated: 'The trust honours existing commitments and initiates new ones through its own contacts rather than responding to unsolicited applications.'

The Lionel Wigram Memorial Trust

General

£14,000 (2005/06)

Beneficial area UK, with a preference for Greater London.

Highfield House, 4 Woodfall Street, London SW3 4DJ

Correspondent A F Wigram, Chair

Trustees *A F Wigram, Chair; Mrs S A Wigram.*

CC Number 800533

Information available Accounts were on file at the Charity Commission.

General The trust makes grants to a wide range of organisations. Its annual report for 2005/06 stated the trustees 'have particular regard to projects which will commemorate the life of Major Lionel Wigram who was killed in action in Italy in 1944'.

In 2005/06 the trust's assets totalled £732,000 and it had an income of £53,000, comprised mainly of rental income. Grants totalled £14,000. They were broken down as follows:

Coping with illness and disability – 15 grants totalling £6,400
All grants were for £425 each and included those to 3H Fund, Access to Art, Break and the James Powell (UK) Trust.

Community projects/helping the disadvantaged – 7 grants totalling £2,500
Beneficiaries included Caring for life and Charterhouse in Southwark Fund (£425 each); Rainbow Development in Africa (£350); and Friends of the Elderly (£50).

Performing arts – 1 grant of £3,000
The sole beneficiary was Newbury Spring Festival.

Historical/restoration – 1 grant of £425
The sole beneficiary was HipART.

Research and prevention of illness – 2 grants totalling £850
Bath Institute of Medical Engineering and Gift of Life Commemorative Trust each received £425.

Conservation – 1 grant of £425
The sole beneficiary was Marine Conservation Society.

Applications In writing to the correspondent.

The Richard Wilcox Welfare Charity

Animal welfare, health, medical research, welfare of patients, hospitals

£321,000 (2004/05)

Beneficial area UK.

Herschel House, 58 Herschel Street, Slough SL1 1PG

Correspondent Richard Oury, Administrator

Trustees *John Ingram; Nick Sargent; Roger Danks.*

CC Number 1082586

Information available Accounts were on file at the Charity Commission without a list of grants.

General Registered with the Charity Commission in September 2000, the objectives of the trust are to:

- prevent cruelty and to relieve the suffering and distress of animals of any species who are in need of care, attention and protection
- relieve sickness and protect and preserve good health
- promote the research and advancement of the causes and treatment of diseases
- relieve patients receiving treatment in hospital or on their discharge
- provide, maintain and improve hospitals and other institutions providing medical treatment
- assist or promote any charitable organisation or charitable purpose.

In 2004/05 it had an income of £378,000 and grants totalled £321,000. Assets stood at £2.3 million. Further information on grants was not included with the accounts filed at the Charity Commission.

Applications In writing to the correspondent. The trustees meet quarterly to assess grant applications.

The Felicity Wilde Charitable Trust

Children, medical research

£55,000 (2005/06)
Beneficial area UK.

Barclays Bank Trust Company Ltd, Estates and Trusts, Osborne Court, Gadbrook Park, Northwich, Cheshire CW9 7UE

Correspondent Rob Taylor

Trustee *Barclays Bank Trust Co. Ltd.*

CC Number 264404

Information available Information had been filed at the Charity Commission.

General The trust supports children's charities and medical research, with particular emphasis on research into the causes or cures of asthma.

In 2005/06 it had an income of £69,000 and gave grants totalling £55,000.

Previous beneficiaries have included Action on Addiction, Asthma UK, Bobath – Glasgow, Breakthrough Breast Cancer, British Epilepsy Association, British Lung Foundation, ChildLine, Children's Liver Disease Foundation, Darlington Association on Disability, East Anglia Children's Hospices, Home-Start Leicester, Honeypot Charity, Kids Out, Meningitis Research Foundation, National Back Pain Association, National Eczema Society, Shooting Star Trust Children's Hospice, Southampton University Development Trust, Sparks, Starlight Children's Foundation, West Midlands Post Adoption Service and Who Cares? Trust.

Exclusions No grants to individuals or non-registered charities.

Applications In writing to the correspondent at any time. Applications are usually considered quarterly.

The Wilkinson Charitable Foundation

Scientific research, education

£57,000 (2004/05)
Beneficial area UK.

c/o Lawrence Graham, 190 Strand, London WC2R 1JN

Correspondent B D S Lock, Trustee

Trustees *B D S Lock; G C Hurstfield.*

CC Number 276214

Information available Full accounts were on file at the Charity Commission.

General The trust was set up for the advancement of scientific knowledge and education at Imperial College, University of London and for general purposes. Grants are only given to academic institutions.

The trustees have continued their policy of supporting research and initiatives commenced in the founder's lifetime and encouraging work in similar fields to those he was interested in.

In 2004/05 the foundation had assets of £1.3 million and an income of £49,000. Grants to 12 organisations totalled £57,000.

The main beneficiary was Wolfson College (£32,000). Other grants included those to University College – London (£8,000), Imperial College of Science, Technology and Medicine, (£5,000), Imperial College (£2,500), Portsmouth Grammar School (£2,000) and Alzheimer's Society, British Heart Foundation, DISCS, Eliminating Leukaemia, Medical Laser Institute – Lasers for Life and University of Cambridge/Darwin Correspondence Project (£1,000 each).

Exclusions No grants to individuals.

Applications In writing to the correspondent.

The Kay Williams Charitable Foundation

Medical research, disability, general

About £37,000 (2005/06)
Beneficial area UK.

BDO Stoy Hayward, Kings Wharf, 20–30 Kings Road, Reading, Berkshire RG1 3EX

Tel. 0118 950 4013

Correspondent R M Cantor, Trustee

Trustees *R M Cantor; D W Graham; Mrs M C Williams.*

CC Number 1047947

Information available Information was obtained from the Charity Commission website.

General The trust was established in 1995 and generally has about £50,000 available to be given in grants. In 2005 the trust had an income of £16,000 and a total expenditure of £49,000. Further information was not available.

Previous beneficiaries have included Royal Opera House Trust, Cancer Research Campaign, Action for Blind People, Help the Aged, Cancer Relief Macmillan Fund, ITGD, NCH Action for Children, the River Thames Boat, the Samaritans and World Cancer Research Fund.

Applications In writing to the correspondent.

Dame Violet Wills Charitable Trust

Evangelical Christianity

£80,000 (2006)
Beneficial area UK and overseas, but there may be a preference for Bristol.

Ricketts Cooper and Co., Thornton House, Richmond Hill, Bristol BS8 1AT

Correspondent H E Cooper, Secretary and Treasurer

Trustees *D G Cleave, Chair; S Burton; H E Cooper; Miss R Daws; J R Dean; G J T Landreth; Mrs M J Lewis; Prof A H Linton; Revd Dr E C Lucas; Mrs J Persson; Mrs R E Peskett; Revd A J G Cooper; D R Caporn; Revd R W Lockhart.*

CC Number 219485

Information available Accounts were obtained from the Charity Commission website.

General The trust continues to operate within the original terms of reference, supporting evangelical Christian activities both within the UK and overseas. It is not the practice of the trustees to guarantee long-term support to any work, however worthy. The trust does not make a practice of supplying funds to individuals or non-registered charities.

Current categories of Christian work for trustee consideration are:

- training and bursaries
- missions – UK
- missions – other countries
- literature
- broadcasts.

In 2006 the trust had assets of £1.8 million and an income of £92,000. Grants were made to 115 organisations totalling £80,000.

Organisation in receipt of amounts over £1,000 each included: WC and SWET – Evangelists Fund (£13,000); Echoes of Service – Bristol Missionaries (£3,600); Christian Ministries – General Purposes (£2,200); Bristol International Student Centre (£2,000); Redcliffe College – overseas student bursary fund – (£1,800); Living Waters Radio Ministry (£1,600); FEBA Radio (£1,500); AWM Media (£1,200); and Christian TV Association, OC Team – NEGST and SAT – 7 Trust (£1,000 each).

Exclusions Grants are not given to individuals.

Applications In writing to the correspondent. Trustees meet in March and September.

The John Wilson Bequest Fund

Health, welfare, women

See below

Beneficial area Mainly Edinburgh.

Messrs J and R A Robertson, 15 Great Stuart Street, Edinburgh EH3 7TS

Tel. 0131 225 5095

Correspondent A D Sheperd

SC Number SC010651

Information available Information was obtained from the Scottish Charity Register.

General The trust supports charities which are concerned with people who are poor or unwell living in Edinburgh, especially those which make special provision for women. It also supports individuals in need in Edinburgh and foreign missionaries of any Protestant church in Scotland while they are at home (for further information on grants to individuals, see *A Guide to Grants for Individuals in Need*).

In 2005 the trust had an income of £66,000, further financial information was not available.

Applications In writing to the correspondent.

Sumner Wilson Charitable Trust

General

£48,000 (2003/04)

Beneficial area UK.

Munslows, Mansfield House, 2nd Floor, 1 Southampton Street, London WC2R 0LR

Tel. 020 7845 7500

Correspondent N A Steinberg

Trustees *Lord Joffe; Mrs A W S Christie; M S Wilson.*

CC Number 1018852

Information available Accounts were on file at the Charity Commission.

General This trust had general charitable purposes, with no preferences or exclusions. In 2003/04 it had assets of almost £2 million, an income of £41,000 and made grants totalling £48,000.

There were 19 grants of £1,000 or more listed in the accounts. Beneficiaries included St James's Place Foundation (£13,000), Kids Company and Prince's Trust (£5,000 each), Jaipur Limb Campaign, Katie and Eloise Memorial Trust, London School and Oxford Brookes (£2,500 each) and Children with AIDS Charity, Hope and Homes for Children, Howard League, Relate – Winchester and District, West London Centre for Counselling and Village Education (£1,000 each).

Unlisted grants under £1,000 each totalled £5,000.

Applications In writing to the correspondent, or to the trustees.

The Benjamin Winegarten Charitable Trust

Jewish

£133,000 to organisations (2005/06)

Beneficial area UK.

25 St Andrew's Grove, Stoke Newington, London N16 5NF

Correspondent B A Winegarten, Trustee

Trustees *B A Winegarten; Mrs E Winegarten.*

CC Number 271442

Information available Accounts were on file at the Charity Commission, but without a list of grants.

General This trust makes grants for the advancement of the Jewish religion and religious education. In 2005/06 it had assets of £514,000 and an income of £149,000, including £100,000 from donations and grants. Grants to organisations totalled £133,000, with £13,000 going to individuals.

Previous beneficiaries have included Hechal Hatovah Institute, the Jewish Educational Trust, the Mechinah School, Merkaz Lechinuch Torani Zichron Ya'akov, Ohr Someach Friends, Or Akiva Community Centre, Yeshivo Hovomo Talmudical College and ZSVT.

Applications In writing to the correspondent.

Wingfield's Charitable Trust

General

£23,000 (2004/05)

Beneficial area UK and overseas, with some preference for the Shrewsbury area.

c/o Dyke Yaxley Limited, 1 Brassey Road, Old Potts Way, Shrewsbury SY3 7FA

Tel. 01743 241281 **Fax** 01743 235794

Correspondent Catherine Helen Thomas, Trustee

Trustees *Marie Claire Wingfield; Helen Margaret Wingfield; Catherine Helen Thomas.*

CC Number 269524

Information available Accounts were available from the Charity Commission, but without a list of grants.

General In 2004/05 the trust had assets of £600,000 and an income of £28,000. Grants totalled £23,000, but unfortunately a list of grants was not available.

The trust informed us that it makes grants to a wide range of causes. The trust implied, however, that some preference is given to causes in Shrewsbury over those from the rest of the UK. The founder also has a special interest in supporting people with exceptional talent in the arts who do not have the financial means to progress – particularly opera and ballet. Grants to individuals are not made direct to the person, but via a supporting charity.

Applications In writing to the correspondent. Applications are usually considered once a month. The trust receives many more applications than it is able to support. Only those applicants who include an sae will receive a reply.

The Francis Winham Foundation

Welfare of older people

£722,000 (2005/06)

Beneficial area England.

41 Langton Street, London SW10 0JL

Tel. 020 7795 1261 **Fax** 020 7795 1262

Email francinetrust@btopenworld.com

Correspondent Mrs J Winham, Trustee

Trustees *Francine Winham; Dr John Norcliffe Roberts; Josephine Winham; Elsa Peters.*

CC Number 278092

Information available Accounts on file at the Charity Commission.

General The foundation makes around 150 grants a year, mostly for amounts under £5,000 and which can be as low as £75. Grants are given to both national organisations (including their local branches) and local charities. Many organisations are regular recipients, although not necessarily on an annual basis.

In 2005/06 the trust had assets of £3.9 million and an income of £1.1 million. Grants were made to 489 organisations totalling £722,000. Some organisations received many payments during the year, which are likely to have gone to local branches.

There were 18 organisations in receipt of £10,000 or more: SSAFA (£48,000); Royal British Legion (£28,000); Friends of the Countess Mountbatten House and wpf Counselling Psychotherapy (£20,000 each); Camden Housebound Link Services, Cotswold Villages Old People's Association, Help the Hospices, the Shakespeare Hospice and Universal Beneficent Society (£15,000 each); British School of Osteopathy and Care and Repair – Bristol (£13,000 each); Lygon Almshouses (£11,000); and Abbeyfield Epping Society, Age Concern Sandwell, Counsel and Care, Goldhill Housing Association, Hospital of the Blessed Trinity – Guildford, and North London Hospice (£10,000 each).

Applications In writing to the correspondent. The trust regrets it cannot send replies to applications outside its specific field of help for older people. Applications should be made through registered charities or social services departments only.

Anona Winn Charitable Trust

Health, medical, welfare

£44,000 (2004)

Beneficial area UK.

Kissingstone Cottage, Edgeworth, Stroud, Gloucestershire GL6 7JQ

Correspondent The Trustees

Trustee *Trefoil Trustees Ltd.*

CC Number 1044101

Information available Accounts were on file at the Charity Commission.

General Registered with the Charity Commission in February 1995, the trustees maintain a list of charitable

organisations which it supports; this list is reviewed periodically.

In 2004 the trust had assets of £1.2 million and an income of £46,000. Grants totalled £44,000 of which £10,000 went to the British Red Cross and £9,000 to the Charities Aid Foundation.

Other beneficiaries included: the British Museum Development Trust, the Initiative Foundation, In Kind Direct, the Royal Academy of Arts and Seven Springs Foundation (£2,000 each); Action on Addiction, Angels International, Arthritis Research, British Heart Foundation, the Children's Hospital Trust Fund, the Metropolitan Police Benevolent Fund, Motor Neurone Disease Foundation, Newmarket Day Centre, RNLI and RAOC Charitable Trust (£1,000 each); Elizabeth Finn Trust, Gloucestershire Kidney Patients' Association, Jubilee Sailing Trust and National Playing Fields Association (£500 each); and Lady Hoare Trust (£250).

Exclusions No applications are considered from individuals.

Applications Applications will only be considered if received in writing and accompanied by the organisation's latest report and full accounts.

The Michael and Anna Wix Charitable Trust

Older people, disability, education, medicine and health, poverty, welfare, Jewish

£60,000 (2005/06)

Beneficial area UK.

Portrait Solicitors, 1 Chancery Lane, London WC2A 1LF

Correspondent The Trustees

Trustees *Mrs J B Bloch; D B Flynn; Miss Judith Portrait.*

CC Number 207863

Information available Full accounts were on file at the Charity Commission.

General In 2005/06 the trust had assets of £1.8 million and an income of £58,000. Grant management and administration costs were high at

£17,000. Grants were made to 227 organisations totalling £60,000.

The largest grants went to: Nightingale House (£6,000); British Technion Society and Jewish Care (£2,000 each); Friends of the Hebrew University of Jerusalem (£1,500); Council of Christians and Jews, Norwood, Weizmann Institute Foundation, World Jewish Aid and World Jewish Relief (£1,000 each).

Remaining grants were in the range of £100 and £500 each. Beneficiaries included Action Medical Research, Action on Addiction, Arthritis Care, Book Aid International, BREAK, Centrepoint, Dial UK, Disabled Living Foundation, Enham Trust, Epilepsy Research Foundation, Hospice of the Valleys, Jewish Marriage Council, Jubilee Sailing Trust, National Eczema Society, Jewish Lads' and Girls' Brigade, Kids Care London, NSPCC, Parents for Inclusion, Pearson's Holiday Fund, Royal School for the Blind – Liverpool, VSO, Who Cares? Trust, Yad Vashem, Wireless for the Bedridden and Women's Link.

Exclusions Applications from individuals are not considered. Grants are to national bodies rather than local branches or local groups.

Applications In writing to the trustees. Applications are considered half-yearly. Only applications from registered charities are acknowledged. Frequent applications by a single charity are not appreciated.

The Maurice Wohl Charitable Foundation

Jewish, health and welfare

£207,000 (2005/06)
Beneficial area UK and Israel.

1st Floor, 7–8 Conduit Street, London W1S 2XF
Correspondent J Houri
Trustees *Maurice Wohl; Mrs Vivienne Wohl; Mrs Ella Latchman; Prof. David Latchman; Martin D Paisner; Daniel Dover; Sir Ian Gainsford.*
CC Number 244519
Information available Accounts were on file at the Charity Commission.

General This foundation has general charitable purposes in the UK and Israel, with a preference for Jewish charities. A wide range of causes are supported, including medical treatment and research, education, disability and older people's organisations, sheltered accommodation, the arts, relief of poverty and so on.

In 2005/06 the foundation had assets of £17.8 million which generated an income of £691,000. Grants were made totalling £207,000.

Beneficiaries of the largest grants during the year were: Manchester Jewish Community Centre (£65,000); Hatzola Northwest (£55,000); Yeshivah Ohel Torah Beth David (£15,000); Jewish Care and Medical Aid Trust (£10,000 each); Western Marble Arch Synagogue (£8,100 in three grants); the Jerusalem Great Synagogue (£5,800); Chai Cancer Care, Community Security Trust, Conference of European Rabbis and St Mark's Hospital Foundation (£5,000 each); and St George Hospital (£1,000).

Exclusions The trustees do not in general entertain applications for grants for ongoing maintenance projects. The trustees do not administer any schemes for individual awards or scholarships and they do not, therefore, entertain any individual applications for grants.

Applications In writing to the correspondent. The trustees meet regularly throughout the year.

The Maurice Wohl Charitable Trust

Jewish, health, welfare, arts, education

£23,000 (2005/06)
Beneficial area UK and Israel.

1st Floor, 7–8 Conduit Street, London W1S 2XF
Correspondent J Houri
Trustees *Maurice Wohl; Mrs Ella Latchman; Prof. David Latchman; Martin Paisner; Daniel Dover; Sir Ian Gainsford.*
CC Number 244518
Information available Full accounts were on file at the Charity Commission.

General This foundation has general charitable purposes in the UK and Israel,

with a preference for Jewish charities. A wide range of causes are supported, including medical treatment and research, education, disability and older people's organisations, sheltered accommodation, the arts, relief of poverty and so on.

In 2005/06 the trust had assets of £2.9 million, which generated an income of £129,000. Out of a total expenditure of £45,000, grants totalled £23,000.

Beneficiaries included Communaute Israelite de Geneve (£4,400); Federation of Jewish Relief Organisation (£4,100); Israel Museum (£1,700); Western Marble Arch Synagogue (£1,500); Jerusalem Great Synagogue (£1,300); and Comet Charities Ltd, the Jersey Association of Youth and Friendship, Yeshivat Beth Abraham Slonim Ltd and Yesodey Hatorah Schools (£1,000 each).

Exclusions The trustees do not administer any schemes for individual awards or scholarships, and they do not, therefore, entertain any individual applications for grants.

Applications To the correspondent in writing. Applications are regularly considered throughout the year.

Women at Risk

Women

£236,000 (2005)
Beneficial area Worldwide.

PO Box 31055, London SW1X 9WD
Tel. 020 7201 9982
Email women.risk@reed.co.uk
Correspondent Louise Kellerman, Manager
Trustees *A Reed; A J Jewitt; Ms M Newham; Ms M Baxter; M J Whittaker.*
CC Number 1059332
Information available Information was provided by the charity.

General The trust supports smaller projects that do not have well developed fundraising campaigns, and which benefit women and people disadvantaged by poverty, psychological abuse, emotional distress and infringement of human rights. Its grantmaking is particularly focused on the relief of poverty and sickness, the preservation of health and advancement of education among women and girls who are in need.

The trust seeks projects that meet its charitable objectives, to work in partnership to fundraise and then to distribute the money raised to the partners.

Its current focus is safe motherhood and violence against women.

In 2005 the trust had an income of £835,000. After management and administration costs of £39,000, grants were made totalling £236,000.

Beneficiaries during the year were Colombo Friend in Need Society (£90,000), ASFU (£20,000), Refuge, WOMANKIND Worldwide and Forward (£15,000 each), Centre for Filipinos, Family Focus, Safehands for Mothers, Sarvodaya Suwasetha Sewa Society, Women in Need, CATAW and Women's Development Centre (£10,000 each), Action on Elder Abuse and Red Mujeres de Condega (£5,000 each) and Working Women's Organisation (£1,000).

Exclusions No grants to individuals. Only charitable/not-for-profit organisations are supported on a long-term basis.

Applications In writing to the correspondent.

Woodlands Green Ltd

Jewish

£319,000 (2004/05)
Beneficial area Worldwide.

19 Green Walk, London NW4 2AL
Correspondent J A Ost, Secretary
Trustees A Ost; E Ost; D J A Ost; J A Ost; A Hepner.
CC Number 277299
Information available Accounts were on file at the Charity Commission, but without a list of grants.

General The trust's objectives are the advancement of the Orthodox Jewish faith and the relief of poverty. It mostly gives large grants to major educational projects being carried out by orthodox Jewish charities.

In 2004/05 the trust had assets of £1.3 million, an income of £166,000 and made grants totalling £319,000.

Previous beneficiaries have included Achisomoch Aid Co., Beis Soro Schneirer, Friends of Beis Yisroel Trust, Friends of Mir, Friends of Seret Wiznitz,

Friends of Toldos Avrohom Yitzchok, JET, Kahal Imrei Chaim, Oizer Dalim Trust, NWLCM, TYY Square and UTA.

Exclusions No grants to individuals, or for expeditions or scholarships.

Applications In writing to the correspondent.

The Woodroffe Benton Foundation

General

£214,000 (2004/05)
Beneficial area UK.

16 Fernleigh Court, Harrow, London HA2 6NA
Tel. 020 8421 4120
Email alan.king3@which.net
Correspondent Alan King, Secretary
Trustees *James Hope, Chair; Mrs Sheila Dickson; Colin Russell; Miss Celia Clout; Peter Foster; Air Commodore Philip Miles.*
CC Number 1075272
Information available Accounts were on file at the Charity Commission.

General This trust makes grants towards:

- people in need, primary care of people who are sick or elderly or those effected by the results of a local or national disaster
- promotion of education
- conservation and improvement of the environment.

The trust rarely donates more than £2,000 and does not normally make more than one grant to the same charity in a 12-month period.

In 2004/05 it had assets of £6.1 million and an income of £184,000. Grants totalled £214,000. Management and administration expenses were high at £38,000.

Ongoing support was given to 26 organisations totalling £106,000. Beneficiaries included Queen Elizabeth's Grammar School (£52,000 in five grants), Ifield Park Housing Society (£15,000 in two grants), Community Links (£10,000), Calibre and Prisoners' Families & Friends Service (£5,000 each), Charity Search and Rye Respite Care Centre (£3,000 each) and Cathedral Camps (£2,000).

There were 121 grants made in response to 324 unsolicited applications. These grants totalled £80,000, the following were for £1,000 or more: Coram Family and Young People's Trust for the Environment (£5,000 each); St Andrew's Club (£2,000); Fareshare, Home From Hospital Care, Manna Society and Medical Engineering Resource Unit (£1,500 each); and Befriending Network, Bognor Fun Bus Company, Carers of Barking & Dagenham, Contact The Elderly, Country Holidays for Inner City Kids, Design and Manufacture for Disability, Edinburgh Young Carers Project, Living Paintings Trust, St Giles' Trust, Shake Trust, Spitalfields City Farm, Step By Step and Turntable Furniture (£1,000 each).

A further £23,000 was given in grants made at the discretion of individual trustees, retired trustees and the foundation secretary.

Exclusions Grants are not made outside the UK and are only made to registered charities. No grants to individuals. Branches of UK charities should not apply as grants, if made, would go to the charity's headquarters.

Applications On a form available from the correspondent. Full guidance notes on completing the form and procedures for processing applications are sent with the form.

The Geoffrey Woods Charitable Foundation

Young people, education, disability, health

£100,000 (2004/05)
Beneficial area UK and overseas.

The Girdlers Company, Girdlers Hall, Basinghall Avenue, London EC2V 5DD
Correspondent The Clerk
Trustees *The Girdlers Company; N K Maitland; A J R Fairclough.*
CC Number 248205
Information available Accounts were on file at the Charity Commission.

General In 2004/05 the foundation had assets of £1.1 million, an income of £174,000 and made grants totalling £100,000.

The foundation is administered by the Girdlers Company and its objectives are the advancement of education and religion and the relief of poverty. The trust is responsible for three funds as shown below:

The Master's Fund is allocated an amount each year for the master of the company to donate to charities of his or her own choice. This amounted to £1,700 in 2004/05.

Christmas Court Donations allow members to nominate charities at Christmas time. Grants totalled £30,000 in 2004/05.

The Jock French Charitable Fund encourages charitable donations from members of the livery of the company. The fund is allocated a sum that is four times the amount covenanted or donated to the foundation by the livery. The subscribing members are invited to nominate charities to receive donations. The total sum allocated is distributed in May and November each year, following ratification by the livery. In 2004/05 grants totalled £68,000.

Applications 'Beneficiaries are nominated by members of the company and outside applications are no longer considered.'

The A and R Woolf Charitable Trust

General

£43,000 (2005/06)

Beneficial area Worldwide; UK, mainly in Hertfordshire.

2 Oak House, 101 Ducks Hill Road, Northwood, Middlesex HA6 2WQ

Correspondent Mrs J D H Rose, Trustee

Trustees *Mrs J D H Rose; C Rose; Dr G L Edmonds; S Rose; A Rose.*

CC Number 273079

Information available Accounts were on file at the Charity Commission.

General The trust supports a range of causes, including Jewish organisations, animal welfare and conservation causes, children and health and welfare charities.

Both UK and overseas charities (through a British-based office) receive support, together with local charities. Most of the grants are recurrent.

In 2005/06 the trust had assets of £2.5 million and an income of £46,000. Grants totalled £43,000.

There were 43 grants listed in the accounts, of which 13 were for £1,000 or more. Beneficiaries included: Diabetes UK, United Nations International Children's Emergency Fund and University of Hertfordshire Charitable Trust (£5,000 each); the Zoological Society of London (£3,700); Apex Charitable Trust, the National Endometriosis Society and WellBeing for Women (£2,000 each); Northwood and Pinner Liberal Synagogue (£1,200); and the Council of Christians and Jews and World Wildlife Fund – UK (£1,000 each).

Other beneficiaries of grants in the range of £130 and £650 included Boys Town Jerusalem, Breast Cancer Campaign, Care for the Wild International, Farms For City Children, Hampstead Synagogue Cultural Fund, I Rescue, the Multiple Sclerosis Society, the National Trust, PHAB England, the Stroke Association, United Jewish Israel Appeal and the World Society for the Protection of Animals.

There were a further 43 single donations under £100 each totalling £3,700.

Exclusions No grants to individuals or non-registered charities unless schools, hospices and so on.

Applications Support is only given to projects/organisations/causes personally known to the trustees. The trust does not respond to unsolicited applications.

The Fred and Della Worms Charitable Trust

Jewish, education, arts

£95,000 (2005/06)

Beneficial area UK.

23 Highpoint, North Hill, London N6 4BA

Tel. 020 8342 5360 **Fax** 020 8342 5359

Email fred@worms5.freeserve.co.uk

Correspondent The Trustees

Trustees *Mrs D Worms; M D Paisner; F S Worms; A D Harverd.*

CC Number 200036

Information available Full accounts were on file at the Charity Commission.

General In 2005/06 the trust had assets of £2.1 million, which generated an income of £144,000. After low administration fees of just £1,000, grants were made totalling £95,000.

Social and healthcare	£45,000
Youth	£12,000
Education	£17,000
The arts	£16,000
Religion	£4,700

Beneficiaries included: Joint Jewish Charitable Trust (£30,000); British Friends of the Hebrew University (£14,000); Child Resettlement Fund (£5,300); Bnai Brith Hillel Foundation, European Jewish Publication Society, Jewish Care and Maccabi Union (£5,000 each); JNF Botanical Gardens (£2,700); Friends of LVOV (£2,600); British Friends of the Art Museum of Israel (£2,200); Duke of Edinburgh Award and London Jewish Culture Centre (£1,500 each); English National Opera Company (£1,200); United Synagogue (£1,300); and Ben Uri Art Gallery and Royal National Theatre (£1,000 each).

Exclusions No grants to individuals.

Applications In writing to the correspondent. The trust stated that its funds are fully committed.

The Diana Edgson Wright Charitable Trust

Animal conservation, welfare, general

£50,000 (2005)

Beneficial area UK with some preference for Kent.

c/o 2 Stade Street, Hythe, Kent CT21 6BD

Correspondent R H V Moorhead, Trustee

Trustees *R H V Moorhead; P Edgson Wright; H C D Moorhead.*

CC Number 327737

Information available Accounts were obtained from the Charity Commission website.

General This trust has general charitable purposes. The policy is to support a small number of charities. In 2005 the trust had assets of £1.4 million and an income of £53,000. Grants were made totalling £50,000.

There were 43 grants made in the year, beneficiaries of larger grants of £1,000 or more included: Kitchen Tables Charitable Trust and Royal British Legion (£4,000 each); British Red Cross for S E Asia Earthquake Appeal (£3,700); Dragon School Trust (£3,000); Caldecott Foundation, Cantoris Charitable Trust, the Dragon School Trust, Dumfries and Galloway Action and Kent Air Ambulance Trust (£2,000 each); Gurkha Welfare Trust (£1,750); St Peter and St Paul's Church (£1,500); and Paula Carr Charitable Trust, Sellindge Parish Church, Wildlife Protection Society of India and YMCA (£1,000 each).

Beneficiaries of smaller grants included Charing Parish Church Council, the Child Bereavement Trust, the Donkey Sanctuary, Folkestone Rainbow Trust, Macmillan Cender Relief, Marine Conservation Society, Merlin, the Natural History Museum and Simon Paul Foundation.

Applications In writing to the correspondent.

The Matthews Wrightson Charity Trust

Caring and Christian charities

£79,000 to organisations (2005)
Beneficial area UK and some overseas.

The Farm, Northington, Alresford, Hampshire SO24 9TH

Correspondent Adam Lee, Secretary and Administrator

Trustees *Miss Priscilla W Wrightson; Anthony H Isaacs; Guy D G Wrightson; Miss Isabelle S White.*

CC Number 262109

Information available Accounts were on file at the Charity Commission.

General 'The trust welcomes applications from charities or individuals undertaking charitable projects. The trustees favour smaller charities or projects, e.g. those seeking to raise under

£25,000 and usually exclude large national charities and those with turnover in excess of £250,000. There is a bias towards innovation, Christian work and organisations helping the disadvantaged particularly to re-integrate into the community; excluded are unconnected local churches, schools and village halls, and animal charities.' [The standard 'unit' donation for 2006 was £400.]

In 2005 it had assets of £1.7 million and an income of £65,000. Grants totalled £93,000 including £14,000 to 33 individuals. They were broken down as follows.

Youth	43 grants	£18,000
Arts	6	£18,000
Individuals	33	£14,000
Disability	28	£11,000
Worldwide	20	£10,000
Christian causes	18	£9,000
Rehabilitation	9	£5,700
Medical	10	£3,900
Older people	6	£2,200
Miscellaneous	4	£1,400

The largest donation was to The Royal College of Art (£15,000) to support students who find their grants and other income inadequate (hardship grants) and for awards to students to further ideas for UK industrial production (starting your own business awards). Other beneficiaries of grants over £1,000 each were Childhood First and Help Tibet (£1,200 each) and Genesis Arts Trust and Premier Christian Radio (£1,000 each).

Aside from 8 grants of £800 to eight, all other gifts, with a few exceptions, were for £400, the Charity's 'unit' for 2005. Beneficiaries included Aid to Russia and the Republics, the Boys' Brigade Paisley, Cancer Research UK, Cherry Trees, Churches Together in Britain and Ireland, DEMAND, Daneford Trust, Friends of Somerset Churches and Chapels, Friends of Wells Cathedral, Harvest Trust, I-CAN, Manna Counselling Service, Nishta Rural Health Clinic and Centre, Pimlico Opera, Shopmobility Worcester, Stepping Stones Trust, Wells for India, Whizz-Kidz, X-Stream Youth Work and Youth for Christ Warrington.

Exclusions No support for individuals (other than visitors from overseas) seeking education or adventure for personal character improvement. No support for unconnected local churches, village halls, schools and animal charities. Charities with a turnover of over £250,000 are generally not considered. Most grants are to organisations seeking, or with a turnover of less than, £25,000. Individuals seeking

funding for 'self-improvement' education are not favoured.

Applications In writing to the correspondent. No special forms are used, although latest financial accounts are desirable. One or two sheets (usually the covering letter) are circulated monthly to the trustees, who meet every six months only for policy and administrative decisions. Replies are only sent to successful applicants; allow up to three months for an answer. Please include an sae if an answer to an unsuccessful application is required. The trust receives over 1,000 applications a year; 'winners have to make the covering letter more attractive than the 90 others received each month'.

Miss E B Wrightson's Charitable Settlement

Music education, inshore rescue, recreation

£19,000 to organisations and individuals (2005/06)
Beneficial area UK.

Swangles Farm, Cold Christmas Lane, Hertfordshire SG12 7SP

Correspondent Mrs N Hickman

Trustees *A Callard; Mrs E Clarke; P Dorkings.*

CC Number 1002147

Information available Accounts were available from the Charity Commission website.

General The trust makes grants for general charitable purposes, with a preference for inshore rescue services, multiple sclerosis causes and young people with musical talent. It primarily supports individuals, but applications can also be made by groups and charities seeking funding for the advancement of music education and recreational charitable objects.

As mentioned in the trust's 2005/06 accounts:

'The Charity exists to make grants out of its income and/or capital in favour of any legally charitable purpose at the trustees' discretion, with specific recognition of inshore rescue services, the help of Multiple Sclerosis and of young individuals with musical talent.'

In 2005/06 the trust had assets of £1.5 million and an income of £30,000. Grants were made totalling £19,000, which was distributed to three organisations and thirty-four individuals. Grants to organisations were made to Frenford Clubs (£4,000), Beslow Loan Scheme (£1,000), and Hill and Company (£300).

Applications In writing to the correspondent. Trustees meet regularly to consider applications and 'all properly completed applications are acknowledged'. Guidelines are provided by the trust for applications by individuals, but not organisations.

Wychdale Ltd

Jewish

£135,000 (2005/06)

Beneficial area UK and abroad.

89 Darenth Road, London N16 6EB

Correspondent The Secretary

Trustees *C D Schlaff; J Schlaff; Mrs Z Schlaff.*

CC Number 267447

Information available Full accounts were on file at the Charity Commission.

General The objects of this charity are the advancement of the Orthodox Jewish religion and the relief of poverty in the UK and abroad. The charity stated in its 2005/06 accounts that it 'invites applications from religious and educational institutions as well as organisations providing services for the relief of poverty both in the UK and abroad'.

In 2005/06 the trust had assets of £895,000 and an income of £451,000, including £438,000 from donations. Grants were made totalling £135,000.

Beneficiaries were: Society of Friends of Torah (£33,000); Kahal Chassidim Bobov and United Talmudical Association (£24,000 each); Forty Ltd (£12,000); and Chevrat Maoz Ladal (£6,000).

Exclusions Non-Jewish organisations are not supported.

Applications In writing to the correspondent.

Wychville Ltd

Jewish, education, general

£249,000 (2005/06)

Beneficial area UK.

44 Leweston Place, London N16 6RH

Correspondent Mrs S Englander, Secretary

Trustees *B Englander, Chair; Mrs S Englander; E Englander; Mrs B R Englander.*

CC Number 267584

Information available Accounts were on file at the Charity Commission, but without a list of grants.

General This trust supports educational, Jewish and other charitable organisations. In 2005/06 the trust had assets of £69,000, an income of £281,000 mostly from donations and made grants totalling £249,000. No further information was available.

Applications In writing to the correspondent.

The Wyseliot Charitable Trust

Medical, welfare, general

£85,000 (2005/06)

Beneficial area UK.

17 Chelsea Square, London SW3 6LF

Correspondent J H Rose, Trustee

Trustees *E A D Rose; J H Rose; A E G Raphael.*

CC Number 257219

Information available Accounts were provided by the trust, but without a narrative report.

General In 2005/06 the trust had assets of £2.2 million, which generated an income of £94,000. Grants were made to 26 organisations totalling £85,000.

Grants included: 5,000 each to Alzheimer's Trust, Cystic Fibrosis Trust, New Avenues Youth Project, Royal Marsden Cancer Fund and St Mungo's Trust; £4,000 each to Macmillan Cancer Relief Fund, MIND and Time & Talents Association; £3,500 to Trinity Hospice; £3,000 each to Brain Research Trust, Defeating Deafness, Earls Court Homeless Families Project and

Musicians Benevolent Fund; £2,000 each to Home Start, National Arts Collection Fund and Vitiligo Society; and £1,000 to Sir John Golding Fund.

Exclusions Local charities are not supported. No support for individuals; grants are only made to registered charities.

Applications In writing to the correspondent; however, note that the trust states that the same charities are supported each year, with perhaps one or two changes. It is unlikely new charities sending circular appeals will be supported and large UK charities are generally not supported.

The Yapp Charitable Trust

Social welfare

£301,000 (2005/06)

Beneficial area England and Wales.

47a Paris Road, Scholes, Holmfirth HD9 1SY

Tel. 01484 683403

Email info@yappcharitabletrust.org.uk

Website www.yappcharitabletrust.org.uk

Correspondent Mrs Margaret Thompson, Administrator

Trustees *Revd Timothy C Brooke; Peter R Davies; Peter G Murray; Mrs Stephanie Willats; David Aeron-Thomas.*

CC Number 1076803

Information available Accounts were on file at the Charity Commission. Detailed and up-to-date guidelines can be found on the trust's website.

General The Yapp Charitable Trust was formed in 1999 from the Yapp Welfare Trust (two-thirds share) and Yapp Education and Research Trust (one-third share). However, rather than combining the criteria for the two trusts, the trustees decided to focus on small charities, usually local rather than UK charities. The trust now accepts applications only from small charities and organisations with a turnover of less than £60,000 in the year of application. The objectives are restricted to registered charities in England or Wales and cover work with:

1 older people
2 children and young people, aged 5 to 25

3 people with disabilities or mental health problems

4 moral welfare – people trying to overcome life-limiting problems such as addiction, relationship difficulties, abuse or a history of offending

5 education and learning (including lifelong learning) and scientific or medical research.

Applications from outside these areas cannot be considered. Grants are given towards running costs and salaries but not for capital equipment.

The trust gives priority to work that is unattractive to the general public or unpopular with other funders, particularly when it helps improve the lives of marginalised, disadvantaged or isolated people. Within these areas the trust gives preference to charities that can demonstrate the effective use of volunteers. Grant-making policies are kept under review – current priorities and exclusions are publicised on the trust's website.

In 2005/06 the trust had assets of £6.4 million, generating an income of £278,000. Grants ranged between £9,000 and £630 and were made to 91 organisations totalling £301,000. Just under half the grants were for more than one year. Since September 2006 the trust has pursued a policy that most grants are for more than one year.

Examples of grants are broken down as follows:

Disability – 28 grants totalling £86,000
BootStrap – Nottingham, Choices for Families of Children with Arthritis and Tools for Self Reliance – Milton Keynes (£6,000 each over two years); Wokingham and West Berkshire Mental Health Association (£6,000 over three years); Pukar Disability Resource Centre (£4,200 over two years); Durham Area Disability Leisure Group, FDM For Disability Mobility and Voluntary Support Scheme (£4,000 each), Lowestoft Shopmobility and National Long-Term Survivors Group (£3,000 each); Cornwall Dyslexia Association, Lancaster District Children's Integration Group and Teesdale Disability Access Forum (£2,000 each); and Eastsiders (£1,000).

Education – 10 grants totalling £30,000
Making A Difference – Tameside and Wolverhampton Inter-Faith Council (£6,000 each over two years); Glenholme Youth Centre (£4,500 over two years); African Women Group (£2,500); African Community School and Thames Bengali Association (£2,000 each); Somali Education Centre (£1,500); and

Redbridge French Speaking African Women (£1,000).

Elderly people – 12 grants totalling £49,000
West Norfolk Befriending (£9,000 over three years); Leeds Chinese Women's Group and Northmoor Live at Home (£6,000 over two years); Shropshire Reminiscence (£5,000 over two years); Lache Park Ltd (£4,000 over two years); Age Concern Chelmsford, First Voice and Ward End Asian Elders Welfare Association (£3,000 each); and Contact (£1,500).

Moral welfare – 19 grants totalling £79,000
Family Awareness Drug Support (£7,000 over two years); Camden Listening and Counselling Centre, Pembrokeshire Counselling Service and Restoring Broken Walls Trust (£6,000 each over two years); Bedford African Community Support Project, Gloucestershire Rape Crisis Centre and Peterborough African Refugees Community Association (£5,000 each over two years); 4Cs Counselling Centre, Hackney Bangladeshi Cultural Association and Volunteer Centre Craven (£4,000 over two years); New Bolton Somali Community Association (£3,000); West Kent Mediation (£1,500); and Nigerian Women's Welfare Association (£1,400).

Young people – 22 grants totalling £58,000
Kidz Klub – Trinity Church Page Moss and Maximum Life Youth Project (£6,000 each over two years); Bognor Fun Bus Co. Ltd, Rochdale Special Needs Cycling Club, Stoke Heath Community Centre and Lancaster Boys' Club (£4,000 over two years); Bullying Online and Focus on Young People in Bassetlaw (£3,000 each); Rainworth and Blidworth Detached Youth Project, Redditch Wheels and Wyndam Boys and Girls Club (£2,000 each); Great Bridge Community Forum (£1,500); and 5th Abbey Wood Brownies, Cardiff Yemeni Community Association and Vallance Community Sports Association (£1,000 each).

Exclusions No applications are accepted from:

- organisations based in Scotland and Northern Ireland – work must be carried out in England or Wales
- charities whose total annual expenditure is more than £60,000
- charities that are not registered with the Charity Commission. Organisations must have their own charity number or be excepted from registration. Industrial and Provident

Societies and Community Interest Companies are not eligible to apply

- new organisations – applying organisations must have been operating as a constituted charity for at least three years.

Grants are not made for:

- new work – funding is given to sustain existing work that has been happening for at least a year, not to create new paid posts nor to launch new activities or put on special events
- capital-type expenditure – buildings, renovations, furnishings, equipment, minibuses
- work with under-5s
- childcare
- holidays and holiday centres
- core funding of general community organisations such as community associations, community centres and general advice services, because some of their work is outside our objects
- bereavement counselling
- debt advice
- community safety initiatives
- individuals – including charities raising funds to purchase equipment for or make grants to individuals
- fundraising groups raising money to benefit another organisation such as a hospital or a school.

Applications On a form available from the administrator. Applicants may request a form by email in Word 2000 format if preferred, although all applications must be sent by post. The trustees meet three times a year to consider applications. Meetings are usually in late March, July and November.

Please phone or email for advice if you are unsure whether to apply or how to complete the form.

The Dennis Alan Yardy Charitable Trust

General
£38,000 (2004/05)

Beneficial area Overseas and UK with a preference for the East Midlands.

PO Box 5039, Spratton, Northampton NN6 8YH

Correspondent Dennis Alan Yardy, The Secretary

Trustees *Dennis Alan Yardy, Chair; Mrs Christine Anne Yardy; Jeffrey Creek; Mrs Joanne Stoney.*

CC Number 1039719

Information available Accounts were on file at the Charity Commission, but without a list of grants.

General This trust was established in 1993. It supports major UK and international charities and those within the East Midlands area.

In 2004/05 the trust had assets of £530,000, an income of £30,000 and made grants totalling £38,000.

Exclusions No grants to individuals or non-registered charities.

Applications In writing to the correspondent.

The John Young Charitable Settlement

Wildlife, general

£61,000 (2003/04)

Beneficial area UK and overseas.

c/o Lee Associates, 5 Southampton Place, London WC1A 2DA

Tel. 020 7025 4600

Correspondent K A Hawkins

Trustees *J M Young; G H Camamile.*

CC Number 283254

Information available Accounts were on file at the Charity Commission.

General In 2004 the trust had assets of £400,000 and an income of £87,000 including £75,000 from donations and gifts. Grants to 22 organisations totalled £61,000.

Beneficiaries included Peter Rice Scholarship – Harvard University (£6,100), Architectural Association Foundation, Forest Guardians, London Open House, RSPB and Toynbee Hall (£5,000 each), Design Museum and Médecins Du Monde UK (£3,000 each), National Hospital Development Foundation (£2,500), Kings Cross Homelessness Project and Prostate Cancer Charitable Trust (£2,000 each), East Anglia Children's Hospice, National Autistic Society, Street Outreach Program and Walk the Walk Worldwide (£1,000 each) and Action Aid (£250).

Applications In writing to the correspondent.

David Young Charitable Trust

General, Jewish

£93,000 (2004/05)

Beneficial area UK.

Harcourt House, 19 Cavendish Square, London W1M 9AB

Correspondent The Trustees

Trustees *M S Mishon; Lady L M Young of Graffham; The Rt Hon Lord Young of Graffham; Claire Watkins.*

CC Number 265195

Information available Accounts were on file at the Charity Commission.

General The trust's accounts state that it 'supports charitable institutions including those engaged in medical and ancillary services (including medical research), education, helping those who are disabled and older, relieving poverty, providing sheltered accommodation and developing the arts, etc'.

In 2004/05 it had assets of £155,000, an income of £227,000 and made grants totalling £93,000.

Nine beneficiaries of amounts over £1,000 each were listed in the accounts: the Prince's Trust (£25,000), Jewish Care (£15,000 in two grants), United Jewish Israel Appeal (£13,000), Chichester Festival Theatre Trust and Tavistock Fund for Aphasia (£10,000 each), Community Security Trust (£7,000), Friends of Lubavitch UK (£5,000), British ORT (£5,000 in two grants) and Welfare Works Charitable Trust (£1,000).

Other donations of less than £1,000 each totalled £2,600.

Applications In writing to the correspondent.

The William Allen Young Charitable Trust

General

£217,000 (2005/06)

Beneficial area UK, with a preference for south London.

Riverside House, 26 Osiers Road, London SW1B 1NH

Correspondent Torquil Sligo-Young

Trustees *T F B Young; J G A Young; T Sligo-Young.*

CC Number 283102

Information available Accounts were on file at the Charity Commission.

General The trust supports humanitarian causes, with a large number of health organisations supported each year. Grants are made to local and national organisations throughout the UK, although there appears to be a preference for south London.

In 2005/06 the trust had assets of £18.4 million with an income of £201,000 and made 143 grants totalling £217,000.

The largest grants went to: Aldenham School, British Benevolent Fund of Madrid, Bruton School For Girls, Gonville and Caius Development Fund and St George's Ophthalmology Research and Education Fund (£10,000 each).

Other beneficiaries included: Anti-slavery International, Church of St Peter Fitzpaine, Heriot-Watt University, St Margaret's Yeovil Hospice and National Society of Epilepsy (£5,000 each); the Ellen McArthur Trust (£4,000); RNLI (£3,000); St Raphael's Hospice (£2,500); and Dorset Somerset Ambulance, LHHP Society and Royal Hospital for Neurodisability Putney (£2,000 each).

Grants of £1,000 each or less included those to: Abbeley Foundation, Battersea Dogs Home, Cancer Research UK, Down's Syndrome Association, Merton Medical Society, Rotary Club of Kew Gardens and Veterinary Benevolent Fund (£1,000 each); Action Medical Research, Battersea Crime Prevention, Clapham Angling Society, Diamond Centre for Disabled Riders, HCPT – Pilgrimage Trust, New Farleigh Hospice Chelmsford, Share Community and the Worshipful Company of Wheelwrights (£500 each); St Joseph's Hospice (£300);

and Red Gates School and Richmond Mencap (£250).

Applications The trust has stressed that all funds are committed and consequently unsolicited applications will not be supported.

Zephyr Charitable Trust

Housing, health, environment, third world

£32,000 to organisations (2005).
Beneficial area UK and worldwide.

New Guild House, 45 Great Charles Street, Queensway, Birmingham B3 2LX
Tel. 0121 212 2222 **Fax** 0121 212 2300
Correspondent R Harriman, Trust Administrator
Trustees *Elizabeth Breeze; Roger Harriman; David Baldock; Donald I Watson.*
CC Number 1003234
Information available Full accounts were available from the Charity Commission website.

General This trust provided help for organisations benefiting disabled people; homeless people; victims of famine, man-made or natural disasters, war and the environment. In 2005 the trust had assets of £1 million and an income of £36,000. Grants were made to 19 organisations totalling £32,000.

The largest grants made to organisations included the Margaret Pyke Memorial Trust for the Population and Sustainability Network Intermediate Technology (£3,000), Pesticides Action Network UK (£2,100) and CRISIS and the Medical Foundation for the Care of Victims of Torture (£2,000 each).

Other grants included Survival International (£1,900), Rainforest Concern and WOMANKIND UK (£1,600), the Hearing Research Trust and the Karuna Trust (£1,500 each), the National Missing Persons Helpline (£1,000), and the Kings Cross Homelessness Project and MIND – Brent and the Paddington Farm Trust (£800 each).

Exclusions No grants to individuals, expeditions or scholarships.

Applications In writing to the correspondent. The trustees meet to consider ongoing grants in June or July

each year. Unsolicited applications are unlikely to be successful, since the trust makes annual donations to a list of beneficiaries. However, the trust stated that unsolicited applications are considered on a quarterly basis by the trustees and very occasional support is given.

Telephone applications are not accepted.

The I A Ziff Charitable Foundation

General, education, Jewish, arts, young and older people, medicine

£488,000 (2005/06)
Beneficial area UK, with a preference for Yorkshire, especially Leeds and Harrogate.

Town Centre House, The Merrion Centre, Leeds LS2 8LY
Tel. 0113 222 1234 **Fax** 0113 242 1026
Correspondent B Rouse, Secretary
Trustees *Mrs Marjorie E Ziff; Michael A Ziff; Edward M Ziff; Mrs Ann L Manning.*
CC Number 249368
Information available Full accounts were on file at the Charity Commission.

General This trust likes to support causes that will provide good value for the money donated by benefiting a large number of people, as well as encouraging others to make contributions to the work. This includes a wide variety of schemes that involve the community at many levels, including education, public places, the arts and helping people who are disadvantaged. Capital costs and building work are particularly favoured by the trustees, as they feel projects such as these are not given the support they deserve from statutory sources.

In 2005/06 the trust had assets of £6.1 million and an income of £384,000. Grants totalled £488,000. The beneficiaries of the two largest grants were Leeds Jewish Welfare Board towards the Marjorie and Arnold Ziff Community Centre in Leeds (£136,000) and United Jewish Israel Appeal towards the Kfar Galim Village (£126,000).

Other beneficiaries included The University of Leeds Foundation (£50,000); Leeds Grammar School

(£35,000); Royal College of Music (£25,000); Leeds Metropolitan University (£20,000); the Chief Rabbinate Charitable Trust and Ezer Mitzion (£10,000 each); World Jewish Relief (£4,000); Mitzvah Association Ltd (£2,500); Leeds Jewish Blind Society and Zionist Council (£1,500 each); British WIZO (£620); the Cure Parkinson's Trust (£500); British Friends of Laniado (£350); Holocaust Survivors Friendship Association and the National Art Fund (£250 each); and Children Number One Foundation (£100).

Exclusions No grants to individuals.

Applications In writing to the correspondent. Replies will only be given to a request accompanied by an sae. Please note that funds available from the trust are limited and requests not previously supported are unlikely to be successful. Initial telephone calls are welcome but please note the foregoing comments.

Stephen Zimmerman Charitable Trust

Jewish

£50,000 (2004/05)
Beneficial area UK.

35 Stormont Road, London N6 4NR
Correspondent S Zimmerman, Trustee
Trustees *Mrs L J Zimmerman; S Hauswirth; S Zimmerman.*
CC Number 1038310
Information available Accounts were on file at the Charity Commission.

General Registered with the Charity Commission in June 1994, this trust distributes mainly to Jewish organisations with some smaller awards made to UK and London-based organisations.

In 2004/05 it had an income of £51,000 and grants to 46 organisations totalled £50,000. Beneficiaries included United Jewish Israel Appeal (£15,000), Jewish Care (£10,000), United Jewish Israel Appeal (£5,000), Jewish Association of Business Ethics (£2,500), RNIB (£2,000), British ORT, London Youth and United Synagogue (£1,500 each), United Synagogue (£1,200) and CIS Development Fun, Cancer Research and Norwood Ltd (£1,000 each).

Applications In writing to the correspondent.

Subject index

The following subject index begins with a list of the categories used. The categories are fairly wide-ranging to keep the index as simple as possible. There may be considerable overlap between some of these categories, particularly children, older people and young people with, for example, the social/moral welfare or medicine and health categories.

The list of categories is followed by the index itself. Before using the index, please note the following:

How the index was compiled

1. The index aims to reflect the most recently recorded grant-making practice. It is therefore based on our interpretation of what each trust has actually given to, rather than what its policy statement says or its charitable objectives allow it to do in principle. For example, where a trust states it has general charitable purposes, but its grants list shows a strong preference for welfare, we have indexed it as welfare.

2. We have tried to ensure that each trust has given significantly in the areas mentioned above (usually at least £30,000), therefore small, apparently untypical grants have been ignored for this classification.

3. The index has been compiled from the latest information available to us.

Limitations

1. It has not been possible to contact all 1,200 trusts specifically in regard to this index so policies may have changed.

2. Sometimes there will be a geographical restriction on the trust's grant giving which is not shown up in this index, or the trust may not give for the specific purposes you require under that heading. It is important to read the entry carefully, you will need to check:
(a) The trust gives in your geographical area of operation.
(b) The trust gives for the specific purposes you require.

(c) There is no other reason to prevent you making an application to this trust.

3. We have omitted the General category as the number of trusts included would make it unusable.

Under no circumstances should the index be used as a simple mailing list. Remember that each trust is different and that often the policies or interests of a particular trust do not fit easily into the given categories. Each entry must be read individually and carefully before you send off an application. Indiscriminate applications are usually unsuccessful. They waste time and money and greatly annoy trusts.

The categories are as follows:

Arts, culture, sport and recreation *page 380*

A very wide category including performing, written and visual arts, crafts theatres, museums and galleries, heritage, architecture and archaeology, sports.

Children and young people *page 381*

Mainly for welfare and welfare-related activities.

Community and economic development *page 382*

This includes employment.

Disability *page 382*

Disadvantaged people *page 387*

This includes people who are:
- socially-excluded
- socially and economically disadvantaged
- unemployed
- homeless
- offenders
- educationally disadvantaged

- victims of social/natural occurrences, including refugees and asylum seekers.

Education and training *page 388*

Environment and animals *page 389*

This includes:
- agriculture and fishing
- conservation
- animal care
- environment and education
- transport
- sustainable environment.

General charitable purposes *page 390*

Housing *page 394*

Illness *page 394*

This includes people who are ill, or who have physical or mental disabilities, learning difficulties, or mental health problems.

Medicine and health *page 398*

Older people *page 400*

Religion (general) *page 401*

This includes inter-faith work and religious understanding.

Christianity *page 403*

Islam *page 404*

Judaism *page 404*

Rights, law and conflict
page 406

This includes:

- citizen participation
- conflict resolution
- legal and advice services
- rights
- equality and justice.

Science and technology
page 406

Social sciences, policy and research *page 406*

Social welfare *page 406*

This is a very broad category including:

- community care and services
- counselling and advice
- social preventative schemes
- community centres and activities.

Voluntary sector management and development *page 408*

Women *page 409*

Arts, culture, sport and recreation

Children and young people

Community and economic development

Disability

Disadvantaged people

Education and training

Environment and animals

General charitable purposes

Mrs S K West's Charitable Trust
The Barbara Whatmore Charitable Trust
The Colonel W H Whitbread Charitable
  Trust
The Whitecourt Charitable Trust
A H and B C Whiteley Charitable Trust
The Lionel Wigram Memorial Trust
The Richard Wilcox Welfare Charity
The Kay Williams Charitable Foundation
Sumner Wilson Charitable Trust
Wingfield's Charitable Trust
The Maurice Wohl Charitable Trust
The Geoffrey Woods Charitable
  Foundation
The A and R Woolf Charitable Trust
The Diana Edgson Wright Charitable
  Trust
Wychville Ltd
The Wyseliot Charitable Trust
The Dennis Alan Yardy Charitable Trust
The John Young Charitable Settlement
The William Allen Young Charitable
  Trust
Zephyr Charitable Trust
The I A Ziff Charitable Foundation

Housing

The Oliver Borthwick Memorial Trust
Henry T and Lucy B Cadbury Charitable
  Trust
The Emmandjay Charitable Trust
The Oliver Ford Charitable Trust
Help the Homeless Ltd
The Horne Trust
The Hyde Charitable Trust – Youth Plus
The Irish Youth Foundation (UK) Ltd
  (incorporating The Lawlor
  Foundation)
The Peter Kershaw Trust
John Laing Charitable Trust
Land Aid Charitable Trust
The Nadezhda Charitable Trust
The Norton Foundation
Richard Rogers Charitable Settlement
The Rowan Charitable Trust
The Audrey Sacher Charitable Trust
The Scurrah Wainwright Charity
The Yapp Charitable Trust

Illness

The A B Charitable Trust
The Keith and Freda Abraham
  Charitable Trust
The Victor Adda Foundation
Adenfirst Ltd
The Adnams Charity
AF Trust Company
The Sylvia Aitken Charitable Trust

The Alabaster Trust
The Alborada Trust
D G Albright Charitable Trust
Alcohol Education and Research Council
Alexandra Rose Day
The Altajir Trust
Altamont Ltd
AM Charitable Trust
Sir John and Lady Amory's Charitable
  Trust
The Ampelos Trust
The André Christian Trust
Anglo-German Foundation for the Study
  of Industrial Society
The Animal Defence Trust
The Annandale Charitable Trust
The Appletree Trust
The John Apthorp Charitable Trust
The Archbishop of Canterbury's
  Charitable Trust
Archbishop of Wales Fund for Children
The John M Archer Charitable Trust
The Ardwick Trust
The Artemis Charitable Trust
The Ove Arup Foundation
The AS Charitable Trust
The Ashe Park Charitable Trust
The Laura Ashley Foundation
The Ashworth Charitable Trust
The Ian Askew Charitable Trust
The Association of Colleges Charitable
  Trust
Astellas European Foundation
The Astor Foundation
The Atlantic Foundation
The Aurelius Charitable Trust
Harry Bacon Foundation
The Bacta Charitable Trust
The Bagri Foundation
The Baker Charitable Trust
Balmain Charitable Trust
The Barbers' Company General Charities
The Barbour Trust
Barchester Healthcare Foundation
Barclays Stockbrokers Charitable Trust
Peter Barker-Mill Memorial Charity
Lord Barnby's Foundation
The Barnsbury Charitable Trust
The Misses Barrie Charitable Trust
The Bartlett Taylor Charitable Trust
The Paul Bassham Charitable Trust
The Batchworth Trust
The Batty Charitable Trust
The Bay Tree Charitable Trust
The Beacon Trust
Bear Mordechai Ltd
The Beaufort House Trust
The Beaverbrook Foundation
The Peter Beckwith Charitable Trust
The Bedfordshire and Hertfordshire
  Historic Churches Trust
The David and Ruth Behrend Fund
Belljoe Tzedoko Ltd

Michael and Leslie Bennett Charitable
  Trust
The Geoffrey Berger Charitable Trust
The Berkeley Reafforestation Trust
The Bestway Foundation
The Billmeir Charitable Trust
The Birmingham Hospital Saturday
  Fund Medical Charity and Welfare
  Trust
Birthday House Trust
The Michael Bishop Foundation
Peter Black Charitable Trust
The Bertie Black Foundation
Sir Alec Black's Charity
The Blair Foundation
Blakes Benevolent Trust
The Neville and Elaine Blond Charitable
  Trust
The Blueberry Charitable Trust
The Boltons Trust
The John and Celia Bonham Christie
  Charitable Trust
The Charlotte Bonham-Carter Charitable
  Trust
Salo Bordon Charitable Trust
The Harry Bottom Charitable Trust
The A H and E Boulton Trust
The M Bourne Charitable Trust
Bourneheights Limited
The Viscountess Boyd Charitable Trust
The William Brake Charitable Trust
The Tony Bramall Charitable Trust
The Breast Cancer Research Trust
The Harold and Alice Bridges Charity
Briggs Animal Welfare Trust
British Humane Association
British Institute at Ankara
The Britten-Pears Foundation
The Broadfield Trust
The Roger Brooke Charitable Trust
R S Brownless Charitable Trust
The T B H Brunner Charitable
  Settlement
Brushmill Ltd
The Buckinghamshire Masonic
  Centenary Fund
Buckland Charitable Trust
The Burden Trust
Burdens Charitable Foundation
The Burry Charitable Trust
The Arnold Burton 1998 Charitable
  Trust
The Geoffrey Burton Charitable Trust
The Bill Butlin Charity Trust
The C B Trust
The C J M Charitable Trust
C J Cadbury Charitable Trust
The Christopher Cadbury Charitable
  Trust
The George W Cadbury Charitable Trust
The Richard Cadbury Charitable Trust
The Edward and Dorothy Cadbury Trust
The George Cadbury Trust

Medicine and health

Older people

Religion

Christianity

Islam

Judaism

The David Uri Memorial Trust
Vivdale Ltd
The Weinstein Foundation
West London Synagogue Charitable
  Fund
The Benjamin Winegarten Charitable
  Trust
The Michael and Anna Wix Charitable
  Trust
The Maurice Wohl Charitable
  Foundation
The Maurice Wohl Charitable Trust
Woodlands Green Ltd
The A and R Woolf Charitable Trust
The Fred and Della Worms Charitable
  Trust
Wychdale Ltd
Wychville Ltd
David Young Charitable Trust
The I A Ziff Charitable Foundation
Stephen Zimmerman Charitable Trust

Rights, law and conflict

The A B Charitable Trust
The Anglian Water Trust Fund
The AS Charitable Trust
The Baltic Charitable Fund
Thomas Betton's Charity for Pensions
  and Relief-in-Need
Henry T and Lucy B Cadbury Charitable
  Trust
The Casey Trust
The Chandris Foundation
J A Clark Charitable Trust
The Elizabeth Clark Charitable Trust
Clover Trust
The Daiwa Anglo–Japanese Foundation
The W G Edwards Charitable
  Foundation
The Edith Maud Ellis 1985 Charitable
  Trust
The Emmandjay Charitable Trust
The EOS Foundation
The Forbes Charitable Foundation
Ford Britain Trust
Sydney E Franklin Deceased's New
  Second Charity
Maurice Fry Charitable Trust
The Gamlen Charitable Trust
The Good Neighbours Trust
The Ireland Fund of Great Britain
The J R S S T Charitable Trust
The Law Society Charity
The Leigh Trust
Mariapolis Limited
The Millfield House Foundation
S C and M E Morland's Charitable Trust
The Nadezhda Charitable Trust
Newby Trust Limited

The Noon Foundation
The Persula Foundation
The Platinum Trust
Prairie Trust
The Monica Rabagliati Charitable Trust
The Eleanor Rathbone Charitable Trust
The Rowan Charitable Trust
The Alan and Babette Sainsbury
  Charitable Fund
The Scott Bader Commonwealth Ltd
David Solomons Charitable Trust
The Stone Ashdown Charitable Trust
Vision Charity
The Scurrah Wainwright Charity
Wallace and Gromit's Children's
  Foundation
The Weavers' Company Benevolent
  Fund
Webb Memorial Trust
The Westcroft Trust
Women at Risk
The Yapp Charitable Trust

Science and technology

The Altajir Trust
The Armourers' and Brasiers' Gauntlet
  Trust
The Baltic Charitable Fund
Thomas Betton's Charity for Pensions
  and Relief-in-Need
The Casey Trust
The Chandris Foundation
The Elizabeth Clark Charitable Trust
Clover Trust
The Robert Clutterbuck Charitable Trust
Lance Coates Charitable Trust 1969
Cobb Charity
William Dean Countryside and
  Educational Trust
The Harry Dunn Charitable Trust
The W G Edwards Charitable
  Foundation
The Beryl Evetts and Robert Luff Animal
  Welfare Trust
The Forbes Charitable Foundation
The Good Neighbours Trust
The Simon Heller Charitable Settlement
The Humanitarian Trust
The Kohn Foundation
The John Spedan Lewis Foundation
The Miller Foundation
The Mountbatten Memorial Trust
The Pet Plan Charitable Trust
The Platinum Trust
The Rowlands Trust
Dr Mortimer and Theresa Sackler
  Foundation
The Alan and Babette Sainsbury
  Charitable Fund

The Andrew Salvesen Charitable Trust
The Simpson Education and
  Conservation Trust
David Solomons Charitable Trust
Vision Charity
Wallace and Gromit's Children's
  Foundation
The Wilkinson Charitable Foundation

Social sciences, policy and research

Anglo–German Foundation for the
  Study of Industrial Society
The Baltic Charitable Fund
Thomas Betton's Charity for Pensions
  and Relief-in-Need
British Institute at Ankara
The Casey Trust
The Chandris Foundation
The Elizabeth Clark Charitable Trust
Clover Trust
EAGA Partnership Charitable Trust
The W G Edwards Charitable
  Foundation
The Elmgrant Trust
The Forbes Charitable Foundation
The Good Neighbours Trust
The Lord and Lady Haskel Charitable
  Foundation
Houblon-Norman/George Fund
The Eleni Nakou Foundation
The Platinum Trust
David Solomons Charitable Trust
Vision Charity
Wallace and Gromit's Children's
  Foundation
Webb Memorial Trust

Social welfare

Access 4 Trust
The Company of Actuaries' Charitable
  Trust Fund
The Green and Lilian F M Ainsworth
  and Family Benevolent Fund
The Sylvia Aitken Charitable Trust
The Alborada Trust
The Alchemy Foundation
Alexandra Rose Day
The Almshouse Association
Alvor Charitable Trust
Viscount Amory's Charitable Trust
The Andrew Anderson Trust
The Appletree Trust
The Archbishop of Canterbury's
  Charitable Trust

Voluntary sector management and development

Women

Geographical index

The following geographical index aims to highlight when a trust gives preference for, or has a special interest in, a particular area: county, region, city, town or London borough. Please note the following:

1. Before using this index please read the following and the introduction to the subject index on page 379. We must emphasise that this index:
   (a) should not be used as a simple mailing list, and
   (b) is not a substitute for detailed research.

When you have identified trusts, using this index, please read each entry carefully before making an application. Simply because a trust gives in your geographical area does not mean that it gives to your type of work.

2. Most trusts in this list are not restricted to one area, usually the geographical index indicates that the trust gives some priority for the area(s).

3. Trusts which give throughout England, Northern Ireland, Scotland and Wales have been excluded as have those which give throughout the UK, unless they have a particular interest in one or more locality.

4. Each section is ordered alphabetically according to the name of the trust.

The categories for the overseas and UK indices are as follows:

England

We have divided England into the following nine categories:

North East *page 412*

North West *page 412*

Yorkshire and the Humber *page 412*

East Midlands *page 412*

West Midlands *page 412*

Eastern England *page 413*

South East *page 413*

South West *page 413*

London *page 414*

Some trusts may be found in more than one category because they provide grants in more than one area i.e. those with a preference for northern England.

Wales *page 414*

Scotland *page 414*

Northern Ireland *page 414*

Overseas categories

Overseas general

Developing world *page 414*

Individual continents *page 415*

These are listed in alphabetical order of continent.

The Middle East has been listed separately. Please note that most of the trusts listed are primarily for the benefit of Jewish people and the advancement of the Jewish religion.

England

North East

The Anglian Water Trust Fund
The Catherine Cookson Charitable Trust
The Dickon Trust
The Eventhall Family Charitable Trust
The GNC Trust
Percy Hedley 1990 Charitable Trust
The Ruth and Lionel Jacobson Trust
(Second Fund) No. 2
The Millfield House Foundation
The Normanby Charitable Trust
The Nigel Vinson Charitable Trust

North West

The Green and Lilian F M Ainsworth &
Family Benevolent Fund
The David and Ruth Behrend Fund
The Harold and Alice Bridges Charity
The Amelia Chadwick Trust
The Robert Clutterbuck Charitable Trust
Coutts and Co. Charitable Trust
The Lord Cozens-Hardy Trust
William Dean Countryside and
Educational Trust
The Dwek Family Charitable Trust
The Eagle Charity Trust
The Eventhall Family Charitable Trust
The Fairway Trust
Florence's Charitable Trust
Ford of Britain Trust
The GNC Trust
The Hammonds Charitable Trust
The M A Hawe Settlement
The S Hodgkiss Charitable Trust
P H Holt Charitable Trust
The Clifford Howarth Charity
Settlement
The J E Joseph Charitable Fund
The P Leigh-Bramwell Trust 'E'
Jack Livingstone Charitable Trust
The Mason Porter Charitable Trust
The Mushroom Fund
The Duncan Norman Trust Fund
Penny in the Pound Fund Charitable
Trust
The Pennycress Trust
The Cecil Pilkington Charitable Trust
The Sir Harry Pilkington Trust
The Col W W Pilkington Will Trusts
The Rainford Trust
The Fanny Rapaport Charitable
Settlement
The E L Rathbone Charitable Trust
The Eleanor Rathbone Charitable Trust

The John Rayner Charitable Trust
The Red Rose Charitable Trust
Riverside Charitable Trust Limited
The Searchlight Electric Charitable Trust
The John Slater Foundation
The Steinberg Family Charitable Trust
TJH Foundation
The Treeside Trust
The Ward Blenkinsop Trust
Mrs Waterhouse Charitable Trust
The Norman Whiteley Trust

Yorkshire and The Humber

The Anglian Water Trust Fund
The Harry Bottom Charitable Trust
R M Burton 1998 Charitable Settlement
H & L Cantor Trust
The Joseph & Annie Cattle Trust
Coutts and Co. Charitable Trust
The Manny Cussins Foundation
The Sandy Dewhirst Charitable Trust
The Emmandjay Charitable Trust
The Eventhall Family Charitable Trust
The A M Fenton Trust
The Earl Fitzwilliam Charitable Trust
The GNC Trust
The Constance Green Foundation
The Hammonds Charitable Trust
May Hearnshaw's Charity
The Linden Charitable Trust
George A Moore Foundation
The W L Pratt Charitable Trust
The Patricia and Donald Shepherd Trust
W W Spooner Charitable Trust
The Hugh and Ruby Sykes Charitable
Trust
The Scurrah Wainwright Charity
The Whitecourt Charitable Trust
The I A Ziff Charitable Foundation

East Midlands

The Anglian Water Trust Fund
The Ashby Charitable Trust
The Benham Charitable Settlement
The Michael Bishop Foundation
The Harry Bottom Charitable Trust
The Christopher Cadbury Charitable
Trust
The Chetwode Foundation
The Coates Charitable Settlement
Coutts and Co. Charitable Trust
The Cripps Foundation
William Dean Countryside and
Educational Trust
The Duke of Devonshire's Charitable
Trust

The Harry Dunn Charitable Trust
The Earl Fitzwilliam Charitable Trust
Ford of Britain Trust
The Forman Hardy Charitable Trust
The GNC Trust
May Hearnshaw's Charity
The Joanna Herbert-Stepney Charitable
Settlement
The P and C Hickinbotham Charitable
Trust
The Charles Littlewood Hill Trust
The Linmardon Trust
The Norton Foundation
The Owen Family Trust
The E H Smith Charitable Trust
The Jessie Spencer Trust
The Hugh and Ruby Sykes Charitable
Trust
The Lady Tangye Charitable Trust
The Constance Travis Charitable Trust
The R D Turner Charitable Trust
The Florence Turner Trust
The Whitaker Charitable Trust
A H and B C Whiteley Charitable Trust
The Dennis Alan Yardy Charitable Trust

West Midlands

The Michael Bishop Foundation
The Richard Cadbury Charitable Trust
The Christopher Cadbury Charitable
Trust
The George Cadbury Trust
The Edward and Dorothy Cadbury Trust
(1928)
The Wilfrid and Constance Cave
Foundation
William Dean Countryside and
Educational Trust
The R M Douglas Charitable Trust
The John Feeney Charitable Bequest
Ford of Britain Trust
The Charles Henry Foyle Trust
The GNC Trust
Mrs H R Greene Charitable Settlement
Grimmitt Trust
The Hammonds Charitable Trust
The Hawthorne Charitable Trust
May Hearnshaw's Charity
The Lillie Johnson Charitable Trust
The Langdale Trust
The Langley Charitable Trust
The Edgar E Lawley Foundation
Limoges Charitable Trust
The Millichope Foundation
The Janet Nash Charitable Trust
The Norton Foundation
The Owen Family Trust
The Park House Charitable Trust
The Bernard Piggott Trust
The Ratcliff Foundation

The Clive Richards Charity Ltd
The Rowlands Trust
The Saintbury Trust
The Sheldon Trust
The E H Smith Charitable Trust
The Stephen R and Philippa H Southall
    Charitable Trust
The Lady Tangye Charitable Trust
C B and H H Taylor 1984 Trust
The R D Turner Charitable Trust
The Westcroft Trust

Eastern England

The Adnams Charity
Alvor Charitbale Trust
The Anglian Water Trust Fund
A J H Ashby Will Trust
The Paul Bassham Charitable Trust
The Bedfordshire and Hertfordshire
    Historic Churches Trust
The Geoffrey Burton Charitable Trust
The Leslie Mary Carter Charitable Trust
The Chapman Charitable Trust
The Robert Clutterbuck Charitable Trust
The Augustine Courtauld Trust
The Lord Cozens-Hardy Trust
The Cripps Foundation
The Earl Fitzwilliam Charitable Trust
Ford of Britain Trust
The Fowler, Smith and Jones Charitable
    Trust
The Horace and Marjorie Gale
    Charitable Trust
Mrs H R Greene Charitable Settlement
The Gretna Charitable Trust
The Haymills Charitable Trust
The Charles Littlewood Hill Trust
The Hudson Foundation
The John Jarrold Trust
The Christopher Laing Foundation
The D C Moncrieff Charitable Trust
The Music Sales Charitable Trust
The Alderman Norman's Foundation
The Panacea Society
The Late Barbara May Paul Charitable
    Trust
The Pennycress Trust
Ranworth Trust
The South Square Trust
The Spurrell Charitable Trust
Annie Tranmer Charitable Trust
The Simon Whitbread Charitable Trust
The A and R Woolf Charitable Trust

South East

Alvor Charitable Trust
The Anglian Water Trust Fund
The Ashe Park Charitable Trust

The Ian Askew Charitable Trust
The Astor of Hever Trust
Peter Barker-Mill Memorial Charity
The Barnsbury Charitable Trust
The Bartlett Taylor Charitable Trust
The Billmeir Charitable Trust
The William Brake Charitable Trust
The Roger Brooke Charitable Trust
The Buckingham and Gawcott
    Charitable Trust
The Buckinghamshire Masonic
    Centenary Fund
The Burry Charitable Trust
The George Cadbury Trust
The Wilfrid and Constance Cave
    Foundation
The Chapman Charitable Trust
The John and Freda Coleman Charitable
    Trust
The Sir Jeremiah Colman Gift Trust
Cowley Charitable Foundation
The Ronald Cruickshanks Foundation
The Alderman Joe Davidson Memorial
    Trust
The Demigryphon Trust
The DLM Charitable Trust
The Dugdale Charitable Trust
East Kent Provincial Charities
The Fawcett Charitable Trust
The Doris Field Charitable Trust
Ford of Britain Trust
The Louis and Valerie Freedman
    Charitable Settlement
The Friarsgate Trust
The GNC Trust
The Grimsdale Charitable Trust
The Bishop of Guildford's Foundation
The H & M Charitable Trust
The Hare of Steep Charitable Trust
The Dorothy Hay-Bolton Charitable
    Trust
The Hobart Charitable Trust
The Hyde Charitable Trust
The Ingram Trust
The Richard Kirkman Charitable Trust
The Lawlor Foundation
The Raymond and Blanche Lawson
    Charitable Trust
The Leach Fourteenth Trust
The Sir Edward Lewis Foundation
The Elaine and Angus Lloyd Charitable
    Trust
The C L Loyd Charitable Trust
Paul Lunn-Rockliffe Charitable Trust
Gerald Micklem Charitable Trust
The Moss Charitable Trust
The Moulton Charitable Trust
The Cecil Pilkington Charitable Trust
The Powell Foundation
The River Trust
The Peter Samuel Charitable Trust
The Bassil Shippam and Alsford Trust

The South Square Trust
St Michael's and All Saints' Charities
The Late St Patrick White Charitable
    Trust
The Swan Trust
Rosanna Taylor's 1987 Charity Trust
The Thompson Fund
The Three Oaks Trust
The Tory Family Foundation
Roger Vere Foundation
The F J Wallis Charitable Settlement
The Diana Edgson Wright Charitable
    Trust
The William Allen Young Charitable
    Trust

South West

The Keith & Freda Abraham Charitable
    Trust
D G Albright Charitable Trust
Sir John and Lady Amory's Charitable
    Trust
The Bisgood Charitable Trust
The John and Celia Bonham Christie
    Charitable Trust
The Viscountess Boyd Charitable Trust
The Bristol Charities
The George Cadbury Trust
The Wilfrid and Constance Cave
    Foundation
The Roger and Sarah Bancroft Clark
    Charitable Trust
Mabel Cooper Charity
Coutts and Co. Charitable Trust
The Harry Crook Foundation
The Wilfrid Bruce Davis Charitable
    Trust
The Elmgrant Trust
The Evangelical Covenants Trust
The Joyce Fletcher Charitable Trust
The GNC Trust
The Grimsdale Charitable Trust
The R J Harris Charitable Settlement
The Dorothy Holmes Charitable Trust
The Marjorie and Geoffrey Jones
    Charitable Trust
The Lawlor Foundation
The Leach Fourteenth Trust
The Macfarlane Walker Trust
The A M McGreevy No. 5 Charitable
    Settlement
Misselbrook Trust
The Moss Charitable Trust
The Mount 'A' Charity Trust
The Norman Family Charitable Trust
The Susanna Peake Charitable Trust
The Mrs C S Heber Percy Charitable
    Trust
The Ratcliff Foundation
The Rowlands Trust

413

The Saintbury Trust
The Peter Samuel Charitable Trust
Philip Smith's Charitable Trust
The Van Neste Foundation
The Wakefield Trust
The Colonel W H Whitbread Charitable
  Trust

London

The Company of Actuaries' Charitable
  Trust Fund
The John Apthorp Charitable Trust
The Armourers' and Brasiers' Gauntlet
  Trust
The Baltic Charitable Fund
The Chapman Charitable Trust
Coutts and Co. Charitable Trust
Ford of Britain Trust
The Hammonds Charitable Trust
The Hyde Charitable Trust
The Ingram Trust
The J E Joseph Charitable Fund
The Lawlor Foundation
Lloyd's Charities Trust
The Mitchell Charitable Trust
The Morris Charitable Trust
The Music Sales Charitable Trust
Salters' Charities
The Shipwrights' Company Charitable
  Fund
The South Square Trust
The Worshipful Company of Spectacle
  Makers Charity
The Adrienne and Leslie Sussman
  Charitable Trust
The Cyril Taylor Charitable Trust
The Lionel Wigram Memorial Trust
The William Allen Young Charitable
  Trust

Wales

The Laura Ashley Foundation
The Atlantic Foundation
Birthday House Trust
The Catholic Trust for England and
  Wales
The Cemlyn-Jones Trust
The Chapman Charitable Trust
CLA Charitable Trust
Peter De Haan Charitable Trust
Ford of Britain Trust
Gwyneth Forrester Trust
The GNC Trust
Leonard Gordon Charitable Trust
Mary Homfray Charitable Trust
The Incorporated Church Building
  Society

J I Charitable Trust
The Jenour Foundation
The Ian Karten Charitable Trust
The Llysdinam Trust
Henry Lumley Charitable Trust
The McKenna Charitable Trust
The Nigel Moores Family Charitable
  Trust
The Noon Foundation
Norwood and Newton Settlement
The Oakdale Trust
The Ouseley Trust
The Owen Family Trust
Penny in the Pound Fund Charitable
  Trust
The Bernard Piggott Trust
The Ratcliff Foundation
The Barbara Ward Children's
  Foundation
A H and B C Whiteley Charitable Trust

Scotland

The Adamson Trust
The Sylvia Aitken Charitable Trust
Alvor Charitbale Trust
James and Grace Anderson Trust
The Appletree Trust
The Astor of Hever Trust
The D W T Cargill Fund
The Craignish Trust
The Demigryphon Trust
The Dickon Trust
Elizabeth Hardie Ferguson Charitable
  Trust Fund
The Gordon Fraser Charitable Trust
The Emily Fraser Trust
The Gamma Trust
The GNC Trust
The Christina Mary Hendrie Trust for
  Scottish and Canadian Charities
The Ian Karten Charitable Trust
The R J Larg Family Charitable Trust
The Miller Foundation
Penny in the Pound Fund Charitable
  Trust
A M Pilkington's Charitable Trust
The Russell Trust
The Andrew Salvesen Charitable Trust
The Peter Samuel Charitable Trust
The Sharon Trust
The Patricia and Donald Shepherd Trust
Talteg Ltd
The Tay Charitable Trust
The James Weir Foundation
The Whitaker Charitable Trust
A H and B C Whiteley Charitable Trust

Northern Ireland

The GNC Trust
The Lawlor Foundation
Lindale Educational Foundation
The Whitaker Charitable Trust

Developing world

The Ardwick Trust
Veta Bailey Charitable Trust
The Bay Tree Charitable Trust
The Viscountess Boyd Charitable Trust
The C B Trust
Henry T and Lucy B Cadbury Charitable
  Trust
The Carpenter Charitable Trust
The Casey Trust
The Catalyst Charitable Trust
The Thomas Sivewright Catto Charitable
  Settlement
Lance Coates Charitable Trust 1969
Cobb Charity
The Muriel and Gershon Coren
  Charitable Foundation
The Cumber Family Charitable Trust
The Dickon Trust
The Eagle Charity Trust
The Emerging Markets Charity for
  Children
The Ericson Trust
Sydney E Franklin Deceased's New
  Second Charity
The Jill Franklin Trust
The Angela Gallagher Memorial Fund
The Constance Green Foundation
Miss K M Harbinson's Charitable Trust
Philip Henman Trust
The Joanna Herbert-Stepney Charitable
  Settlement
The Thomas J Horne Memorial Trust
The Jephcott Charitable Trust
The Langley Charitable Trust
The Marchday Charitable Fund
Mariapolis Limited
Marr-Munning Trust
The Millhouses Charitable Trust
Nazareth Trust Fund
Mr and Mrs F E F Newman Charitable
  Trust
The Philanthropic Trust
The David and Elaine Potter Charitable
  Foundation
Prairie Trust

Africa

Americas

Asia

Alphabetical index

A B: The A B Charitable Trust 1

Abraham: The Keith and Freda Abraham Charitable Trust 1

Abrams: Brian Abrams Charitable Trust 1
Eric Abrams Charitable Trust 1

Acacia: The Acacia Charitable Trust 2

Access: Access 4 Trust 2

Actuaries': The Company of Actuaries' Charitable Trust Fund 2

Adamson: The Adamson Trust 3

Adda: The Victor Adda Foundation 3

Adenfirst: Adenfirst Ltd 3

Adnams: The Adnams Charity 4

AF: AF Trust Company 4

Ainsworth: The Green and Lilian F M Ainsworth and Family Benevolent Fund 4

Aitken: The Sylvia Aitken Charitable Trust 5

Alabaster: The Alabaster Trust 5

Alborada: The Alborada Trust 5

Albright: D G Albright Charitable Trust 6

Alchemy: The Alchemy Foundation 6

Alcohol: Alcohol Education and Research Council 6

Alexandra: Alexandra Rose Day 6

Alexis: The Alexis Trust 7

All: All Saints Educational Trust 7

Allsop: The Pat Allsop Charitable Trust 8

Almond: The Almond Trust 8

Almshouse: The Almshouse Association 8

Altajir: The Altajir Trust 9

Altamont: Altamont Ltd 9

Alvor: Alvor Charitable Trust 9

AM: AM Charitable Trust 9

Ambika: Ambika Paul Foundation 10

Amory's: Sir John and Lady Amory's Charitable Trust 10
Viscount Amory's Charitable Trust 10

Ampelos: The Ampelos Trust 11

Anchor: The Anchor Foundation 11

Anderson: James and Grace Anderson Trust 11
The Andrew Anderson Trust 12

André: The André Christian Trust 12

Anglian: The Anglian Water Trust Fund 12

Anglo-German: Anglo-German Foundation for the Study of Industrial Society 13

Animal: The Animal Defence Trust 13

Annandale: The Annandale Charitable Trust 13

Appletree: The Appletree Trust 14

Apthorp: The John Apthorp Charitable Trust 14

Archbishop: The Archbishop of Canterbury's Charitable Trust 14
Archbishop of Wales Fund for Children 15

Archer: The John M Archer Charitable Trust 15

Ardwick: The Ardwick Trust 15

Armenian: Armenian General Benevolent Union London Trust 16

Armourers': The Armourers' and Brasiers' Gauntlet Trust 16

Artemis: The Artemis Charitable Trust 17

Arup: The Ove Arup Foundation 17

AS: The AS Charitable Trust 17

Ashburnham: Ashburnham Thanksgiving Trust 17

Ashby: A J H Ashby Will Trust 18

Ashe: The Ashe Park Charitable Trust 18

Ashley: The Laura Ashley Foundation 18

Ashworth: The Ashworth Charitable Trust 19

Askew: The Ian Askew Charitable Trust 19

Association: The Association of Colleges Charitable Trust 20

Astellas: Astellas European Foundation 20

Astor: The Astor Foundation 21
The Astor of Hever Trust 21

Atlantic: The Atlantic Foundation 22

Atwell's: Lawrence Atwell's Charity 22

Aurelius: The Aurelius Charitable Trust 22

Bacon: Harry Bacon Foundation 23

Bacta: The Bacta Charitable Trust 23

Bagri: The Bagri Foundation 23

Baker: The Baker Charitable Trust 23

Balmain: Balmain Charitable Trust 24

Balney: The Balney Charitable Trust 24

Baltic: The Baltic Charitable Fund 24

Bancroft: William P Bancroft (No. 2) Charitable Trust and Jenepher Gillett Trust 25

Barbers': The Barbers' Company General Charities 25

Barbour: The Barbour Trust 25

Barchester: Barchester Healthcare Foundation 26

Barclays: Barclays Stockbrokers Charitable Trust 27

Barker-Mill: Peter Barker-Mill Memorial Charity 27

Barnabas: The Barnabas Trust 27

Barnby's: Lord Barnby's Foundation 28

Barnsbury: The Barnsbury Charitable Trust 28

Barrie: The Misses Barrie Charitable Trust 29

Bartlett: The Bartlett Taylor Charitable Trust 29

Bassham: The Paul Bassham Charitable Trust 29

Batchworth: The Batchworth Trust 30

Batty: The Batty Charitable Trust 30

Bay: The Bay Tree Charitable Trust 30

Beacon: The Beacon Trust 31

Bear: Bear Mordechai Ltd 31

Beaufort: The Beaufort House Trust 31

Beauland: Beauland Ltd 31

Beaverbrook: The Beaverbrook Foundation 32

Beckwith: The John Beckwith Charitable Trust 32
The Peter Beckwith Charitable Trust 32

Bedfordshire: The Bedfordshire and Hertfordshire Historic Churches Trust 32

Behrend: The David and Ruth Behrend Fund 33

Belljoe: Belljoe Tzedoko Ltd 33

Benham: The Benham Charitable Settlement 33

Bennett: Michael and Leslie Bennett Charitable Trust 34

Berger: The Geoffrey Berger Charitable Trust 34

417